Footprint Malaysia & Singapore

Dinah Gardner

5th edition

"'Typical,' said Flint, full of approval. 'The Malays are fantastic. You get people like this all over the Federation - plenty of time for small talk, very hospitable, give you the shirt off their back. I got this theory. You ask a guy directions in Malaysia. If the guy's Chinese he knows where you want to go but he won't tell you how to get there. If he's Indian he knows and he'll tell you. If he's Malay he won't know the place but he'll talk for 10 hours about everything else. It's the temperament. Friendly. No hangups. Out-going. All the time in the world.'"

'Dependent Wife', Paul Theroux: The Collected Stories

1 Penang Hill
Take the cable car ride through rainforested slopes

2 Kellie's Castle
The haunted house of a mad Scottish rubber tycoon

3 Cameron Highlands
A hill station patched with tea plantations and tudor lodges

4 Taman Negara National Park
Loiter at a salt lick to spot endangered animal footprints

5 Kuala Terengganu
A sleepy state capital with a thriving kain songket, batik and silverware cottage industry

6 Perhentians
There are no roads on these islands, just forest trails and glorious sands

7 Kuala Selangor Nature Park
Home of the famous fireflies, who perform a synchronized flash dance

8 Kuala Lumpur
A mix of towers, malls, temples and mosques

9 Singapore
A sim city of modernity crossed with colonial elegance

10 Kuching
Cat Kitsch city of sampans, Chinese shophouses, palaces and colonial splendours

Malaysia Highlights

See colour maps at back of book

11 Headhunter's Trail Jungle trek tracing the bloody footsteps of Kayan tribesmens' former skull collecting raids

12 Rejang River Malaysia's longest river where tiny craft bump through rapids to reach forest longhouses

13 Similajau National Park Visit between May and September to catch sight of dolphins

14 Bario Home to the hospitable Kelabit mountain tribe

15 Kemabong Visit this Murut village during a festival to see locals dance their giant trampoline jig

16 Pulau Tiga Wallow in mud volcanoes on this island

17 Gunung Kinabalu Feel on top of the world by climbing this mountain – one of Southeast Asia's tallest peaks

18 Gomantong At dusk, millions of bats cascade through the guano-clogged caves

19 Sipadan Love-making turtles delight snorkellers year-round at this world class scuba site

Contents

Southern Peninsula

East Coast Peninsula

Sarawak

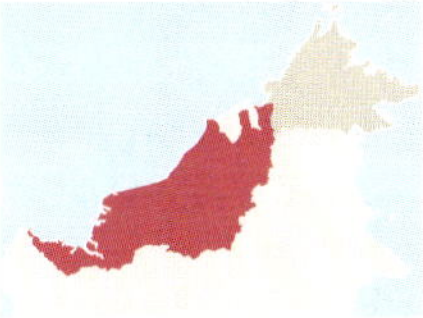

Sabah

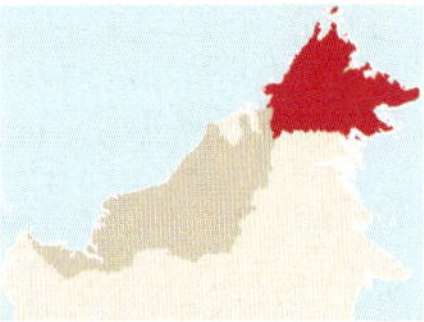

Background

Singapore

Some of the best diving in the world is found at the beautiful Sipadan Island which stands on a coral and limestone stalk rising 200 m from the bed of the Celebes Sea.

Subterranean art
Illuminated cave sculptures are to be found in the Batu Caves, the largest Indian pilgrimage centre in Malaysia during the Thaipusam festival.

A foot in the door

The 'Malay Archipelago' is a term intimately associated with the mystery of the East. It conjures up images of sultans and head-hunters; munificent jungles brimming with exotic wildlife and clippers cutting through the warm waters of the South China Sea. Of course, today's Malay Archipelago is another world – the jungles are contained in national parks or have been ploughed up into rubber and palm oil plantations, the cities of Singapore and Kuala Lumpur are modern metropolises of glass, and container ships, not clippers, now plough through the Strait of Melaka.

Even so, Malaysia retains its cross-cultural stamp with the sharp spices of its Indian markets, its flamboyant red Buddhist temples and the prayer call of the muezzin echoes from a multitude of mosques across the country. Sandwiched between Singapore to the south and Thailand to the north, the Peninsula states support the great bulk of the country's population. And, just as Malaysia itself is a country of two halves, so the Peninsula too can be broadly divided into a vibrant western side and a bucolic east separated by the Barisan Titiwangsa, the Peninsula's jungled spine. Malaysian Borneo - the states of Sabah and Sarawak - dovetails more closely with the romantic vision of 'Malaya'. The countryside remains dominated by tribal groups, collectively known as Dayaks, and much of it is still forested.

Singapore is a world-class city with world-class attractions and only the barest whiff of the East. When the Orient does appear it has invariably been sequestered by New Singapore. Hundred year old shophouses have been converted into drinking holes and edgy studios while the bumboats which used to ferry cargo from freighter to godown now carry tourists up and down the restaurant-lined Singapore River. Renowned for its epicurean delights, Singapore is aiming to become a regional centre for the arts too.

10 Asian fusion

Over the four decades since independence the country has been transformed from a poor, undeveloped British colony, reliant on the export of primary products like rubber and tin, to a self-confident industrializing nation with a burgeoning middle class, an increasingly sophisticated economy and an elected leader of state.

Malaysia is sometimes called the lucky country of Asia because it is so richly endowed with natural resources. It has the world's largest tin deposits, extensive oil and gas reserves and is cloaked in rainforest containing valuable tropical hardwoods. In the late 1980s and early 1990s, a sudden explosion of industrial growth, spearheaded by a surge in manufacturing, changed the complexion of Malaysia's economy beyond recognition. It is now one of the world's biggest producers of computer disk drives and boasts its own car, the Proton.

Twin peaks
The Petronas Towers, once the tallest buildings in the world, dominate the Kuala Lumpur skyline.

Malaysia is a young country; until the end of the last century there was just a collection of divided coastal sultanates around the peninsula and three colonial trading settlements. Today the Federation of Malaysia includes the 11 peninsular states together with Sabah and Sarawak.

A favourite Malaysian dish is rojak, a tossed salad with many different ingredients. It is not uncommon to hear the rojak analogy applied to Malaysia's exotic ethnic mix of Malays, Chinese, Indians and indigenous tribes. The country's cultural blend makes Malaysia interesting, but it is also a potentially volatile mixture. Today, most Malaysians are too young to remember the 1969 race riots, although they have lived with the consequences ever since. The government's affirmative action policies have attempted to lessen the economic disparities between the races and have given the Malays, the economic underdogs, a helping hand.

Spirits in the sky
The summit of Gunung Kinabalu, which towers over Borneo, is home to the spirits of the dead, according to the Kadazans, Sabah's largest ethnic group.

1

2

4

5

7

8

10

11

1 *The cooler climes of the Cameron Highlands, " a fine plateau, shut in by lofty mountains" provide respite to visitors .* *▸▸ See page 124 .*

2 *The night market in Kuala Lumpur.* *▸▸ See page 80 .*

3 *The two-horned Sumatran Rhinoceros is highly endangered. A small crash of rhinoceri live in Sabah.* *▸▸ See page 451 .*

4 *This pied hornbill is one of nine species found in Malaysia. Hornbills love fig trees and are the official emblem of Sarawak.* *▸▸ See page 524 .*

5 *The sharp Pinnacles at Gunung Mulu, home to the largest limestone cave system on earth, are the "the world's most nightmarish surface to travel over".* *▸▸ See page 375 .*

6 *Fraser's Hill. The beauty of the highlands and the cool climate attracted the first British colonials to establish a hill station.* *▸▸ See page 123 .*

7 *Teluk Bahang on Penang's north coast, which used to be home to Malabar fisherman.* *▸▸ See page 165 .*

8 *Colourful trishaws clatter around the historical streets of Melaka.* *▸▸ See page 204 .*

9 *Devotees to Lord Subramanian, pierce their bodies in a day of penance and thanksgiving.* *▸▸ See page 52 .*

10 *Some of Malaysia's shores are welcoming breeding grounds for thousands of Green turtles.* *▸▸ See page 450 .*

11 *The Rafflesia flower, named after the founder of Singapore, Sir Thomas Stamford Raffles, is the largest flower in the world and one of the smelliest plants on earth.* *▸▸ See page 423 .*

12 *A fishing village on Mabul Island, one of the jewels in the aquamarine sea off the south coast of Sabah.* *▸▸ See page 459 .*

Chinatown, the Moorish-style railway station and one or two other notable buildings represent the old in Kuala Lumpur; the new is showcased in the 88-storey, 421-metre-high Petronas Twin Towers, the world's second tallest building.

The venerable town of Melaka has churches and trading houses reflecting its Dutch and Portuguese parentage and also a fine Chinatown. An even better array of colonial-era Chinese shophouses are to be found in Georgetown, Penang. Ipoh is another tin-rush settlement colonised by Chinese with a well preserved Old Town and excellent Chinese restaurants.

The British converted the cooler slopes of Cameron Highlands and Fraser's Hill into a home from home with beamed cottages and rose gardens in the 1920s. It is still possible to settle down to a cream tea or roast beef and Yorkshire pudding.

Penang Island is the west coast's best known and most developed beach resort. Langkawi and Pangkor islands are more rustic although fairly bruised by upmarket resorts. While the west coast may be the industrial and political core of Malaysia, the eastern side is regarded as the heartland of Malay culture and tradition. Malay sports from top-spinning to kite-flying and crafts like batik-making and silverwork remain vibrant.

East coast tropical islands such as Tioman, along with stretches of quiet coastline and beaches, offer far more diving possibilities than the west coast. The coral reefs around the offshore islands like Pulau Lang Tengah and the Perhentian group offer great undersea forests for new divers to learn the ropes. There is also the additional attraction of turtles which

Singapore's urbscape: an ultra-modern city state of gleaming towers, shopping malls, theme parks and food to satisfy all palates.

The orang utan, Asia's great ape, lives among up to 100,000 of his fellow primates in the wilds of Borneo.

come ashore to lay their eggs at numerous locations including Rantau Abang. Inland are the Peninsula's finest national parks, Endau Rompin and Taman Negara. Fishing, hiking, waterfalls, rapids and 1500 m-peaks, along with wildlife from the extremely rare Sumatran rhinoceros to civets, wild boar and hornbills add to their allure.

Across to Borneo, the Skrang, Belaga, Rejang and Baram rivers with their trading settlements, tribal villages, rapids and daredevil speedboats are the entrees into inland Sarawak and the state's magnificent natural heritage. The Gunung Mulu National Park has razor-sharp limestone pinnacles and kilometres of caves including the world's largest cavern.

Kuching supports arguably Malaysia's finest museum, the Sarawak Museum, with an incomparable ethnographic collection. Sabah is a natural wonderland. From Kota Kinabalu it is easy to see Malaysia's highest mountain, Gunung Kinabalu, which rises to more than 4,000m. The world's largest flower, the Rafflesia, grows here. On the east coast the small Sepilok Orang Utan Rehabilitation Centre teaches the semi domesticated primates to live wild so they can be introduced back into the forest. Two of Sabah's most memorable protected areas are marine. The Turtle Islands National Park is Southeast Asia's most important turtle-breeding area. Here it is possible to see the kings of Malaysia's reptile population, Green and Hawksbill turtles, laying their eggs on three tiny islands. The second is the Sipadan Island Marine Reserve off Sabah's northeast coast. When Jacques Couusteau visited Sipadan in 1989 he described it as an untouched piece of art. The diving here is the best in Malaysia indeed, some of the best in the world.

Supreme Bliss
Kek Lok Si Temple (the Monastery of Supreme Bliss), which overlooks central Penang Island, took two decades to build.

Essentials

Footprint features

Planning your trip

Where to go

Getting around Peninsular Malaysia and Singapore is not difficult and even making the trip from Kota Bharu at the northern extremity of the east coast, down to Melaka, towards the southern end of the west coast, need only take a day's travelling by road. Air links between the major towns are, self-evidently, faster still. However, many visitors with only, say, a fortnight in the area wonder whether it is possible to combine a trip to Peninsular Malaysia and the East Malaysia states of Sabah and Sarawak. This requires a little more thought. There are regular domestic air connections between Kuala Lumpur, the capital and Johor Bahru, just across from Singapore to the major cities of East Malaysia, and from there with smaller towns in the Bornean interior. For those intending, for example, to fly to Kota Kinabalu, Sabah, stay a few days at Tanjung Aru Beach, and then return to the Peninsular, taking in East and West Malaysia should pose no difficulties. However, if intending to do more than this, such as climbing Mount Kinabalu, travelling upriver on the Baram, Rejang or Skrang rivers, or hiking through one of the national parks , then a little more leeway in terms of time is required. A minimum period to just scratch the surface would be one week; more preferable would be10 days to two weeks. Of course some people spend many weeks in just one area and still profess to have seen only a fraction of what is on offer.

Hill stations

Fraser's Hill and the Cameron Highlands offer a taste of colonial Malaya, and there are good walks around the Cameron Highlands. The Genting Highlands is more ersatz and kitsch, a favourite haunt of Kuala Lumpur's nouveau riche. Maxwell Hill is the quietest of the hill stations.

Wildlife and jungle

The national parks of the Peninsula do not compare with those of East Malaysia. Nonetheless, Taman Negara and the Endau Rompin National Park are both well worth visiting. Rantau Abang on the east coast is a stretch of shoreline where turtles come to lay their eggs. In East Malaysia, Sarawak and Sabah offer a wealth of parks and conservation areas. Some, like the Semonggoh Orang Utan Sanctuary and the Bako National Park outside Kuching, and the Sepilok Orang Utan Rehabilitation Centre and the Turtle Islands National Park outside Sandakan are accessible as day trips from Kuching and Sandakan respectively. Other parks, like the Niah and Gunung Mulu national parks, require several days to explore properly.

Natural features

The caves at the Niah and Gunung Mulu national parks and Gunung Kinabalu, Malaysia's highest mountain, are stupendous natural features worth visiting in themselves. There are many islands you can visit off both the west and east coasts of the Peninsula, although the east coast islands come closer to popular notions of palm-fringed island idylls. Penang has a wide selection of hotels and facilities, albeit overdeveloped and an historical centre. Langkawi, has also developed rapidly in recent years and is more the haunt of upmarket resorts than budget-friendly guesthouses. Also off the west coast and just a few hours by road from Kuala Lumpur is Pulau Pangkor. Tioman, off the Peninsula's east coast, is less developed than Langkawi and Penang and there are also numerous other islands which are still less touched by the hands of humans. On the Peninsula itself, Kampong Cherating is the best known beach resort, which still has a backpacker feel to it, although it is hardly off the beaten track. There are also other groups of hotels and chalets dotted up and down the east coast. Sabah and Sarawak do not have beach 'resorts' to compare with those – at least in scale – of the Peninsula. However, there are some fine beaches and excellent snorkelling and diving, especially in the Tunku Abdul Rahman National Park and the Sipadan Island Marine Reserve. Small resorts include those at Damai, north of Kuching; Tanjung Aru, outside Kota Kinabalu; and Labuan.

Historical sites

Melaka is one of Malaysia's two historic gems. There are buildings dating from the Portuguese and Dutch periods, as well as some fine Chinese shophouses. Georgetown, the capital of Penang, is Malaysia's second city of architectural and historical note, with probably the finest assembly of Sino-colonial architecture in the region. Both have come under serious development pressure over the years and this may be one reason why they have not yet made UNESCO's list of World Heritage Sites, although they have tried hard to be included.

Culture

Traditional Malay culture is best preserved on the east coast of the Peninsula and especially in the Malay heartland of Kelantan (Kota Bharu), with its rural kampongs, or villages, and thriving craft industry. The Sarawak Cultural Village near Kuching offers an anaesthetized vision of tribal life and culture; the upriver 'tribes' and longhouses give a taste of the real thing. The Rajang, Skrang, and Kinabatangan rivers, dotted with towns and small tribal settlements, are all worth exploring by boat.

For information on visiting longhouses in Sarawak, see page 339

Shopping

KL is the best place to buy the full range of handicrafts from batik to blowpipes, although prices are higher than at their source. The east coast is the centre of the Peninsula's Malay handicraft industry, particularly Kelantan (Kota Bharu). Sabah and Sarawak (especially Kuching) are the places to find tribal handicrafts. Many are on sale in the main towns, although smaller communities potentially offer the best buys.

Museums

KL's museums are less impressive than those in Singapore but are still worth visiting and are getting better all the time – the last few years has seen some extensive upgrading and renovation. The Islamic Arts Museum in KL is, perhaps, the city's best. The best museum in East Malaysia is the Sarawak Museum in Kuching with its superb ethnographic collection.

Itineraries

The above is only a selection of places of interest and is not exhaustive. It is designed to assist in planning a trip to the region. Any 'highlight' list is inevitably subjective. Itineraries for Peninsular Malaysia and Singapore are easy to customise to meet your own needs and interests. Distances are not enormous, transport is good and the seasons rarely put particular places off-limits. (The exception to this is the east coast where the monsoon between November and February brings rough seas and heavy rains. Some islands are difficult or impossible to reach at this time, and some national parks are also closed.) Most travellers arrive either in Singapore or KL, although a good number also enter Malaysia overland across its northern border with Thailand. From all these points of arrival it is possible to reach any of Malaysia's beach resorts, bar some of the islands off the east coast which require a morning boat departure from the mainland. The main question is how to combine, say, a visit to Melaka, to the south, with a few days on the beach in Penang, to the north, or east to Tioman island.

It requires a little more effort to co-ordinate and plan a visit to one of the Peninsular's national parks where two, three or four days may be necessary to explore the area to any degree. And as noted above, for those who want to combine a visit to the Peninsula with a trip to East Malaysia, and particularly if this includes river trips, trekking and longhouse stays, then even more time should be put to one side. As a rule-of-thumb, one week is the minimum length of time to get a taster of Peninsular Malaysia and Singapore, and two weeks if this is to be combined with East Malaysia.

When to go

Climate

When planning a trip to Malaysia, always take into account the rainy seasons; the best time to visit the Peninsula's east coast is between March and September. Trips along the east coast and interior jungles are not advisable between November and February, during the northeast monsoon. The east coast suffers flooding at this time of year, and it is inadvisable and also impossible to take fishing boats to offshore islands such as Pulau Tioman as the sea can be very rough. Taman Negara National Park is closed from November to the end of January. Other parts of Peninsular Malaysia can be visited year round as the rainy season is not torrential, although it is fairly wet during the northeast monsoon period. Rainfall is worst from May to September on the west coast of the Peninsula, but it is never very heavy.

In East Malaysia, March and June are the best times to visit the interior, the worst rains are usually from November to February and some roads are impassable in these months. Conversely, in the dry season, some rivers become unnavigable. In recent years the onset of the wet and dry seasons in both Sabah and Sarawak has become less predictable; environmentalists ascribe this to deforestation and/or global warming, although there is no scientifically proven link. For more information on climate, see page 517.

Festivals and events

Note that school holidays run from mid- to late February, mid-May to early June, mid- to late August and late November to early January. During these periods it is advisable to book hotels. Room rates also increase significantly during these holiday periods. Finally, during Ramadan (see Festivals, page 52) travel can be more difficult and many restaurants close during daylight hours, especially in the east coast states of Kelantan and Terengganu. After dusk many Muslims break their fast at stalls which do a roaring trade, although generally Ramadan is not a period when Muslims eat out, but instead dine at home.

Tour operators

UK

Audley Travel, 6 Willows Gate, Stratton Audley, Oxfordshire, OX27 9AU. T01869 276200, www.audleytravel.com

Eastern Oriental Express, Sea Containers House, 20 Upper Ground, London, SE1 9PF, T0207-8055100, www.orient-express trains.com Offices worldwide. Operates luxury train trips between Thailand, Malaysia and Singapore.

Exodus, Grange Mills, Weir Rd, London, SW12 ONE, T020-8675550, www.exodus.co.uk
Wide range of trips in Southeast Asia including Malaysia. The Borneo Explorer tour includes river journeys and the caves at the Niah National Park.

Explore Worldwide, 1 Frederick Street, Aldershot, Hampshire, GU11 1LQ, T01252-760100, www.explore.co.uk

Arranges small group tours (average 16 people) with any different types of trip offered including cultural excursions, adventure holidays and natural history tours.
Kuoni Travel, Kuoni House, Dorking, Surrey, T01306-747002, www.kuoni.co.uk Consistently high-quality service tour operator which organises trips all over Southeast Asia.
Magic of the Orient, 2 Kingsland Court, Three Bridges Road, Crawley, West Sussex, RH10 1HL, T01293 537700, www.magic-of-the-orient.com Specialists in tailor-made tours to Asia.
realworld-travel, The Foundry, 156 Blackfriars Road, London, SE1 8E, T0870 7364757, http://www.4real.co.uk/ Everything from self-drive tours, to beaches and rainforest treks.
Regaldive, 58 Lancaster Way, Ely, Cambridgeshire, CB6 3NW, T0870-2201777, www.regal-diving.co.uk, offers diving tours around Sipadan and Mabul islands on the south-east coast of Sabah.
Silk Steps, Deep Meadow, Edington, Bridgewater, TA7 9JH, T01278 722460, www.silksteps.co.uk Tours on the Peninsula and Borneo.
Trans Indus, Northumberland House, 11 The Pavement, Popes Lane, Ealing, London W5 4NG, T020-85662729, www.transindus.co.uk Specializes in tailor-made tours, covering Peninsular and East Malaysia.
Travel Mood, 214 Edgware Rd, London W2 1DH; 1 Brunswick Ct, Bridge St, Leeds, LS2 7QU; 16 Reform St, Dundee, DD1 1RG, T08705 001 002, www.travelmood.com 21 years' experience in tailor-made travel to the Far East and specialists in adventure and activity travel.

Malaysia

Borneo Eco Tours, Lot 1, Pusat Perindustrian, Kolombong Jaya, Mile 5.5, Jalan Kolombong 88450 Kota Kinabalu, Sabah, www.borneoecotours.com Specializing in environmentally aware tours.

Australia

Intrepid Travel, 11 Spring Street, Fitzroy, Victoria T1300-360887 www.intrepidtravel.com.au Australian company with agents all over the world. Dozens of different tours of Malaysia, including some that also take in neighbouring countries like Thailand.
Coulter-Goodall Tours, 115a Pt Cartwright Drive, Kawana Waters, Sunshine Coast, 4575 Australia, T1800-655 888 (toll free), http://www.cgtours.com/ Specializes in train tours and stopover trips to KL, Cameron Highlands and Penang.

Finding out more

Useful websites

www.aseansec.org Homepage of the Asean Secretariat, the Southeast Asian regional organization of which Singapore is a founder member. Lots of government statistics, acronyms etc.

www.asiainfo-by-cj.com A good and informative non-commercial website on Malaysia and other parts of Southeast Asia.

headlines.yahoo.com/full_coverage/world/malaysia/ An excellent news site for Malaysian current affairs.

www.journeymalaysia.com A great web resource that covers the majority of Malaysia's tourist sites in an entertaining and factual way. You can also book tours.

www.kiat.net A website set up by a young Malaysian with excellent material on things like Putrajaya, Cyberjaya, KLIA and transport systems in Malaysia.

www.malaysiamydestination.com The website for Tourism Malaysia.

www.sabahtravelguide.com A kick ass travel site with links to the official tourist board. There's interactive maps, tour agents, up-to-date descriptions of destinations, good travel advice and travel features.

www.sarawaktourism.com A newly spruced up site with heaps of information on the state. www.sabahtourism.com A nicely designed but hard to navigate site about Sabah by the state's tourism board.

www.virtualtourist.com A good website with content by other travellers. Put in your destination and find information on hotels, restaurants, things to see and even tourist traps and places to avoid.

Singapore

www.sg/ Links to homepage with good information on events, health, sports, business and more.

http://www.visitorsguide.com.sg/ A guide by the city state's yellow pages with tourist information and business contacts.

Tourist boards

Australia, Level 2, 171 Clarence St, Sydney, NSW 2000, T92994441, mtpb.sydney@tourism.gov.my; 56 William St, Perth, WA 6000, T9-894810400, mtpb.perth@tourism.gov.my

Canada, 1590-1111 W Georgia St, Vancouver, BC, V6 E4, T604-6898899, mtpb.vancouver@tourism.gov.my

France, 29 Rue des Pyramides, 75001 Paris, T331-42974171, mtpb.paris@tourism.gov.my

Germany, Rossmarkt 11 D, 60311 Frankfurt Am Main, T069-283782, mtpb.frankfurt@tourism.gov.my)

Hong Kong, Gd Flr, Malaysia Bldg, 47-50 Gloucester Rd, T2528-5810, mtpb.hongkong@tourism.gov.my

Italy, Via Triviata Della Passarella, No 4, 20122 Milan, T39-02796702.

Japan, 5F Chiyoda Bldg, 1-6-4 Yurakucho Chiyoda-ku, Tokyo 100, T3-3501 8691, mtpb.tokyo@tourism.gov.my; 10th Flr, Cotton Nissay Bldg, 1-8-2 Otsubo-Honmachi, Nishi-ku, Osaka 550-004, T6-444 1220, mtpb.osaka@tourism.gov.my

Singapore, #01-01B/C/D, 80 Robinson Rd, Singapore 068898, T2-5326321/5326351 mtpb.singapore@tourism.gov.my

South Africa, 1st floor, 5 Commerce Sq, 39 Rivonia Rd, Sandhurst, T2711 2680292 mtpb.johannesburg@tourism.gov.my

Sweden, Klarabergsgatan 35, 2tr Box 131, 10122 Stockholm, T46-8-24 99 00 mtpb.stockholm@tourism.gov.my

UK, 57 Trafalgar Square, London, WC2N 5DU, T020-79307932. mtpb.london@tourism.gov.my

USA, 818 Suite 804, West Seventh St, Los Angeles, CA 90017, T213 6899702, mtpb.la@tourism.gov.my; 120 East 56th Street, Suite 810, New York 10022, T001212 754 - 1113/1114/1115/1117 mtpb.ny@tourism.gov.my

Language

Bahasa Melayu (the Malay language, normally just shortened to bahasa) is the national language. It is very similar to Bahasa Indonesia, which evolved from Malay, and can be understood in southern Thailand, throughout Borneo and as far afield as the Moro areas of the southern Philippines. All communities, Malay, Chinese and Indian, as well as tribal groups in Sabah and Sarawak, speak Malay, as most are schooled in the Malay medium. Nearly everyone in Malaysia speaks some English, except in remoter rural areas, although the standard of English declined markedly during the 1980s and 1990s. Realizing this, and because of the general acceptance that good English is essential for business, the government sought to reverse the decline starting from the mid-1990s. The other main languages spoken in Malaysia include the Chinese dialects of Mandarin, Cantonese and Hokkien as well as the Indian languages of Tamil and Punjabi.

For those wanting to get a better grasp of the language, it is possible to take courses in KL (enquire at Tourism Malaysia offices) and other big cities. The best way to take a crash course in Malay is to buy a 'teach-yourself' book; there are several on the market, but one of the best ones is *Everyday Malay*, by Thomas G Oey (Periplus Language Books, 1995), which is widely available. A Malay/English dictionary or phrase book is a useful companion too; these are also readily available in bookshops.

Basic grammar and vowels

Basic grammar is very simple: there are no tenses, genders or articles and the structure of sentences is straightforward. Plurals are also easy: one man, for example is laki, men is laki-laki, often denoted as laki. Pronunciation is not difficult as there is a close relationship between the letter as it is written and the sound. Stress is usually placed on the second syllable of a word. For example restoran (restaurant) is pronounced res-TO-ran. For pronunciation of vowels and consonants: a is pronounced as ah in an open syllable, or as in but for a closed syllable; e is pronounced as in open or bed.; i is pronounced as in feel; o is pronounced as in all; u is pronounced as in foot. The letter c is pronounced as in ch as in change or chat. The r's are rolled.

Specialist travel

Disabled travellers

Disabled travellers are not well catered for in Malaysia (and this stands in contrast with the situation in Singapore (see page 536). Pavements are treacherous for those in wheelchairs, crossing roads is a hazard, and public transport is not well adapted for those with disabilities. This is surprising for a country which in so many other ways presents itself as cutting edge. But it is not impossible for disabled people to travel in Malaysia. For those who can afford to stay in the more expensive hotels, the assistance of hotel staff makes life a great deal easier, and there are also lifts and other amenities. And even those staying in budget accommodation will find that local people are helpful, sometimes heart-warmingly so.

Gay and lesbian travellers

Like Singapore (see page 536), Malaysia – officially at least – is not particularly accommodating of what might be regarded as alternative lifestyles and homosexuality remains a crime. (Bear in mind that even Malaysia's former deputy prime minister, Anwar Ibrahim, was charged with sodomy in 1999.) However there is a bubbling gay scene in KL and, to a lesser extent, in Johor Bahru, Melaka, KK, Kuching and Penang. There are two good websites for gay and lesbian travellers to the region: www.fridae.com has city listings, features on local gay and lesbian issues, an events page and a personals section with a search by region. There is also http://www.utopia-asia.com/tipsmala.htm The website's homepage states: "Gay life in Malaysia is blossoming. However, Muslims, both Malay and visitors, are subject to antiquated religious laws which punish gay or lesbian sexual activity with flogging and male transvestism with imprisonment. Police may arrest and harass any gay person (Muslim or non-Muslim) in a public place (ie cruise spots), so discretion is advised."

The Utopia website provides a listing of gay clubs, bars, discos and gyms in Malaysia (Johor Bahru, KL, KK, Kuching, Melaka and Penang) and also meeting spots for gays in those towns and cities. Other websites for gays in Malaysia http://members.tripod.com/gaycapitalkl/ for KL and http://www.geocities.com/swkgayscene/ for Sarawak.

Student travellers

Anyone in full-time education is entitled to an International Student Identity Card (ISIC). These are issued by student travel offices and travel agencies across the world and offer special rates on all forms of transport and other concessions and services. The ISIC head office is: **ISIC Association**, Box 9048, 1000 Copenhagen, Denmark, T45-33939303.

Students can benefit from discounts on some entrance charges and special deals, for example, on trains (see page 30). However there is no institutionalised system of discounts for students.

Travelling with children

Travelling with children is a touch more difficult than in child-friendly Singapore, but nonetheless is an awful lot easier – and safer – than in most other so-called 'developing' countries. Food hygiene is good, bottled water is sold almost everywhere, public transport is cheap (including taxis) and ubiquitous, most museums and other attractions provide good discounts for children, powdered milk and baby food (as well as all the other baby/child paraphernalia) are widely sold, and high chairs are available in most restaurants (even coffee shops).

Many people are daunted by the prospect of taking a child to a 'developing' country, but Malaysia's level of development is high and if you are thinking of a place in the Asian tropics to travel with your child then Malaysia – and particularly the Peninsula – is one of the easiest and safest bets. Naturally, it is not something to be taken on lightly; travelling is slower and more expensive and there are additional health risks for the child or baby. But it can be a most rewarding experience. Children are excellent passports into a local culture. You will also receive the best service, and help from officials and members of the public when in difficulty.

! Most western baby products are now available in Malaysia.

Children in Malaysia are given 24-hour attention by parents, grandparents and siblings. They are rarely left to cry and are carried for most of the first 8 months of their lives since crawling is considered animal-like. A non-Asian child is still something of a novelty and parents may find their child frequently taken off their hands, even mobbed in more remote areas. This can either be a great relief (at mealtimes, for instance) or most alarming. Some children love the attention, others react against it; it is best simply to gauge your own child's reactions.

Disposable nappies can be bought in most towns in Malaysia but can be expensive. If you are staying any length of time in one place, it may be worth taking Terry's (cloth) nappies. All you need is a bucket and some double-strength nappy cleanse (simply soak and rinse). Cotton nappies dry quickly in the heat and are generally more comfortable for the baby or child.

The advice given in the health section on food and drink should be applied even more stringently where young children are concerned. Be aware that expensive hotels may have squalid cooking conditions; the cheapest street stall can be more hygienic. Where possible, try to watch the food being prepared. Stir-fried vegetables and rice or noodles are the best bet; meat and fish may be pre-cooked and then could be left out before being re-heated. Various fruits can be bought very cheaply right across

Southeast Asia: papaya, banana and avocado are all excellent sources of nutrition, and can be self-peeled ensuring cleanliness. Powdered milk is also available throughout Malaysia, although most brands have added sugar. But if taking a baby, breast feeding is strongly recommended. Powdered food can be bought in most towns; the quality may not be the same as equivalent foods bought in the West, but it is perfectly adequate for short periods. Bottled water and fizzy drinks are also sold widely. If your child is at the 'grab everything and put it in mouth' stage, a damp cloth and some Dettol (or equivalent) are useful. Frequent wiping of hands and tabletops can help to minimize the chance of infection.

At the hottest time of year, air conditioning may be essential for a baby or young child's comfort when sleeping. This rules out many of the cheaper hotels, but air conditioned accommodation is available in all but the most out-of-the-way spots. Guesthouses probably won't have cots, so it is worth bringing a travel cot, but more expensive hotels should be able to provide them (but it is worth emailing or phoning to check). When the child is bathing, be aware that the water could carry parasites, so avoid letting him or her drink it.

Public transport may be a problem; trains are fine but long bus journeys are restrictive and uncomfortable. Hiring a car is undoubtedly the most convenient way to see a country with a small child. Back-seatbelts are fitted in more recent models and it is possible to buy child-seats in capital cities and rent them from larger car hire outfits.

Checklist Baby wipes; child paracetamol; disinfectant; first aid kit; flannel; immersion element for boiling water; Kalvol and/or Snuffle Babe or equivalent for colds; instant food for under-one-year-olds; mug/bottle/bowl/spoons; nappy cleanse, double-strength; ORS/ORT (Oral Rehydration Salts or Therapy) such as Dioralyte, widely available in the countries covered here, and the most effective way to alleviate diarrhoea (it is not a cure); portable baby chair, to hook onto tables – not essential but can be very useful; sarong or backpack for carrying child (and/or light weight collapsible buggy); sterilizing tablets (and an old baby-wipes container for sterilizing bottles, teats, utensils); cream for nappy rash and other skin complaints such as Sudocreme; sunblock, factor 15 or higher; sunhat; Terry's (cloth) nappies, liners, pins and plastic pants; thermometer; zip-lock bags for carrying snacks, powdered food; wet flannel.

Women travellers

Women – if not accompanied by men – usually attract unwarranted attention, particularly in more Islamic areas, such as the east coast

Most male attention is bravado and there have been few serious incidents involving foreign female tourists (or male, for that matter). However women should be sensitive to the fact that Malaysia is a predominantly Muslim country. In the east coast states of Kelantan and Terengganu particularly, women should dress appropriately, avoiding short skirts and singlets. In beach resorts clothing conventions are more relaxed but topless bathing, is beyond the pale as far as most Malaysians are concerned. If swimming outside beach resort areas bear in mind that Malay women usually bathe fully clothed so stripping off and running like a gazelle into the sea with nothing more than a bikini may raise one or two eyebrows.

When travelling it is best to keep to public transport and to travel during the day. Hitching is not advisable for women travelling on their own.

Working in the country

For a website listing jobs and working opportunities in Malaysia, as well as tips (and links) for anyone thinking of working there, see www.escapeartist.com/Malaysia/Malaysia.html The Malaysian government recently began an incentive programme for foreigners to move or retire to the country called, Malaysia: My Second Home. This scheme offers a renewable five year multiple entry visa called a social visit pass. The catch is you need to have RM150,000 banked in Malaysia and a minimum of RM7,000 monthly income. If you are retired you only need one of these. Apply through Malaysian embassies or Tourism Malaysia offices.

The Ministry of Human Resources (MOHR) provides the official view of labour law and practice in Malaysia, details of which can be found on its website, www.mohr.gov.my/

Before you travel

Visas and immigration

No visa is required for a stay of up to three months (provided it is not for the purpose of working) for many countries including the United Kingdom, the United States, Australia, New Zealand, Canada, Ireland and the majority of European countries. If you intend to stay longer, two-month extensions are usually easy to get from immigration offices in KL, Penang or JB. Note that Israeli passport holders are not allowed to enter Malaysia.

Visit passes issued for entry into Peninsular Malaysia are not automatically valid for entry into the East Malaysian states of Sabah and Sarawak. On entry into East Malaysia from Peninsular Malaysia visitors have to go through immigration even though the flight is an internal one. You get a new stamp in your passport and this is usually one month. If you want more, then you must ask the official. (The reason for this odd state of affairs is that Sabah and Sarawak maintain control over immigration and even Malaysian visitors from the 'mainland' are required to obtain a travel permit to come here.) Apply to the immigration offices in Kota Kinabalu and Kuching for a one-month extension; two extensions are usually granted with little fuss. There are certain areas where permits are necessary in East Malaysia – for example for Bario and the Kelabit Highlands in Sarawak; permits are obtained from the residents' offices (see appropriate sections).

Embassies and consulates

Australia, High Commission, 7 Perth Ave, Yarralumla, Canberra, ACT 2600, T06-2731543.
Austria, Prinz Eugenstrasse 18, A-1040 Vienna, T5051042.
Belgium, 414A, Ave de Tervuren, 1150 Brussels, T32-2-7760340.
Brunei, 61, Simpang 336, Jalan Kebangsaan BA 1211 kg. Sungai Akar, PO Box 2826, Bandar Seri Begawan BS8675, Negara Brunei Darussalam, T673-2381095.
Canada, High Commission, 60 Boteler St, Ottawa, Ontario KN 8Y7, T613-241-5182.
France, 2 Bis Rue Benouville, Paris, T45531185.
Germany, Klingelhoefer St 6, D-10785 Berlin, T30-885749-0
Italy, Via Nomentana 297 00162, Rome, T8415764
Japan, 20-16, Nanpeidai-Machi, Shibuya-ku, Tokyo 150, T34763840
Netherlands, Rustenburweg 2, 2517 KE The Hague, T070-3506506
New Zealand, High Commission, 10 Washington Ave, Brooklyn, Wellington, T852439
Singapore, PO Box 9422
Spain, Paseo de La Castellano 91-50, Centro 23, 28046 Madrid, T34-915550684
Sweden, Karlavagen 37, PO Box 26053, 10041 Stockholm, T46-8-7917960.
Switzerland, Jungfranstrasse 1, CH-3005 Berne, T41-0313504700.
UK, High Commission, 45, Belgrave Square, London SW1X 8QT, T020-72358033.
USA, 3516 International Court, NW, Washington DC 20008, USA, T202-572 9700.

Customs

Duty-free allowance 200 cigarettes, 50 cigars or 250 g of tobacco and one litre of liquor or wine. Cameras, watches, pens, lighters, cosmetics, perfumes and portable radio/cassette players are also duty-free in Malaysia. Visitors bringing in dutiable goods such as video equipment may have to pay a refundable deposit for temporary importation. It is advisable to carry receipt of purchases to avoid this problem.

Export restrictions Export permits are required for arms, ammunition, explosives, animals and plants, gold, platinum, precious stones and jewellery (except reasonable personal effects), poisons, drugs, motor vehicles. Unlike Singapore, export permits are also required for antiques (from the Director General of Museums, Muzium Negara, Kuala Lumpur).

Vaccinations

A certificate of vaccination for yellow fever is necessary for those coming from endemic zones except for children under one year of age. See also page 61.

What to take

Travellers usually take too much. Almost everything is available in the main towns and cities – and often at a lower price than in western countries. Remoter areas are inevitably less well supplied.

In terms of clothing, dress in Malaysia (and, but to a lesser extent, Singapore) is relatively casual – even at formal functions. Suits are not necessary except in a few of the most expensive restaurants. However, although formal attire may be the exception, dressing tidily is the norm. Women particularly should note that in many areas of Malaysia, they should avoid offending Muslim sensibilities and dress 'demurely' (ie keep shoulders covered and wear below-knee skirts or trousers). This is particularly true on the east coast of the Peninsula, especially in Kelantan, but does not generally apply in most beach resorts.

There is a tendency, rather than to take inappropriate articles of clothing, to take too many of the same article. Laundry services are cheap, and the turn-around rapid.

The following lists provide an idea of what to take with you on a trip to Malaysia: Bumbag, first aid kit, insect repellent, international driving licence, passports (valid for at least 6 months), photocopies of essential documents, spare passport photographs, sun protection, sunglasses, Swiss Army knife, torch, umbrella, phrase book. Those intending to stay in budget accommodation might also include: cotton sheet sleeping bag, money belt, padlock (for room and pack), soap, student card, towel, travel wash.

For women travellers: a supply of tampons (although these are available in most towns), a wedding ring for single female travellers who might want to help ward off the attentions of amorous admirers.

There is a good smattering of camping grounds in Malaysia, both in Peninsular Malaysia and in Sabah and Sarawak. If intending to camp, then all the usual equipment is necessary: a tent, stove, cooking utensils, sleeping bag etc.

Money

Currency

The unit of currency is the Malaysian dollar, or ringgit (RM), which is divided into 100 cents, or sen. Bank notes come in denominations of RM1, 5, 10, 20, 50, 100, 500 and 1,000. Coins are issued in 1, 5, 10, 20 and 50 sen. The ringgit is one of the world's few currencies still pegged to the US$ at a rate of RM3.80 = US$1. This has been the case since 1998. For the latest exchange rates check www.oanda.com/convert/classic

Credit cards

Most of the bigger hotels, restaurants and shops accept international credit cards, including American Express, BankAmericard, Diners, MasterCard and Visa. Visa and MasterCard are the most widely accepted. Cash advances can be issued against credit cards in most banks, although some banks – notably Bank Bumiputra – limit the amount that can be drawn. A passport is usually required for over-the-counter transactions. It is also possible to draw cash from ATMs (Automatic Teller Machines) if you have a PIN number (Personal Identification Number). Maybank, with branches in most towns, will accept both Visa and MasterCard at its ATMs. Cards with the Cirrus mark will also be accepted at most banks' ATMs.

Traveller's cheques

These can be exchanged at banks and money changers and in some big hotels (often guests only). Money changers often offer the best rates, but it is worth shopping around. Banks charge commission on travellers' cheques. Those from all major issuing companies and denominated in just about any major currency are widely accepted. But, as elsewhere, US dollars are probably best. With the very wide availability of ATMs increasing numbers of visitors are finding that there is no need to arrive with travellers' cheques.

Cost of living

While there is certainly a wealthy middle class emerging in KL - you'll see that many people own their own cars for instance - poverty is still endemic in rural Malaysia, particularly in Kelantan, Terengganu, Kedah and Perlis, where many families struggle on less than RM510 a month. Even so, most surveys have found the poverty gap narrowing with the improving economy. For professionals, salaries are lower than their Singapore peers, but considerably more than their Indonesian compatriots. A doctor will earn around RM4,000 a month, with a teacher a little less than RM2,000.

Cost of travelling

Prices have been relatively stable and because the ringgit has been held down at a lower-than-market exchange rate tied to the ever-plummeting US$, Malaysia is relatively cheap for the overseas visitor. A slump in the tourist industry sparked by 'international terrorism' and the fear of bird flu and Sars has meant hotels and restaurants have kept their prices down.

Having said all this, Malaysia was no longer a cheap place to live even before a recession of 1998 and people wanting to stay in accommodation other than that pitched at the pocket of the budget traveller will find the country more expensive than neighbouring Thailand and Indonesia.

It is still possible to travel on a relatively tight budget, and getting by on US$15-20 (RM60-80) per day – including accommodation, meals and transport – is certainly possible if you stay in the bottom end guesthouses, eat at stalls or in hawker centres, and travel on public transport. Cheaper guesthouses charge around RM20-40 a night for two – which translates into a US dollar figure of about US$5-10. Dorm beds are less common these days, but are available in big towns for around RM10-20, or US$3. It is usually possible to find a simple a/c room for RM40-80 or US$10-20. A room in a top quality, international class hotel will cost RM300-500 or US$80-130, and in a tourist class hotel (with a/c, room service, restaurant and probably a swimming pool), RM100-150 or US$26-40. Eating out is also comparatively cheap: a good curry can be had for as little as RM2-4 (US$0.50-1). Finally, overland travel is a bargain. Although private car ownership is rapidly spreading, many ordinary Malaysians still travel by bus and consequently the bus network is not only extremely good, but fares are very good value.

Getting there

Air

Kuala Lumpur International Airport (KLIA) is at Sepang, 72 km from the city, see page 115. Some international flights go direct to Penang, Langkawi, Kota Kinabalu and Kuching. Smaller airlines also run services between Singapore and island resorts such as Langkawi and Pulau Tioman. Around 40 international carriers serve KL. See Getting around for the Discover Malaysia Airpass.

From Europe The approximate flying time from **London** to KL (non-stop) is 12½ hours. From London Heathrow, *Malaysia Airlines (MAS)*, *Virgin* and *Garuda Indonesia* (the latter two in a codeshare) offer the only direct service. MAS also flies a non-stop connection to KL from **Manchester**. MAS have non-stop services from **Amsterdam, Frankfurt, Paris, Rome, Vienna** and **Zurich**. From **Amsterdam:** *MAS KLM, Northwest Airlines* and *Air France*. From **Frankfurt:** *MASLufthansa* and *Garuda Indonesia*. You can fly from **Zurich** with *MAS* and *Swiss Air*. From **Paris:** *MAS* and *Garuda Indonesia*. From other cities a change of plane is often necessary en route.

From the USA and Canada Approximate flying time from **Los Angeles** International Airport (LAX) is 20 hours. *MAS* flies from LA via Tokyo and Canada.

From Australasia You can fly direct from **Sydney, Melbourne, Brisbane, Darwin, Cairns** and **Perth** (flight times range between five and nine hours), with *MAS, Virgin Atlantic* and *Austrian Airlines*. *MAS* also flies from **Auckland**.

From South and Southeast Asia From **Delhi (India)**, *MAS* and *Air India* fly to KL. *Air Lanka* flys from **Colombo,** while *Biman Bangladesh Airlines* flies from **Dhaka (Bangladesh)**. *Pakistan International Airlines* and *MAS* fly from **Karachi**. Flights via other cities available from Male and Kathmandu. There are flights to KL from all regional capitals in Southeast Asia. *AirAsia* has flights connecting KL with **Singapore, Jakarta** and **Bangkok** and also Bangkok with KK in Sabah. *Bangkok Airways* will fly from June 2005 from Koh Samui to KL and Singapore.

There are numerous flights on many airlines from **Hong Kong, Manila** and **Tokyo.** Flights between **Singapore** and Malaysia cost the same US dollar amount whether bought in Malaysia or Singapore – so it saves money buying a return ticket in Malaysia.

Flight agents

Australia and New Zealand

Flight Centres, 82 Elizabeth St, Sydney, T13-1600; 205 Queen St, Auckland, T09-309 6171. Also branches in other places.

STA Travel, T1300-360960, www.statravelaus.com.au; 702 Harris St, Ultimo, Sydney, and 256 Flinders St, Melbourne. In NZ: 10 High St, Auckland, T09-366 6673. Also in major towns and university campuses.

Travel.com.au, 80 Clarence St, Sydney, T02-929 01500.

UK and Ireland

Council Travel, 28a Poland St, London, W1V 3DB, T020-74377767, www.destinations-group.com

STA Travel, 86 Old Brompton Rd, London, SW7 3LH, T020-74376262, www.statravel.co.uk Other branches across the UK. Specialists in low-cost student/youth flights

and tours, student IDs and insurance.
Trailfinders, 194 Kensington High Street, London, W8 7RG, T020-79383939.

North America

Air Brokers International, 323 Geary St, Suite 411, San Francisco, CA94102, T01-800-883 3273, www.airbrokers.com Consolidator and specialist on RTW and Circle Pacific tickets.
Council Travel, 205 E 42nd St, New York, NY 10017, T1-888-COUNCIL, www.counciltravel.com Student/budget agency with branches in many other US cities.
Discount Airfares Worldwide On-Line, www.etn.nl/discount.htm A hub of consolidator and discount agent links.
International Travel Network/Airlines of the Web, www.itn.net/airlines Online air travel information and reservations.
STA Travel, 5900 Wilshire Blvd, Suite 2110, Los Angeles, CA 90036, T1-800-777 0112, www.sta-travel.com Branches across US.
Travel CUTS, 187 College St, Toronto, ON, M5T 1P7, T1-800-667 2887, www.travelcuts.com Specialist in student discount fares, Ids and other travel services. Branches in other Canadian cities.
Travelocity, www.travelocity.com Online consolidator.

Southeast Asia

Bangkok Airways, Singapore Office, Passenger Terminal Building 1, #041-04F Singapore 819642, T65-6545 8481, bangkokairways@pacific.net.sg, www.bangkokair.com An office is due to open in KL also.

Rail

Keretapi Tanah Melayu (KTM), www.ktmb.com.my, runs express trains daily between Singapore and the major cities on the west coast of Malaysia. There is a daily express train between Bangkok (Thailand) and Butterworth. This connects with the KL service, and from KL onwards to Singapore. Another railway line runs from Gemas (halfway between KL and Johor Bahru) to Kota Bharu, on the northeast coast.

The most luxurious way to travel by train to Malaysia is aboard the **Eastern & Oriental (E&O) Express**. For information call Bangkok T2514862; London T020-79286000; USA T800- 5242420; and Singapore T065-2272068. This a/c train consisting of 22 carriages, including a salon car, dining car, bar and observation deck, and carrying just 132 passengers, runs once a week from Singapore to Bangkok and back. Luxurious carriages, fine wines and food designed for European rather than Asian sensibilities make this not just a mode of transport but an experience. The journey takes 43 hours with stops in Kuala Lumpur, Butterworth and Padang Besar. But such luxury is expensive.

Road

It is possible to travel to and from Malaysia by bus or share-taxi from Thailand and Singapore. Direct buses and taxis are much easier than the local alternatives which stop at the borders. Singapore is six hours by taxi from KL (via Johor Bahru) and about seven hours by bus (see page 116). Taxi fares are approximately double bus fares. There are direct buses and taxis to destinations in Thailand from most major towns in northern Malaysia (see relevant sections) and six border crossing points. For those using the north-south highway – which is most people – the crossing point is at Bukit Kayu Hitam, which links up with the Thai city of Hat Yai. On the western side of the Peninsula there are also crossings at Wang Kelian and Padang Besar. The Wang Kelian crossing (to Satun in Thailand) is convenient if driving oneself; it is quiet and usually pretty rapid. The Padang Besar crossing is easy on foot and makes sense if travelling to or from Pulau Langkawi. In Perak the crossing is at Pengkalan Hulu, and in Kelantan, on the eastern side of the Peninsula there are two more crossing points, the more important at Pengkalan Kubar, and the second from Kota Bahru to Rantau Panjang/Sungai Golok (see page 296). The more popular of these is the Rantau Panjang crossing; few people cross at Pengkalan Kubar. Note that the Thai provinces here were suffering from serious separatist violence in 2004 with bombings and shootings occurring daily, with a death toll in the hundreds. Check the situation if you intend to cross the border at this point. Local buses and taxis terminate at the border crossing points, but there are regular connections to towns and cities from each side.

It is also possible to cross overland from the East Malaysian states of Sarawak and Sabah to Kalimantan (Indonesian Borneo) and Brunei. The main crossing point is in the west, between Kuching in Sarawak and Pontianak in Kalimantan and regular buses run between these two towns.

Sea

Most passenger ships and cruise liners run between Port Klang, west of KL, Georgetown (Penang), Singapore, Kuantan, Kuching and Kota Kinabalu. **Feri Malaysia** connects these Malaysian ports and Singapore. Deluxe cabins are available. Schedules change annually; contact Tourism Malaysia for bookings, see page 32.

There are also regular ferry services from Melaka to Dumai in Sumatra and from Georgetown (Penang) to Medan, also in Sumatra (see relevant sections). Passenger boats connect Langkawi Island with Satun in South Thailand (see page 179). Small boats run between Johor state and Singapore's Changi Point. In East Malaysia, there are connections between Tawau and Tarakan via Nunukan. There is also a regular ferry service between Sandakan in Sabah and Zamboanga in the southern Philippines.

Touching down

Airport information

The new Kuala Lumpur International Airport (KLIA) is at Sepang, 72 km from the city. Glitzy and high-tech, reflecting Malaysia's 2020 vision, it has loads of restaurants, shops, banks and such like. A helpful Tourism Malaysia desk dishes out lots of pamphlets on KL and beyond. The KLIA website is //www.klia.com.my/ The old airport at Subang (sounding confusingly similar to Sepang), 24 km southwest of KL, is now closed, but discussion is underway to open it as a budget airline airport. For details of other international airports, such as Penang, Kota Kinabalu and Kuching, see the relevant regional chapters.

Public buses to KL are available one floor down from the arrivals concourse. From KLIA express coaches operate every 30 minutes to hotels in KL, RM25 one-way. From KLIA the first coach leaves at 0500 and the last departure at 2230. The journey takes around 1 hour. The coach first goes to Hentian Duta bus station, and then passengers change to a shuttle bus for hotel connection. Take the clearly marked signs from the arrivals hall.

The **KLIA Ekspres** train runs from 0500 until midnight between the airport and KL Sentral train station in the centre of the city. From here you will need to take a taxi to your hotel. The non-stop journey takes around half hour and there's a train at least every 20 minutes (35RM one way). Alternatively you can take the KLIA transit which takes around 35 minutes to make the same journey, but still costs RM35. It stops at three intermediate stations and leaves between 0550 and 0100.

Arriving at night

KL's international airport (www.klia.com) is about 70 km from the city centre. While arriving late at night does make things a little more difficult it is nothing to get worried about. The airport is safe, well run and has plenty of facilities.

But the KLIA Exspres train to the city centre only runs between 0500 and 2400, with public buses to KL shuttling between 0530 and 2230 daily. If you arrive outside these hours you will have to either take a taxi or limo into KL or hire a car – most major rental companies have counters open 24 hours. Budget taxis run on a coupon system - after midnight a homegrown proton taxi to the centre will cost RM86.10. The taxi/limo counter is in the arrivals hall near door 3.

Alternatively, opt to spend the time recuperating from your flight. The **Airside Transit Hotel**, T3-87874848, airsidehotel@klia.com.my is situated within the airport at satellite A. The 80 rooms are comfortable and there are also fitness and business centres, a bar and café. **Concorde Inn Hotel**, T3-87833118; 5 mins from the airport, complementary shuttle bus available, with 420 rooms, swimming pool and more. Top of the pile is the stylish **Pan Pacific Hotel**, T3-87873333, http://klairpport.panpacific.com, which is next to the airport's control tower with more than 400 rooms, plenty of good sports facilities, some restaurants and even more besides.

For a **taxi** expect to pay around RM60-80. They operate on a coupon system; make sure you pick up one from the taxi counter at the exit in arrivals; touts charge more than double the official rate. Many hotels provide a pick-up service, but make sure they are aware of your arrival details; there is a hotel pick-up office just outside the terminal exit. Major car rental companies have desks in the arrivals concourse.

Airport tax

Airport departure tax is RM10 for domestic flights, and RM45 for international, but these are almost always included in the ticket price.

Tourist information

Tourism Malaysia (headquarters), 17th Flr, Menara Dato' Onn, Putra World Trade Centre, 45, Jln Tun Ismail, 50480 Kuala Lumpur T3-26158188, www.tourismmalaysia.giv.my. There is an information centre on Level two of the Putra World Trade Centre (in the convention centre). For practical advice, visitors are better advised to contact the Malaysia Tourism Centre (MTC), 109 Jln Ampang, Kuala Lumpur T3-21633664. There are several other tourist information bureaux in KL (see page 73) and regional tourism offices in state capitals, all of which are reasonably efficient.

Tourism Malaysia has a tourist information bureau in most large towns; it is very efficient and can supply further details on tourist sights, advise on itineraries, help place bookings for travel and cultural events and provide updated information on hotels, restaurants and air, road, rail, sea and river transport timetables and prices. If there is no Tourism Malaysia office in a town, travel agents are usually helpful and the best place to head for.

Touching down

Emergencies Ambulance, police or fire, T999.

Business hours Banks For Kelantan and Terengganu banks are open 0930-1130 on Thu, closed Fri. Government offices: 0800-1245, 1400-1615 Mon-Thu, 0800-1200, 1430-1615 Fri, 0800-1245 Sat. Note that offices and banks are shut on the first and third Sat of every month. In the states of Kedah and Terengganu, 0800-1615 Sat-Wed, 0800-1245 Thu, closed Fri. In Kelantan 0800-1645 Sun-Wed, 0800-1245 Thu, closed Fri and Sat. For Kelantan and Tergengganu, banks and offices are also closed on the first and third Thu of every month. Shops: 0930-1900, supermarkets and department stores 1000-2200.

Official time Eight hours ahead of GMT.

Voltage 220-240 volts, 50 cycle AC. Some hotels supply adaptors.

Weights and measures Metric, although road distances are marked in both kilometres and miles.

Local customs and laws

Dress

Malaysians dress for the heat. Clothes are light, cool and casual most of the time, but also fairly smart. Some establishments, mainly exclusive restaurants, require a long-sleeved shirt with tie or local batik shirt and do not allow shorts in the evening.

Those visiting the Cameron Highlands or other upland areas are advised to take a light sweater. For jungle treks, a waterproof is advisable, as are canvas jungle boots, which dry faster than leather. Although many Malaysian business people have adopted the Western jacket and tie for formal occasions, the batik shirt, or baju, is the traditional formal wear for men, while women wear the graceful sarung kebaya.

Malaysians dress smartly, particularly in cities; tourists in vests, shorts and flip-flops look out of place in modern cosmopolitan KL. Dress codes are important to observe from the point of view of Islamic sensitivities, particularly on the Peninsula's east coast. In some places such as Marang, bikinis are banned and wearing them will cause great offence. Topless bathing is completely taboo in Malaysia; this should be remembered even if you see other tourists stripping off. Dress modestly out of respect for Muslim tradition.

Malaysia's cross-cultural differences are most apparent on the streets: many Chinese girls think nothing of wearing brief mini-skirts and shorts, while their Malay counterparts are clad from head to toe. The tudung (or telukung) veil signifies adherence to the puritanical lifestyle of the fervently Islamic dakwah movement; during the 1980s, this almost became a fashion among women at universities as well as among blue-collar workers in factories. Some women dressed in the full black purdah until it was forbidden by the government. Much of this was the result of peer pressure and reflected a revival of strict Islamic values in Malaysia during and after the 1970s.

Conduct

As elsewhere in Southeast Asia, in Malaysia 'losing face' brings shame. You lose face if you lose your temper, and even in a situation like bargaining, using a loud voice or wild gesticulations will be taken to signify anger. By the same token, the person you shout at will also feel loss of face too, particularly if it happens in public. It should also

Malaysian manners - as learned from a princess

In Malaysia's multi-ethnic melting pot, Malays, Chinese, Indians, Eurasians and expatriates have discovered that cross-cultural etiquette and the art of obligiing another's sense of decorum is the essence of racial harmony. The trouble is that for many visitors, commiting a Malaysian-style faux pas is one of life's inevitabilities. Or, it was, until Datin Noor Aini Syed Amir published her practical handbook to Malaysian customs and etiquette in 1991.

As a Malay princess, Datin Noor - Malaysia's Miss Manners - should know. "While the Malays are very generous and forgiving with foreigners who make Malay faux pas, those who do not make such blunders will be highly admired and respected," the Datin said.

Her catch-all advice to visitors is to utter "a profuse apology in advance to the person you may offend." For those who forget to absolve themselves before the slip up, her social observations cover every conceivable situation *mat sellehs* - the local nickname for foreigners - might find themselves in.

When eating with chopsticks, warns Datin Noor, avoid crossing them and never stick them vertically into your ricebowl so they resemble joss sticks. Do not be offended by enthusiastic belches and slurps around the dinner table either: Malaysians live to eat and like to share their appreciation. Visitors mucy also learn to distinguish between flabby handshakes and Malay *salams*. "Unlike the western handshake, which is a rather vigorous up and down movement... the Malay handshake is a simple palm-to-palm touch," she writes. The most important part of the gesture is immediately touching your hand to your heart as a signal of sincerity. And, she adds "Never use your left hand in Malay company!"

Datin Noor goes onto warn newcomers not to touch people's heads, when to take their shoes off and to think before they kiss a lady's cheek - in greeting. Dazzling, long-sleeved batk shirts are what you wear to formal dinners and black is a taboo for happy occasions. She explains what Tunkus, Tuns, Datuks, Datos and Datins are and notes that the King's title 'Yang Di-Pertuan Agong' means He Who is Made Supreme Lord.'

Malaysian Customs & Etiquette A Practical Handbook by Datin Noor Aini Syed Amir. Times Books International, 1991.

be noted that in Muslim company it is impolite to touch others with the left hand and other objects – even loose change. Although men shake hands, for a man to shake a woman's hand is not the norm outside KL. Indeed excessive personal contact should be avoided: Malays, especially, do not tend to slap one another on the back!

A couple of other points of conduct should be remembered when in Malaysia. Using the index finger to point at people, even at objects, is regarded as insulting. The thumb or whole hand should be used to indicate something, or to wave down a taxi. Before entering a private home, remember to remove your shoes; it is also usual to take a small gift for the host.

Eating

When picking up and passing food, do not use the left hand in Muslim company. It is worth remembering that Malays do not make pork satay and that Hindus do not make beef curries. Chinese cooking on the other hand seems to incorporate almost anything.

Death for drug traffickers

Malaysia is well known around the world for its stringent laws against drugs. As they fill in their immigration forms, visitors cannot fail to notice the bold block capitals reading: "BE FOREWARNED – DEATH FOR DRUG TRAFFICKERS UNDER MALAYSIAN LAW". At entry points to Malaysia there are prominent posters repeating this warning, the words emblazoned over an ominous picture of a noose. World attention focuses on Malaysia whenever Westerners go to the gallows, but they represent a tiny fraction of those hanged for drug-trafficking offences. According to Amnesty International between 1970 and June 2001, 353 death sentences were carried out for drug crimes. One of Malaysia's biggest-ever mass-hanging of traffickers took place at Taiping jail in May 1990 when eight Hong Kong people were executed.

The Dadah Act - dadah is the Malay word for drugs – stipulates a mandatory death sentence upon conviction for anyone in possession of 15 or more grams of heroin or morphine, 200g of cannabis or hashish or 40g of cocaine. Those caught with more than 10g of heroin or 100g of cannabis are deemed to be traffickers and face lengthy jail sentences and flogging with a rotan cane.

Following the execution of two Australians in 1986, the then Australian Prime Minister, Bob Hawke, branded the Malaysian government 'barbaric'. A similar outcry resulted from the hanging of a Briton in 1987; the British opposition even called for a trade embargo of Malaysia. But former Malaysian Prime Minister Dr Mahathir Mohamad, who is a medical doctor and as such has taken the Hippocratic Oath, has consistently refused to bow to international pleas for clemency.

In a British television documentary in 1991, The prime minister, the junkie and the boys on death row, he said: "We have to carry out this death penalty because it would not be fair to those who had already been hanged and their families."

Tipping

Tipping is unusual in Malaysia, as a service charge of 10% is automatically added to restaurant and hotel bills, plus a 5% government tax (indicated by the + and ++ signs). Nor is tipping expected in smaller restaurants where a service charge is not automatically added to the bill. For personal services, porterage for example, a modest tip may be appropriate.

Prohibitions

The trafficking of illegal drugs into Malaysia carries the death penalty. While alcohol is not illegal in any part of Malaysia, be aware of Muslim sensibilities, particularly in the East Coast states of Kelantan and Terengganu.

Religion

Remove shoes before entering mosques and Hindu and Buddhist temples; in mosques, women should cover their heads, shoulders and legs and men should wear long trousers.

Responsible tourism

"Tourism is like fire. It can either cook your food or burn your house down". This sums up the ambivalent attitude that many people have regarding the effects of tourism. It is a major foreign exchange earner for Malaysia, and the world's largest single industry; yet many people in receiving countries would rather that tourists stayed home. Tourism is seen to be the cause of polluted beaches, rising prices, loose morals, consumerism, and much else besides.

Most international tourists come from a handful of wealthy countries. This is why many see tourism as the new 'imperialism', imposing alien cultures and ideals on sensitive and less modernized peoples. The problem, however, is that discussions of the effects of tourism tend to degenerate into simplifications – culminating in the drawing up of a checklist of 'positive' and 'negative' effects. Although such tables may be useful in highlighting problem areas, they also do a disservice by reducing a complex issue to a simple set of rather one dimensional 'costs' and 'benefits'. Different destinations will be affected in different ways; these effects are likely to vary over time; and different groups living in a particular destination will feel the effects of tourism in different ways and to varying degrees. At no time or place can tourism (or any other influence) be categorized as uniformly 'good' or 'bad'. Tourism can take a young Australian backpacker on US$10 a day to a guesthouse on the east coast of Peninsular Malaysia, a family to a luxury hotel in Penang where a room can cost over US$200 a night, or a young couple to the forests and longhouses of East Malaysia.

Some tourists are attracted to Malaysia, and particularly East Malaysia, because of its exotic 'tribal' peoples. When cultural erosion is identified, the tendency is to blame this on tourists and tourism who become the so-styled 'suntanned destroyers of culture'. The problem with views like this is that they assume that change is bad, and that indigenous cultures are unchanging. It makes local peoples victims of change, rather than masters of their own destinies. It also assumes that tourism is an external influence, when in fact it quickly becomes part of the local landscape. Cultural change is inevitable and on-going, and 'new' and 'traditional' are only judgements, not absolutes. Thus new cultural forms can quickly become key markers of tradition. Tourists searching for an 'authentic' experience are assuming that tradition is tangible, easily identifiable and unchanging. It is none of these.

Tourist art, both material (for instance, sculpture) and non-material (like dances) is another issue where views over the impacts of tourism sharply diverge. The mass of inferior 'airport' art on sale to tourists demonstrates, to some, the corrosive effects of tourism. It leads craftsmen and women to mass-produce second rate pieces for a market that appreciates neither their cultural or symbolic worth, nor their aesthetic value. Yet tourism can also give value to craft industries that would otherwise be undermined by cheap industrial goods. So, some people argue that the craft traditions of Kelantan and Teregganu, as well as those of Sabah and Sarawak have been given a new injection of vitality by the demands that tourism creates.

The environmental deterioration that is linked to tourism is due to a destination area exceeding its 'carrying capacity' as a result of overcrowding. But carrying capacity, though an attractive concept, is notoriously difficult to pin down. A second dilemma facing those trying to encourage greater environmental consciousness is the so-called 'tragedy of the commons', better described in terms of Chinese restaurants. When a group of people go to a Chinese restaurant with the intention of sharing the bill, each customer will tend to order a more expensive dish than he or she would normally do – on the logic that everyone will be doing the same, and the bill will be split. In tourism terms, it means that hotel owners will always build those few more bungalows or that extra wing, to maximize their profits, reassured in the

How big is your footprint?

- → Learn about the country you're visiting.
- → Start enjoying your travels before you leave by tapping into as many sources of information as you can.
- → Think about where your money goes – be fair and realistic about how cheaply you travel. Try and put money into local people's hands; drink local beer or fruit juice rather than imported brands and stay in locally-owned accommodation.
- → Open your mind to new cultures and traditions. It can transform your holiday experience and you'll earn respect and be more readily welcomed by local people.
- → Think about what happens to your rubbish - take biodegradable products and a water filter bottle. Be sensitive to limited resources like water, fuel and electricity.
- → Help preserve local wildlife and habitats by respecting rules and regulations, such as sticking to footpaths, not standing on coral and not buying products made from endangered plants or animals.
- → Use your guidebook as a starting point, not the only source of information. Talk to local people, then *discover your own adventure!*
- → Don't treat people as part of the landscape, they may not want their picture taken. Put yourself in their shoes, ask first and respect their wishes.
- → This is taken from the Tourism Concern website which also provides further elaboration of the points noted here. The code was developed from a Young Travellers' conference in April 2001 but is not aimed only at young travellers. As they say: "It applies to everybody who loves travelling, whether on a budget holiday or staying in a luxury community run centre".

knowledge that the environmental costs will be shared among all hotel owners. So, despite most operators appreciating that over-development may 'kill the goose that lays the golden eggs', they do so anyway. But many areas of Malaysia have few other development opportunities and those with beautiful landscapes and/or exotic cultures find it difficult not to resist the temptation to market them and attract the tourist dollar. And why shouldn't they?

One of the ironies is that the 'traveller' or 'backpacker' finds it difficult to consider him or herself as a tourist at all. This, of course, is hubris built upon the notion that the traveller is an 'independent' explorer somehow beyond the bounds of the industry. Anna Borzello in an article entitled 'The myth of the traveller' in the journal *Tourism in Focus* (no. 19, 1994) writes that, "Independent travellers cannot acknowledge – without shattering their self-image – that to many local people they are simply a good source of income ... [not] inheritors of Livingstone, [but] bearers of urgently needed money." Although she does, in writing this, grossly underestimate the ability of travellers to see beyond their thongs and friendship bracelets, she does have a point when she suggests that it is important for travellers honestly to appraise their role as tourists, because, "Not only are independent travellers often frustrated by the gap between the way they see themselves and the way they are treated, but unless they acknowledge that they are part of the tourist industry they will not take responsibility for the damaging effects of their tourism."

Pressure groups

Tourism Concern, a UK-based charity, works to resolve in a constructive manner some of the issues sketched out above. As they say on their website: "We look at the way tourism affects the people and environments in tourism destination areas. Tourism Concern raises awareness of tourism's impact with the general public, with government decision-makers and within the tourist industry itself – and we provide a unique information base for campaigners and students of tourism." It is possible to subscribe to their magazine, In Focus by writing to **Tourism Concern**, Stapleton House, 277-281 Holloway Road, London N7 8HN. Subscription rates vary between £12 and £25. Alternatively, visit their website: www.tourismconcern.org.uk

Safety

Normal precautions should be taken with passports and valuables such as cameras; many hotels have safes. Pickpocketing and bag snatching is a problem in some cities (particularly JB, KL and Penang).

Getting around

Transport around the East Malaysian states of Sabah and Sarawak is not as easy as it is on the Peninsula since there are fewer roads and some are not in a good state of repair. There are excellent coastal and upriver express boat services in Sarawak and the national airline, Malaysian Airlines (MAS), and AirAsia have an extensive network in both states; flying is relatively inexpensive.

Air

Non-Malaysian passport holders are eligible for the **Discover Malaysia Pass**, if they fly into (or out of) the country on *Malaysian Airlines* (MAS). The basic pass is US$199 for travel for up to a maximum of 5 flights within the country. The pass must be purchased within 14 days of arrival in Malaysia, and must be used up within 28 days. It offers significant savings on domestic air travel but obviously makes most sense on longer routings. Bear in mind that holders can only cross between Peninsular Malaysia and East Malaysia (Sabah/Sarawak) once (ie a return journey across the South China Sea).

MAS operates an extensive network of flights to domestic destinations. On the Peninsula *MAS* serves Alor Star, Ipoh, Johor Bahru, Kota Bahru, Kuala Lumpur, Kuala Terengganu, Kuantan, Langkawi and Penang. In Sabah *MAS*'s destinations are Kota Kinabalu, Kudat, Labuan, Lahad Datu, Sandakan, Semporna, Tawau and Tomanggong. And in Sarawak *MAS* flies to Bario, Belaga, Bintulu, Kuching, Lawas, Limbang, Long Banga, Long Lelang, Long Seridan, Marudi, Miri, Mukah, Mulu and Sibu. Local *MAS* offices are listed under each town; the head office is at Bangunan *MAS* (opposite Equatorial Hotel), Jln Sultan Ismail, 50250, Kuala Lumpur. For fares, see table. Domestic flights from KL leave either from the international airport, KLIA, 72 km from the city. Flights get very booked up on public holidays.

AirAsia flies to Alor Star, Bintulu, JB, KL, Kota Bharu, KK, Kuala Terengganu, Kuching, Labuan, Langkawi, Miri, Penang, Sandakan, Sibu and Tawau.

For details on fares and schedules see the airlines' websites: **MAS (www.malaysia-airlines.com.my)** and **AirAsia (www.airasia.com)**.

Guide to domestic Malaysian Airlines (MAS) air fares

Destination	One-way (RM)	Destination	One-way (RM)
JB-Ipoh via KL	241	KL-Kuching	262
JB-Kota Bharu via KL	295	KL-Langkawi	205
JB- Langkawi via KL	295	KL-Penang	158
JB-Penang via KL	270	KL-Sandakan	418
Kota Kinabalu-Bintulu	127	KL-Sibu	320
Kota Kinabalu-Johor Bahru	347	Kuantan-JB via KL	141
Kota Kinabalu-Kuching	228	Kuching-Bintulu	117
Kota Kinabalu-Penang via KL	541	Kuching-Johor Bahru	169
Kota Kinabalu-Sandakan	83	Kuching-Labuan	199
Kota Kinabalu-Sibu	180	Kuching-Lahad Datu via K Kinabalu	310
KL-Alor Setar	172	Kuching-Miri	164
KL-Ipoh	100	Kuching-Penang	340
KL-JB	141	Kuching-Sandakan via K Kinabalu	284
KL-Kota Bahru	158	Kuching-Sibu	72
KL-Kota Kinabalu	437	Kuching-Tawau via K Kinabalu	320
KL-Kuala Terengganu	158	Langkawi-Penang	77
KL-Kuantan	112		

Rail

In August 1992 the Peninsular Malaysian Railway System or Keretapi Tanah Melayu (KTM) was privatized and became the **Keretapi Tanah Melayu Berhad** (KTM). The KTM is an economical and comfortable way to travel round the Peninsula. Privatization has pumped much needed investment into the system. However, buses generally make the journey much faster than trains, many of which arrive at awkward times in the middle of the night.

There are two main lines. One runs up the west coast from Singapore, through KL, Ipoh and Butterworth, connecting with Thai railways at Padang Besar (where a half of the extra-long platform is managed by Malaysian officials and the other half by Thais) and from there continues to Hat Yai in Southern Thailand and north to Bangkok. The other line branches off from the west coast line at Gemas (halfway between KL and Singapore) and heads northeast to Kota Bahru. From Kota Bahru it is possible to take buses/taxis to Rantau Panjang/Sungai Golok for connections with Thai railways. (See page 296 for warning on travel to this area). The express service (Ekspres Rakyat or Ekspres Sinaran) only stops at major towns; the regular service stops at every station but is slightly cheaper. All first and second-class coaches have sleeping berths on overnight trains and all classes have a/c. Reservations can be made for both classes. Visitors should note that the a/c on Malaysian trains is very cold. First and second-class carriages are equipped with videos. In East Malaysia there is only one railway line, running from Kota Kinabalu to Tenom, via Beaufort (see page 416).

For KMT fares and schedules, T03-22671200. For booking and ticket delivery, T03-22671200 (0830-1700 Mon-Sat). www.ktmb.com.my See also train tables on page 40 and page 41

Wau Exspres timetable

KL-Tumpat-KL	XW/16 Dep ↓	XW/17 Arr ↑
KL Sentral	1955	0725
Kajang	2028	0652
Seremban	2114	0602
Tampin	2201	0510
Gemas	2307	0410
Bahau	2352	0306
Mentakab	0117	0120
Jerantut	0215	2359
Kuala Lipis	0317	2259
Gua Musang	0449	2129
Dabong	0556	2024
Krai	0654	1931
Tanah Merah	0725	1859
Pasir Mas	0753	1834
Wakaf Bharu (for Kota Bahru)	0811	1819
Tumpat	0829	1800

Timuran Exspres (jungle train) timetable

Singapore-Tumpat-Singapore	XST/14 Dep ↓	XST/15 Arr ↑
Singapore	2000	0905
Johor Bahru	2055	0755
Kulai	2123	0717
Kluang	2208	0631
Labis	2254	0541
Segamat	2318	0516
Gemas	0030	0453
Bahau	0117	0410
Triang	0207	0320
Mentakab	0241	0245
Kuala Krau	0309	0156
Jerantut	0337	0109
Kuala Lipis	0441	0010
Gua Musang	0618	2233
Dabong	0724	2126
Krai	0820	2031
Tanah Merah	0850	1959
Pasir Mas	0916	1934
Wakaf Bahru	0933	1919
Tumpat	0950	1900

Rail passes for 5, 10 and 35 days are available to all foreign visitors, except those from Singapore, for every class and there are no restrictions other than seat

Exspres KL-Singapore fares

	From KL 1st class/2nd class	From Singapore 1st class/ 2nd class
KL Sentral		S$68/34
Seremban	RM19/13	S$58/30
Tampin	RM27/17	S$50/27
Gemas	RM35/20	S$43/23
Segamat	RM38/21	S$38/21
Kluang	RM52/27	
Johor Bahru	RM64/33	
Singapore	RM8/34	

Tambang Exspres train fares

From KL Sentral to Hat Yai (Thailand)	1st class lower/upper berth	2nd class lower/upper berth
Hat Yai		46/43.50
Padang Besar	70/62	41/38.50
Alor Star	70/62	41/38.50
Sungai Petani	70/62	41/38.50
Butterworth	67/59	40/37.50
Bukit Mertajam	65/57	39/36.50
Parit Buntar	62/54	38/35.50
Taiping	53/45	34/31.50
Kuala Kangsar	49/41	32/29.50
Ipoh	40/32	28/25.50
Batu Gajah	38/30	27/24.50
Tapah Road	32/24	25/22.50

availability. Passes are available from railway stations in Singapore, KL, Johor Bahru, Butterworth, Padang Besar, Rantau Panjang, Wakaf Bahru (Kota Bahru). A 15-day pass costs US$70 (adult), US$35 (child); a 10 day pass, US$55 (adult), US$28 (child), and a 5 day pass, US$35 (adult), US$18 (child). There are also concessions offered (including for foreigners) to family groups (4 people or more), 25%; groups of 10 or more, 25%; handicapped persons, 50%; and senior citizens (65 years+), 50%. If travelling overnight, berth charges are RM70 (lower a/c), RM50 (upper a/c) for deluxe; and RM14 (lower a/c), RM11.50 (upper a/c) for second class. There are additional charges for international express services.

Road

Bus

Peninsular Malaysia has an excellent bus system with a network of public express buses and several privately-run services. A/c express buses (and VIP buses on the more popular routes) connect the major towns; seats can be reserved and prices are reasonable. Prices quoted are for a/c buses. The a/c on Malaysian buses is, as on the

Transnasional fares (except Kurnia Bistari for KL to Cameron Highlands)

Depart Kuala Lumpur	
Ipoh	RM11
Johor Bahru	RM20
Mersing	RM20
Kota Bharu	RM26
Kuala Terengganu	RM25
Melaka	RM8
Cameron Highlands	RM13
Penang	RM22
Singapore	RM26
Depart Melaka	
KL	RM8
Singapore	RM11
Mersing	RM15
Kota Bahru	RM32
Ipoh	RM19
Depart Singapore	
Melaka	S$12
Mersing	S$10
KL	S$15
Depart Kota Bahru	
KL	RM26
Penang	RM20
Kuala Terengganu	RM9

trains, often very cold. Prices vary according to whether the bus is express or regular, and between companies. Recommended private companies are *Plusliner* (with super VIP buses) and *Transnasional*. Although these may cost a few ringgit more, it's usually money well spent. In larger towns there may be a number of bus stops; some private companies may also operate directly from their own offices. Note buses are less frequent on the east coast.

During the school holiday period, it can be difficult to get bus tickets and it is worth booking ahead.

Buses in East Malaysia are more unreliable because of the poorer road conditions. Even in East Malaysia roads are a good deal better than in Indonesian Borneo. With heavy rain, the highway connecting KK with Sandakan is sometimes blocked by mud slides.

Car and motorcycle

Car-hire companies are listed in individual towns under transport. Visitors can hire a car provided they are in possession of an international driving licence, are over 23 and not older than 65, and have at least one year's driving experience. Car hire costs from RM100 to RM250 per day approximately depending on the model and the company. Cheaper weekly and monthly rates and special deals are available. Please note that driving in Malaysia carries its risks - local drivers don't always obey traffic lights, road signs and hardly ever give way. Some expats strongly urge visitors not to risk hiring a car because of the dangers of sharing the road with Malaysian drivers.

Driving is on the left; give way to drivers on the right. Within towns the speed limit is 50 km per hour; the wearing of seat belts is compulsory for front seat passengers and the driver. Most road signs are international but awas means caution. Road maps are on sale at most petrol stations; Petronas (the national oil company) produces an excellent atlas: *Touring Malaysia by Road*. Road conditions are good when compared with Indonesia: most are kept in good repair. However, during the monsoon season, heavy rains may make some east coast travel difficult and the west coast roads can be congested. In Sarawak the road network is extremely limited: air or water transport are the only option in many areas. In Sabah, four-wheel-drive vehicles are de rigeur; they are readily available, but expensive. On some islands, such as Penang, Langkawi and Pangkor, motorbikes are available for hire, starting around RM25 per day. If bringing your own car into the country, no carnet or deposit is required. The vehicle is allowed to stay in the country as long as the owner has permission to stay.

Important road signs to note

awas caution
beri laluan give way
berhenti stop
dilarang berhenti no stopping
dilarang meletak kereta no parking
dilarang memotong no overtaking
ikut kiri keep left
jalang bahaya dangerous road ahead
jalan licin slippery road
jalan sehala one way
kawasan kemalangan accident area
kurangkan laju slow down
utara/selatan north/south
timur/barat east/west

Cycling

Bicycles are available for hire from some guesthouses and specialist hire shops, especially on islands such as Pangkor, Penang, Langkawi and Tioman, but also in some towns and hill resorts. Compared with hiring motorbikes, bike hire can seem expensive – around RM10-20 per day and substantially more (hour-for-hour) from those places that hire by the hour. Price also vary a good deal depending on the machine, locally or Chinese-made sit-up-and-beg bikes are cheaper than new mountain bikes.

We have had a number of letters from people who have cycled through various parts of Southeast Asia. The advice below is collated from their comments, and is meant to provide a general guideline for those intending to travel by bicycle. There may be areas, however, where the advice does not hold true, and some of the letters we have received even disagree on certain points.

Here are some points: Touring, hybrid or mountain bikes are fine for most roads and tracks in Malaysia – take an ordinary machine; nothing fancy; Mountain bikes have made a big impact in the country, so accessories and spares are widely available. Less common are components made of unusual materials – titanium and composites; as cycling is becoming more common clubs are springing up across the country. Unlike Indonesia and Thailand, a foreigner on a bike is not such an object of interest; cars and buses rarely give way to a bicycle and so be very wary, especially on main roads; non-a/c, cheaper buses are more accommodating of bicycles, a/c tour-buses may refuse to carry a bike; many international airlines take bicycles free-of-charge, provided they are not boxed. Take the peddles off and deflate the tyres; In general, when cycling avoid major roads and major towns.

In addition to the listing of useful things to take on page 27, bicyclists might in addition consider: pollution mask if travelling to large cities; a basic tool kit including a puncture repair kit; spare inner tubes; spare tyre; pump; a good map of the area; bungee cords; and a water filter.

Hitchhiking

It is easy for foreigners to hitch in Malaysia; look reasonably presentable and it shouldn't be long before someone will stop. Hitching is not advisable for women travelling alone.

Taxi

There are two types of taxi in Malaysia – local and 'out-station' – or long distance. The latter – usually Mercedes or Peugeot – connect all major towns and cities. They operate on a shared-cost basis – as soon as the full complement of four passengers turns up the taxis set off. Alternatively, it is possible to charter the whole taxi for the price of four single fares. Taxi stands are usually next door to major bus stations. If shared, taxi fares usually cost about twice as much as bus fares, but they are much faster. For groups travelling together taking a taxi makes good sense. Note that it is easier to find passengers going your way in the morning than later in the day.

Local taxi fares in Malaysia are fairly cheap, but it is rare to find a taxi with a meter (KL is about the only place you can find this rare breed), you will need your bargaining skills. On the east coast, a/c taxi cost more.

Trishaws

In KL it has long been too dangerous for trishaws, apart from around Chinatown and suburban areas. In towns such as Melaka, Georgetown and Kota Bharu, as well as in many other smaller towns trishaws are still available, but by and large they have become an expensive way to travel for well-heeled tourists.

Sea

On the Peninsula, there are regular scheduled ferry services between the main islands, Pulau Pangkor, Penang and Pulau Langkawi, and the mainland. There are services from Mersing to Pulau Tioman. There are passenger and car ferries between Butterworth and Georgetown, Penang, every 20 minutes. For other offshore islands, mostly off the east coast, fishing boats, and sometimes regular boats, leave from the nearest fishing port.

Local water transport comes into its own in Sarawak, where lack of roads makes coastal and river transport the only viable means of communication. On the larger rivers in Sarawak, such as the Rajang and the Baram, there are specially adapted express boats. If there is no regular boat, it is nearly always possible to charter a local longboat, although this can be expensive. In the dry season the upper reaches of many rivers are unnavigable except by smaller boats. In times of heavy rain, logs and branch debris can make rivers unsafe. Some river transport still operates on rivers on the peninsula's east coast.

Feri Malaysia runs two routes, both on a weekly schedule. (1) Port Klang-Singapore-Kuching-Kota Kinabalu-Singapore-Kuantan-Port Klang. (2) Kuantan-Kota Kinabalu-Kuching-Singapore-Port Klang. Tourism Malaysia offices have information on Feri Malaysia and can place bookings.

Maps

Country maps Bartholomew Singapore and Malaysia (1:150,000); Nelles Malaysia (1:1,500,000); Nelles West Malaysia (1:650,000); Nelles Singapore (1:22,500); Nelles Indonesia (1:4,000,000). City maps Nelles Singapore; Bartholomew Singapore.

Locally available maps Maps are widely available in Malaysia and Singapore. Both the Singapore and Malaysian tourist boards produce good maps of their respective capital cities and in the case of Malaysia a series of state maps, although these are much poorer in quality. The Sabah and Sarawak tourist boards also publish reasonable maps.

Map shops In London, the best selection is available from **Stanfords**, 12-14 Long Acre, London WC2E 9LP, T020-78361321; also recommended is **McCarta**, 15 Highbury Place, London N15 1QP, T020-73541616.

Sleeping

Malaysia offers a good selection of international-standard hotels as well as simpler hotels, rest houses and hostels. Room rates are subject to 5-10% tax. Many of the major international chains have hotels in Malaysia, such as Hilton, Regent, Holiday Inn and Hyatt plus local and regional chains such as Merlin, Ming Court and Mutiara; most of these are on the west coast. Room rates in the big hotels, particularly in KL, have been fairly stable for the last few years. The number of four- and five-star hotel rooms has also multiplied and this, combined with a weak ringgit and generally depressed economy, has helped to keep prices stable. By world standards, even the most expensive hotels are good value for money. It is also possible to rent condominiums in some cities, mainly KL and Georgetown.

For our quick reference price guide to hotels, see the inside front cover of the book.

There are youth hostels in KL, Georgetown (Penang), Port Dickson, Fraser's Hill, Cameron Highlands, Kuantan, Kota Bahru, Kota Kinabalu and Pulau Pangkor. On the east coast of Peninsular Malaysia and in East Malaysia, it is often possible to stay with families in Malay kampongs (villages), the so-called Homestay programme (contact local tourist office or travel agent for more information). The most popular place to do this is at Kampong Cherating, north of Kuantan, although it has become increasingly touristy in recent years; it is also possible to stay in a kampong house in Merang. Along many of Malaysia's beaches and on the islands, there are simple atap-roofed 'A'-frame bungalows and wooden chalets. Towns and cities on the tourist trail also often have guesthouses with dormitory accommodation for the seriously shallow of pocket. These are noted in the detailed comments provided for each establishment.

Accommodation in East Malaysia does not offer such value for money as hotels on the Peninsula but there are some bargains. For accommodation in national parks (see relevant chapters), it is necessary to book in advance. In Sarawak and Sabah it is possible to stay in longhouses, where rates are at the discretion of the visitor (see page 339).

Reflecting Malaysia's enthusiastic embrace of all things high-tech, most hotels, and even many guesthouses, have internet access. Many have websites.

In the more popular holiday destinations like the Cameron Highlands, accommodation can become scarce during the school holidays – April, August and December. During these months it is worth booking ahead. It is also worth noting that many hotels in tourist resorts have two, sometimes three, room tarrifs. One for weekdays, one for weekends and, sometimes, a third for holiday periods. Room rates can vary substantially between these periods.

Camping

There are not many sites in Malaysia, but 'wild camping' is easy. In Sabah camping is a much cheaper option and you get to stay exactly where you want to be, for example at Tunku Abdul Rahman Marine Park.

Food and drink

Cuisine

Malaysians, like their neighbours in Singapore, love their food, and the dishes of the three main communities, Malay, Chinese and Indian, comprise a hugely varied

Hotel prices and facilities

L RM500+ Luxury: hotels at the top of this bracket are few and far between. KL's splendid Carcosa Seri Negara is one such hotel. The Datai on Langkawi is another and the Pangkor Laut Resort on the private island of Pangkor Laut is also in the top league.

AL RM260-499 International class: impeccable service, beautifully appointed, offering an array of facilities and business services. Malaysia's AL grade hotels, most of which are grouped towards the bottom end of the price category, are regarded as among the best value in the region.

A RM130-259 First class: good range of services and facilities, sometimes including a swimming pool, gym and maybe a spa. Very competitively priced, given standards of service.

B RM65-129 Tourist class: hotels in this category provide a basic range of services and facilities including a coffee shop and/or simple restaurant and all rooms should have a/c.

C RM40-64 Economy: while there are some excellent economy hotels in this category, few provide much in the way of services. Guests will usually have the option of a/c or fan-cooled rooms and a choice of attached/shared bathrooms. Backpacker-oriented hostels fall into this category, and usually offer good travel advice, laundry service, breakfast facilities and maybe a common fridge and kitchen and are suitable for families on a budget.

D RM20-39 Budget: most hotels in this class are Chinese-run and located in town centres. They are therefore often noisy and many are pretty scruffy joints with not much in the way of service or facilities. At the upper end, rooms have a/c and attached bathrooms; cheaper rooms have fans and communal bathrooms. Some fine old tumbledown colonial relics in this range offer good value for money. Youth hostels fall into this price range.

E RM10-19 Lodging house/guesthouse/hostel: for this price range you are looking at a simple room with shared bathroom and fan. Some backpacker places will have simple rooms and dorms in this category.

F under RM10: there is little in the way of a bed for the night for this price, except for a space in a dorm at a bottom of the range hostel, or a simple A-frame near the beach, if you're lucky.

national menu. Even within each ethnic cuisine, there is a vast choice; every state has its own special Malay dishes and the different Chinese provincial specialities are well represented; in addition there is North Indian food, South Indian food and Indian Muslim food. Nyonya cuisine is found in the old Straits Settlements of Penang and Melaka. Malaysia also has great seafood, which the Chinese do best, and in recent years a profusion of restaurants, representing other Asian and European cuisines, have set up, mainly in the big cities. In the East Malaysian states of Sabah and Sarawak, there are various tribal specialities to be had.

For restaurant price codes, see the inside front cover. For health matters relating to food, see page 61. For Malay and Asian food glossaries see page 628.

With a large ethnic Indian population, vegetarian food is usually available, especially on the Peninsula. In East Malaysia it can be harder to find vegetarian alternatives. There are also numerous Chinese and Malay vegetarian dishes, although it is not unusual to find slivers of meat even when a vegetable dish is specifically requested. In tourist areas and more cosmopolitan towns vegetarian restaurants are becoming popular.

Malay

The best Malay food is usually found at stalls in hawker centres. The staple diet is rice and curry, which is rich and creamy due to the use of coconut milk. Herbs and spices include chillis, ginger, turmeric, coriander, lemongrass, anise, cloves, cumin, caraway and cinnamon.

Chinese

Each province of China has its own distinct cuisine. A balanced meal should contain the five basic taste sensations: sweet, bitter, salty, spicy and acidic to balance the yin and yang.

Cantonese and Hainanese cooking are the most prevalent Chinese cuisines in Malaysia. Some of the more common Malaysian-Chinese dishes are Hainanese chicken rice (rice cooked in chicken stock and served with steamed or roast chicken), *char kway teow* (Teochew-style fried noodles, with eggs, cockles and chilli paste), or *luak* (Hokkien oyster omelette), dim sum (steamed dumplings and patties) and *yong tow foo* (beancurd and vegetables stuffed with fish). Good Chinese food is available in restaurants, coffee shops and from hawker stalls.

Cantonese Light and delicately flavoured dishes are often steamed with ginger and are not very spicy. Shark's fin and birds' nest soups, and dim sum (mostly steamed delicacies trolleyed to your table, but only served until early afternoon) are Cantonese classics. Other typical dishes include fish steamed with soya sauce, ginger, chicken stock and wine; wan ton soup; blanched green vegetables in oyster sauce; and suckling pig.

Hainanese Simple cuisine from the southern island of Hainan; chicken rice with sesame oil, soy and a chilli and garlic sauce is their tastiest contribution.

Hakka Uses plenty of sweet potato and dried shrimp and specializes in stewed pigs' trotters, *yong tau foo* (deep-fried beancurd), and chillis and other vegetables stuffed with fish paste.

Hokkien Being one of Singapore's biggest dialect groups means Hokkien cuisine is prominent, particularly in hawker centres, although there are very few Hokkien restaurants. Hokkien Chinese invented the spring roll and their cooking uses lots of noodles and in one or two places you can still see them being made by hand. Hokkien cuisine is also characterized by clear soups and steamed seafood, eaten with soya sauce. Fried Hokkien *mee* (yellow wheat noodles stir-fried with seafood and pork), *hay cho* (deep fried balls of prawn) and *bee hoon* (rice vermicelli cooked with prawns, squid and beansprouts with lime and chillies) are specialities.

Hunanese Known for its glutinous rice, honeyed ham and pigeon soup.

Peking (Beijing) Chefs at the imperial court in Peking had a repertoire of over 8,000 recipes. Dumplings, noodles and steamed buns predominate, since wheat is the staple diet, but in Singapore, rice may accompany the meal. Peking duck, shi choy (deep fried bamboo shoots), and hot and sour soup are among the best Peking dishes. Peking duck (with the skin basted with syrup and cooked until crisp) is usually eaten rolled into a pancake and accompanied by hoisin sauce and spring onions. Fish dishes are usually deep-fried and served with sweet and sour sauce.

 Shanghainese Seafood dominates this cuisine and many dishes are cooked in soya sauce. Braised fish-heads, braised abalone (a large shellfish) in sesame sauce, and crab and sweetcorn soup are typical dishes. Wine is often used in the preparation of meat dishes, hence drunken prawn and drunken crab.

Steamboat The Chinese answer to fondue is a popular dish in Singapore and can be found in numerous restaurants and at some hawker centres. Thinly sliced pieces of raw meat, fish, prawns, cuttlefish, fishballs and vegetables are gradually tossed into a bubbling cauldron in the centre of the table. They are then dunked into hot chilli and soya sauces and the resulting soup provides a flavoursome broth to wash it all down at the end.

Sichuan Very spicy (garlic and chilli are dominant), Sichuan is widely considered the tastiest Chinese cuisine. Sichuan food includes heaps of hot red peppers, traditionally considered to be protection against cold and disease. Among the best Sichuan dishes are smoked duck in tea leaves and camphor sawdust; minced pork with beancurd; steamed chicken in lotus leaves; and fried eels in garlic sauce.
Teochew Famous for its muay porridges. This is a light, clear broth consumed with side dishes of crayfish, salted eggs and vegetables.

Indian

Indian cooking can be divided into three schools: northern and southern (neither eat beef) and Muslim (no pork). Northern dishes tend to be more subtly spiced, use more meat and are served with breads. Southern dishes use fiery spices, emphasize vegetables and are served with rice. The best-known North Indian food is tandoori, which is served with delicious fresh naan breads, baked in ovens on-site. Other pancakes include *roti, thosai* and *chapati*. Malaysia's famous mamak-men are Indian Muslims who are highly skilled in everything from teh tarik (see Drink below) to rotis. See also Glossary, page 628.

Nyonya

Through inter-marriage with local Malays a unique culture evolved and with it, a cuisine that has grown out of a blend of the two. Nyonya food is spicier than Chinese food, and it uses pork. Nyonya dishes in Penang have adopted flavours from neighbouring Thailand, whereas Melaka's Nyonya food has Indonesian overtones. In traditional Straits Chinese households, great emphasis was placed on presentation and the fine-chopping of ingredients. See also Glossary, page 628.

New Asia (Fusion)

This is a blending of cuisines and ingredients from East and West. So far, the foodies have not agreed on a single name. It is sometimes termed 'Fusion' cuisine, sometimes Trans-ethnic, and sometimes New Asia. Perhaps this confusion over what to call the food is because people don't seem to be able to agree what constitutes the cuisine(s) in the first place. Some chefs and food critics maintain that it involves cooking Eastern ingredients using Western cooking techniques. Others see it as a combination of two styles of cooking and two sets of ingredients. One chef believes you should be able to drink wine with New Asia cuisine, something that you cannot do with Chinese food, as soy sauce kills the taste of wine. But like most things, you'll know it when you see it. Classic French and other chefs are, of course, appalled by what they see as just a confusion of tastes: the art of good cooking is to bring out the flavour of the fish, meat or vegetables, not to annihilate them with lemon grass, chillies, soy and other herbs and condiments.

Sabahan

The Kadazans form the largest ethnic group in Sabah. Their food tends to use mango and can be on the sour side. See also Glossary, page 628.

Eating out

Malaysia, like Singapore, just about has it all on the restaurant front: from the swankiest restaurants where international cuisine is served at prices that are usually rather less than one would expect, through to stalls and hawker centres where a meal can cost less than a Coke back home. There's also a huge range to choose from because, as noted above, Malaysia is a plural society and home to significant Malay, Chinese and Indian populations that have, at times, intersected in gastronomically interesting ways. Furthermore, and again as in Singapore, good food is not confined to restaurants; some of the best local dishes can be sampled at hawker centres, which are cheap and often stay open late into the night.

The cheapest places to eat are in hawker centres and roadside stalls (often concentrated in or close to night markets) where it is possible to eat well for just RM3-4. Stalls may serve Malay, Indian or Chinese dishes and, even, some food which approximates to 'Western'. Next in the sequence of sophistication and price come the ubiquitous *kedai kopi* (coffee shops) which can be found in every town, and almost every street and where a meal will cost upwards of RM5. Usually run by Chinese or Indian families, rather than Malay, they open at around 0900 and close in the early evening, many are 24-hours. However some open much earlier, at dawn, to serve dim sum to people making their way to work. Chinese-run *kedai kopi* tend to be the last to close - sometimes as late as midnight - and they are also the only coffee shops where it is possible to track down a cold beer. Malay-run *kedai kopi* are good for lunch with their *nasi campur* spreads, while Indian-run coffee shops offer what you would expect them to offer. Above the kedai kopi come a phalanx of restaurants from the basic to the extremely pricey. A special category are the restaurants geared to travellers' culinary needs which tend to be concentrated in beach resorts. Here it is possible to live off banana pancakes, fudge cake, smoothies, jaffles and all the other dishes that backpackers on the move seem to need to keep body and soul together. Hotel restaurants regularly lay on buffet spreads, which are good value at about RM20-30, often much cheaper than the price of a room would suggest.

Many restaurants charge an extra 15% service and tax. During Ramadan many Malay restaurants close during daylight hours.

Drink

Soft drinks, mineral water and freshly squeezed fruit drinks are available. Anchor and Tiger beer are widely sold, except in the more Islamic states of the east coast, especially Kelantan, and is cheapest at the hawker stalls (RM5-7 per bottle). A beer will cost RM8-15 per bottle in coffee shops. Malaysian-brewed Guinness is popular, mainly because Chinese believe it has medicinal qualities as it has been successfully sold on the 'Guinness Stout is good for you' line (Recent studies suggest there is some truth in that). Malaysian tea is grown in the Cameron Highlands and is very good. One of the most interesting cultural refinements of the Indian Muslim community is the Mamak-man, who is famed for *teh tarik* (pulled tea), which is thrown across a distance of about a metre, from one cup to another, with no spillages. The idea is to cool it down for customers, but it has become an art form; mamak-men appear to cultivate the nonchalant look when pouring. Malaysian satirist Kit Leee says a tea-stall mamak "could 'pull' tea in free fall without spilling a drop – while balancing a beedi on his lower lip and making a statement on Economic Determinism". Most of the coffee comes from Indonesia, although some is locally produced. Malaysians like strong coffee and unless you specify *kurang manis* (less sugar), *tak mahu manis* (don't want sugar) or *kopi kosong* (empty coffee, black, no sugar), it will come with lashings of condensed milk.

Shopping

Most big towns now have modern shopping complexes as well as shops and markets. Department stores are fixed-price, but nearly everywhere else it is possible – and necessary – to bargain. In most places, at least 30% can be knocked off the asking price; your first offer should be roughly half the first quote.

What to buy

The islands of Langkawi, Tioman and Labuan have duty-free shopping; the range of goods is poor, however. In addition to the duty-free shops, cameras, watches, pens, lighters, cosmetics, perfumes and portable radio/cassette players are all duty-free in Malaysia. Film and camera equipment are still cheaper in Singapore, which offers a wider selection of most products – especially electronics and computer products. Kuala Lumpur and most of the state capitals have a Chinatown which usually has a few curio shops and nearly always a pasar malam, or night market. Indian quarters, which are invariably labelled 'Little India', are only found in bigger towns; they are the best places to buy sarongs, longis, dotis and saris (mostly imported from India) as well as other textiles. Malay handicrafts are usually only found in markets or government craft centres.

Handicrafts

The Malaysian arts and crafts industry used to enjoy much more royal patronage, but when craftsmen went in search of more lucrative jobs, the industry began to decline. The growth of tourism in recent years has helped to reinvigorate it, particularly in traditional handicraft-producing areas, such as the east coast states of Terengganu and Kelantan. The Malay Arts and Crafts Society has also been instrumental in preventing the decline of the industry. Malaysian Handicraft and Souvenir Centres (Karyaneka centres), were set up to market Malaysian arts and crafts in KL and some state capitals. Typical Malaysian handicrafts which can be found on the Peninsula include woodcarvings, batik, songket (cloth woven with gold and silver thread), pewterware, silverware, kites, tops and wayang kulit (shadow puppets). For more detail on Malaysian crafts, see page 508.

Other than the Peninsula's east coast states, Sarawak is the other place where the traditional handicraft industry is flourishing (see page 395). The state capital, Kuching, is full of handicraft and antique shops selling tribal pieces collected from upriver; those going upriver themselves can often find items being sold in towns and even longhouses en route. Typical Sarawakian handicrafts include woodcarvings, pua kumbu (rust-coloured tie-dye blankets), beadwork and basketry (see page 333). Many handicraft shops on Peninsular Malaysia also sell Sarawakian handicrafts – particularly those in KL – although there is a considerable mark-up.

Entertainment

Bars and clubs

Firstly, it should be said that Malaysia is most certainly not Ibiza. There has never been a really hot club and dance circuit in Malaysia, although KL can now boast some internationally-standard clubs attracting big-name DJs. Karaoke is more the average Malaysians cup of arak than hip-hop. The main towns where there is a nightlife of sorts are KL (for obvious reasons), Johor Bahru (because Singaporeans pop down here to see whether they made the right decision leaving the Federation in the mid-1960s) and Penang (because of all the tourists). The backpacker haunts on the East Coast also have some places that live largely in the past and play Bob Marley back-numbers, while Kuching and Kota Kinabalu, the capitals of the East Coast states of Sarawak and Sabah, also have a fair sprinkling of discos and clubs, usually in the glitzier hotels (so all very sanitised).

Most bars offer happy hours (usually 1700-1900).

Cinema

Most of the big cities have multiplex cinema (tickets around RM10) – these are usually tucked away in shopping malls. Chains to look out for are Golden Screen, Tanjong Golden Village (swanky multiplex in the KLCC Suria among others), and Mega Pavillion which have comfy seats, air conditioning and pop corn. As a general rule, big cities or towns like KL, JB, Ipoh, Melaka, Penang, Kuantan, Kuching, Miri and Kota Kinabalu have a choice of cinemas. Outside those, cinemas are few and far between. Mainstream Hollywood movies are shown along with an Asian selection including local offerings, Bollywood blockbusters and Japanese, Hong Kong and Korean cinema. While Bollywood movies and local films are unlikely to have English sub-titles, East Asian movies often have them. Movies are rated U (general viewing), 18SG (for over 18s with non-excessive horrifying or violent content), 18SX (for over 18s with non-excessive sex scenes), 18PA (for over 18s with political/religious counter-culture elements) or 18PL (for over 18s with a combination of two or more undesirable elements). At the end of 2004, KL's Berjaya Times Square shopping mall launched its IMAX cinema (tickets around RM15).

Comedy

Stand up comedians and comic plays are most likely to perform at the Actor's Studio Theatre in KL. Many shows, however will be in Malay. If you are lucky you may catch a bilingual show which will be half in Malay and half in English. It's unlikely you'll be able to catch any comedy in English outside of KL. During the Mahathir era comedy was an occasional 'safe' outlet for local artists to poke fun at their prime minister.

Dance and theatre

Malaysia is not a mecca for the performing arts. For contemporary dance and theatre you're best bet is KL. You can see productions at the National Theatre (Istana Budaya) T3-40252525, The **Actor's Studio Bangsar**, T3-20940400, www.theactorsstudio.com.my/, and **Plaza Putra** underneath Merdeka Square. International acts are generally staged at the **Genting International Showroom** in the Genting Highlands, 51km away. See www.kakiseni.com/ for more information on Malaysia's arts scene. You are unlikely to see any English-language theatre outside of KL.

For traditional dance performances see Malaysia Tourism. Some of the fancier hotels and restaurants will also have shows while guests eat. Tourism Malaysia also hosts an annual theatre festival, but many of the offerings are in Malay.

Festivals and events

The timing of Islamic festivals is an art rather than a science and is calculated on the basis of local sightings of various phases of the moon. Thus dates are approximations and can vary by a day or two. Muslim festivals move forward by around 9-10 days each year. To check on dates, see www.tourism.gov.my.

Chinese, Indian (Hindu) and some Christian holidays are also movable. To convert the Gregorian calendar to the lunar calendar try http://umunhum.stanford.edu/~lee/chicomp/lunar.html To make things even more exciting, each state has its own public holidays when shops close and banks pull down their shutters. This makes calculating public holidays in advance a bit of a quagmire of lunar events, assorted kings' birthdays, and tribal festivals. Note that most government offices (including some tourism offices) are closed on the first and third Saturday of each month.

Tourism Malaysia has dates of movable holidays and festivals, see page 32 for contact information

Schools in Malaysia have five breaks through the year, although the actual dates vary from state to state. They generally fall in the months of January (one week), March (two weeks), May (three weeks), August (one week), and October (four weeks).

Only sultans' and governors' birthday celebrations are marked with processions and festivities; state holidays can disrupt travel itineraries – particularly in east coast states where they may run for several days.

January-February

New Year's Day (1 January) Public holiday except Johor, Kedah, Kelantan, Perlis and Terengganu).

Thaipusam (movable: public holiday Johor, Negeri Sembilan, Perak, Penang and Selangor only) celebrated by many Hindus throughout Malaysia in honour of their deity Lord Subramanian (also known as Lord Muruga); he represents virtue, bravery, youth and power. Held during full moon in the month of Thai, it is a day of penance and thanksgiving. Devotees pay homage to Lord Subramanian by piercing their bodies, cheeks and tongues with sharp skewers (vel) and hooks weighted with oranges, and carrying kevadis (steel structures bearing the image of Lord Muruga). There are strict rules the devotee must follow in order to purify himself before carrying the kevadi; he becomes a vegetarian and abstains from worldly pleasures. Women cannot carry kevadis as they are not allowed to bare their bodies in order to be pierced. Although a kevadi carrier can have as many as a hundred spears piercing his flesh he only loses a small amount of blood in his trance. Each participant tries to outdo the others in the severity of his torture. At certain temples fire-walking is also part of this ceremony. Many Hindus disapprove of the spectacle and believe that their bodies are a gift from Siva; they shold serve as a temple for the soul and should not be abused. This festival is peculiar to Hindus in Malaysia, Singapore and Thailand and is a corruption of a Tamil ceremony from South India. The biggest gatherings are at Batu Caves just outside KL, when thousands of pilgrims congregate in a carnival-like atmosphere (see page 87); there are also festivals held in Melaka, Penang and Singapore.

Chinese New Year (movable: public holiday, two days in most states, one day in Kelantan and Terengganu) a 15-day lunar festival celebrated in late Jan/early Feb. Chinatown streets are crowded for weeks with shoppers buying traditional oranges which signify luck. Lion, unicorn or dragon dances welcome-in the New Year and, unlike in Singapore, thousands of firecrackers are ignited to ward off evil spirits. Chap Goh Mei is the 15th day of the Chinese New Year and brings celebrations to a close; it is marked with a final dinner, another firecracker fest, prayers and offerings. The Chinese believe that in order to find good husbands, girls should throw oranges into the river/sea on this day. In Sarawak the festival is known as

Guan Hsiao Cheih (Lantern Festival).
Hari Raya Haji (movable: public holiday; in Kedah, Kelantan, Perlis and Terengganu. Hari Raya Qurban is also a public holiday celebrated by Muslims to mark the 10th day of Zulhijgah, the 12th month of the Islamic calendar when pilgrims celebrate their return from the Haj to Mecca. In the morning, prayers are offered and later, families hold 'open house'. Those who can afford it sacrifice goats or cows to be distributed to the poor. Many Malays have the title Haji in their name, meaning they have made the pilgrimage to Mecca; men who have been on the Haj wear a white skull-hat. The Haj is one of the five keystones of Islam.
Sultan of Kedah's birthday (20 Jan, state holiday) Kedah.
Federal Territory Day (1 Feb, state holiday), KL and Labuan.

March-April

Easter (movable) Celebrated in Melaka with candle-lit processions and special services (see page 204). Good Friday is a public holiday in Sabah and Sarawak.
Maal Hijrah (Awal Muharram) (movable: public holiday), marks the first day of the Muslim calendar, marking the Prophet Muhammad's journey from Mecca to Medina on the lunar equivalent of 16 July AD 622. Religious discussions and lectures commemorate the day.
Installation of Sultan of Terengganu Day (4 Mar, state holiday), Terengganu.
Sultan of Selangor's birthday (9 Mar, state holiday), Selangor.
Sultan of Kelantan's birthday (30-31 Mar, state holiday), Kelantan.
Sultan of Johor's birthday (8 April) Johor.
Declaration of Melaka as Historic City (15 April) Melaka.
Sultan of Perak's birthday (19 April), Perak

May

Labour Day (1 May: public holiday).
Kurah Aran (1 May) celebrated by the Bidayuh tribe in Sarawak (see page 390) after the paddy harvest is over.
Wesak Day (movable: public holiday except Labuan) the most important day in the Buddhist calendar, celebrates the Buddha's birth, death and enlightenment. Temples throughout the country are packed with devotees offering incense, joss-sticks and prayers. Lectures on Buddhism and special exhibitions are held. In Melaka there is a procession at night with decorated floats, bands, dancers and acrobatics.
Birthday of the Prophet Muhammad (Maulidur Rasul) (movable: public holiday) to commemorate Prophet Muhammad's birthday in AD 571. Processions and Koran recitals in most big towns.
Wesak Day (movable, public holiday, 26 May).
Pahang Hol Day (7 May, state holiday), Pahang.
Rajah of Perlis' birthday (17 May, state holiday), Perlis.
Harvest Festival (30-31 May, state holiday), Sabah and Labuan.

June

Birthday of His Majesty the King (first Sat of the month: public holiday) mainly celebrated in KL with processions.
Dragon Boat Festival (movable) honours the suicide of an ancient Chinese poet hero, Qu Yuan. He tried to press for political reform by drowning himself in the Mi Luo River as a protest against corruption. In an attempt to save him fishermen played drums and threw rice dumplings to try and distract vultures. His death is commemorated with dragon boat races and the enthusiastic consumption of rice dumplings; biggest celebrations are in Penang.
Dayak Day (1-2 Jun, state holiday), Sarawak.

July

Governor of Penang's birthday (second Sat of the month, state holiday), Penang.
Yang Di-Pertuan Besar of Negeri Sembilan's birthday (19 Jul, state holiday), Negeri Sembilan.
Sultan of Terengganu's birthday (20 Jul, state holiday).

August-September

Hari Kebangsaan or National Day (31 August: public holiday) commemorates

Malaysian independence (merdeka) in 1957. Big celebration in KL with processions of floats representing all the states; best places to see it: on the Padang (Merdeka Square) or on TV. In Sarawak, Hari Kebangsaan is celebrated in a different divisional capital each year. Mooncake or Lantern Festival (movable). This Chinese festival marks the overthrow of the Mongol Dynasty in China; celebrated, as the name suggests, with the exchange and eating of mooncakes. According to Chinese legend secret messages of revolt were carried inside these cakes and led to the uprising. In the evening, children light festive lanterns while women pray to the Goddess of the Moon.

Festival of the Hungry Ghosts (movable) on the seventh moon in the Chinese lunar calendar, souls in purgatory are believed to return to earth to feast. Food is offered to these wandering spirits. Altars are set up in the streets and candles with faces are burned on them.

Governor of Sarawak's birthday (14 Sep, state holiday), Sarawak.

Governor of Sabah's birthday (16 Sep, state holiday), Sabah.

October

Festival of the Nine Emperor Gods or Kiew Ong Yeah (movable) marks the return of the spirits of the nine emperor gods to earth. The mediums whom they are to possess purify themselves by observing a vegetarian diet. The gods possess the mediums, who go into trance and are then carried on sedan chairs whose seats are comprised of razor-sharp blades or spikes. Devotees visit temples dedicated to the nine gods. A strip of yellow cotton is often bought from the temple and worn on the right wrist as a sign of devotion. The ceremonies usually culminate with a fire-walking ritual.

Governor of Melaka's birthday (second Sat of the month, state holiday), Melaka.

Sultan of Pahang's birthday (24 Oct, state holiday) Pahang.

October-November

Deepvali (movable: public holiday except Sarawak and Labuan) the Hindu festival of lights commemorates the victory of light over darkness and good over evil: the triumphant return of Rama after his defeat of the evil Ravanna in the Hindu epic, the Ramayana. Every Hindu home is brightly lit and decorated for the occasion.

Hari Hol Almarhum Sultan Ismail (movable, Johor). Israk and Mikraj (movable, Kedah and Negeri Sembilan).

Awal Ramadan (movable: public holiday Johor and Melaka) the first day of Ramadan, a month of fasting for all Muslims – and by implication, all Malays. During this month Muslims abstain from all food and drink (as well as smoking) from sunrise to sundown – if they are very strict, Muslims do not even swallow their own saliva during daylight hours. It is strictly adhered to in the conservative Islamic states of Kelantan and Terengganu. Every evening for 30 days before breaking of fast, stalls are set up which sell traditional Malay cakes and delicacies. The only people exempt from fasting are the elderly as well as women who are pregnant or are menstruating.

Nuzul Quran (movable, Kelantan, Pahang, Perak, Perlis, Selangor and Terengganu).

December

Christmas Day (25 December: public holiday) Christmas in Malaysia is a commercial spectacle these days with fairy lights and decorations and tropical Santa Clauses – although it does not compare with celebrations in Singapore. Mostly celebrated on the west coast and ignored on the more Muslim east coast. Midnight mass is the main Christmas service held in churches throughout Malaysia.

Hari Raya Puasa or **Aidil Fitri** (movable: public holiday) marks the end of the Muslim fasting month of Ramadan and is a day of prayer and celebration. In order for Hari Raya to be declared, the new moon of Syawal has to be sighted; if it is not, fasting continues for another day. It is the most important time of the year for Muslim families to get together; Malays living in towns and cities balek kampong (return home to their village), where it is 'open house' for relatives and friends, and special Malay delicacies are served. Hari Raya is also enthusiastically celebrated by Indian Muslims.

Festivals in East Malaysia

Besides those celebrated throughout the country, Sabah and Sarawak have their own festivals. Exact dates can be procured from the tourist offices in the capitals. State public holidays are listed on page 52.

Kadazan Harvest Festival or Tadau Keamatan (movable: public holiday, Sabah and Labuan only) marks the end of the rice harvest in Sabah; the magavau ritual is performed to nurse the spirit back to health in readiness for the next planting season. Traditionally, the ritual world would have been performed in the paddy fields by a bobohizan (high priestess). Celebrated with feasting, tapai (rice wine) drinking, dancing and general merry-making. There are also agricultural shows, buffalo races, cultural performances and traditional games. The traditional sumazal dance is one of the highlights of the festivities.

Gawai (movable: public holiday Sarawak only) is the major festival of the year for the Iban of Sarawak; longhouses party continuously for a week. The Gawai celebrates the end of the rice harvest and welcomes the new planting season. The main ritual is called magavau and nurses the spirit of the grain back to health in advance of the planting season. Like the Kadazan harvest festival in Sabah, visitors are welcome to join in, but in Sarawak, the harvest festival is much more traditional. On the first day of celebrations everyone dresses up in traditional costumes, singing, dancing and drinking tuak rice wine until they drop.

Gawai Burung (Sarawak) is biggest of all the gawais and honours the war god of the Ibans. Gawai Kenyalang is one stage of Gawai Burung and is celebrated only after a tribesman has been instructed to do so after a dream.

Gawai Antu (Sarawak), also known as **Gawai Nyunkup** or **Rugan**, is an Iban tribute to departed spirits. In simple terms, it is a party to mark the end of mourning for anyone whose relative had died in the previous six months.

Gawai Batu (Sarawak) is a whetstone feast held by Iban farmers in June.

Gawai Mpijong Jaran Rantau (Sarawak) is celebrated by the Bidayuh before grass cutting in new paddy fields.

Gawai Bineh (Sarawak) is an Iban festival celebrated after harvest. It welcomes back all the spirits of the paddy from the fields.

Gawai Sawa (movable) is celebrated by the Bidayuh in Sarawak to offer thanksgiving for the last year and to make the next year a plentiful one.

Festivals in Sarawak

Most of Malaysia's mainstream festivals are celebrated in Sarwak, including Chinese New Year, Christmas and Hari Raya. But there are also some festivals that are peculiarly Sarawakian.

31 May – 1 June Gawai Dayak
Sarawak's major home-grown festival, marking the end of the rice harvest. Vast quantities of food are prepared and tuak brewed. Urban residents return to their rural roots for a major binge.

Mid-March – early April (moveable) **Kaul**
Celebrated by the Melanau community. Although the Melanu are now largely Muslim and Christian, this animist festival continues to be celebrated – most enthusiatically in the coastal town of Mukah. Fishermen appease the spirits of the sea before the onset of the fishing season by launching miniature wooden boats. Young men compete in a game known as tibou where they see how many can swing from a single rope.

Activities and tours

Birdwatching

Malaysia is home to hundreds of birds including many migratory species and there are great facilities for bird watchers. Popular areas for bird watchers are Fraser's Hill, Maxwell Hill and Taman Negara National Park on the peninsula, and Kinabalu Park and Layang-Layang Island in Sabah. For orgnaised bird-watching holidays see http://www.birdtours.co.uk/tripreports/malaysia/index.htm

Cookery courses (Malay)

For those wishing to learn more about Malaysian cuisine, several state tourist boards offer short courses in curry-making, etc. Enquire at Tourism Malaysia information centres. A wide variety of Malaysian cookery books is available at leading bookshops.

Diving

Malaysia's underwater world is as diverse as anywhere can be: from pristine vistas of immaculate corals with enormous whale sharks or schools of hammerheads to shallow waters rich with tiny and rare marine creatures. Like her land environment, Malaysia's seas are incredibly diverse and it's this diversity that attracts divers from all over the planet. Peninsula Malaysia has the South China Sea to the east and the Straist of Melaka to the west. Borneo's two states, over 500 km away, are surrounded by the South China, Sulu and Celebes Seas. Each has it's own weather patterns and consequent dive styles. Choosing where to dive will be governed by the time of year and where you happen to be, but no matter where that is, there will be a delightful island resort and a friendly dive centre to help you submerge.

Diving seasons and conditions It is hard to be general about seasons across Malaysia. Although it is warm and humid all year round, the mainland and Borneo are governed by very different wind patterns and currents. For example, monsoons from the north east will affect the mainland's east coast, but make little difference to Borneo's east coast. Consequently, best dive seasons are listed after each resort or region.

Water temperature No matter what time of year you visit , or what area, the water is invariably warm. Temperatures hover between 25 and 29 degrees celsius but may occasionally drop as low as 23 degrees celsius. A 3mm wetsuit is as much as you are likely to need unless you plan to do more than 3 dives a day.

Equipment Almost every dive centre will rent good quality equipment but bringing your own will considerably reduce costs. Prior to departure, check your baggage allowance with the airlines and see if you can come to some kind of arrangement for extra weight.

Dive facilities There are masses of world-class dive destinations on almost as many islands - and the good news is that there are just as many operators. In general, dive businesses are extremely professional and run by friendly and helpful staff. Some, on smaller or newer resorts, may have limited facilities. Many work closely with one of the International governing bodies (PADI, NAUI, CMAS, BSAC). It's always worth asking around if you're unsure of what you are being offered.

Recompression facilities As always, there are a few simple rules to avoid getting bent: Don't dive too deep; Don't ascend too quickly; Use - and obey - your computer; Always do a safety stop - 3 mins at 3 m minimum; Drink a lot of water to avoid dehydration. Should you become victim to a suspected decompression attack, contact one of the facilities listed below immediately or the Malaysian Diving Emergency Hotline, T5- 9304114 (24 hours) for advice. **Sipadan Island:** Borneo Divers run a single chamber on Mabul Island, www.borneodivers.info/SecurityFrame.html, no telephone available. **Labuan:** chamber owned and operated by the Malaysian Navy. **Labuan Recompression Chamber**, Labuan Pejabat Selam, Markas Wilayah Laut Dua, 87007, Labuan, Labuan T87-412122. **East Coast:** Kuantan Naval Base. **Kuantan Mawilla Sail Diving Team**, Tg. Gelang, 25990, Kuantan, Pahang T9-433 330/583 3600. **West Coast: Armed Forces Hospital**, RMN Base, 32100 Lumut, Perak, Malaysia T5-683 7090 ext 4071, F5-683 7169, divemed@hatl.gov.my **Singapore: Naval Medicine and Hyperbaric Centre**, 36 Admiralty Rd. West Singapore 759960, T65- 7505544, F65-7505610.

Dive Insurance Note that air evacuation services, if available are extremely expensive and hyperbaric chambers can charge as much as $800 US per hour. Good dive insurance is imperative. It is inexpensive and well worth it in case of a problem, real or perceived. Many general travel insurance policies will not cover diving. Contact DAN (the Divers Alert Network) for more information, www.diversalertnetwork.org. DAN Europe: www.daneurope.org and DAN South East Asia Pacific: www.danseap.org. If you have no insurance you can join on-line.

The outstanding region of Malaysian Borneo is "the" destination for serious divers who travel here for no other reason but to submerge. The State of Sabah has many well established and well run island resorts completely dedicated to diving. Sea and wind conditions vary, so diving can be hard, but there are many places suitable for novices.

Layang Layang Fly an hour north of Sabah's capital, Kota Kinabalu, to find isolated Layang Layang. This tiny, man made island is shared with the Royal Malaysian Navy who built it to ensure their claim over the Spratley Group of islands. There is little more than an airstrip on the edge of a turquoise lagoon. However, around the edge of this lagoon is a large atoll whose steep sided walls drop off to unimaginable depths. Strong currents drag nutrients across the reefs which, in turn, ensures prolific hard coral growth and creates a haven to masses of pelagic - or open water - life. While the corals and reef life alone are worth a visit, most people come for the curious hammerhead phenomena. Every Easter, large schools swarm around Layang then head off again a few weeks later. At other times turtles, reef sharks and schooling fish are common. As the diving here can be challenging - and there is little else to do - it is perhaps not a place for novices. The resort is also a bird sanctuary where rare boobies nest. Open between March and September. Dive Centre: **Layang Layang Island Resort**, A-0-3 Block A, Megan Phileo Avenue II,12, Jalan Yap Kwan Seng, 50450 Kuala Lumpur, T3-21622877, www.layanglayang.com

Lankayan An hour or so by boat from Sandakan into the Sulu Sea, idyllic Lankayan is ringed by an iridescent white beach and covered in a labyrinth of unruly green jungle. Surrounding the island is a set of flat plateaus that gradually shelve and drop off into a healthy reef system. There are no great walls, but gentle slopes covered, primarily, in hard corals. A recent survey confirmed high bio-diversity but visibility can be low at times. This is due to mainland proximity, shallow reef structures and high plankton concentration. However, diving here is about looking for the animals who thrive in these nutrient rich conditions. There are plenty, including rare rhinopias and occasional whalesharks that come to feed. Several shipwrecks ensure good variety, including one straight off the jetty. There is a small turtle hatching programme and black tip reef sharks breed in the shallow waters. You can watch juveniles at just 12-18 inches long hunting in the lagoon. This is a year round resort and dive conditions are mostly gentle. Good shore diving would also make this a great place for trainees or new divers.Dive Centre: **Lankayan Island Resort**, 484 Bandar Sabindo, 91021 Tawau, Sabah. T89-765200, www.lankayan-island.com

Sipadan Most famous of Borneo's dive destinations, this tiny spit of land is an all out magnet for divers. The walls of the island drop to well over 600 metres and this unique geography has created a spectacular marine environment. If you are looking for the big stuff, then is the place for you. Turtles are everywhere, so prolific and curious, that they will follow you around on a dive. One even bit our camera flash! Sharks are easy to spot, white tips always seem to be snoozing on sandy shelves and hammerheads are frequently spotted out on Barracuda Point. Speaking of which, huge schools of barracuda just hang about waiting for a diver with a camera. The wall is quite spectacular yet there are plenty of small and colourful creatures to see as well. The island itself is tiny. Dive conditions are variable yet generally OK for all levels of divers.

 Mabul Sipadan's nearest neighbour and well known as a special place for spotting small creatures, Mabul does not disappoint. The island is quite large compared to Sipadan and nearby Kapalai, and has a village and several resorts. Offshore there is even a hotel housed in a converted oil rig. It is frankly one of the ugliest things you will ever see, until you get beneath it and discover it's also one of the best dives of your life. This one small space has more frogfish, crocodile fish, lions, scorpions and morays than you ever thought you'd see in one place. The pylons are eerie, reminiscent of a wreck dive, and surrounded by schooling fish. Shore dives are equally spectacular - nudibranchs, squid and seahorses are all common no matter what time of year you come. Once again, the island is tailored towards divers but you can enjoy a decent walk on the beach and visit the local village. Conditions are generally easy, although currents can restrict dives sites. Dive Centres: **Sipadan-Mabul Resort**, P.O. Box 15571, 88864 Kota Kinabalu, Sabah, T88-230006, www.sipadan-mabul.com.my **Sipadan Water Village Resort**, P.O. Box No. 62156, 91031 Tawau, Sabah, T89-752996, www.sipadan-village.com.my

Kapalai Although charted on maps, there is only a sand bar remaining from what was once a small island. At low tide you can walk along the beach that emerges, spotting shells and tiny critters caught in puddles. This flat topography is similar underwater, yet visibility here is reasonable as the reef mounds are washed daily by gentle tides. Corals tend to be low lying to the contours of the landscape but they're all pretty healthy and a great haven for masses of weird and whacky critters. Leaf fish appeared in threesomes, hawkfish all over the place, frogfish on virtually every dive. The resort itself is a water village, wooden bungalows perch on stilts over an aquarium-like lagoon and the dive from the jetty is spectacular - resident mating mandarin fish, blue ringed octopus, clown frogfish, batfish and even baby nurse sharks reside within a couple of fin strokes. This is a delightful resort, perfect for romantics. Diving is year-round and suitable for everyone.Dive centres: **Sipadan Kapalai Resort**, 484 Bandar Sabindo, 91021 Tawau, Sabah, T89-765200, www.sipadan-kapalai.com

Mataking As Sipadan Island becomes ever busier, the resorts around her grow and develop. Mataking is the newest and building quite a reputation. The reefs here are shallow and gentle and in the past, there has been some damage. However the resort is working hard to regenerate the reef with the introduction of a well regarded "reef ball" project . These artificial reefs give baby corals a foundation to latch onto and help attract fish species by giving them protection. Meanwhile there is a proliferation of small, colourful creatures plus rays, turtles and so on. The island itself is quite large and ringed by a stretch of white sandy beach. There's even an outdoor spa set under the mangrove trees. Just watch out for the coconut crabs who come to visit at night. Diving is year round and the island perfect for everyone, even non-diving chums.Dive centres: **The Reef Dive Resort**, Mataking Island: No. 193-195 Jalan Bakau, 91000 Tawau, Sabah T89-770022, www.mataking.com

Labuan Federal Territory This small island, just 8 km off the west coast of Sabah, and short a hop from the Sultanate of Brunei, is an intriguing wreck diving destination. The island has a deep water harbour and has always been a busy commercial centre. Now it's a duty free port with waterside markets, hotels, night clubs, and excellent restaurants. The marine park consists of three small islands with pretty beaches and ringed by some shallow reefs that are suitable for snorkelling. However, the real draw is the cluster of accessible wrecks. A couple are WWII (the American and Australian wrecks) while the Blue Water and Cement wrecks are more recent. This last is suitable for beginners, but the others requires more advanced diving experience. Fish and coral growth on the structures are reasonable, a good thing as the local reefs suffer from sediments and low visibility. The best dive season is between May and September. Dive centres: **Borneo Divers**, Menara Jubili 53 Jalan Gaya 88000 Kota Kinabalu, Sabah, T88-222226, www.borneodivers.info

Peninsula or Mainland Malaysia The dive reputation of this area lags far behind highly respected Borneo. It's not that there isn't good diving, it just isn't quite as spectacular. West coast reefs have suffered due to the commercial nature of the region, however, the good news for divers, is that the easily reached and relaxing east coast has a huge variety of resorts and islands. The best time to visit is in the drier season, from April till October, but even then visibility can drop way down to 3 metres - or be as high as 30. All these places are suitable no matter what your experience is, although serious divers may find it not quite enough of a challenge. If no accomodation is listed below it' s because the dive centres work with several. Just tell them your budget and they'll find you somewhere nice to stay.

Perhentian Islands Inside the Terengganu Marine Park, are the two Perhentian Islands. These tiny, pretty and very 'Robinson Crusoe' islands are ringed by dive sites. Mostly, these tend to be rocky outcrops with cracks and crevices to investigate. There's plenty of coral growth and all the typical fish species - angels butterflies, jacks and so on. In July and August bigger pelagics, even whale sharks, may make an appearance... you just never know your luck. Dive centres: **Coral View Island Resort**: on Perhentian Besar, Anjung Holidays S1a, Terminal Pelancongan, Kuala Besut, 22300 Besut, Terengganu, T9-6974095, www.pulauperhentian.com.my **Spice Divers/Chempaka Chalets**, on Pulau Perhentian Kecil, 22300 Kuala Besut, Terengganu, T19-9857329, www.spicedivers.com.my

Redang Island Just below Perhentian and also part of the marine park, Redang consists of a main island surrounded by a cluster of smaller ones. This was Malaysia's first marine park and has the best visibility as there are deeper drop offs. Dive sites circle outcrops which have sandy terrain on the eastern side and rocky on the west. This makes for quite a variety of sites with plenty of hard corals and fans. Occasional mantas and whale sharks have been spotted.Dive centres: **Redang Kalong Resort**, 57 Jalan Sultan Zainal Abidin, 20000 Kuala Terengganu, T9-6221691, www.redangkalong.com

Lang Tengah Regarded as one of the nation's best-kept secrets this little island has pristine beaches and unspoiled tropical jungle interior. It is also very undeveloped, with only two tiny resorts that give it a sense of exclusivity. Diving is, like it's neighbours, gentle and easy going. Dive centres: **Blue Coral Island Resort**, Unit L1-09, Bangunan JOTIC NO. 2, Jalan Ayer Molek, 80000 Johor Bahru, T7-2272901, www.langtengah.com.my

Tenggol Island Further south, this island is regarded it as having some of the best diving on the peninsular It's a bit further offshore and has better visibility. The west of the island is a steep sided wall that descends down to 30 metres where interesting boulders can be found. There's plenty of colour with soft corals and fans, while on the east of the island you may find some intriguing critters lurking in the sand. Dive centres: **Tenggol Aqua Resort**, 77A Jalan Sultan Sulaiman, 20000 Kuala Terengganu T9-6262020, www.myoutdoor.com

Tioman Island The movie, South Pacific, was filmed on Tioman and it is as lovely as you might recall (if you're old enough). At less than an hour's flight from Kuala Lumpur, it is an ideal add-on, but possibly as much for it's jungle walks, bird life and flora as it's diving. The island is a designated marine park, but the water is very shallow so best suited to beginners. In fact, this can be a good place to take a course.

There is more challenging diving a little way off shore, with all the usual suspects to spot, and a couple of small wrecks lurk in the shallows. Dive centres: **Tioman Dive Centre,** Kampong Tekek, 86807 Tioman, Pahang, T/F9- 4191228, www.tioman-dive-centre.com **B&J Diving Centre**, No. 46 Kampong Salang, Pulau Tioman, T9-419 5555, www.divetioman.com

Langkwai and Pulau Payar The west coast of Malaysia's Peninsula is not regarded as a dive specific destination by those in the know. A history of heavy shipping, trade and industry has taken it's toll on the marine realm, but if you are heading this way for another reason, there is diving available. The Payar Marine Park has some reasonable coral reefs and plenty of life in them, but the area tends to suffer from low visibility. Dive centres: **East Marine/Royal Langkawi Yacht Club**, Jalan Dato Syd Omar, 07000 Kuah, Langkawi, T4-9663966, www.eastmarine.com.my

Liveaboards Ocean Rover: this high-class vessel cruises the Peninsula east coast in summer visiting Tioman, Redang, Perhentian and Tenggol. Occasional cruises start in Singapore, travel up the Malay coast, finishing at Koh Samui in Thailand. Or vice versa. **Ocean Rover Cruises,** 3/20 Moo 5, Viset Road, Tambon Rawai, Ampur Muang, Phuket, 83100, Thailand, T66-7628 1387, www.ocean-rover.com **Celebes Explorer**: the only regular sailings around the top of Borneo are on this vessel. Itineraries cover Sipadan and nearby islands, depending on the length of cruise. **Adventure Journey World Travel,** P. O. Box 12248, 88825 Kota Kinabalu, Sabah T88-223918, www.borneo.org/liveaboard **White Manta**: departing Singapore from April to November, this boat travels up to Tioman island and various other Malaysian destinations for trips of around four days. 31 Bishan St 11 ,#14-02 Bishan Loft, Singapore 579819 T65-6552 3544, www.whitemanta.com

Spas

Many luxury hotels have cashed in on the popularity of pamper-yourself holidays by adding spas to their resorts. You'll find spas, aromotherapy and massage centres in most of the upmarket hotels all over the country - on the Peninsula and in East Malaysia - but Langkawi, an island off the west coast has made it into a specialty. On rainy days, there's not much else to do but soak around and get rubbed at a spa. As well as the top notch award-winning spa at *The Datai*, there are plenty of more budget options available.

Trekking and climbing

There are good jungle treks in Taman Negara and in the Endau Rompin National Park and hiking in the Cameron Highlands all on the Peninsula. There are numerous opportunities for climbing, especially in East Malaysia. Most of East Malaysia's parks offer hiking trails, but the best are in the Niah, Gunung Mulu and Gunung Kinabalu national parks. Climbing Mount Kinabalu in Sabah, to be at the summit for sunrise, is one of the most popular hike.

Water Rafting

Wild or white water rafting is not a well established activity in Malaysia although there are some good spots to take to the swirl. Sabah has the Padas (graded 3) and the Kiulu (graded 2) rivers where tour operators can organize rafting. On the Peninsula there are several rivers with rapids accessible from Fraser's Hill.

Spectator sports

The best place to see traditional sports such as **Silat** – the Malaysian art of self defence, **kite-flying** and **top-spinning** is at the Cultural Centre in Kota Bahru on the east coast where performances and competitions are held at fixed times every week.

All over the country, a good way to make friends is by watching village **football** matches – you may be asked to take part. Head to the village green.

There are **horse racing** tracks in Penang, T4-229 3233, www.penangturfclub.com and near KL at Selangor T3-9058 3888.

For **motor racing** there is the state of the art Malaysian F1 Grand Prix stadium with its 15-turn track in Sepang, 60km south of KL. See www.malaysiangp.com.my for information on events and how to get there.

Health

Local populations in Malaysia are exposed to a range of health risks not encountered in the western world. Many of the diseases are major problems for the local poor and destitute and though the risk to travellers is more remote, they cannot be ignored. Obviously five-star travel is going to carry less risk than back-packing on a minimal budget.

The health care in the region is generally of good quality. There are many excellent private and government clinics/hospitals. As with all medical care, first impressions count. If a facility is grubby then be wary of the general standard of medicine and hygiene. It's worth contacting your embassy or consulate on arrival and asking where the recommended (ie those used by diplomats) clinics are. Providing embassies with information of your whereabouts can be also useful if a friend/relative gets ill at home and there is a desperate search for you around the globe. You can also ask them about locally recommended medical do's and don'ts. If you do get ill, and you have the opportunity, you should also ask your medical insurer whether they are satisfied that the medical centre or hospital that you have been referred to is of a suitable standard. Singapore has world-class health facilities and very few infectious disease risks.

Remember that it is risky to buy medicinal tablets abroad because the doses may differ and there may be a trade in false drugs.

Before you go

Ideally, you should see your GP or travel clinic at least six weeks before your departure for general advice on travel risks, malaria and vaccinations. Make sure you have travel insurance, get a dental check (especially if you are going to be away for more than a month), know your own blood group and if you suffer a long-term condition such as diabetes or epilepsy make sure someone knows or that you have a Medic Alert bracelet/necklace with this information on it.

Basic vaccinations include **Polio** if none in the last 10 years; **Tetanus** again if you haven't had one in the last 10 years (after five doses you have had enough for life); Diphtheria if none in the last 10 years; **Typhoid** if nil in the last three years; **Hepatitis A** as the disease can be caught easily from food/water.

Malaria

There is no risk in Singapore. Malaysia has no risk of malaria in most areas, a few rural areas may be affected but seek specialist advice as the situation may change.

Items to take with you

Mosquito repellents. Remember that DEET (Di-ethyltoluamide) is the gold standard. Apply the repellent every four to six hours but more often if you are sweating heavily. If a non-DEET product is used check who tested it. Validated products (tested at the London School of Hygiene and Tropical Medicine) include Mosiguard, Non-DEET

 Jungle formula and non-DEET Autan. If you want to use citronella remember that it must be applied very frequently (ie hourly) to be effective. If you are a popular target for insect bites or develop lumps quite soon after being bitten, carry an Aspivenin kit. This syringe suction device is available from many chemists and draws out some of the allergic materials and provides quick relief. **Sun screen. Pain killers.** Paracetomol or a suitable painkiller can have multiple uses for symptoms but remember that more than eight paracetomol a day can lead to liver failure. **Ciproxin (Ciprofloxacin).** A useful antibiotic for some forms of travellers' diarrhoea. **Immodium.** A great standby for those diarrhoeas that occur at awkward times (ie before a long coach/train journey or on a trek). It helps stop the flow of diarrhoea and in my view is of more benefit than harm. (It was believed that letting the bacteria or viruses flow out had to be more beneficial. However, with Immodium they still come out, just in a more solid form.) **Pepto-Bismol.** Used a lot by Americans for diarrhoea. It certainly relieves symptoms but like Immodium it is not a cure for underlying disease. Be aware that it turns the stool black as well as making it more solid. **MedicAlert.** These simple bracelets, or an equivalent, should be carried or worn by anyone with a significant medical condition.

For longer trips involving jungle treks taking a clean needle pack, clean dental pack and water filtration devices are common-sense measures.

On the road

Diarrhoea and intestinal upset

Symptoms Diarrhoea can refer either to loose stools or an increased frequency; both of these can be a nuisance. It should be short lasting but persistence beyond two weeks, with blood or pain, require specialist medical attention.

Cures Ciproxin (Ciprofloxacin) is a useful antibiotic for bacterial traveller's diarrhoea. It can be obtained by private prescription in the UK. You need to take one 500 mg tablet when the diarrhoea starts and if you do not feel better in 24 hours, the diarrhoea is likely to have a non-bacterial cause and may be viral (in which case there is little you can do apart from keep yourself rehydrated and wait for it to settle on its own). The key treatment with all diarrhoeas is rehydration. Try to keep hydrated by taking the right mixture of salt and water. This is available as Oral Rehydration Salts (ORS) in ready-made sachets or can be made up by adding a teaspoon of sugar and a half teaspoon of salt to a litre of clean water. Drink at least one large cup of this drink for each loose stool. You can also use flat carbonated drinks as an alternative. Immodium and Pepto-Bismol provide symptomatic relief.

Prevention The standard advice is to be careful with water and ice for drinking. Ask yourself where the water came from. If you have any doubts then boil it or filter and treat it. There are many filter/treatment devices now available on the market. Food can also transmit disease. Be wary of salads (what were they washed in, who handled them), re-heated foods or food that has been left out in the sun having been cooked earlier in the day. There is a simple adage that says wash it, peel it, boil it or forget it. Also be wary of unpasteurised dairy products, these can transmit a range of diseases from brucellosis (fevers and constipation), to listeria (meningitis) and tuberculosis of the gut (obstruction, constipation, fevers and weight loss).

Sun protection

Symptoms White Britons are notorious for becoming red in hot countries because they like to stay out longer and do not use adequate sun protection. This can lead to sunburn, which is painful and followed by flaking of skin. Aloe vera gel is a good pain reliever for sunburn. Long-term sun damage leads to a loss of elasticity of skin and the development of pre-cancerous lesions. Years later a mild or a very malignant form of cancer may develop. The milder basal cell carcinoma, if detected early, can be treated by cutting it out or freezing it. The much nastier malignant melanoma may have already spread to bone and brain at the time that it is first noticed.

Prevention Sun screen. SPF stands for Sun Protection Factor. It is measured by determining how long a given person takes to 'burn' with and without the sunscreen product on. So, if it takes 10 times longer to burn with the sunscreen product applied, then that product has an SPF of 10. If it only takes twice as long then the SPF is 2. The higher the SPF the greater the protection. However, do not just use higher factors just to stay out in the sun longer. 'Flash frying' (desperate bursts of excessive exposure), as it is called, is known to increase the risks of skin cancer. Follow the Australians' with their Slip, Slap, Slop campaign referred to earlier

Bites and stings

It is a very rare event indeed for travellers, but if you are unlucky (or careless) enough to be bitten by a venomous snake, spider, scorpion or sea creature, try to identify the creature, without putting yourself in further danger (do not try to catch a live snake). Snake bites in particular are very frightening, but in fact rarely poisonous – even venomous snakes bite without injecting venom. Victims should be taken to a hospital or a doctor without delay. Commercial snake bite and scorpion kits are available, but are usually only useful for the specific types of snake or scorpion. Most serum has to be given intravenously so it is not much good equipping yourself with it unless you are used to making injections into veins. It is best to rely on local practice in these cases, because the particular creatures will be known about locally and appropriate treatment can be given. Certain tropical sea fish when trodden upon inject venom into bathers' feet. This can be exceptionally painful. Wear plastic shoes if such creatures are reported. The pain can be relieved by immersing the foot in hot water (as hot as you can bear) for as long as the pain persists or citric acid juices in fruits such as lemon is reported as useful.

Symptoms Fright, swelling, pain and bruising around the bite and soreness of the regional lymph glands, perhaps nausea, vomiting and a fever. Symptoms of serious poisoning would be: numbness and tingling of the face, muscular spasms, convulsions, shortness of breath or a failure of the blood to clot, causing generalized bleeding.

Treatment of snake bite Reassure and comfort the victim frequently. Immobilize the limb by a bandage or a splint and get the person to lie still. Do not slash the bite area and try to suck out the poison because this sort of heroism does more harm than good. If you know how to use a tourniquet in these circumstances, you will not need this advice. If you are not experienced, do not apply a tourniquet.

Precautions Do not walk in snake territory in bare feet or sandals – wear proper shoes or boots. If you encounter a snake stay put until it slithers away and do not investigate a wounded snake. Spiders and scorpions may be found in the more basic hotels, especially in the Andean countries. If stung, rest and take plenty of fluids and call a doctor. The best precaution is to keep beds away from the walls and look inside your shoes and under the toilet seat every morning.

Hepatitis

Symptoms Hepatitis means inflammation of the liver. Viral causes of the disease can be acquired anywhere in the world. The most obvious symptom is a yellowing of your skin or the whites of your eyes. However, prior to this all that you may notice is itching and tiredness.

 Cures Early on, depending on the type of hepatitis, a vaccine or immunoglobulin may reduce the duration of the illness.

Prevention Pre-travel hepatitis A vaccine is the best bet. Hepatitis B (for which there is a vaccine) is spread through blood and unprotected sexual intercourse, both of these can be avoided. Unfortunately there is no vaccine for hepatitis C or the increasing alphabetical list of other Hepatitis viruses.

Dengue fever

Unfortunately there is no vaccine against this and mosquitoes that carry it bite during the day. You will feel like a mule has kicked you for two to three days, you will then get better for a few days and then feel that the mule has kicked you again. It should all be over in seven to 10 days. Heed all the anti-mosquito measures that you can.

Sexual health

The range of visible and invisible diseases is awesome. Unprotected sex can spread HIV, Hepatitis B and C, Gonorrhea (green discharge), chlamydia (nothing to see but may cause painful urination and later female infertility), painful recurrent herpes, syphilis and warts, just to name a few. You can cut down the risk by using condoms, a femidom or avoiding sex altogether.

Water

There are a number of ways of purifying water. Dirty water should first be strained through a filter bag and then boiled or treated. Bringing water to a rolling boil at sea level is sufficient to make the water safe for drinking, but at higher altitudes you have to boil the water for a few minutes longer to ensure all microbes are killed. There are sterilising methods that can be used and there are proprietary preparations containing chlorine (eg Puritabs) or iodine (eg Pota Aqua) compounds. Chlorine compounds generally do not kill protozoa (eg Giardia). There are a number of water filters now on the market available in personal and expedition size. They work either on mechanical or chemical principles, or may do both. Make sure you take the spare parts or spare chemicals with you and do not believe everything manufacturers say.

Underwater health

Symptoms If you go diving make sure that you are fit do so. The **British Sub-Aqua Club**(BSAC), Telford's Quay, South Pier Road, Ellesmere Port, Cheshire CH65 4FL, UK, T01513-506200, www.bsac.com, can put you in touch with doctors who do medical examinations. Protect your feet from cuts, beach dog parasites (larva migrans) and sea urchins. The latter are almost impossible to remove but can be dissolved with lime or vinegar. Keep an eye out for secondary infection.

Cures Antibiotics for secondary infections. Serious diving injuries may need time in a decompression chamber.

Prevention Check that the dive company know what they are doing, have appropriate certification from BSAC or **Professional Association of Diving Instructors** (PADI), Unit 7, St Philips Central, Albert Rd, St Philips, Bristol, BS2 0TD, T0117-3007234, www.padi.com, and that the equipment is well maintained.

Altitude sickness

Symptoms Acute mountain sickness can strike from about 3,000 m upwards and in general is more likely to affect those who ascend rapidly (for example by plane) and those who over-exert themselves. Teenagers are particularly prone. On reaching heights above 3,000 m, heart pounding and shortness of breath, especially on exertion, are almost universal and a normal response to the lack of oxygen in the air. Acute mountain sickness takes a few hours or days to come on and presents with heachache, lassitude, dizziness, loss of appetite, nausea and vomiting. Insomnia is common and often associated with a suffocating feeling when lying down in bed. You may notice that your breathing tends to wax and wane at night and your face is puffy in the mornings – this is all part of the syndrome.

Cures If the symptoms are mild, the treatment is rest, painkillers (preferably not aspirin-based) for the headaches and anti-sickness pills for vomiting. Should the symptoms be severe and prolonged it is best to descend to a lower altitude immediately and reascend, if necessary, slowly and in stages. The symptoms disappear very quickly with even a few 100 m of descent.

Prevention The best way of preventing acute mountain sickness is a relatively slow ascent. When trekking to high altitude, some time spent walking at medium altitude, getting fit and getting adapted, is beneficial. On arrival at places over 3,000 m a few hours' rest and the avoidance of alcohol, cigarettes and heavy food will go a long way towards preventing acute mountain sickness.

Other problems experienced at high altitude are sunburn, excessively dry air causing skin cracking, sore eyes (it may be wise to leave your contact lenses out) and sore nostrils. Treat the latter with Vaseline. Do not ascend to high altitude if you are suffering from a bad cold or chest infection and certainly not within 24 hours following scuba diving.

Prickly heat

A very common intensely itchy rash is avoided by frequent washing and by wearing loose clothing. It is cured by allowing skin to dry off (through use of powder and spending two nights in an air-conditioned hotel!).

Each year there is the possibility that avian flu or SARS might rear its head. Check the news reports. If there is a problem in an area you are due to visit you may be advised to have an ordinary flu shot or to seek expert advice.

Further information

Websites

Foreign and Commonwealth Office (FCO) (UK), www.fco.gov.uk This is a key travel advice site, with useful information on the country, people, climate and lists the UK embassies/ consulates. The site also promotes the concept of 'Know Before You Go'. And encourages travel insurance and appropriate travel health advice. It has links to the Department of Health travel advice site, see below.

Department of Health Travel Advice (UK), www.doh.gov.uk/traveladvice This excellent site is also available as a free booklet, the T6, from Post Offices. It lists the vaccine advice requirements for each country.

Medic Alert (UK), www.medicalalert.co.uk This is the website of the foundation that produces bracelets and necklaces for those with existing medical problems. Once you have ordered your bracelet/necklace you write your key medical details on paper inside it, so that if you collapse, a medical person can identify you as someone with epilepsy or allergy to peanuts etc.

Blood Care Foundation (UK), www.bloodcare.org.uk The Blood Care Foundation is a Kent-based charity "dedicated to the provision of screened blood and resuscitation fluids in countries where these are not readily available". They will dispatch certified non-infected blood of the right type to your hospital/clinic. The blood is flown in from various centres around the world.

The Health Protection Agency
www.hpa.org.uk This site has up to date malaria advice guidelines for travel around the world. It gives specific advice about the right drugs for each location. It also has useful information for those who are pregnant, suffering from epilepsy or planning to travel with children.
World Health Organisation,
www.who.int The WHO site has links to the WHO Blue Book on travel advice. This lists the diseases in different regions of the world. It describes vaccination schedules and makes clear which countries have Yellow Fever Vaccination certificate requirements and malarial risk.
Fit for Travel (UK),
www.fitfortravel.scot.nhs.uk This site from Scotland provides a quick A-Z of vaccine and travel health advice requirements for each country.
British Travel Health Association (UK), www.btha.org This is the official website of an organization of travel health professionals.
Travel Screening Services (UK),
www.numberonehealth.co.uk This is the health author's website. A private clinic dedicated to integrated travel health. The clinic gives vaccine, travel health advice, email and SMS text vaccine reminders and screens returned travellers for tropical diseases.

Books

The Travellers Good Health Guide by Dr Ted Lankester, ISBN 0-85969-827-0. *Expedition Medicine (The Royal Geographic Society)* Editors David Warrell and Sarah Anderson ISBN 1 86197 040-4.
International Travel and Health World Health Organisation Geneva, ISBN 92 4 158026 7.
The World's Most Dangerous Places by Robert Young Pelton, Coskun Aral and Wink Dulles ISBN 1-566952-140-9.

Keeping in touch

Communications

Internet

Malaysia is one of the most gung-ho places on the planet when it comes to information technology and the internet. In line with this, internet cafés have sprung up all over the place and every town, however small, down-at-heel and apparently forgotten-by-the-wider-world will have, at the very least, a place offering internet services. Rates are cheap too: RM2.50 per hour at the bottom end, with most places charging around RM3-5/hour, but some hotels up to RM10/hour. Generally, internet cafés mainly geared to tourists are more expensive than those largely serving the local market where teenage boys spend hours playing noisy online games.

Post

Malaysia's post is cheap and reasonably reliable, although incoming and outgoing parcels should be registered. To send postcards and aerograms overseas costs RM0.50, while letters cost RM0.90 (under 10 grammes), RM1.40 for letters under 20 grammes. Post-office opening hours are 0830-1700 Monday-Saturday, (closed every the first Saturday every month). Fax services are available in most state capitals. Poste Restante is a reliable service available at general post offices in major cities; as elsewhere, make sure your surname is capitalised and underlined. Most post offices provide a packing service for a reasonable fee (around RM5). You can also buy AirAsia tickets at post offices.

Telephone

There are public telephone booths in most towns; telephones take RM0.10 and RM0.20 coins. Card phones are now widespread and they make good sense if phoning abroad. Telekom Malaysia offers a variety of cards: Kadfon, the Ring Ring card and iTalk (which offers the best IDD rate). There is also the TIMEKontact card (formerly Uniphone). Cards come in denominations from RM20 to RM100. They are available from airports, petrol stations and most outlets of 7-eleven and also from magazine stalls on the street. The stall in front of Kotaraya has a friendly owner and sells a range of cards.

Operator for 'outstation' (trunk) calls: T101
Enquiries: T102
Directory: T103
International IDD assistance: T108

International direct calls can be made from telephones with IDD (international direct dialling) facility (007 plus country code plus area code plus number). Direct international calls can be made from most Kedai Telekom and telephone booths in major towns.

You can use your mobile phone in Malaysia if you have a GSM model. If you want to keep the same number you will need to get roaming before you leave your home country – be aware this service is expensive, you will be paying top rates for outgoing and incoming calls and messages. A better idea is to get a pre-paid SIM card when you arrive. This is useful for making local calls, receiving calls from home and messaging is also fairly inexpensive. The three main service providers are Celcom, Maxis (the best for coverage) and DiGi (the cheapest but the worst for coverage). Pre-paid cards are available from most mobile phone shops.

Media

Newspapers

The main English-language dailies are *The New Straits Times, Business Times, The Star* (best for local news), and *The Malay Mail* (afternoon, basically a gossip rag). The main Sunday papers are *The New Sunday Times, The Sunday Mail* and *The Sunday Star*. *The Sun* is a free English-language daily found in train stations and shopping centres but is generally packed with ads and little else. The English-language dailies are government-owned and this is reflected in their content which tends to be relentlessly pro-government. *Aliran Monthly* is a high-brow but fascinating publication offering current affairs analysis from a non-government perspective. *The Rocket* is the Democratic Action Party's opposition newspaper, and also presents an alternative perspective. Both are available at some news stands. International editions of leading foreign newspapers and news magazines can be obtained at main news stands and book stalls, although some of these are not cleared through customs until mid-afternoon (notably *The Asian Wall Street Journal*). In East Malaysia the main English-language newspapers are the *Sabah Daily News* and the *Sarawak Tribune*.

If you are looking for any alternative line to that of the government's then it would be best to check the welter of opposition websites. For a critical look at the country try www.aliran.com/

For listings of what to do, the best sources are *Night & Day*, published weekly, and the What's On section of the *Malay Mail*.

Radio

There are six government radio stations which broadcast in various languages including English. Radio 1 broadcasts in Bahasa Melayu; Radio 2 is a music station; Radio 3 is Malay; Radio 4 is in English; Radio 5, Chinese; Radio 6, Tamil. In KL you can tune into the Federal Capital's radio station and elsewhere in the country there are local stations. The BBC World Service can be picked up on FM in southern Johor, from the Singapore transmitter. Elsewhere it can be received on short-wave. The main frequencies are (in kHz): 11750, 9740, 6195 and 3915.

The main services that can be picked up on short-wave radio are: British Broadcasting Corporation (BBC, London) Southeast Asian service 3915, 6195, 9570, 9740, 11750, 11955, 15360; Singapore service 88.9MHz; East Asian service 5995, 6195, 7180, 9740, 11715, 11750, 11945, 11955, 15140, 15280, 15360, 17830, 21715; Voice of America (VoA, Washington) Southeast Asian service 1143, 1575, 7120, 9760, 9770, 15185, 15425; Indonesian service 6110, 11760, 15425; Radio Beijing Southeast Asian service (English) 11600, 11660; and Radio Japan (Tokyo) Southeast Asian service (English) 11815, 17810, 21610.

Television

RTM1 and RTM2 are operated by Radio Television Malaysia, the government-run broadcasting station. Apart from locally produced programmes, some American and British series are shown. NTV7 has many imported shows from the US including David Letterman and reality shows and the locally produced Pillow Talk (aired late at night), which is ground-breaking for conservative Malaysia, as it features women hosts discussing taboo subjects such as sex and love. NTV8 is a channel for early 20s and teens which has some imported shows including Baywatch. Channel 9 and TV3 has mainly Malay programmes. Programmes for all channels are listed in daily newspapers. Singapore Broadcasting Service programmes can be received as far north as Melaka and are often listed in Malaysian papers. Satellite TV only recently arrived in Malaysia. Many hotels carry the ASTRO service which offers HBO. STAR movies, ESPN, CNN, BBC, Discovery and MTV as well as a host of Chinese channels.

Kuala Lumpur

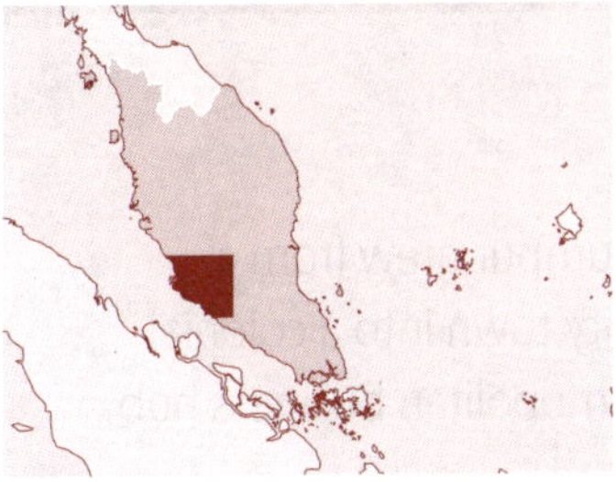

Footprint features

Introduction

In the space of a century, Kuala Lumpur grew from a trading post and tin-mining shanty town into a colonial capital. Today, it is a modern, cosmopolitan business hub and centre of government.

The economic boom that started in the late 1980s has caused a building bonanza that has rivalled Singapore's. In downtown Kuala Lumpur, old and new are juxtaposed. The jungled backdrop of the copper-topped clock tower of the Supreme Court of a century ago has been replaced by scores of stylish, high-rise office blocks, dominated by the soaring, angular-roofed Maybank headquarters. The Victorian, Moorish and Moghul-style buildings, the Art Deco central market, and the Chinese shophouses stand in marked contrast to these impressive skyscrapers. The Petronas Twin Towers offers the most impressive addition to the modern skyline – part of the Kuala Lumpur City Centre (KLCC) development, this is the second tallest building in the world.

Around the city are the intriguing Batu Caves and some good entertainment in the form of the Sunway Lagoon, Mines Wonderland. Seremban, a former tin-mining centre and window on the world of the Minangkabau culture is south of the capital.

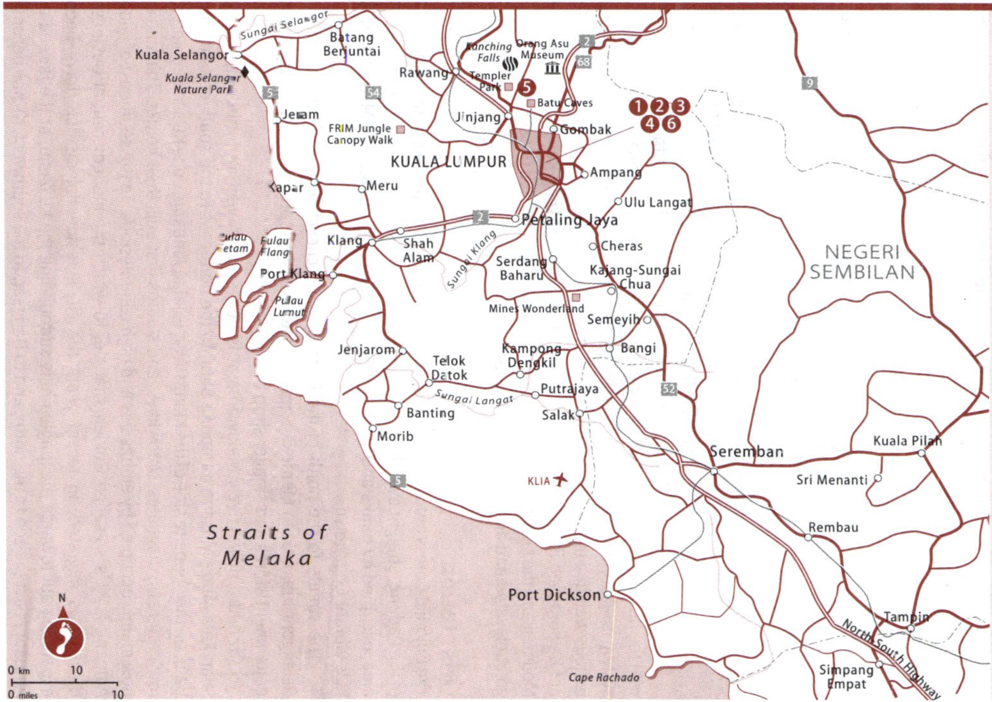

★ Don't miss...

1. **Museum of Islamic Arts Malaysia** Pore through a stunning, sumptuous collection of religious art and artifacts – the best in the world, page 80.
2. **Little India** Shop for saris and South Asian sweetmeats in the bazaar-like streets, page 82.
3. **Petronas Towers** Survey the city from the skies by climbing Malaysia's tallest skyscrapers, page 84.
4. **Bukit Nanas Forest Reserve** Enjoy the surreal experience of trekking through rainforest in the heart of the city, page 85.
5. **Batu caves** Explore these holy Hindu caverns, wreathed in incense and lit by spooky shafts of light, page 87.
6. **Mamak experience** Tuck into a *roti canai* and *teh tarik* breakfast at an Indian Muslim canteen, page 102 .

Ins and outs

→ *Colour map 2, grid A2 Population:1,500,000*

Getting there

As befitting Malaysia's capital, Kuala Lumpur (KL) is well linked both to other areas of Malaysia and to the wider world. The international airport at Sepang provides a slick point of entry to the country. It lies over 70 km to the south, with a KLIA Exspres rail link to the KL Sentral train station in the city centre. Domestic air connections (including to Sabah and Sarawak) also pass through Sepang. KL Sentral is a transport hub – from this gleaming new station you can hop off the KLIA Exspres and onto a KTM train going to Singapore, Penang, Kota Bharu and Bangkok or you can catch a taxi to your hotel or you can change to the underground/overground trains that zip around the city. Lines that have an interchange with KL Sentral are: the Monorail (actually across the road, not in the same building), the KTM Komuter, and the Putra LRT line (only the Star LRT does not go through KL Sentral. These last three are in the KL Sentral building. Puduraya bus station also has international connections south to Singapore and north to Bangkok, as well as to many towns on the Peninsula. » *See also Transport, page 115 and Airport Information, Essentials, page 31.*

This is a good map of the lines: www.kiat.net/malaysia/KL/transit.html The map is up-to-date but ignore the text as it's not.

Getting around

Kuala Lumpur is not the easiest city to navigate, with its sights spread thinly over a wide area. Pedestrians have not been very high on the list of priorities for Malaysian urban planners, with many roads, especially outside the city centre, built without pavements, making walking both hazardous and difficult. In addition, with the exception of the area around Central Market, Chinatown and Dayabumi, distances between sights are too great to cover comfortably on foot, both because of the lack of pavements and because of heavy pollution and the hot and humid climate. Like other Southeast Asian cities, with the notable exception of Singapore, the internal combustion engine rules. The bus system is labyrinthine and congested streets mean that travelling by taxi can make for a tedious wait in a traffic jam. Try to insist that taxi drivers use their meters, although do not be surprised if they simply refuse point blank. The two Light Rail Transit (LRT), the Monorail and the KMT Komuter rail lines are undoubtedly the least hassle and provide a great elevated and air-conditioned view of the city.

See colour maps of KL transport system at the back of the book.

Orientation

The Colonial Core is around the Padang and down Jalan Raja and Jalan Tun Perak. East of the Padang, straight over the bridge on Lebuh Pasar Besar, is the main commercial area, occupied by banks and finance companies. To the southeast of Merdeka Sq is KL's vibrant Chinatown.

The streets to the north of the Padang – the cricket pitch in front of the old Selangor Club, next to Merdeka Square – are central shopping streets with modern department stores and smaller shops.

To find a distinctively Malay area, it is necessary to venture further out, along Jalan Raja Muda Musa to Kampong Baru, to the northeast.To the south of Kampong Baru, on the opposite side of the Klang River, is Jalan Ampang, once KL's 'millionaires' row', where tin magnates, or towkays, and sultans first built their homes. The road is now mainly occupied by embassies and high commissions. To the southeast of Jalan Ampang is KL's so-called Golden Triangle, to which the modern central business district has migrated. In recent years the city's residential districts have been expanding out towards the jungled hills surrounding the KL basin, at the far end of Ampang, past the zoo to the north, and to Bangsar, to the southwest. KL has become

24 hours in the city

Begin the day by heading to the Petronas Twin Towers. Queue for a free ticket to the skybridge (closed Mondays) to survey the city from above. Head back to earth, pick up a copy of the *New Straits Times* and enjoying a leisurely coffee before making a foray for the classic Malay breakfast: *nasi lemak* - rice cooked in coconut milk served with prawn sembal, *ikan bilis* (rather like anchovies), hard boiled egg, cucumber and peanuts.

Make your way to Chinatown and discover two facets of Malaysia's cultural heritage: the Sri Mahamariamman Temple and the Chan See Shu Yuen Temple. For the sake of cultural balance make your way to the Masjid Megara National Mosque, stopping en route at the art deco Central Market to browse handicrafts and souvenirs.

At midday engage with a dim sum buffet lunch which you can work off with a walk in the 90 hectare Lake Gardens before looking around the Islamic Arts Museum near its southern tips. By mid afternoon shake off the past and witness Malaysia's tryst with modernity.

Start the evening with a mouth-tingling cold beer at the Coliseum Café before heading back to Chinatown around 1930 when the copy-watch sellers and all sorts of other hawkers emerge from their work load.

For dinner, sample another slice of this culinary melting pot in the unique Nyonya cuisine of the Straits Malays. Check listings page 602.

While KL is not Ibiza there is still a reasonably hot stock of bars and clubs on Jln Pinang and Jln P Ramlee, and a less touristy congregation in Bangsar baru to the west of the city centre and near the university of Malaya. If your stomach grumbles after midnight, 24-hour mamak canteens are plentiful in Bangsar.

Lie on your bed and reflect on what's in your stomach or in your head: Indian, French, Taoist, Hindu, Chinese, Malay, Muslim and Western. Quite a cultural score for one day.

a city of condominiums, which have sprung up everywhere from the centre of town to these outlying suburbs. Greater KL sprawls out into the Klang Valley, once plantation country and now home to the industrial satellites of Petaling Jaya and Shah Alam.

The most recent – and grandiose – development is Putrajaya, Malaysia's new administrative capital, which has been hacked out of plantations 35 km south of KL. It is estimated that when it is completed, Putrajaya's population will be 330,000. The city will cost a cool US$8 bn. Other developments in this area to the south of KL include the new international airport, which opened in 1998, and the Cyberjaya, the heart of Malaysia's much-vaunted Multimedia Super Corridor.

Best time to visit

The weather in KL is hot and humid all year round with temperatures rarely straying far below 20 degrees celsius or much above 30 degrees. There is also no rainy season per se, you can get rainstorms throughout the year. Try to coincide your trip with one of the festivals (see page 52), one of the most colourful and shocking is the Thaipusam festival (see page 52).

Tourist information

Malaysian Tourism Centre (MTC), ⓘ *109 Jln Ampang, T3-21633664, daily 0700-2400.* Located in an opulent mansion formerly belonging to a Malaysian planter and tin miner it provides information on all 13 states , money-changing facilities, an express

Kuala Lumpur

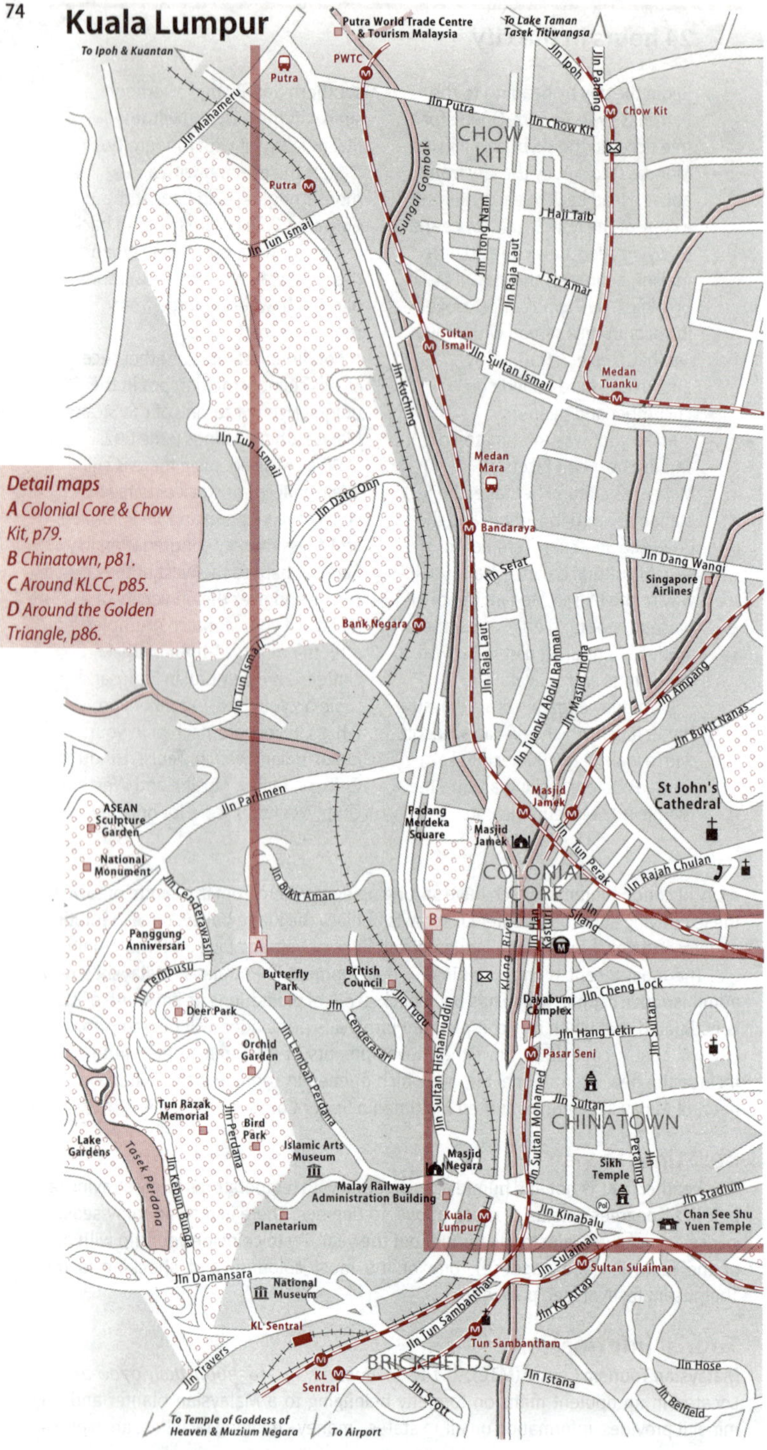

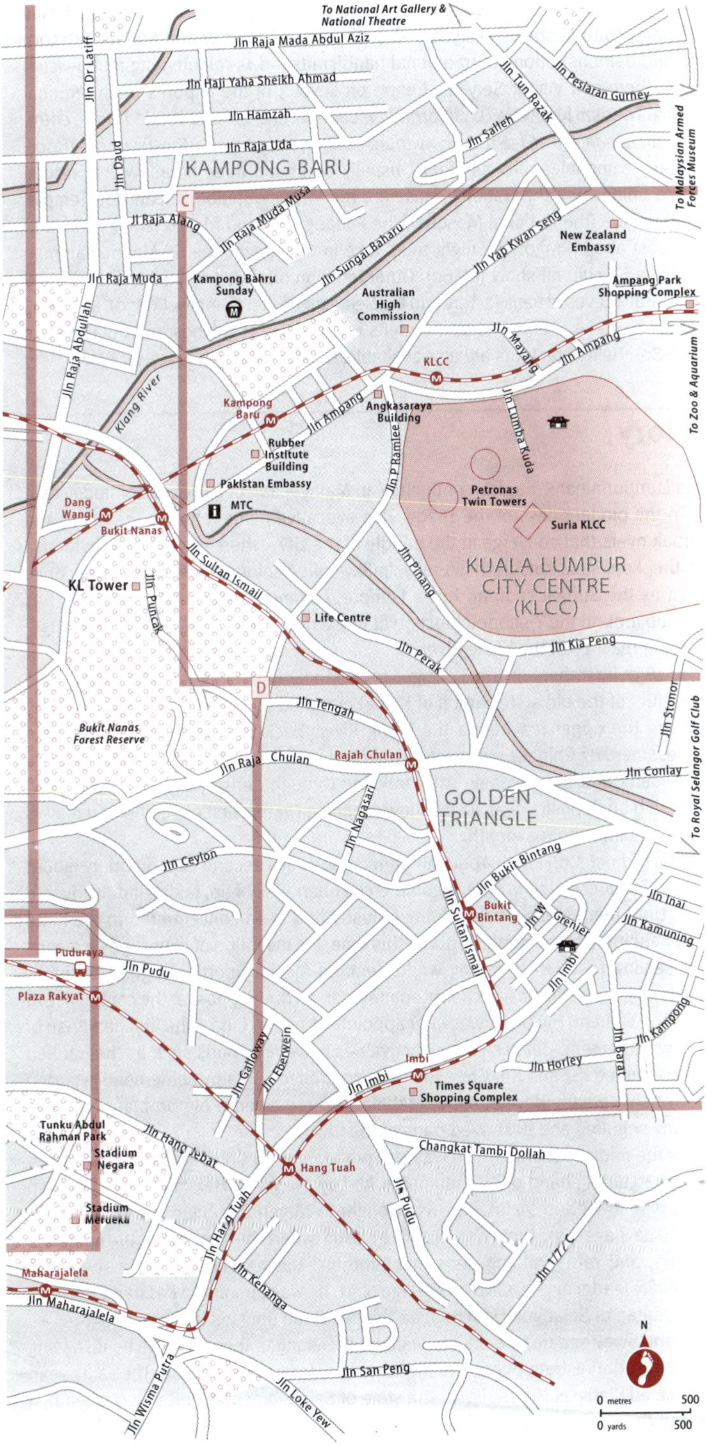
To National Art Gallery & National Theatre
Jln Raja Mada Abdul Aziz
Jln Dr Latiff
Jln Haji Yaha Sheikh Ahmad
Jln Hamzah
Jln Tun Razak
Jln Pesiaran Gurney
Jln Salleh
Jln Raja Uda
Jln Daud
KAMPONG BARU
To Malaysian Armed Forces Museum
C
Jl Raja Alang
Jln Raja Muda Musa
Jln Sungai Baharu
Jln Yap Kwan Seng
New Zealand Embassy
Jln Raja Muda
Kampong Bahru Sunday
Australian High Commission
Ampang Park Shopping Complex
Jln Raja Abdullah
Jln Mayang
Jln Ampang
Klang River
KLCC
Kampong Baru
Jln Ampang
Angkasaraya Building
Jln Lumba Kuda
To Zoo & Aquarium
Rubber Institute Building
Jln P Ramlee
Pakistan Embassy
Petronas Twin Towers
Dang Wangi
MTC
Suria KLCC
Bukit Nanas
Jln Sultan Ismail
Jln Pinang
KL Tower
Jln Puncak
KUALA LUMPUR CITY CENTRE (KLCC)
Life Centre
Jln Perak
Jln Kia Peng
D
Jln Tengah
Jln Stonor
Bukit Nanas Forest Reserve
To Royal Selangor Golf Club
Jln Raja Chulan
Rajah Chulan
Jln Conlay
Jln Nagasari
GOLDEN TRIANGLE
Jln Ceylon
Jln Bukit Bintang
Jln Inai
Bukit Bintang
Jln Sultan Ismail
Jln W
Grenier
Jln Kamuning
Puduraya
Jln Imbi
Jln Pudu
Plaza Rakyat
Jln Kampong
Jln Barat
Jln Galloway
Jln Eberwein
Imbi
Jln Horley
Jln Imbi
Times Square Shopping Complex
Tunku Abdul Rahman Park
Jln Hang Jebat
Changkat Tambi Dollah
Stadium Negara
Hang Tuah
Jln Pudu
Stadium Merdeka
Jln Hang Tuah
Jln 1/77C
Maharajalela
Jln Kenanga
Jln Maharajalela
N
Jln San Peng
Jln Wisma Putra
Jln Loke Yew
0 metres 500
0 yards 500

 bus ticketing counter, reservations for package holidays, a souvenir shop, Malay restaurant, cultural shows every Tuesday, Thursday, Saturday and Sunday at 1500, RM5, and demonstrations of traditional handicraftsand 15-minute-long audio-visual shows. There is a Visitor Services Centre on Level 3 of the airport's main terminal building. **Tourism Malaysia** ⓘ, *Information Centre, Level 2, Putra World Trade Centre, 45 Jln Tun Ismail, T3-26158188, www.tourismmalaysia.gov.my, Mon-Fri 0900-1800.*

Many companies offer city tours, usually of around three hours, which include visits to Chinatown, the National Museum, the Railway Station, Thean Hou Temple, Masjid Negara (the National Mosque), the Padang area and Masjid Jamek – most of which cost about RM30. City night tours take in Chinatown, the Sri Mahmariamman Temple and a cultural show (RM60). Other tours on offer visit sights close to the city such as Batu Caves, a batik factory and the Selangor Pewter Complex (RM30), as well as day trips to Melaka, Port Dickson, Fraser's Hill, Genting Highlands and Pulau Ketam (RM40-80). Helicopter tours are also available. ▸▸ *See also tour operators, page 114.*

History

Kuala Lumpur means 'muddy confluence' in Malay – as apt a description today as it was in the pioneer days of the 1870s. This evocative name refers to the Klang and Gombak rivers that converge in the middle of the city – there is also some evidence that the kopi-susu-coloured (literally 'milky-coffee-coloured') Gombak was once known as the Sungai Lumpur. Kuala Lumpur, commonly known simply as KL, has grown up around the Y-shaped junction of these rivers in the area called Ulu Klang – the upper reaches of the Klang River.

In 1857, members of the Selangor royal family (including Rajah Abdullah, the Bugis chief of the old state capital of Klang) mounted an expedition to speculate for tin along the upper reaches of the Klang River. Backed by money from Melakan businessmen, 87 Chinese prospectors travelled up the river by raft to the confluence of the Klang and the Gombak. After trekking through dense jungle they stumbled across rich tin deposits near what is now Ampang. On this first expedition 69 miners died of malaria within a month.

This did not stop Rajah Abdullah from organizing a second expeditionary labour force, which succeeded in mining commercial quantities of tin, taking it downriver to Klang. Until then, Malaya's tin-mining industry had been concentrated in the Kinta Valley near Ipoh, to the north. At about this time, the invention of canning as a means of preserving food led to strong world demand for tin. Spotting a good business opportunity, two Chinese merchants opened a small trading-post at the confluence in 1859. One of them, Hiu Siew, was later appointed Kapitan Cina – the first headman of the new settlement. But secret-society rivalries between groups such as the Hai San (who controlled KL) and the Ghee Hin (who controlled a nearby settlement) retarded the township's early development. Malaria also remained a big problem and fires regularly engulfed and destroyed parts of the town.

By the mid-1860s, KL, which was still predominantly Chinese, began to prosper under the guiding hand of its sheriff, **Yap Ah Loy**. He was a Hakka gang leader from China, who arrived in Melaka in 1854, fought in Negeri Sembilan's riots at Sungei Ujong (see page 92), then went to KL in 1862 where he became a tin magnate, (towkay), and ran gambling dens and brothels. But he emerged as a respected community leader and in 1868, at the age of 31, he was appointed Kapitan Cina of KL by the Sultan of Selangor. He remained the headman until his death in 1885.

Frank Swettenham, the British Resident of Selangor, then took the reins, having moved the administrative centre of the Residency from Klang in 1880. The same year, KL replaced Klang as the capital of the state of Selangor; shortly after Yap's death, it became the capital of the Federated Malay States. Swettenham pulled down the ramshackle shanties and rebuilt the town with wider streets and brick houses. In the National Museum there is a remarkable photograph of the Padang area in 1884, showing a shabby line of atap (palm thatch) huts where the Sultan Abdul Samad Building is today. By 1887 the new national capital had 518 brick houses and a population of 4,050. By 1910, when the magnificent Moorish-style railway station was completed, the city's population had risen more than 10-fold and nearly four-fifths of the population was Chinese. The town continued to grow in the following decades, becoming increasingly multiracial in character, as the British educated the Malay nobility, then employed them as administrators. The Indian population also grew rapidly; many were brought from South India to work on the roads and railways and the plantations in the Klang Valley.

During the Second World War, the city was bombed by the Allies, but little real damage was incurred. The Japanese surrendered in KL on 13 September 1945. Three years later, with the start of the Communist Emergency, there was a massive influx of squatters into the city. The city area quickly became overcrowded, so in 1952 Petaling Jaya, KL's satellite town (see page 89), was founded to relieve the pressure. It subsequently went on to attract many of Malaysia's early manufacturing industries. Following the end of the Emergency, Malaya became the independent Federation of Malaya on 31 August 1957. Independence was declared by the first prime minister of the independent federation, Tunku Abdul Rahman ('Papa Malaysia'), in the newly built Merdeka Stadium (see page 82). Not until the almagamation of Malaya, Sarawak and Sabah, in 1963 was the name Malaysia given to the new nation.

Modern Kuala Lumpur

In 1974, the 243-sq-km area immediately surrounding the city was formerly declared the Federal Territory of Kuala Lumpur, with a separate administration from its mother state of Selangor. Today, although one of the smallest capitals in Southeast Asia, it is a rapidly growing business centre; with its industrial satellites gaining the lion's share of the country's manufacturing investment. The skyline is dominated by the Petronas Twin Towers, in the Kuala Lumpur City Centre (KLCC) complex, which on completion in 1996 became the tallest building in the world at 452 m and 88 storeys. It has now been knocked back into second place by the Taiwan 101 tower in Taipei. The bridge connecting the two towers claims the title of the highest bridge in the world. When the building was being built in 1995 and 1996 the contractors were completing a floor every four days – and were being paid around RM2.2 million (US$579,000) per day.

There have been efforts to create a 'new Malaysian architecture', to lend the city a more integrated look and a national identity. Such buildings include the modern-Islamic Masjid Negara (the National Mosque), the National Museum and the Putra World Trade Centre (the latter two have Minangkabau-style roofs) and the 34-storey Dayabumi complex, by the river, with its modern-Islamic latticed arches. At the same time, KL has also been trying to cultivate a 'garden city' image like neighbouring Singapore; from the top of its skyscrapers, KL looks green and spacious, although green areas are fast being taken over by building developments.

Once a relatively quiet capital city, KL is becoming increasingly noisy and congested, as well as suffering from serious air pollution – or 'the haze', which is widely thought to be caused by the fires that burn uncontrollably in Sumatra and Kalimantan from July to September. Pollution is sometimes so bad it makes landings at KL's airport difficult. Locals note how convenient it is for the authorities to blame fires in another country for pollution problems at home. Environmentalists' initiatives to reduce pollution have got nowhere. Instead, while KL hospitals fill up with children suffering from bronchial problems, the health ministry feebly recommends that Malaysians wear surgical masks and give up exercising outside.

Sights

KL is a bit of a sprawl of a city. The big shopping malls, trendy restaurants and bars are clustered around The Golden Triangle and the KLCC. Here too are the Petronas Towers, once the tallest in the world, and the KL Tower, another mighty spike on the landscape. The ethnic neighbourhoods lie southwest of here – there's Chinatown a web of bustling streets filled with temples, funeral stores, restaurants and shophouses, and Little India packed with stores selling Bollywood cds, saris and spices. Also here is the colonial core where the remnants of the British empire ring Merdeka Square. You can escape from the hustle a few streets southwest of here in the Lake Gardens which house the fine Islamic Arts museum and a bird and orchid park.

The colonial core

Mederka Square and around

Behind the mosque, from the corner of Jalan Tuanku Abdul Rahman and Jalan Raja Laut, are the colonial-built public buildings, distinguished by their grand, Moorish architecture. All were the creation of AC Norman, a colleague of Hubbock's, and were built between 1894 and 1897. The photogenic former State Secretariat, now called the **Sultan Abdul Samad Building**, with its distinctive clock tower and bulbous copper domes, houses the Supreme Court. To the south of here is another Moorish building, the **Textile Museum**, ⓘ *26 Jalan Sultan Hishamuddin, daily 0930-1800, free*. It has excellent content, with an emphasis on weaving, as well as beadwork, batik and some embroidery. There is a video presentation and a shop.

The Sultan Abdul Samad Building faces on to the **Padang** on the opposite side of the road, next to **Merdeka Square**. The old Selangor Club cricket pitch is the venue for Independence Day celebrations. The centrepiece of Merdeka Square is the tallest flagpole in the world (100 m high) and the huge Malaysian flag that flies from the top can be seen across half the city, particularly at night when it is floodlit. The Padang was trimmed to make way for the square, which is also the venue for impromptu rock concerts, and is a popular meeting place. A shopping complex, the Plaza Putra, has been built underneath the square.

The very British mock-Tudor **Royal Selangor Club** fronts the Padang and was the centre of colonial society after its construction in 1890. Much of the building was damaged by a fire in the late 1960s and the north wing was built in 1970. The Selangor club is still a gathering place for KL's VIPs. It has one of the finest colonial saloons, filled with trophies and pictures of cricket teams. The famous Long Bar (known as 'The Dog') – which contains a fascinating collection of old photographs of KL – is still an exclusively male preserve. On the north side of the Padang is **St Mary's Church**, one of the oldest Anglican churches in Malaysia, built in 1894.

❢ Non-members can only visit if accompanied by a member

The **Bank Negara Money Museum**, ⓘ *on the Ground Floor of the Bank Negara Building, Jalan Dato Onn, Mon-Fri 0900-1630, Sat 0900-1200, free*, is a must for numismatic collectors. Founded in 1989, it houses a collection of Malaysian money.

On the south side of Merdeka Square is the **Museum of National History**, which has only limited displays including rocks, skulls and coins. ⓘ *T2944590, daily 0900-1800, free.*

The Dayabumi Complex and National Market

North of the mosque, back towards the Padang, is the 35-storey, marble **Dayabumi Complex** (see Chinatown map, page 81). Located on Jalan Raya, it is one of KL's most

Colonial core & Chow Kit

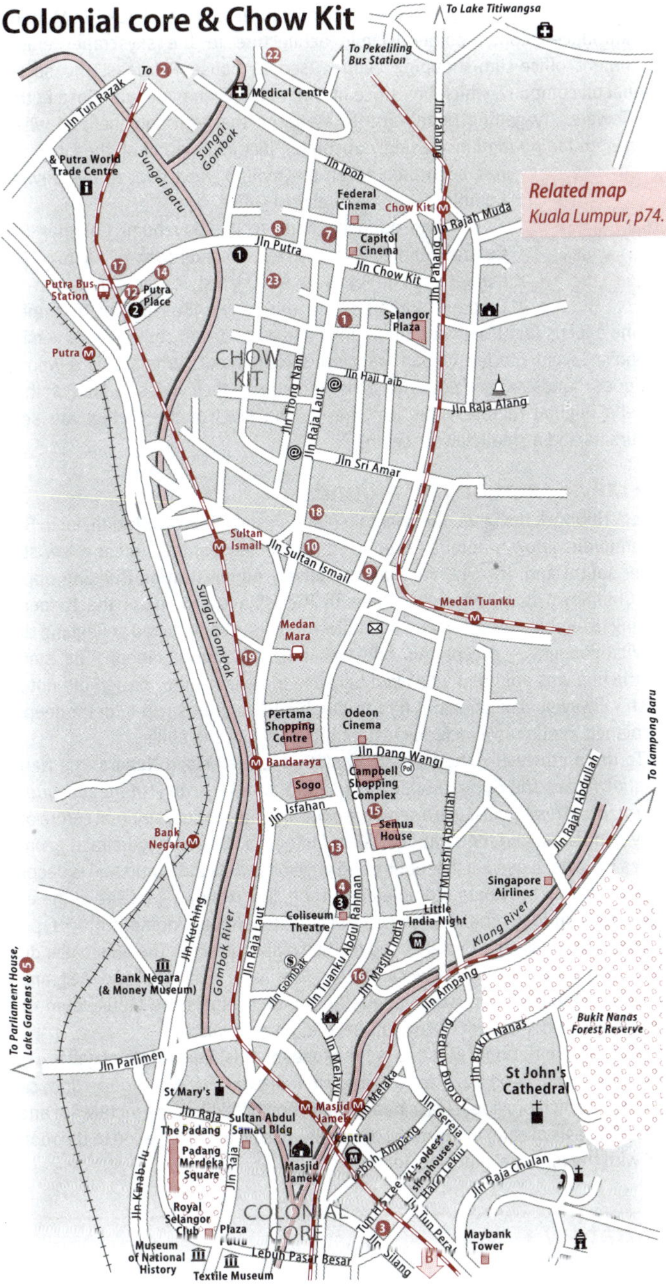

Related map
Kuala Lumpur, p74.

Sleeping
Backpackers' Travellers' Lodge **3**
Carcosa Seri Negara **5**
City **1**
Coliseum **4**
Dynasty **2**
Elegant Inn **7**
Grand Central **8**
Grand Centrepoint **9**
Grand Continental **10**
Kowloon **13**
Legend **14**
Noble **15**
Palace **16**
Pan Pacific **17**
Plaza **18**
Putra **12**
Quality **19**
Vistana **22**
Wira **23**

Eating
Chameleon Vegetarian **1**
Cili Padi Thai **2**
Coliseum Café **3**

striking modern landmarks. It was designed by local architect Datuk Nik Mohamed, and introduces contemporary Islamic achitecture to the skyscraper era. The government office-cum-shopping centre used to house Petronas, the secretive national oil company, which has since moved to the even more grandiose Petronas Twin Towers. Try getting permission to stand on the 30th floor helipad where a superb, but fading (and increasingly obsolete), pictorial map of all the city's sights has been painted on the rooftop. Next door to the Dayabumi Complex is the General Post Office.

The market is now a bit of a tourist trap, although it is definitely worth visiting for a one-stop buying spree.

On the opposite bank to the Dayabumi Complex is the **Central Market**, ⓘ *www.centralmarket.com.my*, a former wet market built in 1928 in Art Deco-style, tempered with 'local Baroque' trimmings. In the early 1980s it was revamped to become a focus for KL's artistic community and a handicraft centre – KL's version of London's Covent Garden or San Francisco's Fisherman's Wharf. It is a warren of boutiques, handicraft and souvenir stalls – some with their wares laid out on the wet market's original marble slabs. On the second level of the market are several restaurants and a small hawker centre.

The railway station and around

In 1910, Hubbock designed the fairy-tale Moorish-style **Railway Station**, Jalan Sultan Hishamuddin (now a hotel and replaced by the new Sentral station a few streets further south) and, in 1917, the **Malaya Railway Administration Building** opposite (see Chinatown map, page 81). Beneath the Islamic exterior of the former, the building resembles the glass and iron railway stations constructed in England during the Victorian era – except this one was built by convict labour. The station's construction was apparently delayed because the original roof design did not meet British railway specifications; it had to be able to support snow a metre deep. The refurbished interior now includes restaurants and souvenir stalls.

To the northwest of the old railway station is the **Masjid Negara** (the National Mosque), ⓘ *Sat-Thu 0900-1800, Fri 1445-1800. Muslims can visit the mosque from 0630-2200. Women must use a separate entrance*, the modern spiritual centre of KL's Malay population and the symbol of Islam for the whole country. Abstract, geometric shapes have been used in the roofing and grillwork, while the Grand Hall is decorated with verses from the Koran. Completed in 1965, it occupies a 5-ha site at the end of Jalan Hishamuddin. The prayer hall has a star-shaped dome with 18 points, representing Malaysia's 13 states and the five pillars of Islam. The 48 smaller domes emulate the great mosque in Mecca. The single minaret is 73 m tall and the grand hall can accommodate 8,000 worshippers. An annex contains the mausoleum of Tun Abdul Razak, independent Malaysia's second prime minister.

Close to the National Mosque is the **Museum of Islamic Arts Malaysia**, ⓘ *Jalan Lembah Perdana, T603 2274 2020, www.iamm.org.my, Tue-Sun, 1000-1800, closed Mon, RM8*, which provides a fascinating collection of textiles and metalware and is a wonderful oasis of calm in the midst of the city. It is possible to get on to the roof, at a level with the mosque's mosaic dome.

Chinatown

Southeast of the Central Market lies Chinatown, roughly bounded by Jalan Tun HS Lee (Jalan Bandar), Jalan Petaling and Jalan Sultan. It was the core of Yap Ah Loy's KL (see page 76) and is a mixture of crumbling shophouses, market stalls, coffee shops and restaurants. This quarter wakes up during late afternoon, after about 1630, and in the evening, when its streets become the centre of frenetic trading and haggling. Jalan Petaling and parts of Jalan Sultan are transformed into an open-air night market, pasar malam, and food stalls selling Chinese, Indian and Malay delicacies, fruit stalls, copy watch stalls, pirate dvds, leather bag stalls and all manner of impromptu boutiques line the streets. Jalan Hang Lekir, which straddles the gap between Jalan Sultan and Jalan Petaling, is full of popular Chinese restaurants with their tables set up on the pavement. Off the north side of Jalan Hang Lekir, there is a lively covered fruit and vegetable market in two intersecting arcades.

Sri Mahamariamman Temple

ⓘ *South of Jalan Hang Lekir, tucked away on Jalan Tun HS Lee (Jalan Bandar)*

The extravagantly decorated **Sri Mahamariamman Temple**, incorporating gold, precious stones and Spanish and Italian tiles. It was founded in 1873 by Tamils from southern India who had come to Malaya as contract labourers to work in the rubber plantations or on the roads and railways. Its construction was funded by the wealthy Chettiar money-lending caste, and it was rebuilt on its present site in 1985. It has a silver chariot dedicated to Lord Murugan (Subramaniam), which is taken in procession to the Batu Caves (see page 87) during the Thaipusam festival, when Hindu

In testament to Malaysia's sometimes muddled ethnic and religious mix, it is not uncommon to find Chinese devotees joining in the Thaipusam festival.

Chinatown

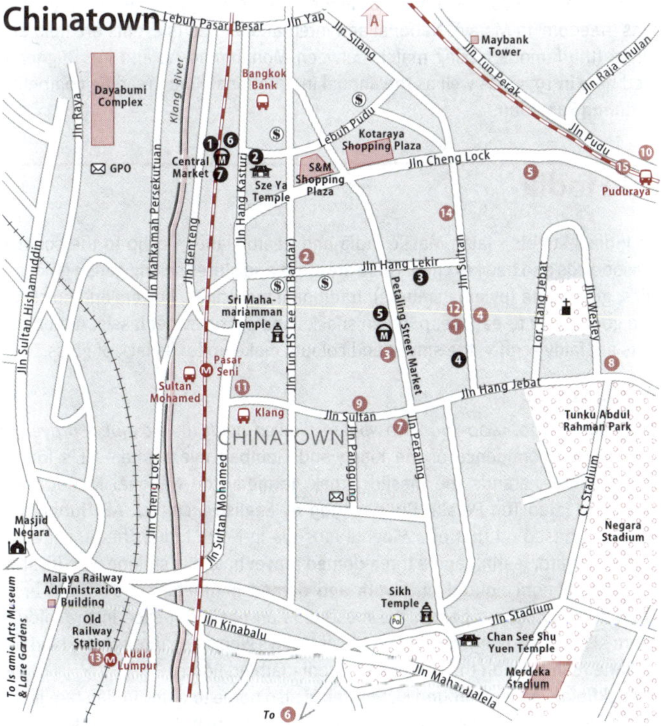

Sleeping
AnCasa 5
Backpackers' Travellers' Inn 1
Backpackers Travellers' Lodge 2
Chinatown Guesthouse 3
Furama 4
Heritage Station 13
Lok Ann 7
Mandarin Pacific 9
Pudu Hostel 10
Puduraya 15
Red Dragon Backpackers 14
Starlight 11
Swiss Inn 12
YMCA 6
YWCA 8

Eating
China Town Pavilion 3
Formosa Vegetarian 4
Gourmet Food Court 5
Hameed's 7
Naili's Place 1
Nam Heong 4
Oriental Bowl 2
Sawah Padi 7
Yusoof Dan Zakhir 6

devotees converge on the temple. Large numbers flock to the temple to participate in the ritual; this is usually preceded by about half-an-hour's chanting, which itself is accompanied by music.

Chinese temples

There are two prominent Chinese temples in the Chinatown area. The elaborate **Chan See Shu Yuen Temple**, at the southernmost end of Jalan Petaling, was built in 1906 and has a typical open courtyard and symmetrical pavilions. Paintings, woodcarvings and ceramic sculptures decorate the façade. It serves both as a place of worship and as a community centre. The older **Sze Ya Temple**, close to the central market on Lebuh Pudu, off Jalan Cheng Lock, was built in the 1880s on land donated by Yap Ah Loy. He also funded the temple's construction and a photograph of him sits on one of the altars. Ancestor worship is more usually confined to the numerous ornate clan houses (kongsis); a typical one is the **Chan Kongsi** on Jalan Maharajalela, near the Chan See Shu Yuen Temple.

Merkeka Stadium

ⓘ *RM1.*

Southeast of Chinatown, off Jalan Stadium, is the 50,000-capacity Merdeka Stadium, the site of Malaysia's Declaration of Independence on 31 August 1957 (merdeka means 'freedom' in Malay). National and international sports events are held at the stadium (the famous boxing match between Mohammad Ali and Joe Bugner was staged here in 1975), as well as the annual international Koran reading competition, held during Ramadan.

Little India

Little India's streets - Jalan Masjid India and nearby lanes - echo to the sounds of Bollywood cds and hawker cries. There are stalls and stores selling garish gold, saris, fabrics, great kurta (pyjama smocks), traditional medicines, flowers and spices. It is also a good place to eat cheap Indian snacks and sip on sweet lassis. Although the streets are fairly scruffy, the smells and colours make up for its lack of gloss.

Masjid Jamek

ⓘ *Daily 0900-1100, 1400-1600. No women allowed inside the mosque at prayer time.*

At the muddy confluence of the Klang and Gombak rivers where KL's founders stepped ashore, stands the Masjid Jamek, formerly the National Mosque (main entrance on Jalan Tun Perak). Built in 1909 by English architect, AB Hubbock, the design was based on that of a Moghul mosque in North India. The mosque has a walled courtyard, (sahn), and a three-domed prayer hall. It is striking with its striped white and salmoncoloured brickwork and domed minarets, cupolas and arches. Surrounded by coconut palms, the mosque is an oasis of peace in the middle of modern KL, as is apparent by the number of Malays who sleep through the heat of the lunchtime rush-hour on the prayer hall's cool marbled floors.

Brickfields, an area around KL Sentral, is also home to many Indian families and traders. There is talk of reinventing Little India as Malay Street, and turning Brickfields into KL's new Little india!

Lake Gardens and around

Muzium Negara (National Museum)

ⓘ *T3-22826255, 0900-1800 daily, RM2.*

Overlooking Jalan Damansara, near the southern tip of the Lake Gardens, is the Muzium Negara, with its traditional Minangkabau-style roof, and two large murals of Italian glass mosaic either side of the main entrance. They depict the main historical episodes and cultural activities of Malaysia.The museum was opened in 1963, and, set on three floors, provides an excellent introduction to Malaysia's history, geography, natural history and culture.

Lake Gardens (Taman Tasek Perdana)

ⓘ *Take bus 21C or 48C from behind Kotaraya Plaza, or bus 18 or 21A from Chow Kit, get off at the old railway station. Taxis away from the park can be difficult to find – it may be worth either chartering one to wait for you or booking one in advance.*

Close to the museum is the south entrance to the 90-ha Lake Gardens (Taman Tasek Perdana). Pedal boats can be hired on the main lake, Tasek Perdana, at the weekend. The gardens also house a Hibiscus Garden (Taman Bunga Raya), with over 500 species; an Orchid Garden (Taman Bunga Orkid), which has over 800 species and is transformed into an orchid market at weekends; as well as children's playgrounds, picnic areas, restaurants and cafés, and a small deer park. At the north end of the Lake Gardens is the **National Monument**. Located at the far side of Jalan Parlimen, it provides a good view of Parliament House. The memorial, over 15 m tall, with its dramatically posed sculpted figures, is dedicated to the heroes of Malaya's 12-year Communist Emergency (see page 488). The state of emergency was lifted in 1960, but members of the banned Communist Party managed to put a bomb under the memorial in 1975. Below the monument is a **sculpture garden** with exhibits from throughout the member countries of the Association of South East Asian Nations (ASEAN).

❢ The man-made park is a joggers' paradise and popular city escape.

The showpiece of the Lake Gardens is the **Bird Park (Taman Burung)**, ⓘ *daily 0900-1830, RM22, child RM15*. Opened in 1991 in an effort to out-do neighbouring Singapore's famous Jurong Bird Park, this aviary is twice the size of Jurong and is billed as the world's largest covered bird park, and encloses more than 2,000 birds from 200 species, ranging from ducks to hornbills. Spread out over 20 ha of landscaped gardens, most of the birds are free and very accustomed to being around people. The hornbill area is particularly exciting. It houses seven varieties of hornbill, most of which are indigenous to Malaysia. There is a reference centre, refreshment kiosk and binoculars for hire.

The **Butterfly Park (Taman Rama-rama)** ⓘ *daily 0900-1800, adult RM10, child RM3*, is a five-minute drive from the main entrance of the Lake Gardens, coming in from Jalan Parlimen. It is a miniature jungle, which is home to almost 8,000 butterflies, from 150 species. There are also small mammals, amphibians and reptiles, and rare tropical insects in the park. There is an insect museum and souvenir shop on the site.

On the southeast edge of the park is **Tun Razak Memorial**, ⓘ *T3-26937740, Tue-Sun 0900-1800, closed Mon*, the former residence of Malaysia's revered second prime minister, the late Tun Abdul Razak, whose great, great, great, great, great grandfather, Sultan Abdullah of Kedah, ceded Penang to the British (see page 159). In recognition of his services – he is popularly known as the father of Malaysia's development – his old home has been turned into a memorial with the aim of preserving his documents, speeches, books and awards, as well as housing his collection of walking sticks and pipes. At the southeastern end of the Lake Gardens is the **National Planetarium**, ⓘ *T3-22735484, Mon-Thu 1000-1600, Sat and Sun 1000-1900, Space Science Show (1100, 1400, 1600), adult RM3, child RM2, Sky* movie, adult RM6, child RM4, exhibition RM1, which has a theatre with a 20-m-diameter domed screen where the Space Science Show and Sky movies are projected. Other facilities include an exhibition hall, an observatory, a viewing gallery and a 14-in telescope.

The modern 18-storey **Parliament House** and its Toblerone-shaped House of Representatives is on the west fringe of the gardens. When parliament is in session, visitors may observe parliamentary proceedings (permission must be formally obtained, and visitors must be smartly dressed). In years gone by, many of the administrative arms of government were housed in the State Secretariat (now renamed the Sultan Abdul Samad Building) on the Padang.

Kuala Lumpur City Centre and Jalan Ampang

Kuala Lumpur City Centre

The old Selangor Turf Club racecourse, which lies to the southeast of this intersection, has been the focus of extraordinary redevelopment in the guise of the Kuala Lumpur City Centre (KLCC), ⓘ *www.klcc.com.my*, a 'city within a city'. High-rise development came late to KL but has rapidly gained a foothold; the city's offices, hotels and shopping complexes are mostly concentrated in the Golden Triangle, on the east side of the city. The complex is one of the largest real estate developments in the world, covering a 40-ha site and including the Petronas Towers, see below. The Ampang Tower, a mere 50-storey office block and the Suria KLCC, a crescent-shaped retail and entertainment centre on the junction of Jalan Ampang and Jalan P Ramlee, the Esso Tower, a 20-ha park with a children's playground and the Mandarin Oriental, a five-star hotel with over 600 rooms are all part of the KLCC project. Jalan Bukit Bintang and Jalan Sultan Ismail was where the first modern hotels and shopping complexes went up – the Regent, the Hilton (now the Mutiara), the Equatorial, Holiday Inn, Shangri-La and Concorde.

Petronas Towers

ⓘ *The sky bridge, which links the two towers on the 41st Floor, is open to the public daily 0830-1700 except Mon. Visitors must queue for a ticket which gives free access to the bridge and some stunning views. Only a limited number of people are allowed up every day, so it is advisable to get there before 0900.*

The Petronas Twin Towers was designed by American architect Cesar Pelli and the surrounding park by the Brazilian landscape artist Roberto Marx Burle. On Level 4, Suria KLCC Petrosains, **The Discovery Centre**, which is really a petroleum promotion exercise, has rides and hands-on computer games all glorifying this industry and is actually a great place for children. ⓘ *T3-23318181, Mon-Thu 0930-1730, Fri 1330-1730, Sat and Sun 0930-1830, RM12, RM7 child.*

Jalan Ampang

Jalan Ampang became the home of KL's early tin-mining millionaires and an important leafy adjunct to the colonial capital. The styles of its stately mansions range from Art Deco and mock-Palladian to Islamic. Today many of these buildings have become embassies and consulates (although the government is trying to persuade foreign missions to decamp to Putrajaya). One of the lovelier **Art Deco-style buildings** now houses the **Rubber Research Institute**. Further into town, another renovated house is now the **Malaysian Tourism Centre (MTC)**. It was the headquarters of the Japanese Imperial Army during the Second World War, but was originally built in 1935 by Eu Tong Seng, a wealthy Chinese rubber planter and tin mogul, see also Ins and Outs. More recently the area around Jalan Ampang and Jalan Tun Razak has been transformed into a commercial centre; several towers have sprung up in the area in recent years, including the extraordinary hour-glass-shaped Pilgrims' Building, which co-ordinates the annual Haj and looks after the pilgrims' funds. There are several further developments including a Sheraton and Hyatt, both five-star tower-block hotels. The area has become a booming shopping area in the shape of Ampang Park and City Square shopping centres.

Menara KL

ⓘ *T3-20205448, for reservations, T3-20205055, www.menarakl.com.my, daily 1000-2200, RM15, RM9 for children. There is no public transport – take a taxi or walk from one of the surrounding roads.*

Near the intersection of Jalan Ampang and Jalan Sultan Ismail atop Bukit Nanas stands the Menara KL (**KL Tower**). This 421-m-high tower is the second tallest telecommunications tower in Asia and the fourth tallest in the world (the viewing tower stands at 276 m). Characteristically, the tower is the brain-child of former Prime Minister Dr Mahathir Mohammed. There are 22 levels and 2,058 stairs, so the lift is recommended! At ground level there are several shops and fast-food restaurants and a mini amphitheatre. Above the viewing platform is the Seri Angkasa revolving restaurant. It has excellent Malay cuisine and revolves once every 60 minutes, so diners get to see the whole city between hors d'oeuvre and ice cream.

Bukit Nanas Forest Reserve

ⓘ *Entry is free.*

Combine a visit to the tower with a walk in the surrounding Bukit Nanas Forest Reserve, a beautiful 11 ha of woodland in the centre of the city with marked trails.

KL is perhaps the only city with a patch of rainforest (Bukit Nanas Forest Reserve) at its heart. There are a couple of entrances into this reserve and various tracks running through it – you can get onto one of these tracks from the road going up to KL Tower. There are also ways in from Jalan Ampang and Jalan Bukit Nanas (off Jalan Raja Chulan) (look for signposts). Butterflies, monkeys, squirrels and birds live in the forest. There are warnings about dangerous snakes.

Around KLCC

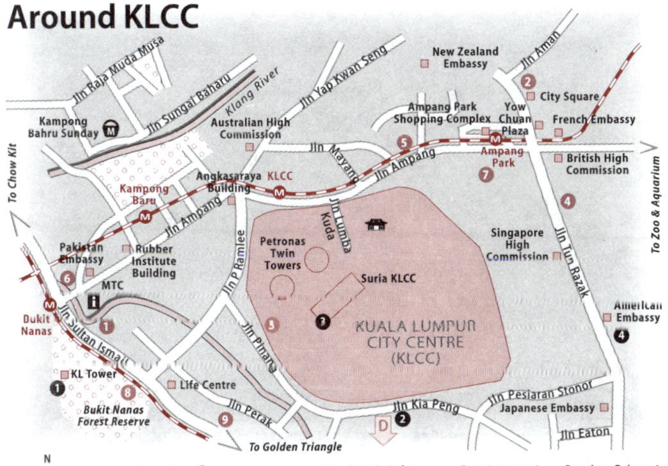

Sleeping
Concorde & Hard Rock Café **1**
Corus **5**
Crown Princess **2**
Equatorial **9**
Hard Rock Cafe **1**
Mandarin Oriental **3**
MiCasa **4**
New World **6**
Nikko **7**
Renaissance **6**
Shangri-La **8**

Eating
Bharath's **3**
Bombay Palace **4**
D'Tandoor **1**
Seri Angkasa **1**
Top Hat **2**

The Golden Triangle

The **Rumah Penghulu Abu Seman,** ⓘ *T3-21627459 for information on exhibitions, Mon to Fri 1000-1600*, on Jalan Stonor, otherwise known as the Heritage Centre of the Badan Warisan Malaysia, is to be found in a mock-Tudor building off Jalan Conloy, on the northern edge of the Golden Triangle. In the garden is a reconstructed headman's house made of timber – it displays detailed carvings and is furnished in the style of a 1930s house. Just to the east of the Heritage Centre is the **Komplex Budaya Kraf**, a local handicraft centre offering visitors the chance to dabble in batik or watch artists at work.

One of the newest shopping plazas in the Golden Triangle is Times Square on Jalan Imbi, which features a roller coaster, an Imax cinema, and hotel complex as well as the usual retail and dining suspects.

The **Karyaneka Handicraft Centre** (Kompleks Seni Budaya) is on Jalan Conlay to the east of the city centre and is popular with tour groups. There is a small museum illustrating the batik, weaving and pottery processes. Craft demonstrations are held from 1000 to 1800, and there are crafts on sale from each of the 13 states of Malaysia. ⓘ *Daily 0900-1800; minibus or Intrakota no 40 from Jalan Tuanku Abdul Rahman.*

South of the Karyaneka Handicraft Centre, on Jalan Bukit Bintang, is the **Jade Museum**. This small museum houses a private collection of 80 jade artefacts from China. Replicas and jade souvenirs are for sale – or so it seems. ⓘ *Daily 1000-1900, RM10; 10-min walk from Bukit Bintang Monorail station.*

Around the Golden Triangle

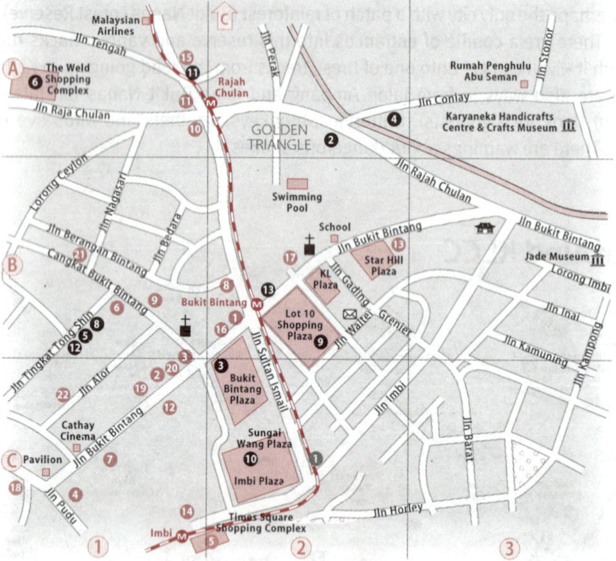

N

0 metres 100
0 yards 100

Sleeping
Agora 1 *B2*
Berjaya Times Square 5 *C2*
Bintang Warisan 2 *C1*
Cardogan 3 *B1*
Century 4 *C1*
Comfort Inn 6 *B1*
Federal 7 *C1*
Fortuna 8 *B2*
Imperial 9 *B1*
Istana 10 *A1*
JW Marriott 13 *B2*
Lodge 11 *A1*
Malaysia 12 *C1*
Melía 14 *C1*
Mutiara 15 *A1*
Nova 22 *C1*
Pondok Lodge 21 *B1*
Putra Bintang 20 *C1*
Regent 17 *B2*
Shuttle Inn 16 *B2*
Swiss Garden 18 *C1*
Tai Ichi 19 *C1*

Eating
Bangkok Jam 3 *C2*
Dondang Sayang 6 *A1*
Eden Village 2 *A2*
Esquire Kitchen 10 *C2*
Koryo-Won 11 *A1*
Nyonya 5 *B1*
Sao Nam 12 *C1*
Satay Anika 3 *C2*
Seri Melayu 4 *A2*
Tarbush 13 *B2*
Teppanyaki 10 *C2*
Unicorn 9 *B2*
Zura Traditional 8 *B1*

Bars & clubs
Delaney's Pub 1 *C2*

Outer Kuala Lumpur

Chow Kit

The US$150 million **Putra World Trade Centre** (Kompleks Seni Budaya, Jalan Conlay), to the north of the city centre on Jalan Tun Ismail, took nearly 15 years to materialize, but when it opened in 1985, Malaysia proudly announced that it was finally on the international convention and trade-fair circuit. The luxurious complex of buildings includes the Pan-Pacific Hotel, a sleek 41-storey office block and an exhibition centre, adorned with a traditional Minangkabau roof. The headquarters of former Prime Minister Dr Mahathir Mohamad's ruling United Malays National Organization (UMNO) occupies the top floor and there is a tourist information centre on the second floor.

Titiwangsa

The **National Art Gallery**, *T3-40254990, http://artgallery.gov.my, daily 1000-1800, free; to get there take the new Monorail to Titiwangsa station. The gallery is a 15-minute walk from the station. Walk eastwards along Jalan Tun Razak, the gallery is on the left hand side*, has moved from its location near the old railway station to north of the city at Jalan Temerloh next to the National Theatre and National Library. The gallery showcases some 2,000 works by Malay artists.

Taman Seputeh

Thean Hou Temple (**Temple of the Goddess of Heaven**), ⓘ *Getting there: minibus 27 from Klang bus terminal to Jalan Syed Putra*, is situated at Jalan Klang Lama (off Jalan Tun Sambathan, to the southwest of the city). Perched on a hill, it has a panoramic view over KL. A contemporary Buddhist pagoda and Buddha images are enshrined in the octagonal hall. It stands between a sacred Bodhi tree and a Buddhist shrine, built by Sinhalese Buddhists in 1894.

Around Kuala Lumpur

The most popular day-trip from KL is the Batu Caves, around half an hour's drive north (1-hour by public bus). This series of caverns, with their entrances wreathed in mist reached by a sweat-inducing flight of steps and with colourful Hindu paraphernalia everywhere, make a fun day out. Closer to the city, the newly-moved National Museum, Art Gallery and Theatre. Further north, Templer Park is a great place for picnics and escaping the city. KL's satellite towns have become destinations in themselves with hotels, restaurants, bars and shopping centres such as Petaling Jaya, Shah Alam and Putrajaya. Petaling Jaya or PJ, in the southwest, also has the Sunway Lagoon, a fun water park, Shah Alam has an impressive mosque, while bustling Port Klang is the country's main port. To the south around the airport are the Mines Wonderland theme park and the Sepang International circuit for world-class motor-racing. Seremban, the state capital of Negeri Sembilan and Port Dickson can also be visited from KL.

North

Batu Caves

ⓘ *Caves stay open until about 2100. RM1. Getting there: Bus 11 or 11D from near Central Market or taxi. The caves are a short walk off the main road.*

This system of caverns set high in a massive limestone outcrop, 13 km north of KL, was 'discovered' by American naturalist William Hornaby in the 1880s. In 1891 Hindu priests set up a shrine in the main cave dedicated to Lord Subramaniam and it has now become the biggest Indian pilgrimage centre in Malaysia during the annual Thaipusam festival (see page 52), when over 800,000 Hindus congregate here.

The main cave is reached by a steep flight of 272 steps. Coloured lights provide illumination for the fantasy features and formations of the karst limestone cavern. There are a number of other, less spectacular caves in the outcrop, including the Museum Cave (at ground level) displaying elaborate sculptures of Hindu mythology. During the Second World War, the Japanese Imperial Army used some of the caves as factories for the manufacture of ammunition and as arms dumps; the concrete foundations for the machinery can be seen at the foot of the cliffs.

Templer Park

The park, covering 500 ha and about 10 km further on up the main road from the turn-off to the Batu Caves, serves as KL's nearest jungle playground, apart from the tiny Bukit Nanas Forest Reserve in the middle of the city. It opened as a park in 1954 and is named after the last British High Commissioner of Malaya, Sir Gerald Templer, 'the Tiger of Malaya', who oversaw the tactical defeat of the Communist insurgents during the Emergency (see page 488). The park is dominated by several impressive 350-m-high limestone hills and outcrops, the biggest being **Bukit Takun** and Bukit Anak Takun (similar to the Batu Caves outcrop).

The park attracts swarms of weekend day-trippers – although most do not venture far beyond the car park and picnic area

There are extensive networks of underground passages and cave systems within the hills, thought to have formed 400 million years ago. Unfortunately, two huge floodlit golf courses have impinged on the boundaries of the park making access to some of these massifs more difficult. The park has a wide variety of jungle flora and fauna and is a popular venue for boy scout and youth camps. Nearby are the **Kanching Falls** (sometimes incorrectly referred to as Templer Park Falls) ⓘ *Buses from Puduraya bus terminal*, dropping 300 m in several stages and a good place for swimming.

Orang Asli Museum

ⓘ *Sat-Thu 0900-1700, free. Getting there: Bus from Lebuh Ampang terminus or it is a 15-minute walk from Titiwangsa Monorail station.*

Situated 25 km north of KL on the old Gombak Road, this museum preserves the traditions of Malaysia's indigenous Orang Asli aboriginals, who number about 60,000 on the peninsula. There are displays giving the background to the 18 different tribes and their geographical dispersal. There are also models of Orang Asli village houses and a souvenir shop attached to the museum selling Orang Asli crafts.

Jungle canopy walk

ⓘ *It is important to book with FRIM (T3-62797525), as it can be closed.*

It is possible to do this walk through the treetops at the Forestry Research Institute of Malaysia (FRIM) at Kepong, some 30 minutes north of KL, on the Jabayan Perhutanan.

East

The **Malaysian Armed Forces Museum,** ⓘ *Jalan Padang Tembak, T3-2312010, 20 mins in taxi*, exhibits pictures, paintings and weapons, including those captured from the so-called Communists Terrorists during the Emergency (see page 488). **Royal Selangor Complex** ⓘ *4 Jalan Usahawan 6, Setapak Jaya, T3-41456122, www.visitorcentre.royalselangor.com, daily 0900-1700, free. Take the Putra LRT to Wangsa Maju station, and then take a taxi (fare around RM3)*. On Jalan Pahang, in Setapak Jaya, to the north of the city, is the biggest pewter factory in the world, employing over 500 craftsmen. Royal Selangor was founded in 1885, using Straits tin (over 95%) which is alloyed with antimony and copper. Visitors can watch demonstrations of hand-casting and pewter working. Visitors can also see jewellery making and the handpainting of bonded porcelain. You can also make your own pewter by enrolling in a day-class at the "school of hard knocks". Call the Centre in advance. One of the most photographed sights at the complex is the massive pewter tankard outside the building – it is in the Guinness Book of Records as the largest in the world. As well as the Setapak Jaya Complex, there are showrooms throughout the city (see page 112).

The **National Zoo and Aquarium** ⓘ *T3-41082219, daily 0900-1700, adult RM10, child RM5. Take the Putra LRT to Wangsa Maju station followed by a taxi*, is 13 km from the centre of KL, down Jalan Ampang to Ulu Klang. The zoo encompasses a forest and a lake and houses 1,000 different species of Malaysian flora and fauna in addition to collections from elsewhere in the world. It also has an aquarium with over 80 species of marine life.

West and southwest

Asian Art Museum

ⓘ *Mon to Fri 0900-1600, Sat 0900-1200, free. To get there, take the LRT to the University and then take a taxi.*

The Asian Art Museum is housed within the university campus, about 4 km southwest of the Lake Gardens. The museum exhibits Asian art objects, sculpture, ceramics, textiles and handicrafts.

Petaling Jaya

Located 15 km southwest of KL, this is a thriving industrial satellite and middle-class dormitory town for the capital and is known as PJ. Initially built to provide low-cost housing for squatter resettlement it is now a satellite city in its own right, with shopping and administration centres. The whole town, with its streets running in semi-circles, was planned on a drawing board, but despite its unimaginative street names (or rather, numbers), is not as sterile as it might sound. In recent years it has become quite lively, with its own nightlife scene and several gourmet restaurants (particularly around Damansara Utama, where clubs stay open until 0300 or 0400), which cater for PJ's expatriate and wealthy Malaysian population. Also nearby is the water theme park **Sunway Lagoon**, ⓘ *T3-56311452, 1200-1800 during the week (closed Tue) and 1000-1800 at the weekends, RM39 for all the park, RM26 children; take the Putra LRT to Kelana Jaya and catch the shuttle service from there. Alternatively, buses to most parts of Petaling Jaya can be boarded at Bangkok Bank stop and Klang bus terminal,* with a variety of watery rides on offer and some dry-land activities too. A new addition at Sunway is the **Extreme Park**, ⓘ *T0182321426*, which offers paintball, watersports including diving lessons on a 50-acre lake, go-karting and golf.

Bandar Utama lays claim to providing the biggest shopping mall in the country, with heaps of restaurants too

Shah Alam

ⓘ *Shah Alam is an hour from KL's Klang bus station or you can take a taxi (RM20).*

The new state capital of Selangor, situated between KL and Port Klang, has the reputation of being Malaysia's best-planned city and is an ultra-modern showpiece town. The skyline is dominated by the State Mosque, **Masjid Sultan Salahuddin Abdul Aziz Shah**, which has a huge, blue aluminium dome, said to be the largest aluminium dome in the world. Completed in 1988, it is reputed to be the largest mosque in Southeast Asia and can accommodate up to 16,000 worshippers. **Wet**

 World ⓘ *daily 1200-2000, except Wed, and 1000-2000 weekend, RM7 adults, RM4 children*, a water theme park provides some entertainment for children, including the Monsoon Buster – a watercoaster, which at one point reaches a height of 220 m.

Klang and its offshore islands

ⓘ *The KTM Komuter line runs to Port Klang, where it's a short walk into town.*

This royal town, 30 kilometres southwest of KL, is also known as Kelang, a name thought to derive from an old Sumatran word for tin. It has a magnificent mosque and attractive royal palace, the **Istana Alam Shah**, set in well-cared-for grounds. The palace is closed to the public, but can be seen from the road. Klang had been the capital of Selangor for centuries before the tin-mining town of Kuala Lumpur assumed the mantle in 1880. Klang was the name for the whole state of Selangor when it formed one of the Negeri Sembilan (the nine states of the Malay Federation).

Today **Port Klang** (previously known as Port Swettenham, after former British Resident Frank Swettenham) is KL's seaport and is a busy container terminal. Klang is also an important service centre for nearby rubber and palm oil plantations, which, in the early decades of the 20th century, spread the length of the Klang Valley to KL.

The **Gedung Rajah Abdullah** warehouse, built in 1857, is one of the oldest buildings in the town. Rajah Abdullah was the Bugis Chief who first dispatched the expedition to the upper reaches of the Klang River, which resulted in the founding of KL. There is a **fort** in Klang, built by Rajah Mahdi (a rival of Raja Abdullah), which guarded the entrance to the Klang valley from its strategic position overlooking the river.

The town is well known for its seafood; most of the restaurants are close to the bus terminal. Ferries leave from Klang for offshore islands such as Pulau Ketam (see below), Pulau Morib (golf course, see page 114) and Pulau Angsa.

Pulau Ketam (Crab Island), ⓘ *about 10 km west of Port Klang. From KL, take the Komuter train to Port Klang and then a ferry, 45 mins, 8 a day, RM5.30*, is like a downmarket Venice, Malaysian-style, with the whole village on stilts over the water. It is a good spot for seafood.

Kuala Selangor

Kuala Selangor is a coastal town on the banks of the River Sungai Selangor, 64 km northwest of KL. In the 19th century, it was a focal point of the Sultanate of Selangor. The Dutch built two fortresses here in 1784, overlooking the Sungai Selangor estuary, to blockade the Sungai Selangor in retaliation for Sultan Ibrahim of Selangor's attacks on Melaka. In 1871, British gunboats bombarded the forts – then occupied by Malays – for several hours, marking the first British intervention in the Selangor Civil War, over the possession of the tin-rich Klang Valley. The larger of the two, **Fort Altingberg**, ⓘ *daily during daylight hours*, on Bukit Melawati, serves as a royal mausoleum and museum.

Kuala Selangor Nature Park

ⓘ *The actual riverside site is around 8 km from Kuala Selangor, near a village called Kampong Kuantan. There are regular direct buses from KL's Puduraya bus terminal to Kuala Selangor. Taxis can be chartered from Kuala Selangor to Kampong Kuantan, a boat trip can then be taken from Kampong Kuantan,RM10 each for four people, each boat costs RM40 to charter and seats 4 people. The Malayan Nature Society, which operates the park, will arrange private transport to Kampong Kuantan and back, for approximately the same price, when pre-arranged with their KL office, T3-22879422.*

Fort Altingberg overlooks the Kuala Selangor Nature Park, 250 ha of coastal mangrove swamp and wetland. It has several observation hides, and more than 156 bird species, including bee eaters, kingfishers and sea eagles have been recorded here. There are also **leaf monkeys**. It is also one of the best places to see Malaysia's

Brand-name Satay from the source

Kajang, about 20 km south of KL on the Seremban road, is named after the palm-leaf canopy of a bullock cart, once ubiquitous and still occasionally seen in Negeri Sembilan.

At hawker centres, there are stalls called 'Satay Kajang': the town long ago gained the reputation for the best satay in the country. There are many satay stalls in Kajang today. Selamat makan!

famous synchronized fireflies – the only fireflies in Southeast Asia that manage to co-ordinate their flashing; they are best observed on a moonless night, from about one hour after sunset.

South

Mines Wonderland

ⓘ Batu 10 1/2, Jalan Sungai Besi, T3-89422163, Mon-Fri 1700-2200, Sat and Sun 1600-2300, RM6 adults and RM10 for the water taxi. Tale KTM Komuter from KL railway station to Serdang station (walkable from here).

This adventure playground, next to the site of Sepang International Airport in Sungai Besi about 20 minutes south of KL, has been constructed on a 60-ha plot, which used to be the largest tin-mining lake in the world. Attractions include a Snow House, where you can see sculptures carved out of ice by artists from China. Alternatively, take a ride on a water taxi or see the Musical Fountain or any of the other sound and light attractions. The whole 'Mines Resort City' consists of a sizeable conference centre set within a five-star hotel, a 'Beach Resort' (although there is no beach here), a shopping mall, a business park, an international-standard golf course, and a new residential development.

From Kuala Lumpur to Seremban and Port Dickson

The drive south from KL through Seremban to Melaka runs on the first stretch of the much-vaunted north-south Highway, and is an easy, pleasant drive through rubber and oil palm plantations. Like the route north from KL, the towns are predominantly Chinese, while the rural kampongs are almost exclusively Malay. Negeri Sembilan, a confederacy of nine small states, is renowned for its Minangkabau-style architecture. This is characterized by buffalo-horn shaped roof peaks, reflecting the influence of the state's first inhabitants who came from Sumatra.

On the coast, southwest of Seremban, off the main highway, is the seaside resort town of Port Dickson (PD), which serves as a popular weekend retreat from KL but is not generally frequented by tourists from abroad. The drive southeast from PD to Melaka is much more interesting along the coastal backroads that run through open countryside and Malay kampongs.

Seremban → Colour map 2, grid B2

ⓘ Tourist information State Economic Planning Unit, 5th floor Wisma Negeri, T6-7622311.

Seremban is the capital of the state of Negeri Sembilan, which translates from Bahasa as 'nine states', and was historically a loose federation of districts, lorded over by four territorial chiefs. Seremban (formerly known as Sungei Ujong) started life as another rough and ready tin-mining centre with a large population of Chinese. A lively town, its major sight is the Teman Seni Budaya (Cultural Complex) which offers an interesting insight into the Minangkabau culture. The town, 62 km south of KL, is easily accessible and can be visited in a day from either KL or Melaka.

Tin mining flourished in the early years of the 19th century – one of the reasons Melaka continued as a thriving trading port. The control of the river, Sungai Linggi, which was the route Sungei Ujong's tin took to the sea, became a great source of contention between the 1820s and 1860s. The Dato Klana, or territorial chief of the Sungei Ujong district, frequenty clashed with other members of the council of chiefs over the highly profitable river taxes and port dues. All wanted a share of the river tolls and erected illegal forts along the river to levy tolls from the Chinese merchants from Melaka and the Chinese miners. In 1857 the British sent an expedition up the river to destroy these fortified toll booths, but this did not work and in no time they were back in business. In 1860 the confrontation came to a tumultous head when the tin miners in Sungei Ujong rebelled against the chiefs; hundreds were killed in the subsequent riots. One of the Chinese ring-leaders was a ruthless young Hakka ruffian named **Yap Ah Loy**, who went on to become headman of a new tin boomtown called Kuala Lumpur in 1862.

Along the fringe of the outstanding **Lake Gardens** (Taman Bunga) is the **State Mosque** (Masjid Negri), with its nine pillars representing the nine old mine-states of Negeri Sembilan. The Cultural Complex (**Teman Seni Budaya**) is on 4-ha site at the junction of Jalan Sungai Ujong and the KL-Seremban road, 2 km from the centre of town. The main building is the Terak Perpatih, originally constructed as the pavilion for an international Koran-reading competition in 1984 and now a museum. On the ground floor are handicraft displays and upstairs there is an exhibition of historical artefacts. Also within the complex is a beautifully carved traditional Minangkabau wooden house, Rumah Contoh Minangkabau, built in 1898 (originally at Kampong Air

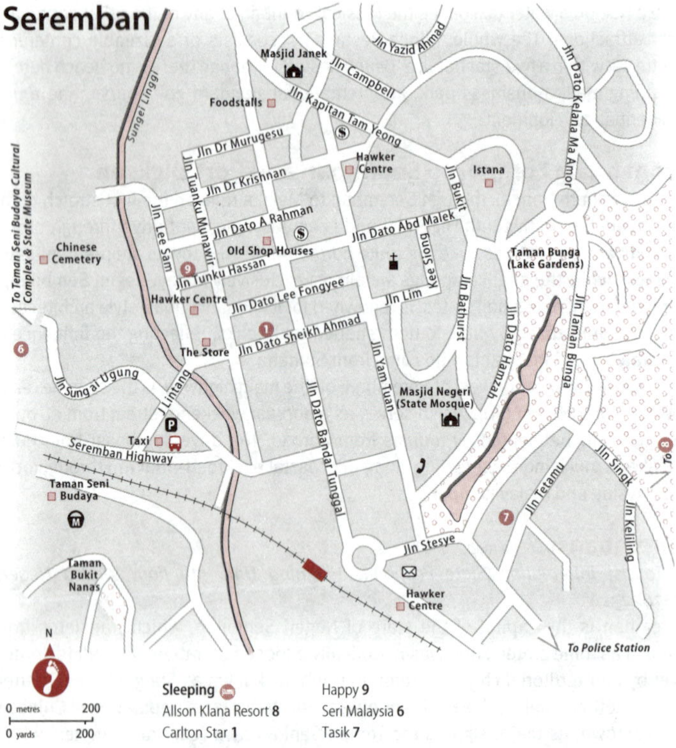

Minangkabau: the buffalo-horn people from across the water

Negeri Sembilan's early inhabitants were immigrants from Minangkabu in Sumatra. They started to settle in the hinerland of Melaka and around Sungai Ujong (modern Seremban) during the 16th and 17th centuries and were skilled irrigated paddy farmers. Minangkabau roughly translates as 'buffalo horns' and the traditional houses of rural Negeri Sembilan and Melaka have magnificent roofs that sweep up from the centre into two peaks. The Minangkabau architetural style has been the inspiration behind many modern Malaysian buildings, notably the Muzium Negara (National Museum) and the Putra World Trade Centre in Kuala Lumpur.

The Minangkabau introduced Islam, a sophisticated legal system and their matrilineal society to the interior of the Malay peninsula. In 1773 they appealed to the Minangkabau court at Pagar Ruyong in Sumatra to appoint a ruler over them and a Sumatran rince - Raja Melewar - was installed as the first king, (Yang di-Pertuan Besar), of the confederacy of mini-states, with his capital at Sri Menanti.

But Negeri Sembilan's four undang (territorial chiefs), saw to it that he wielded no real power. In all there were four kings from Sumatra, all of them ineffectual and the link with Sumatra finally ended in 1824 with the establishment of an indigenous hereditary royal family. The current Sultan of Seremban, educated at Oxford, continues to reside in his palace outside the town.

Garam). In 1924 it was shipped to England and exhibited as an example of Malay architecture. On its return it was reassembled near the Lake Gardens in Seremban before being moved to Taman Seni Budaya.

The **State Museum**, ⓘ *1000-1800 Tue-Wed, 0815-1300 Thu, 1000-1215, 1445-1800 Fri, 1000-1800 Sat-Sun, closed Mon*, is also part of the complex and is itself a good example of Minangkabau architecture; it is a reconstructed 19th-century palace (Istana Ampang Tinggi), a high stilt building with an *atap* roof. The museum houses a small collection of ceremonial weapons and tableaux depicting a royal wedding and some photographs and other memorabilia from the time of the Malayan Emergency.

Sri Menanti

ⓘ *A taxi from Seremban would cost about RM20, or else take a Kuala Pilah bus.*

Sri Menanti, the old Minangkabau capital of Negeri Sembilan, is 30 km east of Seremban, about 10 km before Kuala Pilah. This area is the Minangkabau heartland. *Sri* is the Minangkabau word for 'ripe paddy', and *Menanti* means 'awaiting' – although it is colloquially translated as 'beautiful resting place'. It was also common for early kings to add the Sanskrit honorific 'Sri' to their titles and palaces. The former royal capital is on the upper reaches of Sungai Muar, which meanders through the valley that was known as Londar Naga, or the tail of the dragon. The **Istana Lama Sri Menanti**, ⓘ *1000-1800 Sat-Wed, 0815-1300 Thu, closed Fri*, is a beautifully carved wooden palace built in Minangkabau style in 1908. It has 99 pillars depicting the 99 warriors of the various *luak-luak* (clans). It was, until 1931, the official residence of the Yang di-Pertuan Besar, the state ruler. On the fourth floor is a display of royal treasures. It is not officially a museum but is open to visitors. This royal town also has a large mosque. Most people come here on a day trip from Seremban, but there is a reasonable resort hotel next to the Istana Lama, see Sleeping.

Port Dickson

Port Dickson, typically shortened to PD, is 32 km from Seremban and is one of the most popular seaside resorts in Malaysia, as testified by all the modern condominium developments. The pace of development has given the little fishing port a pollution problem in recent years and many people regard the sea as so toxic that it is best not to swim at all. This is a narrow point of the Melaka Strait and large ships use the deep-water channel, which cuts close to the Malaysian coast. Rarely a month goes by when the Malaysian authorities aren't giving chase to tankers, which have an increasingly alarming tendency to dump thousands of tonnes of sludge, oil and effluent into the strait. Although for KL's residents it may be a convenient destination for a day trip or weekend, it is, frankly, hard to imagine why those with more time on their hands would wish to come here.

The port town, originally called Tanjung Kamuning, was renamed after Sir Frederick Dickson, British Colonial Secretary and acting Governor in 1890. Port Dickson itself is quiet and undistinguished but to the south is a long, sandy beach, stretching 18 km down to the **Cape Rachado** lighthouse, although there are cleaner places to swim in Malaysia. Built by the British on the site of a 16th-century Portuguese lighthouse, Cape Rachado has panoramic views along the coast. At **Kota Lukut**, 7 km from Port Dickson, is Raja Jamaat fort, built in 1847 to control the tin trade in the area.

Sleeping

Room rates in KL's top hotels escalated as the economy boomed in the early 1990s. However, the city's hosting of the Commonwealth Games in 1998 led to the construction of many new hotels and the number of beds available in 3, 4 and 5-star hotels more than doubled between 1997 and 2000. This, along with the economic crisis, the stagnation in tourism arrivals associated with the 'haze' and Sars and the political problems in the region, has led to KL (and Malaysia more generally) facing a glut of rooms, low occupancy levels, and falling room rates.

By international standards KL's hotels are excellent value for money, but because of the city's traffic problems, the location of a hotel has become an increasingly important consideration. Most top hotels are between Jln Sultan Ismail and Jln P Ramlee, in KL's Golden Triangle. South of Jalan Raja Chulan, in the Bukit Bintang area, south of the Golden Triangle, there is another concentration of big hotels. There are also lots of cheap hotels in the Golden Triangle particularly along Jalan Bukit Bintang, convenient for upmarket restaurants, bars and shopping, while the Chinatown area is home to rock bottom budget places which are looking the worst for wear.

If you are staying in the larger, a/c hotels and are a non-smoker, it is possible to request a room on a non-smoking floor. Rooms with a/c generally have non-opening windows, making it difficult to freshen the air. Many of the cheaper hotels are around Jln Tuanku Abdul Rahman, Jln Masjid India and Jln Raja Laut, all of which are within easy walking distance of the colonial core of KL (although these tend to be quite sleazy and run down), northeast of the Padang. Some top hotels drastically reduce their room rates during weekdays.

Homestays It is possible to live with a Malaysian family, sharing their home and eating meals together. At least one member of the family will be able to speak English. Tourism Malaysia has a list of homestays and can advise on how to arrange one. Homestays vary in cost from RM40 a night for all meals and simple bed in a village house to RM100 or more with expensive tour agencies who provide transport and day-trips to sites and activities such as white water rafting, farms and scenic spots etc. Some even offer golf.

You'll probably have a more satisfactory stay if you organize it once you get there and meet locals and ask for their advice than going through a tour agency. www.homestayrelau.cjb.net

For accommodation at the airport, see Airport Information, Essentials.

The colonial core *p78, map p79*

A **AnCasa Hotel**, Jln Cheng Lock, situated next to the Puduraya bus station, T3-20266060, F20313350. International hotel. Well-furnished, clean a/c rooms with televisions, internet access, mini-bar and in-room safe. Restaurant and bar. Breakfast included. Walking tours of KL available. Recommended.

A **Furama**, Komplek Selangor, Jln Sultan, T3-20701777, www.furama.com.my A/c, restaurant, health centre. An uninspired hotel with the benefit of a central location in the heart of Chinatown, reasonable rates with some cut price offers around RM120, geared, as name suggests, mainly to Japanese visitors. Includes a lacklustre breakfast.

B **Lok Ann**, 113A Jln Petaling, T20789544. A/c, clean, large rooms, with televisions and telephones, well-used feel, centrally located in Chinatown.

B **Puduraya**, 4th Flr, Puduraya Bus Station, Jln Pudu, T20721000, F20705567. A/c, restaurant, breakfast included, clean, spacious rooms, some with spectacular views overlooking the city centre. Residents have access to on-site health club, but the gym in this is pitiful. Very convenient for bus station.

B **Quality Hotel**, Jln Raja Laut, T3-26939233, www.quality.com.my A/c, Sichuan restaurant, coffee house, pool, squash, health club, gymnasium, big enough hotel, but inside everything is rather bijou – the lobby is squashed, the swimming pool tiny and the fitness and business centres on the small side.

B **Swiss Inn**, 62 Jln Sultan, T3-20723333, www.swissgarden.com A/c, café, in good position in the heart of Chinatown. Often does backpacker deals. Clean, nicely furnished, and a cared for feeling, unlike other three star hotels in the region which are peeling around the edges. Staff, although not rude, are distracted and unhelpful and standard rooms come without windows.

B-E **Heritage Station**, Banguanan Stesen Keretapi, Jln Sultan Hishamuddin, T3-22721688, www.heritagehotel malaysia.com. Part of the magnificent Moorish-style railway station. After its redevelopment it managed to retain some of its colonial splendour, but disappointingly the standard rooms have been furnished in a contemporary style.It's more of a faded elegance these days, with cranky lifts, saggy floors, lukewarm food. But unbeatable for atmosphere and location. Also backpacker dorms available in a/c rooms with own bathroom.

C **Red Dragon Backpackers**, 83 Jln Sultan, T3-20706000, F3-20701707. Converted from the old Rex cinema and newly opened at the end of 2004. Big complex of nondescript air con doubles, and dorm rooms, all with shared bathrooms. Many of the rooms have no windows. Backpacker friendly café downstairs with book exchange and beer. Good place for breakfast.

C **Starlight**, 90-92 Jln Hang Kasturi, T3-20789811. A/c, spacious rooms with (basic) en-suite facilities. Excellent staff. Well situated for Central Market, Chinatown, bus stations, eateries, shops, places of interest. Being opposite the Klang bus station, it can be noisy. Recommended.

C **YWCA**, 12 Jln Hang Jebat (to the east of Chinatown and south of Jln Pudu), T3-20783225. Fans, hot/cold water, quiet and clean with a friendly atmosphere. Also caters for couples. Restaurant, also access to TV and fridge. Although it looks a bit grim with wire mesh on the windows. Also a bit of a trek into Chinatown.

C-D **Backpackers' Travellers' Inn**, 2nd Flr, 60 Jln Sultan (opposite Furama Hotel), T3-2382473. Some a/c, centrally and conveniently located in Chinatown next to excellent stalls/restaurants, popular and professionally run. Rooms are small but generally clean, ranging from non-a/c dorm rooms to a/c rooms with attached showers, good facilities for the traveller including left luggage, washing and cooking facilities. Also available, book exchange, video, television and laundry. Recommended.

C-D **Backpackers' Travellers' Lodge**, 158 Jln Tun HS Lee, T20710889. Some rooms have a/c and attached bathrooms with unpredictable hot water supply, clean and a good choice in this area, dorms. Internet access (pricey), several windowless rooms. Under same management as Backpackers' Travellers' Inn.

C-D **Chinatown Guesthouse**, 2nd Flr, Wisma BWT, Jln Petaling, in the centre of the pasar malam (night market), T20720417. Right in the middle of Chinatown, travel bulletin board, budget guesthouse, most rooms are quiet and have fans, very friendly. Don't be put off by the grimy entrance stairs!

D **Backpackers Travellers Home**, 23 & 25B Jln Tun Tan Siew Sin, T3-20313546. Simple rooms, backpacker friendly, book exchange, laundry service and balcony roof top.

D-E **Pudu Hostel**, 3rd Floor, Wisma Lai Choon, 10 Jln Pudu (opp. Puduraya bus station), T3-29789600, www.puduhostel.com Big lounge area with pool table, TV, and washing and ironing facilties. 24-hour Internet downstairs. All rooms with shared bathroom. But rooms are cramped and shabby but overall clean. Dorms available.

Little India *p82*

B **Kowloon**, 142-146 Jln Tuanku Abdul Rahman, T3-26934246, F3-26926548, kowloon@po.jar- ing.my A/c, coffee house, clean, value for money, rooms have mini-bar and TV, but those facing the main street are noisy. Residents can use health club on-site at a discounted rate. Recommended.

B **Noble**, 4th Flr, Jln Tuanku Abdul Rahman, T3-27117111, www.hotelnoble.com Modern, clean and tastefully finished. Although without much character, this hotel offers reasonable value. Rooms include TV, have standing showers and a/c. Includes breakfast and a free paper.

B **Palace Hotel**, 40-46 Jln Masjid India, T26986122, F26937528, palacekl@tm.net.my Slightly better quality than others in its genre, good location, offers a/c, bathroom, television, telephone, so nothing new but staff are friendly and the atmosphere less humdrum.

C **Coliseum**, 100 Jln Tuanku Abdul Rahman, T3-26926270. Fans or a/c, restaurant, colonial hotel. If arriving outside hrs, knock on one of the side doors. Large, simply furnished rooms, a famous bar and restaurant (see below) and friendly staff. No attached bathrooms. Rooms facing main street are very noisy. For those on a budget who want a taste of the 1920s, it is certainly worth a try.

Lake Gardens and around *p83*

L **Carcosa Seri Negara**, Taman Tasek Perdana, T3-22821888, F3-22826868. A/c, restaurant, pool, former residence of the British High Commissioner and built in 1896, it is now a luxury hotel, where Queen Elizabeth II stayed when she visited Malaysia during the Commonwealth Conference in 1989 and where other important dignitaries, presidents and prime ministers are pampered on state visits. Situated in a relatively secluded wooded hillside and overlooking the Lake Gardens. Recommended.

KLCC and Jalan Ampang

p84, map p85

L-AL **MiCasa Hotel Apartments**, 368b Jln Tun Razak, T3-2618833, F3-2611186, micasa@po.jaring.my A/c, restaurant, pool, shopping arcade, hair salon, dentist and doctor, children's pool, jacuzzi, tennis, squash, gym, sauna, children's playhouse, business centre, first rate, especially for longer stays. It has 240 suites, which include fully equipped kitchen with utensils and sitting room, Italian restaurant, tapas bar. Recommended.

AL **Corus** , Jln Ampang, T3-21618888, www.corushotelhk.com Upmarket hotel with some rooms enjoying a great view of the Petronas Twin Towers.

AL **Crown Princess**, City Square Centre, Jln Tun Razak, T3-21625522, www.crownprincess.com.my A/c, on the 10th floor is a pool and a restaurant, good for 'High Tea' buffet. The Taj Indian restaurant is on 11th floor, as is the lobby lounge with baby grand piano, and cafés. There is also a business centre, adjacent shopping centre with 168 shops, opulent décor, and over 500 spacious rooms with panoramic views. Recommended.

AL **Mandarin Oriental Hotel**, KLCC (next door to Petronas Twin Towers), T3-33808888, www.mandarinoriental.com Relatively new luxury hotel, with all that you would expect for its prestigious location. Several bars and restaurants, and function rooms named after precious stones. Health spa, swimming pool, tennis, sauna and massage rooms.

AL **Shangri-La**, 11 Jln Sultan Ismail, T3-20322388, www.shangri-la.com A/c, Chinese, Japanese and French restaurants, small, rather old-fashioned pool, health club, sauna, jacuzzi, tennis. With its grand marble lobby and 720 rooms, the 'Shang' has remained KL's ritziest hotel despite the arrival of swish upstart competition. Constantly playing host to political leaders and assorted royalty for dinner, its best feature is its ground floor Gourmet Corner deli, which stocks a great variety of European food. Recommended.

AL-A **Berjaya Times Square**, 1 Jln Imbi, T3-21178000, www.berjayaresorts.com KL's newest 5-star – shares the same building as KL's newest shopping mall – Times Square. 900 suites boasting some fabulous views of the city with kitchenette, separate bathtub and shower, a lounge and bedroom. Great facilties -,big pool, gym, jacuzzi, conference rooms and restaurants. Popular with tour groups. Everything is new and gleaming, but the atmosphere is a bit sterile.

AL-A **Equatorial**, Jln Sultan Ismail, T3-21617777, www.equatorial.com A/c, restaurant (excellent Cantonese), pool, one of KL's earlier international hotels, the Equatorial has had several revamps over the years, its 1960s-style coffee shop has metamorphosed into one of the best hotel coffee shops in town, open 24 hrs (see below), with an international news agency in the basement, the hotel is the favoured repose of visiting journalists. Choose a room at the back to reduce disturbance by traffic noise, two no-smoking floors.

A **New World**, 128 Jln Ampang, T3-21636888, www.renaisaance.com Under the Renaissance management. Recently renovated, a total of 520 rooms in this relatively new horror. Good-sized rooms and nice bathrooms but all a bit ostentatious. Shares its spectacular pool with the Renaissance (see below) next door. Includes breakfast.

A **Nikko**, 165 Jln Ampang, T3-2611111, www.hotelnikko.com.my A/c, pool, Japanese and Chinese restaurants, near city square and Ampang shopping centres. Oriental atmosphere with very Japanese feel to it.

A-B **Concorde**, 2 Jln Sultan Ismail, T3-21442200, www.concorde.net A/c, restaurant, decent sized pool, gym, it is the old Merlin (the first big modern hotel in KL) masquerading behind a face-lift and rather sterile interior décor, 4 good restaurants, coffee shop and the Hard Rock Café attached to it.

The Golden Triangle *p86, map p86*

L **Istana**, 73 Jln Raja Chulan, T3-21419988, www.hotelistana.com.my A/c, Chinese, Japanese and Italian restaurants, pool, this striking, almost grotesquely extravagant hotel is in the heart of KL's business district, all facilities including limousine transfer from airport to hotel.

L **JW Marriott**, 183 Jln Bukit Bintang, T3-27159000, http://marriott.com/property/propertyPage/KULDT Next to KL's most opulent shopping plaza Star Hill, has pool, fitness centre, conference facilities. Magnificent in its extravagance.

L **Regent**, 160 Jln Bukit Bintang, T3-21418000, www.regenthotels.com A/c, Western, Cantonese and Japanese restaurants, beautiful pool, gym with Roman baths, children's pool, a/c squash courts, health club, business centre (open until midnight), the ultimate hotel in KL – it won the 'Best Hotel in Malaysia' award the year it opened in 1990, all suites have butler service and the rooms and bathrooms are lavishly appointed, the enormous lobby is designed around a pool of cascading water. Recommended.

L-AL **Federal**, 35 Jln Bukit Bintang, T3-21489166, www.federalhotel.com.my A/c, Indian restaurant, revolving restaurant, ice-cream bar, cafés, bowling, shopping arcade, business centre, pool. When it opened in the early 1960s it was the pride of KL: its Mandarin Palace restaurant was once rated as the most elegant restaurant in the Far East, and is still good, but does not compare with the world-class glitz that KL has attracted of late.

AL **Century**, 17-21, Jln Bukit Bintang. T3-21439898, F3-27150880, cklhres@pd.jaring.my Opened in 1998, very large, with restaurant, conference facilities and health club.

AL **Renaissance**, corner of Jln Ismail and Jln Ampang, T3-21622233, www.renaissance-kul.com A hotel with more than 900 rooms and an over-the-top lobby of massive black marble pillars. Furnishings in rooms are verging on the pretentious, but the lovely pool makes up for all of this. 2 tennis courts. Also a total of 9 lounges, bars and restaurants. Includes breakfast.

AL Swiss Garden, 117 Jln Pudu, T3-21413333, www.swissgarden.com A/c, Chinese restaurant, tiny pool, fitness centre with limited equipment, business centre, Blue Chip Lounge (a classy bar with live band and a computer terminal linked to the KL Stock Exchange), spa, with 310 good-sized rooms and 15 storeys, but disappointing facilities. Expensive for what you get.

AL-A Mutiara(formerly the Hilton), Jln Sultan Ismail, T3-21482322, www.mutiarahotels.com/mutiara_kl/ A/c, restaurant, pool, all facilities and fairly recently renovated.

A Melía Kuala Lumpur, 16 Jln Imbi, T3-21428333, www.solmelia.com Chinese and Spanish restaurants, over 300 rooms, pool, health centre, hairdresser, florist, business centre, not quite up to the standard of many of the other big hotels charging around the same prices, but nonetheless a very reasonable place to stay.

A-B Hotel Nova, 16-22 Jln Alor (Bukit Bintang), T3-21431818, F3-21429985, novahtl@tm.net.my Quite stylish for the price range and lacking in pretension. A/c rooms with bathroom, TV, telephone, limousine and laundry service.

A-B Wenworth, Jln Yew, southeast of the city, T3-92009999, F3-92009006 A/c, Chinese restaurant, café, roof pool, health spa, simple but comfortable rooms, good location for North-South highway – approaching KL from the south, it is one of the first hotels in the city. The surrounding Pudu area is fast being developed with old shophouses giving way to tower blocks and 2 new shopping centres – Phoenix Plaza and the Leisure Mall. Breakfast is included in room tariff and there is a monthly food promotion. A taxi ride will get you to the city centre and Golden Triangle. Recommended.

B Agora, 106-110 Jln Bukit Bintang, T21428133, F214258133, www.agorahotel.com.my A/c, restaurant, small 50-room hotel, located on busy intersection in shopping area of Golden Triangle, rooms on the front tend to be noisy, interesting design incorporating Greek columns and elegant furnishings. Small and past its prime but functional.

B Bintang Warisan, 68 Jln Bukit Bintang, T3-21488111, www.bintangwarisan.com A/c, coffee house, nice little hotel, limited number of standard-price double bedrooms. Good, clean but quite basic small rooms, only facilities are two small cafés, some rooms have their own garden, prices include breakfast.

B Cardogan, 64 Jln Bukit Bintang, T21444883, F21444865, cardogan@po.jaring.my A/c, coffee house, health centre, business centre, dark wood interior. It has 61 rather bare rooms and small shower rooms attached. Price includes breakfast.

B Fortuna, 87 Jln Berangan, T21419111, F21418237, fortuna@tm.net.my. A/c, coffee house with live band, health centre, just off Bukit Bintang, tucked away and slightly quieter than most, behind McDonalds, good value for money. Recommended.

B Imperial, 76-80 Jln Cangkat Bukit Bintang (Jln Hicks), T3-21481422, F3-21429048. A/c, restaurant, well-priced Chinese hotel in an otherwise pricey part of town, well located for shopping centres but at this price don't expect a gem.

B Lodge, Jln Sultan Ismail, T3-21420122, F3-21416819, kllodge@tm.net.my A/c, restaurant, small pool, small hotel on busy junction, surrounded by tower blocks, large rooms with 1950s fittings.

B Malaysia, 67-69 Jln Bukit Bintang, T3-21428033, F3-21428579. A/c, restaurant, a rather jaded hotel amidst all the glitz, faded wallpaper, limited facilities, but a lot cheaper than many. Iron railings over windows restrict view of the street. Unsuccessful attempt at international style.

B-C Comfort Inn, 65 Cangkat Bukit Bintang, T3-21413636, F3-21434633, comfortinn@pd.jaring.my This is described as a 2-star budget hotel with a/c, coffee shop and laundry facitlies. The same ownership runs a budget guesthouse called Comfort Lodge around the corner on Jalan Tingkat Tong Shin (**C**) offering rooms with shared bathrooms.

C-D Pondok Lodge, 20 Jln Cangkat Bukit Bintang, T21428449, www.pondoklodge.com A stream of backpackers makes its way to this hostel on the basis of a rival guidebook's glowing recommendation. But rooms are nothing to shout about – simple cells with little else and all have shared bathroom, and the price is RM10 – RM15 higher than other guest houses. What sets this place apart is the rooftop garden, and the funky upper floor

lounge area which has a kitchen, big comfy sofas and a breakfast dining area.
C-D Putra Bintang, 72 Jln Bukit Bintag, T3-21419228, F3-21429678. Gleaming new and efficient. Basic rooms with a/c, attached shower and shiny tiles. Popular. 24-hour Internet room downstairs. If it's clean you're after, this is a good budget choice. Best to book ahead.
C-D Tai Ichi, 78 Jln Bukit Bintang, T3-21427533, F3-21486294. A/c. Another little basic hotel in this strip. A bit shabby, but clean and serviceable.
C-D Shuttle Inn, 112 Jln Bukit Bintang, T3-21450828. Friendly little place, with basic, cleanish rooms with attached shower room, TV and a/c.

Chow Kit *p87, map p79*

AL Pan Pacific, Jln Putra, T3-40425555, http://kualalumpur.panpacific.com/ A/c, restaurant, pool, gym, spa, attached to the Putra World Trade Centre, so favoured by convention delegates, good views over the city, excellent dim sum restaurant, next to the PWTC LRT station.
A Grand Continental, Jln Belia/Jln Raja Laut, T3-26939333, F3-26938429, grandcm@tm.net.my. A/c, restaurant, pool, not really in the big league, except insofar as it has 300-odd unremarkable rooms, impersonal atmosphere, but reasonable facilities, similar, but much larger, to nearby Plaza Hotel. Breakfast included.
A Legend, 100 Jln Putra, T3-40429888, F3-40430700, www.legendsgroup.com/legendkl/index.html A/c, Chinese, Japanese and health food restaurants (7 in total), pool, health centre, like a monstrous Lego creation, this hotel is legendary in size, with 600 rooms and apartments, and a lobby on the ninth floor, the hotel was opened by Joan Collins and pursues a film-star image. Next to the PWTC LRT station, a very regal atmosphere. Staff are friendly and helpful.
A-B Wira Hotel, 123 Jln Thamboosamy, T3-40423333, www.kl-hotels.com/wira Off the main street, so slightly quieter than other typical business hotels in the area. Friendly staff, new hotel so clean, a/c, television, telephone and fridge in rooms. Coffee shop.
B City Hotel, 366 Jln Raja Laut, T3-40414466, F3-40415379. A/c, no restaurant, 101 rooms, does not look much from the exterior, but rooms are clean with good hot water showers, professional management, competitively priced, most guests are Malaysians. Recommended.
B City Villa (formerly Asia), 69 Jln Haji Hussein, T3-2926077, F3-2935143. A/c, restaurant – established and popular, karaoke bar, good value for money. Breakfast included.
B Dynasty, 218 Jln Ipoh, T3-40437777, www.dynasty.com.my A/c, pool, Chinese or Mediterranean restaurants, business centre, a short distance from the Putra World Trade Centre, all the luxury you would expect for the price. Does 'The Ultimate Wedding Dynasty' for all religions – very tacky. Good value but inconvenient location.
B Elegant Inn, 164 Jln Raja Laut, T3-40452288, F3-40456973. Situated on busy main street, standard mid-range, a/c rooms, attached bathrooms, television and telephone. Postal and laundry services.
B Grand Central, 63 Jln Putra/Jln Raja Laut, T40413011, F40424758, www.grandhotelsinternational.com.my/central_kl/ A/c, clean but drab middle-market hotel with 138 rooms and little to recommend it but reasonable room rates, very basic restaurant.
B Grand Centrepoint, 316 Jln Tuanku Abdul Rahman, T26933988, F26943688, www.ubb.com.my/hotel A/c, Island Bar, café, two restaurants, 100-room hotel, very clean, stylish primary colour décor, good for business people on a tight(ish) budget. Price includes breakfast.
B Plaza, Jln Raja Laut, T3-26982255, F3-2920959. A/c, restaurant, 160-room hotel offering competitive rates, price includes buffet breakfast and use of sauna.
B Vistana, 9 Jln Lumut, off Jln Ipoh, T3-40428000. A/c, restaurant, coffee house, business centre, pool, classic business hotel of excellent standard but unpretentious, within easy walking distance of Putra World Trade Centre, a RM5 taxi ride from Chinatown, and close to Titiwangsa LRT and Monorail station.
C Hotel Putra, 50-52 Jln Putra, T3-40412232, reservation@hotelputra.com Clean, simple a/c rooms, with attached bathrooms, television and telephone. Internet café adjoining, breakfast included. A little out of town but near the PWTC LRT station.

Outer Kuala Lumpur *p87*

C **YMCA**, 95 Jln Padang Belia, T3-22741439, F3-22740559, www.ymcakl.com Good facilities – fitness centre, language courses, shop – neutralized by inconvenient location in Brickfields district on the southwest outskirts, off Jln Tun Sambathan, it is, however, within sniffing distance of Raju's tandoori ovens (see Eating, page 107), and it's a short walk to KL Sentral train hub.

Mines Wonderland *p91*

AL **Mines Beach Resort and Spa**, Jln Dulang, T3-89436688, sales@mbr.com.my Furnished to a high standard, the resort has even managed to achieve a sandy beach. Low-rise hotel in well-landscaped gardens, a pleasant alternative to the bustle of KL.

AL **Palace of the Golden Horses**, Jln Kuda Emas, T3-89432343, pgh_reservation@signature.com.my Set on the shores of the old tin-minng lake, a hotel with 400-plus rooms hotel, luxury fittings, a range of cuisines, state-of-the-art conference centre, exquisite spa, fitness centre, free-form lagoon pool, and children's camp. The closest 5-star hotel to the new airport.

B **Mint**, 8th Rm, KL-Seremban Highway, T3-89438888, F3-9438889. Ugly block of over 400 rooms, sizeable pool, health and business centre, convenient for Mines Exhibition Centre, Wonderland, and airport.

Petaling Jaya *p89*

AL **Allson Sunway Lagoon Resort**, Jln Lagun Timur, Bandar Sunway, T3-74928000, www.sunway.com.my/hotel New and dazzling resort, the world's largest surf 'n wave pool, health and spa club, 3 tennis courts, squash, 170-m man-made beach, kiddy camp, shuttle service to KL, coffee house, Japanese restaurant, Chinese restaurant, American/Italian restaurant, poolside bar. Recommended.

AL **Hyatt Regency Saujana Hotel & Country Club**, 2km off Sultan Abdul Aziz Shah Airport Highway T3-78461234, http://saujana.regency.hyatt.com/ 5 mins from the airport and 2 mins from the golf course (it has 2 18-hole championship courses), low-rise hotel set in landscaped gardens, it is a particularly convenient stop-over for early morning flights, provides shuttle service to and from airport.

AL **Pan Pacific Glenmarie Resort**, Jln Sultan, T3-78031000, http://glenmarie-kl.panpacific.com/ Resort hotel with 300 rooms set in more than 1,000 ha of grounds, with sports facilities including 2 golf courses, Olympic-sized swimming pool, squash and tennis courts.

AL **Petaling Jaya Hilton**, 2 Jln Barat, T3-79559122. Large white block, about a 45-min drive from the airport. There's a pool, spa, tennis courts and golf course.

A **Shah's Village Hotel**, 3 & 5 Lorong Sultan, T3-79569322, www.shahsresorts.com A/c, restaurant, boutique-style hotel set around a garden and pool.

Klang and its offshore islands *p90*

C **SeaLion Guest House**, T3-31103142. The only guesthouse on the island of Pula Ketam.

Kuala Selangor Nature Park *p90*

C-D **Chalets**, T3-32892294. The Malayan Nature Society runs chalets in Kuala Selangor Nature Park, a short walk from the last bus stop. These must be booked in advance a few days in advance for weekend visitors. Some have bathrooms others have shared bathrooms.

Seremban *p91 map p101*

Seremban has only a few hotels, one of which is among the best of Malaysia's resort hotels, the *Allson Klana*. There are 3 mid-range hotels; the rest are basic, Chinese- run establishments of an almost uniformly poor quality.

AL **Allson Klana Resort**, PT4388 Jln Penghulu Cantik, Taman Tasik Seremban, T6-7627888, www.allsonklana.com.my/. The *Allson* is a good alternative to staying in KL, the airport being only 20 mins from the new site, set in 24 acres of landscaped gardens. The *Allson Klana* is a luxurious and well-established resort hotel, overlooking one of the largest lagoon-shaped pools in Malaysia and has over 200 very comfortable and spacious rooms with a/c, in-house video, shower and bath, mini-bar, other facilities include tennis, health club, sauna, business centre, delicatessen and boutique, outstanding food outlets include *Yuri Japanese Restaurant*, *Blossom Court Chinese Restaurant* as well as a coffee house.

B **Carlton Star**, 47 Jln Dato Sheikh Ahmad, T6-7636663, F6-7620040. Good central position, a/c, coffee house, fitness centre, karaoke lounge. One of the better budget places to stay although rooms are a bit poky.

B **Seri Malaysia**, Jln Sungai Ugung, T6-7644181, www.serimalaysia.com.my. A bit out of the way, but good value for money. Building is topped with a Minangkabau-style roof, but rooms are standard hotel fare.

B **Tasik**, Jln Tetamu, T6-7630994, F6-7635355. Located next to the Lake Gardens, a/c, TV, shower, restaurant, pool, business centre, seen better days but has a good central position and outlook over the Lake Gardens.

D **Happy**, 35 Jln Tunku Hassan, T6-7630172. Probably the best of the budget places to stay, although that is not saying much. The rooms may be dark but at least they are reasonably clean.

D-E **Nam Yong**, 5 Jln Tuanku Munawir, T7620155. Restaurant, grotty hotel, the only plus being the price of the rooms.

Sri Menanti *p93*

B **Sri Menanti Resort**, T6-4970242, with air conditioning, pool and restaurant, and good, well-equipped rooms.

Port Dickson *p94*

Because PD is a favourite family getaway for KL's weekenders, beach hotels are often quite full – and rates are comparatively high. During the week, discounts are often on offer. There is not much selection for the budget-minded traveller, who may be wise to give Port Dickson a miss.

AL **Ilham Resort** Tanjung Biru, T2-6626800, F2-6625646. Resort comprising 59 apartments. All rooms have a/c and phones. Facilities include a pool, tennis court, squash court and spa on site. A babysitting service is available.

AL **Guoman**, km 16, Jln Pantai, T2-6627878, www.guomanhotels.com A top class resort set in 90 acres of grounds and sat on ½ km of beach front. Refurbished in 2003, over 250 rooms & suites, golf course, swimming pool, 7 restaurants and cafes.

A **Bayu Beach Resort**, Batu 4½, Jln Pantai, T2-6473703, www.bayu.com.my. Pool, luxury 300-room beach resort, good watersports facilities, all rooms with a/c, kitchenette, TV, minibar, Chinese restaurant, coffee house, karaoke lounge.

A **Corus Paradise Resort** , 3½ km Jln Pantai, T2-6477600, www.corusparadisepd.com/. Luxury hotel, the best on the strip, over 200 rooms, all with ocean views, bath, TV, in-house video, mini-bar, tea/coffee-making facilities, other amenities include pool, children's playground, tennis, squash, watersports, business centre, coffee house.

A **Regency**, Batu 5, T2-6474090. Minangkabau-style architecture, tennis, squash, children's pool, two restaurants, business centre.

A **Tanjung Tuan Beach Resort**, Batu 5, Jln Pantai, T2-662013. A/c, restaurant, pool, good sports facilities and weekday discounts.

B **Seri Malaysia**, Batu 4, Jln Pantai, T2-6476070, www.serimalaysia.com.my. One of newer additions to this budget chain of hotels, good views across beach and good value. Recommended.

B **Travers Hotel**, Batu 9, T2-6625273. Quiet location facing the sea, charges include breakfast, clean.

B-C **Golden Resort**, Batu 10, Jln Pantai, T2-6625176. Rooms have a/c, mini-fridge and TV. Facilities include restaurant and pool.

C **Beach Point Motel**, Batu 9, Jln Pantai, T2-6625889. Located down a track off main road, a/c, shower, basic but spotlessly clean.

C **Lido**, Batu 8, Jln Pantai, T2-6625273. Restaurant, quiet location, set in large grounds.

D **Kong Meng**, Batu 8, Teluk Kemang, T2-6625683. restaurant, on the beachfront, reasonable for the price.

E **Port Dickson Youth Hostel**, Km 6 Jln Pantai, T2-6472188. YHA card holders only (although some non-members seem to land a room), separate dorm for men and women, dining/cooking area, large compound, camping facilities.

Eating

Many of KL's big hotels in the Jln Sultan Ismail/Bukit Bintang areas serve excellent value buffet lunches and offer a selection of local and international dishes. One of the best ways to sample various cuisines is to graze among the foodstalls. In the past few years, Cangkat Bukit Bintang and Tingkat Tong Shin, a couple of streets sprouting west from Jalan Bukit Bintang have emerged as trendy eating areas.

Chinatown *p80, map p81*

Chinese

Oriental Bowl, 587 Leboh Pudu, T3-22025577. A/c restaurant above Chinese spice shop, convenient location for Central Market, rather formal atmosphere.

Restoran China Town Pavilion, Jln Hang Lekir. One of the open-air restaurants that gets out the tables in the evening. Lively place for a beer. The food is a tad overpriced, good but nothing special. Patronised mainly by tourists.

Formosa Vegetarian, 48 Jln Sultan. Mammoth menu of fake meats and fish, beancurds and other creative veggie dishes. Recommended.

Nam Heong, 54 Jln Sultan, Hainanese chicken rice.

Seng Nam, Lebuh Pasar Besar, Hainanese. The steamboats in the restaurant area of Chinatown are worth sampling at one of the outdoor tables.

The "Gourmet Food Court" on Jalan Petaling, opposite The Swiss Inn has a great vegetarian counter with a dozen choices of tasty vegetables and beancurd to pile on rice. Best cheap breakfast in Chinatown. Recommended.

Yook Woo Hin, 100 Jln Petaling, open until 1400. Cheap dim sum in the middle of Chinatown.

Indian and Pakistani

Hameeds, 1st Flr, Central Market, specialist in fish-head curry.

Restoran Yusoof Dan Zakhir, opposite Central market. Simple food hall with blaring music, and bright yellow and green décor. Cheap and good grazing. Recommended.

Malay

Naili's Place, Central Market Annexe, T3-20265105. Quirky place with waterfalls and a wooden bridge. Also serves western food.

Thai

Sawah Padi, G/F, Central Market, T3-22602218. Elegance inside the bustle of Central Market. Often has traditional dancing shows.

Foodstalls

Puduraya Bus Station, Jln Pudu, a good variety of stalls, open at all hrs.

Little India *p82*

International

Coliseum Café, 100 Jln Tuanku Abdul Rahman (Batu Rd), next door to the old Coliseum Theatre, long-famed for its sizzling lamb and beef steaks, Hainanese (Chinese) food and Western-style (mild) curries, all served by frantic waiters in buttoned-up white suits. During the Communist Emergency, planters were said to come here for gin and curry, handing their guns in to be kept behind the bar; it is easy to believe it. Recommended.

Foodstalls

Jln Masjid India, Little India, has many good Indian and Malay foodstalls.

Lorong Raja Muda Food Centre, off Jln Raja Muda, on the edge of Kampong Baru, has mainly Malay food.

Sunday Market, Kampong Baru (main market actually takes place on Sat night), has many Malay hawker stalls.

Lake Gardens and around *p83*

International

Carcosa Seri Negara, Persiaran Mahameru, Taman Tasek Perdana (Lake Gardens), T3-22821888 (reservations), open daily 1530-1800. Built in 1896 to house the British Administrator for the Federated Malay States, Carcosa offers English-style high tea in a sumptuous, colonial setting, expensive Italian lunches and dinners are also served in the Mahsuri dining hall on fine china plates with solid silver cutlery, Continental cuisine, high tea (recommended).

Malay

Seri Melayu, 1 Jln Conlay, T3-21451833. Open 1100-1500, 1900-2300 (reservations recommended for groups of 4 or more – although it seats 500!). One of the best Malay restaurants in town in traditional Minangkabau-style building, the brain-child of former Malaysian PM Dr Mahatir Mohamad, beautifully designed interior in style of Negeri Sembilan palace, don't be put off by cultural shows or the big groups – the food is superb and amazing in its variety, including regional specialities; it's very popular with locals too. Individual dishes are expensive, the buffet is the best bet (choice of more than 50 dishes), with promotions featuring cuisine from different states each month. Those arriving in shorts will be given a sarong to wear. Recommended.

KLCC and Jalan Ampang

p84, map p85

Indian and Pakistani

Bharath's, Suria KLCC, T3-21632631. Classy South Indian restaurant with great views. Some of the seating is provided by wooden swings. Very kitsch.

D'Tandoor, KL Tower, T3-20212020. Fancy Indian restaurant (part of an international chain) in the KL tower.

Bangles, 270 Jln Ampang, T3-45324100. This is reckoned to be among the best North Indian tandoori restaurants in KL, often necessary to book in the evenings. Recommended.

Bombay Palace, 388 Jln Tun Razak, next to US Embassy, T3-21454241, open 1200-1500, 1830-2300, good-quality North Indian food in tasteful surroundings with staff in traditional Indian uniform, menu including vegetarian section. Tourism award winners for several years.

International

Ciao, 428 Jln Tun Razak, T3-9854827, open 1200-1430, 1900-2230, closed Mon, authentic tasty Italian food served in a beautifully renovated bungalow. Recommended.

Shook, JW Marriot Hotel, T3-27168535. Four open kitchens covering Japanese, Chinese, Italian and a western grill.

Lakshmi Villas, Leboh Ampang, excellent vegetarian food, try the masala dosai – pancakes stuffed with vegetables and accompanied by a lentil sauce.

Japanese

Benkay, Hotel Nikko, Jln Ampang, T3-21611111. Named after a legendary warrior. Has seasonal specials, a teppanyaki room and sushi bar.

Malay

Seri Angkasa, at the top of the KL Tower (see page 85), T3-22085055. A sister restaurant to Seri Melayu. The tower revolves, achieving a full rotation in 60 mins. Good food, booking advisable for the evenings. There is also a good value buffet lunch available (RM55).

Nyonya

Kapitan's Club, 35 Jln Ampang, T3-22010242, open 1100-1500, 1800-2230, spacious restaurant decorated with Straits woodwork, staff in traditional outfits, 'top hats', the house speciality is a tasty pastry and egg dish, Kapitan chicken is popular, Malay dishes also available.

Top Hat , 7 Jln Kia Peng, T3-22413611, open 1200-1500, 1900-2400, good Eastern Nyonya set menu, some Western dishes such as chicken pie, set in a 1930s colonial bungalow, just south of KLCC. Recommended.

Seafood

Studio 123, 159 Jln Ampang. Easily missed – it's opposite the Corus Hotel – this is an unassuming place with friendly staff and excellent, good-value food. Recommended.

Vietnamese

Tamarind Springs, Taman Tun Abdul Razak, Ampang, T3-42569300. Indochinese cuisine served in leafy elegance.

Foodstalls

Ampang Park Shopping Complex, along Jln Tun Razak, is a popular but small centre, with good variety of stalls.

The Golden Triangle *p86, map p86*

Chinese

Golden Phoenix, Hotel Equatorial, Jln Sultan Ismail, T3-21617777. Open 1200-1430, gourmet Chinese establishment, mock Chinese courtyard setting.

Lai Ching Yuen, The Regent Hotel, Jln Bukit Bintang, T3-21418000. Set in mock Chinese pavilion, holder of 4 Malaysian Tourism Gold Awards for consistently fine cuisine, popular with Chinese gourmets, luxury table settings, revolving solid granite table centres.

Shang Palace, Shangri-La Hotel, Jln Sultan Ismail, T3-20322388. Open 1200-1430, 1900-2300, dim sum lunch of over 40 varieties costs around RM50, check food promotions for evening meals.

The Blossom, Swiss Garden Hotel, 117 Jln Pudu, T3-21413333. Open 1130-1430, 1830-2230, around 40 varieties of dim sum, tiger prawns a house speciality, good selection of pork dishes, abalone and birds' nests only for those on hefty expense accounts.

Marco Polo, Wisma Lim Foo Yong, 86 Jln Raja Chulan, T3-21425595. Open 1200-1500, 1900-2300, extensive menu, barbecue roast suckling pig recommended, 1970s-style décor, very busy lunchtimes.

Esquire Kitchen, Level 1, Sungai Wang Plaza, Jln Sultan Ismail. Dumplings and pork dishes good value, Shanghai dishes popular.

International

Lafitte, Shangri-La Hotel, 11 Jln Sultan Ismail, T3-20743900, open 1200-1500, 1900-2300, excellent French restaurant, but very expensive. Recommended.

Sakura Café & Cuisine, 165-169 Jln Imbi, excellent variety of Malay, Chinese and Indian dishes including fish-head curry, located in an area with many other good cheap restaurants. Recommended.

Scalini's, 19 Jln Sultan Ishmail, just down from the Istana Hotel. Wonderful Italian food. Pasta dishes excellent, trendy surroundings and friendly staff. Pricey but recommended.

Delaney's, Parkroyal Hotel, Jln Sultan Ismail, open 1200 until late. The manufactured Irish experience available at most cities around the world. Asian snacks, hearty pies and a pint of Guinness - you can't go wrong.

Hard Rock Café, Ground Flr, Concorde Hotel, 2 Jln Sultan, Ismail, T3-21444062, open 1130-0200. One of the best places for top-quality American burgers, steaks and salads, good value. Recommended.

Tarbush, 138, Jln Bukit Bintang, T3-42534177. Lebanese cuisine served in a simple setting. Locals recommend it for the good service and the authentic Middle Eastern taste with no Malay influence.

The Ship, 40 Jln Sultan Ismail. Very dark interior, extensive menu of steaks, chicken, salads. The stone grills are particularly popular. Open from lunch until 0230.

E'Toile bistro, Basement, Equatorial Hotel, Jln Sultan Ismail. Coffee and pastries with free Internet access to all customers. Nice touch. Recommended.

Federal Hotel Revolving Restaurant, 35 Jln Bukit Bintang. This was once one of KL's tallest buildings, now rather dwarfed but still a good spot for ice-cream sundaes with a view.

Lodge Coffee Shop, Jln Sultan Ismail. Good value for money, particularly local dishes – *nasi goreng*, curries and buffets. Recommended.

Roadhouse Grill, 42 Jln Sultan Ismail, open 1130-2400. Cheap and cheerful American fare.

Japanese

Kampachi, Hotel Equatorial, Jln Sultan Ismail, T3-21617777. Ginza-trained chefs, private tatami rooms and another winner of Malaysian Tourism award.

Zipangu, Shangri-La Hotel, 11 Jln Sultan Ismail, T3-20322388. Regular winner of best restaurant, with a small Japanese garden. Limited menu but highly regarded.

Chikuyo-Tei, Plaza See Hoy Chuan, Jln Raja Chulan, open 1200-1500, 1830-2230. Housed in a basement, good-value set meals, quality teppanyak, seafood and steak.

Munakata, 2nd Flr, Menara Promet, Jln Sultan Ismail.

Teppanyaki, 2nd Flr, Sungai Wang Plaza, Jln Bukit Bintang and Lot 10, Jln Sultan Ismail, basement, excellent Japanese fast food, set meal for RM10.

Korean

Korean Restaurant, 24 Jln Medan Imbi, open 1100-1500, 1800-2300, small restaurant off Jln Imbi, lashings of garlic, friendly staff.

Koryo-Won, Kompleks Antarabangsa, Jln Sultan Ismail, T3-21482322. Excellent barbecues, particularly when washed down with Jung Jong rice wine. Recommended.

Malay

Spices, Concorde Hotel, 2 Jln Sultan Ismail, T3-22442200. Open 1130-1500, 1830-2300, closed Sun. Ironically, considering its name, the food is not overly spicy, eclectic Asian cuisine as well as traditional Malay, 4-piece band background music, a/c indoors or poolside outdoors, setengah (a stiff whisky drink popular in colonial times) features on the varied drinks list.

Estana Restaurant and Garden, 23D Jln Sultan Ismail, opposite The Ship, excellent Malay and north and south Indian cuisine.

Satay Anika, Ground Floor, Bukit Bintang Plaza, Jln Bukit Bintang. Fast-food satay. Recommended.

Nyonya

Restoran Nyonya, 21 Jln Tingkat Tong Shin (just behind Jln Bukit Bintang), T3-21430100. Home recipes seasoned with sour lime and tamarind flavoured sauces.

Dondang Sayang, 12 Lower Ground Floor, The Weld, Jln Raja Chulan, T3-22613831; also at 28 Jln Telawi Lima, Bangsar Baru, T3-22549388. Popular and reasonably priced restaurant with big Nyonya menu.

Zura Traditional, 19 Tingkat Tong Shin (just behind Jln Bukit Bintang), T3-21486466. Arty eatery serving traditional Peranakan cuisine. The spicy coconut fish comes recommended.

Sri Penang, Lower Ground Flr, Menara Aik Hua, Cangkat Raja Chulan (Jln Hicks), variety of Nyonya and North Malaysian dishes.

Thai

Bangkok Jam, BB Plaza, Jln Bukit Bintang, T21423449. Popular Thai eatery, recommended by locals.

Sri Thai, 42 Jln Sultan Ismail, T3-21429915. Well established eatery near Jln Bukit Bintang, although it's looking a bit faded now. It's lasted 25 years in a city where a restaurant's expected life span is often very short, so it must be doing something right.

Johnny's Thai Steamboat, in the basement of Bukit Bintang Plaza. Good value spicy Thai dishes.

Seafood

Eden Village, 260 Jln Raja Chulan. Wide-ranging menu, but probably best known for seafood, resembles a glitzy Minangkabau palace with garden behind, cultural Malay, Chinese and Indian dances every night (less touristy outlet in PJ 25-31 Jln 5322/23, Damansara Jaya).

New Ocean, 29B Medan Imbi (off Jln Imbi and Jln Hoo Teik Ee). Good seafood restaurant just round the corner from the Sungai Wang and Lot 10 shopping complexes.

Unicorn, 1st Flr, Annex Block, Lot 10 Shopping Centre, Jln Sultan Ismail, T3-2441695, open 1100-1500, 1800-0400. Big, smart Chinese seafood restaurant in the Lot 10 complex, just by the footbridge to Sungai Wang, good stop for shoppers.

Vietnamese

Sao Nam, 25 Tingkat Tong Shin, T3-21441225. Choose from the romantic but sweaty outdoor garden area or the yellow-painted canteen inside. Wide range of traditional Vietnamese dishes.

Teahouses

Chinese teahouse. Try out the traditional Chinese teahouse opposite Sungai Wang Hotel on Jln Bukit Bintang.

Foodstalls

Lot 10 Shopping Complex, Jln Sultan Ismail, there is an excellent choice of food here, if you can tolerate the high-volume music.

Chow Kit *p87, map p79*

Chinese

The Museum, The Legend Hotel, The Mall, Putra Pl, 100 Jln Putra, T3-40429888. Open 1200-1500, 1830-2230, aims to look like a museum, with Chinese antiques and columns everywhere. Teochew and Cantonese cuisine, adventurous food promotions, winner of Malaysian Tourism and Promotion best Chinese award.

Hai Tien Lo, Pan Pacific Hotel, Jln Putra, T3-40494510. Open 1200-1500, 1900-2300, excellent dim sum, steamed fish with suet. Recommended.

Cameleon Vegetarian Restaurant, 1 Jln Thamboosamy (off Jln Putra, near The Mall and Pan Pacific), Thai and Chinese, good kway teow, but vegetarians with carnivorous instincts rate the soyabean roast duck and various other ersatz meat and fish dishes whose presentation (and sometimes taste) is convincing.

Indian and Pakistani

The Taj, The Crown Princess Hotel, 11th Flr, City Square Centre, Jln Tun Razak, T3-21625522 ext. 5680, open 1200-1500, 1900-2300, closed Sat lunch Stylish Anglo-Raj décor, live Indian muzak, open view kitchen, New Delhi chefs create first rate Indian cuisine, the vegetable samosas and tandooris – meat and veg – are excellent. Recommended.

Alhmdoolilla, 12 Jln Dang Wangi, rated for its rotis.

International

Lot 253, The Mall, 2nd Flr, 100 Jln Putra, T3-4431988, open 1200-2200. Good set menu and authentic French atmosphere.

Marble Arch, Hotel Grand Continental, Jln Raja Laut, T3-2939333, open 1100-1500, 1800-2300. Good buffet lunches and set meals during food promotions when chefs are on hand from the country being promoted.

Japanese

Keyaki, Pan Pacific Hotel, Jln Putra, T3-40494412, open 1200-1500, 1900-2300. Good set meals, excellent sashimi and sushi made with fish flown in from Japan twice weekly, highly rated, but extremely expensive.

Sushi King, Lower Ground Flr, The Mall, Jln Putra, T3-4428205 and 63 Jln Sultan Ismail, T3-2417312. Spotlessly clean sushi bar, prices from RM0.50 to RM3 per sushi.

Thai

Cili Padi Thai Restaurant, 2nd Flr, The Mall, Jln Putra. Soups and seafood are excellent, a recommended speciality is King Solomon's Treasure (chicken wrapped in pandan leaves). Closes at 2200 sharp. Recommended.

Foodstalls

Chow Kit is the best area for food stalls. On Jln Raja Muda Abdul Aziz there is a food court with great Indian and Afghan food. Jln Haji Hussien has a picturesque collection of superb food stalls. Walk up Jln Haji Hussien and turn right. The food court on the top floor of The Mall, built like rows of old Chinese shophouses, is run-down but has an attractive ambience. The Indian, Malay and Chinese food is all good, but the majority of places to eat here close by 2000. It's cheap too – tandoori chicken, naan, dal and drink, all for just RM8. Jln Raja Alang and Jln Raja Bot stalls, off Jln Tuanku Abdul Rahman, are mostly Malay stalls.

Next to Keramat supermarket there is a South Indian stall with good mutton soup. In the alleyway between Keramat supermarket and the Pakistani mosque there are lots of good food stalls during the day. Kampong Baharu and Kampong Datok Keramat are Malay communities. On the river front behind Jln Mesjid India are good Indian and Malay night stalls.

Medan Hang Tuah, The Mall (Top Floor), Jln Putra (opposite the Pan Pacific Hotel).

Munshi Abdullah Food Complex, off Lorong Tuanku Abdul Rahman (near Coliseum), for good satay.

Scores of rough and ready Chinese pavement restaurants line Jalan Alor, parallel to Jalan Bukit Bintang.

Outer Kuala Lumpur *p87*

Wan Kembang (Cik Siti), 24 Jln 14/22, Petaling Jaya (in front of the mosque), specializing in Kelantanese food.

Chinese

Ampang Yong Tau Foo, 53 Jln SS2/30, Petaling Jaya. Yong tau foo (stuffed beancurd dishes) in a coffee shop. Recommended. Closed Mon.

Halfway to Kajang, near Sungai Besi (take Seremban highway, exit to left at Taman Sri Petaling – before toll gates, right at T-junction, over railway line and past Shell and Esso stations, turn left towards Sungai Besi tin mine, then branch right to Balakong, the restaurant is signposted), it is little more than a tin shed (with a fruit stall outside) but is famed among KL's epicureans for its deep-fried, paper-wrapped chicken, wild boar curry and vinegar pork shank. Recommended.

Indian and Pakistani

¥ **Annalakshmi**, 46 Lorong Maarof, Bangsar Baru, T3-22823799. Excellent Indian vegetarian restaurants run by the Temple of Fine Arts, dedicated to the preservation of Indian cultural heritage in Malaysia, the buffet is particularly recommended.

¥ **Sri Vani's Corner (Raju's)**, Jln Tun Sambathan 4 (next to YMCA tennis courts), overgrown hawker stall rated among its dedicated clientele as the best place for tandooris and oven-baked naan in KL. Recommended.

¥ **Valentine Roti**, 6 Jln Semark (close to the National Library), this place was fortunate enough to be reviewed in the Far Eastern Economic Review and was billed as the best roti restaurant in town. Ilango Arokias-amy's rotis are a treat, light and flaky, and as he says "I think God wanted me to do this".

International

¥¥¥ **Jake's**, 21 Jln Setiapuspa, Medan Damansara, off Jln Damansara, towards PJ, T3-20945677, open 1200-1500, 1830-2300, Jake's steaks are highly rated in KL, served by cowboys and cowgirls. Recommended.

Seafood

¥¥ **Bangsar Seafood Village**, Jln Telawi Empat, Bangsar Baru, open 1200-1430, 1800-2300. Large restaurant complex with reasonably priced seafood, fresh from tanks that line the inside of the restaurant, specialities include crab in butter sauce and Thai-style tiger prawns (and a good satay stall).

¥¥ **Hai Peng Seafood Restaurant**, Taman Evergreen, Batu Empat, Jln Klang Lama (Old Klang Rd). The smallest and least assuming restaurant in a row of Chinese shophouses (red neon sign), but one of the very best seafood restaurants in Malaysia, where the Chinese community's seafood connoisseurs come to eat (the other seafood restaurants in the cluster include Chian Kee, Pacific Sea Foods and Yee Kee, most of which are good, but not as good as Hai Peng). Its specialities include butter crab (in clove and coconut), belacan crab, sweet and sour chilli crab and bamboo clams, the siu yit kum (small gold-leaf tea) – a delicious, fragrant Chinese tea, which is perfect with seafood, open until 0100. Recommended.

Vietnamese

¥¥ **Restoran Sri Saigon**, 53 Jln 552/30, Petaling Jaya, T3-7753681. Genuine Vietnamese dishes.

Foodstalls

Brickfields, Jln Tun Sambathan, has a string of small outdoor restaurants.

Mamaks For a good, cheap eat, Mamaks, canteens runs by Muslim Indians can be found everywhere, many are open 24 hours. The most famous Mamak is Mamak SS2 Mumi, in the SS2 area of Petaling Jaya. It's so well known that taxi drivers know where it is just by its name.

Seremban *p91, map p92*

Chinese

¥¥¥ **Blossom Court**, *Allson Klan Resort*, classy Chinese restaurant, expensive-looking décor, popular for extensive range of *dim sum*, good Peking duck and Cantonese dishes.

¥¥¥ **Happy**, 1 Jln Dato Bandar Tunggal.

¥¥¥ **Regent**, 2391-2 Taman Bukit Labu.

Indian

¥ **Samy**, 120 Jln Yam Tuan, banana leaf.

Japanese

¥¥¥ **Yuri**, *Allson Klan Resort*, excellent quality, traditional Japanese, good, private Tatami rooms, sushi bar, Teppanyaki counter, good-value set meals.

Foodstalls

Jalan Tuanku Antah, near the post office; **Jalan Dr Murugesu**, opposite Masjid Janek mosque.

Port Dickson *p94*

Seafood

¥ **Haw Wah Seafood**, Teluk Kamang, simple but clean coffee shop at end of row of modern shophouses on main road, good seafood.

¥ **Kemang Seafood**, Batu 7, Malay seafood, crab sold by weight (1 kg RM25).

Foodstalls

Scattered around town and along Jln Pantai.

Bars and clubs

Kuala Lumpur now has a vibrant bar scene, several streets have emerged over the past five years or so as hip scenes to be seen. Lines of bars, restaurants, coffee shops and even Mamaks have sprouted along the same street, serving food and drink well into the early hours of the morning. The Golden Triangle is a good place to find bars and clubs – the main bar and club street being Jalan P Ramlee, but a few bars have begun setting up pumps in Cangkat Bukit Bintang, and this area is slated to grow more nightspots. Bangsar and Desi Sri Hartamas are two areas just outside the centre of KL which have developed into popular night-time spots. Bars, restaurants, coffee shops and mamaks stand side by side in a network of streets in these two areas. Most stay open until the early hours of the morning.

The Metro section in *The Star* (Malaysia's most widely read English-language daily) is devoted to what's on and where. Also check out freebie magazines such as *Juice* (available in bars and clubs) or *KL lifestyle*, *KLUE* and *KL Vision* (usually free in hotels, if not they are available in newsagents for about RM5)

Since the mid-1980s, with the rise of the KL yuppy, the city has shaken off its early-to-bed image and now has a slightly more lively club scene. Several old colonial buildings have been converted into night spots. Most nightclubs and discos in KL stay open until 0300 during the week and until 0400 on Fri nights and weekends. Clubs are concentrated in Jalan P Ramlee and Bangsar. International DJs are occasionally lured to Zouk, Atmosphere, Espanada, Liquid and Nouvo.

Gay clubs cannot freely advertise themselves as 'gay' here because of the illegal status of homosexuality. Saying that, however, there are a couple of well established gay clubs – Liquid and Velvet and several gay-friendly venues that host gay functions, including the new Zouk superclub. While some girls will hang out in gay bars, there is no lesbian bar per se. Occasional girls' events will be held at various venues, best to check www.fridae.com or www.forplu.com, which should list upcoming events. The Fridae website also has an up-to-date gay and gay-friendly bar and club listing.

Atmosphere@Twelve SI, 12 Jln Sultan Ismail. A superclub, with a mega dance floor, stage and plenty of seating. International DJs.

Beach Club, Jln P Ramlee. Casual resort-style club playing mostly "oldies". Centrepiece is a tank with baby sharks (which must be uncomfortable for them since sharks 'see' through vibrations). Gets packed and is popular with tourists.

Bistro 1957, 22 Jln 25/70A Desi Sri Hartamas. A patriotic liitle bar-cum-restaurant as the theme is Malaysia's independence. Nice beer garden and reasonable prices.

Budaba, 924 Jln P Ramlee. Giant hands support the sign to this place. Owner seems to have tried too hard to manufacture a chillout ethnic feel but fell short of the required ambience. Even so, it's not a bad place for a drink.

Delaney's Pub, corner of Jln Imbi and Jln Pudu, quite expensive standard Irish pub.

Espanada, 97 Jln Sultan Ismail. Swanky club with a massive dance floor but a bit tacky with giant metal palm trees. However it's popular and hosts many events.

Finnegans, 51 Jln Sultan Ismail. Nice beer garden, no nonsense pub, very popular with expats but the toilets are some of the filthiest in the city.

Frangipani, 25 Cangkat Bukit Bintang, T21443001, is an elegant French restaurant and bar with a premoninantly gay clientele.

Funteque, 102-104 Jln Bukit Bintang. Cavernous bar on the second floor with live cover bands.

Green Lotus Café, 20 & 38 Jln Walter Grenier (off Jln Imbi), T21150377. Gay friendly boutiquey café-cum-bar with smooth music, dim lights and an ethnic feel.

Hard Rock Café, Basement and Ground Flr, Wisma Concorde, 2 Jln Sultan Ismail, T3-21444062. The Hard Rock, with its Harley Davidson chopper poised on the rooftop, opened in 1991 and quickly became one of the most popular and lively bars in town, good atmosphere and small disco floor.

Liquid, Mezzanine, Central Market Annexe. A predominantly gay club and bar - they advertise themselves as the place for those with "an alternative lifestyle". Laid back bar on the first floor with balcony seating.

Upstairs is a thumping club, regularly hosting international Djs.

Nouvo, 16 Jln P Ramlee. Chic club for a youngish crowd. R&B and hard house nights.

Q-bar, Westin Hotel, 199 Jalan Bukit Bintang, T3-2731 8333. Latin grill, wine and cigar lounge. The Latin-American bar has a resident Colombian band. Popular with expats.

Poppy, 18 Jln P Ramlee. Very stylish bar and restaurant with a running water, romantic lighting and incense. Recommended for its ambience. Popular with locals.

Reggae Bar, 158 Jln Tun H S Lee. Large, friendly bar, popular with backpackers as it's the only bar in Chinatown and within staggering distance of dorms. Cheap spirits for ladies on most nights.

The Red Chamber, 33 Jln Telawi 3, Bangsar. Funky bar splashed in red from floor to ceiling.

Velvet, Shahzan Tower, Jln Sultan Ismail. One of the original house clubs that now caters to a gay clientele.

Zino, 20 Cangkat Bukit Bintang. Mon-Fri 1700 till late, 1200-late Sat and Sun. Relaxed, small, chill-out style bar with a little garden out front. Funky, shadowy decor.

Zouk, 113 Jln Ampang. Perhaps KL's newest and trendiest nightclub following in the footsteps of Singapore's Zouk. A glowing domed exterior, with changing hue encapsulates the groovy interior. Hosts occasional gay parties. Attracts international DJs such as Tiesto and has a great chillout bar, Velvet Underground. Recommended.

Entertainment

Art galleries

KL is gradually becoming a centre for local and some international artists, but the art market is not exactly flourishing, and much of the artwork around is mediocre. The following are some of the main galleries. Contemporary Malaysian art can be seen at **Art Salon**, 4 Jln Telawi Dua, Bangsar Baru, open Tue-Sun. All work is by local contemporary artists. Prices range from a few hundred RM to thousands. For information on the latest show, T3-22822601. **AP Art Gallery**, Ground Flr, Central Market, off Jln Hang Kasturi, near Chinatown. **Artfolio Gallery**, 1st Flr City Sq, Jln Tun Razak, T3-21623339. **Art House**, 2nd Flr, Wisma Cosway, Jln Raja Chulan, Golden Triangle district, T3-21482283. Regional work focussing on Chinese, Taiwanese and Tibetan painting and sculpture. Very active in organising exhibitions. **Sandra Knuyt**, Shangri-La Hotel, T3-2032 4073, 0900-2230 daily. Work from around the world including works in porcelain and glass and an expensive shop. **Galeri Petronas**, Suria KLCC, T3-2331 7770, 1000-2000 Tue-Sun. Multimedia terminals to learn about Malaysian art and regular exhibitions of contemporary local and regional work including cartoon art.

Cinemas

Cinemas are open daily from 1100. The first showing is usually a 1300 matinee with the last show at 2115 (midnight show Sat). *The Sun* newspaper's weekly listings magazine *Time Out* publishes details of what's on at the cinemas, and screenings are also listed in *The New Straits Times* and the *Star*. Tickets cost around RM10. Cineplex, small cinema complexes, are increasingly popular and many are incorporated into the shopping plazas.

Alliance Francaise, 15 Lorong Gurney, off Jln Semarak, T3-26947880 hosts art house movies, art exhibitions. **Capitol**, Jln Raja Laut, T3-4429051; **Cathay**, Jln Bukit Bintang, T3-2429942; **Cathay Cineplex**, The Mall, T3-4426122; **Coliseum**, Jln Tuanku Abdul Rahman, T3-2925995; **Federal**, Jln Raja Laut, T3-4425014; **Odeon**, Jln Tuanku Abdul Rahman, T3-2920084; **Odeon Cineplex**, Central Sq, T3-2308548; **President**, Sungai Wang Plaza, Jln Sultan Ismail, T3-2480084; and **Rex**, Jln Sultan, T3-2383021; **Tanjong Golden Village** at the KLCC with 12 screens, T3-74922929.

Classical music

Petronas Philharmonic Hall (KLCC), T3-20517007, www.dfpmpo.com KL Symphony Orchestra and the Malaysian Philharmonic Orchestra perform here.

Cultural shows

Central Market, T3-22746542. During the weekends at 1945, performances of Bangsawan (Malay Traditional Theatre), Nadagam (Indian Traditional Theatre) and Chinese Opera all take place.
Eden Village, 260 Jln Raja Chulan, T3-2141 4027. Malay, Indian and Chinese dancing every night.
Malaysia Tourism Centre (MTC), 109 Jln Ampang, T3-21643929, has shows on Tue, Thu, Sat and Sun at 1500 to 1545 (5RM).
Seri Melayu Restaurant, 1 Jln Conlay. Traditional Malay folk dances and singing in KL's best Malay epicurean experience (see page 103).
Temple of Fine Arts, 116 Jln Berhala, Brickfields, T3-22743709. This organization, set up in Malaysia to preserve and promote Indian culture, stages cultural shows every month with dinner, music and dancing. The temple organizes an annual Festival of Arts (call for details), which involves a week-long stage production featuring traditional and modern Indian dance (free, since "the Temple believes art has no price"), it also runs classes in classical and folk dancing, and in playing traditional musical instruments.

Theatre

Genting International Showroom, Genting Highlands Resort, Genting Highlands, T3-2162 2666, http://mice.genting.com.my. Two theatres with seating for over a 1,000 each; where the majority of international acts play. (51 km away in the Genting Highlands). Major performances including occasional international acts play here.
National Theatre (Istana Budaya) Jln Tun Razak, T3-40252525, www.kakiseni.com/
The Actors Studio, Bangsar, level 3, New Wing, Bangsar Shopping Centre, Jln Maarof, Bangsar, T3-20940400, www.theactorsstudio.com.my Most local theatre is performed here.
Plaza Putra. Occasional performances are performed here, underneath Merdeka Sq.

Shopping

As recently as the early 1980s, Malaysians and KL's expatriates used to go on shopping expeditions to neighbouring Singapore as KL just was not up to it. These days, however, the city has more or less everything, with new shopping complexes springing up every year. They are not concentrated in any particular area and ordinary shopping streets and markets are also dotted all around the city.

Antiques

Oriental Spirit, 1st Flr, Central Market (northern end). A stunning emporium of mostly mainland Southeast Asian treasures. Quite pricey but the interior is an Aladdin's Cave of goodies and is well worth a look for the imaginative way in which it's been laid out.

Artefacts

For a general range of Southeast Asian artefacts, the best areas are Jln Ulu Klang, Jln Pudu and Bangsar Town Centre. **Tibetan Treasures**, 16 Cangkat Bukit Bintang, for antique Tibetan furniture and paintings.

Batik

Aran Novabatika Malaysia, 174 Ground Flr, Ampang Park Shopping Centre, Jln Ampang.
Batik Bintang, Lobby Arcade, Federal Hotel, Jln Bukit Bintang.
Batik Corner, Lot L1.13, The Weld Shopping Centre, 76 Jln Raja Chulan, excellent selection of sarong lengths and ready-mades in batiks from all over Malaysia and Indonesia.
Batik Malaysia, 114 Jln Bukit Bintang, Mun Loong, (also 113 Jln Tunku Abdul Rahman).
Batik Permai, Lobby Arcade, Hilton Hotel, Jln Sultan Ismail.
Central Market, Jln Hang Kasturi. Hand-painted silk batik scarves downstairs, many shops sell batik in sarong lengths.
Evolution, G24, Citypoint, Dayabumi Complex, Jln Sultan Hishamuddin, T3-2913711. Fashionable range of ready-mades and other batik gift ideas by designer Peter Hoe.

Faruzzi Weld Shopping Centre, Jln Raja Chulan (also at 42B Jln Nirwana, just off Jln Tun Ismail), exclusive and original batiks. Recommended.
Globe Silk Store, 185 Jln Tuanku Abdul Rahman. The city's oldest department store, founded in 1930, mainly selling fabrics.
Heritage, 38 1st Flr, has a big selection of very original Kelantanese batiks (RM15-90 per m), most ordinary batiks cost about RM7 per m.
Khalid Batik, 48 Ground Flr, Ampang Park Shopping Centre, Jln Ampang.

Books

There is a second-hand bookshop on the First Floor of Central Market. Guesthouses are good places for second hand books and book exchanges.
Berita Book Centre and **MPH Bookstores**, Bukit Bintang Plaza, 1st Flr and Ground Flr respectively, Jln Bukit Bintang.
Bookazine, Damansara Heights, 8 Jln Batai.
Kinokuniya, Isetan Dept Store, 2nd Flr, 50 Jln Sultan Ismail.
Minerva Book Store, 114 Jln Tunku Abdul Rahman.
Popular Book Co, Jln Petaling, Jln Hang Lekir, Sungai Way Plaza.
Times Books, KLCC, Yow Chuan Plaza, 6-7 Jln Tun Razak and Weld Shopping Complex, has a good selection of English-language books.

Cameras

KL is a good place to buy cameras, as they are very competitively priced here.
Bukit Bintang Plaza and **Sungai Wang Plaza**, Jln Sultan Ismail, Golden Triangle have good choices.

Carpets and rugs

Ampang Park Shopping Complex, Jln Ampang.
City Square, Jln Tun Razak, northeast of Golden Triangle.
KL Plaza, Jln Bukit Bintang, Golden Triangle.

Clothing

A good place to look for custom-made shoes is along Jln Tuanku Abdul Rahman.
Berjama Times Square (KL's newest shopping mall with an indoor roller coaster and due to have an iMax cinema at the end of 2004), Jln Imbi has designer clothing and accessories.
Starhill Shopping Centre, Jln Bukit Bintang, Golden Triangle; located at Lot 10 on the corner of Jln Sultan Ismail and Jln Bukit Bintang, Golden Triangle. Six-stories of upmarket designer brands next to the Marriott Hotel.
Sogo, Jln Tuanku Abdul Rahman. One of Southeast Asia's largest department stores. This Japanese store has international brands spread over eight stories.
Sungai Wang Shopping Plaza, Jln Sultan Ismail, Golden Triangle. For custom-made clothing and discount fashion brands.
Weld Shopping Centre, Jln Raja Chulan, near the KL Tower, and **City Square**, Jln Tun Razak, northeast of Golden Triangle. Good for discount fashion brands.

Fabric

A good place to look for fabrics is along Jln Tuanku Abdul Rahman.
Ampang Point Shopping Centre, Jln Ampang. Lots of boutiques and the Royal Department Store.
Lot 10, Jln Bukit Bintang. Another trendy shopping centre, with the Japanese giant store – Isetan. With sports gear, cosmetics, gift shops and brands.
Semua House, Lorong Tuanku Abdul Rahman (at northern end of Jln Masjid India). Sports stores and electronics.

Furniture

Rattan furniture is available from Bangsar Town Centre and Ampang Point.
Oriental Style, 1st Flr, Central Market (southern end), and at 64 Jln Hang Kasturi, reproduction Asian furniture. Pricey.
Oriental Spirit, 1st Flr, Central Market (northern end), antique furniture. Expensive but beautiful objects.

Gems

Petaling St; **Lot 10**, Jln Bukit Bintang; **City Sq**, Jln Tun Razak. Sell gold, pearls and precious gems.

Semua House, Lorong Tuanku Abdul Rahman (at northern end of Jln Masjid India) also sells gems and stones.
Ampang Shopping Complex, Jln Ampang; **Petaling St**; **Lot 10**, Jln Bukit Bintang; **KL Plaza**, Jln Bukit Bintang. Sell semi-precious gems, jade and porcelain

Handicrafts and home decor

Many of the handicrafts are imported from Indonesia. The areas to look for Chinese arts and handicrafts are along Jln Tuanku Abdul Rahman and in Bangsar Town Centre. Jln Masjid India, running parallel with Jln Tuanku Abdul Rahman, is an Aladdin's Cave of all things Indian, from saris to sandlewood oil, from bangles to brassware incense burners.
Aked Ibu Kota, Jln Tuanku Abdul Rahman. Shopping centre with wide variety of goods including local handicrafts.
Amazing Grace, G-3P Yow Chuan Plaza, Jln Tun Razak.
Andida Handicraft Centre, 10 Jln Melayu.
Borneo Crafts, 1st Flr, Central Market, mostly wooden pieces, good selection of puppets and boxes.
Central Market, Jln Hang Kasturi, the old wetmarket is now full of handicrafts stalls, not always the cheapest but a wide selection.
Golden Triangle, 1st Flr, Central Market. Sells a cornucopia of wooden figures.
Karyaneka Handicraft Village, Kompleks Budaya Kraf, Jln Conlay. Government-run, exhibiting and selling Malaysian handicrafts. Some batik demonstrating goes on on the ground floor.
Lavanya Arts, 116A Jln Berhala Brickfields, run by the Temple of Fine Arts of Annalakshmi vegetarian restaurant fame, which aims to preserve Malaysia's Indian heritage. The shop sells Indian crafts: jewellery, bronzes, wood carvings, furniture, paintings and textiles.
Lum Trading, 123 Jln SS2/24 SEA Park, Petaling Jaya, for baskets and bambooware.
Oriental Style, 1st Flr, Central Market, selection of upmarket baskets, pots, brassware. Quite pricey but worth a look.
Peter Hoe, 139 Jln Tun HS Lee or 2 Jln Hang Lekir. For a range of small items such as candlesticks, mirrors, table decorations. All his products are sourced in the region. He also sells jewellery and some locally printed clothing.

Pewter

Dai-Ichi Arts and Crafts, 122 Mezanine Flr, Parkroyal Hotel, Jln Sultan Ismail/Jln Imbi; **KL Arts & Crafts**, 18 Ground Floor, Central Market, Jln Hang Kasturi; **Royal Selangor Pewter Showrooms**, 231 Jln Tuanku Abdul Rahman, T2986244.

Markets and shopping streets

For apparel, shoes, bags and textiles try Jln Sultan and Jln Tun HS Lee, close to Klang bus station. In Petaling St (Chinatown) you can barter for Chinese lanterns, paintings, incense holders, etc.
Central Market, next to Jln Hang Kasturi, is a purpose-built area with 2 floors of boutiques and stalls selling just about every conceivable craft – pewter, jewellery, jade, wood and ceramics for a start. Stalls of note include one that sells all kinds of moulds and cutters for baking, a wonderful spice stall, another one for nuts and a third for dried fruits.
Jalan Melayu is another interesting area for browsing – Indian shops filled with silk saris and brass pots and Malay shops specializing in Islamic paraphernalia such as songkok (velvet Malay hats) and prayer rugs as well as herbal medicines and oils.
Jalan Tuanku Abdul Rahman (Batu Rd) was KL's best shopping street for decades and is transformed into a pedestrian mall and night market every Sat between 1700 and 2200.
Kampong Baru Sunday Market (Pasar Minggu), off Jln Raja Muda Musa (a large Malay enclave at the north end of KL), is an open-air market which comes alive on Sat nights. Malays know it as the Sunday market as their Sunday starts at dusk on Saturday (so don't go on the wrong night), when a variety of stalls selling batik sarongs, bamboo birdcages and traditional handicrafts compete with dozens of food stalls. However, the Pasar Minggu has largely been superseded by Central Market as a place to buy handicrafts.
Leboh Ampang, off Jln Gereja, was the first area to be settled by Indian immigrants and today remains KL's 'Little India', selling

everything from samosas to silk saris.
Pasar Malam, Jln Petaling, Chinatown is a night market full of 'copy watches', pirate dvds and cheap clothes.
Pudu Market, bordered by Jln Yew, Jln Pasar and Jln Pudu, is a traditional wet market selling food and produce, mainly patronized by Chinese.

Shopping complexes

The majority of KL's shopping complexes are to be found in this area, listings are east to west.
Ampang Park, Jln Tun Razak, opposite City Sq, Ampang, is one of the oldest shopping complexes in town, noted for its jewellery boutiques.
Bukit Bintang Plaza, corner of Jln Bukit Bintang and Jln Sultan Ismail, one of KL's oldest shopping centres, houses the popular department store Metrojaya, Marks & Spencer and a labyrinth of other shops, which lead into Sungai Wang.
Jln Sultan Ismail/Bukit Bintang, Berjaya Time's Square, Jln Imbi, all the usuals, a hotel, a rollercoaster, and scheduled to have an IMAX cinema.
Kota Raya Shopping Complex, Jln Cheng Lock, close to the Pudu Raya bus station, has cut-price goods.
Kuala Lumpur Plaza, Jalan Bukit Bintang. Tower Records is here, also good for watches, bags, jewellery and shoes.
Imbi Plaza, corner of Jln Sultan Ismail and Jln Imbi, good for computer hardware and software.
Lot 10, Jln Sultan Ismail. Distinctive green and blue striped façade, Isetan Department Store, British India, Moschino, Knickerbox, plus an excellent food court.
Low Yat Plaza Shopping Centre, the most recent addition to the Bukit Bintang scene, it houses BB Chinatown and Computer City.
Mid-Valley Megamall, Federal Highway, Lingkaran Syed Putra (a suburb of KL) This is indeed 'mega'. It has a wide range of shops and a choice of restaurants. There is also a multiplex cinema here.
Pertama Shopping Complex, Jalan Abdul Tunku Abdul Rahman. In the Chow Kit area near the Bandaraya LRT station, one of the older complexes and a great place for the bargain hunter. It has a wide range of mid-budget products from souvenirs to fashion and a basement bazaar, as well as photographic and electronic goods. KL's original department store.
Sogo Pernas Department Store, Jln Tuanku Abdul Rahman, Ampang is a huge store on 10 floors.
Star Hill Plaza, next to JW Marriott Hotel, prestigious marble-clad shopping centre housing Tang's Department Store (of Singapore fame) and many designer boutiques.
Sungai Wang Plaza, Jln Sultan Ismail, one of the largest complexes in KL, houses over 500 shops and Parkson Grand Department Store, and a basement food court.
Suria KLCC, in the new KLCC complex, is without doubt the grooviest shopping centre in town, housing, among other things, designer fashions and jewellery shops.
The Mall, Jln Putra, right across from Putra World Trade Centre, is a quite trendy, large shopping mall, good for fashion, housing Yaohan Department Store, Starlight Express indoor theme park, lots of fast food outlets, Delifrance, Pizza Hut etc.
The Weld, on the corner of Jln Raja Chulan and Jln P Ramlee, a Golden Triangle: a large Times Bookstore, Reject Shop, art gallery and a selection of fashion/leather shops, food outlets, etc.
Subang Parade, Subang Jaya, houses Parkson Grand Department Store and Toys 'R' Us, an amusement park and fast-food outlets.
Yow Chuan Plaza, Jln Tun Razak, Ampang, has antiques, curios, souvenirs and designer goods, and is linked to City Sq next door which has a Metrojaya department store and Toys 'R' Us

Watches

Lot 10, Jln Bukit Bintang; **Sungai Wang Plaza**, Jln Sultan Ismail; **KL Plaza**, Jln Bukit Bintang. Jln Petaling is the best place to find a 'genuine copy' watch.

Activities and tours

Bowling

Federal Bowl, Federal Hotel, Jln Bukit Bintang, T3-2489166.
Leisure Mall Bowling, Cheras Leisure Mall, Jln Manis, 6 Taman Segar, T3-9323866.
Miramar Bowling Centre, Wisma Miramar, Jln Wisma Putra, T3-2421863.
Pekeliling Bowl, Yow Chuan Plaza, Jln Tun Razak, T3-2430953.

Golf

Kelab Golf Negara, Subang (near Subang International Airport), 2 18-hole courses, T3-7760388.
Plaza Putra Indoor Golf Centre. Underground complex in Dataran Merdeka, golfers can select from 7 prestigious international courses from a computerized menu, T3-4432541.
Royal Selangor Golf Club, Jln Kelab Golf, off Jln Tun Razak, T3-9848433exclusive championship course (including 2 18-hole courses and a 9-hole course), one of the oldest in the country, non-members can only play at weekdays.
Saujana Golf & Country Resort, Subang (near Subang International Airport), T3-7461466. 2 18-hole championship courses.
Sentul Golf Club, 84 Jln Strachan, Sentul, built in 1928, recently refurbished and a swimming pool added, T3-4435571.
Templer Park Country Club, 21 km north of KL, fully floodlit course for 24-hr golf, frequented by Japanese golf package tourists, developed and part-owned by Japanese company, the more environmentally minded have complained that the course has ruined the north end of Templer Park.

Health centres

Fitness International, Parkroyal Hotel, Jln Sultan Ismail.
Good Friend Health Centre, 33 Jln Tun Sambathan 5.
Recreation Health Centre, 4th Flr, Furama Hotel, Komleks Selangor, Jln Sultan Ismail.

Spectator sports

Merdeka Stadium and the Stadium on Jln Stadium, off Jln Maharajalela. Inter-state Malaysia Cup football matches are played here. The (rather more successful) Selangor team play at the Shah Alam Stadium
Padang. Cricket, rugby and hockey are played here in the centre of KL, most weekends.

Swimming

Bangsar Sports Complex, Jln Terasek Tiga, Bangsar Baru, T3-2546065, Mon-Sat 0800-1300, closed Sun.
KLCC park Has a pleasant swimming pool, which can be used free of charge.

Watersports

Sunway Lagoon and Adventure Park, T3-56311452. Theme park, with plenty of entertainment both in and out of the water, all-park admission RM39 (RM26 for children), open 1100-1800 Mon, Wed, Thu, Fri, 1000-1800 Sat, Sun and public holidays. Take the Putra LRT to Kelana Jaya and catch the shuttle service from there. Alternatively, buses to most parts of Petaling Jaya can be boarded at the Bangkok Bank stop and Klang bus terminal. **The Mines**, Sungai Besi Tin Mine, T9487402 (admission: weekdays adult RM8, child RM4; weekends adult RM12, child RM6), 20 mins' drive from KL, before the toll booths on highway to Seremban, exit on left (at Taman Sri Petaling), turn right at T-junction, over the railway line and past Shell and Esso stations towards Serdang and Kajang, signposted to the left, located in what was the biggest tin mine in the world, in clean, turquoise water and beneath dramatic rocky cliffs. The 200-acre recreational park has a snow house where the temperature is regulated to create all-year-round snow. Other amusements are a roller coaster, water screen, laser show and a musical fountain.

Tour operators

There are plenty of travel agents in the Angkasaraya Building on the corner of Jln

Ampang and Jln Ramlee.
Excellence Holidays, 210 Jln Imbi, T3-2454988, F3-2424366, tour@excellenceho.my
Reliance Travel, 3rd Floor, Sungei Wang Plaza (T3-2486022), for student/cheap outbound tickets.
STA, 5th Flr, Magnum Plaza, Jln Pudu, T3-2489800.
Thomas Cook, Level 18, Menara Lion, Jln Ampang (near Nikko Hotel), T3-2649252.

Tours

Asia Tenggara Aviation Services, T3-77830097, F3-77830095. Helicopter tours of the city are available. 20-min tours in three-seater Piper 28 planes. Each passenger costs RM240; must have three. Note that aerial photography is not allowed.
Asian Spooks Experience, T3-20925626 ext. 137, www.ez2pr.com/ One of the weirdest tours on offer. It is a night city tour, popular with westerners, but not with Asian visitors. For their money, would-be thrill seekers get a steamboat dinner, and a creepy tour of an Indian temple, Chinese cemetery, a drive past Pudu prison, and a getting-to-know the Asian vampire session. At RM168 per person (minimum of 2 people) it's a little pricey.
Utan Bara Adventure Team (UBAT), Suite 284014003, The Heritage, Jln Pahang, T3-40225124, F3-40226125, http://www.ubat.com.my/ For a jungle tour with a difference. The people who run this outfit are ex-security personnel and the names of their tours speak for themselves: 'Practical jungle survival course', 'cross country jungle raid' and a daily tour to an elephant orphanage where you get to scrub clean and feed baby elephants.

Transport

Air

Getting to town from the airport

The **KLIA Ekspres** train (T3-22678000, www.KLIAekspres.com) runs between 0500 and 2400 between the airport and **KL Sentral** train station in the city centre, 30 mins, every 20 mins, 35RM one way.

Alternatively you can take the **KLIA transit**, 35 mins, RM35. It stops at three intermediate stations and leaves between 0550 and 0100. If using the KLIA Ekspres you can check your luggage in at KL Sentral for outgoing flights.

The **KLIA Ekspres Coach Service** (T3-62033064) provides an efficient service from Sepang International Airport into the city centre to Hentian Duta (near the Tun Razak Hockey Stadium), 1 hr, every 30 mins from 0500 to 2230, RM25, with a RM1 shuttle bus service from Hentian Duta to major hotels.

Bargain hard for a **taxi** to the city. For a taxi from the city to KL Airport expect to pay around RM70-90 when you buy a coupon, 1 hr. Hotels can arrange a good fare in the RM60 range. Make sure the taxi fare includes the motorway toll for either direction.

Car-hire firms have desks at the airport terminal. Arrange hotel pick-up service in advance or at the office outside the terminal.

Long distance

KL's relatively new international airport at Sepang (T3-87762000) lies 72 km south of the city. **MAS** and **AirAsia** flights to other Malaysian destinations include connections with **Alor Star, Ipoh, Johor Bahru, Kota Bharu, Kota Kinabalu, Kuala Terengganu, Kuantan, Kuching, Labuan, Lahad Datu, Langkawi, Miri, Penang, Tawau**.

Airline offices

Aeroflot, Ground Flr, Wisma Tong Ah, 1 Jln Perak, T3-21610231.
Air India, Bangunan Ankasa Raya, 123 Jln Ampang, T3-21420166.
AirAsia, Sepang Airport, toll-free T1-300 889933.
American Airlines, Bangunan Angkasa Raya, 123 Jln Ampang, T3-21480644.
Bangladesh Biman, Bang Angkasaraya, T3-21483765.
British Airways, T1800881260.
Cathay Pacific, Level 22, Menara IMC, 8 Jln Sultan Ismail, T3-20783355.
China Airlines, 22 Jln Imbi, T3-21427344.
Czechoslavak Airlines, 12th Flr, Plaza Atrium, 10 Lorong P Ramlee, T3-2380176.
Delta Airlines, UBN Tower, Jln P Ramlee, T3-2324700.

Garuda, Suite 3.01, Level 3, Menara Lion, Jln Ampang, T3-21622811. Opposite Ampang Park Shopping Mall.
Japan Airlines, Menara Citibank, T3-21611722.
KLM, Parkroyal Hotel, T3-27119811.
Korean Air, 17th Flr, MUI Plaza, Jln P Ramlee, T3-21428311.
Lufthansa, 3rd Flr, Pernas International Bldg, Jln Sultan Ismail, T3-21614666.
MAS MAS Bldg, Jln Sultan Ismail, T3-21610555 (1300883000 reservations).
Northwest Airlines, UBN Tower, Jln P Ramlee, T3-21433542.
Philippine Airlines, 104-107 Wisma Stephens, Jln Raja Chulan, T3-21429040.
PIA, Ground Floor, Angkasa Raya Bldg, 123 Jln Ampang, T3-21425444.
Qantas, T1800881260.
Royal Brunei, 2nd Flr, UBN Tower, 10 Jln P Ramlee, T3-20706628 (T3-20707166 reservations).
Royal Jordanian, 8th Flr, Mui Plaza, Jln P Ramlee, T3-21487500.
Saudi, Megan Avenue, 12 Jln Yap Kwan Seng, T3-21660088.
Scandinavian Airlines, Bangunan Angkasa Raya, 123 Jln Ampang, T3-21426044.
Singapore Airlines, Wisma SIA, 2 Jln Sang Wangi, T3-26923122.
Sri Lankan Airlines, MUI Plaza, T3-20723633.
Thai International, Kuwasa Bldg, 5 Jln Raja Laut, T3-26937100.
Turkish Airlines, Wisma Goldhill, T3-20312900.
United Airlines, Bangunan MAS, Jln Sultan Ismail, T3-21611433.
Virgin Atlantic, 77 Jln Bukit Bintang (2nd Flr), T3-21430322/3.

Bus

Local

Intrakota has taken over most routes now but it's not an easy system to grasp. An Intrakota bus map should be available free from the City Hall. Fares are upwards from 70c.

Long distance

KL's main bus terminal is Puduraya (T3-20700145) on Jln Pudu. Buses leave here for destinations across **the Peninsula** as well as to **Singapore** and **Thailand**. Most large bus companies have their offices inside the terminal, above the departure hall. Many hotels and guesthouses will arrange tickets, which saves a journey to Puduraya. There are bus offices opposite the terminal along Jln Pudu and, due to overcrowding within, quite a few buses drop off and pick up along this road. Avoid buying tickets from touts. Inside there is an information desk, post office, tourist police booth, left luggage office (Mon-Sun 0800-2200) and foodstalls. Puduraya serves most travellers needs – the exception being those wishing to visit Taman Negara National Park.

The **Pekeliling Station**, T3-40449022, is in the north of the city, off Jln Tun Razak. Buses to towns in **Pahang State**, including **Jerantut** (for **Taman Negara**) and **Kuala Lipis**, leave from here, not from Puduraya. Other destinations include **Kuantan** and the **Genting Highlands**.

The **Putra Station**, T3-40438984, facing the Putra World Trade Centre, serves the east coast and connections with places in **Kelantan, Terengganu** and **Pahang**, including **Kuantan, Kuala Terengganu** and **Kota Bharu**.

Klang Station in Chinatown, on Jln Hang Kasturi, serves Port Klang and Shah Alam suburb.

Seremban *p91, map p92*

Newish, brightly coloured station on Jln Sungai Ujong. Connections with **JB, Melaka, KL, Kota Bharu** and **Port Dixon.**

Port Dickson *p94*

The station is on Jln Pantai, just outside the main centre, but buses will normally stop on request anywhere along the beach. Regular connections with **KL** and **Melaka**.

Car hire

Apex Rent-A-Car, T3-21421926; **Avis**, T3-92222558; **Hertz**, T3-21486433; **Mayflower**, T3-22791188; **Orix**, T3-21423009; **Sintat**, T3-21452641.

Taxi

Local

KL is one of the cheaper cities in Southeast Asia for taxis and there are stands all over town, but you can hail a taxi pretty much anywhere you like. Most are a/c and metered, but it is a challenge sometimes to get the driver to use the meter: RM2 for the first 1 km and RM0.10 for every 200 m thereafter. Extra charges apply between 2400 and 0600 (50% surcharge), for each extra passenger in excess of 2, as well as RM1 for luggage in the boot. Waiting charges are RM2 for the first 2 mins, RM0.10 for every subsequent 45 secs. During rush hours, shift change (around 1500) or if it's raining, it can be very difficult to persuade taxis to travel to the centre of town; negotiate a price (locals claim that waving a RM10 bill helps) or jump in and feign ignorance.

For 24-hr taxi service try the following: **Comfort**, T3-80242727; **Teletaxi**, T3-92211011; **KL Taxi**, T3-92214241. **Supercab**, T3-78757333; A surcharge of RM1 is made for a phone booking.

Long distance

These leave from Jln Pudu, outside the Puduraya bus station. Share taxis run to most large towns on the Peninsula; fares are about double those of the equivalent bus journeys. There are no scheduled departures, it is a case of turning up and seeing which taxis have space and where they are going.

Seremban *p91, map p92*

Port Dickson, KL, Melaka, T6-7610764.

Port Dickson *p94*

T2-7610764, shared taxis to Melaka, KL and Seremban.

Trains

Local

Within the city there are five rail systems spanning the city: two **LRT** lines, the Putra (pink) and Star (yellow and light green), two **KTM Komuter** lines (blue and red), and the new **monorail** (light blue). Trains leave every 5-15 mins, and tickets cost upwards of RM1.20. Going from one line to the other often means coming out of the station and crossing a road! All lines except the Star LRT go through KL Sentral. The trains are a great way to see the city as they mostly run on elevated rails, some 10 m above street level.

Long distance

The **Sentral Railway Station**, Jln Stesen, T3-27302000, www.klsentral.com.my There is a left-luggage office and information desk. The desk is helpful and can advise on schedules. KL is on the main line from **Singapore** to the south and **Butterworth** (Penang) to the north; some of these trains go on through to Bangkok. To get on the east coastline you have to go to **Gemas**, the junction south of KL or to **Kuala Lipis** or **Mentakab**, 150 km to the west of KL. Regular connections with **Alor Star, Butterworth, Taiping, Ipoh, Tapah Rd (for Cameron Highlands), Tampin, Gemas, Johor Bahru** and **Singapore**. Tourists, on production of their passport, can buy a KTM rail pass, which offers unlimited rail travel, although it is not valid on the Thai system. There are plenty of fast food restaurants inside the station. Visit www.ktmb.com.my/ for more information.

Seremban *p91, map p92*

The blue KTM Komuter line ends in Seremban. The journey takes less than an hour.

Directory

Banks

Money changers are in all the big shopping centres and along the main shopping streets and they generally give better rates than banks. Most branches of the leading Malaysian and foreign banks have foreign exchange desks, although some (for example Bank Bumiputra) impose limits on charge card cash advances.There are bank ATMs everywhere that will provide Ringgit for cards with Cirrus, Visa, MasterCard, Maestro or Plus. **American Express**, 18th Flr, The Weld (near KL Tower), Jln Raja Chulan, T3-20500000.

Seremban *p91, map p92*

Bumiputra, Wisma Dewan Permagaa Melayu; **Maybank**, 10-11 Jln Dato Abdul Rahman; **OCBC**, 63-65 Jln Dato Bandar Tunggal; **Public Bank**, 46 Jln Dato Lee Fong Yee; **Standard & Chartered**, 128 Jln Dato Bandar Tunggal; **UMBC**, 39 Jln Tuanku Munawir.

Port Dickson *p94*
Bumiputra, 745 Jln Bharu; **Public**, 866 Jln Pantai; **Standard Chartered**, 61 Jln Bharu.

Embassies and consulates

Australia, 6 Jln Yap Kwan Seng, T3-21465555.
Austria, 7th Flr, MUI Plaza, Jln P Ramlee, T3-21484277.
Belgium, 8A jln Ampang, T3-20322001.
Canada, 7th Flr, Plaza MBS, 172 Jln Ampang, T3-21612155.
Denmark, 22nd Flr, Bangunan Angkasa Raya, 123 Jln Ampang, T3-20322001.
France, 192 Jln Ampang, T3-21620671.
Germany, 3 Jln U Thant, T3-21480073.
Italy, 99 Jln U Thant, T3-42565122.
Japan, 11 Persiaran Stonor, off Jln Tun Razak, T3-21427044.
Japan, 11 Persiaran Stonor, off Jln Tun Razak, T3-21427044.
Netherlands, 4 Jln Mesra (off Jln Damai), T3-21610148.
New Zealand, 191 Jln Ampang, T3-20782533.
Norway, 11th Flr, Bangunan Angkasa Raya, Jln Ampang, T3-21485317.
Singapore, 209 Jln Tun Razak, T3-21616277.
Spain, 200 Jln Ampang, T3-21484655.
Sweden, 6th Flr, Angkasa Raya Bldg, 123 Jln Ampang, T3-21485433.
Switzerland, 16 Persiaran Madge, T3-21480622.
UK, 185 Jln Ampang, T3-21482122.
USA, 376 Jln Tun Razak, T3-21685000.

Internet

There are internet cafes everywhere, many of them are open 24 hours. There are dozens along Jln Bukit Bintang and a handful around Chinatown. The Chinatown internet venues are often packed with gaming schoolboys which can make it very noisy. Many backpacker places will offer internet. Expect to pay upward of 3RM per hour. For a classier surf, buy a coffee at Hotel Equatorial's Etoile Bistro, and you get half an hour's free broadband access.

Language schools

Available at many places (see Yellow Pages), but not cheap.
Time Spoken Language Centre, 2nd Flr, 226-227 Campbell Complex, T3-26921595. Recommended but not especially, based on 'travelling bahasa', flexible schedules.

Medical facilities

Casualty wards are open 24 hrs
Assunta Hospital, Petaling Jaya, T3-77823433. **Damai Service Hospital**, 115-119 Jln Ipoh, T3-40434900. **Pudu Specialist Centre**, Jln Baba, T3-21429146. **Tung Shin Hospital**, 102 Jln Pudu, T3-20721655.

Port Dickson *p94*
Hospital, on the waterfront by the bus station, Jln Pantai.

Places of worship

Churches: English-language Sunday services at the following churches at the times stated. **Baptist Church**, 70 Cangkat Bukit Bintang, 0830, 0945. **St Andrews International Church**, 31 Jln Raja Chulan, 0900, 1100. **St John's Cathedral** (Roman Catholic), 5 Jln Bukit Nanas, 0800, 1030, 1800. **St Mary's (Anglican) Church**, Jln Raja, 0700, 0800, 0930 (family Eucharist), 1800. **Wesley Methodist Church**, 2 Jln Wesley, 0815, 1030, 1800.

Post

General Post Office Dayabumi Complex, Jln Sultan Hishamuddin (Poste Restante).

Telephone

Overseas telephone service: **Kedai Telekom** at the airport. **Kaunter Telegraf STM**, Wisma Jothi, Jln Gereja; **Syarikat Telekom Malaysia**, Bukit Mahkamah. Assisted International Calls: T108. Directory Enquiries: T103. Trunk Calls Assistance: T101.

Useful information

Fire T994. **Immigration** Jln Pantai Bharu, T3-79578155. **KL Tourist Police** T3-21496593. **Police/ambulance** T999. **Weather Report** T1052. **Wildlife and National Parks Department** Km 10, Jln Cheras, T3-90752872, F3-90752873.

Northern Peninsula

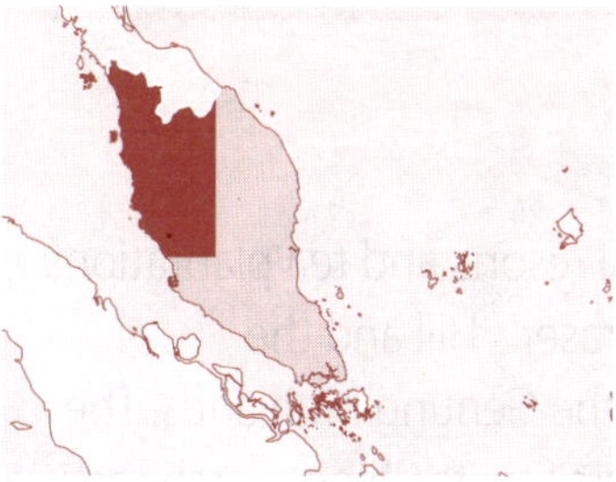

Footprint features

Introduction

North of KL are the temperate hill resorts and tea plantations of the Cameron Highlands and Fraser's Hill and the entertainment gambling hub of the Genting highlands. The former tin-rush town of Ipoh offers Straits Chinese architecture and some superb food. It is off the beaten for many tourists, so makes a welcome break from the travel network.

Offshore there is the 25 km-long island of Penang with its fine capital Georgetown packed with Chinese shophouses, temples and clan houses. On the north shore is an array of beachside hotels. Less developed than Penang are the islands of Pulau Pangkor to the south and Pulau Langkawi to the north, the latter closer to Thailand than to mainland Malaysia. Langkawi has world-class resorts, fine beaches and jungle adventures.

★ Don't miss...

1. **Cameron Highlands** Trek through lush jungle or potter about flower gardens searching for the elusive black rose, page 124.
2. **Smokehouse Hotel** Imagine you are in the English countryside by taking high tea in the garden of this Tudor-style lodge in Tanah Rata, page 131.
3. **Cheong Fatt Tze** Stay the night in this indigo mansion, the beautifully restored home of a 19th century Chinese businessman in Penang, page 164.
4. **Langkawi cable car** Take a ride up Gunung Mat Chinchang for a bird's eye view of the island and a slice of south Thailand, page 190.
5. **Sun worship** Pantai Rhu has the whitest sands of all Langkawi's beaches, page 191.
6. **Spas** Pamper yourself with a Swedish, Indonesian, Thai, hot stone, aromatherapy in Langkawi; for top of range try *The Datai*, page 199.

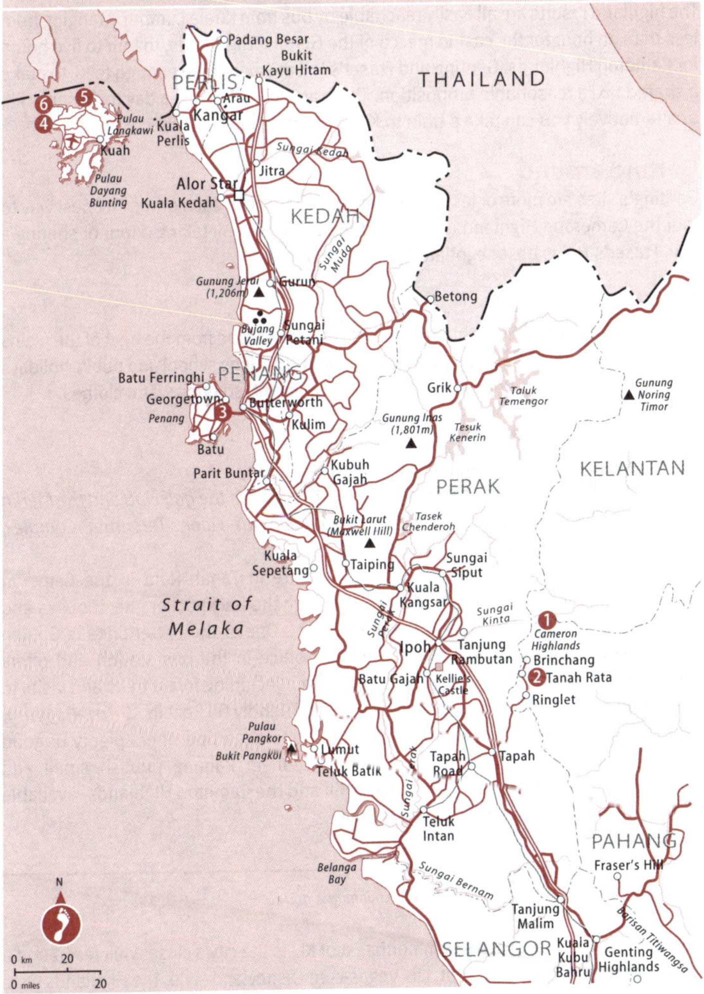

Highlands and Hill Stations

On the road north, Peninsular Malaysia's mountainous jungled backbone lies to the east. It is called the Barisan Titiwangsa or Main Range. It remains largely unsettled apart from the Genting Highlands and the old British hill stations of Fraser's Hill, the Cameron Highlands and Maxwell Hill and some scattered Orang Asli aboriginal villages. During the Malayan Emergency in the late 1940s and early 1950s, the Communist guerrillas operated from jungle camps in the mountains and later used the network of aboriginal trails to infiltrate the peninsula from their bases in southern Thailand. ▸▸ *For Sleeping, Eating and other listings, see pages 130-137.*

Ins and outs

Getting there

The highland resorts are all easily reachable by bus from Kuala Lumpur – ranging from less than an hour for the casino mecca of the Genting Highlands, to four to five hours for Cameron Highlands. Genting and Fraser's Hill are also close enough to KL to make a shared taxi a reasonable proposition. There are several buses a day to Fraser's Hill, or alternatively you can take a train to Kubu Bharu, and then a taxi or bus.

Getting around

Genting's sites are more or less within walking distance of each other. The best way to tour the Cameroon Highlands flower and tea gardens is by taking a tour or sharing a taxi. Fraser's Hill is best negotiated on foot or by taxi.

Best time to visit

Due to their altitiude, the highland resorts are a nice escape from the heat of the plains all year round. However, it might be worth avoiding is during school and public holidays to escape the crowds. Remember, it gets chilly at night, so bring warm clothes.

Tourist information

For more information on Genting: www.genting.com.my

Fraser's Hill Development Corporation Office ⓘ *between the golf club and the Merlin Hotel, maps and general information available, 9th Floor, Terentum Complex, T9-5171623, F9-5171626.*

There is no official tourist information centre in Tanah Rata in the Cameron Highlands and information is best picked up from the backpacker guesthouses and the tour agencies dotted around the main street. One of the better ones is **Golden Highlands Adventure Holidays** which has an office in the bus station and offers inexpensive half-day and full-day tours of the area including forest treks and visits to tea plantations, strawberry, rose and bee farms. Friendly Gil Rozells ⓘ *T0136135109, zeeess1@yahoo.com* mans the office from 1000 to 1930 and offers plenty of good advice on where to stay and what to do. Tourism Pahang publish small and moderately useful guides to both Fraser's Hill and the Cameron Highlands, available free. Also see www.cameronhighlands.com.

Genting Highlands→ *Colour map 2, grid A2*

The Genting Highlands, just 51 km northeast of KL, is the city's closest hill resort and a popular source of entertainment, Las Vegas-cum-Disneyland style. The Highlands were first developed as a resort in the 1960s by a prominent Malaysian businessman, Tan Sri Lim Goh Tong. At the time, investing in construction at an altitude of 2,000 m above sea level was considered a hare-brained idea. Building the tortuous and impossibly steep road through the dense, jungle-covered hills took seven years alone. However, the idea took off, and the government conceded to allow Malaysia's only casino to operate here. The casino attracts an estimated 30,000 clients a day and provides the main source of revenue in the Highlands. The resort's main attraction is the **Casino de Genting**, which is one of the largest casinos in the world, with endless rows of slot machines, games tables and even a computerized racetrack where it is possible to bet on the Royal Ascot. The décor is glitzy; red plush and glittering chandeliers abound. Occasional grand sweeps are made: people still talk of an Indonesian who put a 4-ringgit keno token into a machine and came away with 1.5 million ringgit. Other attractions in the resort include an outdoor and indoor theme park, which is rated among the best in Malaysia and is constantly being expanded. There is a leisure zone to cater for the wet-weather days, particularly frequent in Highlands at the end of the year. It takes at least a day to get around this bonanza of entertainment and at least as long to work out how to get around. Weekends and public holidays are very busy; Chinese New Year and Hari Raya are two of the peak holiday times.

Fraser's Hill → *Colour map 2, grid A2 Altitude: 1,524m*

Fraser's Hill is named after Englishman Louis James Fraser, who ran a gambling den, traded in tin and opium and operated a mule train in these hills at the end of the 19th century. He went on to manage a transport service between Kuala Kubu and Raub. Before Mr Fraser lent his name to it, the seven hills were known as Ulu Tras. The development of the hill station began in the early 1920s. In 1925, British High Commissioner Sir George Maxwell wrote that Fraser's Hill "would always be the most exquisite and most dainty hill station in Malaya", and although he foresaw that development would come to this hitherto remote slice of Pahang he cannot have anticipated the changes that would transform the station over the next three-quarters of a century.

It was along the road from Kuala Bubu Bharu that the British High Commissioner, Sir Henry Gurney, was ambushed and killed by Communist insurgents during the Malayan Emergency in 1951 (see page 488). A few years earlier British soldiers were involved in the massacre of suspected Communist sympathizers near Kuala Kubu. They shot dead a number of rubber tappers from a local village. There are a number of Orang Asli villages along rivers and tracks leading from the twisting road up the hill.

Fraser's Hill is close enough to KL to be a favoured weekend resort. Because it was easily accessible by train from Kuala Kubu Road, it was a popular weekend retreat long before the Cameron Highlands. Most of colonial Malaya's big companies, such as Sime Darby, Guthries' and Harrisons and Crosfield, built holiday bungalows among the hills. More and more luxury bungalows are now being built here to cater for wealthy Malaysians, but it is still more tranquil and attractive than Genting. Although it is not as varied as the Cameron Highlands by way of attractions, there is one trail (a three-hour walk), which starts just to the south of the tennis courts and ends at the *Corona Nursery Youth Hostel*, offering good opportunities for birdwatchers (260 species of migratory and local birds have been identified here) and wild flower enthusiasts, a golf course, tennis courts and gardens. Swimming at **Jeriau waterfalls**, 4km from Fraser's Hill town centre, is limited as the concrete pool has all but silted up so that the water is only knee deep, but standing under the powerful waterfall is very refreshing.

The Orang Asli tribes procured the poison from the ipoh tree for their blowpipe darts from its fabled lethal sap. It was known as the deadliest poison in the world.

Cameron Highlands → *Colour map 1, grid C3*

The biggest and best known of Malaysia's hill stations lies on the northwest corner of Pahang, bounded by Perak to the west, and Kelantan to the north. On the jungle-clad 1,500m-high plateau the weather is reassuringly British – unpredictable, often wet and decidedly cool – but when the sun blazes out of an azure-blue sky, the Camerons are hard to beat.

Cameron Highlands

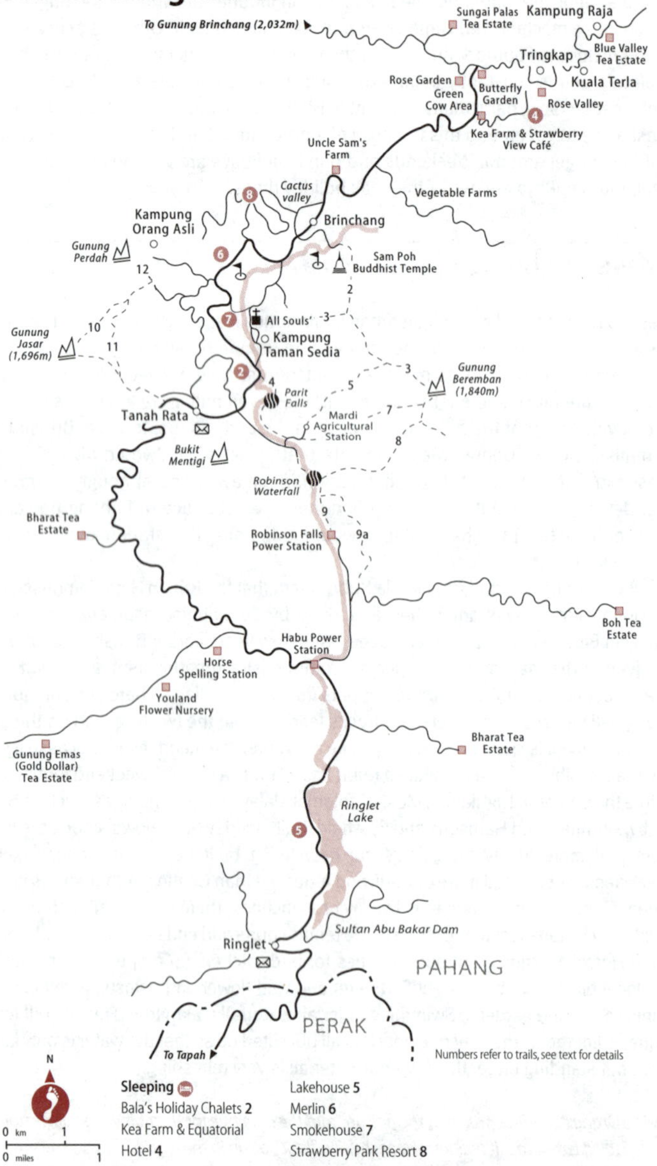

Sleeping
Bala's Holiday Chalets **2**
Kea Farm & Equatorial Hotel **4**
Lakehouse **5**
Merlin **6**
Smokehouse **7**
Strawberry Park Resort **8**

Most of the tourist attractions in the Cameron Highlands are on and around the plateau but there are a handful of sights on the road from Tapah. These are listed in order from the bottom of the mountain up. There are three main townships in the Highlands: **Ringlet**, **Tanah Rata** (literally 'flat land') and **Brinchang**. The latter two are in the plateau area, either side of the golf course.

There are a number of worthwhile forest walks/treks in the Camerons. Good walking boots and a water bottle should be taken (see box, page 126). Because of the danger of attacks by illegal immigrants, it is advisable for women travelling alone only to trek with a guide or with other travellers.

Unfortunately, the Cameron Highlands is no longer a peaceful bolt-hole in the sky. Frenetic development is turning the area, in critics' eyes, into a building site where forest is fast making way for golf courses and luxury tourist developments. A new highway now links Ipoh to the Cameron Highlands and runs to Gua Musang for connections to the east coast promising to bring a wave of development to the area.

Ins and outs

Getting there There are buses from KL's Puduraya terminal and Georgetown (Penang) direct to the Cameron highlands and various tour buses make the journey too. There is a direct taxi service from Georgetown. Alternatively catch a bus to Tapah, the main way station for the Camerons. There are numerous connections from KL to Tapah, as well from Ipoh, Butterworth, Kuantan, Melaka and Singapore. From Tapah there are local buses every two hours to the Highlands. Alternatively, take a train to Tapah Road, Tapah's train station (outside town to the west), a bus or taxi into Tapah town, and a bus from there to the Camerons. There are twice daily rail connections with Tapah Road from KL, Ipoh and Butterworth.

Getting around Buses from Tapah all pass through Tanah Rata and Brinchang and it is usually possible to climb aboard to travel between these centres. There are also taxis available for hire by the hour or for specific journeys.

Best time to visit Daytime temperatures in the Cameron Highlands average around 23°C, and in the evening, when it drops to 10°C and the hills are enveloped in swirling cloud, known as 'the white witch', pine log fires are lit in the hilltop holiday bungalows. The weather has become more unpredictable in the last 50 years – torrential downpours and landslides are no longer confined to the monsoon months of November and December. But the mountain air is still bracing enough to entice thousands of holiday makers to the Camerons from the steamy plains. Today coach-loads of Singaporeans wind their way up the mountain roads and, together with well-heeled KL businessfolk, fork out extortionate sums for weekends in timeshare apartments and endless rounds of golf.

History

In the colonial era this mountain resort was a haven for homesick, overheated planters and administrators. Its temperate climate induced an eccentric collection of them to settle and retire in their Surrey-style mansions where they could prune their roses, tend their strawberries, sip G&Ts on the lawn, stroll down to the golf course or nip over to Mr Foster's mock-Tudor *Smokehouse* for a Devonshire cream tea. The British Army also had a large presence in Tanah Rata until 1971 – their imposing former military hospital (now reverted to a Roman Catholic convent) still stands on the hill overlooking the main street. To the left of the road leading into Tanah Rata from Ringlet are a few remaining Nissen huts from the original British army camp.

While most of the old-timers – the likes of Stanley Foster, Captain Bloxham (who nursed racehorses at his bougainvillaea-fringed 'spelling station' at Ringlet) and Miss Gwenny Griffith-Jones (founder of Singapore's Tanglin School) – have now

Jungle walks: Cameron Highlands

The Cameron Highlands is great walking country, although many of the longer trails were closed in the 1970s when the army found secret food dumps for the Communist Party of Malaya (CPM), which used the Main Range as its insurgency route from its bases near Betong in South Thailand. Despite the CPM calling a halt to hostilities in 1990, the trails have not reopened. There are, however, a handful of not-so-strenuous mountains to climb and a number of jungle walks. Cameronian trails are a great place for people unfamiliar with jungle walks. They are also very beautiful.

Basic sketch maps of trails, with numbered routes, are available at the Tourist Information kiosk in Tanah Rata and from most hotels.

Walkers are advised to take plenty of water with them as well as a whistle, a lighter and something warm. It is very easy to lose your way in jungle – the district officer has had to call out Orang Asli trackers on many occasions over the years to hunt down disoriented hikers. Always make sure someone knows roughly where you are going and approximately what time you are expecting to get back.

There is a centuries-old Orang Asli trail leading from Tanjung Rambutan, near Ipoh, up the Kinta River into the Main Range. One branch of this trail goes north to the summit of Gunung Korbu (2,183 m), 16 km away. When William Cameron and his warrior companion Kulop Riau left on their elephant-back expedition into the mountains, they followed the Kinta River to its source and, from the summit of nearby Gunung Calli, saw Blue Valley 'plateau'. Cameron's view of the plateau that would later bear his name was obscured by two big mountains, Irau (the one shaped like a roller coaster) and Brinchang.

At 2,032 m, Gunung Brinchang is the Highlands' highest peak and the highest point in Malaysia accessible by road. The area around the communications centre on the summit affords a great panorama of the plateau, although it spends most of its life shrouded in cloud. The road up the mountain veers left in the middle of Boh's Sungei Palas tea estate past Km 73. From the top of Brinchang it is possible to see straight down into the Kinta valley, on the other side. Ipoh is only 15 km away, as the hornbill flies.

Gunung Beremban (1,840 m) makes a pleasant hike, although its trails are well worn. It can be reached from Tanah Rata (trail No 7 goes up

gone to rest, they bequeathed an ambience, which the Cameron Highlands has yet to shake off. Miss 'Griff' had been one of the original pioneers, trudging up through the jungle from Tapah on an oxcart, when they first cut the road, with its hairpin bends, in the 1930s.

Fifty years elapsed between the discovery of the highland plateau and the arrival of the first settlers. William Cameron, a government surveyor, first claimed to have stumbled across "a fine plateau, shut in by lofty mountains" while on a mapping expedition in 1885. In a letter in which he gave an account of this trip, he wrote: "[I saw] a sort of vortex in the mountains, while for a wide area we have gentle slopes and plateau land". The irony was that Cameron's name was bestowed on a place he never set eyes on. What he probably came across was the smaller plateau area farthest from Tanah Rata, known as Blue Valley. The highland plateau itself was discovered years later by a Malay warrior named Kulop Riau, who accompanied Cameron on his mapping expeditions. Cameron's report engendered much excitement. Sir Hugh Low, who, 34 years earlier, had made the first attempt at Sabah's Gunung Kinabalu, was by through the experimental tea in the MARDI station past the padang off Jalan Persiaran Dayang Endah), Brinchang (trail No 2 leads up from behind the Sam Poh Buddhist temple) – a more arduous route, or the golf course (follow trail No 3 past the Arcadia bungalow where the road stops) – this is the easiest. Allow about 4 hours to get up and down. There is a good view down Tanah Rata's main street from the top. It is also possible to climb Gunung Beremban from Robinson Falls (trail No 8 leads off trail No 9). The trail heading for the latter is from the very bottom of the road leading past MARDI from Tanah Rata.

Gunung Jasar (1,696 m), between the golf course and Tanah Rata, is a pleasant – but gentler – walk of about 3 hours (trail No 10). The trail goes from halfway along the old back road to Tanah Rata near the meteorological station (the road – Jalan Titiwangsa – leaves Tanah Rata from behind a hotel south of town and emerges at the golf course, on the corner next to the Golf Course Hotel). The Jasar trail also forks off to Bukit Perdah (trail No 12, which branches off the Jasar trail) 2 to 3 hours to the top and back. The path down from the summit comes out on a road leading back into the top end of Tanah Rata.

The trails to Robinson Falls (trail No 9, an hour's walk) and Parit Falls (trail No 4, 30 minutes' walk) are more frequently trampled. The trail branches off to No 9a, which leads down to the Boh tea estate road near Ringlet Lake. The walk to the Boh tea estate is a long one, but it is possible to hitch along the road or catch a bus with great views when you get there. There are tours every hour. The estate is closed on Monday, and closes at 1700 on other days; the last bus leaves the factory at 1730. The short trail to Parit Falls starts behind the Garden Hotel and mosque on the far side of Tanah Rata's padang and ends up below the Slim army camp. Parit Falls is a small waterfall in between the two, with what was once a beautiful jungle pool before it became cluttered with daytrippers and their rubbish.

There are hundreds of other trails through the Camerons, traversing ridges and leading up almost every hill and mountain. Most are Orang Asli paths, some date from the Japanese occupation in the Second World War (these are marked by barbed wire) and some aren't really trails at all – beware!

then the Resident of Perak. He wanted to develop the newly reported Highland area as "a sanatorium, health resort and open farmland". Twenty years elapsed before the first pioneers made their way up to the so-called 'Cameron's Land'.

Hot on the heels of the elderly 'gin and Jaguar' settlers (most of them insisted on solid British cars for the mountain roads) came the tea planters and vegetable farmers. The cool mountain climate was perfect for both. The forested hillsides were shaved to make way for more tea bushes and cabbages and the deforestation appears to have affected the climate. The local meteorological station reports that the average temperature has risen 2°C in the past 50 years.

The Camerons' most talked-about visitor arrived in March 1967 for a quiet sojourn in Moonlight bungalow, perched on a hilltop above the golf course. The disappearance of the US-born Thai silk emperor, art collector and military intelligence agent Jim Thompson from a lonely Cameronian backroad, propelled the hill resort into the headlines. Teams of Orang Asli trackers combed the jungle in vain, while detectives, journalists and film makers toyed with credible explanations: he had been given a new identity by the CIA; he had been kidnapped and smuggled from the Highlands in the boot of a Thai taxi; he had been eaten by a tiger. The fate of Thompson, the Lord Lucan of Southeast Asia, remains a mystery to this day.

Southern Cameron Highlands

Tapah is a centre for making the large bamboo baskets that are used to collect the tea grown in the Highlands. The town itself is very small, a single street of dilapidated shophouses with a couple of basic hotels and a few eating places. The bus station in Tapah is on Jalan Raja, just off the main road. There are connections every two hours with Tanah Rata, as well as occasional departures for KL and Penang. Most long-distance bus departures from Tapah (including for KL, Melaka, Penang, Kuantan, and Ipoh as well as connections with Hat Yai in southern Thailand) are from the Caspian Restaurant on the main highway. The Tapah Road Railway Station is about 10 km from the town. **Kuala Woh**, a jungle park with a swimming pool, fishing and natural hot pools, is only 13 km from Tapah, on the road to the Camerons and has a basic camping area. **Lata Iskandar Waterfall**, 22½ km from Tapah, is a beautiful jungle waterfall, right by the roadside, which has been ruined by commercial ventures capitalizing on the picnic spot. However, it is a good place to pick up the local terracotta pottery, crafted in Kampung Kerayung. The **19th Mile**, further up the hill, is a better spot for a stop-off. To the right of the shop, a path leads along the side of the river, up into the jungle, past Asli villages, waterfalls and jungle pools. Good for birdwatching and butterflies.

Ringlet was the first township on the road to the Cameron Highlands, just inside Pahang state, it was relocated to its present site in the 1960s when the original village was flooded to make way for the Sultan Abu Bakar hydroelectric scheme. Ringlet is the Semai aboriginal word for a jungle tree. The town itself is basically unattractive with shabby 1960s apartment blocks. There is also a cluster of hawker stalls in the town centre and a well-used temple.

After Ringlet, the road follows a wide river to a large, murky brown lake, connected to a hydroelectric dam. The lake is overlooked by the famous **Lakehouse**, a Tudor-style country house, formerly the home of Colonel Stanley Foster and now an 18-room hotel, and food and souvenir stalls. At the Habu power station, a road leads to two of the tea growing estates of the Boh Plantations. The Boh Estate is 6 km from the junction and the Fairlie Estate is 12 km, ⓘ *free guided tours of the factory given almost every hour at the Fairlie Estate, Tue-Sun.The letters BOH stand for "best of the highlands'.*

Youland Flower Nursery is on the road to Gold Dollar tea estate, left off the main road to Tanah Rata from Ringlet (milestone 32). Before reaching Tanah Rata, on the right is a waterfall and picnic spot, on the left is the Cameron Bharat tea shop; which has a fine view over the Bharat tea estate.

Tanah Rata

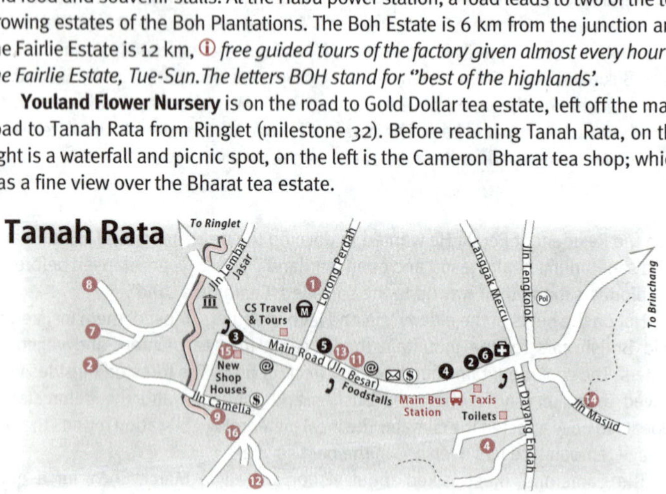

Sleeping
Cameronian Holiday Inn 2
Century Pines Resort 14
Cool Point 4
Daniel's 1
Father's Guesthouse 7
Heritage 8
Highlander 15
Hillview Inn 9
Orient & Restaurant 11
Papillon Guesthouse 12
Seah Meng 13
Twin Pines 16

Eating
Gayatri 4
Mayflower 2
Roselane Coffee House 5
Suria 3
T Café 6

Tanah Rata

A further 5 km up the mountain is Tanah Rata, the biggest of the three Cameronian towns. Having said this, it is still not very large, comprising a row of shophouses straddled along the main road where there are two or three restaurants, imitating British cafés with fish and chips on most menus. It is a friendly little town, with a resort atmosphere rather like an English seaside town. There are also several souvenir shops, including the Yung Seng Souvenir Shop, which is more upmarket than the others and has an interesting selection of well-priced Asli crafts, ranging from blowpipes to woodcarvings. It is also worth looking in local shops for teas from surrounding estates: *Gan Seow Hooi* (seowhooigan@hotmail.com) is the only shop that will let customers sample the high-grade leaf tea grown in the area. It is worth a visit for the traditional tea ceremony as well as the tea itself. The shop also stocks traditional Chinese clay teapots and other Chinese handicrafts.

Brinchang and around

In recent years Brinchang, 7 km beyond Tanah Rata, on the far side of the golf course, has grown fast: since the mid-1980s several new hotels have sprung up, mainly catering for mass-market Malaysian Chinese and Singaporean package tourists. It is not a very beautiful little town, although the central square with its craft centre offers a small ray of interest. **Sam Poh Buddhist Temple**, a popular sight with Chinese visitors who arrive by the coach load, is located just outside Brinchang, along Jalan Pecah Batu, overlooking the golf course. It is backed by the Gunung Beremban hills and comprises both a temple and monastery, which were built here in 1971. Emphasis is on size and grandeur, with monumental double gates with dragons at either side leading into the complex. The inner chamber with its six red-tiled pillars holds a vast golden effigy of a Buddha.

Up the hill from Brinchang the Cameron Highlands becomes one big market garden and the terrain becomes increasingly steep and hilly. **Cactus Valley** is five minutes' walk from the town. The centre grows an amazing variety of the desert plants, some as old as 60 years, as well as a host of flowers including roses, bird of paradise, and an orchard of apples, peaches and passion fruit trees. Just after the army camp on the left, is **Uncle Sam's Farm**. The farm specializes in the cultivation of the kaffir lily, as well as strawberries, oranges, apples and a selection of cacti. Beyond Uncle Sam's, 4 km up the road from Brinchang, there is a large market selling local produce to eager customers from the plains below.

The Cameronian climate is particularly suited to the cultivation of vegetables more usually associated with temperate climates. Cabbages, cauliflowers, carrots and tomatoes, as well as fruit such as strawberries and passion fruit, are taken by truck from the Camerons to the supermarkets of KL and Singapore. **Kea Farm**, with its neatly terraced hillsides, is down the first right turn after the market area. At the Kea turning, on the main road, Kea Farm has a small shop and café and restaurant called the *Strawberry View*. Here, perched on the hillside is the *Equatorial Hill Resort*.

Brinchang

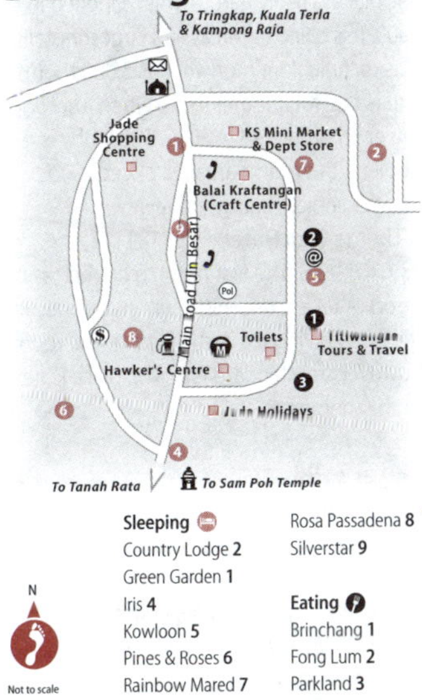

The **Butterfly Garden**, ⓘ *daily 0800-1700, about RM2.50.* is past the Kea Farm turning. There is a large shop attached to the garden, where everything from framed dead butterflies to Cameronian souvenirs (beetles embedded in key rings) is on sale. Outside there are fruit and vegetable stalls – all very popular with Chinese visitors.

The **Rose Garden** is 2 km further up the mountain. To get there, take the first left turn after the butterfly farm, on Jalan Gunung Brinchang, at what is known as the Green Cow area; a village there was burned to the ground by the Communists during the insurgency. A few kilometres beyond the Rose Garden, continue up Jalan Gunung Besar, which is a very picturesque narrow road, on the right is a turning for one of the Boh tea plantations – the**Sungai Palas,** ⓘ *guided tours of the tea processing factory every 10 minx, Tue-Sun; the visitors' centre has a video about tea cultivation that you can watch and a shop, as well as a charming terrace where you can order a pot of tea and enjoy the dramatic view across the steeply terraced tea plantations.*

Back at the Green Cow area, the main road, the C7, continues into the mountains, finally ending at the **Blue Valley Tea Estate**, 13 km from the junction with Jalan Gunung Brinchang. Midway along the C7, at the village of Trinkap, a right turn leads to a large rose-growing establishment, **Rose Valley**, ⓘ *daily 0800-1800, adults RM3, children RM1.50*. It boasts 450 varieties of rose including the thornless rose, the black rose, and the green rose, said to be the ugliest of the rose family. It also has a cactus plantation where some of the plants are 40 years old and lays claim to having the largest flower vase in Malaysia.

Sleeping

Genting Highlands *p122*

The accommodation at Genting Highlands comes under the umbrella of the *Genting Highlands Resorts*. Weekends and holidays have the disadvantage of visitors having to queue at check-in and check-out times. It is best to visit on a weekday if possible.

A **Awana Golf & Country Resort**, T3-64369000, www.awana.com.my/en/ag/index.htm. The 30-storey octagonal tower dominates this resort, which is 10 km below the main resort peak, and overlooks an 18-hole golf course. All rooms have fans (a/c not needed at this altitude), bath, TV and balconies offering panoramic views. Facilities include a heated pool, tennis, gymnasium, sauna, children's library, coffee house, restaurant, cocktail lounge and golf course.

A **Genting Hotel**, T3-27181118, F3-61011888. Located in the heart of the action, deluxe Genting Club rooms, a heated pool and jacuzzi, restaurant, coffee house and easy access to all the resort facilities.

A **Highlands Hotel**, T3-27181118, F3-61011888. Next door to the Genting Hotel. Massive (around 900 rooms), and very smart; calling its décor 'London-style'.

A **Ria Apartments**, T3-27181118, F3-61011888, a 2-room unit sleeps 4 and in low season is priced at the lower end of the A range, a 3-room unit is even more economical and sleeps 6, while the penthouse sleeps 8. All rooms come with bathroom, kitchenette and self-service laundry is available. Service also provides Mahjong tables, a clue to the apartment's popularity with Chinese visitors.

A-B **First World Hotel**, T3-27181118, F3-61011888. Splashed in rainbow colours this place is really hard to miss. Opened in 2000, it is billed as Malaysia's largest hotel. This technicolour monster has 3,000 rooms, and is due for another 4,000 when a second tower is completed in 2005. The lobby is opulent, but rooms are well priced. Good budget choice. Gets good reviews.

B **Theme Park Hotel**, T3-27181118, F3-61011888. The first hotel to be built at the resort. A recent refurbishment has disneyfied the hotel giving it a castle façade. The rooms however, are standard fare. The place is next to the theme park.

Fraser's Hill *p123*

Many of the hotels have facilities for recreations such as tennis, squash, riding and snooker.

AL **Ye Olde Smokehouse Hotel**, T9-3622226, www.thesmokehouse.com.my//fh.htm. Small 16-room hotel in the 'olde

English' style of the Smokehouse Hotel in the Cameron Highlands; with breakfast, a/c, TV, minibar, bath, in-house movie, restaurant and pool. Rooms are spacious, clean, with bathroom and some balconies overlooking the golf course, offering excellent views. Price includes breakfast, which makes it good value.

A **Silverpark Resort**, Jln Lady Maxwell, T9-3622888, www.fraserssilverpark.com Apartments only, no cooking facilities, associated with Fraser's Hill Golf Club golf course, pool, restaurant, children's playground.

A-B **Shahzan Inn** (formely Merlin Inn) , Jln Lady Guillemard, T9-3622300, F9-3622284, shahzan8@tm.net.my Sterile rooms in a rather ugly white block, although some have very nice views.

B **Fraser's Hill Development Corporation**, T9-3622248, F9-3622273. The organization manages the *Puncak Inn*, next to the bus stop, a nondescript 27-room hotel, and a series of 3-4 bedroom bungalows; hiking and birdwatching tours can be arranged.

C **Fraser Hill Travel Lodge** (YHA), MC G/5 Taman Setia (Sg Hijua), Fraser Hill, T9-3622443. Run by Mike Chan who will bend over backwards to help you and is very informative. Definitely the best budget option in town. Bedroom apartment with shared kitchen and bathroom with hot water. Around 15 mins' walk from town or a 5-min shuttle bus ride.

C **Gap Resthouse**, T9-362 2227, 8 km before Fraser's Hill. Large rooms, excellent value and a very characterful place to stay. Restaurant serves good Chinese food but poor Western and Malay-Indian food.

C **Seri Berkat Rest House**, T9-8041026, book through district office at Kuala Kubu Bharu. Another colonial building with high ceilings and big rooms.

Cameron Highlands *p124, map p124*

It should be noted that normally during public holidays, accommodation gets fully booked and prices rise by 30-50%. It is also busy at peak school holiday periods: Apr, Aug and Dec. The most economic form of accommodation is to share a bungalow between a group of people. Most bungalows have gardens, log fires and are away from the centre.

A **Lakehouse**, T5-4956152, www.lakehouse-cameron.com/ This is located a few kilometres outside of Ringlet but has fantastic views. It is a Tudor-style country house, the final brain-child of Colonel Stanley Foster, with 18 rooms of antique furnishings, four-poster beds and en-suite bathrooms, overlooking the lake, restaurant serving English food, *Cameron Bar* and *Highlander Lounge* both have English country pub atmosphere, a great place to stay and reasonable value considering.

Tanah Rata *p129, map p128*

AL **Heritage**, T5-4913888, www.heritage.com.my Located just west of Tanah Rata next to the Convent School. This place has a rather bland international look, out of keeping with its surroundings, although one presumes the intention is to make it look colonial/chalet-esque in appearance. It has 170 spacious rooms, bath, TV, in-house video, Chinese restaurant, coffee house, sauna , health centre, squash, a bar and a chemist.

A **Smokehouse Hotel**, T5-4911215, www.thesmokehouse.com.my/ch.htm This place is modelled on its namesake, the *Smokehouse* in Mildenhall (UK) and it preserves its home counties ethos and 'ye olde English' style of old-time resident Colonel Stanley Foster. Its rooms are first class, there is an original red British telephone box in the garden, restaurant serves expensive English food.

A-C **Bala's Holiday Chalets**, T5-4911660, www.balaschalet.com Located 1 km outside Tanah Rata on road to Brinchang (RM3 taxi ride). Not chalets at all, but a rambling colonial house (one of the oldest in the area, formerly a British school) with some character and a pleasant garden, despite renovation rooms remain dank, private bathrooms with hot water (sporadically available) shower, great view, private cable TV. Common sitting-rooms, log fires, good atmosphere but relying on reputation, overpriced restaurant. Free shuttle service between house and Tanah Rata.

B **Merlin**, 72 Jln Pekeliling Tun Abd Razak, T5-4911211, F5-4911178. Excellent position overlooking the golf course, north of Tanah Rata, but a bit stuck out by itself, and not very atmospheric.

B Strawberry Park Resort, T5-4911166, F5-4911949. Magnificent setting above Tanah Rata, dominating a hilltop with its 8 blocks of walk-up rooms and apartments, built in Tudor/Swiss-chalet style. Interior is starting to look dated, rooms are designed to hold maximum capacity, even the smallest studio rooms and 1-room apartments can sleep 4 people. All rooms with bath (inadequate water heaters), TV, in-house video. Resort facilities include indoor pool (the only one in the Cameron Highlands), tennis, squash, sauna, indoor games rooms, mini-putting green, children's play area, 7 km jogging track, *Monroe's Pub* (with the only disco in the Cameron Highlands and karaoke rooms), coffee house, *Tudor Grill* steakhouse, Chinese restaurant.

B Century Pines Resort, Jln Masjid, T5-4915115, www.thongsin.com Luxury cottages. Although there's no colonial charm, the 59 spanking brand new cottages, reminiscent of an English middle class housing estate, offer excellent value for money at the quiet edge of town and within calling distance of the mosque's minarets. Another 149 rooms in a sandstone building should be ready by the end of 2004. All rooms have five star hotel facilities with VCD players and Internet access.

B Cool Point, Jln Dayang Indah, T5-4914914, F5-4914070. A tacky interpretation of the Tudor style and rather dated décor, recently comfortable (albeit spartan) rooms, TV, breakfast included in room rate, restaurant, overpriced but discounts in low season.

D Cameronian Holiday Inn, 16 Jln Mentigi, T5-4911327, F5-4914966, nasan@pc.jaring.com Restaurant, garden, TV, games, sitting area, 24-hr coffee bar, laundry and internet service Hot showers in more expensive rooms, this is one of the better mid-budget places in town (well, 300m from town) with a large lawn and a suitably relaxing atmosphere, although the beds are a bit saggy. Dorm beds also available (F). Quiet and back from the main road, popular. Recommended.

D Highlander Hotel, 80B Persiaran Camelia 4, T5-4914934, rkup@pd.jaring.my 12 big rooms equipped with bathroom and kettle, a little gloomy but quite kitsch. Good value for money.

D Hillview Inn, 17 Jln Mentigi, T5-4912915, F5-4915212, hillview_inn@hotmail.com Charming house with all rooms with balcony. Facilities include TV, Internet service, laundry, book exchange, beautiful garden and restaurant. Very quiet.

D Orient, 38 Jln Besar, T5-4911633. Located above *The Orient* Chinese restaurant. Price includes own bathroom. If you want to avoid the hostels, it's a great budget choice.

D Papillon Guesthouse, Jln Mentigi, T5-4914069. Close to the Twin Pines Chalet, good-sized rooms (more expensive with own bathrooms) and dorm beds available, friendly and enthusiastic management. Set back from the main road among surrounding huts and houses, this is the non-tourist option.

D Seah Meng, 39 Jln Besar, T5-4911618. On the main street but quiet. Fairly typical Chinese hotel with little atmosphere but the large rooms are kept spotless. Attentive staff. More expensive rooms have showers. Run by a friendly and hospitable family.

D-E Daniel's, 9 Lorong Perdah, T5-4915823, Kand@tm.net.my Once very popular, this place is now trying to contend with some serious black slurs, namely rumours of bed bugs, thieving and police arrests. But, it's not a bad place to stay - it's friendly, the staff are helpful and rooms are cheap. Laundry, internet, movies,jungle bar and nightly log fires. Rooms are very small however, with paper thin walls making them cold and noisy and the shared showers are a bit grubby. There are cleaner, more atmospheric places to stay.

D-E Father's Guest House, Jln Gereja, T5-4912484, www.fathersplace.cbj.net Near the convent, up a long flight of steps. This colonial era set of buildings is a popular backpackers' haunt, and justifiably so. The guesthouse has a very friendly atmosphere and a great communal area with beautiful views. There is also access to cable TV and a number of videos and DVDs are available to watch. Tours to the tea plantations and butterfly garden depart daily (RM15). *Father's* also offers internet access. Dorm beds available (E). The *Secret Garden Café* is a great place for breakfast. The setting is very tranquil, and the staff are very friendly. Many travellers say they are made to feel like part of a family. It offers a free pick up from the bus station. Highly recommended.

D-E **Twin Pines**, 2 Jln Mentigi, T5-4912169, twinpinech@hotmail.com Popular guesthouse a short walk from the bus station. Small, clean rooms and dorm, more expensive rooms have own hot showers. Nice leafy garden, internet, TV room and friendly staff. Good value. Bus tickets and tours bookable here, good source of information (good on transport around Malaysia).

Brinchang and around *p129, map p129*

As for elsewhere in the region, it should be noted that during public holidays, accommodation gets fully booked and prices rise by 30-50%. It is also busy at peak school holiday periods of Apr, Aug and Dec. The cheapest form of accommodation is a shared bungalow between a group of people. Most bungalows have gardens, log fires and are away from the towns.

AL **Equatorial Hill Resort**, near Kea Farm, north of Brinchang, T5-4961777, F5-4961333. This is a monstrosity of more than 500 rooms, very mock Tudor in style, with all the facilities of a four-star hotel – a heated pool, tennis, squash, bowling alley, Cineplex. Not exactly an intimate little place.

A **Rosa Passadena**, T5-4912288, F5-4912688, rosapsch@tn.net.my Large mock-Tudor concrete block, dominating town centre, 120 rooms, bath, TV, in-house video, restaurant, karaoke lounge. Rooms offer superb views of the surrounding Highlands. Restaurant serves everything from steaks to Chinese steamboats.

B **Country Lodge**, T5-4913071, F5-4911396. Located on hillside above Brinchang, typical black and white Tudor-style, decor rather on the severe side, parquet floors and rattan furniture, spacious standard and deluxe rooms as well as suites, restaurant, karaoke lounge. Price is for either hotel room or apartment; great value – dinner is sometimes included free to encourage custom. Recommended as the most tasteful place to stay in Brinchang, away from the noisy karaoke.

B **Hotel Green Garden**, Lot 13, secretary 2, Main Rd. T5-4915834, F5-4915824. Mid-size hotel, a/c, attached bathroom, television. Laundry service, room service and taxis service available. Fairly standard, central location.

B **Iris Hotel** 56, Jln Kuari, T5-4911818, F5-4912828, irish@tm.net.my Although this place looks pretty hideous – a doll's house on a grand scale – it is nonetheless good value. Rather sparsely furnished rooms have hot water and TV. Average restaurant.

B **Rainbow Hotel**, Lot 25, T5-4914628, F5-4914668. Same owner as the Rosa Passadena. Fairly bland corner hotel with 36 good-value comfortable rooms (but don't expect Conran, more like a dentist's waiting room) all with TVs and mini-bar. Good views on one side. Recommended, although there is no restaurant.

C **Kowloon Hotel**, 34-35 Jln Besar, T5-4911366, F5-4911803. Above popular Chinese restaurant, nice rooms with shower, good value for money (under the same management as the Parkland Hotel).

C-D **Pines and Roses**, T5-4912205, F5-4912203 Good value family rooms with TV and water heater although basic furnishings, dorm also available, very clean.

Eating

Genting Highlands *p122*

Eating places are all within the resort, which caters for most tastes and budgets

TTT **Awana Golf and Country Resort**, T3-64369000. This place has a number of places to eat: **Japanese Restaurant**. Recommended for sushi. **Sails Grill**, 2nd Flr, successfully achieves the romantic, candle-lit look combined with dark wood and ethnic masks, excellent quality, international cuisine, 5-star service. Recommended. **Genting Theatre Restaurant**, 2nd Flr, tables arranged around the stage, eat while watching a show. Also **Restaurant Kampong**, Ground Flr, traditional Malay fare, good-value buffet and set lunch, and **Sidewalk Café**, Ground Flr, a 24-hr coffee shop.

TTT **Highlands Hotel**, T3-27181118, has a couple of places to eat: **The Bistro**, continental food, pizza. **Good Friends Restaurant**, Chinese food.

T **Happy Valley Restaurant**, Theme Park Hotel, houses a large and very popular Chinese restaurant.

T **Resort Café**, Resort Hotel, offering an all-day à la carte and buffet breakfast, lunch and dinner.

Fraser's Hill *p123*

ŸŸ **Old Smokehouse**, similar to the *Smokehouse Hotel* in the Cameron Highlands, serving English-style dishes such as beef Wellington and Devonshire cream teas.

ŸŸ **Spices**, Jln Genting, 49000 Bukit Fraser, T9-3622510. Serves Guinness and has a small but interesting menu (Indian, Chinese and Western food). The place has a 1950s feel to it.

Ÿ **Satay's Corner**, Chinese, up the hill from the main town, next to the mosque. Serves a good breakfast.

Cameron Highlands *p124, map p124*

ŸŸŸ **Lakehouse**, traditional English food, typical Sun lunch fare and cream teas.

Tanah Rata *p129, map p128*

ŸŸŸ **Smokehouse**, similar to Lakehouse, favourites include beef Wellington, roast beef, Yorkshire pudding, steak and kidney pie, and Devonshire cream teas.

ŸŸ **Gayatri**, 25 Jln Besar, claypot and Hainam chicken rice and great tandoori. Excellent breakfast *rotis* and murtabak, chairs and tables outside.

ŸŸ **Mayflower**, 22 Jln Besar, specializes in Highland steamboat, seafood, popular with locals.

ŸŸ **Merlin**, international menu, and pleasant atmosphere but not very good value.

ŸŸ **The Orient**, 38 Jln Besar, steamboat and soups are popular, good value set lunch. Vegetarian option is packed with meat and fish.

ŸŸ **Suria**, 66A Jln Perisan Camellia 3, excellent South Indian food served on a banana leaf, good range of vegetarian options, breakfast buffet, friendly staff and open 24 hours.

Ÿ **Bala's**, Bala's Holiday Chalets, good breakfasts and vegetarian dinners, also a popular stop for cream teas.

Ÿ **Roselane Coffee House**, 44 Jalan Besar, T5-4911419, 0800-2200 daily. Western and local food, set meals are good value.

Ÿ **T Café**, 1.F, 4 Jln Besar, T019 57228833. Entry up a flight of steps at the side of the building. Cozy travellers café serving western versions of Chinese and Malay dishes as well as sandwiches, burgers, pasta and a wicked selection of cakes, scones and pies. Very friendly and nice atmosphere. Recommended.

Foodstalls

Next to the bus station, opposite the main row of shops on Jln Besar, serve good selection of Malay, Indian and Chinese food.

Brinchang and around *p129, map p129*

Brinchang, below hotel of same name on Jln Besar, popular for its steamboat, good selection of vegetable dishes. Recommended.

Ÿ **Coco's**, 25 Jln Besar, cheap, good choice and good portions.

Ÿ **Kowloon**, Jln Besar. Busy restaurant, red tablecloths and clean, tiled floors, menu priced according to size of portion, lemon chicken and steamboat are popular. Recommended.

Ÿ **Fong Lum**, 24 Jln Besar. In the same vein as *Kowloon*, very meaty menu, lit with fairy lights after dark.

ŸŸ **Ferns Restaurant**, Rosa Passadena Hotel, Western and oriental, good-value buffet.

ŸŸ **Parkland**, Parkland Hotel. Grill restaurant with steaks, breakfast menu.

Foodstalls

Hawker stalls in the central square, open after 1600, good for satay and roti.

Bars and clubs

Fraser's Hill *p123*

Ye Olde Tavern, above the *Puncak Inn*, Fraser's answer to an English inn, with log fire. Spices Restaurant also, see Eating above.

Tanah Rata *p129, map p128*

Kavy Hotel. The bar under the hotel has a pool table and is a good place for a beer.

Lakehouse and **Smokehouse** hotel bars are also popular venues for their country pub atmosphere and air of exclusivity.

Strawberry Park Resort. The only nightlife as such takes place here where there is the only disco in town, karaoke, and a bar.

Brinchang and around *p129, map p129*

Big Rock Disco Café is the main disco at the resort.

Rosa Passadena Hotel. Apart from a rash of karaoke bars, any nightlife that exists takes place here.

Entertainment

Genting Highlands *p122*

Casino de Genting, *Genting Hotel*. Formal dress required, a tie for men or hire a batik shirt at the door. Blackjack, baccarat, roulette, Tai-Sai are among the table games, along with slot machines, computerized racing. The International Room, for card-holders only, caters for more serious players. *Indoor Theme Park*, the usual video games as well as trains raids, safari expedition, along with plenty of rides for tots. Open Mon-Fri 1000-1800, Sat 0800-2200, Sun 0800-2000. These hours are extended during peak season. Ticket fee adult RM18 (RM22 peak season), child RM15 (RM19 peak season). *Leisure Zone*, 32-lane bowling alley – the second largest in Malaysia – plus table-tennis and snooker.

Outdoor Theme Park, packed with rides including a water flume, go kart track, Rolling Thunder Mine Train roller coaster, double loop Corkscrew roller coaster, gravity drop space shot and the Matahari Ferris wheel. A monorail makes a circuit of the park and offers good views on a clear day, a cable car runs across the park – also good for views. Open Mon-Fri 1000-2400, 0800-0100 Sat, 0800-2400 Sun. These hours are extended during peak season. Ticket fee RM29 (RM33 peak season).

First World Theme Park has a more esoteric bunch of entertainment including a snow slide, RM12, (uses 'real' manufactured snow from Japanese technology), an amazing skydiving simulator, RM50, a branch of the kooky Ripley's Believe It Or Not, RM18, a ghost train and water park.

Activities and tours

Genting Highlands *p122*

Awana Golf & Country Resort, Km 13, T3-64369000, F3-61013535, www.awana.com.my/en/ag/index.htm An 18-hole, international-class course featuring bunkers, ponds and streams, putting green, three-tiered driving range, open daily 0730-1730. Not open to public at weekends.

Awana Horse Ranch, T3-2112026. Open daily 0800-1800, pony rides for children, jumps and horse trekking.

Fraser Hill *p123*

Fraser Golf & Country Club, 18-hole course, T9-3622888.

The Paddock where small bajau ponies are saddled with vast westerners.

Allan's Water. Paddle boats for hire.

Jeram Besu, white water rafting.

Tanah Rata *p129, map p128*

Cameron Highlands Golf Club, T5-4911126. Located north of Tanah Rata, connected by a pleasant footpath, founded in 1885 by the British surveyor William Cameron, the 18-hole course is magnificently appointed, occupying pride of place in the centre of the plateau, surrounded by jungled hills. It is a favourite haunt of Malaysian royalty. Green fee and caddy fee, T4911126. Note that players are expected to wear appropriate clothing, which rules out singlets and revealing shorts. Shoe and club hire available. Tennis courts are across the road from the golf clubhouse, rackets and balls on hire at clubhouse shop.

Tour operators

CS Travel & Tours, 47 Jln Besar, T5-4911200, F5-4912390. For local tours, air/train/bus tickets, and accommodation reservations.

Golden Highlands Adventure Holidays, Main Bus Station T5-4911485. For local tours, good information, ticketing and hotel bookings. It also runs a bus tour from Tanah Rata to Ipoh which takes in sites around Ipoh as well as hot springs and a waterfall in the highlands.

Brinchang and around *p129, map p129*

Cameron Highlands Golf Club, (see Tanah Rata, page 129)

Tour operators

See also Tanah Rata, above.

Jade Holidays, 37a and b Jln Bandar, T5-4912318, F5-4912071, for local tours, air and bus tickets, accommodation bookings, jungle trekking.

Titiwangsa Tours & Travel, 36 Jln Besar, T4912122, F4911246, similar services to Jade Holidays.

Transport

Genting Highlands *p122*

Bus

The Awana resort operates an a/c express bus service between the **KL Puduraya bus station** and Genting Highlands (Genting Skyway Lower Station) from here you must take the cable car or a bus. The express bus service runs every 30 mins from 0700 to 1900, RM6.80. The journey takes 1 hr, inclusive of the cable car, which runs from near the *Awana Hotel* to the resort at the peak. The ticketing office at Puduraya is at counter 43. For advance reservations T20726863. A free shuttle service operates every 2 hrs between the *Awana* and the *Resort Hotel*. An hourly, 24-hr, free shuttle service connects the *Resort Hotel*, *Genting Hotel* and *Ria Apartments*. There is an express bus service between **KL Sentral station** and the **Skyway Lower Station**, operating between 0800-1900, RM6.80. The ticketing office is on level 2 of KL Sentral. There is also a shuttle service to the highlands from **Sepang International Airport**.

Cable car

The 'flying carpet cable car' operates between the resort at the peak and a station near *Awana*. It runs every 20 mins, RM 4. The upward journey runs between 0730-2300 Sun-Fri and 0730-midnight Sat. Going down, the cable run runs from 0915-1930 Mon-Thur, 1115-1930 Fri and Sun, and 0730-1115 Sat. Travelling time is 12 mins. For enquiries T61011118, ext 56138.

Fraser's Hill *p123*

There are two routes to Fraser's Hill. Either take the KL-Karak highway and turn off at Bentong towards Raub and then left again at Tranum for The Gap. (The Gap is an 8-km one-way road that climbs up Fraser's Hill. It's uphill on odd hours, and downhill only on even hours.) If you have more time and would like something a little more scenic, take the road to Ipoh and then turn off at Kuala Kubu Bahru for The Gap. Note the information below regarding traffic on the narrow Gap road, which is one-way at certain times of the day.

Bicycle hire

From Fraser's Hill Development Corporation Office.

Bus

Regular connections from **KL's Puduraya bus station** to **Kuala Kubu Bahru**, at the foothill of Fraser's Hill. Change here to Fraser's Hill. The bus only runs at 0800 and 1200 from Kuala Kubu Bahru to Fraser's Hill, with return buses departing from Fraser's Hill at 1000 and 1400.

Car

A one-way traffic system operates from 0600-1940, 8 km from Fraser's Hill: uphill traffic gets right-of-way on the odd hours, downhill traffic on the even hours (with 40 mins of traffic permitted during those hours).

Taxi

Shared taxis go direct to **Fraser's Hill**. KL (RM10 from Kubu Bahru, or RM40 for the whole cab).

Tanah Rata *p129, map p128*

Those who suffer from travel sickness are advised to take some anti-nausea medication before setting out on the mountain road.

Bus

At the time of writing buses were not using the new highways linking Ipoh in the west and Gua Musang in the east with the Camerons, although they are used by cars and taxis. This is likely to change and cut journey times (from Tanah Rata to Ipoh, 1 ½ hours, and 3 ½ hours to Gua Musang). Currently, **Kurnia Bistari** has five express buses which ply between **KL's Puduraya terminal** and the Cameron Highlands, first one at 0900, last one at 1530 (5 hrs). Leaving from **Tanah Rata**, the first one departs at 0830 and the last one at 1630. Most other buses for the Cameron Highlands leave from **Tapah**, 67 km from Tanah Rata. Connections at least every 2 hours between 0730 and 1730, and regular connections with **Brinchang** and **Tanah Rata** and with **Sungai Palas** and **Kampong Raja** (in the north of the Camerons). Tickets for the return journey can be booked at travel agents or at the bus station in Tanah Rata. From **Tapah** there are express buses to KL every 2 to 2 ½ hours, first one at 1020, last one at 1815. There are three express buses to **Ipoh** and then onto **Georgetown, Penang**, at 0800,

0900 and 1500 (RM19.50). Buses coming down from the Camerons tend to be more expensive. For the east, a minibus runs from Tanah Rata to **Gua Musang** for connections onto **Kota Bharu** and **Kuantan** (RM68) leaving Mon, Wed, Fri, 0700. By the time this book reaches the shelves there should be a daily express bus connection. For all these buses, it is wise to book one day in advance. Note the bus station is open 0730 to 1800.

Nearly all the buses from Tapah (last bus 1730) go through **Ringlet**, **Tanah Rata** and on to **Brinchang** and it is easy enough to climb aboard one of the buses that do this route through the day, every two hours.

Car hire

Because visitors pose a serious insurance problem on the mountain roads, the car rental business is not well developed in the Camerons. The only one available is semi-official: contact **Ravi** at *Rainbow Garden Centre* (between *The Smokehouse* and Tanah Rata), T5-491782. If you are driving, remember to sound your horn at bends and beware of the lorries that hurtle along. If you are wondering why there are lorries on the road it is because there is a large replantation project under way as well as construction work.

Taxi

Taxis are available for local travel – they can be chartered for individual jouneys or by the hour. It is also possible just to take a seat in a taxi, going from Tanah Rata to **Brinchang**, for example. Taxi and local bus station (T5-4911485) on either side of the *Shell* station in Tanah Rata. To order a taxi: T5-4911234.

Train

The nearest station to the Camerons is Tapah Rd in **Tapah**, 67 km from Tanah Rata. There are two connections daily with **Ipoh** and onto **Butterworth** and **Hat Yai** in Thailand leaving at 1107 and 2343 and two south to **KL** leaving at 0315 and 0403.

Brinchang and around *p129, map p129*

See also Tanah Rata, page 136.

Bus

For travel between Tanah Rata, Brinchang and Tapah it is easy enough to climb aboard one of the buses that travels this route through the day or take a taxi (RM4).

Taxis

Taxis are available for local travel and can be chartered for about RM15 per hr.

Directory

Genting Highlands *p122*

Bank Maybank, Genting Hotel. **General Post** Genting Hotel.

Fraser's Hill *p123*

Banks It is possible to change money at Maybank, in the Shahzan Inn, and at the Malaysia Bank, along from the Shahzan Inn entrance in the same complex of shops.

Tanah Rata *p129, map p128*

Banks All the banks are on Jln Besar. Arab-Malaysian Finance, HSBC, Maybank, Sampanian National and Visa Finance Berhad. It is also possible to change money at CS Travel & Tours. **Internet** Almost all backpacker places and the hotels have Internet. Else, Highlands Computer Centre, 39 Jln Besar, a few doors down from Roselane Coffee Shop (0900 to 2200). Pusat Komputer, 1/F, 55B Persiaran Camellia 3 (1000-2200). Both charge around 4RM per hr. **Medical facilities** Hospitals Opposite gardens at north end of town, on Jln Besar, T5-4911966. **Places of worship** Anglican, All Souls' Church, between Kampong Taman Sedia and golf course. Converted army Nissen hut with lich-gate in memory of Miss Griffith-Jones. Services 1030 Sun. **Useful addresses** District office T5-4911455, alert this office if someone you know is long overdue after a jungle walk.
Police T5-4911222, opposite gardens at north end of town.

Brinchang and around *p129, map p129*

Banks Public Bank, next to Garden Lodge. **Internet** There's an internet café next door to the Fong Lum, on the second floor. **Post** opposite the Petronas petrol station at the north end of the town. **Medical services** See Tanah Rata, above. **Useful addresses** Police In central square, next to children's playground.

Ipoh and around

→ Colour map 1, grid C3

The northern state of Perak is known for its tin ore (mainly in the Kinta Valley) and Ipoh, its capital, is Malaysia's third city. The city is situated in the Kinta Valley, between the Main Range and the Keledang Mountains, to the west. There are some fine examples of colonial architecture in the Old Town and outerlying areas housing among other notable sights the Perak Darul Ridzuan Museum which provides an interesting insight into Ipoh's history. Within easy reach of the city is the Sam Poh Tong, the largest cave temple in the area, and Perak Tong, one of the largest Chinese temples in Malaysia.

Close to Ipoh are the Royal town of Kuala Kangsar, the ancient town of Taiping with its strong Chinatown, Lumut, a holiday destination on the coast and the pleasant island of Pulau Pangkor with good beaches and coral. ▸▸ *For Sleeping, Eating and other listings, see pages 146-155.*

Ins and outs

Getting there

Ipoh's airport is 15 km south of town; daily direct fights with KL and international connections with Medan in Sumatra (Indonesia). From the train station on the edge of town there are connections with Butterworth and KL as well as south to Singapore and north to Hat Yai in Thailand. Ipoh is on the main N-S highway and there are regular connections with just about everywhere of any size on the Peninsular. The long-distance bus terminal is several km north of town and requires a taxi or bus ride to reach. Share taxis are available for journeys to KL, Butterworth, Taiping, Alor Star and Tapah.

Getting around

Local car hire firms and taxis are also available (note taxi drivers do not use meters). However, Ipoh is not a large place and it is perfectly possible to walk around the town. The grid layout of the town's streets makes navigation a doddle.

Tourist information

None of Ipoh's three tourist offices offer much in the way of help and assistance, bar a map. **Ipoh City Council Tourist Office,** ⓘ *Jln Abdul Adil, Mon-Thu 0800-1245 and 1400-1615 , Fri 0800-1212 and 1400-1615, Sat 0800-1245.* **Perak Tourist Information Centre,** ⓘ *State Economic Planning Unit, Pejabat Setiausaha Kerajaan, Jln Panglima Bukit Gantang Wahab, Mon-Thu 0800-1245, 1400-1615, Fri 0800-1215, 1445-1615, Sat 0800-1245, closed Sun, T5-2531957, F5-2418173.* **Tourist information,** ⓘ *Casuarina Hotel, 18 Jln Gopeng, T5-2532008. Also see www.perak.gov.my*

Background

Ipoh is named after the abundance of the huge, elusive ipoh (*upas*) trees that once grew there. The city also has an abundance of imposing limestone outcrops. These jungle-topped hills, with their precipitous white cliffs, are riddled with passages and caves, many of which have been made into cave temples.

In its early days, Ipoh's citizens became wealthy on the back of the tin-mining industry. In 1884 the Kinta Valley tin rush brought an influx of Chinese immigrants to Ipoh; many made their fortunes and built opulent town houses. Chinese immigrants have bequeathed what is now one of Malaysia's best-preserved Chinatowns (the 'Old Town'). In the 1880s Ipoh vied with Kuala Lumpur to be the capital of the Federated States of Malaya, and long after KL took the title, Ipoh remained the commercial 'hub of Malaya'. The city has long had an active 'flesh trade': there are frequent round-ups of Thai and Burmese prostitutes who are smuggled across Malaysia's north border.

Few tourists spend long in Ipoh – most are en route to Penang, KL or Pulau Pangkor. Those who do stay rarely regret it: there are excellent Chinese restaurants (a speciality is the rice noodle dish, *sar hor fun*, which literally means 'melts in your mouth'), Buddhist temples and examples of Straits Chinese architecture. It is also a good place to pick up Chinese imported goods, such as baskets and chinaware. The shophouses on and around Jalan Yau Tet Shin make for good browsing. Ipoh also has a handful of very well-established bakers. On Jalan Raja Eleram the two bakeries here have been in the business for well over 50 years. They specialize in French bread, buns and cakes.

Sights

The Kinta River, spanned by the Hugh Low Bridge, separates the old and new parts of town. The **Old Town** is centred on the river between Jalan Sultan Idris Shah and Jalan Sultan Iskander Shah, and is known for its old Chinese and British colonial architecture, particularly on Jalan Sultan Yusuf, Jalan Leech and Jalan Treacher.

Prominent landmarks include the **Birch Memorial**, a clock tower erected in memory of the first British resident of Perak, JWW Birch. His murder in 1875 was one of colonial Malaya's first anti-British incidents and the three perpetrators, after being hanged, promptly became local heroes, which they remain to this day. The four panels decorating the base of the tower depict the development of civilization; the upper part of the tower holds a bust of JWW Birch who was, local history relates, not well-liked in the area. The Moorish-style **railway station** (off Jalan Kelab), built in 1917, bears close resemblance to its Kuala Lumpur counterpart, and is known as the 'Taj

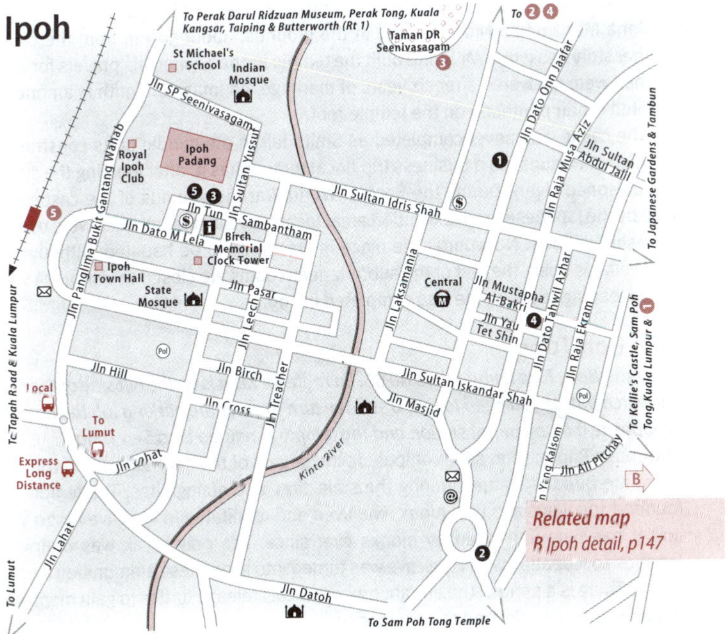

0 metres 100
0 yards 100

Sleeping
Fair Park 4
Grandview 3
Heritage 1
Majestic Station 5
YMCA 2

Eating
Blue Window Café 1
Kafe Abarnaashre 3
Lou Wong Tauge Ayam Kuetiau 4
Rahman 2
Restuncle House 5

Mahal' of Ipoh. The **Station Hotel** is a colonial classic. Both hotel and station were being renovated at the time of writing. **Ipoh Town Hall**, with its Palladian façade, stands opposite. A solitary ipoh tree stands in the centre of **Taman DR Seenivasagam** (a park north of the centre). The park also contains an artificial lake and a children's playground. There are also **Japanese Gardens**, ⓘ *Mon-Fri 1600-2000, Sat-Sun 0900-2000*, complete with a typical Japanese carp pond, nearby on Jalan Tambun. The **Geological Museum**, ⓘ *Mon-Fri 0800-1615, Sat 0800-1245, free, but entry permission from the information counter is necessary*, on Lorong Hariman, out of town centre, was set up in 1957. It is known for its exhibition of tin ore and collection of fossils and precious stones, as well as over 600 samples of minerals. On Jalan SP Seenivasagam there is an old **colonial mission school** with an impressive white stone façade and an Indian mosque next door.

Heading out of town, past **St Michael's School**, on Jalan Panglima Bukit Gantang Wahab, after about 500m on the right is an elegant, white colonial building, which houses the **Perak Darul Ridzuan Museum**, ⓘ *0900-1700 daily, closed Fri, free*. The building, which is over 100 years old, once the home of Malay dignitaries of Kinta, now holds a collection showing the history of Ipoh, and mining and forestry within the state.

Around Ipoh

Kellie's Castle

ⓘ *0830-1930, RM0.50.*

Down the road to Batu Gajah, just to the south of Ipoh (about a 30-minute drive), is the eccentric edifice of Scotsman William Kellie Smith, a late-19th-century rubber tycoon. He shipped in Tamil workers from South India to build his fanciful Moorish-style mansion, and, following an outbreak of fever, allowed them to build the Sri Maha Mariamman Hindu temple in the grounds, about 500 m from the castle. Another story has it that Mr Smith built the temple in 1902, when his prayers for a son and heir were answered after six years of marriage. An image of Smith is among the sculpted Hindu pantheon on the temple roof.

The castle was never completed as Smith left in the middle of its construction and died in Portugal on a business trip (local rumour has it, after inhaling the smoke of a poisoned cigar). During the Second World War the grounds of the castle were used by the Japanese as an execution area; locals say that the tall trees were used as makeshift gallows. No wonder the place is presumed to be haunted: although the wine cellar is open, the rest of the subterranean rooms are closed to visitors. A white bridge leading to the castle was completed in 1994.

Sam Poh Tong

ⓘ *0730-1800. Take Kampar bus No 66. En route for KL, it is on the left side of the road, but watch out, as you need to take a sudden turn to enter the parking lot; the entrance is opposite a Mobil petrol station and the temple is named Ling Sen Tong.*

At Gunung Rapat, 5 km south of Ipoh, is the largest of the cave temples in the area. There are Buddha statues among the stalactites and stalagmites. The temple was founded 100 years ago by a monk who lived and meditated in the cave for 20 years and it has been inhabited by monks ever since. The only break was during the Japanese occupation when the cave was turned into a Japanese ammunition and fuel dump. There is a pond at the entrance where locals release turtles to gain merit while young boys sell turtle food to earn money.

Perak Tong

ⓘ *0900-1600. Take Kuala Kangsar bus or city bus No 3.*

One of the largest Chinese temples in Malaysia is 6½ km north of Ipoh on Jalan

Kuala Kangsar. Built in 1926 by a Buddhist priest from China, the temple houses over 40 Buddha statues and mystical traditional Chinese-style murals depicting legends. It is visited by thousands of pilgrims every year and is the most ornately decorated of the many cave temples at the base of the 122 m limestone hill. A path beyond the altar leads into the cave's interior and up a brick stairway to an opening 100 m above ground with a view of the surrounding countryside. Another climb leads to a painting of Kuan Yin, Goddess of Mercy, who looks out from the face of the limestone cliff. A 15-m-high reinforced concrete statue of the Buddha stands in the compound.

Gua Tambun (Tambun Cave)

ⓘ *Caves open 0900-1600, RM5. Hot springs open 1500-2400. Take Tambun bus, a 15-min drive from Ipoh.*

Traces of a civilization dating back 10,000 years were discovered at these caves, 3 km rom Ipoh near Tambun, in the 1930s. The ochre drawings on the cave walls and the limestone cliffs depict the life of prehistoric man; especially interesting is the 'Degong' fish, a drawing of a large fish that feeds on meat, rather like a piranha. **Tambun Hot Springs** nestle at the foot of this limestone hill. The Japanese were responsible for their initial development during the occupation. Two swimming pools have been built – one filled with lukewarm water and one with hot. There also saunas.

Kuala Kangsar *Colour map 1, grid B2*

Though at first glance, this royal town half-way between Ipoh and Taiping on the Kangsar River seems unassuming, it is a pleasant place to stop off, with plenty of atmosphere.

On the east bank of the Kangsar River lies the **Sultan of Perak's home,** ⓘ *find the main roundabout in the town, which has a distinctive clock tower at its centre, and head southeast towards the gates marking the start of the road to the palace estate. The road twists alongside the Perak River where there is also a back walkway for those on foot.* The first monument you come to is the **Ubudiah Mosque**, built on the slopes of Bukit Chandan. Completed in 1917, it is one of the most beautiful mosques in the country with its golden domes and elegant minarets. Next to it are the graves of the Perak royal family.

Present members of the Perak royal family are resident in the beautiful **Istana Iskandariah** (and south bank of the Perak), which was built in 1930 and sits on the summit of Bukit Chandan, overlooking the Perak River and Ubudiah Mosque. It is a massive marble structure with a series of towers, topped by golden onion domes set among trees and rolling lawns. It is not open to the public, but the former yellow palace, Istana Kenangan (next door to the current Istana), is now the **Museum di Raja** (Perak Royal Museum) ⓘ *0900-1730, closed Fri lunchtime for prayers,* and exhibits royal regalia. It is a fine example of Malay architecture and was built by Sultan Idris of Perak between 1913 and 1917, without recourse to any architectural plans or even a single nail.

In the vicinity of the palaces are several grand **traditional wooden Malay homes,** which used to house court officials. There is also another **former palace** (not open to public) near the Ubudiah Mosque. This imposing white building was erected in 1903 for the 28th Sultan of Perak. For many years it housed the Mazwin School for Ladies, but has now been renovated into the **Sultan Azlan Shah museum** which is due to open in mid-2005. Besides these buildings, in the grounds of the district office near the Agricultural Department, is one of the first three rubber trees planted in Malaysia. HN Ridley, also known as 'Crazy Ridley', was responsible for developing Kuala Kangsar as a rubber planting district. He obtained rubber seeds from London's Kew Gardens and brought them, first to Singapore, and then to Kuala Kangsar where the seeds were sown in 1877, when Sir Hugh Low was British President in Perak. The sole tree to remain is now marked with a memorial plaque to Ridley. Across the road from Kuala Kangsar's famed rubber tree is a charming pavilion, built in 1930 as a viewing gallery from which the sultan could watch polo on the padang. The padang is also overlooked by the attractive red-roofed building of the **Malay College**. Considered the Eton of Malaysia, the school was built in 1905 for the children of the Perak royal family. During the Japanese occupation in the Second World War, the college was turned into administration offices for the Japanese Imperial Army who interrogated and subsequently beheaded anyone found to be a traitor. A school once again in the 1950s, it attracted a celebrated crowd – Anthony Burgess taught here (see Further reading on page 528 for a listing of his novels with a Malaysian theme).

Across the Perak River there is a village where **traditional pottery-making** goes on, mostly within the Handicraft Centre there. The pottery is earthenware and fired in padi husk, which gives it a rich black colour. The traditional product of the potteries is the *labu sayong*, a water pitcher, in the shape of a gourd.

Taiping → *Colour map 1, grid B2*

With a backdrop of the Bintang Mountains, Taiping is the old capital of Perak and one of the oldest towns in Malaysia. Around 1840, Chinese immigrants started mining tin in the area, and it is the only big Malaysian town with a Chinese name. The town is busy and friendly, with a close-knit, community-oriented atmosphere similar to that in the other Chinatowns of Terengganu and Melaka.

In the 1860s and 1870s the Larut district of Taiping, then known as Kelian Pauh, was the scene of the Perak War, caused by bloody feuding between two rival Chinese secret societies, the Hai San and Ghee Hin, over rights to the rich tin deposits. The fighting between these Hakka and Hokkien groups resulted in British armed intervention and, when it subsided, the town was renamed thai-peng, or 'everlasting peace'.

The Japanese built a prison in Taiping during the Second World War (next to the Lake Garden), which was then converted into a rehabilitation centre for captured terrorists during the Communist Emergency. Some of the executions carried out under Malaysia's draconian drugs legislation now take place in Taiping jail (see page 35).

One of the main reasons for coming here is to visit Maxwell Hill (see page 143). There is more colonial-era architecture here than in many of Malaysia's towns; there are some fine examples on Jalan Kota, including the former District Office, and on Jalan Main and Jalan Station. Jalan Iskandar has some fine examples of Chinese shophouse architecture.

Sights

As early as 1890 the **Lake Garden** (Taman Tasik) was set up on the site of an abandoned tin mine by Colonel ESF Walker. It is very lush due to the high rainfall and is the pride of the town. Covering 66 ha, the park lies at the foot of Bukit Larut (Maxwell Hill). At one end of the park is **Taiping Zoo** ⓘ *www.zootaiping.gov.my, 0830-1830 daily, including public holidays. RM4 (adults), RM2 (children), extra charge for camera or video camera*, which is one of the oldest in Malaysia and boasts over 800 animals, including Malaysian elephants, tigers and hornbills, as well as an assortment of animals from Africa. Animals are normally fed between 1000 and 1200. In the early morning locals use the park for their tai chi exercises. Rowing boats are available for hire on lake.

Maxwell Hill is the oldest hill station in Malaysia and the wettest place in the country receiving an average of 5,029 mm of rain a year.

Built in 1883, the lovely colonial **Perak Museum,** ⓘ *out on Jalan Taming Sari (Main Road), opposite the prison, 0930-1700 Sat-Thu, 0900-1215, 1445-1700 Fri, free,* is the oldest museum in Malaysia, dating from 1883. It contains a collection of ancient weapons, aboriginal implements, stuffed animals and archaeological finds. The bull elephant skull on show was extracted from an animal that was killed after derailing a train at Telok Anson in 1894. Near the museum is **All Saints' Church**. Built of wood in 1889, it is the oldest Anglican church in Malaysia. The graveyard contains graves of early settlers and those who died in the Japanese prisoner-of-war camp nearby. Also next to the museum is the **Ling Nam Temple,** worth a visit for the Chinese antiques inside and is said to be the oldest Chinese temple in Perak State. The **railway station** on Jalan Steysen, now a school, is the oldest in Malaysia.

There is a handy pamphlet, available from the Perak Museum that maps out a heritage walking tour with photographs and short descriptions of the many colonial-era buildings.

Around Taiping

Kuala Sepetang lies 16 km west of Taiping and contains a Mangrove Forest Museum, the first of its kind in Malaysia. The site lies in 40,700 ha of mangrove swamp, which is more than half the swamp area in Peninsular Malaysia. The museum aims to highlight forestry operations in Malaysia.

The foot of **Bukit Larut**, formerly known as **Maxwell Hill,** ⓘ *for information phone the superintendent, T5-8077243,* is just 12 km or so east of the Lake Garden. Most people climb the hill, whether on foot or by Land Rover, as a day excursion from Taiping. At an elevation of 1,034 m it was once a tea plantation. Bukit Larut is a small resort with limited facilities compared to the peninsula's other hill stations. The road up was built by prisoners of war during the Japanese occupation in the Second World War. It is in such bad repair that it is virtually inaccessible in anything other than a four-wheel-drive vehicle; in any case private transport is not permitted.

Taiping

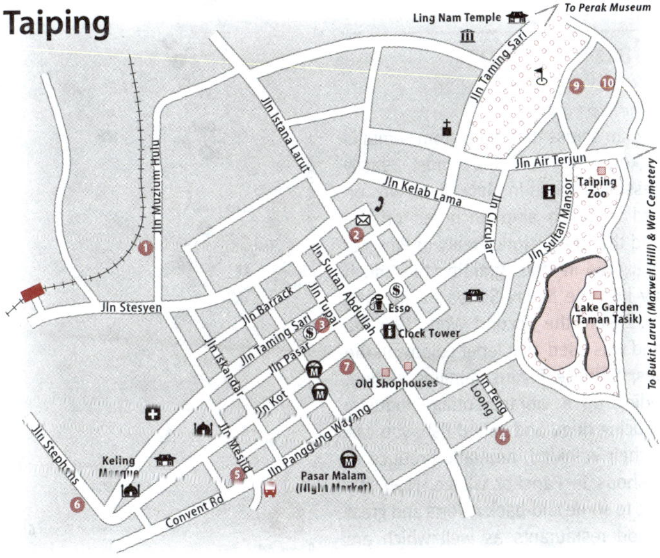

N

0 metres 100
0 yards 100

Sleeping
Fuliyean **2**
Lagenda **1**
Legend Inn **5**
Meridien **6**
Nanyang **3**
New Champagne **4**
Panorama **7**
Rumah Rehat Baru **9**
Seri Malaysia **10**

On the way up you pass a **Commonwealth War Cemetery**. Many of the gravestones here are marked December 1941, which was the date a single company from the Argyle Regiment tried to hold back the Imperial Japanese 42nd Infantry on the road north of Kuala Kangsar. Another stop is the **Tea Gardens** (or what is left of them) at the Batu 3.5 mark. The administration office is at the Batu 6 marker and about 1 km on from here is the end of the road – at the *Gunung Hijau Rest House*. From here travel is on foot. On clear days, from the summit, it is possible to see for miles along the coast. The walk to the top takes about 30 minutes and is a good trail for birdwatchers. There are jungle walks near the top of the hill, but leeches can be a problem. To walk all the way down takes around two to three hours.

Lumut

ⓘ *Lumut Tourist Information Centre, Jln Sultan Idris Shah, opposite the jetty, T5-6834057, 0900-1700 Mon to Fri, 0900-1345 Sat, closed Sun.*

Lumut is primarily a base for the Royal Malaysian Navy, which has a population of around 25,000, compared with a populace of 1,000 in Lumut itself. Lumut is also a transit point for Pulau Pangkor, and in recent years it has also begun tentatively to develop as a holiday destination in its own right. *The Orient Star*, an international-class hotel, looms large on the coast and apartment blocks are rearing their ugly heads on the hilltop of Bukit Engku Busu. The town is at its zenith during the *Pesta Laut*, a sea festival, which takes place every August at nearby Teluk Batik.

Teluk Batik, 7 km south of Lumut, is a popular beach spot (often used by the naval base), with chalets, food stalls and changing rooms backing the sweeping, sandy bay. There is another sandy beach at **Teluk Rubiah** a further 6 km south, near the *Teluk Rubia Royal Golf Club*, which has a pool, tennis courts and golf course. A taxi from Lumut should cost RM20.

Pulau Pangkor

→ *Colour map 1, grid C2*

Just 7 km across the Straits from Lumut is Pangkor, one of the most easily accessible islands in Malaysia. It was on board a British ship anchored off the island that the historic Treaty of Pangkor was signed in 1874, granting the British entry into the Malay States for the first time. Before the Second World War the island was used as a leper colony. In the fifties, Chinese fishing families settled, building up a vibrant cottage industry producing dried and salted fish, you can see their wrinkled, aromatic produce in the shops in Pangkor village. Now, it's home to some laid-back resorts and great seafood restaurants as well which are virtually deserted during the week but packed with holidaying locals during the week. While some of the beaches are a bit grubby, it's possible to hire a motorbike and laze on some fine secluded sands.

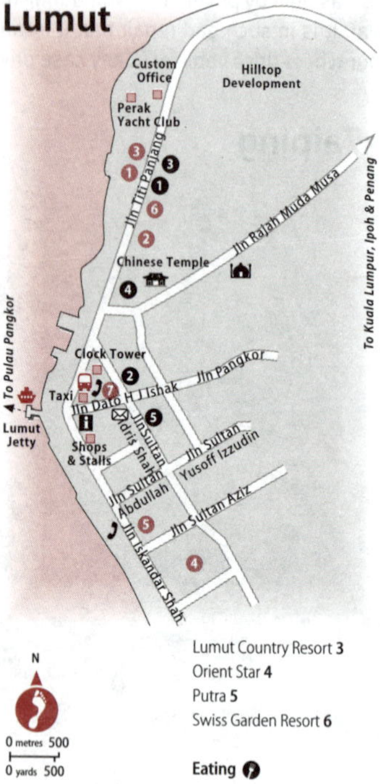

Sleeping
Blue Bay Resort **1**
Era **7**
Harbour View **2**
Lumut Country Resort **3**
Orient Star **4**
Putra **5**
Swiss Garden Resort **6**

Eating
Capri **5**
Makanan Laut Ocean **1**
Nasi Kandar **2**
Ocean Seafood **3**
Phin Lum Hooi **4**

Ins and outs

Getting there and around Pulau Pangkor is accessible by air from KL. Regular half hour departures by boat from Lumut. Taxis and minibuses provide transport on the island. It is also possible to hire motorbikes and bicycles.

Pangkor is one of the largest fish suppliers in Peninsular Malaysia. Old Pangkor has the fishing villages of Sungai Pinang Kecil (the first stop-off for the ferry from Lumut), Sungai Pinang Besar and Pangkor (main village). Modern Pangkor to the north has a modern luxury resort. To the southwest is the tiny island of Pankgor Laut. The main island is pretty but is very busy at weekends and during school holidays, as it is one of the few places on the west coast with good beaches, although on weekdays it can feel deserted. While it does not have the same heady atmosphere of the east coast islands, it has a much more laid-back, local feel, comparable to that of Langkawi but on a smaller scale.

Pulau Pangkor

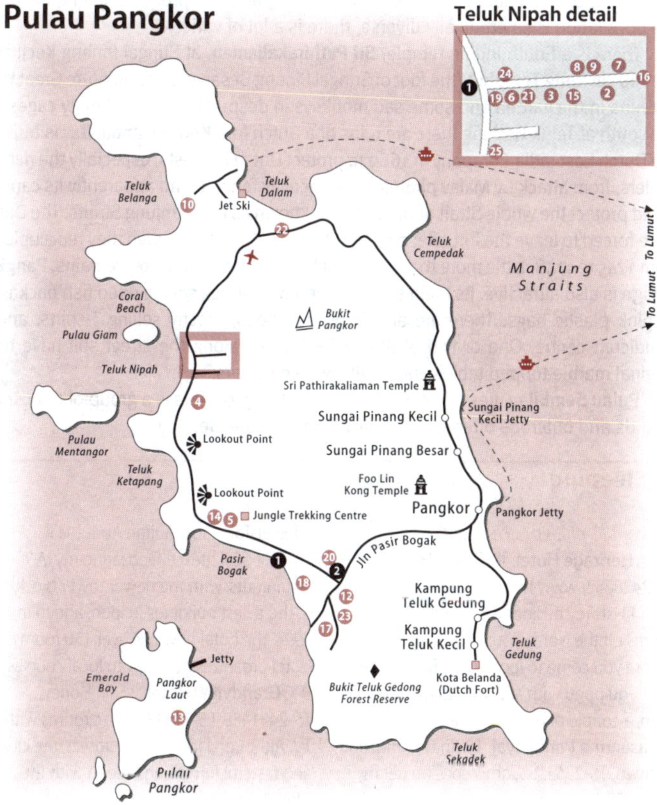

N

0 metres 500
0 yards 500

Sleeping
Coral Beach Camp 2
Coral View Beach Resort 5
Flora Beach Resort 3
Hornbill Resort 4
Joe Fisherman Village 7
Lima Chalets 6
Nipah Bay Villa 8
Nipah Water Front 24
Ombak Inn Resort 9
Pangkor Coral Bay Resort 12
Pangkor Island Beach Resort 10
Pangkor Laut Resort 13
Pangkor Puteri Resort 23
Pangkor Village Beach Resort 14
Purnama Beach Resort 15
Seagull Beach Resort 16
Seaview 17
Sri Bayu Beach Resort 18
Sunshine Beach Resort 25
Suria Beach Resort 19
Teluk Dalam Resort 22
Vikry Resort 20
Zek Pink 21

Eating
Coco 2
Foodstalls 1

Some of the best beaches and coral can be found on nearby islands, such as **Emerald Bay** on Pangkor Laut, a private island only open to guests of the resort (see Sleeping, page 149). Emerald Bay is the spot where F Spencer Chapman escaped from Malaya after three years fighting the Japanese behind enemy lines, all recounted in his book *The Jungle is Neutral*. There are some hidden beaches on the main island. North of **Pasir Bogak**, the most developed beach, turtles lay their eggs right on **Teluk Ketapang** beach, mainly during May, June and July. North of this are two of the best beaches **Coral Bay** (Teluk Nipah) and **Golden Sands** (Teluk Belanga). The most popular beach is at Pasir Bogak. Visitors can also take boats to Pulau Mentangor and Pulau Sembilan.

There are good walks round the island: it takes nearly a day to walk all the way round (although the winding, narrow roads are not very safe for pedestrians); half a day by bicycle; and two to three hours by motorcycle. Note, however, that the route is quite hilly and the parkland past the *Pangkor Island Beach Resort*, a difficult ride for all but the most determined bicyclist. The west coast is comparatively secluded with stretches of quiet beach and the occasional fishing settlement, while the east coast hums with commercial activity, like boat building and fish processing, and because the population is so ethnically diverse, there is a lot of variety.

There is a South Indian temple, **Sri Pathirakaliaman**, at Sungai Pinang Kecil and the **Foo Lin Kong Temple** at the foot of Sungai Pinang Besar, with a miniature Great Wall of China in the garden and some sad monkeys in desperately old and rusty cages. To the south at Teluk Gedung there are ruins of a Dutch fort, **Kota Belanda**. It was built by the Dutch East India Company in 1680 to protect Dutch interests, especially the rich tin traders, from attack by Malay pirates. It was heavily fortified and apparently its cannon could protect the whole Strait of Dinding also known as the Manjung Straits. The Dutch were forced to leave the fort after an assault by the Malays, although they reoccupied it from 1745 to 1748. Little more than a shell of the former building now remains. **Pangkor village** is also attractive. Its main street is lined with stores selling dried fish packaged in pink plastic bags. There are also souvenir shops, mostly selling T-shirts, and a handicraft centre. One or two of the coffee houses along the street still have their original marble-topped tables and Straits wooden chairs.

Pulau Sembilan lies 27 km south of Pulau Pangkor. This is a group of nine small islands and outcrops offering good diving and marine life.

Sleeping

Ipoh *p138, maps p139 and p147*

AL-A Heritage Hotel, Jln Raja DiHilir, T5-2428888, www.heritage.com.my. Fairly new 11-storey business hotel with 265 rooms off the North-South highway just before you come to Ipoh town. Rooms are well-equipped with a/c, mini-bar, sauna, gym, a couple of restaurants and a 'fun' pub.

A Casuarina Park Royal, 18 Jln Gopeng, out of town, T5-2555555, gmcaspr@tm.net.my Over 200 rooms, a/c, restaurant, pool, Ipoh's finest but not central.

A Syuen, 88 Jln Sultan Abdul Jalil, T5-2538889, syuenht@tm.net.my A/c, 10 food and beverage outlets, central hotel with real style, 300 rooms, overlooking the bougainvillea park, a/c, TV, mini-bar, comfortable and well-furbished rooms, disco, pool, business centre, sauna, tennis.

B Excelsior, 43 Jln Sultan Abdul Jalil, T5-2536666, htexcel@po.jaring.my A/c, restaurants; with the newer tower block, one of the tallest buildings in Ipoh, added in 1994, the hotel now has over 150 rooms. Hotel organizes golf trips to local courses.

B-C Grandview Hotel, 36 Jln Horley, T5-2431488, F5-2431811. A/c rooms with TV. Although lacking in character, the clean and tasteful furnishings, along with the friendly and efficient service, make this one of the best value options in town.

B-C Tambun Inn, 91 Jln Tambun, T5-5477211, F5-5467887. Located 4 km from city centre, most rooms are deluxe double, which are priced at upper end of B category but offer good value, TV, a/c, in-house video, health centre, karaoke lounge.

B-C Majestic Station Hotel, Bangunan

Stesyen Keretapi, Jln Panglima Bukit Gantang Wahab, T5-2555605, F5-2553393. A/c, restaurant, 100 rooms. Under renovation, along with the station at time of writing. It's to be hoped that the old-colonial-style décor will be retained, good range of facilities from in-house movies to a health service, great atmosphere, well run and priced. Beautiful location set right in the heart of the old town. Recommended.

C Fair Park, 85 Jln Kamaruddin Isa, T5-5488666, fairpark@tm.net.my One of the newer budget hotels, near DBI Sports Centre.

C New Caspian , 20-26 Jln Ali Pitchay, T5-2439254, F5-2439258. A package of clean and comfortable rooms offering reasonable value for money with TV, fridge, kettle and a/c, although the plumbing is noisy. Recently renovated and a good location with lots of late night cafes and Chinese restaurants.

B-C Merloon, 92-98 Jln Mustapha al-Bakri, T5-25413363, www.pvghotels.com. Big old airy building with large, clean rooms. A tad expensive for the lack of in-room facilities – there's no fridge or TV in standard rooms.

C-D Ritz Kowloon, 92-96 Jln Yang Kalsom, T5-2547778, F5-2533800. Chinese-run with a/c, TV, in-house video, safe, tastefully furnished rooms. Very helpful staff.

C Robin, 106-110 Jln Mustapha al-Bakri, T5-2413755, F5-2541818. Same owner as the Merloon and next door, but about RM10 pricier. Rooms have a/c, TV and fridge. Not bad value. Attached to a restaurant and spa.

C YMCA, 211 Jln Raja Musa Aziz, take a small path along the river to get here, T5-2540809. Tennis courts, dorm beds available (**E**), this place is good value and the grounds as well as the rooms are spacious, but the location is inconvenient.

D Shanghai, 85 Jln Mustapha al-Bakri. Fan only, shower, restaurant, clean and central. Although badly in need of modernizing this is a good budget option.

Ipoh detail

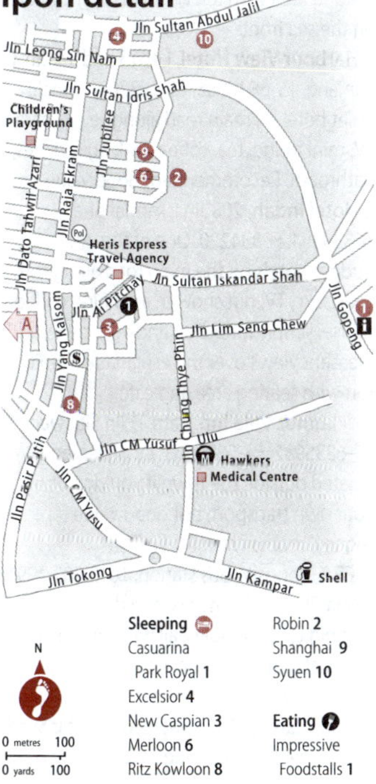

Sleeping
Casuarina Park Royal 1
Excelsior 4
New Caspian 3
Merloon 6
Ritz Kowloon 8
Robin 2
Shanghai 9
Syuen 10

Eating
Impressive Foodstalls 1

Kuala Kangsar *p141*

Although Kuala Kangsar is not a popular stopover spot, due to the limited number of rooms, it is best to book in advance.

There are very few places to stay in Kuala Kangsar; none is particularly desirable apart from the *Rest House*, and all are small – the largest hotel has 14 rooms.

B Rest House (Rumah Rehat Kuala Kangsar), Bukit Candan, T5-7765872. Pleasant position just inside the gates to the palace road, old colonial mansion, huge rooms with a/c, bathroom and hot water, some rooms face the river (fabulous views), friendly, helpful staff.

C-D Double Lion, 74 Jln Kasa, 300 m from the bus station, T5-7768010, some a/c, an alternative to the *Rest House* and a pleasant enough place to stay with large rooms, some overlooking the river.

Taiping *p142, map p143*

B Lagenda Hotel, Jln Residensi (opposite King Edward's School), T5-822044. Well designed with rooms set around a small outdoor pool. Good showers but poor a/c, fans are provided as well. Restaurant.

B Legend Inn, 2 Jln Long Jaafar, T5-8060000, F5-8066666. A hotel block with 88 rooms, bath, TV, video channel, coffee house, plushest place in town with well-equipped rooms.

B Panorama, 61-79 Jln Kota, T5-834111, F5-8085129. A/c, TV, in-house video, bath, mini fridge, coffee-making facilities, joined to a 3-storey supermarket, the *Fajar*, restaurant. The hotel has a central location and 79 pretty ordinary rooms.

B Seri Malaysia, 4 Jln Sultan Mansor, T5-8069502, www.serimalaysia.com.my One of the new chain of budget hotels, located outside the town, near the Lake Garden, spotlessly clean to the point of being sterile.

B-C Meridien, 2 Jln Simpang, T5-8081133. A/c, TV, shower, coffee house, restaurant.

C Fuliyean, 14 Jln Barrack, T5-8068648, F5-8070648. A/c, TV, bath, quite new and good value, rooms kept very clean.

C New Champagne Hotel, 17 Jln Lim Swee aqun, T5-8065060, opposite Cathay Cinema and a big restaurant, and round the block from *Furama Hotel*. Friendly, helpful staff, this Chinese-owned restaurant is a pleasant, clean establishment.

C-D Rumah Rehat Baru (New Resthouse), 1 Jln Sultan Mansor, Taman Tasek, T5-8072044. Fan or a/c, restaurant, situated a little out of town and the new block is hardly attractive but the rooms are large, with attached bathrooms, it overlooks the Lake Garden and is good value. Recommended.

D Nanyang, 129-131 Jln Pasar, T5-8074488. A/c or fan, TV. Clean, simple and friendly.

Around Taiping *p143*

For bungalows it is essential to book in advance (between 0900-1200), T5-8077241 or write to: Officer in charge, Bukit Larut Hill Resort, Taiping.

B Cendana and **Tempinis** both between the 6th and 7th milestones, Bukit Larut.

E Bukit Larut, large bathroom, excellent value.

E-F Rumah Hijau, Bukit Larut, also has a campsite.

Lumut *p144, map p144*

AL Swiss-Garden Resort, 101-107 Jln Titi Panjang, T5-6183333, www.swissgarden.com New, clinical feel, but has good facilities.

AL-A Orient Star, Lot 203 and 366, Jln Iskandar Shah, T5-6834199, tosrlso@po.jaring.my A hotel with 150 a/c rooms, TV, in-house video, mini fridge, free-form pool with swim-up bar, paddling pool, gymnasium, jet-ski hire, bicycle hire, coffee house, bar, palatial in size and décor, pleasantly furnished rooms with balconies and sea views but no beach. A classy place that sometimes offers excellent discounts.

A-B Blue Bay Resort, T5-6836939, F5-6836239. Breakfast included in room rate. TV, tea/coffee-making facilities, complimentary newspaper, late check-out (1500), pool, a/c. Jungle and fishing treks organized, also Island cruises. Two restaurants. Great value although it looks a little spartan.

B Hotel Putra, Jln Iskandar Shah, T5-6838000, dayaent@po.jaring.my New hotel, fully a/c, baths in all bedrooms, TV, telephone, tea/coffee-making facilities, some rooms with lovely view over bay towards Pangkor. Restaurant. Breakfast included in room rate. Good value.

B Lumut Country Resort, 331 Jln Titi Panjang, T5-6835109, F5-6835396. A hotel with 44 a/c rooms, swimming pool, paddling pool, tennis courts, does not quite measure up to the *Orient Star*, but has some attractive features such as hand-printed batik bed covers and wooden floors. Disco, function room. Very good value; one of the best deals in town.

B-C Galaxy Inn, Jln Sultan Idris Shah, T5-6838731, F5-6838732. Clean and simple rooms with attached bathrooms, a/c, apartments available for monthly rental. Seating area with television in foyer. Situated on the sea front.

C Harbour View Hotel, Lot 13 and 14, Jln Titi Panjang, T5-6837888, F5-6837088. Small, quiet hotel on main road along sea front, a/c, TV, mini fridge, tea/coffee-making facilities, bathroom. Recommended. Good value.

C Hotel Indah, 208 Jln Iskandar Shah, T6835064, F6834220. One of the newer budget hotels on the main road along the coast, a/c, TV, hot shower, adjoining coffee house, simply furbished and very clean, with pleasant views over the esplanade. Family run with seating area and café.

C-D Lumut Villa Inn, Batu 1, Jln Sitiawan, T5-6835982, F5-6836563. Inconveniently located outside the town if you do not have your own transport, but good value for money, rooms without a/c (D).

D ERA, opposite bus station, T013 505 4991, sykna@hotmail.com. Six-bed dorm rooms, and big clean doubles, all with shiny tiled floors, shared bathrooms, some with balcony, washing facilities and kitchen. Friendly family atmosphere, owner Mr Syed has a wealth of information for travellers.

Recommended budget option if you have to stay overnight in Lumut.

Pulau Pangkor *p144, map p145*

Room rates are discounted during the week – especially the more expensive hotels. Most of the mid and upper range accommodation is at Pasir Bogak and can be reached from Pangkor village by taxi. Many of the budget places are at Teluk Nipah on the west coast, which requires a rather longer taxi ride in one of the vehicles belonging to Pangkor's taxi mafia. Note that many places increase their room rates by around 50% during public holidays.

L **Pangkor Laut Resort**, Pangkor Laut Island, T5-6991100, reservation T03 21459000, www.pangkorlautresort.com. Malaysia's top resort which is idyllic. The chalets, a blend of Malay and Balinese architecture, are magnificently set, either over the sea (linked by wooden walkways) or on the jungled hillside. Each is beautifully furnished, with carved wood and rattan work. Luxurious bathrooms with recessed tubs and orchids floating on the water's surface greet you upon arrival. A/c, mini-bar, CD player (TV in lounge only), immaculate kimonos, fresh fruit. Other facilities include well-stocked library (books and CDs), 3 swimming pools, squash, watersports, health club, gymnasium, sauna, spa, jacuzzi. A steep hike, or a short shuttle ride, takes you to Emerald Bay, one of the most perfect sandy bays in Malaysia. The wildlife on Pangkor Laut is also remarkably abundant and diverse – from hornbills to macaques – and the jungle treks are recommended. Paradise it may be, but some kayakers who said they had paddled secretly to the island, report seeing dregs of litter along the island's waterline, similar to the detritus that spoils the beaches on the main island. Even so, this place comes highly recommended if you have no limit to your budget.

L-AL **Sri Bayu Beach Resort**, Pasir Bogak, T5-6851929, sribayu_hotels@hotmail.com Chalets, suites and rooms, oriental-style décor, a/c, TV, bath, pool, tennis, karaoke, restaurant, children's club, rather overpriced but a good place to stay on Pasir Bogak.

AL **Pangkor Island Beach Resort**, Teluk Belanga, T5-6851091, www.pangkorislandbeach.com Formerly the Pan Pacific. Secretive resort tucked away in the north corner, serviced by its own ferry with a private 1.2km beach. A/c, restaurants, two pools, limited golf course, tennis courts, watersports, limited business facilities. More expensive rooms have sea views, cheaper ones look on to the garden. Excellent location on wide sandy bay, 240 rooms of varying standard and price.

AL **Teluk Dalam Resort**, T5-685000, www.pangkorresorts.com Unique retreat set in 40 acres of gardens with 160 wooden chalets built to resemble upmarket kampong village homes, but decorated with bland western furniture. Very peaceful and elegant with hornbills in the garden, swimming pool, tennis courts, nursery and video games room.

A-B **Hornbill Resort**, Teluk Nipah, T5-6852005, F5-6852006. All rooms with sea views and balcony, a/c, TV, hot shower, good breakfast menu, seafood restaurant, popular bar with local and imported brews, and recommended at sunset.

A-B **Nipah Bay Villa**, Teluk Nipah, T5-6852198, F5-6852386, A/c, shower, attractive wooden cottages, well equipped. Access to video library and internet, laundry service, motorbike hire, traditional massage, also has a restaurant, breakfast included in room rate. Discounts available for stays of over one night.

A-B **Pangkor Coral Bay Resort**, Pasir Bogak, T5-6855111, www.pangkorcoralbay.com.my Six-storey, tired white building, the only hotel of this size on this part of the island. Great value for money considering the facilities - TV, a/c, pool, small gym, disco/karaoke, jacuzzi, sauna. Two restaurants, and watersports are organised. The interior needs a spruce up though and it's a five minute walk to the beach.

A-B **Pangkor Puteri Resort**, Pasir Bogak, T5-6853409, www.pangkorputeri.com Pasir Bogak's newest offering housed in two incongruous orange box-like buildings. But inside there's big, clean suites with fully-equipped kitchen, living room, bedrooms, balcony and a sea view for rooms in front. Great value for three people sharing on a weekday (RM120).

A-B **Seaview**, Pasir Bogak, T5-6851605, F5-6851970. A/c, restaurant, watersports, fishing, boat trips, pool, tennis and badminton, breakfast included in room rate. (Package for 3 or more people including all meals RM85-120.)

B Coral View Beach Resort, Pasir Bogak, T5-6852190, www.coralviewresort.com.my Formerly Khoo's. Cute chalets on hillside surrounded by trees; a very tranquil spot with hornbills and macaques sneaking around at night to pinch leftover food. Upper level chalets have great sea views. Simple accommodation away from the backpacker crowd, has a core of loyal guests who make return visits spanning decades. Simple restaurant, and rooms in a block, with or without a/c; sea tours arranged. Good views, friendly staff, motorbike hire. Quiet strip of beach out front. Ten minute walk to Pasir Bogak proper makes it a little isolated and hard to find a taxi.

B Flora Beach Resort, Teluk Nipah, T5-7762805, F5-6853878. Chalets similar in style to a number of other places, such as the *Purnama*. Breakfast included.

B-C Nipah Water Front, Teluk Nipah, T5-6855485. Fairly new beachfront place, one of the more upmarket backpacker choices. Big comfy beds, clean and roomy. Same family ownership as Vikry Resort at Pasir Bogak.

B-C Seagull Beach Resort, Teluk Nipah, T5-6852878, F5-6852857. Longhouse, mini-cabins and chalets all with bathroom and television. A/c or fan. Good location and quiet too. Clean, friendly, serves Western breakfast (not included in room rate), games and badminton available.

B-C Sunshine Beach Resorts, Teluk Nipah, T0125641198, jefftan10@hotmail.com. One of the newest budget places. Currently four pleasant chalets, friendly owner, motorbike hire and good seafood restaurant. Recommended by other travellers.

B-C Suria Beach Resort, Lot 4441, Teluk Nipah, T5-6853922, F5-6853921. A/c, shower, rooms here are clean enough but spartan and lacking in character. Overcapacity of rooms makes bargaining possible here. Restaurant serves Malay and Western food. Avoid cycle rental – not good bikes.

B-D Pangkor Village Beach Resort, Pasir Bogak, T5-6852227, F5-6853787. A/c chalet include breakfast and dinner. Also, A-frames and tents. Fairly unfriendly place, and a shade expensive for what's on offer. Basic chalets, huts and tents which get hot during the day, although it has a quiet setting next to the beach with some nice gardens.

B-D Purnama Beach Resort, Teluk Nipah, T5-6853530, pbr2000@tm.net.my Chalets with fan or a/c, breakfast included, some rooms with TV, restaurant, internet access and games, karaoke, mini swimming pool, motorbike hire and laundry service.

C Mizam Resort, Teluk Nipah, T/F5-6853359. A/c chalets with attached bathrooms. Restaurant serving Malay, Chinese and Western dishes. Clean and in a quiet location at the end of a row of resorts. Friendly staff, good value. Recommended.

C Zek Pink, Teluk Nipah,T5-6853529, zek_pink@tm.net.my Curiously named but well-equipped resort popular with Malaysian tourists. Rooms with a/c or fan, attached bathroom, TV, restaurant. Island trips available.

C-D Coral Beach Camp, Teluk Nipah, T5-6852711, F5-6852796. A-frame huts with additional cost for bathroom, family rooms split between 5; organizes watersport, motorbike hire. Dorm available for 8 people sharing. Rather basic.

C-D Lima Chalets, Teluk Nipah, T6852494. Chalets with fan and bathroom. One of a number of resorts with identical chalets. Clean but nothing special.

C-D Ombak Inn Resort, Teluk Nipah, T5-6855223. Small and simple resort comprising a few a/c wood chalets some A-frames and tents. A good-value option for backpackers.

C-D Vikry Resort, Pasir Bogak, T5-6854258. Ten a/c chalets in spacious grounds. Rusty A-frames reserved for school trips. Plans to build beachfront rooms. The Indian restaurant is one of the best places to eat on the island. Friendly staff. Recommended.

D Joe Fisherman Village, Teluk Nipah, T5-6852389. One of the most popular budget places to stay with simple A-frame chalets with 2 mattresses on the floor and a fan, bicycles for hire, meals available.

Eating

Ipoh *p138, maps p139 and p147*

Ipoh is well known for its Chinese food, especially Ipoh chicken rice and *kway teow* – liquid and fried versions. The pomelo and the seedless guava are both grown in the state of Perak, and the state is also known for its delicious groundnuts.

Malay

Kafe Abarnaashre, 27-29 Jln Tun Sambantham. Bustling hall with good, cheap Malay and Indian food.

Chinese

Jalan Yau Tet Shin The place to go for late evening Chinese food with beer.
Foh San, Jln Osbourne, *dim sum*.
Kawan, Jln Sultan Iskandar Shah, also Malay and Indian dishes.
Ming Court, 36 Jln Leong Sin Nam, dim sum.
Mung Cheong, 511 Jln Pasir Putih, Cantonese.
Nam Thim Tong, Mile 3.5 Gopeng Rd, Chinese, vegetarian, serves ersatz meat dishes made of soya bean.
Lou Wong Tauge Ayam Kuetiau, 49 Jln Yau Tet Shin. Big corner restaurant, good for late night Chinese fare with tables spilling onto the street.
Chuan Fong, 175 Jln Sultan Iskandar, speciality is curry *laksa*.
Foh San, 2 Osbourne St, popular for Hong Kong *dim sum*, served 0600-1200.
Woh Heng Coffee Shop, Osbourne St, good rice and noodles.

Indian

Rahman, 78 Jln CM Yussuf, good food, with banana pancakes or *roti* for breakfast. Friendly, chatty owner.
Shal's Curry House, 4 Jln Dato Maharaja Lela, a/c, excellent South Indian food and good vegetarian dishes. Recommended.
Mohamad Ibrahim, 786 Jln Yang Kalsom, speciality is *mee rebus*.

International

Royal Casuarina Coffee House, and **Il Ritrove**, Italian restaurant specializing in nouvelle cuisine, 18 Jln Gopeng
Blue Window Café, 56 Jln Dato Onn Jaafar, Western food, aspires to 'romantic' atmosphere.
Excelsior Hotel Coffee House, 43 Jln Clarke.
Ever Fresh Juice Station, 21 Jln Mustapha al Bakri, good fresh juice bar.
Restuncle House, 13 Jln Tun Sanbatham. Supercheap Malay dishes and great iced drinks (try their ice cappucino mix) served in a Bob Marley inspired café, also tables on the street facing the Padang. Very cheap and good food, beautifully presented. Friendly owner Amy speaks excellent English and can offer traveller advice. Live band on Saturdays. Recommended.

Foodstalls

Jln Clarke, Jln Dewan, Ipoh Garden, Jln Sultan Idris Shah, mainly Chinese stalls. **Railway Station**, Jln Kelab. Recommended. **Wooley Food Centre**, Canning Gardens. On Jln Ali Pitchay is **Restoran Impressive Foodstalls**, cheap and clean. Recommended.

Kuala Kangsar *p141*

Many restaurants only open at lunchtime, it can be a problem eating after dusk. The smartest restaurant seems to be the overpriced *Hotel Seri Kangsar*. In front of here is an Indian restaurant open from early morning until late evening serving good *roti canai* and chapati. The market has foodstalls serving Malay food and there's a bakery beside the Double Lion Hotel. There's a supermarket on Jln Kangsar selling most goods.

Taiping *p142, map p143*

Dragon Phoenix, Jln Kota. Chinese food.
Malaysia Restoran, 36 Jln Eastern. Chinese food.
Nagaria Steak House, 61 Jln Pasar, dark interior, popular for beer drinking.
Panorama, 61-79 Jln Kota, mediocre Western food and steakhouse.
Kedai Kopi Sentosa, Jln Kelab Cina, good Teow Chiew noodles.
Kum Loong, 45-47 Jln Kota, good dim sum 0500-1000, good place to experience local 'bustle'! Recommended.
Prima Restaurant, 21-23 Jln Kota.
Restoran Bumi, Jln Kota (next door to *Kum Loong*). Malay restaurant. Serves some western dishes.

Foodstalls

Large **night market** on Jln Panggung Wayang. **Hawker Centre** in Metro Arcade (Shopping Centre), 54 Medan Simpang (5 km from town centre, on road to Kuala Kangsar). **Malay hawker stalls** on Jln Tupai.

Burger, rice and fried chicken stalls near foot of Bukit Larut (Maxwell Hill).

Around Taiping *p143*

TT **Rumah Hijau** or **Bukit Larut** guesthouses.

Lumut *p144, map p144*

TT **Capri**, 4174 Jln Sultan Idris Shah, T5-6833112. Soups, salads, ice cream and a long list of pastas and oven-baked pizzas.
TT **Ocean Seafood Restaurant**, 115 Jln Tit Panjang, a/c, specializes in Chinese and seafood.
TT **Sin Pinamhui**, 93-95 Jln Titi Panjang, traditional Chinese food.
T **Jook Joint**, Jln Sultan Idris Shah, bistro food for a change from rice and *roti*.
T **Kedai Makan Sin Pinamhui** (**Green House Restaurant**), 95 Jln Titi Panjang. Another worthwhile Malay place to try; open 1030-1445 and 1715-2045, closed Thu.
T **Makanan Laut Ocean Restaurant**, Jln Titi Panjang, fresh fish dishes available.
T **Nasi Kandar**, 46 Jln Sultan Idris Shah, friendly and clean, with excellent rice and *roti*. Serves good vegetarian rice. Recommended.
T **Phin Lum Hooi**, next to Chinese Temple on Jln Titi Panjang, cheap Chinese coffee-shop fare.
T **Restoran Samudera Raya**, 39 Jln Sultan Idris Shah, Indian and Malay food.

Pulau Pangkor *p144, map p145*

Most hotels and chalets have their own restaurants – most end up eating where they are staying. Seafood is always on the menu
TTT **Pangkor Laut Resort**, Pangkor Laut Island, T5-6991100, reservation T03 2145 9000, www.pangkorlautresort.com Eating at the resort is a delight; top-quality seafood at the *Fisherman's Cove*, steamboat at *Uncle Lim's*, or western fare at the *Sumudra* where chimes blow in the breeze.
TT **Coco**, Pasir Bogak. Outdoor seafood restaurant and local dishes. Recommended.
T **Fook Heng**, Pangkor village, simple coffee shop but excellent quality Chinese food, seafood prices are high.
T **Guan Guan**, Pangkor village, specializes in seafood.
T **Juo**, in the same street as the Hornbill Resort, excellent food and fresh fish in this Indonesian restaurant.
T **Vikry Resort**. Excellent home-cooked dishes served on banana leaves. One of Pangkor's best kept secrets. Recommended.
T **Wah Mooi**, Sungai Pinang Kecil, steamed carp recommended by locals. .
T **Ye Lin Seafood Garden**, 200 Jln Pasir Bogak, popular outdoor restaurant, prides itself on its low prices.

Foodstalls

On Pasir Bogak and Teluk Nipah.

Bars and clubs

Ipoh *p138, maps p139 and p147*

Apart from the bars and discos in four-star hotels there are a couple of bars near the train station.
Sixties Coffee Shop, 4, Jln Dato Mahaaraja Lela. A rather gloomy bar that does not serve coffee, filled with sixties memorabilia – old posters and album covers. Quirky.
Miner's Arms, Jln Dato Mahaaraja Lela. A British-themed pub.

Lumut *p144, map p144*

New bars (and restaurants) are springing up along the sea front, possibly due to Navy influence and growing popularity of Pulau Pangkor. Bars serve beer on tap and are more often than not Western – as in Wild West – themed.

Activities and tours

Ipoh *p138, maps p139 and p147*

DBI Sports Complex, Perak Sports Centre, Lebuh Raya Thivy, T5-5460651. Largest swimming complex in Southeast Asia. Other facilities include: tennis, indoor badminton, table tennis, volleyball, basketball, a velodrome rugby pitch, stadium. Admission charge. Open 0900-2100.
Perak Turf Club, Jln Raja Dihilir, 30350 Ipoh, Perak, T5-2540505. Races held every Sat and Sun.
Royal Perak Golf Club, Jln Sultan Azlan Shah, 3 km from town centre, T5-573266 18-hole course laid out over 420 ha, only open to visitors on weekdays, members only at weekends and holidays. Clubhouse facilities include bowling alley, cards and billiards room, and bar.

Tour operators

Deluxe Tours, 58 Jln Dato Tahwil Azhar (Jln Osbourne), T5-2537260, F5-2558969, air ticketing, tours, hotel reservations.
Fiyen Travels, 1-3 Jln Che Tak, T5-2533455, F5-2506709, sightseeing tours, hotel reservations, domestic and international air ticketing.
HWA Yik Tour & Travel, 23 Jln Che Tak, T5-2504060, F5-2530118, tours, hotel reservation, domestic and international air ticketing, mini-bus rental.
K&C Travel, K & C Travel & Tours, 250 Jln Sultan Iskandar, T5-2506999, F5-2502154, airline ticketing, hotel reservation, travel insurance, foreign exchange.
Keris, 4-6 & 13-19 Jln Ali Pitchay, T5-2552666, www.keristravel.com Also has a money exchange.
Khong Bros, 21, Jln Ali Pitchay, T5-2534000, F5-2532076. Ticketing and tours.
Reliance, Lot 1-12 1st Flr, Bangunan Sri Kinta, Jln Sultan Idris Shah, T5-2518711, F5-2538458, ticketing, travel shop, travel insurance.

Kuala Kangsar *p141*

No 3 MDKK, Jln Tebing, T5-7769717. Three-day canoe safaris depart from Kuala Kangsar and follow the Perak for almost its entire length to the Cherendoh dam.

Taiping *p142, map p143*

Bukit Jana Golf & Country Club, Jln Bukit Jana, T5-8837500. Clubhouse has pool, paddling pool, tennis, squash, kids' playground, card room and restaurant.

Tour operators

Fulham Tours, 25 Jln Kelab Cina, T5-8073039, F5-8081330, ticketing, hotel reservation, licensed money changers.
Poly Travels, 53 Jln Mesjid, T5-820155, ticketing, currency exchange, hotel reservation, tours.
Trans Asia Pacific, 112 Jln Barrack, T5-828451, ticketing, hotel reservation, car hire, package tours.

Pulau Pangkor *p144, map p145*

Pangkor Island Beach Resort, Teluk Belanga, Golden Sands, T5-6851091, 9-hole golf course, on the coast.
Pangkor Yacht Club, Teluk Gedong, T5-6853478, watersports facilities, including jet skis, sailing and snorkelling, also organize fishing trips and round-island tours.

Transport

Ipoh *p138, maps p139 and p147*

Air

Sultan Azlan Shah Airport, T5-3122459, approximately 15 km south of town, RM10 taxi ride.
Airline offices MAS, Lot 108 Bangunan Seri Kinta, Jln Sultan Idris Shah, T5-2414155.

Bus

Ipoh is on the main north-south road and is well connected. The bus terminal is on Medan Kidd, a short taxi trip from the town centre. Buses to **Taiping**, **Lumut** and **Kuala Kangsar** leave from the local bus terminal opposite. Regular connections with **Butterworth**, **KL** (3 hrs), **Alor Star**, Kuantan, Sungai Petani, **Johor Bahru**, **Kangar**, **Kuala Perlis**, **Lumut** (1 hr 45 mins, roughly every 30 mins, first bus at 0730, last bus at 1930, RM4.50) and Tapah (90 mins). There are also services to **Kota Bharu** via **Grik/Gerik**. An express coach company has a booking office at 2 Jln Bendahara, T5-535367. It operates a daily service to **Singapore, Johor Bahru, KL, Butterworth, Penang, Lumut, Alor Star** and Kuala Kangsar.

Car hire

Avis, Sultan Azian Shah Airport, T5-206586.
Hertz, *Royal Casuarina Hotel*, 18 Jln Gopeng, T5-2505533, and Sultan Azlan Shah Airport, T5-3127109.

Taxi

Nam Taxi Company, 15 Jln Raja Mus Aziz, T5-2412189.
Radiocab, T5-2540241.
Shared taxis leave from beside the bus station for **KL, Butterworth, Taiping, Alor Star, Tapah**. Connections with **Hat Yai** in southern Thailand.

Train

Ipoh is on the main north-south line. Two daily connections north with **Butterworth and Hat Yai** and two daily going south to **KL**, T5-2540481. See page 40 and 41 for timetable.

Kuala Kangsar *p141*

Bus

The bus terminal is in the centre of town on Jln Raja Bendahara. Regular connections with **Ipoh**, **Butterworth**, **KL**, **Lumut**, **Taiping** and **Kota Bharu**. Taxi: the only local transport available. Taxis leave from close to the bus station for destinations including **Butterworth, KL, Ipoh** and **Taiping**.

Train

The station is out of town to the northeast, on Jln Sultan Idris. Trains on the KL-Butterworth route also stop here.

Around Taiping *p143*

The steep walk from Taiping Lake Gardens takes about 2½-3½ hrs. The road is restricted and private cars are not permitted. A Land Rover service runs from the foot of the hill just above the Lake Garden in Taiping, every hr 0700-1800, T5-827243.

Taiping *p142, map p143*

Bus

The main long-distance bus station is 7 km out of town and getting there means either catching a town bus or a taxi. Regular connections with **Butterworth**, **Ipoh**, **Sungai Petani** and **KL**. There is also a morning bus to **Kuantan** on the east coast. For other connections, change at Ipoh. Local buses for **Ipoh**, **Grik**, **Lumut** and **Kuala Kangsar** leave from the local bus station, which is much more conveniently located in the centre of town at the intersection of Jln Masjid and Jln Iskandar.

Train

The station is on the west side of town. Lying on the north-south railway line, there are twice daily connections with **Ipoh**, **KL** and **Butterworth** (see page 40 and 41 for timetables).

Lumut *p144, map p144*

Bus

The bus station is in the centre of town, a few mins' walk from the jetty. Regular connections with **Ipoh**, **KL** and **Butterworth** and less regular connections with **Melaka**. Bus every 30 mins from Ipoh (1 hr 45 mins). Buses also run between **Lumut** and **Singapore**.

Ferry

Pan Silver Ferry has regular crossings, at least every 30 mins from 0700 to 2100 from Lumut Jetty to **Pangkor village** on **Pangkor Island**. The crossing takes under 30 mins, RM5 one way.. Crossings every 2 hrs from 0845 to 1830 to Pangkor Island Beach Resort at the north end of Pangkor Island.

Taxi

Services to **Ipoh**, **KL** and **Butterworth**.

Pulau Pangkor *p144, map p145*

Air

The airport on the north of the island is used by Berjaya Air's 48-seater Dash-7's to carry passengers between Pangkor and **KL**. The 50-min flight leaves KL for Pangkor 1030, returns at 1130 on Mon, Wed, Fri, Sat and Sun, RM225 one way, RM450 return. T5-6854516.

Boat

Ferries leave from **Lumut** jetty (watch out for the hotel touts). Connections every 30 mins to Pangkor Jetty (RM5 one-way, 30 mins, first boat from Lumut at 0700, last boat at 2100; from Pangkor, first departure at 0640, last one at 2100), also regular connections with Pangkor Island Beach Resort, jetty close to Golden Sands (RM6 one-way). There are plans to build a larger jetty with a tourist information board listing all the resorts on the island with contact information. There are inter-island ferries or it is possible to hire fishing boats from the main villages. Large hotels will organize trips to the islands.

Bus/taxi

There is a fleet of pink taxis, or more accurately minbuses (*Kereta Isewa*), from Pangkor village to **Pasir Bogak,Teluk Nipah** and **Pangkor Island Beach Resort**. There are no meters, and the prices are fixed. You can share a taxi to cut costs. RM8 to Pasir Bogak, RM10 to Coral View Resort, RM18 to Telok Nipah, 25RM to Pangkor Island Beach Resort and RM18 to Teluk Dalam. Cabs wait at the jetty and at the above sites.

Motorbike/bicycle hire

It is possible to hire motorbikes from Pangkor village for RM20-30 per day, while most resorts and chalet operations have both motorbikes and bicycles for hire.

Directory

Ipoh *p138, maps p139 and p147*
Banks Bank Bumiputra, Hock Hua Bank, Malayan Banking and Maybank are all on Jln Sultan Idris Shah; UMBC, Oriental Bank and Public Bank, are on Jln Yang Kalsom; in the new town, along Jln Sultan Yussuf there is a Southern Bank, Hong Kong Bank, Standard Chartered and Bank of Commerce. (see Tour operators) also have foreign exchange facilities. **Internet** Infoweb Station, Jln Dato Onn Jaafar, near Jln Sultan Idris Shah. **Post** Next to the railway station on Jln Panglima Bukit Gantang Wahab. There is another Post Office on Jln Dato Onn Jaafar.

Kuala Kangsar *p141*
Post Jln Taiping, near the clock tower.

Taiping *p142, map p143*
Banks Bank Bumiputra and UMBC on Jln Kota; Standard Chartered at crossroads of Jln Kota and Jln Sultan Abdullah. Poly Travels, 53 Jln Mesjid and Fulham Tours, 25 Jln Kelab Cina, have foreign exchange facilities. **Internet** Discover de Internet, 3 Jln Panggong Wayang, T5-8069487, RM2.50/hr. Services include printing, scanning and faxing. Helm Computer Technology Centre, Jln Kota, T5-8082454, F5-8086525. **Post** Jln Barrack.

Lumut *p144, map p144*
Banks Pengurup Wang Raya, 47 Jln Sultan Idris Shah; Bank BumiputeraJln Sultan Idris Shah. Bank Simpanan Nasional, Jln Sultan Idris Shah. **Post** Jln Dato JK Ishak.

Pulau Pangkor *p144, map p145*
Banks Large hotels will change money and there's a Maybank in Pangkor village.

Penang

Colour map 1, grid B1 Population: 1.2 million

Penang – or, more properly, Pulau Pinang – is the northern gateway to Malaysia and is the country's oldest British settlement. It has been sold to generations of tourists as 'the Pearl of the Orient', but in shape Penang looks more like a frog than a pearl. Although the island is best known as a beach resort, it is also a cultural gem with Chinese, Malay and Indian influences. Georgetown has the largest collection of pre-war houses in all Southeast Asia.

Penang State includes a strip of land on the mainland opposite, Province Wellesley – named after Colonel Arthur Wellesley, later to become the Duke of Wellington, who went on to defeat Napoleon at Waterloo. Covering an area of 738 sq km, Province Wellesley is also known by its Malay name, Seberang Perai. Georgetown's founder, Captain Francis Light, originally christened Penang's Prince of Wales Island. In Malay, pinang is the word for the areca nut palm, an essential ingredient of betel nut. The palm was incorporated into the state crest in the days of the Straits Settlements during the 19th century. Today Pulau Pinang is translated as 'betel-nut island'. Light named Georgetown after George, the Prince of Wales, who later became King George IV as it was acquired on his birthday; most Malaysians know the town by its nickname, Tanjung, as it is situated on a sandy headland called Tanjung Penaga.

▸▸ For Sleeping, Eating and other listings, see pages 169-181.

Ins and outs

Getting there

Penang airport is 20 km south of Georgetown and there are regular connections with KL, JB and Langkawi as well asinternational links with a handful of regional capitals and now MAS flies direct from London (the return trip must be made via KL). Direct bus connections link the island via the 13-km-long Penang Bridge with KL and a host

Penang Riots of 1867

The nine days of fighting started when a member of the White Flag society (a Malay gang) threw a rambutan skin at a Toh-Peh-Kong society member whom he caught peering through his front door. Open warfare ensued and bullet holes can still be seen in the walls of the shophouses in Cannon Square.

The riots were finally put down when troop reinforcements arrived from Singapore.

The societies were fined RM5,000 each, which funded the construction of four new police stations in the different parts of town where the societies operated.

of Peninsula towns as well as international services in Thailand and Singapore. Those wishing to take the train need to alight at Butterworth, see page 168, and make their way across the bridge from there (or take the ferry); taxis also tend to terminate there, with local taxis making the run across the bridge to the island; long-distance taxis will, however, cross the bridge for an extra charge. Ferries leave from Georgetown for Belawan, on Sumatra, Indonesia and for Langkawi and from there to Thailand. ▸▸ *See also Transport, page 179.*

Getting around

There are bus services including a free shuttle bus that does a circuit stopping at most tourist destinations in Georgetown (Mon-Fri 0700-1900, Sat 0700-1400 Sat, every 12 minutes; the stops are marked with red circular signs enclosing a number) around the island and in the tourist areas there are plenty of taxis. It is also possible to hire self-drive cars and motorbikes from local and international firms. In Georgetown there are city buses and taxis as well as a number of trishaws. There are also bicycles for rent.

Orientation

Georgetown, the capital of Penang state, is on the northeast point of the island, nearest the mainland; Bayan Lepas Airport is on the southeast tip. The 13 km Penang Bridge, linking the island to Butterworth, is half-way down the east coast, just south of Georgetown. Batu Ferringhi, now a strip of luxury hotels, is Penang's most famous beach and is on the north coast.,There are still a handful of small, secluded coves with good beaches on the northwest tip of the island. The west of the island is a mixture of jungle-covered hills, rubber plantations and a few fishing kampongs. There are more beaches and fishing villages on the south coast. A short, steep mountain range forms a central spine, which includes Penang Hill, overlooking Georgetown, at 850 m above sea level.

Tourist offices

Penang Tourist Centre, ⓘ *Penang Port Commission Building, Jln Tun Syed Sheikh Barakbah (off Victoria Clocktower roundabout, opposite Fort Cornwallis), T4-2616663, Mon-Fri 0800-1630, Sat 0800-1300, closed 1st and 3rd Sat and every Sun.* This tourist office is known to be unreliably informed on occasions. Often your best bet for finding out information is to ask the locals. Restaurant and café owners are particularly helpful. A monthly tourist freebie newspaper is published, the *Penang Tourist Newspaper*, useful for checking out special deals, restaurants and latest fares and fees. **Tourism Malaysia Northern Regional Office,** ⓘ *10 Jln Tun Syed Sheh Barakbah, round the corner from the Penang Tourist Association, T4-2620066.* One of the best places is the **Tourist Information Centre,** ⓘ *3rd Flr,*

Penang's local newspaper in English can be read at http://penang.thestar.com.my

Boxing Day tsunami batters Malaysia

The Indian Ocean earthquake that triggered a tsunami on 26 December 2004 smashed into the top western coastline of Malaysia. At least 68 Malaysians were killed, dozens injured and thousands made homeless. Estimates put the cost of the disaster for Malaysia at 100 million ringgit.

Most of the victims were picknickers or fishermen in Penang, although several people perished in coastal villages in Kota Kuala Muda in Kedah state, and Langkawi suffered some damage.

The quake-powered waves which crashed into Malaysia were much slower because they were secondary or deflected waves that bent around Indonesia and travelled at around 160 km/h.

Soon after the disaster, Kuala Lumpur was at pains to reassure the international community that it was safe to travel to Malaysia. Four days after the tsunami, the Penang Tourism Council issued a "business as usual" statement, claiming hotels were at 75 per cent occupancy, flights were running as normal and beaches were cleared of debris.

The quake which was triggered at around 9am Malaysia time, generated giant waves which hit Penang's Miami Beach, Batu Ferringhi and Pantai Pasir Panjang, coastal areas in Kedah state and Langkawi's Pantai Cenang and Kuala Teriang almost five hours later at 1:40pm. Langkawi reported no fatalities although a couple of hotels closed for repairs on Pantai Cenang, and several boats and yachts were lost from Telaga harbour.

The government gave RM20,000 to families of the 68 dead Malaysians.

KOMTAR Tower, Jln Penang, T4-2614461, the office is hidden around a bend opposite the McDonald's. Also branch at Batu Ferringhi, outside Eden Seafood Village, and at Bayan Lepas Airport, T4-6430501, Mon-Sat 1000-1800, the information centre has a list of tour companies in Georgetown. You can pick up a copy of the Penang Tourist newspaper here (RM2, else free at hotels and the main tourist office opposite Fort Cornwallis). It is particularly useful for event information.

The three main **tours** offered by companies are: the city tour; the Penang Hill and temple tour; and the round-the-island tour. All cost RM45-85 with two departures a day, usually one around 0900 and one at 1400. See also Tour operators.

History

Before the arrival of Francis Light, who captained a ship for a British trading company, in 1786, Penang was ruled by the Sultan of Kedah. The sultanate had suffered repeated invasions by the Thais from the north and Bugis pirates from the sea. Sultan Muhammad Jawa Mu'Azzam Shah II was also beset by a secession crisis and when this turned into a civil war he requested help from Francis Light, then based at Acheen in Sumatra, whom he met in 1771. Light was in search of a trading base on the north shore of the Strait of Melaka, which could be used by his firm, Jordain, Sulivan and De Souza, and the British East India Company. In 1771, Light sent a letter to one of his bosses, De Souza, in which he first described Penang's advantages, but before De Souza made up his mind, Light struck a private deal with the Sultan of Kedah. The Sultan installed Light in the fort at Kuala Kedah and gave him the title of Deva Rajah, ceding to him control of the Kedah coast as far south as Penang. In turn, Light promised to protect the Sultan from his many enemies.

A frisson between Sultan Muhammad and the East India Company brought developments to a standstill in 1772. Light left Kedah and sailed to Ujung Salang, which English sailors called 'Junk Ceylon' and is now known as Phuket, where he built up a trading network. Eleven years later he finally repaired relations with Kedah and the newly installed Sultan Abdullah agreed to lease Penang to the British – again, in return for military protection. On 11 August 1786, Light formally took possession of Penang. The island was covered in dense jungle and was uninhabited, apart from a handful of Malay fishermen and a few Bugis pirates.

A township grew up around the camp by the harbour. A wooden stockade was built to defend the island on the site of the original camp and the cantonment was called Fort Cornwallis, after Marquis Cornwallis, the then Governor-General of India. Light declared Prince of Wales Island a free port to attract trade away from the Dutch, and this helped woo many immigrant traders to Penang. Penang's status as a free port was only withdrawn in 1969. Settlers were allowed to claim any land they could clear. The island soon became a cultural and religious melting pot. By 1789, Georgetown had a population of 5,000, and by the end of century the number had more than doubled.

Penang

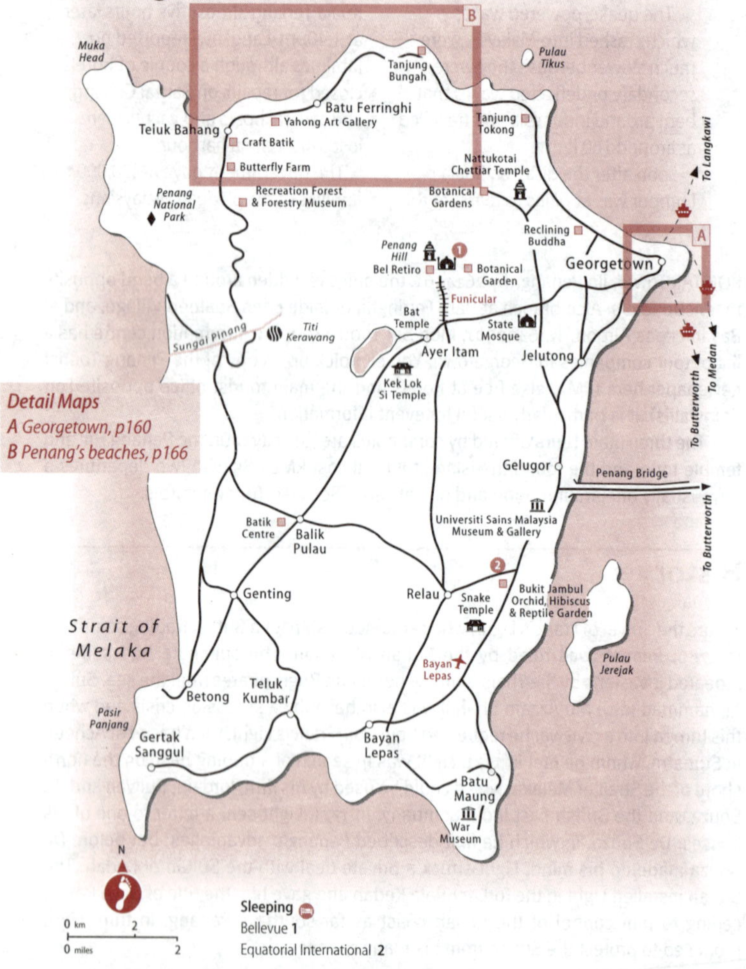

The Sultan of Kedah was upset that the East India Company had not signed a written contract setting out the terms of Penang's lease. When the company began to haggle with him over the price and the military protection he had been promised, Sultan Abdullah believed the British were backing out of their agreement. In alliance with the Illanun pirates, the Sultan blockaded Penang in 1790 and tried to force the Company's hand. Light went on the offensive and quickly defeated the Sultan's forces. The vanquished Sultan Abdullah agreed to an annual fee of 6,000 Spanish dollars for Penang. Francis Light remained the island's superintendent until his death, from malaria, in 1794. The disease, which struck down many early settlers, earned Penang the epithet of 'the White Man's Grave'.

Despite Georgetown's cosmopolitan atmosphere, there remained a strong British influence: the British judicial system was introduced in 1801 with the appointment of the first magistrate and judge, an uncle of novelist Charles Dickens. The previous year, Colonel Arthur Wellesley had signed a new Treaty of Peace, Friendship and Alliance with Kedah's new Sultan Diyauddin, which superseded Light's 1791 agreement and allowed for Penang's annexation of Province Wellesley, on the coast of the peninsula, in return for an annual payment of 10,000 Spanish dollars.

In 1805 Penang's colonial status was raised to that of a Residency. A young administrative secretary, Stamford Raffles, arrived to work for the governor. Georgetown became the capital of the newly established Straits Settlements, which included Melaka and Singapore (see page 483). But the glory was shortlived. Following Raffles's founding of Singapore in 1819, Georgetown was quickly eclipsed by the upstart at the southern tip of the peninsula and by the 1830s had been reduced to a colonial backwater. From an architectural perspective, this proved a saving grace: unlike Singapore, Penang retains many of its original colonial buildings and rich cultural heritage.

Colonial Penang prospered, through tin booms and rubber booms, until the outbreak of the Second World War. When the Japanese raced down the peninsula on stolen bicycles, Penang was cut off, without being formally taken. The British residents were evacuated to Singapore within days, leaving the undefended island in the hands of a State Committee, which, after three days, put down the riots that followed the British withdrawal. The Japanese administration lasted from December 1941 to July 1945; remarkably, Georgetown's buildings survived virtually unscathed, despite Allied bombing attacks.

Today, Chinese make up just over half of Penang's population, while 35% are Malay and 11% Indian. Penang, along with the other two Straits settlements of Melaka and Singapore, was a centre of Peranakan culture. Peranakans, also known as Babas or Straits Chinese, evolved their own unique blend of Malay and Chinese cultures (see page 499). The Babas of Penang, however, have almost disappeared as a distinctive group – although various shops and restaurants play to the Peranakan theme.

Georgetown

The original four streets of Georgetown – Beach (now known as Lebuh Pantai), Lebuh Light, Jalan Masjid Kapitan Kling (previously Lebuh Pitt) and Lebuh Chulia – still form the main thoroughfares of modern Georgetown. Lebuh Chulia was formerly the Cantonese heartland of the Ghee Hin triad, one of the secret societies involved in the 1867 Penang Riots. The older part of town to the west of Weld Quay, in the shadow of Kapitan Kling Mosque, is predominantly Indian.

At 13.5 km, Penang bridge is the longest in Asia and the third longest in the world.

Georgetown is, however, mainly Chinese; the main Chinatown area is contained by Jalan Kapitan Kling Mosque, Lebuh Chulia, Jalan Penang and Jalan Magazine. The shophouses were built by Chinese craftsmen: the rituals, burial customs, clan associations, temples and restaurants make up a self-contained Chinese community. Despite the traffic and a skyline pierced by the Kompleks Tun Abdul Razak (KOMTAR) skyscraper, the streets still have charm. There are an estimated 12,000 pre-war houses still standing in Georgetown, making it an architectural gem in Southeast Asian terms.

Penang has managed to preserve at least some of its heritage while that in other Malaysian towns has been torn down partly because of a rent control act – on the statute books for years – which has frozen rents and therefore made redevelopment

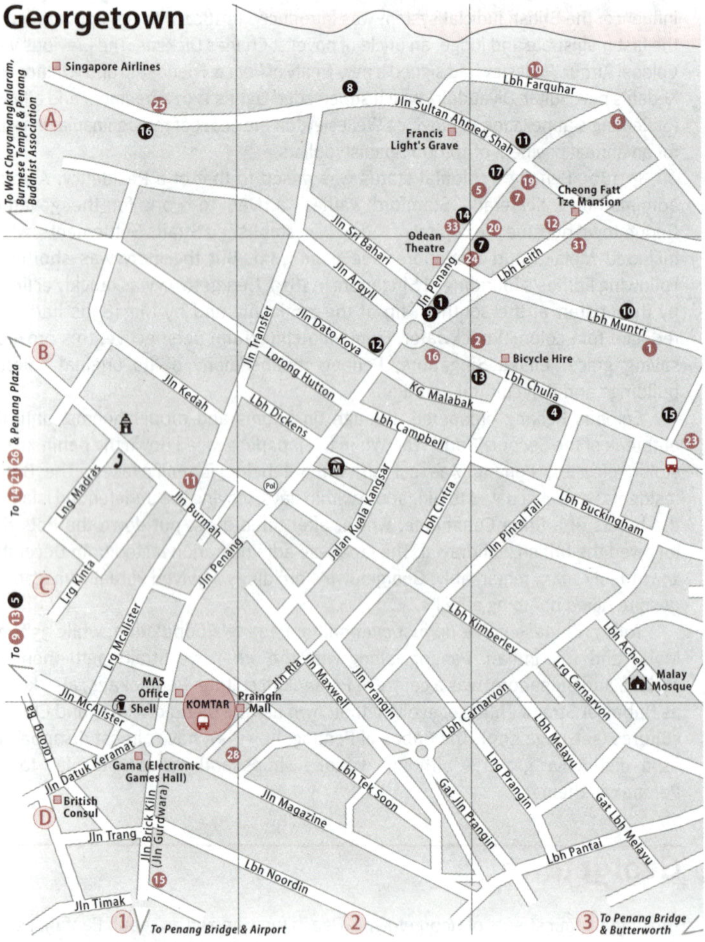

Sleeping

75 Travellers Lodge **1** *B3*
Berjaya Georgetown **21** *B1*
Blue Diamond **2** *B3*
Broadway Hostel **3** *B4*
Cheong Fatt Tze Mansion **12** *A3*
Cititel **5** *A3*
City Bayview **6** *A3*
Continental **7** *A3*
Coral Hostel **4** *C4*
D'Budget Hostel **8** *C5*
Eastern & Oriental **10** *A3*
Embassy **11** *C1*
Grand Continental **15** *D1*
Hang Cheow **16** *B2*
Hong Ping **17** *C4*
Hotel 1926 **14** *C1*
Love Lane Inn **18** *B4*
Malaysia **19** *A3*
Merchant **20** *A3*
Oasis **22** *B4*
Olive Spring & Rainforest Restaurant **23** *B3*
Oriental **24** *B2*
Paramount **25** *A1*

unprofitable. While the houses may be mouldering, at least they aren't (usually) being demolished. This, however, may all change, as this rent control was lifted a few years ago. In an effort to preserve its cultural heritage, Penang has put itself forward for a UNESCO world heritage listing. It is still waiting.

However, not all of the island is worthy of such a status. Pollution and litter have spoiled parts of Penang in recent years. Some beaches are dirty and very few people swim in the sea. The coral that used to line the shore at Batu Feringghi has all gone, mainly due to the silt washed around the headland during the construction of the Penang Bridge. But the sea is not as dirty as in some of the region's other big resorts, as testified by the presence of otters on the beach at Batu Feringghi in the early morning.

Related Map
Penang, p158

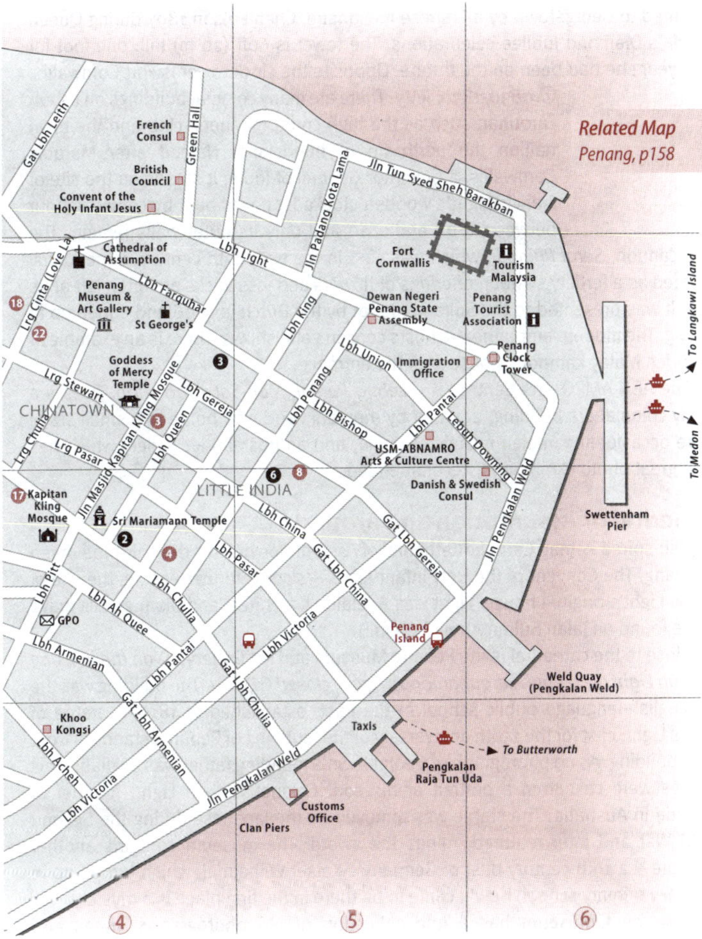

Shangri-La **28** *D1*
Sheraton **26** B1
Sunway **9** C1
Waldorf **31** *B3*
White House **33** *A2*
YMCA **13** *C1*

Eating
Bella Casa **1** *B2*
Datuk Keramat Hawker Centre **5** *C1*
Dawood **2** *C4*
Dragon King **3** *B4*
Ecco Café **15** *B3*
Eng Thye Café **4** *B3*
Green Vege Recipe **9** *B2*
Kaliaman's **6** *C5*
Lum Fong **10** *B3*
Maple **7** *B2*
May Garden **14** *A2*
Ocean-Green **16** *A1*
Passage Thru' India **12** *B2*
Rhak Café **13** *B3*
Sea Palace **17** *A3*
The Garage **11** *A3*
Thirty Two **8** *A2*

Sights

Street names in Georgetown are confusing as many have been rechristened with Malay names; streets are known by both their Malay and English names (for example Jalan Penang/Penang Rd – not to be muddled with Lebuh Penang/Penang Street). Of particular note: Lebuh Pitt (Pitt Street) has been renamed Jalan Masjid Kapitan Kling; Beach Street is now Lebuh Pantai.

Clock Tower, Fort Cornwallis and ABN-AMRO Arts Centre

At the junction of Lebuh Light and Lebuh Pantai is the Penang Clock Tower, which was presented to Georgetown by a Chinese millionaire, Chen Eok, in 1897 during Queen Victoria's Diamond Jubilee celebrations. The tower is 60ft (20 m) tall: one foot for every year she had been on the throne. Opposite the clock tower is Fort Cornwallis, ⓘ *0830-1830, RM3*. There are many colonial buildings on Lebuh Farquhar, such as the high court, mariners' club and the town hall.on the north tip of the island. Named after Marquis Cornwallis, a Governor-General of India, it stands on the site of Francis Light's wooden stockade. It was built by convict labour between 1808 and 1810 and only its outer walls remain. The main cannon, *Serai Rambai*, which was cast in the early 17th century, is popularly regarded as a fertility symbol; offerings of flowers and joss sticks are often left at its base. It was presented to the Sultan of Johor by the Dutch in 1606 and ended up in Penang. The modern amphitheatre hosts concerts and shows. There is an example of a wooden Malay kampong house near the entrance.

Penang's Chinatown is one of the liveliest in Malaysia; its atmosphere and most of its original architecture remain intact.

The ABN-AMRO Arts Centre, ⓘ *9 Lebug Pantai, Mon-Sat 1000-1800, free*, is a stately colonial-era building, donated by the bank, and now home to a small stage where occasional gamelan recitals are held, and an upstairs art gallery which has some great photo exhibitions. Recommended.

Cathedral of Assumption and around

The twin-spired Roman Catholic Cathedral of Assumption houses the only pipe-organ in Penang. The Convent of the Holy Infant Jesus – slightly further east, is the site of Francis Light's original house. Light was Adelaide's architect and planner. His grave can be found on Jalan Sultan Ahmad Shah.

Close to the cathedral is the **Penang Museum and Art Gallery**, ⓘ *on the junction of Lebuh Light and Lebuh Farquhar, 0900-1700, closed Fri, RM1*. The building was the first English-language public school in the east, established in 1816. A statue of Francis Light, cast for the 150th anniversary of the founding of Penang, stands in front of the building. As no photograph of Georgetown's founding father was available, his features were cast from a portrait of his son, Colonel William Light, founder of Adelaide in Australia. The statue was removed by the Japanese during the Second World War and later returned, minus the sword. The museum contains another sculpture – a 19th-century bust of Germany's Kaiser Wilhelm II, which turned up in Wellesley primary school. How it came to be there in the first place is a mystery.

The small museum has a fine collection of old photographs, maps and historical records charting the growth of Penang from the days of Francis Light. There are some fascinating accounts in the History Room of the Penang Riots in August 1867 (see page 156). Downstairs there is a replica of the main hall of a Chinese trader's home and, upstairs, a Straits Chinese exhibition with a marriage chamber and a room of traditional ornamental gowns. The art gallery, also upstairs, has a series of temporary exhibitions.

St George's Church, ⓘ *next door to the museum on Lebuh Farquhar; bus No 4, 7 & 10, also the free shuttle bus stops outside*, was the first Anglican church in

Southeast Asia. It was built in 1817 with convict labour. The building was designed by Captain Robert Smith (some of his paintings are in the State Museum).

The **Goddess of Mercy Temple**, (Kuan Yin Teng), on Jalan Kapitan Kling Mosque/Lorong Steward was built at the beginning of the 1800s by the island's early Chinese immigrants. Kuan Yin is probably the most worshipped of all the Chinese deities, and is revered by Buddhists, Taoists and Confucians. The goddess is a Bodhisattva, one who rejected entry into nirvana as long as there was injustice in the world. The goddess is associated with peace, good fortune and fertility, which accounts for her popularity. Kuan Yin is portrayed as a serene goddess with 18 arms; 2 arms are considered inadequate to rid the world of suffering. The roof-tops are carved to represent waves, on which stand two guardian dragons. Shops in the area sell temple-related goods: lanterns, provisions for the afterlife (such as paper Mercedes cars), joss sticks and figurines.

Although Georgetown is mainly Chinese, it has always had a large population of Indians, living in the city centre. The Hindu **Sri Mariamann Temple**, on Lebuh Queen/Lebuh Chulia, was built in 1883. It is richly decorated and dedicated to the Hindu god Lord Subramaniam. The main statue is strung with gold, silver, diamond and emerald jewellery. It is normally used to lead a chariot procession to the Waterfall Temple during Thaipusam (see page 52). The symbols of the nine planets and the signs of the zodiac are carved into the ceiling. The surrounding area is largely Indian, with money changers and jewellery shops, as well as restaurants and tea-stalls.

There is also a Muslim community in Georgetown and the Indo-Moorish**Kapitan Kling Mosque** (on Jalan Kapitan Kling Mosque) was built by the island's first Indian Muslim settlers around 1800. It was named after the 'kapitan' or headman of the Kling – the South Indian community. As a sight it is rather disappointing.

Clan Piers and Armenian Street

Straight down Lebuh Chulia next to the Kapitan King Mosque is the Chinese water village off Pengkalan Weld. The entrance is through the temple on the quayside. It is known as the **Clan Piers**, as each of the jetties is named after a different Chinese clan. None of the families pays tax as they are not living on land. Rows of junks belonging to the resident traders are moored at the end of the piers.

Armenian Street, ⓘ *one and a half blocks south of Kapitan Kling Mosque*, is worth a wander as this area of the city is being remodelled and conserved because of its historical value; you can see the house of the rich Arab merchant who constructed the mosque opposite the park and a bit further down the road can be found the traditional Chinese house where Dr Sun Yat Sen is said to have planned the Canton uprising (The Canton Uprising started in Canton (modern Guangzhou in China) against the Qing dynasty. The uprising eventually led to the downfall of the child emperor, hence the birth of modern China.)

Khoo Kongsi and Malay Mosque

ⓘ *Mon-Fri 0900-1700, Sat 0900-1300, RM5. The free shuttle bus stops nearby.*

Located on Jalan Acheh, off Lebuh Pitt, Khoo Kongsi is approached through an archway to Cannon Square, and is one of the most interesting sights in Georgetown. A *kongsi* is a Chinese clan house, which doubles as a temple and a meeting place. Clan institutions originated in China as associations for people with the same surname. Today they are benevolent organizations that look after the welfare of clan members and safeguard ancestral shrines. Most of the *kongsis* in Penang were established in the 19th century when clashes between rival clans were commonplace.

The Khoo Kongsi is the most lavishly decorated of the *kongsis* in Penang, with its ornate Dragon Mountain Hall. It was built in 1898 by the descendants of Hokkien-born Khoo Chian Eng. A fire broke out in it the day it was completed, destroying its roof. It was rebuilt by craftsmen from China and was renovated in the 1950s; the present tiled roof is said to weigh 25 tonnes. The *kongsi* contains many fine pieces of Chinese art and sculpture, including two huge carved stone guardians, which ensure the wealth, longevity and happiness of all who came under the protection of the *kongsi*. The interior hall houses an image of Tua Sai Yeah, the Khoo clan's patron saint, who was a general during the Ch'in Dynasty in the 2nd century BC.

There are other kongsis in Georgetown, although none is as impressive as the Khoo Kongsi. The Chung Keng Kwee Kongsi is on Lebuh Gereja and the Tua Peh Kong Kongsi on Lebuh Armenian. The Khaw Kongsi and the modern Lee Kongsi are both on Jalan Burmah; Yap Kongsi on Lebuh Armenian and the combined *kongsi* of the Chuah, Sin and Quah clans at the junction of Jalan Burmah and Codrington Avenue. Every *kongsi has ancestral tablets as well as a hall of fame to honour its 'sons' or clansmen who have achieved fame in various spheres of life. Today women are honoured in these halls of fame too.*

Near the Khoo Kongsi, on Jalan Acheh, is the Malay Mosque. Its most noteworthy feature is the Egyptian-style minaret – most in Malaysia are Moorish. In the past it was better known as the meeting place for the notorious White Flag Malays, who sided with the Hokkien Chinese in street battles against the Cantonese (Red Flags) in the Penang Riots of 1867. The hole halfway up the minaret is said to have been made by a cannonball fired from Khoo Kongsi during the clan riots. The mosque is one of the oldest buildings in Georgetown, built in 1808.

South Georgetown

ⓘ *1030-2230, RM5. All buses stop at Komtar.*

Apart from the RM850-million Penang Bridge and several new hotels, one of the few visible architectural monuments of the 20th century is **Kompleks Tun Abdul Razak** (**KOMTAR**) on Jalan Penang. This cylindrical skyscraper, which houses the state government offices and a shopping centre, dominates Georgetown. There should be spectacular views of the island and across the straits to the mainland from the 58th floor, but unfortunately the windows are filthy and even if they were clean the smog usually prevents a clear view. The viewing gallery encircles the souvenir centre and has coin-operated telescopes.

West of the cathedral

Cheong Fatt Tze Mansion, ⓘ *14 Lebuh Leith, T4-2620006, www.cheongfatttzemansion.com; fully guided restoration tours every 1100 or 1500 daily. RM10.* Winner of the UNESCO Conservation Award 2000, and the National Architectural Award for Conservation 1995, the mansion is now a state monument. Built by Thio Thiaw Siat, a Kwangtung (Guandong) businessman who imported craftsmen from China, this Chinese equivalent of a stately home is one of only three surviving Chinese mansions in this style; the others are in Manila and Medan (Sumatra). There is also a chance to stay in one of the decadent 16 bedrooms.

Jalan Sultan Ahmed Shah (previously Northam Road Mansions) became known as Millionaires' Row as it was home to many wealthy rubber planters in the wake of the boom of 1911-20. Many of the palatial mansions were built by Straits Chinese in a sort of colonial baroque style, complete with turrets and castellations. Many of them have now gone to seed as they are too expensive to maintain; a few have been lavishly done up by today's generation of rich Chinese businessmen. The largest houses are the Yeap family mansion, known as the White House, and the Sultan of Kedah's palace.

West of the town centre

On Jalan Burmah is **Wat Chayamangkalaram,** ⓘ *Bus No 93, 202*, also known as Wat Buppharam, the largest Thai temple in Penang. It houses a 32-m-long reclining Buddha, Pra Chaiya Mongkol. There is a nine-storey pagoda behind the temple. The Thais and the Burmese practise Theravada Buddhism as opposed to the Mahayana school of the Chinese. Queen Victoria gave this site to Penang's Thai community in 1845. Opposite Wat Chayamangkalaram is Penang's only **Burmese temple**. It has ornate carvings and two huge white stone elephants at its gates. The original 1805 pagoda (to the right of the entrance) has been enshrined in a more modern structure.

The **Penang Buddhist Association** ⓘ *168 Jalan Anson; Bus No 202*. The Buddha statues are carved from Carrara marble from Italy, the glass chandeliers were made in what was Czechoslovakia and there are paintings depicting the many stages of the Buddha's path to enlightenment. Next door at No 184 is a 1960s Art Deco-style building, which is a clan hall for the Lee family.

The island

From Georgetown, the round-island trip is a 70-km circuit. It is recommended as a day trip as there is little or no accommodation available outside Georgetown apart from the north coast beaches.

Batu Ferringhi and Teluk Bahang

→ *Colour map 1, grid B1*

The main beach, Batu Ferringhi, whose hot, white sands were once the nirvana of western hippies, has been transformed into an upmarket tropical version of the Costa Brava. There are scores of hotels along the beach strip and graffiti are splashed across the famous Foreigner's Rock. Ferringhi – which is related to the Thai word *farang* (foreigner) – actually means 'Portuguese' in Malay. Portuguese Admiral Albuquerque, who captured Melaka in 1511, stopped off at Batu Ferringhi for fresh water on his way down the Straits. St Francis Xavier is said to have visited Batu Ferringhi in 1545. Towards the end of the 16th century, Captain James Lancaster, who later founded the East India Company in 1600, also came ashore at the beach.

To the majority of today's tourists, Batu Ferringhi is Penang. The beach is just over 3 km long but it has been extended to the fishing village of Teluk Bahang at the west end. Most holidaymakers and honeymooners prefer to stick to their hotel swimming pools rather than risk bathing in the sea which for much of the year looks like coffee. Pollution, siltation and an influx of jellyfish have affected water quality, but of late, the hotels have taken much more care of the beach itself. With its palms and casuarina trees, it retains at least some of its picture-postcard beauty. The hotels offer many different activities: windsurfing, water skiing, diving, sailing and fishing as well as jungle walks and sightseeing tours of the island.

Apart from the string of plush modern hotels, the Batu Ferringhi area also has many excellent restaurants, hawker stalls and handicraft shops, see Shopping.

The small fishing kampong of Teluk Bahang is situated at the westerly end of this northern stretch of beach. It is where the Malabar fishermen used to live and has now been dramatically changed by the *Penang Mutiara Beach Resort*. Beyond Teluk Bahang, around **Muka Head**, the coast is broken into a series of small secluded coves separated by rocky headlands; there are several tiny secluded beaches. Some of these are only accessible by boat, which can be hired either from the beach hotels, or from fishermen in Teluk Bahang, which is much cheaper. Trails also lead over the headland from the fishing kampong. One trail goes along the coast past the University Malaya Marine Research Station to Mermaid Beach and Muka Head lighthouse (one-and-a-half hours); another leads straight over the headland to Pantai Keracut (two hours).

The **Teluk Bahang Recreation Forest** has several well-marked trails and a Forestry Museum. ⓘ Tue-Thu 0900-1300, 1400-1700, Fri 1445-1700, Sat-Sun; 0900-1200. One kilometre up the road from the Teluk Bahang junction, the Butterfly Farm ⓘ *Butterfly House, 830 Jln Teluk Bahang, T4-8851253, tpgoh@butterfly-insects.com*, claims to be the largest tropical butterfly farm in the world. It has around 4,000 butterflies at any one time, representing over 120 species of Malaysian butterflies. The best time to visit the farm is in the late morning or early afternoon when the butterflies are most active. There is a small but excellent reptile and insect museum next door. The farm is also an important research centre and breeding station. Around 20% of the butterflies are released into the wild to help secure the future of the different species. ⓘ Mon-Fri 0900-1730, Sat-Sun 0900-1800, adults RM10, children RM5.

The **Green Orchid Farm**, ⓘ *Jln Sungai Pinang, 0800-1900 daily*, is situated next door to the Butterfly Farm. It is a small place with a wide range of orchids – all for sale, potted, bottled or just cut stems. While it is not a garden as such it is still worth a look if you appreciate orchids. Unfortunately, at the time of writing, there were reports that the farm owner would lose his lease and a Taiwanese International school would be built on the land.

Northern Penang

The **Nattukotai Chettiar Temple**, ⓘ *Bus No 7; get off at the stop before the Botanical Gardens*, on Waterfall Road was built by members of the Indian Chettiar money-lending fraternity and is the biggest Hindu temple on the island. It is a centre of pilgrimage during the Thaipusam festival (see page 52).

The **Botanical Gardens**, ⓘ *T4-2270428, daily, daylight hours; the more interesting plants are kept under lock and key and are open to visitors Mon-Fri 0700-1900; Bus No 7*, also on Waterfall Road, are situated in a valley surrounded by hills 8 km from Georgetown. The gardens are well landscaped and contain many indigenous and exotic plant species. They were established in 1844. A path leads from the gardens' Moon Gate up Penang Hill; see below, the 8-km hike takes about 1½ hours. The resident macaques are a bit frisky, it's wise to watch them from a distance.

Central Penang

A short distance from Kek Lok Si is the funicular railway ⓘ *every 30 mins between 0630 and 2330*, which started operating in 1922. It climbs 850 m up **Penang Hill**, ⓘ *Bus No 130 or 101 to Ayer Itam Station, then shuttle bus No 8 to the railway. Most buses from Stand 3 go to Penang Hill, but if unsure the bus drivers are helpful – provided you have the right change for the fare.* A vintage steam engine is on display at the Penang Museum. The railway was originally completed in 1899, but

Penang's beaches

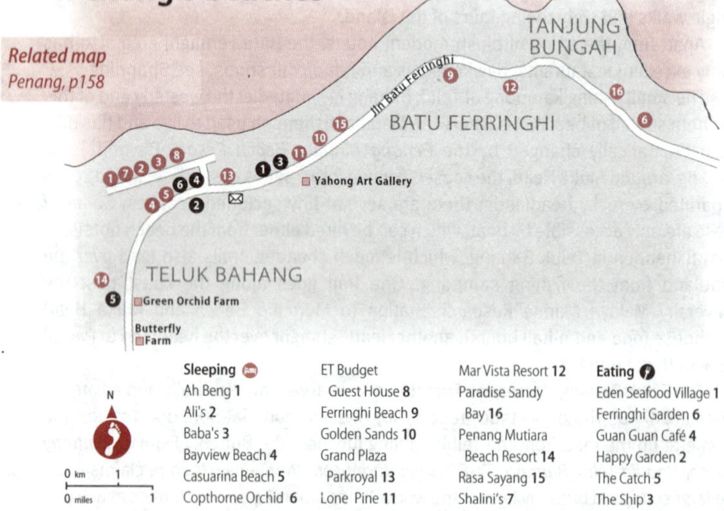

Sleeping
Ah Beng 1
Ali's 2
Baba's 3
Bayview Beach 4
Casuarina Beach 5
Copthorne Orchid 6
ET Budget Guest House 8
Ferringhi Beach 9
Golden Sands 10
Grand Plaza Parkroyal 13
Lone Pine 11
Mar Vista Resort 12
Paradise Sandy Bay 16
Penang Mutiara Beach Resort 14
Rasa Sayang 15
Shalini's 7

Eating
Eden Seafood Village 1
Ferringhi Garden 6
Guan Guan Café 4
Happy Garden 2
The Catch 5
The Ship 3

on its inauguration by the governor it didn't work and had to be dismantled. Penang Hill is about 5°C cooler than Georgetown and was a favoured expatriate refuge before the advent of air-conditioning. Indeed, it was the first colonial hill station developed on Peninsular Malaysia. **Bel Retiro**, designed as a get-away for the governor, was the first bungalow to be built on the hill. There is a small hotel. See Sleeping. The ridge on top of Penang Hill is known as Strawberry Hill after Francis Light's strawberry patch. On a clear day it is possible to see the mountains of Langkawi and North Kedah from the top. There's also a temple, a mosque and a post office and police station on the top. There are also a few restaurants and a small hawker centre. The hill gets very crowded on weekends and public holidays. A well-marked 8-km path leads down to the Moon Gate at the Botanical Gardens (about an hour's walk) from between the post office and the police station; a steep but delightful descent, with plenty of places to sit along the way. The hill supports the last relic patch of tropical rainforest on Penang and as such is deemed of considerable natural value. The flora and fauna here have been protected since 1960.

The absence of a paved road up Penang Hill meants that its essential qualities of seclusion and peace have been preserved on an island otherwise battered by the forces of Communism.

The **State Mosque**, ⓘ *Jalan Ayer Itam/Jalan Masjid Negeri; Bus No 101 or 130.*, is the largest and newest mosque in Penang and can accommodate 5,000. It was designed by a Filipino architect. There are good views from the top of the 57-m-high minaret. You must get permission first from mosque officials.

The **Bat Temple**ⓘ *Bus No 101 or 130*, at Ayer Itam is a sanctuary for fruit bats, which hang from the cave roof. The sacred bats are zealously protected by Buddhist monks. About 60 years ago the wealthy Madam Lim Chooi Yuen, built the bat temple to protect the bats.

A pleasant wooded hilly area to relax in just above the town is the **Ayer Itam Dam**, ⓘ *Bus No 101 or 130. then change to bus No 8*. There are several trails around the lake, originally shortcuts to other parts of the island.

Kek Lok Si Temple (The Monastery of Supreme Bliss),ⓘ *T4-8283317, 0900-1800, free, voluntary contribution to climb the 30-m-high tower; Bus No 101 or 130, followed by a five-minute walk or Transit Link shuttle bus No 8,* south of Ayer Itam, can be seen from some distance away. It took Burmese, Chinese and Thai artisans, who were shipped in specially, two decades to build it. The abbot of the Goddess of Mercy Temple on Lebuh Pitt came from China in 1885 and the landscape around Ayer Itam reminded him of his homeland. He collected money from rich Chinese merchants to fund the construction of the huge temple, modelled on Fok San Monastery in Fuchow, China. On the way up the 'ascending plane' is a pond for turtles, which are a symbol of eternity. The temple sprawls across 12 ha and is divided into three main sections: the Hall of Bodhisattvas, the Hall of Devas and the sacred Hall of the Buddha. The seven-tier pagoda, or Ban Po, the Pagoda of a Thousand Buddhas, is built in three different styles: the lower follows a Chinese design honouring the Goddess of Mercy, Kuan Yin; the middle is Thai-Buddhist and commemorates Bee Lay Hood (the Laughing Buddha); and the upper Burmese levels are dedicated to the Gautama or historic Buddha with thousands of gilded statues. The topmost tier contains a relic of the Buddha, a statue of pure gold and other treasures, but it is closed to visitors. All pretty tacky stuff and more than half the complex has been turned into a shopping centre. All-in-all, an impressive building compromised by tack.

South Penang

Universiti Sains Malaysia Museum and Galleryⓘ *Daily 0900-1700; taxi*, is at Minden near the Penang Bridge interchange. It has a large ethnographic and performing arts sections with a special exhibition on *wayang kulit* (shadow puppets – see Drama, page 505). There is also an art gallery with works by Malaysian artists and visiting temporary exhibitions.

Snake Temple, ⓘ *T4-6437273, 0700-1900, RM1; Bus No 66 or 80*, also known as Temple of the Azure Cloud, was built in 1850 at Bayan Lepas 12 km from Georgetown. Snakes were kept in the temple as they were believed to be the disciples of the deity Chor Soo Kong, to whom the temple is dedicated. The temple was built as the result of a donation from a Scotsman, David Brown, after he was cured by a local priest of an 'incurable disease', using local medicines. Nowadays the reptilian disciples (almost exclusively Wagler's pit vipers) are a bit thin on the ground. The number of snakes in the temple varies from day to day – there are usually more around during festivals. The incense smoke keeps them in a drugged stupor, and most of them have had their fangs extracted. Photographs with (defanged) snakes can be posed for in a new annex next door to the temple (RM4). The temple is surrounded by factories and a highway and most locals say the place is a con, given the paucity of reptiles.

Batu Maung ⓘ*Take minibus No 27*, is a Chinese fishing village near Bayan Lepas and is known for its 'floating' seafood restaurant, built out over the water. Around the south coast, there are a few beaches and a couple of unremarkable fishing kampongs. The southern beaches are more secluded than the beaches along the north coast; the drawbacks are the litter and the absence of accommodation.

It is much easier to explore the kampongs and beaches around the south and west coasts – most of which are off the main road – if you have private transport.

Also here, is Penang's latest tourist venue, the **War Museum**, ⓘ *Mukim 12, Daerah Barat Daya, daily 0900-1900, RM10; shuttle bus from Tourism Malaysia Office 0930 and 1430*, built around a 1930s military fortress. The fort sprawls across 20 acres on Bukit Batu Maung – a supposedly haunted hill. It is gradually being restored, but currently visitors can clamber over a torture chamber, medical infirmary, canon firing bay and scoot along tunnels.

The**Bukit Jambul Orchid and Hibiscus and Reptile Garden,** ⓘ *daily 0930-1830; snake show Sat, Sun, public holidays at 1130 and 1530. RM5 for adults, RM2 for children*, is found along Persiaran Bukit Jambul, close to the Hotel Equatorial and five minutes' drive from the airport. As its name suggests, it specializes in orchids and hibiscus. There is also a reptile house here.

Veering north towards the centre of the island, however, beyond Barat, is **Balik Pulau**, a good *makan* stop with a number of restaurants and cafés. Around the town, which is known as the durian capital of Penang, there are a number of picturesque Malay kampongs.

West Penang

Further up the west side of the island is the **Penang National Park**, formerly the Pantai Acheh Forest Reserve, ⓘ *Entrance to the park is through Telok Bahang at the end of Batu Ferringhi Road; Bus No 93 to Telok Bahang. Either walk from here or take a boat from the fishing jetty. Longer fare stages cost anything up to RM1.5. As the island buses are infrequent, check departure times at each place to avoid being stranded*, which also has well-marked trails into the jungle and to the bays further round; for example, to Pantai Keracut (one hour). After the Pantai Acheh junction, and on up a twisting, forested section of road, there is a waterfall with a pleasant pool, suitable for swimming, just off the road (20th milestone), called **Titi Kerawang**.

Butterworth→ *Colour map 1, grid B2 Phone code: 04*

This industrial and harbour town and base for the Royal Australian Air Force was billeted here under the terms of the Five Powers Pact. It is the main port for ferries to Penang, and most tourists head straight for the island; Butterworth is not a recommended stopping point.

Sleeping

Georgetown *p159, map p160*

In Georgetown, most upmarket hotels are concentrated in the Jln Penang area. Most cheaper hotels are around Lebuh Chulia & Lebuh Leith.

L **Eastern & Oriental (E&O)**, 10 Lebuh Farquhar, T42222000, www.e-o-hotel.com A/c, restaurant, pool, built in 1885 by the Armenian Sarkies brothers, who operated Singapore's Raffles Hotel (see page 562) and the Strand Hotel in Rangoon (Yangon). Noël Coward and Somerset Maugham figured on former guest lists. Stunning hotel, 'restored to its former glory'. Staff are friendly and efficient, atmosphere is luxurious. Endless options for varied cuisine, both international and local, from coffee houses to ballrooms. Shop, business centre, swimming pool and gymnasium.

L-AL **City Bayview Hotel**, 25a Lebuh Farquhar, T4-2633161, www.citybayviewpg.com.my Large top-of-the-range hotel, although less formal atmosphere than others in this category. Facilities include 24-hr room service, laundry, dry cleaning, tour desk, swimming pool, health centre (at additional cost), gym, internet access and a revolving restaurant. All rooms are pleasant, but those in a new wing are slightly more spacious and suites are available for those looking for a luxury stay.

L-AL **Shangri-La**, Jln Magazine, T4-2622622, www.shangri-la.com A/c, restaurant, 24-hr coffee garden, pool, small fitness centre, mostly used by business people rather than tourists, next to KOMTAR. Excellent conference facilities. Good central location.

AL **Berjaya Georgetown Hotel**, T4-2277111, www.berjayaresorts.com/berjaya-georgetown/info.html One of the newest luxury hotels, 330 rooms, part of one-stop Midland Park Complex. All the usual amenities: swimming pool, health centre, several restaurants, business centre.

AL-A **Cheong Fatt Tze Mansion**, 14 Leith St, T4-262006, www.cheongfatttzemansion.com This indigo-blue 19th century mansion, fully restored, has a selection of really elegant, themed rooms all furnished with period pieces and modern facilities. Rate includes breakfast and valet service. A unique, albeit pricey experience. Recommended for those who want to live Penang's history and culture first-hand.

AL-A **Cititel**, 66 Jln Penang, T4-3701188, www.cititelhotel.com Breakfast included in room rate, 24-hr café, Chinese and Japanese restaurants, sports bar with electronic darts and video games. Florist, beauty salon and convenience store. Large hotel in central location. Recommended.

AL-A **Hotel 1926**, 227 Jln Burma, T4-2281926, www.hotel1926.com.my A charming string of newly restored British colonial terraced homes now forms this boutique hotel. A little out of the way on Jln Burma, and rooms a tad twee. Also few facilities - you are paying for the historical ambience.

AL-A **Sheraton**, 3 Jln Larut, T4-2267888, www.starwood.com/sheraton. Five-star hotel with 237 rooms. Special facilities in rooms include direct fax line, electronic safe, iron. For those who get really hungry at unpredictable hours there is a 24-hr restaurant.

AL-B **Continental**, 5 Jln Penang, T4-2636388, hotelconti@po.jaring.my. A/c, restaurant, 18 storeys with great views from higher rooms. New wing, with more expensive rooms. Swimming pool, restaurant, lounge and coffee garden. Not as grand as *Cititel*, but comfortable.

AL-B **Merchant**, 55 Jln Penang, T4-2632828, F4-2625511. A/c, restaurant, marble lobby, TV, in-house video, mini-bar, coffee house, central location. Friendly, helpful staff. Good value.

A **Equatorial International**, 1 Jln Bukit Jambal, T4-6438111, www.equatorial.com/pen/index.html A/c, restaurant, between the airport and town, on a hill with a view over the Penang Bridge, mostly used by visiting business people as it is conveniently located for Penang's duty-free industrial zone, which lies between it and the airport. A monstrous block of 400-plus rooms with good sports facilities and adjacent 18-hole golf course.

A **Malaysia**, 7 Jln Penang, T4-2633311, www.hotelmalaysia.com.my A/c, restaurant, dated high-rise hotel, plush décor with coffee house, disco, health centre.

A-B **Grand Continental**, 68 Brick Kiln Rd (Jln Gurdwara), T4-2636688, www.grandhotelsinternational.com.my A/c, restaurant, pool, health club, coffee lounge, massage centre, karaoke lounge. Good value.

A-B Sunway, 33 New Lane, T4-2299988, sunway@swhtlpg.po.my Pleasant décor, good facilities in rooms, a/c, TV, pulsating shower, in-house video, iron, fridge, complimentary tea/coffee, pool, jacuzzi, restaurant, tea-house, pub, tennis and squash arranged. Breakfast included. Not much character but great value for money.

B Oriental, 105 Jln Penang, T4-2634211/6, www.oriental.com.my A/c, restaurant, dated décor, big rooms and good value (often great promotions), welcoming staff, well-located with good views from the upper floors. Recommended.

C Paramount, 48F Jln Sultan Ahmad Shah, T4-2273649. A/c, restaurant, big rooms in run-down colonial house, right on the sea, but not central. Recommended.

C Waldorf, 13 Leith St, T4-2626140, waldorf@pc.jaring.my A/c, bath, dated décor. This two-star hotel bears little resemblance to its New York namesake. One saving grace is it's opposite the beautiful Cheong Fatt Tze Mansion.

C-D Blue Diamond, 422 Lebuh Chulia, T4-2611089. Restaurant, fan, Chinese nationalist General Chiang Kai Shek once took refuge here, spacious rooms, bar and cheap restaurant downstairs. Pool tables and television in bar. Popular with backpackers, bar can be noisy in the evenings. Central location in China Town.

C-D Embassy, 12 Jln Burmah, T4-2267515. A fossil of a hostel. Rumbling a/c, some hot water showers. Rooms entering their retirement but spacious with old décor. Friendly and clean, not a bad budget option.

C-D YMCA, 211 Jln Macalister, T4-2288211, ymcapg@streamyx.com. Clean and comfortable on a quiet tree-lined street, Also has gym, badminton and laundry. A/c and fan rooms available.

D White House Hotel, 72 Jln Penang, T4-2632385, F4-2641409. Fan and a/c rooms available. Lovely staff, communal eating area, clean attached or common bathroom with hot water, excellent value for money. Recommended.

D-E D'Budget Hostel, 9 Lebuh Gereja, T4-2634794. Some a/c, roof terrace, laundry, money changer, tea-making, TV, hot water shower, near Medan ferry, clean but sterile, soulless place, quiet, friendly and helpful management, dorms also.

D-E Hang Cheow, 511 Lebuh Chulia, T4-2610810. Rates negotiable, friendly owner! Basic budget accommodation. Restaurant.

D-F 75 Travellers Lodge, 75 Lebuh Muntri, T4-2623378, F4-2633378. Penang's newest backpacker offering, and already hugely popular. Very traveller-oriented, with plenty of tourist information, balcony, laundry, ticketing, visas, mail service, cable TV and western café next door. Rooms with shared bathroom and cheap dorms available. Well-run, but don't expect anything fancy.

D-F Broadway Hostel, 35f Jln Masjid Kapitan Kling, T4-2628550, F4-2619525. Clean and basic, some a/c, dorm, one of the best budget options.

D-F Coral Hostel, 99-101 King St, T4-2644909. Very friendly Indian-run place, with simple rooms or dorm close to Little India. Well set-up for travellers with TV lounge, motorbike and bicycle rental, cheap Internet and discounted ferry tickets. Recommended.

D-F Love Lane Inn, 54 Love Lane, T016-4198409, ocean008@hotmail.com Well-established backpacker favourite. Usually friendly staff with both dorms and rooms and shared cold water bathroom. Very popular.

D-F Oasis Hotel, 23 Love Lane, T4-2639710, oasishotel23@hotmail.com. Lovely old building with fishpond and wandering cats in a less frenetic corner of town. Shared bathrooms, fan and basin in room. There is one hot water shower. 'Interesting' atmosphere, set in overgrown garden, dorm beds available. Rooms a bit basic and not always spotless.

D-F Olive Spring, 300-302 Chulia St, above Rainforest Restaurant, T4-2614641. Friendly staff and clean rooms make this a very popular place to stay (so it's often hard to get a room). All rooms with shared bathroom. Nice airy building with creaky staircases, good atmosphere. Avoid rooms at the front because they suffer from a lot of street traffic noise. Dorm beds available too.

D-F Wan Hai, 35 Love Lane, T4-2616853. Fan, restaurant, run-of-the-mill budget hotel, motorcycles for hire, visa applications for Thailand and bus tickets to Thailand organized, dorm, terrace.

E Hong Ping, 273B, Lebuh Chulia, above *Coco Island* restaurant, T4-2625234. A/c, private bath, TV, bare but quiet rooms.

Batu Ferringhi and Teluk Bahang

p165, map p166

The big international hotels all have excellent facilities, including tennis, watersports, sailing and sightseeing tours. They also offer free shuttle services at least once a day to Georgetown. With fewer European customers, many have turned their attention to the incentive travel business and the Asian market, targeting Singaporeans in particular. Hotels are still going up though. While middle-to-upmarket tourists are spoilt for choice, budget travellers' options on the north coast are rather more limited. All the budget guesthouses are in a little strip close to the sea-edge just next to turn-off by the Grandplaza Parkroyal.

L **Penang Mutiara Beach Resort**, Jln Teluk Bahang, Teluk Bahang, T4-8868888, www.mutiarahotels.com A/c, restaurant, pool, luxurious spa, over 400 rooms, the last outpost of 5-star luxury along the beach. The Mutiara (Malay for 'pearl') has landscaped gardens, a great pool with a bar and every conceivable facility including a children's wonderland; a drink at the Mutiara bar costs the same as a huge meal in some nearby restaurants. Recommended.

L-AL **Bayview Beach**, T4-8812123, www.bayiewbeach.com A/c, 2 restaurants, pool, over 400 rooms, pleasant location, away from others on the strip. Plush interior, sophisticated, but not strikingly different from other 5-star hotel here. Staff are friendly.

L-AL **Casuarina Beach**, T4-8811711, reservations@casuarina.com.my Elegant rooms, a/c, restaurant, pool, named after the trees that line Batu Ferringhi beach, particularly nice grounds and a good beach, a variety of watersports arranged, theme parties. Tennis courts and table tennis available. Doctor on-call and laundry service.

L-AL **Copthorne Orchid Penang**, Tanjung Bungah, T4-8903333, copresv@po.jaring.my A/c, 2 restaurants, pool, good business facilities. A very formal atmosphere. A little dated.

L-AL **Crown Jewel**, Tanjung Bungah, T4-8904111, F4-8904777. Over 280 rooms, not as good as Paradise Sandy Beach but sometimes offers good-value promotions.

L-AL **Golden Sands Resort**, T4-8861911, www.shangri-la.com A/c, restaurant, pool, popular and central on the beach, arguably the best swimming pool. Restaurant and bar situated on the beach front. Well equipped and a large resort.

L-AL **Grand Plaza Parkroyal**, T4-8811133, www.grandplaza.penang.parkroyalhotels.com Recently upgraded, a/c, 4 restaurants, attractive pool, gym, tennis court, large 300-room 5-star hotel, with excellent facilities especially for families, including children's play area, special children's programmes and babysitting. Beautiful garden area and large, airy rooms with sea views. Recommended.

L-AL **Lone Pine**, T4-8811511, www.lonepinehotel.com A/c, restaurant, one of the oldest hotels along Batu Ferringhi (opened in 1948), but recently renovated into a smart boutique hotel. TV, mini-bar, pool, reasonably priced, but not up to the standards of its neighbours. Wouldn't win a beauty contest but has 10 ha of landscape gardens. Nightly live band, set back from beach slightly. Quieter, less hectic atmosphere than neighbouring large resorts.

L-AL **Mar Vista Resort**, T4-8903388, mvr@po.jaring.my All 120 suites have kitchenette (utensils extra charge), sea views, a/c, TV. Dated décor, pool, paddling pool, jacuzzi, health club, restaurant. Apartment rental ranges from weekly to yearly.

L-AL **Paradise Sandy Beach**, 527 Jln Tanjung Bungah, T4-8999999, www.paradisehotel.com More than 300 rooms, all of which are suites of varying size with kitchenette, balconies, sea views, TV, complimentary coffee/tea, a/c and bath. The décor is tasteful and facilities are good, free-form pool, paddling pool, watersports, tennis, squash and gym, 24-hr coffee house and lounge overlooking the sea. Stunning views. Recommended.

L-AL **Rasa Sayang**, T4-8811811, www.shangri-la.com A/c, restaurants, pool, another of the *Shangri La* group. Over 500 rooms, probably the most popular along the beach strip, modern interpretation of Minangkabau-style, horse-shoe design around central pool and garden area. More sophisticated style than others on the strip, still welcoming. Recommended.

AL **Ferringhi Beach Hotel**, T4-8905999, ferringhi@po.jaring.my A/c, restaurant, pool, 350 rooms, a/c, mini-bar, TV, in-house video, overhead bridge to beach, offers golf packages, caters mainly for tour groups.

C-D Ah Beng, 54c Batu Ferringhi, right on the beach, T4-8811036. A/c, clean. At the end of the budget hotel road, rooms with a/c, fan. Friendly, family run. Recommended.
C-D Ali's, 53b Batu Ferringhi, T4-8811316, alisguesthouse@hotmail.com Funky, quirky backpacker house with pleasant balcony, round door like a hobbit-hole in the front room and cozy garden bar and restaurant. One of the best budget options, despite the coldness of the staff.
C-D Baba's, 52 Batu Ferringhi, T4-8811686, www.geoctities.com/babaguesthouse2003, babaguesthouse2000@yahoo.com Clean, homely and relaxed. Some rooms have a/c and shower. The owner here is well informed and a good source of information.
C-D ET Budget Guest House, 47 Batu Ferringhi, T4-8811553, wwwgeocities.com/etguesthouse. An offshoot of Baba's. Good tour and bus information, laundry service. Another good value option with travel information and tickets available.
C-D Shalini's, 56 Batu Ferringhi, T4-8811859, ahlooi@pc.jaring.my Lovely little house with balcony overlooking the sea. Clean and homely, mostly cold-water shared bathrooms.
E-F Rama's, 365 Mukim 2, T4-811179. Homestay-type accommodation, dorm or rooms.

Central Penang *p166*

B Bellevue, Penang Hill, T4-8299600, F4-8292052, penbell@tm.net.my A/c, restaurant serving steamboat, colonial-style house, cool retreat up on the hill. Good views over Georgetown. Pleasant accommodation, small and quite isolated from the real action – other than the sites and attractions on Penang Hill.

Butterworth *p168*

Nearly all the hotels are located a good 20 mins' walk from the bus terminal, so a taxi ride is advisable.
B Berlin, 4802 Jln Bagan Luar, T4-3321701, F4-3323388. A/c, TV. Next to *Sayang Coffee House*, which serves meals. The best option, if you are unfortunate enough to require accommodation in Butterworth.
C Apollo, just round corner from Capital, very clean, a/c and fan rooms, private bathroom.

Eating

Georgetown *p159, map p160*

Penang's specialities include *assam laksa* (a hot-and-sour fish soup), *nasi kandar* (curry), *mee yoke* (prawns in chilli-noodle soup) and *inche kabin* (chicken marinated in spices and then fried). Penang and Melaka are the culinary centres of Nyonya cuisine (see page 48). Penang's 'Little India' is bounded by Lebuh Bishop, Lebuh Pasar and Lebuh King, close to the quay. There is a string of good Indian restaurants along Lebuh Penang, in this area. Try the foodstalls for great Malay food, see page 174.

Chinese

TTT **Shang Palace**, Shangri La Hotel, Jln Magazine, T4-2622622, Hong Kong, dim sum brunch, Cantonese dishes.
TT **Goh Huat Seng**, 59A Lebuh Kimberley, Teochew cuisine, best known for its steamboats.
TT **Tower Palace**, Level 58-60 KOMTAR, good-value dim sum.
T **Ang Hoay Loh**, 60 Jln Brick Kiln. Hokkien food: specialities include glass noodles and pork and prawn soups.
T **Green Vege Recipe**, 151A Penang Rd. Family-run vegetarian canteen serving inventive meatless dishes based on Chinese and Japanese recipes. An excellent place to get filled up on cheap and tasty food if you're a vegetarian.
T **Lum Fong**, 108 Muntri St. Lively coffee shop with an arcaded front, old wooden tables and chairs, good noodles.
T **May Garden**, 70 Penang Rd, good food and very popular.
T **Potbless**, Hutton Lane, *nasi lemak*, banana leaf, steamboat.
T **Sin Kheng Hooi Hong**, 350 Lebuh Pantai, Hainanese cuisine, *lor bak* (crispy deep-fried seafood rolls, with sweet-and-sour plum sauce). Recommended.
T **Tropics**, Sunway Hotel, 33 New Lane, good value steamboat buffet.

Fusion

TTT TT **Thirty Two**, 32 Jln Sultan Ahmad Shah, T4-2622232. Chinese-owned Italian mansion built in the 1920s. Beautifully maintained. The restaurant includes a bar and lounge area with live jazz bands, a terrace by the water and a no-smoking room with a/c. Varied menu, referred to as Asian fusion cuisine. Beautiful building, friendly staff and sophisticated ambience.

Indian

ᛘᛘ **Annalakshmi**, Basington Av, T4-2288575, 1800-2130. Serves a great vegetarian curry.
ᛘᛘ **Kashmir**, base of *Oriental Hotel*, 105 Jln Penang (not Lebuh Penang). North Indian food – usually very busy. Recommended.
ᛘᛘ **Passage Thru' India**, 132 Penang Rd, T4-2620263. Award-winning elegant restaurant which promises the "best Indian experience". Offers a tasty crab masala.
ᛘ **Banana Leaf**, Lebuh Penang, about two blocks south of Lebuh Gereja. Serves excellent southern Indian food; an especially good place for a *thali* and the *lassis* are good.
ᛘ **Dawood**, 63 Lebuh Queen (across from Sri Mariamman Temple). Indian Muslim restaurant known for its curries, original 1960s décor, *kari kapitan* (chicken curry) and duck are popular. Recommended.
ᛘ **Hameediyah**, 164A Lebuh Campbell. Indian Muslim food, *murtabak*, *rotis*, large portions.
ᛘ **Kaliaman's**, 43 Lebuh Penang, one of Penang's best Indian restaurants, South Indian food at lunch, northern Indian food in the evening, not very clean.
ᛘ **Kashmir**, Penang Rd, 1200-1430, 1900-2230.
ᛘ **Kassim Mustafa**, 12 Lebuh Chulia, basic coffee shop that prides itself in cooking a handful of dishes very well, most trade done between 0500 and 1200, specialities are *nasi dalcha* (rice cooked with ghee and cinnamon), *ayam negro* and mutton *kurma*. Good *roti bom* and *teh tarik*. Staff are friendly, and this is also an excellent place for breakfast. Recommended.
ᛘ **Kassim Nasi Kandar**, 2-1 Jln Brick Kiln. Hhot Indian Muslim food, open 24 hrs, recommended by locals.
ᛘ **Kedai Kopi Yasmeen**, 177 Jln Penang. Simple open-fronted Indian coffee shop, *murtabak*, *roti* etc. Recommended.
ᛘ **The Tandoori House**, Lorong Hutton. Nicer décor than *Kashmir* (above), evergreen north Indian specialities.

International

ᛘᛘ **Beetle Nuts Fun Café**, 9-11 Leith St, in same old block as 20 Leith St, theme is American, Tex-Mex, trendy.
ᛘᛘ **Bella Casa**, 105a Penang Rd, T4-2642030, a large Italian menu, good lasagne di carne.
ᛘᛘ **Ecco Café**, Love Lane near junction with Lebuh Chulia. Atmospheric bar/Italian café crammed with bizarre objects from Indian tapestries, an electronic organ to a grotesque Japanese she-he pig statue. Very relaxed and friendly hang-out. The owner handmakes his own pizza dough and pasta, to create some of Penang's best Italian food for a reasonable price. Tattoo parlour upstairs. Highly recommended.
ᛘ **Brasserie**, *Shangri La Hotel*, Californian cuisine.
ᛘ **Café Tower Lounge**, 59th Flr, KOMTAR, buffet lunch, good view over the city and afterwards free entrance to viewing gallery.
ᛘ **Coco Island Café**, Lebuh Chulia, good food, popular.
ᛘ **Rainforest Restaurant**, 300 Chulia St, popular with budget travellers, interesting scrapbooks of travellers' experiences, wide selection of food: nachos, sandwiches, steak, pizza, apple crumble (recommended), all home-cooked and no preservatives. Freshly baked bread. Recommended.
ᛘ **Rhak Café**, 451 Lebuh Chulia. Open from 0630. Simple backpacker-style canteen with beer and movies in the evening.

Japanese

ᛘᛘᛘ **Kurumaya**, 269 Burma Rd. Top quality *sushi* and *sashmi*.
ᛘᛘ **Hide No Ya**, 8 Abu Siti Lane, T4-2282359, small, friendly restaurant, especially good for its *tempura chauonmushi*, *karagi* and *sashimi/suishi*. Recommended.
ᛘᛘ **Kong Lung**, 11c Leith St. Immaculate traditional décor, *teppenyaki* and set lunches. Recommended.
ᛘᛘ **Miyabi**, 216 Jln McAlister, well-established Japanese restaurant.
ᛘᛘ **Shin Miyako**, 105 Jln Penang (next to the *Oriental Hotel*). Smart-looking restaurant and reasonably priced for Japanese food.

Malay

ᛘᛘ **City Bayview Hotel**, 14th Flr, 25a Lorong Farquhar, Asian cuisine served while the room gently rotates one circuit in about an hour, giving spectacular views of the city and coast.

Nyonya

ᛘ **Dragon King**, 99 Lebuh Bishop. Family-run

business, probably the best Nyonya food in any of the old Straits Settlements, specializes in fish-head curry, good satay, *otak-otak* (fish marinated in lime and wrapped in banana leaf), *curry kapitan* (chicken cooked in coconut milk) and *kiam chye boey* (a meat casserole). Recommended.

Nyonya Corner, 15 Jln Pahang, excellent *otak-otak*.

Seafood

TTT Eden, 11B Lorong Hutton, popular chain of restaurants, seafood and grills.

TT Grand Garden Seafood, 164 Jln Penan. Seafood market restaurant, outside eating.

T Maple, 106 Jln Penang (near Oriental Hotel), same management as *May Garden* and food is in the same league.

T May Garden, 70 Penang Rd (next to *Towne House*), reckoned to be among the best seafood restaurants in Georgetown, with an aquarium full of fish and shellfish to choose from. The crab is excellent and May Garden's speciality is frogs' legs, fried with chilli and ginger or just crispy. Recommended.

T Ocean-Green, 48F Jln Sultan Ahmad Shah (in quiet alleyway in front of *Paramount Hotel*), specialities include lobster and crab thermidor, drunken prawns and fresh frogs' legs ('paddy chicken'), lovely location, overlooking fishing boats. Recommended.

T Sea Palace, 50 Jln Penang (next to *Peking Hotel*), huge menu, popular, a/c, Chinese tableware, good value. Recommended.

Thai

T Café D'Chiangmai, 11 Burmah Cross, serves an interesting mixture of Thai and local dishes, renowned for its fish-head curry, popular in the evenings.

Coffee shops

Most Chinese coffee shops are along Jln Burmah and Jln Penang, also some in the financial district along Lebuh Bishop, Lebuh Cina and Lebuh Union.

Khuan Kew and **Sin Kuan Hwa**, both in Love Lane are particularly popular – the latter is well known for its Hainan chicken rice.

Maxim Cakehouse and Bakery on Penang Rd is also a popular stop.

Kek Seng (382 Jln Penang), founded in 1906 and still serving *kway teow* soup and colourful *ais-kacangs* .It's the oldest in Georgetown.

Foodstalls

Penang's hawker stalls are renowned in Malaysia and serve some of the best food on the island.

Datuk Keramat Hawker Centre (also called *Padang Brown*), junction of Anson and Perak roads, is one of the venues for Georgetown's roving night market – possible to check if it's on by calling the tourist information centre, T4-2616663. Recommended.

Kota Selera Hawker Centre, next to Fort Cornwallis, off Lebuh Light. Recommended.

Lebuh Keng Kwee, famed locally for its *cendol* stalls (cocktails of shaved ice, palm sugar and jelly topped with *gula melaka* and coconut milk.

Lebuh Kimberley (called noodle-maker street by the Chinese), good variety of hawker food at night.

Lorong Selamat Hawker Stalls, highly recommended by locals.

Padang Kota Lama/Jln Tun Syed Sheh Barakbah (Esplanade), busy in the evenings. Recommended.

Pesiaran Gurney Seawall (Gurney Drive), hawker stalls opposite the coffee shops, good range of Malay, Chinese and Indian food, very popular in the evenings. Recommended.

There are also popular stalls along **Jln Burmah**, **Love Lane** and at **Ayer Itam**. Good *roti-canai* opposite *Golden Plaza Hostel*, Lebuh Ah Quee.

Batu Ferringhi and Teluk Bahang

p165, map p166

Virtually every cuisine is represented along this stretch. Many of the big Batu Ferringhi hotels have excellent restaurants. They have to be good as there is plenty of good quality competition from roadside restaurants.

Chinese

TTT House of Four Seasons, *Penang Mutiara Beach Resort*, Jln Teluk Bahang, closed Tue, good old-fashioned opulence, black marble, silk and carpets, interesting menu, Cantonese and Szechuan dishes. Recommended.

TTT Marco Polo, *Bayview Beach*, Batu Ferringhi, wide selection of Cantonese dishes, shark's fin is popular, bright lighting and typical Chinese décor with tables set around a courtyard.

TT Fok Lok Sow, *Mar Vista Resort*, Batu Ferringhi, good value buffet and 7-course set dinner.

Sin Hai Keng, 551 Tanjung Tokong, overlooks the sea and serves everything from noodles to pork chops, excellent satay.

International

Feringgi Grill, Rasa Sayang Resort, Batu Ferringhi, popular restaurant, aims to imitate an English club, 3-piece band, specialities include prime US rib of beef served with Yorkshire pudding, expensive but memorable.

La Farfalla, *Penang Mutiara Beach Resort*, 1 Jln Teluk Bahang, closed Mon, romantic setting overlooking pool, live string band play in background, authentic Italian chef, specialities include beef carpaccio, scallops and lobster.

Sigi's By The Sea, *Shangri La's Golden Sands Resort*. Waterfront restaurant, includes bar, full cocktail menu and lovely atmosphere. Food is high class as you'd expect. Specialities are the quesadillas and the lamb shanks. Recommended.

The Ship, Batu Ferringhi (next to *Eden Seafood Village*), purpose-built wooden ship with steakhouse inside.

Tiffins, *Grandplaza Parkroyal Hotel*, Batu Ferringhi, very popular with locals, especially business people wishing to impress clients, Nyonya décor, wood carvings and antique furniture, eclectic cooking style, many interesting items, set meal is good value.

Guan Guan Café, Batu Ferringhi (opposite Yahong Art Gallery), where backpackers hang out, good-value snacks;

Kokomo, 1c Jln Sungai Kelian, Tanjung Bungah (opposite *Novotel*), hip meeting place, light meals and snacks, happy hour 1800-2100.

Japanese

Honjin, *Bayview Beach*, Batu Ferringhi, peaceful Japanese-style setting with a garden at centre of restaurant, good quality food, set meals are best value.

Japanese Restaurant, *Rasa Sayang Resort*, Batu Ferringhi, typically spartan Japanese décor, two main areas on menu: sushi and sashimi; and teppanyaki.

Malay

Papa Din's Bamboo, 124-B Batu Ferringhi (turn left after police station and *Eden Restaurant*, 200 m up the Kampong Road by *Happy Garden Restaurant*), home-cooked Malay fish curries made by loveable *bumoh* who prides himself on being able to say 'thank you' in 30 languages, Papa Din Salat is also a renowned masseur.

Seafood

Eden Seafood Village, 69a Batu Ferringhi, if it swims, *Eden* cooks it – priced according to weight – not cheap, nightly cultural shows, *Eden* has now expanded to include two other big, clean red restaurants, adjacent and opposite the original, the *Ferringhi Village* at 157b and *Penang Village*.

Ferringhi Garden, 34 Batu Ferringhi, open courtyard or a/c interior serving lobster and tiger prawns.

The Catch, Jln Teluk Bahang, next to *Mutiara Hotel*, Malay, Chinese, Thai and international seafood dishes, huge fish-tanks for fresh fish, prawns, crabs, lobster etc, 1-hr-long cultural show daily, pleasant setting, one of the best seafood restaurants on the island. Recommended.

End of the World, end of Teluk Bahang beach, huge quantities of fresh seafood, its chilli crabs are superb and its lobster is the best value for money on the island (about RM25 each), pleasant setting on beach, not too many tourists. Recommended.

Happy Garden, Batu Ferringhi, left after police station and *Eden* restaurant, pretty garden, Chinese and Western dishes.

Hollywood, Tanjung Bungah, Batu Ferringhi, great views over the beach, serves *inche kabin* chicken stews and good selection of seafood.

Thai

Dusit Thai, 92 Batu Ferringhi (next to *Lone Pine Hotel*).

Bars and clubs

Georgetown *p159, map p160*

Most of the big hotels have In-house nightclubs and discos. Expect to pay cover charges if you are not a guest.

Leith St, Lbh Leith (next to Waldorf Hotel), pleasant bar, building is 150 years old and many original features have been retained, pitchers of Carlsberg, satay and prawn, and other light snacks.

George's, Sunway Hotel, 33 New Lane, quintessentially English, live music.

Chillout Club, The Gurney Hotel, 18 Persiaran Gurney, Georgetown, T4-3707000. Good dance club with R&B and house music. Very popular with 20-somethings; Wed night ladies night.
The Garage, 2 Penang Rd (opp E&O Hotel), T4-2636868. There are several bars and clubs inside this restored art deco garage including Slippery Senoritas, a tapas and Salsa bar with live South American music and performing bar staff. Recommended. Open 1100-0300.

Batu Ferringhi and Teluk Bahang

p165, map p166

Beers, Grandplaza Parkroyal.
Borsalino, *Grandplaza Parkroyal*, open 2100-0200. Sunken dance floor, fun disco.
Cool Bananas & Sunset Bar, good selection of beers, some draught, low prices, darts and snooker nights.
Ozone, *Mar Vista Resort*, Batu Ferringhi, open 2100-0200. Disco, karaoke and live band area.
Sapphire, *Ferringhi Beach Hotel*, open 2400-0100, 30% discount on pouring brands and draught beer, Ladies' Night Tue.
Swing Pub, *Bayview Beach*, cross between a pub and a disco.

Entertainment

Georgetown *p159, map p160*

Cinemas

All cinemas are now to be found in cineplexes, within the shopping centres.
Prangin Mall, best of the bunch in the new shopping complex opposite KOMTAR.
The old Odean Theatre still shows Indian and southeast Asian offerings. Entrance is via some rather dodgy guys loitering around the entrance.

Batu Ferringhi and Teluk Bahang

p165, map p166

Most of the larger hotels have cultural shows in the evening.
Eden Seafood Village, Batu Ferringhi.

Festivals

Georgetown *p159, map p160*

Feb/Mar Chap Goh Meh, celebrated on the 15th night of the first month of the Chinese lunar calendar; girls throw oranges into the sea for their suitors to catch.
May/Jun **Penang International Dragon Boat Race, Tuen Ng festival** near Penang Bridge; teams from around the region and beyond compete. (Moveable date).
Floral Festival at the Botanic Gardens held at the end of May/Jun. City parades by Malays (at Fort Cornwallis), Chinese (at Khoo Kongsi) and Indians (at Market St). See tourist office for details.
Sep **Penang Lantern Festival** held at the end of Sep, a parade with lanterns. The Mid-Autumn festival. (Moveable).
Oct/Nov **Deepavali Open House**, festivities in Little India. (Moveable).

Shopping

Georgetown *p159, map p160*

This requires a lot of wandering around the narrow streets & alleyways off Jln Penang. The main areas are Jln Penang, Jln Burmah and Lebuh Campbell.

Antiques

An export licence is still required for non-imported goods. Shops are concentrated on and around Jln Penang with the best ones at the top end opposite Eastern and Oriental Hotel. There are also antique shops along Rope Walk (Jln Pintal Tali). Most stock antiques from Burma, Thailand, Indonesia, Malaysia, Sabah and Sarawak, as well as a few local bargains. Another street with a number of crafty-cum-antique shops is Rope Walk or Jln Pintal Tali.
Oriental Arts Co, 3f Penang Rd. Well-established with a fine collection of antiques
Penang Antique House, 27 Jln Patani, showcase of Peranakan (Straits Chinese) artefacts – porcelain, rosewood with mother-of-pearl inlay, Chinese embroideries and antique jewellery.

Art galleries

ABN-AMRO Arts Centre, 9 Lebuh Pantai. Formerly the ABN-AMRO bank building, beautiful colonial house with great photo exhibitions.
College of Art and Music is housed in a grand colonial building on Leith St.
College Gallery, 7 Leith St, T4-2618087. Exhibitions are occasionally on view here.
Galerie Mai, 54 Tung Hing Building, Jln Burmah, T4-377504.

The Art Gallery, 36B Burmah Rd, T4-2298219.
Yahong Art Gallery, Batu Ferrenghi, T4-8811093, open 0930-2100, has a variety of batik exhibits as well as some jewellery and other works of art.

Batik

Asia Co, 314 Jln Penang.
Maphilindo Baru, 217 Penang Rd, excellent range of batiks and sarongs (including songket) from Malaysia, Sumatra and Java.
Sam's Batik House, 159 Jln Penang.
Yuyi Batik House, Level 3, Kompleks Tun Abdul Razak (KOMTAR), Jln Penang. Factory outlet in Teluk Bahang and souvenir shops in Batu Ferringhi.
Ying Yang, 187 Penang Rd. From wooden curios, incense to tie-dyed hippy garb.

Books

There are several bookshops in Lebuh Chulia near *Swiss Hotel*, selling second-hand books.
HS Sam Bookstore, 144 Lebuh Chulia, prides itself on being well organized and runs a sideline in travel services: Thai visas, bus ticketing, car/bike rental and has a luggage storage.
MPH Bookstore, Island Plaza, Jln Tanjong Tokong.
Parvez Book Store, 419 Lebuh Chulia (as well as dealing in books they arrange Thai visas and trips, and car/motorbike hire).
Popular Bookshop, Arked Ria 2, KOMTAR Tower and at Midland Park Complex, Jln Burmah.
Times Bookshop, Penang Plaza, 1st Flr, 126 Burmah Rd.

Camping gear

Tye Yee Seng Canvas, 162 Chulia St, good stock of tents, rucksacks, sleeping bags and beach umbrellas.

Cassettes, electrical and photographic equipment

The best place to look for these items is in the shops along Jln Campbell
Curios and unusual bargains
Many of the curios are imported from China and are very well priced.
Lebuh Chulia, Bishop and Rope Walk (Jln Pintal Tali).
Tan Embroidery Co, 20 Lebuh Pantai. Has a good selection.

Food shops

There are a number of outlets in Georgetown, mostly Chinese-run, selling locally produced specialities.
Cap Jempol Tropiks, either at 17 Leith St (next to *Cathay Hotel*) or 50c Penang Rd (next to *Peking Hotel*). For a selection of unusual pre-packaged products, such as dried mango, jackfruit, nutmeg oil and coconut cookies.
Eu Yan Sang, 156 Chulia St. Chinese teas and ginseng in a variety of forms are the speciality of this shop who offer a herb-boiling service in a cauldron that bubbles inside the doorway.
Gama, behind the KOMTAR Tower, is excellent for stocking up on basics.
Him Heang, 162 Jln Burmah. Similar products to Wee Ling including *pong pneah* (pastry filled with molasses or caramel).
Wee Ling, 132 Chulia St. Dragon Ball biscuits, pastry balls filled with a mung bean paste.

Handicrafts

Jln Penang is a good place to start: **China Handicraft Co**, 3d Jln Penang; **Federation Arts & Crafts**, 3c Jln Penang; **Peking Arts & Crafts** at 3b Jln Penang.
Arts and Culture Information Centre, T2642273, 1200-1400 Thu to Sat.
See Koon Hoe, 315 Lebuh Chulia, sells Chinese opera masks, jade seals and paper umbrellas.
The Garage, 2 Penang Rd (opp E&O Hotel). This bright orange art deco restored garage which formerly serviced Austins, Jags and Morris Minors now houses gift and souvenir stalls.
The Mah Jong Factory in Love Lane sells high-quality Mah Jong sets.

Jewellery

Lebuh Campbell and Lebuh Kapitan Klang. Reasonable quality fake wristwatches can be purchased near the Snake Temple (see page 168).

Markets

The night market changes venue every night and is more often than not out of town. There are illegal street vendors selling CDs etc bargain and you might also happen to beat the odds of receiving a faulty disk. There may be plans in the future to set up a permanent night market in Chinatown but these are as yet unfulfilled. Jln Chulia and the surrounding streets have a busy and friendly atmosphere with good late-night cafés. It is popular with westerners and most bars offer international football games on the television or a film.

Shopping complexes

Midland Park, Jln Burmah, opposite Adventist Hospital, amusement arcades, roller skating, bowling alley, several fast-food outlets, hawker foodstalls. *Popular Bookshop* and shops.
Island Plaza, Jln Tanjung Tokong, on road to Batu Ferringhi, upmarket shops – *East India Company*, *Guess*, *Fila*, *Coca Restaurant*, the *Forum*, a food court and a new cinema.
Bukit Jambul Shopping Complex, close to the airport, good range of shops, food outlets and an ice-rink.
KOMTAR, hundreds of boutiques, two department stores, fast-food restaurants, amusement arcade.
Prangin Mall, new complex opposite KOMTAR. Far more upmarket than the others, with an ice-rink and cineplex. Also on offer is a *Starbucks* for those craving real coffee. There are restaurants, fast-food outlets and a few more upmarket shops.

Batu Ferringhi and Teluk Bahang

p165, map p166

Craft Batik, opposite the Grandplaza ParkRoyal, batik cloth sold by metre and as ready-made garments, demonstrations can be seen to rear of showroom.
Deepee's Silk Shop, 591 Batu Ferringhi, offers a reasonable tailoring service.
Sim Seng Lee Batik and Handicrafts, 391 Batu Ferringhi.
Yahong Art Gallery, 58d Batu Ferringhi Road, T4-8811251, F4-8811093, displays batik paintings by the Teng (born in China in 1914) family. The elder Teng is regarded as the father of Malaysian batik painting. Entrance is free and the batik works are certainly worth it. Also offers packaging and transport of bought goods to any international destination.

▲ Activities and tours

Georgetown *p159, map p160*

Bowling
Midland Park Complex, Jln Burmah.

Golf
Airforce Golf Club, Butterworth, T4-3322632, 9-hole course, green fees weekdays RM20, weekends RM30.
Bukit Jambul Golf & Country Club, Jln Bukit Jambul, T4-6442255, hilly course, green fees weekdays RM100, weekends RM150.
Penang Turf Club, Golf Section, Jln Batu Gantong, T4-2266701, http://penangturfclub.com, 18-hole, RM84 weekdays, RM126 weekends.
Kristal Golf Resort, 364 Jln Valdor, Seberang Perai Selatan, T4-5822280, www.kristalgolf.com.my Green fees weekdays RM105, weekends RM150.
Penang Golf Resort, Lot 2462, Mk6, Jln Bertram, 13200 Kepala Bates, T4-5782002, F4-5750226.

Horse racing
Penang Turf Club, Jln Batu Gantung, T4-2293233.

Snorkelling and diving
While Pulau Payar (Payar Island) is usually accessed from Langkawi, it is possible to organise diving and snorkelling day-trips out there from Penang.
East Marine Holidays, 5 Lengkok Nun, Penang (for the office), T4-2263022, www.eastmarine.com.my Costs around RM220 for snorkelling, RM320 for diving including the return ferry and buffet lunch.

Tour operators
Most of the budget travel agents are along Lebuh Chulia. There are quite a few agencies around the Swettenham Pier.
Everrise Tours & Travel, Lot 323, 2nd Flr, Wisma Central, 202 Jln, T2264329.
Georgetown Tourist Service, Jln Imigresen, T4-2295788 city island tours; **MSL Travel**, Ming Court Inn Lobby, Jln Macalister, T4-2272655 or 340 Lebuh Chulia, T4-2616154, student and youth travel bureau.
MS Star Travel Agencies, 475 Lebuh Chulia, T4-2622906.
Renae Agency, 2 Penang Port Commission Complex, T4-2622369.
Tour and Incentive Travel, Suite 7B, 7th Flr Menara BHL, Jln Sultan Ahmad Shah, T4-2274522.

Batu Ferringhi and Teluk Bahang

p165, map p166

Boat trips

Trips can be arranged through fishermen at Teluk Bahang. Negotiate the price in advance.

Traditional massage

Simple on-the-beach foot reflexology place opposite *Baba's*. Nice setting for a foot massage. Health clubs, such as the **Do-Club** in the Mar Vista Resort, Batu Ferringhi, in all major hotels offer massage.

Transport

Georgetown *p159, map p160*

Air

Bayan Lepas Airport is an international airport, 20 km south of Georgetown and 36 km from Batu Ferringhi, T4-6434411. Transport to town: taxis operate on a coupon system from the airport (30 mins to Georgetown, RM25). Regular connections with **Johor Bahru**, **KL**,and **Langkawi**. The once-daily Langkawi flight takes 30 mins (leaving Penang 1215). Worldwide international connections on *MAS*, most via KL except for direct London to Gerogetown route, return is via KL. Regular direct connections to **Singapore**, **Bangkok** and **Medan**, Sumatra.

Airline offices AirAsia. Just behind the MAS office in KOMTAR, T4-2615642; **Cathay Pacific**, AIA Building, Lebuh Farquhar, T4-2260411; **Emirates**, T4-2631100; **MAS**, Kompleks Tun Abdul Razak (KOMTAR), Jln Penang, T4-2620011 (the ticket office is on the ground floor, at the southern side of KOMTAR, and can only be entered from outside the complex) or at the airport, T4-6430811; **Singapore Airlines**, Wisma Penang Gardens, 42 Jln Sultan Ahmad Shah, T2263201; **Thai International**, Wisma Central, 202 Jln Macalister, T4-2266000. **United Airlines**, T4-2636020.

Bicycle hire

Rental from *Swiss Hotel*, Lebuh Chulia, RM20 per day.

Boat

Passenger and car ferries operate from adjacent terminals, Pengkalan Raja Tun Uda, T4-3315780. Ferry service between Georgetown and **Butterworth**. Ferries leave every 20 mins 0600-2400. less than RM1 return. **Selasa Express Ferry Company** has its office by the Penang Clock Tower, next to the Penang Tourist Office, T4-2625630. **Sejahtera** and **Fast Ferry Ventures** operate boats between Georgetown and **Langkawi** daily, two departures from each company a day, one around 0900 and another at 1430 (3 hrs), RM35 one way, RM60 return. Tickets can be bought from travel agents all over town. Boats leave from Swettenham Pier. It is possible to take a motorcycle or bicycle aboard.

International boat connections Several ferry companies including **Fast Ferry Ventures** operate a service between Penang and Belawan (Medan's port), **Sumatra**, from Swettenham Pier. Usually two departures daily, one around 0800 and another around 1430, RM90 one-way, RM160 return, journey time 4½ hrs. Note that the Sat departure is often full, so book a ticket beforehand if possible. Tickets can be bought from most guesthouses and travel agents. You will need to get a visa for Indonesia in advance before you arrive in the country.

Bus

City buses leave from Lebuh Victoria near the Butterworth ferry terminal and serve **Georgetown** and the surrounding districts. All buses leave for various points around the island from Pengkalan Weld (Weld Quay) – next to the ferry terminal, and all buses stop at KOMTAR. At the time of writing, the bus service was in some disarray as companies went out of business, and new ones started. Your best bet is to ask at the Tourist Office, or get a copy of the *Penang Tourist* Newspaper, which carries a copy of the bus routes.

The **long distance bus terminal** is beside the ferry terminal at Butterworth. Booking offices along Lebuh Chulia and inside KOMTAR. Some coaches operate from Pengkalan Weld direct to major towns on the peninsula (see Butterworth, page 168). **Masa Mara Travel**, 54/4 Jln Burmah, is an agent for direct express buses from Penang to **Kota Bharu** and **KL** (5 hrs). Minibus companies now organize an early morning pick-up from your hotel, to **Hat Yai**, from where there are connections north to Thailand. Pick ups at 0500, 0800, 1200, 1600 and 2200 . There are also regular bus connections to **Bangkok, Phuket** and **Surat Thani**. Also some hotels (eg *New Asia* and *Cathay*) organize minibuses to destinations in Thailand. There is an overnight bus to **Singapore**.

Car hire

The journey from Penang to KL is reasonably painless, at 4½ hrs. There is a RM7 toll to drive across the Penang Bridge to the mainland. No payment required for the inbound journey.
Budget, 28 Jln Penang, T4-6436025 and Bayan Lepas Airport.
Hawk Rent-a-car, T4-8813886.
Hertz, 38 Lebuh Farquhar, T4-2635914 and Bayan Lepas Airport.
Orix, City Bayview Hotel, 25A Lebuh Farquhar, T1 800 881555.
New Bob Rent-a-Car, 7/F Gottlieb Rc, T2291111 and Bayan Lapas Airport.

Motorcycle hire

In Georgetown there are several motorbike rental shops, many of them along Lebuh Chulia. It costs from around RM35 per day to hire a motorcycle depending on size.

Taxi

Long-distance taxis to all destinations on the peninsula operate from the depot beside the Butterworth ferry on Pengkalan Weld.
There are taxi stands on Jln Dr Lim Chwee Leong, Pengkalan Weld and Jln Magazine. Fares are not calculated by meter, so agree a price before you set off; short distances within the city cost RM5-7. A trip to the airport costs RM25.
Radio taxis, T4-8909918 (at ferry terminal).
CT Radio Taxi Service, T4-2299467.

Direct taxis from Penang to Thailand: overnight to **Hat Yai; Surat Thani** for Koh Samui, **Krabi** (for Phuket).

Train

The station is by the Butterworth ferry terminal, T4-2610290. Advance bookings for onward rail journeys can be made at the station or at the ferry terminal, Pengkalan Weld, Georgetown. From Butterworth: two daily connections with **Alor Star**, **Taiping**, **Ipoh**, **KL** (6 hrs), **JB** (see page 40 and 41 for timetable). See also Butterworth, page 181.

Trishaw

Bicycle rickshaws that carry 2 people are one of the most practical and enjoyable ways to explore Georgetown. Cost RM1 per half mile or RM15 per hour; if taking an hour's trip around town, agree on the route first, bargain and set the price in advance.

Batu Ferringhi and Teluk Bahang

p165, map p166

Bus

Blue bus No 93 goes to Batu Ferringhi/Teluk Bahang from Pengkalan Weld (Weld Quay) or KOMTAR in Georgetown, every 30 mins, RM2, 30-40 mins.

Car hire

Avis, *Rasa Sayang Hotel*; **Hertz**, *Casuarina Beach Hotel*; **Kasina Baru**, 651 Mukim 2, Teluk Bahang (opposite *Mutiara Beach Resort*), T4-8811988; **Mayflower**, *asuarina Beach Hotel*; **Ruhanmas**, 157B Batu Ferringhi, T4-8811576; **Sintat Rent-a-Car**, *Lone Pine Hotel*.

Motorbike hire

Quite a few places along Batu Ferringhi offer motorbike hire, all of them clearly signposted on the road and most of the guesthouses also hire bikes. Expect to pay around RM110 per day for a car, RM35 for a motorbike.
Saber Holidays, Batu Ferringhi Beach, T4-8811882.

Taxi

Stands on Batu Ferringhi (opposite *Golden Sands Hotel*). The big hotels along the strip are well served by taxis. Be warned though that some taxis operate on commission for certain resorts and guesthouses. Try and work out roughly where you want to stay before you get there and ring up your destination in advance to check rates. Of course not all taxi drivers are quite so manipulative; many are friendly, honest and a good source of information. Taxi from airport to Batu Ferringhi, 40 mins, 45RM.

Butterworth *p168*

Butterworth is the main transport hub for **Penang**, and buses and trains operate into **Thailand**, and down to **KL** and **Singapore**.

Bus

The bus station is next to the ferry terminal. There are regular connections with **KL**, **Taiping**, **Kuala Kangsar**, **Melaka**, **Johor**

Bahru, **Kota Bharu**, **Kuala Terengganu**, **Kuantan** and **Ipoh** (2 hrs). Buses leave at least every hour from Butterworth for **Kuala Kedah** (Langkawi ferry). There are also buses to **Keroh**, on the border with Thailand, from where it is possible to get Thai taxis to Betong.

Ferry

Ferries for pedestrians and cars and leave for **Georgetown** every 15-20 mins. The 20-min trip (little used now the bridge is built) is free from Penang to Butterworth, while the journey from Butterworth to Penang is under RM1 (60 sen; RM7 for a car).

Taxi

Taxis these leave from next to the ferry terminal. If you take a taxi to Penang you must pay the taxi fare plus the toll for the bridge.

Train

The railway station is beside the Penang ferry terminal. There are two daily connections with **Alor Star**, **Taiping**, **Ipoh**, **KL** and **JB** (see page 40 and 41 for timetable), and trains to **Bangkok**, (19 hrs) and **Singapore** (14 hrs). Butterworth is one of the main stopovers on the Eastern and Orient Express, which travels in style from Singapore to Bangkok. Passengers disembark here to make the 3-hr trip by ferry and rickshaw to Georgetown.

Directory

Georgetown *p159, map p160*

Banks

Most banks in Georgetown are in or around the GPO area and Lebuh Pantai. Most money changers are in the banking area and Jln Masjid Kapitan Keling and Lebuh Pantai, close to the Immigration Office. **Bank Bumiputra**, 37 Lebuh Pantai; **Citibank**, 42 Jln Sultan Ahmad Shah; **HSBC**, Lebuh Pantai; **Maybank**, 9 Lebuh Union (branches everywhere!); **Standard Chartered**, 2 Lebuh Pantai.

Internet

The Global Net, 94 Love Lane, also sells cut-price ferry tickets to Medan and Langkawi, but the owner wouldn't let on how he can sell them that cheap! **Ginza Internet Café**, 428 Jln Chulia, T4-2644309; **Omegactec**, 50 Lebuh Lieth,T/F4-2643750, sells teaching software and internet services, friendly and helpful staff. There are also a number of other internet cafés along Lebuh Chulia, all offering similar rates of RM3/hr. There are also internet cafes off Jln Burma, down Jln Macalister, which cater for the more hardened computer games addict.

Post

Lebuh Pitt, efficient poste restante, also provides a parcel-wrapping service, T4-2618973.

Consulates

Denmark, Bernam Agencies, Hong Kong Bank Chambers, Lebuh Downing, T4-2624886; **France**, 82 Bishop St, Wisma Rajab, T4-2629707; **Germany**, Bayan Lepas Free Trade Zone, T4-6471288; **Indonesia**, 467 Jln Burmah, T4-2275141; **Japan**, 2 Jln Biggs, T4-2263030; **Netherlands**, Algemen Bank Nederland, 9 Lebuh Pantai, T4-2616471; **Thailand**, 1 Jln Ayer Raja, T4-2268029 (visas arranged in 2 days); **UK**, Birch House, 73 Jln Datuk Keramat, T4-2625333.

Libraries

Alliance Francaise, 46 Jalan Phuah Hin Leong T4-2276008, **The British Council**, 3 Weld Quay, T4-2620330. **Penang Public Library**, Dewan Sri Pinang, Lebuh Light, T4-2293555.

Medical services

General Hospital (government), Jln Residensi, T4-2293333; **Lam Wah Ee Hospital** (private), 141 Jln Batu Lancang, T4-6571888.

Places of worship

St George's Church, Lebuh Farquhar, services in English 0830 and 1830 every Sun.

Telephone

Telecoms office (international calls; fax and telex facilities): Jln Burmah.

Useful addresses

Immigration Office, on the corner of Lebuh Light and Lebuh Pantai, T4-2615122.

Butterworth *p168*

Banks Maybank, UMBC and HSBC on Jln Bagan Luar. Internet **Genesys**, 4922 Jln Bagan Luar, T3243710. RM6 per hr.

Alor Star and around

→ Colour map 1, grid A2

Alor Star is the capital of Kedah State on the road north to the Thai border. It is the home town of former Prime Minister Dr Mahathir Mohamad and is the commercial centre for northwest Malaysia. Its name, which has been corrupted from Alor Setar, means 'grove of setar trees' (which produce a sour fruit). Kedah is now Malaysia's most important rice-growing state; together with neighbouring Perlis, it produces 44% of the country's rice, and is known as jelapang padi (rice-barn country).

Nearby is the Bujang Valley Historical Park, where the remains of an ancient Hindu kingdom lie, Gunung Jerai, the highest mountain in the northwest and Kuala Perlis a small fishing port, the jumping off point for Pulau Langkawi, see page 188. *» For Sleeping, Eating and other listings, see pages 185-187.*

Ins and outs

Getting there

Alor Star's airport is 10 km north of town. Direct domestic connections with KL. Both MAS and AirAsia fly from here. From the railway station near the town centre trains connect with KL and Singapore (and points between) and north to the border with Thailand and Hat Tai. Alor Star is also on the main N-S highway and there are bus connections with all the major destinations on the Peninsular as well as Singapore and Hat Yai. The bus terminal is several kilometres ouside town. For Kuala Kedah and the ferry to Langkawi catch bus no 106 from the local bus station. Share taxis leave from the stand near the centre of town.

Getting around

Taxis are available for out of town trips from the stand on Jln Langgar in Alor Star and the town bus station is not far away on Jln Stesyen, also close to the train station. It's easy enough to walk around the town centre.

Tourist information

Kedah State Tourist Office, ⓘ *2nd Flr, State Secretariat Building, Jln Sultan Badlisah, Alor Star, T4-7333302*. Limited selection of brochures, not much information on Alor Star or Kedah.

History

Kedah is the site of some of the oldest settlements on the peninsula and the state's royal family can trace its line back several centuries. The ancient Indian names for the state are Kadaram and Kathah, and archaeologists believe the site of the 5th century kingdom of Langkasuka was just to the southeast of Kedah Peak (Gunung Jerai), in the Bujang River valley, half-way between Butterworth and Alor Star.

Sights

Alor Star has some interesting buildings, most of which are clustered round the central Padang Besar (Jalan Pekan Melayu/Jalan Raja); apart from them, the town is unremarkable. The most interesting building is the State Mosque, the Moorish-style Masjid Zahir, completed in 1912 and designed by state architect James Gorman. Almost directly opposite is the Thai-inspired **Balai Besar**, (audience hall), built in 1898, which is still used by the Sultan of Kedah on ceremonial occasions; it houses the royal throne. Close to the mosque is the **Balai Seni Negeri**, (State Art Gallery), ⓘ *1000-1800 Sat-Thu, 1000-1200 1430-1800 Fri*, which contains a collection of historical paintings and antiques, including Malay handicrafts and colonial collections. The building was formerly the High Court and was built in the early 20th century. Further down Jalan Raja is the 400-year-old **Balai Nobat**, an octagonal building topped by an onion-shaped dome. This building houses Kedah's *nobat* (royal percussion orchestra); it is said to date back to the 15th century. Again, it is not open to the public.

Royal Museum Kedah, (Muzium Di Raja), is next to the Baslai Besar and gives an insight into the heritage and traditions of the Sultans of Kedah. ⓘ *Sat-Thu 1000-1800, Fri 1000-1200 and 1430-1800, free.*

The **State Museum**, (Muzium Negeri) ⓘ *1000-1800 Sat-Thu, 0900-1200, 1500-1800 on Fri*, situated around 2 km north of the centre, is styled on the Balai Besar and was built in 1936. The museum houses exhibits on local farming and fishing practices, a collection of early Sung Dynasty porcelain and some finds from the archaeological excavations in the Bujang Valley (see below).

The **Pekan Rabu** (Wednesday market), which is now held all week long, is a good place to buy local handicrafts and try some of the traditional food of Kedah. It does not cater for tourists, and is therefore a good place to find local foods and see everyday Malay life.

Two other places of interest are the **Royal Boat House**, near the Sungai Anak Bukit, west of the clock tower. It houses boats belonging to former rulers of Kedah.

For prime minister-watchers, the house where former Prime Minister Dr Mahathir Mohamad was born on 20 December 1925, has been opened as a **museum**, ⓘ *18 Lorong Kilang Ais, off Jalan Pegawai, 0900-1800 Sat-Thu, 0900-1200, 1500-1800 Fri*, giving an insight into his early days of 'simple' living. Photographs and various bits-and-pieces of Mahathir memorabilia including his 'favourite' bicycle are on display.

Bujang Valley

ⓘ *To get there, change buses at Bedong; it is easier to take a taxi from Alor Star.*

Situated near the small town of **Sungai Petani**, to the southeast of Kedah Peak (Gunung Jerai), is this site of some of Malaysia's most exciting archaeological discoveries: finds there have prompted the establishment of the **Bujung Valley Historical Park**, under the management of the National Museum. The name Bujang is derived from a Sanskrit word, *bhujanga*, meaning serpent. It is thought to be the site of the capital of the 5th-century Hindu kingdom of Langkas, the hearthstone of Malay fairytale romance. While the architectural remains are a far cry from those of Cambodia's Angkor Wat, they are of enormous historical significance.

The city is thought to represent one of the very earliest Hindu settlements in Southeast Asia, several centuries before Angkor, and at least 200 years before the founding of the first Hindu city in Java. The capital of Langkasuka is thought to have been abandoned in the 6th century, probably following a pirate raid. There have been some remarkable finds at the site, including brick and marble temple and palace complexes of both Hindu and Buddhist origin - coins, statues, Sanskrit inscriptions, weapons and jewellery. In 1925 archaeologists stumbled across "a magnificent little granite temple near a beautiful waterfall" on a hillside above the ancient city. One of them, Dr Quarith Wales, the director of the Greater-India Research Committee wrote of the temple: "It had never been robbed, except of images, although the bronze trident of Shiva was found. In each of the stone post-holes were silver caskets containing rubies and sapphires." More than 50 temples have now been unearthed in the Bujang area, most of them buried in soft mud along the river bank.

For several centuries, Indian traders used the city as an entrepôt in their dealings with China. Rather than sail through the pirate-infested Melaka Strait, the traders stopped at the natural harbour at Kuala Merbok and had their goods portered across the isthmus to be collected by ships on the east side. There is speculation that the area of the Sungai Bujang was later used as a major port of the Srivijaya Empire, whose capital was at Palembang, Sumatra. But recent findings by Malaysian archaeologists have begun to contradict some of the earlier theories that Hinduism was the earliest of the great religions to be established on the Malay peninsula. Recently excavated artefacts suggest that Buddhism was introduced to the area before Hinduism. The local archaeologists maintain that the Buddhist and Hindu phases of Bujang Valley's history are distinct, with the Hindu period following on much later, in the 10th-14th centuries. This is at odds with previous assertions by archaeologists that the remains of the temples' "laterite sanctuary towers are of the earliest type and not yet suggestive of pre-Angkorian architecture".

Many of the finds can be seen in the museum at Bukit Batu Pahat near Bedong; alongside the museum is a reconstruction of the most significant temple unearthed so far, **Candi Bukit Batu Pahat**, Temple of the Hill of Chiselled Stone. Eight sanctuaries have been restored and a museum displays statues and other finds. ⓘ *0900-1600 Mon-Thu, 1445-1600 Fri, 0900-1215 Sat-Sun.*

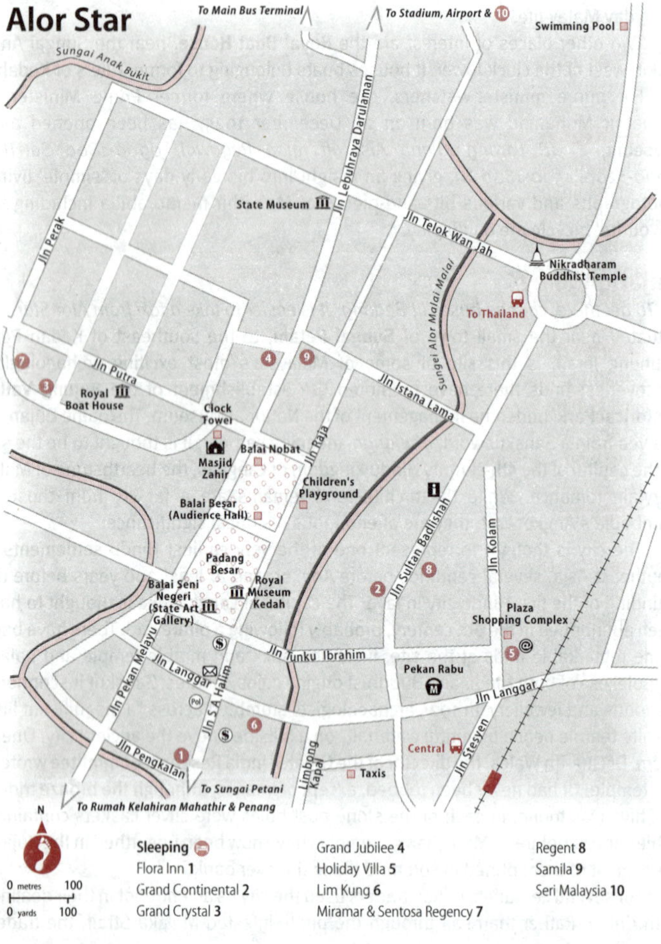

Gunung Jerai → *Altitude: 1,206m*

ⓘ Gunung Jerai is about 4 km north of Garun. Jeeps from Gurun to the resort run 0900-1700. Gurun is 33 km south of Alor Star and 60 km north of Butterworth. Northbound buses to Alor Star and southbound buses to Butterworth will all pass through Gurun where you can hop off and take a taxi. Alternatively, take a bus to Sungei Petani where there's a bus every 30 mins to the bottom of the hill. There are also local buses every 45 mins from Alor Star to the base of the hill. For more information see Tourism Malaysia, the Kedah State Tourist Office in Alor Star or the Gunung Jerai Resort.

Otherwise known as Kedah Peak, Gunung Jerai is the highest mountain in the northwest and is part of the **Sungai Teroi Forest Recreation Park**. This park is managed by the state government, and visitors to the park will be accompanied by a guide. A jeep meets visitors at the foot of the mountain and transports them to the summit. The peak has been used as a navigational aid for ships heading down the Strait of Melaka for centuries. It is between the main road and the coast, north of Sungai Petani. In 1884 the remains of a 6th- century Hindu shrine were discovered on the summit. It had been hidden under a metre-thick layer of peat, which caught fire, revealing the brick and stone construction, thought to be linked with the kingdom of Langkasuka. Archaeologists speculate that the remains may originally have been a series of fire altars. But they are destined to remain a mystery as a radio station has now been built on top. About 3 km north of Gurun, between Sungai Petani and Alor Star, a narrow road goes off to the left and leads to the top of the mountain (11 km). There is even a small hotel just below the summit and the Museum of Forestry on top. There are good views out over Kedah's paddy fields and the coast.

Kuala Kedah

Historically the town has been an important port for trade with India and there are the ruins of an old fort, built between 1771 and 1780. The fort was built for defence of the state capital from pirate attacks. It fell into the hands of the Siamese army, under the leadership of Raja Ligor in 1821 and was occupied by Siam until 1842, after which it was abandoned. Kuala Kedah, 12 km W of Alor Star, is renowned for its seafood stalls. It is also a departure point for Langkawi (see page 188).

Kuala Perlis

This small fishing port, 14 km from Kangar, (the capital of the state of Perlis, the smallest in Malaysia) at the delta of the Sungai Perlis is mainly a jumping-off point for Pulau Langkawi and Phuket (in Thailand). It is noted for its local fast-food, *laksa*, and there are foodstalls by the jetty. There is a night market every Tuesday.

Sleeping

Alor Star *p182, map p184*

AL Holiday Villa, 162/163 Jln Tunku Ibrahim (contained in the large Plaza shopping centre), T4-7349999, hbas@pd.jaring.my Large luxury hotel in the centre of town, with a great swathe of facilities including IDD telephone, in-house video, and 24-hr restaurant. Guests have access to the Villa Recreational Centre with fitness centre, sauna, pool and steambath.

AL Sentosa Regency Hotel, 250 Jln Putra, T4-7303999, regency@po.jaring.my A new hotel with spacious rooms, some semi-suites also available. Facilities include restaurant, tea/coffee-making facilities in room, gym, laundry service, satellite TV. Pleasant and not too impersonal.

A Grand Continental, Lot 134-141, Jln Sultan Badlishah, T4-7335917, www.grandhotelsinternational.com.my/ A/c, 138 rooms, bath, TV, in-house movies, coffee house, business centre, car rental, central location and great-value discounts from the rack rate usually available.

B Grand Crystal, 40 Jln Kampong Perak, T4-7313333, www.grandhotelsinternational.com.my/crystal_asetar A/c, TV, bath, pool, coffee house – like the *Grand*

Continental (it is part of the same chain), discounts often on offer, includes breakfast.

B Samila, 27 Jln Lebuhraya Darulaman, T4-7318888, F4-7339934. A/c, restaurant, nightclub, a step down from the *Grand Crystal* in terms of price. Dark wood 1970s décor creates a stylish and rather retro interior, plus it has a friendly and comfortable atmosphere.

B Seri Malaysia, Mukim Alor Malai, Daerah Kota Setar, Jln Stadium, T4-7308738, F4-7307594. A 100-room hotel, one of the 'amazingly affordable' chains, a/c, TV, shower, tea/coffee-making facilities, in-house video, café, clean, functional and good value, located between stadium and public swimming pool at north end of town.

C Flora Inn, 8 Kompleks Medan Raja, Jln Pengkalan Kapal, T4-7322375, F4-7308058. Overlooking the Kedah River, a/c, TV, food court, coffee-making facilities, laundry service available. Rather tired décor but spacious. Not the best-value option in town, although at the bottom end of their range of rooms they have some reasonably priced 'eco' (ie economy rather than ecological) rooms.

C Regent, 1536 Jln Sultan Badlishah, T4-7311900, F4-7311291. All 25 rooms with a/c, great value for money. Recently refurbished, new TVs with cable channels and movies available, new bathrooms and entire hotel repainted to give bright, friendly atmosphere. Recommended.

C-D Grand Jubilee Hotel, 429 Jln Kancut, T4-7330055, F4-7330197. Clean and well managed. Rooms with shower, some with a/c and TV. Simple but friendly.

E Lim Kung, 36A Jln Langgar, T4-722459. Fan only, good value. Recommended.

C Miramar, 246 Jln Putra, T4-7338144, F4-7311668. Simple and clean rooms with a/c and attached bathrooms. Some cheaper fan rooms. Standard budget option.

Bujang Valley *p183*

B Sungai Petani Inn, Jalan Kolam Air, Sungai Petani, T4-4213411. The plushest in town with air conditioning and pool.

B-D Hotel Duta, 7 Jalan Petri. The best of the budget hotels.

Gunung Jarai *p185*

B Gunung Jerai Resort, T04414311. A 1920s resthouse, rooms and chalets, garden.

B Peranginan Gunung Jerai, Sungai Teroi Forest Recreation Park, T4-4223345. A/c, restaurant, attached bathrooms with showers, slightly worn but reasonable.

Kuala Perlis *p185*

B Hotel Seaview, T4-9852171 is across from the taxi rank with plain rooms and a coffee house if you miss the boat to Langkawi.

Eating

Alor Star *p182, map p184*

Chinese

Sri Pumpong, Jln Pumpong. It's speciality is barbecued fish.

Indian

Bunga Tanjong, Jln Seberang, Indian Muslim food, seafood curries.

Thai

Café de Siam, Jln Kota, lashings of Thai-style seafood.

Kway Teow Jonid, Jln Stadium (next to the police station), fried *kway teow*, washed down with teh tarik.

Malay

Rose Restaurant, Jln Sultan Badishah, local café serving good *roti* and *nasi*. Recommended.

Foodstalls

'Garden' Hawker Centre, Jln Stadium, good range of cuisines, next to stadium, Jln Langgar (in front of cinema); **Old Market** (*Pekan Rabu*), Jln Tunku Ibrahim.

Shopping

Alor Star *p182, map p184*

An extensive shopping plaza can be found in the multi-storey building at the end of Jln Tunku Ibrahim (it also houses the *Holiday Villa Hotel*). **Handicrafts** can be found in the Old Market, Pekan Rabu, on Jln Tunku Ibrahim.

Transport

Alor Star *p182, map p184*

Air

The airport is 10 km north of town. Daily connections on MAS and AirAsia with **KL**.

Airline offices AirAsia office at the airport; MAS, 180 Kompleks Alor Star, Lebuhraya Darulaman, T4-711106; also next to *Flora Inn*, Jln Pengkalan.

Bus

Alor Star has rather a confusion of bus stations. The main bus terminal is about 2 km north of the town centre, off Jln Bakar Bata, and most long-distance buses leave from here. Destinations include KL, **Melaka**, **Ipoh**, **JB** , **Kota Bharu**, **Kuantan** and **Kuala Terengganu**. There are connections with KL every 2 hours (RM26) and one bus to JB at 0830 (RM47). Local southbound buses, including buses to **Butterworth** and **Kuala Kedah** (for Langkawi), leave from the central bus station in front of the railway station on Jln Stesyen in the centre of town and also the express bus station. Local buses also leave from the station by the taxi stop off Jln Langgar; long-distance connections eastwards with **Kota Bharu** also leave from here; two departures daily (0900 and 2100, RM23.60).

International connections the northern section of the north-south Highway runs to the Malaysian border crossing at Bukit Kayu Hitam, from where it is easy to cross to **Sadao**, the nearest Thai town on the other side of the border. Most of the buses leave from Penang/Butterworth for **Bangkok** and other destinations on the Kra Isthmus. There are, though, two direct connections a day between Alor Star and **Hat Yai** in Thailand following the north-south highway through Changlun to Bukit Kayu Hitam – the easiest way to cross the border. These leave from the small station on Jln Sultan Badlishah, north of the town centre. Alternatively, catch a bus or taxi from Alor Star, following the north-south highway, to Bukit Kayu Hitam, on the border with Thailand. It is then a shortish walk past the paraphernalia of border-dom to the bus and taxi stop where there are connections with the Thai town of Sadao (a few kilometres on) and Hat Yai. A less popular alternative is to travel to Padang Besar (accessible from Kangar in Perlis), where the railway line crosses the border. From here it is an easy walk to the bus or train station for connections to Hat Yai. The other option is to take a taxi from Sungai Petani to Keroh and cross the border into Thailand's red-light outpost at Betong.

There are also bus connections with **Singapore** from the main long-distance terminal, or Express Bus Station, 1 km north of town. Share taxis also available. A shuttle bus also goes here, from Jln Langar in the centre.

Taxi

These leave from the stand just south of Jln Langgar, near the town centre, for Penang, Kuala Kedah (for Langkawi) and Kangar (Perlis).

Train

Station is off Jln Langgar. There are two trains a day (at 1851 and 2119) to KL and Butterworth, see page 40 and 41 for timetable. There is an express train from Alor Star to Hat Yai departing daily at 1617. The slower Ekspres Langkawi train leaves for Hat Yai at 0815.

Kuala Kedah *p185*

Bus

Buses leave at least every hour from **Alor Star** to Kuala Kedah. For long-distance bus connections you must change at Alor Star.

Boat

Regular connections with **Langkawi**. Langkawi ferry leaves at least every hour between 0800 and 1900, 1½ hrs, RM15.

Kuala Perlis *p185*

Bus and taxi

Both leave from the ferry terminal. Regular connections by bus and taxi with **Butterworth**, less-regular links with **Alor Star, KL** (around every hour between 0900 and 2200), **Kota Bharu** (0800 and 1945, RM26) and **Padang Besar** (for connections with Thailand, see below) and local buses to **Kangar**. High-speed ferry: departs from Kuala Perlis jetty approximately every hr between 0800 and 2000 to Pulau Langkawi, 45 mins, RM12. Last ferry back to Kuala Perlis leaves at 2000.

Directory

Alor Star *p182, map p184*

Banks Bank Bumiputra, Jln Tunku Ibrahim; Chartered Bank, Overseas Union Bank and UMBC are all on Jln Raja. **Internet** There are cafés in the Plaza shopping centre at the end of Jln Tunku Ibrahim. **Post**, GPO, Jln Langgar, opposite the Police Station.

Pulau Langkawi

→ *Colour map 1, grid A1*

The Langkawi group is an archipelago of 99 islands around 30 km off the west coast of Peninsular Malaysia, and Pulau Langkawi itself, by far the largest of the group, is a mountainous, palm-fringed island with scattered fishing kampongs, paddy fields and sandy coves. Some of the islands are nothing more than deserted limestone outcrops rearing out of the turquoise sea, cloaked in jungle, and ringed by coral.

The name Langkawi is the last surviving namesake of the ancient kingdom of Langkasuka, known as negari alang-kah suka, or 'the land of all one's wishes'. Langkasuka, whose capital is thought to have stood at the base of Kedah Peak, south of Alor Star, is mentioned in Chinese accounts as far back as AD 500. According to a Chinese Liang Dynasty record, the kingdom of 'Langgasu' was founded in the first century and its Hindu king, Bhagadatta, paid tribute to the Chinese Emperor. The names of its kings – known as daprenta-hyangs – resurface in Malay legends and fairytales.

The main settlement of locals is in the dusty town of Kuah, while upmarket resorts are at Pantai Cenang, Pantai Tengah, Burau Bay, Datai Bay and Pantai Rhu. Panta Canang and Tengah also have a smattering of cheaper guesthouses. » *For Sleeping, Eating and other listings, see pages 192-200.*

Ins and outs

Getting there

Langkawi's airport is 20 km from Kuah (the main town and location of the jetty). Regular connections with KL, JB, KK, Kuching and Penang. There are also flights direct from London and Singapore. Ferries from Kuala Perlis and Kuala Kedah leave roughly every hour to Langkawi and there are three to four daily departures from Penang by sea.

Getting around

Taxis offer reasonably priced travel around the island (prices are fixed according to the distance). Cars, motorcycles and bicycles are also available for hire. Boats are also available for hire to explore the neighbouring islands.

Best time to visit

Langkawi's wet season usually spans the months between April to October. The water clarity is poor between July and September, the months of the monsoon, and the sea can be rough.

Tourist information

It is easy to drive round the island at a fairly leisurely pace within a day.

Langkawi Tourist Information Centre, ⓘ *Jln Pesiaran Putra, Kuah, T4-9667789, F4-9667889, 0900-1300, 1400-1700, daily.* The monthly magazine, *Senses of Langkawi*, which you can pick up from hotels and touristy restaurants has some articles on Langkawi life and some ideas of things to do and where to eat on the island. The privately-run www.langkawi-online.com and www.mylangkawi.com websites have some good information.

Background

In January 1987 the Malaysian government conferred duty-free status on Langkawi to promote tourism on the island. The promotion campaign and improved transport links to the mainland means the islands can no longer be touted as 'Malaysia's best-kept secret'. New hotels, shopping centres and restaurants have sprouted with

Kuah means 'gravy', and derives from a legend about a fight that broke out between two families who fell out over the breaking of a betrothal. Kitchen pots and pans were thrown around and a cooking pot smashed on to Belanga Pecah ('broken pot'); its contents splashed all over Kuah.

typical Southeast Asian speed and, for some former visitors at least, the Langkawi of old is just a memory. But development has been concentrated in a handful of places, so much of the island remains relatively unspoilt. Budget accommodation is still available and the construction of upmarket hotels and resorts means that a broader spectrum of tourists is being attracted.

Kuah

The main town is strung out along the seafront, and is the landing point for ferries from Satun (Thailand), Kuala Perlis, Kuala Kedah and Penang. The jetty is 2 km from Kuah itself. The town is growing fast and developers have reclaimed land along the shoreline to cope with the expansion. There is a rather stark park area overlooked by a giant effigy of an eagle on Dataran Lang (Eagle Square), symbol of the island's flight to prosperity. The park area itself, Chogm Park, was built to commemorate the Commonwealth Heads of Government Meeting (CHOGM) in 1989. The old part of Kuah has several restaurants, a few grotty hotels, banks, plenty of coffee shops and a string of duty-free shops, which do a roaring trade in cheap liquor, cigarettes and electronics. There is also an attractive mosque.

The town's name *Kuah*, meaning 'gravy', is said to derive from a legend about a fight that broke out between two families who fell out over the breaking of a betrothal. Kitchen pots and pans were thrown around and a cooking pot smashed on to *Belanga Pecah* ('broken pot'); its contents splashed all over Kuah. A saucepan of boiling water landed at *Telaga Air Hangat* (the motley hot springs on the north of the island).

Makam Mahsuri

The road west to the golf course goes to Makam Mahsuri, the tomb of the legendary Princess Mahsuri, in the village of Mawat 12 km from Kuah. The beautiful Mahsuri was condemned to death for alleged adultery in 1355. She protested her innocence and several attempts to execute her failed. According to the legend, the sentence was finally carried out using her own *tombak* (lance) and her severed head bled white blood, thus confirming her innocence. Before Mahsuri died she cursed the island, saying it would remain barren for seven generations. Shortly afterwards, the Thais attacked, killing, plundering, looting and razing all the settlements to the ground. At the time of the Thai attacks, villagers buried their entire rice harvest on Padang Matsirat in Kampong Raja, but the Thais found it and set fire to it too, giving rise to the name Beras Terbakar, the 'field of burnt rice', nearby. The legend is far more interesting than the field, which is just a field! ⓘ *0800-1700, RM1.*

Pantai Cenang

Southwest of Mahsuri's tomb, past some beautiful paddy fields and coconut groves, are the two main beaches, Pantai Cenang and Pantai Tengah. Pantai Cenang is a strip about 2 km long, with accommodation that runs the gamut from budget through mid-range chalet operations to a couple of more upmarket resorts. It is also possible to hire boats to the islands off Pantai Cenang from the beach. Pantai Cenang also has a range of watersport facilities on offer and boasts the **Langkawi Underwater World** ⓘ *1000-1800 daily, RM15 (RM10 for children), T4-9556100,* one of the largest aquariums in Asia, stocked with more than 100 tanks and over 5,000 types of marine life. The highlight of the aquarium is the 15-m-long walk-through tunnel tank. Plans are afoot to build a penguinarium and import 30 penguins to waddle around in it.

Pantai Cenang is still one of the nicest beaches on the island and there is accommodation to suit all budgets.

Just north of Pantai Cenang the **Muzium Laman Padi**, (rice museum garden) ⓘ *0700-1200, free*, has a gallery explaining all the stages of rice farming, a multi-tiered rooftop rice garden, ducks and buffalo. Of course, you can also taste cooked rice at their restaurant, *Café d'Padi*.

Pantai Tengah

Most of the new beach chalet development is along the 3-km stretch of coast from Pantai Cenang to Pantai Tengah, which is at the far southern end, around a small promontory. Pantai Tengah is less developed and quieter and not as nice as Pantai Cenang. Although, the beaches can get crowded at weekends and during school and public holidays.

Pantai Kok and Burau Bay

The road west leads past the airport to Pantai Kok, once a magnificent unspoilt bay with a dramatic backdrop of the forested Gunung Mat Chinchang. The area is now spotted with upmarket resorts and a fancy marina. Ever proud of their Hollywood connections, irrespective of whether it offended their neighbour Thailand or not, Malaysia has recreated part of the set of *Anna and the King* at Pantai Kok, ⓘ *1000-1900 daily, RM3.50 adults (RM2 children)*. Much of the movie was filmed here and on the mainland, as Thailand, who found the story offensive to the memory of its royal family, refused to have anything to do with it. Some of the buildings, however, have collapsed, and there is no explanation for how the movie was made in the ones still standing. Essentially it's just some wooden huts filled with props and costumes. Of little interest to anyone except hardened fans of the movie.

There are several isolated beaches along the bay, accessible by boat from either Pantai Kok itself, Pantai Cenang (12 km away) or Kampong Kuala Teriang, a small fishing village *en route*. On the west headland, the **Telaga Tujuh** waterfalls used to be the island's so-called 'most wonderful natural attraction'. It can no longer claim to be that, as the area has been bought by *Berjaya Leisure Berhad*, 'mother' of the *Berjaya Hotels Group*. A pipeline running next to the pools, and the waterfall, goes all the way to the *Berjaya Langkawi Beach Resort* on nearby Burau Bay, reducing the falls to a trickle in dry season and a modest cascade in wet. The falls run down the steep hillside, between huge rocks and through a series of seven (*tujuh*) pools (*telaga*); so much for development.

Also near Burau Bay is Langkawi's newest attraction, a cable car station that jerks passengers to 709 m above sea level to the top of **Gunung Mat Chinchang** (Langkawi's second tallest mountain), ⓘ *T4-9594225, F4-9594121, 1000-2000 daily, RM15 adults (RM5 children)*, where you can have a buffet dinner. The views are truly spectacular - on a clear day you can see the mainland and South Thailand as well as the forested and craggy sides of Mount Mat Chinchang. Best to call first to arrange a ride as the cable car does not operate on windy days.

East of Pantai Kok is Kuala Muda which has a few hotel resorts.

North coast

Right on the northwest tip of Langkawi is **Datai Bay**, which has a beautifully landscaped golf course and -two of the most sophisticated resorts in Malaysia – *The Datai* and *The Andaman*, each with their own private stretch of beach, They are accessible via a road which cuts up through the hills to the coast from the Pantai Kok to Pasir Hitam road. On the way to *The Andaman*, the **Ibrahim Hussein Museum**, ⓘ *T4-9594669, www.ihmcf.org, 0900-1800 daily, RM12 adults (children free)*, is a funky art gallery showcasing the work of one of Malaysia's well known artists.

Crocodile Adventureland Langkawi, ⓘ *0900-1800, RM8 (RM5 for children), daily shows at 1115 and 1445, T4-9592559*, houses over 1,000 crocodiles. Along with the usual array of caged crocodilia that consume 1,000 kg of meat daily, this gruesome place has pythons and other shows and delights to tantalise the discerning visitor.

Pantai Rhu is a beautiful white-sand cove, enclosed by a jungled promontory with **Gua Cerita**, (Cave of Legends), at the end of it. Within the cave, Koranic verse has been written on the walls. Beneath the sheer limestone cliff faces, there are a couple of small beaches accessible by boat. The Thai island Koh Turatao is just 4 km north. Past the *Tanjung Rhu Resort*, there is a collection of foodstalls and small shops next to the beach. It is possible to hire boats and canoes from the beach, which is backed by a small lagoon. Another sign of encroaching development – a branch of the *Four Seasons Hotel* is due to open here in early 2005.

Telaga Air Hangat, ⓘ *0900-1800, RM4 (children RM2), T4-9591357*, 14 km northwest of Kuah, is centred on some hot springs. Activities include displays of traditional crafts, elephant and snake 'displays', performances of traditional dance, as well as an 18-m-long, hand-carved river stone mural. There is a restaurant and a shop here. At the ninth milestone, a 3-km-long path branches off to the Durian Perangin waterfall, on the slopes of Gunung Raya, which rises to 911 m, the island's tallest mount. This is the area for forest and mangrove trekking. For a tarzan-like

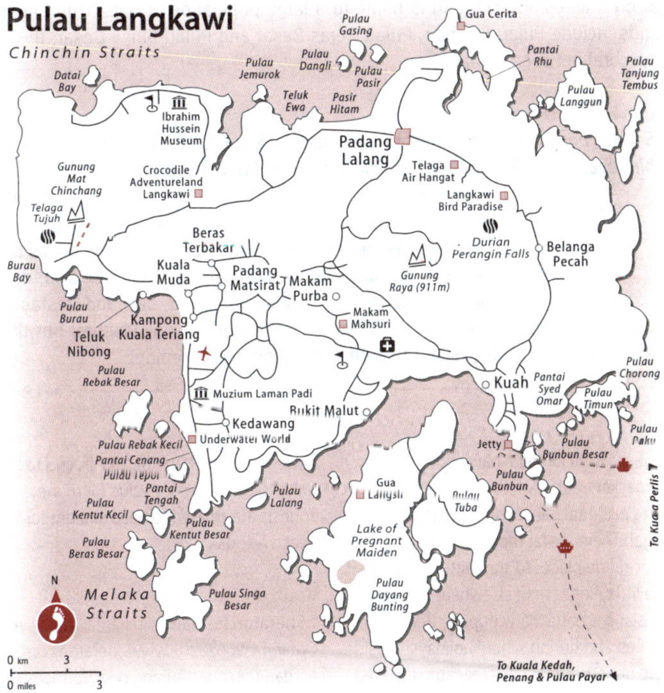

experience, Langkawi Canopy Adventures offer airtrekking tours of the forest here – definitely not for the faint-hearted. Helmets and safety ropes are involved for a 120 m flying fox slide through the canopy followed by a 30 m abseil down. Phone Jurgen on T4848744, RM150. Not far away, on the seaward side of the road, is the **Galeria Perdana**, ⓘ *1000-1700 Mon-Thu, 1000-1415 and 1500-1700 Fri, 0900-1800 Sat and Sun, RM3 (RM1 children), T4-9591498*, which houses around 2,500 gifts given to long-serving former Prime Minister Dr Mahathir Mohamad (he held the top post from 1981 to 2004). Just past this is Taman Burung, **Langkawi Bird Paradise**, ⓘ *0900-1800 daily, RM12 adults (RM6 children)*, housing 150 feathered species. It has a covered walkway, peacocks, and a flamingo pond.

Neighbouring islands

Pulau Dayang Bunting

ⓘ *Boat trips are organized to Pulau Dayang Bunting by many of the larger hotels and travel agents; or boats can be chartered privately from Pantai Cenang. Most trips also include a chance to snorkel off Pantai Singa Besar.*

This island, whose name means 'Island of the Pregnant Maiden', is the second-largest island in the archipelago, and lies just south of Langkawi. Separated from the sea by only a few metres of limestone is a freshwater lake renowned for its powers to enhance the fertility of women; unfortunately it is also said to be inhabited by a big white crocodile, although most people swim there unmolested. The myth surrounding this lake involves a beautiful girl named Telani, who became pregnant by the king's son. This indiscretion so angered the god Sang Kelembai that he brought a drought upon the land and turned the new-born baby into a white crocodile. Telani was turned into a rock and the king's son was transformed into an island. To the north of the lake is the intriguingly named **Gua Langsir**, or 'Cave of the Banshee'. The cave is high on a limestone cliff and is home to a large population of bats. Other nearby islands include Pulau Bunbun, Pulau Beras Besar and Pulau Singa Besar; there is some coral between the last two.

Pulau Payar

ⓘ *Several hotels and companies run day trips to Pulau Payar. These islands are also within reach of Kuala Kedah, on the mainland and Pulau Penang.*

Just to the south of Payar there is a good coral reef, reckoned to be the best off Malaysia's west coast.

This tiny island, 2 km long and 250 m wide, about 45 minutes southeast of Langkawi, is part of a marine park. The other islands are **Segantan**, Kala and Lembu. A reef platform has been built with an underwater observation chamber and diving facilities (see Activities and tours). a bar and restaurant, souvenir shop. There are basic facilities on the island for day visitors, but those intending to camp on the island require permission, see Sleeping.

Sleeping

Langkawi is no longer a haven for backpackers, although there some budget places in Pantai Cenang and Pantai Tengah.There are far more mid- and upper-range places to stay, although prices are a little higher than elsewhere in Malaysia. The island is particularly popular during Nov-Feb and during school holidays. Outside these periods, room rates are often reduced.

Most of the hotels in Kuah itself tend to be rather seedy and poor value for money. Tourists are advised to head straight for the beach resorts.

Kuah *p189, map p193*

L **Sheraton Perdana**, Jln Pantai Dato' Syed Omar, T4-9662020, www.sheraton.com/perdana A/c, restaurant, pool, formerly the

Langkawi Island Resort, has its own private beach with watersports facilities, and all the comforts you would expect of a *Sheraton*.

AL Tiara Langkawi, Pusat Dagangan Kelana Mas, T4-9662566, F4-9662600. Dubious and over-the-top pink castle-like creation. The hotel has been suffering from 'management problems' and is sometimes open and sometimes not. Locals predict its imminent demise. If it is open, rooms have a/c, shower, TV. There are also restaurants and a disco as well as an assortment of sports including fishing trips, jet skiing and diving. Breakfast included. Its grand scale make it feel slightly isolating.

A Beringin Beach Resort, round the corner from the *Sheraton Perdana*, T4-9666966, F4-9667970. A/c, restaurant, own private beach. Recommended.

A-B City Bayview, Jln Pandak Mayah, T4-9661818, F4-9663888. Newish block dominating Kuah town, 280 rooms with 4-star facilities, including a pool and health centre, two restaurants (Chinese and coffee house), breakfast included in the room rate. Central location.

B Eagle Bay (formerly Hotel Central), 33 Jln Persiaran Putra, T4-9668585, www.eaglebay.com.my Over 100 rooms in this rather ugly multi-storey block (don't come here if you're looking for a slice of traditional serenity), a/c, comfortable, discounts sometimes available. Breakfast included.

B Grand Continental, Lot 398, Mk Kuah, T4-9660333, www.grandhotelsinternational.Com.my A/c, TV, in-house movies, tea/coffee-making facilities, restaurant, pool, gymnasium and health club. Although it is slightly out of the centre of town – and also a rather ugly block – the hotel does have good views over surrounding islands.

B Twin Peaks Island Resort, Jln Kelibang, T4-9668255, F4-9667458, wooden chalets surrounding shadeless pool, children's playground, island tours.

C Asia, 3A-4A Jln Persiaran Putra, T4-9666216. A/c, reasonable place with attached bathrooms as well as some dorm beds, 15 mins' walk from the jetty. Clean and quiet in a good location. Recommended.

Pantai Cenang *p189, map p194*

The most popular of the 3 main beaches, with plenty of hotels and chalets to choose from; some are cramped a little too closely together. Despite the development, it is a picturesque beach.

L-AL Bon Ton, T4-9556787, www.bontonresort.com.my. Langkawi's "something different". Australian owner Narelle has rebuilt five 100-year-old Malay houses, largely using the original woodwork and stocked with Indonesian furniture and modern facilities including hot showers, fridge and kettle (TV on request). The homes have a unique atmosphere and are very comfortable although they do let in a lot of the wildlife as the windows are glass-free. Animal lovers will be especially happy as Narelle also runs an animal shelter, and lazy cat residents of this drape themselves around the resort. If you're lucky the boldest will curl up on your bed. There's a pool jacuzzi, fantastic fusion restaurant and Chinese bar. The resort has its own mini-guide to Langkawi and staff are very helpful. Although it doesn't face the beach, the reedy lake makes a romantic setting at

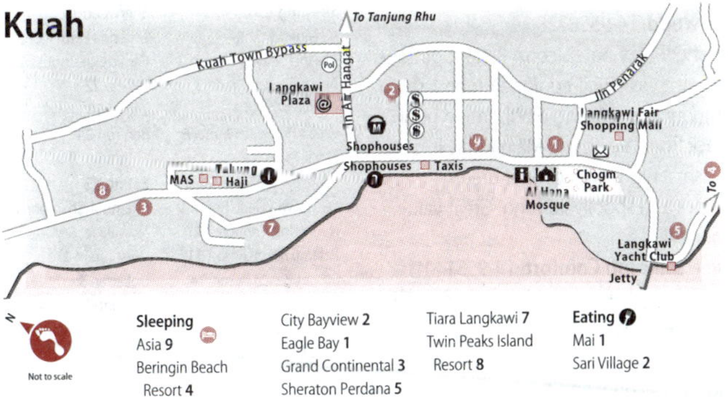

sunset. Unbeatable for its atmosphere. Highly recommended.

L-AL Casa del Mar, T4-9552388, www.casadelmar-langkawi.com. One of the nicest resorts on this stretch of the beach. Mediterranean-style building with deep-terracotta coloured walls. 24 elegant rooms with nice touches like dvd player, cold milk in the fridge and separate bath and shower. Sits astride the beach making it a great place for a sunset cocktail. The resort has a RM1,700 royal suite – owned by the Sultan, and only rented out with his permission - complete with a dress-up room and private jacuzzi.

AL Pelangi Beach Resort, T4-9528888, www.meritus-hotels.com. A/c, restaurant, pool, chalet-styled 5-star resort. Guests and their baggage are whisked around in electric cars, holiday camp atmosphere, with daily activities.

A Beach Garden Resort, T4-9551363, combeer@pd.jaring.my A/c, restaurant, pool, apart from the *Casa del Mar and Pelangi* this is the nicest hotel along this stretch, with thatched roofs, a tiny swimming pool and a wonderful restaurant on the beach. Good value. Recommended.

B Lagenda Permai Chalet, T4-9552806, http://lagendapermai.tripod.com/lagenda1.html Rows of prim little chalets set back from the beach but in pleasant plots, some with a/c, TV and fridge. Dorm rooms also available for 4 sharing. RM50 for each group of 4. Clean. Dorm rooms offer good value, although small.

B Langkapuri Beach Resort, T4-9551202, F4-9551959. Oldish but well-maintained chalets with TV and fridge. Right on the beach, although the sands here are not particularly nice.

B Sherwood, T4-9558228, www.sherwood-hotels.com 3-star boutique hotel with plush well-equipped rooms set in a compound and facing a swimming pool, set back from the beach. Main lobby is quite ghoulish at night with copper green staircases and spooky lighting. Great value for money.

B The Nadias Inn Comfort, T4-9551401, F4-9551405 Clean place with 96 large and characterless rooms. The hotel has a swimming pool, restaurant and karaoke lounge. No alcohol on site.

C AB Motel, T4-9555278, www.geocities.com/abmotel By far the most highly recommended budget option on Langkawi. Clean rooms with fan or a/c, and showers.

Pantai Cenang & Pantai Tengah

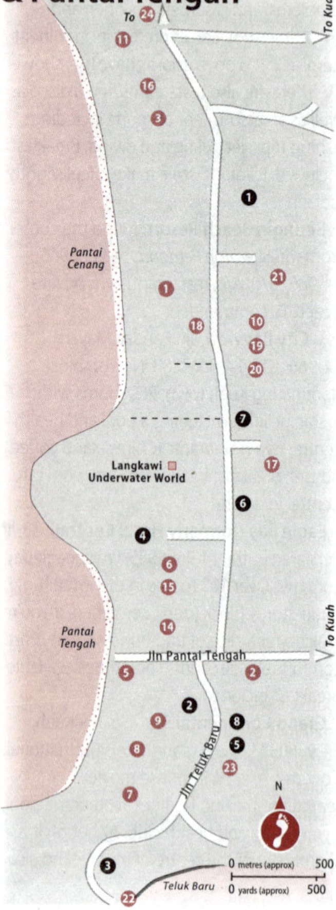

Sleeping

AB Motel **1**
Aseania Seaview Resort **2**
Beach Garden Resort **3**
Charlie's Motel **5**
Green Hill Beach Motel **6**
Lanai **7**
Langkawi Holiday Villa **8**
Langkawi Village Resort **9**
Nadias Inn Comfort **10**
Pelangi Beach Resort **11**
Sunset Beach Resort **14**
Tanjung Malie Beach Motel **15**
Casa Del Mar **16**
Irish Bar **17**
Langkapuri Beach Resort **18**
Sherwood **19**
Lagenda Permai Chalet **20**
Gecko Guesthouse **21**
Awana **22**
Zackry **23**
Bon Ton **24**

Eating

Champor Champor **1**
Sunvillage & Matahari Malay Restaurant **2**
Unkaizan **3**
The Lighthouse **4**
Tang Lung Seafood **5**
T-Jay's **6**
Red Tomato Garden Cafe **7**
Sheela's **8**

Organizes island hopping and sightseeing tours. Also has a restaurant and Internet.

C Irish Bar, T4-9558151, in Pantai Cenang, inland opposite Underwater World. Run by Yorkshireman Derek, he also has some **(C)** rooms out the back with crisp sheets, a/c or fan.

D Gecko Guesthouse, T0194283801. Tucked away up a lane on the other side of the main road to the beach. Nicely-decorated rooms, albeit simple with wooden floors and attached cold water showers. Bar and very traveller friendly. Lots of long-term stayers. Run by English woman, but local staff a tad strange. Not a bad choice.

Pantai Tengah *p190, map p194*

A Awana, T4-9555111, F4-9555222. Right next to the Star Cruise terminal on the headland. Fantastic views of the bay and islands. Over 200 four-star rooms, a bit heavy on the pine furniture. Very popular with Chinese tourists.

A Lanai, T4-9558462, F4-9558459, www.lanaibeach.com. Situated at the end of the beach, with a spacious set-up. Two pools (one for kids) and a games room. Rooms have a/c, TV. Hotel organizes island tours, friendly staff. Bicycles for rent. Good value, especially good for families.

A Langkawi Holiday Villa, T4-9551701, www.holidayvillalangkawi.com Over 250 rooms, 2 pools, tennis, restaurants and all the amenities you would expect of a first-class resort, including a health centre and squash courts.

A Langkawi Village Resort, Jln Teluk Baru, T4-9551511, www.langkawi-villageresort.com A resort with 100 bunglows with sea views. A/c, bath and shower, cable TV and fridge. Tennis courts and a pool, and from 2200 onwards there is the dubious 'Coco Jam' disco.

A Sunset Beach Resort, T/F9556200, www.sunvillage.com.my. Beautiful setting romantic chalets filled with Balinese furniture and frangipani flowers scattered about the gardens. Large, clean bathrooms. Honeymoon suites available. Stunning. Highly recommended.

B Aseania Seaview Resort, Jln Pantai Tengah, T4-9552020, F4-9552115. This large pink and white building resembles a strawberry gateau, but with a pool complete with waterfalls it is a good option for those looking to relax. Rooms with TV, a/c, shower and fridge. Two restaurants and a business centre. Watersports organized and bikes can be hired. Breakfast included.

B-C Charlie's Motel, T4-9551200, F4-9551316. A/c and fan, restaurant, chalets, at the end of Pantai Tengah. Good location but expensive for tacky huts – walls peeling, grubby carpet. Not the best budget option and staff a bit standoffish.

C Green Hill Beach Motel, T4-9559935. F4-9558935. Fan or a/c, restaurant. Grubby and uncared for huts, better budget options around, although it's close to the beach.

C-D Tanjung Malie Beach Motel, T4-9551891, tmbm@tm.net.my Mosquito-filled huts near the beach with cold-water showers, both a/c and fan available. Place appears to be falling apart at the seams. Only plus points are that it's cheap and on the beach.

D-E Zackry, right at the south end of Pantai Tengah, T4-9557595, www.langkawinetworks.com. Great budget option. Basic rooms, some with shared shower, dorms available. All clean and tiled. Although it doesn't face the sea, the beach is just across the road. Friendly owner, and quiet location. Bicycle hire for free. Recommended.

Pantai Kok and Burau Bay *p190*

Having once been the most popular place for those on a lower budget to stay, it now has a number of exclusive resorts and a few top-class hotels as well as Telaga Harbour Park Marina with a clock tower, shops and restaurants.

Most of the resorts that did spring up at Kuala Muda have now closed down, probably something to do with the rather disappointing beach, which does not offer any of the more spectacular views than can be found in other areas of the island. The area is close to the airport.

AL Berjaya Langkawi Beach Resort, Burau Bay, T4-9591888, www.berjayaresorts.com.my Malaysian-style chalets spread over 170 ha of tropical rainforest, some on stilts over water, some on jungled hillside, all serviced by minibuses. Each chalet has a/c, TV, cable TV, in-house movies, mini-bar, balcony, massage shower and is very comfortably furbished with oriental carpets and classical furniture. Excellent facilities include pool, jacuzzi, Japanese restaurant, tennis, watersports, daily organized activities, white-sand beach, beach restaurant, Chinese restaurant and good-value buffet served in Dayang café, inside vast main lobby overlooking sea. Surprisingly, this 400-room resort manages to feel friendly and not impersonal. Recommended.

AL **Sheraton Beach Resort**, Teluk Nibong, T4-9551901, www.sheraton.com/langkawi Pool overlooking the islands, restaurants, children's centre, health club and spa, watersports activities, rooms arranged in individual Malay-style chalets serviced by resort bus. Total of 6 lounges and bars to choose from. Beautiful hotel, but its beach is a disappointment.

A **Mutiara Burau Bay**, Jln Teluk Burau, T4-9591061, www.mutiarahotels.com A/c, restaurant, at the far end of Pantai Kok, with Gunung Mat Chinchang behind it, away from other chalets. A fun hotel that's good for families with a swimming pool , children's play area and forest or beach horse riding. Its Seashell Beach Café has won an entertainment award. Recommended.

A **Tanjung Sanctuary**, Teluk Nibong, T4-9552977, www.tanjungsanctuary.com.my. Tucked away down a forested road on the way to Pantai Kok, this intimate resort is at the lower end of the price bracket making it good value for money. It has a little beach, small pool and large chalets tastefully furnished.

B **Langkasuka Resort**, Kauala Muda, T4-9556888, F4-9555888. Large hotel with 214 rooms aimed primarily at the Japanese and Korean tourist market. Rooms with a/c, shower, TV. Hotel has pool and several restaurants. Little to offer.

The bay has a great view of Thailand's Koh Turatao and other islands and arguably the best stretch of beach on Langkawi. There are just 2 hotels.

North coast *p191*

L **Andaman**, Datai Bay, T4-9591088, www.theandaman.com Luxury resort with its own stretch of beach, spa and beautiful pool set among mature trees. Very friendly and helpful staff. Resident naturalist takes guests on nature walks and jungle treks. Great Malay restaurant in Kampong-style house.

L **Datai**, Datai Bay, T4-9592500, www.ghmhotels.com/thedatai/index.asp. Two pools, health club, 40 individual 'villas' each with private sun-bathing terrace, spacious marble bathroom, a/c, bar, minimalist décor offset by Jim Thompson silks from Bangkok, connected by walkways set in 400 ha of primary jungle where hornbills and flying squirrels roam. There are a further 60 rooms, designed with panache, large rooms with sitting areas and cool wooden floors, own balcony with jungle (and some sea) views, private beach, fine white sand, a wealth of watersports.

Beach Restaurant serves top-quality buffet in the evening, idyllic setting under *atap*-roofed structure, supported on trunks of original trees that were cleared to make way for the resort. *Pavilion Restaurant* on stilts among treetops serves Thai food, *Dining Room*, a/c serves Malay and Western food, 18-hole golf course adjacent, attractive, very luxurious resort. Recommended.

L **Tanjung Rhu Resort**, Mukim Air Hangat, T4-9591033, www.tanjungrhu.com.my Exquisitely laid-out resort of only 100 rooms with understated décor, beautifully presented, dining on the beach, luxurious facilities, a honeymooners' paradise.

Neighbouring islands *p192*

B-E **Sunrise Beach Homestay**, Pulau Tuba (the island opposite Kuah), T4-9669752, F4-9669264, sunriseresort.tripod.com. Wooden chalets along Pasir Panjang beach, a stretch of secluded sands on Tuba Island. RM10 tents for two also available with kitchen facilities. Call to arrange transport from Kuah jetty. Quite isolated.

E **Camping**, Pulau Payar. Permission is required from of the Fisheries Management and Protection Office, Wisma Tani, Jalan Mahameru, KL, T4-2982011, or Wisma Persekutuan, Jalan Kampong Baru, Alor Star, T4-725573.

L-AL **Rebak Marina Resort**, T4-9665566, www.rebakmarina.com On Pulau Rebak Besar, the island just opposite Pantai Cenang. 150 chalets, and berthing docks for 200 leisure boats.

Eating

Langkawi's speciality is *mee gulong* – fried noodles cooked with shredded prawns, slices of beef, chicken, carrots, cauliflower rolled into a pancake and served with a thick potato gravy. Langkawi is also known for its Thai cuisine. Being close to the border, Thai influences even creep into the Malay dishes with the use of hot and spicy ingredients. Thai-styled seafood is also fairly commonplace.

Virtually all of the beach hotels have their own restaurants, some of which are excellent; seafood is an obvious choice on Langkawi.

Kuah *p189, map p193*

While Kuah is not much to look at it does have some great Chinese seafood restaurants along the main street, all quite reasonable value for money.

TT **Sari Village**, Kompleks Pasar Lama, T4-9667515, built out on stilts over the sea – which is now being reclaimed – vast selection of seafood. Beautifully designed restaurant with good views over bay and surrounding islands. Owned by globe-trotting architect and landscape architect Ridzuan Aziz. Menu influenced by Pakistani cuisine. Specialities include vegetable curry and fish tandoori. Recommended.

T **Prawn Village**, Jln Persiaran Putra (near *Asia Hotel*), good seafood. Large open restaurant where diners can play God and choose their own fish for the chop-and-wok.

T **Orchid**, 3 Dundong Kuah, Chinese. Large and popular with the locals.

T **Naga Emas Restaurant**, 31 Pusat Bandar, Jln Pandak Mayah, Thai seafood and steamboat.

T **Sangkar Ikan**, Jln Pantai Penarak, seafood restaurant and fish farm where you can hire rods and catch fish for your own dinner.

T **Mai**, 131 Langkawi Mall, T4-9660255, F4-9660254. Stylish restaurant serving modern Thai and Malay food. Excellent and original menu. Serves set lunch for RM10, from 1000-1500. Mai-blend fruit shake recommended.

Foodstalls

The roadside foodstalls in Langkawi, particularly those just down from the *Langkasuka Hotel* in Padang Matsirat are highly recommended. Try to eat as much as you can and your bill still won't rise above RM5. There is also a collection of stalls behind Langkawi Duty Free.

Pantai Cenang *p189, map p194*

TTT TT **Casa del Mar** and the **Beach Garden Restaurant** next door, which offer a good international selection, beautifully prepared. The latter is right on the beach and is highly recommended.

TT **Champor Champor**, T4-9551449. International food in fantastically decorated restaurant.

TT **Nam**, inside the Bon Ton Resort just north of Pantai Cenang. Beautiful restaurant overlooking a lake serving funky fusion food. Try the rock lobster and baked snapper on mango rice. Highly recommended.

TT **Sunvillage Restaurant** and **Matahari Malay Restaurant**, T4-9556200, F4-9551751. Two spectacular restaurants set in exquisite landscaped surroundings. The extensive menus at each offer traditionally prepared dishes. Recommended.

TT **Red Tomato Garden Café**. Great place for breakfast (they have homemade bread) or a pizza for a dinner. At night it gets very cozy with fairy lights. German Tania runs this place with her Malay husband. Very friendly. Recommended.

TT **The Lighthouse**, T4-9552586. Minimalist place, inspired by its name, right on the beach. Has a varied menu, and the satay is particularly recommended.

TT **T-Jay's**. Friendly Italian restaurant with homemade pasta, pizzas, ice cream and coffee.

Pantai Tengah *p190, map p194*

TTT **Unkaizan**, T4-9554118, Great views from the balcony from this upmarket Japanese joint. Chef formerly worked at *The Andaman*. Expensive but recommended.

TT **Sheela's**. Closed Mon. Garden restaurant serving European and Malay cuisine although the menu is quite limited.

TT **Tang Lung Seafood**, T4-9558818. Chinese seafood garden, pretty at night with red lanterns. Offers shuttle service from major hotels.

Pantai Kok *p190*

Oriental Pearl, *Berjaya Langkawi Beach Resort*, Buran Bay, upmarket Chinese restaurant, simple a/c restaurant with ocean views, steamboat recommended.

The North Coast *p191*

Pavillion, *The Datai*, Datai Bay, stunning setting on a high terrace in jungle tree-tops, top-class Thai chefs, papaya salad, excellent seafood.

The Dining Room, *The Datai*, Datai Bay, quintessentially tasteful in the style of the resort, overlooking turquoise pool and spotlit jungle, French chef combines Malay and Western cuisine, interesting menu.

Barn Thai, Kampong Belanga Pecah, Mukim Kisap, T9666699. Around 9 km from Kuah on the road to Padang Lalang, this is a unique restaurant set in mangrove swamp, reached along a 450-m wooden walkway, housed in a fine wooden building that blends with its natural surroundings. There have been mixed reviews about the Thai food, but the setting is memorable and they often have live Jazz.

Bars and clubs

Nightlife in Langkawi mainly centres on the larger hotels, which offer bars, discos, karaoke and live music.

Kuah *p189, map p193*

Malaysians recommend the disco and live band at the Sheraton Perdana's **Someplace Else bar**.

Pantai Cenang *p189, map p194*

Pantai Cenang now has a few standalone bars, but they tend to close by 0100. The big yellow **Go Slow Café** in Pantai Cenang opposite Nadia's is right on the beach and is a good place for a sunset beer. An unpretentious bar that also serves Malay food and fish and chips. They occasionally hold laser parties. A great place to go if you're hunkering after TV sports or Irish food with your beer is the **Irish Bar**, T4-9558151, in Pantai Cenang, inland opposite Underwater World. Run by Yorkshireman Derek, it's a surreal slice of Britain on the Island.

Pantai Tengah *p190, map p194*

Tammy's Bar in Pantai Tengah which stays open until the early hours and caters to a lot of the Island's expats. Otherwise there's the **Coco Jam Disco** at the *Langkawi Village Resort*, a slightly trashy bar with pool table, that is usually open until 0300.

Pantai Kok and Burau Bay *p190*

Mutiara Burau Bay has the award-winning **Seashell's** which is fun pub and restaurant with dancing on the beach.

Shopping

Kuah *p189, map p193*

Duty free shops line the main street in Kuah, and alcohol is especially good value. There is a duty free shopping complex at the jetty. The only shop selling alcohol here, **Sime Duty Free**, is on the first floor. Although Langkawi enjoys duty free status there is not much reason to come here for the shopping. At least on a cursory appraisal, the range seems to be limited and the prices not that great, although alcohol is quite cheap. There is also: **Cenang Duty Free** next to Underwater World; the **Langkawi Fair Shopping Centre**, Persiaran Putra, Kuah (near the jetty); **Langkawi Mall**; the **Saga Shopping Centre**; and **Zone Shopping Paradise**.

Fishing tackle There is a fishing shop opposite the *Langasuka Hotel* in Kuah.

Handicrafts Many small shops in Kuah sell textiles. The best-stocked handicraft shop is in front of the *Sari Restaurant* in Kuah, **Batik Jawa Store**, 58 Pekan Pokok Asam. Also recommended is **Sunshine Handicraft**, Jln Pandak Mayah (left turning before the Duty Free) stocks a range of *songket* products, particularly *songket* sarongs; open daily. **Flint Stones Handicraft**, Jln Pandak Mayah, offers a good range of Asian handicrafts. Both these places offer 30% discount during the low season.

Pantai Kok and Burau Bay *p190*

The **Oriental Village** is a new shopping development overlooking Burau Bay. Lots of themed restaurants to go with the duty free shopping. Open 1000-2200, daily. All-in-all, lots of shopping – although for visitors from outside Malaysia and Singapore it seems a long way to come to hole up in some surreal tropical shopping paradise.

Activities and tours

North Coast *p191*

Golf

Datai Bay Golf Club, Teluk Datai, T4-9592620, F4-9592216. Green fees RM150, 18-hole course, magnificent fairways, sea views. Tee-off times, 0730-1630 daily.

Gunung Raya, Jln Air Hangat, Kisap, T4-9668148. Designed by Max Wexler on a 750-ha former rubber plantation, this is an 18-hole course. There is also a driving range. Open 0700-1700 daily.

Langkawi Golf Club, Jln Bukit Malut, T4-9666187.

Go-karting

Morac International Karting Circuit, Pantai Cenang, near the airport, T4-9555827, open daily 1000-1900, RM70 for 10mins (RM5 for racing suit hire).

Spas

Langkawi has become a centre for pampered holidaymakers with a great range of spas from the severely upmarket at *The Datai*, to backpacker friendly outlets at Pantai Cenang. It's also a good option when it rains, as there's not much else to do in inclement weather.

The Spa, *The Datai*, T4-9592500. Nothing but the best – a luxurious spa set in the rainforest.

Teratai Spa , *Pelangi Beach Resort*, T4-9528888.Part of the Aspara chain, with Swedish, Indonesian Thai, hot stone and Yin and Yang massages for around RM300 an hour.

Gentle Touch Aromatherapy, Pantai Tengah, T4-9559245. Offers a traditional Malay massage for RM100 an hour.

Indian Ayurvedic Massage, Pantai Cenang, T4 9559078. Indian treatments with aromatic oils for around RM125 an hour.

Watersports

The big resorts and hotels all offer watersports facilities.

Cabana Watersports, T0124705325, offers the most extensive range of watersports activities on the island, including scuba diving and snorkelling, jet and water skiing, parasailing, banana boat rides and island hopping. Friendly staff. Café attached.

Tour operators

Organized tours around Langkawi and neighbouring islands can be booked through almost all the hotels and resorts. There are also scores of agents at the ferry pier. Popular tours include jungle trekking (including canopy trekking), paddling through mangrove swamps, island hopping, eagle spotting and feeding (operators throw chicken guts to swooping sea eagles and kites – a dubious practice which you may not want to support) and a round island trip to take in the waterfalls, mountains and other sites of interest.

Trips to Pulau Rebak Besar (opposite Pantai Cenang) leave from the beach next to Pelangi Resort (signposted from the road).

Langkawi Canopy Adentures, T0124848744, juergzim@yahoo.com for air trekking at 30m.

East Marine, T4-9663966, www.eastmarine.com.my, leaves Kuah for Pulau Payar (for snorkelling and scuba diving) daily at 0930 (returning at 1500). The journey each way takes one hour and the package costs RM 220adult, RM140 child.

Mutiara Burau Bay, can organize guided horse riding trips through kampongs, forest and a gallop along the beach. Call Hamzah on 0194379783.

Neighbouring islands *p192*

A reef platform has been built at Pulau Payar with an underwater observation chamber and diving facilities (tank and weights RM50, full diving gear RM70, introductory dive RM100), bar and restaurant, souvenir shop. Contact **East Marine**, see above.

Transport

Air

The international airport is the other side of Pantai Cenang, about 20 km from Kuah and 8 km from Pentai Cenang, at Padang Matsirat.

Transport to town

A taxi to Kuah is RM12 and around RM10 to Pantai Kok. Prices are fixed – coupons on sale in the airport building. Daily connections with **JB, KL,** and **Penang** on MAS. Air Asia flies between Langkawi and **KL** only. MAS and Silk Air operate frequent connections with **Singapore**. MAS also has a twice-weekly

London-Langkawi service. There are also direct flights from **Hong Kong**.
Airline offices MAS, Ground Floor, Langkawi Fair Shopping Mall, Persiaran Putra, Kuah, T4-7463000; **Silk Air**, c/o *MAS*, T4-2923122; **Air Asia**, T4-2027777.

Bicycle hire
On the main beaches, RM10-15 per day.

Boats
It is well worth hiring a boat if you can get a large group of people together, otherwise it tends to be expensive – approximately RM150 per day. Many of the beach hotels run boat trips to the islands as well as one or two places in Kuah (see Tour operators above).

Ferries to Langkawi leave from both **Kuala Perlis** and **Kuala Kedah**. Timetables subject to seasonal change (fewer boats during the monsoon months, Apr-Sep), journey time from Kuala Perlis is 14 mins, RM12 adults, RM7 children and from Kuala Kedah, 1½ hrs, RM15. **Fortune Express**, Seraya Bayu; and **Labuan Express**. Regular connections with Kuala Perlis at least every hr from 0800-1900, RM12. To Kuala Kedah there are boats at least every hr, 0730-1900, RM15. There are three to four departures daily for **Penang**. Usually two in the morning around 1100 and one at 1430, RM35. **Langkawi Ferry Services** and **Labuan Express** both run connections with **Satun** in Thailand, RM20, 1 hr. There are four to five ferries a day, with the first leaving at 0930 and the last at 1600.

Bus
There are no local buses.

Car hire
Mayflower Acme, *Pelangi Beach Resort*, Pantai Cenang, T4-911001.
Tomo Express, 14 Jln Pandak Maya 4, Pekan Kuah, T4-9669252. Expect to pay about RM80 per day.

Motorcycle hire
Motorbikes are reasonably cheap to hire (RM20-35 per day) and are far-and-away the best way to scoot around the island. There are rental shops in Kuah and on all the main beaches. Although Langkawi's roads are wide and not very busy, be warned to drive with extra special care since monkeys and buffalo frequently dart or lumber onto the tarmac.

Road and boat
it is a 6-hr journey from KL to Kuala Kedah; from there catch the boat to Langkawi. Note, leaving Langkawi, there are bus ticket agents at the ferry if you want to book a connection from Kuala Perlis or Kuala Kedah. Connections with KL are easiest from Kuala Kedah, while if you're heading east to Kota Bharu take a ferry to Kuala Perlis. **Qudrat Bistari Agency**, which sells bus tickets, at counter nine at the Kuah jetty is friendly and helpful.

Taxi
Fares around the island are fixed. From the jetty to **Kuah** is RM4, to **Pantai Cenang** RM16, to Datai Bay, RM25.

Directory

Kuah *p189, map p193*
Banks Maybank and **United Malayan Banking Corporation** are just off the main street in Kuah in the modern shophouse block. Banks are open all day Mon-Thu and Sun, but only in the morning on Fri and Sat. There are several money changers along the main street (ferry terminal has poor rates), mainly in textile shops. Also in Kuah, **Noorul Ameen**, at 15 Jln Pandak Mayah on the corner opposite the taxi stand, go to the 2nd floor, offers some of the best rates on the island. **Post** General Post Office, at the jetty end of the main street in Kuah.
Internet There are a number of cafés in Kuah, including **Langkawi Online**, Ground floor, Langkawi Plaza, open daily 0930 to midnight. Useful addresses Customs office T9666227, Immigration Office T9694005.

Pantai Cenang and Pantai Tengah *p189 and p190, map p194*
There are also a couple of money changers at Pantai Cenang and Pantai Tengah. There is one opposite the *Aseania*, open daily 1100-2130, and another opposite *Underwater World*, open 1000-2000 daily. **Internet** Max Gen2 , next to the *Sunset Beach Resort*, 4RM per hour. **AB Motel** has internet, open 1000-2300 daily, 5RM per hour.

Southern Peninsula

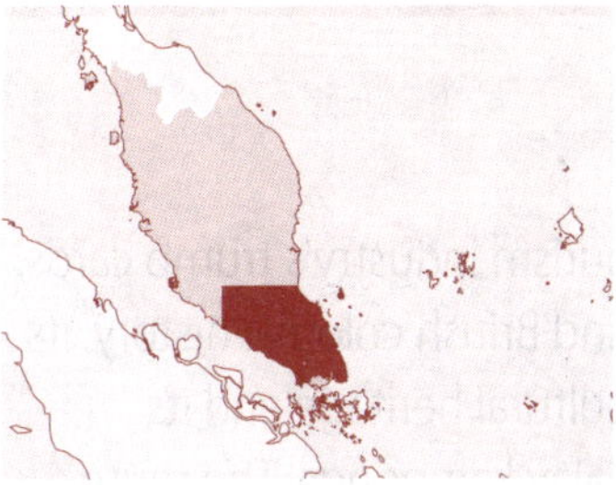

Footprint features

Introduction

Melaka is one of the Malaysian tourism industry's trump cards, thanks to its Portuguese, Dutch and British colonial history, its rich Peranakan (Straits Chinese) cultural heritage and its picturesque hinterland of rural Malay kampongs. The route south from Melaka is a pleasant but unremarkable drive through plantation country to Johor Bahru (JB), on the southernmost tip of the peninsula.

It is a short hop across the causeway from JB to Singapore, and Malaysia's east coast islands and resorts are within easy reach. One of the most famous of these is Tioman Island, a large volcanic outcrop on the east coast with perfect strips of sandy beaches, good diving and snorkelling, forest trails, mountain hikes and, for the most part, a laid-back atmosphere. Inland lies Peninsula Malaysia's second largest national park – Endau Rompin, 800 square-km of lowland forest. Although facilities are limited and access trickier than Taman Negara, the park offers more possibilities of catching a glimpse of rare rhinos, tigers and boars because of the paucity of tourists.

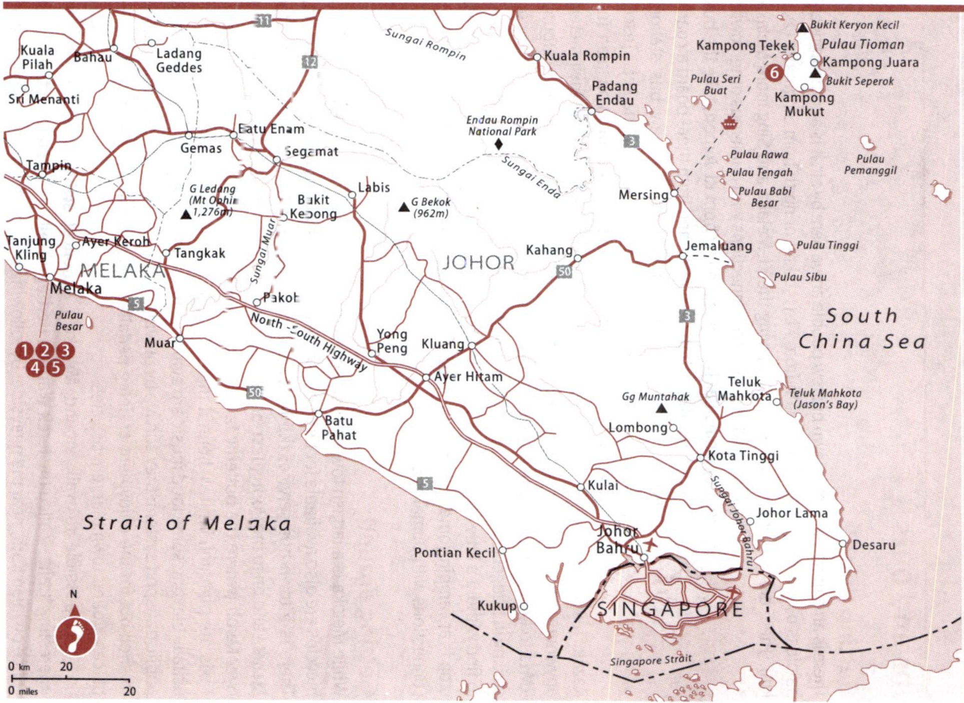

★ Don't miss...

1. **Melaka town square** The funky red terracotta Dutch buildings and the Armenian-style Christ Church make fantastic photos, page 212.
2. **Chinatown** Amble the network of streets for temples, mahjong games, art galleries and Melaka's millionaire's row, page 214.
3. **Baba Nyonya Heritage Museum** Step back in time with a tour around this beautifully-preserved Peranakan Straits Chinese townhouse in Melaka, page 214.
4. **Nyonya cuisine** Sample Malaysia's spicy fusion forerunner of Chinese and Southeast Asian flavours, page 223.
5. **Trishaw ride** Covered in tinsel, fake garlands and blasting out pop tunes, trishaws are a kitsch way to pedal round Melaka's historical streets, page 226.
6. **Fan Canyon** Many divers rate the experience of swimming through gigantic gorgonian sea fans as one of their scuba highlights in Tioman, page 237.

Melaka and around

→ Colour map 2, grid B3

Thanks to its strategic location on the strait that bears its name, Melaka was a rich, cosmopolitan port city long before it fell victim to successive colonial invasions. Its wealth and influence are now a thing of the past, and the old city's colourful history is itself a major money-spinner for Malaysia's modern tourism industry. The Jerak Warison Heritage Trail is a great introduction to historical Melaka with its striking Dutch colonial core and bustling, although somewhat manufactured,Chinatown which houses the oldest Chinese temple in Malaysia.

After you've exhausted the rich historical sites of Melaka, 11km up the road towards the north-south highway is Ayer Keroh, a kind of contrived holiday camp with golf, a zoo, night safari, butterfly park and go-kart racing. Tanjung Kling, 9km northwest is well-known for its seafood although the waters around here are, as the tourist bureau put it, "kind of milky". For serious trekkers, there's the myth-enshrouded Mount Ledang which is a tough scramble at 1,276m. » *For Sleeping, Eating and other listings, see pages 219-226.*

Ins and outs

Getting there

There is an airport 9 km from town but few people arrive here by air. It is a comparatively painless overland journey either south from KL (150 km) or north from Singapore (250 km). There are numerous express buses plying the KL-Melaka and Singapore-Melaka routes and there are also connections with numerous other towns on the peninsula. Travelling directly from KL Airport, take the bus to Nilai, then through to Seremban and from there board a coach direct to Melaka. The town has a swanky new bus station, opposite a big branch of the British supermarket, Tesco, inconveniently located a few kilometres out of town on Jalan Tun Razak. Taxis are notorious for ripping off tourists as drivers refuse to use their meters anywhere in town. The fare from the bus station to the centre of town should be around RM12 to RM15. Guest house touts often hassle new arrivals but If you are planning on staying in budget accommodation they are worth paying attention to as places are hard to find without a little help. The railway line does not run through Melaka – the nearest stop is at Tampin some 40 km north of town. There are daily express international ferry connections with Dumai in Sumatra. » *See also Transport, page 225.*

Arriving in Melaka by road it is not immediately apparent that the city is Malaysia's historical treasure-trove.

Getting around

While Melaka is a largish town it is still possible to enjoy many of the sights on foot; bicycles are also available for hire from some of the guesthouses and shops in town. There is a town bus service; the No 17 bus runs from the bus station to historical Melaka and on to the Portuguese area while the No 19 runs from the bus station out to Ayer Keroh (where the butterfly farm, reptile park and 'Mini Malaysia' are situated). Taxis are plentiful. While colourful trishaws daubed in tinsel and fake flowers and usually blasting some loud music are available for rent these are not part of Melaka's public transport system: they survive by providing a service to tourists who are willing to shell out for the enjoyment of being pedalled around town. There are also many places around town that rent bicycles.

It is possible to walk around Melaka's historical sights. There is now an interesting 'trail' – called the **Jerak Warisan Heritage Trail**, which starts at the Tourist Office on Jalan Kota, near the quayside; by following this trail the visitor gets to see all the major cultural sights of interest. The route crosses the bridge, to the Baba Nyonya Heritage Museum, takes in all the temples on Jonkers Street and then back across the bridge to Stadthuys, St Paul's Church, St Paul's Hill and the Porta de Santiago Independence Monument. For a 'handout' on the trail, ask at the Tourist Office.

There are boat tours down the river through the original port area and past some of the old Dutch houses, see Tours and activities. .The river is a little pungent, but the 16th-century sanitation adds to the realism.

Tourist information

Tourism Malaysia, ⓘ *Jln Kota (opposite Christ Church), T6-2814803, F6-2849022. 0845-1700 Sat-Thu, 0845-1215 and 1445-1700 Fri.* Also tourist information desk at Ayer Keroh, ⓘ *T6-3125811. www.melaka.gov.my*

Background

The city was founded by Parameswara, a fugitive prince from Palembang in Sumatra. According to the 16th-century *Sejara Melayu* (the Malay Annals), he was a descendant of the royal house of Srivijaya, whose lineage could be traced back to Alexander the Great. Historians, however, suspect that he was really a Javanese refugee who, during the 1390s, invaded and took Temasek (Singapore), before he himself was ousted by the invading Siamese. He fled up the west coast of the peninsula and, with a few followers, settled in a fishing kampong.

The Malay Annals relate how Parameswara was out hunting one day, and while resting in the shade of a tree watched a tiny mouse deer turn and kick one of his

Melaka

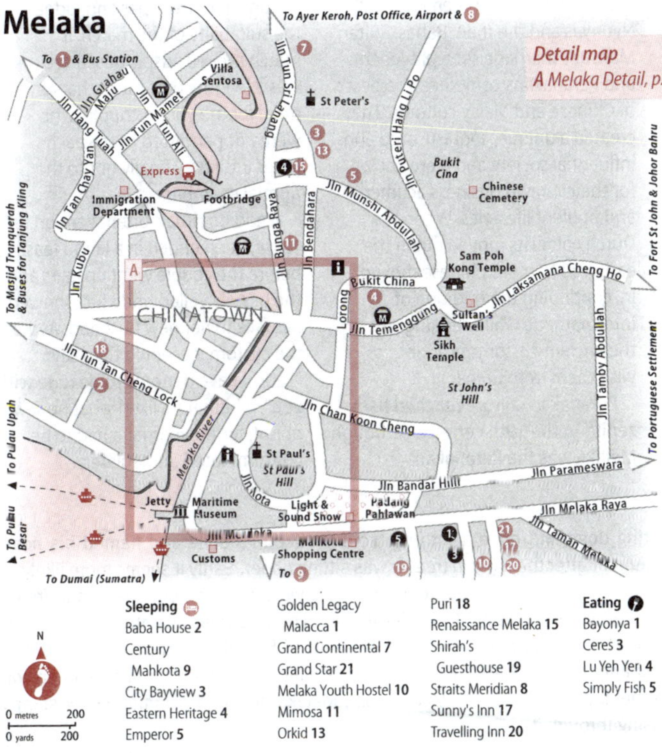

Detail map
A Melaka Detail, p210

Sleeping
Baba House **2**
Century Mahkota **9**
City Bayview **3**
Eastern Heritage **4**
Emperor **5**
Golden Legacy Malacca **1**
Grand Continental **7**
Grand Star **21**
Melaka Youth Hostel **10**
Mimosa **11**
Orkid **13**
Puri **18**
Renaissance Melaka **15**
Shirah's Guesthouse **19**
Straits Meridian **8**
Sunny's Inn **17**
Travelling Inn **20**

Eating
Bayonya **1**
Ceres **3**
Lu Yeh Yen **4**
Simply Fish **5**

The Nyonyas and the Babas

By the early 1400s Melaka was one of the most important ports of call for Chinese trade missions. They arrived between November and March on the northeast monsoon winds and left again in late June on the southwest monsoon; giving them plenty of time to settle down and start families.

Melaka's early sultans made several visits to China, paying obeisance to the Ming emperors to ensure Chinese imperial protection for the sultanate. When Sultan Mansur Shah married the Ming Chinese princess Hang Li Poh in 1460, she brought with her a retinue of 500 'youths of noble birth' and handmaidens who settled around Bukit Cina – or Chinese Hill.

Subsequent generations of Straits Chinese came to be known as Peranakans – from the Bahasa word *anak* (offspring), and means 'born here'. Peranakan women were called Nyonyas and the men, Babas. Sultan Mansur's marriage set a precedent and Peranakans combined the best of Chinese and Malay cultures. They created a unique, sophisticated and influential society and were known for their shrewd business acumen and opulent lifestyles. When the Dutch colonists moved out in the early 1800s, more Chinese moved in, continuing the tradition of intermarriage while clinging to the ancient customs brought with them from China.

Peranakan culture reached its zenith in the 19th century. Although Melaka was the Peranakan hearthstone, there were also large Straits Chinese communities in Penang and Singapore. The Nyonyas adopted Malay dress and were known for their fastidiousness when it came to clothes. The women were renowned for their intricate jewellery and glass beadwork – which are now prized antiques. The Nyonyas imported colourful porcelain from China for ceremonial occasions, which became known as Nyonya-ware and was typically emblazoned with phoenix and peony flower motifs. They also imported craftsmen from China to make their intricate silver jewellery, including elaborate belts and hairpins.

Peranakan weddings were elaborate affairs; couples were paired off by marriage-brokers, contracted by the groom's parents to consult horoscopes and judge the suitability of the match. If a match proved auspicious, there was a lengthy present-exchanging ritual for the young couple, who were not permitted to see each other until they finally got to the nuptial chamber.

Wedding rituals often went on for 12 days and ended in a lavish feast before the couple went upstairs and the heavily veiled bride first showed her face to her new husband. As was the custom, he would then say: "Lady, I have perforce to be rude with you", whether he liked what he saw or not, for the marriage had to be consummated immediately.

hunting dogs and drive it into the sea. He liked its style and named his nearby settlement after the *malaka* tree he was sitting under. Sadly it seems more likely that the name Melaka is derived from the Arabic word *malakat*, or market, and from its earliest days the settlement, with its sheltered harbour, was an entrepôt. Melaka was sheltered from the monsoons by the island of Sumatra, and perfectly located for merchants to take advantage of the trade winds. Because the Strait's deep-water channel lay close to the Malayan coast, Melaka also had command over shipping passing through it.

Peranakan architecture is exemplified in the Chinese Palladian townhouses – the best examples of which are in Melaka – with their open courtyards and lavish interiors, dominated by heavy dark furniture, inlaid with marble and mother-of-pearl.

Aside from their magnificent homes, one of the Peranakans' most enduring endowments is their cuisine, the result of the melding of cultures. The food is spicy but uses lots of coconut milk and is painstakingly prepared – Nyonya-Baba restaurants are difficult business propositions. For details of particular dishes, see page 628).

The cliquey Peranakan upper-class assimilated easily into British colonial society, following the formation of the Straits Settlements in 1826. The billiard-playing, brandy-swilling Babas, in their Mandarin dresses, conical hats, pigtails and thick-soled shoes successfully penetrated the commercial sector and entered public office. Many became professionals, such as lawyers, doctors and teachers, although they were barred from entering government above the clerical level.

"Strange to say," wrote Vaughan, "that although the Babas adhere so loyally to the customs of their progenitors they despise the real Chinamen and are exclusive fellows indeed; [there is] nothing they rejoice in more than being British subjects..." In Penang they were dubbed 'the Queen's Chinese'. Over the years they evolved their own Malay patois, and, in the 19th century, English was also thrown into their linguistic cocktail. They even devised a secret form of slang by speaking Baba Malay backwards.

Although they chose not to mix with immigrant Chinese, they retained a strong interest in events in China. The Straits Settlements provided a refuge for exiled reformers from the motherland – most notably Dr Sun Yat-sen, who lived in both Singapore and Penang in the early 1900s and became the first president of the Republic of China in 1911.

The Baba community's most famous son was Tan Cheng Lock, who was born into a distinguished Melakan Baba family in 1883. He lent his name to the Peranakans' architectural treasure, Jalan Tun Tan Chen Lock (formerly Heeren Street) in Melaka's Chinatown. Tan served in local government in colonial Melaka from 1912-1935 and vociferously fought British discrimination against the Straits and Malayan Chinese. He charged that the British had done nothing to "foster and strengthen their spirit of patriotism and natural love for the country of their birth and adoption". Tan was the spokesman for Malaya's Chinese community and fought for equality among the races; he founded the Overseas Chinese Association and became a prominent reformist politician in the years leading up to Malaysian independence.

In 1405 a Chinese Muslim Admiral, the eunuch Cheng Ho, arrived in Melaka bearing gifts from the Ming Emperor (including a yellow parasol, which has been the emblem of Malay royalty ever since) and the promise of protection from the Siamese. Cheng Ho (Zheng Ho) made seven voyages to the Indian Ocean over the next three decades and used Melaka as his supply base. The Chinese gained a vassal state and Melaka gained a sense of security: Parameswara was wary of possible Siamese encroachment. Court rituals, ceremony and etiquette were formalized and an exclusive royal court language evolved. In 1411, three years before his death,

The Flor de la Mar: sunken treasure beyond measure

From the early years of the first millennium, Chinese junks were plying the Nanyang, or South Seas, and by the 1400s a sophisticated trade network had built up, linking Asia to India, the Middle East and Europe. For three centuries, Melaka was at the fulcrum of the China trade route and even before the Europeans arrived, hundreds of merchants came each year from Arabia, Persia, India, China, Champa, Cambodia, Siam, Java, Sumatra and the eastern Isles. By the early 1500s, more than 100 large ships were anchoring at Melaka every year. It was known as the emporium of the east.

But this trade was not without its casualties and the sunken wrecks littering the coastal waters of the South China Sea and the Strait of Melaka have given rise to a new, highly profitable industry: treasure-hunting. Divers, in league with marine archaeologists and maritime historians, have flocked to the region in recent years. The most publicized find was the 1987 salvage of a cargo of Chinese porcelain from a vessel that sank off the Riau Islands in 1752; the booty was auctioned by Christie's in Amsterdam two years later for US$16 million. But treasure hunting carries with it political sensitivities over the ownership of wrecks. Salvage operators have been jailed in Indonesia and salvaged antiquities have been confiscated in Thailand.

The ultimate sunken treasure trove lies in what remains of the wreck of the *Flor de la Mar*, at the bottom of the Strait of Melaka. The Portuguese vessel, commanded by Admiral Alfonso d'Albuquerque, is thought to be the richest ship ever lost. Having left Lisbon in 1503, Albuquerque plundered his way from Mozambique, the Red Sea and India to the coastal regions of Burma and Thailand. By July 1511, when he anchored off Melaka, he had amassed untold riches. After capturing the city, he plundered it.

In his book *The Search for Sunken Treasure*, the treasure hunter Robert F Marx wrote: "The spoils the Portuguese took from Malacca stagger the imagination." They included more than 60 tonnes of gold booty in the form of solid gold statues of elephants, tigers, birds and monkeys, all studded with gemstones. There was gilded furniture, gold ingots, gold coins, gold-plated royal litters, chests full of diamonds, rubies and sapphires and several tonnes of Chinese and Arabic coins. And this was just the loot from Sultan Ahmad's palace".

In London, Sotheby's auction house tentatively valued the treasure at US$9 billion; by far the world's richest wreck. Albuquerque stole so much gold that Melaka was left without any coinage. Tin coins were minted instead, for the first time.

Two days after setting off for Portugal, his fleet of four ships ran into

Parameswara sailed with Cheng Ho to China with a large retinue and was received by the third Ming Emperor, Chu Ti. Melaka's next two rulers continued this tradition, making at least two visits each to China.

But China began to withdraw its patronage in the 1430s, and to make sure Melaka retained at least one powerful friend, the third ruler, Sri Maharaja, married the daughter of the sultan of the flourishing maritime state of Samudra-Pasai in Sumatra. Historian Mary Turnbull says "he embraced Islam and hitched Melaka's fortunes to the rising star of the Muslim trading fraternity". He adopted the name Mohamed Shah, but retained the court's long-standing Hindu rituals and a storm at the northeastern tip of Sumatra. Two ships went down, then the *Flor de la Mar* itself hit a reef. Albuquerque survived the shipwreck and managed to salvage a gold sword, a jewel-encrusted crown, a ruby bracelet and a ring, which today are on display in a Lisbon museum. The rest was lost in 37 m of water. The admiral returned to Portugal on his one remaining ship. With his pilot, who also survived, he drew up a chart indicating where the ship went down – 8 km off Tanjung Jambu Air in Aceh.

It lay there, forgotten, for nearly 500 years. In 1988 an Italian specialist in underwater wrecks and an Australian marine historian claimed to have located the *Flor de la Mar*, hidden under several metres of mud, using satellite imaging. The Indonesian government , in whose territorial waters the wreck lay, then awarded a salvage contract to PT Jayatama Istikacipta, a company linked to the family of President Suharto, which sub-contracted the diving operation to an Australian, arrested in Indonesia the previous year for illegal treasure-hunting. He hired former divers from the British Navy's Special Boat Squadron to join the search. In 1989 they found a couple of wrecked Chinese junks but no *Flor de la Mar* and, in frustration, the operation was called off.

The same year, the Indonesians granted a search permit to a Singapore salvage firm. After a year's fruitless exploration, they hired Robert Marx, who, with the aid of a facsimile of Albuquerque's chart, located the reef that the ship had struck. Numerous artefacts were recovered, but, he wrote "a thorough sonar and magnetometer survey revealed that the main section of the wreck lies in an area the size of five football fields at a depth of 37 m under 15 m of concrete-like mud."

The discovery sparked a political row. Malaysia and Portugal contested Indonesia's claim to the booty and the matter was passed to the International Court in The Hague for adjudication. Meanwhile, an endless stream of conspiracy stories – none of them confirmed – surrounds the fate of the *Flor de la Mar*.

In 1991, it was reported that "powerful interests linked to President Suharto" had harassed other treasure-hunters researching the location of the wreck and had privately tried to force them to help mount a covert salvage operation. In late 1991, following further reports that Indonesian Navy divers had tried again, Jakarta and Kuala Lumpur reportedly entered a joint-venture agreement. Under it, Malaysia agreed to bear the entire cost of the operation and split the booty 50/50. There are constant rumours about secret salvage operations circulating among Singapore's commercial diving community, but the matter is so sensitive and the stakes potentially so high that lips are firmly sealed.

ceremonies. He died without a child from his marriage to the Pasai princess and a succession crisis followed. The rightful royal heir, the young Rajah Ibrahim, was murdered in a palace coup after a year on the throne and Kasim, one of Mohamed's sons by a non-royal marriage, declared himself Sultan Muzaffar Shah. Melaka's first proper sultan made Islam the state religion and beat off two Siamese invasions during his reign. Islam was also spreading through the merchant community. In the latter half of the 15th century the faith was taken from Melaka to other states on the peninsula as well as to Brunei and Javanese port cities that were breaking away from the Hindu kingdom of Majapahit.

In the late 15th century, Malay power reached its pinnacle. Muzaffar's successor, Sultan Mansur Shah, extended Melaka's sway over Pahang, Johor and Perak, the Riau archipelago and Sumatra. Contemporary European maps label the entire peninsula 'Malacca'. According to the Malay Annals, the sultan married a Chinese princess in 1460. This marriage and the arrival of the princess and her followers marked the formal beginning of the unique and prosperous Straits Chinese *Peranakan* culture (see page 206).

Another cultural blend that had its roots in medieval Melaka was the Chitty Indian community, the result of Indian merchants inter-marrying with local women, including the Malay nobility. Because foreign traders had to wait several months before the winds changed to allow them to return home, many put down roots and Melaka, 'the city where the winds met', had hundreds of permanent foreign residents. There were no taboos concerning cross-cultural marriage: the polygamous Muslim Sultan Mansur Shah even visited the crumbling Majapahit court in East Java where he cemented relations by his second royal marriage, to the Hindu ruler's daughter.

By the beginning of the 16th century Melaka was the most important port in the region. Foreign merchants traded in Indian and Persian textiles, spices from the Moluccas (Maluku), silk and porcelain from China as well as gold, pepper, camphor, sandalwood and tin. The Malay language subsequently became the *lingua franca* throughout the region.

Tales of luxuriance and prosperity attracted the Portuguese who came in search of trading opportunities, with the aim of breaking the Arab merchants' stranglehold on trade between Europe and Asia. Spices from the Moluccas came through the Strait and whoever controlled the waterway determined the price of cloves in Europe. The Portuguese – known to Melakans as 'the white Bengalis' – combined their quest for

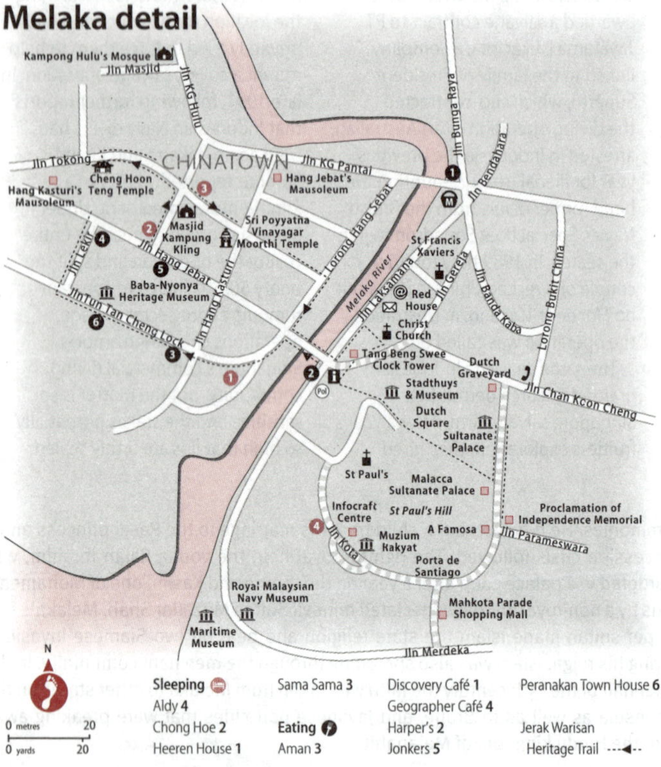

riches with a fervent anti-Muslim crusade, spurred by their hatred of their former Moorish overlords on the Iberian peninsula. They arrived in 1509, received a royal welcome and then fled for their lives when Gujerati (Indian) traders turned the sultan against them. Alfonso d'Albuquerque, the viceroy of Portuguese India, returned two years later with 18 ships and 1,400 men. After an initial attempt at reconciliation, he too was beaten off. D'Albuquerque then stormed and conquered the city in July 1511, the year after he seized Goa on India's west coast. The Melakan court fled to Johor where Sultan Ahmad re-established his kingdom.

The foreign merchants quickly adapted to the new rulers and under the Portuguese the city continued to thrive. Tomé Pires, a Portuguese apothecary who arrived with d'Albuquerque's fleet and stayed two years, wrote in his account, *Suma Oriental*: "Whoever is lord of Melaka has his hand on the throat of Venice," adding that "the trade and commerce between different nations for a thousand leagues on every hand must come to Melaka". The port became known as the 'Babylon of the Orient'. Despite the two-year sojourn of Spanish Jesuit priest St Francis Xavier, Christianity had little impact on the Muslim Malays or the hedonistic merchant community. A large Eurasian population grew up, adding to Melaka's cosmopolitan character; there are still many Pereiras, D'Cruzes, de Silvas, da Costas, Martinezes and Fernandezes in the Melaka phone book.

Back in Lisbon in the early 17th century, the Portuguese monarchy was on the decline, the government in serious debt and successive expeditions failed to acquire anything more than a tenuous hold over the Spice Islands, to the east. The Portuguese never managed to subdue the Sumatran pirates, the real rulers of the Strait of Melaka. As Dutch influence increased in Indonesia, Batavia (Jakarta) developed as the principal port of the region and Melaka declined. The Dutch entered an alliance with the Sultanate of Johor and foreign traders began to move there. This paved the way for a Dutch blockade of Melaka and in 1641, after a six-month siege of the city, Dutch forces, together with troops from Johor, forced the surrender of the last Portuguese governor.

Over the next 150 years the Dutch carried out an extensive building programme; some of these still stand in Dutch Square. Melaka was the collecting point for Dutch produce from Sumatra and the Malay peninsula, where the new administration attempted to enforce a monopoly on the tin trade. They built forts on Pulau Pangkor and at Kuala Selangor, north of Klang, to block Acehnese efforts to muscle in on the trade, but the Dutch, like the Portuguese before them, were more interested in trade than territory. Apart from their buildings, the Dutch impact on Melaka was minimal. Their tenure of the town was periodically threatened by the rise of the Bugis, Minangkabaus and Makassarese, who migrated to the Malay peninsula, having been displaced by the activities of the Dutch East India Company in Sulawesi and Sumatra. In 1784 Melaka was only saved from a joint Bugis and Minangkabau invasion by the arrival of the Dutch fleet from Europe.

By the late 18th century, the Dutch hold on the China trade route was bothering the English East India Company. In 1795 France conquered The Netherlands and the British made an agreement with the exiled Dutch government, allowing them to become the caretaker of Dutch colonies. Four years later the Dutch East India Company went bankrupt, but just to make sure that they would not be tempted to make a comeback in Melaka, the British started to demolish the fortress in 1807. The timely arrival of Stamford Raffles, the founder of modern Singapore, prevented the destruction from going further, and in 1824, under the Treaty of London, Melaka was surrendered to the British in exchange for the Sumatran port of Bencoolen (Bengkulu).

In 1826 Melaka became a part of the British Straits Settlements, along with Penang and Singapore. But by then, its harbour had silted up and it was a town of little commercial importance. In 1826 it had a population of 31,000 and was the biggest of the settlements; by 1860, although its population had doubled, it was the smallest and least significant of the three. In 1866, a correspondent for the *Illustrated London News* described Melaka (which the British spelled *Malacca*) as "a land where it is 'always afternoon' – hot, still, dreamy. Existence stagnates. Trade pursues its operations invisibly. It has no politics, little crime, rarely gets even two lines in an English newspaper and does nothing towards making contemporary history". In 1867 the Straits Settlements were transferred to direct colonial rule and Melaka faded into obscurity. Strangely, it was the town's infertile agricultural hinterland that helped reinvigorate the local economy at the turn of the 20th-century. The first rubber estate in Malaya was started by Melakan planter Tan Chay Yan, who accepted some seedlings from 'Mad' Henry Ridley, director of Singapore's Botanic Gardens, and planted out 1,200 ha in 1896. The idea caught on among other Chinese and European planters and Melaka soon became one of the country's leading rubber producers.

Sights

Jalan Munshi Abdullah, which runs through the middle of the more recent commercial district, is like any Malaysian main street. While the old city is quite compact, the town itself is neither as small or as medieval-looking as visitors are led to suppose. The historical sights from the Portuguese and Dutch periods are interesting because they are in Malaysia – not because they are stunning architectural wonders. That said, the old red Dutch buildings on the east bank of the river and the magnificent Peranakan architecture and stuccoed shophouses on the west side, lend Melaka an atmosphere unlike any other Malaysian town. It also lays claim to many of the country's oldest Buddhist and Hindu temples, mosques and churches.

The most interesting parts of the old town are close to the waterfront.

Town Square

The Dutch colonial architecture in the town square is the most striking feature of the riverfront. The buildings are painted a bright terracotta red and are characterized by their massive walls, chunky doors with wrought-iron hinges and louvred windows. The most prominent of these is the imposing **Stadthuys**. Completed in 1660, it is said to be the oldest-surviving Dutch building in the East, and served as the official residence of the Dutch governors. The renovated building now houses a good **history museum**, ⓘ *0900-1730, Sat-Thu 0900-1245, 1445-1800 Fri, RM5,* detailing in maps, prints and photographs the history and development of Malacca/Melaka. Also here are a cultural museum and a literature museum, which are of less obvious interest to the average visitor. Just southwest from Stadthuys, on the river is a half-size replica of the galley that the viceroy of Portuguese India arrived in. The **Tang Beng Swee Clock Tower** looks Dutch but was built by a wealthy Straits Chinese family in 1886. **Christ Church**, ⓘ *Thu-Tue*, was built between 1741 and 1753 to replace an earlier Portuguese church, which was by then a ruin (church records date back to 1641). Its red bricks were shipped out from Zeeland in Holland. It is Malaysia's oldest Protestant church and the floor is still studded with Dutch tombstones. The original pews are intact – as are its ceiling beams, each hewn from a single tree trunk more than 15 m long. On the altar there is a collection of sacramental silverware bearing the Dutch coat-of-arms and there is a beautiful altar carving of the Last Supper.

On Jalan Kota, which runs in a curve round St Paul's Hill from the square is the Muziam Islam Melaka (Islamic Museum), ⓘ *Tue-Sun 0900-1730, closed Mon,* a new addition to the spread of museums. A rather average display of Islamic cultural pieces.

St Paul's Hill

From behind the gate, a path leads up to the ruins of **St Paul's Church**, built on the site of the last Melakan sultan's *istana*. The small chapel was originally built by the

Portuguese in 1521 and called *Nossa Senhora da Annunciada*, Our Lady of the Annunciation. The body of St Francis Xavier (the 16th-century Jesuit missionary who translated the catechism into Malay and visited the church regularly), was temporarily interred in the church vault following his death off the coast of China in 1552. His remains were later sent to Portuguese Goa on the west coast of India. An armless marble statue, erected in 1953, now commemorates Malaysia's best-known missionary. The Portuguese added gun turrets and a tower to the church and it became a fortress between 1567 and 1596. During the Dutch seige of Melaka in 1641, it was badly damaged but the invaders repaired it and renamed it St Paul's. It became a Protestant church and remained so until Christ Church was completed in 1753. St Paul's ended its life as a cemetery; it was used as a special burial ground for Dutch nobles, whose tombs line the walls. There are good views of the city and over the sea from the top of Saint Paul's Hill. The ruins now host buskers and souvenir sellers.

Head down the hill the other side and you reach the **Porta de Santiago**, the remains of the great Portuguese fort A Famosa, said to have been built in four months flat under Admiral Alfonso d'Albuquerque's supervision in 1511. What remains is largely a Dutch reconstruction, the result of repair work carried out following the siege in 1641; it prominently displays the Dutch East India Company's coat-of-arms. The fort originally sprawled across the whole hill and housed the entire Portuguese administration, including their hospitals and five churches. It was flattened by the British between 1806 and 1808 when they occupied Melaka during the Napoleonic Wars. They wanted to ensure that the fort was not reclaimed by the Dutch. Stamford Raffles arrived for a holiday in Melaka just in time to forestall the destruction of its last remaining edifice.

A wooden replica of Sultan Mansur Shah's 15th-century *istana* is below St Paul's. The **Sultanate Palace** has been painstakingly reconstructed from a description in the 16th-century *Serjarah Melayu* (Malay Annals) and was built in 1985 using traditional construction techniques and materials. Mansur – who came to the throne in 1459 – inherited what was reputed to be the finest royal palace in the world, with a roof of copper and zinc in seven tiers, supported by wooden carved pillars. According to the Annals, his magnificent *istana* was destroyed by fire after being struck by lightning the year after his accession. ⓘ *0900-1730 daily, RM2.*

The **Proclamation of Independence Memorial** was built in 1912 and formerly housed the Malacca Club. The old Dutch colonial building was the social centre of British colonial Melaka. Perhaps appropriately, it now houses an extensive timeline exhibition covering Malaysia's journey to independence. There are lots of photographs – interesting to those who like that sort of thing – and it also represents a fine example of nation-building. ⓘ *0900-1800 Sat-Thu, 0900-1200 and 1500-1800 Fri, closed Mon, free.*

East bank

The **Maritime Museum** is housed in a full-scale reconstruction of the Portuguese trading vessel *Flor de la Mar*, on the riverbank, 200 m downstream from the river boat embarkation point. Of all the museums in Melaka, this is one of the better ones – many of the other museums are rather repetitive, but as Melaka's history is the history of sea-trade, this is a more interesting option. It has a collection of models of foreign ships that docked at Melaka during its maritime supremacy from the 14th century to the Portuguese era. The *Flor de la Mar* itself ended its days on the sea bed just off-shore, laden with treasure that was bound for Portugal (see box, page 208). ⓘ *0900-1730, closed Fri 1215-1445, RM2.* Entry to the Maritime Museum also gives access to the **Royal Malaysian Navy Museum**, across the road, ⓘ *Jalan Kota, T2830926, 0900-1730, closed Fri 1215-1445, RM2*, which displays the salvaged remains of 19th-century vessels that have foundered or been sunk in the Melaka Strait, as well as more contemporary bits and pieces.

Chinese cobblers

One of Melaka's most significant cultural assets was removed from 92 Jonker Street as part of the project to lure tourists.

Elderly Mr Yeo, the proprietor, was given three days to move out. For two generations the Yeo family, at **Wah Aik Shoemaker Shop**, have been the only cobblers catering for the country's dwindling population of ageing Chinese women with bound feet. The practice, which was considered *de rigeur* for women of noble stock during the Ch'ing Dynasty (1644-1912), was rekindled among the families of nouveau riche Chinese tin towkays during the days of the British Straits Settlements.

The process involved binding the feet firmly with bandages before they were fully formed; it was supposed to add to a woman's sensuality, but in reality it just caused a lot of pain. In China, the practice was outlawed in 1912. There are only a handful of women in Malaysia with bound feet, most of them in Melaka and all of them in their 80s or 90s. Mr Yeo Sing Guat made these *san choon chin lian* (3-in golden lotus feet) shoes – with brocade on authentic Shanghai Hang Chong silk – for them and as tourist souvenirs; he also makes the Peranakan *kasut manik* 'pearl shoes', sewn with miniature pearl beads.

Chinatown

A concrete bridge from the south end of Dutch Square leads to Chinatown, the oldtrading section of Melaka. **Jalan Hang Jebat**, formerly known as **Jonker Street**, was once famous for its antique shops: Nyonya porcelain, Melakan-style 'red and gold' carved furniture, wooden opium beds, Victorian mirrors, antique fans and Peranakan blackwood furniture inlaid with mother-of-pearl. There are some good examples of Peranakan architecture along the street – notably the renowned Jonkers Melaka Restoran. But none of these Peranakan houses compare with the picturesque **Jalan Tun Tan Cheng Lock**. Named after a leading Melakan Baba, instrumental in pre-independence politics (see box, page 206), it is lined with the Straits Chinese community's ancestral homes and is Melaka's 'Millionaires' Row'. Many of the houses have intricately carved doors that were often specially built by immigrant craftsmen from China. Today tour buses exacerbate the local traffic problem, which clogs the narrow one-way street, but many of its Peranakan mansions are still lived in by the same families that built them in the 19th century.

One of the most opulent of these houses has been converted into the **Baba Nyonya Heritage Museum**, ⓘ *48-50 Jalan Tun Tan Cheng Lock, 1000-1230 and 1400-1600, closed all day Tue; RM8, children RM4*. It is in a well-preserved traditional Peranakan town house, built in 1896 by millionaire rubber planter Chan Cheng Siew. Today it is owned by William Chan and his family, who conduct tours of their ancestral home. The interior is that of a typical 19th-century residence and all the rooms are still as they would have been 100 years ago. The house contains family heirlooms and antiques, including Nyonyaware porcelain and blackwood furniture with marble or mother-of-pearl inlay, and silverware. There is also a collection of traditional wedding costumes, photographs and kitchen utensils. The kitchen sink has the name of William Chan's great grandfather carved on it. The information-packed tours are run regularly throughout the day.

Although at first glance, tourists may be impressed by the streets around Chinatown, the sad truth is that the desire to attract mass tourism to this 'heritage' town has probably destroyed more heritage than it has protected. Over 20 buildings have been demolished and many traditional trades evicted in the interests of bigger business. False 'heritage' façades and trinket shops have taken the place of the authentic article. 'Jonker Walk' – the renaming of Jonker Street (Jalan Hang Jebat) – has led to the pedestrianization of the street over the weekends. There are two ways of looking at Jonker Walk. Most visitors come away thinking that the night market here is fun and zingy, they like the shophouse architecture, the hawkers sell tasty snacks, and the pedestrianization of the street makes it all more human, The alternative view is that the street has been transformed from a place with real people running traditional businesses to a contrived and ersatz place geared to the needs of tourists. No local residents were consulted about the project, the original traders and guilds have been displaced, and an accumulation of rubbish and associated rats and cockroaches has created health problems.

The **Cheng Hoon Teng Temple**, on Jalan Tokong, was built in 1645, although there were later additions in 1704 and 1804 and is the oldest Chinese temple in Malaysia. The name literally means 'Temple of the Evergreen Clouds' and was founded by Melaka's Kapitan Cina, Lee Wi King from Amoy, a political refugee who fled from China. All the materials used in the original building were imported from China, as were the craftsmen who built it in typical South Chinese style. The elaborate tiled roofs are decorated with mythological figures, flowers and birds, and inside there are wood carvings and lacquer work. The main altar houses an image of Kuan Yin, the Goddess of Mercy (cast in solid bronze and bought from India in the 19th century), who is associated with peace, good fortune and fertility. On her left sits Ma Cho Po, the guardian of fishermen and on her right, Kuan Ti, the god of war, literature and justice. The halls to the rear of the main temple are dedicated to Confucius and contain ancestral tablets.

Nearby, on Jalan Tukang Emas, is the **Sri Poyyatha Vinayagar Moorthi Temple**, built in 1781 and the oldest Hindu temple in use in Malaysia. It is dedicated to the elephant-headed god Vinayagar (more usually known as Ganesh). Near to this Hindu temple on Jalan Tukang Emas is the **Masjid Kampong Kling**, a mosque built in 1748 in Sumatran style, with a square base surmounted by a three-tiered roof and pagoda-like minaret. Another 18th-century mosque in the same style is the **Masjid Tranquerah**, Jalan Tengkerah, 2 km out of town on the road to Port Dickson. Next door is an unusual free-standing octagonal minaret with Chinese-style embellishments, in marked contrast to Malaysia's traditional Moorish-style mosques. In the graveyard is the tomb of Sultan Hussein Shah of Johor who, in 1819, signed the cession of Singapore to Stamford Raffles.

West bank

On the west bank is **Kampong Morten**, a village of traditional Melakan houses. It was named after a man who built Melaka's wet market and donated the land to the Malays. The main attraction here is Kassim Mahmood's hand-crafted house.

North Melaka

St Peter's Church ⓘ *Jalan Taun Sri Lanang, daily until 1900.*on was built in 1710 by descendants of the early Portuguese settlers when the Dutch became more tolerant of different faiths. Iberian design is incorporated in the interior, where Corinthian pillars support a curved ceiling above the aisle, similar to churches in Goa and Macau. It is the centre of the Roman Catholic faith in Malaysia. Easter candlelit processions to St Peter's seem strangely out of context in Malaysia.

Bukit Cina is the largest traditional Chinese burial ground outside China, containing more than 12,000 graves. Chinese graveyards are often built on hillsides because the hill is said to protect the graves from evil winds; this hill has the added advantage of overlooking water and the ancestral spirits are said to enjoy the panoramic view over the city and across the Strait of Melaka.

In 1460 when Sultan Mansur Shah married Li Poh, a Ming princess, she took up residence on Melaka's highest hill, **Bukit Cina**, which became the Chinese quarter. The Malay Annals do not record what became of the princess's palace but the hill, off Jalan Munshi Abdullah/Jalan Laksamana Cheng Ho, remained in the possession of the Chinese community and because of its good *feng shui* – its harmony with the supernatural forces and the elements - it was made into a graveyard. The cemetery now sprawls across the adjoining hills of Bukit Gedona and Bukit Tempurong. Some of the graves date back to the Ming Dynasty, but most of these are now overgrown or in the process of disintegrating.

At the foot of the hill is an old Chinese temple called **Sam Poh Kong**, built in 1795 and dedicated to the famous Chinese seafarer, Admiral Cheng Ho (see page 207). It was originally built to cater for those whose relatives were buried on Bukit Cina. This temple has a peaceful and relaxed atmosphere and is interesting to explore. Next to the temple is the **Sultan's Well** (*Perigi Rajah*), also called the **Hang Li Poh Well**, said to have been sunk in the 15th century. It is believed that drinking from this well ensures a visitor's return to Melaka – but anyone foolhardy enough to try this today is liable to contract dysentery and instead stay rather longer than they anticipated. However, while the water may be off-limits to all but the most foolhardy, there is a small market situated beside the well where the visitor can sample the local fruits.

The ruined **Fort St John**, another relic of the Dutch occupation, is southeast of Bukit Cina. Its hilltop location affords some excellent views although its aspect has been spoiled by the water treatment plant and high-rise apartment block on either side of it.

Portuguese Settlement

ⓘ *Take a No 17 bus from outside the Equatorial Hotel.*

About 3 km from the town centre is the Portuguese Settlement (Medan Portugis) at Ujong Pasir, where the descendants of the Portuguese occupiers settled. A Portuguese community (of sorts) has managed to survive here for nearly five centuries; unlike the subsequent Dutch and British colonial régimes, the Portuguese garrison was encouraged to intermarry and generally treat the Malays as social equals. Today these Malaysians of Portuguese descent number around 4,500 (although other estimates are much lower). In the country as a whole, there are thought to be some 20,000. The process of integration was so successful that when the Dutch, after capturing the city in 1641, offered Portuguese settlers a choice between amnesty and deportation to their nearest colony, many chose to stay. In the 1920s, as their distinctive culture was threatened with extinction, the leaders of the community pleaded with the British to allot them a piece of land on which they could settle. A small area of swampland was duly allocated and the neat and well-planned settlement visible today was built, its street named after Portuguese heroes largely unrecognized in Malaysia. The main square, built only in 1985, is a concrete replica of a square in Lisbon – and is visibly ersatz.

Today there are just a few tourist-oriented restaurants and shops in the modern Portuguese Square, and cultural shows are staged on Saturday nights (see Eating page 223). Other than tourism, the residents of the Portuguese settlement earn their livelihoods by fishing and through a small number of cottage industries including shrimp paste production. The central role that the sea plays in the community's coherence and identity is threatened by a land reclamation project that will cut off its access to the sea. This will destroy the settlement's fishing industry, its fish-based cottage industries and undermine its attraction to tourists. Resident Gerard Fernandis said, "Our history, our culture, songs, dances and food are all linked to the sea", adding that without the sea the "settlement will become an island in a sea of concrete."

The descendants of the original settlers still speak a medieval Portuguese dialect called Cristao (pronounced 'Cristang'), spoken nowhere else in the world.

Crouching princess, hidden passion

The fairy princess of Gunung Ledang magicked her way into an epic movie in 2004, stirring the country's hopes for its first Oscar nomination.

The film industry wanted *Puteri Gunung Ledang* (The princess of Mount Ophir) to do to Malaysian cinema what Oscar-winning *Crouching Tiger, Hidden Dragon* did for Chinese-language movies.

The epic, known locally as *PGL*, wound up being the most expensive movie ever made in Malaysia, costing around US$4 million and took three years to make.

Scriptwriters cooked two legends together for the storyline which is set in 15th century Melaka. Simply told, a Javanese princess falls in love with Malay warrior Hang Tuah.

But the Sultan of Melaka is determined to wed the princess himself and Hang is sent to fetch her from Mount Ledang where she has fled. Hang is forced to choose between his love for the runaway beauty and loyalty to his leader.

To waylay the Sultan, the princess agrees to marry him if he can first solve seven very tricky riddles.

The movie is packed with flying warriors, fight scenes (all choreographed to the moves of silat, a Malaysian martial art), mighty explosions and telepathic characters. During scenes shot in the Cameron Highlands, the filmmakers got into trouble with green groups for chopping down trees without permits and trashing the environment.

Local audiences, tempted by a lush marketing campaign, flocked to see it, and, largely liked it. It's a long, long movie however, 145 minutes all told; many reviews griped about the length - prompting one unkind reviewer to comment that the movie had sent some in the audience to sleep.

Others moaned at the lack of passion. Considering PGL is a love story, there's no flesh, no sex - Hang and the princess never even get to kiss. The most racy scene has the princess showing a flash of cleavage in a wet robe. But conservative Malaysia demands the film industry keep it clean. One reviewer complained, "there was as much chemistry between the two [lead lovers] as a neutered rottweiler and a spayed poodle". The song and dance routines inspire comparisons with Bollywood (Malaysian cinema is sometimes unkindly dubbed Mallywood).

Even so, the movie is now doing the rounds of international film festivals, and it won good reviews at the Venice film festival. When it screened in Singapore in December 2004, it was the first Malay movie to open there for 30 years. *PGL*'s makers had had their fingers crossed for nomination status in Best Foreign Language Movie at the 2005 Oscars, but to no avail.

You can catch a bit of the movie's drama at its official website on //www.pglthemovie.com/

Around Melaka

Tanjung Kling

About 9 km northwest of Melaka, it is a pleasant drive past beachside kampongs despite the muddy sea and dirty beach from passing tankers that have a habit of swilling out their tanks. This does not seem to affect the taste of the seafood – or perhaps it improves it – and there are several restaurants and hawker stalls along the roadside at **Pantai Kundor**, where there are a number of hotels. Kampong Kling is thought to have got its name from Tamils who originally settled there, having come

Tanjung Kling is a much more relaxing place to stay than Melaka itself.

Peranakan Table Manners

Local food is served with local superstition. The heritage of the Babas and the Nyonyas includes a detailed etiquette of what to do and what to avoid at mealtimes. Food is considered a symbol of *jerki*, meaning luck or fortune. For this reason food should not be squashed, dropped or trodden upon and anything spilt must be picked up. If food is not treated with due respect this is known as sway, and brings bad fortune. Meals should be eaten at a circular table; sitting at a corner is to be avoided. Once seated diners should not sit with their chin in their hand, nor should they move from seat to seat as this will lead to a restless life. Other acts of sway include farting or crying at the dinner table, discussing depressing topics while eating, breaking or using chipped crockery, and piling plates one on top of one another. If cutlery is clashed together, sibling squabbles will follow.

For women there are yet further complications. If a woman drinks too much soup it will rain on her wedding day; if she leaves food on her plate she will marry an ugly husband; and if she sings at the table her husband will be old.

These traditions reach out to a wider belief system that sees inanimate objects as potential habitats for spirits. Thankfully they are not followed to the letter by Perankan restaurants in Melaka, although the proprietors are often happy to offer further insights into this culture.

from Kalingapatam, north of Madras. For the less geographically confident, local tour companies offer organized tours on foot or by car, including visits to the plantation and to Ayer Keroh. Ask at the tourist office in Melaka for details.

Ayer Keroh

ⓘ *Take bus 19 from Melaka.*

Situated just off the highway to KL, 11 km northeast of Melaka, Ayer Keroh has a lake, jungle, a golf course and a country club. It is also the site of **Melaka Zoo** ⓘ *T6-2324053, daily 0900-1800, RM7, RM4 for children*. The zoo now has a night viewing safari, ⓘ *2000-2400, Fri and Sat, adults RM10, children RM5*, where guests are driven around lit-up exhibits by tram. Elephant and horse rides ⓘ *RM2/RM1 just Sat and Sun 1000-1200, 1400-1600*. Ayer Keroh also has the **Butterfly and Reptile Sanctuary**, ⓘ *daily 0900-1800, RM5, RM3 children*, a go-kart track ⓘ *daily 0900-1800*,and a **Mini Malaysia Complex**, ⓘ *daily 0900-1800, RM4, RM2 children*, where the various states of Malaysia are represented by 13 traditional houses containing works of art and culture (similar to the Karyaneka Handicraft Centre in KL) as well as an Orang Asli village. All the houses look remarkably alike, except the Borneo one. It also stages cultural shows. It is, however, overstaffed and badly managed. Mini-ASEAN is next door and is more varied (and included in the ticket price). The **Ayer Keroh Golf and Country Club** ⓘ *T6-2322000*, off the main road past the Ayer Keroh Lake is the longest golf course in Malaysia, take note that handicap cards must be produced.

Pulau Besar

Contrary to its name, Pulau Besar is a small, quiet island, about 8 km southeast of Melaka, which is popular at weekends. According to local legend, a princess became pregnant by a Melakan commoner and was banished to the island to die. There is a shrine on the island dedicated to an early Muslim missionary, who is said to have come to Melaka in the 1400s. The island has good beaches (although the sea is not clean and most of the coral is dead) and there are jungle walks. See also Sleeping.

Gunung Ledang → *Altitude: 1,276 m*

This is one of the peninsula's best-known mountains, also called Mount Ophir, located on the east side of the North-South Highway, equidistant from Melaka and Muar and just inside Johor state. It is isolated from the mountains of the Main Range and is sacred to the Orang Asli of Melaka. A Straits Chinese and Malay rumour has it that the mountain is the domain of a beautiful fairy endowed with the local version of the Midas Touch: she has a habit of turning Gunung Ledang's plant-life into gold. The mountain is said to be guarded by a sacred tiger, which is possessed by the fairy.

Would-be climbers are strongly recommended to refer to the detailed trail-guide in John Briggs', 'Mountains of Malaysia', available in Singapore and KL bookshops.

Gunung Ledang is a strenuous climb involving some very steep scrambles, particularly towards the top. In 1884 an expedition reached the summit while trying to demarcate the boundary between Johor and Melaka. Most climbers of Gunung Ledang choose to camp overnight on the summit, although, at a push, it can be done in a day, from dawn to dusk. The mountain is surrounded by and covered in virgin jungle, and rises through mossy forest (where there are several varieties of pitcher plant), to the rocky summit. Climbers are strongly advised to stick closely to the trails. The trail is complex in places and the climb should be carefully planned. There are two main trails up the mountain; the best route starts 15 km from Tangkak, just beyond Sagil. Waterfalls (*Air Terjun*) are signposted off the road that leads to Air Penas, an over-popular local picnic spot. The trail begins just beyond the rubber factory. Climbers can enquire about guides at the Gunung Ledang Resort, see Sleeping below.

Sleeping

Melaka *p204, maps p205 and p210*

There's plenty of choice in Melaka with some charming places to stay right in the heart of town. There are several good hotels around Tanjung Kling; several good budget hotels at Taman Melaka Raya and one excellent budget hotel in the heart of Chinatown.

L Century Mahkota, Jln Merdeka, T6-2812828, www.centuryhotel.com On the waterfront next to the Mahkota Parade Shopping and Entertainment Complex, this is one of Melaka's first resort hotels. Two pools, health centre, tennis court, two squash courts, mini golf, children's playground, spread out over several towers, the 20 'rooms' are actually suites and apartments, with the usual facilities plus kitchen.

L Renaissance Melaka, Jln Bendahara, T6-2848888, www.renaissancehotels.com/mkzrn The only 5-star hotel in Melaka, 24 storeys high, it is the tallest building in the town, with 300 rooms all of which are spacious and elegantly appointed with Malaccan wood furniture, a/c, mini-fridge, TV, in-house video and grand views either over the town or to the sea, other amenities include coffee shop, restaurants, fitness centre, pool on the 9th floor. Recommended.

AL City Bayview, Jln Bendahara, T6-2839888, cbviewmk@tm.net.my A/c, restaurant, pool, the rooms visitors are shown are not always like the ones they will end up with. Directly opposite the hospital. The most hideous crystal chandelier greets you as you enter the hotel. This poor taste is in keeping with much of the hotel. Overpriced.

AL Golden Legacy Malacca, 146 Jln Hang Tuah, T6-2840777, F6-2838989 Newish sophisticated hotel with 250 plus rooms (although billed as 'boutique'), business facilities, gymnasium, pool and more. Well designed and popular with business visitors.

A-B Heeren House, 1 Jln Tun Tan Cheng Lock, T6-2814241, F6-2814239. A/c, restaurant, rates include breakfast, 5 a/c nicely furnished rooms in colonial and Peranakan style, with canopied 4-poster beds (booking recommended) co-owned by a British lecturer from Singapore and his Chinese partner, afternoon tea, pleasant position in front of the river. Timber floors and 4-poster beds add to the charm of this riverside hotel. Expensive for what you get (rooms are small), but it's a quiet, family-run establishment. Breakfast included. There have been some reports of poor service.

A-B **Mimosa hotel**, 108 Jln Bunga Raya, T6-2821113, www.mimosahotel.com Newish hotel – decent, fully carpeted rooms with a/c, TV and shower. Its restaurant is curiously only open between 0700-1400. Popular with Japanese tours.

B **Aldy Hotel**, 27 Jln Kota, T6-2833232, www.aldyhotel.com.my. Brand new spanking hotel offering spacious rooms tastefully stocked with rattan furniture. Great location alongside the river just next to the tourist office. Only downside is it straddles a bar and restaurant, so could be a bit noisy at night.

B **Emperor**, 123 Jln Munshi Abdullah, T6-2840777, www.theemperorhotel.com A/c, restaurant, pool, health centre, reasonably clean. Great sea views and excellent value at present prices. Breakfast included and special offers on meals, but the hotel is looking a little tired now. Needs a spruce up.

B **Grand Continental**, 20 Jln Tun Sri Lanang, T6-2840088, F6-2848125. Consists of 150 a/c rooms, restaurant, large rooms, good service, buffet for all meals, at a good price. Recommended. Breakfast included.

B **Hotel Orkid** 138 Jln Bendahara, T6-2825555, F6-2827777. Smart hotel at an affordable price. A/c, shower, TV. Facilities include a spa, restaurant and bar. Primarily a business visitor's stopover but good value for tourists except for the nightly karaoke warblings from across the street.

B **Straits Meridian**, 1 Jln Malinja, Taman Malinja, towards Ayer Keroh, T6-2841166, www.sherwoodhotels.com All suite accommodation. Many special deals on both meals and accommodation available here so worth checking it out.

B **Puri**, 118 Jln Tun Tan Cheng Lock, T6-64686154, www.hotelpuri.com. Beautiful hotel set in a restored Peranakan house. There's a bird room with nesting starlings in the ceiling's covings, a tiny museum depicting the restoration work, a serene Chinese garden café, and a lobby with a piano and spiral staircase. The rooms don't have as much character unfortunately, although they are clean and tastefully furnished. Several come with balconies. Recommended.

B-C **Baba House** 125-127 Jln Tun Tan Cheng Lock, T6-2811216, www.melaka.net/babahouse. In the centre of Chinatown, 60 a/c rooms, no restaurant, TV, attractive traditional Baba house, beautiful design, rooms quite plain and some overly small but clean, mostly without windows.

D **Chong Hoe**, 26 Jln Tukang Emas, T6-2826102. A/c, good location opposite the Masjid Kampong Kling mosque.Reasonable value.

D **Eastern Heritage**, 8 Jln Bukit China, T6-2833026, eastern_heritage@hotmail.com. Great old Chinese building with carved wood and gold inlay, spacious rooms on 2nd floor, dorm on 3rd floor, small dipping pool on 1st floor, batik lessons available, six friendly cats, and closer to the heart of the city than other low budget places. Extremely popular, with an authentic feel.

D **Grand Star Hotel**, 256b & 257b, Taman Melaka Raya Jalan 3, T6-2818199. An extensive guesthouse, a little grubby but with friendly staff and good facilities. Internet access, TV, video, kitchen, open 24 hours. Smokers welcome.

D **Sama-Sama**, 26 Jln Tukang Besi (Blacksmith's Street), T6-3051980, www.sama-sama-guesthouse.com/ Chilled-out budget choice right in the heart of Chinatown in a 300-year-old shop house. Owner Soon has furnished the place in a gentle hippy style with a Bob Marley influence. Dorms, doubles and singles are centered around a serene courtyard with a fish pond and hammocks. Laundry facilities, great sound system in the hall, and the very friendly Soon. Towels and sarongs provided. Recommended. Melaka's only budget choice with character.

D **Sunny's Inn**, 270 Jln Taman Melaka Raya, T6-2265446, www.geocities.com/sunny_

For an explanation of the sleeping and eating price codes used in this guide, see inside the front cover. Other relevant information is found in Essentials, pages 45-49.

inn2002 A couple of single and double rooms and a dorm (F), kitchen, bikes for hire, nightly video, good information, friendly staff, bus tickets. Very similar to most budget hotels in this area – in other words, pretty basic.

D-E **Shirah's Guest House**, 207 Taman Melaka Raya, T6-2861041, www.shirahguesthouse.com. Owner Din is super friendly and organises trips and bbqs for guests. Rooms are clean and simply furnished with a few nice touches like 4-poster beds in some rooms. Internet, bikes for hire and kitchen facilities. Din is a great source of information on Melaka.

D-E **Travelling Inn**, 238 & 239 Jln Melaka Raya, T6-2866697. Very friendly staff and a variety of dorms, single and double rooms available. Rooms are clean but very bare. Whole place has a 'plastic chair and vinyl floor' feel. Opened in 2002. Not a bad budget choice.

E **Melaka Youth Hostel**, 341 Taman Melaka Raya, T6-2827915. Clean and well run with doubles and dorms, all recently renovated. Friendly staff, clean rooms but sterile environment., laundry service available but no kitchen. Spacious common room with TV.

Tanjung Kling *p217*

A **Klebang Beach Resort**, 92-1, km 9, Batang Tiga, Tanjung Kling, T6-3155888, F6-3151713. Small hotel, clean and comfortable, but unimaginative decor, small free-form pool, paddling pool, children's playground, 2 restaurants.

A **Riviera Bay Resort**, 10 km Jln Tanjung Kling, T6-3151111, riviera.rbm@meritus-hotels.com. Classical architecture on a palatial scale, takes the form of a U-shaped building on 14 floors with 450 spacious suites, tastefully decorated in shades of green and all sea-facing, with a/c, TV, in-house movies, mini-bar, other amenities include 3 restaurants under a top Swiss chef, the Buccaneer pub, hair salon, children's playground, watersports, tennis, pool with swim-up bar, paddling pool. Just 15 mins' drive from Melaka's town centre.

B **Shah's Beach Resort**, 9 km, Tanjung Kling, T6-3152120. A/c, restaurant, pool, 1950s front with two lines of a/c chalets behind, tennis court and pool can be used by non-guests for a fee. Breakfast included.

C **Straits View Lodge**, C-7886, Pantai Kundur, Batu 9, Tanjung Kling, T6-514627, F6-325788. Simple chalets, friendly atmosphere, boat, bike and fishing equipment for hire.

Ayer Keroh *p218*

A **Malacca Village Paradise Resort**, oppoiste Ayer Keroh Lake, T6-2323600, F6-2325955. Formerly the *Park Plaza*, this is a recent addition to the Paradise chain, popular with Singaporeans at weekends, but reduced rates often available during week, over 500 rooms in imposing Malaccan-red buildings, 2 swimming pools, 2 tennis courts, gymnasium, 2 squash courts, recreation centre, health club (good value shiatsu massage), beauty salon, jogging track, children's playground and sand-pit, 2 restaurants, all rooms with a/c, bath, mini-bar, tea and coffee-making facilities, TV, in-house video. Breakfast included, great value. Recommended.

B-C **Ayer Keroh Country Resort**, Lebuh Ayers Keroh, next to Mini Malaysia, T6-2325211, F6-2320422. Motel-like atmosphere, a/c, restaurant, pool.

E **Ayer Keroh Recreational Forest** (Call Malacca Forest Department, T6-5291244, F6-5294176), off the main road opposite Mini Malaysia. Camping, chalets and tree houses.

Pulau Besar *p218*

B **Panda Nusa Resort**, located on 22 ha of the 133-ha island is that 37 Jalan Chan Koon Cheng, T6-2818007, a deluxe beach resort designed to look like a traditional Melakan village. It has air conditioning, a restaurant, and a pool complex complete with open-air Jacuzzi.

Gunung Ledang *p219*

A-B **Gunung Ledang Resort**, 91-a, Jln Sutera, Taman Sentosa, (Sales office. 28, Jln Segamat, 84020 Sagil, T6-9772888, http://www.ledang.com/ This place has 60 chalets and 30 jungle huts set in the jungle, facilities and activities include a swimming pool, gym, health centre, restaurant and convention centre. The resort is about 2 hrs' drive on the North-South Express through Tangkak Town to Sagil; from there drive up the mountain.

Eating

Melaka *p204, maps p205 and p210*

Chinese

Good New World Restoran, Taman Melaka Raya, T6-2842528, large and modern, specializes in Cantonese dishes. Locally recommended.

Bee Bee Hiong, City Park, Jln Bunga Raya, for fish-ball fans.

Ceres, 256-257 Jln Melaka Raya. A heaven for veggies and health freaks. Tasty cuisine made from beancurd in its various guises, alfalfa sprouts and vegetables. A mix of Chinese cooking and western snacks. Recommended.

Chop Teo Soon Leng, 55 Jln Hang Tuah, Teochew cuisine.

Dragon Village Restaurant, 1 Jln Kubu Melaka, T6-2815678, in charming old building, popular, although out of the hub of things at the edge of Chinatown.

Hoe Kee Chicken Rice, Jln Hang Jebat, Hainanese chicken rice in Chinatown coffee shop, incredibly popular with workers at lunchtime. Recommended.

Keng Dom, 148 Taman Melaka Raya, T2826409, locally renowned for its steamboats.

Kim Swee Huat, 38 Jln Laksamana, big menu with staple western fillers (include travellers' food) as well as local food.

Lu Yeh Yen, 154 Jln Bunga Raya. Chinese staples. Best to come here at night when tables are set up in the temple courtyard. Bustling and popular. Service, albeit friendly, is slow and erratic.

New Oriental Satay and Mee, 82 Jln Tengkera (road to Tanjung Kling), being a Chinese stall, serves pork satay and other variations such as cuttlefish (*sotong*) satay, also well known for its *yee kiow mee*.

UE Teahouse, 20 Lorong Bukit Cina, *dim sum* from early morning until 1200. Recommended.

Indian

Banana Leaf, 42 Jln Munshi Abdullah, South Indian meat curries and vegetarian dishes, biriyani specials on Wed and Sat evenings.

Kerala, Jln Melaka Raya, good value.

Mitchell Raaju Nivaas, Jln Laksamana, aside from its good curries, this restaurant also offers cooking lessons, RM2, for those who want to make Indian breads and basic curries.

Sri Lakshmi Villas, intersection of Bendahara and Temenggong, fabulous *dosai masalas* and other good value Indian dishes. International

Veni, 34 Jln Temenggong, banana leaf restaurant with good selection of meat curries and vegetarian dishes, *roti canai* breakfasts.

International

Taming Sari Grill, *Renaissance Melaka Hotel*, Jln Bendahara, T6-2848888, seafood and meat cooked on marble with a little olive oil, served with bread, baked potato and salad.

Harper's, 2 Lorong Hang Jebat. Charming riverside eatery with high ceilings opposite tourist office on the other side of the river. Serves western and nyonya fare. Good place to catch sight of monitor lizards as they dodge the floating gunk in the river.

Aman, 101 Jln Tun Tan Cheng Lock. Atmospheric bar and café at night, filled with candles and comfy sofas. Also a furniture shop.

Café Sixties, 12 Jln Melaka Raya 23, Taman Melaka Raya, T6-2819507, rock 'n' roll interior, fish 'n' chips, steak, curry and others.

Coconut House, 128 Heeren St, a townhouse that now serves excellent woodfire pizzas, houses an art gallery and bookshop and is also a venue for art films. The restaurant also serves fresh fruit juices, beers, a selection of coffees and fresh cakes. Patrons can choose music from the owners' CD collection. Friendly welcoming staff, recommended. Closed Thur.

Discovery Café, 3 Jln Bunga Raya, discovery_café@hotmail.com A little haven for backpackers. A small friendly café and bar situated just along from the tourist office. It has a terrace, pool table, darts board, television, Internet access and a library of travel guides (this one included!). Recommended.

Geographer Café, 83 Jonkers St, www.geographer.com.my A friendly establishment with a good choice of local and western food. Internet access. Recommended if only for Mr Burns,

Malaysia's answer to Frank Sinatra, singing live with his keyboard. Pleasant dining area upstairs.

Simply Fish, 206, Jln Melaka Raya. Spotlessly clean café serving an interesting range of mainly European-style fish dishes.

Malay

Anda, 8b Jln Hang Tuah, popular modern coffee shop, specialities include *ikan bakar* (grilled fish), *sayur masak lemak* (deep-fried marinated prawns) and *rendang*.

Mini, 35 Jln Merdeka, good for *ikan panggang* (grilled fish with spicy sauce) and *nasi campur*.

Taman, 10 Jln Merdeka, on the sea front, known for its *ikan assam pedas* – hot (chilli-hot) fish curry. *Cendol* can be drunk all over Malaysia – sample it at the Clock Tower, near Bukit St Paul. It is made up of crushed ice, coconut milk, *gula melaka* – glutinous rice beads and strips of green jelly – delicious!

Nyonya

Jonkers, 17 Jln Hang Jebat. Old Nyonya house, with restaurant in the old ancestral hall. Good atmosphere and excellent food – Nyonya and international, set menu good value at RM20 (changes regularly), worth a visit for the house alone but the food is also excellent. Closes around 1600. Recommended.

Nam Hoe Villa (*Restoran Peranakan*), 317c Klebang Besar (6 km towards Port Dickson), T6-3154436. Open 1100-1500, 1830-2300; cultural show at 2000 (except Sat). Originally the house of a Chinese rubber tycoon, now a restaurant and Peranakan showpiece, all the best-known Nyonya dishes are served; buffet.

Ole Sayang, 1988199 Taman Melaka Raya, T6 2831966, serves all the favourites, including chicken *pongteh* (in sweet and sour spicy sauce). Recommended.

Restoran Manis Sayang, 617-618 Taman Melaka Raya, T6-2813393, traditional Nyonya chicken and fish dishes.

Restoran Peranakan Town House, 107 Jln Tun Tan Cheng Lock, T6-2845001, same management and concept as *Nam Hoe Villa*. Only opens for dinner on weekends, weekdays last orders at 1530. Authentic atmosphere – eating here will recreate the feelings of dining in an upper-class Straits Chinese house about 100 years ago.

Bayonya, 164 Taman Malaka Raya, bayonyarest@hotmail.com Excellent Peranakan cuisine. The establishment is owned by a real enthusiast who will provide a culture lesson with your meal. Recommended.

Heeren House, 1 Jln Tun Tan Cheng Lock, good value set lunch, cakes, appeals to western tastes, some Peranakan and Portuguese dishes, a/c, attractive Peranakan furniture.

Nancy's Kitchen, 15 Jln Hang Lekir, housed in the *Old China Cafe*. Excellent, authentic Nonya food classics such as 'chicken candlenut curry'. Small range of local cakes and biscuits available to take out. Open lunchtimes, closed Wednesdays. Robert and his family are great hosts and Nancy, the chef, occasionally emerges from the kitchen. Recommended.

Nyonya Makko, 124 Taman Melaka Raya, T6-2840737, located near the bottom of St Paul's Hill, good selection, cheap and friendly. Recommended.

Portuguese

Most restaurants in the *Medan Portugis* are expensive tourist traps but some of the spicy seafood dishes are worth trying.

Restoran de Lisbon, Portuguese Square, run by Senhor Alcantra, this places comes recommended with its dishes that blend Malaysian and Portuguese cuisines – including devil chicken curry and sea bass roasted in a banana leaf, all washed down with ice-cold Portuguese lager or wines, cultural shows Sat evenings.

San Pedro, Portuguese Settlement (just off the square), family run and probably the best at the Portuguese settlement, specialities include spicy baked fish, wrapped in banana leaf.

Thai

My Place, 357 Jln Melaka, also some Malay, Chinese and Indian dishes.

Seafood

Pengkalan Pernu (Pernu Jetty), 10 km south on the way to Muar, has several fish restaurants and stalls where you can pick your own fish and have it grilled. North of

Melaka, towards Tanjung Kling, there are a few Chinese seafood restaurants along the beach.

Bunga Raya Restaurant, 39-40 Jln Taman, T6-2836456, crab, prawn and lobster are house specialities.

Bakeries and ice cream

Outlets for both in **Mahkota Parade shopping mall** (try Parkson Grand Department Store), the mall is opposite the Sound & Light Show arena on Jalan Merdeka; *Renaissance Melaka Hotel* has a good bakery shop in lobby.

Foodstalls

Glutton's Corner, along the old esplanade on Jln Merdeka/Jln Taman: excellent choice of food, although the stalls now face a painted wall rather than the sea, thanks to a land reclamation project. **Prince Satay Celup**, at No 16. Recommended. **Jalan Bendahara**, several noodle stalls and a Mamak man (Indian Muslim) who serves *sup kambing* (mutton soup) and the bits – for marrow suckers (opposite the *Capitol*), Chinese food. **Jalan Bukit Baru**, just off the main road past the state mosque, mostly Chinese food. **Jalan Bunga Raya**, stalls (next to Rex Cinema), seafood recommended. **Jalan Semabok** (after Bukit Cina on road to JB), Malay-run fish-head curry stall, which is a local favourite. **Klebang Beach**, off Jln Klebang Besar, Tanjung Kling – stalls, with several *ikan panggang* (grilled fish) specialists.

Tanjung Kling *p217*

Roti John, Pantai Kundor, on the seafront, Melaka's Roti John specialist.

Yashika Traveller Hostel, Batu 8, Pantai Kundor, beach restaurant, international.

Entertainment

Melaka *p204, maps p205 and p210*

Cinemas

There's a **Golden Screen Multiplex** in Mahkota Parade.

Clubs

Cosmopolitan Club, 14 Hang Lekir is the site of a club, which was formerly the Malayan Chinese Literary Association, exclusively for the Babas of Heeren St. Today, it is patronized by locals playing mah-jong and snooker. Non-members may participate in the games for a small fee. The club is run by a friendly, English-speaking, family with insiders' knowledge of their home town.

Cultural shows

At the Portuguese Settlement in Portuguese Square, every Sat at 2030. Songs and dances, an excuse for a sing-along and knees-up.

Nam Hoe Villa (Restoran Peranakan), 317c Klebang Besar (6 km towards Port Dickson), T6-3154436, 2000 Sun-Fri.

Taman Mini Malaysia, Ayer Keroh, 1120 and 1430 Sat, Sun and public hols.

Son et Lumière

Melaka Light and Sound Show, on the Padang, opposite St Paul's Hill, T011-664166, chronological history of Melaka, an hour-long show with a distinctly Malay nationalist perspective, 5 mins' mention of European rule and no mention of the contribution by the Chinese and Indian ethnic communities, not expertly presented. Daily 2000 (Malay), 2030 (English), RM 10.

Festivals and events

Melaka *p204*

March/April Easter Procession (movable), on Good Friday and Easter Sunday, starts from St Peter's Church.

May Saint Sohan Singh's Prayer Anniversary (movable) thousands of Sikhs from all over Malaysia and Singapore congregate at the Melaka Sikh temple, Jalan Temenggong, to join in the memorial prayers.

June 29 Pesta San Pedro (Feast of St Peter) (movable) celebrated at the Portuguese Settlement by fishermen. The brightly decorated fishing boats are blessed and prayers offered for a good season; **Mandi Safar** (movable) bathing festival at Tanjung Kling; **Kite Festival** (movable) on the sea front.

Shopping

Melaka *p204, maps p205 and p210*

Melaka is best known for its antique shops, which mainly sell European and Chinese items.

Antiques

Jalan Hang Jebat (formerly Jonker St) is the best place for antiques, from shadow puppets to Melakan furniture inlaid with mother-of-pearl.

Books

Boon Hoong Sports and Bookstore, 13 Jln Bunga Raya; **Jln Taman Melaka** Raya for a good number of English language books.
Times Bookshop, Jaya Jusco Stores, Mukim Bukit Baru.

Clothes

Orang Utan House, 59 Lorong Hang Jebat. Artist Charles Cham sells very original T-shirts from his shop. His place is hard to miss – a huge orange orang utan is painted on the outside of the building.

General

Main shopping centres on Jln Hang Tuah and Jln Munshi Abdullah.
Mahkota Parade Shopping and Entertainment Complex, including **Parkson Grand Department Store and Supermarket**, 1 Jln Merdeka, just south of the river mouth, a good choice of shops – the centre won an award for the best shopping centre in the country. Has a very western feel with many international chain stores.

Handicrafts

Crystal D'beaute, 18 Medan Portugis.
Dulukala, Jln Laksamana. A varied collection including prints and batiks. **Karyaneka (handicraft) centres** at 1 Jalan Laksamana and **Mini Malaysia Complex**, Ayer Keroh.

Paintings

Jonker Art Collection, 76 Jalan Hang Jebat T6-2836578, a small shop selling prints by local artists, in particular the work of Titi Kwok, son of the well-known Macau-based artist Kwok Se and owner of the Cheng Hoon Art Gallery situated a couple of streets away on Jln Tokong. He is often in the shop selling his own beautiful Chinese-style ink paintings and has plenty of time for his customers. Recommended.
Orang Utan House, 59 Lorong Hang Jebat, paintings by local artist Charles Cham.

Woodwork

Malacca Woodwork, 312c Klebang Besar, T6-3154468, specialist in authentic reproduction antique furniture including camphor wood chests.

Activities and tours

Melaka *p204, maps p205 and p210*

Boat tours

Boat tours of Melaka's docks, go-downs, old Dutch trading houses, wharves and seafront markets run from the quay close to the Tourism Malaysia office. Predictably this area is known as Melaka's 'Little Venice', but it does not live up to the description. However, the guides are generally informative, pointing out settlements and wildlife. There are views of the giant lizards on the banks and plenty of rubbish floating downstream. Boats leave when full and usually there is a departure every hour or so between 1000 and 1400, although departures do vary according to the tides. Tickets for the river boat can be purchased from the tourist office (45 minutes, RM8). For reservations, T062-865468.

Golf

"A" Famosa Golf Resort, Jln Kemus, Pulan Sebang, T010-6010333, near the Alor Gajah interchange of the north-south expressway, 18-hole course.

Tour operators

Annah (Melaka) Tours & Travel, 27 Jln Laksamana, T6-2835626; **AR Tours**, 302a Jln Tun Ali, T6-2831977; **Satik Tour & Travel**, 143 Jln Bendahara, T6-2835712. **Stadthuys Tours & Travel**, T6-2846373. **Falcon Travel Service**, 53 Lorong Bukit China, T6-2820478.

Ayer Keroh *p218*

Golf

Ayer Keroh Golf & Country Club, 14 km from Melaka, T6-2332000.

Transport

Melaka *p204, maps p205 and p210*

Air

Airport is at Batu Berendam, 9 km out of town. **Merpati Airways** runs a four-weekly flight to Pekan Baru in Indonesia. It is necessary to secure a visa from the Indonesian Embassy in KL (see page 181) before departing for Sumatra from Melaka.

Bicycle hire
Many of the cheaper hotels/hostels rent out bikes, as do one or two shops in town, RM5-8 per day.

Boat
Express ferries to **Dumai** (Sumatra), leave daily from the public jetty on Melaka River, 2 hrs. Tickets from travel agents. Try **Atlas Travel Service**, Jln Hang Jebat, T6-2820777. Service leaves Malacca at 0900 and at 1500, one-way adult fare RM 80; return RM 150. Ferries also leave for **Bukan Baru** (Sumatra) from the public jetty on Tue, Thu and Sat, 6 ½ hours (RM120) at 0950. Note tourists now need to get a visa in advance for travel into Indonesia.

Buses
Local buses leave from the long distance bus distance, out of town. Less than RM1 round town. Long distance buses leave from the terminal on Jln Tun Razak. Regular connections with **KL**, **Seremban**, **Port Dickson**, **Ipoh**, **Butterworth**, **Lumut** (Pulau Pangkor), **Kuantan**, **Kuala Terengganu**, **Kota Bharu**, **Johor Bahru** and **Singapore** (direct, 4 hrs).

Car hire
Avis, 124 Jln Bendahara, T6-2846710; **Hawk**, T6-2837878; **Sintat**, *Renaissance Melaka Hotel*, Jln Bendahara, T6-2848888; **Thrifty**, G-5 Pasar Pelancong, Jln Tun Sri Lanang, T6-2849471.

Taxi
Taxi drivers in Melaka refuse to use their meters. Bargain hard. When directing a taxi be careful not to confuse street names with general district areas; use the former whenever possible. There are stands outside major hotels and shopping centres, or T6-2823630. Between 0100 and 0600, there is a 50% surcharge.

There is a taxi station at the long distance bus station on Jln Tun Razak. Vehicles leave for **KL, Seremban, Penang, Mersing, Johor Bahru**. Passengers for Singapore must change taxis at the long distance terminal in JB.

Train
Nearest station is at Tampin, 40 km north; Tampin railway station, T6-4411034. See page 40 and 41 for timetables.

Trishaws
Mostly for the tourist trade, they congregate at several points in town (there are usually a number near the the tourist information centre on the town square) – RM2 for single destination or RM10-15 per hour.

Tanjung Kling *p217*
Patt Hup buses 51, 18, 42 and 47 buses can be caught from Jln Tengkera (at the north end of Jln Tun Tan Cheng Lock, in Melaka); there are also taxis.

Directory

Melaka *p204, maps p205 and p210*
Banks Bumiputra, Jln Kota; HSBC, Jln Kota. Several banks on Jln Hang Tuah near the bus station and Jln Munshi Abdullah. **Post** General Post Office, just off Jln Kota next to Christ Church. Sells a range of cards, in addition to stamps. **Internet** These are many in number, easy to come across and very inexpensive. Internet café, beside the Youth Museum in Historical Melaka, RM3 per hour; Red House, 16 Jln Laksamana, T6-2926080. RM3 per hour, The Geographer Café and The Discovery Café. **Medical services** Straits Hospital, 37 Jln Parameswara, T6-2835336. **Useful addresses** Central Police Station, Jln Kota, T6-2825522; Immigration office, Bangunan Persekutaan, Jln Hang Tuah, T6-2824958/2824955 (for visa extensions); Tourist Police, Jln Kota, T6-2703238 (close to the Tourism Malaysia office).

Johor Bahru

→ Colour map 2, grid C5

Modern Johor Bahru – more commonly called JB – is not a pretty town. It lies on the southernmost tip of the peninsula and is the gateway to Malaysia from Singapore. JB is short on tourist attractions but has for many years served either as a tacky red-light reprieve for Singaporeans and/or as a large retail outlet. There is little reason to stay here, most travellers pass through on their way from or to Singapore. ▸▸ *For Sleeping, Eating and other listings, see pages 229-232.*

Ins and outs

Getting there

Senai airport, www.senaiairport.com, is 20 km from town and there are connections with KL and several other destinations in East and Peninsular Malaysia. There are international air links with several destinations in Indonesia and with Bangkok. A shuttle bus service runs from the airport to town. There is a regular bus service between Singapore and KL, and links with most other towns on the Peninsula. Outstation taxis provide a service to KL, Melaka, and Kuantan. The KL-Singapore railway line runs through JB and there are trains to both destinations including commuter trains to Singapore. There is a FerryLink service between Changi Point in Singapore and Tanjung Belungkor. ▸▸ *See also Transport, page 231.*

Getting around

Hiring cars in JB is considerably cheaper than in Singapore.
Cheap taxis (meters not an option) provide the main form of transport for most visitors.

Tourist information

Johor Tourist Information Centre (JOTIC), ⓘ *T7-2249960, www.johortourism.com.my*, and **Tourism Malaysia Information Centre**, *T7-2223591, both located at 2 Jln Air Molek, 0900-1700 Mon-Sat, 1000-1600 Sun*, but neither is very helpful.

Safety

While JB is reasonably safe, at the time of writing there was a spate of street theft by snatch and grab motorcyclists. The newspapers carried the story of one local mother who died after sustaining injuries from one of these robbers.

Background

At weekends JB is jammed with Singaporeans, here, it would seem, largely for sex and/or shopping – and, perhaps, the chance to escape for a few hours from the stultifying atmosphere of their own clean and green country.

The Royal Abu Bakar Museum is one of Malaysia's best museums and makes a stay in otherwise unexciting JB worth while.

There are two links with Singapore: the old causeway across the Selat Tebrau (Strait of Johor), built in 1924, is overburdened with road traffic and also carries the railway and water pipelines (Singapore relies on Johor for most of its water supply). A bridge to the east of the causeway, known as the Second Link is 30 km out of town to the west at Gelang Patah.

History

The Sultanate of Johor was founded to the east of modern JB in the 16th century by the stepson of Sultan Ahmad who had been forced to flee from Melaka by the Portuguese. Next was to follow almost two hundred years of upheaval at the hands of the Achenese, the rival Sumatran kingdom on Jambi, infighting and also squabbling with the Dutch.

Abu Bakar, the grandson of Singapore's Temenggon Abdur Rahman moved his headquarters to the small settlement of Tanjong Putri in Johor, which he renamed Johor Bahru in 1866. In the early 20th century, Johor attracted many European rubber planters. Johor was the last state to join the colonial Malay Federation, in 1914.

Johor Bahru

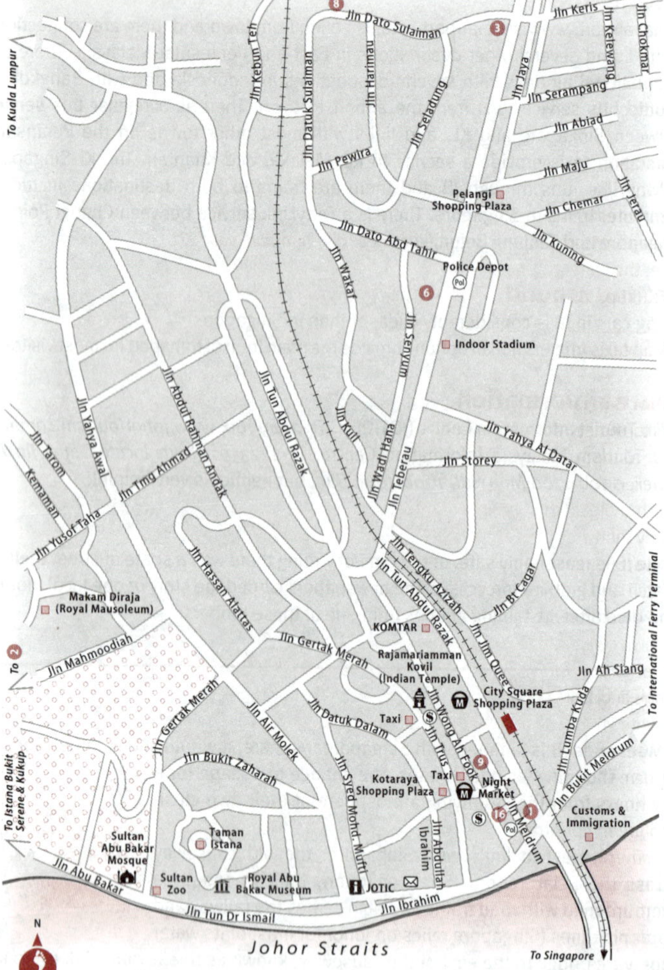

Sleeping
Causeway Inn 1
Crystal Crown 3
Grand Continental 6
Hyatt Regency 2
JB 9
Mutiara 8
Top 16

Sights

The renovated **Istana Besar**, the Sultan's former residence on Jalan Tun Dr Ismail (built by Sultan Abu Bakar in 1866). It is now a royal museum, the **Royal Abu Bakar Museum**. Today the Sultan lives in the Istana Bukit Serene, which is on the west outskirts of town (it is not open to the public) and locals say the Sultan enjoys great feng shui with his new residence. The Istana Besar is a slice of Victorian England set in beautiful gardens, overlooking the strait. In the north wing is the throne room and museum containing a superb collection of royal treasures, including gruesome hunting trophies such as hollow elephant feet and an array of tusks and skulls, as well as Chinese and Japanese ceramics. ⓘ *0900-1800 Mon-Sun, closed Fri, US$7 (payable in ringgit at a very poor exchange rate), children under 12 US$3.*

Not far away, on Jalan Abu Bakar, is the **Sultan Abu Bakar Mosque**, which faces the Strait of Johor. It was finished in 1900 and clearly reflects the Victorian climate of the period. The mosque can accommodate 2,500 worshippers.

The 32-m-high tower of the 1930s **Istana Bukit Serene** on Jalan Skudai – the home of the Sultan of Johore and not open to the public – is only outdone by the 64-m tower of the State Secretariat, on Bukit Timbalan, which dominates the town.

Kukup

On the Strait of Melaka 40 km southwest of Johor, this small Chinese fishing kampong renowned throughout the country, and in Singapore, for its seafood, especially prawns and chilli crab. Most of the restaurants, known as *kelong*, are built on stilts over the water. To get there, take bus No 3 to Pontian Kecil, and from there take a taxi to Kukup; alternatively take a taxi the whole way.

Sleeping

Johor Bahru *p227, map p228*

JB's top hotels cater for businesspeople and have all the 5-star facilities. Most budget travellers don't stop in JB so there really isn't much choice at the bottom end, except for seedy short-stay hotels.

A Hyatt Regency, Jln Sungai Chat, T7-2221234, www.hyatt.com/Malaysia/ Over 2 km west of town centre, all the comforts you would expect of the *Hyatt* chain including pool, tennis and an internet room. 10 mins from downtown JB.

A Mutiara, Jln Dato Sulaiman, Century Garden, T7-3323800, www.mutiarahotels.com A/c, restaurants, pool, gym, 24-hr coffee house. Formerly the *Holiday Inn*, the hotel is due for a refurbishment. Good views of the city, and complimentary shuttle service between hotel and main shopping plazas. Rooms are large and comfortable.

B Crystal Crown, 117 Jln Harimau, 117 Jln Tebrau, T3334422, F3343582. A/c, restaurants, TV, business centre, tea and coffee-making facilities, minibar, pool, organizes car hire. Breakfast included. A tourist-class hotel geared to business visitors.

B Grand Continental, 799 Jln Tebrau, T7-3323999, F7-3321999. Part of the *Grand Continental Chain*, 4-star hotel geared to the business visitor, rates include breakfast, rooms with a/c, TV, mini-bar, pool, health centre and business centre. Breakfast included.

B Meldrum Hotel, 1 Jln Siu Nam (entrance on Jln Meldrum), T7-2278988, hotel_meldrum@po.jaring.my Very friendly, large hotel with spacious a/c rooms with TV and hot shower. Unsleazy compared with many of the other hotels in the area.

B-C JB Hotel, 80a Jln Wong Ah Fook, T7-2246625. Some a/c, clean, reasonably spacious rooms and at this price.

C Causeway Inn, 6 Jln Meldrum, T7-2248811, F7-2248820. A/c, unlike neighbouring premises, this is a clean, quiet, well-run hotel that looks smart and does not overcharge with TV, excellent bathroom (bath). Check the room though because some have no view. Recommended.

C **Hawaii**, 23 Jln Meldrum, T7-2240633, F7-2240631. Average Malay-run hotel; much better value on weekdays when rates are slashed. Cheaper than most but by no means outstanding. No hot water.

C **Top Hotel**, 12 Jln Meldrum, T7-2244755. Much better value than most of the mid-range hotels in this area. Large rooms with huge beds. Bathrooms of a very good standard. Recommended.

Eating

Johor Bahru *p227, map p228*

Chinese

TTT **Grand Court Restaurant**, *Hotel Grand Continental*, 3rd flr, T7-3345578, good selection including some Cantonese and Nyonya dishes.

Japanese

TT **Kinsahi**, Plaza Pelangi, T7-3323288. Japanese served in relaxing settings for inside a shopping mall.

T **Yamani Café**, a tiny streetside café in Plaza Seni. Serves a mixture of Arabic, Malay and western food. Good atmosphere opposite stage where evening traditional dance performances are often held.

Malay

T **Sedap Corner**, Good chain of Chinese, Malay food. Branches among others in Plaza Kotaraya, Plaza Pelangi and City Square.

Seafood

JB is best known for its seafood, which is considerably cheaper than in Singapore.

TTT **Meisan**, Mutiara, Jln Dato Sulaiman, Century Garden, superb but expensive spicy Sichuan restaurant.

TT **George & Dragon Café**, 1 Jln Glsier, far out on the western edge of town. Family run restaurant serving English and Irish pub grub including pies and steaks. Also serves afternoon tea with scones and cream.

TT **Marina Seafood**, 1d Jln Skudai, very popular, Specialities include drunken prawns, frogs' legs and chilli crabs, diners may find flashing neons and revolving stage unsettling. Good views across the Singapore straits. Recommended.

TT **Newsroom Café**, Puteri Pan Pacific, The Kotaraya, offering reasonably priced local/continental dishes.

TT **Seasons Café**, branches in City Square and Plaza Pelangi. Café serving a mixture of western snacks and breads and some Asian rice dishes.

Coffee shops

There are branches of **Coffee Bean** and **Starbucks** in City Square.

Foodstalls

The night market on Jln Wong Ah Fook is also a great place to sample the full array of stall dishes.

Tepian Tebrau, Jln Skudaí (facing the sea beside the *General Hospital*) good for Malay food – satay and grilled fish. There is also good stall food at the long distance bus terminal and outside the railway station. There is a sprawling outdoor hawker centre right in the centre of town, adjacent to the Plaza Kotaraya on Jln Trus. **Pantai Lido** is another well-known hawker centre and there is a 'food court' in the *Kompleks Tun Abdul Razak*, Jln Wong Ah Fook as well as the Plaza Kotaraya on Jln Trus.

Shopping

Johor Bahru *p227, map p228*

Handicrafts

Craftown Handicraft Centre, Jln Skudai; **Jaro**, Jln Sungai Chat; **Johorcraft**, **Kompleks Kotaraya** and **Kompleks Tun Abdul Razak**, Jln Trus; **Karyaneka Centre** at Kompleks Mawar, 562 Jln Sungeai Chat; **Mawar**, Jln Sultanah Rogayah, Istana Besar.

Shopping complexes

Large shopping complexes include the upmarket **City Square** (once inside you could be in Singapore) on Jalan Wong Ah Fook, www.city-square.com/; **Holiday Plaza**, Jln Datuk Sulaiman, 3 floors of retails outlets as well as a cinema, night club, hawker centre and various fast food outlets; **Kompleks Tun Abdul Razak** (KOMTAR), Jln Wong Ah Fook; **Plaza Pelangi**, Jln Tebrau, billed as JB's 'most exciting mall'; shops include fashion goods, souvenirs, handicrafts and there is also the usual range of food and beverage outlets; **Sentosa Complex**, Jln Sutera; **Kotaraya**, off Jln Trus, a pink building situated in the centre of the city, opposite the night market – possibly the best place to shop with a hawker centre upstairs; **Johor Bahru Duty Free Complex**, this place is next to the International Ferry Terminal and is said to be one of the largest such complexes in the world (ugh!) – better known as ZON; and the tiny Plaza Seni which sells handicrafts and Arabic hookah pipes.

Activities and tours

Johor Bahru *p227, map p228*

Golf

Royal Johor Country Club, Jln Larkin, T7-2233322; **Palm Resort Golf and Country Club**, Jln Persiaran Golf, off Jln Jumbo (near airport), Senai, T7-5996222, F7-5996001, course is part of a 5-star resort, which includes tennis, squash, bowls, pool, fitness centre, sauna, Japanese baths and luxury hotel and bungalows.

Transport

Johor Bahru *p227, map p228*

Air

MAS and **AirAsia** fly into Senai, JB's airport, 20 km north of the city. Transport to town: buses at least every hour and taxis. Regular connections on *MAS* and *AirAsia* with **KL, Kota Bharu, Kota Kinabalu, Kuching, Miri** and **Penang** . *AirAsia* also has direct flights to **Bangkok** and **Jakarta.**

Airline offices MAS, 1st flr, Plaza Pelangi, Menara Pelangi, Jln Kuning, Taman Pelangi, T7-3341003/3341001 – a little over 2 km from the town centre. **AirAsia**, JOTIC, 2 Jln Ayer Molek, T7-2224760.

Boat

JB's ferry terminal to the east of the causeway is operating ferry services to **Tanjung Belungkor**. Bumboats leave from various points along Johor's ragged coastline for **Singapore**; most go to **Changi Point** (Changi Village), on the northeast of the island, where there is an immigration and customs post. The boats run from 0700-1600 and depart when full (12 passengers). There is a passenger ferry from Tanjung Belungkor (JB) to Changi Ferry Terminal 3 times a day, T653236088. JB's ferry terminal east of the causeway offers connections with **Batam** in Indonesia.

Bus

Local buses leave from the main bus terminal on Jln Wong Ah Fook.

The Larkin bus terminal is inconveniently located 4 km north of the town centre. Book tickets at agents opposite railway station on Jln Tun Abdul Razak or its cheaper at the station itself. Regular connections with **Melaka, KL** (RM12.50), **Lumut, Ipoh** (RM40), **Butterworth** (RM45), **Mersing** (RM12), **Kuantan, Kuala Terengganu**, and **Alor Star** (RM45).

International connections From **Singapore** there are three bus services. The non a/c **SBS** No 170 runs every 15 mins from Singapore's Ban San Terminal between Queen St and Rochor Canal Rd. Tickets are all priced around RM2 from JB, or S$2 (twice as much) from Singapore. The **Johor Singapore Express** is a/c and is slightly more frequent and also leaves from Ban San. Both buses end up at the JB Larkin terminal. The yellow Causeway Link bus with a smiley face runs between Kranji MRT station in Singapore and the Larkin terminal. It only takes 20 mins from the border to the MRT station. All three buses require you to get off twice - for the Malay border point and its Singaporean counterpart. You have to take all your luggage with you since the bus does not wait for you. You wait for the next bus to come along; each bus has its own stop after exiting immigration. Keep your ticket or you will have to buy a new one. Also have a pen handy to fill in immigration forms as they are not provided. If you plan on staying in JB, you don't need to board the bus again after passing Malay immigration. Just walk out of immigration, through the underpass and you're already in town. The streets here have lots of budget hotels, or you can catch a taxi. There's little point in going to Larkin bus terminal unless you plan on taking a bus out of JB.

Car hire

It is much cheaper to hire a car in JB than it is in neighbouring Singapore but check whether the car hire company allows the car to go to Singapore. The causeway between JB and Singapore should be avoided at all costs during public holidays. It gets particularly jammed at rush hours. **Avis**, *Tropical Inn Hotel*, 15 Jln Gereja, T7-2244824;

Budget, Suite 216, 2nd flr Orchid Plaza, T7-2243951; **Calio**, *Tropical Inn*, Jln Gereja, T7-2233325; **Halaju Selatan**, 4M-1 Larkin Complex, Jln Larkin; **Hertz**, Room 646, Puteri Pan Pacific Hotel, Jln Salim, T7-2237520; **National**, 50-B ground flr Bangunan Felda, Jln Sengget, T7-2230503 (and at the airport); **Thrifty**, *Holiday Inn*, Jln Dato Sulaiman, T7-3332313; **Sintat**, 2nd Flr, Kompleks Tun Abdul Razak (KOMTAR), Jln Wong Ah Fook, T7-2227110.

Taxis

Taxis, minus the meter are plentiful. The main long-distance taxi station is attached to the Larkin bus terminal 4 km north of town. Taxis from here to destinations including **KL, Melaka, Mersing** and **Kuantan**.

Malaysian taxis leave, when full, for Singapore from the taxi rank on the 1st flr of the car park near the KOMTAR building on Jln Wong Ah Fook and go to the JB taxi rank on Rochor Canal Rd in Singapore. Drivers provide immigration forms and take care of formalities, making this a painless way of crossing the causeway. Touts also hang around JB's taxi rank offering the trip to Singapore in a private car. They will take you directly to your address in Singapore, although their geography of the island is not always expert. This is also a fairly cost-effective way to travel and is reliable.

Train

The station is on Jln Campbell, near the causeway, off Jln Tun Abdul Razak. Regular connections with **KL** and all destinations on the west coast, see page 40 and 41 for timetable. Malaysian and Singapore immigration desks are actually in the Singapore railway station, so for those wanting to avoid delays on the causeway, this is a quick way to get across the border.

Directory

Johor Bahru *p*

Banks Bumiputra, HSBC and United Asia are on Bukit Timbalan. Several money changers in the big shopping centres and on/around Jln Ibrahim/Jln Meldrum. **Internet** There are some internet cafés opposite City Square shopping plaza on Jalan Wong Ah Fook. There's also nternet on the second floor of Larkin Bus Station. **Post** Jln Tun Dr Ismail. **Medical services** Sultanah Aminah General Hospital, Jln Skudai. **Useful addresses** Immigration office, 1st flr, Block B, Wisma Persektuan, Jln Air Molek, T7-2244253.

Pulau Tioman and around

→ *Colour map 2, grid B5*

There are a total of 64 islands off Mersing in the Seribuat archipelago; many are inaccessible and uninhabited. The most accessible of these is Tioman, made famous by the Hollywood movie, South Pacific, *and which has scores of resorts, simple beach huts and any number of dive operators. It is also possibly to island hop to bask on deserted beaches or snorkel in coves – Pulau Rawa, Pulau Tengah and Pulau Besar are nearest the coast. Further afield, the islands mainly cater to serious divers.* ▸▸ *For Sleeping, Eating and other listings, see pages 239-248.*

Ins and outs

Getting there and around

There is accommodation available and boats to Pulau Rawa, Pulau Babi Besar (Big Pig Island), Pulau Tinggi, Pulau Sibu, Pulau Aur (Bamboo Island) and Pulau Pemanggil. The main departure point is Mersing, see below. ▸▸ *See also Transport, page 247.*

Best time to visit

If you plan on visiting any of the beaches or islands on the east coast, and especially if you're hoping to dive, the best time to visit is between February and September to avoid the rainy season. During the winter monsoon, the seas are very rough and many island resorts are closed and boat operators pack up business. Between May and September is the best time for turtle spotting.

Mersing

ⓘ *Mersing Tourist Information Centre, Jln Abu Bakar (about 5 mins from the jetty walking into town), T7-7995212. Friendly and useful source of information. Mon-Thu 1400-1600, Fri 1445-1630, although it's often closed during these times.*

This small fishing port is a pleasant little town distinguished only by the Masjid Jamek, a green-tiled mosque, half a kilometre out of town on the top of a hill. Most people are in a hurry to get to the islands, namely Pulau Tioman, the best known of the East Coast's islands, and spend as little time as possible in the town.

As ferry times can sometimes be erratic, it's possible to get stuck here overnight if you don't arrive early enough. In recent years a number of good little restaurants have sprung up and Mersing is not an unpleasant place to spend a day or two. The town is evidently prospering, thanks to the flow of tourists to the islands. There is a plethora of tour and ticketing agencies as well as a shiny shopping plaza.

Pantai Air Papan, ⓘ *Take Mersing-Endau bus to Simpang Air Papan (turn-off); there is no bus service connecting with the beach, although it is possible to hitchhike. Chartered taxi available. Arrangements can be made for pick-ups later in the day*, 9 km north of Mersing, is the best mainland beach in the area. Formerly, the most popular beach was **Sri Pantai**, but it is now stony and unpleasant. Pantai Air Papan is 5 km off the main road north and the beach is about 2 km long, between two headlands. The beach is quite exposed but is backed by lines of casuarina and coconut palms. There is a liberal scattering of rubbish among the trees. There are a number of places at the end of the road offering budget accommodation, see Sleeping, and a few beach shelters dotted along the beach.

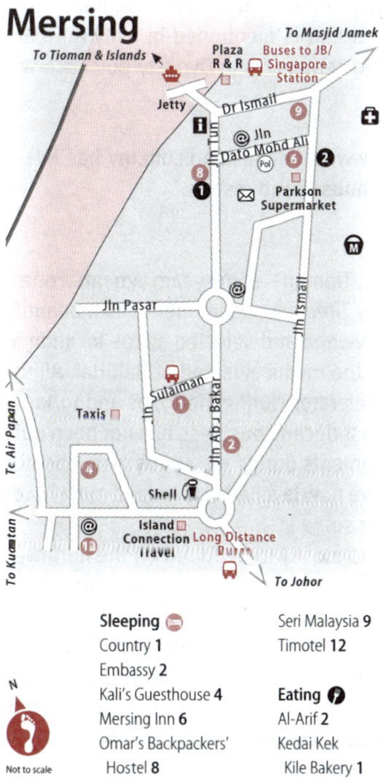

Pulau Tioman

→ *Colour map 2, grid B6 Phone code: 07*

Tioman, 56 km off Mersing, is the largest island in the volcanic Seribuat Archipelago at 20 km by 12 km. The island is dominated by several jagged peaks, notably the twin peaks of Nenek Semukut and Bau Sirau towards the southern end of the island, and in Malay legend its distinctive profile is the back of a dragon whose feet got stuck in the coral. It is densely forested and is fringed by white coral-sand beaches; with kampongs around the coast.

Ins and outs

Getting there The airport is in the centre of Tekek. The *Berjaya Tioman Beach Resort* (see page 239) sends a bus to meet each plane and various touts approach likely looking passengers. The jetty is just 100 m or so away where you can catch a sea taxi or ferry to other spots or walk to your hotel. Daily connections with KL and Singapore. Most people arrive on Tioman by ferry from Mersing. The jetty at Mersing is 5 minutes' walk out of Mersing next to the blue-roofed R&R Plaza. Tickets can be bought from one of the many ticket offices at the R&R Plaza. The variety can be confusing and slightly concerning but in fact all licensed vendors comply with the regulation price. The ferry timetable is only drawn up a month in advance because it depends on tides.

! Many locals are unhappy with the sale of alcohol on the island. However, the upmarket resorts generally cater to alcohol drinking guests and there is plenty of cheap booze at the duty free stores. Many of the simpler chalet operations do not allow alcohol on their premises, a few others will quietly serve beer or wine at their restaurant.

Getting around There are very few trails around the island and only one road, a 2 km stretch from the airstrip at Tekek to the Berjaya Tioman Beach Resort although amid much controversy, a new road is being built from Tekek to Juara on the eastern coast. However, you can still walk from the west side of the island to the east by a beautiful jungle trail. To get from one kampong to another, the best way is to go by boat and a 'sea bus' service works its way around the island. To get to Mukut and Nipah you must get off at Genting from where you can hire a boat to the beach. For Paya you need to ask the boat to make the stop.

Best time to visit Many guesthouses and resorts close down between November and February when it is wet and can be windy and rough. Chinese New Year seems to be a popular time for places to open, cashing in on the Singapore market, but as Chinese New Year is a moveable feast the date varies from year to year. Transport from Mersing also becomes more difficult during the off season; ferries will only leave if there is sufficient demand to make it worth their while.

The highest peak is Gunung Kajang (1,049 m) or Palm Frond Mountain. It has been used as a navigational aid for centuries and is mentioned in early Arab and Chinese sailing charts. In the mid-1970s, 12th-century Sung Dynasty porcelain was unearthed on the island.

Tourist information The Tioman website, www.tiomanisland.com.my has lots of local information and pictures of many guesthouses and resorts.

Background

Despite the growth in hotels and guesthouses, Tioman – some years ago rated one of the world's 10 best 'desert island escapes' by *Time* magazine – remains a beautiful island. In the 1950s it was discovered by Hollywood and selected as the location for the musical *South Pacific* where it starred as the mythical island of Bali Hai. All this attention put Tioman on the map; tourism accelerated during the 1970s and 1980s as facilities were expanded. However, over the last decade business has not been quite so brisk and prices, which for some establishments during the 1980s were absurdly high, given the level of amenities on offer, have now levelled out. Indeed most hotels have not increased their rates for five years or so.

The cheaper beach-hut accommodation is mostly to be found on the northwest side of the panhandle, and despite a growth in the number of places to stay, these little kampongs have retained their charm and are still very laid back, making them an idyllic retreat for anyone who is looking for a deserted beach, a touch of snorkelling or diving and some great seafood, although Kampong Salang has developed a brash and concrete atmosphere. Thankfully, as yet, there are no nightclubs or fast-food restaurants and the tourist trinket shops are very low key.

Kampong Tekek

Kampong Tekek is the kampong-capital of Tioman and, frankly, is nothing special. However because boats from Mersing first call at Tekek's large concrete jetty, and the airport is also here, many visitors decide to stay put rather than face another journey. Tekek has the longest beach on the island, but for a large stretch north of the jetty it is rather dirty and with an ugly concrete breakwater. Almost all the coral is dead and broken, the river is polluted and there are rusting oil drums and other paraphernalia littering the town. There are many places to stay at Tekek, mostly south of the jetty or towards the northern end of the bay. However, much of the accommodation is run down and the place doesn't have much of a tropical island resort atmosphere. It feels like a small service centre, which is what it is. Tekek has a couple of duty free shops, small post office, a police post, an excellent clinic, a couple of money changers, the administrative HQ for the island, a few mini-marts, and an immigration post. The main area of accommodation is a 5-10 minute walk south of the jetty.

The island

Kampong Lalang is not really a kampong at all but a beach devoted solely to the Berjaya Tioman Beach Resort and its sister condotel.

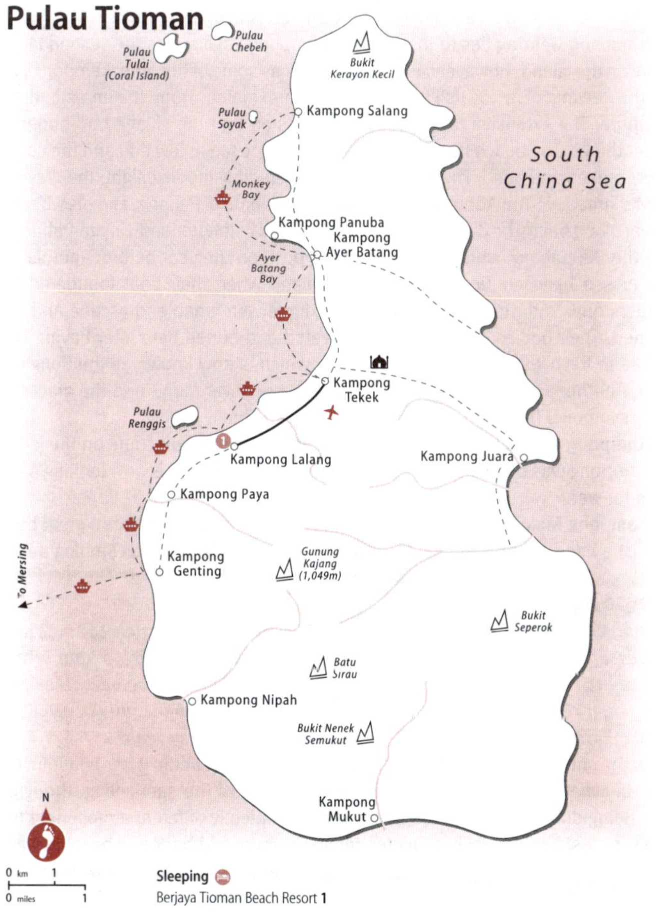

The beach is rocky at low tide at **Ayer Batang** (also known as ABC) and the sandy area quite small. The better portion of the beach is south of the jetty. Monitor lizards roam freely and the tall coconut palms are home to scores of bickering fruit bats that are nosiest during dusk. There are a couple of mini markets for supplies and souvenirs, a small beach bar and internet at Bamboo Hill guesthouse. **Kampong Panuba** is a tiny stretch of beach with a single resort just north of Ayer Batang.

Kampong Salang is the northernmost development on the island and is set in a sheltered cove with a beautiful beach. The beach is more rowdy than Ayer Batang, with concrete development and more of a party scene. The mangrove swamp to the south of the jetty, though dirty, still holds plenty of monitor lizards which cruise around like primeval monsters. Some are getting on for 2 m in length. There are minimarts at *Salang Indah* and at *Khalid's Place* for basic supplies such as drinks, toilet paper, nibbles, fruit, etc. A 150-room resort lies unused and now decomposes on the south end of the Bay, testament to the fact that Tioman cannot pull the kind of numbers developers had dreamed of. Salang's laidback atmosphere is already falling prey to European backpackers and a big pink concrete food court stands sadly at the jetty.

Kampong Paya is south of Tekek. A quiet place with a small *surau* (prayer hall) and a couple of restaurants The jetty here has now been upgraded and the ferries from Mersing stop here. The beach is attractive enough but at low tide a belt of dead and broken coral makes swimming difficult and there have been reports that sandflies are sometimes a major nuisance on this beach.

Kampong Genting lies to the south of Kampong Paya and is the second largest village on the island. However it is not as popular as some of the other kampongs and has the feeling of a locals' resort; tourists are mainly from the mainland and Singapore. The extensive jetty gives an impression that the village had hoped for greater things. The beach here is poor; rocks are exposed at low tide and the coral is largely broken and dead. There is, though, an incredibly modest sight: the graves of Tun Mohamad bin Tun Adbul Majid, the sixth Bendahara of Pahang, and his wife, also of royal blood being the daughter of Sultan Mahmud of Johore-Riau-Lingga-Pahang. In 1803 the Bendahara (who had assumed the position the year before) and his wife were at sea between Tioman and the mainland when their boat foundered in a thunderstorm. With their cabin locked the couple were unable to escape and both drowned. Their bodies, though, were recovered and buried here after having been washed in fresh water from the local river – which is now known as the Sungai Air Rajah. Another version has it that the bodies were never found and the graves are purely symbolic. There is a *surau* (prayer hall), by the jetty.

Kampong Nipah is one of the most secluded and tranquil spots on the island. The Kampong was badly damaged by a monsoon in 2003 and is now looking a little worse for wear.

Kampong Mukut is in a tiny, isolated rocky bay and doesn't have a great beach and just a handful of resorts but there are plenty of good treks and climbing trails.

Kampong Juara

ⓘ *Being on the east side of the island, the ferries from Mersing rarely call here and it is necessary to catch one of the sea buses that circle the island, RM50 from Tekek to Juara, 2 hrs. To walk from Tekek to Juara is a tough 3-hr walk. The new Tekek-Juara road, under construction in 2004, should be finished by the time this book goes to press, allowing visitors to reach the other side of the island by vehicle.*

This is the only kampong on the east coast with accommodation. It has beautiful long white beaches which sometimes have good breakers. The snorkelling, though, is poor. Being on the seaward side, Juara has a completely different atmosphere from the west coast kampongs; it is quieter, friendlier, more laid-back and bucolic, thanks mainly to its seclusion. However, because of its reputation, it is occasionally subject to waves of tourists who pass through, and unfortunately building activity indicates that its relative seclusion is soon to be shattered. A new paved road will soon link Kamung Tekek with Juara. There is also a path from Kampong Tekek, through the jungle, to Juara. Alternatively, it is possible to take a boat from Tekek. The Sungai Baru which flows into the sea here is home to some monitor lizards.

Trails

ⓘ *For mountain climbing and forest trekking, guides are available from Berjaya Tioman Beach Resort. Also ask around at the larger resorts, and the dive centres as they occasionally arrange trips. Nipah Beach Chalets and some of the resorts on Kampong Juara will hire guides. The trek from Ayer Batang to Kampong Salang and the cross-island walk to Kampong Juara can both be done without a guide, although the first trek is rather hard going.*

The **cross-island trail**, from the mosque in Kampong Tekek to Kampong Juara, on the east coast, is a two to three-hour hike (around 4 km), which is quite steep in places. The trail is reasonably well marked: follow the path past the airport and then turn inland towards the mosque. From Juara, the trail begins opposite the pier. It is a great walk, although for those planning to stay at Juara, it is a tough climb with a full pack. The section from Tekek is part natural path, part concrete steps. Three-quarters of the way up from Tekek there is a small waterfall, really just a jumble of rocks and water, just off the path to the right. It can be wonderfully refreshing after the arduous climb, but check for leeches when you emerge. Shortly after the waterfall the route levels out and works it way through an upland plateau. This is the most enchanting part of the walk: massive trees and dense forest, strangling figs – a real taste of jungle. It is not unusual to see squirrels, monkeys monitor lizards, shrews and various tropical insects. Just as the path begins to descend towards Juara there is a small drinks stop, the *Rest Cross*, incongruously located amongst the giant trees. This marks the beginning of the concrete trail which winds down to Juara. A motorcycle taxi service is available for the truly exhausted as well as fruit juices and soft drinks. The section down to Juara is less dramatic and more cultivated with rubber trees and banana groves, but even here it is common to see some wildlife, including monkeys and squirrels. To return to the west coast, there is a daily sea bus service from Juara leaving in the afternoon.

The trail from Kampong Juara, on the east coast, is longer and more arduous.

There are also many easier jungle and coastal walks along the west coast: south from Tekek, past the resort to kampongs **Paya** and **Genting** and north to **Salang**. The walk from Ayer Batang to Salang is a difficult one of more than 3 hours, with a trail that snakes over rocky outcrops, fallen trees and sometimes peters out altogether. About an hour into the walk you will hit **Monkey Bay**, which is a beautiful white sandy beach. If you get fed up with the trek you can always shout down a passing boatman to get you back to civilization. **Gunung Kajang** can be climbed from the east or west sides of the island; an unmarked trail leads from the Tioman Island golf course (advisable to take a guide). It is also possible to trek to **Bukit Nenek Semukut** (Twin Peaks) and **Bukit Seperok**. The trail up Semukut starts from Pasir Burong, the beach at Kampong Pasir.

Diving

ⓘ *There are dive shops based in most of the kampongs: at Salang, Tekek, Genting, Paya, Ayer Batang and at the Berjaya Tioman Beach Resort, see Activities and tours.*

Tioman's coral reefs are mainly on the western side of the island, although sadly large areas have been killed off. This is in part due to fishing boats dragging anchor, partly through nimble-fingered snorkellers pilfering coral stalks (this kills neighbouring corals), partly because all the boat activity kicks up sand and retards the growth or kills the coral, and partly because of the crown-of-thorns starfish (see page 289). Wholesale coral 'harvesting' has also been going on, to feed the increasingly lucrative trade in salt-water aquaria. Live coral specimens are loaded into water-filled bags, having been hacked off reefs with pick axes. This practice has more or less ended around Tioman now, but is still reported to be going on off other east coast islands. Pollution is also said to be a coral-killer. Both sewerage and effluent from building sites can alter water salinity levels, killing coral and resulting in the proliferation of harmful algae.

The best time to dive is mid-March to May, when visibility is at its best, but it is possible to dive through to the end of October.

There are still some magnificent coral beds within easy reach of the island. **Pulau Renggis**, just off the *Berjaya Tioman Beach Resort*, is the most easily accessible coral from the shore, with a depth of up to 12 m and a good place for new divers to find their flippers. For more adventurous dives, the islands off the northwest coast are a better bet. There is cave diving off **Pulau Chebeh**, (up to 25 m), and varied marine life off the cliff-like rocks of **Golden Reef** (depths up to 20 m) and nearby **Tiger Reef** (for 9 to 24 m dives). Off the northeastern tip of the island is **Magicienne Rock** (20-24 m dives) – where bigger fish have been sighted. Off the southwestern coast is **Bahara Rock** (20 m), considered one of the best spots on the island.

Boat tours

Boats leave from Kampong Tekek to Pulau Tulai (or Coral Island) Turtle Island; to a waterfall at Mukut, or an around-island trip. All boats must be full otherwise prices increase. Boat trips can also be arranged to other nearby islands. See also Activities and tours.

Other islands

Pulau Rawa

A small island 16 km off Mersing, Pulau Rawa is owned by a nephew of the Sultan of Johor and was one of the first resorts built in the area; it remains highly rated by lots of travellers. The island has a fantastic beach and for those in need of a desert island break Rawa is perfect, for there is absolutely nothing to do except mellow out. Unfortunately the coral reef is disappointing, but more active visitors can windsurf, canoe, and fish. The island gets busy at weekends as it is close enough for day visitors; it is also a popular getaway for Singaporeans.

Pulau Babi Besar, Pulau Tinggi and Pulau Sibuh Tengah

Pulau Babi Besar is larger and closer to the mainland than Rawa. It is a very peaceful island and is particularly well known for its beaches and coral. Pulau Tinggi is probably the most dramatic-looking island in the Seribuat group, with its 650-m volcanic peak but is less popular than neighbouring Sibuh Tengah. Pulau Sibuh Tengah, formerly a refugee camp for Vietnamese boat people, is an hour away from Mersing. The government has declared it a marine park because of its reef and the fact that giant leatherback turtles (see page 274) lay their eggs there between June and August.

Pulau Sibu and Pulau Pemanggil

Pulau Sibu, otherwise known as the Island of Perilous Passage (and includes Pulau Sibu Besar, Pulau Sibu Tengah, Pulau Sibu Kukus and Pulau Sibu Hujung) because it used to be a pirate haunt, has been recommended by many travellers for its beaches and watersports. Sibu is frequented more by Singaporeans and expatriates than by western tourists. It is popular for fishing and diving and because it is larger than the other islands there is more of a sense of space and there are also some good walks. The best beaches on Pulau Pemanggil are at kampongs Buan and Pa Kaleh, which is fortunately where the accommodation is sited. Landmarks include the Harimo (Tiger) Caves which is a good location for snorkelling.

There is no alcohol on Pulau Penamggil (you can bring your own from the mainland but be discreet).

Pulau Aur

Pulau Aur, at 80km from the mainland, is one of the furthermost islands of the Seribuat Archipelago. It is only really accessible by buying a fairly expensive dive package. Once home to hundreds of fishermen, traders and slaves, and the favourite hunting ground of pirates, the island now only caters to tourists, for the main part divers hungry for wreck dives.

Sleeping

Mersing *p233, map p233*

B **Mersing Inn**, 38 Jln Ismail, T7-7991919, F7-7991919. Discounts are available (10% off all rooms on weekdays), clean and bright, a/c, with telephones and televisions in every room, all rooms en suite, with a bath in the triple and deluxe rooms. Very helpful staff. Recommended.

B **Seri Malaysia**, Jln Ismail, T7-7991876, www.serimalaysia.com.my A/c, tea and coffee-making facilities, pool, restaurant, no charge for children under 12, situated just out of the centre.

B **Timotel**, 839 Jln Endau, T7-7995898, www.timotel.com.my. Looks like a set of offices from the outside but offers huge, luxurious rooms. Just out of the centre of town.

C **Kali's Guesthouse**, No 12E Kampong Sri Lalang, T7-7993613. Fan only, restaurant, arguably the best-kept, friendliest and most relaxed place to stay in Mersing area, rooms range from longhouse dorm to 'A'-frames and bungalows; atap-roofed bar and small Italian restaurant in garden next to beach. Highly recommended. To get there take a bus heading for Endau.

D **Country Hotel**, 11 Jln Sulaiman, T7-7991799. A/c or fan, clean and has a convenient location near the market and the bus and taxi stands.

C-D **Embassy**, 2 Jln Ismail, T7-7993545/7991301, F7-7995279 Some a/c, restaurant, very well-kept hotel – scrupulously clean, rooms without TVs considerably cheaper. Recommended.

C-E **Teluk Godek Chalet** (Lani's Place), Pantai Air Papan, T7-7994469, which looks the newest and best. A/c rooms with cable TV and telephone.

D **Golden City**, 23 Jln Abu Bakar, T7-7995028, F7-7991723. Bathroom (shower), near the bus station, some cheaper rooms with outside shower (RM10), free mineral water and a bike/motorcycle storage facility (RM1.50), friendly.

D **Omar Backpackers' Hostel**, Jln Abu Bakar (opposite the post office), T7-7995096. Clean and well looked-after but only 10 beds, excellent information on Sibu and other less visited islands, treks and river cruises. Relaxed place where Omar, the owner seems to let the guests run things. Very basic rooms (2 doubles and 1 dorm). Recommended. Omar has a souvenir shop, and runs tours around the islands for RM70.

Pulau Tioman *p233, map p235*

Sandflies can be a problem on Tioman and mosquito coils are recommended

The *Berjaya Tioman Beach Resort* and most of the cheaper places to stay are scattered along the west coast (the island is virtually uninhabited on the southeast and southwest sides and north of Juara Beach on the east coast, apart from a few fishing kampongs). Most of the accommodation on the island is simple: they are often individually owned by locals who may offer home-cooked meals and it is often hard to distinguish between them in terms of facilities and quality: atap or tin-roofed chalets/huts (C-E categories), 'A'-frames (E-F) or dorms (F). Chalets with attached bathrooms fall into the C-D categories and upwards. Rooms are fairly spartan; expect to pay more for mosquito nets and electricity. Inevitably, beachfront chalets cost more. Due to stiff competition, many prices are negotiable depending on the season.

Kampong Tekek

A-C **Babura Sea View**, T7-4191139. Some a/c, restaurant, the last place at the south end of the beach with 23 varied rooms. It consists of 3 separately owned businesses – the resort, a good Chinese restaurant, and *Tioman Reef Divers*, a PADI/NAUI dive shop. The rooms are clean and well maintained although some can be dark; the best are in the new block on the beach front. Recommended.

B **Persona Island Resort**, T/F7-4191213. Some a/c, restaurant, turn right at jetty and this place is a 5 minute walk. It is the flashest place to stay in Tekek with 24 clean and functional rooms in 2-storey buildings but it is not on the beach. Large restaurant.

B-C **Peladang**, T7-4191249, F011950852. Some a/c, a well-kept little place with clean and comfortable chalets. Its big drawback is that it is on the opposite side of the road some distance from the beach so it is neither possible to watch the sun go down over the horizon nor dash headlong from your chalet into the water.

B-D **Coral Reef Seaview**, T7-4191137. Some a/c, restaurant, a group of chalets all looking rather jaded and dusty, some facing onto the sea, others set back and facing one another.

B-D **Sri Tioman Beach Resort**, T7-4191189. Some a/c, restaurant, a popular place and one of the better places to stay in this price range in Tekek. Sea-facing chalets shaded beneath casuarina trees, good restaurant with prawn, squid and fish dishes as well as the usual range of pancakes etc.

C **Monte Chalets**, T013 3412266. Restaurant (American breakfast included in room rate) on the beach and run by Zuki. Much the same as *Tekek Inn* and *Sri Tioman Beach Resort* (the three actually share guests when they are full) although *Monte* suffers from being next to what looks like an oil storage depot.

D **Tekek Inn**, T011358395. This is perhaps the best of the cheaper places to stay. It is on the beach, rooms are OK with attached showers, the management is suitably relaxed and there are snorkels and canoes for hire. No restaurant here, just a drinks station. Recommended.

Kampong Lalang

AL **Berjaya Tioman Beach Golf & Spa Resort**, Lalang, T7-4191000, www.berjayaresorts.com. A hotel with 400 rooms set in 200 acres of land, built on the site of the old Kampong Lalang. This tourist class hotel is by far the biggest and most expensive resort on Tioman, with a good range of facilities and a lovely stretch of beach. This is not the place to come if you are hoping for a quiet retreat; during holiday periods, the whole place is heaving with activity. Rooms are adequately equipped but furnishings are a little dated. Choice of rooms; the cheapest have garden views and are the older 1-storey chalets. The deluxe and superior 2-storey chalets are bigger and are more suitable for families, some overlook the sea (if you crane your neck). All rooms have wooden floors and balconies, a/c, TV and mini-bar. Rather shabby bathrooms, with hot water shower only (bath tubs in deluxe rooms only). The suites are very forgettable. Several restaurants (see Eating

Kampong Tekek

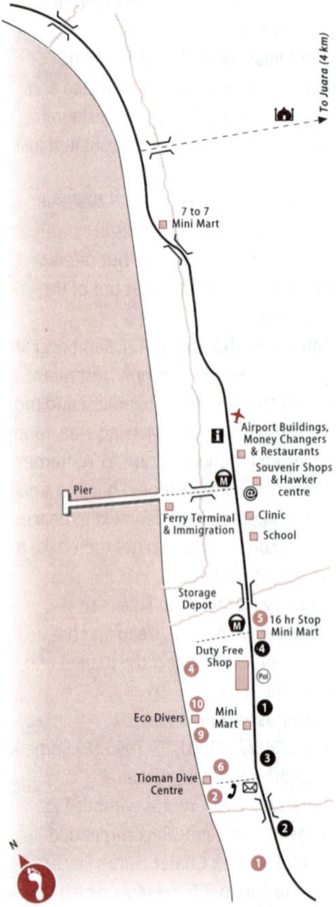

Sleeping
Babura Sea View, Chinese Restaurant & Tioman Reef Divers **1**
Coral Reef Seaview **2**
Monte Chalets **4**
Peladang **5**
Persona Island Resort **6**
Sri Tioman Beach Resort **9**
Tekek Inn **10**

Eating
Kontiki Bar & Café **3**
Liza **1**
Malay No Name **2**
Shady Bakery **4**

below). Rather cramped area for the freeform pool with children's slides and Jacuzzi. Watersports centre with boats for diving and snorkelling parties to nearby islands (it is possible to snorkel 100 m out from the northern end of the bay and at the very southern end, near the beach), jet skis, windsurfers, 18-hole golf course, gym – with good range of (underused) equipment, donkey and horse riding, tennis courts.

Ayer Batang

This lies just north of Tekek. Accommodation here is spread out around the bay and is generally quite good and is mainly simple chalets.

B **Bamboo Hill Chalets**, T7-4191339, www.geocities.com/bamboosu. The flashiest place on the beach tucked into the hills on the northern edge. Beautiful wood-floored huts with plenty of space. Hot water showers, fridge, kettle, sofas and balconies facing the sea. One fan room. There's internet here and a small library of books. Recommended.

B-D **Nazri's**, T7-4191329. The most southerly of the guesthouses in Ayer Batang. This has a range of accommodation. There's a newly built concrete block with more upmarket (for this beach) tiled rooms with a/c. Some rooms in rows with a running verandah

Kampong Ayer Batang (ABC)

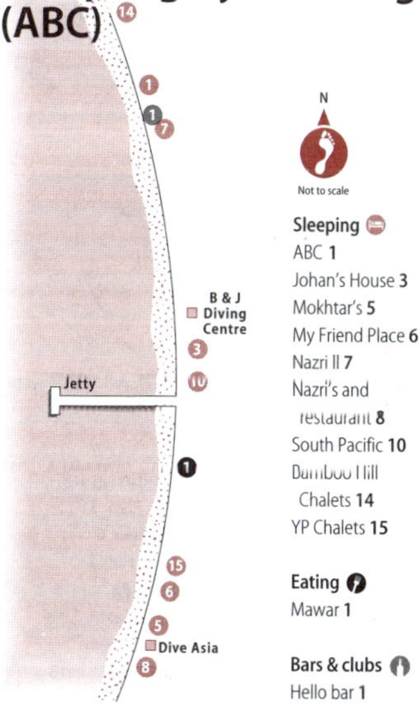

(5 with a seaview), some simple 'A' frames at the back of the plot, among the mango trees. Spartan but clean rooms, restaurant on seafront, friendly management, good discounts available during low season. Recommended.

C **Nazri II** Decent, clean and not too cramped rooms with wooden floors and seaviews. A raised restaurant provides a spectacular view of the bay. Laundry service, jet ski, fishing and snorkelling available. Recommended.

C-D **ABC**, T013 9220263. Very popular place to stay at northern end of stretch, with some good snorkelling just off the beach. Small 'A'-frames, attractive rather intimate little plot with family atmosphere, good cheap food, hammocks, volleyball, friendly service. Recommended.

C-D **Johan's House**, T7-4191359. Big plot with small chalets on the beach and some newer and bigger rooms with a/c on the hill. Extensive travellers' food menu, snorkelling equipment for hire, library, speedboat available.

C-E **Mokhtar's**, T9-4191148. Simple huts, fan and mosquito nets provided, basic restaurant.

D **South Pacific**, T7-4191176. The first bunch of chalets to the north of the jetty. Simple wooden huts with cold water showers and mosquito nets in a small grassy garden.

D **YP Chalets**, simple huts with mosquito nets and fan. No restaurant, but bikes for hire.

E **My Friend Place**, 10 very small rooms, fan and mosquito net.

Kampong Panuba

C-D **Panuba Inn**, T013 7720454, panuba@hotmail.com, situated just to the north of Kampong Ayer Batang, on the next promontory, and has its own jetty, but there's a small forest trail so guests can walk into Ayer Batang. The ferry from Mersing will stop here if you ask the boatmen in advance. Attractively laid out chalets built on stilts on the hillside, wall with seaviews. Rocky beach, snorkelling in front of resort, restaurant, rather idyllic being so secluded, homely atmosphere.

Kampong Salang

B-D **Khalid's Place (also known as Salang Pusaka Resort)** , T094195317/034. 44 fairly basic rooms in a pleasant garden setting. Family room and a/c room available.

B-D **Salang Beach Resort**, T7-4195015, F7-4192024. Chinese restaurant, spacious chalets with verandahs set in well-kept grounds, some with a/c. This resort is quiet and the beach is virtually a private one. The management can be brusque.

B-D **Salang Indah** T7-4195915, www.salangindah.com. Large, rather garish, restaurant with some delicious seafood specialities. Variety of chalets in all price brackets, some with attached bathrooms right on the sea, others with a/c and private stairs down to the sea, plus the original rather drab rooms in a U-shaped barrack of a building. There's a minimart and internet café. It is hard to avoid the conclusion that it has over-expanded.

C **Zaid's Place**, a popular place, with fairly switched-on management. There's a choice of rooms, some with seaview, others which face onto a little garden, all are clean and have fans. Money changer, library, good restaurant. Recommended.

C-D **Ella's Place**. At the northern end of the beach, so very quiet. Simple chalets with fan.

C-D **Paklong**, T7-4195000. 13 rooms with fan, some with a/c, no sea view, but friendly family management, rather fetid swamp close by.

D **Salang Huts**. A really isolated choice right at the northern end near a rocky bay. If you don't mind the abandoned air, there's plenty of hammocks and very cheap simple huts.

Kampong Paya

A **Paya Beach Resort**, T077991432, www.payabeach.com/ Small resort 30 a/c chalets, all sea-facing. Pool and spa. There is a PADI dive school attached to the hotel.

D **Sri Paya Holiday**, T011716196. 26 small bungalows in the middle of the village by the pier, little character.

Kampong Genting

A-B **Island Reef Resort**, set back on hillside behind jetty, with chalets side on to beach, so no views except in the restaurant.

B **Sun Beach Resort**, T9-4197043, about 50 rambling bungalows built too close together, some on the seafront, others piled up the hill behind. Monstrous restaurant on stilts and bar.

B-C **Bayu Chalets**, T012-3871309 (for reservation in KL), http://gbayuc.tioman.tripod.com/index.htm, at the north end of the beach, quiet and secluded. Upmarket wooden chalets with some attempt to give them a Malaysian village feel. Some fan, some a/c, some larger rooms can sleep four. There's also a restaurant and games room.

D **Damai**, bookable in Mersing at Jln Abu Bakar, T7-4197055. About 80 rather grotty looking double chalets with balconies, restaurant, minimarket and 24-hr electricity, speedboat to Mersing.

Kampong Nipah

B-D **Nipah Beach Chalet**. Funky place with simple wooden huts decorated with bamboo and colourful batiks. One chalet sleeps five, four on beds, and one in a rooftop annexe.

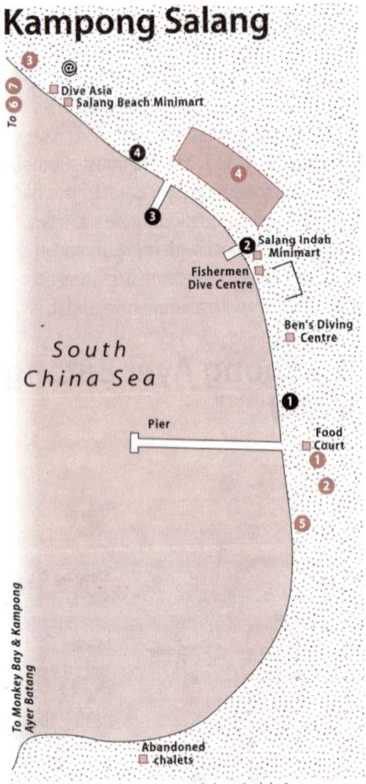

N

Not to scale

Sleeping
Khalid's Place **1**
Paklong **2**
Salang Beach Resort **3**
Salang Indah **4**
Zaid's Place **5**
Ella's Place **6**
Salang Huts **7**

Eating
Amin's Café **1**
Salang Dreams **2**
Sunset Boulevard **3**
Warung **4**

Kampong Mukut

C Mukut Coral Resort, T7-7992535, restaurant, traditional-style atap-roofed chalets with balconies, a/c, secluded and beautiful location with magnificent backdrop.

C Mukut Harmony Resort, T7-7993440. Simple rows of chalets with fan and bathroom.

Kampong Juara

B Juara Beach, T7-4193188, F4193231, the swankiest place in Juara north of the pier mainly geared at package tourists. This new place has massive rooms set back from the beach, with wooden floors, hot water showers and comfortable beds.

C Bushman, T7-4192109, near the southern end of the beach, simple huts practically on the sands. There's a restaurant and bar and a dive shop (www.bushman-diving.com) and the staff are friendly. More huts to come.

D Lagoon Bay Resort, the last place to stay at the southern end of the bay. It is quite a walk from the jetty over the headland. It is run by British guy, John, who has been living on the island for some years. He is helpful with info on treks. Accommodation here is simple chalets all with fan. He mainly caters to Singaporean outward bound school trips, but the place makes a nice quiet retreat.

D Rainbow Chalets, T7-4193140. Simple colourful chalets next to Bushman's on the beach. Run by a Dutch woman and her Malay husband. No mosquito nets. The husband runs the Sunrise Dive Centre (www.sunrisedivecentre.com).

D-E Juara Mutiara, T7-792309, organizes diving trips or island tours, booking office in Mersing, 6 Jln Abu Bakar, near *Plaza R&R*. The more expensive rooms sleep 4, all have attached showers, clean and popular, some chalets right on the beach, can be noisy (for Juara) as there are other chalet operations on both sides.

E Paradise Point, restaurant with extensive menu, one of only three places to stay on the northern side of the beach. Simple rooms, attached showers, the chalets siding onto the beach get the breeze, a quiet place with a relaxed atmosphere. Recommended.

E Riverview Place. The cheapest yet the most scenic place to stay next to an aquamarine mangrove swamp at the northern edge of the bay. Simple chalets right on the beach. Also rumoured to serve the best seafood. Recommended.

E-F Mizani's place, over the headland at the southern end of the beach, isolated and quiet.

Kampong Juara

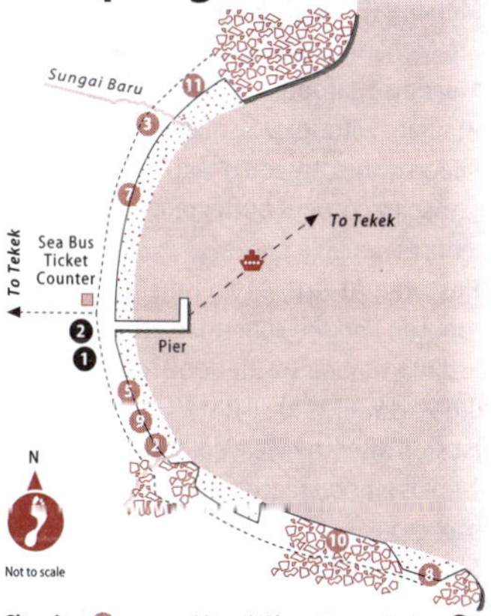

Sleeping
Bushman 2
Busong 3
Juara Mutiara 5
Lagoon Bay Resort 8
Mizani's Place 10
Paradise Point 7
Rainbow Chalets & Sunrise Dive Centre 9
Riverview Place 11

Eating
Happy Café 1
Mini Café 2

Pulau Rawa

Rawa has no kampongs on it.

A-B Rawa Safaris Island Resort, Tourist Centre, Jln Abu Bakar, Mersing T7-7991204, www.rawasfr.com Some a/c, restaurant (Malay and international dishes), bungalows, chalets and 'A'-frames, watersports. Sahid mixes some powerful cocktails in the bar; drink more than two Rawa specials and you'll be on the island for good.

A Le Club Rawa, 'A'-frame chalets on the beach. Expensive for basic amenities on offer.

Pulau (Babi) Besar

A D'Coconut Island Resort, T0342965753,T0342911808, www.dcoconut.com. Built on the land of an old coconut plantation, with chalets, a large restaurant, pool and watersports.

A Radin Island Resort, 9 Tourist Information Centre, Jln Abu Bakar, Mersing, T7-7994152. Restaurant (some a/c) stylish traditional chalets with jungle hillside backdrop.

A-C Nirwana Beach Resort, T7-7995929,

choice of chalets, some with a/c, restaurant attached, dorms available.

B **Hillside Beach Resort**, 5B Jln Abu Bakar, Mersing or book through Suite 125, 1st Flr, Johor Tower, 15 Jln Gereja, Johor Bahru, T077994831, F7-2244329. Restaurant, very attractively designed Kampong-style resort, nestling on jungled slopes above beach, watersports.

C-E **Batu Kembar**, 18 large chalets on a hillside, for 4 people each in bunks, a/c, hot showers and balconies.

E **Bluewater Resort**, chalet or longhouse accommodation in this place in Aur village.

Pulau Tinggi

A-F **Nadia Comfort Inn**, c/o 17 Tingkat 2, Tun Abdul Razak, Kompleks (KOMTAR), Jln Wong Ah Fook, Johor Bahru, T072231694. Booking office in Mersing opposite *Plaza R&R*, Jln Abu Bakar, restaurant, pool, luxurious Malay-style wooden chalets. Also 'A'-frames, chalets and bungalows on the island.

Pulau Sibu

A **Twin Beach Resort**, T607-3322122. 40 chalets, no a/c or hot water but good sports facilities.

A-D **Sibu Island Cabanas** (c/o G105 *Holiday Plaza*, Century Garden JB), T073317216. Restaurant, chalets and deluxe bungalows.

C **Sibu Island Resorts**, Suite 2, 14th Flr, KOMTAR, Jln Wong Ah Fook, Johor Bahru, T072231188. More than 100 well-appointed chalets on Pulau Sibu Tengah with a/c, cable TV. Coffee house, restaurant and pool and bar.

C-D **O & H Kampong Huts** (c/o 9 Tourist Information Centre, Jln Abu Bakar, Mersing), T7-7993124/7993125. Good restaurant, chalets, some with attached bathrooms, clean and friendly, trekking and snorkelling. Recommended.

C-D **Sea Gypsy Village Resort**, 9 Tourist Information Centre, Jln Abu Bakar, Mersing, T7-7993124. Restaurant, chalets and bungalows. Recommended.

Pulau Pemanggil

There is a small agent at the very front of Mersing's *Plaza R&R* dealing exclusively with Pemanggil travel and accommodation.

A **Lanting Beach Resort**, T607-7993973, www.lantingresort.com.my Pleasant chalets built on a big rocky platform at the far end of the beach, making the resort very secluded. Staff have good English.

C-E **Dagang Chalets and Longhouse**, Kampong Buau (1 longhouse room sleeps 8 at RM10 per person), restaurant serving local food, *Mara Chalet* at Kampong Pa Kaleh, on southwest side. Contact *Tioman Accommodation & Boat Services*, 3 Jln Abu Bakar, Mersing, T7-7993048.

Pulau Aur

F **Longhouse** provides basic accommodation.

Eating

Mersing *p233, map p233*

Chinese

Yung Chuan Seafood, 51 Jln Ismail, big open coffee shop with vast selection, speciality: seafood steamboat.

Malay

Golden Dragon Restaurant, 2 Jln Ismail, big Chinese seafood menu, reasonably priced, chilli crabs, drunken prawns, wild boar and *kang-kong belacan*. Excellent banana/pineapple pancakes for breakfast. Recommended.

Malaysia, opposite the bus stop, open all night. Staple Malay fare of *nasi campur*.

Mersing (Ground Floor, *Mersing Hotel*), Jln Dato Mohammed Ali, excellent seafood.

Mersing Seafood, 56 Jln Ismail, a/c restaurant with spicy Sichuan or Cantonese seafood dishes, try squid with salted egg yoke, spicy coconut butter prawns. Big menu, reasonable prices.

Restoran Al-Arif, 44 Jln Ismail (opposite *Parkson* supermarket), cheap Muslim restaurant with good rotis and curries as well as local dishes. If this is your first stop after the west coast or Singapore, Al-Arif is a good place to get into the east coast groove.

Sin Nam Kee Seafood, 387 Jln Jemaluang (1 km out of town on Kota Tinggi road), huge seafood menu and reckoned by locals to be the best restaurant in Mersing; occasional karaoke nights can be noisy.

Bakeries

Kedai Kek Kile, Jln Abu Bakar (next to Omar's). A good selection of cakes and pastries cooked on the premises.

Foodstalls

There are a number of upmarket stalls and coffee shops in the new *Plaza R&R* next to the river. There are also a smattering of more traditional stalls alongside the fresh fruit and vegetables in the market on Jln Ismail.

Pulau Tioman *p233, map p235*

Most restaurants are small family run kitchens attached to groups of beach huts. All provide western staples such as omelettes and French toast, as well as Malay dishes. On the whole, the food is of a high standard. Understandably it makes most sense to eat seafood: superb barbecued barracuda, squid, stingray and other fish. Not all restaurants sell beer.

Kampong Tekek

ꝉ **Babura Sea View Chinese Restaurant** (separate ownership from the guesthouse) is recommended by ex-pats.

ꝉ **Liza Restaurant**, which is the most sophisticated place to have a meal and serves delicious Malay food.

ꝉ **Malay Restaurant** (no name), north of the *Babura* and before the bridge is a small restaurant, also recommended.

ꝉ **Sri Tioman Beach Resort** The food at this restaurant is worth trying, especially the squid and chilli prawns.

ꝉ **The Shady Bakery** has cheese slices and baguettes.

Kampong Lalang

ꝉꝉ **Berjaya Tioman Beach Resort Restaurant** offers a choice of restaurants, none of which are outstanding. The best bet is the buffet meal, which is quite good value and a huge spread is on offer. The other restaurants offer barbecue and steamboat. Service for à la carte meals is painfully slow and pretty inefficient. The golf club offers a snack bar with good pizzas and sandwiches.

Kampong Ayer Batang

ꝉ **Mawar**. Tables in the scrubby sand. But the Malay dishes are very good and cheap here, especially the fish.

ꝉ **Nazri's Place**. The seafront restaurant is one of the best on this stretch with good seafood and western backpacker staples like chips and sandwiches. Sometimes wine is available. Great view of the ocean. Possible to carry tables onto the sand. Cheap but food a couple of ringgit more than the other places – but worth it.

Kampong Salang

This is a sizeable hamlet, so there are a number of restaurants independent of the guesthouses.

ꝉ **Amin's Café** Another good option right by the jetty; it provides breakfast, lunch and dinner, simple, low key place.

ꝉ **Salang Dreams** next to the *Salang Indah Minimart* has good Malay food and a good evening seafood barbecue.

ꝉ **Sunset Boulevard** is built over the sea north of the *Salang Indah*. Good seafood and the best spot for a cold beer.

ꝉ **Warung** Among the best of the warungs is the place just north of the *Sunset Boulevard* – simple dishes, breakfast served.

Kampong Paya

ꝉ **Mekong Restaurant** at the south end of the bay produces good Chinese seafood dishes.

Kampong Juara

All the guesthouses serve roughy the same dishes: curries, noodle and rice dishes, pancakes, fish, omelettes etc.

ꝉ **Happy Café**. Open-air restaurant with great views of turquoise ocean. Malay dishes, seafood the best.

ꝉ **Mini Café** Good Malay seafood, try the chilli fish, sweet and sour or simply grilled.

ꝉ **Riverview Place** Expats recommend this simple place as the best in the village. Serves Malay and seafood.

Bars and clubs

Kampong Tekek

ꝉ **Dolphin Bar**, next to Tekek Inn, T9-4191779. Beachside bar (said to be Tekek's only beachside bar; recommended by expats. Cheap beer.

ꝉ **Kontiki Café**. Another bar popular with expats, gets a bit rowdy.

Kampong Ayer Batang

Hello Bar, just in front of Nazri's II is a tiny beachside open air bar full of character. Run by the charming, 'K' it's a great place for a beer at sunset. Watch out for Henry the bat's aerial dance when the Bob Marley CD gets played.

Shopping

Mersing *p233, map p233*

Arts Souvenir, 1 Gerai MDM, Jln Tun Dr Ismail, next to Malay restaurants on the corner after *R&R Plaza*. Artist Sulaiman Aziz specializes in colourful t-shirts, shorts and beachware and hand-painted batiks. There are some knick-knack souvenir shops in the *R&R Plaza*.

The **market** on Jln Ismail offers more authentic batiks and is worth wandering around.

Pulau Tioman *p233, map p235*

Kampong Tekek

There are a number of minimarts in the Kampong. There is a very small market area next to the *Peladang Restaurant*.

Pak Ali Nasir's stall is the best place for fruit. There are a handful of souvenir shops in Tekek selling the usual range of sea-derived knick-knacks.

Activities and tours

Mersing *p233, map p233*

Boats for fishing trips can be chartered by groups of 12 or more from the jetty. Owners may be reluctant to take the long journey out to the far off shore islands.

Tour operators

Competition is intense at peak season and tourists can be hassled for custom Ticketing and travel agents all over town are much of a muchness and visitors are unlikely to be ripped off – although use licensed agents (usually displayed on the door). Agencies tend to promote their own business so expect the truth to be warped, bent and generally polished to a high and unlikely sheen. Many agents are now located in the *R&R Plaza* on Jln Tun Dr Ismail, next to the river. They also promote package deals to specific chalet resorts; sometimes they are good value, but buying a boat ticket puts you under no obligation to stay at a particular place.

Dee Travel & Tours, T7-77992344, 8 Jln Abu Bakar; **Golden Mal Tours**, 9 Jln Sulaiman, T7-7991463; **Island Connection Travel & Tours**, 2 Jln Jemaluang, T7-7992535, tours and ticketing. Recommended; **Kebina**, Jln Abu Bakar, T7-7993123, F7-7995118; **Omar's**, opposite the Post Office, T7-7995096.

Boat tours

Boats can be booked from many of the guesthouses.

Diving

Most beaches have dive centres attached to at least one guesthouse. PADI, NAUI and SSI (Scuba Schools International) certification available, but PADI is by far the most popular.

Pulau Tioman *p233, map p235*

Kampong Tekek

Diving **Tioman Reef Divers** attached to *Babura Sea View*. This is reputedly the best dive shop. **Tioman Dive Centre** and **Eco Divers** are also highly regarded.

Kampong Ayer Batang

Diving **B&J Diving Centre**, next to *Johan's House* has a small pool for diving practice and can provide PADI certification.

Kampong Salang

Salang is sold as a snorkellers' haven but, sadly, that is history – the coral is disappointing. It does, however, get better further out, and where the coral cliff drops off to deeper water, there is a more interesting variety of marine life including the odd reef shark. Snorkels and fins can be hired just about everywhere, about RM7-10 per day.

Diving **Ben's Diving Centre**, next to *Salang Indah* hires out equipment and can organize PADI certification and diving trips to nearby islands.**B&J Diving Centre**, T011717014, F011954247. **Dive Asia** by the *Salang Beach Resort* also offers PADI certification.

Fishermen Dive Centre near the *Salang Indah* offers courses and lessons in underwater photography.

Kampong Paya

Diving Dive shop at the *Paya Resort* with PADI certification courses.

Kampong Genting

Diving **Sharkeys**, the *Tropical Coral Inn*, runs SSI certificated courses.

Kampong Juara

Diving Snorkelling and fishing gear can be hired from most guesthouses. For diving there's **Bushman's**, T7-4192109, www.bushman-diving.com, at the Bushman resort and **Sunrise Dive Centre**, www.sunrisedivecentre.com next door at *Rainbow Chalets*.

Golf **Tioman Island Golf Club**, T7-445445, F7-445716, most club-members are weekend trippers from KL and Singapore, beautiful 18-hole course. Equipment including clubs, golf shoes, and buggy available for hire.

Tour operators

The majority of resorts can organize trips around the island and boat tickets back to the mainland. Note, though, bus tickets cannot be bought on the island.
Guides are available from Berjaya Tioman Beach Resort and in Kampong Tekek.

Transport

Mersing *p233, map p233*

Boat

The jetty is a 5-min walk from the long distance bus stop. Most of the ticket offices are by the jetty but boat tickets to the islands are also sold from booths near the bus stop. The boat trip to the islands from Mersing can be extremely rough during the monsoon season; boats will sometimes leave Mersing in the late afternoon, on the high tide, but rough seas can delay the voyage considerably. During peak monsoon all ferry services are cancelled and the ferry companies move to the west coast to find work there. It is advisable only to travel during daylight hours. There are several companies offering speedboats (RM35, just under 2 hours) and slow boats (RM30, three hours plus). They stop at Genting, Berjaya, Tekek, Ayer Batang, and Kampong Salang, and you must tell the boat workers where you want to get off in advance.

Bus

The local bus station is on Jln Sulaiman opposite the *Country Hotel*.

Long-distance buses leave from two locations: those not originating in Mersing leave from the roundabout by the *Shell Station* and those that start from Mersing leave from Jln Abu Bakar, from the car park next to the Plaza R&R. Tickets can be bought from *Plaza R&R* or from tour agents in town. Regular connections with **KL**, **JB**, RM9), **Kuantan**, **Cherating**, RM22, **Terengganu**, RM22, **Ipoh Penang** and **Singapore KB**, RM29.

Taxi

Taxis leave from Jln Sulaiman opposite the *Country Hotel*, next to the local bus station; **KL**, **JB** (RM100) (for Singapore, change at JB), **Melaka Kuala Terengganu** and **Kuantan** (RM100-120).

Pulau Tioman *p233, map p235*

Air

Berjaya Air flies from **Singapore** and **KL** daily to the airstrip on the island. Baggage allowance is 10 kg. A bus from the *Berjaya Tioman Resort* meets each arrival and transports guests to the hotel. Alternatively walk to the pier and catch one of the sea-buses or ferries to the other beaches.

Airline offices Berjaya Air operates out of *Berjaya Resort*, T7-4191303, www.berjaya-air.com

Boat

Fast boats from Mersing to **Tioman** leave around every hour to two hours (journey time just under 2 hours, speedboat, RM35 one way; slow boat, RM30) and there are one or two slow boat departures (more than 3 hours) daily. During the monsoon season (Nov-Feb) departures can be erratic; boats may not run if there are insufficient passengers and the sea can get quite rough. All boats land on the west coast of Tioman and call at each of the main kampongs so you need to tell the boatman where you want to disembark.

Beaches and kampongs are connected by an erratic sea-bus service, which runs roughly every hour or so from 0800 to 1600. The early-morning sea-bus goes right round the island; otherwise it is necessary to charter a boat to get to the waterfalls (on the south coast) and Kampong Juara. Sea-bus fares (per person, children half price) from Kampong Tekek to **Kampong Ayer Batang**/ABC, RM10, **Panuba**, RM12, **Salang**, RM20, **Lalang**, RM10, **Juara**, RM50. The east coast will be accessible by road when a concrete trail is finished, by (very slow) boat or by the jungle trail.

Boats to some of the smaller islands leave daily from Mersing, usually around 1100 and return in the afternoon, else arrange boat transfer through resort. Boats to Tioman sometimes stop off at **Rawa** on the way. Boats to **Rawa**, RM35, *DCoconut* has a boat connection for US$15 return to **Pulau (Babi) Besar**. No regular boats to Pulau Aur or Pulau Pemanggil. Getting to **Pulau Aur** takes 4 hrs or more. Also boats to **Sibu** from Tanjung Sedili Besar at Teluk Mahkota (23 km off the Kota Tinggi-Mersing road), south of Mersing.

Pulau Pemanggil

The boat trip to Pemanggil is long. 4-5 hours – 64 nautical miles offshore.

Directory

Mersing *p233, map p233*

Banks Maybank, Jln Ismail; UMBC, Jln Ismail, no exchange on Sat. Money changer on Jln Abu Bakar and Giamso Safari, 23 Jln Abu Bakar also changes TCs. **Post** Jln Abu Bakar. **Internet** Mersing EasyNet Café, Jln Dato Mohd Ali (just off the roundabout). open 1000-2300. **Medical services** Dentists Klinik Pergigian, 28 Jln Mohd, Ali, T7-7993135. **Doctors** Klinik Grace, 48 Jln Abu Bakar, T7-7992399.

Pulau Tioman *p233, map p235*

Kampong Tekek

Banks There are 2 money changers at Tioman Airport in the blue-roofed shopping plaza. **Internet** Internet café on the second floor of the souvenir shop and food court building opposite the jetty at Tekek. **Medical services** There is a small clinic in Tekek which is good for minor illnesses. The nearest decompression chamber is at Kuantan. **Post** Mini-post office in Kampong Tekek. **Telephone** Public phones in all villages, IDD calling from *Berjaya* and some guesthouses. There are card phones in Tekek next to the Mini Pos (cards available at Post Office).

Kampong Lalang

Banks TCs can be changed at the *Berjaya Resort* (large surcharge). Recently, some smaller resorts have begun to accept them.

Ayer Batang

Internet Bamboo Hill Chalets, and there's Internet at the Dive Asia shop.

Kampong Salang

Banks Some shops will also change money. **Internet** Salang Indah at Kampong Salang.

Endau Rompin National Park

→ Colour map 2, grid B5 Phone code: 09

The endangered Sumatran rhino, tigers, wild boars, tapir, elephant deer and mousedeer roam in this park, one of the biggest remaining tracts of virgin rainforest on the peninsula. Birdlife includes hornbills and the argus pheasant. Amongst the flora there are fan palms (Endau ensis), walking stick palm (Phychorapis singaporensis) and climbing bamboo (Rhopa loblaste), pitcher plants and orchids The 80,000 ha park straddles the border of Johor and Pahang states and in the late 1980s Endau Rompin was upgraded to the status of a national park to protect the area from the logging companies who ravaged the park through the 1970s. *» For Sleeping, Eating and other listings, see pages 250-250.*

Ins and outs

Getting there

There are two ways of getting to the park; either via Rompin, Pahang, (paved road to Selanding and then a rough track for 25 km to the park boundary at Kinchin). The other route is from Johor in the south, on route 50 from Kahang; its 48 km on a logging route to Kampong Peta (the visitors' centre and entry point to the park). From the visitors' centre it's another 15 km to base camp at Kuala Jasin (3 hrs on foot or 45 mins by boat, RM10/person upon request). For arrivals to the park by boat, travel to Endau, 33 km up the coast from Mersing, and from there, take a 6-hr motorboat ride upstream to Kampong Peta (RM200 one way).

Getting around

Both Johor and Pahang state authorities recommend that visitors come on an organised tour, given the convoluted travel instructions and excessive fees, this is a sensible option.

Park essentials and tourist information

The park is managed by the **Johor National Parks Corporation**, ⓘ *T607 2237471*, a private body set up by local government which has made access to the park easier and has allowed some new accommodation. Because of privatisation, prices for entry and accommodation are relatively high. Unlike Taman Negara National Park, trips to Endau require careful planning and are best organized by tour agents who can usually do it up cheaper than arranging it independently. Some guides do offer one-day treks but this should not be attempted alone. Entry permits are required and these must be secured in advance from the forestry department in Kuala Rompin, T09 4145204. A tour operator will take care of this for you. If you do decide to travel independently the costs are RM50 per day for a guide (compuslory) – one guide can be shared between 10 people, RM20 entry permit at each zone (there is a zone A and a zone B), RM10 for a camera, RM20 fishing permit.

❢ Due to the extended travel time required to reach the park, visitors should consider a visit of around three nights

If arriving via Endau by boat, at the junction of the Endau and Jasin rivers (9 hours from Endau) is a good campsite and base for trekking and fishing expeditions. Boats go further upstream, but it is advisable to take a guide from Endau or the Orang Asli kampongs (RM20-30 per day). At present it is necessary to take all provisions and camping equipment with you.

Most package trips involve a 70-km jeep trip from Mersing to Kampong Peta followed by a 1½-hour longboat ride to the first campsite. Visitors to the park can trek around the Asli trails and visit spectacular waterfalls, the biggest of which is the Buaya Sangkut waterfall on Sungai Jasin.

Entrance fees must be paid at the Park Headquarters in Kampong Peta where the officer on duty will provide a briefing of rules and regulations that apply in the park. See www.pahangtourism.com.my/tropical/attractions/endau_rompin.html for more information on the park.

Best time to visit

The park is closed during monsoon season, November-March and during the rainy season you will need a four-wheel drive to negotiate the tracks thick with mud. Fishing trips are best organized between February and August.

Sleeping

Endau Rompin National Park *p248*

There is no accommodation available in the park; camping only (including tent hire_ is RM12.50 per person) at Kuala Jasin, Batu Hampar, Upih Guling and Kuala Marong, which have a combined capacity of 250-300 visitors. Base camp is at Kampong Peta – place to set up your tent, and simple A frames. At headquarters there is running water and flush toilets and a small grocery shop.You can contact **Malaysian Nature Society** in KL (03-22879422, natsoc@po.jaring.my for information on tours and accommodation at the Park. Or **Johor Park Corporation**, T7-2237471, www.johorpark.com There are several other campsites Kuala Jasin has running water, a few A-frames and fire pits. Even more basic are those at Kuala Marong, Batu Hampar (no toilets, water from the river)

Activities and tours

Endau Rompin *p248*

Hotels and guesthouses in Kuala Rompin also usually organize trips into the park.

Tour operators

Organized expeditions, which cost anything from RM90-200 per person per day, include return vehicle and boat transfer, camping equipment, cooking utensils and permits.

Eureka Travel, 277A Holland Ave, Holland Village, Singapore, T65-4625077, F65-4622853. Offers ecologically orientated tours. Recommended.

Giamso Travel, 23 Jln Abu Bakar, Mersing, T077992253. The company can supply camping equipment.

Ping Anchorage, 77A Jalan Sultan Sulaiman, Kuala Terengganu, T09 6262020. One of Malaysia's most successful tour companies.

Shah Alam Tours, 138 Mezz Flr, Jln Tun Sambanthan, Kuala Lumpur T032307161, F032745739.

Wilderness Experience, 6B Jln SS 21/39, Damansara Utama, Petaling Jaya, T037178221.

Transport

Endau Rompin *p248*

Boat

Speed boats to first Orang Asli village (**Kampong Punan**). This can cost anything from RM200-400 for a 2-day trip. It is possible to charter longboats (carrying up to 6 passengers) from Kampong Punan to go further upstream.

Bus

Connections with **JB**, **Terengganu** and **Kuantan**. Buses from JB and Kuantan stop on demand at **Endau**, or regular local buses from Mersing to Endau. There is a 56-km jungle road from Kahang town to Kampong Peta where there is a visitors' centre and the entry point to the park.

Taxi

From Mersing.

East Coast Peninsula

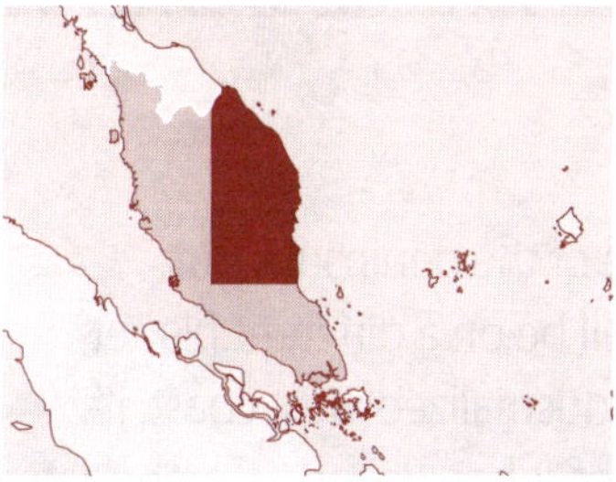

Footprint features

Introduction

It might just be on the other side of the peninsula, but Malaysia's east coast could as well be on a different planet than the populous, hectic and industrialized west coast. Its coastline, made up of the states of Johor, Pahang, Terengganu and Kelantan, is lined with coconut palms, dotted with sleepy fishing kampongs and interspersed with rubber and oil palm plantations, paddy fields, beaches and mangroves. The string of Islands stretching all along the coast offer a mix of lazy getaways – Pulau Kapas, acclaimed snorkelling and diving sites – Pulau Tenggol and Pulau Lang Tengah, to parties and barbecues on the beach at Pulau Perhentian.

For an insight into Malay traditions and artistry, Kota Bahru in the north stages almost daily events from kite flying to drumming sessions, while Kuala Terengganu is a souvenir hunting ground with fine silverware and handicraft markets.

★ Don't miss...

1. **Taman Negara** Swing through the jungle on the world's longest treetop bridge, page 268.
2. **Batiks** Hand dye or paint your own cloth in laid-back Cherating, page 272.
3. **Diving** For the best diving head to Pulau Tenggol, page 275.
4. **Rantau Abang** Watch giant leatherback turtles bulldoze up the beach to lay their eggs, page 275.
5. **Fisherman's breakfast** Start the day the local way with a plate of *nasi dagang* - sticky rice with fish curry and pickles - at a hawker stall in Kuala Terengganu, page 286.
6. **Perhentians** Learn to scuba dive or just splash and snorkel in the turquoise seas around this undeveloped island getaway, page 291.
7. **Kota Bahru** Enjoy the traditional crafts of Kelantan from silver-making and shadow puppets to kung fu and kite-flying, page 296.

Ins and outs

Getting there and around

The east coast can be reached from various points on the west coast. Routes from Butterworth (Penang) and Kuala Kangsar in the north, lead across to Kota Bharu on the northeast coast. There's a new highway from KL to Kuantan (halfway down the east coast) and the railway cuts north from Gemas (south of KL) to Kota Bharu. There is a new highway from Ipoh to Gua Musang in Kelantan via the Cameron Highlands.

Best time to visit

If you plan on visiting any of the beaches or islands on the east coast, and especially if you're hoping to dive, the best time to visit is between February and September to avoid the rainy season. During the winter monsoon, the seas are very rough and many island resorts are closed and boat operators pack up business. Between May and September is the best time for turtle spotting.

Background

Until the 19th century, the narrow coastal plain between the jungled mountains and the sea was largely bypassed by trade and commerce and its 60-odd coral-fringed (and largely uninhabited) offshore islands were known only to local fishermen. The mountainous interior effectively cut the east coast off from the west coast, physically, commercially and culturally. The east coast did not have the tin deposits which attracted Chinese speculators and miners to the towns on the other side of the Main Range in the 19th century; and in more recent decades it was left behind as Malaysia joined the development race. The rural parts have been buffered from Western influence; traditional kampong lifestyles have been tempered only by the arrival of the electric lightbulb, the outboard motor and Japanese motorbikes. The east coast's fishermen and paddy farmers are Malaysia's most conservative Muslims.

In the 1990 general election, the people of Kelantan voted a hardline Islamic opposition party into power –Parti Islam Se Malaysia (PAS). Several elections on, the PAS still holds Kelantan, although in the interim they have won and lost the state of Terengganu. The rural Malays of the east coast have not enjoyed much in the way of 'trickledown' from Malaysia's new-found economic prosperity. Although they are *bumiputras* ('sons of the soil', see page 497) – few have reaped the benefits of more than two decades of pro-Malay policies.

The September 11 atrocities in the US and the war in Afghanistan would seem, however, to have stopped the PAS's expansion in its tracks, for the time being at least (see page 491). Party leaders rather short-sightedly called for a jihad in support of the Taliban, they organised a rather bad-tempered demonstration outside the US embassy in KL, and also refused to rule out violence. Former Prime Minister Mahathir played all this to his advantage. In reality, however, while some members of the PAS are pretty extreme in the main the party has managed Kelantan and, more latterly, Terengganu, pretty sensibly. However, the people of Terengganu who voted and then ousted the party in the ballot of 2004, realised that with PAS they will also be denied the economic support that states loyal to the Barsian Nasional (BN) ruling party enjoyed. They opted out and voted in the BN.

During the Second World War, the Japanese Imperial Army landed at Kota Bharu and sped the length of the peninsula within six weeks on stolen bicycles (see page 485). The east coast did not figure prominently during the war, except in the realm of literary fiction, starring in Neville Shute's *A Town Like Alice*.

Before and after the war, rubber and oil palm plantations sprang up – particularly in the south state of Johor – which changed the shape of the agricultural economy. But the most dramatic change followed the discovery of large quantities of high-grade crude oil and natural gas off the northeast coast in the 1970s. By the mid-1980s, huge storage depots, gas processing plants and refineries had been built in Terengganu, and the battered old coast road was upgraded to cater for Esso and Petronas tankers. The town of Kerteh, halfway between Kuantan and Kuala Terengganu, is a refinery town, built along one of the best beaches on the peninsula. The construction boom and the rig work helped boost the local economy and provide employment, but the east coast states (bar Johor, which straddles the entire south tip of the peninsula) have singularly failed to attract much industrial investment in the way their west coast neighbours have. Oil money has, however, helped transform the fortunes of Terengganu.

On the whole, the east coast has been less sullied by industrial pollution; the South China Sea is a lot cleaner than the Strait of Melaka. Despite the oil, the East Coast is still the rural backwater of the peninsula (95% of state revenues from oil go straight into federal coffers in KL).

Kuantan and around

→ *Colour map 2, grid A5*

The modern capital of Pahang has a population of around 280,000 and is a bustling, largely Chinese, town at the mouth of the Kuantan River. Kuantan is the main transport and business hub for the east coast; most visitors spend at least a night here as a base to explore the mystical lake of Tasek Chini, the Semelai aboriginal kampongs of lake Tasek Bera, the Charah Caves and the adventure sports of the Gunung Tapis Park. ▸▸ *See Sleeping, Eating and other listings, pages 260-265.*

Ins and outs

Getting there

Kuantan's airport is 20 km from town. There are connections with KL. There are bus connections with all towns up and down the east coast as well as with key destinations on the west, including KL. Outstation taxis travel to Kuala Terengganu, KL and Mersing. ▸▸ *See also Transport, for further information, page 264.*

Getting around

Kuantan is not a large town, despite its importance as a centre for transport connections to regions across the country. City buses provide a regular service to the beach and hotels at Teluk Chempedak and there are also a number of car hire firms in town.

Tourist information

Padang Tourist Information Centre, ⓘ *Jalan Mahkota, 25000 Kuantan, Pahang Darul Makmur, T609 5161007, www.pahangtourism.com.my, Mon-Fri 0800-1630, closed for lunch, Sat 0800-1245, Sun closed.* Really pleasant staff, very helpful, up-to-date information covers a large proportion of Malaysia, specifically Pahang state.

Sights

While many tourists pass through Kuantan not many seem to stay longer than it takes to wipe their feet and take a couple of breaths before moving on, and wandering around the centre you are unlikely to meet many westerners. It is noticeable, for example, that local people, while not unfriendly, do not speak very good English. When people do remain in the Kuantan area for any length of time they seem to stay in the fishing villages to the north and south of town.

Kuantan's fairly new **Sultan Ahmad Shah** mosque (Masjid Negeri), in the centre of town, is worth wandering around. Visitors are asked to don oversized hooded cloaks. These enormous cloaks, the time limits given to non-Muslim visitors by the stern yet surprisingly amused guards, and the restrictions placed on females, do not detract from the cool and calming beauty of the building. Freshly decorated in blue, green and white, with a cool marbled interior, the mosque can be seen across the town. It has blue and yellow stained-glass windows and the morning sun projects their coloured patterns on the interior walls. Kuantan has several streets of old shophouses which date from the 1920s. Most of the oldest buildings are opposite the padang on **Jalan Mahkota**. The 300-km stretch of coast between Kuantan and Kota Bharu is comprised of long beaches, interspersed with fishing kampongs and the occasional natural gas processing plant and oil refinery.

Teluk Chempedak→ *Colour map 2, grid A5*

ⓘ *There are regular connections with the Rah Matalan bus company from the local bus station. A taxi should cost RM5-8. A short walk north of Teluk Chempedak are Methodist Bay and Teluk Pelindong, which are beyond the range of most picknickers.*

This beach resort is just 4 km east of Kuantan and marks the beginning of the beaches. The Pahang state government has reserved the 30 km stretch of coast from Teluk Chempedak beach north to the Terengganu state border exclusively for tourism-related projects, so there is likely to be much more development. Teluk Chempedak was once the site of a quiet kampong, and is now a beach strip with a range of hotels, a string of bars and restaurants. There is a government-run handicraft shop (*Kedai Kraf*) beside the beach, specializing in batik. A short walk north of Teluk Chempedak are Methodist Bay and Teluk Pelindong, which are beyond the range of most picknickers.

Pekan→ *Colour map 2, grid A5*

The old royal capital of Pahang, Pekan has a languid feel to it. It has a reasonably picturesque row of older wooden shophouses on the busy street along the river, but

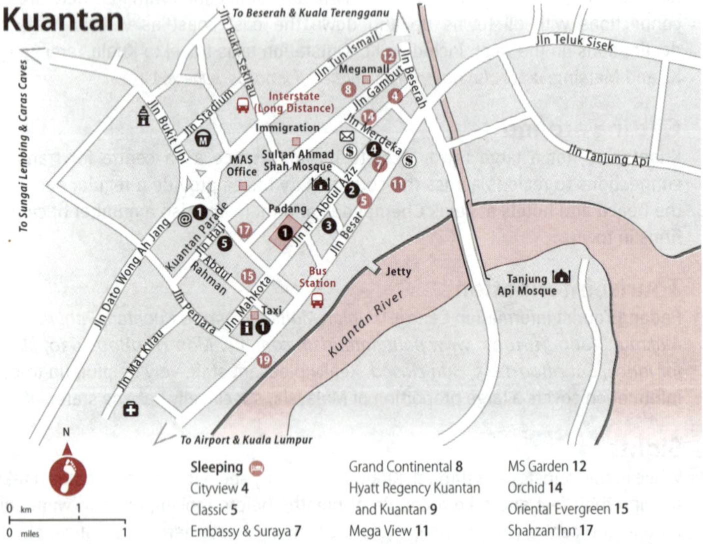

is otherwise not a particularly photogenic town. Aside from its mosques, Pekan's most distinguishing feature is its bridge, which straddles the Pahang River, the longest river on the peninsula.

Pekan means 'town' in Malay. It used to be known as Pekan Pahang, the town of Pahang. Even before the Melakan sultanate was established in the late 14th century, it was known by the Sanskrit name for town: *Pura*. It is divided into Old Pekan (Pekan Lama) and New Pekan (Pekan Bharu); the former was the exclusive abode of the Malay nobility for centuries.

There are two mosques in the centre of Pekan: the **Abdullah Mosque**, Jalan Sultan Ahmad (beyond the museum), and the more modern **Abu Bakar Mosque** next door. On the north outskirts of the town is the **Istana Abu Bakar**, the royal palace, just off Jalan Istana Abu Bakar. Its opulent trimmings are visible from the road, but it is closed to the public. The small but interesting **Sultan Abu Bakar Museum**, ⓘ *Jalan Sultan Ahmad, 0930-1700 Tue-Thu, Sat-Sun; 0930-1215, 1445-1700 Fri, RM1*, is housed in a splendid colonial building and has a jet-fighter mounted Airfix-style in the front garden. The museum includes a collection of brass and copperware, royal regalia, porcelain from a wrecked Chinese junk and an exhibition of local arts and crafts. In the back garden there is a depressing mini-zoo which rarely gets visited. It is home to Malayan honey bears, a tapir, a collection of monkeys, a black panther and a fish eagle, all squeezed into tiny cages. A good map of Pekan is provided.

Tasek Chini→ *Colour map 2, grid A4*

ⓘ *Getting there is not easy on public transport. A taxi should cost about RM80 and take 1½ hrs.*

Tasek Chini is an amalgam of 13 freshwater lakes, whose fingers reach deep into the surrounding forested hills, 100 km southwest of Kuantan. The lake and the adjoining mountain are sacred to the Malays; legend has it that Lake Chini is the home of a huge white crocodile. The Jakun proto-Malay aboriginals, who live around Tasek Chini, believe a *naga* (serpent), personifying the spirit of the lake, inhabits and guards its depths. Some commentators believe that as tourism begins to pick up there, Tasek Chini will acquire similar status to that of Scotland's Loch Ness, although Lake Chini's monster has not been spotted now for more than a decade. Locals call their monster 'Chinnie'.

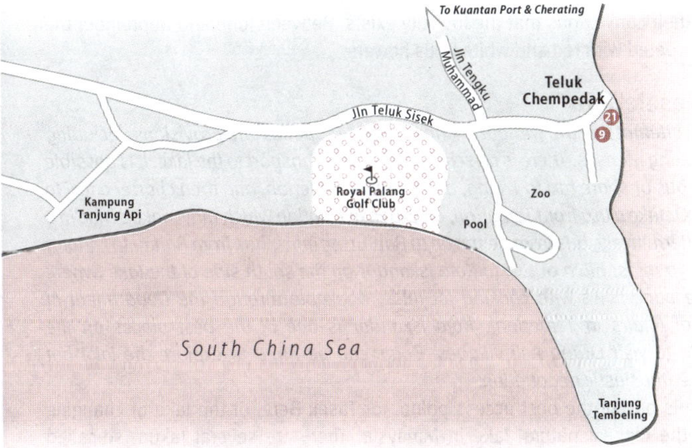

Tong Nam Ah **19**
Hyatt **21**

Eating
Foodstalls **1**
Tjantek Art Bistro **2**
Kheng Hop **3**
Z&Z **4**
Ming Teck **5**

Dateline Kuantan: Churchill's Malayan nightmare

"In all the war, I never received a more direct shock," wrote former British wartime Prime Minister Winston Churchill in his memoirs. "As I turned and twisted in bed, the full horror of the news sank in upon me." On 10 December 1941 Churchill got the news that a Japanese air strike force operating from Saigon (South Vietnam) had destroyed and sunk two of the most powerful warships in the Royal Navy.

HMS Prince of Wales, a 35,000-ton battleship, and *HMS Repulse*, a 32,000-ton battle cruiser, sank within an hour of each other, with the loss of 1,196 lives, 95 km off Kuantan. A few days earlier the ships had arrived in Singapore, then the biggest naval operations base in the world, to underscore Britain's commitment to protecting its colonies in the East. They were soon speeding north in an effort to pre-empt and disrupt Japan's amphibious invasion of Malaya, but the flotilla, which had no air cover, was spotted by a Japanese submarine. The first wave of Japanese fighter-bombers arrived at 1100; by 1233, the *Repulse*, its thick armour-plated hull holed by five torpedoes, was sunk. The *Prince of Wales* went down 47 minutes later in about 60m of water. Accompanying destroyers rescued 1,900 men from the two vessels before retreating to Singapore, which fell to the Japanese Imperial Army eight weeks later.

The wrecks of the two ships were declared war graves and in 1991, on the 50th anniversary of the Japanese attack, a team of British Navy divers laid white ensign flags on both ships to commemorate the dead.

More intriguing still are tales that the lake covers a 12th-14th century Khmer walled city. The rather unlikely story maintains that a series of aquaducts were used as the city's defence and that when under attack, the city would be submerged. In late-1992, however, the *Far Eastern Economic Review* reported that recent archaeological expeditions had uncovered submerged stones a few metres underwater at various points around the lake. But the Orang Asli fishermen do not need archaeologists to support their convictions that the lost city exists. Between June and September the lake is carpeted with red and white lotus flowers.

Lake Tasek Bera

ⓘ *Do not attempt this trip without taking adequate supplies and provisions, including basic cooking utensils. There is no scheduled public transport to the lake. It is possible to take a bus or share taxi to Triang, due south of Temerloh, and then charter a taxi to the lake. Or take a taxi from Temerloh, an expensive option which may make sense in a group. Alternatively, bus from Kemayan to Bahau, 45 mins; bus from Bahau to Ladang Geddes, 30 mins; hitch or taxi to Kota Iskandar on the south side of the lake (where there are bungalows with cooking facilities, bookable through the Department of Aboriginal Affairs in Temerloh). Kota Iskandar is one of the best places on the peninsula to visit Orang Asli villages. Boats can be hired to explore the lake but requires enthusiastic negotiation.*

Temerloh is one of the best access points for Tasek Bera, or the lake of changing colours, the biggest natural lake in Malaysia. There are several Jakun, so-called proto-Malays, and Semelai aboriginal kampongs (including the largest Kota Iskandar) around the lake, once a major centre for the export of jelutong resin, used as a sealant on boats and as jungle chewing gum. Similar to Tasek Chini (see page 257), Tasek Bera is a maze of shallow channels connecting smaller lakes, in all about

5 km wide and 27 km long. During the dry season it is little more than a swamp, but in the wet it becomes an interconnected array of shallow lakes. The Semelai traditionally exploited the expansion and contraction of the lake(s), fishing during the wet season and collecting non-timber forest products during the dry. When the waters reached their peak, and wild pigs became stranded on the many islands that dot the lake, the Semelai would hunt. One of the lake's resident species is the rare fish-eating 'false' gharial crocodile *(Tomistoma schlegeli)*.

Charah Caves

ⓘ *These lie 25 km northwest of town; take a right fork at the 24 km mark. Catch a Sungai Lembing-bound bus from the local bus station and get off at Panching, from here it is 3 km to the caves, although it may be possible to catch a lift on the back of a motorbike. Alternatively, Pahang Tourism runs tours to the caves.*

In 1954, the Sultan of Pahang gave a Thai Buddhist monk permission to build a temple in a limestone cave at Pancing, known as the 'yawning skull' cave. A steep climb up 200 stone steps leads into the cave which contains shrines and religious icons cut into the rock. The collection is dominated by a 9 m-long reclining Buddha, set among the limestone formations. There is always a monk in residence in the cave.

Beyond the caves is **Sungai Lembing**, ⓘ *T609-541 2377, Tue-Sun 0900-1800, RM1*, an old tin mine and the site of some of the oldest tin workings on the peninsula. It claims to be the deepest tin mine in the world. A museum has now opened to visitors.

Gunung Tapis Park

ⓘ *Permits can be obtained from the Sungai Lembing Tapis Resort (T9-5411339) or made through Pahang Tourism in Kuantan. It is only accessible by jeep via Sungai Lembing; from here accessible via a 12 km track.*

This state park, 49 km from Kuantan, offers rafting, fishing (the local fish, ikankelah, is said to be delicious) and trekking. The park is centred on Gunung Tapis which rises to 1,500 metres and can be climbed in three days. However facilities are still poorly developed although there are camp sites.

Beserah and Sungai Karang→ *Colour map 2, grid A5*

ⓘ *To get there, take a bus, hourly, from the main bus terminal in Kuantan.*

Once a picturesque fishing kampong, 10 km north of Kuantan, Beserah now sprawls and is not much more than a suburb of Kuantan. Beserah is a friendly place but aesthetically it bears little comparison with villages further north. Like Teluk Chempedak to the south it does provide a slightly quieter place to stay. There is, however, a local handicraft industry still; there is a batik factory to the north of the village. The village's speciality is *ikan bilis* (anchovies), which are boiled, dried and chillied on the beach and end up on Malaysian breakfast tables, gracing *nasi lemak* (rice cooked in coconut milk). Beserah's fishermen use water buffalo to cart their catch directly from their boats to the kampong, across the middle of the shallow lagoon. The kampong has become rather touristy in recent years, but there is a good beach, just to the north, at Batu Hitam.

Kampong Sungai Ular (Snake River Village)

ⓘ *Catch a bus running up the east coast road and asked to be dropped off at Kampong Sungai Ular.*

Sungai Ular, 31 km north of Kuantan, is a typical laid-back and very photogenic Malay fishing village. There is a small island, Pulau Ular, just offshore. The beach is usually deserted, is backed by coconut palms and has fine white sand. The Kampong is signposted to the right, just off the main road.

Temerloh

Situated on the Pahang River, Temerloh is the halfway point on the KL-Kuantan road and a popular makan stop. The Karak Highway tunnels through the Genting Pass, to the northeast of KL and the road then runs east through Mentakab (where there is a railway station) to Temerloh. From Temerloh it is possible to take a river trip to **Pekan**, the old royal capital of Pahang (see page 256) and to **Tasek Bera** (page 258). Frankly, there's not much to bring people to Temerloh, although it is emerging as an important administrative and service centre.

Sleeping

Kuantan *p255, map p256*

The upmarket hotels are mostly at Teluk Chempedak (4 km north of Kuantan, see page 256). There are plenty of cheap Chinese hotels in Kuantan itself, mostly on and around Jln Teluk Sisek and Jln Besar. Several smart new hotels have sprung up in the B-C range which offer excellent value for money.

A **Mega View Hotel**, 567 Jalan Besar, T9-5171888, F9-5563999. Large (150 rooms) and multi-storey hotel on the banks of the Kuantan River. Conveniently situated, offering comfortable rooms with telephones and televisions, some with views over the river. Services include restaurant, coffee shop, drinks lounge and karaoke. Aimed at businessmen, it offers a health centre to help unwind.

A **MS Garden Hotel**, Jln Lorong Garnbut T9-5177899, msgarden@tmnet.com.my. An enormous hotel, which is very elegant inside, at the business end of town. Restaurant and coffee garden. Includes breakfast. Promotional offers available.

B **Cityview Hotel**, Jln Haji Abdul, T9-5553888, cityview@pd.jaring.my Quite bare, with few extras but comfortable rooms. Good value. Breakfast included.

B **Hotel Grand Continental**, Jln Gambut, T9-5158888, www.grandcontinental.com.my Part of the *Grand Continental* chain, not much character but comfortable and smart, over 200 rooms all with a/c, TV, in-house movie, tea and coffee-making facility, other facilities include pool, coffee house, Chinese restaurant, health centre, business centre. Promotional rates available.

B **Shahzan Inn**, 240 Jln Bukit Ubi, T9-513668, F9-5135588. Plain-looking tower with snooty staff. Two-star facilities and a small shelterless pool. On the plus side, it's just around the corner from the spectacular Sultan Ahmad Shah mosque.

C **Classic**, 7 Bangunan LKNP, Jln Besar, T9-5554599, F9-5134141. A/c, extremely clean, big rooms and spacious attached bathrooms, certainly represents good value – recommended.

C **Hotel Orchid** 11 Jalan Merdeka, T9-5555570. Family-run hotel, very clean, rooms are large with attached bathrooms. Friendly and helpful owners, a/c, special group rates and 24 hrs service. Although small, highly recommended.

C **Suraya**, 55-57 Jln Haji Abdul Aziz, T9-5164266, F9-5126728. A/c, coffee area, simple, well-appointed rooms, attached bathrooms, video, catering mainly for business people and domestic tourist market, good value and nice staff.

D **Embassy**, 60 Jln Teluk Sisek, T9-5127486. A/c, well looked after, all rooms have attached bathroom, good value, above *Tanjung Ria* coffee shop, some rooms rather noisy because of main road.

D **Oriental Evergreen**, 157 Jln Haji Abdul Rahman, T9-5130168. A/c, Chinese restaurant, prominently advertised hotel. The décor leaves a bit to be desired, but it is clean and comfortable, great value. Recommended.

E **Tong Nam Ah**, 98 Jln Besar, T9-5144204. Fan, conveniently located for bus station and hawker stalls. Rooms are very basic (with a fan and basin).

Teluk Chempedak *p256*

Teluk Chempedak provides a more relaxed alternative to the noisier hotels in Kuantan.

AL **Hyatt Regency Kuantan**, Telok Chempedak, T9-5661234, www.kuantan.regency.hyatt.com/ A/c, several restaurants and bars, 2 pools, fitness centre, low-rise hotel in landscaped gardens and a beautiful setting on the beach, good sports (including watersports) facilities, well-stocked craft shop, well-managed with good views, Sampan Bar, an extension with new rooms. Friendly and efficient staff. Recommended.

B-C Annex Rest House, Jln Teluk Sisek, 2 km before Teluk Chempedak. Restaurant (rather inadequate), spacious grassy grounds.

B-C Kuantan, opposite *Hyatt*, T9-5680026. A/c, restaurant, very clean, cheaper rooms fan only but all have attached bathroom, noisy television lounge, very pleasant terrace for sundowners, although it now faces the Hyatt extension. The manager here is very helpful and friendly, and the place has a relaxed atmosphere. Recommended.

C Hill View, a/c, restaurant in block of karaoke lounges, bars and restaurants, not good value for money.

Pekan *p256*

There is a poor selection of hotels in Pekan; the government rest house is the best bet.

D Pekan, 60 Jln Tengku Ariff Bendahara, T9-71378. A/c, restaurant, badly run, but quite friendly people.

D Rumah Rehat (rest house), beside the football field (*padang*), off Jln Sultan Abu Bakar, T9-421240. A big, low-slung colonial building in need of a lick of paint with a cool, spacious interior and big, clean rooms, restaurant. It is advisable to try to book accommodation in advance if visiting during the Sultan's birthday celebrations.

Tasek Chini *p257*

C-F Lake Chini Resort, T4778000, F4772008. Ten chalets, some with attached bathrooms, a 10-bed dorm and camping, small restaurant attached to the resort serving simple dishes.

E Rajan Jones Guest House, this is the cheapest place to stay situated 30 mins' walk from the *Lake Chini Resort*, room rate includes all meals but the accommodation is very basic, no running water or electricity, tours and treks arranged.

Beserah and Sungai Karang *p259*

Most of the resort hotels are around Sungai Karang, 3-6 km N of Beserah village itself.

AL Swiss Garden Resort & Spa, Balok beach, Mukim Sungai Karang, T9-5447333, www.swissgarden.com/hotel. An international class hotel on the beach with over 300 rooms, gardens and a good pool, business facilities, health club and sauna, and much more.

A Coral Beach Resort (formerly *Ramada*), 152 Sungai Karang (about 6 km north of Beserah), T9-5447544, F9-5447543. A/c, restaurants, pool, paddling pool, playground, good range of facilities including tennis, squash, badminton, gymnasium, jacuzzi and watersports. Adjacent to fine white-sand beach, popular stop-over for cruises, hence its amphitheatre which can seat 800 people for cultural shows, all rooms spacious, a/c, TV, in-house video, mini-bar, tea and coffee-making facilities, non-smoking rooms available; *Reliance tour agency* in arcade.

A Le Village Beach Resort, Lot 1260 Sungai Karang, 8 km north of town, T9-5447900, fal@tm.net.my Indian management, a pleasant enough place with a pool and tennis, getting popular with tour groups.

B Blue Horizon Beach Resort, Kampong Balok (5 km north of Beserah), T9-5448119, F9-5448117. North of Beserah on a good beach, pool, clean and spruce with big wooden chalet rooms, built around central area, garden a bit of a wilderness, discounts often available.

B Gloria Maris Resort (1 km north of Beserah), T9-5447788, F9-5447619. A/c, restaurant, watersports, very small pool, sandwiched between road and Pasir Hitam (not such a good stretch of beach), small chalets and friendly management.

B Tiara Beserah Beach Resort, 812 Jln Beserah, T9-5448101, F9-5141979. Thirty-two rooms in new atap-roofed chalets, a/c, TV, pool, café.

E La Chaumiere, T9-5447662. This is the most popular of the budget places to stay, it is well run and pleasant, to get here ask to be let off at Kampong Pantai Beserah and walk towards Kampong Pelidong and the sea, about 1 km.

E-F Jaffar's Place, very rudimentary kampong accommodation, room rate includes all meals, away from the beach.

Temerloh *p260*

The accommodation in Temerloh is basic.

B Hotel Green Park, Lot 373, Jln Serendit, T2963055, F2962517. A/c, complimentary tea/coffee, TV, smartly furbished. Recommended.

B Seri Malaysia Temerloh, Lot 370/6/92, Jln Hamzah, T2965788, F2965711. One of the new budget chain, a/c, TV, money changer, restaurant, good value. Recommended.

C Rumah Rehat (*Rest House*), Jln Datuk Hamzah, T2963254, F2963431. Some a/c, restaurant, great position on the river, large rooms. Recommended.

C-D Ban Hin, 40 Jln Tangku, T2962331. Some a/c, better rooms with attached bathrooms, reasonable.

D-E Isis, 12 Jln Tengku Babar, T2963136. Some a/c, the best of the cheaper places to stay, more expensive rooms with attached bathrooms.

Eating

Kuantan *p255, map p256*

Eating out may present difficulties due to the language barrier and the apparent reluctance of locals to accommodate the uninitiated.

Cheun Kee, Jln Mahkota, large open-air Chinese restaurant, good selection of seafood.

Tjantek Art Bistro, 46 Jln Besar (opposite *Classic Hotel*). A funky art-cum-coffee shop also serving pasta, steaks, seafood, teas and juices. There's an art gallery on the first floor.

Cantina, 16 Lorong Tun Ismail 1 (off Jln Bukit Ubi), smart a/c restaurant with waiters in batik bajus, Indonesian-style seafood and curries. Recommended by locals.

Choo Kong, Jln Mahkota, Chinese noodles, cold beer, marble top tables, basic but good. Recommended.

Kheng Hop, 17 Jln Mahkota (on corner), opposite the playing field, big, lively old coffee shop with marble-top tables and good *nasi lemak* and *nasi daggang* in the mornings, unchanged for 50 years.

Kuantan Seafood, Jln Wong Ah Jong, opposite *BKT* (*Restoran Malam*), hawker-style stalls in big open restaurant, very popular.

Ming Teck, 253 Lorong Tun Ismail. Simple Chinese vegetarian place open 0700-1800 serving seriously genuine-looking fake meats and good meatless versions of Malay favourites such as *nasi lemak*.

Sri Patani, 79 Bangunan Udarulaman, Jln Tun Ismail, excellent Malay/South Thai food. Recommended.

Z & Z, 60 Jln Teluk Sisek (below *Embassy Hotel*), good breakfasts (especially *nasi lemak*), bright, sunny and friendly.

Zul Satay, junction of Jln Teluk Sisek and Jln Beserah (known as Kuantan Garden, between Kuantan and Teluk Chempedak), upmarket satay joint. All the usual plus rabbit and offal. Recommended.

Foodstalls

Malay cafés and foodstalls along the river bank, behind the long distance bus station, busy and popular. Recommended, especially for seafood. There are more hawker stalls on junction of Jln Mahkota and Jln Masjid (Taman Salera), next to the local bus station. **Kuantan Garden**, junction of Jln Teluk Sisek and Jln Beserah (between Kuantan and Teluk Chempedak), large number of Chinese stalls.

Teluk Chempedak *p256*

Chempedak Seafood, A-1122, Jln Teluk Sisek, big Chinese restaurant at the crossroads on the way to Teluk Chempedak, specialities: chilli crab and freshwater fish.

Pattaya, on the beach front, good views of the beach, serves crab priced by weight, good food and good value.

Selera Warisan, next door to the *Pattaya*. Good sea food and pleasant situation overlooking the beach.

Taj Mahal Curry House, 13 Teluk Chempedak, North Indian cuisine plus fish-head curry.

Foodstalls

Group of *gerai makan* in newish brick kiosks, next to the beach alongside the Handicraft centre. They serve Malay,Thai, Chinese and western food.

Pekan *p256*

There are a couple of reasonable coffee shops in the new town. The foodstalls on Jln Sultan Ahmad, near the bus/taxi stands, are the best Pekan has to offer.

Beserah and Sungai Karang *p259*

Pak Su Seafood Restaurant, popular Chinese restaurant on terrace next to the beach. Recommended.

Beserah Seafood, Malay/Chinese, speciality: buttered prawns.

Gloria Maris Golden Cowrie Restaurant, near the chalets, Malay/Indian/Thai and traditional Sun lunch at fixed price, seafood salad by weight.

Bars

Kuantan

Boom Boom Bar, 236 Jalan Teluk Sisik. Pool, bands and restaurant. Also on site, Mini Boom Boom, outdoor café.

Teluk Chempedak

The best bars and nightlife are along the beachfront at Teluk Chempedak. New karaoke bars and pubs have sprouted up in town, most with a distinctly Western theme. **Lips** and **Urban Beach**, situated on the main road into Chempedak, opposite the Hyatt carpark, both offer beer and karaoke, possibly a bad combination, but they are friendly enough, and make up for the general absence of night life in Kuantan where many restaurants close early in the evening.
Ranch Pub (formerly the Country Ranch), not far from the *Hyatt Hotel*. This pub comes recommended.
The Sampan Bar, on the *Hyatt Hotel* beachfront, is in the atap-roofed shell of a junk which beached in 1978 with 162 Vietnamese refugees aboard. The bar capitalizes on this slightly perverse novelty by charging more.

Shopping

Kuantan *p255, map p256*

Books Hamid Brothers, 23 Jln Mahkota (this place is also a money changer, recommended locally for efficiency and reasonable rates). **Syarikat Ganesh**, 18C Jln Besar; **Teruntum Enterprise**, Wakil Dewan Bahasa, Jln Mahkota. Several craft shops along Jln Besar, expensive and touristy.
Kuantan Parade, corner of Jalan Penjara and Jalan Haji Abdul Rahman. Fully air conditioned shopping plaza, offers western chain stores to those experiencing consumer cold turkey. Berjaya Megamall (between the *Grand Continental* and *MS Garden* hotels) with a cinema, Starbucks and boutiques.

Festivals and events

Pekan *p256*

October **Sultan's Birthday** (24th: state holiday) celebrated with processions, dancing and an international polo championship which the sultan hosts on his manicured polo ground at the istana.

Activities and tours

Kuantan *p255, map p256*

Golf

Royal Pahang Golf Club, KM5, Jln Telok Sisek, T9-5675811-2, F9-5671170, 18-hole course.
Astana Golf & Country Club, KM 13, Off Jln Sungai Lembing, T9-5687311, F9-5672519. 27-hole championship-standard course, and night golfing at this swanky resort.

Boat trips

Kuantan River Cruise. For information and booking, Jabatan Perhubugan Awam, Majilis Perbandaran Kuantan, Jalan Tanah Putih, T9-5121555/5121666, amjpa2@mpk.gov.my Leaving from the jetty at the IBU Pejabat MPK, this cruise takes in the mangrove swamps and jungle surrounding the Kuantan River. Boats leave at 1100 and 1430 and the excursion takes between 1-2 hrs.

The following operators include trips around the Kuantan area and river tours. **East Coast Holidays**, 13 Telok Cempedak, T9-5665228; **Reliance**, 66 Jln Teluk Sisek, T9-5102566. **SMAS Travels**, 1st Flr, Kompleks Teruntum, Jln Mahkota, T9-5113888.
Syarikat Perusahaan, 38, 2nd Flr, Bangunan DPMP, Jln Wong Ah Jang. **Taz Ben Travel & Tours**, 2nd Flr, Kompleks Teruntum, Jln Mahkota, T9-5102255.

Teluk Chempedak *p256*

Tour operators

East Coast Holidays, 13 Teluk Chempedak, T9-5665228/5676839, helpful staff; they offer tours to Lake Chini, the Panching caves and waterfall, Kapas Island, Kuala Trengganu and a Turtle watching tour. The company also offers services such as flight reconfirmation, hotel reservation and car rental.
Mayflower Acme Tours, *Hyatt Kuantan*, Teluk Chempedak, T9-5121469.
Morahols Travel, 11 Teluk Chempedak, T9-5100851.

Pekan *p256*

Polo

Matches are held in season; Prince Charles is said to have played here. The polo field is surrounded by traditional Malay houses.

Tasek Chini *p257*

Tour operators

There are a few tour companies which run package tours to the lake.

Malaysian Overland Adventures, Lot 1.23, 1st Flr, Bangunan Angkasaraya, Jalan Ampang, Kuala Lumpur, T03-2413569, is recommended.

Transport

Kuantan *p255, map p256*

Air

Sultan Ahmad Shah Airport is 20 km south of town. Regular connections with **KL** (MAS only). Taxis available for the journey to town (RM20).

Airline offices **MAS**, Ground Floor, Wisma Bolasepak Pahang, Jln Gambut, T9-5157055, F9-5157870.

Bus

Local bus station is on junction of Jln Besar and Jln Abdul Rahman. Regular connections with Teluk Chempedak; and Cherating.

Since the new highway linking KL and Kuantan the journey to capital only takes 2 ½ hours by road. The long distance bus station is on Jln Stadium and companies have their offices on the second floor. Regular connections with **KL**, **Mersing**, **JB**, **Singapore**, **Melaka**, **Penang**, **Kuala Terengganu Kota Bharu** and **Jeruntot** for Taman Negara. To get to **Cherating** take a bus from the local bus station on Jln Besar.

Car hire

Budget, 59 Jln Haji Abdul Aziz, T9-5126370 or *Coral Beach Resort*, 152 Sungai Karang, Beserah, T9-5447544. **Hertz**, *Samudra River View Hotel*, Jln Besar, T9-5122688. **National**, 49 Jln Teluk Sisek, T9-5127303.

Taxi

Taxi station on Jln Besar, next to the local bus station. **KL**, **Mersing** (RM140 for 4 people) and **Kuala Terengganu**.

Teluk Chempedak *p256*

Bus

Regular connections from **Kuantan**.

Car hire

Avis, *Hyatt Hotel*, Teluk Chempedak, T9-5661234, and Ground Floor, Loo Bros Bldg, 59 Jln Haji Abdul Aziz, T9-5123666; **Mayflower**, *Hyatt Kuantan*, Teluk Chempedak, T9-5131234; **Sinat**, Lot 3, *Merlin Inn*, Teluk Chempedak, T9-5141388.

Pekan *p256*

Bus

Bus stop on Jln Sultan Ahmad in the centre of town. Regular connections with **Kuantan** and from there onward although there are direct buses to **Mersing**.

Taxi

Taxis for **Kuantan** and elsewhere stand between Jln Sultan Ahmad and the waterfront, opposite the indoor market.

Tasek Chini *p257*

Bus and boat

Take the KL highway (Rt 2) from Kuantan towards **Maran**; 56 km down the road, Tasek Chini is signposted to the left and onwards to Kampong Belimbing. There are no buses, you will have to charter a taxi or use a tour agency. At Belimbing it is possible to hire a boat across the Pahang River and onto the waterways of Tasek Chini. It is also possible to be dropped off at the resort and picked up at an arranged time. An alternative way to get to Tasek Chini is by catching a bus from **Kuantan** or **Pekan** for **Kampong Chini** (12 km from the resort). From here there is a sealed road to the resort but, again, no public transport – although people have managed to persuade local motorcyclists to take them pillion.

Beserah *p259*

Bus

Several local buses from **Kuantan**'s main bus terminal all pass through Beserah, departures at least every hour.

Termeloh *p260*

Bus

The bus terminal is close to the centre of town. Daily connections with **KL**'s Pekeliling terminal, **Melaka**, **Penang**, **Kota Bharu**, **Kuantan**, **Alor Setar**, **Seremban**, **Kuala Lipis**, **Kangar** and **Ipoh**. Taxis run to **KL**, **Kuantan**, **Mentakab** and **Jerantut**.

Train
The nearest railway station is at **Mentakab**, 12 km west of Temerloh. Connections south with **Singapore** and north to **Kota Bharu**, see page 40 and41 for details of timetabling.

Directory

Kuantan *p255, map p256*
Banks Along Jln Mahkota and Jln Besar, between GPO and bus station. **Post** Jln Mahkota (east end). **Medical services** Hospital, Jln Mat Kilau. **Useful addresses** Immigration Office, Wisma Persektuan, Jln Gambut, T9-5142155.

Pekan *p256*
Banks Bumiputra, 117 Jln Engku Muda Mansur. **Post** In the middle of town.

Pahang's National Parks

→ *Colour map 1, grid C5, Altitude: 2,187 m*

Taman Negara is in a mountainous area (it includes Gunung Tahan, the highest mountain on the peninsula) and lays claim to some of the oldest rainforest in the world. This area was left untouched by successive ice ages and has been covered in jungle for about 130 million years which makes it older than the rainforests in the Congo or Amazon basins.

Kenong Rimba Park is home to the Batik Orang Asli tribe. It does not have the variety of wildlife but is less touristy and cheaper. *See Sleeping, Eating and other listings, see pages 269-272.*

Taman Negara National Park

Once known as King George V Park, Taman Negara was gazetted as a national park in 1938 when the Sultans of Pahang, Terengganu and Kelantan agreed to set aside a 43,000 ha tract of virgin jungle where all three states meet.

www.taman-negara.com for an overview on the park run by NKS travel.

The range of vegetation in the park includes riverine species and lowland forest to upland dwarf forest on the summit of Gunung Tahan. Over 250 species of bird have been recorded in Taman Negara, and wildlife includes wild ox, sambar, barking deer, tapir, civet cat, wild boar and even the occasional tiger and elephant herd. However, the more exotic mammals rarely put in an appearance, particularly in the areas closer to Kuala Tahan.

Ins and outs

Getting there Taman Negara straddles the mountainous interior of three states. Because it is one of the most popular destinations on the peninsular there are lots of ways to get here - by bus, by bus and boat and by train. *See Transport for further information, page 271.*

Best time to visit Between March and September, during the dry season. The park may be closed at the height of the monsoon season from the beginning of November to the end of December, when the rivers are in flood, although this isn't always the case.

Tourist information The Department of Wildlife has a bureau at the Kuala Tembeling jetty (see below) and issues permits and licences. You will need to get your permit before entering the park (bring photocopies of your passport). Park permit RM1; fishing licence RM10; camera licence RM5. Those who risk turning up at the Kuala Tembeling jetty without booking may be turned away if boats are full.

The park headquarters, ⓘ *daily 0800-2200*, are at Kuala Tahan, on the south boundary of the park, accessible by boat from Kuala Tembeling, a two-to three-hour beautiful journey. At Kuala Tahan all visitors are required to check in at the reception desk. Various companies run tours to Taman Negara. It is sometimes cheaper to do this than going it alone, but it does cut down on your options. Many visitors, particularly those unfamiliar with travelling in Malaysia, have recommended tours for their logistical advantages, although the park is also easy to visit independently. The disadvantage of independent travel is that tour groups tend to book up the hides. See Activities and tours for further information.

Equipment For trekking it is worth having walking boots for even the shortest of excursions as rain turns mud paths into skid patches, a thick pair of socks and long (loose) trousers. Leeches are common in the park after rain, spraying clothes and boots with insect repellent and wearing leech socks helps. Having said this, minimal clothing is needed, as it's hot work. A good torch is essential equipment for those going to hides and a water bottle is also essential on longer walks and treks. A raincover may be useful. Visitors are not permitted to carry glass into the park. The shop at Park HQ hires out torches, tents, water bottles, cooking equipment and fishing tackle - even jungle boots. A camera permit is RM5.

Hides Some hides *(bumbun)* are close to the park headquarters, as close as a five-minute walk, and nearly all are within a day's walk or boat ride. Visitors can stay

Taman Negara

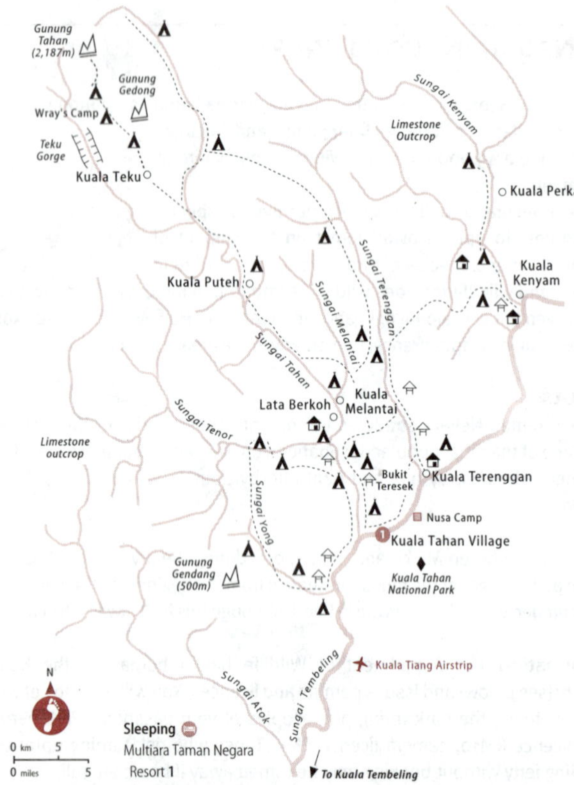

overnight, but there are no facilities other than a sleeping space (sheets can be borrowed from Kuala Tahan for RM5 per night) and a pit latrine. Take a powerful torch to spotlight any animals that visit the salt-licks. You are more likely to see wildlife at the hides further from the Park HQ, as the numbers of people now visiting Taman Negara have begun to frighten the animals away. Rats are not frightened: food bags must be tied securely at night. During popular periods and on weekends it is best to book your spot at a salt-lick.

Background

Gunung Tahan is the highest of three peaks on the east side of the park, and marks the Pahang-Kelantan border. Its name means 'the forbidden mountain': according to local Asli folklore the summit is the domain of a giant monkey, who guards two pots of magic stones. The first expeditions to Gunung Tahan were despatched by the Sultan of Pahang in 1863 but were defeated by the near-vertical-sided Teku Gorge, the most obvious approach to the mountain, from the Tahan River. The 1,000 m-high gorge ended in a series of waterfalls which came crashing 600 m down the mountain. Several other ill-fated European-led expeditions followed, before the summit was finally reached by four Malays on another British expedition in 1905.

Until the park was set up, **Kampong Kuala Tahan**, now the site of the park headquarters, was one of the most remote Orang Asli villages in North Pahang, at the confluence of the Tembeling and Tahan rivers. This area of the peninsula remained unmapped and mostly unexplored well into the 20th century. These days, Kuala Tahan is sometimes over-run with visitors; park accommodation has expanded rapidly under private sector management. But most visitors do not venture more than a day or two's walk from headquarters, and huge swathes of jungle in the north and east sections of the park remain virtually untouched and unvisited. Taman Negara now has scores of trails, requiring varying amounts of physical exertion; the toughest walk is the nine-day Gunung Tahan summit trek.

Treks

Trails are signposted from Park HQ. Tours are conducted twice daily by guides and these include night walks, cave treks and other treks and walks. Because most visitors tend to stick to the trails immediately around the Park HQ, even a modest day's outing will take you away from the crowds. A full listing and details on various routes can be obtained at Park HQ. Independent day treks/walks can be taken to caves, swimming holes, waterfalls, along rivers (again with swimming areas), to salt-licks and hides, and, of course, through forest. Longer overnight treks are also possible but guides must be taken on all these longer forays. The most demanding is climbing Gunung Tahan.

Gunung Tahan → *Altitude: 2,187 m*

This is a nine-day trek to the summit and back. It is best climbed in February and March, the driest months. **Day 1**: Kuala Tahan to Kuala Melantai (four to five hours). **Day 2**: Kuala Melantai to Kuala Puteh (eight hours). No streams en route; succession of tough climbs along the ridge, final one is Gunung Rajah; 1½ hours descent to campsite by Sungai Tahan. **Day 3**: Kuala Puteh to Kuala Teku (2½-4½ hours). Route follows Sungai Tahan, which must be crossed several times. The campsite is at the Sungai Teku confluence and was the base camp for the first successful Gunung Tahan expedition in 1905. **Day 4**: Kuala Teku to Gunung Tangga Lima Belas (seven hours). Long uphill slog (4½ hours) to Wray's Camp (named after 1905 expedition member). This is a good campsite; alternatively climb through mossy forest to Gunung Tangga Lima Belas campsite, which has magnificent views, but is very exposed. **Day 5**: Gunung Tangga Lima Belas to summit, returning to the Padang. After a scramble up the side of a rockface on Gunung Gedong, the trail leads to the Padang – a plateau area (three to four hours). Set up tents and leave equipment at campsite; route to summit follows ridge and takes 2½ hours. Essential to take raincoat; summit often shrouded in mist. Begin descent to the Padang by 1600. **Days 6-9**: Padang to Kuala Tahan, following the same route.

Gunung Gagau and Canopy Walk

ⓘ *A guide is necessary for this climb (around RM400 per week, RM50 for each additional day); maximum 12 people with one guide. A Sleeping bag and a tent are vital; all of the camps have water and firewood.*

Another mountain in Taman Negara that is less frequently climbed is **Gunung Gagau** (1,377 m), far to the northeast of Kuala Tahan. It is a six to seven day trek of which one day is spent travelling up river on Sungai Sat. This area of the park is rarely visited and it is advisable to take a guide.

The **Canopy Walk**, ⓘ *1100-1500 Sat-Thu and 0900-1200 Fri, RM5*, half an hour from headquarters, is worth a visit in order to take in jungle life at close proximity. The walkway is suspended about 30 m above the forest floor and stretches for over 400 m.

Fishing

Fishing is better further from Kuala Tahan (be aware that fishing is often prohibited); there are game-fishing lodges near the confluence of the Tenor and Tahan rivers, at Kuala Terenggan (up the Tembeling from Kuala Tahan) and at Kuala Kenyam, at the confluence of the Kenyam and the Tembeling. The best months to fish are February-March and July-August; during the monsoon season. At the height of the monsoon, in November and December travel can be difficult and the park sometimes closed. The rivers Tahan, Kenyam and the more remote Sepia (all tributaries of the Tembeling) are reckoned to be the best waters. There are more than 200 species of fish in the park's rivers including the *kelasa* which is a renowned sport fish. A permit costs RM10, rods for hire (see also Booking, Equipment and Sleeping, below).

River trips

Boat trips can be arranged from Park HQ to the Lata Berkoh rapids on Sungai Tahan (near Kuala Tahan), Kuala Terenggan (several sets of rapids to be negotiated), and to Kuala Kenyam (from where a trail leads to the top of a limestone outcrop). A trip to the rapids, misleadingly called a waterfall, by park authorities, on a boat that holds four passengers will cost RM80. Although this is a comparatively expensive way to see the park it is probably the most enchanting and when split between a number of people (boats carrying up to 12 people can be booked) is worthwhile.

Jerantut

The nearest town to Kuala Tembeling, the most popular entry point into Taman Negara, is Jerantut some 16 km away; a trip that costs RM15 by taxi. For those travelling to the park on public transport it may be necessary to spend a night here and there is a range of accommodation on offer.

Kenong Rimba National Park → *Colour map 1, grid C4*

Kenong Rimba Park is 1½ hours east of Kuala Lipis by boat down the Jelai River to Kampong Kuala Kenong. The park, which encompasses the Kenong River valley and encompasses some 120 sq km, is the home of the Batik Orang Asli tribe, who are shifting cultivators. There is a network of Asli trails around the park and several caves and waterfalls. There are two campsites along the river and chalets.

The park is a good alternative to Taman Negara. Though it may not have the same variety of animal life (and especially large mammals) it is less touristed and trekking here is cheaper.

Ins and outs

The park is managed by **Kuala Lipis District Forest Office** ⓘ *Government Office Complex, Kuala Lipis, T9-3121273*. Both a guide and permit are needed before you will be allowed into the park. For tours and treks to Kenong Rimba, see Activities and Tours, Kuala Lipis. Entrance to the park is from Batu Sembilan, jetty (20 mins) or an hour's boat ride from the jetty in Kuala Lipis.

Kuala Lipis

Kuala Lipis is a pleasant and relaxed town on the Jelai and Lipis rivers, 100 km north east of Fraser's Hill. Unlike other Malay towns it has not been thoughtlessly redeveloped and many colonial buildings still survive. This is probably because Malaysia's development has passed by Kuala Lipis. At the end of the 19th century it grew to prominence as a gold mining town and, for a short period, was the area's administrative capital. However, gold fever has passed (although the mines have been re-opened since) and the town's administrative role passed to Kuantan in 1955. Today, as well as being a good base from which to trek to Kenong Rimba, it has not inconsiderable charms.

Sleeping

Taman Negara National Park *p265*

Accommodation ranges from the resort, small hotels across the river, fishing lodges, chalets, visitor lodges for hides, hides and campsites.

A **Mutiara Taman Negara Resort**, Kampong Kuala Tahan, T9-2662200, www.malaysiaforestresorts.com. Accommodation, which must be booked in advance, runs the gamut from 8-bed dorms with fans, lockers and shared bath, to timber chalets and bungalows, some of them self-catering. Camping is also offered. The resort also runs a lodge in Kuala Terenggan with chalets and a restaurant.

An alternative to the park is to stay in **Kampong Kuala Tahan**, on the other side of the river (which can be crossed by a small boat throughout the day), where accommodation is much cheaper – albeit slightly less convenient:

B **Teresek Hill View**, T9-2663065, range of places to stay including dorm beds, basic chalets and more sophisticated bungalows with attached bathrooms.

D-C **Ekotown Chalets**, fan and a/c rooms, generally good reviews, but some plumbing worries.

E **Argoh Chalets**, basic doubles with fan and shower, dorm beds also available.

E **Liana Hostel**, T9-2669322, basic with 4 beds per room.

D-F **Nusa Camp**, T9-2662369, F9-2664369, restaurant, across the river from Park HQ and then 15 mins upriver, Offers a range of accommodation including dorms with two bunk beds per room, bungalows with attached bathrooms, and also tents for hire, the owner 'Byoing' is keen to help and will organize trips to the rapids (not particularly exciting), various hikes and trips to an Orang Asli village. To get to *Nusa Camp* take one of the longboats from Park HQ (there is a shuttle boat every 2 hrs); they also run a direct service from Kuala Tembeling with boats leaving at 0900 and 1400 daily (Fri 1445).

E-F **Tembeling Hostel**, much like *Liang* in price and standard, but 2 beds per room.

Fishing lodges

C-D There are a number of fishing lodges in the park, in which beds and mattresses are provided; there is no bedding or cooking equipment however. These can be booked at Kuala Tahan HQ.

Chalets

C-D There are chalets in various villages around the park, usually booked for tour agencies guests.

Visitor lodges for hides

B Visitor Lodges for hides at Kuala Terenggan and Kuala Kenyam can also be booked from Kuala Tahan HQ. These are right away from the crowds but are surprisingly comfortable with attached bathrooms and restaurant. There is no charge for staying in the hides themselves.

Hides

It is possible to spend a night in one of the wildlife observation hides. These are raised up among the trees at Tabang, Belau, Yong, Cegar Anjing and Kumbang.

Camping

F The *Mutiara Taman Negara Resort* rents out tents (2/3/4-person). There is an additional RM1 fee for use of their campsite. The landscaped campsite can accommodate up to 200, but fortunately never does. Tents, once hired, can be taken with you on treks. See map for campsite locations. There are communal toilet facilities and lockers are available.

Jerantut *p268*

B-E **Camp Nusa**, 16 LKNP Building, New Town Jerantut, T9-2662369, www.macroworld.com/tnegara/ 15 mins by boat from park headquarters. Wooden chalets through to A-frames and dorm rooms, as well as tent hire.

B-F **Sri Emas Hotel**, T9-2664499, www.taman-negara.com Some a/c, shower, the most sophisticated hotel in town, excellent source of information on the park, free transport to and from bus/rail station. *NKS Hotel & Travel* who run the hotel will also organize trips to the park and will book your accommodation there, dorm beds available – as well as a storeroom to leave your luggage while you are in the park. Internet cafe, movies and a (poor) restaurant here. Recommended.

C-D **Jerantut Guesthouse**, T9-2666200 (also run by *NKS*). Some a/c, restaurant, popular place with range of options including a/c rooms with attached bathrooms, simple fan rooms, they organize daily trips to the park.

E **Chet Fatt Hotel**, T9-2665805 adequate.

Kuala Lipis *p269*

C **Persona Rimba Resort Kenong**, Kuala Lipis, T9-3125032, F9-3121421. Simple wooden huts. Tours organised.

D **Hotel Jelai**, 44 Jln Jelai, T9-3121562. Near the Jelai River, convenient for boats to Rimba. Small, clean rooms, shared bathrooms with hot water and reasonable value.

D **Hotel Kuala Lipis** (aka *Appu's Guesthouse*), 63 Jln Besar, T9-3123142. Four rooms and two dorms, convenient for the train station. Some a/c, shared bathrooms run by Mr Appu who runs highly recommended tours to Kenong Rimba, good source of information. Recommended.

E **Gin Loke**, 64 Jln Besar, T9-3121388. Simple rooms, shared facilities, organizes treks into Kenong Rimba.

E **Hotel Tiong Kok**, Jln Besar, T9-3122044. Clean, good value.

Eating

Taman Negara National Park *p265*

Because of the cost of food at the resort, many tourists prefer to bring their own. The resort operates one restaurant and bar – the *Seri Mutiara*. On the other side of the river at Kampong Kuala Tahan are a number of floating restaurants which serve unremarkable food but at prices considerably lower than those in the park complex.

Jerantut *p268*

There are a number of Malay-style coffee shops in town as well as the usual stalls in the market area.

Activities and tours

Taman Negara National Park *p265*

Tour operators

Mutiara Taman Negara Resort, Kuala Tahan, T9-2662200, www.malaysiaforestresorts.com The Mutiara runs the only luxury resort in the park, their package deals include a stay (3 days, 2 nights for RM400 which includes two treks). It also runs a shuttle service from KL to Kuala Temberling jetty.

Jerantut *p268*

Tour operators

NKS Hotel & Travel, Hotel Sri Emas, Jerantut, T9-2664499, www.taman-negara.com Can also book shuttle bus and tour package at the *Pudu Hostel* in KL, T3-20789600 (see page 96). This company seems to have Taman Negara for the budget traveller all wrapped

For an explanation of the sleeping and eating price codes used in this guide, see inside the front cover. Other relevant information is found in Essentials, pages 45-49.

up. It arranges bus and boat transfers, hotel or guesthouse stay in Jeruntut, package tours, 4 days, 3 nights for RM350. Tours include boat trips, camping, trekking, stay at Orang Asli village and cave exploring.

Kuala Lipis *p269*

Tour operators

Mr Appu Annandaraja who runs the *Kuala Lipis Hotel* comes highly recommended as a trek organizer. He organizes a four-day trek including food and boat transport in and out of Kenong Rimba. Another guesthouse which organizes trips to the park for much the same price is the **Gin Loke Hotel**, 64 Jalan Besar. Organized treks into Kenong Rimba are also run by **Tuah Travel & Tours**, 12 Jalan Lipis, Kuala Lipis, T9-312144. There are other registered freelance guides who can be hired from Kuala Lipis.

Transport

Bus and Boat

Most visitors get a bus or taxi to **Kuala Tembeling** jetty via Jerantut. There are regular connections from **KL** via **Temerloh** and Kuantan. In addition, most guesthouses in **KL** can arrange tickets and also some tour companies – NKS Travel shuttle bus leaves from Petaling Street in KL's Chinatown (0745, RM30 oneway, 3 hrs). The Mutiara Taman Negara Resort's bus leaves outside the Hotel Istana in KL (0800, RM35). Both buses connect with a boat to the park. If you want to take a public bus, departures are from Pekeling bus station in **KL** (access via Titiwangsa LRT and Monorail station). You will need to catch the first bus to make the boat connection to the park in time.

At Kuala Tembeling there are boats to the Park HQ at **Kuala Tahan**, a 2½-hour upriver trip. The boats leave around 0900 and 1400 (1445 only on Fri) so if you are coming from KL, you will need to leave before 0900 to make sure you get the boat or you will have to stay in Jeruntut overnight. The return boat trip takes 2 hrs; departures at 0900 and 1400.

Nusa Camp also operates a boat service from Kuala Tembeling to their own resort.

Bus

Although it is now possible to go by road all the way to Kampong Kuala Tahan from **Jerantut** the boat journey is far more interesting and enjoyable. The road is rough and requires 4WD – transport is provided by guesthouses in Jerantut. There is a shuttle service from **Jerantut** to Kuala Tahan inside the park but these leave at 0830 and 1330.

Train

It is also possible to take the jungle train to **Tembeling Halt** via Tumpat (but tell the guard as it is an unscheduled stop!. It is accessible from KL, Kota Bharu and Singapore. There are two trains a day from KL, 1815 and 1955, both arrive around 0800); from here it is a 30-min walk to the jetty. This is probably the best way if you are coming from Singapore. Because the train from KL arrives in the early hours of the morning, you are better off disembarking at **Jerantut** and staying there. Trains from **KL** leave at 1815 and 1955 to arrive in Jerantut at 0102 and 0213. There is a daily mail train from **Singapore** that leaves at 0935 to get to Jerantut at 1749, where you will have to spend the night. There is also an express train that leaves at 2000 from Singapore and gets into Jerantut at 0336. From Kota Bharu you must take a taxi to Wakaf Bharu station (about 6 km outside). Trains from here leave at 1719, 1819, and 1919 to get to Jerantut in the late evening (the journey takes around six hours).

Jerantut *p268*

Bus and taxi

The bus and taxi station in Jerantut is in the centre of town. Regular connections from **KL**'s Pekeliling terminal via Temerloh. Taxis direct to Jerantut from KL leave from the Puduraya bus terminal. From the east coast, there three daily buses from **Kuantan** to Jerantut (0830, 1300 and 1500) as well as taxis. See also Taman Negara, Transport.

Kuala Lipis *p269*

Bus

Regular Transnasional bus connections with **Kuala Lumpur** leave from the Pekeliling bus terminal in KL (roughly every 90 mins between 0830 and 2030). Daily connections from **Kuala Lipis** with **Kota Bharu** and **Kuantan**. There are also connections with **Fraser's Hill**.

Train
There are two daily trains to Kuala Lipis from **KL**; the 1815 gets in at 0216, while the 1955 arrives at 0312. The 0935 mail train from Singapore arrives at 2000, and t he 1857 gets in at 0436. From **Kota Bharu** (leave from Wakaf Bharu station, 6 km outside), the 1719, 1819, and 1919 trains get into Kuala Lipis at 2154, 2254 and 0005. There are connections with **Jerantut/Tembeling Halt** (for Taman Negara).

Directory

Taman Negara National Park *p265*
Useful services Mutiara Taman Negara Resort has an expensive mini-market (selling goods for trekking and camping, 0800-2230), a clinic (0800-1615 Mon-Sun; hospital attendant on call 24 hrs, for emergencies), a mini-post office and a library. There is also a jungle laundry service. In the 'Interpretative Room', there is a thrice daily film and slide-show on the park's flora and fauna.

Kampong Cherating and around

Colour map 1, grid C6 Phone code: 09

A quiet seaside village, set among coconut palms, a short walk from the beach, Kampong Cherating has become a haven for those who want to sample kampong life or just hang out in a simple chalet-style budget resort. Over the years it has metamorphosised into something a little more sophisticated and upmarket.

Kemasik is the best beach close to Cherating but the highlight of the area is Rantau Abang, the nesting site for five different species of turtle. *See Sleeping, Eating and other listings, pages 276-279.*

Ins and outs

Getting there

It is a 40-minute drive from Kuantan's airport (regular connections by MAS to KL). Bus stop on the main road around 500 m from the kampong itself, down two lanes. Connections with most destinations on the east coast as well as with Singapore and KL. There are buses to Kemasik. Rantau Abang is also accessible by bus. *See Transport for further information, page 279.*

Tourist information

Badgerlines Information Services ⓘ *about 20 m down on left from lane leading from main road bridge, 0900-1700 and 2000-2200*, a good source of local information, independently run. **Cherating Travel Post** (next to *Mimis*), ticketing (buses, taxis, minibuses), car, motorbike, mountain bike, and boat hire, foreign exchange (including TCs, poor rate), book rental, newspapers and tourist information; organizes tours to Tasek Chini, night market, turtle hatching Terengganu National Park, batik factories and night-time jungle trek. Internet, overseas telephone calls and flight confirmation.

Sights

Cherating never was much of a kampong until the tourists arrived – there was a small charcoal 'factory', using *bakau* mangrove wood, but the local economy is now entirely dependent on sarong-clad Westerners and, more recently, growing numbers of Malaysian and Singaporean tourists. The beach at Cherating is big, but not brilliant for swimming because the sea is so shallow.

Cherating is named after the sand-crabs which are very common along the beach. They may look like heavily armoured tanks, but they are not dangerous. There are a couple of very private and extremely beautiful little beaches tucked into the rocky headland dividing Cherating beach and the *Club Med* next door. These are more easily accessible from the sea (boats can be hired from the kampong) than from the steep trail leading over the promontory. This path goes right over to the *Club Med* Beach which is private. Bathers and sun-bathers should be prepared for periodic low-level fly-pasts by the Royal Malaysian Army whose helicopters swoop over the beaches.

Cherating has grown explosively in recent years. Big, modern resort complexes have sprung up 3-km south of the original kampong; it is known as Cherating Bharu, (New Cherating). The old roadside village (together with the string of atap-roofed chalet resorts) is called Cherating Lama, or Old Cherating. Although the old kampong atmosphere has been irreversibly tempered by the arrival of *Anchor* Beer and the population explosion, Cherating is still a peaceful haunt with some excellent places to stay and one or two of the best bars in Malaysia. Cherating's Malay residents have taken the boom stoically – although their obvious prosperity has helped them tolerate the 'cultural pollution'.

It is possible to hire boats to paddle through the mangroves of the Cherating River, to the south side of the kampong, where there is a good variety of **birdlife** as well as monkeys, monitor lizards and otters. For a price there are also demonstrations of **silat**, the Malay martial art, top-spinning, kite-flying and batik-printing in the village. There are some monkeys in the kampong which are trained to pluck coconuts. A couple of kilometres up the road, on Cendor Beach, **green turtles** come ashore to lay their eggs; they are much smaller than the leatherbacks which lay their eggs at Rantau Abang, further north.

Cherating is also a good base to visit some of the sights in and around this part of the east coast including Tasek Chini (see page 257) and the Charas Caves (see page 259), for example.

Kampong Cherating

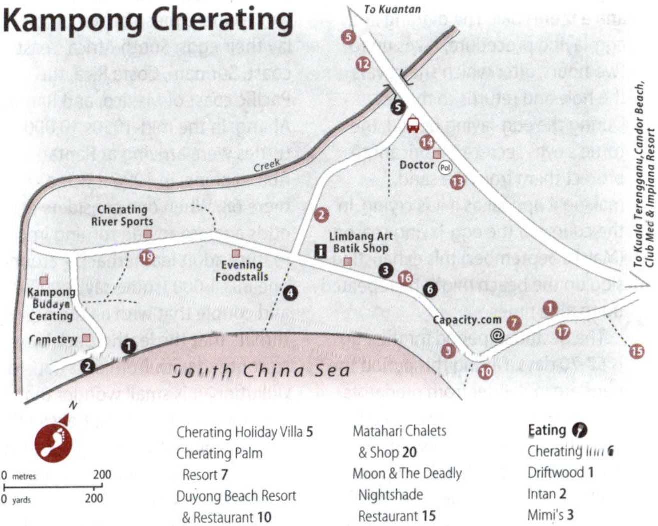

Sleeping
Cherating Bay Resort **1**
Cherating Beach Mini Motel **3**
Cherating Holiday Villa **5**
Cherating Palm Resort **7**
Duyong Beach Resort & Restaurant **10**
Legend **12**
Mak De's House **13**
Mak Long Teh's Guesthouse **14**
Matahari Chalets & Shop **20**
Moon & The Deadly Nightshade Restaurant **15**
Ranting Resort **16**
Residence Inn **17**
Tanjung Inn **19**

Eating
Cherating Inn **6**
Driftwood **1**
Intan **2**
Mimi's **3**
Seaside Seafood **4**
Sunrise Seafood **5**

The giant leatherback turtle

The giant leatherback turtle is so-called for its leathery carapace (shell). It is the biggest sea turtle and one of the biggest reptiles in the world. The largest grow to 3m in length and most of the females who lumber up Rantau Abang's beach to lay their eggs are over 1½m long. On average they weigh more than 350 kg, but are sometimes more than double that. They spend most of their lives in the mid-Pacific Ocean, although they have been sighted as far afield as the Atlantic, and return to this stretch of beach around Rantau Abang each year to lay their eggs.

The beach shelves steeply into deeper water, allowing turtles to reach the beach easily. They are not well designed for the land. It requires huge effort to struggle up the beach, to above the high-tide mark. After selecting a nesting site, the turtle first digs a dummy hole before carefully scooping out the actual nest pit, in which she lays up to 150 soft white eggs between the size of a golf ball and a tennis ball. The digging and egg-laying procedure, takes up to two hours, after which she covers the hole and returns to the sea. During the egg-laying period, the turtle's eyes secrete a lubricant to protect them from the sand, making it appear as if it is crying. In the course of the egg-laying season (May to September) this exhausting slog up the beach might be repeated up to nine times.

The gestation period for the eggs is 52-70 days. During this period the eggs are in danger from predators, so the Fisheries Department collects up to 50,000 eggs each season for controlled hatching in fenced-off sections of beach. The eggs are also believed to be an aphrodisiac and can be bought in wet markets for about RM1 each (a small quota is set aside for public consumption). Young hatchlings are regularly released into the sea from the government hatchery. Many are picked off by predators, such as gulls and fish, and few reach adulthood. The turtles have been endangered by drift-net fishing and pollution. It is also prized for its shell which is thought to have the most beautiful markings of any sea turtle. In nature it is used to camouflage, it is thought, the turtle against a dappled coral background. The 'tortoiseshell' is fashioned into combs and cigarette boxes.

In 1990 the government started fitting radio transmitters to leather-backs to enable satellites to monitor their movements in international waters. French satellite information is providing a stronger database on turtle populations and movements allowing the formulation of a more effective conservation strategy.

Even so, the leatherback turtle appears to be fighting a losing battle against extinction. There are just five main places in the world where these behemoths lay their eggs: South Africa's east coast, Surinam, Costa Rica, the Pacific coast of Mexico, and Rantau Abang. In the mid-1950s 10,000 turtles were arriving at Rantau Abang alone; in 1996 it was a mere 68. When one considers the odds against an egg turning into a mature adult leatherback – around one in a 1,000 (some say, 10,000) – and couple that with all the new threats that the leatherback has to contend with from drift nets to pollution, it is small wonder that some marine biologists believe this magnificent creature could, by the end of the millennium, be on the verge of extinction.

Green turtles come ashore to lay their eggs later in the season. For more details on these, see page 450.

Kemasik

On the road north from Cherating there are several stretches of beach, among the best of which is Kemasik. It is off the main road to the right (85 km north of Kuantan, 28 km north of Cherating), just before the oil and gas belt of Kerteh. Ask buses to stop shortly after windy stretch through hills. At Kemasik, the beach is deserted; there is a lagoon, some rocky headlands and safe bathing. There are no facilities.

Kuala Abang, Kuala Dungun and Pulau Tenggol

Turtles also come ashore at Kuala Abang, a few kilometres north of Dungun, which is much quieter than Rantau Abang, although there are still a few hotels. There are also several places to stay, although not right on the beach, at the small port of Kuala Dungun, famed for its *kuini*, a local mango. There is a weekly night market (*pasar malam*) in Dungun on Thursdays. From there it is possible to hire a boat to Pulau Tenggol, 29 km out, rumoured to be the best diving site on the East coast.

Pulau Tenggol is a small island renowned for having some of the best dive sites off the east coast of Malaysia. To get there head to Kuala Dungun, then take a speed boat (RM50, 45 mins) to the island. A boat trip is usually arranged via the Tenggol Island Resort, see Sleeping.

Rantau Abang → *Colour map 1, grid B6*

This strung-out beachside settlement owes its existence to turtles. Every year between May and September, five different species of **turtle** (*penyuin Malay*) come to this long stretch of beach to lay their eggs, including the endangered giant leatherbacks.

Every year, tens of thousands of tourists also make the pilgrimage. During the peak egg-laying season, in August (which coincides with Malaysia's school holidays), the beach gets very crowded. Up until the mid-1980s the egg-laying 'industry' was poorly controlled; tourists and locals played guitars around bonfires on the beach and scrambled onto turtles' backs for photographs as they laid. Conservationists became increasingly concerned about the declining number of giant leatherbacks that chose to nest on the beach and began to press for stricter policing and management.

Parts of the beach have now been set aside by the government, and access is prohibited; there are also sections of beach with restricted access, where a small admission charge is levied by guides. The Fisheries Department does not charge. Local guides, who trawl the beach at night for leatherbacks coming ashore, charge tourists RM2 a head for a wake-up call. Turtle-watching is free along the stretch around the Turtle Information Centre. The Fisheries Department also runs three hatcheries to protect the eggs from predators and egg-hunters: they are a local delicacy. The closest is five minutes' walk from *Awang's*. Officers from the department patrol the beach in three-wheeler beach buggies.

Do not interfere with the turtles while they are laying. There is now a ban on flash photography and unruly behaviour is punishable by a RM1,000 fine or six months' imprisonment. Camp fires, loud music, excessive noise and littering are all illegal, although the latter is not well enforced.

Rantau Abang Turtle Information Centre, ⓘ *13th Mile Jalan Dungun, T9-8441533, F9-8442653, Sat-Thu 0900-1300, 1400-1900, 2000-2300, Fri 0900-1200, 1500-2300 (Jun-Aug); 0800-1245, 1400-1600 Sat-Wed, 0800-1245 Thu, closed Fri (Sep-Apr)*, opposite the big *Plaza R&R*, has an excellent exhibition and film presentation about sea turtles, focusing on the giant leatherback. The Fisheries Department at the centre is very helpful and friendly.

Sleeping

Kampong Cherating *p272, map p273*

Many new bungalows and chalets have sprung up along the beach in the past decade; larger developments including the *Impiana* resort which has gone up about 2 km north of Cherating Lama. There is a good range of accommodation available, from simple kampong-style stilt-houses and 'A'-frame huts to upmarket chalets. Some of the accommodation in the kampong proper is family run; 'A'-frame and chalet accommodation is along the beach. The smarter, plusher hotels 3 km down the road at Cherating Bharu are much closer to the sea –and have a much nicer stretch of beach. 'A'-frame huts start at about RM10-15 while the more salubrious chalets cost from RM30-60. Note that the mid- and upper-range places whose guests are predominantly Malaysians and Singaporeans on weekend breaks, usually offer discounts during the week.

L-A **Cherating Holiday Villa**, Lot 1303, Mukim Sungai Karang, T9-5819500, www.holidayvillacherating.com/. A/c, restaurant, disco (boasts to be largest in town), pool, 2 rooms and 13 Malaysian chalets – corny but nice inside. Also offer 12 "Malaysia-style boutique villas' at the Eastern Pavilion, which come with their pool and Jacuzzi. Recommended.

AL **Impiana Resort Cherating**, Km 32, Jln Kuantan, T9-5819000, F9-5819090, www.impiana.com. A hotel with 250 rooms in spacious buildings elegantly decorated with wood and rattan, good range of facilities including pool, kid's pool, outdoor Jacuzzi, tennis, children's playground and playhouse with caretaker. Two restaurants, pub with happy hour, all rooms have balconies facing sea, a/c, fan, TV, in-house movies, CNN, minibar, four-poster wooden beds with nets. Recommended.

AL **Legend**, Lot 1290, Mukim Sungai Karang (Cherating Bharu), T9-5819818, www.legendcherating.com/. A/c, Italian and Thai restaurant, huge pool, villas near the beach with smartly appointed rooms, sports centre, tennis courts, watersports facilities, disco, rooms, which overlook big garden and beach, are pleasant and bright. Recommended.

A **Club Med** (round the headland from Kampong Cherating), T9-439131/591131, www.clubmed.com.au/. Renovated 2004-2005. A/c, restaurant, totally self contained resort designed to resemble a Malay village – private beach, watersports facilities, body-building classes, bungee bounce and yoga and evening entertainment, minimum stay: two nights. Closed Nov-Jan. The 'Circus Village' teaches children and adults to juggle, walk a tightrope or fly a trapeze – will be familiar to those who know Club Meds elsewhere.

A-B **Cherating Bay Resort**, T0193523836. Large new place with pool and children's play area, all rooms a/c. Five minute walk from the beach.

B **Cherating Bayview Resort**, Cherating Lama, T9-5819248, F9-5819415. Modern chalets on beach front, some with a/c and TV, restaurant, a good mid-range place to stay. Slightly overpriced for the fan rooms, shower and breakfast included in the room rate (although the owner warns that breakfast is not always guaranteed!).

B **Residence Inn Cherating**, T9-5819333, www.ric.com.my Located on the same lane as *The Moon*, at the northern end of the village, between the main road and the 'village street', pool, kid's pool, Jacuzzi, restaurant, disco, karaoke, comfortable rooms with a/c, minibar, TV. Breakfast included, attractive hotel which is also host to various cultural events.

C **Cherating Palm Resort**, T9-5819378 F9-5819328. Clean, modern chalets with TV, a/c, bathroom all set in an immaculately maintained garden. Good value.

C **Duyong Beach Resort**, Batu 28, T9-5819189 (left at end of lane from main road, at far end). A large number of modern chalets on the beach next to jungled hillside, mainly attracts Malaysian and Singaporean tourists, some rooms with a/c and TV.

C **Ranting Resort**, T9-5819068 (turn left at bottom of lane from main road bridge). Popular restaurant (Western and local dishes), extra for a/c and 2-room chalets on stilts, no TV, quite smart.

C **Tanjung Inn**, turn right at bottom of lane down from main road, after *Coconut Inn*, T9-5819081. Attractive choice of accommodation ranging from first class big bungalows for families to budget chalets (with communal shower and toilet), restaurant, set in carefully tended and landscaped grounds with palms and two ponds, has a good restaurant which serves excellent breakfasts. This is a charming place to stay. Recommended.

D Cherating Beach Mini Motel, T9-5819335. Under same management as neighbouring *Duyong Beach Resort*. Decent chalets on the beach, which is a pretty unique set up in Cherating, rooms have fan and bathroom.

D Cherating Ria Garden (opposite the *Coconut Inn*), T9-5819263. A small number of chalets and A-frames attached to a picturesque restaurant (see below), some with a/c, new bar and reception gives the impression that there has been some investment.

D Mak De's House, in the old village, next to police station, T9-5819316. *Mak De* has been offering kampong accommodation since the late-1970s but his chalets are now only available for long-stays so are not recommended for the average visitor. The proprietor has a long-standing reputation for hospitality and good food, quiet chalets in good condition.

D Mak Long Teh Guesthouse, T9-503290. Like *Mak De*, this family-run operation was up-and-running long before Cherating was discovered by main-stream tourists, friendly, with excellent Malay home cooking – again, and like *Mak De's*, it can be noisy.

D Matahari Chalets, T9-5819835. On the southern of the two lanes from the main Juantan-Kemaman road, no phone. Two rows of attractive bungalows facing each other, with a lawn of about 30 m in between. Some bungalows (with spacious verandahs) have fridges. One of the more pleasant places to stay here. Recommended.

D-E Moon, T9-5819186 or T0109077564 (the northernmost chalet resort on the loop off the main road). 'Come up, be welcome but beware, we are different, even a bit peculiar'. Fan and bathroom, attractive, more rustic chalets in spacious leafy grounds, up a hillside, excellent bar (see below) and restaurant, chalets and longhouse, much more tranquil surroundings than chalet resorts along the beach. Recommended.

Kemasik *p275*

AL Awana Kijal Beach and Golf Resort, Kijal, just south of Kerteh Airport, T603262 3555, F603261 6611, opened in 1996, same management as Genting Highlands, 5-star resort and 18-hole golf course, rather monstrous design, with extensive facilities, surrounded by golf course and the beach.

Kuala Abang, Kuala Dungun and Pulau Tenggol *p275*

AL-A Tanjung Jara Beach Hotel, Tanjung Jara, 6 km north of Dungun, T9-8441801, F9-8442653, www.tanjongjararesort.com A/c, restaurant, pool, the best known 5-star beach resort on the east coast, its Malay-inspired design won it the Aga Khan award for outstanding Islamic architecture, tour excursions, windsurfing, golf and tennis facilities, also offers local tours.

A Tenggol Island Resort, Pulau Tenggol, T9-8484862, tenggol@tm.net.my. A resort aimed at divers. Wooden chalets with attached bathrooms. As well as a first-class dive centre it offers windsurfing and sailing.

B Merantau Inn, T9-8441131. At the south end of the turtle beach, some a/c, restaurant, big, clean chalets above old fish ponds, past its prime, but 3 decent chalets on the beach. Not outstanding but reasonable value.

Rantau Abang *p275*

Rantau Abang's accommodation is strung-out along the main road; there are many overpriced, unpleasant little hovels. New places are opening and old ones closing all the time. Security is a problem here: it is inadvisable to leave valuables in rooms. The only upmarket place to stay near here is the beautiful *Tanjung Jara Beach Hotel* which is roughly halfway between Rantau Abang and Kuala Dungun, see above for details. Most hotels have their own restaurants.

B-E Ismail's, T9-8441054. Next to *Awang's*, good restaurant (only open in peak season), south of the Visitor's Centre, average beach-side set-up, similar to *Awang's*.

C-D Awang's, T9-8443500. Restaurant, some a/c, some rooms are very poor, the best are only average. Not good value for money.

C-D Dahimah's, T9-8452483. 1 km south of Visitor's Centre, restaurant, clean rooms in Malay wooden chalets. Some a/c.

Eating

Kampong Cherating *p272, map p273*

A few new restaurants have sprung up along the main road. Since most chalet hotels have restaurants there's few outside food outlets, but there are plenty of foodstalls.

Sunrise Seafood Restaurant, one of the new restaurants on main road, pleasant terrace set back from road, Western and local dishes.

Cherating Inn Restaurant, a small place that produces unusually good roti and the Cherating Inn Pancake (made with coconut).

Intan Restaurant, along from the Cherating Bayview. A Malay seafood restaurant with local touches and an extensive menu.

Mimi's Restaurant, Services and Tours (left at end of lane from main road, on left), restaurant inefficient, and tours par for the course, but *Mimi's* offers useful laundry service.

Restoran Duyong, T9-5819578 (inside the *Duyong Beach Resort*), lovely setting on raised wooden terrace at edge of beach, lobster and prawns sold by weight, good selection of Western and local dishes.

Seaside Seafood, opposite *Cherating Cottages*, on the beach. Good Chinese/Malay seafood restaurant where you can choose your own fish and it will be grilled on banana leaves. One of the most popular restaurants in Cherating. Recommended.

The Deadly Nightshade (part of *The Moon* chalet resort at northwest end of loop off main road), also known as 'the restaurant at the end of the universe', enchantingly vague menu, mainly Western with some concessions to local tastes, great atmosphere.

Rantau Abang *p275*

There are roadside stalls and coffee shops near the bus stop

Awang's, right on the beach, Awang was formerly the chef at the *Tanjung Jara Beach Hotel*.

Ismail's also has a restaurant and there are some stalls in the **Plaza R&R; Mikinias**, just down from *Awang's*. Big menu but service is slow if it gets busy.

Bars

Kampong Cherating *p272, map p273*

The Moon (part of chalet resort of same name at northwest end of loop off main road), great bar amid atap and leafy foliage. Recommended.

The Driftwood, at southern end of beach, very laid back, serves Western food.

Entertainment

Kampong Cherating *p272, map p273*

Kampong Budaya Cherating (Cherating Cultural Centre), western end of the village street, before the *Cherating Bay View Resort*, pavilion-style attraction, in landscaped garden with a big rather uncosy restaurant, where shows take place. Batik painting, top spinning, songkhet weaving and other typical east coast activities can be seen.The work of artist Ayam is particularly worth a look.

Shopping

Kampong Cheratang *p272, map p273*

Batik

There are several batik shops in Cherating; all the artists offer classes; prices (which include tuition) T-shirt RM30-35, sarong RM35, singlet RM20. **Limbang Art** (left at bottom of lane down from main road bridge), mainly shirts, t-shirts painted by *Munif Ayu Art* (on lane down from main road bridge); **Cherating Collection** (in old village, next to main road and *Mak De's*), designs more colourful and abstract than its two local competitors; **Matahari Chalets** local artist Ayu sells his batik t-shirts here and does batik painting classes.

Handicrafts

Next to *Cherating Cottages* is a large craft superstore endorsed by Club Med. Endorsement of this type, of course, may do more harm than good and some visitors will want to keep the place at a sarong's length. Certainly, a fair proportion of the products do have that mass-produced look, but it does stock some unusual woodwork and good batik.

Activities and tours

Kampong Cherating *p272, map p273*

Cherating River Sports Centre, T0199653591, opposite Tanjung Inn. Organises kayaking, river trips, Snake Island trip, fishing, snorkelling and turtle watching. Boat trips are organized from here and from the two other tourist information centres and by several beach hotels/chalets. Six people are needed to fill a boat, with a full boat approximately RM8 per person, depending on distance up river.

Golf

Kelab Golf Desa Dungun, T9-8441041, Dungun, 18 holes.

Watersports

Cherating Beach Recreation Centre, arranges water skiing and windsurfing. **Club Med**, Mile 29, Jalan Kuantan. T9-5819133, F9-5819172. Watersports facilities and body-building classes open to non-guests.

Transport

Kampong Cherating *p272*

Air

Kuantan Airport is about a 45 min-drive from Cherating.

Bus

Regular buses from Kuantan (Kemaman bus). Bus stops at both ends of the kampong. Regular connections with **Rantau Abang**, **Kuala Terengganu**, **Marang**, **Kota Bharu**. Buses also depart for **KL** and **Singapore**.

Kuala Abang, Kuala Dungun and Pulau Tenggol *p275*

Bus

Express buses leave for **Kuantan, Mersing, KL** and **JB/Singapore**.

Rantau Abang *p275*

Bus

Regular connections with **Kuala Terengganu** and **Kuala Dungun** from opposite *Turtle Information Centre*. From Kuala Dungun connections with Kuantan and other destinations.

Directory

Kampong Cherating *p272*

Banks See *Cherating Travel Post*, below. The nearest bank is at Kemaman, 12 km north.

Internet Cheráting Travel Post (next to *Mimis*, see below); Cherating Library and Cyber Café ('Capacity.com'), T095819330, closed Wed.

Kuala Terengganu and around

→ *Colour map 1, grid B6*

The royal capital of Terengganu state was a small fishing port (the state accounts for about a quarter of all Malaysia's fishermen) until oil and gas money started pumping into development projects in the 1980s. The town has long been a centre for arts and crafts, and is known for its kain songket, *batik, brass and silverware. The focal point of the town is the Pesar Besar Kedai Payang market place. The town's colourful history is revealed in the chinese shophouses and temple, in the Zainal Abdin Mosque and the ceremonial house of Istana Maziah, once home to the Terengganu royal family.*

Around Kuala Terengganu numerous kampongs specialise in handicrafts. Marang is a colourful Malay fishing village and Pulau Kapas has some laidback beaches. » *See Sleeping, Eating and other listings, pages 283-287.*

Ins and outs

Getting there and around

The airport is 18km from town. A taxi costs RM15 from the airport to town. Buses also connect with major destinations across the country. There are plenty of taxis in the area. ▸▸ *See also Transport, page 287.*

Tourist information

Tourism Malaysia, ⓘ *5th Flr, Menara Yayasan Islam Terengganu, Jln Sultan Omar, T9-6221433, F9-6221791.* **State Tourist Information Centre (TIC),** ⓘ *Jln Sultan Zainal Abidin, near the Istana Meziah on the jetty, T9-6221891.0900-1700, Sat-Thu,* impressive looking place bursting with information. See also www.terengganutourism.com, website for the state tourism industry.

Background

Like neighbouring Pahang, Terengganu state was settled at least as far back as the 14th century, and over the years has paid tribute to Siam and, in the 15th century, to the sultanate of Melaka. When the Portuguese forced the Melaka royal house to flee to Johor, Terengganu became a vassal of the new sultanate. In the 18th century, Terengganu is recorded as having a thriving textile industry; it also traded in pepper and gold with Siam, Cambodia, Brunei and China. A Chinese merchant community grew up in Kuala Terengganu. In 1724, the youngest brother of a former sultan of Johor, Zainal Abidin, established Terengganu as an independent state and declared himself its first sultan. Today's sultan is a direct descendant. The state has always been known for its ultra-conservative Islamic traditions.

Sights

The **Pasar Besar Kedai Payang,** (Pasar Payang or central market), ⓘ *0700-1800,* the main market place on Jalan Sultan Zainal Abidin, is the busiest spot in town – particularly in the early morning, when the fishing fleet comes in. On the second floor, the market sells batik, brocade, songket, brassware, and basketware as well as fruit and vegetables on the first floor. **Jalan Bandar,** leading off from the market, is a street of old Chinese shophouses and there is also a busy and colourfully painted Chinese temple. Nearby is the imposing **Zainal Abdin Mosque,** on Jln Masjid. Not far from the mosque (on the other side of Jalan Kota) is the apricot-coloured **Istana Maziah,** the old home of Terengganu's royal family, built in French style. It is now only used on ceremonial occasions and is not open to the public.

Some of Kuala Terengganu's older buildings have fine examples of traditional Malay carvings. Another of these traditional houses was taken apart and reassembled in Kuala Lumpur in the grounds of the National Museum as an example of classical Malay architecture.

The **State Museum,** ⓘ *0900-1700 (closed Fri), RM5. Take a local bus from the local bus station (15-minute journey),* one of the largest in the country, is situated in Losong, a town 5 km southwest of the city. The museum is at the end of Jalan Losong Feri, facing Pulau Sekati. It exhibits rare Islamic porcelain, silver jewellery, musical instruments and weaponry – including a fine selection of *parangs* and *krises*. It is an eclectic collection, erratically labelled. **Bukit Puteri,** near the Istana, has fortress remains on it and provides excellent views of the town.

Around Kuala Terengganu

There is a thriving cottage industry and many of Malaysia's best-known handicrafts are made locally. Surrounding kampongs practise silverwork, batik-printing, songket-weaving and *wau* kite-building, but the best way to see these under one roof is in the **Cendering handicraft centres** (see below). Cendering lies 7 km south of Kuala Terengganu. *Kraftangan Malaysia,* ⓘ *0800-1630 Sat-Wed, 0830-1200 Thu; take Marang-bound buses from Jalan Syed Hussin. The turning is clearly signposted off the main road,* with a beautifully displayed selection of silver, woodwork, silk, batik, brass and basketware as well as handicrafts from elsewhere in Malaysia, is very classy compared with Rusila (see below). Next door to *Kraftangan Malaysia* is the huge *Nor Arfa Batik Factory,* ⓘ *T9-6175700*, producing modern and traditional designs and readymades. Behind *Kraftangan Malaysia* is the *Sutera Semai* silk factory.

Pulau Duyung Besar ⓘ *take a minibus from the local station. Or take a boat (RM0.50) to the island from the little jetty behind the Seri Malaysia,* is the largest island in the Terengganu Estuary and famed for its boat-building. It mainly survives by custom-building yachts.

The **Floating Mosque** ⓘ *take any southbound bus*, is situated on the estuary of the Ibai River. Its name is a slight misnomer; it has been built in such a way that it gives the illusion of floating. Located 6 km from town.

Kampong Pulau Rusa, ⓘ *take a boat from the jetty on Jalan Sultan Zainal Abidin. The village can also be reached by bus from the bus station on Jalan Syed Hussin*, is a songket-weaving and batik centre, 6 km upriver, and is known for its traditional Petani-Terengganu wooden houses.

Batu Buruk beach, running down the northeast side of KT, is not safe for swimming. But there are some good beaches near Kuala Terengganu: Merang 30 km (see page 288) and Batu Rakit 20 km north. There is a guesthouse at the latter. There are regular buses to both beaches from Jalan Syed Hussin.

Numerous **islands** lie off shore from Kuala Terengganu including **Pulau Redang** (see page 288) . Boats leave for the islands from Merang and from the Shah Bandar

Kuala Terengganu

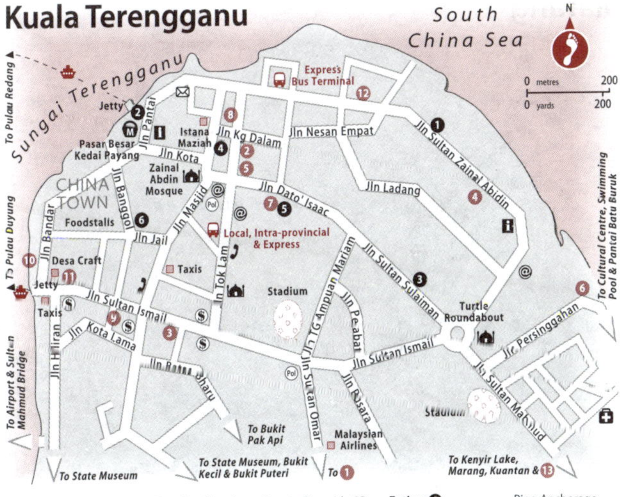

Sleeping
Gran Continental 12
Grand Paradise 2
Kenangan 3
KT Mutiara 3
KT Travellers' Inn 4
Midtown 5
Motel Desa 1
Ping Anchorage 7
Primula Parkroyal 6
Qurata Riverside 13
Seaview 8
Seri Hoover 9
Seri Malaysia 10
Terengganu 11

Eating
Chef's Steak House 1
Kt Wok 3
Mali 6
Ping Anchorage Traveller's Café 5
Taufik 4
Terapung Puteri 2

 jetty in Kuala Terengganu, from which there are now scheduled departures (you'll need a booking at a resort to take the boat from here). **Pulau Lang Tengah** also has good diving. Boats from Merang jetty are arranged via a resort booking. The best diving, reportedly, off the east coast of Malaysia is off **Tenggol Island**. Boats leave from Kuala Dungun, about a 1 ½ hour drive from Kuala Terengganu.

Peladang Setiu Agro Resort, ⓘ *83 km west of Kuala Terengganu, T609-6977136, http://welcome.to/agrosetiuis* set in the midst of tropical forest and offers a 280-ha plot, complete with lakes, arboretum, mini bird park, swimming pool and, for the enthusiast - an obstacle course. Popular with groups, if also provides a campsite.

Marang → *Colour map 1, grid B6*

ⓘ *To get into the town from the main road, follow signs to LKIM Komplex from the north end of the bridge. Half-day river tours, fishing and snorkelling trips are organized by MGH (Marang Guest House), little office by the small jetty, daily 0900-1700, T9-6181976, F9-6181976.*

This is a colourful Malay fishing kampong at the mouth of the Marang River, although it is not as idyllic as the tourist literature suggests. Marang has been buffeted by the vagaries of the tourist industry over the last couple of decades. In the 1980s and 1990s there was a rush to put up budget accommodation, placing it firmly on the tourist map for the first time. Then, by the mid-to late-1990s the kampong began to acquire a bit of a run-down look as the early developments lost their sheen. Now, a number of new, plusher developments along the shorefront in Marang Town have instilled a slightly more chi-chi atmosphere to the place. Notwithstanding all these twists and turns, it is still a very lovely village, with its shallow lagoon full of fishing boats. The best beach is opposite Pulau Kapas at Kampong Ru Muda. It was the centre of a mini-gold-rush in 1988 when gold was found 6 km up the road at Rusila. On the road north of Marang there are a number of batik workshops, all of which welcome visitors.

Pulau Kapas

ⓘ *Many hotels in Marang offer day trips to the islands. Several companies run boats throughout the day to the island, the prices are the same (fast boat, RM25 return, 20 mins, from 0930 until 1700). Their offices are crowded around the jetties and they can also arrange accommodation on the island, although this is easy to do yourself once you get there. Zack at the Suria Link Boat Service is very helpful and his office is a good place to buy boat tickets. Zack also dispenses with unequivocal travel advice. MGH is also recommended. When you pay for your ticket you must tell them what time and day you want to be picked up, or else you can get your resort to phone for you, so remember to keep the number of the agency you booked your boat with.*

Pulau Kapas is 6 km (20 minutes) off the coast, with some good beaches and with a very low key, laid back atmosphere. Those wanting a quiet beach holiday should avoid weekends and public holidays when it is packed. The coral here has been degraded somewhat and there is much better snorkelling at **Pulau Raja**, just off Kapas, which has been declared a marine park. All the guesthouses organize snorkelling and the *Kapas Garden Resort* also has scuba equipment. There is a new resort on the privately-owned Pulau Gemia (Gem Island), just under 1 km from Kapas.

Sleeping

Kuala Terengganu *p279, map p281*

There are only a couple of hotels at the top end of the market but there are several cheaper hotels scattered round town, mainly at the jetty end of Jln Sultan Ismail and on Jln Banggol, but the selection is not great.

AL Hotel Grand Continental, Jln Sultan Zainal Abidain, T9-6251888, www.grandhotelsinternational.com.my Not too far from the express bus station. The swankiest in Kuala Terengganu. A typical plush chain hotel with huge rooms. The best thing about this place is the great view of the coast. There's all the usual facilities – swimming pool, restaurants, cable TV.

A Primula Parkroyal, Jln Persinggahan, T9-6222100, www.primulaparkroyal.com A/c, restaurant (good Malay-food buffet), nice pool, highrise hotel with all mod-cons but rooms are shabby and not soundproofed, they do have a sea view though, also organizes island excursions. Great value for money.

B Kenangan, 65 Jln Sultan Ismail, T9-6222688. A/c, restaurant, bathroom. Slightly cheaper than the *KT Mutiara* next door and not nearly as nice.

B KT Mutiara, 67 Jln Sultan Ismail, T9-6222655, F9-6236895. A/c, shower (hot water), TV. Good value.

B Midtown, Jln Tok Lam, T9-6235288, ythotel@po.jaring.my Two-star hotel in greyish block on corner. A/c, laundry, business centre, tea/coffee-making facilities, fridge, restaurant, serves good breakfast. In the centre of town with good facilities.

B Seri Malaysia, Lot 1640, Jln Hiliran, T9-6236454, www.serimalaysia.com.my A/c, restaurant (good, inexpensive), another in the well-run modern *Seri Malaysian* chain, a/c, TV, minibar, light airy rooms overlooking the river. Recommended.

B-C Grand Paradise, 28 Jln Tok Lam, T9-6228888, www.paradisegroup.com.my A/c, shower (hot water), TV. Quite good value although the bathrooms are matchbox size and not all rooms have windows. Tired-looking now.

C KT Travellers Inn, 201, 1st Flr, Jln Sultan Zainal Abidin, T9-6223666, F9-6232692. Stuck out on busy road downtown, a/c, TV, clean rooms. Quite expensive for what you get. Very busy.

C Motel Desa, Bukit Pak Api, T9-6223033, F9-6223863. A/c, TV, in-house video, minibar, restaurant, pool, set in gardens on a small hill overlooking the town, a possibility for those with own transport.

C Qurata Riverside, Lot 175K Kuala Ibai, T9-6175500, F9-6175511. Small and friendly hotel, 7 km south of Kuala Terengganu, 21 rooms in individual wooden chalets on stilts near the Kuala Ibai River. Designed by a nephew of the local royal family to resemble a Malay village, set in meticulous garden, only marred by proximity of main road, comfortable rooms with wood floors, a/c, ceiling fans, TV and shower room. At low tide it is possible to walk across the river mouth to nearby sand beach. Recommended.

C **Seaview Hotel**, 18a Jln Masjid Abidin, T9-6221911, svhotel@yahoo.com. Slightly overpriced but near the jetty with clean, comfortable rooms, a/c, centrally located opposite Istana Maziah, good mid-range place to stay.

C **Seri Hoover**, 49 Jln Sultan Ismail, T9-6233833, F9-6225975. A/c, restaurant, large, rather ugly hotel with 71 rooms but they are big and clean, bathrooms with hot water, although slightly musty smell.

C-D **Terengganu**, 12 Jln Sultan Ismail, T9-6222900. A/c, cheaper with fan, rooms could do with lick of paint but clean and reasonable value. Staff not particularly friendly or helpful.

E **Ping Anchorage**, 77A Jln Sultan Sulaiman, T9-6262020. The most popular traveller place to stay in town with dorms and fan rooms, one room has a/c and hot water bathroom, the rest share cold water showers. The company is now a very successful tour company, but the rooms here, while functional, cheap and clean are very uninspiring and the mattresses a bit squashy.

F **Awi's Yellow House**, Pulau Duyung Besar, T9-6245046, rohanilongvet@hotmail.com Built out over the river on stilts and is very popular with budget travellers. Dorm and atap-roofed huts, some with balconies over the river, pleasant location with cool breezes, there are some stalls at the bus stop near the bridge, but most travellers bring their own food from KT and have use of kitchen facilities, *Awi's Yellow House* is not yellow and can be hard to find but is well enough known to sniff out. Take a boat from jetty on Jln Bandar – last boat around 2200 – or by road, via the new Sultan Mahmud bridge (taxis or bus from KT).

Marang *p282, map p282*

There are hotels and guesthouses in Marang itself and in Kampong Rhu Muda, about 2 km before the bridge over the Marang River.

B **Seri Malaysia Marang**, Lot 3964, Kampong Paya, T9-6182889, F9-6181289. One of the *Seri Malaysia* chain, opened in 1995, good value, views of Pulau Kapas, a/c, TV, restaurant, launderette, organizes island trips, the best option along this row of accommodation although not extravagant, breakfast included. However the restaurant is overpriced, the variety of food available limited, and the service slap-dash.

B-D **Angullia Beach House**, 12¼ milestone, Kampong Rhu Muda, T9-6181322, F9-6181322. Some a/c, restaurant (with good set meal), extremely friendly, family run chalet resort on lovely stretch of beach opposite Pulau Kapas (therefore sheltered), leafy, well-kept grounds and very clean chalets (no alcohol served), some visitors reckon it is overpriced. Recommended.

C **Island View**, opposite the lagoon, T9-6182006. Some a/c, free bicycles, chalets with attached bathrooms and some simpler rooms, popular. Very attractive setting with a central bougainvillea garden to relax in. However be prepared to share your room with various visitors from the animal kingdom. A little run down now.

C-D **Travellers Check Point**, (aka *Marang Guest House and Restaurant*). On the hill top above Kamal. Scenic views of the lagoon and sea beyond. Clean and friendly, good restaurant, with TV lounge and seating area with games. Well-built chalets with a/c or fan, excellent value for money. Connected to MGH Travel Centre.

C-E **Mare Nostrum Holiday Resort**, Kampong Rhu Muda, T9-6182417. A/c, restaurant, clean and hospitable, boat trips, pleasant little resort next door to *Angullia*, well-kept compound (if a little cramped) and clean chalets. Recommended.

D-E **Nusantara Hostel**, Kompleks Pelancongan, T9-6185733. Opposite the park between the two jetties. Basic rooms, including small dorms (RM10) all with shared cold water showers. The place has a friendly family environment while the odd furniture gives it some character. Fishing trips, tours and general travel advice offered.

E **Green Mango Inn**, A-71 Bandar Marang, T019 9469409. Fan, small, bare A-frame chalets but cheap. Double rooms available. Excellent atmosphere, good views over the bay, a small garden, and sitting area with library and games. Recommended.

E **Zakaria Guesthouse**, Kampong Rhu Muda, T9-6182328. Basic and further out of the village, dorm or rooms.

E-F **Kamal's**, T9-6182181. Opposite the lagoon, very popular, dormitory and chalets, now very rundown but still popular with friendly staff. Tours and activities organized.

Pulau Kapas *p283*

A Gem Island Resort, Pulau Gemia, T9-6245110, F9-6245109, www.gemresorts.com. 52 chalets on a private island.

A-B Duta Puri, T9-6246090. The most upmarket resort on the island. Charming wooden and brick chalets set in nice gardens hung with batiks and stocked with dark wood furniture. Beach facing chalets are more expensive. All rooms have TV and minibar and wooden floors. Recommended.

B Kapas Garden Resort, T012-4302411, www.kapas-resort.com. Owned by the entrepreneurial Fred from Holland, this place offers cozy bungalows and is the only official beer seller on the island. Fred also runs the "Easy Dive Centre".

B-D Makcik Gemuk Resort, T9-6245120. Largest outfit on the island with a range of rooms from simple huts with shared facilities through to larger chalets with attached bathrooms. The name Mac Cik Gemuk means big, fat Auntie! Very popular with local tourists.

D-E The Lighthouse, T019- 2153558. Owner Din is a real character. The best budget place to stay on the island. All rooms are inside an atmospheric Long House. Very mellow place, staff make guests feel like part of the family. Lots of beach games, BBQs and the Tropical Hut bar. Highly recommended.

B-C Yellow Beach Resort , T9-6243005, F9-6313008. 16 chalets, all painted yellow, some with shared toilet. Simple inside but nicely decorated with batiks. Unfortunately the carpeted floor doesn't bode well for wet, sandy feet. Very good restaurant.

Eating

Kuala Terengganu *p279, map p281*

Nasi dagang – known as 'fishermen's breakfast' – is a speciality of the area. It is aromatic or glutinous rice, served with *gulai ikan tongkol* (tuna fish with tamarind and coconut gravy). *Keropok* – or prawn crackers – are another Terengganu speciality.

Chinese

TTT KT Wok, 1081 Block W, Jln Sultan Sulaiman, T9-6243825, ultra modern décor, black and pink colour scheme, specialize in *dim sum*.

T Golden Dragon Restaurant, 198 Jln Bandar, good pork, interesting vegetable dishes, some tables on street. Recommended.

T One-Two-Six, 102 Jln Kampong Tiong 2 (off Jln Sultan Ismail), big open-air restaurant with hawker stalls, good seafood menu, special: fire chicken wings (comes to table in flames). Recommended.

Indian

T Kari Asha, 1-H Jln Air Jermh, good range of curries (including fish heads, dosai and rotis).

T Taufik, 18 Jln Masjid Abidin (opposite Istana Maziah), North and South Indian dishes, well-known for its rotis.

International

TT Chef's Steak House, attached to *The Grand Paradise Hotel*, T9-6230899, F9-6238899. The chef here recommends the tenderloin steak and crème caramel.

TT Husni, 954 Jln Sultan Mohammed, Thai, Malay and Western dishes, vast menu.

T Midtown Café, Jln Tok Lam, a broad selection of Western and Eastern cuisine, should suit all tastes.

T Ping Anchorage Traveller's Café, Jln Dato'Isaac. Friendly, pleasant atmosphere, good breakfast menu, small souvenir shop with some items less tacky than found elsewhere. The place to go for western breakfasts and iced coffees. Check out the guest books to find objective comments on the nearby islands, resorts and tours.

Malay

T Keluarga IQ, 74 Jln Banggol, good place for *nasi dagang* breakfast, also excellent *nasi campur* (curry buffet), open 0630-0300, closed Fri.

T Restoran Terapung Puteri, Jln Sultan Zainal Abidin, T9-6235396, New floating restaurant opposite the tourist information centre, serving a wide range of Malay and western food, good fresh fruit drinks available.

T Mali, 77 Jln Banggol, near the bus station, popular, cheap coffee shop – *nasi lemak*, *nasi campur*, satay and good rotis.

T Nik, 104 Jln Sultan Ismail, standard curries.

T Sri Intan, 14 Taman Sri Intan, Jln Sultan Omar, well-appointed restaurant serving standard Malay dishes.

Seafood

Nil, Jln Pantai Batu Buruk (near the *Pantai Primula Hotel*), view of the beach, good selection of seafood and renowned for its butter crabs in batter.

Foodstalls

Gerai Makanan (foodstalls) opposite the bus station; Malay; **Kampong Tiong** (off Jln Bandar), excellent hawker centre with Malay food on one side, Chinese and indian on the other, open 8 till late; *Jalan Batu Buruk*, near the Cultural Centre, some excellent Malay food and seafood stalls. Recommended. Also **Warung Pak Maidin**, nearby on Jln Haji Busu, which is good on seafood; **Kompleks Taman Selera Tanjung** (1st Flr), huge area of stalls with good variety of dishes, open-air terrace; **Majlis Perbandaran** stalls, Jln Tok Lam; **Pasar Besar Kedai Payang** (Central Market), 1st Flr, Malay snacks, good views over the river. There are also some stalls next to *Stadium Negeri*.

Marang *p282, map p282*

Most hotels have good restaurants serving Malay and international dishes. There are cheap food stalls along the waterfront next to the market. Stalls at Taman Selera, Kampong Rhu Muda, along the roadside are well known, particularly by long-distance bus and taxi drivers, for their Malay and Thai-style seafood (closed Fri).

Pulau Kapas *p283*

All the chalet operations have attached restaurants. Long-stayers recommend the dining at the *Yellow Beach Resort*. Paying Café, next to the main jetty is a good spot for a *roti canai* breakfast.

Shopping

Kuala Terengganu *p279, map p281*

Batik

Some of the best batik in Malaysia can be found in the central market (*Pasar Besar Kedai Payang*). **Wan Ismail Tembaga & Batik**, near turtle roundabout, off Jln Sultan Zainal Abidin – a small, old-fashioned batik factory. There are a number of small craft and batik factories in Kampong Ladang – the area around Jln Sultan Zainal Abidin; **Desa Craft**, 73 Jln Sultan Ismail, in the centre of town, has a good selection of silk and batik readymades and sarongs. Other shops selling batik can be found on Jln Bandar, including the **Batik Gallery** at number 194 and **Yuleza** (Chinese for batik) at number 208. **Noor Arfa**, A3 Jln Sultan Zainal Abidin, T9-6235173, an established producer of batik for many years. Cloth and ready made clothes available and will take orders. **Teratai Arts and Crafts Shop**, 151 Jln Bandar, T9-6252157. High quality craft shop, with batik, woodwork, metalwork and jewellery. Also sells numerous prints and postcards my Malaysian artist Chang Fee Ming. He depicts the colourful nature of local life with stunning watercolours, well worth a visit just to see his work.

Handicrafts

The Central Market is touristy, but offers a range of handicrafts, textiles, brassware etc. **Desa Craft**, on Jln Sultan Ismail, is another good centre.

Marang *p282, map p282*

Handicrafts

Market in Marang has a craft market upstairs and there are several handicraft shops along the main street. **Balai Ukiran Terengganu** (Terengganu Woodcarving Centre), Kampong Rhu Rendang, near Marang, master-carver Abdul Malek Ariffin runs the east coast's best-known woodcarving workshop, makes wide range of intricately carved furniture from cengal wood, carved with traditional floral geometric and Islamic calligraphic patterns, the varnished cengal wood is not to everyone's taste, but everything from mirrors to beds can be ordered for export, because most pieces are made to order there is little on show in Abdul's chaotic workshop, but carvers can be seen at work during the day.

Activities and tours

Kuala Terengganu *p279, map p281*

Golf

Badariah Golf Club, south of town, T9-632456. 9 holes, requires special permission from the Sultan's private secretary's office.

Tour operators

Hedaco Travel, Ground Floor, Terengganu Foundation Bldg, Jln Sultan Ismail, T9-631744; **Ping Anchorage Travel & Tours**, 77A Jln Sultan Sulaiman, T9-6262020, www.pinganchorage.com.my A very well organised and efficient tour service (islands, jungle trekking, Kenyir Lake), offering tours, accommodation, ticketing, and seemingly everything. Recommended. **Turtleliner** (a Reliance franchise), Jln Sultan Masjid Abidin, T9-6237000, F9-6231122, services include flight booking and confirmation, individual and group tours. Helpful staff. **WLO Travel & Air Cargo**, Ground Floor, *Hotel Pantai Primula*, Jln Persinggahan, T9-635844

Pulau Kapas p283

Diving

Aqua Sport, T019 9835879, next to *Duta Puri* runs scuba trips.

Easy Dive Centre at *Kapas Garden Resort*. Snorkelling gear can be hired at all the resorts. There's some coral in front of the *Kapas Garden Resort* just off the beach. The resorts run snorkelling and fishing trips around the island, and kayaks can be hired.

Transport

Kuala Terengganu *p279, map p281*

Air

Sultan Mahmud airport lies 18 km northwest of town, T9-6664204 for information. Regular connections with **KL**.

Airline offices MAS, 13 Jln Sultan Omar, T9-6221415.

Bus

Kuala Terengganu has two bus stations. The express, long distance bus terminal is on Jalan Sultan Zainal Abidain Medan Selera, on the northern edge of the city centre. Connections to **KL**, 7 hrs, **JB**, 9 hrs, **Kota Bharu, Kuantan, Rantau Abang, Mersing, Singapore, Melaka, Butterworth**, 9 hrs and **Alor Star** leave from the long distance terminal. Express buses to **KL** leave 0900, 0930, 1000 and then 2130 and 2200. To **Kuantan** every 90 mins until 2200. To **Mersing**, there are two buses, one at 1230 and one at 2200.

Local buses leave from the MPKT station on Jln Syed Hussin which runs off Jln Masjid. From here you can catch buses to **Merang, Marang** and **Kuala Besut.**

Car hire

South China Sea, *Permai Park Inn*, T9-6224903.

Taxi

Taxis operate from next to the bus station on Jln Masjid and from the waterfront. Destinations include **Kota Bharu, Rantau Abang, Marang, Kuantan, KL, JB** and **Penang**. Taxi, T9-621581.

Marang *p282, map p282*

Bus

Bus stop on the main road up the hill from Marang. Tickets can be bought from the kiosk nearby on Jln Tg Sulong Musa, however, this runs very unpredictable hours so book in advance. Connections with **Kuala Terengganu** every 90 mins, and with **Kuala Dungun** for Pulau Tenggol via **Kuala Abang**. If you're stuck without a ticket you will have to head to Kuala Terengganu's express bus station (taxi RM15, local bus, RM1.50 – one every 90 mins). Taxis wait near the jetty.

Directory

Kuala Terengganu *p279, map p281*

Banks There are several banks along Jln Sultan Ismail. **Bumiputra, UMNO**, Jln Masjid Zainal Abidin; **Hong Kong Bank**, 57 Jln Sultan Ismail; **Maybank**, 69 Jln Paya Bunga; **Public**, 1 Jln Balas Baru; **Standard Chartered**, 31 Jln Sultan Ismail; **UMBC**, 59 Jln Sultan Ismail. There are virtually no money changers in Kuala Terengganu. **Post** General Post Office, Jln Sultan Zainal Abidin. **Telephone** Telekom, Jln Sultan Ismail. **Internet** Golden Wood Internet Café, 59 Jln Tok Lam, opposite the *Midtown Hotel*. **Medical services** Hospital, Jln Peranginan (Just off Jln Sultan Mahmud), T9-6233333.

Marang *p282, map p282*

Internet There are a couple of Internet cafes on Jln Hakaf Tapai past the school on the other side of the main highway to the jetties.

Redang archipelago

Colour map 1, grid B6

The biggest and best-known of the islands is Pulau Redang, but Pulau Lang Tengah is also catching up. Pulau Bidong was the base for a Vietnamese refugee camp in the 1970s and 1980s and as many as 40,000 were once crammed on this island. The boat people have long gone now, and most of the camp's buildings have rotted away. Tour agencies in Kuala Terengganu offer day-trips to the island, where there are few memorials to the refugees and some good snorkelling. The only islands with accommodation are Pulau Redang and Pulau Lang Tengah. *See Sleeping, Eating and other listings, pages 289-290.*

Ins and outs

Getting there There is a daily flight to Pulau Redang from KL. Boats leave from Merang twice daily. *See Transport for further information, page 290.*

Tourist information An independently-run website offering news and reviews of places and diving on Pulau Redang and Lang Tengah is at www.redang.org Tourist information from Tourism Malaysia in Kuala Terenggau.

Merang

Merang is a small fishing kampong with a long white sandy beach; it is also the departure point for the many offshore islands

The nine islands

Redang archipelago is made up of nine islands – the main Redang Island, Lima Island, Paku Besar Island, Paku Kecil Island, Kerengga Besar Island, Kerengga Kecil Island, Ekor Tebu Island, Ling Island and Pinang Island. A number of islands are accessible from Merang, most notably Pulau Redang. Other islands, most of which are uninhabited and all of which are endowed with a good selection of coral, include Pulau Pinang, Pulau Lima and Pulau Ekor Tebu; fishing boats are usually happy to stop off on request.

Pulau Redang is 27 kilometres off Merang in this archipelago, a marine park of nine islands with some of **Malaysia's best reefs**, making it one of the most desirable locations for divers. In the months after the monsoon, visibility increases to at least 20 m but during the monsoon the island is usually inaccessible. Line-fishing is permitted and squid fishing, using bright lights, is popular between June and September; the fishermen use a special hook called a *candat sotong*. The lamps light the surrounding waters, attracting the squid.

Pulau Lang Tengah

Lang Tengah (whose name apparently means eagle resting on middle island) is a tiny rocky island protected by a coral reef that sits between Pulau Perhentian and Pulau Redang and is accessible from both by a boat day-trip. The five resorts on Lang Tengah are spread over two beaches on the western side of the island, Pasir Air and Pasir Mathasaan. This number could well rise. However, the island is less developed than Pulau Redang and is much more tranquil, although the effect of tourists can be seen on the white beaches – visitors report some sands marred with dead coral and litter. There are more than a dozen dive sites around the island and good snorkelling.

The crown-of-thorns – the terminator on the reef

The crown-of-thorns starfish (*Acanthaster planci*) – a ruthlessly efficient, cold-blooded killing machine – launched an invasion of the Pulau Redang Marine Park in the early 1990s. The destructive starfish, which did serious damage to Australia's Great Barrier Reef in the 1980s, can regenerate and multiply rapidly leading to sudden infestations on coral reefs. The crown-of-thorns grazes on staghorn coral (*Acropora*) in particular and if population explosions are left unchecked, the starfish can reduce rich coral colonies into blanched skeletal debris. One crown-of-thorns can suck the living tissues from a coral in a matter of hours and, if present in large numbers, they can eat their way across a reef, devastating it in a matter of weeks.

The crown-of-thorns is aptly named. It measures about 50 cm across and is covered in thousands of poisonous spines, each 3-5 cm long. The spines are extremely sharp and toxic – if they puncture human skin, they cause a severe reaction, including nausea, vomiting and swelling. These short spines grow on the starfish's legs, of which it has more than 20. But marine conservationists, concerned about the threat to the coral and fish breeding grounds, face a daunting task in ridding reefs of the unwelcome echinoderms. Because of their amoeba-like regenerative abilities, the crown-of-thorns cannot simply be chopped in half in situ, because this would create two of them. Instead, each one has to be prised off the coral, taken to the surface and buried on land.

The Malaysian Fisheries Department, with private sector backing, mounted a reef-rescue expedition to Redang in 1992 to do exactly this. The department's marine biologists were unsure as to what had triggered the infestation of crown-of-thorns starfish; it could be that they invade in natural cycles or human interference could have something to do with it. The last major infestation was in the early 1970s. Following their difficult task of picking the starfish off the reef, the divers buried them on shore, as instructed. Perhaps they should have driven wooden stakes through their hearts too: the starfish can go for as long as nine months without food.

Sleeping

Merang *p288*

L-AL The Aryani Resort, Jln Rhu Tapai Merang, Pantai Peranginan Merang, 21010 Setiu, T9-6532111, www.thearyani.com The original heritage timber suites have private courtyards with outdoor bath, elevated restaurant, pool, luxurious.

A-B Sutra Beach Resort, Kampong Rhu Tapai, T9-6531111, www.sutrabeachresort.com.my. A/c, restaurants, pool, 124 chalets, good sports facilities, 20 mins from Kuala Terengganu's airport. Malaysian Tourism award winner.

C Stingray Beach Chalet, T019-3278855, F9-6532018. Built in 1997, directly on the beach, fan, bathroom, immaculately run and offers a dive service. Recommended.

D Kembara Resort, 474 Pantai Peranginan Merang, 21010 Setiu, T9-6238771, F9-6248772. Situated on an endless palm-fringed deserted white beach, running south from the jetty, set in a beautiful garden compound, relaxed atmosphere, just 8 bungalows and 8 rooms all with attached shower and toilet, and fans. Cheap dorm accommodation. No restaurant but there's a large kitchen in the court which is well equipped and can be used freely, a little-known paradise. Recommended.

E Sugi Man's Homestay, 500 m beyond junction, on road to Penarek (signposted from the road). Restaurant, basic kampong farm house, quite a walk from the beach, cooking lessons and kite making, including meals.

Redang archipelago *p288*

Resorts on Redang offer competitive and flexible package deals – check with *Tourism Malaysia*. A typical 2-day/2- night trip costs around RM300 per person; all food, camping and snorkelling equipment included. As always, if you value a measure of privacy and seclusion, avoid weekends and public holidays.

A Berjaya Redang Beach Resort, T9-6973988, F9-6973899. 120 pretty cottages chalets with red roofs. The resort has good reviews but some criticise it (and the rest of the island) for overdeveloping.

A Berjaya Redang Spa Resort, T9-6971111, F9-6971000. A hotel with 152 rooms with a/c, TV, minibar, pool, restaurants, health spa, gym, 18-hole golf course, popular destination for business visitors wishing to combine work and golf (limited business facilities), dive centre, gym, tennis courts, health spa. Not popular with locals or environmentalists.

A Laguna Redang Island Resort, Pasir Panjang, T9-6977888, www.lagunaredang.com.my A new luxury resort, with swimming pool, own stretch of beach, dive shop, restaurants, beach bar, and even mahjong – a subtle sign that there are plenty of Chinese tourists on Pulau Redang.

A Redang Beach Resort, T9-6238188, www.redang.com.my Full range of facilities, package deals available. Newly upgraded.

A Redang Pelangi Resort, T9-6223158, F9-6235282. Pleasant wooden huts on stilts traditional Malay style all with a/c and own bathroom. The resort has a popular disco and karaoke so not recommended if it's tranquillity you're after.

Pulau LangTengah *p288*

There are now five resorts on Lang Tengah spread over two beaches on the western side of the island, Pasir Air and Pasir Mathasaan. This number could well rise.

A Square Point Resort, Pasir Mathasaan , T9-6235333, F9-6239533, A/c chalets, dive centre and restaurant.

A D'Coconut Lagoon, Pasir Mathasaan , T03 42526686, www.dcoconutlagoon.com. Smaller resort with a/c chalets, swimming pool and dive centre.

A-B Blue Coral Island Resort, Pasir Air, T03 7805277, www.malaysiaislandresorts.com. 70 a/c rooms, swimming pool, western and Asian restaurant, reading rooms and dive cente.

Transport

Merang *p288*

Bus

Two buses a day from **Kuala Terengganu** to Merang (RM2.50), and then on to **Penarek**. Minibus connections also available from **Kuala Terengganu**, from Jln Masjid.

Taxi

Taxis from **Merang** to **Penarek**. An a/c taxi from **Kuala Terengganu** to **Merang** should cost RM20-30.

Redang archipelago *p288*

Air

There is now a small air strip on Pulau Redang operated by **Berjaya Air** which flies a 48-seater Dash 7 between **KL** and the strip at 1230 to arrive at 1345. The return flight leaves at 1405 to arrive back in KL at 1520. You do not have to stay at *Berjaya* to use this service.

Boat

These leave for the islands from Merang as well as from the jetty in Kuala Terangganu (but boats leaving from here are only for *Berjaya* customers, two departures, at 1000 and 1500). It has, however, become very expensive to charter boats from Merang. *Tourism Malaysia* in Kuala Terengganu recommends that tourists take advantage of the package deals offered by the island's resorts; further details can be obtained from the *Tourism Malaysia* office.

Pulau Lang Tengah *p288*

Boat

You can also get to the island by booking with a resort on Lang Tengah – they will direct you to a speedboat pick-up at Merang jetty.

The Perhentian Islands

→ Colour map 1, grid A5

Two more beautiful east coast islands, Pulau Perhentian Besar (big) and Pulau Perhentian Kecil (small), just over 20 km off the coast are separated by a narrow sound with a strong current. Despite considerable development in recent years, with more hotels, restaurants, bars, diving outfits and much more noise, the Perhentian islands still remain a paradise, with excellent diving and snorkelling, magnificent beaches and some of the best places for swimming on the east coast. ▸▸ *For Sleeping, Eating and other listings, see pages 291-295.*

Ins and outs

It is important to get to the islands, 20 km offshore, as early as possible on the day of arrival due to high demand for accommodation. Boats leave throughout the day from Kuala Besut which is connected to other towns by regular buses. There are boats between the two islands. ▸▸ *See also Transport, page 295.*

The islands

Of the two islands, Perhantian Besar (big island) is generally more more popular with families as it houses slightly more upmarket resorts, although huts on the beach are also available. Perhentian Kecil (small) is simpler and attracts a younger crowd of party-going backpackers. There is a fishing village and a turtle hatchery in the middle of Long Beach (Pasir Panjang) on Perhentian Kecil. Both islands however, are still only developed to a low key stage and offer beautiful beaches, good snorkelling, and great diving as well as forested trails inland. Despite the low level of development, there is enough tourist activity to worry environmentalists, in particular damage to the reef from irrepsonsible divers, litter (although boats come daily to ship it away in bags from the resorts) and the pollution from the genrators (almost every resort has their own oil-powered generator).

! Travellers should be wary of risking the boat trip too close to the beginning or end of the Dec-Feb monsoon season.

Kuala Besut

It is possible to spend the night in Kuala Besut. This small fishing village has one main place to stay. Business in this little fishing village has expanded to cater for those tourists passing through and good food can be found at a series of small restaurants along the waterfront. Kuala Besut has lots of travel agents which sell boat and bus tickets and book accommodation on the island. Taxis however seem to favour dropping you off at **Pelangi Travel & Tours.**

Sleeping

Perhentian Islands *p291, map p292*

All the resorts and chalets now have their own generators; and all have fresh water from wells. Competition for accommodation is fierce due to the ever increasing popularity of the Perhentians; this must be one of the few places in the world where demand regularly outstrips availability – strict planning laws ensure development is restricted. As the islands are not on the main phone system many of the numbers provided are mobile numbers which are liable to change. Bookings are therefore difficult to make, besides most of the guesthouses do not accept bookings. Upmarket resorts, though, do and during peak season will only accept people who have reservations. Upmarket resorts employ booking agents on the mainland. It's advisable to take the earliest boat possible (particularly Kecil) and accept the first accommodation offer (see Transport page 295).

Perhentian Besar

There are a number of bays with accommodation on the larger island. The majority of it is located on the west coast, which is divided into 3 small beaches by outcrops of rock. There is more accommodation in the secluded bay of Telok Dalam.

AL-A Perhentian Island Resort (bookings c/o 25 Menara Promet, Jln Sultan Ismail, KL, T3-2448530, www.jaring.my/perhentian Some of the 103 rooms have a/c, licensed but expensive restaurant, some watersports facilities, diving equipment and courses available. Chalets have hill view or sea view, each with verendahs.

A Coral View Island Resort, (bookings from Kuala Besut, T9- 6974276, T9- 030943, www.coralview.com.my A/c, shower. Quite an exclusive resort with 72 chalets at northern end of beach, rooms close together, bathroom attached. Sea views more expensive. Diving courses.

A Tuna Bay Island Resort, T9-6979779, www.tunabay.com.my. Pretty wooden chalets and a lovely open air restaurant. One of the nicest of the new resorts. Has its own dive centre, Internet and travel agency.

A-C Flora Bay Chalet, Telok Dalam, T9-6977266/T011-977266, www.florabayresort.com. Everything from swanky chalets to A-frames.

B-C Mama's, T010-9813359. Fan, shower. Selection of chalets for families or couples. Like every other hostel a daily snorkelling trip is organized.

B-D Abdul's, T9-6977058. Decent looking chalets on the beach, fan and shower, with popular restaurant. Good local reputation.

C ABC, T019-6977568. Eight cheap and basic huts, on the beach.

C Coco Hut Chalets, T019-9105019. Restaurant, unspecial 'A'-frames, although new ones with showers are being constructed.

C-D Perhentian Paradise Resort, T010-9810930/T019-9125151. Family or doubles available. Nice location set slightly back from the beach.

Pulau Perhentian

Sleeping
ABC **1**
Abdul's **28**
Chempaka **4**
Coco Hut Chalets **3**
Coral View Island Resort **5**
D'Lagoon **7**
Fatimah's/Aur Beach **26**
Flora Bay Chalet **9**
Lemongrass **23**
Lily Chalet **8**
Mama's **10**
Matahari **11**
Maya Beach Resort **12**
Mohsin **27**
Moonlight **14**
Panorama **15**
Pasir Petani Resort **16**

E Seahorse Chalets, T010-9841181. Affiliated to a dive centre, also offers internet access. Run-down 'A'-frames; cheap.
F Camping. RM5 at *Perhentian Island Resort*; camping is permitted on the island but not on the beach; anybody found sleeping on the beach will be moved on. Restaurant and dive shop floors go for RM10.

Perhentian Kecil

There is more budget accommodation on Kecil although the arrival of the red-roofed concrete *Bubu* resort, which has angered guesthouse operators, has made a stab at making the island more upmarket. Accommodation is split, with some huts on the beautiful white sandy beach of Pasir Panjang (Long Beach), on the east side of the island, and some on Coral Bay, on the west. Long Beach is the place for parties, while Coral Bay is quieter but with less eating choice. The stretch of beach at Coral Bay doesn't have such nice coral but is quieter and the chalets are cheaper and give you more for your money. The two are separated by a 10-minute walk through the forest which is easy by day but not so simple at night! There are a couple of places at the southern tip, not far from Perhentian village and an isolated spot at Teluk Kerma.

Perhentian Island Resort **17**
Perhentian Paradise Resort **18**
Seahorse Chalets **19**
Simfony Village **20**
Suria Resort **25**
Tuna Bay Island Resort **22**

A-B Lily Chalet, Long Beach, T019-2224365. One of the pricier places. Chinese-run fancy (for this beach) chalets. Big and airy with own shower, some with a/c some with fan.
B-C Maya Beach Resort, Coral Bay, T019-9241644. 12 chalets with fan and attached bathrooms in the centre of the beach. Restaurant. Friendly owner.
B-C Suria Resort , T9- 6797960. Swankiest place on this part of the island. Elevated restaurant with good sea views and 24 hr electricity. Hot water (rare) bathrooms. Also A frames with bathroom available. Breakfast included in price.
B-D Mohsin, T010-3338897, mohsinchalets@yahoo.com. Blue-roofed huts on a hill behind *Champaka*, steep stairs to get to the restaurant where there are great views. 30 rooms, mostly in rows. Considered one of the best places on the island, with attached bathrooms and 24-hr electricity. Slightly pricey but worth it if you want a good night's sleep. There's a 20-bed dorm. Recommended.
B-E D'Lagoon, Teluk Kerma, T019-9857089, www.geocities.com/d_lagoon_my Very remote position at the northern end of the island, some rooms in a longhouse, chalets have attached bathrooms, restaurant, a secluded, quiet spot with great snorkelling.
C Pasir Petani Resort, T019-9571624. At the southern end of the island, chalets with fans and attached bathrooms.
C-D Matahari, T019-9568726. Excellent restaurant, often full, proof of its popularity. Set back slightly from the beach but central.
C-D Moonlight, T019-9858222. Simple wooden huts, with fan, shared bathroom which can get dirty. Best point is its location which is on the end of the beach away from the rabble, with lovely views.
C-D Panorama, T010-9122518. Attractive chalets with attached showers and toilets, fans and mosquito nets set in nice garden. Good value with dinner included in room rate which is a great deal as the restaurant is the best on this stretch of the island. Very helpful staff, tours arranged and Internet available. Recommended.

D Chempaka, T019-9857329. Southern end, pleasantly uncramped site with sea views for all the 12 chalets, 12-hours of electricity, charcoal for cooking is provided, shared bathroom. Run down but functional.

D Fatimah's/Aur Beach, T9-6977694. Simple wooden chalets with bathroom inside. Very friendly staff. Best budget option here.

D Lemongrass, T012-9562392. Next to *Rock Garden*. Pretty standard place, simple fan chalets with shared showers and toilet of varying cleanliness. Can get very noisy as popular place for rave-style parties.

D Simfony Village, T019-9104236. Simple chalets with common showers and toilets, with fan and 24 hr electricity. Seriously run-down, with very dubious toilets and showers. One couple said the roof of their hut fell in while they were sleeping, dumping two love-making iguanas and a bunch of sand on their bed. Others report leaks in their huts in the rain. The owner runs the only ferry service to the island from Tok Bali.

Kuala Besut *p291*

C-D Nan's Guest House, T9-6974892, just around the corner from the jetty. They have a/c rooms with TV or simpler fan rooms all with attached bathrooms. (Recommended).

Eating

Perhentian Islands *p291*

There are a couple of restaurants on Perhentian Besar serving simple food – banana pancakes, etc. Particularly popular are the restaurants attached to *Coral View Island Resort*, *Coco Hut Chalets* and *Tuna Bay*. There are also coffee shops in the kampong on Perhentian Kecil and almost all the chalets here have restaurants at very similar prices. Milkshakes, fruit juices and pancakes are particularly recommended. On Long Beach, *Panorama's* is particularly good, the food is nicely presented and you can have dinner and watch movies at the same time. *Shake Shack* is a nice place for breakfast inland along the path towards Coral Bay. There are lots of good seafood BBQs, although avoid eating shark. In order to compete with restaurants on the beach, resorts further back have increased the price of their accommodation to include meals. Although this is not bad value it does limit choice at mealtimes. Note alcohol is not freely available on the island. Some restaurants discreetly offer beer and some spirits but you need to ask first.

Activites and tours

Perhentian Islands *p291*

Diving and snorkelling

The coral around the Perhentian islands is some of the best off the east coast. Most guesthouses arrange snorkelling trips and provide masks, snorkels and fins. It's around RM30-40 for a half day including the boat trip to 3 or so spots and gear. RM10 to hire gear on the beach.

There are also heaps of dive shops (PADI) on both islands which run courses and arrange dives for beginners to old hands, including night dives. Some of the cheapest diving can be found here, with dives for as little as RM50 including gear. The long-running **Turtle Bay Divers** and **Spice Divers**, both on Perhentian Kecil have been recommended. Some dive shops offer day trips to Redang Island. It should be about RM800 to charter a boat. If enough people want to go (say 8-10), then it would work out around RM100 per person. The diving trip is more expensive; if enough people are going it will cost around RM200 per person for dive equipment and trip to Redang. It is advisable to shop around for the best deal, and seek other tourists' advice to get an idea about the quality of the instructors who tend to vary from season to season. Many divemasters and instructors are European and so dive shops offer tuition in a variety of languages. If you are snorkelling off Long Beach, head for the patch near *Moonlight*.

Kuala Besut *p291*

Pelangi Travel & Tours, www.perhentianpelangi.com.my, which is nearest the jetty. Staff here are quite brusque

For an explanation of the sleeping and eating price codes used in this guide, see inside the front cover. Other relevant information is found in Essentials, pages 45-49.

and not really helpful, although they do offer a comprehensive travel service. You are by no means obliged to use them

Transport

Perhentian Islands *p291*

Boat

Fast and some slow boats leave at irregular hours throughout the day, all are booked through travel agents in Kuala Besut. More boats leave in the morning, so the earlier you can get there the better. Fast boats (RM60 return) leave **Kuala Besut** generally every hour from 0700-1600 (at peak periods), 30 mins, boats carry 8-10 people. These small boats drive very fast and the ride can get bumpy, try to sit near at the back near the driver. The same boats leave **Pulau Perhentian** for **Kuala Besut** between 0800-1600. Slow boats (RM40 return) leave Kuala Besut at approximately 1000 and 1500, 1-1½ hrs and carry 12 people. They return from the islands at 0800 and noon. Both boats cannot land at the beach. The posher resorts have makeshift jetties which the boats can drop you off at, but for the rest, you'll have to transfer yourself and your luggage to a tiny 13-foot boat (RM5) for a short scoot to the sands. Those staying at the more remote *Pasir Petani Resort* on Perhentian Kecil should pre-arrange a pick-up time. Travellers should be wary of risking the boat trip too close to the beginning or end of the Dec-Feb monsoon season. The fishing boats are not best equipped for rough seas and life jackets are rarely available. If you want to travel between the islands once you are there you will have to hire a water taxi. These motorised dinghies have fixed rates, ask at the guesthouse. A single trip between Long Beach and the opposite beach is RM20.

Bus

Main express buses go from the station at Jerteh, about 20 mins by taxi. From **Kuala Terengganu** (Jln Masjid): Kota Bharu-bound bus to Jerteh. Regular connections between **Jerteh** and **Kuala Besut**. From **Kota Bharu**: Bus 3, south-bound to **Pasir Puteh** (36 km south). Regular connections between **Pasir Puteh** and **Kuala Besut**. To **Kuala Lumpur**: **Mahligia Express** bus company, T9-6903699 leaves twice a day, one around 0830 and one at 2030. Buses from KL leave around a similar time. Boats leave from Kuala Besut to **Perhentian**.

Taxi

Kuala Terengganu (RM48); **Merang Jetty** (RM35, for Redang), **Kota Bharu** (RM25). Taxis from **Pasir Puteh** or **Jerteh** to **Kuala Besut** (RM10). Some taxis will offer to drive you to Tok Bali for access to Perhentians. The problem with this is there's only one kind of ferry run by the owner of Simfony Village on Long Beach and so the times are inconvenient. Better option is to head to Kuala Besut, make sure the taxi driver knows this, as some will try and take you there anyway as its closer to Kota Bharu than Kuala Besut.

Directory

Perhentian Islands *p291*

Banks There are no banks or ATM machines on the islands or in Besut and very few of the hotels accept credit cards. If you arrive in Besut short on cash, the nearest bank is a half-hour bus journey away, in Jerteh; buses leave every half hour. Most guesthouses will change money, but at a poor rate. Note that most dive centres accept credit cards and some will let you have cash on them, but expect to be fleeced. **Internet** Upmarket resorts have Internet. Connection is slow and expensive - around RM12 for 30 mins. On Long Beach, there's Internet at **Panorama** for RM10 for 30 mins. At Coral Bay, **Perhentian Pro-Diver** has IDD and Internet for RM9 for 30 mins.

Kota Bharu and around

→ Colour map 1, grid A5

Kota Bharu is the royal capital of Kelantan, 'the land of lightning', and is situated near the mouth of the Kelantan River. The city is one of Malaysia's Malay strongholds, despite its proximity to the Thai border. This was reinforced during the latest general elections when the opposition PAS once again managed to secure KB and Kelantan (now the only PAS state in the country). While some people react against the state government's enthusiastic support for an Islamic interpretation of public (and private) morals, Kota Bharu is one of Malaysia's more culturally interesting and colourful towns with many eclectic museums, mosques and grandiose royal palaces, including the Istana Batu, Istana Balai and Istana Jahar.The city's wet market is an unmissable experience and an architectural delight, and the Kampong Kraftangan handicraft village forms part of the impressive Kelantan cultural zone.

The crafts for which Kelantan is renowned – such as silverware, weaving and metal-working – were in part the result of the state's close relations with the Siamese kingdom of Ayutthaya in the 17th century. The makyung, a traditional Malay court dance, is still performed in Kelantan and wayang kulit (shadow puppet plays) still provide entertainment on special occasions in the kampongs. Kota Bharu is the centre for Malay arts and crafts, although batik printing, woodcarving, songket-weaving and silver working are more often confined to the villages.

Around KB are Kong Mek, a 100-year-old Chinese temple and KB's most famous beach, Pantai Cahaya Bulan. There are also waterfalls, a Thai village and one of Malaysia's oldest mosques. » For Sleeping, Eating and other listings, see pages 302-279.

Ins and outs

Getting there

KB's airport is 8 km from town. There are direct links on **MAS** with KL, and with KL and JB on **AirAsia**. Unusually, the train station is 6 km out of town at Wakaf Bharu. The line runs south to KL and Singapore. There is a confusion of 3 bus terminals in KB but the majority of express buses depart from the most central. There are connections with all major destinations on the Peninsula. Buses also run to Rantau Panjang and Pengkalan Kubor, both on the Thai border. Outstation taxis also offer a service to many larger towns. » See also Transport, page 305.

Getting around

The trishaw used to be the backbone of the town's public transport system, but taxis have just about elbowed them out of the scene. There is also a city bus service and a number of local and international car hire firms.

Tourist information

Tourist Information Centre, ⓘ *Jln Sultan Ibrahim, T9-7485534, F9-7486652, 0800-1700, closed Fri.* A helpful office, with a good map of the town. It will arrange taxis and ferries to the islands, as well as booking accommodation on the islands.

Safety

Since 2004, southern Thailand has been plagued by separatist violence which has in some cases been brutally put down by the Thai police and army. Almost 80 Muslim protesters were suffocated to death in Thai army trucks in October 2004. Militants regularly bomb Buddhist temples and gunmen attack non-Muslims in motorbike drive-by shootings almost daily. It is not recommended for tourists to travel here. At the time of writing more than 500 people have been killed by the unrest. The affected Thai states are Narathiwat (adjoins Kelantan), Patani and Yala.

History

The fertile alluvial soils of the Kelantan River valley and the coastal plain have supported mixed farming and a thriving peasant economy for centuries.

Kelantan may have been part of the second-century kingdom of Langkasuka (see page 183), but from early in the first millennium AD, it was an established agricultural state which adopted the farming practices of the kingdom of Funan on the lower Mekong River. Because it was effectively cut off from the west coast states of the peninsula, Kelantan always looked north: it traded with Funan, the Khmer Empire and the Siamese kingdom of Ayutthaya.

By the 14th century, Kelantan was under Siamese suzerainty, although at that time it also fell under the influence of the Javanese Majapahit Empire. For a while, during the 15th and 16th centuries, Kelantan joined other peninsular states in sending tribute to the Sultanate of Melaka, and its successor, Johor. By then the state had splintered into a number of small chiefdoms; one local chief, Long Mohammed, proclaimed himself Kelantan's first sultan in 1800.

When a succession dispute erupted on the death of the heirless Sultan Mohammed, Siam supported his nephew, Senik the 'Red-Mouth' who reigned for 40 peaceful years. On the next succession crisis, in 1900, Bangkok installed its own nominee as sultan. But in 1909, a treaty between Siam and Britain pushed Bangkok to cede its suzerainty over Kelantan to the British. This severed the state from its Islamic neighbour, the former sultanate of Petani, in Southeast Thailand. British interference caused much resentment and provoked a brief revolt in 1912. After using Kota Bharu as one of their beachheads for the invasion of Malaya in December 1941, the Japanese Imperial Army won support for restoring Kelantan to Thailand. In October 1945 however, Kelantan reluctantly joined the Malayan Union, under the British colonial administration.

Modern Kelantan

Today Kelantan is Malaysia's most conservative and traditional state and since October 1990 it has been ruled by the hard-line Parti Islam – or *PAS*, its Malay acronym. On several occasions the PAS-led state government have voted to introduce strict Islamic – or Sharia – law. Non-Muslims in the state – mainly in Kota Bharu, where one-third of the population is Chinese or Indian – were alarmed by the prospect of the *hudud* criminal code being implemented. It dictates that for crimes such as theft, fornication, intoxication and apostasy, 'criminals' should have their hands and/or legs severed or should be lashed until death if unrepentant. When Islamic officials broke up a rowdy Chinese New Year party in Kota Bharu in 1994, the local Chinese community thought their fears had been realized and that this was a taste of things to come.

Hudud can't become law until it's passed by a two-thirds majority in Federal Parliament, but the whole matter has become a conundrum for Muslim politicians in KL. The government does not want to be seen as un-Islamic by opposing Kelantan's move, but it cannot feasibly support Sharia law, so it polishes its own Islamic credentials by building new mosques and sponsoring Koran-reading competitions. Sharia law totally conflicts with the vision of Islamic moderates and modernists. The battle between Kelantan and the government in KL continues. In the most recent general elections the opposition PAS once again managed to hold onto Kelantan despite the most fervent efforts by BN (Barisan Nasional) to secure a victory here and the promise of massive development funds. The state is a hotbed of opposition politics.

This highly charged political and religious atmosphere contrasts with the Kelantanese people's laid-back, gentle manner. Tourists visiting the state should be particularly aware of Islamic sensitivities, but the trappings of Islam rarely impinge on the enjoyment of the state's rich cultural heritage.

Sights

The heart of Kota Bharu is the **central market** ⓘ *off Jalan Temenggong, daily 0900-2000*, which is one of the most vibrant and colourful wet markets in the country. It is housed in a three-storey octagonal concrete complex painted green which has a glass roof and, because it's so bright, is a photographer's paradise. In the modern Buluh Kubu complex across the road on Jalan Tengku Petra Semerak, there are many shops selling Kelantanese batik and other handicrafts. Nearby is the **Istana Balai Besar**, ⓘ *not usually open to the public*, the 'palace with the big audience hall',

Kota Bharu

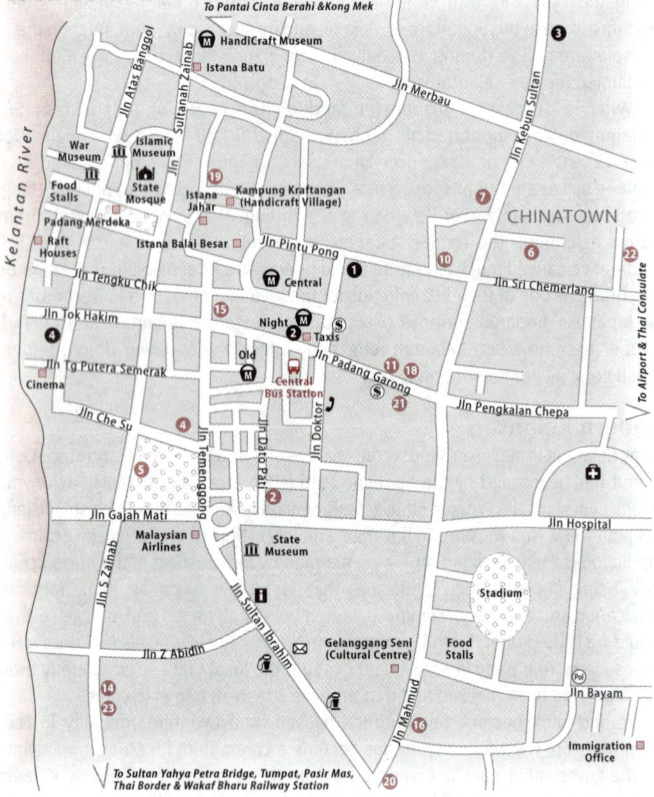

N

0 metres 200
0 yards 200

Sleeping
Ansar 2
Crystal Lodge 4
Dynasty Inn 5
Hostel Pantai Timor 6
Ideal Travellers' House 7
Juita Inn 10
KB Inn 11
Menora 14
Tokyo Baru 15
Perdana 16
Sabriena Court 18
Safar Inn 19
Sentosa 20
Yee 21
Zeck Traveller's Inn 22
De 999 23

Eating
Mubihah Vegetarian Cake House 1
Neelavathy 2
Ambassador & Kow Lun 3
Meena Curry House 4

built in Patani-style in 1844 by Sultan Mohammed II. The istana, with its decorative panels and wood-carvings is still used on ceremonial occasions. The palace contains the throne-room and the elaborate royal barge, which the sultan only ever used once for a joy ride on the Kelantan River in 1900. Beside the old istana is the single-storey **Istana Jahar,** ⓘ *0830-1645, RM3,* constructed in 1889 by Sultan Mohammed IV; it is now the 'centre for royal customs' and is part of the new cultural complex (see below). It exemplifies the skilled craftsmanship of the Kelantanese woodcarvers in its intricately carved beams and panels. There is a small craft collection including songket and silverware.

Kampong Kraftangan (Handicraft Village) is close to the central market. It aims to give visitors a taste of Kelantan's arts and crafts all under one roof. The large enclosure, in which merbuk birds (doves) sing in their bamboo cages, contains four buildings, all wooden and built in traditional Malay style. They are part of the Kelantan cultural zone area which includes several museums, including the Istana Jahar. The complex is quite impressive, but visitors appear few and far between, giving the sprawling place a slightly empty, lackadaisical feel. The **Handicraft Museum** ⓘ *Sat-Thu 1000-1800, closed Fri, RM1,* contains exhibits and dioramas of traditional Kelantanese crafts and customs. There is also a batik workshop and demonstration centre where local artists produce hand-painted batiks. There are several stalls, stocked with handicrafts such as batik, silverware and *songket*, for sale. At ground level there is a pleasant restaurant serving Kelantanese delicacies. Opposite the new complex is the **Istana Batu**, the sky-blue Stone Palace, which was built in 1939 and was one of the first concrete buildings in the state. The former royal palace was presented to the state by the Sultan for use as a royal museum and contains many personal possessions of the royal family.

A little north of the commercial centre is **Padang Merdeka**, built after the First World War as a memorial. Merdeka Square is also where the British hanged Tok Janggut, 'Father Long-beard', who led the short-lived revolt against British land taxes in 1915. Opposite, on Jalan Sultan Zainab, is the **State Mosque**, which was completed in 1926. Next door is the State Religious Council building, dating from 1914. Next to the mosque on Jalan Merdeka is a magnificent two-storey green-and-white mansion with traditional Islamic latticework carving on eaves, which houses the **Islamic Museum,** ⓘ *0830-1645 Sat-Thu*; donations only. The building itself is more noteworthy than its eclectic contents. The **War Museum,** ⓘ *0830-1645, RM2 adult, RM1 child,* next to the Islamic Museum gives visitors an informative account of the Second World War in Southeast Asia. Beginning with Pearl Harbor, it tells the story of the Japanese invasion of Kelantan in December 1941 and the subsequent conquest of Malaya. It includes many pictures and items from the period.

Directly west of the mosque, running north-south along the riverbank is **Jalan Pasar Lama**, off Jalan Post Office Lama. This is an interesting area for a gentle stroll; there are many beautiful but rapidly decaying old Chinese shophouses (there's a large Chinese community in this part of town). Most of the buildings date to the early 1900s. Some have been rendered completely uninhabitable because vast trees have taken root inside them.

At the **Gelanggang Seni** (Cultural Centre), on Jalan Mahmud, opposite the stadium, many traditional arts are regularly performed. The centre tends to get rather touristy but it is the best place to see a variety of cultural performances in one place. For more detail on each of these traditional forms of entertainment, see page 475. These include: Demonstrations of *silat* (the Malay art of self-defence); *Drumming* competitions on Sat and Mon using the *rebana ubi* Kelantan drums, made from hollowed-out logs; *Top-spinning* competitions on Sat and Mon; *Wayang kulit* (shadow-puppet) performances on Wed; *Kite-flying* competitions (Sat afternoons) with the famous paper-and-bamboo *wau bulan* – or Kelantan moon-kites, the symbol of *MAS*. This has been a Kelantanese sport for centuries;

the aim is to fly your kite higher than anyone else's and, once up there, to defend your superiority by being as aggressive as possible towards other competitors' kites. Kite-flying, according to the Malay Annals, was a favourite hobby in the heyday of the Melaka sultanate in the15th century.

Other cultural performances include traditional dance routines such as the royal *Mak Yong* dance and the *Menora*, both of which relate local legends. Coconut-Husk Percussion is on Wed.

The **State Museum,** ⓘ *T9-7482266, 0830-1645, Sat-Thu, RM2,* is situated on Jalan Sultan Ibrahim near the clock tower.

Kong Mek

ⓘ *From KB follow road to PCB; after 500 m, on sharp right bend, turn left at vegetable market; go down dirt track and turn right through Chinese gateway at bottom.*
Also known as Tin Heng Keong, this Chinese temple is 1 km out of town, on the road to PCB (see below). It is about 100 years old and is particularly colourful; best time to visit is 0900-1000 each day when the temple is particularly lively. There is another smaller temple with a grotesque laughing Buddha and a grotto on the riverbank, closer to town.

Pantai Cahaya Bulan and other beaches

ⓘ *To get there take a minibus 10, which leaves every 20 minutes from Bazaar Buluh Kubu, off Jalan Tengku Chik or from Jalan Padang Garong, or take a taxi.*
This is KB's most famous beach, formerly **Pantai Cinta Berahi**, but still known as **PCB**, 10 km north of the city. It is really only famous for its name, meaning the 'Beach of Passionate Love'. In 1994 the Islamic state government, which takes a dim view of passionate love, rechristened it the Beach of the Shining Moon, which conveniently retains the old acronym, PCB. In comparison with some other east coast beaches, it is an unromantic dump. In Malay, the word *berahi* is, according to one scholar, "loaded with sexual dynamite ... a love madness". Local Malays, alluding to this heated innuendo, used to euphemistically call it *pantai semut api* – the beach of the fire ants. Today, young Malay lovers do not even dare to hold hands on the beach, for fear of being caught by the religious police and charged with *khalwat*, the crime of 'close proximity', under Sharia Islamic law. The origin of the name *cinta berahi* is lost. One theory is that it was used as a code word by Malay and British commandos during the Japanese wartime occupation: the site of the Imperial Army's invasion, in 1941, is nearby, on Pantai Dasar Sabak (see page 300). Despite being rather over-rated, there are several resorts along the beach. It gets crowded on weekends and room rates rise accordingly.

Pantai Dalam Rhu, also known as Pantai Bisikan Bayu ('Beach of the Whispering Breeze'), lies 40 km southeast of KB. **Pantai Irama,** the 'Beach of Melody', 25 km south of KB, is the best of the nearby beaches for swimming. **Pantai Dasar Sabak** is 13 km northeast of KB. Nearby Kampong Sabak is a good place to watch the morning fishing boats come in. To get there, take a bus 8 or 9 from old market terminal.

Other excursions

In the area round Pasir Puteh there are several waterfalls: Jeram Pasu, Jeram Tapeh and Cherang Tuli. **Jeram Pasu** is the most popular, 35 km from Kota Bharu, ⓘ *It is most easily accessible by taxi or bus 3 to Padang Pak Amat and taxi to the waterfalls.*

Around **Tumpat**, next to the border, are small Thai communities where there are a few Thai-style buildings and wats; they do not, however, compare with the Thai architecture on the other side of the border. **Wat Phothivian** at Kampong Berok 12 km

Pantai Dasar Sabak is where the Japanese troops landed on 7 December 1941, 90 minutes before they bombed Pearl Harbor.

east of KB, on the Malaysian side of Sungai Golok, has a 41 m reclining Buddha statue, built in 1973 by chief abbot Phra Kruprasapia Chakorn, which attracts thousands of Thai pilgrims every year, ⓘ *take bus 27 or 19 to Chabang Empat and then a taxi the last 3-4 km to Kampong Jambu. This last part of the journey also makes for a pleasant enough rural stroll.*

Masjid Kampong Laut at Kampong Nilam Puri, 10 km south of KB, ⓘ *Bus 44 or express bus 5 leaves every 30 mins*, was built 300 years ago by Javanese Muslims as an offering of thanks for being saved from pirates. Having been damaged once too often by monsoon floods, it was dismantled and moved inland to Kampong Nilam Puri, which is an Islamic scholastic centre. It was built entirely of cengal, a prized hardwood, and constructed without the use of nails. It vies with Masjid Kampong Kling (in Melaka) for the title of Malaysia's oldest mosque.

From Kuala Kerai (a 1½-hour bus trip south from Kota Bharu, bus 5), it is possible to take a boat upriver to Dabong, a small kampong nestled among the jungled foothills of the Main Range (two hours, departs in the morning but not on Friday), where there is a resthouse and restaurant. Dabong, in the centre of Kelantan state, is on the north-south railway, so it is possible to catch the train back to Wakaf Bharu (across the river from KB). Alternatively, take a taxi.

Gua Musang

Gua Musang is the largest town on Route 8, the road through the interior, and lies in Kelantan state close to the border with Pahang. It began life as little more than a logging camp but has now expanded into a thriving administrative centre. The jungle is studded with limestone outcrops in this area of the Peninsula and a particularly impressive one overshadows Gua Musang. There have been reports of large mammals including wild elephants, tigers and tapirs along the roads near here and this is about as wild as Peninsular Malaysia gets outside the national parks and wildlife reserves.

Coast to coast

The East-West highway makes for a memorable journey. It runs from Kota Bharu to Penang, straight across the forested backbone of the peninsula and was one of the biggest civil engineering projects ever undertaken in Malaysia. During its 11-year construction, contractors had to push their way through densely jungled mountains, coping with frequent landslides and even hit-and-run-attacks by Communist insurgents.

Grik can be reached from Kuala Kangsar in Perak (see page 142) or from Butterworth via either Kulim (directly east of the town) or Sungai Petani (35 km north of town) which lead first to Keroh, on the Thai border, then on to Grik. The Kuala Kangsar route is a particularly scenic drive along a 111 km road which winds its way up the Perak River valley, enclosed by the Bintang mountains to the west and the Main Range to the east. En route, the road passes Tasek Chenderoh, a beautiful reservoir, surrounded by jungled hills. At **Kota Tampan**, just north of the lake, archaeologists have unearthed the remains of a Stone Age workshop, with roughly chiselled stone tools dating back 35,000 years. The road cuts through the jungle and there are some spectacular viewpoints. There are landslides along this stretch of road during the wet season).

To the east of Grik, the highway runs close to the former bases of the Communist Party of Malaya, which, until 1989, operated out of their jungle headquarters near Betong, just across the Thai border. The area was known as 'Target One' by the Malaysian security forces. The construction of the road opened the previously inaccessible area up to timber companies; there has been much illegal logging – and cross-border drug-smuggling – in this 'cowboy country' of North Perak and Kelantan. The 200 km-long highway opened in 1982, and for the first few years was closed to traffic after 1600 because of the security threat posed by Communist insurgents; this threat has now ended. However, road maintenance is something of a hazard, and the journey is slow going with a whole series of road works and places where the road has subsided.

The train trundles along the railway line which cuts a diagonal through the peninsula, running due north from Gemas (south of KL on the KL-Singapore line) to Kota Bharu. Much of the route is through the jungle, and the track skirts the west boundary of Taman Negara, the national park (see page 265). The train is slow, but it is an interesting journey. From Gemas the line goes through Jerantut, Kuala Lipis, Gua Musang, Kuala Kerai and on to Kota Bharu. It is possible to catch the train at Mentakab (along the Karak Highway, east of KL) or at Kuala Lipis, which can be reached by road via Fraser's Hill and Raub. It is also possible to drive from Kuala Lipis via Gua Musang to Kota Bharu. There are buses from Kuala Lipis to Gua Musang and Kuala Kerai.

Sleeping

Kota Bharu *p296, map p298*

None of the hotels except for the *Murni* serves alcohol so minibars are usually a bleak sight. Budget travellers are spoilt for choice in KB; there are some very pleasant cheaper hostels and guesthouses (most of them in secluded alleyways with gardens) and they are locked in fearsome competition. As a result, new ones start up all the time as old ones fold; the State Tourist Information Centre has a list of budget accommodation and is happy to make recommendations. Homestays can also be arranged with local people. See under Activities and tours for details.

A Perdana, Jln Mahmud, T9-7485000, F9-7447621. A/c, restaurant, pool, tennis and squash courts, bowling alley, best in town, central location, babysitting, gym, sauna, traditional massage. Broad spectrum of tour information available and also a travel agent on site.

A-B Crystal Lodge, 124 Jln Che Su, T9-7470888, F9-7470088. A/c and attached bathroom, breakfast with morning newspaper provided. Attractive and good open-air roof restaurant. Karaoke and mini-cinema.

A-B Dynasty Inn, 2865 D and E Jln Sultan Zainab, T9-7473000, dynasty@hotmail.com A hotel with 47 rooms, a/c, TV, hot shower, good views, rooftop coffee house, Chinese seafood restaurant.

B Ansar, Jln Maju, T9-7474000, F9-7461150. Clean hotel, conveniently located near the night market, it is an Islamic hotel, so no shoes, prayers in the hallways and signs mentioning Allah in the elevators, basic breakfast included, overpriced. Very comfortable with decent rooms and business centre.

B Juita Inn, Jln Pintu Pong, T9-7446888, hotel@tm.net.my Attractive hotel with 70 rooms, a/c, TV, minibar, restaurant, room rates include breakfast. Rooms are small but clean and well furnished – note that the superior rooms have no windows, not particularly good value.

B Safar Inn, Jln Hilir Kota, T9-7478000, F9-7479000. A hotel with 31 rooms, a/c, TV, carefully furnished rooms with wall-to-wall carpets. Good location, in the heart of town.

B Sentosa, 3180-A Jln Sultan Ibrahim, T9-7443200/7443292. A/c, restaurant (formerly *Irama Baru & Apollo Hotel*), all spruced up, very clean and car rental organized. Great value.

B-C Tokyo Baru, 3945 Jln Tok Hakim, T9-7449488/7444511. A/c, well-maintained place, friendly. Recommended.

B-D Sabriena Court, Jln Padang Garong, T9-7447944, SabrienaCourt@hotmail.com A/c, restaurant, reasonable value for money, also offers some backpacker accommodation; do not confuse with sister hotel, *Hotel Sri Kencana*.

D Hostel Pantai Timor, Lot 391 Jln Pengkalan Chepa, behind Safra Jaya supermarket, T9-7483753. Well kept, friendly, also dorms.

D Ideal Travellers' House, 5504a Jln Padang Garong, T9-7442246, idealtrahouse@hotmail.com Quiet, friendly, pleasant verandah, rooms and dormitory. This family run, popular hostel also helps with onward transport to Thailand and the Perhentians. Offers free pick-up from early morning bus arrivals (0500) from KL and Penang, but often staff do not show up! However, most travellers have a good experience here and get lots of help with travel arrangements from this place.

D **KB Inn**, 1872 Jln Padang Garong, T7441786. Very close to bus station and night market, breakfast and hot drinks free, small sitting area with TV, typical of centre of town budget accommodation.

D-F **Town**, 286 Jln Pengkalan Chepa, T9-7432521. Some rooms with a/c and own bathroom, travel information and booking available here. Friendly, helpful management.

E-F **Menora**, Wisma Chua Tong Boon, (1st Flr) Jln Sultanah Zainab, T9-7481669. Well kept, facilities include TV and powerful showers, dorm. Recommended.

E **Zeck Traveller's Inn**, 7088-G Jln Sri Cemerlang, T9-7473423, ztraveller_Inn@hotmail.com Some rooms with private shower, dorm rooms, verandah, free pick-up from bus station, one of the most popular places to stay.

E-F **Yee**, Jln Padang Garong, 2nd Flr, T7441944. Everything you need: laundry, breakfast, showers, travel information, bicycles for hire, dorm but unfortunately, the rooms are dirty.

F **DE 999**, next to *Menora*, Jln Sultanah Zainab, T9-7481955. Cheap and clean rooms, close to the Cultural Centre, price including breakfast, free bicycles, dorm and rooms. Popular with Japanese tourists.

Pantai Cinta Berahi and other beaches *p300*

A **Perdana Resort** (also known as *PCB Resort*), Jln Kuala Pa'Amat, Pintai Cinta Berahi, T9-7744000, F9-7744980. A/c, restaurant, pool, watersports, more pleasant stretch of beach, dotted with white chalets colour schemed blue, green and pink according to room type, not very well maintained, popular with business conventions and meetings.

B-C **Motel Irama Bachok**, Bachok, T9-7788462, is clean and reasonable value. To get there, take a bus 2A or 2B to Bachok, which leaves every 30 mins.

C-D **Long House Beach Motel**, Pantai Cinta Berahi, T9-7731090. Some a/c, restaurant (Thai food), not bad value really but it doesn't have a great deal of charm.

D-E **HB Village**, Pinta Cinta Berahi, T9-7734993. Very clean, very friendly and very big crocodiles in attached farm.

E **Dalam Rhu Homestay**, Pantai Dalam Rhu, which has simple kampong-style accommodation and is well looked after. Take bus 3, southbound, and change at Pasir Puteh.

Gua Musang *p301*

C **Kesedar Inn**, T099121229. On the edge of town, attractive lawn, clean rooms, friendly.

E **Rest House**, rather run down but an attractive place to stay, shared facilities.

Eating

Kota Bharu *p296, map p298*

Beer and other alcoholic beverages are only available in certain Chinese coffee shops, notably along Jln Kebun Sultan.

The Kelantan speciality is *ayam percik* – roast chicken, marinated in spices and served with a coconut-milk gravy. *Nasi tumpang* is a typical Kelantanese breakfast; banana-leaf funnel of rice layers interspersed with prawn and fish curries and salad.

TT **Ambassador**, 7003 Jln Kebun Sultan, big Chinese coffee shop next to *Kow Lun*, Chinese dishes including pork satay and other iniquitous substances – like beer.

TT **Kow Lun**, 7005 and 7006 Jln Kebun Sultan, good lively Chinese coffee shop with large variety of dishes and lots of beer.

TT **Malaysia**, 2527 Jln Kebun Sultan, Chinese cuisine, speciality: steamboat.

T **Meena Curry House**, 3377 Jln Gajah Mati, Indian curry house, banana leaf restaurant. Recommended.

T **Neelavathy**, Jln Tengku Maharani (behind *Kencana Inn*), South Indian banana-leaf curries. Recommended.

T **Qing Liang**, Jln Zainal Abidin, excellent Chinese vegetarian, also Malay and Western dishes. Recommended.

Bakeries

Mubihah Vegetarian Restaurant and Cake House, opposite *Kentucky Fried Chicken*, 157 Jln Pintu Pong. Eat in or takeaway; excellent breads, pastries, cakes etc – one of the best '*kek and roti*' shops in Malaysia.

Foodstalls

Night market (in car park opposite local bus station, in front of Central Market), exclusively Malay food, satays and exquisite array of curries; for a delectable sweet dish to round off the evening, try the banana *murtabak*. Colour-coded tables – if you eat from a certain stall and sit at a blue table, you are obliged to buy your drink from a stall in the blue area; excellent fruit juices, no alcohol. Open every night from 1800, but closes from 1900-2000 for evening prayers. More choice and atmosphere at the weekends. Recommended.

Nasi Padang Osman Larin (otherwise known as *Nasi Hoover* as it is outside *Hotel Hoover*) is a stall on Jln Datuk Pati (between the Tourist Information Centre and the bus station) famed locally for its curries. By the stadium in Jln Muhamud.

Entertainment

Kota Bharu *p296, map p298*

Cultural shows

Regular cultural shows at the **Gelanggang Seni** (cultural centre), Jln Mahmud.

Festivals

Kota Bharu *p296*

Ask the tourist office or phone Kelantan State Government who organise the kite festival, T9-7481957, for information on all festival dates.

May/June Malaysia International Kite Festival, Pantai Seri Tujuh (Beach of the Seven Lagoons), Turnport (adjacent to Thai border), 7 km from KB. To get there take bus 43.

July (movable) Drum festival a traditional east coast pastime; **10-12**, Sultan's birthday celebrations.

August (movable) Bird Singing Contest when the prized *merbuk* (doves) or *burong ketitir* birds compete on top of 8 m-high poles. Bird singing contests are also held on Fri mornings around Kota Bharu.

September (movable) Top-spinning contest. Another traditional east coast sport which is taken very seriously.

Shopping

Kota Bharu *p296, map p298*

Antiques

Lam's, Jln Post Office Lama (in contrast to the modern town walk there are several old bamboo raft houses along this street).

Batik

Astaka Fesyer, 782K (3rd floor). Recommended; **Bazaar Buluh Kubu**, Jln Tengku Petra Semerak, just across the road from the Central Market, houses scores of batik boutiques; also in the building are tailors' shops which can turn out very cheap shirts, blouses and dresses within 24 hrs.

Handicrafts

The Central Market is cheapest for handicrafts. There are numerous handicraft stalls, silver-workers, kite-makers and wood-carvers scattered along the road north to Pantai Cinta Berahi. At Kampong Penambang, on this road, just outside KB, there is a batik and songket centre.

Silverware

On Jln Sultanah Zainab (near the bridge across the Kelantan River), before junction with Jln Hamzah, there are 3 shops selling Kelantan silver including **KB Permai**, a family business which works the silver on the premises. The **Kampong Kraftangan** (Handicraft Village) contains many stalls with a huge range of batik sarongs and ready-mades, silverware, songket, basketry and various Kelantanese knick-knacks.

Activities and tours

Kota Bharu *p296, map p298*

Golf

Royal Kelantan Golf Club, 5488 Jln Hospital, 18-hole course.

Tour operators

Batuta Travel & Tour, 1st Flr, Bangunan PKDK, Jln Dato' Pati, T9-7442652; **Boustead Travel**, 2833 Jln Temenggong, T9-7449952; **Kelmark Travel**, Kelmark House, 5220 Jln Telipot, T9-7444211; **KTIC** (Kelantan State Tourist Information Centre) organizes a number of tours – river and jungle-safari trips, staying in kampongs and learning local crafts. It also organizes three-day 'Kampong Experience' tours which are not as contrived as their name suggests. Full board and lodging provided by host families which can be selected from list including potters, fishermen, batik-makers, kite-makers, silversmiths, dance instructors, top-makers and shadow puppet-makers. All only available by request. Cost from RM285 (all in); minimum two people. It also runs short Kelantanese cooking courses; **Pelancongan Bumi Mars**, Tingkat Bawah, Kompleks Yakin, Jln Gajah Mati, T9-7431189. The **Tourist Information Centre** also arrange tours as do several of the guesthouses in town.

Transport

Kota Bharu *p296, map p298*

Air

The airport is 8 km from town; RM12 per taxi. Regular connections with **KL**, and **JB**. Transport to town: by taxi RM10 per person or town bus No 9.

Airline offices AirAsia office at the airport. MAS, Ground Floor, Komplek Yakin, Jln Gajah Mati (opposite the clock tower), T9-7447000 and T9-7440557 at the airport.

Bus

City buses and long-distance express buses leave from the Central Bus Station, Jln Hilir Pasar. Regional buses to places like **Gua Musang** and **Pasir Puteh** also depart from this station. Regular connections with **Grik**, **Kuala Terengganu**, **Jerantut**, **Kuantan, KL**, **JB**, **Penang**, **Alor Star**, **Kuala Lipis**, **Butterworth**, **Melaka**, **Mersing**, **Temerloh**, and many other destinations.

Car hire

Avis, *Hotel Perdana*, Jln Sultan Mahmud, T9-7484457, South China Sea, airport, T9-7744288, F9-7736288; from *Perdana Hotel*, Pacific, T9-7447610.

Taxi

Taxi station next to the Central Bus Station, Jln Hilir Pasar. Destinations include **Kuala Terengganu**, **Kuantan**, **KL**, **JB**, **Butterworth**, **Grik**. Also taxis to **Rantau Panjang** (for **Sungai Golok**, **Thailand**).

International connections The Thai border is at the Malaysian town of Rantau Panjang; on the other side is the Thai settlement of Sungai Golok. Bus no 29 for **Rantau Panjang** leaves on the hr through the day from the central bus station, off Jln Hilir Pasar (1½ hrs). From here it is a shortish 1-km walk across the border to **Sungai Golok's** train and bus stations where there are connections to other destinations in Thailand including Hat Yai, Surat Thani (for Koh Samui) and Bangkok. Trishaws and motorbike taxis wait to assist people making the crossing.

Another route into Thailand is via **Pengkalan Kubor**, a quieter and much more interesting crossing to **Ta Ba** (Tak Bai). Bus nos. 27, 27a and 43 go to **Pengkalan Kubor**. Small boats cross the river regularly and there is also a car ferry. Long-tails cater for the clientele of the cross-border prostitution industry only. There are also regular bus connections with **Singapore**.

Train

Wakaf Bharu station is 6 km out of town, across the Kelantan River. Bus 19 or 27. Several daily connections with **Singapore** and **KL** via **Gua Musang**, **Kuala Lipis**, and **Jerantut**. The railway is slow but the scenery makes the journey worthwhile. Trains to KL leave at 1719 and 1819 to arrive between 0600 and 0700. The daily service to Singapore leaves at 1919 and arrives at around 0900.

Gua Musang *p301*

Bus

Daily buses from **Kuala Lipis** to Gua Musang (0800 and 1300) and **Kuala Kerai** (1430) with onward connections to Kota Bharu. There is a new road linking Gua Musang to Tanah Rata in the Cameron Highlands and through to Ipoh on the west coast. At the time of writing there was a minibus connection between Gua Musang and **Tanah Rata**. This is likely to expand to fully fledged bus services in the near future.

Coast to coast *p301*

Bus

Grik has connections with **Butterworth, KL**, **Taiping** and **Ipoh**. For **Kota Bharu** change at Tanah Merah. It is possible to cross the border into Thailand from **Keroh**, 50 km north of Grik. There are regular taxis from Keroh to the border post and Thai taxis and *saamlors* (trishaws) on the other side. There are Thai taxis to **Betong** which is 8 km from the border.

Directory

Kota Bharu *p296, map p298*

Banks Money changers in main shopping area. Bumiputra, Jln Maju; D & C, Jln Gajah Mati; Hongkong & Shanghai, Jln Sultan. **Post** General Post Office Jln Sultan Ibrahim. **Embassies and consulates** Royal Thai Consulate, Jln Pengkalan Chepa, T9-7440867 (open 0900-1200, 1330-1530, Mon-Thu and Sat). **Medical services** Hospital Jln Hospital, T9-7485533. **Useful addresses** Immigration Office 3rd Flr, Federal Bldg, Jln Bayam, T9-7482120.

Sarawak

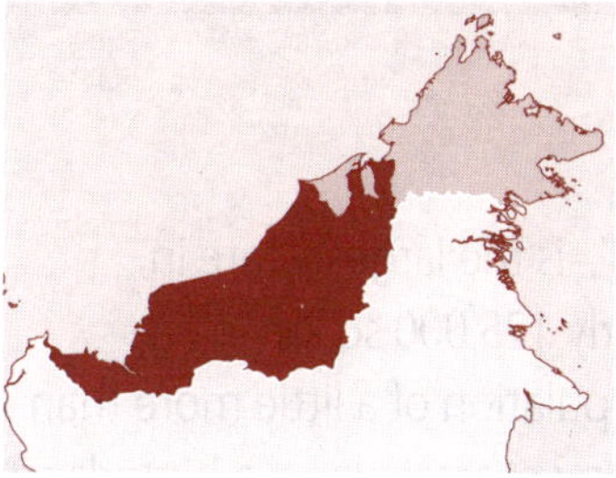

Footprint features

Introduction

Sarawak, the 'land of the hornbill', is the largest state in Malaysia covering an area of nearly 125,000 sq km in Northwest Borneo and with a population of a little more than two million. Sarawak has a swampy coastal plane, a hinterland of undulating foothills and an interior of steep-sided, jungle-covered mountains.The lowlands and plains are dissected by a network of broad rivers that are the main arteries of communication and where the majority of the population are settled.

In the mid-19th century, Charles Darwin described Sarawak as "one great wild, untidy, luxuriant hothouse, made by nature for herself". Sarawak is Malaysia's great natural storehouse,where little more than half a century ago great swathes of forest were largely unexplored and where tribal groups, collectively known as the Dayaks, would venture downriver from the heartlands of the state to exchange forest products of hornbill ivory and precious woods. Today the Dayaks have been gradually incorporated into the mainstream and the market economy has infiltrated the lives of the great majority of the population. But much remains unchanged. The grandeur of the forests, although much reduced by a rapacious logging industry, are still some of the most species-rich on the globe; more than two-thirds of Sarawak's land area, roughly equivalent to that of England and Scotland combined, is still covered in jungle, although this is declining.

★ Don't miss ...

1. **Sarawak Museum** Wince at the palang display - Dayak bamboo tool for piercing the glans of the penis - in Kuching, page 312.
2. **Bako National Park** One of the best places in Sarawak to get nose to nose with the proboscis monkey, page 324.
3. **Kuching waterfront** Amble along the promenade, snacking on *ais goreng* (fried ice cream), page 331.
4. **Longhouse stay** Secure an overnight invite at an Iban, Bidayuh or Orang Ulu village, page 339.
5. **Rejang River** Ride the rapids on a boat trip to Kapit or Belaga, page 346.
6. **Caving** Become a spelunker and admire the prehistoric cave art in Niah National Park, page 359.
7. **Pinnacles** It's a challenging trek to Mulu's forest of razor sharp limestone needles on Fire Mountain, page 375.

Kuching and around

→ *Colour map 3, grid C1 Population: around 425,000*

Because of Kuching's relative isolation, and the fact that it was not bombed during the Second World War, Sarawak's state capital has retained much of its 19th-century dignity and charm, despite the increasing number of modern high-rise buildings. Chinese shophouses still line many of the narrow streets. Kuching is a great starting point to explore the state and there are many sights within it's compact centre, including the renowned Sarawak Museum and the Petra Jaya State Mosque.

Within easy reach is the Semenggoh Orang Utan Sanctuary and the national parks of Gunung Gading, Kubah and Tanjung Datu National Park. North of Kuching is the Damai Peninsula and Bako National Park on the Muara Tebas Peninsula. ▸▸ *For Sleeping, Eating and other listings, see page 326-337.*

Ins and outs

Getting there

There are daily connections with KL and also regular flights to other destinations in Peninsular and East Malaysia including Kota Kinabalu and JB. International connections are limited to Bandar Seri Begawan (Brunei), Singapore, Hong Kong (via Kota Kinabalu), and Perth. The airport is 10 km south of Kuching. A taxi from the airport is paid for by a fixed-price coupon (RM17.50) to city centre. There are several out-of-town bus companies and they provide services to destinations along the Sematan. Interior towns are sometimes difficult to access by road. There is also a bus service to Pontianak in Kalimantan (Indonesia, 10 hours) and to Brunei, via Miri. Express boats serve Sibu and Sarikei. See also Transport page 335.

! If you are inside Sarawak you don't need to dial the prefix. If you are calling from outside Sarawak but inside Malaysia you need to use the prefix.

Getting around

The central portion of the city, which is the most interesting, can be negotiated on foot. Sampans, (*perahu tambang*), provide cross-river transport and operate as river taxis. There are 2 city bus companies that provide a cheap and fairly efficient service. Taxis are found outside many of the larger hotels and at designated taxi stands. There are also several international as well as local self-drive car hire firms in Sarawak.

Best time to visit

Kuching is hot and humid year-round. While heavy showers can happen at any time, they are more likely during the rainy season (from November to February), which could make trekking difficult. May and June is also the time for Gawai Dayak (see page 55) a kind of harvest festival – a time for feasting and partying.

Tourist information

Sarawak Tourism Board, ⓘ *Visitors' Information Centre, Old Courthouse, Sarawak Tourism Complex, Jln Tun Abang Haji Openg, T82-410944, www.sarwaktourism.gov, 0800-1800 Mon-Fri, 0800-1500 first and third Sat of the month, 0800-1600 for other Sat, closed Sun*. The centre is housed in the beautiful Old Courthouse Complex. It has a good stock of maps and pamphlets, but the staff can be abrupt and give conflicting advice. The smaller branch office of the Sarawak Tourism Association on the waterfront has infinitely more helpful and courteous staff. Sarawak Tourism Association, ⓘ *waterfront, Main Bazaar, T82-240620, F82-427151, 0800-1245 and*

Tom Harrisson: life in the fast lane

Reputed to be one of the most important figures in the development of archaeology in Southeast Asia, Tom Harrisson, the charismatic 'egomaniac', put Borneo and Sarawak on the map.

Tom Harrisson loved Sarawak and, it would seem, Sarawak loved him. It was only appropriate that when he was killed in a traffic accident in 1976 it was in Thailand and not in Malaysia.

He first visited Sarawak in 1932 as part of a Royal Geographical Expedition sent, along with around 150 kg of Cadbury's chocolate, to collect flora and fauna from one of the world's great natural treasure stores. Instead Harrisson found himself entranced by the territory's human populations and so the love affair began.

By all accounts, Harrisson was a difficult fellow – the sort that Imperial Britain produced in very large numbers indeed. He was a womaniser with a particular penchant for other people's spouses, he could be horribly abusive to his fellow workers, and he apparently revelled in putting down uppity academics. But he was also instrumental in putting Sarawak, and Borneo more generally, on the map and in raising awareness of the ways in which economic and social change was impacting on Sarawak's tribal peoples.

Before taking up the curatorship of the Sarawak Museum in 1947 Harrisson also distinguished himself as a war hero, parachuting into the jungle and organising around 1,000 headhunters to terrorize the Japanese. All-in-all, Tom Harrisson led life in the fast lane.

(For those wanting to read a good biography of Harrisson get hold of *The most offending soul alive* by Judith M Heimann, Honolulu: Hawaii University Press, 1998)

1400-1645 Mon-Thu, 0800-1130 and 1430-1645 Fri, and 0800-1245 Sat, closed first and third Sat in the month, closed Sun. There is also a desk at Kuching International Airport, ⓘ *T82-450944*; good for information on bus routes, approved travel agents and itineraries. **Tourism Malaysia,** ⓘ *Bangunan Rugayah, Jln Song Thian Cheok, T82-246575, F82-246442*, information on Sarawak and rest of Malaysia – good stock of brochures. The state and national tourism organizations are both well informed and helpful; they can offer advice on itineraries, travel agents and up-to-date information on facilities in national parks.

National parks information

For information and advance accommodation booking for the national parks of Bako, Gunung Gading, Kubah and Matang Wildlife Centres, contact the **National Parks and Wildlife Booking office** ⓘ *Inside the tourist information centre in the Old Court House, Sarawak Tourism Complex, Jln Tun Abang Haji Openg, T82-248088, F82-248087*. You can also book through www.forestry.sarawak.gov.my, click on online services, and then 'booking of national park'. Also npbooking@sarawak.net.gov.my

History

Shortly after dawn on 15 August 1839 British explorer James Brooke sailed round a bend in the Sarawak River and, from the deck of his schooner, *The Royalist*, had his first view of Kuching. According to the historian Robert Payne, he saw "...a very small town of brown huts and longhouses made of wood or the hard stems of the nipah palm, sitting in brown squalor on the edge of mudflats." The settlement, 32 km upriver from the sea, had been established less than a decade earlier by Brunei chiefs who had come to oversee the mining of antimony in the Sarawak River valley. The antimony – used as an alloy to harden other metals, particularly pewter – was exported to Singapore where the tin-plate industry was developing.

By the time James Brooke had become Rajah in 1841, the town had a population of local Malays and Dayaks and Cantonese, Hokkien and Teochew traders. Chinatown dominated the south side of the river while the Malay kampongs were strung out along the riverbanks to the west. A few Indian traders also set up in the bazaar, among the Chinese shophouses. Under Charles Brooke, the second of the White Rajahs, Kuching began to flourish; he commissioned most of the town's main public buildings. Brooke's wife, Ranee Margaret, wrote: "The little town looked so neat and fresh and prosperous under the careful jurisdiction of the Rajah and his officers, that it reminded me of a box of painted toys kept scrupulously clean by a child."

Like other cities in East Malaysia, Kuching's population is predominantly Chinese and Malay and they easily outnumbered the Dayaks who live here.

Background

Sarawak's capital is divided by the Sarawak River; the south is a commercial and residential area, dominated by Chinese while the north shore is predominantly Malay in character with the old kampong houses lining the river. The **Astana**, **Fort Margherita** and the **Petra Jaya area**, with its modern government offices, are also on the north side of the river. The two parts of the city are very different in character and even have separate mayors. Kuching's cosmopolitan make-up is immediately evident from its religious architecture: Chinese and Hindu temples, the imposing state mosque and Protestant and Roman Catholic churches.

Of all the cities in Malaysia, Kuching has been the worst affected by the 'smog' - euphemistically known as the 'haze' - that periodically engulfs large areas of Borneo and the Indonesian island of Sumatra, largely blamed on slash and burn deforestation in Kalimantan. This was most severe in mid-1997 (see page 527), but occurs to some extent every year, although to a lesser degree. At the peak of the 'emergency' in late September 1997 – for that is what it became – Kuching came to a stop. It was too dangerous to drive and, seemingly, too dangerous to breathe. People were urged to remain indoors. Schools, government offices and factories closed. The port and airport were also closed. Tourism traffic dropped to virtually zero and for 10 days the city stopped. At one point there was even discussion of evacuating the population of the State of Sarawak. People began to buy up necessities and the prices of some commodities rose 500 per cent.

Sights

Sarawak Museum

ⓘ *Daily 0900-1700, closed on first day of public holidays, free. There is a library attached to the museum as well as a giftshop, the Curio Shoppe, all proceeds of which go to charity, and a bookshop. Permits to visit the Niah's Painted Cave can be obtained, free of charge, from the curator's office.*

Kuching's biggest attraction is this internationally renowned museum, housed in two sections on both sides of Jalan Tun Haji Openg. The old building to the east of the main road is a copy of a Normandy town hall, designed by Charles Brooke's French valet. The Rajah was encouraged to build the museum by the naturalist Alfred Russel Wallace, who spent over two years in Sarawak, where he wrote his first paper on natural selection. The museum was opened in 1891, extended in 1911, and the 'new' wing built in 1983. Its best known curators have been naturalist Eric Mjoberg, who made the first ascent of Sarawak's highest peak – Gunung Murud (see page 368) – in 1922, and ethnologist and explorer Tom Harrisson, whose archaeological work at

A town called Cat

There are a number of explanations as to how Sarawak's capital acquired the name 'Cat'. (Kuching means 'cat' in Malay – although today it is more commonly spelt kucing as in modern Bahasa 'c' is pronounced 'ch'.)

Local legend has it that James Brooke, pointing towards the settlement across the river, inquired what it was called. Whoever he asked, mistakenly thought he was pointing at a passing cat. If that seems a little far-fetched, the Sarawak museum offers a few more plausible alternatives. Kuching may have been named after the wild cats (*kucing hutan*) which, in the 19th century, were commonly seen along jungled banks of the Sarawak River. Another theory is that it was called after the fruit *buah mata kucing* ('cat's eyes'), which grows locally. Most likely, however, is the theory that the town may originally have been known as Cochin – port – a word commonly used across India and Indochina.

Niah made world headlines in 1957. The museum overlooks pleasant botanical gardens and the Heroes Memorial, built to commemorate the dead of the Second World War, the Communist insurgency and the confrontation with Indonesia. Across the road, and linked by an overhead bridge, is the Dewan Tun Abdul Razak building, a newer extension of the museum.

The museum has a strong ethnographic section, although some of its displays have been superseded by the Cultural Village (see page 323), Sarawak's 'living museum'. The old museum's ethnographic section includes a full-scale model of an Iban longhouse, a reproduction of a Penan hut and a selection of Kayan and Kenyah woodcarvings. There is also an impressive collection of Iban war totems (*kenyalang*) and carved Melanau sickness images (*blum*), used in healing ceremonies. The museum's assortment of traditional daggers (*kris*, see page 486) is the best in Malaysia. The Chinese and Islamic ceramics include 17th-20th century Chinese jars, which are treasured heirlooms in Sarawak (see page 317).

Check the website www.museum.sarawak.gov.my for information on Sarawak's museums.

The natural science collection, covering the flora and fauna of Sarawak, is also noteworthy. The new Tun Abdul Razak ethnological and historical collection includes prehistoric artefacts from the Niah Caves, Asia's most important archaeological site (see page 359); there is even a replica of Niah's Painted Cave – without the smell of guano.

Nearby is the Heroes Memorial which commemorates those who died in the Second World War, the Communist Insurgency and the confrontation with Indonesia.

Sarawak Islamic Museum

ⓘ *Sat-Thu 0900-1700, closed Fri.*

Not far from the Sarawak Museum is this museum, located on Jalan P Ramlee in the restored Maderasah Melayu Building, an elegant, single-storey colonial edifice. As its name suggests, the museum is devoted to Islamic artefacts from all the ASEAN countries, with the collection of manuscripts, costumes, jewellery, weaponry, furniture, coinage, textiles and ceramics spread over seven galleries, each with a different theme, and set around a central courtyard.

Waterfront

Around Main Bazaar are some other important buildings dating from the Brooke era; most of them are closed to the public. The **Supreme Court** on Main Bazaar was built in 1874 as an administrative centre. State council meetings were held here from the

1870s until 1973, when it was converted to law courts. In front of the grand entrance is a memorial to Rajah Charles Brooke (1924) and on each corner there is a bronze relief representing the four main ethnic groups in Sarawak – Iban, Orang Ulu, Malay and Chinese. The clock tower was built in 1883. The **Square Tower**, also on Main Bazaar, was built as an annex to Fort Margherita in 1879 and was used as a prison. Later in the Brooke era it was used as a ballroom. The square tower marks one end of Kuching's waterfront esplanade which runs alongside the river for almost 900 m to the Hilton.

The **Waterfront** has been transformed into a landscaped esplanade through restoration and a land reclamation project. It has become a popular meeting place, with foodstalls, restaurants and entertainment facilities including an open-air theatre. There is a restored Chinese pavilion, an observation tower, a tea terrace and musical fountains, as well as a number of modern sculptures. During the day, the waterfront offers excellent views of the Astana, Fort Margherita and the Malay kampongs which line the north bank of the river. At night, the area comes alive as younger members of Kuching's growing middle class make their way down here to relax.

A good way to see the Sarawak River is to take a **cruise**, ⓘ *RM35. Tickets can be bought at the waterfront at booths around half-way down the esplanade, else tourist agencies sell them. Day and night cruises of around 90 mins are on offer.*

The **General Post Office**, with its majestic Corinthian columns, stands in the centre of town, on Jalan Tun Haji Openg. It was built in 1931 and was one of the few

Kuching

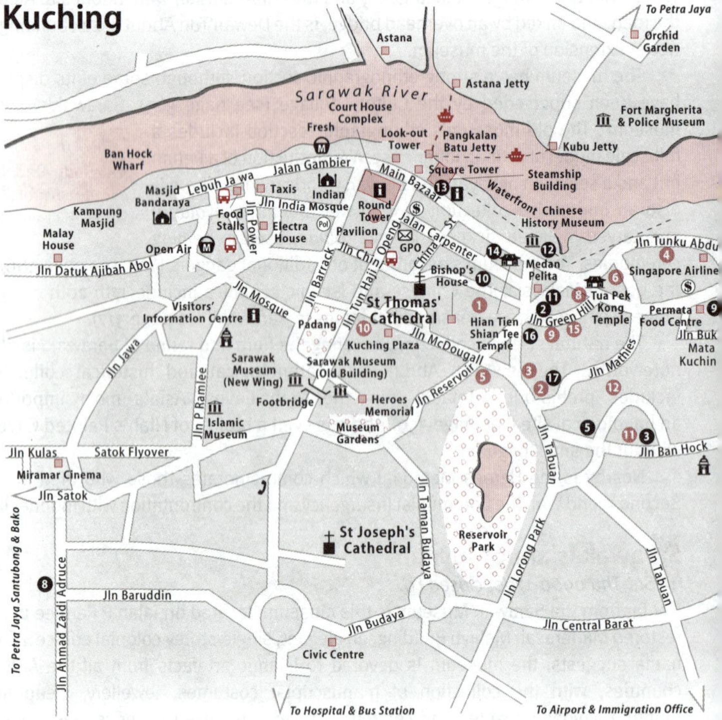

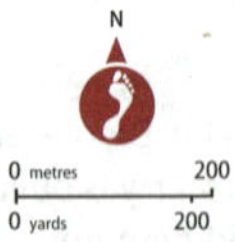

Sleeping
Anglican Guesthouse **1**
B&B Inn **2**
Borneo **3**
Borneo B&B **9**
Crown Plaza Riverside **4**
Fata **5**
Grand Continental **14**
Green Mountain Lodging House **15**
Harbour View **8**
Hilton **6**
Holiday Inn **7**
Merdeka Palace **10**
Supreme **11**
Telang Usan **12**
Kingwood Inn **13**

Eating
Aunty Mary's Kitchen **14**
D'Alif **13**

buildings built by Vyner Brooke, the last Rajah. It has been renovated and there have been long-term plans to make it the home of the **Sarawak Art Museum**.

The **Court House** complex, which now houses the Sarawak Tourism Board's Visitors Cente, was built in 1871 as the seat of Sarawak's government and was used as such until 1973. It remains one of Kuching's grandest structures. The buildings have belian (ironwood) roofs and beautiful detailing inside and out, reflecting local art forms. It also continues to house the state's high court and magistrate's court as well as several other local government departments. The colonial-baroque **clock tower** was added in 1883 and the **Charles Brooke Memorial** in 1924. The complex also includes the **Pavilion Building** which was built in 1907 as a hospital. During the Japanese occupation it was used as an information and propaganda centre and it is now undergoing renovation with a view to making it the home of a new **textile museum**. Opposite the court house is the **Indian Mosque** (**Mesjid India**) on Lebuh India, originally had an atap roof and *kajang* (thatch) walls; in 1876 belian-wood walls were erected. The mosque was built by South Indians and is in the middle of an Indian quarter where spices are sold along the Main Bazaar. When the mosque was first built only Muslims from South India were permitted to worship here; even Indian Muslims from other areas of the subcontinent were excluded. In time, as Kuching's Muslim population expanded and grew more diversified, so this rigid system was relaxed. It is hard to get to the mosque as it is surrounded by buildings. However a narrow passage leads from Lubuh India – between shop numbers 37 and 39.

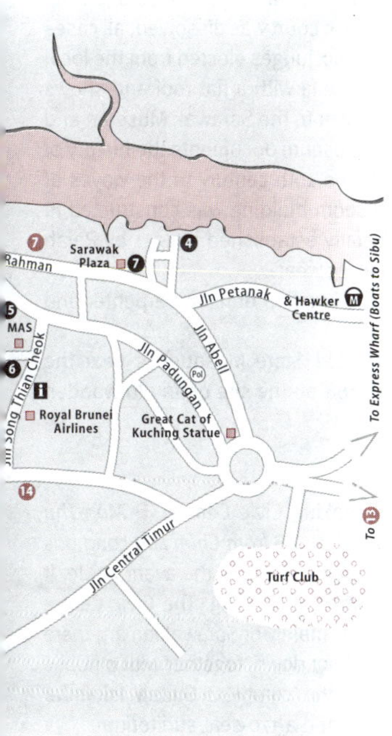

Green Hill Corner **2**
Hornbill Corner **3**
Khatulistiwa Café **12**
KTS Seafood Canteen **4**
Lan Ya Keng **10**
Perfect Vegetarian **11**
San Francisco Grill **5**
See Good **6**
Suan Chicken Rice **7**
The Junk **16**
The Tapanga Tree **15**
Thompson's Corner **8**
Top Spot Food Court **9**
Tsui Hua Lau **17**

The **Round Tower** on Jalan Tun Abang Haji Openg (formerly Rock Road) was originally planned as a fort (1886) but was never fully completed. The whole area is undergoing restoration for future art galleries and cultural exhibits. The **Steamship Building**, 52 Main Bazaar, was built in 1930 and was previously the offices and warehouse of the Sarawak Steamship Company. It has been extensively restored and now houses a restaurant, souvenir stalls, a handicrafts gallery and an exhibition area.

The **Bishop's House**, off Jalan McDougall, near the Anglican Cathedral of St Thomas, is the oldest surviving residence in Sarawak. It was built in 1849, entirely of wood, for the first Anglican Bishop of Borneo, Dr McDougall. The first mission school was started in the attic – developed into St Thomas's and St Mary's School, which is now across the road on Jalan McDougall.

Chinatown

Kuching's Chinese population, part of the town's community since its foundation, live in the shophouses lining the narrow streets around **Main Bazaar**. This street, opposite the waterfront, is the oldest in the city, dating from 1864. The Chinese families who live here still pursue traditional occupations such as tin smithing and woodworking. Kuching's highest concentration of antique and handicraft shops is to be found here. **Jalan Carpenter**, parallel to Main Bazaar, has a similar selection of small traders and coffee shops, as well as foodstalls and two small Chinese temples. Off **Leboh China** (Upper China Street), there is a row of perfectly preserved 19th-century Chinese houses. The oldest Chinese temple in Kuching, **Tua Pek Kong** (also known as Siew San Teng), in the shadow of the Hilton on Jalan Tunku Abdul Rahman, was built in 1876, although it is now much modernized. There is evidence that the site has been in use since 1740 and a Chinese temple was certainly here as early as 1770. The first structure was erected by a group of Chinese immigrants thankful for their safe journey across the hazardous South China Sea. New immigrants still come here to give thanks for their safe arrival. The Wang Kang festival to commemorate the dead is also held here. Just to the east of here, **Jln Padungan** has some of Kuching's finest Chinese shophouses. Most were built during the rubber boom of the 1920s and have been restored. There are also some great coffee shops in this quarter of town. Further east still, the kitsch statue of the **Great Cat of Kuching** – the sort of thing to induce nightmares in the aesthetically inclined – mews at the junction of Jln Padungan and Jln Central.

The **Chinese History Museum**, ⓘ *Daily 0900-1800, T82-231520, free*, stands on the Waterfront, opposite Tua Pek Kong Temple. The building itself is of interest: it was completed in 1912 and became the court for the Chinese population of Kuching. The Third Rajah was keen that the Chinese, like other ethnic groups, should settle disputes within their community in their own way and he encouraged its establishment. From 1912 until 1921, when the Chinese court was dissolved, all cases pertaining to the Chinese were heard here in front of six judges elected from the local Chinese population. The building itself is a simple cella with a flat roof and shows English colonial influences. In 1993 it was handed over to the Sarawak Museum and was turned into the Chinese History Museum. The museum documents the history of the Chinese in Sarawak, from the early traders of the 10th century to the waves of Chinese immigration in the 19th century. The museum building was constructed in the early 20th century as the Chinese court, officially established in 1911 by Rajah Charles Brooke. The exhibits are now a little worse for wear.

Hian Tien Shian Tee (Hong San) temple, at the junction of Jalan Carpenter and Jalan Wayang, was built in 1897.

The Moorish, gilt-domed **Masjid Bandaraya** (Old State Mosque) is near the market, on the west side of town; it was built in 1968 on the site of an old wooden mosque dating from 1852.

Civic Centre and Planetarium

On the south side of the river the extraordinary-looking Civic Centre, ⓘ *Mon-Thu 0915-1730, Sat and Sun 0915-1800; bus 14A, 14B, 14C and 8 from Chim Lan Long bus station on Jln Masjid*, on Jalan Taman Budaya, is Kuching's stab at the avant garde. It has a viewing platform, ⓘ *0900-2100*, for panoramas of Kuching. The Civic Centre complex houses an art gallery with temporary exhibits, mainly of Sarawakian art, there is also a restaurant and a pub-cum-karaoke bar one floor down, together with a public library. Malaysia's first planetarium is also within the complex: **Sultan Iskandar Planetarium** ⓘ *shows, RM3*, which has a 15-m dome and a 170-seat auditorium.

Astana

ⓘ *Take a sampan across the river from the Pangkalan Batu jetty next to Square Tower on The Waterfront to the Astana and fort; less then RM1 one way; the boats can be hired quite cheaply at an hourly rate, around RM30 per hour.*

Apart from the Sarawak Museum, the White Rajahs bequeathed several other architectural monuments to Kuching. The Astana, a variant of the usual spelling istana (palace), was built in 1870, two years after Charles Brooke took over from his

A ceramic inheritance

Family wealth and status in Sarawak was traditionally measured in ceramics. In the tribal longhouses upriver, treasured heirlooms include ancient glass beads, brass gongs and cannons and Chinese ceramic pots and beads (such as those displayed in the Sarawak Museum). They were often used as currency and dowries. Spencer St John, the British consul in Brunei, mentions using beads as currency on his 1858 expedition to Gunung Mulu. Jars, (*pesaka*), had more practical applications; they were (and still are) used for storing rice, brewing *tuak* (rice wine) or for keeping medicines.

Their value was dependent on their rarity: brown jars, emblazoned with dragon motifs, are more recent and quite common while olive-glazed dusun jars, dating from the 15th-17th centuries are rare. The Kelabit people, who live in the highlands around Bario, treasure the dragon jars in particular. Although some of the more valuable antique jars have found their way to the Sarawak Museum, many magnificent jars remain in the Iban and other tribal longhouses along the Skrang, Rejang and Baram rivers. Many are covered by decoratively carved wooden lids.

Chinese contact and trade with the north coast of Borneo has gone on for at least a millennium, possibly two. Chinese Han pottery fragments and coins have been discovered near the estuary of the Sarawak River and from the 7th century, China is known to have been importing birds' nests and jungle produce from Brunei (which then encompassed all of North Borneo), in exchange for ceramic wares. Chinese traders arrived in the Nanyang (South Seas) in force from the 11th century, particularly during the Sung and Yuan dynasties. Some Chinese pottery and porcelain even bore Arabic and Koranic inscriptions – the earliest such dish is thought to have been produced in the mid-14th century. In the 1500s, as China's trade with the Middle East grew, many such Islamic wares were traded and the Chinese emperors presented them as gifts to seal friendships with the Muslim world, including Malay and Indonesian kingdoms.

uncle. It stands on the north bank of the river almost opposite the market on Jalan Gambier. The Astana was hurriedly completed for the arrival of Charles' new bride (and cousin), Margaret. It was originally three colonial-style bungalows, with wooden shingle roofs, the largest being the central bungalow with the reception room, dining and drawing rooms. The crenellated tower on the east end was added in the 1880s at her request. Charles Brooke is said to have cultivated betel nut in a small plantation behind the Astana, so that he could offer fresh betel nut to visiting Dayak chiefs. Today it is the official residence of the governor of Sarawak and is only open to the public on Hari Raya Puasa, a day of prayer and celebration to mark the end of Ramadan (see page 54). To the west of the Astana, in the traditionally Malay area, are many old wooden kampong houses.

Fort Margherita

ⓘ *1000-1800 Tue-Sun, closed public holidays, free. Take a sampan across the river from the Pangkalan Batu jetty next to Square Tower on The Waterfront to the Astana and fort; less then RM1 one way; the boats can be hired quite cheaply at an hourly rate, around RM30 per hour.*

Not far away from the Astana, past the Kubu jetty, is this fort, now the **Police Museum**, on Jalan Sapi. It was also built by Rajah Charles Brooke in 1879 and named after

Ranee Margaret, although there was a fort on the site from 1841 when James Brooke became Rajah. It commanded the river approach to Kuching, but was never used defensively, although its construction was prompted by a near-disastrous river-borne attack on Kuching by the Ibans of the Rejang in 1878. Even so, until the Second World War a sentry was always stationed on the lookout post on top of the fort; his job was to pace up and down all night and shout 'All's well' on the hour every hour until 0800. The news that nothing was awry was heard at the Astana and the government offices.

After 1946, Fort Margherita was first occupied by the Sarawak Rangers and was finally converted into a police museum in 1971, which is a lot more interesting than it sounds. There is a large collection of armour and weaponry on the ground floor, including weapons captured during the Indonesian konfrontasi from 1963-65 (see page 386). Up the spiral staircase, on the second floor, there is a display of police uniforms and communications equipment used by jungle patrols. The third floor houses an exhibition on drugs, counterfeit currency and documents, supplies and weapons captured from Communist insurgents in the 1960s and 1970s. From the top, there are good views across the city and up and down the Sarawak River. En route to the courtyard at the bottom, former prison cells have been set up to recreate an opium den – complete with emaciated dummy – and to reinforce the dangers of *dadah*, (drugs) the courtyard itself contains the old town gallows complete with hanging dummy. During the rule of the White Rajahs, however, death sentences were carried out by a slash of the *kris* (traditional Malay sword) through the heart.

The **Malay kampongs** along the riverside next to Fort Margherita are seldom visited by tourists – however, they have some beautiful examples of traditional and modern Malay architecture. The **Kuching Orchid Garden** ⓘ *T82-446688, Tue-Sun 1000-1800, free; take a sampan across the river as for the fort*, was redeveloped close by to Fort Margharita, and opened in 2000, the park is divided into two; the Orchid Nursery and a garden, with more than 100 species of orchids.

Petra Jaya

The new **State Mosque**, is situated across the river at Petra Jaya and was completed in 1968. It stands on the site of an older mosque dating from the mid-19th century. Its interior is of Italian marble.

Kuching's architectural heritage did not end with the White Rajahs; the town's modern buildings are often based on local styles. The new administration centre is in Petra Jaya, on the north side of the river. The **Bapak** (father) **Malaysia** building is named after the first Prime Minister of Malaysia and houses government offices; the **Dewan Undangan Negeri**, (State Legislative Assembly of Sarawak) next door, is based on the Minangkabau style. Kuching's latest building is the ostentatious **Masjid Jamek**. Also in Petra Jaya, like a space launch overlooking the road to Damai Peninsula, is the **Cat Museum** ⓘ *Daily 0900-1700 (closed public holidays), free, camera RM3; take Petra Jaya Transport No 2B or 6*, which houses everything you ever wanted to know about cats.

The **Timber Museum** nearby, on Wisma Sumber Alam (next to the stadium), ⓘ *Mon-Thu 0830-1600, Fri 0830-1130, 1430-1630, Sat 0830-1230, closed Sun and public holidays; take a taxi, RM15, (no bus); the museum has a research library attached to it*, is meant to look like a log. It was built in the mid-1980s to try to engender a bit more understanding about Sarawak's timber industry. The museum, which has many excellent exhibits and displays, toes the official line about forest management and presents facts and figures on the timber trade, along with a detailed history of its development in Sarawak. The exhibition provides an insight into all the different forest types. It has background information on and examples of important commercial tree species, jungle produce as well as many traditional wooden implements. The final touch is an air-conditioned forest and wildlife diorama, complete with leaf-litter; all the trees come from the Rejang River area. While the museum sidesteps the more delicate moral issues involved in the modern logging business, its detractors might do worse than to brush up on some of the less emotive aspects of Sarawak's most important industry.

Around Kuching

Semenggoh Orang Utan Sanctuary

ⓘ *Daily 0800-1245, 1400-1615, RM3; Sarawak Transport Co bus 6 from Ban Hock Wharf, Jawa St or from the stop opposite the post office on Jln Tun Haji Openg, RM2. There's approximately one bus every hour (the last bus going back to Kuching from the main entrance leaves just before 1600). Tell the bus conductor you want to go to Semenggoh and you'll be dropped off just outside the main entrance. It's a pleasant 20-minute walk through the park to the centre. Tour operators also run trips here, but you'll have more time to explore if you make your own trip there. Taxi one-way RM25.*

Semenggoh, 32 km from Kuching, on the road to Serian, became the first forest reserve in Sarawak when the 800 ha of jungle was set aside by Rajah Vyner Brooke in 1920. It was turned into a wildlife rehabilitation centre for monkeys, orang utans, honey bears and hornbills in 1975. All were either orphaned as a result of logging or were confiscated having been kept illegally as pets. The aim has been to reintroduce as many of the animals as possible to their natural habitat. In late 1998 many of the functions which previously attracted visitors to Semenggoh were transferred to the Matang Wildlife Centre (see page 321). However, there are a few trails around the park including a plankwalk and a botanical research centre, dedicated to jungle plants with medicinal applications, and orang utans still visit the centre for food handouts. Even when Semenggoh was operating as an orang utan rehabilitation centre, it did not compare with Sepilok in Sabah (see page 451), which is an altogether more sophisticated affair.

Gunung Penrissen → *Altitude: 1,329 m*

ⓘ *100 km from Kuching to Anna Rais; take an STC bus No 9 from Kuching's Lebuh Jawa. There are two buses a day. Guides – some of whom were former border scouts during konfrontasi – can be hired through the headman at Kampong Padawan; prospective climbers are advised to consult the detailed trail-guide in John Briggs' Mountains of Malaysia. The book is usually obtainable in the Sarawak Museum bookshop.*

This is the highest peak in the mountain range south of Kuching running along the Kalimantan border. The mountain was visited by naturalist Alfred Wallace in 1855. Just over 100 years later the mountain assumed a strategic role in Malaysia's konfrontasi with Indonesia (see page 386) – there is a Malaysian military post on the summit. Gunung Penrissen is accessible from Kampong Padawan; it lies a few kilometres south of Anna Rais, right on the border with Kalimantan. It is a difficult mountain to climb requiring two long days, but affords views over Kalimantan to the south and Kuching and the South China Sea to the north.

Gunung Gading National Park

ⓘ *T82-735714, RM10; 5-mins' drive from Lundu, taxi RM5. From Kuching take STC Bus EP07 from the Express Bus Terminal outside of town to Lundu.*

National park accommodation booking: Sarawak Tourist Information Centre, T82-248088, or the NP office in Petra Jaya, Wisma Sumber Alam, T82-442180.

Gunung Gading National Park was constituted in 1983 and covers 411,1060 ha either side of Sungai Lundu, 65 km north-west of Kuching. There are some marked trails, the shortest of which takes about two hours and leads to a series of waterfalls on the Sungai Lundu. Gunung Gading and Gunung Perigi summit treks take seven to eight hours; it is possible to camp at the summit. The park is made up of a complex of mountains with several dominant peaks including Gunung Gading (906 m). The **Rafflesia,** the largest flower in the world, is found in the park but if you are keen to see one in bloom, it might be worth phoning the Park HQ first, since it has a very short flowering period.

Lundu and Sematan

ⓘ *Bus 2B goes to Lundu via Bau, 2 hrs; a permit from the Forest Department in Kuching, is needed to visit Talang Talang: Wisma Sumba Alam, Jln Stadium, Petra Jaya, Kuching, T82-442180, www.forestry.sarawak.gov.my/forweb/homepage/contact.html.*

These villages have beautiful, lonely beaches and there is a collection of deserted islands off Sematan. One of the islands, **Talang Talang**, is a turtle sanctuary and permission to visit it must be obtained.

Bau

ⓘ *Take bus No 2B from the Chin Lan Long bus station, the journey takes around an hour. Tour companies organize trips also.*

About 60 km from Kuching is **Bau,** which had its five minutes of fame during the 19th century as a small mining town. Today, it is a market town and administrative centre. There are several caves close by; the **Wind Cave** is a popular picnic spot. The **Fairy Cave,** about 10 km from Bau, is larger and more impressive, with a small Chinese shrine in the main chamber and varied vegetation at the entrance. A torch is essential. Another reason to go to Bau is to see the Bindayuh celebrating their *gawai padi*, a festival with animistic roots that thanks the gods for an abundant rice harvest. Singing, dancing, massive consumption of *tuak* (rice wine) and colourful shamans make this a highlight. Held end of May/beginning of June. Ask at the tourist office in Kuching for exact details.

Kubah National Park

ⓘ *RM10; take the Matang Transport Company bus No 11 that departs from outside the Saujana Car Park (first bus departs at 0630 and last return bus at 1640). Buses no longer drop off at the Matang Wildlife Centre; ask to be dropped of at the Park HQ. Travel agents also arrange tours to the park. T82-225003 but the National Parks and Wildlife Booking office in Kuching is likely to be more helpful.*

This is a mainly sandstone, siltstone and shale area, 20 km west of Kuching, covering some 2,230 ha with three mountains: Gunung Serapi, Gunung Selang and Gunung Sendok; there are at least seven waterfalls and bathing pools. Flora include mixed dipterocarp and kerangas (heath) forest; the park is also rich in palms (93 species) and wild orchids. Wildlife includes bearded pig, mouse deer and hornbills and numerous species of amphibians and reptiles. Unfortunately for visitors, Kubah's wildlife tends to stay hidden; it's not really a park for 'wildlife encounters'. There are four marked trails, ranging from 30 minutes to three hours; one, the **Rayu Trail**, passes through rainforest that contains a number of bintangor trees (believed to contain two chemicals which have showed some evidence of being effective against HIV). Visitors may be able to see some trees which have been tapped for this potential rainforest remedy. The park is easy to visit in a daytrip.

The **Matang Wildlife Centre** ⓘ *T82-225012; animal feeding times: orang utans, 0900 and 1500 daily; hornbills, 0830 and 1500 daily; sambar deer, 0900 and 1500 daily; and crocodiles, 1430 Sun only; Matang Transport Company bus No 11 departs infrequently from outside the Saujana car park (see Kubah National Park, above, for details). However this bus does not go all the way to the Matang Wildlife Centre; ask to be deposited at the turning for the Polytechnic and wait for a lift. Alternatively take a taxi from Kuching RM35 one-way and ask the taxi to wait; travel agents also arrange tours to the park*, is part of the Kubah National Park. It houses endangered wildlife in spacious enclosures which are purposefully placed in the rainforest. The key attraction are the orang utans which are rehabilitated for release back into the wild. Other animals include sambar deer, sun bears, civets and bear cats. There is an Information Centre and education programmes, which enable visitors to learn more about the conservation of Sarawak's wildlife. The Centre has also established a series of trails.

Pulau Satang Besar

ⓘ *Inquire at the Visitor Information Centre, overlooking the Padang, Kuching, T82-410942 for departures from Santubong or Kampong Telaga Air.*

North of Kampong Telaga Air, Pulau Satang Besar has been designated a Turtle Sanctuary to protect the green turtles which come ashore here to lay their eggs.

Tanjung Datu National Park

ⓘ *Take a bus to Lundu (see Gunung Gading National Park page 320) and on to Sematan. At the jetty in Sematan, hire a boat, 40 mins (RM100 to hire the whole boat; there is no scheduled service) and the seas are too rough for the journey October to February. The boat will drop you off at the Park headquarter's jetty. You can also jump in a boat to Teluk Melano (more regular) from Sematan (that takes about 40 minutes), and then hire a 10-minute boat trip to the park.*

This is the newest and smallest park in Sarawak, first gazetted in 1994, at the westernmost tip, 100 km from Kuching. It is covered with mixed dipterocarp forest, rich flora and fauna, and beautiful beaches with crystal clear seas and coral reefs.

Damai Peninsula → *Colour map 3, grid C1*

The peninsula, 35 km north of Kuching, is located at the west mouth of the Sarawak River and extends northwards as far as **Mount Santubong**, a majestic peak of 810 m. Its attractions include the **Sarawak Cultural Village**, trekking up Mount Santubong, sandy beaches, a golf course, adventure camp and three resorts which are particularly good value off season when promotional rates are available.

The Penan – museum pieces for the 21st century?

Economic progress has altered many Sarawakians' lifestyles in recent years; the oil and natural gas sector now offers many employment prospects and upriver tribespeople have been drawn into the logging industry. But it is logging that has directly threatened the 9,000-strong Penan tribe's traditional way of life.

Sarawak's nomadic hunter-gatherers have emerged as 'the noble savages' of the late 20th century, as their blockades of logging roads drew world attention to their plight. In 1990, Britain's Prince Charles' remarks about Malaysia's "collective genocide" against the Penan prompted an angry letter of protest from former Prime Minister Dr Mahathir Mohamad. He is particularly irked by western environmentalists – especially Bruno Manser, who lived with the Penan in the late 1980s. "We don't need any more Europeans who think they have a white man's burden to shoulder," Dr Mahathir said.

Malaysia wants to integrate the Penan into mainstream society, on the grounds that it is morally wrong to condemn them to a life expectancy of 40 years, when the average Malaysian lives to well over 60. "There is nothing romantic about these helpless, half-starved, disease-ridden people," Dr Mahathir said. The government has launched resettlement programmes to transform the Penan from hunters into fishermen and farmers. One of these new longhouses can be visited in Mulu (see page 373); it has failed to engender much enthusiasm from the Penan, although 4,000-5,000 Penan have now been resettled. Environmentalists countered that the Penan should be given the choice, but, the government asks, what choice do they have if they have only lived in the jungle?

The Cultural Village, opened by Dr Mahathir in 1990, offered a compromise of sorts – but the Penan had the last laugh. One tribal elder, called Apau Madang, and his grandson were paid to parade in loincloths and make blowpipes at the Penan hut while tourists took their snapshots. The arrangement did not last long as they did not like posing as artefacts in Sarawak's 'living museum'. They soon complained of boredom and within months had wandered back to the jungle where they could at least wear jeans and T-shirts. Today, the Penan hut is staffed by other Orang Ulu. There are thought to be only 400 Penan still following their traditional nomadic way of life.

Ins and outs

Getting there It's a 40-minute bus ride to Buntal, which is east from Kuching. Take bus No 26 from the Petra Jaya terminal. Buses depart every 40 minutes throughout the day. From here, buses continue to Santubong, winding through the foothills.

Santubong and Buntal

The village of Santubong itself, located at the mouth of the Sarawak River, is small and quiet. Formerly a fishing village, most of the villagers now work in one of the nearby resorts. However, some fishing still goes on, and the daily catch is still sold every morning at the quayside. Near the quayside are two or three Chinese-run grocery stores and a coffee shop. The rest of the village is made up of small houses strung out along the road, built in the Malay tradition on stilts – many are wooden and painted in bright colours. Another village here is Buntal which is just off the Kuching-Santubong road. Popular with local Kuchingites who visit at the weekends for the seafood restaurants.

Sarawak Cultural Village

ⓘ Daily 0900-1730, cultural show 1130-1215 and 1630-1715, adult RM45, child (6-12 years) RM22.50, prices include cultural show, T82-846411, www.sarawakcultural village.com; special application must be made to attend heritage centre workshops where courses can be requested in various crafts such as wood-carving, mat-weaving, batik-painting; also intensive day and three to four day courses. There is a restaurant and craft shop, Sarakraf; there is a regular shuttle bus service from the Holiday Inn in Kuching to resort hotels and the Cultural Village (RM10, first bus at 0730, last bus 2200, last bus back from Damai is at 2100).

The Sarawak Cultural Village (Kampong Budaya Sarawak) was the brainchild of the Sarawak Development Corporation which built Sarawak's 'living museum' at a cost of RM9.5m to promote and preserve Sarawak's cultural heritage. With increasing numbers of young tribal people being tempted from their longhouses into the modern sectors of the economy, many of Sarawak's traditional crafts have begun to die out. The Cultural Village set out to teach the old arts and crafts to new generations. For the state development corporation, the concept had the added appeal of creating a money-spinning 'Instant Sarawak' for the benefit of tourists lacking the time or inclination to head into the jungle. While it is rather contrived, the Cultural Village has been a great success and contains some superb examples of traditional architecture. It should be on the sightseeing agenda of every visitor to Kuching, if only to provide an introduction to the cultural traditions of all the main ethnic groups in Sarawak.

Each tribal group is represented by craftsmen and women who produce handicrafts and practise traditional skills in houses built to carefully researched design specifications. Many authentic everyday articles have been collected from longhouses all over Sarawak. In one case the village has served to preserve a culture – pickled – that is already effectively dead: today the Melanau people all live in Malay-style kampongs, but a magnificent traditional wooden Melanau house has been built at the Cultural Village and is now the only such building in Sarawak. Alongside it there is a demonstration of traditional sago processing. A resident Melanau craftsman makes sickness images (*blum*) – each representing the spirit of an illness, which were floated downriver in tiny boats as part of the healing ritual.

There are also Bidayuh, Iban and Orang Ulu longhouses, depicting the lifestyles of each group. In each there are textile or basket-weavers, wood-carvers or sword-makers. There are exhibits of beadwork, bark clothing, and *tuak* (rice wine) brewing. At the Penan hut there is a demonstration of blowpipe making and visitors are invited to test their hunting skills. There is a Malay house and even a Chinese farmhouse with a pepper garden alongside. The tour of the houses, seven in all (you can collect a stamp from each one for your passport!) is capped by an Andrew Lloyd Webber-style cultural show which is expertly choreographed, if rather ersatz. It is held in the on-site theatre which is fully air conditioned.

The Cultural Village is also the venue for the fabulous annual **Rainforest Music Festival** ⓘ *www.rainforestmusic-borneo.com*, which takes place sometime between June and August. Food stalls are laid on, jamming sessions are held in the different sections culminating in a great stage show in the grounds for the evening.

The Cultural Village employs 140 people, including dancers, who earn around RM300 a month and take home the profits from handicraft and *tuak* sales.

Gunung Santubong → *Altitude: 810m*

ⓘ Guides are not necessary (but can be provided), check with hotel recreation counters or at the Santubong Mountain Trek Canteen, T82-846153. The official Damai guide provides a more detailed description of the trek. Take food and water supplies; there is a bus to Damai Beach or (more regularly) to Santubong from Petra Jaya terminal, take No 2b (RM3.30, 40-min journey, first bus 0700, last one 1800) but this will not go unless there are enough passengers. A taxi to Damai should cost around RM35 one-way.

 Situated on the Santubong Peninsula, Gunung Santubong's precipitous southern side provides a moody backdrop to Damai Beach. The distinctive mountain is most accessible from the east side, where there is a clear ridge trail to the top. There are two trails to the summit, one begins opposite the *Palm Beach Seafood Restaurant* and Resort, about 2½ km before the *Holiday Inn Damai Beach*. The conical peak – from which there are spectacular views – can be reached in seven to nine hours (the last stretch is a tough scramble.)

Salak River

ⓘ *Contact hotel recreation counters or tour operators for details.*
Trips up the Salak River depart from the terminal at Santubong village, a 10-minute drive from the resort hotels. River tours last three hours. The journey goes into smaller rivers and a creek and it is a good introduction to the mangrove forest ecosystem.

Bako National Park

Bako is situated on the beautiful Muara Tebas Peninsula, a former river delta which has been thrust above sea level. Its sandstone cliffs, which are patterned and streaked with iron deposits, have been eroded to produce a dramatic coastline with secluded coves and beaches and rocky headlands. Millions of years of erosion by the sea has resulted in the formation of wave-cut platforms, 'honeycomb' weathering, solution pans, arches and sea stacks. Bako's most distinctive feature is the westernmost headland – **Tanjung Sapi** – a 100-m high sandstone plateau, which is unique in Borneo. Established in 1957, Bako was Sarawak's first national park. It is a very small park (2,742 ha) but it has an exceptional variety of flora and guaranteed wildlife spotting! Its beaches and accessible trails make it a wonderful place to chill out for a few days.

Ins and outs

Getting there Bako lies 37 km north of Kuching, an hour's bus journey from Petra Jaya Terminal; a longboat needs to be rented to reach Park HQ. Travelling by car, the drive from Kuching takes about 40 mins, parking is safe at Kampong Bako (from where you rent a boat).

Getting around It is possible to hire boats around the park: speed boats RM40 (can accommodate 5-6).

Tourist information ⓘ *National Parks and Wildlife Booking Office, c/o Visitors' Information Centre, Sarawak Tourism Complex, Old Court House, T82-248088, F82-248087, RM10 per adult, RM5 per child or student. Photography permit RM5, video camera RM10, professional camera RM200. On arrival visitors are required to register at the Park HQ. The information centre is next to Park HQ, with a small exhibition on geology, flora and fauna within the park. Visitors can request to see an introductory video to Bako National Park, duration 42 mins. Open 0800-1245 (0800-1100 on Fri) 1400-1615 Mon-Sun. The Park HQ has a canteen.*

Flora and fauna

There are seven separate types of vegetation in Bako. These include mangroves (*bakau* is the most common stilt-rooted mangrove species), swamp forest and heath forest – known as *kerangas*, an Iban word meaning 'land on which rice cannot grow'. Pitcher plants (*Nepenthes ampullaria*) do however grow in profusion on the sandy soil. There is also mixed dipterocarp rainforest (the most widespread forest type in Sarawak, characterized by its 30-40m-high canopy), beach forest, and padang vegetation, comprising scrub and bare rock from which there are magnificent views of the coast. The rare *daun payang* (**umbrella palm**) is also found in Bako Park; it is a litter-trapping plant as its large fronds catch falling leaves from the trees above and funnel them downwards where they eventually form a thick organic mulch enabling the plant to survive on otherwise infertile soil. There are also wild durian trees in the forest, which can take up to 60 years to bear fruit.

Bako is one of the few areas in Sarawak inhabited by the **proboscis monkey** (**Nasalis larvatus**), known by Malays as 'Orang Belanda', or Dutchmen, or even 'Pinocchio of the jungle', because of their long noses (see page 522). Bako is home to approximately 150 rare proboscis monkeys. They are most often seen in the early morning or at dusk in the Teluk Assam, Teluk Paku and Teluk Delima areas (at the far west side of the park, closest to the headquarters) or around Teluk Paku, a 45-minute walk from the Park HQ. The park also has resident populations of squirrels, mousedeer, sambar deer, wild pigs, long-tailed macaques, flying lemur, silver leaf monkeys and palm civet cats. Teluk Assam, in the area around the Park HQ, is one of the best places for birdwatching: over 150 species have been recorded in the park, including pied and black hornbills. Large numbers of migratory birds come to Bako between September and November. Other inhabitants of the park are the blue fiddler crab, which has one big claw, and is forever challenging others to a fight and mudskippers, evolutionary throw-backs (half-fish, half-frog), which are common in mangrove areas. Also in the park there are two species of **otter**: the oriental small-clawed otter and the hairy-nosed otter (the best area to see them is at Teluk Assam). The **Bornean bearded pig** is the largest mammal found Bako and is usually seen snuffling around the Park HQ. There are many lizards too, the largest being the **water monitor** which is often found near the accommodation. The only poisonous snake occasionally seen is the **Wagler's pit viper**. Nocturnal animals include flying lemur, pangolin, mousedeer, bats, tarsier, slow loris and palm civet (the beach by the Park HQ is a great place for a night time stroll).

Treks

There is a good range of well-marked trails throughout the park – over 30 km in total; all paths are colour coded, corresponding to the map available from Park HQ. The shortest trek is the steep climb to the top of **Tanjong Sapi**, overlooking Teluk Assam, with good views of Gunung Santubong, on the opposite peninsula, across Tanjong

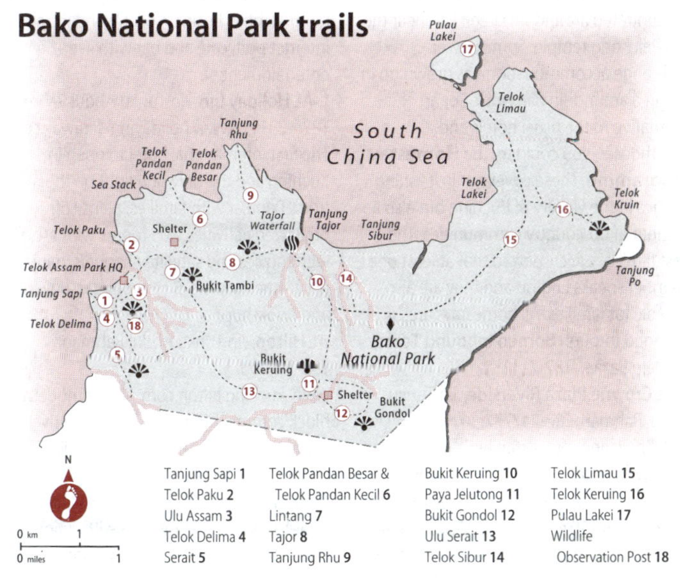

 Sipang, to the west. The 3.5-km trek to Tajor waterfall is among the most popular with varied walking – some steep climbs – spectacular views and a chance of a refreshing swim at the waterfall. The longest trek is to Telok Limau; a five-to seven-hour walk through a variety of terrain. You can arrange with Park HQ to lay on a boat to bring you back (around RM200). Some trails are temporarily closed – check with Park HQ. Full-day treks and overnight camping expeditions can be arranged. There are plank walkways with shelters at intervals to provide quiet watching spots particularly required for viewing the proboscis monkey in the early morning.

Beaches

There are seven beaches around the park, but some are rather inaccessible, with steep paths down to the cliffs. The best swimming beach is at **Teluk Pandan Kecil**, about 1½ hours' walk, northeast from the Park HQ. It is also possible to swim at **Teluk Assam** and **Teluk Paku**. Enquire about jellyfish at the Park HQ before swimming in the sea; it is advisable not to swim in March and April. In the monsoon season, between November and February, the sea can be rough.

Sleeping

Kuching *p310, map p314*

It is possible to negotiate over room rates and many of the hotels seem to have special deals. There is a good choice of international standard hotels in Kuching. Most of them are along Jln Tunku Abdul Rahman with views of the river and the Astana and Fort Margherita on the opposite bank. For a listing of hotels and resorts with websites see the listing on the Sarawak Tourism Board site (www.sarawaktourism.com). The choice at the lower end of the market is limited, except for the Anglican Guesthouse; the cheaper hotels and lodging houses are concentrated around Jln Green Hill, near the Tua Pek Kong temple. Some newer, mid-range accommodation has grown up in the area around Jln Ban Hock. For an alternative to the usual hotels and guesthouses, you could try the **Homestay Programme**. These cover not just fishing villages in the vicinity of Kuching but also a number of up-country communities. The host families are chosen so that at least one member speaks English and they are also suitable for families. All homestays are arranged through **Borneo Inbound Tours**, 98 Main Bazaar, T82-711152.

L-AL **Crowne Plaza Riverside**, Jln Tunku Abdul Rahman, T82-247777, cprk@po.jaring.my 5-star, high-rise glitz hotel with an adjoining, 5-storey shopping complex complete with bowling alley and cineplex. All 250 rooms have a/c, mini-bar, personal safe, TV, in-house movies, en suite bathroom with marble vanity and good shower, plush carpets, wood furnishings carved with Sarawak designs. Facilities include pool, fitness centre, squash court, pâtisserie, 3 restaurants including the Sri Sarawak on the 18th floor which has panoramic views and serves Malay and international food, regular shuttle (RM10) to sister hotel, Damai Lagoon, on the Damai Peninsula. Recommended.

L-AL **Harbour View Hotel**, Lorong Temple, T82-274666, www.harbourview.com.my/ Good position overlooking the Waterfront next to Tua Pek Kong Temple. Business centre and in-room internet port, café and bar with live entertainment.

L-AL **Holiday Inn**, Jln Tunku Abdul Rahman, T82-423111, www.holidayinn-sarawak.com The first international hotel to open in Kuching and the only one right on the river front. Popular with families, plenty of organized activities, 305 rooms with a/c, TV with movies and satellite channels, mini-bar, pool, fitness centre, 3 restaurants, souvenir and bookshop.

AL **Hilton**, Jln Tunku Abdul Rahman, T82-248200, www.kuching.hilton.com White modern block commanding superb views of river and town. Lives up to its name in providing quality and exclusive atmosphere. All 322 rooms have a/c, TV, in-room movies, mini-bar. Very pleasant pool with swim-up bar, shaded by palms, and separate children's pool and playground, tennis, fitness centre. Four restaurants including good steak house (air-freighted meat from Australia), boutique, hair salon, travel agent. Recommended.

AL-A **Grand Continental**, Jln Ban Hock, T82-230399, www.grandhotelsinternational.com.my/ Small pool and business centre. Rooms have TV, IDD, minibar, and tea and coffee-making facilities.

AL-A **Merdeka Palace** Jln Tun Abang Haji Openg, T82-258000, www.merdekapalace.com Central location overlooking playing field. Pool, health-club and business facilities, and broadband in every room. The 214 rooms have mini-bar, satellite TV. Six bars, restaurants on site. Great value. Recommended.

A-B **Borneo**, 30 Jln Tabuan, T82-244122, F82-254848. Chinese atmosphere in this hotel located about a 10 min walk from the centre of town. Rooms with a/c and bath. Good value restaurant, breakfast included. Has old world charm.

A-B **Kingwood Inn**, Jln Padungan, T82-330888, kingwd@po.jaring.my Rooms have TV. Facilities include a pool, coffee house and bar. Late checkout available. Out of town but pleasant.

A-B **Telang Usan**, Jln Ban Hock (next to Supreme), T82-415588, tusan@po.jaring.my The best of these 2 hotels located in an untidy area of town. A/C, TV, bath, restaurant, in-house travel agent, orang ulu owned and managed hotel, friendly with traditional kenyah decor, karaoke and bar, conference rooms, smart and comfortable, quiet location, excellent value.

B-C **Fata**, Jln McDougall, T82-248111, F82-428987. Clean hotel with a 1970s feel. A/c, restaurant, rooms in the older part are cheaper and better value for money.

B-C **Supreme**, Jln Ban Hock, T82-255155, F82-252522, 74 rooms, a/c, en suite bath or shower, mini-bar, TV, in-house videos. Evening entertainment; bands or karaoke. A little run down.

C-D **Green Mountain Lodging House**, 1 Jln Green Hill, T82-416320, F82-412457. The best and cleanest of the groups of hotels located in the Jln Green Hill area. Friendly management, hot water, secure atmosphere, and rooms on the third floor have nice views onto a small wooded hill. Rooms have a/c, TVs, are airy and clean.

C-E **Borneo Bed & Breakfast**, 2/F, 3 Jln Green Hill, T82-246292/T013 8434 200, borneobedbreakfast@yahoo.com. Kuching's newest one-stop backpacker guesthouse run by the friendly Mr Buan. Sixteen rooms ranging from doubles and triples to dorms. All rooms have shared bathroom. There's laundry, breakfast included in room rate and a lounge. Lots of travel information. Phone and book ahead as this place is always packed out. Recommended.

C-E **B&B Inn**, Tabuan Rd (next to the Borneo Hotel), T82-237366, gohyp@pb.jaring.my Although popular and central, not particularly cheap. Tours organized, clean and safe, dorms beds available, although recent rumours of bed bugs.

D-E **Anglican Guesthouse**, back of St Thomas' Cathedral (path from Jln Carpenter), T82-414027. Fan, old building set in beautiful gardens on top of the hill, spacious, pleasantly furnished rooms, with basic facilities, far and away the best of the cheaper accommodation in town. More expensive family rooms are big with sitting room and attached bathroom. Best to book in advance. Recommended.

D-E **Kuching**, Lebuh Temple, T82-413985. Adequate Chinese-run hotel, reasonable rates for rooms with fan and wash-hand basin, shared bathrooms.

Gunung Penrissen *p320*

L-AL **Hornbill Golf & Jungle Club, Borneo Highlands Resort,** Jln Borneo Heights, Padawan, T82-790800, F82-790100, www.hornbillgolf.com As its name suggests, this is a mountain hideaway for golf fanatics. There are luxurious chalets and suites beautifully furnished with golfing touches like paintings of greens. The resort lies at an altitude of 1,000 m and so the weather is cooler and more spring-like. Apart from golf, jungle treks are organised as well as a longhouse tour, a rabbit farm, spas and flower gardens.

Gunung Gading National Park *p320*

A-E **National park accommodation** Bookings taken through the National Parks and Wildlife Booking office inside the Visitor Information Centre, Kuching, T82-248088.

2, 3-bedroom chalets and a hostel (RM15/person) are available.

Lundu and Sematan *p320*

A **Ocean Resort**, 176 Siar Beach, Jln Pandan, Sematan, T82-452245 (Kuching office) or T011-225001 (resort), some rooms in hostel, 2 bedroom chalets with attached kitchen also available. The plushest place to stay in Sematan.

C **Lundu Gadung Hotel**, Lot 174 Lundu Town District, T82-735199, (a/c but shared bathroom).

Kubah National Park *p320*

A-F **National park accommodation**. Bookable through the National Parks and Wildlife Booking office inside the Visitors' Information Centre in Kuching, Old Court House, T82-248088. There are chalets and an eight-room hostel block and 5 huge bungalows at the park HQ with full kitchen facilities, 4 beds (2 rooms), a/c, hot water, TV and verandah.

Damai Peninsula *p321, map p319*

L-AL **Holiday Inn Resort Damai Lagoon**, Teluk Penyu, Santubong, T82-846900, www.holidayinn-sarawak.com Superbly located at the foot of Mount Santubong, on a small, well-kept, sandy beach, its 256 rooms and 30 chalets are in stylish buildings with steep, wood-shingled roofs. There are polished wood floors and decorative woodcarving throughout; a monumental, timber-roofed lobby open to the sea, and pleasant gardens dotted with tribal wooden effigies surrounding a lagoon-style pool (the largest in Sarawak) which has a sandy slope for kids at one end and a man-made cave, complete with cascade and stage for shows, at the other. The lagoon also has a circular, swim-up bar, shaded by colonial, wood-shingled roof, all rooms have a/c, TV, in-house movies, mini-bar, tea and coffee-making facilities, balcony and personal safe. Other facilities include restaurant, tea-house (excellent for sunset views), bar, health club (with spa), tennis, boutique, bicycle hire, canoe hire, watersports and children's playground. Sterling competition for the Holiday Inn and definitely better in terms of access to beach and general tranquillity. Recommended.

AL-A **Holiday Inn Resort Damai Beach**, Teluk Bandung, Santubong, PO Box 2870, T82-846999, www.holidayinn-sarawak.com/ The resort calls itself the 'Crown Jewel of Sarawak', although the real jewel in the crown is the large, private, wooden mansion at the top of the resort which belongs to the Sultan of Brunei. The hill-top extension, directly below the Sultan's mansion, has chalets modelled on ethnic designs, such as the circular Bidayuh buildings which make this a better than average Holiday Inn. The beach is bigger than that at Damai Lagoon Resort, but less accessible if you are staying at the hill-top site. All 302 rooms, including 179 chalets, have a/c, colour TV, in-house movie, coffee and tea-making facilities. Other facilities including 2 pools, tennis, spa pool, watersports, kids' club, bicycle/scooter hire, games room, restaurant (good value buffet), PV Fun Pub (a popular night spot for Kuchingites), children's playground and lobby shops.

A-B **Damai Rainforest Resort (Camp Permai)**, Pantai Damai, Santubong, PO Box B91, Satok Post Office, T82-321498, F82-321500. Located at the foot of Mount Santubong, near the Damai Lagoon Resort, this is an outward-bound centre which offers a number of courses including adventure training and leadership development. Other facilities include artificial climbing wall, obstacle course, abseiling, sailing, canoeing, paintball competitions. Sleeping in 10 a/c tree houses or log cabins, cafeteria, tents and camping equipment for hire.

A **Santubong Kuching Resort**, Jln Santubong, PO Box 2364, T82-846888, F82-846666. Surrounded by the Damai Golf Course, 380 rooms all with a/c, restaurant, large pool, chalets with jacuzzis, tennis, basketball, volleyball, gym, mountain biking, etc. Nestling beneath Mount Santubong, a low-rise resort popular with golfers, it also has the largest conference and banquet facilities in Sarawak. Price includes breakfast.

For an explanation of the sleeping and eating price codes used in this guide, see inside the front cover. Other relevant information is found in Essentials, pages 45-49.

Bako National Park *p324, map p325*
All bookings to be made at the **National Parks and Wildlife Booking Office**, c/o Visitors' Information Centre, Sarawak Tourism Complex, Old Court House, T82-248088. The hostels are equipped with mattresses, kerosene stoves and cutlery. Resthouses have refrigerators and electricity until 2400. The recommended length of stay is 2 days/1 night. Resthouses and the hostel have fans. Accommodation is always booked out, it's recommended to make a reservation several days before you want to go. A Bako visit can be made in a day trip although an overnight stay is preferable.
Lodge, RM157 per house , RM105 per room.
Hostel, RM42 per room, RM15.75, check-out time 1200.
Camping For those not intending to trek to the other side of the park, it is not worth camping as monkeys steal anything left lying around and macaques can be aggressive. In addition, the smallest amount of rain turns the campsite into a swimming pool. It is however necessary to camp if you go to the beaches on the northeast peninsula. Tents can be hired for RM8 (sleeps 4); campsite RM5.

Eating

Kuching *p310, map p314*
Kuching, with all its old buildings and godowns along the river, seems made for open-air restaurants and cafés – but good ones are notably absent. However, the town is not short of hawker centres. Local dishes worth looking out for include *Umai* – a spicy salad of raw marinated fish with limes and shallots. Other distinctive Sarawakian ingredients are *midin* and *paku* – jungle fern shoots. For information on local specialities see Food glossaries, Footnotes.

Chinese
All the major hotels have Chinese restaurants; most open for lunch and dinner, closing in between.
TT **Hornbill Corner Café**, 85 Jln Ban Hock. All-you-can-eat steamboat and barbecue, popular.
TT **Red Eastern Café**, Jln Ban Hock, specializes in steamboat.
TT **River Palace**, Crowne Plaza Majestic Hotel, first-class Chinese restaurant, offers regular food promotions.
T **Hot and Spicy House**, Lot 303, Section 10, Rubber Rd, T82-250873. Closed Tue, Chinese cooking with West Malaysian influence. Speciality is Ipoh-style *yong tau hoo* (vegetables stuffed with beancurd), just outside the city centre.
T **Lan Ya Keng**, Jln Carpenter, opposite old temple, specializes in pepperfish steak.
T **Lok Thian**, 1st floor, Bangunan Beesan, Jln Padungan, T82-331310. Good food, pleasant surroundings and excellent service, booking advisable, especially at the weekends.
T **Meisan**, Holiday Inn, Jln Tunku Abdul Rahman, dim sum, set lunch; Sun eat-as-much-as-you-can dim sum special, also Sichuan cuisine. Recommended.
T **Min Kong Kee**, 157 Jln Pandungan. A good selection of dishes with authentic Chinese and Malay breakfasts.
T **Minsion Canteen**, end of Jln Chan Chin Ann, on right, speciality is *daud special* (thick noodles in herbal soup with chunks of chicken).
T **Perfect Vegetarian Food Centre**, Jln Green Hill. Great inexpensive canteen serving Malay and Chinese food and western breakfasts, all meatless. Tables outside. Fantastic noodle in pumpkin sauce dish. Highly recommended.
T **Tsui Hua Lau**, Lot 321-324, Jln Ban Hock, T82-414560. Shanghai-style dishes.

Malay
Malay food here seems to be less spicy than on the Peninsula. Sarawak specialities available include *laksa* (spicy noodles – a Malaysia wide dish, but especially good here), and *umai*.
TTT **Sri Sarawak**, Crowne Plaza Riverside Hotel, gourmet food, good views.
TT **Khatulistiwa Café**, Waterfront, (opposite the Crowne Plaza) in a circular pavilion-style building. Great views from this café open 24 hours serving Malay and International dishes. There's an R&B music café on the 2/F open at 2300.
TT **Home Cook**, Jln Song Thian Cheok, clean and good value, speciality Assam fish.
TT **Suan Chicken Rice**, Jln Tunku Abdul Rahman, next to Sarawak Plaza, steamed or curried chicken.

ŸŸ **D'Alif**, Waterfront, just in front of the Steamship. Big airy restaurant with riverside seats. They specialise in Malay seafood, no alcohol. Very popular with locals.

Ÿ **Aunty Mary's Kitchen**, 2&4 Bishopsgate Street (just off Main Bazaar before China Street). Sells the perfect Malay breakfast, *Laksa Mee*. Good and cheap. Closed Sun.

Indian

There are several cheap Indian Muslim restaurants along Lebuh India.

ŸŸ **Banana Leaf**, 7G Lorong Rubber 1, T82-239404. Open all day, specializes in Indian banana leaf meals.

ŸŸ **Bismillah**, Leboh Khoo Hun Reang (near Central Police Station), North Indian Muslim food, good tandoori chicken.

ŸŸ **Lyn's Tandoori**, Lot 62, 10G Lg 4, Jln Nanas, a worthwhile taxi-ride from the centre – genuine North Indian tandoori cuisine, excellent naan, locals recommend it, closed Sun evenings.

ŸŸ **Pots 'n' Buns,** Taman Sri Sarawak Mall, opposite rear store entrance, good *roti canai, murtabak*, plus usual hawker stall food.

ŸŸ **Rahamath Café**, 19 Jln Padungan, good *roti canai*.

ŸŸ **Serapi**, Holiday Inn, specializes in North Indian tandoori, good vegetable dishes, also serves air-freighted steak. Recommended.

Indonesian

ŸŸ **Minangkabau Nasi Padang**, 168 Chan Chin Ann Rd, spicy Padang food including such classics as beef rendang, lunch time only.

Japanese

ŸŸŸ **Ten-Ichi**, 315-319 Bangunan Bee San, Jln Pandungan, T82-331310. Elegant surroundings.

ŸŸ **Kikyo-Tei**, Jln Crookshank, in front of Government Resthouse, also some Chinese and western dishes, large main room with separate Teppanyaki and Tatami rooms. The set lunch is a good deal. Recommended by locals.

ŸŸ **Minoru**, Lot 493, Section 10, Rubber Rd, T82-251021. Set lunch and dinner as well as an extensive menu and good service.

International

ŸŸ **San Francisco Grill**, 76 Jln Ban Hock, steak house, cosy atmosphere, live piano, largely Chinese clientele which means steak is seasoned with 5 spices, meat is air-freighted, chips mediocre, but nice atmosphere.

ŸŸŸ **Serapi**, Holiday Inn, imported steaks, excellent selection of grills and seafood, North Indian tandoori, elegant surroundings, open lunch and dinner but not between times.

ŸŸ **Orchid Garden**, Holiday Inn, Jln Tunku Abdul Rahman, good breakfast and evening buffets, international and local cuisine. Recommended.

ŸŸ **The Junk Restaurant**, 80 Wayang St, T82-259450, closed Tue. Intimate little gem of a restaurant filled with crazy antiques like old cash registers and lit by lanterns. Serves good but not fantastic pasta, steaks and other western and Asian dishes. Recommended.

ŸŸ **The Tapanga Tree**, Taman Letak Kereta, Jln Padungan (off Jln Tunku), T82-248773. Very funky place with open-air seating and cozy indoor restaurant on the fourth floor of this block. Very friendly staff and cute gecko logo. Cuisine is described as fusion – there's lamb kebab, grilled seafood and plenty of Asian choices. Nice use of local woodcrafts. Mon-Sat live music. The outdoor terrace has no view, but a pleasant place nonetheless.

ŸŸ **Waterfront**, Hilton Hotel, Jln Tunku Abdul Rahman, reasonably priced for the venue, the best pizzas and a family brunch buffet on Sun which is very popular.

ŸŸ **Hani's Bistro**, Jln Chan Chin Ann (near Holiday Inn), reasonably priced café, good mix of eastern and western cuisine, generous helpings, tasty haricot oxtail, good background music. Recommended.

Ÿ **Dulit Coffee House**, Telang Usan Hotel, Jln Ban Hock, pleasant terrace café, mix of western and eastern food, specializes in French oxtail stew and the only genuine chicken kebabs in Kuching.

Seafood

Excellent seafood is to be found in Kuching. On Kampong Buntal are several seafood restaurants on stilts over the sea, 25 km north of Kuching, very popular with Kuchingites.

ŸŸ **Benson Seafood**, Lot 122/3, Section 49, Jln Abell, T82-255262. Full range of Sarawak seafood.

🍴 **Ah Leong**, Lot 72, Jln Pandungan, near Kingwood Inn, good choice of seafood.
🍴 **KTS Seafood Canteen**, 157 Jln Chan Chin Ann, excellent butter prawns and grilled stingray.
🍴 **See Good**, Jln Bukit Mata Kuching, behind MAS office, extensive range of seafood. Recommended by locals. Strong flavoured sauces, lots of herbs, extensive and exotic menu, unlimited free bananas, closed 4th and 18th of every month.

Thai

🍴 **Bangkok Thai Seafood Restaurant**, 318-319 Jln Padungan, T82-335043. In a complex with Japanese and Chinese restaurants. Fine dining. Booking advisable for weekends.

Coffee shops

There are a handful of Malay/Indian coffee shops on India St including Madinah Café, Jubilee and Malaysia Restaurant.
Many Chinese coffee shops serve excellent *laksa* (breakfast) of curried coconut milk with a side plate of *sambal belacan* (chillied prawn paste).
Fook Hoi, Jln Padungan, old-fashioned coffee shop, famous for its *sio bee* and *ha kau* (pork dumpling). **Life Café**, 108 Ewe Hai St (near Carpenter St, behind Main Bazaar), T82-411954. Closed Tue, attractive café serving mostly vegetarian food plus a good range of teas and coffees (including Sarawak tea), friendly staff and pleasant atmosphere.
Cozy Corner Cafe, Borneo Hotel, Jln Tabuan, selection of coffees, teas, cakes and pastries in a relaxing atmosphere. **Tiger Garden**, opposite Rex Cinema, Lebuh Temple. **Coffee Master**, 13 China St, T82-250958. Western snacks and iced Sarawak coffee. A trendy modern drinking place in a quiet street off the waterfront. Try a hot cup of Dong Ding Oolong tea.

Foodstalls and food centres

There are great open-air informal places along the waterfront selling everything from kebabs to ais cream goreng (fried ice cream) that start opening towards the evening. It makes a great place for an evening meal. Most of the food stalls are clustered around the Hilton end of the promenade selling Malay dishes and fruit juices (no alcohol). Beautiful views of the river and accompanied by popular Malay love songs.
Hock Hong Garden, Jln Ban Hock, opposite Grand Continental, finest hawker stall food in Kuching, little English spoken but definitely worth trying to be understood. **Chinese Food Centre**, Jln Carpenter (opposite temple), Chinese foodstalls offering hot and sour soups, fish balls and more. **King's Centre,** Jln Simpang Tiga (bus No 11 to get there), large range of foodstalls, busy and not many tourists. **Kubah Ria Hawker stalls**, Jln Tunku Abdul Rahman (on the road out of town towards Damai Beach, next to Satok Suspension Bridge), specialities *sop kambling* (mutton soup). **Petanak Central Market**, Jln Petanak, above Kuching's early morning wet market, light snacks, full seafood selection, good atmosphere, especially early in the morning. **Satok Bridge**, under the suspension bridge, very good barbecued chicken and seafood. **Saujana Food Centre**, 5th floor of the car park near the mosque (take the lift), mostly Malay food but also seafood. **Song Thieng Hai Food Centre**, between Jln Padungan and Jln Ban Hock, every type of noodle available.

Some of the best food centres are located in the suburbs; a taxi is essential.
Permata Food Centre, behind MAS office, purpose-built alternative to the central market, prices are higher but the choice is better, bird-singing contests (mainly red-whiskered bulbuls and white-rumped sharmas) every Sun morning, excellent range of fresh seafood. Recommended. **Batu Lintang Open-Air Market**, Jln Rock (to the south of town, past the hospital). **Capital Cinema Hawker Centre**, Jln Padungan. **Jln Palm Open-Air Market**. Lau Ya Keng, Jln Carpenter, opposite temple, specializes in Chinese dishes. **Rex Cinema Hawker Centre**, Jln Wayang/Jln Temple, squashed down an alleyway, satay. Recommended. **Thompson's Corner**, Jln Palm/Jln Nanas. **Top Spot Food Court**, Jln Bukit Mata Kuching, top floor of a car park, wide range of stalls, popular. **Tower Market**, Lebuh Market.

Damai Peninsula *p321, map p319*

🍴 **New Dolphin Seafood Restaurant**, Kampong Buntal, T82-846441, great position on the coast, about 5km east of Santubon, good food, above average prices.

Santubong Mountain Trek Canteen, T82-846153, 5 mins' walk from hotels, rice and noodle dishes, in nearby Buntal village there are excellent seafood restaurants.

Bako National Park *p324*

The canteen is open 0700-2100. It serves local food at reasonable prices and sells tinned foods and drinks. No need to take food, there is a good seafood restaurant near the jetty.

Bars

Kuching *p310, map p314*

Expect to pay around RM8-10 for a beer, slightly more in the swisher hotel bars. Most places have happy hours, and two-for-one offers. Bars tend to close around 0100-0200, a little later in hotels. Most bars are centered along Bukit Mata off Jln Pandungan and along Jln Borneo next to the Hilton.

The main centres of evening entertainment are: Jln Tunku Abdul Rahman, Jln Mendu, Jln Padungan, and Jln Borneo. There are enough clubs, pubs and bars to keep most people reasonably happy. Clubs and discos usually have a cover charge although there is usually a drink or 2 thrown in with the price. Expect to pay around RM10-15 for a beer, and RM20-25 for a spirit.

Casablanca Lounge, Crowne Plaza Riverside Hotel, cocktail lounge and karaoke.

Cat City, Jln Chan Chin Ann (turn left at Pizza Hut), happy hour 2030-2215, followed by live bands (usually Filipino) playing a mixture of Western rock covers and Malay and Chinese ballads, open late.

De Tavern, Taman Sri Sarawak Mall (facing Hilton car park), friendly kayan-run corner pub, serves good rice wine, open 1630-0130, happy hour until 2030.

Eagle's Nest & The Cottage, 16-20 Jln Bukit Mata. Great selection of wines, good party atmosphere, occasional karaoke nights which should probably be avoided.

Earthquake, 21 & 22 Jln Bukit Mata. Silver spaceship interior, looks like a thumping Asian club joint.

Hornbill's Corner Café, Jln Ban Hock, breezy open air pub.

Margerita Lounge, Hilton Hotel, the best cocktails and good live music.

Marina Fun Pub and Disco, Jln Ban Hock, live band until 0200, then a DJ until 0330, crowded at weekends.

Monsoon, Riverside Complx, Jln Tunk Abdul Rahman. Nice local and tourist mix here with a balcony jutting out over the river.

Rejang Lobby Lounge, Holiday Inn, small but popular.

The Fisherman's Pub, 1st floor, Taman Sri Sarawak Mall, karaoke, friendly staff and a pleasant crowd of regulars.

Tribes, downstairs at Holiday Inn, ethnic food, tribal decor and a variety of live music, open 1600-0100.

Tropical Pub & Bar, Jln Abell. The place to go for a lively local disco (Malaysian music).

Jupiters, Jln Ban Hock. Only open on Fri, Sat and eve of public holidays – top 40 hits played.

Damai Peninsula *p321, map p319*

PV The Fun Pub at Holiday Inn Damai Beach is Damai's main night spot and very popular – an open-air pub with pool and karaoke and live bands.

Entertainment

Kuching *p310, map p314*

Cinemas

Riverside Cineplex, Riverside Complex, Jalan Tunku Abdul Rahman, in the base of the Crowne Plaza Hotel, T82-427061, check local press for details of programme. **Star Cineplex**, Level 9, Medan Pelita, top floor of car park on Temple St.

Cultural shows

Cultural Village, Damai Beach, cultural shows, with stylized and expertly choreographed tribal dance routines, 1130 and 1630, daily.

Festivals and events

Bau *p320*

May/June The Bindayuh celebrate **gawai padi**, a festival with animistic roots that thanks the gods for an abundant rice harvest. Ask at the tourist office in Kuching for exact details.

Shopping

Kuching *p310, map p314*

When it comes to choice, Kuching is the best place in Malaysia to buy tribal handicrafts, textiles and other artefacts, but they are not cheap. In some of Sarawak's smaller coastal and upriver towns, you are more likely to find a better bargain, although the selection is not as good. If buying several items, it is a good idea to find one shop which sells the lot, as good discounts can be negotiated. It is essential to shop around: the best-stocked handicraft and antique shops in and near the big hotels are usually the most expensive. It is possible to bargain everywhere. Most shops are closed Sun.

It is illegal to export any antiquity without a licence from the curator of the Sarawak Museum. An antiquity is defined as any object made before 1850. Most things sold as antiquities are not; some very convincing weathering and ageing processes are employed.

Antiques and curios

Most of these shops are scattered along Main Bazaar, with a few in the Padungan area.

Artwork

Galleri M, Hilton Lobby, paintings from a wide range of Sarawakian artists. **Artrageouslyramsayong**, 94 Main Bazaar, T82-424346, www.artrageouslyasia.com. Art gallery of Sarawak artiste extraordinaire Ramsay Ong who made fame with his tree bark works. Now showing an eclectic collection of contemporary Malaysian art. Recommended.

Birds' nests

Mostly exported to China.
Teo Hoe Hin Enterprise (next to McDonalds) is worth visiting to view the delicacies.

Books and maps

Berita Book Centre, Jln Haji Taha, has a good selection English-language books. **HN Mohd Yahia & Sons**, Holiday Inn, Jln Tunku Abdul Rahman, and in the basement of the Sarawak Shopping Plaza, sells a 1:500,000 map of Sarawak. **Times Books**, 1st floor, Riverside Shopping Complex, Jln Tunku Abdul Rahman, best and biggest bookshop for foreign language books.

Handicrafts

Most handicraft and antique shops are along Main Bazaar, Lebuh Temple and Lebuh Wayang. Telang Usan Hotel, some Orang Ulu and Penan crafts, including good modern beadwork and traditional headgear. **Sarakraf**, Upper Ground Floor, Sarawak Plaza Shopping Complex, sarakraf@tm.net.my Wide range of souvenirs and handicrafts with outlets in major hotels in Kuching, Damai, Sarawak Cultural Village and Miri airport (chain set up by the Sarawak Economic Development Corporation). **Galleri M**, Hilton Lobby, 26 Main Bazaar. Exclusive jewellery, bead necklaces and antiques, best available Iban hornbill carvings. **Bong & Co**, 78 Main Bazaar. **Borneo Art Gallery**, Sarawak Plaza, Jln Tunku Abdul Rahman. **Borneo Arts & Crafts**, 56 Main Bazaar. There is a Sunday market (which starts on Sat afternoon) on Jln Satok, to the southwest of town, with a few handicraft stalls. Sat evening or Sun early morning are the best times to visit. **Eeze Trading**, Lot 250, Section 49, Ground floor, Jln Tunku Abdul Rahman. **Karyaneka (handicrafts) Centre** at Cawangan Kuching, Lot 324 Bangunan Bina, Jln Satok. **Loo Pan Arts**, 83 Jln Ban Hock. **Native Arts**, 94 Main Bazaar. **Sarawak Batik Art Shop**, 1 Lebuh Temple. **Sarawak House**, 67 Main Bazaar. More expensive but better qualitycrafts, carvings, fabrics and pots. **Atelier Gallery**, 104 Main Bazaar. **Syarikat Pemasarah Karyaneka**, Lot 87, Jln Rubber. **Tan & Sons**, 54 Jln Padungan. **Thian Seng**, 48 Main Bazaar (good for pua kumbu); **Art Gallery**, 5 Wayang St, designer T-shirts with Sarawak motifs amongst other crafts. **Fabriko**, Main Bazaar in beautifully restored Chinese shophouse, interesting souvenirs and gallery. **Arts of Asia**, 68 Main Bazaar.

Markets

The **Vegetable and Wet market** are on the riverside on Jln Gambier; further up is the **Ban Hock Wharf market**, now full of cheap imported clothes. The **Sunday Market** on Jln Satok sells jungle produce, fruit and vegetables (there are a few handicraft stalls) and all sorts of intriguing merchandise; it starts on Sat night and runs through Sun morning and is well worth visiting. There is a jungle produce market, **Pasar Tani**, on Fri and Sat at Kampong Pinang Jawa in Petra Jaya.

Postcards
Adventure Images showroom, 55 Main Bazaar, good range of both colour and black and white postcards, also sell greetings cards and posters.

Pottery
Rows of pottery stalls along Jln Penrissen, out of town, take a bus (3, 3A, 9A or 9B) or taxi to Ng Hua Seng Pottery bus stop. Antique shops sell this pottery too.
Shopping complexes
Sarawak Plaza, next to the Holiday Inn, Jln Tunku Abdul Rahman; **Riverside Shopping Complex**, next to Crown Plaza Riverside Hotel, best complex in Kuching, has Parkson Department Store and good supermarket in basement.

Activities and tours

Kuching *p310, map p314*

Bowling
Riverside Complex, Jln Tunku Abdul Rahman, 24-lane bowling alley.

Diving
While Kuching is no Sipadan, you can go diving here. **Borneo Inbound Tours**, 98 Main Bazaar organises scuba trips to the Tanjung Datu National Park from Telok Melano. There are dive sites at Batu Mandi and artificial reefs off Talang Talang islands. Only available from April to September because of the monsoon. The package includes a homestay with a Malay family in the traditional fishing village of Telok Melana (RM650, 2 days, 1 night) which includes transport there and back.

Fishing
Offshore from Santubong or deep sea game fishing at Tanjung Datu (near Indonesian border), contact Mr Johnson, **Fui Lip Marketing**, 15 Ground floor, Wisma Phoenix, Jln Song Thian Cheok.

Golf
Damai Golf Course, Jln Santubong, T82-846088, F82-846044. Due to its popularity bookings should be made 3 days in advance, designed by Arnold Palmer, right on the sea, a very long 18 holes - with electric buggies to prevent your expiring through perspiring. Swimming, tennis and squash courts are among the other facilities available here.
Kelab Golf Course, Petra Jaya, 18 holes, T82-440966.
Hornbill Golf & Jungle Club, Borneo Highlands Resort, Padawan, T82-790800. 18-hole golf course at 1,000 m alititude.
Sarawak Golf and Country Club, Petra Jaya, T82-440966.

Mountain biking
Good trails from Kamppung Singgai, about 30 mins from Kuching (across the Batu Kawa bridge). Beginners to intermediate – good trail near Kampong Apar. Advanced trail – Batang Ai.
Borneo Adventure, T82-245175 on Main Bazaar rents mountain bikes and can arrange specialized tours. **Power Action Cycles**, 64 Carpenter St, T82-421387 also rents mountain bikes for RM30 a day. Alternatively, hire a bike from Kuching and tour the Malay villages adjacent to the Astana and Fort Margherita. Cross the Sarawak River by sampan (around RM1 for you and your bike) and then follow the small road that runs parallel to the river.

Outward bound
Camp Permai Sarawak, PO Box 891, Satok Post Office, T82-321497, F82-321500. An 18-ha site of tropical rain forest including its own beach. It is aimed at families with kayaking, wind surfing, sailing, rafting, and trekking. **Rock Climbing 'Batman Wall'** at the Fairy Caves outside Bau has 20 routes and rises to 40 m.

Spectator sports
Malaysia Cup football matches are held in the Stadium Negeri Sarawak, Petra Jaya. **The Turf Club** on Serian Rd is the biggest in Borneo (see newspapers for details of meetings).

Swimming
Kuching Municipal Swimming Pool, next to Kuching Turf Club, Serian Rd, open mornings only.

Tour operators
Most tour companies offer city tours as well as trips around Sarawak: to Semenggoh, Bako, Niah, Lambir Hills, Miri, Mulu and Bario. There are also competitively priced packages to longhouses (mostly up the Skrang River – see page 338). It is cheaper and easier to take organized tours to Mulu, but these should be arranged in Miri (see page 361) as they are much more expensive if arranged from Kuching. Other areas are easy enough to get to independently.

Borneo Adventure, No 55 Main Bazaar, T82-245175, www.borneoadventure.com Known for its environmentally friendly approach to tourism. Offers tours all over Sarawak. Recommended. **Borneo Exploration**, 76 Jln Wayang, T82-252137, ckkc@tm.net.my **Borneo Fairyland**, 18 Main Bazaar, T82-420194, aimed at backpackers. **Borneo Inbound Tours & Travel**, 98 Main Bazaar, T82-237287. The only agency currently organising scuba diving around Kuching and the only agency for homestay programs. Call Mr Abang Zainudin (T013 8273711), manager of Borneo Inbound to arrange a homestay in the Kuching area. **Borneo Interland Travel**, 63 Main Bazaar, T82-413595, www.bitravelcom.my. Helpful staff. The only agency licensed to sell bus and boat tickets in town. There's another branch in the Merdeka palace hotel. **Borneo Transverse**, Ground floor, 16 Jln Green Hill, T82-257784, bttt@po.jaring.my **Gaya Holidays**, 37 Main Bazaar, T82-415476, sales@interworld-borneo.com, for river cruises (RM30/person/hr). **Harrisons Travel**, 28 Jln Green Hill, T82-240977. Advice on tours as well as air, bus and boat tickets. **Ibanika Expeditions**, Lot 435, Ground floor, Jln Ang Cheng Ho, T82-424022, ibanika@po.jaring.my Long-established company offering longhouse and more general tours, also offers French and German-speaking guides. **Interworld**, 1st floor, 161/162 Jln Temple, T82-252344, F82-424515. **Journey Travel Agency**, Lobby Floor, Kuching Hilton Hotel, Jln. Borneo, T82-424934, dolores@pd.jaring.my **Pan Asia Travel**, 2nd floor, Unit 217-218, Sarawak Plaza, Jln Tunku Abdul Rahman, T82-419754, half-day excursions from Kuching. **Saga Travel**, Level 1, Taman Sri Sarawak Mall, Jln Tunku Abdur Rahman, T82-418705, F82-426299. **Tropical Adventure**, 1st floor, 17 Main Bazaar, T82-413088, F82-413104.

Damai Peninsula *p321, map p319*
Golf
Damai Golf Course, Jln Santubong, PO Box 400, T82-846088, F82-846044, international standard, 18-hole golf course designed by Arnold Palmer, laid out over approximately 6½ km, 10-bay driving range. Caddies, clubs and shoes for hire, spacious club house, restaurant, bar, pro shop, tennis, squash, pool.

Mountain biking
Close to the Damai Rainforest Resort is the purpose-built **Damai Cross Country Track** where visitors can get very hot, sweaty and dirty as they career around the 3.5-km track; bikes can be hired from hotels.

Watersports
Holiday Inn Resort Damai Beach and the **Holiday Inn Resort Damai Lagoon** both offer a range of watersports from jetskiing through to sailing. Snorkelling trips also arranged. The **Damai Rainforest Resort** has a slightly more restricted range of watersports on offer.

Transport

Kuching *p310, map p314*
Air
Airport information: T82-457373.
Transport to town: Green bus Sarawak Transport Co, 12A (RM1) to **Lebuh Jawa** (45-min journey, departing every 50 mins) which operate between 0710 (0630 from Kuching) and 2000, or taxi to town (RM17.50 – buy a coupon from the counter in the arivals lounge).

Regular connections with **KL** (8-10 flights daily) **JB, KK, Bintulu, MiriSibu Penang, Labuan Mulul, Bandar Seri Begawan** and **Brunei**. AirAsia flies between Kuching and KL and Kuching and JB, it doesn't fly between KK and Kuching. **MAS Rural Air Service** operates Twin Otters to a large number of airfields across the state including Miri-Bario (for the **Kelabit highlands**), Miri-Mulu (for **Gunung Mulu**) and Sibu-Kapit-Belaga (for the **Rejang River**). MAS has direct flights to **Singapore**, **Perth** and **Pontianak** (Indonesia) and via Kota Kinabalu, **Hong Kong**, **Taipei**, **Manila**, **Seoul** and **Tokyo**.

Airline offices Air Asia, Wisma Ho Ho Lim, Ground Floor, 291 Jln Abell, T82-283222. **MAS**, Lot 215, Jln Song Thian Cheok, T82-246622, F82-244563. **Sin Hwa Travel Service**, 8 Lebuh Temple, T82-246688. **Royal Brunei**, 1st floor, Rugayah Building, Jln Song Thian Cheok, T82-243344, F82-244563. **AirAsia** office at the airport.

Boat

Local Sampan cross the Sarawak River from next to the Square Tower on Main Bazaar to **Fort Margherita** and the **Astana** on the north bank, less then RM1. Small boats and some express boats connect with outlying kampongs on the river. Sampans can also be hired by the hour (RM30 per hour) for a tour up and down the river.

International Express boats leave from the Sin Kheng Hong Wharf, 6km out of town. Take a taxi (RM8). Tickets for **Kuching-Sibu** are only for sale at two places in town; **Borneo Interland**, 63 Main Bazaar, T82-413595 and **Lim Magazine bookshop**, 19 Ban Hock Lane T82-410076. Else turn up half hour at the ferry before departure to get a ticket. Two daily departures for **Sibu** via Sarakei at 0830 and 1230 (4 hrs, RM30).

Bus

There are 2 bus companies around town: blue and white **Chin Lian Long** buses serve the city and its suburbs. Major bus stops are at Jln Mosque and opposite the Post Office. The green and yellow **Sarawak Transport Company** (STC) buses leave from the end of Lebuh Jawa, next to Ban Hock Wharf and the market. STC buses operate on regional routes; bus 12A (RM1) airport service starts at 0630, departs every 40 mins until 1915.

Buses depart from the **Regional Express Bus Terminal** on Jln Penrissen at mile 3.5 (a taxi ride costs around RM10). You either have to buy tickets at the bus station itself a few km outside of the centre, or from **Borneo Interland** (63 Main Bazaar, T82-413595, closed Sun). Buses to Sibu (RM40, 7 hours, first departure 0645, last 2200) **Bintulu** (RM60) and **Miri** (RM80, 15 hours, first 0100 last 2100).

International connections There are express bus departures to **Pontianak** in Kalimantan, Indonesia, 8 hours (first at 0730, last at 2300, RM45, bus only departs if full). It is necessary to have a valid Indonesian visa (see Embassies and consulates below). Buses leave from the Regional Express Bus Terminal. There are several departures daily from Kuching via Miri and Kuala Belait to **Bandar Seri Begawan** (Brunei; RM130). It is possible to enter Sarawak from Indonesia driving a private vehicle (including rental vehicles) so long as it has international insurance cover.

Car hire

Cat City Holidays, Lot 2537, 1st flr, Central Park, Commercial Centre, T82-412500, www.catcityholidays.com They also have a counter at the airport; **Pronto Car Rental**, 1st floor, 98 Jln Padungan, T/F82-236889. **Mayflower Car Rental**, Lot 4.24A, 4th floor, Bangunan Satok, Jln Satok, T82-410110; **Wah Tung Travel Service**, counter at Kuching International Airport, T82-616900.

Taxi

Local taxis congregate at the taxi stand on Jln Market, or outside the big hotels, they do not use meters so agree a price before setting off. 24-hr radio taxi service T82-480000/348898. Short distances around town should cost RM5-8.

Damai Peninsula *p321, map p319*

Bus

There are shuttle buses from the Holiday Inn in **Kuching** (RM10, RM5 for children, 40 mins, first bus at 0730 from Kuching, last return bus at 2200) or take the public bus No 2B, operated by **Petra Jaya Transport** (yellow buses with black and red stripes) to **Santubong** at a fraction of the price (RM3.30) from the market place at the end of Jln Gambier. Tour companies offer packages for various prices including transport, entrance to the Sarawak Cultural Village and lunch.

Taxi

From **Kuching** costs RM35.

Bako National Park *p324, map p325*

Bus and boat

Petra Jaya (yellow/red/black stripes) bus 6 or 2B every hour from Electra House on Lebuh Market to Kampong Bako, 45 mins (RM3.50); also minibuses (no fixed schedule) from Lebuh Market RM3. The last buses returning to **Kuching** depart around 1800. From **Kampong Bako**, charter a private boat to **Sungai Assam** (30 mins) which is a short walk from park HQ, RM40 per boat each way – ask price before boarding (up to 5 people).

Directory

Kuching *p310, map p314*

Banks

Money changers in the main shopping complexes usually give a much better rate for cash than the banks – although if changing TCs the rates are much the same. ATMs are two-a-penny. Note that the first and third Sat of every month is a bank holiday. **Standard Chartered**, Wisma Bukit Mata Kuching (opposite Holiday Inn), Jln Tunku Abdul Rahman. **HSBC**, Bangunan Binamas (near Cat Statue) **American Express**, 70 Jln Padungan (assistance with Amex traveller's cheques) T82-252600. **Majid & Sons Money Changer**, 45 Jln India. **Mohamed Yahia & Sons** (money changer), GF3, Sarawak Plaza – some of the best rates in Kuching.

Embassies and consulates

Indonesian Consulate, 111 Jln Tun Abang Haji Openg, T82-241734; **Australian Honorary Consul**, T82-233350; **British Honorary Representative**, T012 3220011; **French Honorary Consul**, c/o Telong Usan Hotel, T82-415588. **New Zealand Honorary** Consul, T82-482177.

Internet

Cyber City, Taman Sri Sarawak (opposite the Hilton and behind Parkson Grande), open 1000-2200 (RM4 per hr). **Waterfront Cyber** Cafe, Steamship Building open 0900-2100 (RM4 per hr). **Dot.com**, Wayang St (next to Ting & Ting supermarket and Borneo Hotel) open 0900 to 2100, RM2 per hour. International calls can also be made from most public cardphones. Major hotels all have cardphones in their lobbies.

Medical services

Sarawak General Hospital, Jln Tan Sri Ong Kee Hui, off Jln Tun Haji Openg, T82-257555. **Normah Medical Centre**, across the river on Jln Tun Datuk Patinggi Hj. Abdul Rahman Yakub, T82-440055, private hospital with good reputation. **Doctor's Clinic**, Main Bazaar, opposite Chinese History Museum is said to be excellent and is used to treating travellers' more minor ailments (RM20 for consultation). **Timberland Medical Centre**, Rock Rd, T82-234991. Recommended. **Apex Pharmacy**, 125 1st floor, Sarawak Plaza, open 1000-2100; **YK Farmasi**, 22 Main Bazaar, open 0830-1700; UMH, Ban Hock Rd, open 0900-2030, Sat 0900-1800.

Places of worship

Christian churches conduct services in a number of languages. The **Muslim Council of Sarawak** provides details of Muslim prayer times throughout the state, T82-429811. **St Thomas' Anglican Cathedral**, Jln McDougall, T82-240187 for times of services. **Sarawak Baptist Church**, Setampak, Stampin, T82-413462. **Evangelical services**: Lot 1863 Block 10, 26 Iris Gardens, T82-425212. **Trinity Methodist Church**, 57 Jln Ellis, T82-411044. **Roman Catholic**: St Joseph's Cathedral, Jln Tun Abang Hj, T82-423424.

Post

General Post Office, Jln Tun Haji Openg, open Mon-Sat 0800-1800, Sun 1000-1300. Operates a poste restante service.

Useful addresses

Immigration 1st floor, Bangunan Sultan Iskandar (Federal Complex) Jln Simpang Tiga, T82-245661. **Tourist Police** T82-241222. Office located opposite Padang Merdeka.

Bandar Sri Aman and around

→ *Colour map 3, grid C2*

Previously called Simmanggang, Bandar Sri Aman lies on the Batang Lupar, a three- to four-hour journey from Kuching, and is the administrative capital of the Second Division. The river is famous for its tidal bore; several times a year, a wall of water rushes upstream wreaking havoc with boats, small and large alike, and divides into several tributaries: the Skrang River is one of these (see below). It is possible to spend the night in longhouse homestays on the river.

The Batang Ai National Park is home to hornbills, orang utan and gibbons. ▸▸ *For Sleeping, Eating and other listings, see pages 342.*

Ins and outs

Getting there and around Bandar Sri Aman is accessible from Kuching and Sibu by bus. To reach the Skrang longhouses, buses and then chartered boats must be arranged. There is one hotel in Batang Ai National Park. It arranges transport for its guests. Trips to longhouses and the national park can be organised through Borneo Adventure Travel Company, see page 342. ▸▸ *See also Sleeping and Transport, page 342.*

Sights

The major sight in Bandar is the defensive **Fort Alice**. Most tourists do not stop in Bandar but pass through on day trips from Kuching to visit the traditional **Iban longhouses** sited along the Skrang River.The route to Bandar goes through pepper plantations and many 'new' villages. During Communist guerrilla activity in the 1960s (see page 386), whole settlements were uprooted in this area and placed in guarded camps.

Fort Alice was constructed in 1864. It has small turrets, a central courtyard, a medieval-looking drawbridge, and is surrounded by a fence of iron spikes. Rajah Charles Brooke lived in the Batang Lupar district for about 10 years, using this fort – and another downriver at Lingga – as bases for his punitive expeditions against pirates and Ibans in the interior. The fort is the only one of its type in Sarawak and was built commanding this stretch of the Batang Lupar River as protection against Iban raids. The original fort here was built in 1849 and named Fort James; the current fort was constructed using much of the original material. It was renamed Alice in honour of Ranee Margaret Brooke (it was her second name). It is said that every evening at 2000, until the practice was ended in 1964, a policeman would call from the fort (in Iban): "Oh ha! Oh ha! The time is now 2000. The steps have been drawn up. The door is closed. People from upriver, people from downriver are not allowed to come to the fort anymore." (It probably sounded better in Iban.)

Skrang longhouses

The Skrang River, was one of the first areas settled by Iban immigrants in the 16th-18th centuries. The slash-and-burn agriculturalists originally came from the Kapual River basin in Kalimantan. They later joined forces with Malay chiefs in the coastal areas and terrorized the Borneo coasts; the first Europeans to encounter these pirates called them 'Sea Dayaks' (see page 389). The Ibans took many heads. Blackened skulls – which local headmen say date back to those days – hang in some of the Skrang longhouses. In 1849, more than 800 Iban pirates from the Batang Lupar

Visiting longhouses: house rules

There are more than 1,500 longhouses in Sarawak. They are usually situated along the big rivers and their tributaries, notably the Skrang (see page 338), the Rejang (see page 346) and the Baram (see page 361). The Iban, who are characteristically extrovert and hospitable to visitors, live on the lower reaches of the rivers. The Orang Ulu tribes – mainly Kayan and Kenyah – live further upriver, and are generally less outgoing than the Iban. The Bidayuh live mainly around Bau and Serian, near Kuching. Their longhouses are usually more modern than those of the Iban and Orang Ulu, and are less often visited for that reason. The Kelabit people live in the remote plateau country near the Kalimantan border around Bareo (see page 377).

The most important ground rule is not to visit a longhouse without an invitation. People who arrive unannounced may get an embarrassingly frosty reception. Tour companies offer the only exception to this rule, as most have tribal connections. Upriver, particularly at Kapit, on the Rejang (see page 346), such 'invitations' are not hard to come by; it is good to ensure your host actually comes from the longhouse he is inviting you to. The best time to visit Iban longhouses is during the gawai harvest festival at the beginning of June, when communities throw an open house and everyone is invited to join the festivities.

On arrival, visitors should pay an immediate courtesy call on the headman (the *tuai rumah* in Iban longhouses). It is normal to bring him gifts; those staying overnight should offer the headman between RM10 and RM20/head. The money is kept in a central fund and saved for use by the whole community during festivals. Small gifts such as beer, coffee, biscuits, whisky, batik and food (especially rice or chicken) go down well. It is best to arrive at a longhouse during late afternoon after people have returned from the fields. Visitors who have time to stay the night generally have a much more enjoyable experience than those who pay fleeting visits. They can share the evening meal and have time to talk and drink.

If you go beyond the limits of the express boats, it is necessary to charter a longboat. Petrol costs RM2-4/litre, depending on how far upriver you are. Guides charge approx RM40-80 a day and sometimes it is necessary to hire a boatman or front-man as well. Prices increase in the dry season when boats have to be lifted over shallow rapids. Permits are required for most upriver areas; these can be obtained at the resident's or district office in the nearest town.

Visitors should note the following:

- On entering a longhouse, take off your shoes.
- Accept food and drink with both hands. If you do not want to eat or drink, the accepted custom is to touch the brim of the glass or the plate and then touch your lips as a symbolic gesture; sit cross legged when eating.
- When washing in the river, women should wear a sarong and men, shorts.
- Ask permission to take photographs. It is not unusual to be asked for a small fee.
- Do not enter a longhouse during *pantang* (taboo), a period of misfortune – usually following a death. There is normally a white (leaf) flag hanging near the longhouse as a warning to visitors. During this period (normally one week) there is no singing, dancing or music, and no jewellery is worn.
- Bow your head when walking past people older than you.

The first Europeans to encounter the Iban pirates called them 'Sea Dayaks'. The Ibans took many heads. Blackened skulls – which local headmen say date back to those days – hang in some of the Skrang longhouses...

and Skrang River were massacred by Rajah James Brooke's forces in the notorious Battle of Beting Marau. Four years later the Sultan of Brunei agreed to cede these troublesome districts to Brooke; they became the Second Division of Sarawak.

There are many traditional Iban longhouses along the Skrang River, although those closer to **Pias** and **Lamanak** (the embarkation points on the Skrang) tend to be very touristy – they are visited by tour groups almost every day. **Long Mujang**, the first Iban longhouse, is an hour upriver. Pias and Lamanak are within five hours' drive of Kuching. Jungle trekking is available (approximately two hours). The guide provides an educational tour of the flora and fauna. See Sleeping.

Batang Ai and Batang Ai National Park

The Batang Ai River, a tributary of the Batang Lupar, has been dammed to form Sarawak's first hydro-electric plant which came into service in 1985; it provides 60% of Sarawak's electricity supply, transmitting as far as Limbang. The area was slowly flooded over a period of six months to give animals and wildlife a chance to escape, but it has affected no less than 29 longhouses, 10 of which are now completely submerged. The re-housing of the longhouse community has been the topic of fierce controversial debate. The communities were moved into modern longhouses and given work opportunities in local palmeries. However, it now seems that the housing loans that were initially given are not commensurate with local wages and will be very difficult for the longhouse communities ever to pay off. In addition, the modern longhouses were not provided with farmland, so many local people have returned to settle on the banks of the reservoir. Near the dam there is a freshwater fish nursery. These fish are exported to South Korea, Japan and Europe. Those families displaced by the flooding of the dam largely work here and many of the longhouses surrounding the dam depend upon this fishery for their own fish supply.

The Batang Ai dam has created a vast and very picturesque man-made lake which covers an area of some 90 sq km, stretching up the Engkari and Ai rivers. Beyond the lake, more than an hour's boat ride upriver from the dam, it is possible to see beautiful lowland mixed dipterocarp forest.

The **Batang Ai National Park**, ⓘ *250 km from Kuching and two hours from the jetty by boat*, covers an area of over 24,040 ha and was inaugurated in 1991. It protects the much endangered **orang utan**, and is home to a wide variety of other wildlife, including **hornbills** and **gibbons**. As yet there are no visitor facilities, but four walking trails have been created, one of which takes in an ancient burial ground. Trips to one of the 29 longhouses surrounding the dam and to Batang Ai National Park are organized by the *Borneo Adventure Travel Company*, see Activitives and Tours.

The Batang Lupar River provided Somerset Maugham with the inspiration for his short story 'Yellow Streak' in 'Borneo Tales'. It was one of the few stories he wrote from personal experience: he nearly drowned after being caught by the bore in 1929.

The longhouse – prime-site apartments with river view

Most longhouses are built on stilts, high on the riverbank, on prime real estate. They are 'prestigious properties' with 'lots of character', and with their 'commanding views of the river', they are the condominiums of the jungle. They are long-rise rather than high-rise, however, and the average longhouse has 20-25 'doors' (although there can be as many as 60). Each represents one family. The word long in a settlement's name – as in Long Liput or Long Terawan – means 'confluence' (the equivalent of kuala in Malay), and does not refer to the length of the longhouse.

Behind each of the doors – which even today, are rarely locked – is a bilik (apartment), which includes the family living room and a loft, where paddy and tools are stored. In Kenyah and Kayan longhouses, paddy (which can be stored for years until it is milled) is kept in elaborate barns, built on stilts away from the longhouse, in case of fire. In traditional longhouses, the living rooms are simple atap roofed, bamboo-floored rooms; in modern longhouses – which are designed on exactly the same principles – the living rooms are commonly furnished with sofas, lino floors, a television and an en suite bathroom.

At the front of the bilik is the dapur, where the cooking takes place. All biliks face out onto the ruai, (gallery), which is the focus of communal life, and is where visitors are usually entertained. The width of the wall which faces onto the ruai indicates the status of that family. Attached to the ruai there is usually a tanju (open verandah), running the full length of the house – where rice and other agricultural products are dried. Long ladders – notched hardwood trunks – lead up to the tanju; they can get very slippery and do not always come with handrails.

Sleeping

Bandar Sri Aman and around *p338*

There is only a limited selection of hotels.

B **Bukit Saban Resort** is located on the rarely visited Paku River, just north of the Skrang and Lemnak rivers, about 4½ hrs from Kuching. T082-477145, F082-477103 Kuching sales office and T083-648949 at the resort. 50 rooms in longhouse style with traditional sago palm thatch, restaurant, a/c, TV, hot water, seminar facilities.

B **Champion**, 1248 Main Bazaar, T320140. A small but central establishment.

Skrang Longhouses *p338*

All longhouses along the Skrang River are controlled by the Ministry of Tourism so all rates are the same – RM40 inclusive of all meals. Resthouses at most of the longhouses can accommodate 20-40 people, mattresses and mosquito nets are provided in a communal sleeping area with few partitions, basic conditions, with flush toilet, shower, local food (visitors are sometimes allowed to sleep on the communal area), phone available and clinic nearby. If the stay is 3 days/2 nights, on the second night it is possible to camp in the jungle and then get a return boatride to the longhouse.

Batang Ai and Batang Ai National Park *p340*

A **Hilton International Batang Ai Longhouse Resort**, T83-584388, www.hilton.com On the eastern shore of the lake. Opened in 1995, the resort is made up of 11 longhouses, built of the local belian (ironwood) to traditional designs; despite its lakeside location there are no views, except from the walkways, as longhouses are built, for purposes of defence, to face landwards – in this case over the buggy track. However, compromises to modern comforts have been made; the rooms are cluttered with furniture and TV sets. One hundred rooms all with a/c, fan, TV, shower room, mini-bar, other facilities include a pool and paddling pool, restaurant, 18-km jogging track, shuttle from Kuching Hilton International, tour desk. If the Hilton is not your style (or your pocket cannot stretch to it), there is, unfortunately, not much else. The hotel arranges transport.

Private tour companies provide accommodation in the longhouses here, in a much more central location within the park than the Hilton.

Eating

Bandar Sri Aman and around *p338*

Alison Café & Restaurant, 4 Jln Council, Chinese cuisine.

Chuan Hong, 1 Jln Council, Chinese coffee shop, also serves Muslim food.

Melody, 432 Jln Hospital, Chinese and Muslim food.

Activities and tours

Bandar Sri Aman and around *p338*

Borneo Adventure Travel Company, 55 Main Bazaar, Kuching, T82-410569, F82-422626 and at the *Hilton Batang Ai Longhouse Resort*. Many of the restaurant staff in the resort are locals and discreet enquiries may get you a trip to a longhouse and/or Batang Ai National Park for considerably less than the Borneo Adventure Travel Company charge.

Transport

Bandar Sri Aman and around *p338*

Bus

Regular connections with **Kuching**, RM15, (135 km to Kuching) and **Sibu** (via Sarikei).

Skrang Longhouses *p338*

Bus

Buses 14 and 19 to **Pias** and bus 9 to **Lemanak**. Self-drive car rental (return) or minibus (8-10 people, return) from **Kuching** to **Entaban**. From these points it is necessary to charter a boat to reach the nearest longhouses. Many of the Kuching-based tour agencies offer cut-price deals for 1 to 2-day excursions to Skrang (see page 335). Unless you are already part of a small group, these tours work out cheaper because of the boat costs.

Sibu, Kapit and Belaga

→ *Colour map 3, grid B3*

The third largest town in Sarawak, Sibu is sited at the confluence of the Rejang and the Igan rivers 60 km upstream from the sea. It is the starting point for trips up the Rejang to the towns of Kapit and Belaga. The Rejang is an important thoroughfare and Malaysia's longest river at 563 km. Tours to upriver longhouses can be organized from Sibu, or more cheaply from Kapit and Belaga. » *For Sleeping, Eating and other listings, see pages 348-354.*

Ins and outs

Getting there

The airport is 25 km from town; flights to KL, Kuching, Bintulu, Miri, and KK. The new bus station is about 3 km out of town (take a taxi - RM10 - or a Lorong Rd bus (no number) or Sungei Merah bus 12 or 17 from the local bus station just outside the ferry terminal. There are daily connections with Bintulu and Miri, and Kuching via Sarikei. Boats for Kuching and Sarikei dock at 2 wharfs close to the centre of town. See also Transport, page 353. » *See also Transport, page 353.*

Getting around

Although Sarawak's third largest town, it is still possible to see most of Sibu's sights on foot.

Tourist information

Visitors' Information Centre, ⓘ *Ground floor, 32 Jln Tukang Besi (around the corner from the Methodist Church), T84-340980, www.sarawaktourism.com, 0800-1700 Mon-Fri, 0800-1250 Sat, closed first and third Sat of the month, Sun closed*, very friendly and helpful office. As well as information on Sibu they can advise for trips onwards to Kapit and Belaga.

Background

Thanks to the discovery of the Kuala Paloh channel in 1961, Sibu is accessible to boats with a sizeable draft. Sibu is a busy Chinese trading town – the majority of the population came originally from China's Foochow Province – and is the main port on the Rejang (also spelt 'Rajang'). In 1899, Rajah Charles Brooke agreed with Wong Nai Siong, a Chinese scholar from Fukien, to allow settlers to Sibu. Brooke had reportedly been impressed with the industriousness of the Chinese: he saw the women toiling in the paddy fields from dawn to dusk and commented to an aide: "If the women work like that, what on earth must the men be like?"

The Kuching administration provided these early agricultural pioneers with temporary housing on arrival, a steamer between Sibu and Kuching, rice rations for the first year and tuition in Malay and Iban. The town grew rapidly, (its expansion is documented in a photographic exhibition in the Civic Centre) but was razed to the ground in 'the great fire' of 1828. The first shophouses to be constructed after the fire are the three-storey ones still standing on Jalan Channel. At the beginning of the 20th century, Sibu became the springboard for Foochow migration to the rest of Sarawak. Today it is an industrial and trading centre for timber, pepper and rubber, and home to some of Sarawak's wealthiest families, mostly timber towkays (merchants).

Sights

The old trading port has now been graced with a pagoda, a couple of big hotels and a smart esplanade. The 1929 **shophouses** along the river are virtually all that remains of the old town. The seven-storey **pagoda**, adjacent to Tua Pek Kong Temple, cost RM1.5m to build; there are good views over the town from the top, you'll need to ask for the key. The pagoda and temple are well worth visiting for the caretaker, Tan Teck Chiang, alone. Chiang speaks great English and gives impromptu animated lectures filled with unique interpretations and humour on the temple, Chinese culture and Taoism. Just turn up and ask for Chiang. In the **Sibu Civic Centre,** ⓘ *2½ km out of town on Jalan Tun Abang Haji Openg, 1030-1730 Tue- Sun; take Sungei Merah bus No 4 from the bus terminal and ask for the Civic Centre.* There is an exhibition of old photographs of Sibu and a mediocre tribal display. This serves as Sibu's municipal museum. Five aerial photographs of the town, taken every five years or so since 1947, chart the town's explosive growth.

Kapit

→ *Colour map 3, grid C4* *Population: 100,000*

Kapit, which means 'twin' in local dialect, is the 'capital' of Sarawak's Seventh Division, through which flows the Rejang River and its main tributaries, the Batang Balleh, Batang Katibas, Batang Balui and Sungai Belaga. In a treaty with the Sultan of

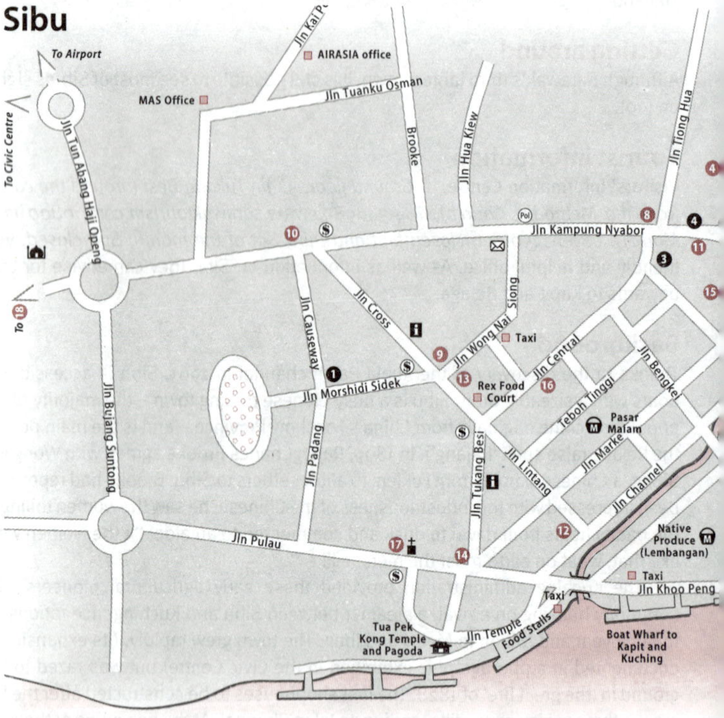

Sleeping
Eden Inn **1**
Emas **4**
Garden **5**
Hoover House **17**
Kingwood **6**
Li Hua **7**
Mandarin **8**
New World **9**
Paramount **18**
Phoenix **10**
Premier & Sarawak House Shopping Centre **11**
Ria **12**
Sarawak **13**
Sentosa Inn **14**
Tanahmas **15**
Villa **16**

Brunei, Rajah James Brooke acquired the Rejang Basin for Sarawak in 1853. Kapit is the last 'big' town on the Rejang and styles itself as the gateway to 'the heart of Borneo' – after Redmond O'Hanlon's book (*Into the Heart of Borneo*) which describes his adventure up the Batang Balleh in the 1980s. Kapit is full of people who claim to be characters in this book.

The main sights in the town are Fort Sylvia and the Kapit Museum but, like O'Hanlon and his journalist companion James Fenton, most visitors coming to Belaga venture into the interior to explore the upper Rejang and its tributaries, where there are many **Iban** and **Orang Ulu longhouses**.

Background

There are only a few tens of kilometres of metalled road in and around Kapit, but the little town has a disproportionate number of cars. It is a trading centre for the tribespeople upriver and has grown enormously in recent years with the expansion of the logging industry upstream. Logs come in two varieties – 'floaters' and 'sinkers'. Floaters are pulled downstream by tugs in huge chevron formations. Sinkers – like belian (ironwood) – are transported in the Chinese-owned dry bulk carriers which line up along the wharves at Kapit. When the river is high these timber ships are able to go upstream, past the Pelagus Rapids. The Rejang at Kapit is normally 500 m wide and in the dry season, the riverbank slopes steeply down to the water. When it floods, however, the water level rises more than 10 m, as is testified by the high water marks on Fort Sylvia.

Eating
Blue Splendour 4
Esplanade Seafood & Café 5
New Capital 3
Metropol 1
Sri Meranti 2

Sights

Fort Sylvia near the wharves was built of belian (ironwood) by Rajah Charles Brooke in 1880, and is now occupied by government offices. It was originally called Kapit Fort but was renamed in 1925 after Rajah Vyner Brooke's wife. Most of the forts built during this time were designed to prevent the Orang Ulu going downriver; Fort Sylvia was built to stop the belligerent Iban headhunters from attacking Kenyah and Kayan settlements upstream.

The other main sight is the **Kapit Museum**, ⓘ *0900-1200, 1400-1600 Mon-Fri, 0900-1200 Sat and Sun. The museum is often closed during opening hours and it may be necessary to actively search for the curator to open it; all exhibits are labelled in English*, enlarged in the 1990s, and moved to Fort Sylvia. It exhibits on Rejang tribes and the local economy. Set up by the Sarawak Museum in Kuching it includes a section of an Iban longhouse and several Iban artifacts including a wooden hornbill. The Orang Ulu section has a reconstruction of a longhouse and mural, painted by local tribespeople. An Orang Ulu salong (burial hut), totem pole and other wood carvings are also on display. The museum also has representative exhibits from the small Malay community and the Chinese. Hokkien traders settled at Kapit and Belaga and traded salt, sugar and ceramics for pepper, rotan and rubber; they were followed by Foochow traders. Appropriately, the Chinese exhibit is a shop! In addition, there are also displays on the natural history of the upper Rejang and modern industries such as mining, logging and tourism.

Kapit has a particularly colourful daily **market** in the centre of town. Tribeswomen bring in fruit, vegetables and animals to sell; it is quite normal to see everything from turtles, frogs, birds and catfish to monkeys, wild boar and even pangolin and pythons.

Pelagus Rapids

These are 45 minutes upstream from Kapit on the Rejang River. The 2.5-km long series of cataracts and whirlpools are the result of a sudden drop in the riverbed, caused by a geological fault-line. Express boats can make it up the Pelagus to Belaga in the wet season (September-April), but the rapids are still regarded with some trepidation by the pilots. When the water is low (May-August), the rapids can only be negotiated by the smallest longboats. There are seven rapids in total, each with local names such as 'The Python', 'The Knife' and one, more ominously, called 'The Grave'.

Longhouses

ⓘ *To go upriver beyond Kapit it is necessary to get a permit (no charge) from the offices in the State Government Complex. The permit is valid for travel up the Rejang as far as Belaga and for an unspecified distance up the Balleh. For upriver trips beyond Belaga another permit must be obtained there; however, these trips tend to be expensive and dangerous. See also Activities and tours for further information. Longhouses between Kapit and Belaga are accessible by the normal passenger boats but these boats only go as far as Sungai Bena on the Balleh River (2½ hrs). To go further upriver it is necessary to take a tour or organize your own guides and boatmen. The sort of trip taken by Redmond O'Hanlon and James Fenton (as described in O'Hanlon's book Into the Heart of Borneo) would cost more than RM1,500 a head.*

Some longhouses are accessible by road and several others are within an hour's longboat ride from town. In Kapit you are likely to be invited to visit one of these. Visitors are strongly advised not to visit a longhouse without an invitation, ideally from someone who lives in it. As a general rule, the further from town a longhouse is,

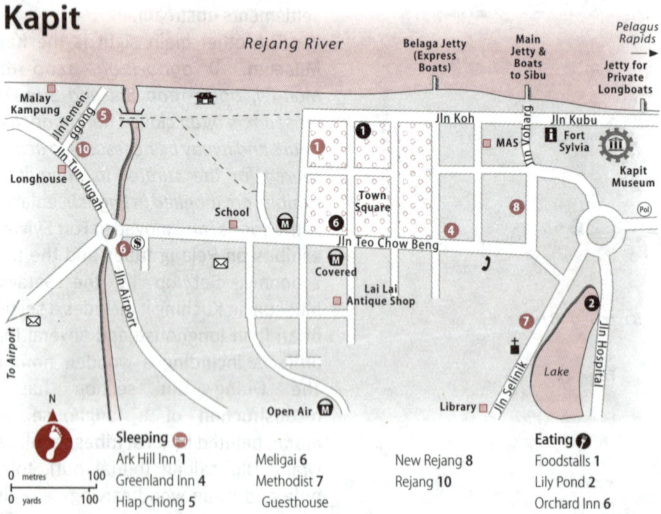

the more likely it is to conform with the image of what a traditional longhouse should be like. That said, there are some beautiful traditional longhouses nearby, mainly Iban. One of the most accessible, for example, is **Rumah Seligi**, about 30 minutes' drive from Kapit. Cars or vans can be hired by the half-day. Only a handful of longhouses are more than 500 m from the riverbanks of the Rejang and its tributaries. Most longhouses still practise shifting cultivation; rice is the main crop but under government aid programmes many are now growing cash crops such as cocoa. Longhouses are also referred to as Uma (Sumah) and the name of the headman, ie Long Segaham is known locally as Uma Lasah, Lasah being the chief.

The vast majority of the population, about 68%, in Sarawak's Seventh Division is Iban. They inhabit the Rejang up to, and a little beyond, Kapit as well as the lower reaches of the Balleh and its tributaries. The Iban people are traditionally the most hospitable to visitors, but as a result, their longhouses are the most frequently visited by tourists. Malays and Chinese account for 3.4% and 7% of the population respectively. The Orang Ulu live further upriver; the main tribes are the Kayan and the Kenyah (12%) and a long list of sub-groups such as the Kejaman, Beketan, Sekapan, Lahanan, Seping, and Tanjong. In addition there are the nomadic and semi-nomadic Penan, Punan and Ukit. Many tribal people are employed in the logging industry, and with their paid jobs, have brought the trappings of modernity to even the remotest longhouses.

Rumah Tuan Lepong Balleh Only enter this longhouse with the local policeman called Selvat Anu who lives there; ask for him at Kapit Police Station. During the day Selvat and some members of the longhouse can take visitors on various adventure tours: river trips, visiting longhouses, jungle treks, fishing, pig-hunting, camping in the jungle, trips up to logging areas, swimming in rivers, mountain trekking. Selvat is very knowledgeable and has good relations with the longhouse communities. Visitors can eat with the family and occasionally have the chance to experience a traditional Iban ceremony. See Sleeping.

Belaga → *Colour map 3, grid B5*

This is the archetypal sleepy little town; most people while their lifetime in coffee shops. They are the best place to watch life go by, and there are always interesting visitors in town, from itinerant wild honey-collectors from Kalimantan to Orang Ulu who have brought their jungle produce downriver to the Belaga bazaar or those who are heading to the metropolis of Kapit for medical treatment. At night, when the neon lights flicker on, Belaga's coffee shops are invaded by thousands of cicadas, beetles and moths.

A few Chinese traders set up shop in Belaga in the early 1900s, and traded with the tribespeople upriver, supplying essentials such as kerosene, cooking oil and shotgun cartridges. The Orang Ulu brought their beadwork and mats as well as jungle produce such as beeswax, ebony, gutta-percha (rubbery tree gum) and, most prized of all, bezoar stones. These are gall-stones found in certain monkeys (the wah-wahs, jelu-merahs and jelu-jankits) and porcupines. To the Chinese, they have much the same properties as rhinoceros horn (mainly aphrodisiacal) and even today, they are exported from Sarawak to Singapore where they fetch S$300 per kg.

Belaga serves as a small government administration centre for the remoter parts of the Seventh Division as it is the last settlement of any size as you venture up the Rejang. It is also a good place to arrange visits to the Kayan and Kenyah longhouses on the Linnau River. There is a very pretty **Malay kampong** (Kampong Bharu) along the esplanade downriver from the Belaga Bazaar. The Kejaman **burial pole** on display outside the Sarawak Museum in Kuching was brought from the Belaga area in 1902.

Up river

ⓘ *To go upriver beyond Belaga it is necessary to obtain a permit from the Resident's office and permission from the police station.*

When the river is high, express boats go upstream as far as **Rumah Belor** on the Batang Balui, but for the purpose of visiting longhouses in the Belaga area, it is best to hire a boat in Belaga. Many of the longhouses around Belaga are quite modern, although several of the Kenyah and Kayan settlements have beautifully carved wooden *salongs* (tombstones) nearby. All the longhouses beyond Belaga are Orang Ulu. Even longhouses which, on the map, appear very remote (such as Long Busang), are now connected by logging roads from Kapit, only four hours' drive away. To get well off the beaten track, into Penan country, it is possible to organize treks from Belaga towards the Kalimantan border, staying in longhouses en route.

About 2 km up the Batang Belaga from Belaga are the **Pasang Rapids** rapids, ⓘ *hire a boat from Belaga*, which are certainly the biggest in Sarawak. It appears that no one has purposely tried to shoot them as they are too dangerous. Boats can get reasonably close, however, and in the dry season, it is possible to climb up to a picnic area, overlooking the white water.

Sleeping

Sibu *p343, map p344*
Cheaper hotels tend to be around the nightmarket in Chinatown but there is also a selection within each walk of the jetty.

A **Kingwood**, 12 Lorong Lanang 4, T84-335888, kingwood@tm.net.my Largest hotel in Sibu with 168 rooms, more expensive ones have views of the Rejang River. All rooms with a/c, TV, mini-bar, Riverfront Cafe, Chinese restaurant, pool, health centre.

Upper Rejang

Build and be (Bakun) Dammed: an ecological time bomb

The Bakun Dam, upriver from Belaga on the Upper Rejang and 400 km east of Kuching, has had more twists and turns than the river on which it (may be) built.

The RM9.12 billion project, one of the largest in Southeast Asia, will flood a tract of virgin rainforest that supports at least 43 species of endangered mammals and birds. It will also displace thousands of longhouse-dwelling tribespeople.

The dam is going to be twice the height of the Aswan Dam in Egypt and will flood 69,000 hectares – an area bigger than Singapore. Former prime minister Mahathir described it as "a project whose time has come". Environmentalists say it will be an ecological time bomb in the heart of Borneo.

The project has been on and off the books countless times. In 1990 it was scrapped for environmental reasons, but was back on again in 1993. Again, in late 1997, in the midst of Malaysia's economic crisis, when money was scarce, it was shelved only to be restarted in 2001. In 2004, with the government struggling to find buyers for the dam's electricity, it was rumoured the project would again be scrapped or postponed. But Prime Minister Badawi says he is determined to see the project through, although its original completion date of 2003 has been pushed back to 2007, a date, which observers say, is also unlikely to be met. Even during the hiatus, preparations for the eventual flooding went on. Thousands of locals were moved from their villages and jungle longhouses and rehoused elsewhere.

The plan is for Bakun to generate 2,400 MW of electricity. The power will be consumed within Sabah and Sarawak, and possibly Brunei and Kalimantan, and involve the construction of 800 km of high voltage power lines. Plans for a 600+ km undersea cable have been shelved. The cable was to pipe power to the peninsular where energy needs are rising, unlike Borneo where there does not seem to be the growth in demand to warrant the dam's construction.

Roads need to be carved through dense jungle to bring building materials and engineering equipment to the remote site, above the Bakun Rapids. Malaysian lobby groups such as the Environmental Protection Society predict the project will cause severe soil erosion in an area already suffering from the effects of logging. In the early 1990s the riverwater was clear and fish abundant; now the river is a muddy brown and water levels fluctuate wildly. Nor is the project a long-term one: even the government admits its productive life is likely to be in the region of 25 years before it silts up. Friends of the Earth Malaysia say: "This project is going to have a tremendous effect on the lives of natives, plants and animals and bio-diversity of the pristine forests where it is going to be built".

The local tribespeople, whose ancestors battled for decades against the White Rajahs, have, it seems, finally met their match, in Malaysia's relentless thrust towards modernity. See www.irn.org/programs/bakun, homepage of the International Rivers Network – for more information on the dam.

A Paramount, 3 Lorong 9A, Jln Kampong Dato, T84-331122, paramounthtlrsv@myjaring.net. Sibu's newest high-end hotel a little bit out of town on the western edge facing the river. A/c, TV, kettle and other 2-star room amenities, but have little atmosphere.

A Premier, Jln Kampong Nyabor, T84-323222, F84-323399. Restaurant, clean rooms with a/c, TV, own bath, some with river view. Helpful staff, adjoins the Sarawak House Shopping Centre, discounts often available. Recommended.

A Tanahmas, Jln Kampong Nyabor, T84-333188, www.tanahmas.com.my A/c, very high-standard restaurant, well-appointed modern hotel with swimming pool, Blowpipe Lounge bar and conference facilities. Recommended.

B Garden, 1 Jln Hua Ping, T84-317888, F84-330999. A/c, restaurant, well-kept and efficiently run with a good central location and a serviceable coffee shop.

B Li Hua, Long Bridge Commercial Centre, T84-324000, F84-326272. Slightly out of town, but located along the river. TV, a/c, restaurant, coffee house and roof-top swimming pool. Good value.

C Phoenix, 1 & 3 Jln Kai Peng (off Jln Kampong Nyabor), T84-313877, F84-320392. TV, a/c. A very well-run hotel with spacious rooms and decent bathrooms.

C Sarawak, 34 Cross Rd, T84-333455, F84-320536. A/c, attached bathroom, TV. Centrally located and a well-furnished place, good value.

C-D Eden Inn, 1 Jln Lanang, T84-337277. Opposite the Sacred Heart Catholic Church. Massive rooms in a big solid building. TV and a/c make this place excellent value. Recommended.

C-D Sentosa Inn, 12 Jln Pulau, T84-349875, F84-311706. A/c, TV, run of the mill but clean and quiet. Military style beds but nice extras like toilet paper, towel and soap.

D Emas, 3A Foochow Lane, T84-310877, F320848. Some a/c, clean.

D Hoover House, Methodist Church, Jln Pulau, T84-332491 or call Tony T016 869 2491. Six rooms attached to the Methodist Church with attached bathroom. Must book ahead as almost always full. Safe and recommended.

D Mandarin, 183 Jln Kampong Nyabor, T84-339177, F84-333425. A/c, standard rooms, cheap.

D New World, 1 Jln Wong Nai Siong, T84-310311. A/c, clean rooms with attached bathrooms.

D Ria, 21 Jln Channel, T84-326622. A/c, reasonable value.

D Villa, 2-4 Lebuh Central, T84-337833. Good location next to travel agencies. Threadbare rooms, a little shabby, but clean and cheap.

Kapit *p344, map p346*

All hotels are within walking distance of the wharf.

B Greenland Inn, 463 Jln Teo Chow Beng, T84-796388, F84-797989. A/c, well-maintained small hotel with good rooms. Recommended. Although it charges an inflated rate for what is offered, it is comfortably the smartest hotel in town.

B-C New Rejang Hotel, clean rooms in a modern mid-range hotel. Rooms with a/c, bathroom with fantastic showers, desk and satellite TV. This is where you can find Joshua Muda, who can help arrange longhouse tours.

C Meligai, 334 Jln Airport, T84-796817/796611. Full range of accommodation from VIP suite to dingy standard rooms, has some of the trappings of a city hotel but rooms are generally poor. Also home to a cheap restaurant and the Meligai pub.

D Ark Hill Inn, 451 Jln Airport, T84-796168, F84-796337. A/c, bathroom, friendly, clean rooms. It is also situated on the river and there are great views from some of the rooms. Recommended.

D Hiap Chiong, 33 Jln Temenggong Jugah, T84-796314. Some a/c, no attached bath, top floor best bet.

D Rejang, 28 New Bazaar, T84-796709. Some a/c, basic but clean – if you can afford the extra cash its slightly newer sister hotel is a better option.

E Methodist Guesthouse. Sometimes budget rooms available here.

Pelagus Rapids *p346*

A-B Pelagus Resort, set on the banks of the Rejang overlooking the rapids,T84-799050, F84-799060, www.theregencyhotel.com.my/pelagus/. 40 longhouse-style rooms, with restaurant, pool, bar and sun-deck, deluxe rooms have a/c, otherwise there are fans. Trips organized from resort to longhouses, nature treks and river safaris, whitewater rafting on the rapids. Regular express boats pass through the rapids upstream.

Longhouses *p346*

D Rumah Tuan Lepong Balleh You can stay in this longhouse, RM30, inclusive of meals, generator until 2300, basic. It is about one hour's drive from Kapit; take a minibus and ask for 'Selvat and Friends Traditional Hostel and Longhouse'.

Belaga *p347*

C-D Belaga Hotel, 14 Belaga Bazaar, T86-461244. Some a/c, restaurant, no hot water, particularly friendly proprietor, good coffee shop downstairs, in-house video and cicadas. Best option.

D Bee Lian Hotel, 11 Belaga Bazaar, T86-461439. A/c, rooms are fine, 9 rooms.

D Belaga Budget Hotel, 4 Belaga Bazaar, (upstairs from MAS office), T86-461512. Just four rooms in this place with fan or a/c. Restaurant and internet.

Eating

Sibu *p343, map p344*

Chinese

TT Jhong Kuo, 13 Jln Wong Nai Siong, Foochow.

TT New Capital, 46 Jln Kampong Nyabor. You can tell this place is something fancy in Sibu with its pink tablecloths, lazy susan's and faux chandeliers. Extensive menu.

TT Sri Meranti, 1A Jln Hardin. Friendly staff, good seafood, nice sitting out area with cold beer and tablecloths.

T Blue Splendour, 1st floor, 60-62 Jln Kampong Nyabor (opposite Premier Hotel), recommended by locals.

T Esplanade Seafood & Café, on the Rejang esplanade. Great al fresco dining, with tables facing the river. Open evening only when the place is strung with red lanterns. Excellent Chinese food and western dishes including fish'n'chips, barbecued meats, burgers and omelettes. Recommended, best in town.

T Golden Palace, Tanahmas Hotel, Jln Kampong Nyabor, Cantonese and Schezuan.

International

T Peppers Café, Tanahmas Hotel, Jln Kampong Nyabor, western and local food, curries particularly recommended, popular.

Malay

T Metropol, 1st floor, 20 Jln Morshidi Sidek, also serves Melanau curries.

T Sheraton, Delta Estate (out of town), Malay (and some Chinese), fish head curries recommended by locals.

Foodstalls

There is a hawker centre on Jln Market, in the centre of town.

Rex Food Court, 28 Jln Cross, is new and clean.

Kapit *p344, map p346*

Kapit's cuisine is predominantly Chinese.

Chinese

T 99, Jln Pedral, fresh air, clean local and Chinese food.

T Hua Hua, Jln Airport/Jln Court, Chinese food.

T Jade Garden, Jln Pedral, local and Chinese food, smart.

T Lily Pond, in the middle of the lily pond, off Jln Hospital, pleasant setting, plenty of mosquitoes and an unimaginative menu.

T S'ng Ee Ho Restaurant, next to Metox supermarket, happy to cook anything you ask for.

International

TT Orchard Inn, 64 Jln Airport, T84-796325. The most upmarket restaurant in Kapit, food well presented but the coffee shops taste just as good, disco from 2200-0100.

Malay

T MI, Jln Pedral, Malay Muslim food.

Bakeries and breakfast

Ung Tong Bakery, opposite the market, bakery and café, good continental-style breakfasts – big selection of rolls and good coffee, fresh bread baked twice daily (0600 and 1100). Recommended.

Chuong Hin, opposite the Sibu wharf, best-stocked coffee shop in town.

Foodstalls

Stalls at the top end of the road opposite the market (dead-end road; brightly painted on the outside). Good satay stall on Jln Hospital, next to the lily pond.

For an explanation of the sleeping and eating price codes used in this guide, see inside the front cover. Other relevant information is found in Essentials, pages 45-49.

Belaga *p347*

Several small, cheap coffee shops along Belaga Bazaar and Main Bazaar.

Entertainment

Sibu *p343, map p344*

Cinema King's Theatre in Sarawak House Complex shows Hollywood movies.

Shopping

Sibu *p343, map p344*

Handicrafts

Stalls along express boat wharves at Jln Channel, mainly selling basketware. **Chop Kion Huat**, Jln Market, just behind the tourist information office has Sarawak handicrafts including batiks, basketware, tshirts and carvings

Markets

Pasar Malam, along High St, Jln Market and Lembangan Lane (Chinatown). **Native market** (Lembangan market), on Lembangan River between Jln Mission and Jln Channel, sells jungle produce.

Pottery

Two potteries at Km 7 and 12 Ulu Oya Rd.

Supermarket

Sarawak House Shopping Complex, Jln Kg Nyabor, has Premier Department Store. There's a good minimarket opposite Chop Kion Huat handicraft shop on Jln Market that has fruit juice, wine, spirits, marmite and a good place to stock up on shampoo and shower gel. There's a book and magazine shop on the ground floor of Sarawak House Complex that sells English magazines.

Kapit *p344, map p346*

Handicrafts

Lai Lai Antique Shop, next road along on the right from the Putena Jaya (see below), small selection of woven rugs/sarongs, prices are high but they are similar to the starting prices at the longhouses. **Din Chu Café,** next to Methodist Resthouse, sells antiques and handicrafts.

Belaga *p347*

Handicrafts

Chop Teck Hua, Belaga Bazaar, has an intriguing selection of tribal jewellery, old coins, beads, feathers, woodcarvings, blowpipes, parangs, tattoo boards and other curios buried under cobwebs and gekko droppings at the back of the shop, although the owner is noticeably uninformed about the objects he sells.

Activities and tours

Sibu *p343, map p344*

Bowling

Sibu Superbowl, 2 Lorong Perpati (off Jln Wong King Huo), T84-331111, F84-318980. Open Mon-Sat 1000-0000, Sun 0900-0000.

Golf

Sibu Golf Club, Km 17 Ulu Oya Rd.

Tour operators

Most companies run city tours plus tours of longhouses, Mulu National Park and Niah Caves. It is cheaper to organize upriver trips from Kapit or Belaga than from Sibu.

Equatorial Tour & Travel Centre, 11 Raminway, T84-331599, F84-330250. **Golden Horse Travel**, 62 Jln Kampong Nyabor, T84-323288, F84-310600. **Metropolitan Travel**, 72-74 Jln Market, T84-313155, F84-345486. **RH Tours & Travel**, 11 Jln Mission, T84-316767, F84-316185. **Sazhong Trading & Travel**, 4 Jln Central, T84-336017, F84-334222, www.geocities.com/sazhong Director Frankie Ting can arrange budget stays for groups in a longhouse in Kapit and beyond. Recommended. **Sibu Golden Tours**, 1D, Lorong Foochow T84-316861, F84-318606. **Sitt Travel**, 147 ground floor, Jln Kampong Nyabor, T84-320168. **Travel Consortium**, 14 Jln Central, T84-334455, F84-330589. Good for air ticketing. **WTK Travel**, Ground floor, Bangunan Hung Ann, 1 Jln Bujang Suntong, T84-319393, F84-319933.

Kapit *p344, map p346*

Tour operators

Sibu's tourist office and travellers recommend local expert **Joshua Muda**, T84-796600, joshuamuda@hotmail.com, he usually can be found in the *New Rejang Inn*. He arranges sensitive and authentic longhouse trips. Some hotels will help organize trips, or inquire at the police station. There are some guides in Kapit who overcharge for very unsatisfactory tours.

Belaga *p347*

Tour operators

The **Belaga Hotel** will contact guides for upriver trips and the District Office can also recommend a handful of experienced guides. In this part of Sarawak, guides are particularly expensive – sometimes up to RM80 a day, mainly because there are not enough tourists to justify full-time work. It is necessary to hire experienced boatmen too, because of the numerous rapids. Sarawak Tourism recommended guides include **John Belakirk**, T86-461512/013 6331527, johneddie1@hotmail.com; **Hamdani Louis**, T86-461039/013 8365850, hamdani@hotmail.com. Prices for trips to longhouses upriver vary according to distance and the water level, but are similar to those in Kapit. English is not widely spoken upriver, basic Bahasa comes in handy.

Transport

Sibu *p343, map p344*

Air

The airport is 25 km north of town. Sibu airport information centre, T84-307755. To get to the airport take a taxi (RM26) or Lanang Bus No 3A which leaves every two hours between 0630 and 1600. From the airport to Sibu you need to buy a taxi coupon (RM28). Regular connections with **Kuching** (RM86, around 10 flights a day), **Bintulu** (RM78, 4 flights a day), **Miri** (RM126, up to 4 flights a day), **Belaga** (RM49, one flight only on Wed and Sat), **KK** (RM194, 3 flights a day) and **KL** (MAS fly once a day, as do **AirAsia**, RM334 for MAS, as low as RM100 by AirAsia).

Airline offices MAS, 61 Jln Tunku Osman, T84-326166. **AirAsia**, Jln Kai Peng.

Bus

Local buses leave from Jln Khoo Peng Loong. Long-distance buses leave from the new Sibu bus terminal at Jalan Pahlawan. To get there take a taxi (RM10), or bus No 12 or No 17 from the local bus station. There are three main long-distance bus companies: **Biaramas Express, Borneo Highway Express** and **Suria Express** which all have routes from Sibu to **Bintulu, Miri** and **Kuching**. Regular connections with **Bintulu**, RM20, 3-4 hrs, and Miri RM40, 6-7 hours, along a surfaced road. First bus leaves around 0630, and then last bus at 0100, departures every hour or more. Best to purchase tickets the day before departure – there are ticket offices for the different companies around the jetty or else buy from the bus station. The early morning buses to Bintulu connect with the buses direct to **Batu Niah** (see Bintulu). There are also daily connections with **Kuching** via **Sarikei** (2 hrs to Sarikei, RM8, 8 hours to Kuching, RM40). There are around 10 daily departures from 0700 to midnight.

Boat

These leave from the wharf. The time of the next departure is shown by big clockfaces on whiteboards, just buy the ticket at the jetty. There are 2 express boats a day between Sibu and **Kuching**. Sejahtera Pertama (T84-321424) boats leave at 0730. **Ekspress Bahagia** (T84-319228) leave a little later at 1130. These boats stop off at Sarekei. Regular express boats to **Kapit** 2-3 hrs and in the wet season, when the river is high enough, they continue to **Belaga**, 5-6 hrs. If travelling from Sibu through Kapit to Belaga, take one of the early morning boats (the first leaves at 0530) which connects all the way through. The last Sibu-Kapit boat departs at around 1300. In the dry season passengers change on to smaller launches to get up-river to Belaga (see below). Some of the Sibu-Kapit boats stop off at **Kanowit** and **Song** on their journey up-river.

Kapit *p344, map p346*

Boat

All 3 wharves are close together. Regular connections with **Sibu** from 0500-1500, 2-3 hrs. **Belaga** is not accessible by large express boats during the dry season. Prices for the express boats start at RM15. In the dry season sometimes smaller speed boats go upriver (RM60-RM100 per person).

Belaga *p347*

At the moment Belaga is comparatively isolated and overland links are poor. During the dry season it is possible to travel by 4WD overland to **Bintulu** (see below), but it is drawn out and expensive. It is likely that road links will improve, particularly with the controversial Bakun Dam project underway (due to be finished in 2007). The road between Bakun and Bintulu has been gradually upgraded and is now surfaced along almost its full length. Journeys take about 3 hrs and you have to arrange travel yourself or hitch. To charter a 4WD for the whole journey to Bintulu costs RM400 for 5 people and the journey takes 5 hours. The Belaga Hotel can help with 4WD or try Peter Ho at *Soon Soon Café*, T86 461085). He has a car that leaves Belaga for Bintulu at 0800, and back to Belaga at 1500.

Air

Connections on Wed and Sat only **Bintulu** (RM40). The airport can be reached by boat (RM8, 30 mins). Contact Hasbee Enterprise (near the jetty), 4 Belaga Bazaar, T86-461240 for help with flights and getting to the airport.

Airline offices MAS, c/o Lau Chun Kiat, Main Bazaar.

Boat

There is a daily boat from **Kapit** leaving early in the morning, which costs RM30-RM25 only in the west season, the journey takes around 5 hours. In the dry season speedboats leave from Kapit at RM60 upwards per person. When the river is very low the only option is to fly or drive to Belaga from Bintulu.

To **Tabau** and on to **Bintulu**: it is possible to hire a boat from Belaga to Kestima Kem (logging camp) near Rumah Lahanan Laseh (RM60 per person in a group or RM260 for 2-3 people); from there logging trucks go to Tabau on the Kemena River. Logging trucks leave irregularly and you can get stuck in logging camps. It is a 3-hr drive to Tabau; this trip is not possible in the wet season. There are regular express boats from Tabau to Bintulu (RM12). This is the fastest and cheapest route to Bintulu, but not the most reliable. It is necessary to obtain permission from the Resident's office and the police station in Belaga to take this route.

Directory

Sibu *p343, map p344*

Banks Standard Chartered, Jln Cross. HSBC, 17 Jln Wong Nai Siong Hock Hua, Jln Pulau. Apart from the banks, cash can be exchanged at good rates at goldsmiths around town. **Internet** PCShop, Sarawak House Complex, Ground Floor. Fast connection. **Post** General Post Office, Jln Kampong Nyabor. **Useful addresses** Police Jln Kampong Nyabor, T84-322222. Residents' Office T84-321963.

Kapit *p344, map p346*

Banks There are 2 banks which will accept TCs, one in the New Bazaar and the other on Jln Airport, but it is easier to change money in Sibu. **Libraries** On the other side of the road from first floor State Government Complex. Good selection of books on history and natural history of Borneo. There's also reportedly Internet access here. Open 1615-2030 Mon-Sat, 0900-1115, 1400-1630 Sat, closed Sun. **Useful addresses** Land Survey Department, Jln Beletik on Jln Airport. Maps of Kapit Division and other parts of Sarawak. Resident's Office, 1st floor State Government Complex (opposite the lily pond), T84-796963/796445, open 0800-1200, 1400-1600, Mon-Fri. Permits for upriver trips. Tourists going to Baleh or Upper Rejang areas must sign a form saying they fully understand they are travelling at their own risk.

Belaga *p347*

Internet Hasbee Enterprises, 4 Belaga Bazaar (RM6 per hour), open 0700-1900. **Post** In the District Office building. **Useful addresses** District Office (for upriver permits) on the far side of the basketball courts.

The North Coast → Colour map 3, grid B4

The North Coast of Sarawak is fairly remote with Bintulu, Miri and Marudi being the only significant towns. Close to Bintulu is Similajau National Park where green turtles lay their eggs. Niah National Park boasts famous limestone caves and is home to jungle birds and primates. Miri is the launch pad for river trips into the interior and Marudi is an upriver trading post and the start of a cross-border trek. ➡➡ *For Sleeping, Eating and other listings, see pages 364-370.*

Ins and outs

Getting there and around Bintulu is accecssible by air, boat and bus. Miri is accessible by air and bus and Marudi by air and boat. ➡➡ *See also Transport, page 369.*

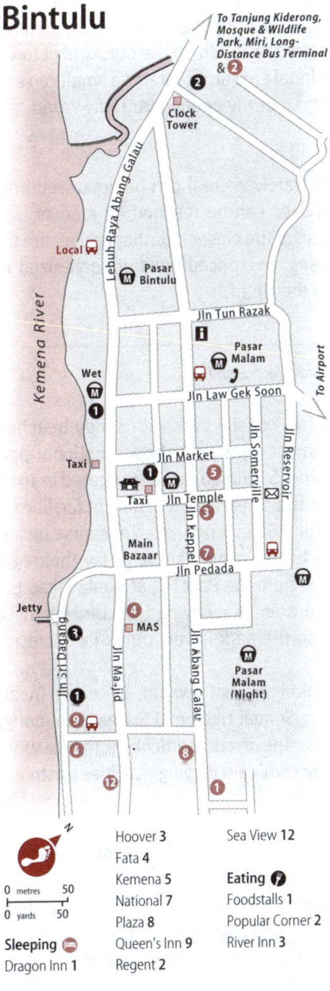

Bintulu

The word Bintulu is thought to be a corruption of Mentu Ulau, which translates as 'the place for gathering heads'. Bintulu, on the Kemena River, is in the heart of Melinau country and was traditionally a fishing and farming centre until the largest natural gas reserve in Malaysia was discovered offshore in the late 1970s, making Bintulu a boomtown overnight. Shell, Petronas and Mitsubishi moved to the town in force. In 1978 the town's population was just 14,000.

Few tourists stay long in Bintulu, although it is the jump-off point to the Similajau National Park and the Niah Caves. The longhouses on the Kemena River are accessible, but tend not to be as interesting as those further up the Rejang and Baram rivers. The Penan and Kayan tribes are very hospitable and eager to show off their longhouses and traditions to tourists.

Ins and outs

Tourist information ⓘ *www.sarawak.forestry.gov.my* for the Sarawak Forestry Department's (rose tinted) view of it all

Background

The remnants of the old fishing village at Kampong Jepak are on the opposite bank of the Kemena River. During the Brooke era the town was a small administrative centre. The **clock tower** commemorates the meeting of five representatives from the Brooke government and 16 local chieftains, the birth of Council Negeri, the state legislative body.

The first project to break ground in Bintulu was the RM100-m crude oil terminal at Tanjong Kidurong from which 45,000 barrels of petroleum are exported daily. A deep-water port was built and the liquefied natural gas (LNG) plant started operating in 1982. The abundant supply of natural gas also created investment in related downstream projects. The main industrial area at Tanjong Kidurong is 20 km from Bintulu. The **viewing tower** at Tanjong Kidurong gives a panoramic view of the new-look Bintulu, out to the timber ships on the horizon. They anchor 15 km offshore to avoid port duties and the timber is taken out on barges.

Sights

Bintulu has a modern **Moorish-style mosque** called the **Masjid Assyakirin**; visitors may be allowed in when it is not prayer time. There is a new, colourful, centrally-located Chinese temple called **Tua Pek Kong**. **Pasar Bintulu** is also an impressive recently-constructed building in the centre of town, built to house local jungle produce market, foodstalls and limited handicrafts stalls. A landscaped **wildlife park, Taman Tumbina,** ⓘ *0800-1800 Mon-Sun, RM2, www.bda.gov.my/tamantumbina.htm*, has been developed on the outskirts of town, on the way to Tanjong Batu. It is a local recreational area and contains a small zoo and a botanic garden (the only one in Sarawak) and a newly opened Butterfly World.

Longhouses

Trips to the longhouses on the Kemena River (rarely visited) can be organized from Bintulu. More than 20 Kemena River longhouses can be reached by road or river within 30 minutes of Bintulu. Iban longhouses are the closest; further upriver are the more traditional Kayan and Kenyah longhouses. Overpriced tours are organized by *Similajau Adventure Tours* or hire a boat from the wharf.

Similajau National Park

→ *Colour map 3, grid B4*

Lying 20 km northeast of Bintulu, Similajau is a coastal park with sandy beaches, broken by rocky headlands. It is Sarawak's most unusually shaped national park being more than 32 km long and only 1.5 km wide. Similajau was demarcated in 1978, but has only really been open to tourists since the construction of decent facilities in 1991. **Pasir Mas,** (Golden Sands), is a beautiful 3½ km long stretch of coarse beach, to the north of the Likau River, where green turtles come ashore to lay their eggs between July and September. A few kilometres from the Park HQ at **Kuala Likau** is a small coral reef, known as **Batu Mandi**. The area is renowned for birdwatching. Bintulu is not on the main tourist track and so the park is very quiet. Its seclusion makes it a perfect escape.

The **beaches** are backed by primary rainforest: peat swamp, kerangas (heath forest), mixed dipterocarp and mangrove (along Sungai Likau and Sungai Sebubong). There are small rapids on the Sebulong River. The rivers, particularly the beautiful **Sungai Likau,** have sadly been polluted by indiscriminate logging activities upstream.

Ins and outs

Permits are available from the **Bintulu Development Authority**. The **information centre** at is at Park HQ, ⓘ T86-332011, at the mouth of Sungai Likau, across the river from the park. A boat is needed to cross the 5m of crocodile-infested river. Because the facilities to the park are actually outside the park, visitors do not need a permit to stay there. This has led to the 'park' becoming very popular with Bintulites at the weekend.

The massacre at Long Nawang

The Japanese Imperial Army invaded the country 100 years and three months after James Brooke was proclaimed Rajah of Sarawak. On Christmas Day 1941, when Rajah Vyner Brooke was visiting Australia, they took Kuching; a few days earlier they had occupied the Miri oilfields. Japanese troops, dressed for jungle warfare, headed upriver. They did not expect to encounter such stiff resistance from the tribespeople. The Allies had the brainwave of rekindling an old tribal pastime – headhunting, which successive Brooke administrations had tried to stamp out. Iban and Orang Ulu warriors were offered 'ten-bob-a-knob' for Japanese heads and many of the skulls still hanging in longhouses are said to date from this time.

The years of occupation were marked by terrible brutality, and many people fled across the border into Dutch Borneo – now Kalimantan. The most notorious massacre in occupied Sarawak involved refugees from Kapit. Just a month after the Japanese invasion, a forestry officer stationed on the Rejang heard that a group of women and children from Kapit were planning to escape across the Iran Range into Dutch territory. He organized the evacuation, and led the refugees up the rivers and over the mountains to the Dutch military outpost at Long Nawang. The forester returned to Kapit to help organize resistance to the Japanese. But when the invading forces heard of the escape they dispatched a raiding party upriver, captured the Dutch fort, lined up the fifty women and ordered the children to climb into nearby trees. According to historian Robert Payne: "They machine-gunned the women and amused themselves by picking off the children one by one... Of all those who had taken part in the expedition only two Europeans survived."

Flora and fauna

One of the first things a visitor notices on arrival at Kuala Likau is the prominent sign advising against swimming in the river, and to watch your feet in the headquarters' area: Similajau is well known for its **saltwater crocodiles** (*Crocodylus perosus*). Similajau also has 24 resident species of **mammals** (including gibbons, Hose's langurs, banded langurs, long-tailed macaques, civets, wild boar, porcupines, squirrels) and 185 species of birds, including many migratory species. Marine life includes **dolphins**, **porpoises** and **turtles**; there are some good coral reefs to the north. Pitcher plants grow in the kerangas forest and along the beach.

Treks

Several trails have been cut by park rangers from the Park HQ; longish but not too difficult. One path follows undulating terrain, parallel to the coast. It is possible to cut to the left, through the jungle, to the coast, and walk back to Kuala Likau along the beach. The main trail to **Golden Beach** is a three- to four-hour walk crossing several streams and rivers where estuarine crocodiles are reputed to lurk. Most of these crossings are on 'bridges', which are usually just felled trees with no attempt made to assist walkers (some 'bridges' have drops of around 5 m) – a good sense of balance is required. Another enjoyable and rewarding walk is the trail to **Selansur Rapids**, around two-and-a-half hours in total. Start off by following the trail to the Golden Beach; after about an hour a marked trail leads off into the forest. The walk ends at the rapids where it is possible to take a dip and cool off.

How to make a swift buck

The Malay name for Niah's Painted Cave is Kain Hitam – or 'black cloth' – because the profitable rights to the birds' nests were traditionally exchanged for bolts of black cloth.

The Chinese have had a taste for swiftlets' nests for well over 1,000 years, and the business of collecting them from 60 m up in the cavernous chamber of the Great Cave is as lucrative – and as hazardous – a profession now as it was then. The nests are used to prepare birds' nest soup – blended with chicken stock and rock salt – which is a famous Chinese delicacy, prized as an aphrodisiac and for its supposed remedial properties for asthma and rheumatism.

Birds' nests are one of the most expensive foods in the world: they sell for up to US$500/kilo in Hong Kong, where about 100 tonnes of them (worth US$40m) are consumed annually. The Chinese communities of North America import 30 tonnes of birds' nests a year. Locally, they fetch RM150-600/kg, depending on the grade.

Hundreds of thousands – possibly millions – of swiftlets (of the Collocalia swift family) live in the caves. Unlike other parts of Southeast Asia, where collectors use rotan ladders to reach the nests (see Gomantong Caves, Sabah, page 452), Niah's collectors scale belian (ironwood) poles to heights of more than 60 m. They use bamboo sticks with a scraper attached to one end (called penyulok) to pick the nests off the cave roof. The nests are harvested three times each season (which run from August to December and January to March). On the first two occasions, the nests are removed before the eggs are laid and a third left until the nestlings are fledged. Nest collectors are now all supposed to have licences, but in reality, no one does. Although the birds' nests are supposed to be protected by the national park in the off-season, wardens turn a blind eye to illegal harvesting – the collectors also know many secret entrances to the caves. Officially, people caught harvesting out of season can be fined RM2,000 or sent to jail for a year, but no one's ever caught. Despite being a dangerous operation (there are usually several fatal accidents at Niah each year), collecting has become so popular that harvesters have to reserve their spot with a lamp. Nest collecting is run on a first-come, first-served basis. Nests of the white nest swiftlets and the black nest swiftlets are collected – the nests of the mossy-nest and white-bellied swiftlets require too much effort to clean. The nests are built by the male swiftlets using a glutinous substance produced by the salivary glands under the tongue which is regurgitated in long threads; the saliva sets like cement producing a rounded cup which sticks to the cave wall. In the swifts' nest market, price is dictated by colour: the best are the white nests which are without any plant material or feathers. Most of the uncleaned nests are bought up by middlemen, agents of traders in Kuching, but locals at Batu Niah also do some of the cleaning. The nests are first soaked in water for about three hours, and when softened, feathers and dirt are laboriously removed with tweezers. The 'cakes' of nests are dried overnight: if left in the sun they turn yellow.

Niah National Park → *Colour map 3, grid A5*

Niah's famous caves, tucked into a limestone massif called Gunung Sabis, made world headlines in 1959, when they were confirmed as the most important archaeological site in Asia. The park is one of the most popular tourist attractions in Sarawak and attracts more than 15,000 visitors every year. The caves were declared a national historic monument in 1958, but it was not until 1974 that the 3,000 ha of jungle surrounding the caves were turned into a national park to protect the area from logging.

The Niah National Park primarily comprises of alluviai or peat swamp as well as some mixed dipterocarp forest. Long-tailed macaques, hornbills, squirrels, flying lizards and crocodiles have all been recorded in the park. There are also bat hawks which provide an impressive spectacle when they home in on one of the millions of bats which pour out of the caves at dusk.

Ins and outs

Getting there The nearest town to the park is Batu Niah. There are regular bus connections with Miri (just under 2 hours), Bintulu (2 hours) and Sibu. From Batu Niah it is around 3 km to the Park HQ and the caves. Either walk through the forest (45 mins), take a longboat, or catch a taxi. See page 247 for further details.

Getting around From Park HQ there are well-marked trails to the caves. Longboats can be chartered for upriver trips.

Tourist information The park HQ are at Pangkalan Lubang next to Sungai Subis. The park and caves are open daily, the park 0800-1700, with the caves closing 30 mins earlier. Entrance fee is RM10 for each person (RM5 for children) and RM5 for camera, RM10 for video and RM200 for professional photography. A guide is not essential but they provide information and can relate legends about the paintings. But even with a guide, visitors cannot cross the barrier 3 m in front of the cave wall. A guide will cost RM35 for groups of up to 20 and can be hired from the Park HQ. From Park HQ, longboats can be hired for upriver trips (maximum of eight people per boat). Visitors are advised to bring a powerful torch for the caves. Walking boots are advisable during the wet season as the plankwalk can get very slippery. For more information on the park, contact Deputy Park Warden, Niah National Park, PO Box 81, Miri Post Office, Batu Niah, T85-737454.

Background

About 40,000 years ago, when the Gulf of Thailand and the Sunda Shelf were still dry ground, and a land-bridge connected the Philippines and Borneo, Niah was home to Homo sapiens. It was the most exciting archaeological discovery since Java man (*Homo erectus*).

Scientist and explorer A Hart Everett led expeditions to Niah Caves in 1873 and 1879, after which he pronounced that they justified no further work. Seventy-nine years later, Tom Harrisson, ethnologist, explorer and conservationist and curator of the Sarawak Museum, confirmed the most important archaeological find at that time in Southeast Asia at Niah. He unearthed fragments of a 37,000-year-old human skull – the earliest evidence of *Homo sapiens* in the region – at the west mouth of the Niah Great Cave itself. The skull was buried under 2.4 m of guano. His find debunked and prompted a radical reappraisal of popular theories about where modern man's ancestors had sprung from. A wide range of Palaeolithic and Neolithic tools, pottery, ornaments and beads were also found at the site. Anthropologists believe Niah's caves may have been permanently inhabited until around AD 1400. Harrisson's excavation site, office and house have been left intact in the mouth of the Great Cave. A total of 166 burial sites have been excavated, 38 of which are Mesolithic (up to 20,000 years ago) and the remainder Neolithic (4,000 years ago). Some of the finds are now in the Sarawak Museum in Kuching.

Park Information Centre

ⓘ *0800-1230, 1400-1615 Mon-Fri; 0800-1245 Sat; 0800-1200 Sun.*
At the Park HQ is this centre, with displays on birds nests and flora and fauna. The exhibition includes the 37,000-year-old human skull which drew world attention to Niah in 1958. Also on display are 35,000-year-old oyster shells, as well as palaeolithic pig bones, monkey bones, turtle shells and crabs which were found littering the cave floor. There are also burial vessels dating from 1600 BC and carved seashell jewellery from around 400 BC.

The caves

To reach the caves, take a longboat across the river from Park HQ at Palangkalan Lubang to the start of the 4 km belian (ironwood) plankwalk to the entrance of the **Great Cave**. Take the right fork 1 km from the entrance. The remains of a small kampong, formerly inhabited by birds' nest collectors (see below) and guano collectors, is just before the entrance, in the shelter of overhanging rocks. It is known as **Traders' Cave**. Beware of voracious insects; wear long trousers and plenty of repellent. There are no lights in the Great Cave (see below), so torches are needed.

The **Painted Cave** is beyond the Great Cave. Prehistoric wall paintings – the only ones in Borneo – stretch for about 32 m along the cave wall. Most of the drawings are of dancing human figures and boats, thought to be associated with a death ritual. On the floor of the cave, several 'death-ships' were found with some Chinese stoneware, shell ornaments and ancient glass beads. These death-ships served as coffins and have been carbon-dated to between 1 and AD 780. By around AD 700 there is thought to have been a flourishing community based in the caves, trading hornbill ivory and birds' nests with the Chinese in exchange for porcelain and beads. But then it seems the caves were suddenly deserted in about 1400. In Penan folklore there are references to 'the ancestors who lived in the big caves' and tribal elders are said to be able to recall funeral rites using death boats similar to those found at Niah.

Niah National Park

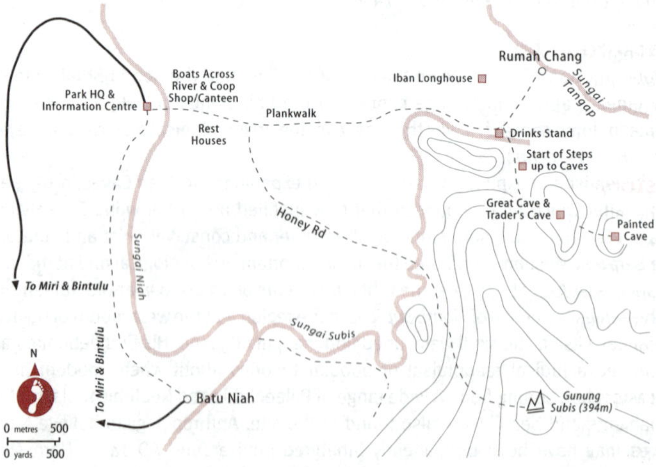

Niah's guano collectors: scraping the bottom

Eight bat species live in the Niah Caves, some are quite common such as the horseshoe bat and fruit bats. Other more exotic varieties include the bearded tomb bat, Cantor's roundleaf horseshoe bat and the lesser bent-winged bat.

The ammonia-stench of bat guano permeates the humid air. People began collecting guano in 1929 and it is used as a fertilizer and to prevent pepper vines from rotting. Guano collectors pay a licence fee for the privilege of sweeping up *tahi sapu* (fresh guano) and digging up tahi timbang (mature guano) which they sell to the Bat Guano Co-operative at the end of the plankwalk.

Treks

A lowland trail called **Jalan Madu** (Honey Road), traverses the peat swamp forest and up Gunung Subis; it is not well marked. Return trips need a full day. The trail leads off the plankwalk to the right, about 1 km from Pangkalan Lubang (Park HQ). The left fork on the plankwalk, before the gate to the caves, goes to an Iban longhouse, Rumah Chang (40 minutes' walk), where cold drinks can be bought.

Miri and the Baram River → *Colour map 3, grid A5*

Miri is the starting point for adventurous trips up the Barani River to Marudi, Bario and the Kelabit Highlands. Also accessible from Miri and Marudi is the incomparable Gunung Mulu National Park with the biggest limestone cave system in the world and one of the richest assemblages of plants and animals. The capital of Sarawak's Fourth Division is a busy, prosperous town, with more than half its population Chinese. One newer project is a waterfront development with a marina – there is a pleasant walk on the peninsula here across the Miri River, and some good fishing.

Ins and outs

Tourist information **Tourist Information Centre,** ⓘ *Jln Malay (next to bus station and just across from the Park Hotel), T85-434181, www.sarawaktourism.com, open 0800-1800 Mon-Fri, 0800-1600 Sat (closed first and third Sat of each month), and 0900-1500 Sun. Accommodation booking, T85-434184.* For information on Tours see Tours and activities.

Permits are now only required for travel to Bario. Apply at the **Resident's office,** ⓘ *Jalan Kwantung, T85-433202 – with passport photocopy*. After acquiring a permit, the police station will need to stamp it. If travelling with a tour company it will take care of the bureaucracy.

History

In the latter years of the 19th century, a small trading company set up in Sarawak, to import kerosene and export polished shells and pepper. In 1910, when 'earth oil' was first struck on the hill overlooking Miri, the little trading company took the plunge and diversified into the new commodity – making, in the process, Sarawak's first oil town. The company's name was Shell. Together with the Malaysian national oil company, *Petronas*, Shell has been responsible for discovering, producing and refining Sarawak's offshore oil deposits. Oil is a key contributor to Malaysia's export earnings and Miri has been a beneficiary of the boom. There is a big refinery at Lutong to the north, which is connected by pipeline with Seria in Brunei. Lutong is the next town on the Miri River and the main headquarters for Shell.

The oil boom in this area began on Canada Hill, behind the town (where, incidentally, this limestone ridge provides excellent views of the town). **Oil Well No 1** was built by Shell and was the first oil well in Malaysia, spudded on 10 August 1910. The well was still yielding oil 62 years later, but its productivity began to slump. It is estimated that a total of 600,000 barrels were extracted from Well No 1 during its operational life. It was shut off in 1972. There are now 624 oil wells in the Miri Field, producing 80 million barrels of oil a year.

Sights

Juxtaposed against Miri's modern boom-town image is **Tamu Muhibba**, the native jungle produce market, ⓘ *open 24 hours*, opposite the *Park Hotel* in a purpose-built concrete structure with pointed roofs on the roundabout connecting Jalan Malay and Jalan Padang. The Orang Ulu come downriver to sell their produce, and a walk around the market provides an illuminating lesson in jungle nutrition. Colourful characters run impromptu 'stalls' from rattan mats, selling yellow cucumbers that look like mangoes, mangoes that look like turnips, huge crimson durians, tiny loofah sponges, sackfuls of fragrant Bario rice (brown and white), every shape, size and hue of banana, *tuak* (rice wine) in old Heineken bottles and a menagerie of jungle fauna – including mousedeer, falcons, pangolins and the apparently delicious long-snouted tupai (jungle squirrel). There is a large selection of dried and fresh seafood – fish and *bubok* (tiny prawns), and big buckets boiling with catfish or stacked with turtles, there are also some handicrafts.

Taman Bulatan is a scenic, centrally located park with foodstalls and boats for hire on the manmade lake.

Miri

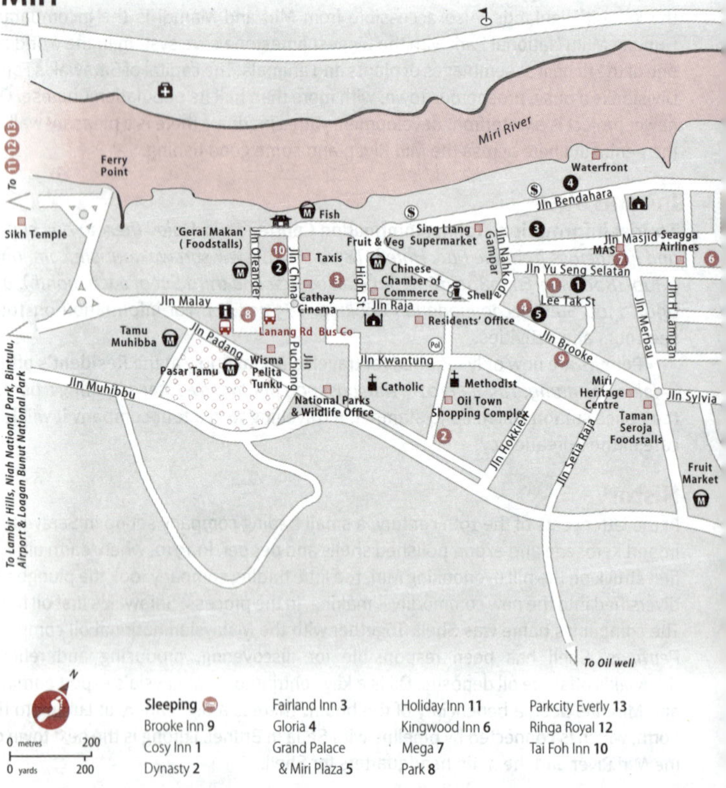

Around Miri

Hawaii Beach ⓘ, *15 min taxi ride from Miri (RM15-RM20) or else take bus No 13 (RM2)*, is a pristine, palm-fringed beach, popular for picnics and barbecues.

Lambir Hills ⓘ *Lambir Hills National Park, T85-491030; RM10 (RM5 for children), photography RM5, video camera RM10, professional camera RM200. The Park HQ is close to the Miri-Niah road, there is an audio visual room with seating for 30 here. From Park Hotel take Bintulu or Bakong bus (RM3, 40 minutes) or by taxi (RM40, 30 minutes)*, is a park mainly consisting of a chain of sandstone hills bounded by rugged cliffs, 19 km south of Miri and just visible from the town; the main attractions are the beautiful waterfalls. Kerangas (heath forest) cover the higher ridges and hills while the lowland areas are mixed dipterocarp forest. Bornean gibbons, bearded pigs, barking deer and over 100 species of bird have been recorded in the park. There is only one path across a rickety suspension bridge at present, but there are numerous waterfalls and tree towers for birdwatching, and several trails which lead to enticing pools for swimming. The park attracts hordes of daytrippers from Miri at weekends. It is possible to stay overnight, see Sleeping.

> *The National Parks Office and Visitor Information Centre are closed on the 1st and 3rd Saturday of the month.*

Loagan Bunut National Park ⓘ *Logan Bunut National Park, T85-779410*, is located in the upper reaches of the Sungai Bunut and contains Sarawak's largest natural lake at approximately 650 ha. The water level in the lake is totally dependent on the water level of the rivers Bunut, Tinijar and Baram. The level is at its lowest in the months of February, May and June and sometimes, for a period of about two to three weeks, the lake becomes an expanse of dry cracked mud. The main cultural attraction at the lake is the traditional method of fishing (*selambau*), which has been retained by the Berawan fishermen. The surrounding area is covered with peat swamp forest. The common larger birds found here are the darters, egrets, herons, bittern, hornbill and kites. Gibbons are also common.

Luconia Island is surrounded by a pristine coral reef. The Luconia Shoals are approximately 150 nautical miles north of Miri and it is only possible to dive here from a live-aboard boat. The reef covers around more than 300 sq km and is said to be untouched with large pelagics from mantas and tuna to black-tip sharks. The best months for diving are between April and August. Some dive sites are easy while others, with strong currents and deep walls, require experience and care. The better known sites are Hayes Reef (excellent wall diving) and Atken Reef (very good drift diving with large pelagics). Night diving, with many large morays, is reported to be excellent.

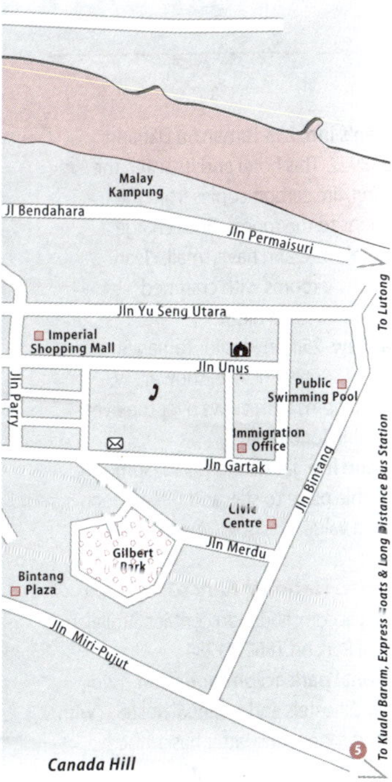

Eating
Apollo 1
Aseanika 2
Bilal 3
Café Bavaria 4
Nyonya's Family Café 5

Marudi

Four major tribal groups – Iban, Kelabit, Kayan and Penan – come to Marudi to do business with the Chinese, Indian and

 Malay merchants. Marudi is the furthest upriver trading post on the Baram and services all the longhouses in the Tutoh, Tinjar and Baram river basins. Most tourists only stop long enough in Marudi to down a cold drink before catching the next express boat upriver; as the trip to Mulu National Park can now be done in a day, not many have to spend the night here. Because it is a major trading post, however, there are a lot of hotels, and the standards are reasonably good.

Trips can be organized through tour operators in Miri. For details of dive spots, see www.borneo.com.au/diving/

Fort Hose was built in 1901, when Marudi was still called Claudetown, and has good views of the river. It is named after the last of the Rajah's residents, the anthropologist, geographer and natural historian Dr Charles Hose. The fort is now used as administrative offices. Also of note is the intricately carved **Thaw Peh Kong Chinese Temple** (diagonally opposite the express boat jetty), also known as Siew San Teen. It was shipped from China and erected in Sarawak in the early 1900s, although it was probably already 100 years old by the time the temple began life in its new location.

The **Marudi-Kampong Teraja log walk** is normally done from the Brunei end, as the return trek, across the Sarawak/Brunei border takes a full day, dawn to dusk. It is, however, possible to reach an Iban longhouse inside Brunei without going the full distance to Kampong Teraja. The longhouse is on the Sungai Ridan, about 2½ hours down the jungle trail. The trail starts 3 km from Marudi, on the airport road. There is no customs post on the border; the trail is not an official route into Brunei. Trekkers are advised to take their passports in the unlikely event of being stopped by police, who will probably turn a blind eye. Kampong Teraja in Brunei is the furthest accessible point which can be reached by road from Labi.

Three **longhouses**, Long Seleban, Long Moh and Leo Mato, are accessible by four-wheel drive vehicle from Marudi.

Sleeping

Bintulu *p355, map p355*

B **Hoover**, 92 Jln Keppel, T86-337166. Restaurant, cable TV, smallish rooms, but well-kept place. A great deal better than the slightly cheaper hotels nearby.

B **Plaza**, Jln Abang Galau, 116 Taman Sri Dagang, T86-335111, F86-332742. A/c, restaurant, pool, very smart hotel, and, compared with other upmarket hotels in Sarawak, excellent value for money. Recommended. Very popular, so worth booking.

B **Regent**, Kemena Commercial Complex, Jln Tanjong Batu, T86-335511, F86-333770. 47 rooms with a/c, TV, mini-bar, restaurant, coffee house.

C **Fata Inn**, 113 Taman Sri Dagang, Jln Masjid, T86-332998. A/c, TV, bathroom. Reasonable.

C **Kemena**, 78 Jln Keppel, T86-331533. A/c, refurbished and on a quiet street, good quality room with TV, fridge. Recommended.

C **National**, 2nd floor, 5 Jln Temple, T86-337222, F86-334304. A/c, clean and well kept. Recommended.

C **Queen's Inn**, 238 Taman Sri Dagang, T86-338922. This hotel and its sister, the *King's Inn*, are carbon copies from the receptions to the rooms. Both charge a reasonable rate and have small, clean, carpeted a/c rooms with cramped bathroom. OK for a night.

C **Sea View**, 254 Jln Masjid, Taman Sri Dagang, T86-339118. A/c, shower, TV, spacious rooms with views over the river. Good value for Bintulu.

D **Dragon Inn**, Jln Abang Galau. Some a/c, a reasonable place to stay and the a/c rooms are good value.

Similajau National Park *p356*

To book accommodation contact Similajau National Park on T86-391284.

C **National park accommodation**. Two chalets, 2 hostels and a 'mega' hostel – with 27 4-bed rooms. The latter has attractive polished hardwood decor. It can get block-booked. There is 24-hour electricity. The canteen at Park HQ serves basic food. Picnic shelters at park HQ.

Niah National Park *p359*

Call Miri National Park & Wildlife Office, at the Old Forestry Building, Jln Angkasa, T85-436637. It's recommended to book accommodation at least two to three days in advance. Do this through the National Parks office, not through the tourist information office. **Niah National Park**, T85- 737454, **National Parks Booking Office**, T85- 434184. You can also book over the internet - www.forestry.sarawak.gov.my, click on online services, and then booking of national park. Also npbooking@sarawak.net.gov.my. All accommodation has 24-hr electricity and treated water

Family Chalet, similar to hostel but with cooker and a/c, 2 rooms with 4 beds in each, RM157.50 per chalet.

Hostels Five hostels each with 4 rooms of 4 beds each, all rooms have private bathrooms, clean and western-style with shower, toilet, electric fans, fridges, large sitting area and kitchen. No cooking facilities but kettle, crockery and cutlery can be provided on request. RM42 for 1 room, 4 beds, or RM15.75 for 1 bed.

VIP Resthouse, RM236.25 per room, a/c, TV, hi-fi.

There are also 4 small hotels in Batu Niah (4 km from Park HQ).

C **Niah Caves Inn**, T85-737333, F85-737332. A/c, shower, spacious, fully-carpeted rooms. Reasonable value.

C **Park View Hotel**, T85-737023. Range of comfortable rooms with TV, a/c, bath but no shower. Some rooms face inwards, discounts often available.

D **Niah Caves Hotel**, T85-737726. Some a/c, shared facilities, 6 rooms (singles, doubles and triples available). Basic, but light and clean, next to the river. A fair budget option.

Camping Tents can be hired from Park HQ (RM8) or from the site (RM5).

Miri and the Baram River

p361, map p362

Most people going to Mulu will have to spend at least a night in Miri. The town has a growing selection of mid-to-upmarket hotels with discounts of 30-40% off quoted prices as a matter of course. Many of the mid-range hotels are around Jln Yu Seng Selatan. Being an oil town, and close to Brunei, Miri has a booming prostitution industry.

A **Dynasty**, Jln Miri-Pujut, T85-421111, dyhlmyy@ po.jaring.my A/c, restaurants, pool, health centre, next to Oil Town Shopping Complex.

A **Grand Palace**, 2 km Jln Miri-Pujut, Pelita Commercial Centre, T85-428888, jrobson@ pc.jaring.my Imposing peach and pastel building on town outskirts next to Miri Plaza Shopping Centre, 125 comfortable, carpeted rooms with a/c, TV, bathroom, mini-bar, pool, fitness centre, karaoke, restaurant.

A-B **Parkcity Everly**, Jln Temenggong Datuk Oyong Lawai, T85-418888, F85-419999. Formerly Holiday Inn, situated 2 km from town centre, at mouth of the Miri River, this 5-storey, modern, white block, curves around the South China Sea, very popular with families at weekends (check for special weekend rates, 168 rooms all with a/c, TV, bathroom, mini-bar, balcony, thick carpets and comfy beds, sunsets over sea, colourful but noisy river traffic, free-form pool, pleasantly surrounded by plants and palms with swim-up bar in form of traditional boat (popular with kids), Jacuzzi and baby pool, sandy area for kids to play, beach too near town to be clean and sea not safe for swimming but pleasant for sunset strolls, coffee house, Chinese restaurant, bar and bakery/delicatessen, fitness centre, sauna. Recommended.

A **Mega,** Jln Merbau, T85-432432, www.megahotel.net The tallest and largest hotel in Miri town centre, 228 rooms with a/c, TV, bathroom, Chinese restaurant, coffee house, swimming pool with jacuzzi, health centre, business centre, internet, shopping mall attached.

A **Rihga Royal**, Jln Temenggong Datuk Oyong Lawai, T85-421121, F85-425057. Japanese-managed hotel on coast south of Miri, 5-star comforts, 225 rooms, all rooms with a/c, mini-bar, TV, Japanese restaurant, Chinese restaurant and coffee house, pool, tennis, health centre.

B **Gloria**, 27 Jln Brooke, T85-416699, F85-418866. A/c, restaurant, 42 rooms, better than it looks from outside, although the economy rooms are windowless, comparatively expensive.

B **Kingwood Inn**, Jln Yu Seng Utara, T85-415888, F85-415009. A/c, restaurant, one of the smaller mid-range places to stay.

C **Brooke Inn**, 14 Brooke Rd, T85-412881,

brookeinn@hotmail.com. Big. Clean carpeted rooms in a lazy motel-style block. Rooms have a/c TV and big windows. Good value.

C **Cosy Inn**, 545-547 Jln Yu Seng Selatan, T85-415522, F85-415155. A/c, restaurant. Looks better from the outside than it is, nevertheless better than others in its class.

C **Park**, Jln Raja, T85-414555, F85-414488. A/c, Chinese restaurant. Ranked a 3-star hotel, although now rather run down, it is good value for money and convenient for the bus station. Despite or maybe because of it's slighty sleazy sheer, the place has shabby charm. Not bad value for money.

C-D **Fairland Inn**, Jln Raja, T85-413981. Somewhat of a favourite among Borneo travellers, this place offers tiny dirty rooms with dribbling cold-water showers and a guaranteed bad night of sleep with the warblings and gigglings from the karaoke girls in neighbouring buildings. It does however have a veneer of cleanliness, just don't look underneath the beds. The place appears safe and the owner is used to travellers. Perhaps the best of a bad bunch.

C-D **Tai Foh Inn**, 19 Jln China, T012-8700530. Arriving by plane, the taxi coupon service will direct you to this establishment if you ask for budget accommodation. While budget it certainly is, whether it fulfils the definition of accommodation is debatable. Dorms and rooms are a mess, with dripping taps, malfunctioning toilets and mattresses long past their expiry date. They do appear, though, to cater for tourists with TV, bag storage, travel info and laundry. Anyway, it's cheap.

Around Miri *p363*

Book accommodation through the National Parks Booking Office, T85-434184 for Lambir Hills.

A-C **Lambir Hills**. If you want to stay overnight there are chalets, one with 2 rooms, 3 beds, 4 units with 2 rooms, 2 beds, RM100 per room or RM150 per house; a/c chalet, 2 rooms with 3 beds, RM50 per room or RM75 per house.

D **Logan Bunut National Park accommodation**. To book accommodation call the National Parks Booking Office, T85-434184. There is one forest hostel with four rooms each with 7 double bunk beds with fan and own toilet. RM15 per bed. The park has a canteen.

F **Campsite** Rental RM5. A canteen is provided, no cooking allowed in chalet, you can cook at campsite or take food into canteen.

Marudi *p363*

A-C **Grand**, Lot 350 Backlane, T85-755711, F85-775293. Some a/c, large but good hotel, restaurant, 30 clean rooms with cable TV, close to jetty and plenty of information on upriver trips.

B **Mount Mulu Hotel**, Lot 80 & Lot 90, Marudi Town District, T85-756671, F85-756670. A/c, discounts are available making this place very good value.

C **Victoria**, Lot 961-963 Jln Merdeka, T85-756067, T85-7556864. All 21 rooms have cable TV.

D **Mayland**, 347 Mayland Building, T85-755106, F85-755333. A/c, 41 rooms, slightly rundown but a good range of accommodation.

Eating

Bintulu *p355, map p355*

Umai, raw fish pickled with lime or the fruit of wild palms (assam) and mixed with salted vegetables, onions and chillies is a Melanau speciality. Bintulu is famed for its belacan – prawn paste – and in the local dialect, prawns are urang, not udang. Locals quip that they are 'man-eaters' because they makan urang.

TT **Marco Polo**, on the waterfront on the edge of town, locals recommend pepper steak.

T **Fook Lu Shou**, Plaza Hotel, Jln Abang Galau, Taman Sri Dagang, seafood and Chinese cuisine, including birds' nest soup, boiled in rock sugar.

T **Kemena Coffee House**, Western, Malay and Chinese, open 24 hrs.

T **Popular Corner**, opposite Hospital, Chinese.

T **River Inn**, opposite wharf, Western and local food.

T **Sarawak**, 160 Taman Sri Dagang (near Plaza Hotel), cheap Malay food.

Foodstalls

Pantai Ria, near Tanjong Batu, mainly seafood, only open in the evenings.

Recommended. Chinese stalls behind the Chinese temple on Jln Temple. Stalls at both markets.

Miri and the Baram River

p361, map p362

Chinese

Apollo, Lot 394 Jln Yu Seng Selatan (close to Gloria Hotel), good seafood, very popular.
Sea View Café, Jln China.

Indian

Bilal, Jln Persiaran Kabor, excellent curries and rotis, coffee house.

International

Café Bavaria, Miri Waterfront, T85-4294959. Pricey German dishes, cheaper Malay food. Run by Monikka from Germany, this place is a quaint slice of Bavaria pasted into Miri. Unfortunately, despite being close to the river, there are no views. But it's open-walled which makes it a pleasant place for an iced coffee.
Park View Restaurant (coffee house of Park Hotel), Jln Malay, most sophisticated menu in town, jellyfish, good selection of seafood and grill. But gloomy surroundings.
Bonzer Garden Steak House, Jln Yu Seng Utara, local dishes much cheaper than burgers.
Cosy Garden (and in Mega Hotel block), pleasant restaurant, but the a/c inhibits any cosiness, limited menu but reasonable prices, steak.

Malay

Aseanika, Jln China, also serves good Indian and Indonesian food.
Nabila's, 1st floor, 441 DUBS Building, Jln Bendahara, also serves Indonesian and Oriental, curries, good rendang.
Nyonya's Family Café, 21 Jln Brooke, T85-429727. Cheap Nyonya fare in a traditional style coffee house with marble-topped tables, curtained dividers and Sarawak noodles. Busy at lunchtimes. Recommended. Closed Sun.

Foodstalls

Gerai Makan, near Chinese temple at end of Jln Oleander, Malay food. Taman Seroja, Jln Brooke, Malay food, best in the evenings.
Tamu Muhibba (Native Market), opposite Park Hotel on roundabout connecting Jln Malay and Jln Padang, best during the day.
Tanjong Seafood stalls, Tanjung Lobung (south of Miri), best in evening.

Marudi *p363*

There are several coffee shops in town.
Rose Garden, opposite Alisan Hotel, a/c coffee shop serving mainly Chinese dishes.

Shopping

Bintulu *p355, map p355*

Handicrafts

Dyang Enterprise, Lobby floor, Plaza Hotel, Jln Abang Dalau, Taman Sri Dagang. The latter is rather overpriced because of the Plaza's more upmarket clientele; the best handicrafts are to be found at Li Hua Plaza, near the Plaza Hotel, in a 4-storey building.

Niah National Park *p359*

Emergency rations recommended.
The **Guano Collectors' Co-operative** shop at the beginning of the plankwalk sells basic food and cold drinks and camera film. There is another basic **shop/restaurant** just outside the park gates. There is a **canteen** at Park HQ, which serves good local food and full western breakfast, good value, barbecue site provided, the canteen is supposed to be open from 0700-2300, but is a little erratic.

Miri and the Baram River

p361, map p362

Books

Parksons Department Store, Bintang Plaza; **Pelita Book Centre**, 1st floor, Wisma Pelita Tunku.

Handicrafts

Borneo Arts, Jln Yu Seng Selatan (Next to Cosy Inn). Open 0900-2100 daily. T-shirts, handicrafts, wood carvings, pottery, Chinese porcelain, batik, Iban textiles, kris daggers, Dayak warrior swords and shields; **Joy art and fashion House**, M floor, Wisma Pelita Tunju; **Longhouse**, 2nd floor, Imperial Mall, the best in town; Miri's council has recently built a small centre on Jalan Brooke (about 15 mins' walk from the local bus station) with space for stalls and a cafe and slapped the label **Miri Heritage Centre** on its side. There's a small stage for dance performances (rare) and local artists have space to sell their work including batiks, beads, basketry, musical instruments and inevitably some tourist tack; **Morsjaya Commercial Centre**, Jln Miri; **Royal Selangor**, 28F, High St; **Sarawak Arts**, Level 3, Miri Square Shopping Complex; **Sarawak Handicrafts**, 2nd floor, Soon Hup Centre; **Syarikat Unique arts and handicrafts centre**, Lot 2994.

Shopping malls

Boulevard (BSC), Jln Pujut Lutong, Miri's largest shopping complex, foodcourt on the top floor, supermarket, department store and boutiques; **Soon Hup Tower**, next to Mega Hotel with Parkwell's supermarket and department store; **Wisma Pelita Tunku**, near bus station, department store.

Supermarket

Parkson Grand, Bintang Plaza; **Pelita**, Ground floor, Wisma Pelita Tunku, useful for supplies for upriver expeditions; **Sing Liang Supermarket** on Jln Nakhoda Gampar – Chinese store; **Ngiukee**, moving from Pelita to Imperial Mall.

Activities and tours

Bintulu *p355, map p355*

Golf

Tanjong Kidurong, 18-hole course, north of Bintulu, by the sea (regular buses from town centre).

Sports complex

Swimming pool (RM2), tennis, football. To get there, fork right from the Miri road at the Chinese temple, about 1 km from town centre.

Tour operators

Deluxe Travel, 30 Jln Law Gek Soon, T86-331293, F86-334995; **Hunda Travel Services**, 8 Jln Somerville, T86-331339, F86-330445. There are half a dozen other agents in town; **Similajau Travel and Tours**, Plaza Hotel, Jln Abang Dalau offers tours around the city, to the Niah caves, longhouses and Similajau National Park.

Miri *p361, map p362*

Golf

Miri Golf Club, Jln Datuk Patinggi, T85-416787, F85-417848, by the sea. Because this is the only golf course in this area of Sarawak, with a large membership, it is worth phoning beforehand to book a tee-off slot.

Swimming

Public pool off Jln Bintang, close to the Civic Centre, RM1.

Tours

Although most tour companies specialize in trips up the Baram River to Mulu National Park, some are much better than others – in terms of facilities and services offered. Every agency in Miri has a Mulu National Park itinerary covering the caves, pinnacles and summits. It is also possible to trek to Bario and Mount Murud, as well as to Limbang from Mulu. Most of the agencies employ experienced guides who will be able to advise on longer, more ambitious treks. The Mulu National Park is one destination where it is usually cheaper to go through a tour company than to try to do it independently. Costs vary considerably according to the number of people in a group. For a three-day Mulu trip, a single tourist can expect to pay RM500; this drops to RM400 a head for a group of four and about RM350 each for a group of 10, all accommodation, food, travel and guide costs included. An eight day tour of Ulu Baram longhouses would cost RM1,800 for one person and RM1,200 per person in a group of 10. A 20-day trek will cost two people (minimum number) around RM2,000 each, and a group of 6-10, RM1,300 a head. For those who want to visit remote longhouses, tour companies present by far the best option. Tour fees cover 'gifts' and all payments to longhouse headmen for food, accommodation and entertainment.

Tour operators

Borneo Mainland, Jln Merpati, T85-433511, F85-434289. **JJ Tour Travel**, Lot 231, Jln Maju Taman, Jade Centre, T85-418690, F85-413308. Ticketing agents. **KKM Travel & Tours**, 236 Jln Maju, T85-417899, F85-414629. **Limbang Travel Service**, 1G Park Arcade (Near Park Hotel), T85-413228. Efficient ticketing service. **Seridan Mulu**, Lobby Arcade of Parkcity Everly Hotel, T85-414300, F85-416066, private accommodation within park, recommended by National Parks Office. Also can do diving trips. **Transworld Travel Service**, 2nd floor Wisma Pelita Tunku, T85-422226, F85-415277. **Tropical Adventure**, Ground floor, Mega Hotel, Jln Merbau, T85-19337, F85-414503. Recommended.

Transport

Bintulu *p355, map p355*

Air

The airport is in the centre of town. Regular connections with **Kuching, Miri, Sibu**. There are also some connections with **Kota Kinabalu**. Twice weekly flights to **Belaga**.

Airline offices MAS, Jln Masjid, T86-331554.

Boat

Enquire at the wharf for times and prices. Regular connections with Tabau, 2½-3 hrs, last boat at 1400 (RM18). Connections with **Belaga**, via logging road, see page 354; this route is popular with people in Belaga as it is much cheaper than going from Sibu.

Bus

There are two stations in town. The terminal for local buses is in the centre of town. The long-distance Medan Jaya station is 10 mins by taxi from the centre, on the road towards Miri (RM8). Regular connections with **Miri** (RM18), **Sarikei** (RM32), **Batu, Niah** (RM10) and **Sibu** (RM16). There are several bus companies but the main one is the **Syarikat** Bas Suria, T86-334914.

Taxi

For **Miri** and **Sibu**, taxis leave from Jln Masjid. Because of the regular bus services and the poor state of the roads, most taxis are for local use only and chartering them is expensive.

Similaju National Park *p356*

There is no regular bus service to the park. Taxis travel the route (30 mins). Rm 40 Bintulu-Similajau trip. RM 60 for a return trip. Bintulu taxi station, T86-332009. Boats are available from the wharf or arrange through *Similajau Tours* in Bintulu.

Niah National Park *p359*

From Batu Niah (near the market) to Park HQ at Pengkalan Lubang, Niah National Park by boat, (RM10 per person or if more than 5 people, RM2 per person) or 45 mins' walk to Park HQ.

Bus

Every two hours for a connection with **Miri** (RM10), 2 hrs, 6 buses a day to **Bintulu** and Sibu via Bintulu to Batu Niah.

Taxi

From **Miri** to Park HQ, will only leave when there are 4 passengers. From **Bintulu** to Batu Niah (RM30). RM10 to Park HQ, however the river boat is far more scenic.

Miri *p361, map p362*

Air

Regular connections on MAS with **Kuching** (5 flights, RM164), **Sibu, Marudi** (RM29, 18-passenger plane), **Bario** (one flight a day, at 0930am, usually full, book ahead), **Bintulu** (RM70), **Limbang, Mulu** (RM58, two flights daily) and **Labuan**. Also connections with **Kota Kinabalu** (3 direct flights daily, RM118). Both MAS and AirAsia have three flights daily to KL. There are no flights between Miri and Brunei. You need to fly first to Kuching or KK.

Transport to town Airport information, T85-615433. Taxi coupon from airport into town costs RM14. Bus No 30 and 28 roughly every hour go to the airport. You need to ask the driver to drop you off outside the airport, otherwise you will be dropped off on the highway, requiring a 10-min trek to the terminal.

Airline offices MAS, 239 Halaman Kabor, off Jln Yu Seng Selatan, T85-414144. AirAsia, T85-438022.

Bus

The new bus terminal at Pujuk Padang Kerbau, Jln Padang is around 4 km from the town centre. A taxi to the terminal should cost around RM10 – watch out for inflated pricing! Or take bus No 33 from outside the tourist centre. Regular connections from early morning to early/mid-afternoon with **Batu Niah** 2-3 hrs, **Bintulu** 4 hrs, **Sibu** 7 hrs, and **Kuching, 13 hrs**. There are ticket booths for the long distance buses next to the Park Hotel.

To **Kuala Baram** and the express boat upriver to Marudi. Regular bus connections with Kuala Baram; there are also taxis to Kuala Baram, either private or shared. Express boats upriver to **Marudi** from Kuala Baram, 3 hrs. Roughly 1 boat every hr from 0715. Last boat 1430. This is the first leg of the journey to Mulu and the interior.

Several departures a day to **Kuala Belait** in Brunei, 2 hrs, RM12, via Sungai Tujuh checkpoint, with onward connections to Bandar Seri Begawan. From the checkpoint you need to change buses at Kuala Belait for Seria (B$1) and then onwards to Bandar Sri Begawan (B$6). You can use Singapore dollars in Brunei – at the exchange rate of one to one. Note the last bus from Seria leaves at 1520 which means you need to catch a morning bus from Miri (0700, 0900 or 1030) to make the connection or you will need to stay the night in Kuala Belait or Seria. Biaramas have a direct service to Brunei's capital which is rumoured to depart Miri at 1000. Travelling by your own means of transport from Miri it is necessary to take the car ferry across the Baram River, then pass through immigration, before another ferry across the Belait River. At weekends and public holidays there are long queues for the ferries as well as at immigration – so be prepared for a long, hot wait. Be warned also that the ferry across the Belait River takes an unscheduled 1-hr break for lunch. Distance itself is nothing – the ferry crossings take no more than 10 mins each and Miri to Kuala Belait is just 27 km. Bus passengers bypass the queues because they board the ferry as foot passengers and then hop on another bus the other side of the river. From Kuala Belait regular connections with Seria, 1 hr and from Seria regular connections with Bandar Seri Begawan ($1 Brunei), 1-2 hrs. It takes minimum 5 hrs to reach Bandar Seri Begawan.

Car hire

Avis, Permaisuri Rd, T85-430222; Lee Brothers, 17 River Rd, T85-410606; Mega, No 3, Lorong 1, Sungai Krokop, T85-431885. Fleet of Proton Sagas available. RM120-150 per day.

Taxi

T85-432277.

Marudi *p363*

Air

The airport is 5 km from town. Connections with **Miri** (RM29), **Bario, Sibu**.

Boat

These leave from opposite the Chinese temple. Connections with **Kuala Baram**; 8 boats a day from 0700-1500 (RM18), **Tutoh**, for longboats to Long Terawan, 1 boat at 1100, (RM22 express boat or RM32 speed boat), **Long Lama**, for longboats to **Bario**, 1 boat every hr 0730-1400. From Long Terawan the long boat journey takes up to 2 hours (RM45 per person for group of 5 or more). From Miri to Kuala Baram take Bus No 1 (RM2.50, first bus 0530) or a shared taxi (RM22).

Directory

Bintulu *p355, map p355*

Banks Bank Bumiputra and Bank Utama on Jln Somerville; Standard Chartered, Jln Keppel. **Post** General Post Office. Far side of the airport near the Resident's office, 2 km from town centre – called Pos Laju. **Useful addresses** National Parks Booking Office T86-331117, ext 50, F86-331923.

Miri *p361, map p362*

Internet Cyberworld, 1st floor Wisma Pelita Tunku (RM3 per hr), Cyber Corner, Wisma Pelita Tunku (RM3 per hr). Planet Café, 1st floor, Bintang Plaza, (RM4 per hr) open 1000-2200 daily. **Banks** All major banks are represented in Miri. **Medical services** Hospital, opposite Ferry Point, T85-420033. **Post** General Post Office, just off Jln Gartak. **Telephone** Telecom Office, Jln Gartak, open daily 0730-2200. **Useful addresses** Immigration Office Jln Unus, T85-442105. National Parks and Wildlife Office, Jln Puchong, T85-432277, F85-431975 (note that it is closed every first and third Sat of the month). Police Station, Jln Kingsway, T85-432533. Resident's Office, Jln Kwantung, T85-433203.

Marudi *p363*

Banks There are 2 local banks with foreign exchange facilities. **Post** Post Office, Airport Rd. **Useful addresses** Police station On Airport Rd.

Northern Sarawak

The impressive peak of Gunung Mulu is the centrepiece of the eponymous national park. The luscious jungle, home to orchids and hornbills, also boasts the largest limestone cave system on the planet. The cooler climes of the Kelabit Highlands provide good walking opportunities around Bario. Limbang is frontier country and the start of a cross-border trek. ►► *For Sleeping, Eating, and other listings, see pages 378-380.*

Gunung Mulu National Park → *Colour map 3, grid A6*

Tucked in behind Brunei, this 52,866 ha park lays claim to **Gunung Mulu**, which at 2,376 m is the second highest mountain in Sarawak, and the **biggest limestone cave system in the world**. In short, Mulu is essentially a huge hollow mountain range, sitting on top of 180-million-year-old rainforest. Its primary jungle contains astonishing biological diversity.

Ins and outs

Park essentials RM10 (RM5 for children), RM5 for camera, RM10 for video, RM200 for professional filming.

Equipment There is a small store at the Park HQ that sells basic necessities; there is also a small shop just outside the park boundary, at Long Pala. A sleeping bag is essential for Gunung Mulu trips; other essential equipment includes good insect repellent, wet weather gear and a powerful torch.

Guides No visitors are permitted to travel in the park without an authorized guide which can be arranged from Park HQ or booked in advance from the national parks office in Miri. Most of the Mulu Park guides are very well informed about flora and fauna, geology and tribal customs. Tour agencies organize guides as part of their fee. Guide fees: RM20 per cave (or per day) and an extra RM10 per night. Mulu summit trips: around RM1,000 for a group of 5 (4 days, 3 nights); Melinau Gorge and Pinnacles: minimum RM400 for five people (3 days, 2 nights). Ornithological guides cost an additional RM10 a day. Porterage: max 10 kg and RM30 per day. RM1 for each extra kilo. Mulu summit: minimum RM90; Melinau Gorge (Camp 5): minimum RM65. It is usual to tip guides and porters.

Tourist information For up-to-date information on Mulu see www.mulupark.com. It is illegal to fish at Clearwater, although it is possible to fish anywhere else in park waters with a hook and line.

For cavers wishing to explore caves not open to the public (those open to visitors are known as 'show' caves) there are designated 'adventure caves' within an hour of Park HQ. Experienced cave guides can be organized from headquarters. The most accessible of these is the one-hour trek following the river course through Clearwater Cave. Cavers should bring their own equipment.

Just outside the national park boundary on the Tutoh River there are rapids which are possible to shoot; this can be arranged through tour agencies.

Best time to visit It is best to avoid visiting the park during school and public holidays. In December the park is closed to locals, but remains open to tourists.

In Robin Hanbury-Tenison's book *The Rain Forest*, he says of Mulu: "All sense of time and direction is lost." Every scientific expedition that has visited Mulu's forests has encountered plant and animal species unknown to science. In 1990, five years after it was officially opened to the public, the park was handling an average 400 visitors a month. Numbers have increased markedly since then – the area is now attracting more than 12,000 tourists a year – and as the eco-tourism industry has extended its foothold, local tribespeople have been drawn into confrontation with the authorities. In the early 90s, a series of sabotage incidents were blamed on the Berawan tribe, who claim the caves and the surrounding jungle are a sacred site.

Gunung Mulu National Park

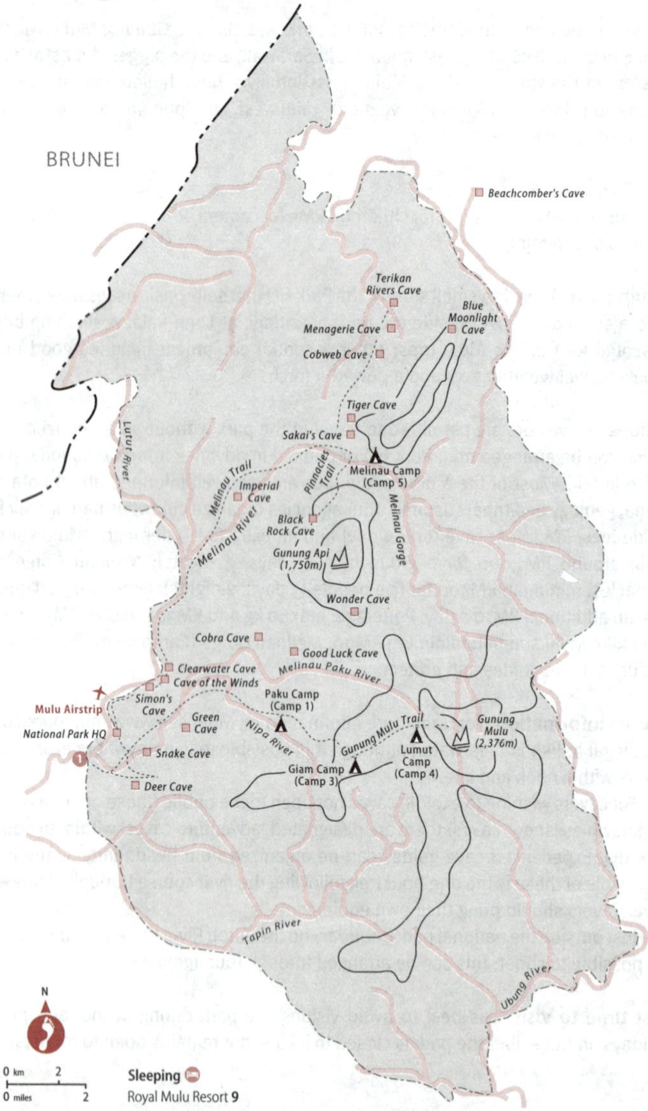

In 1974, three years after Mulu was gazetted as a national park, the first of a succession of joint expeditions led by the British Royal Geographical Society (RGS) and the Sarawak government began to make the discoveries that put Mulu on the map. In 1980 a cave passage over 50 km long was surveyed for the first time. Since then, a further 137 km of passages have been discovered. Altogether 27 major caves have now been found – speleologists believe they probably represent a tiny fraction of what is actually there. The world's biggest cave, the **Sarawak Chamber**, was not discovered until 1984.

The first attempt on Gunung Mulu was made by Spencer St John, the British consul in Brunei, in 1856 (see also his attempts on Gunung Kinabalu, Sabah, page 436). His efforts were thwarted by "limestone cliffs, dense jungle and sharp pinnacles of rock". Dr Charles Hose, Resident of Marudi, led a 25-day expedition to Gunung Mulu in 1893, but also found his path blocked by 600-m high cliffs. Nearly 50 years later, in 1932, a Berawan rhinoceros hunter called Tama Nilong guided Edward Shackleton's Oxford University expedition to the summit. One of the young Oxford undergraduates on that expedition was Tom Harrisson, who later made the Niah archaeological discoveries, see page 359. Tama Nilong, the hunter from Long Terawan, had previously reached the main southwest ridge of Mulu while tracking a rhinoceros. The cliffs of the Melinau Gorge rise a sheer 600 m, and are the highest limestone rockfaces between North Thailand and Papua New Guinea

The limestone massifs of Gunung Api and Gunung Benarat were originally at the same elevation as Gunung Mulu, but their limestone outcrops were more prone to erosion than the Mulu's sandstone. Northwest of the gorge lies a large, undisturbed alluvial plain which is rich in flora and fauna. Penan tribespeople (see page 322) are permitted to maintain their lifestyle of fishing, hunting and gathering in the park. At no small expense, the Malaysian government has encouraged them to settle at a purpose-built longhouse at **Batu Bungan**, just a few minutes upriver from the Park HQ, but its efforts have met with limited success because of the desire of many Penan to maintain their travelling lifestyle. Penan shelters can often be found by river banks.

Reeling from international criticism, the Sarawak state government set aside 66,000 ha of rainforest as what it called 'biosphere', a reserve where indigenous people could practise their traditional lifestyle. Part of this lies in the park. In Baram and Limbang districts, the remaining 300 Penan will have a reserve in which they can continue their nomadic way of life. A further 23,000 ha has reportedly been set aside for 'semi-nomadic' Penan.

In 1961 geologist Dr G Wilford first surveyed Deer Cave and parts of the Cave of the Winds. But Mulu's biggest subterranean secrets were not revealed until the 1980s.

Flora and fauna

In the 1960s and 1970s, botanical expeditions were beginning to shed more light on the Mulu area's flora and fauna: 100 new plant species were discovered between 1960 and 1973 alone. Mulu park encompasses an area of diverse altitudes and soil types – it includes all the forest types found in Borneo except mangrove. About 20,000 animal species have been recorded in Mulu Park, as well as 3,500 plant species and 8,000 varieties of fungi (more than 100 of these are endemic to the Mulu area). Mulu's ecological statistics are astounding: it is home to 1,500 species of flowering plant, 170 species of orchid and 109 varieties of palm. More than 280 butterfly species have been recorded. Within the park boundaries, 262 species of birds (including all eight varieties of hornbill), 67 mammalian species, 50 species of reptile and 75 amphibian species have been recorded.

Mulu's caves contain an unusual array of flora and fauna too. There are three species of swiftlet, 12 species of bat, and nine species of fish, including the cave flying fish (*Nemaaramis everetti*) and blind catfish (*Silurus furnessi*). Cave scorpions (*Chaerilus chapmani*) – which are poisonous but not deadly – are not uncommon.

 Other subterranean species include albino crabs, huntsman spiders, cave crickets, centipedes and snakes (which dine on swiftlets and bats). These creatures have been described as "living fossils...[which are] isolated survivors of ancient groups long since disappeared from Southeast Asia."

Gunung Mulu

The minimum time to allow for the climb is four days, three nights; tents are not required if you stay at Camps 1 and 2. The main summit route starts from the plankwalk at Park HQ heading towards Deer Cave. The Mulu walkway forks left after about 1 km. From the headquarters it is an easy four- to five-hour trek to Camp 1 at 150 m, where there is a shelter, built by the RGS/Sarawak government expedition in 1978. The second day is a long uphill slog (eight to 10 hours) to Camp 4 (1,800 m), where there is also a shelter. Past Camp 3, the trail climbs steeply up Bukit Tumau, which affords good views over the park, and above which the last wild rhinoceros in Sarawak was shot in the mid-1940s. There are many pitcher plants (*Nepenthes lowii*) along this stretch of trail. From Camp 4, known as 'The Summit Camp', the path passes the helicopter pad, from where there are magnificent views of Gunung Benarat, the Melinau Gorge and Gunung Api. The final haul to the summit is steep; there are fixed ropes. Around the summit area, the *Nepenthes muluensis* pitcher plant is common – it is endemic to Mulu. From Camp 4 it takes 1½ hours to reach the summit, and a further seven hours back down the mountain to Camp 1.

! The views from the summit are best during April and May.

Equipment Camp 1 has water, as does Camp 4 if it has been raining. Water should be boiled before drinking. It is necessary to bring your own food; in the rainy season it is wise to bring a gas cooking stove. A sleeping bag and waterproofs are also necessary and spare clothes, wrapped in a plastic bag, are a good idea.

Treks from Camp 5

ⓘ *For a three-day trip, a longboat will cost about RM400. It takes 2-3 hrs, depending on the river level, from Park HQ to Kuala Berar; it is then a 2-3 hr trek (8 km) to Camp 5. Visitors to the Camp 5 area are also advised to plan their itinerary carefully as it is necessary to calculate how much food will be required and to carry it up there. There is a basic shelter which can house about 30 people. The camp is next to the Melinau River; river water should be boiled before drinking.*

Camp 5 is located in the Melinau Gorge, facing Gunung Benarat, take about four to six hours upstream from the Park HQ. From the camp it is possible to trek up the gorge as well as to the Pinnacles, on Gunung Api. It is advisable to hire a longboat for the duration of your time at and around Camp 5. The boat has to be abandoned at Kuala Berar, at the confluence of the Melinau and Berar rivers. It is only used for the first and last hours of the trip, but in the event of an emergency, there are no trails leading back to the Park HQ and there are stories of fever-stricken people being stuck in the jungle.

Melinau Gorge

Camp 5 nestles at the south end of the gorge, across a fast-flowing section of the Melinau River and opposite the unclimbed 1,580 m Gunung Benarat's stark, sheer limestone cliffs. The steep limestone ridges, that lead eventually to Gunung Api, comprise the east wall of the gorge. Heading north from Camp 5, the trail fizzles out after a few minutes. It takes an arduous two to three hours of endless river crossings and scrambles to reach a narrow chute of white water, under which is a large, deep and clear jungle pool with a convenient sandbank and plenty of large boulders to perch on. Alfred Russel Wallace's *Troides brookiana* – the majestic Rajah Brooke's birdwing – is particularly common at this little oasis, deep in undisturbed jungle. The walk involves criss-crossing through waist-deep, fast-flowing water and over stones that have been smoothed to a high polish over centuries: strong shoes are recommended – as is a walking stick. Only occasionally in the walk upstream is it possible to glimpse the towering 600 m cliffs. Mulu can also be climbed from the south ridge of Melinau Gorge – it is three hours to Camp 1, five hours to Camp 3, a steep four to five hour climb to Camp 4, and finally two hours to the top.

The Pinnacles

The Pinnacles are a forest of sharp limestone needles three-quarters of the way up Gunung Api. Some of the pinnacles rise above tree-tops to heights of 45m. The trail leaves from Camp 5, at the base of the Melinau Gorge. It is a very steep climb all the way and a maximum time of three to four hours is allowed to reach the pinnacles (1200 m); otherwise you must return. There is no source of water en route. It is not possible to reach Gunung Api from the pinnacles. It is strongly recommended that climbers wear gloves as well as long-sleeved shirts, trousers and strong boots to protect themselves against cuts from the razor-sharp rocks. Explorers on Spenser St John's expedition to Mulu in 1856 were cut to shreds on the pinnacles: "three of our men had already been sent back with severe wounds, whilst several of those left were much injured," he wrote, concluding that it was "the world's most nightmarish surface to travel over".

Gunung Api (Fire Mountain)

The vegetation is so dry at the summit that it is often set ablaze by lightning in the dry season. The story goes that the fires were so big that locals once thought the mountains were volcanoes. Some of the fires could be seen as far away as the Brunei coast. The summit trek takes a minimum of three days. At 1,710 m, it is the tallest limestone outcrop in Borneo and, other than Gunung Benarat (on the other side of the gorge), is probably the most difficult mountain to climb in Borneo. Many attempts to climb it ended in failure; two Berawans from Long Terawan finally made it to the top in 1978, one of them the grandson of Tama Nilong, the rhinoceros-hunter who had climbed Gunung Mulu in 1932. It is impossible to proceed upwards beyond the Pinnacles.

From Camp 5, cross the Melinau River and head down the Limbang trail towards Lubang Cina. Less than 30 minutes down the trail, fork left along a new trail which leads along a ridge to the south of Gunung Benarat. Climbing higher, after about 40 minutes, the trail passes into an area of leached sandy soils called kerangas (heath) forest. This little patch of thinner jungle is a tangle of many varieties of pitcher plants.

It is possible to trek from Camp 5 to **Limbang**, although it is easier to do it the other way. (See page 377.)

Clearwater Cave

ⓘ *Clearwater can be reached by a 30-minute longboat ride from the Park HQ. Individual travellers must charter a boat for a return trip. Tour agents build the cost of this trip into their package, which works out considerably cheaper.*

This part of the Clearwater System, on a small tributary of the Melinau River, is 107 km long. The cave passage – 75 km of which has been explored – links Clearwater Cave (Gua Ayer Jernih) with the **Cave of the Winds** (Lubang Angin), to the south. It was discovered in 1988. Clearwater is named after the jungle pool at the foot of the steps leading up to the cave mouth, where the longboats moor. Two species of monophytes – single-leafed plants – grow in the sunlight at the mouth of the cave. They only grow on limestone. A lighting system has been installed down the path to Young Lady's Cave, which ends in a 60 m-deep pot hole.

The longest underground cavity in SE Asia and the 7th longest in the world.

On the cave walls are some helictites – coral-like lateral formations – and, even more dramatic, are the photokarsts, tiny needles of rock, all pointing towards the light. These are formed in much the same way as their monstrous cousins, the pinnacles (see above), by vegetation, in this case algae, eating into and eroding the softer rock, leaving sharp points of harder rock which 'grow' at about half a millimetre a year. Inside Clearwater it is possible to hire a rowing boat for RM10 – the river can be followed for about 1½ km upstream, although the current is strong.

Deer Cave

ⓘ *An hour's trek along a plank walk from Park HQ.*

This is another of Mulu's record-breakers: it has the world's biggest cave mouth and the biggest cave passage, which is 2.2 km long and 220 m high at its highest point. Before its inclusion in the park, the cave had been a well-known hunting ground for deer attracted to the pools of salty water running off the guano. The silhouettes of some of the cave's limestone formations have been creatively interpreted; notably the profile of Abraham Lincoln. Adam's and Eve's Showers, at the east end of the cave, are hollow stalactites; water pressure increases when it rains. This darker section at the east end of Deer Cave is the preferred habitat of the naked bat. Albino earwigs live on the bats' oily skin and regularly drop off. The cave's east entrance opens onto 'The Garden of Eden' – a luxuriant patch of jungle, which was once part of the cave system until the roof collapsed. This separated Deer Cave and Green Cave, which lies adjacent to the east mouth; it is open only to caving expeditions.

The west end of the cave is home to several million wrinkle-lipped and horseshoe bats. Hundreds of thousands of these bats pour out of the cave at dusk. Bat hawks can often be seen swooping in for spectacular kills. The helipad, about 500 m south of the cave mouth, provides excellent vantage points. VIPs' helicopters, arriving for the show, are said to have disturbed the bats in recent years. From the analysis of the three tonnes of saline guano the bats excrete every day, scientists conclude that they make an 80 km dash to the coast for meals of insects washed down with seawater. Cave cockroaches eat the guano, ensuring that the cavern does not become choked with what locals call 'black snow'.

Lang's Cave

Part of the same hollow mountain as Deer Cave, Lang's Cave is less well known but its formations are more beautiful, and contains impressive curtain stalactites and intricate coral-like helictites. The cave is well lit and protected by bus stop-style plastic tunnels.

The Sarawak Chamber

Discovered in 1984, this chamber is 600 m long, 450 m wide and 100 m high – big enough, it is said, to accommodate 40 jumbo jets wing-tip to wing-tip and eight nose-to-tail. It is the largest natural chamber in the world. Unfortunately it is not open to the public as it is considered too dangerous.

Bario and the Kelabit Highlands → *Colour map 4, grid C2*

Bario (Bareo) lies in the Kelabit Highlands, a plateau 1,000m above sea level close to the Kalimantan border (Indonesia). The highlands are Sarawak's answer to the hill stations on the peninsula. The undulating Bario valley is surrounded by mountains and fed by countless small streams which in turn feed into a maze of irrigation canals.

Ins and outs

Getting there Bario is only accessible by air or via a 7-day trek from Marudi.

Tourist information For information on Bario and the Kelabits log onto www.kelabit.net

Best time to visit Between March and October.

Background

The local Kelabits' skill in harnessing water has allowed them to practise wet rice cultivation rather than the more common slash-and-burn hill rice techniques. Fragrant Bario rice is prized in Sarawak and commands a premium in the coastal markets. The Kelabit Highlands' more temperate climate also allows the cultivation of a wide range of fruit and vegetables.

The plateau's near-impregnable ring of mountains effectively cut the Kelabit off from the outside world: it is the only area in Borneo which was never penetrated by Islam. In 1911 the Resident of Baram mounted an expedition which ventured into the mountains to ask the Kelabit to stop raiding the Brooke Government's subjects. It took the expedition 17 days to cross the Tamu Abu mountain range, to the west of Bario. The Kelabit were then brought under the control of the Sarawak government.

The most impressive mountain in the Bario area is the distinctive twin peak of the sheer-faced 2,043 m **Bukit Batu Lawi** to the northwest of Bario. The Kelabit traditionally believed the mountain had an evil spirit and so never went near it. Today such superstitions are a thing of the past since locals are mostly evangelical Christians.

In 1945, the plateau was selected as the only possible parachute drop zone in North Borneo not captured by the Japanese. The Allied Special Forces which parachuted into Bario were led by Tom Harrisson, who later became curator of the Sarawak Museum and made the famous archaeological discoveries at Niah Caves (see page 359). His expedition formed an irregular tribal army against the Japanese, which gained control over large areas of North Borneo in the following months.

Treks around Bario

Because of the rugged terrain surrounding the plateau, the area mainly attracts serious mountaineers. There are many trails to the longhouses around the plateau area, however. Treks to Bario can be organized through travel agents in Miri, see page 361. Guides can also be hired in Bario and surrounding longhouses for RM30-40 per day. It is best to go through the Penghulu, Ngiap Ayu, the Kelabit chief. He goes round visiting many of the longhouses in the area once a month. It is recommended that visitors to Bario come equipped with sleeping bags and camping equipment. There are no formal facilities for tourists and provisions should be brought from Miri or Marudi. There are no banks or money changers in Bario.

It is necessary to have a permit to visit the Bario area, obtainable from the Resident's offices in Miri or Marudi.

Several of the surrounding mountains can be climbed from Bario, but they are, without exception, difficult climbs. Even on walks just around the Bario area, guides are essential as trails are poorly marked. The lower ('female') peak of **Bukit Batu Lawi** can be climbed without equipment, but the sheer sided 'male' peak requires proper rock-climbing equipment – it was first scaled in 1986. **Gunung Murudi** (2,423 m) is the highest mountain in Sarawak; it is a very tough climb.

Limbang

→ Colour map 4, grid D2

Limbang is the administrative centre for the Fifth Division and was ceded to the Brooke government by the Sultan of Brunei in 1890. The Trusan Valley, to the east of the wedge of Brunei, had been ceded to Sarawak in 1884. Very few tourists reach Limbang or Lawas but they are good stopping-off points for more adventurous routes to **Sabah** and **Brunei**. Limbang is the finger of Sarawak territory which splits Brunei in two.

Sights

Limbang's **Old Fort** was built in 1897, renovated in 1966, and was used as the administrative centre. During the Brooke era half the ground floor was used as a jail. It is now a centre of religious instruction, Majlis Islam. Limbang is famous for its **Pasar**

 Tamu every Friday, where jungle and native produce is sold. Limbang also has an attractive small museum, **Muzium Wilayah,** ⓘ *400 m south of the centre along Jalan Kubu, 0900-1800, Tue-Sun*. Housed in a wooden villa, painted beige and white, the museum has a collection of ethnic artefacts from the region, including basketry, musical instruments and weapons. To the right of the museum, a small road climbs the hill to a park with a man-made lake.

Trek to Gunung Mulu National Park Take a car south to Medamit; from there hire a longboat upriver to Mulu Madang, an Iban longhouse (three hours, depending on water level). Alternatively, go further upriver to Kuala Terikan (six to seven hours at low-water, four hours at high-water) where there is a simple zinc-roofed camp. From there take a longboat one hour up the Terikan River to Lubang China, which is the start of a two-hour trek along a well used trail to Camp 5. There is a park rangers' camp about 20 minutes out of Kuala Terikan where it is possible to obtain permits and arrange for a guide to meet you at Camp 5. The longboats are cheaper to hire in the wet season.

Lawas

Lawas District was ceded to Sarawak in 1905. The Limbang River, which cuts through the town, is the main transport route. It is possible to travel from Miri to Bandar Seri Begawan (Brunei) by road, then on to Limbang and Lawas. From Lawas there are direct buses to Kota Kinabalu in Sabah.

Sleeping

Gunung Mulu National Park

p371, map p372

Sleeping in the park chalets must be booked in advance at the National Parks and Wildlife Office Forest Department in Miri or Kuching or through Borsarmulu Park Management, T85-424561, brianclark@mulupark.com, www.mulupark.com. Booking fee is RM20 per party and the maximum party size is 10 people. Bookings must be confirmed 5 days before visit.

AL **Royal Mulu Resort**, Sungai Melinau, Muku, Miri, a 20-min (RM5) boat ride downstream from Park HQ, T85-790100, www.royalmuluresort.com. A/c, restaurants, owned by Japan's Royal Hotel Group Rihga the resort currently has 188 rooms from chalets to executive suites. The resort has sparked much resentment among local tribespeople. The Berawan claim the resort's land as theirs by customary right.

The park also has its own accommodation at headquarters. Top of the range are the B **longhouses** which have attached bathroom, a/c, and four single beds, or a twin share. For four people sharing, it works out to be RM30 per pax. Then, the C **Rainforest Rooms** are fan rooms with attached bathroom, sleeping up to four people, working out to be just over RM20 per pax. There is also a E **hostel** with 18 dorm beds, shared toilet and fan for RM18 per pax. At camp 5, the park has an E **open-air hostel** with mats for sleeping and shared bathrooms. There are also simple wooden shelters for sleeping on the summit trail. For both of these, bring your own sleeping bag. F **Camping**. This is only allowed at the campsite at park headquarters (RM5) - bring your own sleeping bag.

There are several hostels just outside the park including: D **Melinau Canteen**, T011291641/ T85-657884, a privately owned hostel with dorm beds about 5 mins' walk downstream from the Park HQ, on the other bank of the river.

Bario *p376*

D **De Plateau Lodge**. Pretty wooden house, offer forest guides at RM65 per day.

D **JR Lodge** (Barview Lodge), T085-791038, well set up for travellers, with airport transfer, restaurant, electricity in the evening, western toilets, board games, motorbike, 4WD, bike rental and trekking offered. Rooms are simple but cheery.

D **Tarawe**. A recommended place to stay with a good source of information and well run. Most visitors camp.

Limbang *p377*

Limbang has become a sex stop for Bruneians whose government takes a more hardline attitude to such moral transgressions and consequently many hotels and guesthouses have a fair share of short-time guests.

B Centre Point Hotel, T85-212922. Newish place with a/c and restaurant which tops Limbang's limited bill of hotels.

B-C Metro, Lot 781, Jln Bangkita, T85-211133, F85-211051. A fairly new addition to Limbang's mid-range accommodation, under 30 rooms, all with a/c, TV, fridge, good quality beds, small but clean rooms. Recommended.

B-C Muhibbah, Lot T790, Bank St, T85-213705, F85-212153. Located in town centre, has seen better days, but rooms are fairly clean with a/c, TV and bathroom.

B-C National Inn, 62a Jln Buangsiol, T85-212922, F85-212282. Probably the best of the 3 hotels along the river here, comfortable a/c rooms with TV, mini-bar, higher rates for river view.

Lawas *p378*

A-B Country Park Hotel, Lot 235, Jln Trusan, T85-85522, A/c, restaurant.

C Lawas Federal, 8 Jln Masjid Baru, T85-85115. A/c, restaurant.

D Hup Guan Lodging House, T85-85362. Some a/c, above a pool hall so can be noisy but the rooms are clean and spacious and reasonable value for money.

Eating

Gunung Mulu National Park *p371, map p372*

There are stoves and cooking utensils available and the small store at Park HQ also sells basic supplies. There is a small canteen at Park HQ but the menu is limited and the food rather boring. As an alternative, cross the suspension bridge and walk alongside the road to the first house on the left; down the bank from here is the **Mulu Canteen**, which fronts onto the river (so there is no sign on the road). There is also the **Melinau Canteen**, just downriver from the Park HQ.

There is a small shop with basic supplies at Long Pala. All tour companies with their own accommodation offer food.

Limbang *p377*

TT Tong Lok, a/c Chinese restaurant next to National Inn, gruesome pink table cloths and fluorescent lighting, but good quality Chinese food.

T Hai Hong, 1 block south of Maggie's, a simple coffee shop – good for breakfast with fried egg and chips on the menu.

T Maggie's Café on the riverside near National Inn, Chinese coffee shop, pleasant location, tables outside next to river in evening – braziers set up in evening for good grilled fish on banana leaf. Recommended.

Festivals and events

Limbang *p377*

May The movable **Buffalo Racing festival** marks the end of the harvesting season.

Activities and tours

Gunung Mulu National Park *p371*

Visitors are recommended to go through one of the Miri-based travel agents (see page 368). The average cost of a Mulu package (per person) is RM350-400 (4 days/3 nights) or RM500 (6 days/5 nights). Independent travellers will find it more expensive arranging the trip on their own.

Limbang *p377*

Sitt Travel, T085-420567, specializes in treks in this area and is the ticketing agent for Miri tour operators.

Transport

Gunung Mulu National Park *p371, map p372*

Within the park Longboats can be chartered privately from Park HQ, if required (maximum 10 people per boat). The cost is calculated on a rather complicated system which includes a rate for the boat, a charge for the engine based on its horsepower, a separate payment for the driver and

For an explanation of the sleeping and eating price codes used in this guide, see inside the front cover. Other relevant information is found in Essentials, pages 45-49.

front-man, and then fuel on top of that. The total cost can be RM100+. How far these boats can actually get upriver depends on the season. They often have to be hauled over rapids, whatever the time of year.

Air

Daily flights from **Miri** to Mulu, 20 mins. The airstrip is just downriver from Park HQ. Currently 2 flights per day from Miri, and 2 daily from **Marudi** and **Limbang**. The price of a flight is only marginally more expensive than taking the bus and boat from Miri and infinitely faster.

Bus/taxi/boat

Bus or taxi from Miri to Marudi express boat jetty near Kuala Baram at mouth of the Baram River (see page 370). Regular express boats from **Kuala Baram** to **Marudi**, 3 hrs (RM18) from 0700 until about 1500. One express boat per day (leaves at 1100) from Marudi to **Long Terawan** on the Tutoh River (tributary of the Baram), via Long Apoh. During the dry season express boats cannot reach Long Terawan and terminate at Long Panai, on the Tutoh River, where longboats continue to Long Terawan (RM20). Longboats leave Long Tarawan for Mulu Park HQ: this used to be regular and comparatively cheap; now that most people travel to Mulu by air, longboats are less frequent and sometimes need to be privately chartered – an expensive business. Mulu Park HQ is 1½ hrs up the Melinau River (a tributary of the Tutoh) (RM45). As you approach the park from Long Tarawan the Tutoh River narrows and becomes shallower; there are 14 rapids before the Melinau River, which forms the park boundary. When the water is low, the trip can be very slow and involve pulling the boat over the shallows, this accounts for high charter rates. For a group of 9 or 10 it is cheaper to charter a boat (RM250 one way). The first jetty on the Melinau River is Long Pala, where most of the tour companies have accommodation. The Park HQ is another 15 mins upriver. Longboats returning to Long Terawan leave the headquarters at dawn each day, calling at jetties en route.

Bario *p376*

Air

The only access to Bario is by air on MAS. Bario's airstrip is very small and because of its position, flights are often cancelled because of mist and clouds. Flights are always booked up. There is one flight a day on MAS from **Miri** at 0930. During school holidays flights are also often booked up. There are is also one connection a day via Marudi.

Foot

It is a 7-day trek from **Marudi** to Bario, sleeping in longhouses en route. This trip should be organized through a Miri travel agent (see page 368).

Limbang *p377*

Air

Daily connections with **Miri, Mulu** and **Lawas**; weekly flights to **Labuan**; and twice weekly connections with **KK**. The airport is about 5 km from town and taxis ferry passengers in.

Boat

Regular connections with **Lawas**, departs early in the morning (2 hrs, RM15). There is also an early morning express departure to **Labuan**.

International connections with Brunei Regular boat connections with **Bandar Seri Begawan**, Brunei (30 mins, RM15).

Directory

Limbang *p377*

Useful addresses Residents' Office, T85-21960.

Lawas *p378*

Air

Connections with **Miri, Limbang, Kuching, Labuan** and **Kota Kinabalu**.

Boat

Regular connections to **Limbang**, 2 hrs. Daily morning boat departures for **Brunei**.

Bus

Connections with Merapok on the Sarwak/Sabah border (RM5). From here there are connections to **Beaufort** in Sabah. Twice-daily connections with **Kota Kinabalu**, 4 hrs (RM20).

Sarawak Background

About a third of the population is made up of Iban tribespeople – who used to be known as the 'Sea Dayaks' – former headhunters, who live in longhouses on the lower reaches of the rivers. Chinese immigrants, whose forebears arrived during the 19th century, make up another third. A fifth of the population is Malay; most are native Sarawakians, but some came from the peninsula after the state joined the Malaysian Federation in 1963. The rest of Sarawak's inhabitants are indigenous tribal groups, of which the main ones are the Melanau, the Bidayuh and upriver Orang Ulu such as the Kenyah, Kayan and Kelabits; the Penan are among Southeast Asia's few remaining hunter-gatherers.

For over 150 years, Sarawak was under the rule of the 'White Rajahs' who tried to keep the peace between warring tribes of headhunters. The Brooke family ran Sarawak as their private country and their most obvious legacies are the public buildings in Kuching, the state capital, and the forts along the rivers. Outside Kuching, the towns have little to offer; most are predominantly Chinese and are mainly modern, without much grace or character. One or two are boom-towns, having grown rich on the back of the logging and oil and gas industries. From a tourist's point of view, the towns are just launching-pads for the longhouses and jungle upriver.

History

Sarawak earned its place in the archaeological textbooks when a 40,000-year-old human skull belonging to a boy of about 15 was unearthed in the Niah Caves in 1958 (see page 359), predating the earliest relics found on the Malay peninsula by about 30,000 years. The caves were continuously inhabited for tens of thousands of years and many shards of Palaeolithic and Neolithic pottery, tools and jewellery as well as carved burial boats have been excavated at the site. There are also prehistoric cave paintings. In the first millennium AD, the Niah Caves were home to a prosperous community, which traded **birds' nests, hornbill ivory, bezoar stones, rhinoceros horns** and other jungle produce with Chinese traders in exchange for porcelain and beads.

Some of Sarawak's tribes may be descended from these cave people, although others, notably the Iban shifting cultivators, migrated from Kalimantan's Kapuas River valley from the 16th-19th centuries. Malay Orang Laut, sea people, migrated to Sarawak's coasts and made a living from fishing, trading and piracy. At the height of Sumatra's Srivijayan Empire in the 11th and 12th centuries, many Sumatran Malays migrated to North Borneo. Chinese traders were active along the Sarawak coast from as early as the seventh century: Chinese coins and Han pottery have been discovered at the mouth of the Sarawak River. Most of the coins and ceramics, however, date from the Chinese Song and Yuan periods in the 11th-14th centuries.

From the 14th century right up to the 20th century, Sarawak's history was inextricably intertwined with that of the neighbouring Sultanate of Brunei, which, until the arrival of the White Rajahs of Sarawak, held sway over the coastal areas of North Borneo. For a more detailed account of how Sarawak's White Rajahs came to whittle away the sultan's territory and expand into the vacuum of his receding empire, see Robert Payne's *The White Rajah's of Sarawak*, see page 529.

Enter James Brooke

As the Sultanate of Brunei began to decline around the beginning of the 18th century, the Malays of coastal Sarawak attempted to break free from their tributary overlord. They claimed an independent ancestry from Brunei and exercised firm control over the Dayak tribes inland and upriver. But in the early 19th century Brunei started to reassert its power over them, dispatching Pangiran Mahkota from the Brunei court to govern Sarawak in 1827 and supervise the mining of high-grade antimony ore, which was exported to Singapore to be used in medicine and as an alloy. The name 'Sarawak' comes from the Malay word serawak, meaning 'antimony'.

Mahkota founded Kuching, but relations with the local Malays became strained and Mahkota's problems were compounded by the marauding Ibans of the Saribas and Skrang rivers who raided coastal communities. In 1836 the local Malay chiefs, led by Datu Patinggi Ali, rebelled against Governor Mahkota, prompting the Sultan of Brunei to send his uncle, Rajah Muda Hashim to suppress the uprising. But Hashim failed to quell the disturbances and the situation deteriorated when the rebels approached the Sultan of Sambas, now in Northwest Kalimantan, for help from the Dutch. Then, in 1839, James Brooke sailed up the Sarawak River to Kuching.

Hashim was desperate to regain control and Brooke, in the knowledge that the British would support any action that countered the threat of Dutch influence, struck a deal with him. He pressed Hashim to grant him the governorship of Sarawak in exchange for suppressing the rebellion, which he duly did. In 1842 Brooke became Rajah of Sarawak. Pangiran Mahkota – the now disenfranchised former governor of Sarawak – formed an alliance with an Iban pirate chief on the Skrang River, while another Brunei prince, Pangiran Usop, joined Illanun pirates. Malaysian historian J Kathirithamby-Wells wrote: "... piracy and politics became irrevocably linked and Brooke's battle against his political opponents became advertised as a morally justified war against the pirate communities of the coast."

The suppression of piracy in the 19th century became a full-time occupation for the rulers of Sarawak and Brunei – although the court of Brunei was well known to have derived a substantial chunk of its income from piracy. Rajah James Brooke believed that as long as pirates remained free to pillage the coasts, commerce would not pick up and his kingdom would never develop; ridding Sarawak's estuaries of pirates – both Iban ('Sea Dayaks') and Illanun – became an act of political survival. In his *The White Rajahs of Sarawak*, Robert Payne wrote: "Nearly every day people came to Kuching with tales about the pirates: how they had landed in a small creek, spread out, made their way to a village, looted everything in sight, murdered everyone they could lay their hands on, and then vanished as swiftly as they came. The Sultan of Brunei was begging for help against them."

Anti-piracy missions afforded James Brooke an excuse to extend his kingdom, as he worked his way up the coasts, 'pacifying' the Sea Dayak pirates. Brooke declared war on them and with the help of Royal Naval Captain Henry Keppel (of latter-day Singapore's Keppel Shipyard fame), he led a number of punitive raids against the Iban 'Sea Dayaks' in 1833, 1834 and 1849. "The assaults", wrote DJM Tate in Rajah Brooke's *Borneo*, "largely achieved their purpose, and were applauded in the Straits, but the appalling loss of life incurred upset many drawing-room humanitarians in Britain." There were an estimated 25,000 pirates living along the North Borneo coast when Brooke became Rajah. He led many punitive expeditions against them, culminating in his notorious battle against the Saribas pirate fleet in 1849.

In that incident, Brooke ambushed and killed hundreds of Saribas Dayaks at Batang Maru. The barbarity of the ambush (which was reported in the Illustrated London News) outraged public opinion in Britain and in Singapore – a commission of inquiry in Singapore acquitted Brooke, but badly damaged his prestige. In the British parliament, he was cast as a 'mad despot' who had to be prevented from committing further massacres. But the action led the Sultan of Brunei to grant him the Saribas and Skrang districts (now Sarawak's Second Division) in 1853, marking the beginning of the Brookes' relentless expansionist drive. Eight years later, James Brooke persuaded the sultan to give him what became Sarawak's Third Division, after he drove out the Illanun pirates who had disrupted the sago trade from Mukah and Oya, around Bintulu.

In 1857, James Brooke ran into more trouble. Chinese Hakka goldminers, who had been in Bau (further up the Sarawak River) longer than he had been in Kuching, had grown resentful of his attempts to stamp out the opium trade and their secret societies. They attacked Kuching, set the Malay kampongs ablaze and killed several European officials; Brooke escaped by swimming across the river from his astana. His nephew, Charles, led a group of Skrang Dayaks to chase after the Hakka invaders, who fled across the border into Dutch Borneo; about 1,000 were killed by the Ibans on the way; 2,500 survived. Historian Robert Payne writes: "The fighting lasted for more than a month. From time to time Dayaks would return with strings of heads, which they cleaned and smoked over slow fires, especially happy when they could do this in full view of the Chinese in the bazaars who sometimes recognized people they had known." Payne says Brooke was plagued by guilt over how he handled the Chinese rebellion, for so many deaths could not easily be explained away. Neither James nor Charles ever fully trusted the Chinese again, although the Teochew, Cantonese and Hokkien merchants in Kuching never caused them any trouble.

The second generation: Rajah Charles Brooke

Charles Johnson (who changed his name to Brooke after his elder brother, Brooke Johnson, had been disinherited by James for insubordination) became the second Rajah of Sarawak in 1863. He ruled for nearly 50 years. Charles did not have James Brooke's forceful personality, and was much more reclusive – probably as a result of working in remote jungle outposts for 10 years in government service. Historian Robert Payne noted that "in James Brooke there was something of the knight errant at the mercy of his dream. Charles was the pure professional, a stern soldier who thought dreaming was the occupation of fools. There was no nonsense about him." Despite this he engendered great loyalty in his administrators, who worked hard for little reward.

Charles maintained his uncle's consultative system of government and formed a Council Negeri, or national council, comprised of his top government officials, Malay leaders and tribal headmen, which met every couple of years to hammer out policy changes. His frugal financial management meant that by 1877 Sarawak was no longer in debt and the economy gradually expanded. The country was not a wealthy one, however, and had very few natural resources – its soils proved unsuitable for agriculture. In the 1880s, Charles' faith in the Chinese community was sufficiently restored to allow Chinese immigration, and the government subsidized the new settlers. By using 'friendly' downriver Dayak groups to subdue belligerent tribes upriver, Charles managed to pacify the interior by 1880.

When Charles took over from his ailing uncle in 1863 he proved to be even more of an expansionist. In 1868 he tried to take control of the Baram River vall2ey, but London did not approve secession of the territory until 1882. It became the Fourth Division; in 1884, Charles acquired the Trusan Valley from the Sultan of Brunei, and in 1890, he annexed Limbang ending a six-year rebellion by local chiefs against the sultan. The two territories were united to form the Fifth Division, after which Sarawak completely surrounded Brunei. In 1905, the British North Borneo Chartered Company gave up the Lawas Valley to Sarawak too. "By 1890," writes Robert Payne, "Charles was ruling over a country as large as England and Scotland with the help of about 20 European officers." When the First World War broke out in 1914, Charles was in England and he ruled Sarawak from Cirencester.

The third generation: Charles Vyner Brooke

At the age of 86, Charles handed the reins to his eldest son, Charles Vyner Brooke, in 1916 and died the following year. Vyner was 42 when he became Rajah and had already served his father's government for nearly 20 years. "Vyner was a man of peace, who took no delight in bloodshed and ruled with humanity and compassion," wrote Robert Payne. He was a delegator by nature, and under him the old paternalistic

James Brooke: the white knight errant

James Brooke lived the life of a Boy's Own comic-book hero. To the socialites of London, he was the king of an exotic far-away country, on a mysterious jungled island, inhabited by roving tribes of headhunters. It was a romantic image, but while it was also a tough life, it was not far from the truth. The Brookes were a family of benevolent despots. There were three White Rajahs, who ruled for over a century, but it was James Brooke, with his forceful personality, violent temper, vengeful instincts but compassion for his people, that set the tone and created the legend.

James was born in India in 1803, the son of a High Court judge in Benares. He joined the Indian army, and fought in the First Anglo-Burmese War as a cavalry officer, where he was mentioned in dispatches for "most conspicuous gallantry." But in 1825 he was hit in the chest by a bullet and almost left for dead on the battlefield. He was forced to return to England where any military ambitions he might have had were dashed by the severity of his injury. He recovered enough to make two trips to the East in the 1830s, on one of which he visited Penang and Singapore where he became an admirer of Sir Thomas Stamford Raffles, Singapore's founding father. Back in England, he bought a schooner, *The Royalist*, and drew up plans to sail to Maurdu Bay (North Sabah), to explore the fabled lake at Kini Ballu (see page 432). His trip did not work out as planned.

The Royalist arrived in Singapore in 1839 and the governor asked Brooke to deliver a letter of thanks to Rajah Muda Hashim, the ruler in Kuching, who had rescued some shipwrecked British sailors. He called in briefly, as promised, was intrigued with what he found, but sailed on. When he returned a year later, the Rajah Muda was still struggling to contain the rebellion of local Malay chiefs. Hashim said that if Brooke helped suppress the rebellion, he could have the Sarawak River area as his and the title of Rajah. Brooke took him up on the offer, quelled the revolt and after leaning heavily on Hashim to keep his word, became acting Rajah of Sarawak on 24 September 1841.

The style of Brooke's government – which also characterized that of his successors – is described by historian Mary Turnbull as "a paternal, informal government based upon consultation with local community chiefs". Brooke realized the importance of maintaining tribal laws and observing local customs; he also recognized that without his

style of government gave way to a more professional bureaucracy. On the centenary of the Brooke administration in September 1941, Vyner promulgated a written constitution, and renounced his autocratic powers in favour of working in co-operation with a Supreme Council. This was opposed by his nephew and heir, Anthony Brooke, who saw it as a move to undermine his succession. To protest against this, and his uncle's decision to appoint a mentally deranged Muslim Englishman as his Chief Secretary, Anthony left for Singapore. The Rajah dismissed him from the service in September 1941. Three months later the Japanese Imperial Army invaded; Vyner Brooke was in Australia at the time, and his younger brother, Bertram, was ill in London.

Japanese troops took Kuching on Christmas Day 1941 having captured the Miri oilfield a few days earlier. European administrators were interned and many later died. A Kuching-born Chinese, Albert Kwok, led an armed resistance against the Japanese in neighbouring British North Borneo (Sabah) – see page 472 – but in protection, the people of Sarawak would be open to exploitation by Europeans and Chinese. In 1842, shortly after he was confirmed as Rajah, he wrote: "I hate the idea of a Utopian government, with laws cut and dried ready for the natives... I am going on slowly and surely basing everything on their own laws, consulting all the headmen at every stage, instilling what I think is right – separating the abuses from the customs." Like his successors, James Brooke had great respect for the Dayaks and the Malays, whom he treated as equals. In the 1840s he wrote: "Sarawak belongs to the Malays, Sea Dayaks, Land Dayaks, Kenyahs, Milanos, Muruts, Kadayans, Bisayahs, and other tribes, and not to us. It is for them we labour, not for ourselves."

Unlike most colonial adventurers of the time, Brooke was not in it for the money. He had a hopeless head for figures and his country was constantly in debt; it would have gone bankrupt if it were not for an eccentric English spinster, Angela Burdett-Coutts, who lent him large amounts of money. In his history of The White Rajahs of Sarawak, Robert Payne wrote that "He had the large view always and large views incline dangerously towards absolute power, and he had seized power with all the strength and cunning that was in him. He possessed the Elizabethan love for power, believing that some Englishmen are granted a special dispensation by God to wield power to the uttermost."

By pacifying pirate-infested coastal districts, Brooke persuaded the Sultan of Brunei to cede him more and more territory, so that towards the end of his reign, Sarawak was a sizeable country. An attack of smallpox, combined with the emotional traumas of a Chinese rebellion in 1857 and the public inquiry into his punitive ambush on the Saribas pirates, seems to have broken his spirit, however. His illness aged him, although an old Malay man, who knew him well, said his eyes remained "fierce like those of a crocodile". Rajah Sir James Brooke (he was knighted by Queen Victoria) visited Sarawak for the last time in 1863 following a succession dispute in which he disinherited his heir, Brooke Johnson. He retired to Dorset in England a disillusioned and embittered man. On Christmas Eve 1867 he had a stroke, and died six months later. When news of his death reached Sarawak, guns sounded a thunderous salute across the Sarawak River.

Sarawak, there was no organized guerrilla movement. Iban tribespeople instilled fear into the occupying forces, however, by roaming the jungle taking Japanese heads, which were proudly added to much older longhouse head galleries. Despite the Brooke régime's century-long effort to stamp out head-hunting, the practice was encouraged by Tom Harrisson (one of Sarawak's most famous 'adopted' sons) who parachuted into the Kelabit Highlands towards the end of the Second World War and put together an irregular army of upriver tribesmen to fight the Japanese. He offered them 'ten-bob-a-nob' for Japanese heads. Australian forces liberated Kuching on September 11 1945 and Sarawak was placed under Australian Military Administration for seven months.

After the war, the Colonial Office in London decided the time had come to bring Sarawak into the modern era, replacing the anachronous White Rajahs, introducing an education system and building a rudimentary infrastructure. The Brookes had become an embarrassment to the British government as they continued to squabble among themselves. Anthony Brooke desperately wanted to claim what he felt was his, while the Colonial Office wanted Sarawak to become a crown colony or revert to Malay rule. No one was sure whether Sarawak wanted the Brookes back or not.

The end of empire

In February 1946 the ageing Vyner shocked his brother Bertram and his nephew Anthony, the Rajah Muda (or heir apparent), by issuing a proclamation urging the people of Sarawak to accept the King of England as their ruler. In doing so he effectively handed the country over to Britain. Vyner thought the continued existence of Sarawak as the private domain of the Brooke family an anachronism; but Anthony thought it a betrayal. The British government sent a commission to Sarawak to ascertain what the people wanted. In May 1946, the Council Negri agreed – by a 19-16 majority – to transfer power to Britain, provoking protests and demonstrations and resulting in the assassination of the British governor by a Malay in Sibu in 1949. He and three other anti-cessionists were sentenced to death. Two years later, Anthony Brooke, who remained deeply resentful about the demise of the Brooke Dynasty, abandoned his claim and urged his supporters to end their campaign.

As a British colony, Sarawak's economy expanded and oil and timber production increased which funded the much-needed expansion of education and health services. As with British North Borneo (Sabah), Britain was keen to give Sarawak political independence and, following Malaysian independence in 1957, saw the best means to this end as being through the proposal of Malaysian Prime Minister Tunku Abdul Rahman, who suggested the formation of a federation to include Singapore, Sarawak, Sabah and Brunei as well as the peninsula. In the end, Brunei opted out, Singapore left after two years, but Sarawak and Sabah joined the federation, having accepted the recommendations of the British government. Indonesia's President Sukarno denounced the move, claiming it was all part of a neo-colonialist conspiracy. He declared a policy of confrontation – Konfrontasi. A United Nations commission which was sent to ensure that the people of Sabah and Sarawak wanted to be part of Malaysia reported that Indonesia's objections were unfounded.

Communists had been active in Sarawak since the 1930s. The Konfrontasi afforded the Sarawak Communist Organization (SCO) Jakarta's support against the Malaysian government. The SCO joined forces with the North Kalimantan Communist Party (NKCP) and were trained and equipped by Indonesia's President Sukarno. But following Jakarta's brutal suppression of the Indonesian Communists, the Partai Komunis Indonesia (PKI), in the wake of the attempted coup in 1965, Sarawak's Communists fled back across the Indonesian border, along with their Kalimantan comrades. There they continued to wage guerrilla war against the Malaysian government throughout the 1970s. The Sarawak state government offered amnesties to guerrillas wanting to come out of hiding. In 1973 the NKCP leader surrendered along with 482 other guerrillas. A handful remained in the jungle, most of them in the hills around Kuching. The last surrendered in 1990.

Politics and modern Malaysia

Politics

In 1957 Kuala Lumpur was keen to have Sarawak and Sabah in the Federation of Malaysia and offered the two states a degree of autonomy, allowing their local governments control over state finances, agriculture and forestry. Sarawak's racial mix was reflected in its chaotic state politics. The Ibans dominated the Sarawak National Party (SNAP), which provided the first Chief Minister, Datuk Stephen Kalong Ningkan. He raised a storm over Kuala Lumpur's introduction of Bahasa Malaysia in schools and complained bitterly about the federal government's policy of filling the

Sarawakian civil service with Malays from the peninsula. An 'us' and 'them' mentality developed: in Sarawak, the Malay word *semenanjung* (peninsula) was used to label the newcomers. To many, *semenanjung* was Malaysia, Sarawak was Sarawak.

In 1966 the federal government ousted the SNAP, and a new Muslim-dominated government led by the Sarawak Alliance took over in Kuching. But there was still strong political opposition to federal encroachment. Throughout the 1970s, as in Sabah, Sarawak's strongly Muslim government drew the state closer and closer to the peninsula: it supported *Rukunegara* – the policy of Islamization – and promoted the use of Bahasa Malaysia. Muslims make up less than one-third of the population of Sarawak. The Malays, Melanaus and Chinese communities grew rich from the timber industry; the Ibans and the Orang Ulu (the upriver tribespeople) saw little in the way of development. They did not reap the benefits of the expansion of education and social services, they were unable to get public sector jobs and to make matters worse, logging firms were encroaching on their native lands and threatening their traditional lifestyles.

It has only been in more recent years that the tribespeoples' political voice has been heard at all. In 1983, Iban members of SNAP – which was a part of former Prime Minister Dr Mahathir Mohamad's ruling Barisan Nasional (National Front) coalition – split to form the Party Bansa Dayak Sarawak (PBDS), which, although it initially remained in the coalition, became more outspoken on native affairs. At about the same time, international outrage was sparked over the exploitation of Sarawak's tribespeople by politicians and businessmen involved in the logging industry. The plight of the Penan hunter-gatherers came to world attention due to their blockades of logging roads and the resulting publicity highlighted the rampant corruption and greed that characterized modern Sarawak's political economy.

The National Front remain firmly in control in Sarawak. But unlike neighbouring Sabah, or indeed any other state in the country with the exception of Kelantan (ruled by opposition PAS) on the Peninsula's east coast, Sarawak's politicians are not dominated by the centre. The chief minister of Sarawak is Taib Mahmud, a Melanau, and his Parti Pesaka Bumiputra Bersatu is a member of the UMNO-dominated National Front. But in Sarawak itself UMNO wields little power.

While the Anwar case (see page 492) dominated political debate on the Peninsula in the months leading up to the elections in 1999 and led many voters – especially the young – to vote against UMNO, this was not the case in Sarawak which, even in political terms, can seem a world apart. Furthermore, Sarawak survived the economic crisis relatively unscathed, so even this did not carry much influence in the campaign. The ruling National Front easily won the election in Sarawak, successfully playing on voters' local concerns and grievances. The problem for the opposition was that local people think it is the state legislature which can help, not the federal parliament in KL which seems distant and ineffective. For this reason, UMNO does not have a presence and it is the Parti Pesaka Bumiputra Bersatu which represents Sarawak in the National Front.

The challenge of getting the voters out in the most remote areas of the country was clearly shown in Long Lidom. There it cost the government RM65,000 to provide a helicopter to poll just seven Punan Busang in a longhouse on the Upper Kajang, close to the border with Indonesia. Datuk Omar of the election Commission said that mounting the general election in Sarawak, with its 28 parliamentary seats, was a "logistical nightmare". Along with a small air force of helicopters, the Commission used 1,032 long boats, 15 speed boats and 3,054 land cruisers. The Commission's workforce numbered a cool 13,788 workers in a state with a population of just two million.

Today there are many in Sarawak as well as in Sabah, who wish their governments had opted out of the Federation like Brunei. Sarawak is of great economic importance to Malaysia, thanks to its oil, gas and timber. The state now accounts for more than one-third of Malaysia's petroleum production (worth more than US$800m per year) and more than half of its natural gas. As with neighbouring Sabah however, 95% of Sarawak's oil and gas revenues go directly into federal coffers.

Skulls in the longhouse

Although headhunting has been largely stamped out in Borneo, there is still the odd reported case, once every few years. But until the early 20th century, headhunting was commonplace among many Dayak tribes and the Iban were the most fearsome of all.

Following a headhunting expedition, the freshly taken heads were skinned, placed in rattan nets and smoked over a fire, or sometimes boiled. The skulls were then hung from the rafters of the longhouse and they possessed the most powerful form of magic.

The skulls were considered trophies of manhood (they increased a young bachelor's eligibility), symbols of bravery and they testified to the unity of a longhouse. The longhouse had to hold festivals – or gawai – to appease the spirits of the skulls. Once placated, the heads were believed to bring great blessing – they could ward off evil spirits, save villages from epidemics, produce rain and increase the yield of rice harvests. Heads that were insulted or ignored were capable of wreaking havoc in the form of bad dreams, plagues, floods and fires. To keep the spirits of the skulls happy, they would be offered food and cigarettes and made to feel welcome in their new home. Because the magical powers of a skull faded with time, fresh heads were always in demand. Tribes without heads were considered spiritually weak.

Today, young Dayak men no longer have to take heads to gain respect. They are, however, expected to go on long journeys (the equivalent of the Australian aborigines' Walkabout), or *bejalai* in Iban. The one unspoken rule is that they should come back with plenty of good stories, and, these days, as most *bejalai* expeditions translate into stints at timber camps or on oil rigs, they are expected to come home bearing video recorders, TV sets and motorbikes.

Many Dayak tribes continue to celebrate their headhunting ceremonies. In Kalimantan, for example, the Adat Ngayau ceremony uses coconut shells, wrapped in leaves, as substitutes for freshly cut heads.

A famous cartoon in a Sarawak newspaper once depicted a cow grazing in Sarawak and being milked on the peninsula. While Sarawak has traditionally been closer to federal government than Sabah (there has never been any hint of a secessionist movement), discontent surfaces from time to time.

Culture

People

For those intending to visit any of Sarawak's tribal peoples, see page 339.

About 30% of Sarawak's population is Iban, another 30% Chinese, 20% is Malay and the remaining 20% is divided into other tribal groups. The total population of the state is almost 2.2 million. The people of the interior are classified as Proto-Malays and Deutero-Malays and are divided into at least 12 distinct tribal groups including Iban, Murut (see page 479), Melanau, Bidayuh, Kenyah, Kayan, Kelabit and Penan. In upriver Dayak communities, both men and women traditionally distend their earlobes with brass weights – long earlobes are considered a beauty feature – and practise extensive body tattooing. For the longhouse communities, the staple diet is hill rice, which is cultivated with slash-and-burn farming techniques.

Malay About half of Sarawak's 300,000-strong Malay community lives around the state capital; most of the other half lives in the Limbang Division, near Brunei. The Malays traditionally live near the coast, although today there are small communities far upriver. There are some old wooden Malay houses, with carved façades, in the kampongs along the banks of the Sarawak River in Kuching. In all Malay communities, the mosque is the centre of the village, but while their faith is important to them, the strictures of Islam are generally less rigorously enforced in Sarawak than on the peninsula. Of all the Malays in Malaysia, the Sarawak Malays are probably the most easy going. During the days of the White Rajahs, the Malays were recruited into government service, as they were on the Malay peninsula. They were renowned as good administrators and the men were mostly literate in Jawi script. Over the years there has been much intermarriage between the Malay and Melanau communities. Traditionally, the Malays were fishermen and farmers.

Chinese Hakka goldminers had already settled at Bau, upriver from Kuching, long before James Brooke arrived in 1839. Cantonese, Teochew and Hokkien merchants also set up in Kuching, but the Brookes did not warm to the Chinese community, believing the traders would exploit the Dayak communities if they were allowed to venture upriver. In the 1880s, however, Rajah Charles Brooke allowed the immigration of large numbers of Chinese – mainly Foochow – who settled in coastal towns like Sibu. Many became farmers and ran rubber smallholdings. The Sarawak government subsidized the immigrants for the first year. During the Brooke era, the only government-funded schools were for Malays and few tribal people ever received a formal education. The Chinese, however, set up and funded their own private schools and many attended Christian missionary schools, so they formed a relatively prosperous, educated élite. Now the Chinese comprise nearly a third of the state's population and are almost as numerous as the Iban; they are the middlemen, traders, shopkeepers, timber towkays (magnates) and express-boat owners.

Iban Sarawak's best known erstwhile headhunters make up nearly a third of the state's population and while some have moved to coastal towns for work, many remain in their traditional longhouses. But with Iban men now earning good money in the timber and oil industries, it is increasingly common to see longhouses bristling with television aerials, equipped with fridges, self-cleaning ovens and flush-toilets, and with Land Cruisers in the car park. Even modern longhouses retain the traditional features of gallery, verandah and doors. The Iban are an outgoing people and usually extend a warm welcome to visitors. Iban women are skilled weavers; even today a girl is not considered eligible until she has proven her skills at the loom by weaving a ceremonial textile, the *pua kumbu* (see page 394). The Ibans love to party, and during the harvest festival in June, visitors are particularly welcome to drink copious amounts of *tuak* (rice wine) and dance through the night.

The Iban are shifting cultivators who originated in the Kapuas River basin of West Kalimantan and migrated into Sarawak's Second Division in the early 16th century, settling along the Batang Lupar, Skrang and Saribas rivers. By the early 19th century, they had begun to spill into the Rejang River valley. It was this growing pressure on land as more and more migrants settled in the river valleys that led to fighting and headhunting (see page 388). Probably because they were shifting cultivators, the Iban remained in closely bonded family groups and were a classless society. Historian Mary Turnbull said "they retained their pioneer social organization of nuclear family groups living together in longhouses and did not evolve more sophisticated political institutions. Long-settled families acquired prestige, but the Ibans did not merge into tribes and had neither chiefs, rakyat class, nor slaves".

The Ibans joined local Malay chiefs and turned to piracy – which is how Europeans first came into contact with them. They were dubbed Sea Dayaks as a result – which is really a misnomer as they are an inland people. The name stuck, however, and in the eyes of Westerners, it distinguished them from Land Dayaks, who were the Bidayuh people from the Sarawak River area (see page 390). While Rajah James Brooke only won the Ibans' loyalty after he had crushed them in battle (see page 382), he had great admiration for them, and they bore no bitterness towards him. He once described them as "good-looking a set of men, or devils, as one could cast eye on. Their wiry and supple limbs might have been compared to the troops of wild horses that followed Mazeppa in his perilous flight." The Iban have a very easygoing attitude to love and sex, which is best explained in Redmond O'Hanlon's book *Into the Heart of Borneo*. Free love is the general rule among Iban communities which have not become evangelical Christians, although once married, the Iban divorce rate is low and they are monogamous.

Melanau The Melanau are a relaxed and humorous people. Rajah James Brooke, like generations of men before and after him, thought the Melanau girls particularly pretty. He said that they had "agreeable countenances, with the dark, rolling, open eye of the Italians, and nearly as fair as most of that race". The Melanau live along the coast between the Baram and Rejang rivers; originally they lived in magnificent communal houses built high off the ground, like the one that has been reconstructed at the Cultural Village in Kuching, but these have long since disappeared. The houses were designed to afford protection from incessant pirate raids (see page 382), for the Melanau were easy pickings, being coastal people. Their stilt-houses were often up to 12m off the ground. Today most Melanau live in Malay-style pile-houses facing the river. Hedda Morrison, in her classic 1957 book *Sarawak*, wrote: "As a result of living along the rivers in swamp country, the Melanaus are an exceptionally amphibious people. The children learn to swim almost before they can walk. Nearly all progress is by canoe, sometimes even to visit the house next door."

The traditional Melanau fishing boat is called a *barong*. Melanau fishermen employed a unique fishing technique. They would anchor palm leaves at sea as they discovered that shoals of fish would seek refuge under them. After rowing out to the leaves, one fisherman would dive off his *barong* and chase the fish into the nets which his colleague hung over the side. The Melanaus were also noted for their sago production – which they ate instead of rice. At Kuching's Cultural Village there is a demonstration of traditional sago production, showing how the starch-bearing pith is removed, mashed, dried and ground into flour. Most Melanau are now Muslim and have assimilated with the Malays through intermarriage. Originally, however, they were animists (animist Melanau are called Likaus) and were particularly famed for their elaborately carved **'sickness images'**, which represented the form of spirits which caused specific illnesses (see page 396).

Bidayuh In the 19th century, Sarawak's European community called the Bidayuh Land Dayaks, mainly to distinguish them from the Iban Sea Dayak pirates. The Bidayuh make up 8.4% of the population and are concentrated to the west of the Kuching area, towards the Kalimantan border. There are also related groups living in West Kalimantan. They were virtually saved from extinction by the White Rajahs. Because the Bidayuh were quiet, mild-mannered people, they were at the mercy of the Iban headhunters and the Brunei Malays who taxed and enslaved them. The Brookes afforded them protection from both groups.

Most live in modern longhouses and are dry rice farmers. Their traditional longhouses are exactly like Iban ones, but without the tanju verandah. The Bidayuh tribe comprises five sub-groups: the Jagoi, Biatah, Bukar-Sadong, Selakau and Lara, all of whom live in far West Sarawak. They are the state's best traditional plumbers, and are known for their ingenious gravity fed bamboo water-supply systems. They are bamboo specialists, making everything from cooking pots and utensils to finely

Tribal tattoos

Tattooing is practised by many indigenous groups in Borneo, but the most intricate designs are those of the upriver Orang Ulu tribes.

Designs vary from group to group and for different parts of the body. Circular designs are mostly used for the shoulder, chest or wrists, while stylized dragon-dogs (*aso*), scorpions and dragons are used on the thigh and, for the Iban, on the throat.

Tattoos can mean different things; for the man it is a symbol of bravery and for women, a good tattoo is a beauty feature. More elaborate designs often denote high social status in Orang Ulu communities – the Kayans, for example, reserved the *aso* design for the upper classes and slaves were barred from tattooing themselves at all. In these Orang Ulu groups, the women have the most impressive tattoos; the headman's daughter has her hands, arms and legs completely covered in a finely patterned tattoo.

Designs are first carved on a block of wood, which is then smeared with ink. The design is printed on the body and then punctured into the skin with needles dipped in ink, usually made from a mixture of sugar, water and soot. Rice is smeared over the inflamed area to prevent infection, but it usually swells up for some time.

carved musical instruments (see page 395) from it. Among other tribal groups, the Bidayuh are renowned for their rice wine and sugar cane toddy. Henry Keppel, who with Rajah James Brooke fought the Bidayuhs' dreaded enemies, the Sea Dayaks, described an evening spent with the Land Dayaks thus: "They ate and drank, and asked for everything, but stole nothing."

Orang Ulu The jungle, or upriver, people encompass a swathe of different small tribal groups. Orang Ulu longhouses are usually made of belian (ironwood) and are built to last. They are well known swordsmiths, forging lethal parangs from any piece of scrap metal they can lay their hands on. They are also very artistic people, are skilled carvers and painters and are famed for their beadwork – taking great care decorating even simple household utensils. Most Orang Ulu are plastered with traditional tattoos (see box, page 391).

Kenyah and Kayan These two closely related groups were the traditional rivals of the Ibans and were notorious for their warlike ways. Historian Robert Payne, in his history *The White Rajahs of Sarawak* described the Kayans of the upper Rejang as "a treacherous tribe, [who] like nothing better than putting out the eyes and cutting the throats of prisoners, or burning them alive". They probably originally migrated into Sarawak from the Apo Kayan district in East Kalimantan. Kenyah and Kayan raids on downriver people were greatly feared, but their power was broken by Charles Brooke, just before he became the second White Rajah, in 1863. The Kayans had retreated upstream above the Pelagus Rapids on the Rejang River (see page 346), to an area they considered out of reach from their Iban enemies. In 1862 they killed two government officers at Kanowit and went on a killing spree. Charles Brooke led 15,000 Ibans past the Pelagus Rapids, beyond Belaga and attacked the Kayans in their heartland. Many hundreds were killed. In November 1924, Rajah Vyner Brooke presided over a peace-making ceremony between the Orang Ulu and the Iban in Kapit (there is a photograph of the ceremony on display in the Kapit Museum).

The Kenyahs and Kayans in Sarawak live in pleasant upriver valleys and are settled rice farmers. They are very different from other tribal groups, have a completely different language (which has ancient Malayo-Polynesian roots) and are class-conscious, with a well-defined social hierarchy. Traditionally their society was composed of aristocrats, noblemen, commoners and slaves (who were snatched during raids on other tribes). One of the few things the Kayan and Kenyah have in common with other Dayak groups is the fact that they live in longhouses, although even these are of a different design, and are much more carefully constructed, in ironwood. Subgroups include the Kejamans, Skapans, Berawans and Sebops. Many have now been converted to Christianity.

In contrast to their belligerent history, the Kenyahs and Kayans are much more introverted than the Ibans; they are slow and deliberate in their ways, and are very artistic and musical. They are also renowned for their parties; visitors recovering from drinking *borak* rice beer have their faces covered in soot before being thrown in the river. This is to test the strength of the newly forged friendship with visitors, who are ill-advised to lose their sense of humour on such occasions.

Their artwork is made from wood, antlers, metal and beads. They use a lot of wooden statues and masks to scare evil spirits at the entrances to their homes.

Penan Perhaps Southeast Asia's only remaining true hunter-gatherers live mainly in the upper Rejang area and Limbang. They are nomads and are related, linguistically at least, to the Punan, former nomadic forest dwellers who are now settled in longhouses along the upper Rejang. The Malaysian government has long wanted the Penan to sedentarise too, but has had limited success in attracting them to expensive new longhouses. Groups of Penan hunter-gatherers still wander through the forest in groups to hunt wild pigs, birds and monkeys and search for sago palms from which they make their staple food, sago flour. The Penan are considered to be the jungle experts by all the other inland tribes. Because they live in the shade of the forest, their skin is relatively fair. They have a great affection for the coolness of the forest and until the 1960s were rarely seen by the outside world. For them sunlight is extremely unpleasant. They are broad and much more stocky than other river people and are extremely shy, having had little contact with the outside world. Most of their trade is conducted with remote Kayan, Kenyah and Kelabit longhouse communities on the edge of the forest.

In the eyes of the West, the Penan have emerged as the 'noble savages' of the late 20th century for their spirited defence of their lands against encroachment by logging companies. But it is not just recently that they have been cheated: they have long been the victims of other upriver tribes. A Penan, bringing baskets full of rotan to a Kenyah or Kayan longhouse to sell may end up exchanging his produce for one bullet or shotgun cartridge. In his way of thinking, a bullet will kill one wild boar which will last his family 10 days. In turn, the buyer knows he can sell the same rotan downstream for RM50-100. Penan still use the blowpipe for small game, but shotguns for wild pig. If they buy the shotgun cartridges for themselves, they have to exchange empties first. Some of their shotguns date back to the Second World War, when the British supplied them to upriver tribespeople to fight the Japanese. During the Brooke era, a large annual market would be held which both Chinese traders and Orang Ulu (including Penan) used to attend; the district officer would have to act as judge to ensure the Penan did not get cheated.

Those wishing to learn more about the Penan should refer to Denis Lau's *The Vanishing Nomads of Borneo* (Interstate Publishing, 1987). Lau has lived among the Penan and has photographed them for many years; his photographs appear in *Malaysia – Heart of Southeast Asia* (published by Archipelago Press, 1991).

Kelabit The Kelabits, who live in the highlands at the headwaters of the Baram River, are closely related to the Murut (see page 479) and the Lun Dayeh of Kalimantan. It was into Kelabit territory that Tom Harrisson parachuted with Allied Special Forces towards the end of the Second World War. The Kelabit Highlands around Bario were chosen because they were so remote. Of all the tribes in Sarawak, the Kelabits have the

The palang

One of the more exotic features of upriver sexuality is the *palang*, (penis pin), which is the versatile jungle version of the French tickler.

Traditionally, women suffer heavy weights being attached to their earlobes to enhance their sex appeal. In turn, men are expected to enhance their physical attributes and entertain their womenfolk by drilling a hole in their organs, into which they insert a range of items, aimed at heightening their partner's pleasure on the rattan mat.

Tom Harrisson, a former curator of the Sarawak Museum, was intrigued by the *palang*; some suspect his authority on the subject stemmed from first-hand experience. He wrote: "When the device is put into use, the owner adds whatever he prefers to elaborate and accentuate its intention. A lively range of objects can so be employed – from pigs' bristles and bamboo shavings to pieces of metal, seeds, beads and broken glass. The effect, of course, is to enlarge the diameter of the male organ inside the female."

It is said that many Dayak men, even today, have the tattoo man come and drill a hole in them as they stand in the river. As the practice has gone on for centuries, one can only assume that its continued popularity proves it is worth the agony.

sturdiest, strongest builds, which is usually ascribed to the cool and invigorating mountain climate. They are skilled hill-rice farmers and their fragrant Bario rice is prized throughout Sarawak. The climate also allows them to cultivate vegetables. Kelabit parties are also famed as boisterous occasions, and large quantities of *borak* rice beer are consumed – despite the fact that the majority of Kelabits have converted to Christianity. They are regarded as among the most hospitable people in Borneo.

Dance, drama and music

Dance

Dayak tribes are renowned for their singing and dancing, and the most famous is the hornbill dance. In her book *Sarawak*, Hedda Morrison wrote: "The Kayans are probably the originators of the stylized war dance which is now common among the Ibans but the girls are also extremely talented and graceful dancers. One of their most delightful dances is the hornbill dance, when they tie hornbill feathers to the ends of their fingers which accentuate their slow and graceful movements. For party purposes everyone in the longhouse joins in and parades up and down the communal room led by one or two musicians and a group of girls who sing." On these occasions, drink flows freely. With the Ibans, it is *tuak* (rice wine), with the Kayan and Kenyah it is *borak*, a bitter rice beer. After being entertained by dancers, a visitor is under compunction to drink a large glassful, before bursting into song and doing a dance routine themselves. The best guideline for visitors on how to handle such occasions is provided by Redmond O'Hanlon in his book *Into the Heart of Borneo*. The general rule of thumb is to be prepared to make an absolute fool of yourself, throwing all inhibition to the wind. This will immediately endear you to your hosts.

The most common dances in Sarawak are: Kanjet Ngeleput (Orang Ulu) dance performed in full warrior regalia, traditionally celebrating the return of a hunter or headhunters. Mengarang Menyak (Melanau) dance depicting the processing of sago from the cutting of the tree to the production of the sago pearls or pellets. Ngajat Bebunuh (Iban) war dance, performed in full battle dress and armed with sword and shield. Ngajat Induk (Iban) performed as a welcome dance for those visiting longhouses. Ngajat Lesong (Iban) dance of the lesong or mortar, performed during gawai. Tarian Kris (Malay) dance of the kris, the Malay dagger, which symbolizes power, courage and strength. Tarian Rajang Beuh (Bidayuh) dance performed after the harvesting season as entertainment for guests to the longhouse. Tarian Saga Lupa (Orang Ulu) performed by women to welcome guests to the longhouse, accompanied by the sape (see below). Ule Nugan (Orang Ulu) dance to the sound of the kerebo bulo, or bamboo slates. The music is designed to inspire the spirit of the paddy seeds to flourish. The male dancers hold a dibbling stick used in the planting of hill rice.

Music

Gongs range from the single large gong, the *tawak*, to the *engkerumong*, a set of small gongs, arranged on a horizontal rack, with five players. An *engkerumong* ensemble usually involves five to seven drums, which include two suspended gongs (*tawak* and *bendai*) and five hour-glass drums (*ketebong*). They are used to celebrate victory in battle or to welcome home a successful headhunting expedition. Sarawak's Bidayuh also make a bamboo gong called a *pirunchong*. The *jatang uton* is a wooden xylophone which can be rolled up like a rope ladder; the keys are struck with hardwood sticks.

The Bidayuh, Sarawak's bamboo specialists, make two main stringed instruments: a three-stringed cylindrical bamboo harp called a *tinton* and the *rabup*, a rotan-stringed fiddle with a bamboo cup. The Orang Ulu (Kenyah and Kayan tribes) play a four-stringed guitar called a *sape*, which is also common on the Kalimantan side of the border. It is the most common and popular lute-type instrument, whose body, neck and board are cut from one piece of softwood. It is used in Orang Ulu dances and by witch doctors. It is usually played by two musicians, one keeping the rhythm, the other the melody. Traditional *sapes* had rotan strings, today they use wire guitar strings and electric pick-ups. Another stringed instrument, more usually found in Kalimantan, or deep in Sarawak's interior, is the *satang*, a bamboo tube with strings around the outside, cut from the bamboo and tightened with pegs.

One of the best known instruments is the *engkerurai* (or *keluri*), the bagpipes of Borneo, which is usually linked with the Kenyahs and Kayans, but is also found in Sabah (where it is called a *sompoton*). It is a hand-held organ in which four bamboo pan-pipes of different lengths are fixed to a gourd, which acts as the wind chamber. Simple *engkerurai* can only play one chord; more sophisticated ones allow the player to use two pipes for the melody, while the others provide an harmonic drone. The Bidayuh are specialists in bamboo instruments and make flutes of various sizes; big thick ones are called *branchi*, long ones with five holes are *kroto* and small ones are called *nchiyo*.

Crafts

Textiles

The weaving of cotton *pua kumbu* is one of the oldest Iban traditions, and literally means 'blanket' or 'cover'. Iban legend recounts that 24 generations ago the God of War, Singalang Burong, taught his son how to weave the most precious of all *pua*, the *lebor api*. Dyed deep red, this cloth was traditionally used to wrap heads taken in battle.

The weaving of *pua kumbu* is done by the women and is a vital skill for a would-be bride to acquire. There are two main methods employed in making and decorating pua kumbu: the more common is the ikat tie-dyeing technique, known as *ngebat* by the Iban. The other method is the *pileh*, or floating weft. The Ibans use a warp-beam loom which is tied to two posts, to which the threads are attached. There is a breast-beam at the weaving end, secured by a back strap to the weaver. A pedal, beneath the threads, lowers and raises the alternate threads which are separated by rods. The woven material is tightly packed by a beater. The material is tie-dyed in the warp.

Because the *pua kumbu* is made by the warp-tie-dyeing method, the number of colours is limited. The most common are a rich browny-brick-red colour and black, as well as the undyed white sections; blues and greens are used in more modern materials. Traditionally, *pua kumbu* were hung in longhouses during ceremonies and were used to cover images during rituals. The designs and patterns are representations of deities which figure in Iban myths and are believed to protect individuals from harm; they are passed down from generation to generation. Such designs, with deep spiritual significance, can only be woven by wives and daughters of chiefs. Other designs and patterns are representations of birds and animals, including hornbills, crocodiles, monitor lizards and shrimps, which are either associated with worship or are sources of food. Symbolic representations of trees, plants and fruits are also included in the designs as well as the events of everyday life. A typical example is the zigzag pattern which represents the act of crossing a river – the zigzag course is explained by the canoe's attempts to avoid strong currents. Many of the symbolic representations are highly stylized and can be difficult to pick out.

Malay women in Sarawak are traditionally renowned for their *kain songket*, sarongs woven with silver and gold thread.

Woodcarvings

Many of Sarawak's tribal groups are skilled carvers, producing everything from huge burial poles (like the Kejaman pole outside the Sarawak museum in Kuching) to small statues, masks and other decorative items and utensils. The Kenyah's traditional masks, which are used during festivals, are elaborately carved and often have large protruding eyes. Eyes are always emphasized, as they are to frighten the enemy. Other typical items carved by tribal groups include spoons, stools, doors, walking sticks, *sapes* (guitars), ceremonial shields, tops of water containers, tattoo plaques, and the hilts of *parang ilang* (ceremonial knives). The most popular Iban motif is the hornbill, which holds an honoured place in Iban folklore (see page 524), being the messenger for the sacred Brahminy kite, the ancestor of the Iban. Another famous Iban carving is the sacred measuring stick called the *tuntun peti*, used to trap deer and wild boar; it is carved to represent a forest spirit. The Kayan and Kenyahs' most common motif is the *aso*, a dragon-like dog with a long snout. It also has religious and mythical significance. The Kenyah and Kayan carve huge burial structures, (*salong*), as well as small ear pendants made of hornbill ivory. The elaborately carved masks used for their harvest ceremony are unique.

Bamboo carving

The Bidayuh ('Land Dayaks') are best known for their bamboo carving. The bamboo is usually carved in shallow relief and then stained with dye, which leaves a pattern in the areas which have been scraped out. The Bidayuh carve utilitarian objects as well as ceremonial shields, musical instruments and spirit images used to guard the longhouse. The Cultural Village (Kampong Budaya) in Kuching is one of the best places to see demonstrations of Bidayuh carving.

Blowpipes

Blowpipes are made by several Orang Ulu tribes in Sarawak and are usually carved from hardwood – normally belian (ironwood). The first step is to make a rough cylinder about 10 cm wide and 2.5m long. This rod is tied to a platform, from which a hole is bored through the rod. The bore is skilfully chiselled by an iron rod with a pointed end. The rod is then sanded down to about 5cm in diameter. Traditionally, the sanding was done using the rough underside of macaranga leaves. The darts are made from the nibong and wild sago palms and the poison itself is the sap of the upas (Ipoh) tree (Antiaris toxicari) into which the point is dipped.

Beadwork

Among many Kenyah, Kayan, Bidayuh, and Kelabit groups, beads have long been symbols of status and wealth; necklaces, skull caps and girdles are handed down from generation to generation. Smaller glass or plastic beads, usually imported from Europe, are used to decorate baby carriers, baskets, headbands, jackets, hats, sheaths for knives, tobacco boxes and handbags. Beaded baby carriers are mainly used by the Kelabit, Kenyah and Kayan and often have shells and animals' teeth attached which make a rattling sound to frighten away evil spirits. Rounded patterns require more skill than geometric patterns, the quality of the pattern used to reflect the status of the owner. Only upper-classes are permitted to have beadwork depicting 'high-class' motifs such as human faces or figures. Early beads were made from clay, metal, glass, bone or shell (the earliest have been found in the Niah Caves). Later on, many of the beads that found their way upriver were from Venice, Greece, India and China – even Roman and Alexandrian beads have made their way into Borneo's jungle. Orang Ulu traded them for jungle produce. Tribes attach different values to particular types of beads.

Sickness images

The coastal Melanau, who have now converted to Islam, but used to be animists, have a tradition of carving sickness images (*blum*). They are usually carved from sago or other soft woods. The image is believed to take the form of the evil spirit causing a specific illness. They are carved in different forms according to the ailment. The Melanau developed elaborate healing ceremonies; if someone was struck down by a serious illness, the spirit medium would perform the berayun ceremony, using the *blum* to extract the illness from the victim's body. Usually, the image is in a half-seated position, with the hands crossed across the part of the body which was affected. During the ceremony, the medium tries to draw the spirit from the sick person into the image, after which it is set adrift on a river in a tiny purpose-made boat or hidden in the jungle. These images are roughly carved and can, from time to time, be found in antique shops.

Basketry

A wide variety of household items are woven from rotan, bamboo, bemban reed as well as nipah and pandanus palms. Malaysia supplies 30% of the world's demand for *manau rotan* (rattan). Basketry is practised by nearly all the ethnic groups in Sarawak and they are among the most popular handicrafts in the state. A variety of baskets are made for harvesting, storing and winnowing paddy as well as for collecting and storing other items. The Penan are reputed to produce the finest rattan sleeping mats – closely plaited and pliable – as well as the *ajat* and *ambong* baskets (all-purpose jungle rucksacks, also produced by the Kayan and Kenyah). Many of the native patterns used in basketry are derived from Chinese patterns and take the form of geometrical shapes and stylized birds. The Bidayuh also make baskets from either rotan or sago bark strips. The most common Bidayuh basket is the *tambok*, which is simply patterned and has bands of colour; it also has thin wooden supports on each side.

Hats

The Melanau people living around Bintulu make a big colourful conical hat from nipah leaves called a *terindak*. Orang Ulu hats are wide-brimmed and are often decorated with beadwork or cloth appliqué. Kelabit and Lun Bawan women wear skullcaps made entirely of beads, which are heavy and extremely valuable.

Pottery

Malaysia's most distinctive ceramic designs are found in Sarawak where Iban potters reproduce shapes and patterns of Chinese porcelain which was originally brought to Borneo by traders centuries ago (see page 317). Copies of these old Chinese jars are mostly used for brewing *tuak* rice wine.

Sabah

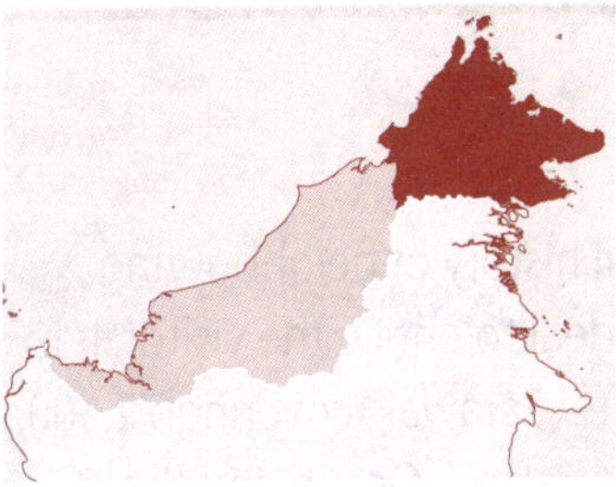

Footprint features

Introduction

Sabah may not have the colourful history of neighbouring Sarawak, but there is still a great deal to entice the visitor. It is second largest Malaysian state after Sarawak, covering 72,500 sq km, making it about the size of Ireland. Occupying the northeast corner of Borneo it is shaped like a dog's head, the jaws reaching out in the Sul and Celebes seas, and the back of the head facing onto the South China Sea.

The highlights of Sabah are natural and cultural, from caves, reefs, forests and mountains to tribal peoples. The Gunung Kinabulu National Park is named after Sabah's (and Malaysia's) highest peak and is one of the state's most popular destinations. Also popular is the Sepilok Orang-utan Rehabilitation Sanctuary outside Sandakan. Marine sights include the Turtle Islands National Park and Sipadan Island, one of Asia's finest dive sites. While Sabah's indigenous tribes were not cossetted in the way that they were in Sarawak by the White Rajahs, areas around towns such as Kudat, Tenom, Keningau and Kota Belud still provide memorable insights in the peoples of the area.

★ Don't miss ...

1. **Seafood** Have a beach bbq on the sands of Manukan Island off Kota Kinabalu, page 417.
2. **Rafflesia** Stroke the fleshy red petals of the world's largest, if stinky, flower at the Tambunan Rafflesia Reserve, page 422.
3. **Murut villages** Watch blowpipes being made while cheering the locals with *tapai* – a fiery cassava wine in kampongs around Tenom, page 424.
4. **Mount Kinabalu** Catch sunrise on the summit of Malaysia's tallest peak, page 440.
5. **Kinabatangan** A guided river cruise is your best chance to spot orang utans in the wild, page 454.
6. **Sipadan** Snorkel with turtles at this world class diving site, page 458.

Kota Kinabalu

→ *Colour map 4, grid B3 Population: 354,000*

KK is most people's introduction to Sabah for the simple reason that it is the only town with extensive air links to other parts of the country as well as with a handful of regional destinations. KK is a modern state capital with little that can be dated back more than 50 years. Highlights include the State Museum and the town's markets. Out of town, within a day's excursion, are beaches such as Tanjung Aru Beach and those near Tuaran, as well as a number of Kadazan and Bajau districts, with their distinctive markets. While it is necessary to go further afield to get a real view of tribal life, this is better than nothing.

The city is strung out along the coast, with jungle-clad hills as a backdrop. Two-thirds of the town is built on land reclaimed from the shallow Gaya Bay; and during the spring tides it is possible to walk across to Gaya Island. Jalan Pantai, or Beach Road, is now in the centre of town. Successive land reclamation projects have meant that many of the original stilt villages, such as Kampong Ayer, have been cut off from the sea and some now stand in stinking, stagnant lagoons. The government is cleaning up and reclaiming these areas and the inhabitants of the water villages are being rehoused. ▸▸ *For Sleeping, Eating and other listings, see pages 408-416.*

Ins and outs

Getting there

KK's airport is 5 km from town. There are connections with other towns in East Malaysia and the Peninsula as well as with various destinations in the Asian region. For buses into town, there is a bus stop 5-mins walk from the airport, RM1 to city centre. Taxis from the airport cost RM13.50 to the city centre. There is a limited railway line with trains to Beaufort and Tenom and an extensive network of bus, minibus and taxi links to destinations in Sabah. Ferries throughout the day for Labuan. Getting to Brunei overland takes around 5 hrs and 2 ferry crossings at Temburong and Terusan (in Brunei), or a 45-minute flight. ▸▸ *See Transport, page 414 for further details.*

Getting around

City buses and minibuses provide a service around town and to destinations in the vicinity of KK. The bus system is being overhauled and a temporary local bus station is now in front of the post office and next to the city park. Buses slightly further afield but still in the KK region leave from next to Plaza Wawasan, while long-distance buses wait in the scruffy carpark at the base of Signal Hill. Red taxis are unmetered, dark blue taxis have a meter. There is a good number of international and local car hire firms.

Tourist information

Sabah Tourism Board, ⓘ *51 Jln Gaya, T88-212121, www.sabahtourism.com, 0800-1700 Mon-Fri, 0800-1400 Sat (office is open every Sat unlike other states), closed Sun*. Sabah Tourism is well-stocked with leaflets and information and has very courteous and helpful staff. Great first point for help when arriving in KK. **Tourism Malaysia,** ⓘ *Ground Flr, Uni. Asia Building, 1 Jln Sagunting, T88-211732, mtpbki@tourism.gov.my* Not so useful for Sabah, but still does its best. A great tourist website for Sabah is at www.sabahtravelguide.com

Tours that are widely available include: Kota Belud tamu (Sunday market), Mount Kinabalu Park (including Poring Hot Springs), Sandakan's Sepilok Orang-utan Rehabilitation Centre, train trips to Tenom through the Padas Gorge and tours of the islands in the Tunku Abdul Rahman National Park. Several companies specialize in scuba-diving tours.

Parks offices All accommodation and trekking at Mount Kinabalu and Poring Hot Springs is now organised through **Sutera Sanctuary Lodges**, Ground Floor, Wisma Sabah, KK, T88-243629, www.suterasanctuarylodges.com. Open 0900-1830, Mon-Fri, 0900-1630 Sat, and 0900-1500 Sun. For Danum Valley and Maliau Basin, contact **Sabah Foundation**, Likas Bay, T88-326327, rosejkj@icsb-sabah.com.my. **Sabah Parks**, Lot 3, Block K, Sinsuran Complex, T88-211881, www.sabahparks.com

Best time to visit

Sabah's equatorial climate means that temperatures rarely exceed 32 degrees celsius or fall below 21 degrees, making it fairly pleasant year-round. However, October to March is the rainy season which pretty much spoils any plans for the beach and makes cimbing Mount Kinabalu or trekking in Sabah's national parks an unpleasant and slippery experience. If you plan on heading to the islands of the east coast to spot turtles, your best chance is between May and September. Sabah Fest, a big carnival of dancing, music and cow races when the Kadazun/Dusun celebrate their harvest festival takes place in May (see page 55).

History

Kota Kinabalu started life as a trading post in 1881 by the British North Borneo Charter Company under the directorship of William C Cowie, see page 445; not on the mainland, but on Gaya Island, opposite the present town, where a Filipino shanty town is today. On 9 July 1897 rebel leader Mat Salleh (see box on page 404),

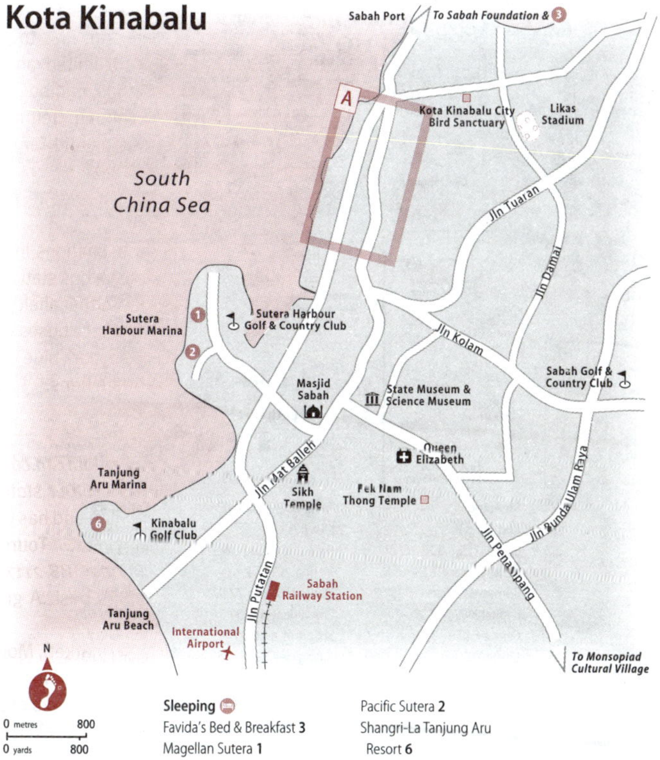

Kota Kinabalu centre

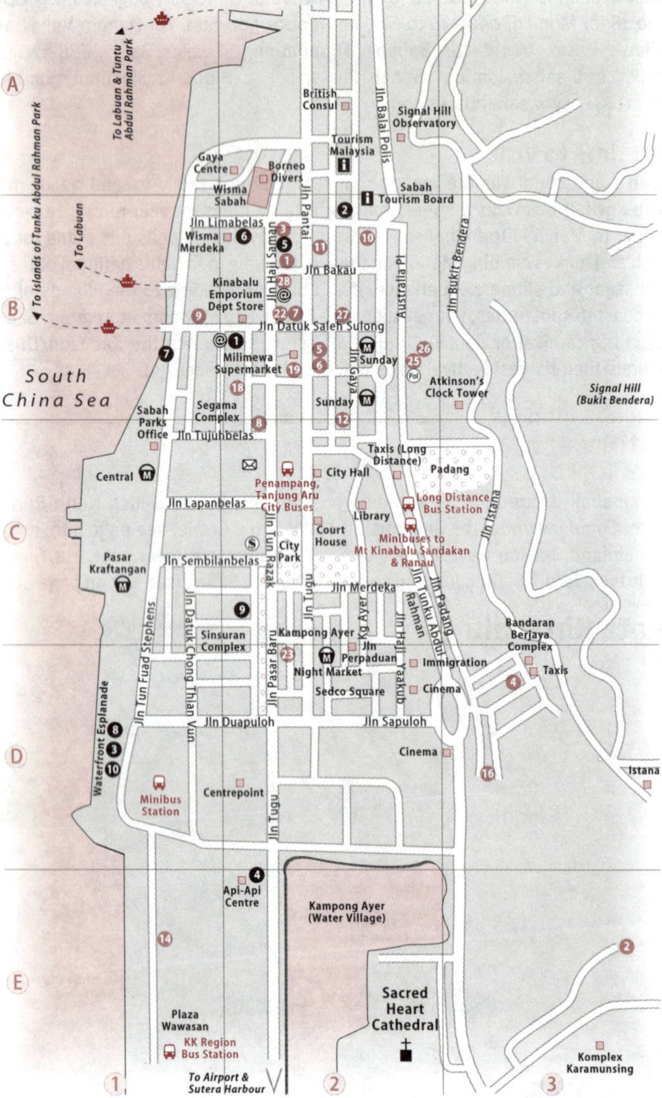

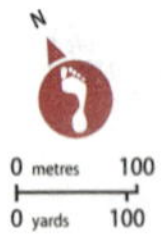

Sleeping
Ang's **1** *B2*
Beach Lodge **6** *B2*
Berjaya Palace **2** *E3*
Borneo Backpackers **25** *B2*
Capital **3** *B2*
Century **4** *D3*
City Inn **5** *B2*
High Street Inn **7** *B2*
Holiday **8** *C2*
Hyatt Regency **9** *B1*
Jesselton **10** *B2*
Kinabalu Daya **11** *B2*
KK **6** *B2*
Lucy's Homestay **26** *B2*
Mandarin **12** *C2*
Planet Kinabalu **27** *B2*
Promenade **14** *E1*
Shangri-L a **16** *D3*
Suang Hee **18** *B2*
Town Inn **19** *B2*
Trekkers Lodge **28** *B2*
Wah May **22** *B2*
Winner **23** *D2*

Eating
Aesha Corner **3** *D1*
Bilal **1** *B2*
Jothy's Curry **4** E2
Little Italy **5** *B2*
Merdeka **6** *B2*
Nan Xing **7** *B1*
Nishiki **2** *B2*
Penang Nyonya **10** D1
Portview **8** *D1*
Sri Sempelang **9** *C2*

who engaged in a series of hit-and-run raids against the British North Borneo Chartered Company's administration, landed on Pulau Gaya. His men looted and sacked the settlement and Gaya township was abandoned.

Two years later the Europeans established another township but this time located on the mainland, opposite Pulau Gaya, adjacent to a Bajau stilt village. The kampong was called 'Api Api' – meaning 'Fire! Fire!' – because it had been repeatedly torched by pirates over the years. After the Gaya experience, it was an inauspicious name. The Chartered Company rechristened it Jesselton, after Sir Charles Jessel, one of the company directors. However, for years, only the Europeans called it Jesselton; locals preferred the old name, and even today Sabahans sometimes refer to their state capital as 'Api'.

Jesselton owed its raison d'être to a plan that backfired. William C Cowie, formerly a gun-runner for the Sultan of Sulu, became managing director of the Chartered Company in 1894. He wanted to build a trans-Borneo railway and the narrow strip of land just north of Tanjung Aru and opposite Pulau Gaya, with its sheltered anchorage, was selected as a terminus.

Photographs in the Sabah State Museum chart the town's development from 1899, when work on the North Borneo Railway terminus began in earnest. By 1905, Jesselton was linked to Beaufort by a 92-km narrow-gauge track. By 1911 it had a population of 2,686, half of whom were Chinese and the remainder Kadazans and Dusuns; there were 33 European residents. Jesselton was of little importance in comparison to Sandakan, the capital of North Borneo.

When the Japanese Imperial Army invaded Borneo in 1942, Jesselton's harbour gave the town strategic significance and it was consequently completely flattened by the Allies during the Second World War. Jesselton followed Kudat and Sandakan as the administrative centre of North Borneo, at the end of the Second World War and the city was rebuilt from scratch. In September 1967 Jesselton was renamed Kota Kinabalu after the mountain; its name is usually shortened to KK.

Sights

Only three buildings remain of the old town: the old **General Post Office** on Jalan Gaya, **Atkinson's Clock Tower** (built in 1905 and named after Jesselton's first district officer) and the old red-roofed **Lands and Surveys building**. The renovated post office now houses the **Sabah Tourism Board.**

Masjid Sabah and Sabah State Museum

The golden dome of Masjid Sabah, on Jalan Tunku Abdul Rahman, is visible from most areas of town, although it is actually about 3 km out of town. Regular minibuses connect it with the town centre. Completed in 1975, it is the second biggest mosque in Malaysia and, like the Federal Mosque in Kuala Lumpur, a fine example of contemporary Islamic architecture. It can accommodate 5,000 worshippers.

Perched on a small hill overlooking the mosque is the relatively new purpose-built Sabah State Museum (and State Archives) ⓘ *on Jalan Mat Salleh/Bukit Istana Lama (Old Palace Hill), www.mzm.sabah.gov.my, 0900-1700 Sat-Thu, closed Fri. RM5, guided tours available; minibuses stop near Wisma Kewangan on the Kota Kinabalu - Tanjung Aru road and near Queen Elizabeth Hospital on the Kota Kinabalu – Penampang road, designed to resemble a Rungut longhouse. The museum is divided into ethnography, natural history, ceramics, history and archaeology. The ethnographic section includes an excellent exhibition on the uses of bamboo. Tribal brassware, silverware, musical instruments, basketry and pottery are also on display. On the same floor is a collection of costumes and artefacts from Sabah tribes like the Kadazan/Dusun, Bajau, Murut and Rungus.*

Mat Salleh – fort-builder and folk hero

Mat Salleh was a Bajau, and son of a Sulu Chief, born in the court of the Sultan of Sulu. He was the only native leader to stand up against the increasingly autocratic whims of the North Borneo government as it sequestrated land traditionally belonging to tribal chiefs. Under the British North Borneo Chartered Company and the subsequent colonial administration, generations of school children were taught that Mat Salleh was a rabble rouser and trouble maker. Now Sabahans regard him as a nationalist hero.

In the British North Borneo Herald of 16 February 1899, it was reported that when he spoke, flames leapt from his mouth; lightening flashed with each stroke of his parang (cutlass) and when he scattered rice, the grains became wasps. He was said to have been endowed with 'special knowledge' by the spirits of his ancestors and was also reported to have been able to throw a buffalo by its horns.

In 1897 Mat Salleh raided and set fire to the first British settlement on Pulau Gaya (off modern-day Kota Kinabalu). For this, and other acts of sabotage, he was declared an outlaw by the Governor. A price tag of 700 Straits dollars was put on his head and an administrative officer, Raffles Flint, was assigned the unenviable task of tracking him down. Flint failed to catch him and Mat Salleh gained a reputation as a military genius.

Finally, the managing director of the Chartered Company, Scottish adventurer and former gun-runner William C Cowie, struck a deal with Mat Salleh and promised that his people would be allowed to settle peacefully in Tambunan, which at that time was not under Chartered Company control.

Half the North Borneo administration resigned as they considered Cowie's concessions outrageous. With it looking less and less likely that the terms of his agreement with Cowie would be respected, Mat Salleh retreated to Tambunan where he started building his fort; he had already gained a fearsome reputation for these stockades. West Coast Resident G Hewett described it as "the most extraordinary place and without [our] guns it would have been absolutely impregnable". Rifle fire could not penetrate it and Hewett blasted 200 shells into the fort with no noticeable effect. The stone walls were 2.5 m thick and were surrounded by three bamboo fences, the ground in front of which was studded with row upon row of sharpened bamboo spikes. Hewett's party retreated having suffered four dead and nine wounded.

Mat Salleh had built similar forts all over Sabah, and the hearts of the protectorate's administrators must have sunk when they heard he was building one at Tambunan. A government expedition arrived in the Tambunan Valley on the last day of 1899. There was intensive fighting throughout January, with the government taking village after village, until at last, the North Borneo Constabulary came within 50 m of Mat Salleh's fort. Its water supply had been cut off and the fort had been shelled incessantly for 10 days. Mat Salleh was trapped. On 31 January 1900 he was killed by a stray bullet which hit him in the left temple.

One of the most interesting items in this collection is a *sininggazanak* – a sort of totem pole. If a Kadazan man died without an heir, it was the custom to erect a *sininggazanak* – a wooden statue supposedly resembling the deceased – on his land. There is also a collection of human skulls – called a *bangkaran* – which before the tribe's wholesale conversion to Christianity, would have been suspended from the rafters of Kadazan longhouses. Every five years a magang feast was held to appease the spirits of the skulls.

The museum's archaeological section contains a magnificently carved coffin found in a limestone cave in the Madai area. Upstairs, the natural history section, provides a good introduction to Sabah's flora and fauna. Next door is a collection of jars, called *pusaka*, which are tribal heirlooms. They were originally exchanged by the Chinese for jungle produce, such as beeswax, camphor and birds' nests.

Next door is the **Science Museum**, containing an exhibition on Shell's offshore activities. The **Art Gallery and Multivision Theatre**, within the same complex, are also worth a browse. The art gallery is small and mainly exhibits works by local artists; among the more interesting works on display are those of Suzie Mojikol, a Kadazan artist, Bakri Dani, who adapts Bajau designs and Philip Biji who specializes in burning Murut designs onto chunks of wood with a soldering iron. The ethnobotanical gardens are on the hillside below the museum complex. There is a cafeteria at the base of the main building.

Sabah has a large Christian population and the **Sacred Heart Cathedral** has a striking pyramidal roof which is clearly visible from the Sabah State Museum complex.

Viewpoints

Further into town and nearer the coast are a series of water villages, including **Kampong Ayer**, although its size has shrunk in recent years. **Signal Hill** (Bukit Bendera), just southeast of the central area, gives a panoramic view of the town and islands. In the past, the hill was used as a vantage point for signalling to ships approaching the harbour.

Likas Bay

There is an even better view of the coastline from the top of the **Sabah Foundation (Yayasan Sabah) Complex**, 4 km out of town, overlooking Likas Bay. This surreal glass sculpture has circular floors suspended on high-tensile steel rods and houses the Chief Minister's office. The Sabah Foundation was set up in 1966 to help improve Sabahans' quality of life. The foundation has a 972,800 ha timber concession, which it claims to manage on a sustainable-yield basis (achievement of a high level annual output without impairing the long-term productivity of the land). Two-thirds of this concession has already been logged. Profits from the timber go towards loans and scholarships for Sabahan students, funding the construction of hospitals and schools and supplying milk, textbooks and uniforms to school children. The Foundation also operates a 24-hour flying ambulance service to remote parts of the interior. See also www.ysnet.org.my

The fact that between the Yayasan Sabah and the core of the city is one of Borneo's largest squatter communities visibly demonstrates that not everyone is sharing equally in the timber boom.

Over in Likas Bay, is the new **Kota Kinabalu City Bird Sanctuary**, ⓘ *0800-1800 Tue-Sun, closed Mon, entrance fee RM10 adults, RM5 children*, a 24-hectare spread of mangrove forest with a 1 5-km boardwalk that snakes inside. Possible sightings include egrets, kingfishers, green pigeons, purple herons, plover and redshanks. A pair of binoculars is recommended.

Markets

Gaya street market is held every Sunday from 0800, selling a vast range of goods from jungle produce and handicrafts to pots and pans. The market almost opposite

The federal government has viewed the spread of Christianity in Sabah with some displeasure and there are financial incentives for anyone converting back to Islam.

 the main minibus station on Jalan Tun Fuad Stephens is known as the **Filipino market** (Pasar Kraftangan), as most of the stalls are run by Filipino immigrants. A variety of Filipino and local handicrafts are sold in the hundreds of cramped stalls, along winding alleyways which are strung with low-slung curtains of shells, baskets and bags. The Filipino market is a good place to buy cultured pearls (about RM5 each) and has everything from fake gemstones to camagong-wood salad bowls, fibre shirts and traditional Indonesian medicines. Further into town, on the waterfront, is the **central market** selling mainly fish, fruit and vegetables. The daily fishing catch is unloaded on the wharf near the market. There is a lively evening market selling cheap t-shirts and jewellery just in front of the City Park.

Tanjung Aru Beach

ⓘ *Take the Tanjung Aru (beach) bus from the station in front of City Hall.*

This is the best beach near KK, after those in Tunku Abdul Rahman National Park, and is close to Tanjung Aru Resort, 5 km south of KK (see page 410). It is particularly popular at weekends and there is a good open-air food court that looks onto the beach.

Penampang

ⓘ *Take a green and white Union Transport bus from just in front of City Hall.*

The old town of Donggongon, 13 kilometres southeast of KK, was demolished in the early 1980s and the new township built in 1982. The population is mainly Kadazan or Sino-Kadazan and about 90% Christian. The oldest church in Sabah, **St Michael's** Roman Catholic church, is on a steep hill on the far side of the new town. Turn left just before bridge – and after turn-off to the new town – through kampong and turn left again after school. It's a 20-minute walk; a granite building with a red roof. It was originally built in 1897 but is not dramatic to look at and has been much renovated over the years. Services are conducted in Kadazan but are fascinating to attend and visitors are warmly welcomed; hymns are sung in Kadazan and Malay. The social focus of the week is the **market** every Sunday.

There are many **megaliths** in the Penampang area which are thought to be associated with property claims, particularly when a landowner died without a direct heir. Some solitary stones, which can be seen standing in the middle of paddy fields, are more than 2 m tall. The age of the megaliths has not been determined. Wooden figures, called *sininggazanak* can also be seen in the ricefields (see page 404). Yun Chuan, Penampang New Town (also known as Donggongon Township), specializes in Kadazan dishes, such as *hinava* – or raw fish, the Kadazan equivalent of sushi. Tapai chicken is also recommended. See page for details on Kadazan cuisine.

The Monsopiad Cultural Village

ⓘ *From 0900-1700, daily. Cultural shows at 1100, 1400 and 1600, RM50. For more information, Borneo Legends and Myths (they manage the village), 5 km Ramaya/Putaton Rd, Penampang, T88-761336, mcv@tm.net.my; the house is hard to find; from new town take the main road east, past Shell station and turn right at sign to Jabatan Air; past St Aloysus Church, house on left about 1½ km from turn-off; minibus from Donggongon Township, 10 km south of KK, to Kampong Monsopaid. Take a bus to Donggongon Town and then change to bus for Monsopiad Cultural Village. Taxi from KK should be about RM20. For RM65 you can catch a shuttle bus from the Sutera Magellan and back, and get entrance to the village. Buses leave for the village at 0930 and 1400 on Mon, Wed, Fri and Sun, and 0900 and 1400 on Tue, Thu and Sat from Sutera Magellan.*

This is in Kampong Monsopiad (named after a fearsome Kadazan warrior-cum-headhunter – Siou do Mohoing, the so-called Hercules of Sabah) just outside Penampang. There are 42 fragile human skulls in the collection, some of which are said to be 300 years old and possess spiritual powers. They are laced together with leaves of the hisad palm, which represents the hair of the victims. For those who have already visited longhouses in Sarawak, this collection of skulls, in the rafters of an ordinary little kampong house overlooking the village and the Penampang River, is a bit of an anti-climax. But Dousia Moujing and his son Wennedy are very hospitable and know much about local history and culture. They preside over their ancestor's dreaded sword (although Wennedy reckons it's not the original, even though there are strands of human hair hanging off it). A three-day, three-night long feast is held at the house in May, in the run-up to the harvest festival. Visitors should remove footwear and not touch the skulls or disturb the rituals or ceremonies in progress. A reconstruction of the original Monsopiad main house gives the visitor an insight into the life and times of the warrior and his descendants. There is a good restaurant here serving traditional dishes; the *kadazandusun hinara* is recommended. It consists of fresh, sliced, raw fish marinated in lime juice and mixed with finely sliced chilli, garlic, gourd and shallots.

Tampuruli

ⓘ *Buses marked Tampuruli leave from the long-distance bus station at the bottom of Signal Hill.*

This popular stop for tour buses is 32 km north of KK at the junction of the roads north and east. It has a suspension bridge straddling the Tuaran River which was built by the British Army in 1922. There is a good handicraft shopping centre here.

Around Kota Kinabalu

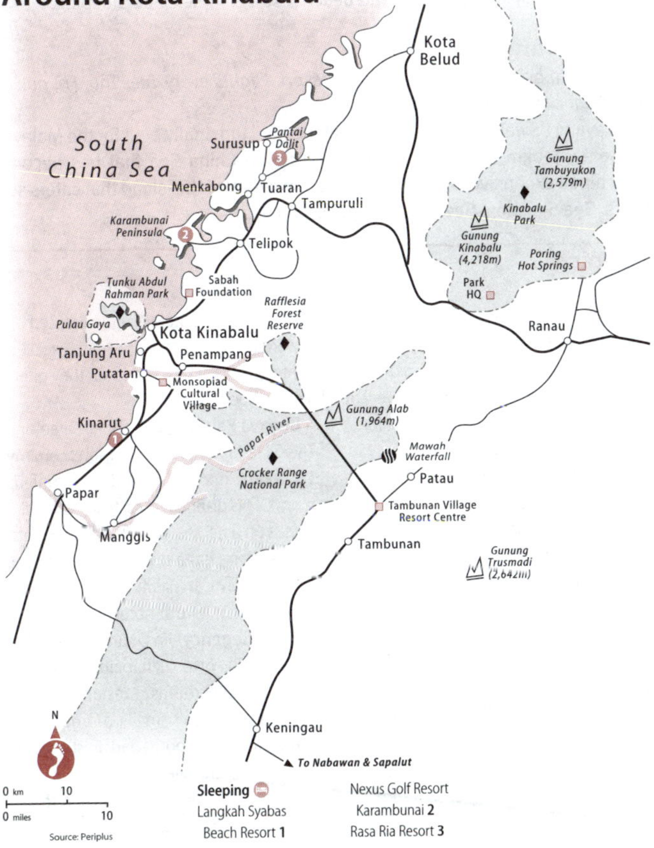

Mengkabong Water Village and Tuaran

ⓘ *Take a Tuaran marked bus from the long distance bus station at the foot of Signal Hill, then change to a local minibus to Mengkabong Water Village. Taxi would cost about RM30, or take a tour.*

This Baja, or sea gypsy, fishing stilt village is within easy reach of KK (see page 400) and is likened to an Asian Venice. The village is particularly photogenic in the early morning, before Mount Kinabalu – which serves as a dramatic backdrop, is obscured by cloud. The fishermen leave Mengkabong at high tide and arrive back with their catch at the next high tide. They use sampan canoes, hollowed out of a single tree-trunk, which are crafted in huts around the village. Some of the waterways and fields around Menkabong are choked by water hyacinth, an ornamental plant that was originally introduced by Chinese farmers as pig-fodder from South America.

For visitors wanting to escape the popular beaches close to KK, **Tuaran**, 45 minutes north of KK, offers a quieter alternative and is a good access point for several different destinations including Mengkabong.

Karam Bunai Beach

The nearby Karam Bunai Beach has a good picnic area, clean beach and sea. Close by is the Mimpian Jadi Resort, see Sleeping.

Karambunai Peninsula

The scenic Karambunai Peninsula 30 km north of KK has been transformed by a sprawling multi-million dollar golf and beach resort complex. See Sleeping.

Layang Layang

ⓘ *You need to book a flight through the resort. Flights every Tue, Thu, Fri, and Sun leaving KK at 0630, 1 hr, RM770.*

Layang Layang ('Swallow Reef') is a man-made atoll (originally built for the Malaysian navy), some 300km northwest of KK in the South China Sea that has become a famous, albeit expensive, dive site. There is one resort on the island that caters solely to divers. See Sleeping. See also Diving, Essentials.

Sleeping

Kota Kinabulu *p400, maps p401 and p402*
Well-heeled tourists will seek the more refined out-of-town resorts; but in KK itself, mid-range hotels have improved immeasurably in recent years. The best bets, offering good value for money, are those catering for itinerant Malaysian businessmen, such as the Mandarin Palace and Shangri-La.

AL **Sutera Harbour Resort**, www.suteraharbour.com/ 384-acre resort created out of reclaimed land which was previously the South China Sea, it lies to the south of the city centre. Opened in July 2000, the Harbour consists of 2 hotels, the **Magellan Sutera**, and the **Pacific Sutera**, 1 Sutera Harbour Boulevard, Sutera Harbour Resort, 88100 Kota Kinabalu, T88-318888. The Magellan Sutera offers the more relaxed resort, with much in the way of sporting activities, including 27 holes of golf and a spa. The Pacific Sutera is more focused towards businessmen, providing excellent conference facilities. Together, they offer almost 1,000 rooms.

A **Berjaya Palace**, 1 Jln Tangki, Karamunsing, T88-211911, www.berjayaresorts.com.my 160 rooms, pool, sauna and gym, conference rooms. This distinctive, castellated hotel stands on a hill south of KK. The proprietor James Sheng has a small resort, with chalets, on Pulau Gaya, at Maluham Bay, east of Police Bay, enquire at hotel.

A **Hyatt Regency**, Jln Datuk Salleh Sulong, T88-221134, http://kinabalu.regency.hyatt.com/ A/c, 288 rooms, 3 restaurants, pool and children's small pool, good central location, rooms vary in standard, business centre, live entertainment (*Shenanigan's Fun Pub*). Tours and treks organized. Good value.

A Jesselton, 69 Jln Gaya, T88-223333, www.jesseltonhotel.com The first hotel to open in KK, this classic hotel dates from 1954. With just 32 rooms, it was upgraded in the mid-1990s and is now considered KK's premier 'boutique'-style hotel. Old establishment, with everything from a London taxi to shoe-shining at your service.

A Langkah Syabas Beach Resort, Kinarut, 21km south of KK, T88-752000, lsr@po.jaring.my A resort with 16 detached and semi-detached chalets encircling the swimming pool, a/c, fans, TVs, tennis and riding centre close by, attractive garden.

A Promenade, 4 Lorong Api-Api 3, Api-Api Centre, T88-265555, www.promenade.com.my/ Attractive seafront position. Several restaurants, business facilities, gym with good range of equipment, pool.

B Capital, 23 Jln Haji Saman, T88-231999, F88-237222. A/c, TV, 102 rooms, coffee shop, central position. Newly renovated in 2004.

B Century, Jln Masjid Lama, T88-242222, F88-242929. A/c, 54 rooms, good seafood restaurant.

B Holiday, Block F, Segama Shopping Complex, off Jln Tun Razak, T88-213116, F88-215576. A/c, quite good with central location, but overpriced.

B Hotel Shangri-La, 75 Bandaran Berjaya, T88-212800, kkshang@po.jaring.my A/c, restaurant, not in the international Shangri-La group; reasonable hotel though and the haunt of business visitors.

B Kinabalu Daya, 9 Jln Pantai, T88-240000, F88-263909. 68 rooms, a/c, the top floor restaurant serves Asian and western food, seminar room. Breakfast included.

B Mandarin, 138 Jln Gaya, T88-225222, F88-225481. A/c, restaurant, marble floors, well-fitted rooms, excellent central location, friendly staff, 6th flr rooms with good view over town, deluxe and super-deluxe particularly spacious. Recommended.

C Ang's, 28 Lorong Bakau, off Jln Pantai, T88-234999, F88-217867. A/c, 35 rather threadbare rooms, try to get a room at the front with windows else you'll be stuck in a windowless box. Not bad value for money, rooms are clean and there's satellite TV but don't expect anything fancy. Central location.

C City Inn, 41 Jln Pantai, T88-218933, F88-218937. A/c, bathroom and TV; good for the price, often full.

C High Street Inn, 38 Jln Pantai, T88-218111, F88-219111. A/c, TV, in-house films, hot water, small but comfortable rooms – very typical of the characterless hotels in this price range.

C Suang Hee, Block F, 7 Segama Shopping Centre, T88-254168, F88-217234. A/c, restaurant, 24 rooms, clean Chinese hotel, reasonable value for money, a/c, TV and bathroom.

C Town Inn, 31-33 Jln Pantai, T88-225823, F88-217762. A/c, 24 rooms, clean with excellent facilities, central location, good for the price. Recommended.

C Wah May, 36 Jln Haji Saman, T88-266118, F88-266122. Modern Chinese hotel, 36 clean rooms kitted out with a/c, TV, fridge. Tight security with CCTV in operation.

C Winner, 9 & 10 Jln Pasar Baru, Kampong Ayer, T88-243222, F88-217345. A/c, 36 rooms, restaurant, pleasant, central hotel, friendly staff, good restaurant.

C-E Beach Lodge, 46 Jln Pantai, T88-213888, beach_lodge@hotmail.com Cute little guesthouse with friendly staff, if a little laid back (prime example of laid backness is second-in-command Razak!). Only has a handful of double rooms, all with shared hot water showers, so need to book ahead about a week in advance. Also two 8-bed dorms available. Breakfast included, and free airport pickup. Lots of tour info and little breakfast/lounge area. Very clean with tiled floors. Recommended.

C-E Farida's Bed & Breakfast, 413 Jln Saga, Mile 4.5 Jln Tuaran, Likas, T88-428733, www.homeaway.com.my/farida.htm. A friendly, whitewashed lodge with 12 rooms, from dorms to doubles with attached bathroom. They offer internet, kitchen, laundry and free breakfast. It's a 10-minute drive from KK to the B&B in Likas. They may be able to offer free pick-up, phone in advance, else take a Likas bus from Plaza Wawasan and get off before the mosque. It's a five minute walk from there. The place is run by Home Away from Home, a tour company.

C-E Trekkers Lodge, 30 Jln Haji Saman, T88-252263, www.trekkerslodge.com. Very popular place, so need to book ahead by several days to get a/c or fan double room. Rooms with attached bathroom are in the B category, not good value. Well set up for travellers with helpful staff, sitting-out area, library, tour information (they can do good deals with Borneo Divers). But because it's so popular it feels cramped and can get a bit grubby, particularly the dorms.

D **Borneo Backpackers**, 24 Lorong Dewan, at the foot of Signal Hill on the corner with the roundabout, T88-234 009, www.borneobackpackers.com. This is a new concept backpackers opened in Jan 2005 in a renovated three-storey building that dates back to the 1950s when it was used as a printing works. 50 beds, internet, laundry, lounge, roof garden, and tourist information. The ground floor houses a post war-era coffee shop stacked with war-time photos and antique-style furniture.

D **KK**, 46 Jln Pantai, 1st floor, T88-248587. Just two floors down from Beach Lodge, this place has cheap doubles with shared bathroom, but is not set up for travellers. There's no travel info or communal lounge, simply a cheap, basic place to stay if all the guesthouses are full.

D-E **Lucy's Homestay (Backpacker Lodge)**, Australia Pl, 25 Lorong Dewan, T88-261495, welcome.to/backpackerkk. Friendly, clean dorms and doubles with a good breakfast included in the room rate. In a quiet location near Signal Hill, this is the nicest and most relaxed of all the backpacker places. Lucy is friendly and offers tour info, simple kitchen, library and little balcony. Due to its popularity you will need to book some days in advance. Recommended.

E **Planet Kinabalu**, 98 & 100 Jln Gaya, T88-319168, planetkinabalu@hotmail.com. Dorm-only place well set up for travellers. Lots of facilities, smartcard entry, laundry, TV and VCDs, tour info and free breakfast at the Malay café downstairs (best free budget breakfast in KK). Nice, casual place.

Homestays in Sabah are now organised through **Nature Heritage Travel and Tours**, ground floor, Wisma Sabah, T88-318747, nhtt@nature-heritage.com

Tanjung Aru Beach *p406*

AL **Shangri-La Tanjung Aru Resort**, Tanjung Aru, T88-225800, www.shangri-la.com A/c, 500 rooms, pool, one of the best hotels in Sabah, although it is now in competition with its sister hotel the Rasa Ria at Tuaran. Tanjung Aru is a public beach, frequented by kite-flyers, swimmers, joggers, and lovers, the hotel is noticeably on the European honeymoon circuit. Recommended.

Mengkabong Water Village and Tuaran *p408*

AL **Rasa Ria Resort**, overlooking Pantai Dalit Beach, near Tuaran T88-792888, www.shangri-la.com/eng/hotel/23/ Top-class Shangri-La resort with 330 rooms, free-form pool, watersports, 18-hole golf course, driving range, spacious gardens, conference facilities, horse-riding cultural events, several restaurants including an Italian and a seafood beach-front restaurant, torch lighting ceremony, and 30 ha of forest nature reserve with semi-tame orang utans. There have been some complaints about the integrity of an orang utan fostering programme run by the resort and the cleanliness of the surrounding beach away from the resort. To get there, take a local bus to Tuaran. Recommended.

Karam Bunai Beach *p408*

A-B **Mimpian Jadi Resort**, No 1 Kuala Matinggi, Kampong Pulau, Simpangan, T88-787799, F88-787775. It has chalets, a private beach, watersports, fishing, mini zoo, karaoke bar, horseriding, volleyball, children's playground, Malay/Chinese and Western food. Getting there: take a bus to Menggatal, then change to a bus to Karam Bunai. Surusup is another 10-15 mins beyond Tuaran. Ask at the store in Surusup for Haji Abdul Saman, who will take visitors by boat to the lesser known Bajau fishing village, Kampong Penambawan, also likened to an Asian Venice, on the north bank of the river. Nearby there is a suspension bridge and rapids where it is possible to swim.

Karambunai Peninsula p408

LL-A **The Nexus Golf Resort Karambunai**, Menggatal, T88-411222, www.nexusresort.com The complex is built on 3,335 acres of land sprawling along the coast and has 490 ocean-view rooms, along with all the usual facilities including an 18-hole golf course, three swimming pools and a host of other sporting activities. It is popular for conferences and is patronised by businessmen from the region.

Layang Layang *p408*

AL Layang Layang Island Resort, T88-709121/141, www.layanglayang.com. This three-star resort has 76 rather plain rooms and 10 suites, with a movie room, swimming pool, bar and restaurant. Besides the resort the atoll is rather bleak with only an airstrip.

Eating

Kota Kinabulu *p400, maps p401 and p402*

The new waterfront has a whole range of restaurants with outdoor seating facing the South China Sea. Seafood is seasonally prone to red tide. Locals will know when it's prevalent. Avoid all shellfish if there is any suspicion.

Chinese

Hyatt Poolside Hawker Centre, Hyatt, Jln Datuk Saleh Sulong, steamboat (minimum 2 people).

Aesha Corner, Anjung Perdana (The Waterfront), Cheap Malay canteen facing the sea.

Avasi Cafeteria & Garden Restaurant, EG 11 Kompleks Kuwasa, steamboat and seafood.

Nan Xing, Jln Datuk Saleh Sulong, opposite the Hyatt and emporium, dim sum and Cantonese specialities.

Phoenix Court, Hyatt, Jln Datuk Saleh Sulong, dim sum, 0700-1400.

Sri Sempelang, Sinsuran 2 (on the corner with Jln Pasar Baru). Great Malay canteen with enormous fruit juices and tables outside. Locals recommend it.

Tioman, Lot 56 Bandaran Berjaya, good claypot and lemon chicken.

Malay

Copelia, Jln Gaya, *nasi lemak* for breakfast, also does takeaway.

Restoran Ali, Segama Complex, opposite Hyatt Hotel, best in a string of coffee shops, all of which are good value for money.

Nyonya

Penang Nyonya, Anjung Perdana (The Waterfront), Good, fair priced Nyonya dishes as spicey as you like.

Sri Melaka Restoran, 9 Jln Laiman Diki, Kampong Ayer (Sedco Complex, near Shiraz). Popular with the fashionable KK set, serves great Malay and Nonya food.

Other Asian cuisine

Jaws, 4th Flr, Gaya Centre, Jln Tun Fuad Stephens, Thai/Chinese cuisine, such as tom yam steamboat.

Nagisa, Hyatt, Jln Datuk Salleh Sulong, T88-221234. Fancy Japanese place with tables facing the South China Sea. Open kitchen, sushi bar, teppanyaki counters and a tatami room for the rich and private.

Nishiki, Jln Gaya (opposite Wing On Life Building), Japanese. Friendly staff and good-sized portions.

Bilal, Block B, Lot 1 Segama Complex, Indian Muslim food, rotis, chapatis, curries. Recommended.

Islamic Restoran, Kampong Ayer, the best roti in town.

Jothy's Curry Restaurant, Api-Api Centre. 1000-2200. Giant curries and banana leaf offerings.

Korean, Jln Bandaran Berjaya, next to *Asia Hotel*, large selection, barbecues are a speciality.

Shiraz, Lot 5, Block B, Sedco Square, Kampong Ayer, Indian. Recommended.

Sri Sakthi, Mile 4.5, Jln Penampeng (opposite Towering Heights Industrial Estate), South Indian banana-leaf – good value.

International

Fat Cat, Jln Haji Saman, cheap slap-up breakfasts.

Gardenia Grill Room, Jesselton Hotel, 69 Jln Gaya, T88-223333. Elegant dining.

Little Italy, Ground Flr, *Hotel Capital*, 23 Jln Haji Saman, T88-232231. Award-winning pizza and pasta place with Italian chef. If you're craving for some European food, this is the place to come. Open for lunch and dinner. Recommended.

Peppino, Tanjung Aru Beach Resort, T88-225800, tasty but expensive, Italian, good Filipino cover band.

Seafood

Garden Terrace, Tanjung Aru Beach Resort, T88-225800, 0600-2300. Asian and western buffet (dim sum available) and a la carte, with tables facing pretty gardens.

Kampong Nelayan Floating Seafood Market, Taman Tun Fuad, Bukit Padang, T88-269991. Popular with tour groups. Chinese and Malay dishes accompanied by traditional dancing.

Merdeka, 11th Flr, Wisma Merdeka, reasonably good seafood, but the view is better in this restaurant which offers 'karaoke at no extra charge'.

Port View, The Waterfront, T88-221753, huge selection of fresh seafood and delicious chilli crab. Massive clattering restaurant, very popular.

Seafood Market, Tanjung Aru Beach, T88-238313, pick your own fresh seafood and get advice on how to have it cooked.

Golf Field Seafood, 0858 Jln Ranca-Ranca (better known by taxi-drivers as *Ahban's Place*), excellent marine cuisine, local favourite. Recommended.

Foodstalls

Stalls above central market. **Sedco Square**, Kampong Ayer, large square filled with stalls, great atmosphere in the evenings, ubiquitous *ikan panggang* and satay. Night market on Jln Tugu, on the waterfront at the Sinsuran Food Centre and at the Merdeka Foodstall Centre, Wisma Merdeka. **Tanjung Aru Beach**, mainly seafood – recommended for *ikan panggang* – and satay stalls: very busy at weekends, but on weekdays it is rather quiet, with only a few stalls to choose from.

Bars and clubs

Kota Kinabalu *p400, maps p401 and p402*

Many of the more popular bars are along The Waterfront. Beach Street is a pedestrianised lane between Jln Pantai and Jln Gaya with restaurants and bars all with outdoor seating. **Shamrock Irish Bar** (there has to be an Irish bar!) has a Thursday ladies' night. A popular late-night club is **The Beach Club** at the end of The Waterfront, with a big dance floor, a bear theme, DJ, quite funky for KK. **Café Upperstar**, Segama Complex (opposite The Hyatt) has fried food and sandwiches, and jugs of long island ice teas for RM45. There's the rough and ready **BB Café Beach Street**, which has cheap beer, a pool table and closes at 0300.

Discos **Shennanigan's**, Hyatt Hotel, Jln Datuk Salleh Sulong, the smartest in town. **Next Door**, Tanjung Aru Beach Hotel. **Tiffiny**, Tanjung Aru, opposite Sacred Heart Church. **Rockies**, Promenade Hotel.

Karaoke Very popular in KK; found in Damai, Foh Sang and KK centre.

Entertainment

Kota Kinabalu *p400, maps p401 and p402*

Cinemas

Cinema in Centrepoint.

Cultural shows

Kadazan-Dusun Cultural Centre (Hongkod Koisaan), KDCA Building, Mile 4.5, Jln Penampang, restaurant open year-round, but at the end of May, during the harvest festival, the cultural association comes into its own, with dances, feasts and shows and lots of tapai (RM15). **Tanjung Aru Beach Hotel** on Wed and Sat, 2000. **Cultural Palace Theatre Restaurant**, Jln Tanjung Lipat, T88-251844, dance shows by Dusun-Kadazan, Bajaus and Muruts. Dinner and show RM42 (from 1845, closed Mon). Need a taxi to get here. Kampong Nelayan (see above) also has dance shows during dinner.

Festivals and events

Kota Kinabalu *p400, maps p401 and p402*

May **Magavau** (see page 55), a post-harvest celebration, carried out at Hongkod Koisaan (cultural centre). Mile 4.5, Jalan Penampang. To get there, take a green and white bus from the MPKK Building, next to state library.

Shopping

Kota Kinabalu *p400, maps p401 and p402*

Antiques

Good antiques shop at the bottom of the Chun Eng Building on Jln Tun Razak, a couple also on Jln Gaya. **Merdeka Complex** and **Wisma Wawasan 2020** hold a number of antique shops. It is necessary to have an export licence from the Sabah State Museum if you intend to export rare antiques.

Books

Arena Book Centre, Lot 2, Ground Floor, Block 1, Sinsuran Kompleks. **Borneo Books**, Wisma Merdeka, Eco-friendly books on Borneo. Wisma Merdeka is the best place to go for the widest range of books. **Borneo Crafts**, Ground Floor, Wisma Merdeka, T88-233757, selection of English language books and magazines. **Rahmant Bookstore**, Hyatt Hotel, Jln Datuk Salleh

Sulong. **Zenithway**, 29 Jln Pantai. Some English books and magazines, also stocks books by the Penguin publisher.

Clothes

The House of Borneo Vou'tique Lot 12A, First Flr, Lorong Bernam 3, Taman Saon Kiong, Jln Kolam, T88-268398, for that ethnic, exotic and exclusive look for men and women – corporate uniforms, souvenir items, tablecloths, cushion covers etc. **Centrepoint Mall** provides the biggest selection of 'designer' clothing.

Electronic goods

VCDs, DVDs and stereo equipment is considered the cheapest in the country here. Both **Karamunsing Complex** and **Centrepoint** are the places to go.

Handicrafts

Mainly baskets, mats, tribal clothing, beadwork and pottery. **Api Tours**, Lot 49, Bandaran Berjaya also has a small selection of handicrafts. **Borneo Gifts**, Ground Floor, Wisma Sabah. **Borneo Handicraft**, 1st Flr, Wisma Merdeka, local pottery and material made up into clothes. **Elegance Souvenir**, 1st Flr, Wisma Merdeka, lots of beads of local interest (another branch on Ground Floor of Centre Point). **Kaandaman Handicraft Centre** below Seafood Market Restaurant, Tanjung Aru Beach. **Kampong Air Night Market**, mainly Filipino handicrafts. **Kraftangan Kompleks/ Filipino Market**, Jln Tun Fuad Stephens (see page 405). **Malaysian Handicraft**, Cawangan Sabah, No 1, Lorong 14, Kg Sembulau, T88-234471, Mon-Sat 0815-1230 and Fri 0815-1600. **Sabah Art and Handicraft Centre**, 1st Flr, Block B, Segama Complex (opposite New Sabah Hotel). **Sabah Handicraft Centre**, Lot 49 Bandaran Berjaya (next to Shangri-La) good selection (also has branches at the museum and the airport). **The Crafts**, Lot AG10, Ground Floor, Wisma Merdeka, T88-252413. There are also several handicraft shops in the arcade at the Tanjung Aru Beach Hotel and one at the airport.

Jewellery

Most shops in Wisma Merdeka.

Shopping complexes

Kinabalu Emporium, Wisma Yakim, Jln Daruk Salleh Sulong is the main department store. **Likas Square**, Likas, pink monstrosity with 2 floors of shopping malls, foodstalls and restaurants. Cultural shows in central lobby. **Segama**, Jln Tun Fuad Stephens and **Sinsuran**. Beware of pickpocketing during the day and more particularly at night.

Activities and tours

Kota Kinabalu *p400, maps p401 and p402*

The sports complex at Likas is open to the general public. It provides volleyball, tennis, basketball, a gym, badminton, squash, aerobics and a swimming pool. To get there take a Likas-bound minibus from Plaza Wawasan. Likas Square, the monstrous pink shopping complex north of Likas Sports Complex, has a Recreation Club within it providing tennis, squash, jogging, golf, driving range, a pool and a children's playground.

Bowling

Merdeka Bowl, 11th Flr, Wisma Merdeka.

Diving

Do not believe dive shops when they say you must book diving through their KK office. It is cheaper to book your dive or dive courses through dive shops in Semporna. Snorkelling and scuba diving in Tunku Abdul Rahman National Park. Tour operators specializing in dive trips also organize dives all over Sabah, their offices are mostly in Wisma Sabah.

Golf

Green fees are considerably higher over the weekend – as much as double the weekday rate. Fees range from about RM50 during the week at the cheaper courses, to as much as RM200 or more over the weekend at flasher clubs. **Golf Booking Centre Malaysia** provides escorted golf tours, nbtt@tm.net.my Courses around KK include the **Sabah Golf and Country Club** at Bukit Padang, T88-247533, the oldest course in the state, this18-hole championship course affords magnificent views of Mt Kinabalu on clear days. **Sutera Harbour Golf & Country Club**, a 27 hole layout on reclaimed land just to south of the city. Great views across the to the islands of Tunku Abdul Rahman Park.

Horse riding

Kindawan Riding Centre, 21 km south of KK at Kinarut, www.kindawan.com. Call Dale Sinidal, an Australian who has run this school for over 10 years, T88-225525. There are trail rides of approximately two hours through villages and paddy fields or along the beach and across to an island at low tide. The surroundings are stunning and the horses are well kept and good tempered. It is RM50 for an hour. Call Ms Sinidal and she will organize transport from KK. For places to stay near Kinarut, see the Papar entry on page 418.

Roller blading Centre Point, 3rd Floor, Jln Gaya.

Sailing

Yacht club at Tanjung Aru, next to the hotel. **Watersports Tanjung Aru Marina**, snorkelling RM10 per day, water skiing RM120 per hr, fishing RM12-25 per day, sailing RM20-40 per hr, water scooter RM60 per hr.

Whitewater rafting

Papar River (Grades I & II), Kadamaian River (Grades II & III), Padas River (Grade IV). Usually requires a minimum of 3 people. Main operators including *Api Tours, Borneo Expeditions* and *Discovery Tours*.

Tour operators

The Sabah Tourism Board has a full list of tour agents operating in the state, and also on its website, www.sabahtourism.com **Adventure Journey World Travel**, Ground Floor, Lot 5, Block A, Taman Fortuna Shoplots, Jln Penampang, T88-223918, www.borneo.org **Api Tours** (Borneo), No 13 Jln Punai Dekut, Mile 5, Jln Tuaran, P O Box 12851, T88-424156, www.jaring.my/apitours Offers a wide variety of tours, including some more unusual ones such as overnight stays in longhouses. Recommended. **Borneo Divers**, Ground Floor, Wisma Sabag, T88-222227, www.borneodivers.info, operates exotic scuba diving trips all over Borneo including around Sipadan, has accommodation on Mamutik Island (Tunku Abdul Rahman). (see page 458), the company also has an office in Tawau T089761214. Dives trips are well organised but expensive, it's possible to bargain. Trekker's Lodge can sometimes help with good deals with this dive shop. **Borneo Eco Tours**, Lot 12A, 2nd Floor, Lorong Bernam 3, T88-234009, www.borneoecotours.com Adventure and culture tours, ecotourist specialists – their Sukau Rainforest Lodge on the Kinabatangan River is highly recommended. **Borneo Sea Adventures**, 1st Flr, 8a Karamunsing Warehouse, T88-230000, www.bornsea.com Also conducts scuba diving courses and runs diving and fishing trips all around Sabah. (see page 458). **Borneo Ultimate**, Ground floor, Wisma Sabah, www.borneoultimate.com. Hard adventure tours including whitewater rafting, mountain biking, jungle trekking, and sea kayaking. **Borneo Wildlife Adventures**, Lot F, 1st Floor, General Post Office Building, T88-213668, www.borneo-wildlife.com Specializing in nature tours, wildlife and cultural activities. **Diethelm Borneo Expeditions**, Suite 303, 2nd Floor, EON-CMG Life Building, 1 Jln Sagunting, T88-222271, T88-260353, dbex@tm.net.my **Discovery Tours**, Ground Floor, Wisma Sabah, Jln Haji Saman, T88-221244, www.infosabah.com.my/discovery/. Run by experienced tour operator Terry Lim. Recommended. **Exotic Borneo**, Likas Post Office, Likas, T88-245920, www.exborneo.com/ Organizes well-run theme tours including culture, adventure and nature, at a price. **Pan Borneo Tours & Travel**, 1st Floor, Lot 127, Wisma Sabah, T88-221221, www.jaring.my/panborn Sightseeing, diving, wildlife tours. **Sipadan Dive Centre**, 11th Flr, Wisma Merdeka, Jln Tun Razak, T88-240584, www.sipadandivers.com Experienced tour outfit, running dives and courses at Sipadan and Tunku Abdul Rahman Park. They also own the new Proboscis Lodge at Sukau. **Tanjung Aru Tours**, The Marina, Tanjung Aru Beach Hotel, T88-214215, F88-240966, Fishing and island tours – particularly to Tunku Abdul Rahman National Park.

Transport

Kota Kinabulu *p400, maps p401 and p402*

Air

The airport is 6 km from town, T88-238555. Air is the most widely used form of transportation between the major towns of Sabah (and it's cheap) (**Sandakan, Tawau,**

Lahad Datu). Taxi RM13.50- to town centre; coupon can be purchased in advance from the booths outside the arrivals hall. Regular connections with **KL**. There are also connections from KK with **Bintulu, Johor Bahru, Kuching, Labuan, Miri** and **Sibu**. International connections are with **Singapore, Brunei, Hong Kong, Philippines, South Korea, Japan**, various cities in China including **Shanghai** and **Taiwan**. AirAsia now have cheap fares between KK and Bangkok.

Airline offices AirAsia, Office on Jln Gaya, T88-438222. **British Airways**, Jln Haji Saman, T88-428057/428292. **Cathay Pacific**, Ground Floor, Block C, Lot CG, Kompleks Kuwasa, 49 Jln Karamunsing, T88-428733. **Dragonair**, T88-254733. **Garuda Airways**, Wisma Sabah. **MAS**, Ground Flr, Karamunsing Kompleks (off Jln Tunku Abdul Rahman, south of Kampong Ayer), Jln Kemajuan, T88-213555, F88-240135, also have an office at the airport. **Philippine Airlines**, 3rd Flr, Karamunsing Complex, Jln Kemajuan, T88-239600. **Qantas**, T88-216998. **Royal Brunei Airlines**, Ground Flr, Kompleks Kowasa, T88-242193, **Sabah Air**, KK Airport, T88-256733. **Singapore Airlines**, Ground Flr, Block C, Kompleks Kowasa, T88-255444. **Thai Airways**, T88-232896, Lot CG14, Block C, Ground Flr, Kompleks Kowasa.

Boat

There is a ferry service between KK and **Labuan** every day between 0800 and 1500, the journey takes two hours (RM31 one way). Ferries to **Serasa Muara** (Brunei) leave from the Labuan jetty between 0830 and 1630 (RM24), the trip takes one hour.

Bus

The bus system is being overhauled and a temporary local bus station is now in front of the post office and next to the city park. Buses slightly further afield but still in the KK region leave from next to Plaza Wawasan, while long-distance buses wait in the scruffy carpark at the base of Signal Hill. **Minibuses**: all minibuses have their destinations on the windscreen, most rides in town are less than RM1 and they will leave when full. You can get off wherever you like.

Buses around the state are cheaper than minibuses but not as regular or efficient. The large buses go mainly to destinations in and around KK itself.

Minibus and taxi There is no central bus station in KK. Taxis and minibuses bound north for **Kota Belud, Tamparuli** and **Kudat** and those going south to **Papar, Beaufort, Keningau** and **Tenom** leave from Bandar Berjaya opposite the Padang and clocktower. Taxis and minibuses going west to **Kinabalu National Park, Ranau** and **Sandakan** leave from Jln Tunku Abdul Rahman, next to the Padang and opposite the State Library. Tamparuli, a few kilometres east of Tuaran, serves as a mini-terminus for minibuses heading to **Kinabalu National Park**. Minibuses leave when full and those for long-distance destinations leave in the early morning. There are lots of bus companies and when you arrive at the bus station touts will try to get you to use their company. All the prices should be the same, and it's advisable to buy your ticket the day before. The time on the ticket is a rough guide only. Get there 10 mins before to guarantee your seat, but you may have to wait until the bus is full. Buses to **Tenom** (0800, 1200, 1600, RM16), **Keningau** (7 departures daily, RM12.15), **Beaufort** (more than 10 every day, RM7), **Tawau** (0730, 0800, RM45), **Sandakan** (0730, 0930, 1300, 2000, RM29.25), **Semporna** (0730, RM45), **Lahud Datu** (0730, RM13.50). Long-distance taxis also leave when full from in front of the clocktower on Jln Tunku Abdul Rahman. Minibus services from KK to **Tuaran** 45 mins, **Kota Belud** 2 hrs, **Kudat** 4-5 hrs, **Beaufort** 2-3 hrs, **Keningau** 2-3 hrs, **Tenom** 4 hrs, **Kinabalu National Park** 1½ hrs, **Ranau** 2 hrs, **Sandakan** 8-10 hrs.

Car hire

Not all roads in the interior of Sabah are paved and a 4WD vehicle is advisable for some journeys. However, car hire is expensive and ranges between RM30-80/hour. Rates often increase for use outside a 50 km radius of KK. All vehicles have to be returned to KK as there are no agency offices outside KK, although local car hire is usually available. Drivers must be between the ages of 22 and 60 and be in possession of an international driving licence. **ABAN-D Rent a Car**, Lot 22, 1st Flr, Taman Victory, Mile 4.5, Jln Penampang,

T88-722300, F88-721959. **Adaras Rent-a-Car**, Lot G03, Ground Floor, Wisma Sabah, T88-2166671, F88-216010. **Hertz**, Level 1, Lot 39, Kota Kinabalu airport, T88-317740. **Kinabalu Rent-a-Car**, Lot 3.61, 3rd Flr, Kompleks Karamunsing, T88-232602, F88-242512, www.kinabalurac.com/**Samzain Rent a Car**, Lot 10, Tingkat 2 Putatan Point, putatan 88200, Penampang, T88-765805.

Taxis

Red taxis are not metered, dark blue ones are not. There are taxi stands outside most of the bigger hotels and outside the General Post Office, the Segama complex, the Sinsuran complex, next to the DPKK building, the Milemewah supermarket, the Capitol cinema and in front of the clocktower (for taxis to **Ranau, Keningau** and **Kudat**). Approximate fares from town: RM10 to **Tanjung Aru Beach Resort**, RM10 **Sabah Foundation**, RM8 to the museum, RM14 airport.

Train

The station is 5 km out of town in Tanjung Aru. There is only one train line on Sabah, and rolling stock dates from the colonial era. Diesel trains run 3 times daily to **Beaufort**, 2 hrs and on to **Tenom**, a further 3 hrs. Departure times are subject to change, T88-254611. There is also a steam train which operates along this same line. For transport from the railway station to town: long distance buses stop near the station.

Directory

Kota Kinabalu *p400, maps p401 and p402*

Banks There are money changers in main shopping complexes. **HSBC**, 56 Jln Gaya. **Maybank**, Jln Kemajuan/ Jln Pantai. **Sabah Bank**, Wisma Tun Fuad Stephens, Jln Tuaran. **Standard Chartered**, 20 Jln Haji Saman. **Embassies and consulates** British **Consul**, Hong Kong Bank Building, 56 Jln Gaya. **Indonesian Consulate**, Jln Karamunsing, T88-428100. **Japanese Consulate**, Wisma Yakim, T88-428169. **Internet** **Touch Surf**, 1/F Segama Complex (opposite Burger King). Fast and cheap. 0900-0000, RM2 per hour. **City Internet Cafe**, Ground Floor, Centrepoint (entrance outside). Slow connection. There's also a traveller's internet café on Jln Pantai next door to Beach Lodge. **Medical facilities** One of the better private clinics is the **Damai Specialist Centre**. **Places of worship** St Simon's Catholic **Church**, Likas, Sun 1700, in English. **Stella Maris** (Tanjung Aru) Sun 0700 in English. **SIB**, Likas (Baptist), Sun 0800, in English. **Post** General Post Office Jln Tun Razak, Segama Quarter (poste restante facilities). **Telephone** Telekom Block C, Kompleks Kuwaus, Jln Tunku Abdul Rahman, international calls as well as local, fax service. **Useful addresses** Immigration 4th Flr Government Building, Jln Haji Yaakub. Visas can be renewed at this office, without having to leave the country.

West and South of Kota Kinabalu

West of KK is the Tunku Abdul Rahman Park, a reef and coral marine park. Travelling south from KK, the route crosses the Crocker Range to Tambunan. Continuing south the road passes through the logging town of Keningau and on to Tenom, where it is possible to take the North Borneo railway, which snakes down the Padas Gorge to Beaufort. The Padas River is the best place to go whitewater rafting in Sabah. Few towns are worth staying in for long on this route but it is a scenic journey.

Pulau Tiga National Park is a forest reserve where the pied hornbill can be spotted and Pulau Labuan is a tax-free haven off the coast. ▸▸ *For Sleeping, Eating and other listings, see pages 425-431.*

Tunku Abdul Rahman Park→ *Colour map 4, grid A3*

The five islands in Gaya Bay, which make up Tunku Abdul Rahman Park (TAR), lie 3-8 km offshore. Coral reefs fringe all the islands in the park. The best reefs are between **Pulau Sapi** and **Pulau Gaya**, although there is also reasonable coral around **Manukan**, **Mamutik** and **Sulug**. Named after Malaysia's first Prime Minister, they became Sabah's first national park in 1923 and were gazetted in 1974 in an effort to protect their coral reefs and sandy beaches. Geologically, the islands are part of the Crocker Range formation, but as sea levels rose after the last ice age, they became isolated from the massif. The islands can be visited all year round.

Ins ans outs

Getting there Boats for the park leave from the main ferry terminal 10 minutes walk north of the town. Ferries to Labuan also leave from here. There are also frequent boats from the Tanjung Aru Beach Resort.

Tourist information Park HQ is on Pulau Manukan; ranger stations on Gaya, Sapi and Mamutik.

Flora and fauna

Some of the only undisturbed coastal dipterocarp forest left in Sabah is on Pulau Gaya. On the other islands most of the original vegetation has been destroyed and established secondary vegetation predominates, such as ferns, orchids, palms, casuarina, coconut trees and tropical fruit trees. Mangrove forests can be found at two locations on Pulau Gaya. Animal and bird life includes long-tailed macaques, bearded pig and pangolin (on Pulau Gaya), white-bellied sea eagle, pied hornbill, green heron, sandpipers, flycatchers and sunbirds.

There is a magnificent range of marine life because of the variety of the reefs surrounding the islands. The coral reefs are teeming with fish-tank exotica such as butterfly fish, Moorish idols, parrot fish, bat fish, razor fish, lion fish and stone fish, in stark contrast to the areas which have been depth-charged by Gaya's notorious dynamite fishermen.

The islands

By far the largest island, **Pulau Gaya**, was the site of the first British North Borneo Chartered Company settlement in the area in 1882. The settlement lasted only 15 years before being destroyed in a pirate attack. There is still a large settlement on the island on the promontory facing KK – but today it is a shanty town, populated mainly by Filipino immigrants. On Pulau Gaya there are 20 km of marked trails including a plank-walk across a mangrove swamp and many beautiful, little, secluded bays. Police Bay is a popular, shaded beach. Gayana Island EcoResort is a big chalet development on the island with its own ferry from the KK jetty. **Pulau Sapi**, the most popular of the island group for weekenders, also has good beaches and trails. It is connected to Pulau Gaya at low tide by a sandbar. Good day use facilities but no accommodation available here, although there are camping facilities.

Pulau Mamutik is the smallest island but closer to the mainland and has a well-preserved reef off the northeast tip. **Pulau Manukan** is the site of the Park HQ and most of the park accommodation. It has good snorkelling to the south and east and a particularly good beach on the east tip. It is probably the best of all the islands but is heavily frequented by day trippers and rubbish is sometimes a problem. There is accommodation here, book through Sutera Sanctuary Lodges, see page 401. Marine sports facilities stretch to the hire of mask, snorkel and fins (RM15 plus RM50 deposit for the day), no sub-aqua gear available, swimming pool, watersports centre for sailing, banana boat, windsurfing etc. Glass-bottom boat trips available. Fish feeding off the jetty attracts large shoals of fish - it is possible to snorkel amongst them when this is going on. The best reefs are off **Pulau Sulug**, which is less developed being a little bit further away. This small island has a sand spit, making it good for swimming. There are dive facilities and a restaurant here now. You can also camp here.

Papar→ *Colour map 4, grid B3*

Formerly a sleepy Kadazan village, about 40 km south of KK, Papar is developing fast. In bandar lama (the old town) there are several rows of quaint wooden shophouses, painted blue and laid out along spacious boulevards lined with travellers' palms. There is a large market in the centre of town. The Papar area is famous for its fruit and there is a good tamu every Sunday.

There is a scenic drive between Papar and KK, with paddy fields and jungle lining the roadside. The nearby beach at Pantai Manis is good for swimming and can be reached easily from Papar. It is also possible to make boat trips up the Papar River, which offers gentle rapids for less-energetic whitewater-rafters. Whitewater rafting trips can be organized through tour agents in KK (see page 414).

The **Klias Wetlands** is a 'new' destination being promoted by Sabah Tourism, popular with visitors who do not have time to visit the east coast of Sabah. It provides the experience of taking a boat through a mangrove swamp. As boats take visitors down the Klias River, wildlife on offer include the proboscis monkey, long-tailed macaques, silver languor monkeys and an abundance of birdlife. ⓘ To get there, the Klias Peninsula lies 120 km south of KK. Trips down the Klias River depart from the Kota Klias jetty. Engaging a tour operator is recommended (Beringgis Marina and Tours, Comfort Paradise, Diethelm Borneo Expeditions or Suniland Travel and Tours, all in KK).

Pantai Manis, just outside Papar, is a 3-km long stretch of golden sand, with a deep lagoon.

Pulau Tiga National Park

Pulau Tiga National Park is 48 km south of KK. Declared a forest reserve in 1933, the 15,864 ha park is made up of three islands: Pulau Tiga, Kalampunian Damit and Kalampunian Besar.

Ins and outs

Getting there and around Either drive 140 km to Kuala Penyu (2 hrs, you can travel by minibus from KK to Beaufort and then change to another minibus for Kuala Penyu, each trip roughly RM7), at the tip of the Klias Peninsula and then take a 30- min boat ride (scheduled departure at 1000 and 1500 from Kuala Penyu), or charter a speedboat from KK; contact **Sipadan Dive Centre**, 11 floor, Wisma Merdeka, Jln TunRazak, KK, T88-240584 who run the island's resort, to organize transport to the island. Sabah Parks Office can help arrange the boat trip, or else contact Pulau Tiga Resort, see Sleeping. Speedboats cost RM350 for 10 people, but possible to bargain down to RM250 for the boat if less people.

Tourist information The Park HQ, on the south side of Pulau Tiga, is mainly used as a botanical and marine research centre and tourism is not vigorously promoted, as a result there are no special facilities for tourists. The best time to visit is between February and April, when it is slightly drier and the seas are calmer

National Park

Pulau Tiga has achieved notoriety as being the location for the reality TV series 'Survivor', chosen for its unspoilt natural landscape. Pulau Tiga's three low hills were all formed by mud volcanoes. The last big eruption was in 1941, which was heard 160 km away and covered the island in a layer of boiling mud. The dipterocarp forests on the islands are virtually untouched and they contain species not found on other west coast islands, such as a **poisonous amphibious sea snake** (*Laticauda colubrina*), which comes ashore on Pulau Kalampunian Damit to lay its eggs. Rare birds such as the **pied hornbill** (*Anthracoceros convexus*) and the **megapode** (*Megapodus freycinet*) are found here, as well as flying foxes, monitor lizards, wild fruit trees and mangrove forest. A network of trails, marked at 50 m intervals leads to various points of interest.

Pulau Labuan→ *Colour map 4, grid B2 Population: 80,000*

Labuan is one of the historically stranger pieces of the Malaysian jigsaw, and so it remains such. Originally part of the Sultanate of Brunei, the 92 sq km island, 8 km off the coast of Sabah, was ceded to the British in 1846 – who were enticed to take it on because of the discovery of rich coal deposits. It joined the Malaysian Federation in 1963, along with Sabah and Sarawak. In 1984 it was declared a tax-free haven – or an 'International Offshore Financial Centre' – and hence this small tropical island with just 80,000-odd inhabitants has a plethora of name plate banks and investment companies. For the casual visitor – rather than someone wanting to salt away their million but in somewhere other than Switzerland – it offers some attractions, but not many. There are good hotels, lots of duty-free shopping, a golf course, sport fishing and diving plus a handful of historic and cultural sights.

Ins and outs

Getting there From the airport, 5 km from town, there are flights to KK, Miri, Kuching and KL (both MAS and AirAsia have daily flights between KL and Labuan). By boat there are regular speedboats to KK and Menumbok (used by those who want to take their car onto Labuan, an hour's drive from KK) and several daily boat connections with Lawas and Limbang (Sarawak) and Sipitang. There's also a regular ferry service with Brunei.

Getting around There is a reasonable island bus network , a few car hire firms and a small number of taxis.

Tourist information **Tourist Information,** ⓘ *Lot 4260, Jln Dewan/Jln Berjaya, T87-423445*. For more information on Pulau Labuan go to www.labuantourism.com.my

History

With a superb, deep water harbour, Labuan promised an excellent location from which the British could engage the pirates which were terrorizing the Northwest Borneo coast. Labuan also had coal, which could be used to service steamships. Sarawak's Rajah James Brooke became the island's first governor in 1846. Two years later it was declared a free port. It also became a penal colony: long-sentence convicts from Hong Kong were put to work on the coal face and in the jungle, clearing roads. The island was little more than a malarial swamp and its inept colonial administration was perpetually plagued by fever and liver disorders. Its nine drunken civil servants provided a gold mine of eccentricity for the novelists Joseph Conrad and Somerset Maugham. In *The Outstation*, Maugham describes the desperate attempt by the resident Mr Warburton to keep a grip on civilization in the wilds of Malaysia: "The only concession he made to the climate was to wear a white dinner jacket; but otherwise, in a boiled shirt and high collar, silk socks and patent leather shoes, he dressed as formally as though he was dining at his club in Pall Mall. A careful host, he went into the dining room to see that the table was properly laid. It was gay with orchids, and the silver shone brightly... Mr Warbuton smiled his approval....".

By the 1880s ships were already bypassing the island and the tiny colony began to disintegrate. In 1881 William Hood Treacher moved the capital of the new territory of British North Borneo from Labuan to Kudat. And eight years later, the Chartered Company was asked to take over the administration of the island. In 1907 it became part of the Straits Settlements, along with Singapore, Malacca (Melaka) and Penang.

Modern Labuan

In 1946 Labuan became a part of British North Borneo and was later incorporated into Sabah as part of the Federation of Malaysia in 1963. Datuk Harris is thought to own half the island (including the Hotel Labuan). As Chief Minister, he offered the island as a gift to the federal government in 1984 in exchange for a government undertaking to bail out his industrial projects and build up the island's flagging economy. The election of a Christian government in Sabah in 1986 proved an embarrassment to then Prime Minister Doctor Mahathir Mohamad: making it Malaysia's only non-Muslim-ruled state. Labuan has assumed strategic importance as a Federal Territory, wedged between Sabah and Sarawak. It is used as a staging post for large garrisons of the Malaysian army, navy and air force.

In declaring Labuan a tax haven – or, more properly, an International Off-shore Financial Centre – the Malaysian government set out its vision of Labuan becoming the Bermuda of the Asia-Pacific for the 21st century; 4,065 off-shore firms had set up on the island by end-2003, and in 2000, the Labuan International Financial Exchange (LFX), a wholly owned subsidiary of the Kuala Lumpur Stock Exchange was established on the island. This, together with several five star hotels such as the Sheraton and the Waterfront, makes it seem that Labuan's days of being a sleepy rural backwater are over.

Port Victoria

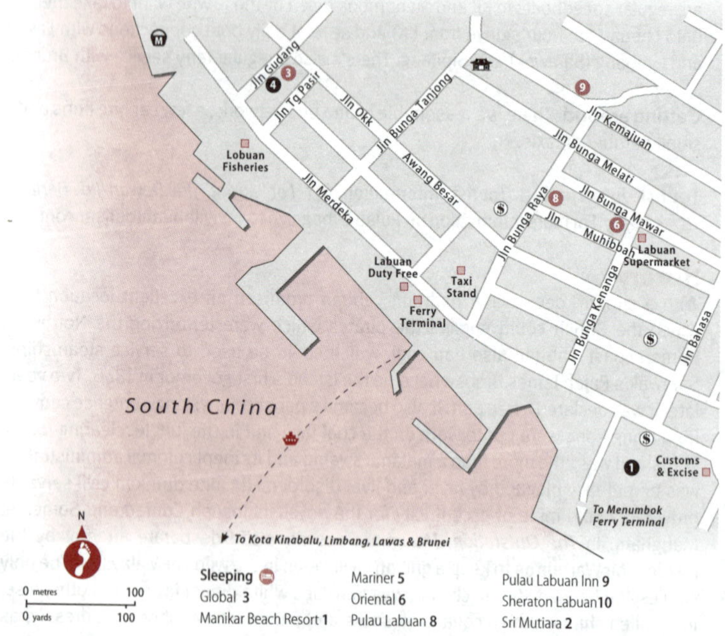

Included in the island's population of about 80,000 are 10,000 Filipino refugees, with about 21 different ethnic groups. The island is the centre of a booming 'barter' trade with the South Philippines; the island is home to a clutch of so-called string vest millionaires, who have grown rich on the trade. In Labuan, 'barter' is the name given to smuggling. The Filipino traders leaving the Philippines simply over-declare their exports (usually copra, hardwood, rotan and San Miguel beer) and under-declare the imports (Shogun jeeps, Japanese hi-fi and motorbikes), all ordered through duty-free Labuan. With such valuable cargoes, the traders are at the mercy of pirates in the South China Sea. To get round this, they arm themselves with M-16s, bazookas and shoulder-launched missiles. This ammunition is confiscated on their arrival in Labuan, stored in a marine police warehouse, and given back to them for the return trip.

Sights

Away from the busy barter jetty, Labuan Town, a name largely superseded by its name of Port Victoria, is a dozy, unremarkable Chinese-Malaysian mix of shophouses, coffee shops and karaoke bars. The **Labuan An'Nur Jamek State Mosque** is an impressive site, whilst the manicured **golf course** provides some light relief for tired businessmen. Illegal cockfights are staged every Sunday afternoon. There is an old brick **chimney** at Tanjung Kubong, believed to have been built as a ventilation shaft for the short-lived coal mining industry which was established by the British in 1947 to provide fuel for their steamships on the Far Eastern trade route. Remnants of the industry, which had petered out by 1911, are to be found in the shape of a maze of **tunnels** in this area. Near to Tanjung Kubong is a **Bird Park**.

On the west coast there are pleasant beaches, mostly lined with kampongs. There is a large **Japanese war memorial** on the east coast and a vast, well tended, **Allied war cemetery** between the town and the airport with over 3,000 graves, most of which are unknown soldiers. The **Peace Park** at Layang Layangan marks the Japanese surrender point on 9 September, 1945, which brought the Second World War to an end in Borneo.

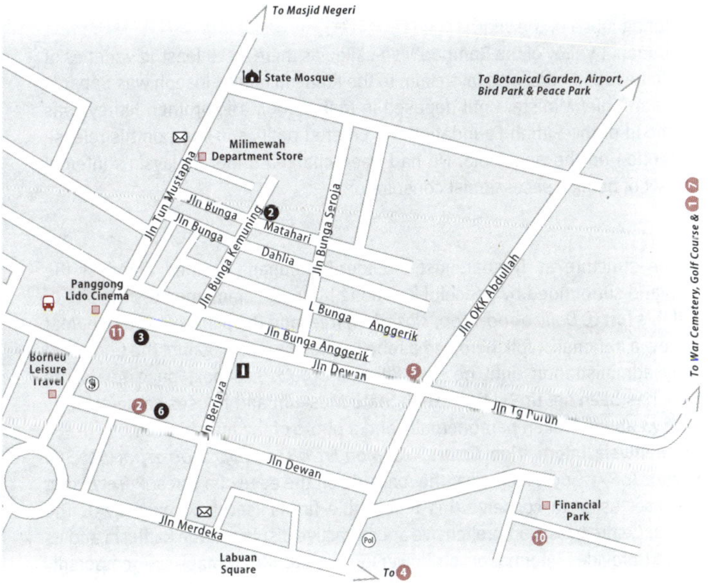

Tiara Labuan 7
Victoria 11
Waterfront Labuan Financial 4

Eating
Café Imperial 3
Foodstalls 1
New Sung Hwa Seafood 4
Seri Malindo 6
Wong Kee 2

Boat trips can be made to the small islands around Labuan, although only by chartering a fishing vessel. The main islands are Pulau Papan (a boring island between Labuan and the mainland), Pulau Kuraman, Pulau Rusukan Kecil (known locally as 'the floating lady' for obvious reasons) and Pulau Rusukan Besar ('floating man'). The latter three have good beaches and coral reefs but none has any facilities.

Off the south coast of the island is the **Marine Park**; a great place to dive, especially as there are four shipwrecks scattered in these waters. The park boasts 20 dive sites. See Activities and tours.

Tambunan→ *Colour map 4, grid B3 Population: 28,000*

The twisting mountain road that cuts across the **Crocker Range National Park** (see page 423) and over the Sinsuran Pass at 1,649 m is very beautiful. There are dramatic views down over Kota Kinabalu and the islands beyond and glimpses of Mount Kinabalu to the northeast. The road itself, from KK to Tambunan, was the old bridle way that linked the west coast to the interior. Inland communities traded their tobacco, rattan and other jungle produce for salt and iron at the coastal markets. The road passes through Penampang. Scattered farming communities raise hill rice, pineapples, bananas, mushrooms and other vegetables which are sold at road-side stalls, where wild and cultivated orchids can also be found. After descending from the hills the road enters the sprawling flood plain of Tambunan – the Pegalam River runs through the plain – which, at the height of the paddy season, is a magnificent patchwork of greens.

The Tambunan area is largely Kadazan/Dusun, Sabah's largest ethnic group, and the whole area explodes into life each May during the harvest festival when copious quantities of *lihing*, the famed local rice wine, are consumed and the Bobolians (high priestesses) are still called upon to conduct various rituals (see page 475). There is a *lihing* brewery inside the Tambunan Village Resort Centre. The Tambunan District covers an area of 134,540 ha. At an altitude of 650 m to 900 m, it enjoys a spring-like climate during much of the year.

Tambunan, ('Valley of the Bamboo'), so-called as there are at least 12 varieties of bamboo to be found here, also lays claim to the Kitingan family. Joseph was Sabah's first Christian Chief Minister until deposed in March 1994. His brother, Jeffrey, was formerly head of the Sabah Foundation. He entered politics in 1994 on his release from detention on the peninsula. He had been charged under Malaysia's Internal Security Act of being a secessionist conspirator.

Sights

A concrete structure at Tibabar, just outside Tambunan, situated amongst the ricefields and surrounded by peaceful kampong houses, commemorates the site of **Mat Salleh's fort** ⓘ *Daily 0900-1700, closed Fri, free*, and the place of his death. Mat Salleh, now a nationalist folk hero, led a rebellion for six years against the Chartered Company administration until he was killed in 1900 (see box, page 404). The memorial has been set up by the Sabah State Museum and houses some exhibits including weapons, Salleh paraphernalia and a photo of the man himself.

The Rafflesia Information Centre, ⓘ *Mon-Fri 0845-1245, 1400-1700, Sat-Sun 0800-1700, T087774691*, located at the roadside on the edge of a Forest Reserve that has been set aside to conserve this remarkable flower (see box, page 423). The Information Centre has a comprehensive and attractive display on the Rafflesia and its habitat and provides information on flowers in bloom. If trail maps are temporarily unavailable, ask the ranger to point out the site blooms seen on the large relief model of the Forest Reserve at the back of the Information Centre. The blooming period of the flower is very short so to avoid disappointment, it may be worth phoning the centre first.

Rafflesia: the largest flower in the world

The rafflesia (*Rafflesia arnoldi*), named after Stamford Raffles, the founder of modern Singapore, is the largest flower in the world. The Swedish naturalist Eric Mjoberg wrote in 1930 on seeing the flower: "The whole phenomenon seems so amazing, so unfamiliar, so fantastic, that we are tempted to explain: such flowers cannot be real!"

Stamford Raffles, who discovered the flower for Western science 100 years earlier during his first sojourn at Bengkulu on the west coast of Sumatra, noted that it was "a full yard across, weighs 15 pounds, and contains in the nectary no less than eight pints [of nectar]...". The problem is that the rafflesia does not flower for very long – only for a couple of weeks, usually between August and December. Out of these months there is usually nothing to see. The plant is in fact parasitic, so appropriately its scent is more akin to rotting meat than any perfume. Its natural habitat is moist, shaded areas.

Ahir Terjan Sensuron is a waterfall 4 km from Rafflesia Information Centre on the Tambunan-KK road (heading towards KK). From the road, it is a 45- minute walk to the waterfall. A large **market** is held here every Thursday morning – on sale are tobacco, local musical instruments, clothing, strange edible jungle ferns and yeast used to make fermented rice wine. There are also bundles of a fragrant herb known as *tuhau*, a member of the ginger family that is made into a spicy condiment or sambal redolent of the jungle. A smaller market is held every Sunday in Kampong Toboh, north of Tambunan.

Crocker Range National Park ⓘ *No visitors' facilities have yet been developed. To get there, see Transport below, as for Tambunan*, incorporates 139,919 ha of hill and montane forest, which includes many species endemic to Borneo. It is the largest single totally protected area in Sabah. Private development is taking place along the narrow strips of land each side of the KK-Tambunan road, which were unfortunately overlooked when the park was gazetted. The **Mawah Waterfall** is reached by following the road north towards Ranau to Kampong Patau, where a sign beside the school on the left indicates a gravel road leading almost to the waterfall (Mawah Airterjun). It is 15 minutes down the road by car and between five and ten minutes' walk along the trail.

Gunung Trusmadi, 2,642 m, 70 km southeast of KK, is the second highest mountain in Malaysia, but very few people climb it: the climb is difficult and facilities, compared with Gunung Kinabalu, few. There are two main routes to the top: the north route, which takes four days to the summit (and three days down) and the south route, which is harder but shorter; two days to the summit. Trusmadi is famous for its huge, and very rare, pitcher plant *Nepethes trusmadiensis*, which is only found on one spot on the summit ridge. It is also known for its fantastic view north, towards Gunung Kinabalu, which rises above the Tambunan Valley. There is a wide variety of vegetation on the mountain as it rises from dipterocarp primary jungle through oak montane forest with mossy forest near the summit and heath-like vegetation on top. An expedition to Trusmadi requires careful planning – it should not be undertaken casually. A more detailed account of the two routes can be found in *Mountains of Malaysia – A Practical Guide and Manual*, by John Briggs.

The best time to climb is in March and it is advisable to take guides and porters for the tough climb (ask the District Officer in Tambunan).

Keningau→ *Colour map 4, grid B3*

The Japanese built fortifications around their base in Keningau during the Second World War. It is now rather a depressing, shabby lumber town, smothered in smoke from the sawmills. The timber business in this area turned Keningau into a boom town in the 1980s and the population virtually doubled within a decade. The felling continues, but there is not much primary forest left these days. There are huge logging camps all around the town and the hills to the west. Logging roads lead into these hills off the Keningau-Tenom road which are accessible by four-wheel drive vehicles. It is just possible to drive across them to Papar, which is a magnificent route. Anyone attempting the drive should be warned to steer well clear of log-laden trucks on their way down the mountain.

Sapulut is deep in Murut country and is accessible from Keningau by a rough road via Kampong Nabawan (four-wheel drive required). At Sapulut, follow the river of the same name east through Bigor and Kampong Labang to Kampong Batu Punggul at the confluence of Sungai Palangan, a two-and-a-half-hour journey. **Batu Punggul** is a limestone outcrop protruding 200 m above the surrounding forest, 30-minutes' walk from the kampong; it can be climbed without any equipment, but with care. It is quite a dangerous climb, but there are plenty of handholds, and the view of the surrounding forest from the top is spectacular. Both the forest and the caves in and around Batu Punggul are worth exploring. Nearby is the less impressive, limestone outcrop, **Batu Tinahas**, which has huge caves with many unexplored passages. It is thought to have at least three levels of caves and tunnels. Some tour operators in KK offer trips out here.

Leeches can be a problem here, so take salt.

From Sapulut, it is a fairly painless exercise to cross the border into Kalimantan. A short stretch of road leads from Sapulut to Agis which is just a four-hour boat ride from the border. There is even an immigration checkpoint at Pegalungan, a settlement en route. One particular longhouse is **Kampong Selungai**, only 30 minutes from Pegalungan. Here it is possible to see traditional boat builders at work, as well as weaving, mat making and beadwork. There are many rivers and longhouses in the area worth exploring. Given the luxury of time, it is a fascinating area where traditional lifestyles have not been much eroded. It is possible to charter a minibus along the Nabawan road to Sapulut, where you can hire boats upriver. At Sapulut, ask for Lantir (the headman, or *kepala*). He will arrange the boat trip upriver, which could take up to two days depending on the river, and accommodation in Murut longhouses, through the gloriously named **Sapulut Adventurism Tourism Travel Company,** run by Lantir. As in neighbouring Sarawak, these long upriver trips can be prohibitively expensive unless you are in a decent-sized group.

Tenom→ *Colour map 4, grid B3*

Situated at the end of the North Borneo Railway, southwest of Keningau on the banks of the Sungei Lapas, Tenom is a hilly inland town, with a population of about 46,000, predominantly Chinese. Although it was the centre of an administrative district under the Chartered Company from the turn of the century, most of the modern town was built during the Japanese occupation in the Second World War. It is in the heart of Murut country, but do not expect to see longhouses and Murut in traditional costume; many Murut have moved into individual houses, except in the remoter parts of the interior, and their modernized bamboo houses are often well equipped.

The surrounding area is very fertile and the main crops here are soya beans, maize and a variety of vegetables. Cocoa is also widely grown. The cocoa trees are often obscured under shade trees called *pokok belindujan*, which have bright pink flowers. The durians from Tenom (and Beaufort) are reckoned to be the best in Sabah. Tamu (market) is on Sunday.

There are many **Murut villages**, ⓘ *Irregular minibuses to the Murut villages; catch a bus from Tenom heading for Kuela Tomani*, surrounding Tenom all with their own churches. In some villages there is also an over-sized mosque or surau. The Murut Cultural Centre lies 10 km out of town. Run by the Sabah Museum, it displays something of the material culture of the Murut people including basketry, cloth and the famous Murut trampolines of lansaran. The best local longhouses are along the Padas River towards Sarawak at Kampong Marais and Kampong Kalibatang where blowpipes are still made. At Kemabong, about 25 km south of Tenom, the Murut community, who are keen dancers, have a lansaran dancing trampoline; a wooden platform sprung with bamboo which can support about 10 Murut doing a jig.

Sabah Agricultural Park, ⓘ *0900-1630, Tue-Sun, closed Mon, RM25 adult, RM10 children*, 15 km northeast of Tenom, is an initiative developed by the Sabah State Government for research. This is also the site of Tenom's **orchid farm**, which has been developed into an agrotourism park.

Beaufort

→ *Colour map 4, grid B3*

This small, sleepy, unexciting town is named after British Governor P Beaufort of the North Borneo Company, who was a lawyer and was appointed to the post despite having no experience of the East or of administration. He was savaged by Sabahan historian KG Tregonning as "the most impotent Governor North Borneo ever acquired and who, in the manner of nonentities, had a town named after him." Beaufort is a quaint town, with riverside houses built on stilts to escape the constant flooding of the Padas River. The Tamu (market) is on Saturday.

Sipitang

Located on the coast, Sipitang is a sleepy town with little to offer the traveller apart from a supermarket and a few hotels. See Sleeping.

Sipitang is south of Beaufort and the closest town in Sabah to the **Sarawak border**. It is possible to take minibuses from Beaufort to Sipitang and on to Sindumin, where you can connect with buses bound for Lawas in Sarawak by walking across the border to Merapok. There is an immigration checkpoint here and month-long permits are given for visitors to Sarawak.

Sleeping

Tunku Abdul Rahman Park *p417*

Rooms are significantly discounted during the week.

A **Gayana Island EcoResort** , Lot 16, Ground Floor, Wisma Sabah, Jln Tun Razak, Pulau Gaya, T88-245150, www.gayana-ecoresort.com Set on the east coast of the island, 44 a/c chalets, restaurant (serves Asian and Western food, T88-245158), barbecue site, private beach, activities include diving, snorkelling, windsurfing, trekking in the jungle, fishing, yachting and a reef rehabilitation research centre. Some reports of dirty water around the resort from nearby shanty town.

A-B **Chalets**, Pulau Manukan, restaurant, pool, facilities including tennis and squash courts, football field, 1,500-m jogging track and a diving centre. Contact **Sutera Sanctuary Lodges**, ground floor, Wisma Sabah, T88-243629, www.suterasanctuarylodges.com for bookings on Manukan.

Camping It is possible to camp on any of the islands. Obtain permission from the Sabah Parks Office in KK, Lot 3, Block K, Sinsuran Complex, T88-211881, www.sabahparks.com. As the island gets packed with tourists during the day, if you camp you can enjoy a practically deserted island after 1700 when the rabble leaves.

Beware of leaving your clothing unattended at the edge of the forest, as monkeys have been known to run off with it!

Papar *p418*

A **KRK 'Mai Aman Country Rest House**, KM 35, off Old Papar Rd, Kinarut. T88-912580, verus@pc.jaring.my 6-room country resthouse and 12 room bush hostel. Luxurious place, with fishing on site in spacious grounds with an orchard.

B **Beringgis Beach Resort**, Km 26, Jln Papar, Kampong Beringgis, Kinarut, T88-752333, ketlee@bigfoot.com A/c, hot baths, car rental, conference halls, private beach, pool, watersports, tours and sports facilities.

B-E **SeaSide Travellers Inn**, Km 20 Papar-KK Highway, Kinarut, T88-750555, www.infosabah.com.my/seaside Restaurant, range of a/c or fan accommodation from dorm to detached bungalows, breakfast included, pleasant location off the beach. Tennis court, pool. Horse-riding and tours can be organized.

Pulau Tiga National Park *p418*

A-D **Pulau Tiga Resort**, T88-240584, www.pulau-tiga.com Wholly owned by Sipadan Dive Centre. There are standard chalets and more budget triples in a longhouse. As well as diving, the resort organizes watersports, treks, and trips to nearby islands. There's a games rooms, 'Survivor Bar' and a restaurant. There is also a hostel that can accommodate 32 people (RM30 per night). Accommodation must be booked in advance through the Sabah Parks Office in KK; there is also an attached canteen. It is also possible to camp.

Pulau Labuan *p 419, map p420*

There is plenty of choice here, but very little at budget lvel.

AL **Sheraton Labuan**, Lot TL 462, Jln Merdeka, T87-422000, www.sheraton.com/labuan Situated opposite the Financial Park complex, this deluxe city hotel has 183 rooms and suites all with spacious bathrooms, and all the trimmings you would expect. Other facilities include pool with whirlpool and swim-up bar, business centre (in-room personal computer also available). Decor has all the opulence of a Sheraton with a vast lobby, clad in marble and dripping with chandeliers, and classy food outlets including *Victoria's Brasserie* for European fare and *The Emperor Chinese Restaurant* which specializes in Cantonese food. Staff are professional and offer top service with a smile. Recommended.

A **Manikar Beach Resort**, Jln Batu Manikar, T87-418700, manikar@tm.net.my. On the northwest tip of Labuan, 20 mins from town centre (complimentary shuttle). A stylish resort built with polished wood (the owner is a timber tycoon), set in 15 ha of gardens, dotted with tall palms which reach down to the beach. The 250 rooms, all sea-facing with generous balconies, are very spacious, paved with stone, tastefully furnished, complete with a/c, mini-bar, TV, in-house video. Large pool set at sea level with swim-up bar, separate children's pool, fitness centre, tennis, play-room, business centre, duty-free shop. The beach is regularly cleaned and sprayed so sandflies are not a problem, but the sea is not recommended for swimming due to jellyfish. Restaurant with indoor and outdoor dining areas, excellent quality food, good value theme buffet nights.

A **Tiara Labuan**, Jln Tanjung Batu, T87-414300, F87-410195. On the west coast next to the golf course, 5-min taxi ride from town centre, beautiful hotel and serviced apartments surrounding a large lotus pond and deep blue pool complete with Jacuzzi. Built onto Adnan Kashoggi's old mansion, the property has an Italian feel with terracotta tiles, putty pink stone, a glorious gilt fountain, and long shady arcades. The original mansion now holds the reception, restaurant (food mediocre), and acres of opulent lounge including an Arab lounge which has low sofas, hubbly-bubbly pipes and a marble fountain. All 25 rooms, and also the 48 serviced apartments (1 or 2 bedroom) are complete with a/c, TV, mini-bar, ring electric hob, cooker hood and sink, and a living room. The Tanjung Batu beach, just across the road, is rather muddy, but good for walks when the tide is out. The *Labuan Beach Restaurant* is here too. On the whole, holiday makers opt for the larger hotels, especially families, as the Tiara has no organized activities or kiddy pool, but this is partly what makes it a haven of tranquillity. Recommended.

A Waterfront Labuan Financial Hotel, 1 Jln Wawasan, T87-418111, F87-413468. This property, overlooking the new yacht marina (and also an industrial seascape) has cultivated a marina-look combined with the atmosphere of being on a luxury cruise. It has over 200 rooms, all with a/c, mini-bar, TV and opulent fittings. The main restaurant, in seafaring spirit, called the *Clipper*, serves Western and local food, there is also a bar, the *Anchorage*, which has live entertainment nearly every evening. Other facilities include pool, tennis and health centre. The hotel also manages the marina with its total of 50 berthing spaces each of which has internationally rated facilities. The Harbour Master also organizes yacht charters and luxury cruises. Recommended.

B Sri Mutiara, Jln Dewan, T87-417811, F87-417996. Smart hotel, clean and reasonable, 39 rooms with a/c, attached bathroom, TV, in-house video and mini-bar.

B Global, U0017, Jln OKK Awang Besar (near market), T87-425201, F87-425180. Best value for money in town, a/c, mini-bar, TV, in-house video, complimentary shuttle to ferry and airport. Recommended.

B Mariner, Jln Tg Purun (on crossroads opposite police HQ), T87-418822, F87-418811. A/c, restaurant, rooms well-equipped (including mini fridge, a/c, TV, in-house video and attached bathroom), good coffee house. Generous discounts available on request.

B Oriental, U0123-4, Lot 33 and 34, Jln Bunga Mawar, T87-419019, F87-419408. Reception on first floor, clean, tiled rooms with a/c, TV, private bathroom.

B Pulau Labuan, 27-28 Jln Muhibbah, T87-416288, F87-416255. A/c, restaurant (Golden Palace Restaurant downstairs).

B-C Pulau Labuan Inn, Lot 8, Jln Bunga Dahlia, T87-416833, F87-441750. The downmarket sister of the Pulau Labuan, spotlessly clean but small a/c rooms.

C Federal Hotel, Jln Bunga Kesuma, T87-411711, F87-411337. A/c, restaurant, all rooms have a/c, TV, in-house video, mini-bar fridge, pink and pastels colour scheme, Chinese-run catering mainly for business people, clean, good value, run by same management as *Sri Mutiara*.

C Kelab Golf, Jln Tanjung Batu, a/c, restaurant, 6 simple but pleasant rooms in the clubhouse, 3 have a view down the manicured fairways.

C Victoria Hotel, Jln Tun Mustapha, T87-218511, F87-218077. One of the oldest hotels in Labuan, pale pink exterior with white stucco decorated lobby, 46 rooms, a/c, private bath. Recommended.

Tambunan *p422*

The area is renowned for its rice wine (lihing) – watch it being brewed at the TVRC factory

C Tambunan Village Resort Centre (TVRC), signposted off the main road before the town located on both sides of the Pegalam River, T88-774076, F88-774205. Collection of chalets and a 'longhouse' dormitory made of split bamboo. Restaurant, motel and entertainment centre (with karaoke and slot machines), hall and sports field. There are also a couple of retreat centres located about 10 mins' walk away.

C-E Gunung Emas Highlands Resort, Km 52 (about 7 km from the Rafflesia Centre). Also some dorm rooms, some very basic tree houses, a fresh climate and good views. Mini zoo and restaurant serving local food. To get there take the Rabunan or the Keningau minibus and then another bus from Tambunan.

Keningau *p424*

A-L Juta, T87-337888, www.sabah.com.my/juta
Marble lobbied business tower, deluxe rooms have mini bar and circular beds. Nice wooden theme throughout. Bar with live crooners and restaurant. Without a doubt, the swankiest pad in town.

B Hillview Garden Resort, PO Box 210, T87-333678 hillview@tm.net.my Newer place with 25 rooms. Good option.

B Perkasa, Jln Kampong Keningau, T88 331045, www.perkasahotel.com.my/. On the edge of town, a/c, Chinese restaurant, coffee house, health centre, comfortable rooms.

C Kristal Hotel, Pegalan Shopping Complex, T88-338888, F88-736134. Reasonable place, void of any real character, but a relatively

For an explanation of the sleeping and eating price codes used in this guide, see inside the front cover. Other relevant information is found in Essentials, pages 45-49.

cheap option in a town short on decent cheap accommodation.

Tenom *p424*

Orchid Hotel and Sri Jaya Hotel are both within walking distance of the bus stop.

AL-B **Perkasa**, top of the hill above the town, PO Box 225, T87-735811, F87-736134. A/c, restaurant, the *Tenom Perkasa* (one of a chain of three – the others are at Keningau and Ranau) is a large, modern hotel, 7 storeys high, commanding superb views over Tenom and surrounding countryside. Rooms are spacious, carpeted, attractively furnished, with a/c, en suite bathroom, TV. As guests are few and far between, the restaurant has a limited but well-priced selection of Chinese and Western dishes. Staff are friendly and helpful in organizing local sightseeing. Recommended.

C **Orchid Hotel**, Block K, Jln Tun Mustapha, T87-737600, excelng@tm.net.my Small but friendly with clean, well-maintained rooms.

D **Hotel Sri Jaya**, PO Box 47, T87-735007. The cheapest option, with 12 a/c rooms, shared bathroom, basic but clean.

C-D **Hotel Sri Perdana**, Lot 71, Jln Tun Mustapha, T87-734001, cheap, standard rooms.

E **Rumah Rehat Lagud Sebren (Orchid Research Station Resthouse)** is 5 km from the agricultural park and has a/c. Take a minibus from the main road and if driving, take the road over the railway tracks next to the station and head down the valley.

Beaufort *p425*

A poor selection of hotels, all roughly the same and slightly overpriced. Rooms are a/c and have bathrooms.

C **Beaufort Hotel**, Lot 19-20, Lochung Park, T87-211911, F87-212590. Centre of town, a/c, 25 rooms.

D **Mandarin Inn**, Lot 38, Jln Beaufort Jaya, T87-212800. A/c. Garners better reviews than the Beaufort.

Sipitang *p425*

B-C **Hotel Asanol**, T87-821506, offers value for money rooms with bathrooms.

B-C **Shangsan Hotel**, T88-821800, which has fairly comfortable rooms with a/c and TV. There is the ubiquitous coffee shop in the same street as the Shangsan.

Eating

Tunku Abdul Rahman Park *p417*

Excellent restaurant on Pulau Manukan. Pulau Mamutik and Pulau Sapi each have a small shop selling a limited range of very expensive food and drink, and Sapi has some hawker-style food. For Pulau Sulug, Sapi and Mamutik take all the water you need – there is no drinkable water supply here, shower and toilet water is only provided if there has been sufficient rain.

Papar *p418*

There are several run-of-the-mill coffee shops and restaurants in the old town.

† **Seri Takis**, Papar New Town (below the lodging house), Padang food

† **Sugar Buns Bakery**, old town. Sweet bread and thick coffee.

Pulau Labuan *p419, map p420*

Chinese

Several basic places to be found along Jln Merdeka and Jln OKK Awang Besar.

††† **The Emperor Chinese Restaurant**, Sheraton Labuan, top-class Chinese cuisine, Cantonese specialities, fresh seafood, special dim sum on Sun and public holidays. Recommended.

†† **Wong Kee**, Lot 5 and 6, Jln Kemuning, large, brightly lit restaurant with a/c, good steamboat. Recommended.

† **Café Imperial**, Chinese coffee shop behind Federal Hotel, better than average coffee shop fare.

International

†† **Country Deli Restaurant and Wine Bar**, Lot 25, Block D, Jati Commercial Centre, T87-410410. Malaysian pizza, take-aways possible.

†† **Labuan Beach**, Jln Tanjung Batu, T87-415611. International and local cuisine, breezy location on sea shore, food not special but ambience makes up for it, as does very well chilled draft Carlsberg. Recommended.

RR **The Clipper**, Waterfront Labuan Financial Hotel, 24-hour up-market coffee shop with local and Western cuisine. Recommended.

†† **Victoria's Brasserie**, Sheraton Labuan, European brasserie-style, good theme buffets as well as á la carte, prides itself on its 'show kitchen concept'. Recommended.

Malay

Restoran Zainab, Jln Merdeka (opposite duty-free shop), Indian/Muslim.
Seri Malindo, next to *Hotel Sri Mutiara*, mixture of Malay and Western food.

Seafood

Restaurant Pulau Labuan, Lot 27-28, Jln Muhibbah, smart interior complete with chandeliers, a/c, fresh fish sold by weight – good tiger prawn). Recommended.
New Sung Hwa Seafood, Jln Ujong Pasir, PCK Building, amongst best value seafood restaurants in Malaysia, chilli prawns, grilled stingray steak recommended, no menu. Recommended.

Foodstalls

Above wet market and at the other end of town, along the beach next to the Island Club. There is an area of stalls on Jln Muhibbah opposite the end of Jln Bahasa, west of the cinema and there are a few hawker stalls behind Hotel Labuan.

Keningau *p424*

Seri Wah Coffee Shop, on the corner of the central square and a selection of foodstalls.

Tenom *p424*

Jolly, near the station, serves Western food (including lamb chops) and karaoke.
Restaurant Curry Emas, specializes in monitor lizard claypot curries, dog meat and wild cat.
Restoran Chi Hin, another Chinese coffee shop.
Sabah, Jln Datuk Yaseen, Muslim Indian food, clean and friendly.
Sapong, Perkasa Hotel, local and Western.
Y&L (Young & Lovely) Food & Entertainment, Jln Sapong (2 km out of town), noisy but easily the best restaurant in Tenom. It serves mainly Chinese food: freshwater fish (steamed *sun hok* – also known as *ikan hantu*) and venison, these can be washed down with the local version of *air limau* (or *kitchai*) which comes with dried plums. There is a giant screen which was shipped in to allow Tenomese to enjoy the 1990 Football World Cup. Recommended.
Yong Lee Restaurant, coffee shop serving cheap Chinese fare in town centre.

Beaufort *p425*

Beaufort Bakery, behind Beaufort Hotel, "freshness with every bite".
Ching Chin Restaurant, Chinese coffee shop in town centre.
Jin Jin Restaurant, behind Beaufort Hotel, Chinese, popular with locals.

Shopping

Pulau Labuan *p419, map p420*

Duty free

If you plan to take duty-free goods into Sabah or Sarawak, you have to stay on Labuan for a minimum of 72 hrs. **Labuan Duty Free**, Bangunan Terminal, Jln Merdeka, T87-411573. This opened in Oct 1990, 142 years after Rajah James Brooke first declared Labuan a free port. The island's original duty-free concession did not include alcohol or cigarettes, but the new shop was given special dispensation to sell them. Two months later the government extended the privilege to all shops on the island, which explains the absurd existence of a duty-free shop on a duty-free island. The shop claims to be the cheapest duty-free in the world, however, you will find competitively priced shops in town too, including **Monegain**. It can undercut most other outlets on the island due to the volume of merchandise it turns over: more than RM1m a month. The shop owes its success to Filipino 'barter traders' who place bulk purchase orders for electronic goods or hundreds of thousands of dollars' worth of Champion cigarettes. These are smuggled back to Zamboanga and Jolo and find their way onto Manila's streets within a week. Brunei's alcohol-free citizens also keep the shop in business – they brought nearly RM2m-worth of liquor from Labuan into Brunei within the first 3 months of the shop opening. Behind Jln Merdeka and before the fish market, there is a congregation of corrugated tin-roofed shacks which houses a small Filipino textile and handicraft market and an interesting Wet market.

Supermarkets

Milimewah, Lot 22-27, Lazenda Commercial Centre, Phase II, Jln Tun Mustapha, department store with supermarket on ground floor. **Financial**

Park, Jln Merdeka, shopping complex with Milimewah supermarket. **Thye Ann Supermarket**, central position below Sri Mutiara. **Labuan Supermarket**, Jln Bunga Kenanga, centre of town.

Tambunan *p422*

Handicrafts

Handicraft Centre, just before the Shell petrol station, for traditional weaving and basketry from the area.

Market

Tamu on Thu.

Activities and tours

Pulau Labuan *p419, map p420*

Diving

There are at least 10 popular dive sites around the TAR islands, with reef depths ranging from 3-21 m, providing a great variety of dive experiences. It is possible to dive throughout the year with an average visibility of about 12 m. The water is cooler from Nov to Feb, when visibility is not as good. For extensive information on the various coral/fish/dive sites, contact Borneo Divers.

Fishing

Fishing with a hook and line is permitted but the use of spearguns and nets is not. Permits are not necessary.

Snorkelling

Snorkel, mask and fins can be rented from boatmen at the KK jetty beforehand (although snorkelling equipment is for hire on Sapi and Manukan).

Pulau Labuan *p419, map p420*

Diving

Borneo Divers, 1 Jln Wawasan, Waterfront Labuan Financial Hotel, T87-415867, www.borneodivers.info Specializes in 2-day packages diving on shipwrecks off Labuan for certified scuba divers, there are 4 wrecks in total, each wreck costs about RM100.

Golf

Kelab Golf, Jln Tanjung Batu, T87-421810. Magnificent 9-hole golf course. Visitors may be asked to see proof of handicap or a membership card from your own club. There are also tennis courts at the golf club and a swimming pool which can be used by visitors for a modest fee.

Horse riding

Labuan Horse Riding Centre, T87-466828. for a different way to sightsee. It offers beach and paddock rides plus lessons.

Sipitang *p425*

Tour operators

Sipitang Tours & Services, Lot 5, Tingkat 1, Kedai SEDCO, T6013-8691570, T6019-8809492.

Transport

Tunku Abdul Rahman Park *p417*

Boat

All boats leave from the main jetty 10 mins walk north of town. Small boats carry six people and will leave to any of the islands (RM15 per person fixed price) when full, but everyone needs to agree to a destination and a return time. It will cost an extra RM10 if you want to return the next day. There's a regular service for **Gayana** between 0800 and 2300, roughly every two hours, RM10 return fare), 38 km. If you want to visit more than 1 island, a boat needs to be chartered, at a cost of about RM280 for a 3 island tour or RM360 for a 5 island tour, taking 12 passengers. It is possible to negotiate trips with local fishermen. Boats also leave from Tanjung Aru Beach Hotel.

Papar *p418*

Minibus

Leaves from Bandar Lama area. Regular connections with **KK**, 1 hr, **Beaufort**, 1 hr.

Pulau Labuan *p419, map p420*

Air

The airport is 5 km from town. Regular connections with **KK**, **Miri**, **Kuching** and **Kuala Lumpur**.

Airline offices MAS, airport, T87-412263. AirAsia, c/o HMD Tours & Travel, T87-416117.

Boat

From the Bangunan Terminal Feri Penumpang next to the duty-free shop on

Jln Merdeka. All times are subject to change, tickets are sold at arrival points at the ferry terminal, but can be bought in town at **Duta Muhibbah Agency** , T87-413827. Two connections a day with **Menumbok** (RM10, the nearest mainland point) by speedboat (30 minutes) or car ferry. It's a 2-hr bus ride from here to **KK**. At present there are 7 boats a day to **Kota Kinabalu**, 2½ hrs, RM31, first boat at 0830, last boat at 1500. There are two daily boats to **Limbang** at 1230 and 1400 (1 ½ hours, RM20) and one to **Lawas** (both Sarawak), at 1230 (1 ½ hours, RM20).

To Brunei: on weekends and public holidays in Brunei the ferries are packed out and it is a scramble to get a ticket. It is possible to reserve tickets to Brunei at the following agents: **Victoria Agency House**, T87-412332, (next to the Federal Hotel in Wisma Kee Chia), **Borneo Leisure Travel**, T87-410251, F87-419989 (opposite Standard Chartered) and the booking office at the back of the Sports Toto on Jln Merdeka all deal with advanced bookings to Brunei. 7 boats leave Labuan for Brunei (Serasa Muara) first departure at 0830, last one at 1630, 1½ hrs, RM24.

Bus
Local buses around the island leave from Jln Bunga Raya.

Car hire
Adaras Rent-a-Car, T87-421590. **Travel Rent-a-Car**, T87-423600.

Taxi
Old Singapore NTUC cabs are not in abundant supply, but easy enough to get at the airport and around hotels. It is impossible to get a taxi after 1900 but minibuses abound.

Tambunan *p422*

Minibus
Buses marked Tabunan go from the long distance bus station at the bottom of Signal Hill in **KK** (1 ½ hours).

Taxi
To **KK** for RM100.

Keningau *p424*

Air Connections with **KK**.

Minibus Minibuses leave from the centre of town, by the market. Regular connections with **KK** and **Tenom**.

Taxi **KK** costs around RM180.

Tenom *p424*

Minibus
Minibuses leave from centre of town on Jln Padas. Regular connections with **Keningau** and **KK** 4 hrs. Minibuses to **Keningau** leave from rail station after a train has arrived.

Taxi
To **KK** costs around RM200 or shared taxis are available for a fraction of the price; they leave from the main street (Jln Padas).

Train
The journey through the **Padas River** gorge is particularly spectacular. Leaves 4 times a day and takes about 3 hrs to **Beaufort** and another 2½ hrs to **Tanjung Aru**, T87-735514.

Beaufort *p425*

Minibus
Minibuses meet the train, otherwise leave from centre of town. Regular connections with **KK**, 2 hrs.

Train
The KK-Tenom line passes through Beaufort: **Tenom**, 2½ hrs, **KK**, 3 hrs.

Sipitang *p425*

There is a line of minibuses and taxis along the waterfront. The jetty for ferries to **Labuan** (daily departures) is a 10-minute walk from the centre.

Directory

Beaufort *p425*

Banks HSBC & Standard Chartered in centre of town. **Post** General Post Office & Telekom, next to Hongkong Bank.

Pulau Labuan *p419, map p420*

Banks HSBC, Jln Merdeka. Standard Chartered, Jln Tanjung Kubang (next to Victoria Hotel). **Syarikat K Abdul Kader**, money changer. **Post** General Post Office Jln Merdeka.

North of Kota Kinabalu

From KK, the route heads north to the sleepy Bajau town of Kota Belud which wakes up on Sunday for its colourful tamu market (open-air trade fair). Near the northernmost tip of the state is Kudat, the former state capital. The region north of KK is a more interesting area with Gunung Kinabalu always in sight. From Kota Belud, the mountain looks completely different. It is possible to see its tail, sweeping away to the east and its western flanks, which rise out of the rolling coastal lowlands. ▸▸ *For Sleeping, Eating and other listings, see pages 434-435.*

Kota Belud → *Colour map 4, grid A3*

This busy little town is in a beautiful location, nestling in the foothills of Mount Kinabalu on the banks of the Tempasuk River, but has little to recommend it save its market. It is the heart of Bajau country – the so-called 'cowboys of the East' but is of little obvious interest to most tourists.

The first Bajau to migrate to Sabah were pushed into the interior, around Kota Belud. They were originally a seafaring people but then settled as farmers in this area. The famed Bajau horsemen wear jewelled costumes, carry spears and ride bareback on ceremonial occasions. The ceremonial headdresses worn by the horsemen, called dastars, are woven on backstrap looms by the womenfolk of Kota Belud. Each piece takes four to six weeks to complete. Traditionally, the points of the headdress were stiffened using wax; these days, strips of cardboard are inserted into the points.

The **largest market (tamu) in Sabah** is held every Sunday in Kota Belud behind the mosque, starting at 0600. A mix of races, Bajau, Kadazan/Dusun, Rungus, Chinese, Indian and Malay, come to sell their goods and it is a social occasion as much as it is a market. Aside from the wide variety of food and fresh produce on sale, there is a weekly water buffalo auction at the entrance to the tamu. Visitors are strongly recommended to get there early, but don't expect to find souvenirs at these markets. However the 'tamu besar', or big market, is held in November, when cultural performances take place and handicrafts are on sale.

This is the account of a civil servant, posted to the KB district office in 1915: "The tamu itself is a babel and buzz of excitement; in little groups the natives sit and spread their wares out on the ground before them; bananas, langsats, pines and bread-fruit; and, in season, that much beloved but foul-smelling fruit the Durian. Mats and straw-hats and ropes; fowls, ducks, goats and buffaloes; pepper, gambia sirih and vegetables; rice (padi), sweet potatoes, ubi kayu and indian-corn; dastars and handkerchiefs, silver and brassware. In little booths, made of wood, with open sides and floors of split bamboos and roofs of atap (sago palm-leaf) squat the Chinese traders along one side of the Tamu. For cash or barter they will sell; and many a wrangle, haggle and bargain is driven and fought before the goods change hands, or money parted with."

Tempasuk River, ⓘ *hire small fishing boats in town to go down the Tempasuk River (RM10 per hour)*, has a wide variety of migrating birds and is a proposed conservation area. More than 127 species of birds have been recorded along this area of the coastal plain and over half a million birds flock to the area every year, many migrating from north latitudes in winter. These include 300,000 swallows, 50,000 yellow longtails and 5,000 water birds. The best period for birdwatching is from October to March. Between Kota Belud and the sea, there are **mangrove swamps** with colonies of proboscis monkeys.

Tamus – Sabah's markets and trade fairs

In Sabah, an open trade fair is called a tamu. Locals gather to buy and sell jungle produce, handicrafts and traditional wares. Tamu comes from the Malay word 'tetamu', to meet, and the biggest and most famous is held at Kota Belud, north of Kota Kinabalu in Bajau country.

Tamus were fostered by the pre-war British North Borneo Chartered Company, when district officers would encourage villagers from miles around to trade among themselves. It was also a convenient opportunity for officials to meet with village headmen. They used to be strictly Kadazan affairs, but today tamus are multiracial events. Sometimes public auction of water buffalo and cattle are held. Some of the biggest tamus around the state are:

Monday: Tandek
Tuesday: Kiulu, Topokan
Wednesday: Tamparuli
Thursday: Keningau, Tambunan, Sipitang, Telipok, Simpangan
Friday: Sinsuran, Weston
Saturday: Penampang, Beaufort, Sindumin, Matunggong, Kinarut
Sunday: Tambunan, Tenom, Kota Belud, Papar, Gaya Street (KK)

Kudat

Colour map 4, grid A4

Kudat town, surrounded by coconut groves, is right on the northern tip of Sabah, 160 km from KK. The local people here are the Rungus, members of the Kadazan tribe. Gentle, warm and friendly, Rungus have clung to their traditions more than other Sabahan tribes and some still live in longhouses, although many are now building their own houses. Rungus longhouses are built in a distinctive style with outward-leaning walls; the Sabah State Museum incorporates many of the design features of a Rungus longhouse. The Rungus used to wear coils of copper and brass round their arms and legs and today the older generation still dress in black. They are renowned for their fine beadwork and weaving. A handful of Rungus longhouses are dotted around the peninsula, away from Kudat town.

The East India Company first realized the potential of the Kudat Peninsula and set up a trading station on Balambanganan Island, to the north of Kudat. The settlement was finally abandoned after countless pirate raids. Kudat became the first administrative capital of Sabah in 1881, when it was founded by a Briton, AH Everett. William Hood Fletcher, the protectorate's first governor, first tried to administer the territory from Labuan, which proved impossible, so he moved to the newly founded town of Kudat which was nothing more than a handful of atap houses built out into the sea on stilts. It was a promising location, however, situated on an inlet of Marudu Bay, and it had a good harbour. Kudat's glory years were shortlived: it was displaced as the capital of North Borneo by Sandakan in 1883.

Today it is a busy town dominated by Chinese and Filipino traders (legal and illegal) on the coast, and prostitutes trading downtown. Kudat was one of the main centres of Chinese and European migration at the end of the 19th century. Most of the Chinese who came to Kudat were Christian Hakka vegetable farmers: 96 of them arrived in April 1883, and they were followed by others, given free passages by the Chartered Company. More Europeans, especially the British, began to arrive on Kudat's shores with the discovery of oil in 1880. Frequent pirate attacks and an inadequate supply of drinking water forced the British to move their main administrative offices to Sandakan in 1883.

Tamus (markets) in Kota Belud District

Tuesday: Pandasan (along the Kota Belud to Kudat road).
Wednesday: Keelawat (along the Kota Belud to KK road).
Thursday: Pekan Nabalu (along the Kota Belud to Ranau road).
Friday: Taginambur (along the Kota Belud to Ranau road, 16 km from Kota Belud).
Monday and Saturday: Kota Belud.
Market time: 0600-1200. All tamus provide many places to eat.

Sights

Kudat is dotted with numerous family farms cultivating coconut trees, maize, ground nuts and keeping bees. Being surrounded by the sea, seafood is also an important element in the diet and fisheries an important industry. Kudat is inhabited by many other ethnic groups: Bonggi, Bajau, Bugis, Kadazandusun, Obian, Orang Sungei and Suluk. The market is on Mondays.

There are some beautiful and extensive unspoilt white sand **beaches** north of town, the best known is **Bak-Bak**, ⓘ *11 km north of Kudat; take a minibus, but they are irregular. The best option is a taxi but this is expensive*. This beach, however, can get crowded at weekends and there are plans to transform it into a resort. It is signposted off the Kota Belud-Kudat road.

Sikuati ⓘ *23 km west of Kudat; take a minibus*, with a good beach. Every Sunday (0800) the Rungus come to the market in this village, on the northwest side of the Kudat peninsula. Local handicrafts are sold.

Between Kota Belud and Kudat there is a marsh and coastal area with an abundance of birds. Costumed Bajau horsemen can sometimes be seen here.

The **'Longhouse Experience'** is possibly the most memorable thing to do in Kudat, ⓘ *for more information in visiting longhouses, enquire at Sabah Tourism, T88-212121, www.sabahtourism.com* A stay at a longhouse enables visitors to observe, enjoy and take part in the Rungus' unique lifestyle. There are two Baranggaxo longhouses with 10 units. Nearby there are the village's only modern amenities, toilets and showers. During the day, the longhouse corridor is busy with Rungus womenfolk at work stringing elaborate beadworks, weaving baskets and their traditional cloth. Visitors can experience and participate in these activities. (Look at the box, page 339, for advice on visiting longhouses. Longhouse meals are homegrown; fish and seafood come from nearby fishing villages, drinks consist of young coconuts and local rice wine. Evening festivities consist of the playing of gongs with dancers dressed in traditional Rungus costume. Tour companies organize trips for visitors.

For those wanting a less touristy visit to a longhouse, **Matunggong** is an area found on the road south of Kudat best known for its longhouses, though they are rather dilapidated now.

At **Kampong Gombizau**, visitors get to see bee-keeping and the process of harvesting beeswax, honey and royal jelly; while **Kampong Sumangkap**, an enterprising little village, offers visitors traditional gong-making and handicraft-making by the villagers.

Sleeping

Kota Belud *p432*

C-D Impian Siu Motel, Kg Sempirai, Jln Kuala Abai, T88-976617. Just 10 rooms in this reasonable place. You get what you pay for.

Homestay programme in Kota Belud village: there is no limit to your length of stay. Live with and be treated as part of the family, getting invited to celebrations such as weddings, etc. Activities include buffalo riding, jungle trekking, river swimming, cultural dancing, visits to local tamus, padi planting. Contact **Nature Heritage Travel and Tours**, ground floor, Wisma Sabah, KK, T88-318747, nhtt@nature-heritage.com, or **Taginambur Homestay**, T88-423993, T013-8528753, hopfans@tm.net.my. Very affordable for young travellers and an excellent way to learn the language and gain an in-depth knowledge of the culture.

Kudat *p433*
The Sunrise and Oriental hotels are within walking distance of the bus stop.
A-B **Kudat Golf & Marina Resort**, off Jln Urus Setia, T88-611211, www.kudatgolfmarinaresort.com. A spanking new orange monster next to a marina. Main attraction is the 18-hole championship golf course.
C **Greenland**, Lot 9/10, Block E, Sedco Shophouse (new town), T88-613211, F88-611854. A/c, standard rooms, shared bath.
C **Kinabalu**, Kudat Old Town, Jln Melor, T88-613888, F88-615388. A/c, clean enough, average value.
D **Southern Hotel**, Kudat Old Town, T88-613133. Only 10 rooms, but quite cheap and represents reasonable value in comparison to its competitors.

Eating

Kota Belud *p432*
There are several Indian coffee shops around the main square.
ǂ **Bismillah Restoran**, 35 Jln Keruak (main square), excellent roti telur.
ǂ **Indonesia Restoran**, next to the car park behind the Kota Belud Hotel.

Entertainment

Kota Belud *p432*
The annual **Tamu Besar** includes a parade and equestrian games by the Bajau Horsemen, a very colourful event, held in **Nov** (Sabah Tourism has more info).

Shopping

Kota Belud *p432*
Market in main square every day, fish market to the south of the main market. Large tamu every Sun and an annual Tamu Besar, both provide a wide variety of local handicrafts amongst the day-to-day items.

Transport

Kota Belud *p432*
Minibus
Leaves from main square. Regular connections with **KK**, **Kudat** and **Ranau**. It takes 90 minutes for **KK** to **Kudat** and **Kota Belud** could be a stop along the way, as connections are easy.

Kudat *p433*
Air
Connections with **KK**, **Sandakan**.

Minibus
Minibuses leave from Jln Lo Thien Hock. Regular connections with **KK**, 4 hrs.

Directory

Kota Belud *p432*
Banks Public Bank Berhad, Jln Kota Kinabalu. **Sabah Finance**, Jln Ranau. Bank Pertanian, Jln Kudat. **Places of worship** There are no English churches but people are happy to interpret. **Catholic Church**, Jln Ranau, **Basel Christian Church of Malaysia**, off Jln Kota Kinabalu, **SIB (Evangelical Church of Borneo)**, off Jln Ranau, **SIB Taginambur**, Jln Ranau (20 mins' drive from Kota Belud and the centre of a religious revival).

Kudat *p433*
Banks Standard Chartered, Jln Lo Thien Hock.

For an explanation of the sleeping and eating price codes used in this guide, see inside the front cover. Other relevant information is found in Essentials, pages 45-49.

Gunung Kinabalu Park

→ Colour map 4, grid A3

Gunung Kinabalu is the pride of Sabah, the focal point of the national park and probably the most magnificent sight in Borneo. In recognition of this, in 2000 the park was declared a World Heritage Site by UNESCO – a first for Malaysia. Although Gunung Kinabalu has foothills, its dramatic rockfaces, with cloud swirling around them, loom starkly out of the jungle. The view from the top is unsurpassed and on a clear day you can see the shadow of the mountain in the South China Sea, over 50 km away. » For Sleeping, Eating and other listings, see pages 443-444.

Ins and outs

Best time to visit

The average rainfall is 400 cm a year, with an average temperature of 20°C at Park HQ but at Panar Laban it can drop below freezing at night. With the wind chill factor on the summit, it feels very cold. The best time to climb Gunung Kinabalu is in the dry season between March and April when views are clearest. The worst time has traditionally been November to December during the monsoon, although wet or dry periods can occur at any time of the year. Avoid weekends, school and public holidays if at all possible.

The park is occasionally closed to climbers. Contact the **Sutera Sanctuary Lodges**, T88-243629, info@suterasanctuarylodges.com, to check the mountain is open for climbing at the time of your visit.

Permits, entrance fees and accommodation

RM100 per person to climb Gunung Kinabalu, an entry fee costing RM15 must be purchased on arrival by all park visitors and compulsory insurance costs RM3.50. The park is run by **Sutera Sanctuary Lodges**. All accommodation in the park must be booked in advance through its office: ground floor of Wisma Sabah, KK, T88-242629, www.suterasanctuarylodges,com, open 0900-1830, Mon-Fri, 0900-1630 Sat, and 0900-1500 Sun. See also Sleeping.

Equipment

A thick jacket is recommended, but at the very least you should have a light waterproof or windcheater to beat the windchill on the summit. You can hire jackets from Laban Rata but you need to book ahead as there are limited numbers. There are small shops at Park HQ and Laban Rata that sell gloves, hats, raincoats etc. It is also best to bring a sweater or thick shirts. Walking boots are recommended, but not essential – many people climb the mountain in trainers. It's a good idea to stock up on warm clothes, chocolate, drinking water and a torch (essential) in KK the day before (try the shops in Wisma Merdeka for cheap woollies). It's also best to carry a dry sweater and socks in your backpack and change just before you get to the peak - if it's raining the damp chill is worse than the actual cold. Sleeping bags are provided free of charge in the **Laban Rata Resthouse**; they are crucial for a good sleep. Carry food and chocolate as a precaution. Essential items include: torch, toilet paper, water bottle, plasters, headache tablets and suntan lotion. A hat is also a good idea – to guard against the sun and the cold. Gloves, balaclavas and torches can be bought at the shop at Park HQ, which also sells a food and drink suitable for the climb (but it's cheaper if you stock up in KK). Lockers are available, RM1 per item, at the Park HQ reception office. The Laban Rata Resthouse has welcome hot water showers, but soap and towels are not provided. Some of the rooms are well heated, cheaper ones leave you to freeze.

! Mount Kinabalu is a tough, steep climb but requires no special skills or equipment.

Guides

Hiring a guide is compulsory: RM70 for the round trip (one to three people), RM80 for the Mesilau trail. Porters available at a charge of RM60 (for 10 kilogram carried). Guides and porters should be reserved at least a day in advance at the Park HQ or at at Sutera Sanctuary Lodges. On the morning of your climb, go to the HQ and a guide will be assigned to you. While a tour will cost around RM500 each, a group of you can hire a taxi, book heated accommodation, and share a guide for the climb for less than RM250 each including all the fees. If you are doing it by yourselves it is best to get to the park a day in advance, stay at park HQ to get up early for the first part of the climb to Lanah Rata. Alternatively you can scramble out of bed at 0600 and make a dash from KK to the Park HQ to be there before 0900, after which time there might not be any guides left. A third option for those who are desperate to go, short of time, and have been informed that there is no accommodation available on the mountain in the next few days (as can

Gunung Kinabalu Trail

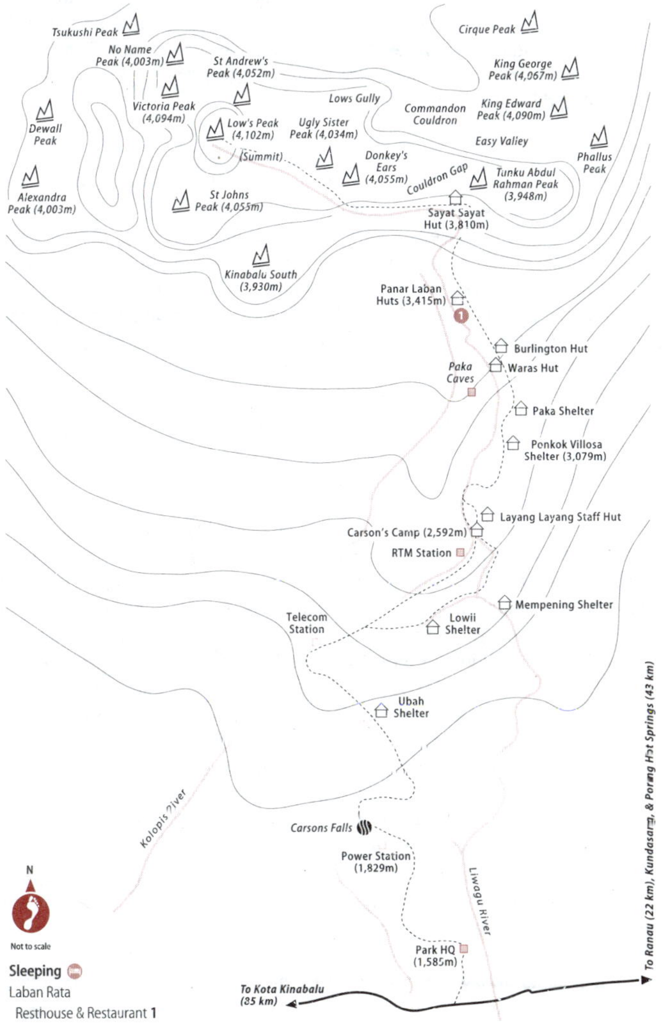

 happen all too often at busy periods such as school holidays) is to try your luck and turn up in person! A bus to the park leaves KK at 0700, and will drop you outside park HQ around 0900 – arrive no later if you are hoping to climb the mountain that day. Reports suggest that once someone has turned up in person to enquire, beds/mattresses up the mountain are often available. You should also be able to pick up a guide if you are there before 1000, although you will be unlikely to find anyone else to share with at this time, and the climb should begin around 1100, time enough to reach Laban Rata. This method should be an absolute last resort, and it is by no means guaranteed to work. If things don't work out, accommodation will probably be available at park HQ, or there are a number of good places within 2 km of the park.

Park headquarters

A short walk from the main Ranau-KK road and all the accommodation and restaurants are within 15 minutes walk from the main compound. There is a Souvenir and bookshop next to the Park HQ which has good books on the mountain and its flora and fauna. Slide and film shows are held in the mini-theatre in the Administration Building at 1400 during the week and at 1930 on weekends and public holidays, while naturalists give escorted trail walks every morning. The museum displays information on local flora and fauna. Beetles "as large as Tom Jones' medallions" and foot-long stick insects.

Treks

A small colour pamphlet, *Mount Kinabalu/A Guide to the Summit Trail*, published by Sabah Parks and widely available, serves as a good guide to the wildlife and the trail itself. Most treks are well used and are easy walks, but the Liwagu Trail is a good three- to four-hour trek up to where it joins the summit trail and is very steep and slippery in places; not advised as a solo trip. There is a daily guided trail walk at 1100, from the park administration building. This is a gentle walk with a knowledgeable guide, although the number of participants tends to be large. The climb to the summit of Mount Kinabalu is not something which should be undertaken lightly. It can be perishingly cold on the summit and altitude sickness is a problem. Some points of the trail are steep and require adequate footware. Changeable weather conditions add to the hazards.

History

In the first written mention of the mountain, in 1769, Captain Alexander Dalrymple of the East India Company, from his ship in the South China Sea, wrote: "Though perhaps not the highest mountain in the world, it is of immense height." During the Second World War Kinabalu was used as a navigational aid by Allied bombers – one of whom was quoted as saying "That thing must be near as high as Mount Everest". It's not, but at 4,095 m, Gunung Kinabalu is the highest peak between the Himalayas and New Guinea. It is not the highest mountain in Southeast Asia: peaks in Northern Burma and the Indonesian province of Irian Jaya are higher.

Gunung Kinabalu is an important watershed with eight major rivers originating on the mountain. It has been gazetted to protect the mountain and its remarkably diverse flora and fauna

There are a number of theories about the derivation of its name. The most convincing is the corruption of the Kadazan Aki Nabulu – 'the revered place of the spirits'. For the Kadazan, the mountain is sacred as they consider it to be the last resting place of the dead, and the summit was believed to be inhabited by their ghosts. In the past the Kadazan are said to have carried out human sacrifices on Mount Kinabalu, carrying their captives to the summit in bamboo cages, where they would be speared to death. The Kadazan guides still perform an annual sacrifice to appease the spirits. Today they make do with chickens, eggs, cigars, betel nuts and rice, on the rock plateau below the Panar Laban Rockface.

The Chinese also lay claim to a theory. According to this legend, a Chinese prince arrived on the shores of Northern Borneo and went in search of a huge pearl on the top of the mountain, which was guarded by a dragon. He duly slew the dragon, grabbed the pearl and married a beautiful Kadazan girl. After a while he grew homesick, and took the boat back to China, promising his wife that he would return. She climbed the mountain every day for years on end to watch for her husband's boat. He never came and in desperation and depression, she lay down and died and was turned to stone. The mountain was then christened China Balu – or Chinaman's widow.

In 1851, Sir Hugh Low, the British colonial secretary in Labuan made the first unsuccessful attempt at the summit. Seven years later he returned with Spencer St John, the British Consul in Brunei. Low's feet were in bad shape after the long walk to the base of the mountain, so St John went on without him, with a handful of reluctant Kadazan porters. He made it to the top of the conical southern peak, but was "mortified to find that the most westerly [peak] and another to the east appeared higher than where I sat." He retreated, and returned three months later with Low, but again failed to reach the summit, now called Low's Peak (standing at 4,095 m above sea level). It remained unconquered for another 30 years. The first to reach the summit was John Whitehead, a zoologist, in 1888. Whitehead spent several months on the mountain collecting birds and mammals and many of the more spectacular species bear either Low's or Whitehead's name. More scientists followed and then a trickle of tourists but it was not until 1964, when Kinabalu Park (encompassing 75,000 ha) was gazetted, that the 8½ km trail to the summit was opened. Today the mountain lures around 200,000 visitors a year. Although the majority are day visitors who do not climb the peak, the number of climbers is steadily increasing, with around 30,000 making the attempt each year.

In plan, the top of the mountain is U-shaped, with bare rock plateaux. Several peaks stand proud of these plateaux, around the edge of the U; the space between the western and eastern arms is the spectacular gully known as Low's Gully. No one has ever scaled its precipitous walls, nor has anyone climbed the Northern Ridge (an extension of the eastern arm) from the back of the mountain. From Low's Peak, the eastern peaks, just 1½ km away, look within easy reach. As John Briggs points out in his book *Mountains of Malaysia*, "It seems so close, yet it is one of the most difficult places to get to in the whole of Borneo."

Flora and fauna

The range of climatic zones on the mountain has led to the incredible diversity of plant and animal life. Kinabalu Park is the meeting point of plants from Asia and Australasia. There are thought to be more than 1,200 species of orchid alone, and this does not include the innumerable mosses, ferns and fungi. These flowering plants of Kinabalu are said to represent more than half the families of flowering plants in the world. Within the space of 3 km, the vegetation changes from lowland tropical rainforest to alpine meadow and cloud forest. The jungle reaches up to 1,300 m; above that, to a height of 1,800 m, is the lower montane zone, dominated by 60 species of oak and chestnut; above 2,000 m is the upper montane zone with true cloud forest, orchids, rhododendrons and pitcher plants. Above 2,600 m, growing among the crags and crevices of the summit rock plateau are gnarled tea trees (*Leptospermums*) and stunted rhododendrons. Above 3,300 m, the soil disappears, leaving only club mosses, sedges and Low's buttercups (*Ranunculus lowii*), which are alpine meadow flowers.

> *It has one of the richest assemblages of flora in the world, with more than 2,000 species of flowering plants.*

Among the most unusual of Kinabalu's flora is the world's largest flower, the rust-coloured **Rafflesia** (see box on page 423). They can usually only be found in the section of the park closest to Poring Hot Springs. Rafflesia are hard to find as they only flower for a couple of days; the main flowering season is from May to July.

Kinabalu is also famous for the **carnivorous pitcher plants**, which grow to varying sizes on the mountain. A detailed guide to the pitcher plants of Kinabalu can be bought in the shop at Park HQ. Nine different species have been recorded on Kinabalu. The largest is the giant Rajah Brooke's pitcher plant; Spencer St John claimed to have found one of these containing a drowned rat floating in four litres of water. Insects are attracted by the scent and when they settle on the lip of the plant, they cannot maintain a foothold on the waxy, ribbed surface. At the base of the pitcher is an enzymic fluid which digests the 'catch'.

Rhododendrons line the trail throughout the mossy forest (there are 29 species in the park), especially above the Paka Cave area. One of the most beautiful is the copper leafed rhododendron, with orange flowers and leaves with coppery scales underneath. There are an estimated 1000 species of orchid in the park, along with 621 species of fern and 52 palm species.

It is difficult to see wildlife on the climb to the summit as the trail is well used, although tree shrews and squirrels are common on the lower trails. There are, however, more than 100 species of mammal living in the park. The Kinabalu summit rats, which are always on cue to welcome climbers to Low's Peak at dawn, and nocturnal ferret badgers are the only true montane mammals in Sabah. As the trees thin with altitude, it is often possible to see tree-shrews and squirrels, of which there are more than 28 species in the park. Large mammals, such as flying lemurs, redleaf monkeys, wild pigs, orang-utan and deer, are lowland forest dwellers. Nocturnal species include the slow loris (*Nycticebus coucang*) and the mischievous-looking bug-eyed tarsier (*Tarsius bancanus*).

More than half of Borneo's 518 species of bird have also been recorded in Kinabalu Park, but the variety of species decreases with height. Two of the species living above 2,500 m are endemic to the mountain: the Kinabalu friendly warbler and the Kinabalu mountain blackbird.

More than 61 species of frogs and toads and 100 species of reptile live in the park. Perhaps the most interesting frog in residence is the horned frog, which is virtually impossible to spot thanks to its mastery of the art of camouflage. The giant toad is common at lower altitudes; he is covered with warts, which are poisonous glands. When disturbed, these squirt a stinking, toxic liquid. Other frogs found in the park include the big-headed leaf-litter frog, whose head is bigger than the rest of its body, and the green stream shrub frog, who has a magnificent metallic green body, but is deadly if swallowed by any predator.

The famous flying tree snake has been seen in the park. It spreads its skin flaps, which act as a parachute when the snake leaps blindly from one tree to another.

There are nearly 30 species of fish in the park's rivers, including the unusual Borneo sucker fish (Gastomyzon borneensis), which attaches itself to rocks in fast-flowing streams. One Sabah Parks publication likens them to 'underwater cows', grazing on algae as they move slowly over the rocks.

Walkers and climbers are more likely to come across the park's abundant insect life than anything else. Examples include pill millipedes, rhinoceros beetles, the emerald green and turquoise jewel beetles, stick insects, 'flying peapods', cicadas, and a vast array of moths (including the giant atlas moth) and butterflies (including the magnificent emerald green and black Rajah Brooke's birdwing).

Mount Kinabalu

The climb to the summit and back should take two days; four to six hours from park HQ at 1,585 m to the *Laban Rata Resthouse* (3,550 m) on the first day (note a second slightly tougher trail has opened from Mesilau which takes 2 to 3 hours longer to get to Laban Rata, but which has far less tourists) and then three hours to the summit for dawn, returning to the Park HQ at around 1200 hours on the second day. Gurkha soldiers and others have made it to the summit and back in well under three hours.

For the really keen, or the really foolhardy, depending on one's perspective and inclination, there is also the annual Kinabalu Climbathon which is held in early October. Having said that the climb to the top 'requires no special skills', the death of a British teenage girl on the mountain in 2001 highlights the hazards of climbing an unfamiliar mountain where changes in the weather can be sudden and dramatic. Keep to the trails and avoid parting company with your group.

A minbus for 12 people can take groups from headquarters to the power station at 1,829 m where the trail starts (RM5 per person). It is a 25-minute walk from the power station to the first shelter. The trail splits in two soon afterwards, the left goes to the radio station and the helipad and the right towards the summit. The next stop is **Layang Layang staff headquarters** (drinking water, cooking facilities, accommodation) – also known as **Carson's Camp** (2,621 m), named after the first warden of the park. There is one more shelter, **Ponkok Villosa** (2,942 m, and about 45 minutes from Carson's Camp) before the stop at the path to **Paka Caves** – really an overhanging rock on the side of a stream. Paka is a 10-minute detour to the left, where Low and St John made their camps.

From the cave/fifth shelter the vegetation thins out and it is a steep climb to **Panar Laban huts** – which includes the well-equipped Laban Rata Resthouse, affording magnificent views at sunset and in the early morning. The name Panar Laban is derived from Kadazan words meaning 'place of sacrifice': early explorers had to make a sacrifice here to appease the spirits and this ritual is still performed by the Kadazan once a year. **Sayat Sayat** (3,810 m) hut – named after the ubiquitous shrubby tea tree – is an hour further on, above the Panar Laban Rockface. Most climbers reach Panar Laban (or the other huts) in the early afternoon in order to rest up for a 0300 start the next morning in order to reach the summit by sunrise. This second part of the trail – 3-km long – is more demanding technically, but the trail is well laid out with regular half mile resting points. Ladders, hand-rails and ropes are provided for the steeper parts (essential in the wet, as the granite slabs can be very slippery). The final 1 km has no hand rails or ropes but is less steep. The first two hours after dawn are the most likely to be cloud-free. For enthusiasts interested in alternative routes to the summit, John Briggs's *Mountains of Malaysia* provides a detailed guide to the climb.

Mountain Garden

ⓘ *Tours leave at 0900, 1200, 1500 and cost RM4 – the garden is closed at other times.* Situated behind park administration building, this landscaped garden has species from all over the mid-levels of the mountain, which have been planted in natural surroundings.

Mesilau Nature Resort

This rainforest resort nestles at the foot of Mount Kinabalu at 2,000 m. The main attractions are the cool climate and the superb views up the mountain and across the plains toward Ranau and the sea. It is possible to scale the peaks of the mountain using the resort as a base, providing an alternative route from which to launch any assault on Low's Peak. Taking this new trail, one would join the main trail at Layang Layang. Alternatively there are a number of walks to be made around the reserve, in this secluded location.

Poring Hot Springs

→ *Colour map 4, grid A4*

ⓘ *If you've already paid the entrance fee to the national park keep your ticket for entrance to the hot springs. If staying at Poring then there is no charge, and the baths can be used all night long. Permits not necessary. An Information Centre has been built here, plus a rafflesia centre, orchid centre, aviary and tropical garden. It is better not to visit the Hot Springs at the weekend or on public holidays, if you want to*

 relax in a peaceful atmosphere; minibuses to the springs leave park HQ at 0900, 1300, 1600; alternatively flag down a bus/minibus to Ranau on the main road a two-minutes' walk from HQ and taxi from there to Poring.
Poring lies 43 km from Gunung Kinabalu Park HQ and is actually part of the national park. The **hot sulphur baths** ⓘ *sulphur bath, RM15 per hour, sulphur bath and Jacuzzi, RM20 per hour*, were installed during the Japanese occupation of the Second World War, for the jungle-weary Japanese troops. There are individual concrete pools with taps which can fit two people, one for the hot spring mineral water and the other for cold; once in your bath you are in complete privacy. However, many visitors now complain that the water is no longer hot, more like lukewarm. The springs are on the other side of the Mamut River, over a suspension bridge, from the entrance. They are a fantastic antidote to tiredness after a tough climb up Gunung Kinabalu. There is also a cold water rock pool. The pools are in a beautiful garden setting of hibiscus and other tropical flowers, trees and thousands of butterflies. There are some quite luxurious private cabin baths available. There are also large baths which hold up to eight people. The deluxe cabins have lounge areas and Jacuzzis. The Kadazans named the area Poring after the towering bamboos, of that name, nearby. (These big bamboos were traditionally used as water carriers and examples can be seen in the museum in KK.)

The **jungle canopy walk** at Poring is a rope walkway 35 m above the ground, which provides a monkey's eye view of the jungle; springy but quite safe. ⓘ *0900-1600 daily, RM5, RM5 charge for camera, RM30 charge for video. Guides are available. You'll need to pay RM30 if you want to use a camera.* The entrance is five minutes' walk from the hot springs and the canopy walkway is 15 minutes' walk from the entrance. The canopy walkway at Danum Valley is far more exciting. If the weather is clear at Ranau, it is generally safe to assume that the canopy walk will also be clear.

Kipungit Falls are only about 10 minutes' walk from Poring and swimming is possible here. Follow the trail further up the hill and after 15 minutes you come to bat caves; a large overhanging boulder provides shelter and a home for the bats.

The **Langanan Waterfall** trail takes 90 minutes one way, is all uphill, but is worth it. There is another hard, 90-minute trail to **Bat Cave** (inhabited by what seems to be a truly stupendous number of bats) and a waterfall. The **Butterfly Farm** ⓘ *0900-1600 Tue-Sun, RM5*, was established, close to the springs, by a Japanese-backed firm in 1992 and is very educational in the descriptions of butterflies and other insects.

Ranau and Kundasang → *Colour map 4, grid B4*

The Ranau plateau, surrounding the Kinabalu massif, is one of the richest farming areas in Sabah and much of the forest not in the park has now been devastated by market gardeners. Even within the national park's boundaries, on the lower slopes of Mount Kinabalu itself, shifting cultivators have clear-felled tracts of jungle and planted their patches. More than 1,000 ha are now planted out with spinach, cabbage, cauliflower, asparagus, broccoli and tomatoes, supplying much of Borneo.

Kundasang and Ranau are unremarkable towns a few kilometres apart; the latter is bigger. The **war memorial**, behind Kundasang, which unfortunately looks like Colditz, is in memory of those who died in the 'death march' in the Second World War (see page 448). In September 1944, the Japanese marched 2,400 Allied prisoners of war through the jungle from Sandakan to Kundasang. The march took 11 months and only six men survived to tell the tale. The walled gardens represent the national gardens of Borneo, Australia and Britain.

Mentapok and Monkobo are southeast of Ranau. Both are rarely climbed. Mentapok, 1,581 m, can be reached in 1½ days from Kampong Mireru, a village at the base of the mountain. A logging track provides easy access halfway up the south side of the mountain. Monkobo is most easily climbed from the northwest, a logging track from Telupid goes up to 900 m and from here it is a two-hour trek to the top. It is advisable to take guides, organized from Ranau or one of the nearby villages.

Sleeping

Gunung Kinabalu Park *p436*

Management of the park is privatized. It is currently being managed by Sutera Sanctuary Lodges, all accommodation in the park must be booked in advance through its office: ground floor of Wisma Sabah, KK, T88-242629, www.suterasanctuarylodges,com, open 0900-1830, Mon-Fri, 0900-1630 Sat, and 0900-1500 Sun.

Park HQ Each cabin is provided with a fireplace, kitchen, shower, gas cooker, refrigerator and cooking and eating utensils. Electricity, piped water and firewood are all provided free of charge. The rates quoted below are reduced on weekdays: The most expensive option at the Park HQ is the **Rajah Lodge**, sleeping 10 people (RM1,150 for the whole lodge). **Kinabalu Lodge**, 8 people, RM414 per night. **Nepenthes Lodge**, 4 people, RM288 per night. **Twin-bedded cabins**, 2 people, RM92 per night, great views. **Four person chalets**, RM230 per night. There are also unheated dorm rooms with shared bathroom for RM12 per bed.

Gunung Kinabalu Laban Rata Resthouse, Panar Laban, 54 rooms (space is often made for extra bodies by laying out matresses on the restaurant floor), a good quality though pricey canteen (but sometimes rather limited food – it all has to be walked up the mountain) and hot water shower facilities plus electricity and heated rooms, bedding provided. Most expensive rooms are the heated deluxe Buttercup rooms at RM230 or RM115 per room, heated dorm rooms for RM34 per bed, while chilly unheated dorms are RM17 per bed.

Close to Park HQ.

A **Haleluyah Retreat Centre**, Jln Linouh, Km 61, Tuaran-Ranau Highway, T88-423993, kandiu@tm.net.my This Christian centre is open to all and is located at 1,500 m close to the foot of Mount Kinabalu. It makes a good stop off point before climbing the mountain. Set amidst 2 acres of natural jungle and approximately 15 mins' walk from the Park HQ, it is isolated but safe, clean, friendly and with a relaxing atmosphere. Cooking and washing facilities, camping area, multi-purpose hall and meeting rooms makes it a suitable venue for seminars, meetings, youth camps or family holidays. Food is available at a reasonable price from a canteen, dorm beds also available.

A-C **Sonny's Cottage**, T88-750555, T88-750479. 6 bedrooms with spectacular views.

A-E **Rina Ria Lodge**, Batu 36, Jln Tinompok, Ranau, T88-889282. About 1 km from the Kinabalu National Park, rooms have attached kitchen and basic bathroom, arm chairs and beautiful views. There is also a shop. Prices increase at weekends. Dorms also available.

B **Kinabalu Rose Cabin**, Km18, Ranau-Kinasaraban Rd, Kundasang, T88-889233 F88-889800, A/c, restaurant, 2 km from the park, towards golf course (30% discount to golfers); range of rooms, suites.

C **Mountain View Motel**, located 5 km east of the Kinabalu National Park on the Ranau-Tamparuli Highway, T88-875389, bbmtkinabalu@hotmail.com Price includes breakfast, hot water, restaurant, laundry facilitites, local tours, climbing gear available for rent. The corrugated iron roof can be loud when it rains.

E **Mountain Resthouse and Restaurant**, T88-771109. Located just outside the park, this has small 4 person dorms that are cheaper, newer, cleaner and warmer than the park dorms. Also spectacular views. This is arguably preferable to the park accommodation.

Mesilau Nature Resort *p441*

L-C **Mesilau Nature Resort**, managed by Sutera Sanctuary Lodges, T88-871733, www.suterasanctuarylodges.com Mesilau provides a range of tasteful wooden chalets that blend neatly into the environment housing groups of up to 6 people (RM400 per room). There is also more budget accommodation provided in dorms in the hostel (RM30 per bed).

Other services available include laundry, gift shop and regular educational talks. The nature reserve is situated close to the Mt Kinabalu Golf Club, just a few mins' drive away.

Poring *p441*

Booking is recommended, see Ins and outs, page 436.

E **Serindit hostel**, 24 people in a dorm, RM12 adult; **Tempua Lodge**, 4 people,

RM92 per chalet; **Enggang Lodge**, 6 people, RM115 per night; **Rajawali Lodge**, 6 people, RM288 per night.
Camping RM6.

Ranau and Kundasang *p442*

L-B **Zen Garden Resorts**, Km 2, Jln Mohimboyan Kibas, T88-889242, F88-889251, cable TV, hot showers and pleasant restaurant.
B **Kinabalu Pine Resort**, Kampong Kundasang, T88-889388, F88-889288. A/c, great views in this attractive but isolated area, 6 km from the national park. Great value.
A-B **Perkasa**, visible on the hill above Kundasang (a further 1 km down the road from Kinabalu Pine), T88-889511, www.perkasahotel.com.my A/c, terrace restaurant, slightly run down but a good view of the mountain, organizes tours to Kinabalu National Park and surrounding area. Oriented towards business travellers.

Eating

Gunung Kinabalu Park *p436*

Park HQ The best places to stay are here but the restaurants are rather spread out requiring a walk between buffet and bed.
ꝉ **Balsam Cafeteria**, 0600-1800, is the cheaper option for Malay staples.
ꝉꝉ The fancier **Liwagu restaurant**, 0600-2200, has beer, chips and curries. Both open early for climbers to stock up on high carb breakfasts. Cooking facilites at the hostels plus **Rajah Lodge, Nepenthes Lodge** and **Kinabalu Lodge.**

Mesilau Nature Resort *p441*

ꝉꝉ **The Kedamaian Restaurant** will provide the 3 main meals. The alternative is the
ꝉ **Malaxi Café**, which has a stunning verandah offering great views of the mountain.

Poring *p441*

ꝉ **Restaurant**, quite good Chinese and Malay food at the springs and stalls outside the park.

Ranau and Kundasang *p442*

There are several restaurants along the roads serving simple food in Kundasang, open 0600-2100.
ꝉꝉ **Perkasa Hotel Restaurant**, Kundasang, local and Western dishes, service good and food excellent.
ꝉ **Five Star Seafood Restaurant**, Ranau. Chinese, opposite the market
ꝉ **Sin Mui Mui**, top side of the square near the market, closed Fri afternoons.

Shopping

Ranau and Kundasang *p442*

Cheap sweaters and waterproofs for the climb from **Kedai Kien Hin**, Ranau. A tamu is held near Ranau on the first of each month and every Sat. Kundasang tamu is held on the 20th of every month and also every Fri.

Activities and tours

Ranau and Kundasang *p442*

Golf

Kundasang Golf Course, 3 km behind Kundasang, one of the most beautiful courses in the region. Club hire from the *Perkasa Hotel*, Kundasang. The Perkasa offer golfing packages to include golf fees, accommodation, breakfast and lunch, transfer from hotel to course.

Transport

Gunung Kinabalu Park *p436*

Bus

All buses heading to Sandakan and Ranau will drop you off at the turn-off to the park.

Minibus

Regular connections from **KK** to **Ranau**, ask to be dropped at the park, 2 hrs. Return minibus must be waved down from the main road (one roughly every hour).

Taxi

RM60 fixed price, taxi from long distance bus station in Kota Kinabalu.

Poring *p441*

Minibuses can be shared from **Ranau** for RM5. **Buses** running between **KK** and **Sandakan** stop in town on Jln Kibarambang.
Taxi Available (RM25).

Ranau and Kundasang *p442*

Minibus

Minibuses leave from the market place. Regular connections to **Park HQ**, to **KK**, to **Sandakan** 8 hrs.

The East Coast

From Ranau it is possible to reach Sandakan by road. Several key sights are within reach of Sandakan: the Turtle Islands National Park, 40 km north in the Sulu Sea, Sepilok Orang-utan Rehabilitation Centre and the Kinabatangan Basin, to the southeast. From Sandakan, the route continues south to the wilds of Lahad Datu and Danum Valley and on to Semporna, the jumping off point for Pulau Sipadan (an island which has achieved legendary status among snorkellers and scuba divers). Tawau Hills State Park has some unusual natural features which draw visitors at weekends. ▸▸ *For Sleeping, Eating and other listings, see pages 460-470.*

Sandakan→ *Colour map 4, grid B5*

Sandakan is at the neck of a bay on the northeast coast of Sabah and looks out to the Sulu Sea. It is a post-war town, much of it rebuilt on reclaimed land and is Malaysia's biggest fishing port; it even exports some of its catch to Singapore. Sandakan is often dubbed 'mini Hong Kong' because of its Cantonese influence; its occupants are well-heeled and the town sustains many prosperous businesses, despite the town as a whole being rather scruffy. It is now also home to a large Filipino community, mostly traders from Mindanao and the Sulu Islands. Manila still officially claims Sabah in its entirety – Sandakan is only 28 km from Philippines' territorial waters.

Ins and outs

Getting there The airport is around 10 km north of town. There are daily connections with KK and several lesser destinations in Sabah, minibuses travel from the airport to the station at the southern end of Jln Pelabuhan. From the long distance bus terminal 5 km (mile 2.5) to the west of town, there are connections with KK, Tawau, Ranau, Lahad Datu, Semporna and several other destinations. See also Transport, page 468.

Getting around Sandakan is not a large town and it is easy enough to explore the central area on foot - although it does stretch some way along the coast. Minibuses provide links with out-of-town places of interest.

Tourist information The privately run **Tourist Information Centre,** ⓘ *T89-22975, 0800-1230, 1330-1630 Mon-Fri, 0800-1230 Sat (closed first and third Sat every month), closed Sun,* next to the municipal council building opposite Lebuh Empat is staffed by the enthusiastic Elvina who does her best to answer all questions with limited resources. The centre was opened by the owner of the Sepilok Jungle Resort but it provides impartial advice.

History

For the Sulu traders, the Sandakan area was an important source of beeswax and came under the sway of the Sultans of Sulu. William Clarke Cowie, a Scotsman with a carefully waxed handlebar moustache who ran guns for the Sultan of Sulu across the Spanish blockade of Sulu (and was later to become the managing director of the North Borneo Chartered Company), first set up camp in Sandakan Bay in the early 1870s. He called his camp, which was on Pulau Timbang, 'Sandakan', which had been the Sulu name for the area for about 200 years, but it became known as Kampong German as there were several German traders living there, and early gun-runners tended to be German. The power of the Sulu sultanate was already on the wane when Cowie set up. In its early trading days, there were many nationalities living in Sandakan: Europeans, Africans, Arabs, Chinese, Indians, Javanese, Dusun and Japanese. It was an important gateway to the interior and used to be a trading centre for forest produce like rhinoceros horn, beeswax, and hornbill ivory along with marine products like pearls and sea cucumbers (tripang, valued for their medicinal properties). In 1812, an English visitor, John Hunt, estimated that the Sandakan/Kinabatangan area produced an astonishing 37,000 kg of wild beeswax and 23,000 kg of bird's nests each year.

The modern town of Sandakan was founded by an Englishman, William Pryer, in 1879. Baron von Overbeck, the Austrian consul from Hong Kong who founded the Chartered Company with businessman Alfred Dent, had signed a leasing agreement for the territory with the Sultan of Brunei, only to discover that large tracts on the east side of modern-day Sabah actually belonged to the Sultan of Sulu. Overbeck sailed to Sulu in January 1878 and on obtaining the cession rights from the Sultan, dropped William Pryer off at Kampong German to make the British presence felt. Pryer's wife Ada later described the scene: "He had with him a West Indian black named Anderson, a half-cast Hindoo named Abdul, a couple of China boys. For food they had a barrel of flour and 17 fowls and the artillery was half a dozen sinder rifles." Pryer set about organizing the three existing villages in the area, cultivating friendly relations with the local tribespeople and fending off pirates. He raised the Union Jack on 11 February 1878.

Cowie tried to do a deal with the Sultan of Sulu to wrest control of Sandakan back from Pryer, but Dent and Overbeck finally bought him off. A few months later Cowie's Kampong German burned to the ground, so Pryer went in search of a new site, which he found at Buli Sim Sim. He called his new settlement Elopura, meaning 'beautiful city', but the name did not catch on. By the mid-1880s it was recalled Sandakan and,

in 1884, became the capital of North Borneo when the title was transferred from Kudat. In 1891 the town had 20 Chinese-run brothels and 71 Japanese prostitutes; according to the 1891 census there were three men for every one woman. The town quickly established itself as the source of birds' nests harvested from the caves at Gomantong and shipped directly to Hong Kong, as they are today.

Timber was first exported from this area in 1885 and was used to construct Beijing's Temple of Heaven. Sandakan was, until the 1980s, the main east coast port for timber and it became a wealthy town. In its heyday, the town is said to have boasted one of the greatest concentrations of millionaires in the world. The timber-boom days are over: the primary jungle has gone, and so has the big money. In the mid-1990s the state government adopted a strict policy restricting the export of raw, unprocessed timber. The hinterland is now dominated by cocoa and oil palm plantations.

Following the Japanese invasion in 1942, Sandakan was devastated by Allied bombing. In 1946 North Borneo became a British colony and the new colonial government moved the capital to Jesselton (later to become Kota Kinabalu).

Sights

Sandakan is strung out along the coast but in the centre of town is the riotous **daily fish market**, which is the biggest and best in Sabah. The best time to visit is at 0600 when the boats unload their catch. The **Central Market** along the waterfront, near the local bus station, sells such things as fruit, vegetables, sarongs, seashells, spices and sticky rice cakes.

The **Australian war memorial**, ⓘ *take Labuk bus service nos 19, 30 and 32*, near the government building at Mile Seven on Labuk Rd, between Sandakan and Sepilok, stands on the site of a Japanese prison camp and commemorates Allied soldiers who lost their lives during the Japanese occupation. The Japanese invaded North Borneo in 1942 and many Japanese also died in the area. In 1989 a new **Japanese war memorial**, ⓘ *walk 20-minutes up Red Hill*, was built in the Japanese cemetery, on Red Hill (Bukit Berenda), financed by the families of the deceased soldiers.

St Michael's Anglican church is one of the very few stone churches in Sabah and is an attractive building, designed by a New Zealander in 1893. Most of Sandakan's stone churches were levelled in the war and, indeed, St Michael's is one of the few colonial-era buildings still standing. It is just off Jalan Singapura, on the hill at the south end of town. In 1988 a big new **mosque** was built for the burgeoning Muslim population at the mouth of Sandakan Bay. The main Filipino settlements are in this area of town. The mosque is outside Sandakan, on Jalan Buli Sim Sim where the town began in 1879, just after the jetty for Turtle Islands National Park and is an imposing landmark. There is also a large water village here, offering a glimpse of traditional culture and life.

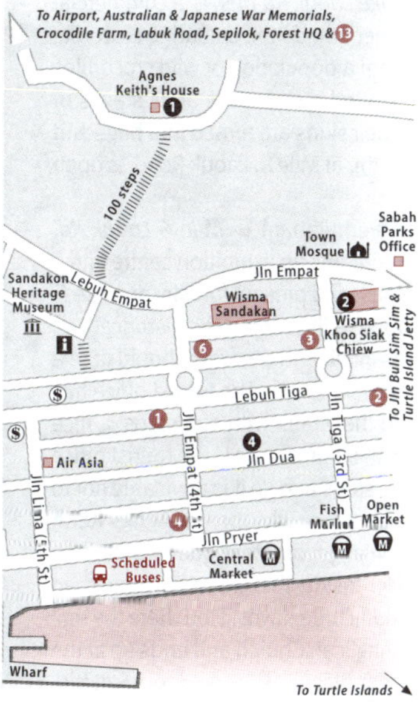

Eating
English Tea House 1
Jiaman 2
Ocean King Seafood 3
Penang Curry House 4
XO Steak House 5

The Borneo Death March

The four years of Japanese occupation ended when the Australian ninth division liberated British North Borneo. Sandakan was chosen by the Japanese as a regional centre for holding Allied prisoners. In 1942 the Japanese shipped 2,750 prisoners of war (2,000 of whom were Australian and 750 British) to Sandakan from Changi Prison, Singapore. A further 800 British and 500 Australian POWs arrived in 1944. They were ordered to build an airfield (on the site of the present airport) and were forced to work from dawn to dusk. Many died, but in September 1944 2,400 POWs were force-marched to Ranau, a 240-km trek through the jungle which only six Australians survived. This 'Death March', although not widely reported in Second World War literature, claimed more Australian lives than any other single event during the war in Asia, including the notorious Burma-Siam railway.

There are a couple of other notable Chinese temples in Sandakan. The oldest one, the **Goddess of Mercy Temple** is just off Jalan Singapura, on the hillside. Originally built in the early 1880s, it has been expanded over the years. Nearby is **Sam Sing Kung Temple** which becomes a particular focus of devotion during exam periods since one of its deities is reputed to assist those attempting examinations. The **Three Saints Temple**, further down the hill at the end of the padang, was completed in 1887. The three saints are Kwan Woon Cheung, a Kwan clan ancestor, the goddess Tien Hou (or Tin Hau, worshipped by seafarers) and the Min Cheong Emperor.

The only **Crocodile Farm** in Sabah ⓘ *daily 0800-1730, RM2, weekday showtimes at 1145 and 1600, feeding times throughout the day; take Labuk Rd bus*, is a commercial licensed enterprise, set up in 1982 when the government made the estuarine crocodile a protected species. The original stock was drawn from a population of wild crocodiles found in the Kinabatangan River. Visitors can see around 2,000 crocs at all stages of maturity waiting in concrete pools for the day when their skins are turned into bags and wallets and their meat is sold to local butchers. The farm, at Mile 8, Labuk Road, is open to the public and has about 200 residents.

The **Forest Headquarters** (Ibu Pejabat Jabatan Perhutanan) ⓘ *Mile 6 Labuk Rd, T89-660811*, next to the Sandakan Golf Course and contains an exhibition centre and a well laid out and interesting mini-museum showing past and present forestry practice.

The **Sandakan Heritage Trail** is a loop which supposedly takes in the historical and cultural gems of this scruffy town – there are 11 sites in all, and the walk should take a leisurely 90 minutes including a good lookout point over the city. The tourist office has trail maps. It starts off at the town mosque, nips up the 'stairs with 100 steps' a nice shady climb with good views from the top. However, in summer 2004, the tourist office warned that several visitors had been mugged on the steps and so it is advisable not to climb them alone. From here the trail passes through the newly-opened **Agnes Keith House** (see box page 449), the restored British colonial government quarters built on the site of her home, ⓘ *0900-1700 Sat-Thu, RM5*. Inside the grounds, there's an **English Tea House** serving scones and pastries on manicured lawns. From here the trail takes in the Goddess of Mercy Temple, St Michael's Anglican Church and ends up at the **Sandakan Heritage Museum** (next door to the tourist office), ⓘ *0900-1700 Sat-Thu, closed Fri, free*, a rather slipshod affair of some early photos of the town and an unexplained mannequin dressed in a kilt. There is, however, a good wall photo of Sandakan razed to the ground taken in 1945.

Agnes Keith's house

American authoress Agnes Keith lived with her English husband in Sandakan from 1934 to 1952. He was the Conservator of Forests in North Borneo and she wrote three books about her time in the colony. *The Land Below the Wind* relates tales of dinner parties and tiffins in pre-war days; *Three Came Home* is about her three years in a Japanese internment camp during the war on Pulau Berhala, off Sandakan, and in Kuching and was made into a film. *White Man Returns* tells the story of their time in British North Borneo. The Keiths' rambling wooden house on the hill above the town was destroyed during the war but was rebuilt by the government to exactly the same design when Harry Keith returned to his job after the war.

Tanah Merah

Pertubuhan Ugama Buddhist (Puu Jih Shih Buddhist temple) overlooks Tanah Merah town. The US$2m temple was completed in 1987 and stands at the top of the hill, accessible by a twisting road which hairpins its way up the hillside. The temple is very gaudy, contains three large Buddha images and is nothing special, although the 34 teakwood supporting pillars, made in Macau, are quite a feature. There is a good view of Sandakan from the top, with Tanah Merah and the log ponds directly below, in Sandakan Bay. The names of local donors are inscribed on the walls of the walkway.

Pulau Lankayan

Pulau Lankayan is a fairly new dive resort on a virtually uninhabited island, one and half hour's boat trip from Sandakan in the Sulu Sea. The resort, Lankayan Island Dive Resort, see Sleeping, offers more than 40 dive sites including a couple of wrecks. Sightings of whale sharks are said to be common here in April and May.

Pulau Berhala

ⓘ *To get to the beach charter a boat from the fish market. You can camp on the island.* This island is ideal for picnicking and swimming. It has 200-m rust-coloured sandstone cliffs on the south end of the island, with a beach at the foot, within easy reach by boat. The island was used as a leper colony before the Second World War and as a prisoner of war camp by the Japanese. Agnes Keith was interned on the island during the war.

Turtle Islands National Park → *Colour map 4, grid A5*

Forty kilometres north of Sandakan, the Turtle Islands are at the south entrance to Labuk Bay. The park is separated from the Philippine island of Bakkungan Kecil by a narrow stretch of water. These eight tiny islands in the Sulu Sea are among the most important turtle breeding spots in all Southeast Asia. The turtle sanctuary is made up of three tiny islands (Pulau Selingan, Pulau Bakkungan Kecil and Pulau Gulisan) and also encompasses the surrounding coral reefs and sea, covering 1,700 ha. On Pulau Bakkungan Kecil there is a small mud volcano.

Ins and outs

Best time to visit The driest months and the calmest seas are between March and July. The egg laying season is between July and October. Seas are rough between October and February.

 Tourist information The numbers of visitors are restricted to 50 per night in an effort to protect the female turtles, which are easily alarmed by noise and light when laying. Visitors are asked not to build campfires, shine bright torches or make noise at night on the beach. The turtles should be watched from a distance to avoid upsetting the nesting process. The park is managed by **Sabah Parks**, Sabah Parks Office Room 906, 9th Flr, Wisma Khoo, Lebuh Tiga, T89-273453. Entrance fee, RM10. All accommodation must be booked through *Crystal Quest*. See Sleeping. This is booked up weeks, sometimes months in advance.

The islands

The islands are famous for their green turtles (*Chelonia mydas*), which make up about four-fifths of the turtles in the park, and hawksbill turtles (*Eretmochelys imbricata*), known locally as sisik. Most green turtles lay their eggs on Pulau Selingan. The green turtles copulate 50-200 m off Pulau Selingan and can be seen during the day, their heads popping up like submarine periscopes. Hawksbills prefer to nest on Pulau Gulisan.

Both species come ashore, year-round, to lay their eggs, although the peak season is between July and October. Even during the off-season between four and 10 turtles come up the beach each night to lay their eggs. Pulau Bakkungan Kecil and Pulau Gulisan can only be visited during the day but visitors can stay overnight on Pulau Selingan to watch the green turtles.

Only the females come ashore; the male waits in the sea nearby for his mate. The females cautiously come ashore to nest after 2000 or with the high tide. The nesting site is above the high tide mark and is cleared by the female's front and hind flippers to make a 'body pit', just under a metre deep. She then digs an egg chamber with her powerful rear flippers after which she proceeds to lay her eggs. The clutch size can be anything between 40 and 200; batches of 50-80 are most common.

When all the eggs have been laid, she covers them with sand and laboriously fills the body pit to conceal the site of the nest, after which the exhausted turtle struggles back to the sea, leaving her Range Rover-like tracks in the sand. The egg-laying process can take about an hour or two to complete. Some say the temperature of the sand effects the sex of the young, if it is warm the batch will be mostly female and if cold, mostly male. After laying her eggs, a tag reading "If found, return to Turtle Island Park, Sabah, East Malaysia" is attached to each turtle by the rangers, who are stationed on each island. Over 27,000 have been tagged since 1970; the measurements of each turtle are recorded and the clutches of eggs are removed and transplanted to the hatchery where they are protected from natural predators – such as monitor lizards, birds and snakes.

The golf ball-sized eggs are placed by hand into 80 cm-deep pits, covered in sand and surrounded by wire. They take up to 60 days to hatch. The hatchlings mostly emerge at night when the

Small and hairy: the Sumatran rhinoceros

Although not as rare as its Javan brother, the Sumatran, or lesser two-horned rhino (*Didermoceros sumatrensis*) is severely endangered. It was once widespread through mainland and island Southeast Asia but has now been hunted to the point of extinction; there are probably less than 1,000 in the wild, mostly in Sumatra but with small populations in Borneo, Peninsular Malaysia and Vietnam. It is now a protected species. Only on Sumatra does it seem to have a chance of surviving. The situation has become so serious that naturalists have established a captive breeding programme as a precaution against extinction in the wild. Unfortunately this has been spectacularly unsuccessful. Around one-third of animals have died during capture or shortly thereafter and, according to naturalists Tony and Jane Whitten, the only recorded birth was in captivity in Calcutta in 1872. The species has suffered from the destruction of its natural habitat, and the price placed on its head by the value that the Chinese attach to its grated horn as a cure-all. Should the Sumatran rhino disappear so too, it is thought, will a number of plants whose seeds will only germinate after passing through the animal's intestines.

The Sumatran rhino is the smallest of all the family, and is a shy, retiring creature, inhabiting thick forest. Tracks have been discovered as high as 3,300 m in the Mount Leuser National Park in Sumatra. It lacks the 'armoured' skin of other species and has a soft, hairy hide. It also has an acute sense of smell and hearing, but poor eyesight.

temperature is cooler, breaking their shells with their one sharp tooth. There are hatcheries on all three islands and nearly every night a batch is released into the sea. Millions of hatchlings have been released since 1977. They are released at different points on the island to protect them from predators: they are a favoured snack for white-bellied gulls and sadly only about 1% survive to become teenage turtles.

Sepilok Orang-utan Sanctuary and Rehabilitation Centre → *Colour map 4, grid B5*

Sepilok, a reserve of 43 sq km of lowland primary rainforest and mangrove, was set up in 1964 to protect the orang-utan, (*Pongo pygmaeus*), from extinction. It is the first and largest of only four orang-utan sanctuaries in the world and now welcomes around 40,000 visitors a year. Logging has seriously threatened Sabah's population of wild orang-utan, as has their capture for zoos and as pets. The orang-utan (see page 521) lives on the islands of Borneo and Sumatra and there are estimated to be perhaps as few as 10,000 still in the wild. In Sabah there are populations of orang-utan in the Kinabatangan basin region (see page 454) and in the Danum Valley Conservation Area as well as in a few other isolated tracts of jungle.

Ins and outs

Getting there There are several buses a day from Sandakan.

Park information The park is open from 0900-1230, 1400-1630, RM30, camera RM10. It is worth getting to the park early. The **Information Centre**, next to the Park HQ, runs a nature education exhibition with replicas of jungle mammals and educational videos. Video viewing times are at 1100, 1200 and 1530. If you want to do the walks you'll need to arrive at the centre in the morning so you can get a permit. The pass is valid all day so you can see both feeds if you arrive early enough. Feeding times: Platform A, 1000 and 1500. Note, the morning feeds are packed with tour groups, the afternoon feed is generally more calmer. Further information about Sepilok can be obtained from the Co-ordinator, Sepilok Orang-Utan Rehabilitation Centre, Sabah Wildlife Department, WDT 200, 95000 Sandakan, T89-531180, F89-531189.

The sanctuary

Sepilok is an old forest reserve, that was gazetted as a forestry experimentation centre as long ago as 1931, and by 1957 logging had been phased out. Orphaned or captured orang-utans which have become too dependent on humans through captivity are rehabilitated and protected under the Fauna Conservation Ordinance and eventually returned to their natural home. Many, for example, may have been captured by the oil palm planters, because they eat the young oil palm trees. Initially, the animals at the Centre and in the surrounding area are fed every day but as they acclimatize, they are sent further and further away or are re-released into the Tabin Wildlife Reserve near Lahad Datu. In 1996, researchers placed microchip collars on the orang-utans enabling them to be tracked over a distance of up to 150 km so that a better understanding of their migratory habits and other behaviour could be acquired.

After an initial period of quarantine at Sepilok, newly arrived orang-utans are moved to Platform A and taught necessary survival skills by the rangers. At the age of seven they are moved deeper into the forest to Platform B, about half an hour's walk from Platform A and not open to the public. At Platform B, they are encouraged to forage for themselves. Other animals brought to Sepilok include Malay sun bears, wild cats and baby elephants.

Sepilok also has a rare Sumatran rhinoceros, (*Didermoceros sumatrensis*), also known as the Asian two-horned rhinoceros, see box page 451. This enclosure is sometimes closed to the public.

The **Mangrove Forest Trail** takes two to three hours one way. The walk takes in transitional forest, pristine lowland rainforest, a boardwalk into a mangrove forest, water holes and a wildlife track. All enquiries at the Visitors' Reception Centre.

Rainforest Interpretation Centre

ⓘ Mon-Thu 0815-1215, 1400-1600, Fri 0815-1135, 1400-1600, Sat 0815-1215, free. A free booklet is available. For more information contact the Forest Research Centre, PO Box 14-07, T89-531522, F89-531068.

The Rainforest Interpretation Centre on the road to Sepilok provides detailed and informative displays about the vegetation in the area. It is run by the Forest Research Centre, which is also found on this road. Great emphasis is given to participation, with questionnaires, games and so on; it offers a wide range of information about all aspects of tropical rainforests and the need for their conservation. The centre is located in the Forest Research Centre's arboretum and in addition to the exhibits there is an 800-m rainforest walk around the lake.

Gomantong Caves

The Gomantong Caves are 32 km south of Sandakan Bay, between the road to Sukau and the Kinabatangan River, or 110 km overland on the Sandakan-Sukau road. The name Gomantong means 'tie it up tightly' in the local language and the caves represent the largest system in Sabah. They are contained within the 3,924 ha Gomantong Forest Reserve.

Edible nests

The edible nests of black and white swiftlets are collected from the cave chambers, but the trade is now strictly controlled by Wildlife Department wardens. The white nests (of pure saliva) fetch more than US$500 per kg in Hong Kong; black nests go for around US$40 per kg. The nest collectors pick about 250 kg a day in the lower chamber and about 50 kg a day in the upper chamber. They earn about RM25 a day. The collectors use 60 m-long rotan ladders. Heavy bundles of wood are lashed to the ladders to minimize swaying – but fatal accidents do occur. On average, a collector is killed once every four or five years in a fall. Bat guano is not collected from the floor of the cave so that it can act as a sponge mattress in the event of a serious fall.

The nests, which are relished as a delicacy by the Chinese are harvested for periods of 10 days, twice a year. The nests are first harvested just after the birds have made them (between February and April). The birds then build new nests, which are left undisturbed until after the eggs have been laid and hatched; these nests are then gathered, sometime between July and September. Harvesting contracts are auctioned to wholesalers who export the nests to Hong Kong, where their impurities are taken out and they are sold at a huge mark-up. Of the profits, about half go to the state government, and more than a third to the contractor. Less than a fifth goes to the collectors. It is possible to buy the birds' nests in Sandakan restaurants, although they are all re-imported from Hong Kong.

Ins and outs

ⓘ *Daily 0800-1600, RM30*; at the Park HQ there is an information centre, a small cafeteria where drinks and simple dishes are sold, and a pit latrine. Good walking shoes are essential as is a torch. If you're squeamish about cockroaches give this cave a miss. If you arrive independently then one of the nest workers, a person from the information centre, or a ranger will show you around. The bats can be seen exiting from the caves between 1800 and 1830; to request to see this it is necessary to ask at the **Gomantong Wildlife Department**, at the information centre, T011-817529/T88-666550.

The caves and reserve

There are sometimes orang-utan, many deer, mouse deer, wild boar and wild buffalo in the reserve, which was logged in the 1950s. There are several cave chambers. The main limestone cave is called Simud Hitam, or the Black Cave. This cave, with its ceiling soaring up to 90 m overhead, is just a five-minute walk from the registration centre and picnic area. The smaller and more complex White Cave (or Simud Putih) is above. It is quite dangerous climbing up as there is no ladder to reach the caves and the rocks are slippery. Two to three hundred thousand bats of two different species are thought to live in the caves: at sunset they swarm out to feed. Sixty-four species of bat have been recorded in Sabah, most in these caves are fruit and wrinkled-lipped bats whose guano is a breeding ground for cockroaches. The squirming larvae make the floor of the cave seethe. The guano can cause an itchy skin irritation. The bats are preyed upon by birds like the bat hawk, peregrine falcon and buffy fish owl.

There are also an estimated one million swiftlets which swarm into the cave to roost at sunset, the birds of birds' nest soup fame (see box). The swiftlets of Gomantong have been a focus of commercial enterprise for perhaps 400 or 500 years. However, it was not until 1870 that harvesting birds' nests became a serious industry here. The caves are divided into five pitches and each is allocated to a team of 10-15 people. Harvesting periods last 15 days and there are two each year (March-April and August-September). Collecting the nests from hundreds of feet above the ground is a dangerous business and deaths are not uncommon. Before each harvesting period a chicken or goat is sacrificed to the cave spirit; it is thought that deaths are not the result of human error, but an angry spirit. The birdlife around the caves is particularly rich, with crested serpent eagles, kingfishers, Asian fairy bluebirds, and leafbirds often sighted. Large groups of richly coloured butterflies are also frequently sighted drinking from pools along the track leading from the forest into the caves.

Kinabatangan River

At 560 km, this river is Sabah's longest. Much of the lower basin is gazetted under the Kinabatangan Wildlife Sanctuary and meanders through a flood plain, creating numerous ox-bow lakes and an ideal environment for some of the best wildlife in Malaysia.

Ins and outs

Visitors who prefer an in-depth look at the area's wildlife can stay overnight at Sukau, two hours by road from Sandakan, where accommodation is provided by local tour operators, see Sleeping. Tour operators take visitors by boat in the late afternoon through the freshwater swamp forest to see proboscis monkeys and other wildlife. There are also walks through the jungle. Because of the lack of public transport to Sukau, the only way to visit the area is with a tour; all tours must be booked in Sandakan or KK. See Sleeping, page 460.

Kinabatangan Riverine Forest area

One of the principal reasons why the Kinabatangan has remained relatively unscathed by Sabah's rapacious logging is because much of the land is permanently waterlogged and the forest contains only a small number of commercially valuable trees. Just some of the animals include: tree snake, crocodile, civet cat, otter, monitor lizard, long-tailed and pig-tailed macaque, silver-, red- and grey-leaf monkey and proboscis monkey. It is the most accessible area in Borneo to see the proboscis monkeys which are best viewed from a boat in the late afternoon, when they converge on tree tops by the river banks to settle for the night. Sumatran rhinoceros have also been spotted (see box page 451) and herds of wild elephant often pass through the park. The birdlife is particularly good and includes oriental darter, egret, storm's stork, osprey, coucal owl, frogmouth, bulbul, spiderhunter, oriole, flowerpecker and several species of hornbill, see page 524.

❢ The Kinabatangan River is one of the best places to see orang utans in the wild.

Because of the diversity of its wildlife, the Kinabatangan riverine forest area has been proposed as a forest reserve. In addition, there has been little disturbance from human settlements: the Kinabatangan basin has always been sparsely inhabited because of flooding and the threat posed by pirates. The inhabitants of the Kinabatangan region are mostly Orang Sungai or people of mixed ancestry including Tambanua, Idahan, Dusun, Suluk, Bugis, Brunei and Chinese. The best destination for a jungle river safari is not on the Kinabatangan itself, but on the narrow, winding Sungai Menanggol tributary, about 6 km from Sukau. The Kinabatangan estuary, largely mangrove, is also rich in wildlife, and is a haven for migratory birds. Boats can be chartered from Sandakan to Abai (at the mouth of the river).

Batu Tulug, also known as Batu Putih (White Stone), on the Kinabatangan River 100 km upstream from Sukau, is a cave containing wooden coffins dating back several hundred years. Some of the better examples have been removed to the Sabah State Museum in KK. The caves are about 1 km north of the Kinabatangan Bridge, on the east side of the Sandakan-Lahad Datu road.

Lahad Datu and around → *Colour map 4, grid B5*

Lahad Datu is Malaysia's 'wild East' at its wildest, and its recent history testifies to its reputation as the capital of cowboy country. The population is an intriguing mixture of Filipinos, Sulu islanders, migrants from Kalimantan, Orang Bugis, Timorese and a few Malays. Most came to work on the oil palm plantations. Nowadays there are so many migrants few can find employment in this grubby and uninteresting town. There are reckoned to be more illegal Filipino immigrants in Lahad Datu than the whole official population put together. Piracy in the Sulu Sea and the offshore islands in Kennedy Bay is rife; local fishermen live in terror. In October 2003, a band of Abu Sayyaf rebels grabbed six Filipino and Indonesian workers from the Borneo Paradise Resort near Kunak. Eight months later, four of the hostages were freed. It was thought a Malaysian businessman had paid a ransom.

During the Second World War, the Japanese made Lahad Datu their naval headquarters for East Borneo. After the war, the timber companies moved in: the British Kennedy Bay Timber Company built Lahad Datu's first plywood mill in the early 1950s. Oil palm plantations grew up in the hinterland after the timber boom finished in the 1970s. As for the town, what it lacks in aesthetic appeal is made up for by its colourful recent history.

Kampong Panji is a water village with a small market at the end of Jalan Teratai, where many of the poorer immigrant families live.

The only good **beaches** are on the road to Tungku; Pantai Perkapi and Pantai Tungku.They can be reached by minibus from Lahad Datu or by boat from the old wharf. It is possible to get to the nearby **islands** from the old wharf behind the Mido Hotel, but because of lawlessness in the area, particularly at sea, a trip is not advisable. In April 2000, the Philippines-based radical Islamic group Abu Sayyaf kidnapped 21 people from Sipadan (see page 458).

Madai Caves ⓘ *Your own transport is required for this trip as it doesn't really cater for tourists*, are about 2 km off the Tawau-Lahad Datu road, near Kunak. The caves are an important archaeological site; there is evidence they were inhabited over 15,500 years ago. The birds' nests are harvested three times a year by local Idahan people whose lean-to kampong goes right up to the cave mouth.

Another 15 km west of Madai is **Baturong**, another limestone massif and cave system in the middle of what was originally Tingkayu Lake. The route is not obvious, so it is advisable to take a local guide. Stone tools, wooden coffins and rock paintings have been found there. Evidence of humans dating from 16,000 years ago, after the lake drained away, can be found at the huge rock overhang. ⓘ *Take a torch. It is possible to camp here, take a minibus from Lahad Datu.*

Gunung Silam, 8 km from Lahad Datu on the Tawau road, a track leads up the mountain to a Telekom station at 620 m and from there, a jungle trail to the summit. There are good views over the bay, when it isn't misty, and out to the islands beyond. It is advisable to take a guide. There is the Silam Lodge, see Sleeping.

Gazetted in 1984, as a protected forest area, **Tabin Wildlife Reserve**, according to the WWF, is one of the last reserves for the critically endangered **Sumatran Rhino**. It's also home to the Borneo Pygmy Elephant. The reserve is about 50 km or an hour's drive from Lahad Datu. Since 2002, it's been possible to stay inside the privately run reserve at the Tabin Jungle Resort, see Sleeping. There are several huge bubbling mud volcanoes an easy trek from the resort.

Danum Valley Conservation Area

→ Colour map 4, grid B5

Danum Valley's 438 sq km of virgin jungle is the largest expanse of undisturbed lowland dipterocarp forest in Sabah. The Segama River runs through the conservation area and past the field centre. The Danum River is a tributary of the Segama joining it 9 km downstream of the Field Centre. Gunung Danum (1,093 m) is the highest peak, 13 km southwest of the Field Centre. Within the area is a Yayasan Sabah timber concession, which is tightly controlled.

Ins and outs

The field centre, which is 65 km west of Lahad Datu and 40 km from the nearest habitation, was set up by the Sabah Foundation (Yayasan) in 1985 for forest research, nature education and recreation; the centre is not open for tourists, but does accept visiting scientists and researchers. If you are a biologist or an educator you may be able to get permission to visit the centre, contact the Sabah Foundation for permission. Guides costs RM5 per hour. **Sabah Foundation**, Likas Bay, T88-326327, rosejkj@icsb-sabah.com.my. Tourists are allowed to visit **only** through the Borneo Rainforest Lodge, see Sleeping and Transport. For more information on Danum Valley see www.maliaubasin.org

The valley

This area has never really been inhabited, although there is evidence of a burial site which is thought to be for the Dusun people who lived here about 300 years ago. There is also growing evidence of pre-historic cave dwellers in the Segama River area. Not far downstream from the field centre, in a riverside cave, two wooden coffins have been found, together with a copper bracelet and a tapai jar, all of uncertain date. There is evidence of some settlement during the Japanese occupation; townspeople came upstream to escape from the Japanese troops. The area was first recommended as a national park by the World Wide Fund for Nature's Malaysia Expedition in 1975 and designated a conservation area in 1981. The field centre was officially opened in 1986.

The main reason for this large conservation area is to undertake research into the impact of logging on flora and fauna and to try and improve forest management, to understand processes which maintain tropical rainforest and to provide wildlife management and training opportunities for Sabahans. Many are collaborative projects between Malaysian and foreign scientists.

Flora and fauna

Leech socks are essential here.

Because of its size and remoteness, Danum Valley is home to some of Sabah's rarest animals and plants. The dipterocarp forest is some of the oldest, tallest and most diverse in the world, with 200 species of tree per hectare; there are over 300 labelled trees in the conservation area. The conservation area is teeming with wildlife: Sumatran rhinoceroses have been recorded, as have elephants, clouded leopards, orang-utans, proboscis monkeys, crimson langur, pig-tailed macaques, sambar deer, bearded pigs, western tarsier, sunbears and 275 species of bird including hornbills, rufous picolet, flowerpeckers and kingfishers. A species of monkey, which looks like an albino version of the red-leaf monkey, was first seen on the road to Danum in 1988, and appears to be unique to this area. There are guided nature walks on an extensive trail system. Features include a canopy walkway, a heart-stoppingly springy platform, 107 metres long and 27 metres above the ground, ancient Dusun burial site, waterfalls and a self-guided trail.

The gentler beast of Borneo

It was dung that eventually solved the mystery surrounding Borneo's rare elephants. For a long time scientists couldn't decide whether the animals were native to the island, or introduced by human settlers. One argument suggested that the British East India Company gave the beasts as gifts to the Sultan of Sulu in the 17th century.

Using evidence gleaned from DNA analysis of the mucus which sticks to elephant droppings, scientists from Columbia University in the United States discovered the pachyderm is indeed indigenous. From genetic data they concluded the Borneo variety is a distinct sub-species of Asian elephant having been isolated from its cousins 300,000 years ago. In recognition of its new status, the animal was rechristened the Borneo Pygmy Elephant in 2003.

The animals are smaller than the Asian elephant, with larger ears, longer tails and straighter tusks. They are also said to be gentler in temper. Scientists believe elephants trooped across swampy land joining Borneo with Sumatra when sea levels were lower during the ice ages.

Conservation groups estimate there are only around 2,000 of the endangered elephants left, which are threatened by ivory poachers and loss of habitat.

Semporna

→ *Colour map 4, grid B6*

Semporna is a small fishing town at the end of the peninsula and is the main departure point for Sipidan Island. Semporna has a lively and very photogenic market, spilling out onto piers over the water. It is a Bajau town and is known for its seafood. There are scores of small fishing boats, many with outriggers and square sails. There is a regatta of these traditional boats every March. The town is built on an old coral reef, said to be 35,000 years old, which was exposed by the uplift of the seabed. Many illegal Filipino immigrants pass through Semporna, as it is only two hours from the nearest Philippine island, which gives the place quite a different feel to other Malay towns.

The islands off Semporna stand along the edge of the continental shelf, which drops away to a depth of 200 m to the south and east of Pulau Ligitan, the outermost island in the group. Darvel Bay, and the adjacent waters, are dotted with small, mainly volcanic islands all part of the 73,000 acre **Semporna Marine Park**. The bigger ones are Pulau Mabul, Pulau Kapalai, Pulau Si Amil, Pulau Danawan and Pulau Sipadan. The coral reefs surrounding these islands have around 70 genera of coral, placing them, in terms of their diversity, on a par with Australia's Great Barrier Reef. More than 200 species of fish have also been recorded in these waters.

Locals live in traditional boats called lipa-lipa or in pilehouses at the water's edge and survive by fishing. In the shallow channels off Semporna, there are three fishing villages, built on stilts: Kampong Potok Salu, Kampong Potok Dua and Kampong Larus. There are many more islands than are marked on the map; most are hilly, uninhabited and have beautiful white sandy beaches.

Reefs in Semporna Marine Park include Bohey Dulang, Sibuan Ulaiga, Tetugan, Mantabuan Bodgaya, Sibuan, Maigu, Selakan and Sebangkat. Pulau Bohey Dulang is a volcanic island with a Japanese-run pearl culture station. Visitors can only visit if there is a boat from the pearl culture station going out. The Kaya Pearl company leases part of the lagoon and Japanese pearl oysters are artificially implanted with a core material to induce pearl growth. The oysters are attached to rafts moored in the lagoon. The pearls are harvested and exported direct to Japan. The islands can be reached by local fishing boats from the main jetty by the market, including Sibun, Sibankat, Myga and Selakan.

Sipadan Island Marine Reserve

→ *Colour map 4, grid C6*

The venerable French marine biologist Jacques Cousteau 'discovered' Sipadan in 1989 and after spending three months diving around the island from his research vessel *Calypso* had this to say: "I have seen other places like Sipadan 45 years ago, but now no more. Now we have found an untouched piece of art." Since then Sipadan has become a sub-aqua shangri-la for serious divers. Sipadan is regularly voted one of the top dive destinations in the world by leading scuba magazines. The reef is without parallel in Malaysia. But Sipadan Island is not just for scuba divers: it is a magnificent, tiny tropical island with pristine beaches and crystal clear water and its coral can be enjoyed by even the most amateur of snorkellers.

Ins and outs

The island's tourist facilities are run by four tour companies, who control everything, see Activities and tours. In 2004, after much legal wrangling, the tour operators agreed to close all resort facilities on the island to protect the environment, although dive boats can still take visitors around the island, numbers will be limited. Tourists can still stay on Mabul, Kapalai and Mataking. It's expected that other islands will soon be developed.

Best time to visit The best diving season is from mid-February to mid-December when visibility is greater (20-60 m); mostly drift diving; the night diving is said to be absolutely spectacular.

Background

But while Sipidan may win lots of points from dive enthusiasts, it has also been in the news for less savoury reasons. In April 2000 Abu Sayyaf, a separatist group in the Philippines, kidnapped 21 people including 10 foreign tourists from the island. Abu Sayyaf, linked to Osama bin Laden's al-Qaeda, spirited the hostages to the Philippine island of Jolo. Here they remained under guard and threat of execution while the Armed Forces of the Philippines tried, sometimes incompetently, to rescue them. The hostages were freed in dribs and drabs with the final batch being released in September 2000, but it wasn't the sort of publicity that Sipadan was looking for. There is a heavy Malaysian navy presence on the island and around Semporna.

Since the end of 2004, resorts on Sipadan have been closed for environmental reasons.

The island is disputed between the Indonesian and Malaysian governments. Indonesia has asked Malaysia to stop developing marine tourism facilities on Sipadan. Malaysia's claim to the island rests on historical documents signed by the British and Dutch colonial administrations. Periodically the two sides get around the negotiating table, but it appears that neither is prepared to make a big issue of Sipadan. Occasionally guests on the island see Indonesian or Malaysian warships just offshore. A third party also contests ownership of Sipadan: a Malaysian who claims his grandfather, Abdul Hamid Haji, was given the island by the Sultan of Sulu. He has the customary rights to collect turtles eggs on the island, although the Malaysian government disputes this.

Pulau Sipadan

Pulau Sipadan is the only oceanic island in Malaysia; it is not attached to the continental shelf, and stands on a limestone and coral stalk, rising 200 m from the bed of the Celebes Sea. The limestone pinnacle mushrooms out near the surface, but a few metres offshore drops off in a sheer underwater cliff to the seabed. The reef comes right into the island's small pier, allowing snorkellers to swim along the

> Pulau Sipadan stands on a limestone and coral stalk, rising 200 m from the bed of the Celebes Sea. The limestone pinnacle mushrooms out near the surface, but a few metres offshore drops off in a sheer underwater cliff to the seabed...

edge of the coral cliff, while remaining close to the coral-sand beach. The edge is much further out around the rest of the island. The tiny island has a cool, forested interior and it is common to see flying foxes and monitor lizards. It is also a stop-over point for migratory birds, and was originally declared a bird sanctuary in 1933. It has been a marine reserve since 1981 and three Wildlife Department officials are now permanently stationed on the island. In addition, the island is also a breeding ground for the green turtle; August and September are the main egg-laying months.

Sipadan is known for its underwater overhangs and caverns, funnels and ledges, all covered in coral. Five metres down from the edge of the precipice there is a coral overhang known as the Hanging Gardens, where coral dangles from the underside of the reef. The cavern is located on the cliff right in front of the island's accommodation area. Its mouth is 24-m wide and the cave, which has fine formations of stalactites and stalagmites, goes back almost 100 m, sometimes less than 4 m below the surface. Visibility blurs where fresh water mixes with sea water. Inside, there are catacombs of underwater passages.

Mabul Island

Located between Semporna and Sipadan, this island of 21 ha is considerably larger than Sipadan and is partly home to Bajau fishermen who live in traditional, palm-thatched houses. In contrast to Sipadan's untouched forest, the island is predominantly planted with coconut trees. Diving has been the most recent discovery; an Australian diver claims it is "one of the richest single destinations for exotic small marine life anywhere in the world". It has already become known as the world's best 'muck diving' – so called because of the silt-filled waters and poor visibility (for this area, though still reasonable, at least 12 m usually, compared with many other places). The island is surrounded by gentle sloping reefs with depths from 3-35 m and a wall housing numerous species of hard corals.

Mataking and Kapalai

This island has only been open as a dive-resort spot for a few years, but with the closure of Sipadan its popularity is almost guaranteed to rocket. There are around 30 good dive sites around the island including various reefs (plenty of good shallow ones making it an ideal spot for beginner divers), a sea fan garden, a 100-m crevice called Alice Channel which runs to Pulau Sipadan and Sweet Lips rock, a good night diving spot. Accommodation is provided by the upmarket Mataking Island Reef Dive Resort. See Sleeping, page 460.

Kapalai is basically a sandbar, heavily eroded and sat on top of the Litigan Reefs between Sipadan and Mabul islands. *Uncle Chang's* will take guests diving around Sipadan as well as the shallow waters around Kapalai.

Tawau→ *Colour map 4, grid C5*

Tawau is a timber port in Sabah's southeastern corner. It is a busy commercial centre and the main channel for the entry of Indonesian workers into Sabah. Kalimantan is visible, just across the bay.

The town was developed in the early 19th century by the British who planted hemp. The British also developed the logging industry in Sabah, using elephants from Burma. The Bombay Burma Timber Company became the North Borneo Timber Company in 1950; a joint British and Sabah government venture.

Tawau is surrounded by plantations and smallholdings of rubber, copra, cocoa and palm oil. The local soils are volcanic and very fertile and palm oil has recently taken over from cocoa as the predominant crop. Malaysian cocoa prices dropped when its quality proved to be 20% poorer than cocoa produced in Nigeria and the Ivory Coast, and coupled with disease outbreaks in the crop, many of the cocoa growers emigrated to the Ivory Coast. KL is now an established research centre for palm oil where there are studies on using palm oil as a fuel.

Now that the Sandakan area has been almost completely logged, Tawau has taken over as the main logging centre on the east coast. The forest is disappearing fast but there are ongoing reforestation programmes. At Kalabakan west of Tawau there is a well established, large-scale reforestation project with experiments on fast-growing trees such as Albizzia falcataria, which is said to grow 30 m in five years. There are now large plantation areas. The tree is processed into, among other things, paper for paper money.

Around Tawau

ⓘ *RM2, for more information, contact Ranger Office, Tawau Hills Park, T89-810676, F11-884917. Access to the park is via a maze of rough roads through the Borneo Abaca Limited agricultural estates. It is advisable to hire a taxi.*

Tawau Hills State Park lies 24 km northwest of Tawau; it protects Tawau's water catchment area. The Tawau River flows through the middle of the 27,972-ha park and forms a natural deep water pool, at Table Waterfall, which is good for swimming. There is a trail from there to some hot water springs and another to the top of Bombalai Hill, an extinct volcano. Most of the forest in the park below 500 m has been logged. Only the forest on the central hills and ridges is untouched. The park is popular with locals at weekends. Camping is possible but bring your own equipment.

Sleeping

Sandakan *p445, map p446*

A **Sabah Hotel**, Km 1, Jln Utara, T89-213299, www.sabahhotel.com.my With a/c, restaurants, attractive pool, Sandakan's only 4-star hotel, with 108 rooms, fitness centre, tennis, pool and squash courts.

A **Sanbay**, Mile 1.25, Jln Leila, T89-275000, F89-275575, Spacious rooms with bathrooms in this three-star hotel.

A **Hotel Sandakan**, 4th Ave, T89-221122, tengis@tm.net.my A/c, coffee house, Cantonese restaurants, bar with live music, business centre (has a lot of business clients). Centrally located, this is not cheap but provides excellent service.

B **City View**, Lot 1, Block 23, 3rd Ave, T89-271122, F89-273112. Restaurant, bath and shower, TV, fridge, a/c. For a little more than the standard guesthouses this is a considerable step up. Recommended.

B **Hsiang Garden**, Km 1, T89-273122, F89-273127. A/c, restaurant, all facilities, good bar.

B **Ramai**, Km 1.5, Jln Leila, T89-273222, F89-271884. A/c, restaurant, all 44 rooms are a good size, with bathrooms. Recommended.

B **Sepilok Inn**, Block 46, Lot 9, Tingkat 1,2,3, Jln Sekolah, T89-271222, F89-273231. A/c, clean rooms with attached bathrooms and TVs, good value.

C Hung Wing, Lot 4, Block 13, Jln Tiga, T89-218855, F89-271240. Some a/c, shower, a wide variety of rooms and prices available. Rooms are spacious, clean and light with bathrooms. The owner is very helpful and speaks excellent English. Probably the best of the mid-range hotels.

C London, Lot D1, Block 10, Jln Empat, T89-216366. A/c, shower and bath, TV, light rooms although not large.

C Mayfair, 24 Jln Pryer, T89-219855. A/c, shower, each room has a TV, and the owner has a vast collection of dvds free to watch. As there's little to do in Sandakan after 2100, the Mayfair offers some welcome entertainment. The decor leaves something to be desired but there's a very friendly atmosphere and is in a central location with views of the market and the sea, good value. Recommended, but book ahead as often full.

D B&B, T89-218328 A simple guesthouse at the bus station if you get stuck here overnight or if you need to be up very early for a connection. RM20 for a dorm bed.

D Uncle Tan's, Mile 16, Jln Gum Gum (5 km beyond Sepilok junction), T89-531639, www.uncletan.com A simple bed & breakfast usually putting up those heading for Uncle Tan's Wildlife Adventure Camp in the Kinabatangan (see Tour operators below). Very cheap but not very clean and being on the main road, it's noisy from the logging trucks which continue to thunder past all night long. A popular stop for travellers.

D-E Travellers Rest Hostel, 2nd Flr, Apt 2, Block E, Jln Leila, Bandar Ramai-Ramai, T89-221460. Some a/c, no attached bathrooms and limited toilet facilities, friendly with lots of travel information. Cooking and washing facilities.

Pulau Lankayan *p449*

AL Lankayan Island Dive Resort, run by Pulau Sipadan Resort & Tours, 1st floor, Bandar Sabindo, Tawau, T89-765200, www.lankayan-island.com The resort offers quiet chalets by the beach and more than 40 dive sites including a couple of wrecks. Sightings of whale sharks are said to be common here in April and May.

Turtle Islands National Park *p449*

The number of visitors to the islands is restricted, even at peak season. There are 3 chalets (one with 2 double bedrooms, two with 6 double bedrooms) on Pulau Selingan (RM255-370 per person. You have to book in advance through **Crystal Quest**, Sabah Park Jetty, Jln Buli Sim Sim, T89-212711, cquest@tm.net.my. Tour agencies can also organise trips to the island.

Sepilok Orang-utan Sanctuary and Rehabilitation Centre *p451*

B-D Sepilok Jungle Resort (and Wildlife Lodge), KM22 Labuk Rd, Sepilok Orang-Utan Sanctuary, 100 m behind the Government Resthouse, T89-533031, www.borneo-online.com.my/sjungleresort This resort is the realization of a dream for John and Judy Lim, who have gradually purchased all the land on the edge of the forest and have landscaped the area surrounding three manmade lakes and cleared the fruit orchards they inherited. They have planted lots of flowering and fruiting trees, attracting butterflies and birds in the process. Pleasant restaurant, great setting, clean and comfortable, boats for fishing available. Recommended. The resort is split into two, the Wildlife Lodge is the older with more budget accommodation offering six-bed dorms RM18 per bed, and plain doubles with own hot water showers and a/c. More luxurious wood-paneled rooms with TV, a/c are in the Jungle Resort next door. The owners are actively involved in Sandakan tourism and opened the tourist information office in the town.

It is due to open Bilit Adventure Camp in 2005, which will offer mid-range rooms along the Kinabantangan River.

B-D Sepilok Resthouse, Mile 14 Labuk Rd, T89-534900. Nice wooden house next to the Orang-utan Centre. A government-owned house, although now privately run. Big rooms, with bathtub and balcony. Clean dorms for RM20 per bed.

C Sepilok B&B, Jln Sepilok, of Mile 14, PO Box 155, T89-532288, F89-217668. Breakfast included. Around 1 km from the Orang-Utan sanctuary. Fairly good value although there is no hot water.

Camping

F Campsite at Sepilok Jungle Resort, but you must bring your own gear.

Kinabatangan River *p454*

Most companies running tours to the Kinabatangan put their guests up in Sukau or in camps along the river.

A **Sukau Rainforest Lodge**, (Borneo Eco-Tours, 2nd flr, Lorong Bernam, Taman Soon Kiong, Kota Kinabalu, T88-234009, www.borneoecotours.com) accessible by boat from Sukau, provides eco-friendly accommodation for 40 visitors, in traditional Malaysian-style chalets, on stilts. All 20 rooms have solar-powered fans, twin beds, mosquito netting, and attached tiled bathroom with hot water. Other facilities include an open dining and lounge area (good restaurant), garden and sundeck overlooking the rainforest, and gift shop. Friendly and efficient service. All in all, a shining example of eco-tourism at its best, highly recommended.

D **The Jungle Sanctuary** , Traveller's Rest Hostel, second floor, Bandar Ramai Ramai, Jln Leila, Sandakan, T019 8004939, junglesanctuary@hotmail.com. This place is modelled on Uncle Tan's but according to reports is far inferior. One group that went said their guides did not seem to know much about the wildlife, and at one point guests were left stranded in the camp after the staff left them overnight. (They did return the next day!). Cheaper than Uncle Tan's at RM220 for a three day two night package, but the saving is not worth it by all accounts.

D **Proboscis Lodge**, run by Sipadan Dive Centre, 10th floor, Wisma Merdeka, Kota Kinabalu, T88-240584. A more upmarket Kinabatangan experience. The resort is located near Sukau not in the heart of the jungle like the jungle camps. Accommodation is in chalets with hot water showers and windows, transport in landcruisers.

E **Uncle Tan Wildlife Adventures**, Mile 16, Jln Gum Gum, T89-531639, www.uncletan.com. A long-established budget option to explore the lower Kinabatangan Valley. Accommodation is in simple three-sided huts with a floor mattress, mosquito net and shared cold water bucket showers. A three-day, two-night package which includes van transport to the river from the B&B on Jln Gum Gum, several river cruises including an amazing night cruise, jungle treks and all meals (simple but hearty) costs RM240 (extra nights can be bought for RM20 each). Prepare to get very muddy, Wellington boots are available. The camp is on the edge of an ox-bow lake and very remote in the middle of the jungle. It is run by enthusiastic young locals who speak pretty good English, love to mix with the guests, and while not naturalist experts, are very knowledgeable about the wildlife. Some of the staff have been working there for more than five years. The camp was started by Uncle Tan, who began taking tourists out to the jungle in 1988. A colourful character, he fought stridently for conservation issues in the region. He died of a heart attack in 2002, and the running of the resort has been taken over by his brother who is based in Singapore. This place is very popular and rightly so, book ahead. Bring raincoat and torch. Very common to see proboscis monkeys and wild orang utan sightings are also not rare. Perhaps your best hands on chance of seeing Sabah's wildlife. Recommended.

Lahad Datu and around *p455*

Lahad Datu is not a popular tourist spot and accommodation is poor and expensive. Avoid the Perdana and Venus hotels on Jln Seroja.

A-D **Tabin Jungle Resort**, Tabin Wildlife Reserve, which has lodges and chalets with a/c and hot showers or more budget-priced tented platforms. Book accommodation through Intra Travel Services, T88-264071, www.tabinwildlife.com.my

B **Executive**, Jln Teratai, T89-881333, F89-881777. A smart 53-room hotel that is easily the priciest in town. An uninspiring place and overpriced.

B **Silam**, Gunung Silam, T88-243245, F88-254227, which is owned by the Borneo Rainforest Lodge and is mostly used by people in transfer to the Danum Valley. Minibuses run from Lahad Datu.

B-C **Jagokota**, Jln Kampong Panji, T89-882000, F89-881526, well-furnished establishment.

C **Mido**, 94 Jln Main, T89-881800, F89-881487. A/c, restaurant, the façade (facing the Standard Chartered Bank) is pock-marked with M-16 bullet holes, the result of over-curious residents watching the 1986 pirate raid on the bank; the Mido comes with all the sleaze of the 'wild East' and fails miserably to live up to its reputation as the best hotel in town.

C **Permaisaba**, Block 1, Lot 3, 1/4 Jln Tengah Nipah, T89-883800, F89-883681. 5 mins' drive from the airport and town, seafood restaurant, Malaysian and Indian food, conference hall, free transfers to/from the airport and town. Big rooms with bathroom attached and hot water, information on the Danum Valley, characterless but convenient.

Danum Valley Conservation Area *p456*

AL **Borneo Rainforest Lodge**, c/o Borneo Nature Tours, Block 3, Ground Floor, Fajar Centre, Lahad Datu, T89-880207, F089885051. KK office: Block D, Lot 10, 3rd Floor, Sadong Jaya Complex, T88-243245, ijl@po.jaring.my One of the finest tourism developments in Sabah. 18 bungalows in a magnificent setting beside the Danum River, built on stilts from belian (ironwood) and based on traditional Kadazan design with connecting wooden walkways. There are 28 rooms, each with private bathroom and balcony overlooking the Danum River, good restaurant, jacuzzi (solar-heated water). Designed by naturalists, the centre aims to combine a wildlife experience in a remote primary rainforest with comfort and privacy and provide high quality natural history information. There is a conference hall, excellent guides, who pre-plan their routes so that visitors don't bump into each other while thinking they are latter day Indiana Jones; day visits to a forest management centre, an adequate library of resource books, after dinner slide shows, a gift shop, rafting is available and night drives can be organized. Mountain bikes, fishing rods and river tubes all available for hire. Electricity available all day. Expensive but well worth it. Price includes meals and guided jungle excursions.

If you get permission to stay at the centre, the **Sabah Foundation** has dorm rooms for 45RM per night, or RM80 for a single room.

Semporna *p457*

A-B **Seafest Hotel**, Jln Kastam, T89-782333, www.seafesthotel.com. Six-storey monster on the waterfront. The only 'real' hotel in Semporna, which markets itself as a business establishment. Characterless two-star hotel rooms with a/c, TV, bathroom, kettle. Facilities include in-house tour office, gym (for which guests need to pay RM5 for each use), and restaurant. Front-facing rooms will have great views of the bay.

C **Arung Hayat Resort**, Jln Pinggir Bakau, T/F89-782526. A traditional Bajau home, a 10-minute trek from town in quiet countryside. Rooms are rickety and simple with lino floors and ill-fitting doors, but the place has charm and the staff are very friendly. They organize snorkelling trips to Sipadan and have a homestay on Mabul Island. The resort might need to relocate as there are plans to build a road through the current site.

C **Lee's Resthouse and Cafe**, Pekau Baru, Semporna New Town, T/F89-784491, leesrest@tm.net.my. Some rooms without windows but rooms appear clean and fresh with nice attached shower. Great value but poor location in the scruffy town. Helpful staff.

C **Seafest Inn**, Jln Kastam, T89-782399, F89-781282. Big comfortable rooms although rather plain. Rooms at the front will have views of the bay.

C-D **Damai Traveller's Lodge**, TL 89, 3rd floor, town centre, T89-782011, F89-781525. Recently refurbished budget hostel with big clean rooms, some with views of the market and ocean. More expensive rooms have TV and hot water. Stuck in town, but not a bad choice.

C-E **Dragon Inn**, Jln Kastam (next to the jetty), T89-781088, F89-781099. Stands out as the hotel built on stilts over the sea, a/c, restaurant, quite a novel setting and great value. Family rooms, doubles with attached bathroom, hot water, a/c, TV. Very rustic. Budget longhouse dorm for RM15 a night. Great experience to have a shower and look down at the green ocean through the wooden slatted floor. You can get a discount if you stop off at *Uncle Chang's dive shop* at the entrance and get a voucher. Recommended.

D **Semporna Lodging House,** Lot 33, Seafront, T019 8233564. Not really facing the sea, but a concrete car park at right angles to the bay. It's a five minute walk to the jetty. Staff here do not speak English and rooms are hot little hutches with brightly painted doors, with shared toilet and shower. Cheap but very simple.

Mabul *p459*

For people diving off Sipadan, Mabul is a convenient place to stay. There are 2 resorts on the island.

AL **Sipadan Water Village**, for reservation PO Box 62156, T89-751777, swvill@tm.net.my General sales agent: *Pan Borneo Tours and Travel*, constructed on several wharves in Bajau water village-style on ironwood stilts over the water. 35 chalets with private balconies, hot water showers, restaurant serving good range of cuisine, dive shop and centre, deep sea fishing tours available. Budget or student travellers are sometimes given large discounts. Prices range from RM470 for divers, including equipment, to RM370 for non-divers.

L **Sipadan Mabul Resort**, located at the southern tip of the island, overlooking Sipadan, PO Box 14125, T88-8823000, mabul@po.jaring.my 25 beach chalets with a/c, hot water showers, balcony, pool and Jacuzzi, restaurant serving Chinese and Western food in buffet style, all-inclusive price, PADI diving courses, snorkelling, windsurfing, deep sea fishing, volleyball, private diving boats.

B **Arung Hayat Resort homestay**. Mabul's only budget option is a 'homestay' run by this resort. Simple mattresses in a hut with 3 meals for RM70. Contact Arung Hayat on T89-782526.

Just offshore is a dilapidated sea platform (some flotsam from an oil rig apparently) which is run as a resort by Sea Ventures Dives. However it appears to be abandoned. With the closure of Sipadan this may well open up again. Sea Ventures Dives, T088 261669, F088 251667, 4th floor, Wisma Sabah, Kota Kinabalu.

Mataking and Kapalai *p459*

L **Mataking Island Reef Dive Resort**. Bookings through Tawau office, 193-195 Jln Bakau, Tawau, T89-770022, F89-763270, or KK counter office, Ground Floor, Wisma Sabah, KK, T/F88-318022, www.mataking.com. It also has a counter in Semporna at the jetty on Jln Kastam. The resort has three daily speedboats from Semporna jetty, journey takes 45 mins. The resort has chalets and deluxe rooms some with sea view and balconies, all with a/c. Facilities at the resort include a spa, satellite TV, internet, bar and restaurant.

AL **Sipadan-Kapalai Dive Resort.** Run by *Pulau Sipadan Resort & Tours*, 1st floor, Bandar Sabindo, Tawau, T89-765200, http://sipadan-kapalai.com/index.htm, www.sipadan-resort.com

Straddling the sandbank on stilts is this resort on Kapaali. The sand spit has no shelter, but hardened sun-bathers can roast here. The resort, modelled as a water village, has twin-sharing chalets,with attached bathrooms, balconies and amazing sea views all round connected by a network of wooden platforms.

Tawau *p460*

Hotels here are not great value for money. Avoid the cheaper lodging houses around Jln Stephen Tan, Jln Chester and Jln Cole Adams.

A **Belmont Marco Polo**, Jln Abaca/Jln Clinic, T89-777988, F89-763739. A/c, restaurant, best hotel in Tawau although considerably more expensive than the competition.

B **Emas**, Jln Utara, T89-762000, F89-763569. A/c, restaurant.

B **Merdeka**, Jln Masjid, T89-776655, F89-761743. A/c, restaurant.

B **Millennium**, 561 Jln Bakau, T89-771155, F89-755511. A/c, spacious rooms. Considerably cheaper than the Marco Polo and very acceptable.

B **North Borneo**, 52-53 Dunlop St, T89-763060, F89-773066. A/c, TV, hot shower, reasonable but expensive for Tawau.

C **Loong**, Jln Abaca, T89-765308. A/c, fully carpeted, clean and light.

C **Pan Sabah**, Jln Stephen Tan, behind local minibus station, T89-762488. A/c, TV, attached bathrooms, clean rooms and very good value compared to other options in town.

C **Sanctuary**, Jln Chester, T89-751155. A/c, clean, central and spacious, but sterile and characterless.

For an explanation of the sleeping and eating price codes used in this guide, see inside the front cover. Other relevant information is found in Essentials, pages 45-49.

Eating

Sandakan *p445, map p446*

p445, map p446

Sandakan is justifiably renowned for its inexpensive and delicious seafood.

Chinese

¥¥ **Golden Palace**, Trig Hill (2 km out of town), fresh seafood, specializes in drunken prawns, crab and lobster, and steamboats (owners will provide transport back to Sandakan if there are no taxis available). Recommended.

¥¥ **Japanese Corner**, Hsiang Garden Hotel , Jln Leila, Hsiang Garden Estate, T89-273122. Lobster and tiger prawns, good value and a popular local lunch venue.

¥¥ **Trig Hill Ming Restaurant**, Sabah Hotel, T89-213299. Km 1, Jln Utara. Cantonese and Szechuan cuisine, particularly renowned for dim sum (breakfast).

¥¥ **See Lok Yum**, next door to Sea View Garden, also very popular with locals.

Fast food

¥ **Fairwood Restaurant**, Jln Tiga, an inexpensive, a/c fast-food place with all the local favourites, situated in the centre of town.

Indian

¥ **Penang Curry House**, 15 Jln Dua. Fabulous Indian food for rock bottom prices. Simple canteen with friendly Filipina waitresses but a real gem in Sandakan. Try their dosa masala. Recommended.

International

¥¥ **English Tea House & Restaurant**, Agens Keith House, T89-222544, www.englishteahouse.org. Indoor and outdoor seating with crisp white tablecloths, pots of tea and scones. There's also a weekend BBQ. Good views of the town nearby.

¥¥ **XO Steak House**, Lot 16, Hsiang Garden Estate (opposite the *Hsiang Garden Hotel*), Mile 1.5, Jln Leila, lobster and tiger prawns and a good choice of fresh fish as well as Australian steaks, buffet barbecue on Fri nights. Recommended.

¥ **Apple Fast Food**, Lorong Edinburgh, good spot for breakfasts.

¥ **Fat Cat**, 206 Wisma Sandakan, 18 Jln Haji Saman, several branches around town, breakfasts recommended.

¥ **Hawaii**, City View Hotel, Lot 1, Block 23, 3rd Ave, Western and local food, set lunch. Recommended.

¥ **Seoul Garden**, Hsiang Garden Estate, Mile 1.5, Leila Rd, Korean.

Malay

¥ **Jiaman**, 1st Flr, Wisma Khoo Siak Chiew, serves interesting selection of Malay and Bajau dishes, no alcohol.

¥ **Perwira**, Hotel Ramai, Jln Leila, Malay and Indonesian, good value. Recommended.

Seafood

In the semi-outdoor restaurants situated at the top of Trig (Trigonometry) Hill (see entries under 'Chinese' cuisine).

¥¥ **Ocean King Seafood**, Mile 2.5, Jln Batu Sapi, T89-618111. Great seafood place built on stilts over the water. Big, over-the-top statues of lobster and marine life Disney up the place. But unbeatable for a relaxing sunset meal, great views.

¥¥ **Pesah Putih Baru**, on the coast, nearly at the end of Sandakan Bay, about 5 km from the port, great views of Sandakan and good food, recommended.

Vegetarian

¥ **Supreme Garden Vegetarian Restaurant**, Block 30, Bandar Ramai Ramai, Jln Leila (west of town), well priced and excellent range of dishes, open for lunch and dinner.

Coffee shops

New Bangsawan, next to New Bangsawan cinema, just off Jln Leila, Tanah Merah, no great shakes, but best restaurant in Tanah Merah (where there are stacks of coffee shops). **Silver Star Ice Cream and Café**, 3rd Ave, popular coffee shop with on-site satay stall in the evenings, particularly friendly and helpful management. Recommended.

Union Coffee Shop, 2nd Flr Hakka Association Building, Third Ave, budget.

Foodstalls

Next to minibus station, just before the community centre on the road to Ramai Ramai, also at summit of Trig Hill.

Sepilok Orang-utan Sanctuary and Rehabilitation Centre *p451*
By far the best place to eat is the verandah restaurant at the **Sepilok Jungle Resort** which serves international and Malaysian food. The food is merely okay but the setting is lovely.

Lahad Datu and around *p455*
Seafood

Melawar, 2nd Flr, Block 47, off Jln Teratai (around the corner from the Mido Hotel), seafood restaurant, popular with locals.
Ping Foong, 1½ km out of Lahad Datu, on Sandakan Rd, open-air seafood restaurant, highly recommended by locals.
Evergreen Snack Bar and Pub, on 2nd Flr, Jln Teratai, opposite the Hap Seng Building, a/c, excellent fish and chips and best-known for its tuna steaks. Recommended.
Golden Key, on stilts over the sea opposite the end of Jln Teratai, it is really just a tumble-down wooden coffee shop, but is well known for its seafood.
Good View, just over 500 m out of town on Tengku Rd. Recommended by locals.
Restoran Ali, opposite Hotel New Sabah, Indian, good roti.
Seng Kee, Block 39, opposite Mido Hotel and next to Standard Chartered Bank, cheap and good.

Foodstalls

Pasar Malam behind Mido Hotel on Jln Kastam Lama. Spicy barbecued fish (*ikan panggang*) and skewered chicken wings recommended. The new market has foodstalls upstairs with attractive views out to sea.

Semporna *p457*
Pearl City Restaurant, attached to Dragon Inn, pilehouse with good seafood, verify prices before ordering. Great setting.
Seafest Restaurant, next to the Seafest Inn, Malay food predominantly with some excellent fish dishes. Good standard for very reasonable prices.
Anjung Paghalian, next to police station near bridge to jetty. Simple outdoor place with good cheap seafood and giant iced avocado juices. Recommended.

Tawau *p460*
Chinese

Dragon Court, 1st Flr, Lot 15, Block 37 Jln Haji Karim, Chinese, popular with locals, lots of seafood.

International

Dreamland, 541 Jln Haji Karim. Good local selection.
Kublai Khan, Marco Polo Hotel, Jln Abaca/Jln Clinic. Cantonese food in cavernous dining hall
The Hut, Block 29, Lot 5, Fajar Complex, Town Extension II, Western, Malay and Chinese, large menu.

Malay

Asnur, 325B, Block 41, Fajar Complex. Thai and Malay, large choice.
Venice Coffee House, Marco Polo Hotel, Jln Abaca/Jln Clinic, 'hawker centre' for late night eating, Malay and Chinese.
Yun Lo, Jln Abaca (below the Hotel Loong), good Malay and Chinese. A popular spot with the locals, this has a good atmosphere. Recommended.

Seafood

May Garden, 1 km outside town on road to Semporna, outside seating.
Maxims, Block 30, Lot 6 Jln Haji Karim.

Foodstalls

Along the seafront.

Entertainment

Sandakan *p445, map p446*
There is a karaoke parlour on just about every street. **Tiffany Discotheatre and Karaoke**, Block C, 7-10, Ground and first floors, Jln Leila, Bandar Ramai-Ramai.

Tawau *p460*
Cinema is on Jln Stephen Tan, next to central market. There are **karaoke** bars on every street corner. Several of the hotels have nightclubs and bars.

Shopping

Sandakan *p445, map p446*
Almost everything in Sandakan is imported. There are some inexpensive batik shops and

some good tailors. **Wisma Sandakan**, next to the town mosque offers 3 floors of dimly lit shopping. Centre Point, near the bus station is even more down-at-heel. **Handicrafts Sabakraf**, opp Hotel Sandakan has basketry, pearls, and souvenirs.

Lahad Datu and around *p455*

The **Central Market** is on Jln Bungaraya and a spice market off Jln Teratai where Indonesian smugglers tout Gudang Garam cigarettes and itinerant dentists and *bumohs*, (witchdoctors), draw large crowds.

Semporna *p457*

Cultured pearls are sold by traders in town. Filipino handicrafts.

Tawau *p460*

General and fish market at the west end of Jln Dunlop, near the Customs Wharf.

Activities and tours

Sandakan *p445, map p446*

Bowling

Champion Bowl, Jln Leila, Bandar Ramai Ramai. Jln Leila is the main road that heads out of Sandakan, Champion Bowl is just out of town at Mile 1 ¼, T089-211396.

Golf

Sandakan Golf Club, Jalan Kolam, Bukit Padang, T88-247533, 10 km out of town, open to non-members.

Recreation clubs

Sepilok Recreation Club, Bandar Ramai Ramai, with snooker, sauna and darts as well as karaoke.

Tour operators

Many tour operators have their offices in Wisma Khoo Siak Chiew.

Borneo Ecotours, c/o Hotel Hsiang Garden, PO Box 02, Jln Leila, T89-220210, F89-213614. **Crystal Quest**, Sabah Park Jetty, Jln Buli Sim Sim, T89-212711, cquest@tm.net.my, the only company running accommodation on Pulau Selingan, Turtle Islands National Park. **Capac Travel Service**, ground floor, Rural District Building, Jln Tiga, T89-217288. Ticketing, tour and hotel services. **Discovery Tours**, Room 908 10th Flr, Wisma Khoo Siak Chiew, T89-274106, F89-274107. **S.I. Tours**, 1st floor, Wisma Khoo Siak Chiew, T89-213501, www.sitours.com.my. Well established company running tours to Gomantong Caves, Kinabantangan, and Turtle Islands National Park. Recommended.**Wildlife Expeditions**, Room 903, 9th Flr, Wisma Khoo Siak Chiew, Lebuh Tiga, Jln Buli Sim-Sim, T89-219616, F89-214570 (branches in Sabah Hotel), the most expensive, but also the most efficient, with the best facilities and the best guides.

Turtle Islands National Park *p449*

The average cost of a one night tour including one night's accommodation and boat transfer is RM360 up. An expedition to the islands needs to be well planned; vagaries such as bad weather, which can prevent you from leaving the islands as planned, can mess up itineraries. Most visitors book their trips well in advance.

Gomantong Caves *p452*

It is easiest on a tour, see under Sandakan. The caves are accessible by an old logging road, which can be reached by bus from the main Sandakan-Sukau Rd. The timing of the bus is inconvenient for those wishing to visit the caves. Alternatively take a taxi (around RM150 from Sandakan). It is a good idea to visit the caves on the way to Sukau, where you can stay overnight.

Lahad Datu and around *p455*

Tour operators

Borneo Nature Tours, Block 3, Fajar Centre, T89-880207, F89-885051.

Semporna*p457*

Tour operators

Today Travel Services, No 90, Lot 2, Tingkat Bawah, T89-781112. Sells AirAsia and MAS flights to KK and KL from Tawau, the nearest airport. Book well in advance.

Sipadan Island Marine Reserve *p458*

Tour operators

Each operator rents out equipment (RM75-100 per day) and provides all food and accommodation. Pre-arranged packages operated by the companies sometimes include air transfer to and from Kota Kinabalu. 'Walk-in' rates are cheaper.

Borneo Divers, Rooms 401-412, fourth floor, Wisma Sabah, Kota Kinabalu, T88-222226, bdivers@po.jaring.my Major Sipadan player, it organises trips from KK to Sipadan with accommodation on Mabul. However, some tourists complain the operation has gone downhill. Three day package with 10 dives and stay on Mabul around RM1,200.

Pulau Sipadan Resort, 484, Block P, Bandar Sabindo, Tawau, T89-765200, F89-763575, www.sipadan-resort.com Organizes dive tours, food and lodging and diving instruction, snorkelling equipment is also available, maximum of 30 divers at any one time. It also runs accommodation on Pulau Kapalai.

Sipadan Dive Centre, A1103, 11th Flr, Wisma Merdeka, Jalan Tun Razak, Kota Kinabalu, T88-240584, sipadan@po.jaring.my Packages (all in) approx: US$740 (5 days/4 nights). Recommended. Most dive centres offer PADI courses here.

Uncle Chang's, entrance to Dragon Inn, Semporna, T019 8030988/89-781002. Uncle Chang, entrepreneur extraordinaire, offers the budget traveller everything. He can get discount bus tickets, offers shuttle service to the airport, gets discounts for the Dragon Inn, has an efficient laundry service and runs some great dive trips out to Sipadan including courses. 3 boat dives including all equipment hire and lunch for RM270.

Tawau *p460*

Diving

Borneo Divers, 46 1st Flr, Jln Dunlop, T89-762259, F89-761691.

Pulau Sipadan Resort & Tours, 1st floor, Bandar Sabindo, Tawau, T89-765200, F89-763563.

Golf

9-hole golf course, modest green fees, even cheaper during the week.

Tour operators

GSU, T89-772531, booking agent for Kalimantan.

Transport

Sandakan *p445, map p446*

Air

The airport is 10 km north of the town centre (RM15 by taxi into town). Early morning flights from **KK** to **Sandakan** allow breath-taking close-up views of Mt Kinabalu as the sun rises. Connections with **Lahad Datu**, **Kudat**, **Tawau** (RM87) and **KK** (RM96). There are also connections between **KL** and Sandakan by **MAS** and **AirAsia**.

Airline offices MAS, Ground Flr, Sabah Building, Jln Pelabuhan, T89-273966; **AirAsia** office on Jln Dua.

Boat

There's a ferry service to Zamboanga in the southern **Philippines**. The journey takes eight hours and leaves at 1700 on Tues and Thu from Sandakan (RM58-RM150, for a suite).

Bus and minibus

Local minibuses from the bus stop between the Esso and Shell stations on on Jln Pryer.

Sandakan's a/c long distance buses leave from the bus station at mile 2.5. Sometimes buses, and all minibuses here, wait until they are full before they depart, so be prepared for a long wait. Regular connections with most towns in Sabah including **Kota Kinabalu**, 8 hrs (RM29.25), **Ranau**, 3½ hrs, **Lahad Datu** (RM15, 3-4 hours). Buses start at 0715, and then several departures until 1100. After this you will have to take a Tawau bus, get off at Simpang Assam and take a minibus into Lahad Datu (RM0.50) **Tawau** (RM28.05, 6 hours). Buses from 0630, every half hour until 1100. Also one bus at 1400. **Semporna** (RM30), one departure around 0800.

Turtle Islands National Park *p449*

Boat

Daily speedboat at 0930, returning 1900, RM100, 40 km NE of Sandakan at Sabah Parks Jetty. Tour operators have their own boats and the fee is included with the package price, so times will vary.

Sepilok Orang-utan Sanctuary and Rehabilitation Centre *p451*

Bus

8 daily public buses from **Sandakan**, from the central minibus terminal in front of Nak

Hotel. Ask for the Sepilok Batu 14 line. From the airport, the most convenient way to reach Sepilok is by **taxi**. Sepilok is 1.9 km from the main road. A taxi should cost around RM25 into Sandakan. You can charter a car for RM30 into Sandakan from the Sepilok Jungle Resort.

Lahad Datu *p455*

Air

Connections with **Tawau**, **Sandakan**, **Semporna**, **KK** and **Kudat**.

Airline offices MAS, Ground Flr, Mido Hotel, Jln Main, T89-881707.

Boat

Fishing boats take paying passengers from the old wharf (end of Jln Kastam Lama) to **Tawau** and **Semporna**, although time-wise (and, more to the point, safety wise) it makes much more sense to go by road or air.

Minibus

Minibuses and what are locally known as wagons (basically 7-seater, 4WD Mitsubishis) leave from the bus station on Jln Bunga Raya (behind Bangunan Hap Seng at the mosque end of Jln Teratai) and from opposite the Shell station. Regular connections with **Tawau**, 2½ hrs, **Semporna**, **Sandakan**, **Madai**.

Danum Valley Conservation Area *p456*

From Lahad Datu, turn left along the logging road at Km 15 on the Lahad Datu-Tawau road to Taliwas and then left again to field centre, 85 km west of Lahad Datu. The Borneo Rainforest Lodge is 97 km (not an easy trip) from **Lahad Datu**; it provides a transfer service (2 hrs), telephone the Lodge for details.

Semporna *p457*

Minibus and bus

Minibus station in front of USNO headquarters. Regular connections with **Tawau** (RM5, 1 ½ hrs) and **Lahad Datu**, most of these leave in the morning. Minibus to Tawau airport.
One daily bus to **KK** (1930, RM48, 10 hrs).

Mataking and Kapalai *p459*

Air and sea

Flight to Tawau, minibus, taxi, or resort van to Semporna (1½ hrs), from where speed boats depart for the islands (between 30mins and 60 mins). Boats to the islands are taken either with dive companies or as a transfer to a resort. Lots of boats leave daily but generally only in the morning between 0700-1000 for the day-trip departure.

Tawau *p460*

Air

The airport is 2 km from town centre. Regular connections with **KK**, **Lahad Datu** and **Sandakan**. AirAsia and MAS both run daily flights between Tawau and KL.

To Tarakan, Indonesia It is necessary to obtain a visa in advance. You can try your luck at the Indonesian consulate in Tawau and in KK. It is possible to fly to Tarakan from Tawau; Indonesian Bouraq and MAS operate flights.

Airline offices MAS, Lot 1A, Wisma SASCO, Fajar Complex, T89-765533. Merdeka Travel, 41 Jln Dunlop, T89-772534/1, booking agents for Bouraq (Indonesian airline). Merpati, 47A Jln Dunlop, 1st Flr, next to Borneo Divers, T89-752323. Sabah Air, Tawau Airport, T89-774005. AirAsia office at the airport.

Boat

Packed boats leave Tawau's Customs Wharf (behind Pasar Ikan) twice daily at 0800 and 1600 for **Pulau Nunukan Timur**, in **Kalimantan**, Indonesia, 2 hrs. It is possible to get a direct boat from **Tawau** to **Tarakan, Indonesia**. Tickets available from the offices opposite Pasar Ikan. From there it is possible to get a boat to Tarakan the next day, or a direct boat to **Pare Pare** (Sulawesi), 48 hrs. There are no longer direct boats to Tarakan and travellers must stop over at Nunukan. All visitors now need to get a visa before arriving in Indonesia.

Bus

Station on Jln Wing Lock (west end of town). Minibus station on Jln Dunlop (centre of town). Direct service from **Tawau** to **Kota Kinabalu** leaving at 2000 to arrive 0500 in KK.

It is possible to drive from **Sapulut** (south of **Keningau**) across the interior to **Tawau** on logging roads but a 4WD vehicle is required.

Directory

Sandakan *p445, map p446*
Banks Most around Lebuh Tiga and Jln Pelabuhan. HSBC, Jln Pelabuhan/Lebuh Tiga. Standard Chartered, Sabah Building, Jln Pelabuhan. **Internet** Sandakan Cybercafe, 2nd Flr, Wisma Sandakan; also internet cafes in Centre Point mall. **Post** General Post Office Jln Leila, to the west of town. Parcel post off Lebuh Tiga. **Places of worship** St Michael's (Anglican) and St Mary's (RC) are on the hill at the south end of Sandakan town. There is also the True Jesus Church, St Joseph's Catholic Church, the SIB Baptist Church, the All Saints Anglican Church and the Basel Church. **Useful addresses** Immigration Federal Building, Jln Leila. Sabah Parks Office Room 906, 9th Flr, Wisma Khoo, Lebuh Tiga, T89-273453. Bookings for Turtle Islands National Park.
Telephone Telecom Office, 6th Flr, Wisma Khoo Siak Chiew, Jln Buli Sim-Sim.

Kinabatangan River *p454*
Tour operators will transport their guests to the lodge or camp as part of the package, some of them offer tours of Gomantong and/or Sepilok en route. Uncle Tan's take you from their B&B just outside Sandakan (buses from KK to Sandakan and Sandakan to Lahad Datu stop outside). The others have transport from Sandakan, Tawau, Danum Valley and Semporna.

Lahad Datu *p455*
Banks Standard Chartered, in front of Mido Hotel. **Post** Post Office, Jln Kenanga, next to the Lacin cinema. **Useful** addresses Danum Coorindinator, Rakyat Berjaya, ground floor, Fajar Centre, T89-881092/881688, danum@care2.com, for permits to Danum Valley. Bookings can also be made for the Danum Valley from Kota Kinabalu at the Sabah Foundation headquarters, Likas Bay, Jln Sulaman, T88-326327/T, rosejkj@ocsb-sabah.com.my.

Semporna *p457*
Internet Several places in town. Cyber planet (opposite Damai), first floor, open 0800-2200, RM3 per hour. Zanna Computer, next to Maybank, first floor. @DCCN opposite the bus station, RM2 per hour (this place is often closed). **Post** General Post Office next to minibus station.

Tawau *p460*
Banks Bumiputra, Jln Nusantor, on seafront. HSBC, 210 Jln Utara, opposite the padang. Standard Chartered, 518 Jln Habib Husein (behind HSBC). Exchange kiosk at wharf. **Post** Post Office off Jln Nusantor, behind the fish market. **Embassies and consulates** Indonesian Consulate, Jln Apas, mile 1.5. **Useful** addresses Immigration Jln Stephen.

Sabah Background

The name 'Sabah' probably derives from the Arabic Zir-e Bad, meaning 'the land below the wind'. Appropriately, as the state lies just to the south of the typhoon belt. Officially, the territory has only been called Sabah since 1963, when it joined the Malay federation, but the name appears to have been in use long before that. When Baron Gustav Von Overbeck was awarded the cession rights to North Borneo by the Sultan of Brunei in 1877, one of the titles conferred on him was 'Maharajah of Sabah'. And in the Handbook of British North Borneo, published in 1890, it says: "In Darvel Bay there are the remnants of a tribe which seems to have been much more plentiful in bygone days – the Sabahans". From the founding of the Chartered Company until 1963, Sabah was known as British North Borneo.

Sabah has a population of almost 2.5 million, and a good number of illegal immigrants on top of that. The inhabitants of Sabah can be divided into four main groups: the Murut, the Kadazan, the Bajau and the Chinese, as well as a small Malay population. These main groups are subdivided into several different tribes (see page 475).

History

Prehistoric stone tools have been found in eastern Sabah, suggesting that people were living in limestone caves in the Madai area 17,000-20,000 years ago. The caves were periodically settled from then on; pottery dating from the late Neolithic period has been found, and by the early years of the first millennium AD, Madai's inhabitants were making iron spears and decorated pottery. The Madai and Baturong caves were lived in continuously until about the 16th century, and several carved stone coffins and burial jars have been discovered in the jungle caves, one of which is exhibited in the Sabah State Museum. The caves were also known for their birds' nests; Chinese traders were buying the nests from Borneo as far back as AD 700. In addition, they exported camphor wood, pepper and other forest products to Imperial China.

There are very few archaeological records indicating Sabah's early history, although there is documentary evidence of links between a long-lost kingdom, based in the area of the Kinabatangan River, and the Sultanate of Brunei, whose suzerainty was once most of North Borneo. By the start of the 18th century, Brunei's power had begun to wane in the face of European expansionism. To counter the economic decline, it is thought the Sultan increased taxation, which led to civil unrest. In 1704 the Sultan of Brunei had to ask the Sultan of Sulu's help in putting down a rebellion in Sabah, and in return, the Sultan of Sulu received most of what is now Sabah.

The would-be white rajahs of Sabah

It was not until 1846 that the British entered into a treaty with the Sultan of Brunei and took possession of the island of Labuan; in part to counter the growing influence of the Rajah of Sarawak, James Brooke. The British were also wary of the Americans; the US Navy signed a trade treaty with the Sultan of Brunei in 1845 and in 1860 Claude Lee Moses was appointed American Consul-General in Brunei Town. He was only interested in making a personal fortune and quickly persuaded the sultan to cede him land in Sabah. He sold these rights to two Hong Kong-based American businessmen who formed the American Trading Company of Borneo. They styled themselves as Rajahs and set up a base at Kimanis, just south of Papar. It was a disaster. One of them died of malaria, the Chinese labourers they imported from Hong Kong began to starve and the settlement was abandoned in 1866.

But the idea of a trading colony on the North Borneo coast interested the Austrian consul in Hong Kong, Baron Gustav von Overbeck, who, in turn, sold the concept to Alfred Dent, a wealthy English businessman also based in Hong Kong. With Dent's money, Overbeck bought the Americans' cession from the Sultan of Brunei, and extended the territory to cover most of modern-day Sabah. The deal was clinched on 29 December 1877, and Overbeck agreed to pay the sultan 15,000 Straits dollars a year. A few days later Overbeck discovered that the entire area had already been ceded to the Sultan of Sulu 173 years earlier, so he immediately sailed to Sulu and offered the sultan an annual payment of 5,000 Straits dollars for the territory. On his return, he dropped three Englishmen off along the coast to set up trading posts; one of them was William Pryer, who founded Sandakan (see page 446). Three years later, Queen Victoria granted Dent a royal charter and, to the chagrin of the Dutch, the Spanish and the Americans, the British North Borneo Company was formed. London insisted that it was to be a British-only enterprise however, and Overbeck was forced to sell out. The first managing director of the company was the Scottish adventurer and former gun-runner William C Cowie. He was in charge of the day-to-day running of the territory, while the British government supplied a governor.

The new chartered company, with its headquarters in the City of London, was given sovereignty over Sabah and a free hand to develop it. The British administrators soon began to collect taxes from local people and quickly clashed with members of the

Sabah's ethnic breakdown

	Population	%
Kadazan/Dusun	561,000	17.8%
Other Muslim	415,400	13.2%
Bajau	353,200	11.3%
Chinese	327,900	10.5%
Others	275,600	8.8%
Malay	204,700	6.5%
Murut	92,000	2.9%
Non-Malay	906,800	28.9%

Total population (Malay and non-Malay – Filipino and Indonesian etc)
3.14 million

Source: July 2000 estimates from Monthly Statistical Bulletin, Sabah.

Brunei nobility. John Whitehead, a British administrator, wrote: "I must say, it seemed rather hard on these people that they should be allowed to surrender up their goods and chattels to swell even indirectly the revenue of the company". The administration levied poll-tax, boat tax, land tax, fishing tax, rice tax, tapai (rice wine) tax and a 10% tax on proceeds from the sale of birds' nests. Resentment against these taxes sparked the six-year Mat Salleh rebellion (see page 404) and the Rundum Rebellion, which peaked in 1915, during which hundreds of Muruts were killed by the British.

Relations were not helped by colonial attitudes towards the local Malays and tribal people. One particularly arrogant district officer, Charles Bruce, wrote: "The mind of the average native is equivalent to that of a child of four. So long as one remembers that the native is essentially a child and treats him accordingly he is really tractable." Most recruits to the chartered company administration were fresh-faced graduates from British universities, mainly Oxford and Cambridge. For much of the time there were only 40-50 officials running the country. Besides the government officials, there were planters and businessmen: tobacco, rubber and timber became the most important exports. There were also Anglican and Roman Catholic missionaries. British North Borneo was never much of a money-spinner – the economy suffered whenever commodity prices slumped – but it mostly managed to pay for itself until the Second World War.

The Japanese interregnum

Sabah became part of Dai Nippon, or Greater Japan, on New Year's Day 1942, when the Japanese took Labuan. On the mainland, the Japanese Imperial Army and Kempetai (military police) were faced with the might of the North Borneo Armed Constabulary, about 650 men. Jesselton (Kota Kinabalu) was occupied on 9 January and Sandakan, 10 days later. All Europeans were interned and when Singapore fell in 1942, 2,740 prisoners of war were moved to Sandakan, most of whom were Australian, where they were forced to build an airstrip. On its completion, the POWs were ordered to march to Ranau, 240 km through the jungle. This became known as 'The Borneo Death March' and only six men survived (see page 448).

The Japanese were hated in Sabah and the Chinese mounted a resistance movement which was led by the Kuching-born Albert Kwok Hing Nam. He also recruited Bajaus and Sulus to join his guerrilla force which launched the 'Double Tenth Rebellion' (the attacks took place on 10 October 1943). The guerrillas took Tuaran, Jesselton and Kota Belud, killing many Japanese and sending others fleeing into the jungle. But the following day the Japanese bombed the towns and troops quickly retook the towns and captured the rebels. A mass execution followed in which 175 rebels were decapitated. On 10 June 1945 Australian forces landed at Labuan, under the command of American General MacArthur. Allied planes bombed the main towns and virtually obliterated Jesselton and Sandakan. Sabah was liberated on 9 September, and thousands of the remaining 21,000 Japanese troops were killed in retaliation, many by Muruts.

A British Military Administration governed Sabah in the immediate aftermath of the war, and the cash-strapped chartered company sold the territory to the British crown for £1.4m in mid-1946. The new crown colony was modelled on the chartered company's administration and set about rebuilding the main towns and war-shattered infrastructure. In May 1961, following Malaysian independence, Prime Minister Tunku Abdul Rahman proposed the formation of a federation incorporating Malaya (ie Peninsular Malaysia), Singapore, Brunei, Sabah and Sarawak (see page 489). Later that same year, Tun Fuad Stephens, a timber magnate and newspaper publisher formed Sabah's first-ever political party, the United National Kadazan Organisation (UNKO). Two other parties were founded shortly afterwards – the Sabah Chinese Association and the United Sabah National Organization (USNO). The British were keen to leave the colony and the Sabahan parties thrashed out the pros and cons of joining the proposed federation. Elections were held in late-1962 in which a UNKA-USNO alliance (the Sabah Alliance) swept to power and the following August, Sabah became an independent country...for 16 days. Like Singapore and Sarawak, Sabah opted to join the federation, to the indignation of the Philippines and Indonesia which both had claims on the territory. Jakarta's objections resulted in the konfrontasi – an undeclared war with Malaysia (see page 386) which was not settled until 1966.

Modern Sabah

Politics

Sabah's political scene has always been lively and never more so than in 1994 when the then Malaysian Prime Minister, Doctor Mahathir Mohamad, pulled off what commentators described as a democratic coup d'état. With great political dexterity, he out-manoeuvered his rebellious rivals and managed to dislodge the opposition state government, despite the fact that it had just won a state election.

Following Sabah's first state election in 1967, the Sabah Alliance ruled until 1975 when the newly formed multi-racial party, Berjaya, swept the polls. Berjaya had been set up with the financial backing of the United Malays National Organization (UMNO), the mainstay of the ruling Barisan Nasional (National Front) coalition on the Peninsula. Over the following decade that corrupt administration crumbled and in 1985 the opposition Sabah United Party (PBS), led by the Christian Kadazan Datuk Joseph Pairin Kitingan, won a landslide victory and became the only state government in Malaysia that did not belong to the UMNO-led coalition. It became an obvious embarrassment to then Prime Minister Doctor Mahathir Mohamad to have a rebel Christian state in his predominantly Muslim federation. Nonetheless, the PBS eventually joined Barisan Nasional, believing its partnership in the coalition would help iron things out. It did not.

When the PBS came to power, the federal government and Sabahan opposition parties openly courted Filipino and Indonesian immigrants in the state, almost all of whom are Muslim, and secured identity cards for many of them, enabling them to vote. Doctor Mahathir has made no secret of his preference for a Muslim government in Sabah. Nothing, however, was able to dislodge the PBS, which was resoundingly returned to power in 1990. The federal government had long been suspicious of Sabahan politicians, particularly following the PBS's defection from Doctor Mahathir's coalition in the run-up to the 1990 general election, a move which bolstered the opposition alliance. Doctor Mahathir described this as "a stab in the back", and referred to Sabah as "a thorn in the flesh of the Malaysian federation". But in the event, the Prime Minister won that national election convincingly without PBS help, prompting fears of political retaliation. Those fears proved justified in the wake of the election.

Sabah paid heavily for its 'disloyalty'; prominent Sabahans were arrested as secessionist conspirators under Malaysia's Internal Security Act, which provides for indefinite detention without trial. Among them was Jeffrey Kitingan, brother of the Chief Minister and head of the Yayasan Sabah, or Sabah Foundation (see page 405). At the same time, Joseph Pairin Kitingan was charged with corruption. The feeling in Sabah was that the men were bearing the brunt of Doctor Mahathir's personal political vendetta.

As the political feud worsened, the federal government added to the fray by failing to promote Sabah to foreign investors. As investment money dried up, so did federal development funds; big road and housing projects were left unfinished for years. Many in Sabah felt their state was being short-changed by the federal government. The political instability had a detrimental effect on the state economy and the business community felt that continued feuding would be economic lunacy. Politicians in the Christian-led PBS, however, continued to claim that Sabah wasn't getting its fair share of Malaysia's economic boom. They said the agreement which enshrined a measure of autonomy for Sabah when it joined the Malaysian federation had been eroded.

The main bone of contention was the state's oil revenues, worth around US$852m a year, of which 95% disappeared into federal coffers. There were many other sore points too and as the list of grievances grew longer, the state government exploited them to the full. By 1994, anti-federal feelings were running high. The PBS continued to promote the idea of 'Sabah for Sabahans', a defiant slogan in a country where the federal government was working to centralize power. Because Doctor Mahathir likes to be in control, the idea of granting greater autonomy to a distant, opposition-held state was not on his agenda. A showdown was inevitable.

It began in January 1994. As Datuk Pairin's corruption trial drew to a close, he dissolved the state assembly, paving the way for fresh elections. He did this to cover the eventuality of his being disqualified from office through a 'guilty' verdict: he wanted to have his own team in place to take over from him. He was convicted of corruption. But the fine imposed on him was just under the disqualifying threshold, and, to the Prime Minister's fury, he led the PBS into the election. Doctor Mahathir put his newly appointed deputy, Anwar Ibrahim, in charge of the National Front alliance campaign.

Datuk Pairin won the election, but by a much narrower margin than before. He alleged vote-buying and ballot rigging. He accused Doctor Mahathir's allies of whipping up the issue of religion. He spoke of financial inducements being offered to Sabah's Muslim voters, some of whom are Malay, but most of whom are Bajau tribes people and Filipino immigrants. His swearing-in ceremony was delayed for 36 hours: the governor said he was sick; Datuk Parin said his political enemies were trying to woo defectors from the ranks of the PBS, to overturn his small majority. He was proved right.

Three weeks later, he was forced to resign; his fractious party had virtually collapsed in disarray and a stream of defections robbed him of his majority. Datuk Parin's protestations that his assemblymen had been bribed to switch sides were ignored. The local leader of Doctor Mahathir's ruling party, Tan Sri Sakaran Dandai, was swiftly sworn in as the new Chief Minister.

In the 1995 general election the PBS did remarkably well, holding onto eight seats and defeating a number of Front candidates who had defected from the PBS the previous year. Sabah was one area, along with the East Coast state of Kelantan, which resisted the Mahathir/BN electoral steamroller.

The March 1999 state elections pitted UMNO against Pairin's PBS. Again the issues were local autonomy, vote rigging, the role of national politics and political parties in state elections, and money. A new element was the role that Anwar Ibrahim's trial might play in the campaign (see page 492) but otherwise it was old wine in mostly old bottles.

The outcome was a convincing win for Mahathir and the ruling National Front who gathered 31 of the 48 state assembly seats – three more than the Prime Minister forecast. Mahathir once again used the lure of development funds from KL to convince local Sabahans where their best interests might lie. "We are not being unfair" Mahathir said. "We are more than fair, but we cannot be generous to the opposition. We can be generous to a National Front government in Sabah. That I can promise."

But worryingly for the National Front, the opposition Parti Bersatu Sabah (PBS) still managed to garner the great bulk of the Kadazan vote and in so doing won 17 seats. As in Sarawak, the election, in the end, was more about local politics than about the economic crisis and the Anwar trial.

However, in the 2004 state and federal elections, the PBS rejoined the National Front, and faced only with the disunity of opposition parties, the BN-PBS coalition won resounding victories in both polls. A legitimate alternative to KL's ruling steamroller has all but died. The BN gave itself half the seats, and distributed the rest between Chinese representatives and one third to other non Malays. The message is that Sabahans accept dominace by the Malay minority from KL in return for money and development.

Culture

People

Sabah's main tribal communities comprise the Kadazan, who mostly live on the west coast, the Murut, who inhabit the interior, to the south, and the Bajau, who are mainly settled around Gunung Kinabalu. There are more than 30 tribes, more than 50 different languages and about 100 dialects. Sabah also has a large Chinese population and many illegal Filipino immigrants.

Kadazans

The Kadazans are the largest ethnic group in Sabah comprising about a third of the population and are a peaceful agrarian people with a strong cultural identity. Until Sabah joined the Malaysian Federation in 1963, they were known as 'Dusuns', meaning 'peasants' or 'orchard people'. This name was given to them by outsiders, and picked up by the British. It became, in effect, a residual category including all those people who were not Muslim or Chinese. Most Kadazans call themselves after their tribal names. They can be broken into several tribes including the Lotud of Tuaran, the Rungus of the Kudat and Bengkoka Peninsula, the Tempasuk, the Tambanuo, Kimarangan and the Sanayo. Minokok and Tengara Kadazans live in the upper Kinabatangan River basin while those living near other big rivers are just known as Orang Sungai, or 'river people'. Most Kadazans used to live in longhouses; these are virtually all gone now. The greatest chance of coming across a longhouse in Sabah is in the Rungus area of the Kudat Peninsula; even there, former longhouse residents are moving into detached, kampong-style houses while one or two stay for the use of tourists.

But Kadazan identity is not that simple. The 1991 census lists both Kadazans (110,866) and Dusuns (229,194). The 1970 census listed all as Kadazan, while the 1960 census listed all as Dusun. In 1995 the Malaysian government agreed to add the common language of these people(s) to the national repertoire to be taught in schools. This they named Kadazandusun. The others are Malay, Chinese, Tamil and Iban.

All the Kadazan groups had similar customs and modes of dress (see below). Up to the Second World War, many Kadazan men wore the chawat loin cloth. The Kadazans used to hunt with blowpipes, and in the 19th century, were still head-hunting. Today, however, they are known for their gentleness and honesty; their produce can often be seen sitting unattended at roadside stalls, and passing motorists are expected to pay what they think fair. The Kadazans traditionally traded their agricultural produce at large markets, held at meeting points, called tamus (see box, page 433). The Kadazan are farmers, and the main rice-producers of Sabah. They used to be animists, and were

Dance

Name of dance	Tribe	District
Sumazau Penampang	Kadan/Dusun	Penampang, west coast
Angalang	Murut	Pensiangan and Tenom Interior and south
Mangiluk	Suluk	East coast
Magunatip	Murut and	Interior and south
Adai Adai	Brunei Malay	Sipitang and Membakut,
Mongigol Sumundai	Rungus	Kudat and Pitas, north of Sabah
Limbai	Bajau	Kota Belud, west coast
Dansa	Cocos	Lahad Datu, east coast
Bolak Bolak	Bajau	Semporna, east coast
Mongigol Sumayan	Lotud	Tuaran, west coast
Umang-Umang Ting-Ting	Brunei Malay	Bongawan, west coast
Daling-Daling	Suluk	East coast
Sumazau Papar	Kadazan, Dusun	Paper, west coast
Titikas	Orang Sungai	Kinabatangan, east coast
Liliput	Bisaya	Beaufort, west coast
Kuda Pasu	Bajau	Kota Belud, west coast

said to live in great fear of evil spirits; most of their ceremonies were rituals aimed at driving out these spirits. The job of communicating with the spirits of the dead, the tombiivo, was done by priestesses, called bobohizan. They are the only ones who can speak the ancient Kadazan language, using a completely different vocabulary from modern Kadazan. Most Kadazans converted to Christianity, mainly Roman Catholicism, during the 1930s, although there are also some Muslim Kadazan.

The big cultural event in the Kadazan year is the Harvest Festival which takes place in May. The ceremony, known as the Magavau ritual, is officiated by a high priestess, (Bobohizan). These elderly women, who wear black costumes and colourful headgear with feathers and beads, are now rarely seen. The ceremony ends with offerings to the Bambaazon (rice spirit). After the ceremonies Catholic, Muslim and animist Kadazans

Description

Performed during Annual harvest Pemanpang Festival (Pesta Kaamatan) to honour the rice spirit (*Bambaazon*). Sumazau means dancing.

A solo warrior dance, accompanied by a group of women dancers (*angalong*). Originally performed after a victorious battle or head-hunting trip.

Performed at weddings and social events.

These dancers need skill and agility to dance among bamboo poles which are hit Kwijau Dusun together to produce the rhythm of the dance.

Evolved from a song; it tells of the activities of the local fishermen and farmers southwest of Sabah

Can be performed as part of certain ritual festivals. For instance, Thanksgiving to rice spirit for a bountiful harvest or moving into a new house.

Performed at weddings, characterized by graceful wrist rotations. Accompanying music is called bertitik.

Performed at weddings. It features energetic foot stomping.

Bolak Bolak is Malay for *castanets*. The dancers hold the castanets and create the rhythm of the music.

Ritual dance performed during *Rumaha* ceremony to honour spirits of skulls, or the *Mangahau* ceremony for the spirits of sacred jars.

Celebrates the birth of a newborn child

A 'courting' dance said to be derived from the English 'darling'. Usually accompanied by a love song.

Performed at similar occasions to Sumazau Penampang. Distinctive foot work.

Titikas is based on the Ingki-Ingki game, similar to hopscotch.

Liliput means 'go around'. A dance to cast away evil spirits in a possessed person.

Originally performed by horsemen or escort a bridegroom and his entourage to the bride's home. The female dancers hold handkerchieves as a sign of welcome.

all come together to play traditional sports such as wrestling and buffalo racing. This is about the only occasion when visitors are likely to see Kadazan in their traditional costumes. In the Penampang area a woman's costume consists of a fitted, sleeveless tunic and ankle-length skirt of black velvet. Belts of silver coins (himpogot) and brass rings are worn round the waist; a colourful sash is also worn. Men dress in a black, long-sleeved jacket over black trousers; they also wear a siga, colourful woven head gear. These costumes have become more decorative in recent years, with colourful embroidery. Villages send the finalists of local beauty contests to the grand final of the Unduk Ngadau harvest festival queen competition in Penampang, near Kota Kinabalu.

It is the Kadazans who dominate the Pasti Bersatu Sabah (PBS), the critical piece in Sabah's political jigsaw.

Tapai – Sabah's rice wine

Tapai, the fiery Sabahan rice wine, is much loved by the Kadazan and the Murut. It was even more popular before the two tribal groups' wholesale conversion to Christianity in the 1930s. Writer Hedda Morrison noted in 1957 that: "The squalor and wretchedness arising from [their] continual drunkenness made the Murut a particularly useful object of missionary endeavour. In the 1930s missionaries succeeded in converting nearly all the Murut to Christianity. The Murut grasped at this new faith much as the drowning man is said to grasp at a straw. From being the most drunken people in Borneo, they became the most sober." In the Sabah State Museum (see page 403) there is a recipe for tapai, also known as buffalos' blood, which was taken down by an administrator during chartered company days:

"Boil 12lbs of the best glutinous rice until well done. In a wide-mouthed jar, lay the rice in layers of no more than two fingers deep, and between layers, place a total of about 20½-oz yeast cakes. Add two cups of water, tinctured with the juice of six beetroots. Cover jar with muslin and leave to ferment. Each day, uncover it and remove dew which forms on the muslin. On the fifth day, stir the mixture vigorously and leave for four weeks. Store for one full year, after which it shall be full of virtue and potence and most smooth upon the palate."

Tapai is drunk from communal jars, which were also used as burial urns, through bamboo straws. The jar is filled nearly to its brim with tapai. Large leaves are placed on the top just under the lower edge of the rim. These leaves are pierced with straws for sucking up the liquid and the intervening space between the leaves and the top of the jar is filled with water. Etiquette demands that one drinks till the water has been drained off the leaves. They are then flooded again and the process is repeated. There is also the distilled form of tapai, called montaku, which is even more potent. When North Borneo became a British crown colony after the Second World War, the administration was concerned about the scourge of tapai drinking on three counts. First, it was said to consume a large portion of the natives' potential food crop, second, it usually caused a crime wave whenever it was drunk, and thirdly, it was blamed for the high rate of infant mortality as mothers frequently gave their babies a suck at the straw.

Oscar Cook, a former district officer in the North Borneo Civil Service, noted in his 1923 book Borneo: the Stealer of Hearts, that tapai was not to everyone's fancy and certainly not to his. "As an alternative occupation to head-hunting, the Murut possess a fondness for getting drunk, indulged in on every possible occasion. Tapai, or pengasai, as the Murut calls it, is not a nice drink. In fact, to my thinking it is the very reverse, for it is chiefly made from fermented rice... is very potent, and generally sour and possessed of a pungent and nauseating odour. Births, marriages, deaths, sowing, harvesting and any occasion that comes to mind is made the excuse for a debauch. It is customary for Murut to show respect to the white man by producing their very best tapai, and pitting the oldest and ugliest women of the village against him in a drinking competition." Cook admits that all this proved too much for him and when he was transferred to Keningau, he had to employ an 'official drinker'. "The applicants to the post were many," he noted.

Bajau

The Bajau, the famous 'cowboys' of the 'wild East', came from the South Philippines during the 18th and 19th centuries and settled in the coastal area around Kota Belud, Papar and Kudat, where they made a handsome living from piracy. The Bajau who came to Sabah joined forces with the notorious Illanun and Balinini pirates. They are natural seafarers and were dubbed 'the sea gypsies'; today they form the second largest indigenous group in Sabah and are divided into subgroups, notably the Binadan, Suluk and Obian. They call themselves 'Samah'; it was the Brunei Malays who first called them Bajau. They are strict Muslims and the famous Sabahan folk hero, Mat Salleh, who led a rebellion in the 1890s against British Chartered Company rule, was a Bajau (see page 404). Despite their seafaring credentials, they are also renowned horsemen and (very occasionally) still put in an appearance at Kota Belud's tamu (see page 434). Bajau women are known for their brightly coloured basketry – tudong saji. The Bajau build their atap houses on stilts over the water and these are interconnected by a network of narrow wooden planks. The price of a Bajau bride was traditionally assessed in stilts, shaped from the trunks of bakau mangrove trees. A father erected one under his house on the day a daughter was born and replaced it whenever it wore out. The longer the daughter remained at home, the more stilts he got through and the more water buffalo he demanded from a prospective husband.

Murut

The Murut live around Tenom and Pensiangan in the lowland and hilly parts of the interior, in the southwest of Sabah and in the Trusan Valley of North Sarawak. Some of those in more remote jungle areas retain their traditional longhouse way of life, but many Murut have opted for detached kampong-style houses. Murut means 'hill people' and is not the term used by the people themselves. They refer to themselves by individual tribal names. The Nabai, Bokan and Timogun Murut live in the lowlands and are wet-rice farmers, while the Peluan, Bokan and Tagul Murut live in the hills and are mainly shifting cultivators. They are thought to be related to Sarawak's Kelabit and Kalimantan's Lun Dayeh people, although some of the tribes in the South Philippines have similar characteristics. The Murut staples are rice and tapioca, they are known for their weaving and basketry and have a penchant for drinking tapai (rice wine – see page 478). They are also enthusiastic dancers and devised the lansaran, a sprung dance floor like a trapeze. The Murut are a mixture of animists, Christians and Muslims and were the last tribe in Sabah to give up head-hunting, a practice stopped by British North Borneo Chartered Company administrators.

Chinese

The Chinese accounted for nearly a third of Sabah's population in 1960; today they make up just a fifth. Unlike Sarawak, however, where the Chinese were a well-established community in the early 1800s, Sabah's Chinese came as a result of the British North Borneo Chartered Company's immigration policy, designed to ease a labour shortage. About 70% of Sabah's Chinese are Christian Hakkas, who first began arriving at the end of the 19th century, under the supervision of the Company. They were given free passage from China and most settled in the Jesselton and Kudat areas; today most Hakka are farmers. There are also large Teochew and Hokkien communities in Tawau, Kota Kinabalu and Labuan while Sandakan is mainly Cantonese, who originally came from Hong Kong.

Filipinos

Immigration from the Philippines started in the 1950s and refugees began flooding into Sabah when the separatist war erupted in Mindanao in the 1970s. Today there are believed to be upwards of 700,000 illegal Filipino immigrants in Sabah (although their migration has been undocumented for so long that no one is certain), and the state government fears they could soon outnumber locals. There are many in Kota Kinabalu, the state capital and a large community – mainly women and children – in Labuan, but the bulk of the Filipino population is in Semporna, Lahad Datu, Tawau and Kunak (on the east coast) where they already outnumber locals 3:1. One Sabah government minister, referring to the long-running territorial dispute between Malaysia and the Philippines, was quoted as saying "We do not require a strong military presence at the border any more: the aliens have already landed".

Although the federal government has talked of its intention to deport illegal aliens, it is mindful of the political reality: the majority of the Filipinos are Muslim, and making them legal Malaysian citizens could ruin Sabah's predominantly Christian, Kadazan-led state government. The Filipino community is also a thorn in Sabah's flesh because of the crime wave associated with their arrival: the Sabah police claim 65% of crime is committed by Filipinos. The police do not ask questions when dealing with Filipino criminal suspects; about 40-50 are shot every year. Another local politician was quoted as saying: "The immigrants take away our jobs, cause political instability and pose a health hazard because of the appalling conditions in which some of them live".

There are six different Filipino groups in Sabah: the Visayas and Ilocano are Christian as are the Ilongo (Ilo Ilo), from Zamboanga. The Suluks are Muslim; they come from South Mindanao and have the advantage of speaking a dialect of Bahasa Malaysia. Many Filipinos were born in Sabah and all second generation immigrants are fluent in Bahasa. Migration first accelerated in the 1950s during the logging boom, and continued when the oil palm plantation economy took off; the biggest oil palm plantation is at Tungku, east of Lahad Datu. Many migrants have settled along the roadsides on the way to Danum Valley; it is easy to claim land since all they have to do is simply clear a plot and plant a few fruit trees.

Crafts

Compared with neighbouring Sarawak and Kalimantan, Sabah's handicraft industry is rather impoverished. Sabah's tribal groups were less protected from Western influences than Sarawak's, and traditional skills quickly began to die out as the state modernized and the economy grew. In Kota Kinabalu today, the markets are full of Filipino handicrafts and shell products; local arts and crafts are largely confined to basketry, mats, hats, beadwork, musical instruments and pottery.

The elongated Kadazan backpack baskets found around Mount Kinabalu National Park are called wakids and are made from bamboo, rattan and bark. Woven food covers, or tudong saji, are often mistaken for hats, and are made by the Bajau of Kota Belud. Hats, made from nipah palm or rattan, and whose shape varies markedly from place to place, are decorated with traditional motifs. One of the most common motifs is the nantuapan, or 'meeting', which represents four people all drinking out of the same tapai (rice wine) jar. The Rungus people from the Kudat peninsula also make linago basketware from a strong wild grass; it is tightly woven and not decorated. At tamus, Sabah's big open-air markets (see box on page 433), there are usually some handicrafts for sale. The Kota Belud tamu is the best place to find the Bajau horseman's embroidered turban, the destar. Traditionally, the Rungus people, who live on the Kudat Peninsula, were renowned as fine weavers, and detailed patterns were woven into their ceremonial skirts, (tinugupan). These patterns all had different names, but, like the ingredients of the traditional dyes, many have now been forgotten.

Background

Footprint features

History

Precolonial Malaya

With the arrival of successive waves of Malay immigrants about five millennia ago, the earliest settlers – the Orang Asli aboriginals (see page 501) – moved into the interior. The Malays established agricultural settlements on the coastal lowlands and in riverine areas and from very early on, were in contact with foreign traders, thanks to the peninsula's strategic location on the sea route between India and China. Although the original tribal inhabitants of Malaya were displaced inland, they were not entirely isolated from the coastal peoples. Trade relations in which 'upriver' tribal groups exchanged forest products for commodities like salt and metal implements with 'downstream' Malays, were widespread. Malay culture on the peninsula reflected these contacts, embracing Indian cultural traditions, Hinduism among them. In the late 14th century, the centre of power shifted from Sumatra's Srivijayan Empire across the Strait to Melaka (see page 204). In 1430, the third ruler of Melaka embraced Islam, and became the first sultan; the city quickly grew into a flourishing trading port. By the early 1500s, it was the most important entrepôt in the region and its fame brought it to the attention of the Portuguese, who, in 1511, ushered in the colonial epoch. They sacked the town and sent the sultan fleeing to Johor, where a new sultanate was established. But because of internal rivalries and continued conflict with the powerful trading sultanate of Aceh in north Sumatra as well as the Portuguese, Johor never gained the prominence of Melaka, and was forced to alternate its capital between Johor and the Riau archipelago.

For an historical introduction to Sarawak see page 381and for Sabah, page 470.

The colonials arrive

The Portuguese were the first of three European colonial powers to arrive on the Malay peninsula. They were followed by the Dutch, who took Melaka in 1641 (see page 205 for a history of Melaka). When Holland was occupied by Napoleon's troops at the end of the 18th century, Britain filled the vacuum, and the British colonial era began. Historian John M Gullick writes: "The main effects of European control were, firstly, to break the sequence of indigenous kingdoms and to disrupt the trade system upon which they had been based; secondly to delimit colonial spheres of influence and thereby to fix the subsequent boundaries of the national states which are heirs to colonial rule; and lastly to promote economic development and establish the infrastructure of government and other services which that development required; mass immigration from India and China was an incidental consequence of economic development."

During the 17th century, the Dutch came into frequent conflict with the Bugis, the fearsome master-seafarers who the Dutch had displaced from their original homeland in South Sulawesi. In 1784, in league with the Minangkabau of West Sumatra, the Bugis nearly succeeded in storming Melaka and were only stymied by the arrival of Dutch warships. The Bugis eventually established the Sultanate of Selangor on the west coast of the peninsula and, in the south, exerted increasing influence on the Johor-Riau sultans, until they had reduced them to puppet-rulers. By then however, offshoots of the Johor royal family had established the sultanates of Pahang and Perak. The Minangkabau-dominated states between Melaka and Selangor formed a confederacy of nine states, or Negeri Sembilan (see page 91). To the northeast, the states of Kelantan and Terengganu came under the Siamese sphere of influence.

Putting Malaya on the map

The names of most of Malaysia's states are older than the name Malaya; until the 1870s the scattered coastal sultanates were independent of each other. Many of the Malay areas were colonized by Sumatrans long ago and it is possible that the word 'Melayu' – or 'Malay' – derives from the Sungai Melayu (Melayu River) in Sumatra. The name in turn is derived from the Dravidian (Tamil) word malai, or 'hill'. As the Malays are coastal people, the paradox is explained by their pre-Islamic religion, which is thought to have been based on a cult in which a sacred mountain took pride of place.

The Graeco-Roman geographer Ptolemy called the Malay peninsula Aurea Chersonesus, or the 'The Golden Chersonese': it was the fabled land of gold. By the early 1500s, European maps were already marking Melaka and Pulau Tioman, which were well known to Chinese mariners. During the Portuguese and Dutch colonial periods, the whole peninsula was simply labelled 'Malacca', and the town was the only significant European outpost until the British took possession of Penang in 1786. There was very little mapping of the peninsula until the early 19th century, and the names of states only gradually appeared on maps over the course of the 17th and 18th centuries.

According to cartographic historian RT Fell, the first maps of the interior of the peninsula, beyond the bounds of the British Straits Settlements, did not appear until the late 19th century. In 1885 the Survey Department was founded and charged with mapping the interior – one of the tasks William Cameron was undertaking when he stumbled across the highland plateau named after him that same year. But right into the 20th century, large tracts of mountainous jungle were still unexplored.

British Malaya emerges

The British occupied Dutch colonies during the Napoleonic Wars, including the Dutch East Indies (now Indonesia), following France's invasion of the Netherlands in 1794. Dutch King William of Orange, who fled to London, instructed Dutch governors overseas to end their rivalry with the British and to permit the entry of British troops to their colonies in a bid to keep the French out. Historian William R Roff writes: "From being an Indian power interested primarily ... in the free passage of trade through the Malacca Straits and beyond to China, the East India Company suddenly found itself possessor not merely of a proposed naval station on Penang island but of numerous other territorial dominions and responsibilities. Nor were some of the company's servants at all reluctant to assume these responsibilities and, indeed to extend them."

The British had their own colonial designs, having already established a foothold on Penang where Captain Francis Light had set up a trading post in 1786 (see page 155). The Anglo-Dutch Treaty of London, which was signed in 1824, effectively divided maritime Southeast Asia into British and Dutch spheres of influence. Britain retained Penang, Melaka (which it swapped for the Sumatran port of Bengkulu) and Singapore – which had been founded by Stamford Raffles in 1819 – and these formed the Straits Settlements. The Dutch regained control of their colonial territories in the Indonesian archipelago. Britain promised to stay out of Sumatra and the Dutch promised not to meddle in the affairs of the peninsula, thus separating two parts of the Malay world whose histories had been intertwined for centuries.

The British did very little to interfere with the Malay sultanates and chiefdoms on the peninsula, but the Straits Settlements grew in importance – particularly Singapore, which soon superceded Penang, which in turn, had eclipsed Melaka. Chinese immigrants arrived in all three ports and from there expanded into tin mining which rapidly emerged as the main source of wealth on the peninsula. The extent of the tin rush in the mid-19th century is exemplified in the town of Larut in northwestern Perak. Around 25,000 Chinese speculators arrived in Larut between 1848 and 1872. The Chinese fought over the rights to mine the most lucrative deposits and organized into secret societies and kongsis, which by the 1860s were engaged in open warfare. At the same time, the Malay rulers in the states on the peninsula were busily taxing the tin traders while in the Straits Settlements, British investors in the mining industry put increasing pressure on the Colonial Office to intervene in order to stabilize the situation. In late 1873 Britain decided it could not rule the increasingly lawless and anarchic states by remote control any longer and the western-central states were declared a British protectorate. In his account of British intervention, William R Roff quotes a Malay proverb: 'Once the needle is in, the thread is sure to follow'.

In 1874, the Treaty of Pangkor established the Residential system whereby British officers were posted to key districts; it became their job to determine all administrative and policy matters other than those governing Islam and Malay custom. This immediately provoked resentment and sparked uprisings in Perak, Selangor and Negeri Sembilan, as well as a Malay revolt in 1875. The revolts were put down and the system was institutionalized; in 1876 these three states plus Pahang became the Federated Malay States. By 1909 the north states of Kedah, Perlis, Kelantan and Terengganu – which previously came under Siamese suzerainty – finally agreed to accept British advisers and became known as the Unfederated Malay States. Johor remained independent until 1914. The British system of government relied on the political power of the sultans and the Malay aristocracy: residents conferred with the rulers of each state and employed the aristocrats as civil servants. Local headmen (known as penghulu) were used as administrators in rural areas.

Meanwhile, the British continued to encourage the immigration of Chinese, who formed a majority of the population in Perak and Selangor by the early 1920s. Apart from the wealthy traders based in the Straits Settlements, the Chinese immigrants were organized (and exploited) by their secret societies, which provided welfare services, organized work gangs and ran local government. In 1889 the societies were officially banned, and while this broke their hold on political power, they simply re-emerged as a criminal underworld. In the Federated Malay States, there was an eight-fold population increase to 1.7 million between 1891 and 1931. Even by 1891 the proportion of Malays had declined to a fraction over a third of the population, with the Chinese making up 41.5 per cent and Indians – imported as indentured labourers by the British (see page 500) – comprising 22 per cent. To the south, Johor, which in the late 1800s was not even a member of the federation, had a similar ethnic balance.
For the most part, the Malay population remained in the countryside and were only gradually drawn into the modern economy. But by the 1920s Malay nationalism was on the rise, partly prompted by the Islamic reform movement and partly by intellectuals in secular circles who looked to the creation of a Greater Malaysia (or Greater Indonesia), under the influence of left-wing Indonesian nationalists. These Malay nationalists were as critical of the Malay élite as they were of the British colonialists. The élite itself was becoming increasingly outspoken for different reasons – it felt threatened by the growing demands of Straits-born Chinese and second-generation Indians for equal rights.

The first semi-political nationalist movement was the Kesatuan Melayu Singapura (Singapore Malay Union), formed in 1926. The Union found early support in the Straits Settlements where Malays were outnumbered and there was no sultan. They gradually spread across the peninsula and held a pan-Malayan conference in

1939. These associations were the forerunners of the post-war Malay nationalist movement. In the run-up to the Second World War the left wing split off to form the Kesatuan Melayu Muda – the Union of Young Malays, which was strongly anti-British and whose leaders were arrested by the colonial authorities in 1940. The Chinese were more interested in business than politics and any political interests were focused on China. The middle class supported the Chinese nationalist Kuomintang (KMT), although it was eventually banned by the British, as it was becoming an obvious focus of anti-colonial sentiment. The KMT allowed Communists to join the movement until 1927, but in 1930 they split off to form the Malayan Communist Party (MCP) which drew its support from the working class.

Japanese occupation

Under cover of darkness on the night of 8 December 1941, the Japanese army invaded Malaya, landing in South Thailand and pushing into Kedah, and at Kota Bharu in Kelantan (see page 300). The invasion, which took place an hour before the attack on Pearl Harbor, took the Allies in Malaya and 'Fortress' Singapore completely by surprise. The Japanese forces had air, land and sea superiority and quickly overwhelmed the Commonwealth troops on the peninsula. Militarily, it was a brilliant campaign, made speedier by the fact that the Japanese troops stole bicycles in every town they took, thus making it possible for them to outpace all Allied estimates of their likely rate of advance.

By 28 December they had taken Ipoh and all of northern Malaya. Kuantan fell on the 31st, the Japanese having sunk the British warships *Prince of Wales* and *Repulse* (see page 258) and Kuala Lumpur on 11 January 1942. They advanced down the east coast, centre and west coast simultaneously and by the end of the month had taken Johor Bahru and were massed across the strait from Singapore. By 15 February they had forced the capitulation of the Allies in Singapore. This was a crushing blow, and, according to Malaysian historian Zainal Abidin bin Abudul Wahid, "the speed with which the Japanese managed to achieve victory, however temporary that might have been, shattered the image of the British, and generally the 'whiteman', as a superior people". Right up until the beginning of the Second World War, the British had managed to placate the aristocratic leaders of the Malay community and the wealthy Chinese merchants and there was little real threat to the status quo. The Japanese defeat of the British changed all that by altering the balance between conservatism and change. Because Britain had failed so miserably to defend Malaya, its credentials as a protector were irrevocably tarnished.

For administrative purposes, the Japanese linked the peninsula with Sumatra as part of the Greater East Asia Co-prosperity Sphere. All British officials were interned and the legislative and municipal councils swept aside. But because the Japanese had lost their command of the seas by the end of 1942, nothing could be imported and there was a shortage of food supplies. The 'banana' currency introduced by the Japanese became worthless as inflation soared. Japan merely regarded Malaya as a source of raw materials, yet the rubber and tin industries stagnated and nothing was done to develop the economy.

After initially severing sultans' pensions and reducing their powers, the Japanese realized that their co-operation was necessary if the Malay bureaucracy was to be put to work for the occupation government. The Indians were treated well since they were seen as a key to fighting the British colonial régime in India. But Malaya's Chinese, while they were not rounded up and executed as they were in Singapore, were not trusted. The Japanese, however, came to recognize the importance of the Chinese community in oiling the wheels of the economy. The Chinese Dalforce militia (set up by the Allies as the Japanese advanced southwards) joined the Communists and

The kris: martial and mystic masterpiece of the Malay world

The kris occupies an important place in Malay warfare, art and philosophy. It is a short sword – the Malay word keris means dagger – and the blade may be either straight or sinuous (there are over 100 blade shapes), sharpened on both edges. Such was the high reputation of these weapons that they were exported as far afield as India.

Krisses are often attributed with peculiar powers; one was reputed to have rattled violently before a family feud. Another, kept at the museum in Taiping, has a particularly bloodthirsty reputation. It would sneak away after dark, kill someone, and then wipe itself clean before miraculously returning to its display cabinet. Because each kris has a power and spirit of its own, they must be compatible with their owners. Nor should they be purchased; a kris should be given or inherited.

The fact that so few kris blades have been unearthed has led some people to assume that the various Malay kingdoms were peaceful and adverse to war. The more likely explanation is that pre-Muslim Malays attributed such magical power to sword blades that they were only very rarely buried. The art historian Jan Fontein writes that "the process of forging the sword from clumps of iron ore and meteorite into a sharp blade of patterned steel is often seen as a parallel to the process of purification to which the soul is subjected after death by the gods".

The earliest confirmed date for a kris is the 14th century; they are depicted in the reliefs of Candi Panataran and possibly also at Candi Sukuh, both on Java. However, in all likelihood they were introduced considerably earlier, possibly during the 10th century.

Krisses are forged by beating nickel or nickeliferous meteoritic material into iron in a complex series of laminations (iron from meteors is particularly prized because of its celestial origin). After forging, ceremonies are performed and offerings made before the blade is tempered. The empu (swordsmith), was a respected member of society, who was felt to be imbued with mystical powers. After forging the blade, it is then patinated using a mixture of lime juice and arsenicum. Each part of the sword, even each curve of the blade, has a name and the best krisses are elaborately decorated. Inlaid with gold, the cross-pieces carved into floral patterns and animal motifs, grips made of ivory and studded with jewels, they are works of art.

But they were also tools of combat. In the Malay world, a central element of any battle was the amok. Taken from the Malay verb mengamok, the amok was a furious charge by men armed with krisses, designed to spread confusion within the enemy ranks. Amok warriors would be committed to dying in the charge and often dressed in white to indicate self-sacrifice. They were often drugged with opium or cannabis. It was also an honourable way for a man to commit suicide.

Alfred Russel Wallace in *Malay Archipelago* (1869) writes: "He grasps his kris-handle, and the next moment draws out the weapon and stabs a man to the heart. He runs on, with the bloody kris in his hand, stabbing at everyone he meets. 'Amok! Amok!' then resounds through the streets. Spears, krisses, knives and guns are brought out against him. He rushes madly forward, kills all he can – men, women and children – and dies overwhelmed by numbers...". The English expression 'to run amok' is taken from this Malay word.

Recommended reading: Frey, Edward (1986) *The Kris: mystic weapon of the Malay world*, OUP: Singapore.

other minor underground dissident groups in forming the Malayan People's Anti-Japanese Army. British army officers and arms were parachuted into the jungle to support the guerrillas. It was during this period that the Malayan Communist Party (MCP) broadened its membership and appeal, under the guise of a nationwide anti-Japanese alliance.

The brutality of the Japanese régime eased with time; as the war began to go against them, they increasingly courted the different communities, giving them more say in the run of things in an effort to undermine any return to colonial rule. But the Japanese's favourable treatment of Malays and their general mistrust of the Chinese did not foster good race relations between the two. A Malay paramilitary police force was put to work to root out Chinese who were anti-Japanese, which exacerbated inter-communal hostility. The Japanese never offered Malaya independence but allowed Malay nationalist sentiments to develop in an effort to deflect attention from the fact they had ceded the North Malay states of Kedah, Perlis, Kelantan and Terengganu to Thailand.

The British return

During the war, the British drew up secret plans for a revised administrative structure in Malaya. The plan was to create a Malayan Union by combining the federated and unfederated states as well as Melaka and Penang, leaving Singapore as a crown colony. Plans were also drawn up to buy North Borneo from the Chartered Company and to replace the anachronous White Rajahs of Sarawak (see page 384) with a view to eventually grouping all the territories together as a federation. As soon as the Japanese surrendered in September 1945, the plan was put into action. Historian Mary Turnbull noted that "Malaya was unique [among Western colonies] because the returning British were initially welcomed with enthusiasm and were themselves unwilling to put the clock back. But they were soon overwhelmed by the reaction against their schemes for streamlining the administration and assimilating the different immigrant communities."

A unitary state was formed on the peninsula and everyone, regardless of race or origin, who called Malaya 'home', was accorded equal status. But the resentment caused by British high-handedness was the catalyst which triggered the foundation of the United Malays National Organization (UMNO) which provided a focus for opposition to the colonial régime and, following independence, formed the ruling party. Opposition to UMNO, led by the Malay ruling class, forced the British to withdraw the Union proposal. The sultans refused to attend the installation of the governor and the Malays boycotted advisory councils. Mary Turnbull noted that the Malayan Union scheme was "conceived as a civil servant's dream but was born to be a politician's nightmare". Vehement Malay opposition prompted negotiations with Malay leaders which hammered out the basis of a Federation of Malaya which was established in February 1948. It was essentially the same as the Union in structure, except that it recognized the sovereignty of the sultans in the 11 states and the so called 'special position' of the Malays as the indigenous people of Malaya. The federation had a strong central government (headed by a High Commissioner) and a federal executive council.

In this federal system, introduced in 1948, non-Malays could only become Malaysian citizens if they had been resident in Malaya for a minimum of 15 out of the previous 25 years, were prepared to sign a declaration of permanent settlement and were able to speak either Malay or English. This meant only three million of Malaya's five million population qualified as citizens, of whom 78 per cent were Malay, 12 per cent Chinese and seven per cent Indian. Historian Mary Turnbull said that while the British believed they had achieved their objective of common citizenship (even on more restricted terms), they had, in reality "accepted UMNO's concept of a Malay nation into which immigrant groups would have to be integrated, and many difficulties were to develop from this premise".

The rise of Communism

The Chinese and Indian communities were not consulted in these Anglo-Malay negotiations and ethnic and religious tensions between the three main communities were running high, unleashing the forces of racialism which had been lying dormant for years. Because their part in the political process had been ignored, many more Chinese began to identify with the Malaysian Communist Party (MCP) which was still legal. It was not until the Communist victory in China in 1949 that the Chinese began to think of Malaya as home. During the war the MCP had gained legitimacy and prestige as a patriotic resistance movement. The MCP's de facto military wing, the MPAJA, had left arms dumps in the jungle, but the Communist leadership was split as to whether negotiation or confrontation was the way forward. Then in 1947 the MCP suffered what many considered to be a disastrous blow: its Vietnamese-born secretary-general, Lai Teck, absconded with all the party's funds having worked as a double agent for both the Japanese and the British. He was suspected of having betrayed the entire MCP central committee to the Japanese in 1942. The new 26-year- old MCP leader, former schoolmaster Chin Peng, immediately abandoned Lai's soft approach.

In June 1948 he opted for armed rebellion, and the Malayan Communist Emergency commenced with the murder of three European planters. According to John Gullick, the historian and former member of the Malayan civil service, it was called an 'Emergency' because the Malayan economy was covered by the London insurance market for everything other than war. Premiums covered loss of stock, property and equipment through riot and civil commotion, but not through civil war, so the misnomer continued throughout the 12 year insurrection. Others say it got its name from the Emergency Regulations that were passed in June 1948 which were designed to deny food supplies and weapons to the Communists.

The Emergency was characterized by indiscriminate armed Communist raids on economic targets – often rubber estates and tin mines – and violent ambushes which were aimed at loosening and undermining central government control. Chinese 'squatters' in areas fringing the jungle (many of whom had fled from the cities during the Japanese occupation) provided an information and supply network for the Communists. In 1950 the British administration moved these people into 500 'New Villages', where they could be controlled and protected. This policy, known as 'The Briggs Plan' after the Director of Operations, Lieutenant-General Sir Harold Briggs, was later adopted (rather less successfully) by the Americans in South Vietnam.

In much the same way as they had been caught unprepared by the Japanese invasion in 1941, the British were taken by surprise and in the first few years the MCP (whose guerrillas were labelled 'CTs' – or Communist Terrorists) gained the upper hand. In 1951 British morale all but crumbled when the High Commissioner, Sir Henry Gurney, was ambushed and assassinated on the road to Fraser's Hill (see page 123). His successor, General Sir Gerald Templer, took the initiative, however, with his campaign to 'win the hearts and minds of the people'. Templer's biographer, John Cloake, gave him Japanese General Tomoyuki Yamashita's old sobriquet 'Tiger of Malaya', and there is little doubt that his tough policies won the war. In his book *Emergency Years*, former mine-manager Leonard Rayner says the chain-smoking Templer "exuded nervous energy like an overcharged human battery". Within two years the Communists were on the retreat. They had also begun to lose popular support due to the climate of fear they introduced, although the Emergency did not officially end until 1960.

Historians believe the Communist rebellion failed because it was too slow to take advantage of the economic hardships in the immediate aftermath of the Second World War and because it was almost exclusively Chinese. It also only really appealed to the Chinese working class and alienated and shunned the Chinese merchant community and Straits-born Chinese.

The road to Merdeka

The British had countered the MCP's claim to be a multi-racial nationalist movement by accelerating moves towards Malayan independence, which Britain promised, once the Emergency was over. The only nationalist party with any political credibility was UMNO. Its founder, Dato' Onn bin Jaafar wanted to allow non-Malays to become members, and when his proposal was rejected, he resigned to form the Independence of Malaya Party. The brother of the Sultan of Kedah, Tunku Abdul Rahman, took over as head of UMNO and to counter Onn's new party, he made an electoral pact with the Malayan Chinese Association (MCA) and the Malayan Indian Congress (MIC). With the MCP out of the picture, the Chinese community had hesitantly grouped itself around the MCA. The Alliance (which trounced Onn's party in the election) is still in place today, in the form of the ruling Barisan Nasional (National Front). After sweeping the polls in 1955, the Alliance called immediately for merdeka, or independence, which the British guaranteed within two years.

With independence promised by non-violent means, Tunku Abdul Rahman offered an amnesty to the Communists. Together with Singapore's Chief Minister, David Marshall and Straits-Chinese leader Tan Cheng Lock (see page 206), he met Chin Peng in 1956. But they failed to reach agreement and the MCP fled through the jungle into the mountains in southern Thailand around Betong. While the Emergency was declared 'over' in 1960, the MCP only finally agreed to lay down its arms in 1989, in a peace agreement brokered by Thailand. The party had been riven by factionalism and its membership had dwindled to under 1,000. In 1991, the legendary Chin Peng struck a deal with the Malaysian government allowing the former guerrillas to return home. Historian Mary Turnbull wrote: "When Malaya attained independence in 1957 it was a prosperous country with stable political institutions, a sound administrative system and a good infrastructure of education and communications – a country with excellent resources and a thriving economy based on export agriculture and mining". Under the new constitution, a king was to be chosen from one of the nine sultans, and the monarchy was to be rotated every five years. A two-tier parliament was set up, with a Dewan Rakyat (People's House) of elected representatives and a Dewan Negara (Senate) to represent the state assemblies. Each of the 11 states had its own elected government and a sultan or governor.

Politicians in Singapore made it clear that they also wanted to be part of an independent Malaya, but in Kuala Lumpur, UMNO leaders were opposed to a merger because the island had a Chinese majority (a straight merger would have resulted in a small Chinese majority in Malaya.) Increasing nationalist militancy in Singapore was of particular concern to UMNO and the radical wing of the People's Action Party, which was swept to power with Lee Kuan Yew at its head in 1959, was dominated by Communists. Fearing the emergence of 'a second Cuba' on Malaysia's doorstep, Tunku Abdul Rahman proposed that Singapore join a greater Malaysian Federation, in which a racial balance would be maintained by the inclusion of Sarawak, Brunei and British North Borneo (Sabah). Britain supported the move, as did all the states involved. Kuala Lumpur was particularly keen on Brunei joining the Federation on two scores: it had Malays and oil. But at the eleventh hour, Brunei's Sultan Omar backed out, mistrustful of Kuala Lumpur's designs on his sultanate's oil revenues and unhappy at the prospect of becoming another sultan in Malaya's collection of nine monarchs.

Prime Minister Tunku Abdul Rahman was disheartened, but the Malaysia Agreement was signed in July 1963 with Singapore, Sarawak and Sabah. Without Brunei, there was a small Chinese majority in the new Malaysia. The Tunku did not have time to dwell on racial arithmetic, however, because almost immediately the new federation was plunged into an undeclared war with Indonesia – which became known as Konfrontasi, or Confrontation (see page 386) – due to President Sukarno's objection to the participation of Sabah and Sarawak. Indonesian saboteurs were landed on the peninsula and in Singapore and there were Indonesian military incursions along the borders of Sabah and Sarawak with Kalimantan. Konfrontasi was finally ended in 1966 after Sukarno fell from power. But relations with Singapore – which had been granted a greater measure of autonomy than other states – were far from smooth. Communal riots in Singapore in 1964 and Lee Kuan Yew's efforts to forge a nation-wide opposition alliance which called for 'a democratic Malaysian Malaysia' further opened the rift with Kuala Lumpur. Feeling unnerved by calls for racial equality while the Malays did not form a majority of the population, Tunku Abdul Rahman expelled Singapore from the federation in August 1965 against Lee Kuan Yew's wishes.

Racial politics in the 1960s

The expulsion of Singapore did not solve the racial problem on the peninsula, however. Because the Malay and Chinese communities felt threatened by each other - one wielded political power, the other economic power - racial tensions built up. Resentment focused on the enforcement of Malay as the medium of instruction in all schools and as the national language and on the privileged educational and employment opportunities afforded to Malays. The tensions finally exploded on 13 May 1969, in the wake of the general election.

The UMNO-led Alliance faced opposition from the Democratic Action Party (DAP) which was built from the ashes of Lee Kuan Yew's People's Action Party. The DAP was a radical Chinese-dominated party and called for racial equality. Also in opposition was Gerakan (the People's Movement), supported by Chinese and Indians, and the Pan-Malayan Islamic Party, which was exclusively Malay and very conservative. In the election, the opposition parties - which were not in alliance – deprived the Alliance of its two-thirds majority in parliament; it required this margin to amend the constitution unimpeded. Gerakan and DAP celebrations provoked counter-demonstrations from Malays and in the ensuing mayhem hundreds were killed in Kuala Lumpur.

The government suspended the constitution for over a year and declared a State of Emergency. A new national ideology was drawn up – the controversial New Economic Policy, which was an ambitious experiment in social and economic engineering aimed at ironing out discrepancies between ethnic communities. The Rukunegara, a written national ideology aimed at fostering nation-building, was introduced in August 1970. It demanded loyalty to the king and the constitution, respect for Islam and observance of the law and morally acceptable behaviour. All discussion of the Malays' 'special position' was banned as was discussion about the national language and the sovereignty of the sultans. In the words of historian John Gullick, "Tunku Abdul Rahman, whose anguish at the disaster had impeded his ability to deal with it effectively," resigned the following month and handed over to Tun Abdul Razak. Tun Razak was an able administrator, but lacked the dynamism of his predecessor. He did, however, unify UMNO and patched up the old Alliance, breathing new life into the coalition by incorporating every political party except the DAP and one or two other small parties into the newly named Barisan Nasional (BN), or National Front. In 1974 the Barisan won a landslide majority.

Tun Razak shifted Malaysia's foreign policy from a pro-Western stance to non-alignment and established diplomatic relations with both Moscow and Beijing.

But within Malaysia, Communist paranoia was rife: as Indochina fell to Communists in the mid-1970s, many Malaysians became increasingly convinced that Malaysia was just another 'domino' waiting to topple. There were even several arrests of prominent Malays (including two newspaper editors and five top UMNO politicians). But when Chin Peng's revolutionaries joined forces with secessionist Muslims in South Thailand, the Thai and Malaysian governments launched a joint clean-out operation in the jungle along the frontier. By the late 1970s the North Kalimantan Communist Party had been beaten into virtual submission too (see page 386). In 1976 Tun Razak died and was succeeded by his brother-in-law, Dato' Hussein Onn (the son of Umno's founding father). He inherited an economy which was in good shape, thanks to strong commodity prices, and in the general election of 1978, the BN won another comfortable parliamentary majority. Three years later he handed over to Dr Mahathir Mohamad.

Modern Malaysia

Politics

On the face of it, Malaysia's political landscape is remarkably unchanging. Abdullah Ahmad Badawi, who succeeded Dr Mahathir Mohamad in October 2003, and won a landslide victory in elections in 2004 heads the Barisan Nasional (BN), or National Front coalition. (Mahathir had ruled for 22 years as Asia's longest-serving elected leader.) Since the first general election was held back in 1959 the largest number of parliamentary seats won by an opposition party has been 27 – by the PAS in 1999. In the latest election in 2004, the ruling coalition expanded their mandate by winning 198 out of the 219 parliamentary seats and 452 out of the 505 state seats. It won control of 11 of the 12 state governments. The opposition secured only 20 parliamentary seats and lost control of Terengganu state and kept control of Kelantan by a wafer-thin margin. The ruling coalition are very much in control and have been over all 11 general elections held since 1959.

With the rapid expansion of Malaysia's economy, and notwithstanding the recession associated with the Asian economic crisis of 1997-99 and a global slump 2001-2002, there has emerged a substantial nouveau riche middle class. There has, in turn, been the expectation in some quarters that a more open political system might evolve as prosperous, and increasingly well educated, people demand more of a political say. But the government does not readily tolerate dissent and during the premiership of Dr Mahathir power has, in fact, become increasingly concentrated in the hands of the government. However, many Malaysians hope that Badawi, who is seen as the 'nice guy' in Malaysian politics, (at least he is a lot more diplomatic than Mahathir)will open up the arena. One sign of Badawi's potential was the release of Anwar Ibrahim (see below) who had been jailed on corruption and sodomy charges six years previously. His release would have been unthinkable under Mahathir.

The 2004 general election

The 11th general election was the first one since 1981 not contested by Mahathir who had tearfully resigned and handed over to his deputy Abdullah Ahmad Badawi in October 2003. Unlike the elections of 1999, the sacking and imprisonment on allegedly trumped up charges of Anwar Ibrahim was not an issue. The public had forgotten him despite efforts by the opposition to revive his case. Also Badawi's face was on the election posters, and it was Mahathir who was associated with Anwar's treatment.

Most observers agree, BN's landslide victory came because it played the Islamic fundamentalism card. Many of Malaysia's Muslims follow a more moderate form of the religion and do not support the idea of an Islamic state. The Islamist PAS wanted to ban rock concerts, make dress even more conservative and separate sexes on beaches and even supermarkets.

The party also relied on good economic data, hoping the electorate would vote for stability and more of the same. The Kuala Lumpur stock exchange hit highs days before polling day.

And to top it all, as the country's media is under government control, the BN easily dominated newspapers and TV. Badawi's promise to tackle corruption may also have won him voters.

Anwar Ibrahim: Malaysia's trial of the century

It may have become commonplace in Malaysia for opposition politicians, free-thinking jurists, environmentalists and other assorted annoyances to be hounded, arrested, tried and jailed, but not mainstream Malay politicians. It is this which rocked Malaysia's political establishment when Anwar Ibrahim, former deputy prime minister and Mahathir's successor in waiting, was arrested in late 1998. Anwar was sacked by Mahathir on 2 September 1998. This was preceded by a series of murky allegations impugning Anwar's morals. In particular, there were whispers that he was bisexual. Not only is this beyond the pale in a largely Muslim country like Malaysia, but homosexuality remains a crime. Anwar's supporters saw this whispering campaign as politically motivated and the result of a widening gulf between Mahathir and his deputy over how to manage the economy.

A few days after he was sacked, Anwar was arrested and charged with five counts of sodomy and five charges of abuse of power. But before his second appearance in court Anwar appeared with bruised arms and a black eye, and accused the police of beating him. Mahathir seemed to imply that the injuries were self-inflicted. Anwar's treatment at the hands of the police as well as the crude and one-sided coverage in the government-controlled press angered many Malaysians. They did not believe the charges, and as the trial continued they became less and less credible. Nonetheless, on 14 April 1999, Anwar was convicted of corruption with a jail sentence for six years and convicted of sodomy and sentenced to nine years in jail. Anwar appealed against both convictions. In 2002, he lost his final appeal against the corruption charges in the federal court. In September 2004, a federal court of three judges overturned the sodomy conviction at 2 to 1 because of inconsistencies in the prosection's evidence. As Anwar had already served the six years for corruption, he was freed. Shortly after he was freed Anwar tried to have the corruption conviction lifted, but he failed in his appeal. The court found Anwar fairly convicted on those charges. Because his conviction was not lifted, Anwar cannot return to politics until April 2008. Directly after Anwar was freed he flew to Germany for back treatment. He alleged the injuries came from abuse during his arrest and jail time. Prime Minister Badawi cautioned overseas leaders not to visit Anwar.

In the immediate aftermath of the Anwar affair it seemed as though it might, in retrospect, prove to be a turning point in Malaysia's political fortunes. It brought demonstrators onto the streets of Kuala Lumpur. It created demands for *reformasi*. It led to the creation of a new opposition party, the Justice Party (Keadilan), led by Anwar's wife Wan Azizah. It even brought the US ambassador to remark that Anwar was the world's "newest and most famous political prisoner". But following the September 11th attacks in the US and the failure of the PAS to produce a measured response to those events (see below) the Anwar affair was pushed very much into the background.

Whether the court had exerted its independence or the order for his release came from above, Anwar's freedom would have been unthinkable under Mahathir.

Money, politics and corruption

The entrenched position of UMNO and the BN has, in the eyes of the government's critics, allowed money politics and political patronage to flourish. It is argued that the use of political power to dispense favours and make money has become endemic, so much so that it is accepted as just another part of the political landscape. In 1995 Datuk Rafidah Aziz, the highly respected minister of International Trade and Industry, revealed in court that her son-in-law, a son of Prime Minister Mahathir, and a brother of Anwar Ibrahim had all benefited from share allocations which fell under her largesse. Such allocations are permitted – indeed encouraged – as part of the effort to increase bumiputra (Malay and indigenous groups) representation in the economy. But the scale to which relatives and political supporters benefit is questioned.

Badawi has made stamping out corruption one of his main aims, and although it is early days, observers note after one year in power the prime minister has gone some way to achieving them. He has strengthened a number of anti-corruption agencies and arrested some Mahathir-era cronies.

Many suggested that Mahathir worsened the corruption problem. They blamed his style and his emphasis on wealth creation. Chandra Muzaffar, a political scientist at the Science University of Malaysia in Penang, for example, argued that "He's created a culture that places undue emphasis on wealth accumulation for its own sake. The new heroes are all corporate barons."

Social ills

Another challenge for the government is how to curb the growth of so-called 'social ills'. For a country which has argued that 'Asian values' have permitted it to modernize without the social and moral degradation evident in the West, this is a sensitive subject. Research has revealed a surge in drug taking (particularly recreational drugs like Ecstasy), illegitimate pregnancies, wife abuse, gangsterism and incest. Moreover, this research seems to show that the problem is predominantly concentrated among Malays.

Racial relations in the New Malaysia

Since the race riots of 1969 relations between Malaysia's Malay and Chinese populations have dominated political affairs. Now that Malaysia is fast attaining economic maturity a debate is beginning to emerge about whether it is time to consign racial politics, and racial quotas, to the dust heap. Former Prime Minister Mahathir's Vision 2020 (see page 496), which sets out a path to developed country status by 2020, significantly talks of a 'Malaysian race working in full and equal partnership'. There is no mention here of 'bumiputras' and 'Chinese Malaysians', but of a single Malaysian identity which transcends race.

Not everyone agrees with this vision. There are those who note that the communal peace which has descended on the nation since 1969 has been based on a fast-growing economy in which everyone has gained even while the portions of the cake allotted to each group have changed. They worry that a slowing economy could bring racial conflicts to the fore again, although this did not happen to any significant degree during 1998 when the economy contracted by 7.5 per cent.

Foreign relations

In foreign affairs Malaysia follows a non-aligned stance and is fiercely anti-Communist. This, however, has not stopped its enthusiastic investment in Indochina and Myanmar (Burma). Malaysia is a leading light in the Association of Southeast Asian Nations (ASEAN).

Malaysia's most delicate relations are with neighbouring Singapore, a country with which it is connected by history and also by water pipelines and a causeway. For a few years Singapore was part of the Malaysian Federation, until it was ejected in

 1965, and Singapore's status as a largely Chinese city state makes for an uneasy relationship with Malay-dominated Malaysia. In 1997 mutual sensitivities were made all too clear in a spat which threatened to escalate into a major diplomatic conflict. The cause? A dispute over whether Johor Bahru was a safe place or not.

Malaysia, Islam and September 11

Like neighbouring Indonesia, the events of September 11 and, more significantly, the reaction by the US, has caused Malaysia to tread a fine line between slavishly supporting the US government on the one hand, and appearing to side with the Osama bin Laden and the Taliban on the other. Former Prime Minister Mahathir warned against the dangers posed by Muslim extremists but was also aware that 60% of Malaysians are Muslim and that there has been something of an Islamic resurgence in recent years.

Mahathir immediately condemned the attacks in New York and Washington. Furthermore, he expressed his concern that the US should respond in a measured manner. But the events also offered Mahathir an opportunity to paint the country's Islamic opposition party, the PAS, as extreme. In September 2001 the DAP left the Alternative Front – which links the PAS, DAP and Keadilan – because of the PAS's desire to make Malaysia an Islamic state. As DAP member Chen Man Hin said at the time, "We are alarmed by the calls of those who preach martyrdom and those who are prepared to die for an Islamic state". Certainly some moderate Muslim voices in Malaysia believe that the PAS has overstepped the mark and revealed its true colours. Following the September 11 atrocities an editorial in the PAS mouthpiece Harakah was titled 'The coming war is a crusade against Islam'.

Economy

Malaysia has an abundance of natural resources. Today, though, tin mining, rubber and palm oil are declining in importance, and while the country's oil, gas and timber wealth are valuable sources of revenue, the manufacturing sector, particularly electronics, has become the powerhouse of the economy. At the same time, the service sector is booming, and tourism is now the third largest foreign exchange earner. Over recent years, Malaysia has been one of the fastest-growing economies in the world. The World Bank defines Malaysia as an upper-middle-income country. There is a Malay saying which goes: *ada gula, ada semut* ('where there's sugar, there's ants') and from the late 1980s foreign investors swarmed to Malaysia, thanks to its sugar-coated investment incentives as well as its cheap land and labour, its good infrastructure and political stability.

Until 1997, and despite one banker likening Malaysia's economic policies to 'Noddyomics', the country's economy grew extraordinarily rapidly. It was this, of course, which played a large part in the World Bank including Malaysia in its list of 'Miracle Economies' (rather more prosaically called High Performing Asian Economies by the World Bank). But the Asian economic crisis, which began in Thailand in mid-1997 and then spread to Malaysia and other Asian countries, put a spanner in the spokes of Malaysia's fast moving economy.

The evolution of the Malaysian economy

In the late 1800s, as the British colonial government developed the infrastructure of the Federated Malay States, they built a network of roads, railways, telephones and telegraphs which served as the backbone of the export economy. In the 50 years following 1880, export earnings rose 30-fold. Most of the tin mines and plantations were in the hands of British-owned companies and remained foreign-owned until the Malaysian government restructured foreign equity holdings in the 1970s.

On independence in 1957, resource-rich Malaysia's future looked bright and foreign investment was encouraged, the capitalist system maintained and there was no threat to nationalize industry. The first national development plan aimed to expand the agricultural sector and begin to reduce dependence on rubber, which, even then, was beginning to encounter competition from synthetic alternatives. But rubber and tin remained the main economic props. In 1963, when the Federation of Malaysia was formed, only six per cent of the workforce was employed in industry and 80 per cent of exports were contributed by tin, rubber, oil palm, timber, and oil and gas.

The structure of Malaysia's economy has been radically altered since independence, and particularly since the 1980s. Commodity exports such as rubber and palm oil, which were the mainstay of the post-colonial economy, have declined in significance and, within 30 years, this sector is unlikely to contribute more than six per cent of Malaysia's export earnings. A turning point was 1987, when agriculture was overtaken by the manufacturing sector in terms of contribution to GDP. Manufacturing output has almost tripled in 25 years, thanks mainly to the fact that Malaysia has been the darling of foreign investors. The value of manufactured exports is growing even faster; today they are approaching three-quarters of Malaysia's export earnings. The country that used to be the world's biggest producer of rubber and tin is now the world's leading producer of semiconductors and air-conditioning units. In May 1993, another landmark was created in Malaysia's economic history: the Malaysia Mining Corporation, one of the country's biggest remaining tin producers, pulled out of tin mining.

But the type of products Malaysia manufactures is also undergoing rapid change. One of the main reasons for this is Malaysia's labour squeeze. The main industrial boom zones (the Klang Valley around Kuala Lumpur, Johor and Penang) are already suffering shortages, and while infrastructural developments have just about kept pace with the flood of foreign manufacturing investment, the labour pool is drying up. In 1996 the unemployment rate was, in practical terms, zero and the government was forced to recruit blue-collar migrant labourers from Thailand, Bangladesh, Myanmar (Burma) and Indonesia. But even with this flow of legal migrant labour it was not sufficient to fill the labour void and there has been a much larger flow of illegal migrant labour.

Transforming the economy

A key element in Malaysia's development strategy is how to manage the transition from a production centre where comparative advantage is based on labour cost to an economy where high levels of education and skills provide the industrial impetus. Malaysia invariably looks across to Singapore as both a role model in this regard and as a competitor.

One of former Prime Minister Mahathir's favoured programmes is the so-called MSC or 'Multimedia Super Corridor' – an attempt to build an Oriental Silicon Valley on a 15 km-by-50 km stretch of land south of KL. This is linked to the new administrative capital of Putrajaya and the associated international airport at Sepang. When you add these developments to the technological centre of Cyberjaya and the bill comes to a breath-taking US$20bn. As Daniel Ng of Sun Microsystems was quoted as saying when the plans for Cyberjaya were in their infancy: "It's as if someone said, 'What would be the perfect Silicon Valley?' and then built it."

There are critics and sceptics aplenty. In particular there are those who say Malaysia lacks the human resources to justify such grandiose plans. Part of the problem is perceived to be the culture of education in the country. Malaysian students are not expected to challenge or contradict their teachers, but to conform. This is perceived to be unhealthy if Malaysia is to become a thinking economy where people are creative and innovative. More practically, Malaysian graduates are often not sufficiently fluent in English to take full advantage of the IT revolution. This dates back to the 1970s when the government switched from English to Bahasa Malaysia as the medium of instruction in secondary schools. Further, the tertiary level enrolment rate in Malaysia is low: just 7.2 per cent of the relevant age group are in higher education. But these sort of criticisms have also be levelled at neighbouring Singapore, and that can hardly be counted an economic failure.

Tourism

Tourism has grown to assume a critical role in Malaysia's economy in the past few years. In 1990, Malaysia launched itself into big league tourism with a bang, joining the swelling ranks of Southeast Asian countries to host 'tourism years'. Visit Malaysia Year (VMY) was a big success: 7.4 million tourists arrived – half as many again as in 1989 and receipts rose 61 per cent to US$1.5bn. This made tourism Malaysia's third biggest earner after manufacturing and oil – up from sixth position the previous year. The latest catchy slogan is the banal 'Malaysia: truly Asia'. Now, it seems, one marketing campaign follows on seamlessly from the last.

While the vast majority of tourists still come from neighbouring Singapore and Thailand, the government is targeting the big spenders – the 'high-yield markets' like the Japanese, who spend 70 per cent more than the average tourist. Smart new hotel and resort complexes have been built and scores of golf courses are being carved out of the jungle. Until fairly recently, the government paid scant regard to the lower-middle end of the tourism market, favouring sparkling new five-star complexes to, in their view, grotty little low-return guesthouses. While 2003 was a bad year for tourism because of the outbreak of Sars in Southeast Asia and repercussions of the Iraq War, figures for the first six months of 2004 picked up 71 per cent year-on-year, with 7.9 million people visiting the country. The majority of these, or 4.8 million, came from Singapore alone. Among European countries the most enthusiastic visitors to Malaysia were the British, with 98,000 arrivals (equalled by the Australians). The Japanese, though, appear to have lost interest and now holiday either at home or in South Korea. Just 147,000 Japanese visited Malaysia in the first six months of 2004.

Mapping out the future: Vision 2020

Mahathir's long term economic blueprint, continued by Badawi, appropriately labelled 'Wawasan 2020' or 'Vision 2020' aims to quadruple per-capita income, double the size of the economy and make Malaysia a fully developed industrialized country by the end of the second decade of the century. Vision 2020 is full of lofty ambitions, grand goals and fuzzy rhetoric and it reads more like a corporate mission statement than a well-defined policy. But while it was undeniably ambitious, few people questioned whether Malaysia could not achieve the annual average economic growth rate of seven per cent necessary to meet the plan's targets. That, though, was before the economic crisis which saw the economy contract by 7.5 per cent in 1998 and grow by just five per cent in 1999.

However 2000 saw a bounce-back as the economy expanded by 8.6 per cent, largely on the back of strong export growth and high government spending. The undervaluation of the ringgit was seen, at the time, to have helped turn the economy around, boosting the country's competitiveness. Consumer confidence recovered with a surge in demand for luxury items. Because all this was linked to Prime Minister Mahathir's decision to go against the IMF (and most economists') recommendations, he personally gained considerable prestige from the economy's robust recovery.

In 2001, Malaysia's economy stalled from reduced demand for its exports (the IT sector shrank markedly that year) and the effect of September 11, GDP grew only 0.5 per cent. The economy picked up again in 2002 and 2003, with 4.1 per cent growth in 2002 and 4.9 per cent in 2003, despite pressure from Sars and the Iraq War.

Falling tigers

Malaysia's economic crisis came quick on the heels of Thailand's fall from economic grace in July 1997, which led to the devaluation of the baht and a US$15bn IMF rescue package. Though Thailand's problems were uniquely serious there were enough commonalities to cause concern in KL's financial district: a high current account deficit; a currency linked to the US$; a booming property sector; and a lack of transparency in some aspects of financial management. It was these similarities with Thailand – and perhaps also a sense that the economies of Asean, having boomed together would also fall together – which led currency speculators to attack the ringgit.

Former Prime Minister Mahathir, predictably, blamed perfidious currency speculators and in particular George Soros, the Hungarian-born billionaire. Mahathir allegedly compared speculators to drug dealers, labelling them anarchists, saboteurs and rogues (*The Economist*, 2 August 1997). In July 1997 at their annual meeting, the nine Asean foreign ministers released a joint communiqué stating that the currency crisis was due to the "well co-ordinated efforts [by speculators] to destabilize ASEAN currencies for self-serving purposes". *The Economist* opined that blaming Soros for Thailand's plight was "rather like condemning an undertaker for burying a suicide".

Unlike the other countries of the region, Mahathir did not stick with the IMF's medicine. Instead he imposed tight currency controls in September 1998. While his actions were widely condemned in the international press, the recovery of the Malaysian economy by mid-1999, in Mahathir's eyes at least, vindicated his actions. Of course, opponents of the controls maintained that the country's economic recovery had little to do with the controls per se. Indeed, they say that of all the countries of the region Malaysia was best placed to deal with the crisis and that the currency controls were an irrelevance in the broader economic context. The danger, these critics of Malaysian economic policies maintain, is that because the country was affected least by the crisis it also did the least to confront the structural problems that created the conditions for the crisis in the first place. In other words they wonder whether it could all happen again.

Culture

People

Visitors sometimes get confused over the different races that make up Malaysia's population. All citizens of Malaysia are 'Malaysians'; they are comprised of Malays, Chinese and Indians as well as other 'tribal' groups, most of whom live in the East Malaysian states of Sabah and Sarawak.

Malaysia had a total population in 2000 of 23.27 million, of whom more than 8 in 10 live on the peninsula, eight per cent in Sabah and nine per cent in Sarawak. Statistics on the ethnic breakdown of Malaysia's multi-racial population tend to differ and because politics is divided along racial lines, they are sensitive figures. For Malaysia as a whole, Malays and other indigenous groups make up roughly 65 per cent of the population, Chinese 26 per cent and Indians eight per cent. The Malays and indigenous groups are usually lumped together under the umbrella term bumiputra – or 'sons of the soil'. This includes both Malays and tribal groups such as the assorted Dayaks of East Malaysia. On the peninsula the Chinese make up a rather large share of the population, amounting to some 31 per cent, while bumis comprise 58 per cent and Indians nine per cent.

In theory being a bumi bestows certain advantages. The New Economic Policy or NEP introduced after the race riots in 1969, discriminates in favour of the indigenous population – mostly the Malays, but also the non-Malay tribal peoples of East Malaysia and the Orang Asli of the peninsula. They receive preferential treatment when it comes to university places, bumi entrepreneurs have an inside track securing government contracts, and they also benefit from discounts on houses. However there have been stories of non-Malay bumiputras not being accorded the affirmative action rights of Malay bumis. In 1997, for example, it was revealed that an Iban ('tribal' Dayak from East Malaysia) man was refused the five to seven per cent discount which bumis are entitled to when he tried to buy a house in Melaka. The federal government was appalled but many commentators were not altogether surprised. What it means to qualify as a bumi has never been adequately defined. It appears that for some people being a bumi not only means being indigenous, it also means being Muslim, and many of the non-Malay bumis are Christian.

Malaysia's population is growing by just over 2 per cent per annum and the total fertility rate – the number of children born to each woman – stands at 3.24. This fertility rate, however, is not equally distributed between the ethnic groups. Since 1970, the bumiputra population has grown fastest, and, on the peninsula, their proportion of the total population has increased from 53 per cent. In the same period, the proportion of the Chinese population has declined from 36 per cent while the proportion of Indians has remained roughly the same. The higher average fertility rate of the Malay compared with the Chinese population means that the delicate racial balance that was such a potential source of instability at independence is becoming less of a worry. It has been estimated that by 2020 the bumiputra population will comprise 70 per cent of the total population of the country. The fear that the Chinese might represent a political threat to Malay domination is receding as each year passes.

Malays

The Malay people probably first migrated to the peninsula from Sumatra. Anthropologists speculate that the race originally evolved from the blending of a Mongoloid people from Central Asia with an island race living between the Indian and Pacific oceans. They are lowland people and originally settled around the coasts. These 'Coastal Malays' are also known as 'Deutero-Malays'. They are ethnically similar to the Malays of Indonesia and are the result of intermarriage with many other racial groups, including Indians, Chinese, Arabs and Thais. They are a very relaxed, warm-hearted people who had the good fortune to settle in a land where growing food was easy. For centuries they have been renowned for their hospitality and generosity as well as their well-honed sense of humour. When Malays converted to Islam in the early 15th century, the language was written in Sanskrit script which evolved into the Arabic-looking Jawi.

Because Malays were traditionally farmers and were tied to rural kampongs, they remained insulated from the expansion of colonial Malaya's export economy. Few of them worked as wage labourers and only the aristocracy, which had been educated in English, were intimately involved in the British system of government, as administrators. "... In return for the right to develop a modern extractive economy within the negeri [states] by means of alien immigrant labor," writes historian William R Roff, "the British undertook to maintain intact the position and prestige of the ruling class and to refrain from catapulting the Malay people into the modern world". Rural Malays only began to enter the cash economy when they started to take up rubber cultivation on their smallholdings – but this was not until after 1910. In 1921, less than five per cent of Malays lived in towns.

On attaining independence in 1957, the new constitution allowed Malays to be given special rights for 10 years, enabling them to become as prosperous as the Chinese 'immigrants'. To this end, they were afforded extra help in education and in securing jobs. The first economic development plan focused on the rural economy, with the aim of improving the lot of the rural Malays. It was the Malay community's sense of its own weakness in comparison with the commercial might of the Chinese that led to ethnic tensions erupting onto the streets in May 1969. Following the race riots, the Malays were extended special privileges in an effort to increase their participation in the modern economy. Along with indigenous groups, they were classed as bumiputras, usually shortened to 'bumis' – a label many were able to use as a passport to a better life.

Chinese

The Chinese community accounts for about a third of Malaysia's population. In 1794, just eight years after he had founded Georgetown in Penang, Sir Francis Light wrote: "The Chinese constitute the most valuable part of our inhabitants: ... they possess the different trades of carpenters, masons, smiths, traders, shopkeepers and planters; they employ small vessels. They are the only people from whom a revenue may be raised without expense and extraordinary effort by the government. They are a valuable acquisition ..." Chinese immigrants went on to become invaluable members of the British Straits Settlements – from the early 1820s they began to flood into Singapore from China's southern provinces. At the same time they arrived in droves on the Malay peninsula, most of them working as tin prospectors, shopkeepers and small traders.

Although the great bulk of Chinese in Malaysia arrived during the massive immigration between the late 19th and early 20th centuries, there has been a settled community of Chinese in Melaka since the 15th century. Many arrived as members of the retinue of the Chinese princess Li Poh who married Melaka's Sultan Mansur Shah in 1460 (see page 216). Over the centuries their descendants evolved into a wealthy and influential community with its own unique, sophisticated culture (see page 206). These Straits Chinese became known as Peranakans (which means 'born here'); men were called Babas and women, Nyonyas. When Peranakans began to be known as such is not known. Baba came into common usage during the 19th century and it is thought that Peranakan was already a well-established label at that time. 'Baba' does not seem to be of Chinese origin but is probably derived from Arabic, or perhaps Turkish, roots. To begin with Baba was used to refer to all local-born foreigners in Malaya, whether they were ethnic Chinese, Indians or Europeans. However, before long it became solely associated with the Straits Chinese.

The centres of Peranakan Chinese culture were the Straits Settlements of Melaka, Penang and Singapore. There were, however, significant differences between the communities in the three settlements. For example, Nyonya food in Penang shows culinary influences from Thailand, while food in Melaka and Singapore does not. The Peranakans of Malaysia and Singapore saw their futures being intimately associated with the British. They learnt English, established close links with the colonial administration system and colonial businesses, and even their newspapers were written in English rather than Chinese. With the massive infusion of new Chinese blood from the mainland beginning at the end of the 19th century there emerged a two-tier Chinese community. The Peranakans were concentrated in the commercial and professional sectors, and the 'pure' Chinese in the manual sectors. But as the 20th century progressed so the influence of the Peranakans declined. Competition from non-Baba Chinese became stronger as their businesses expanded and as sheer weight of numbers began to tell. The Straits Chinese British Association (SCBA) was eclipsed by the Malaysian Chinese Association (MCA) as a political force and the Peranakans found themselves marginalized. As this occurred, so the Babas found themselves the object, increasingly, of derision by non-Baba Chinese. They were regarded as having 'sold out' their Chinese roots and become ridiculous in the process. Today the Straits Chinese, in terms of political and economic power, have become – to a large extent – an irrelevance.

Today Peranakan culture is disappearing. Few Baba Chinese identify themselves as Baba; they have become Chinese Malaysians. Only in Melaka (and to some extent in Singapore) does the Baba cultural tradition remain strong. In Penang the numbers of people who see their Baba roots as anything but historical are dwindling. But although Peranakan culture is gradually disappearing, it has left an imprint on mainstream Malaysian culture. For example the custom among Peranakan women of wearing the sarong and kebaya has become subsumed within Malay tradition and has, in the process, become inter-ethnic. Baba cuisine has also been incorporated within Malay/Chinese cuisine.

The Peranakans may be the most colourful piece in Malaysia's Chinese mosaic, but the vast majority of modern Malaysia's prosperous Chinese population arrived from China rather later, as penniless immigrants. They left China because of poverty, over-population and religious persecution – and were attracted by the lure of gold. In the mid-19th century, these newly arrived immigrants came under the jurisdiction of secret societies and kongsis (clan associations). Some of the most striking examples of the latter are in Penang (see, for example the Khoo Kongsi, page 163). The secret societies sometimes engaged in open warfare with each other as rival groups fought over rights to tin mining areas.

The overseas Chinese have been described as possessing these common traits: the ability to smell profits and make quick business decisions; a penchant for good food (they prefer to sit at round tables to facilitate quicker exchange of information); and a general avoidance of politics in favour of money-making pursuits. Like most stereotypes, these characteristics break down when put to the detailed test but at a certain level of generalization, hold true. It is also true to say – broadly speaking – that the Chinese population felt little loyalty to their host society. At least, that is, until the 1949 Communist take-over in China, which effectively barred their return. Despite the community's political and economic gripes and traumas in the intervening years, Chinese culture has survived and the community enjoys religious freedom; Chinese cuisine is enthusiastically devoured by all races and the mahjong tiles are still clacking in upstairs rooms. Today about 80 per cent of Chinese schoolchildren attend private Chinese primary schools – although all secondary and tertiary education is in Malay.

Indians

Indian traders first arrived on the shores of the Malay peninsula more than 2,000 years ago in search of Suvarnadvipa, the fabled Land of Gold. There was a well established community of Indian traders in Melaka when the first sultanate grew up in the 1400s – there was even Tamil blood in the royal lineage. But most of the 1½ million Indians in modern Malaysia – who make up nearly eight per cent of the population – are descendants of indentured Tamil labourers shipped to Malaya from South India by the British in the 19th century. They were nicknamed 'Klings' – a name which today has a deeply derogatory connotation. Most were put to work as coolies on the roads and railways or as rubber tappers.

About 100 years on, four out of five Indians are still manual labourers on plantations or in the cities. This has long been explained as a colonial legacy, but as modern Malaysia has grown more prosperous, the Tamils have remained at the bottom of the heap. Other Indian groups – the Keralans (Malayalis), Gujeratis, Bengalis, Sikhs and other North Indians, who came to colonial Malaya under their own volition, are now well represented in the professional classes. The South Indian Chettiar money-lending caste, which was once far more numerous than it is today, left the country in droves in the 1930s. Their confidence in British colonial rule was shaken by events in Burma, where anti-Indian riots prompted tens of thousands of Chettiars to return to India. While most of Malaysia's Indian community are Hindus, there are also Indian Muslims, Christians and Sikhs. In Melaka there is a small group of Indians with Portuguese names – known as Chitties.

Today the chanted names of the Hindu pantheon echo around the cool interior of the Sri Mariamman Temple in the heart of the capital Kuala Lumpur as they have since its construction in 1873. But large numbers of Tamils still live in the countryside, where they still make up more than half the plantation workforce. Because the estates are on private land, they fall outside the ambit of national development policies and Malaysia's economic boom has passed them by. The controversial New Economic Policy gave the Malays a helping hand, and although it was aimed at eradicating poverty generally, it did not help the Indians much – who often, and justifiably, feel that they are the group who have missed out most. They lack the economic clout of the Chinese, and the political might of the Malays, and can, it seems, conveniently be forgotten.

The new policy document which replaced the NEP in 1991 officially recognizes that Indians have lagged behind in the development stakes. Education is seen as the key to broadening the entrepreneurial horizons of Tamils, getting them off the plantations, out of the urban squatter settlements and into decent jobs. But in the privately run Tamil shanty schools on the estates, the drop-out rate is double the national average. Critics accuse the Malaysian Indian Congress (MIC), which is part of the ruling coalition, of perpetuating this system in an effort to garner support. Because Indians are spread throughout the country and do not form the majority in any constituency, the plantations have been the MIC's traditional support base. It is not in the MIC's interests to see them move off the estates.

But things are beginning to change on the plantations – an unprecedented national strike in 1990 guaranteed plantation workers a minimum wage for the first time. Workers are becoming more assertive and aware of their individual and political rights. A new party, the Indian Progressive Front, has drawn its support from working class Indians. It seems that these stirrings of new assertiveness represent rising aspirations on the estates – which will have to continue to rise if the Tamils are ever going to escape from their plantation poverty trap, which one prominent Indian leader refers to as 'the green ghetto'. In 1970 ethnic Indians controlled about 1.1 per cent of the country's wealth. By 1992, at the end of the 20-year NEP, this figure had declined to one per cent. It has been estimated that two-thirds of Indians still live in poverty and for the Indians the NEP has been largely irrelevant. While Malays have enjoyed cumulative gains from the NEP and the Chinese have seen their slice of the cake grow in size if not in proportion, the Indian community have been left trailing and marginalized – a classic 'excluded' community.

Orang Asli (Aboriginals)

While the Malay population originally settled on the coasts of the peninsula, the mountainous, jungled interior was the domain of the oldest indigenous groups – the aboriginals. They are a sinewy, dark-skinned race, characterized by their curly hair and are probably of Melanesian origin – possibly related to Australian aborigines. During the Pleistocene ice age, when a land-bridge linked the Philippines to Borneo and mainland Southeast Asia, these people spread throughout the continent. Today they are confined to the mountains of the Malay peninsula, Northeast India, North Sumatra, the Andaman Islands and the Philippines. The **Negrito** aboriginals – who in Malay are known as Orang Asli, or 'Indigenous People' – were mainly hunter-gatherers. As the Malays spread inland, the Orang Asli were pushed further and further into the mountainous interior. Traditionally, the Negritos did not build permanent houses – preferring makeshift shelters – and depend on the jungle and the rivers for their food.

A second group of Orang Asli, the **Senoi** – who are also known as the **Sakai** – arrived later than the Negritos. They practised shifting cultivation to supplement their hunting and gathering and built sturdier houses. The third aboriginal group to come to the peninsula were the **Jakuns** – or **proto-Malays** – who were mainly of Mongoloid stock. They were comprised of several subgroups, the main ones being the Mantera and Biduanda of Negeri Sembilan and Melaka and the Orang Ulu, Orang Kanak and Orang Laut ('Sea People') of Johor. Their culture and language became closely linked to that of the coastal Malays, and over the centuries many of them assimilated into Malay society. Most practised shifting cultivation; the Orang Laut were fishermen. Malaysia's aborigines have increasingly been drawn into the modern economy. Along with the Malays, they are classified as bumiputras and as such, became eligible, as with other tribal groups in East Malaysia, for the privileges extended to all bumiputras following the introduction of the New Economic Policy (NEP) in 1970. In reality, however, the NEP offered few tangible benefits to the Orang Asli, and while the government has sought to integrate them – there is a Department of Aboriginal Affairs in Kuala Lumpur – there is no separate mechanism to encourage entrepreneurism among the group.

Art and architecture

Unlike the countries of mainland Southeast Asia and its neighbour, Indonesia, Malaysia is not known for its art and architecture. Arriving at Kuala Lumpur's Sabang International Airport and driving into town, there is apparently scarcely anything worth an aesthetic second glance. Many of Malaysia's artistic treasures have either been torn down to make way for modern buildings with scarcely a concrete ounce of artistic merit, or have simply rotted away through sheer neglect. However, the country is far from being the artistic desert that a cursory glance might suppose. The sadness, though, is that much of what is deemed to be 'worth seeing' (ie a 'sight') is not Malaysian per se, but colonial. The most attractive towns – notably Georgetown (Penang) and Melaka – are notable mainly for their Chinese shophouses, and Dutch, Portuguese and English colonial buildings. Vernacular Malay houses must be sought out more carefully; few are preserved, and most are being demolished to make way for structures perceived to be more fitting of a thrusting young country on the verge of developed nation status.

In his book *The Malay House*, architect Lim Jee Yuan wrote that traditional houses, which are built without architects, "reflect good housing solutions, as manifested by the display of a good fit to the culture, lifestyle and socio-economic needs of the users; the honest and efficient use of materials; and appropriate climatic design". Classic Malay houses are built of timber and raised on stilts with wooden or bamboo walls and an atap roof – made from the leaves of the nipah palm. It should have plenty of windows and good ventilation – the interior is usually airy and bright. It is also built on a prefabricated system and can be expanded to fit the needs of a growing family. Malay houses are usually simple, functional and unostentatious, and even those embellished by woodcarvings blend into their environment. Lim Jee Yuan said "the Malay house cannot be fully appreciated without its setting – the house compound and the kampong". Kampong folk, he says, prefer "community intimacy over personal privacy" which means villages are closely knit communities.

Most Malays on the peninsula traditionally lived in pile houses built on stilts along the rivers. The basic design is called the bumbung panjangi ('long roof'), although there are many variations and hybrids; these are influenced both by the Minangkabau house-forms (of West Sumatra) and by Thai-Khmer designs. The differences in house-styles between regions is mainly in the shape of the roof. The bumbung panjang is the oldest, commonest, simplest and most graceful, with a long gable roof, thatched with atap. There are ventilation grills at either end, allowing a throughflow of air. From the high apex, the eaves slope down steeply, then, towards the bottom, the angle lessens, extending out over the walls. Bumbung panjang are most commonly found in Melaka, but the design is used widely throughout the peninsula.

These days it is more usual to find the atap replaced with corrugated zinc roofs which require less maintenance and are a measure of status in the community. But zinc turns houses into ovens during the day, makes them cold at night and makes a deafening noise in rainstorms. On the east coast of the peninsula, the use of tiled roofs is more common. Towards the north, Thai and Khmer influences are more pronounced in roof style. As in Thai houses, walls are panelled; there are also fewer windows and elaborate carving is more common. Because Islam proscribes the use of the human figure in art, ornamental woodcarvings depict floral and geometric designs as well as Koranic calligraphy. Most are relief-carvings on wood panels or grilles. In Melaka, colourful ceramic tiles are also commonly used as exterior decoration.

The oldest surviving Malay houses date from only the 19th century. The traditional design is the rumah berpanggung, which is built high off the ground on stilts with an A-shaped roof. The basic features include: Anjung: covered porch at the top of entranceway stairs where formal visitors are entertained; Serambi gantung: verandah, where most guests are entertained; Rumah ibu ('the domain of the mother of the house'): private central core of the house, with raised floor level, where the family talks, sleeps, prays, studies and eats (particularly during festivals); Dapur: kitchen, always at the back, and below the level of the rest of the house; most meals are taken here. The dapur is connected to the rumah ibu by the selang, a closed walkway. Near the dapur, there is usually a pelantar, with a washing area for clothes, a mandi and a toilet.

The best places to see traditional Malay houses are Melaka and Negeri Sembilan, on the west coast, and Terengganu and Kelantan states to the northeast. Minangkabau influence is most pronounced in Negeri Sembilan state, between Kuala Lumpur and Melaka. There, houses have a distinctive, elegant, curved roofline, where the gable sweeps up into 'wings' at each end – the so-called Minangkabau 'buffalo horns'.

Today the traditional Malay house has lost its status in the kampong – now everyone wants to build in concrete and brick. Many planned modern kampongs have been built throughout Malaysia, with little regard for traditional building materials or for the traditional houseforms. Many like-minded architects despair of the 'vulgarization' of the Malay houseform, which has been used as an inspiration for many modern buildings (notably in Kuala Lumpur, see page 77). The curved Minangkabau roof, for example, which has been borrowed for everything from modern bank buildings to toll-booths, has merely become a cultural symbol, and has been deprived of its deeper significance.

Peranakan

The Straits Chinese (Peranakan) communities of Melaka, Penang and Singapore developed their own architectural style to match their unique cultural traditions (see page 206). The finest Peranakan houses can be seen along Jalan Tun Tan Cheng Lock in Melaka (see page 214), notably the Baba-Nyonya Heritage Museum. Typical Peranakan houses were long and narrow, and built around a central courtyard. Their interiors are characterized by dark, heavy wood and marble-topped furniture, often highly decorated, and made by Chinese craftsmen who were brought over from China.

Language and literature

Bahasa Melayu (literally, 'Malay Language') – or to give the language its official title, Bahasa Kebangsaan ('National Language') – is an Austronesian language which has been the language of trade and commerce throughout the archipelago for centuries. It is the parent language of – and is closely related to – modern Indonesian. In 1972, Indonesia and Malaysia came to an agreement to standardize spelling – although many differences still remain.

Modern Malay has been affected by a succession of external influences – Sanskrit from the seventh century, Arabic from the 14th and English from the 19th century. These influences are reflected in a number of words, most of them of a religious or technical nature. All scientific terminology is directly borrowed from the English or Latin. However, there are many common everyday words borrowed from Arabic or English: pasar, for example, comes from the Arabic bazaar (market) and there are countless examples of English words used in Malay – particularly when it comes to modern modes of transport – teksi, bas and tren. Where a Malay term has been devised for a 20th century phenomenon, it is usually a fairly straightforward description. An alternative word for train, for example is keretapi (literally 'fire car') and the word for aeroplane is kapalterbang (flying ship).

From the seventh century, the Indian Pallava script was in restricted use, although few examples survive. The Jawi script, adapted from Arabic, was adopted in the 14th century, with the arrival of Muslim traders and Sufi missionaries in Melaka. To account for sounds in the Malay language which have no equivalent in Arabic, five additional letters had to be invented, giving 33 letters in all. Jawi script was used for almost all Malay writings until the 19th century, and romanized script only began to supplant Jawi after the Second World War. Many older Malays still read and write the script and it is not uncommon to see it along the streets. Some Chinese-owned banks, for example, have transliterated their names into Jawi script so as to make Malays feel a little more at home in them.

Malay literature is thought to date from the 14th century – although surviving manuscripts written in Jawi only date from the beginning of the 15th century. The first printed books in Malay were produced by European missionaries in the 17th century. The best known of Malay literary works are the 16th-century Sejara Melayu or Malay Annals; others include the romantic Hikayat Hang Tuah and the 19th century Tuhfat al-Nafis.

The first of Malaysia's 'modern' authors was the 19th century writer Munshi Abdullah – who has lent his name to a few streets around the country. Although he kept to many of the classical strictures, Abdullah articulated a personal view and challenged many of the traditional assumptions underlying Malay society. His best known work was his autobiography, Hikayat Abdullah. However, it was not until the 1920s that Malayan authors began to write modern novels and short stories. Among the best known writers are Ahmad bin Mohd. Rashid Talu, Ishak Hj. Muhammad and Harun Aminurrashid. Their work laid the foundations for an expansion of Malaysian literature from the 1950s and today there is a prodigious Malay-language publishing industry.

Since independence, the government has promoted Bahasa Melayu at the expense of Chinese dialects and English. However in 1994 then Prime Minister Mahathir signalled a switch in strategy when he declared that university courses in the sciences and technology would be taught in English rather than Bahasa. The emphasis on Bahasa is regarded to some extent as yesterday's battle – the battle to build a national, Malaysian identity. Today's battle is to produce an educated workforce conversant and at home in the world of international business – in other words, people who can use English. When comparisons are made between Malaysian and other overseas students, Malaysian students come out poorly. This is one reason why so many wealthy Malays and Chinese send their children to private English language schools. Now the government appears to have realized the necessity for state schools and universities to reintroduce English. I And in mid-1997 the government ruled that Islamic civilization would become a mandatory course for all university students – they would need to take and pass it in order to graduate. Needless to say, non-Muslim Malaysians, and some Muslim Malaysians, thought this a step backwards and going against the trend towards a modern, outward-looking, and inclusive Malaysia. Later it was announced that the course would also include study of other Asian civilizations.)

Drama, dance and music

Drama

Wayang Kulit Wayang means 'shadow', and the art form is best translated as 'shadow theatre' or 'shadow play'. Shadow plays were the traditional form of entertainment in Malay kampongs. Although film and television have replaced the wayang in many people's lives – especially the young – they are still performed in some rural parts of the peninsula's east coast and are regular fixtures at cultural events. Some people believe that the wayang is Indian in origin, pointing to the fact that most of the characters are from Indian epic tales such as the Ramayana and Mahabharata.

By the 11th century wayang was well-established in Java. A court poet of the Javanese King Airlangga (1020-1049), referred to wayang in The meditation of King Ardjuna: There are people who weep, are sad and aroused watching the puppets, though they know they are merely carved pieces of leather manipulated and made to speak. These people are like men, thirsting for sensual pleasures, who live in a world of illusion; they do not realize the magic hallucinations they see are not real. It seems that by the 14th century the art form had made the crossing from the Javanese Majapahit Empire to the courts of the Malay Peninsula and from there spread to kampongs across the country.

There are many forms of wayang – and not all of them are, strictly speaking, shadow plays – but the commonest and oldest form is the wayang kulit. Kulits are finely carved and painted leather, two-dimensional puppets, jointed at the elbows and shoulders and manipulated using horn rods. In order to enact the entire repertoire of 179 plays, 200 puppets are needed. A single performance can last as long as nine hours. The plays have various origins. Some are animistic, others are adapted from the epic poems. The latter are known as 'trunk' tales or pondok and include the Ramayana. Others have been developed over the years by influential puppet masters. They feature heroic deeds, romantic encounters, court intrigues, bloody battles, and mystical observations, and are known as carangan or 'branch' tales.

The gunungan or Tree of Life, is an important element of wayang theatre. It represents all aspects of life, and is always the same in design: shaped like a stupa, the tree has painted red flames on one side and a complex design on the other (this is the side which faces the audience). At the base of the tree are a pair of closed doors, flanked by two fierce demons or yaksas. Above the demons are two garudas and within the branches of the tree there are monkeys, snakes and two animals – usually an ox and a tiger. The gunungan is placed in the middle of the screen at the beginning and end of the performance – and sometimes between major scene changes. During the performance it stands at one side, and flutters across the screen to indicate minor scene changes.

Traditionally, performances were requested by individuals to celebrate particular occasions – for example the seventh month of pregnancy (tingkep) – or to accompany village festivities. Admission was free, as the individual commissioning the performance would meet the costs. Of course, this has changed now and tourists invariably have to pay an entrance charge.

In the past, the shadows of the puppets were reflected onto a white cotton cloth stretched across a wooden frame using the light from a bronze coconut oil lamp. Today, electric light is more common – a change which, in many people's minds, has meant the unfortunate substitution of the flickering, mysterious shadows of the oil lamp, with the constant harsh light of the electric bulb. There are both day and night wayang performances. The latter, for obvious reasons, are the more dramatic, although the former are regarded as artistically superior.

The audience sits on both sides of the screen. Those sitting with the puppet master see a puppet play; those on the far side, out of view of the puppet master and the accompanying gamelan orchestra, see a shadow play. It is possible that in the past, the audience was segregated according to sex: men on the to' dalang's side of the screen, women on the shadow side.

The puppet-master is known as the to' dalang; he narrates each story in lyrical classical Malay and is accompanied by a traditional gamelan orchestra of gongs, drums, rebab (violins) and woodwind instruments. He slips in and out of different characters, using many different voices throughout the performances, which lasts as long as three to four hours. The words to' dalang are said to be derived from galang, meaning bright or clear, the implication being that the to' dalang makes the sacred texts understandable. He sits on a plinth, an arm's length away from the cloth screen. From this position he manipulates the puppets, while also narrating the story. Although any male can become a to' dalang, it is usual for sons to follow their fathers into the profession. The to' dalang is the key to a successful performance: he must be multi-skilled, have strength and stamina, be able to manipulate numerous puppets simultaneously, narrate the story, and give the lead to the accompanying gamelan orchestra. No wonder that an adept to' dalang is a man with considerable status.

Chinese classical street operas (wayang) date back to the seventh century. They are performed in Malaysia by troupes of roving actors during Chinese festivals, particularly during the seventh lunar month, following the Festival of the Hungry Ghosts. For more details on the wayang, see box, page 509.

Dance

Silat (or, more properly, bersilat) is a traditional Malay martial art, but is so highly stylized that it has become a dance form and is often perfomed with the backing of a percussion orchestra. Pencak silat is the more formal martial art of self-defence; seni silat is the graceful aesthetic equivalent. A variety of the latter is commonly performed at ceremonial occasions – such as Malay weddings – it is called silat pulut. Silat comprises a fluid combination of movements and is designed to be as much a comprehensive and disciplined form of physical exercise as it is a martial art. It promotes good blood circulation and deep-breathing, which are considered essential for strength and stamina. The fluidity of the body movements require great suppleness, flexibility and poise.

Malaysia's best-known silat gurus live along the east coast.

The **Mak Yong** was traditionally a Kelantanese court dance-drama, performed only in the presence of the sultan and territorial chiefs. Performed mainly by women (the mak yong being the 'queen' and lead dancer), it is accompanied by an orchestra of gongs, drums and the rebab (violin). There are only ever two or three male dancers who provide the comic interludes. The dance is traditionally performed during the Sultan of Kelantan's birthday celebrations. Unlike the wayang kulit shadow puppet theatre (above), the stories are not connected to the Hindu epics; they are thought to be of Malay origin. Other Kelantanese court dances include: the garong, a lively up-tempo dance by five pairs of men and women, in a round (a garong is a bamboo cow bell). The payang, a folk dance, is named after the distinctive east coast fishing boats; traditionally it was danced on the beach while waiting for the kampong fishing fleet to return.

The joget dance is another Malay art form which is the result of foreign cultural influence – in this case, Portuguese. It has gone by a variety of other names, notably the ronggeng and the branyo. It is traditionally accompanied by the gamelan orchestra. Arab traders were responsible for importing the zapin dance and Indonesians introduced the inang. Immigrants from Banjarmasin (South Kalimantan), who arrived in Johor in the early 1900s, brought with them the so-called Hobbyhorse Dance – the Kuda Kepang – which is performed at weddings and on ceremonial occasions in Johor. The hobbyhorses are made of goat or buffalo skin, stretched over a rotan frame. There are countless other local folk dances around Malaysia, usually associated with festivals – such as the wau bulan kite dance in Kelantan.

The Lion Dance is performed in Chinese communities, particularly around Chinese New Year, and is accompanied by loud drums and cymbals – hard to miss. The lion dance originated in India, where tamed lions were led around public fairs and festivals as entertainment, but because lions were in short supply, dancers with lion masks took their place. The dance was introduced to China during the Tang Dynasty. The lion changed its image from that of a clown to a symbol of the Buddha and is now regarded as 'the protector of Buddhism'. The lion dance developed into a ceremony in which demons and evil spirits are expelled (hence the deafening cymbals and drums).

Bharata Natyam (Indian classical dance) is performed by Malaysia's Indian community and is accompanied by Indian instruments such as the tambura (which has four strings), the talam (cymbals), mridanga (double-headed drum), vina (single stringed instrument) and flute. In Malaysia, the Temple of Fine Arts in Kuala Lumpur is an Indian cultural organization which promotes Indian dance forms. The Temple organizes an annual Festival of Arts (see page 110).

Music

Traditional Malay music, which accompanies the various traditional dances, offers a taste of all the peninsula's different cultural influences. The most prominent of these were Indian, Arab, Portuguese, Chinese, Siamese and Javanese – and finally, Western musical influence which gave birth to the all-pervasive genre 'Pop Melayu' – typically melancholic heavy rock. Traditional musical instruments reflect similar cultural influences, notably the gambus or lute (which has Middle Eastern origins and is used to accompany the zapin dance), the Indian harmonium, the Chinese serunai (clarinet) and gongs, the rebana drums, also of Middle Eastern origin, and the Javanese gamelan orchestra. Because Malays have traditionally been so willing to absorb new cultural elements, traditional art forms have been in danger of extinction. Most traditional Malay instruments are percussion instruments; there are very few stringed or wind instruments. There are six main Malay drums, the most common of which is the cylindrical, double-headed gendang, which is used to accompany wayang kulit performances and silat. Other drums include the geduk and the gedombak; all three are played in orchestras.

Rebana, another traditional Malay drum, is used on ceremonial occasions as well as being a musical instrument. Traditionally, drumming competitions would be held following the rice-harvesting season (in May) and judges award points for timing, tone and rhythm. The best place to see the rebana in action is during Kelantan's giant drum festivals at the end of June. The drums are made from metre-long hollowed-out logs and are brightly painted. In competitions, drummers from different kampongs compete against each other in teams of up to 12 men. Traditionally the rebana was used as a means of communication between villages, and different rhythms were devised as a sort of morse code to invite distant kampongs to weddings or as warnings of war. Kertok are drums made from coconuts whose tops are sliced off and replaced with a block of nibong wood (from the sago palm) as a sounding board; these are then struck with padded drumsticks.

There are three main gongs; the biggest and most common, the tawak or tetawak is used to accompany wayang kulit shadow puppet theatre and Mak Yong dance dramas. The other smaller gongs are called canang and also accompany wayang kulit performances. The only Malay stringed instrument is the rebab, a violin-type instrument found throughout the region. The main wind instrument is the serunai, or oboe, which is of Persian origin and traditionally accompanies wayang kulit and dance performances. Its reed is cut from a palm leaf.

The**Nobat** is the ancient royal orchestra which traditionally plays at the installation of sultans in Kedah, Perak, Selangor, Terangganu and Brunei. It is thought to have been introduced at the royal court of Melaka in the 15th century. The instruments include two types of drums (negara and gendang), a trumpet (nafiri), a flute (serunai) and a gong. The Nobat also plays at the coronation of each new king, every five years.

Crafts

The Malay heartland, on the east coast of Peninsular Malaysia, is the centre of the handicraft industry – particularly Kelantan. An extensive variety of traditional handicrafts, as well as batiks, are widely available in this area, although they are also sold throughout the country, notably in Kuala Lumpur and other main towns (see individual town entries). In East Malaysia, Sarawak has an especially active handicraft industry (see page 395).

Kites Kite-making and kite-flying (or main wau) are traditional pursuits in the northern Malaysian states of Perlis, Kedah, Kelantan and Terengganu. (Most kite-flying competitions take place after the rice harvest in May, when kampongs compete against each other.) Malaysia's most famous kite is the crescent-shaped Kelantanese wau bulan (moon kite) which has a wingspan of up to 3 m and a length of more than 3 m; they can reach altitudes of nearly 500 m. Bow-shaped pieces of bamboo are often secured underneath, which make a melodious humming noise (dengung) in the wind. Wau come in all shapes and sizes however, and scaled-down versions of wau bulan and other kites can be bought. It is even possible to find batik-covered wau cantik or wau sobek, which are popular wall-hangings but make for awkward hand-luggage. There are often kite-flying competitions on the east coast, where competitors gain points for height and manoeuvering skills. Kites are also judged for their physical attributes, their ability to stay in the air and their sound. On the east coast, all kites are known as wau, a word which, it is said, is derived from the arabic letter of the same sound, which is shaped like a kite. Perhaps the most recognizable one is Terengganu's wau kucing (cat kite), which Malaysia Airlines adopted as its logo. There are also wau daun (leaf kites) and wau jala budi (which literally means 'the net of good deeds kite'). Elsewhere in Malaysia, kites are known as layang-layang (literally, 'floating objects').

Tops Top spinning (main gasing) is another traditional form of entertainment, still popular in rural Malay kampongs – particularly on the east coast of the peninsula. There are two basic forms of tops. The heart-shaped gasing jantung and the flattened top, gasing uri. The biggest tops have diameters as big as frisbees and can weigh more than 5 kg; the skill required in launching a top is considerable. Top-making is a precision-craft, and each one can take up to three days to make; they are carved from the upper roots and stem-bases of merbau and afzelia trees.

Woodcarving Originally craftsmen were commissioned by sultans and the Malay nobility to decorate the interiors, railings, doorways, shutters and stilts of palaces and public buildings. In Malay woodcarving, only floral and animal motifs are used as Islam prohibits depiction of the human form. But most widely acclaimed are the carved statues of malevolent spirits of the Mah Meris, an Orang Asli tribe.

Batik (Batek) The word batik may be derived from the Malay word tik, meaning 'to drip'. It is believed that batik replaced tatooing as a mark of status in the Malay archipelago. (In eastern Indonesia the common word for batik and tattoo are the same.) Although batik-technology was actually imported from Indonesia several centuries ago, this coloured and patterned cloth is now a mainstay of Malaysian cultural identity. Traditionally, the wax was painted onto the woven cloth using a canting (pronounced 'janting'), a small copper cup with a spout, mounted on a

Making a wayang kulit puppet

Wayang kulit puppets are made of buffalo hide, preferably taken from a female animal of about four years of age. The skin is dried and scraped, and then left to mature for as long as 10 years to achieve the stiffness required for carving. After carving, the puppet is painted in traditional pigments.

In carving the puppet, the artist is constrained by convention. The excellence of the puppet is judged according to the fineness of the chisel-work and the subtlety of painting. If the puppet is well made it may have guna – a magical quality which is supposed to make the audience suspend its disbelief during the performance.

Puppets accumulate guna with age; this is why old puppets are preferred to new ones.

Each major character has a particular iconography, and even the angle of the head and the slant of the eyes and mouth determine the character. Some puppets may perform a number of minor parts, but in the main a knowledgeable wayang-goer will be able to recognize each character immediately.

The cempurit or rods used to manipulate the puppet are made of buffalo horn while the studs used to attach the limbs are made of metal, bone or bamboo. Court puppets might even be made of gold, studded with precious stones.

bamboo handle. The cup is filled with melted wax, which flows from the spout like ink from a fountain pen – although the canting never touches the surface of the cloth. Batik artists have a number of canting with various widths of spout, some even with several spouts, to give varied thicknesses of line and differences of effect. The cap speeded-up production, but it also took the artistry out of waxing: waxers merely stamp the design onto the cloth.

In the mid-19th century the 'modern' batik industry was born with the invention (in Java, but quickly adopted in Malaysia) of the cap (pronounced 'jap'). This is a copper, sometimes a wooden stamp which looks something like a domestic iron, except that it has an artistically patterned bottom, usually made from twisted copper and strips of soldered tin. Dripping with molten wax, the jap stamps the same pattern across the length and breadth of the cloth, which is then put into a vat of dye. The waxed areas resist the dye and after drying, the process is repeated several times for the different colours. The cracking effect is produced by crumpling the waxed material, which allows the dye to penetrate the cracks. The cloth is traditionally printed in 12 m lengths.

Recent years have seen a revival of hand-painted batiks (batik tulis), particularly on silk. Price depends on the type of material, design, number of colours used and method employed: factory-printed materials are cheaper than those made by hand. Batik is sold by the sarung-length or made up into shirts – and other items of clothing. **Kain songket** is Malaysia's 'cloth of gold', although it is also woven in other parts of the region, particularly coastal southern Sumatra. Originally cloth made from a mix of cotton and silk was interwoven with supplementary gold or silver thread. Today imitation thread is generally used although the metallic thread from old pieces is also removed to provide yarn for new lengths.

The songket evolved when the Malay sultanates first began trading with China (where the silk came from) and India (where the gold and silver thread derived). Designs are reproduced from Islamic motifs and Arabic calligraphy. It was once exclusive to royalty, but is used today during formal occasions and ceremonies (such as weddings). In Kelantan, Terengganu and Pahang the cloth can be purchased directly from workshops. Prices increase with the intricacy of the design and the number of threads used. Each piece is woven by hand and different weavers specialize in particular patterns – one length of cloth may be the work of several weavers.

Pewterware Pewter-making was introduced from China in the mid-19th century; it was the perfect alloy for Malaysia, which until recently, was the world's largest tin-producer: pewter is 95 per cent tin. Straits tin is alloyed with antimony and copper. The high proportion of tin lends to the fineness of the surface. It is made mainly into vases, tankards, water jugs, trays and dressing table ornaments. The dimpling effect is made by tapping the surface with a small hammer. Selangor Pewter is the world's biggest and best pewter manufacturer, there are factories in KL and Singapore.

Wayang kulit (shadow puppets – see box, page 509) are crafted from buffalo-hide and represent figures from the Indian epic tales. They are popular handicrafts as they are light and portable.

Silverware Silverwork is a traditional craft and is now a thriving cottage industry in Kelantan. It is crafted into brooches, pendants, belts, bowls and rings. Design patterns incorporate traditional motifs such as wayang kulit (see above) and hibiscus flowers (the national flower). The Iban of Sarawak also use silver for ceremonial headdresses and girdles, and some Iban silvercraft can be found for sale on the peninsula.

Religion

Islam

Malays are invariably Muslims and there is also a small population of Indian Muslims in Malaysia. The earliest recorded evidence of Islam on the Malay peninsula is an inscription in Terengganu dating from 1303, which prescribed penalties for those who did not observe the moral codes of the faith. Islam did not really gain a foothold on the peninsula, however, until Sri Maharaja of Melaka – the third ruler – converted in 1430 and changed his name to Mohamed Shah (see page 208). He retained many of the ingrained Hindu traditions of the royal court and did not attempt to enforce Islam as the state religion. The Arab merchant ships which made regular calls at Melaka probably brought Muslim missionaries to the city. Many of them were Sufis – belonging to a mystical order of Islam which was tolerant of local customs and readily synthesized with existing animist and Hindu beliefs. The adoption of this form of Islam is one reason why animism and the Muslim faith still go hand in hand in Malaysia (see below). Mohamad Shah's son, Rajah Kasim, was the first ruler to adopt the title 'Sultan', and he became Sultan Muzaffar; all subsequent rulers have continued to preserve and uphold the Islamic faith. The Portuguese and Dutch colonialists, while making a few local converts to Christianity, were more interested in trade than proselytizing.

The British colonial system of government was more 'progressive' than most colonial régimes in that it barred the British residents from interfering in 'Malay religion and custom'. So-called Councils of Muslim Religion and Malay Custom were set up in each state answerable to the sultans. These emerged as bastions of Malay conservatism and served to make Islam the rallying point of nascent nationalism. The Islamic reform movement was imported from the Middle East at the turn of the 19th century and Malays determined that the unity afforded by Islam transcended any colonial authority and the economic dominance of immigrant groups. The ideas spread as increasing numbers of Malays made the Haj to Mecca, made possible by the advent of regular steamer services. But gradually the sultans and the Malay aristocracy – who had done well out of British rule – began to see the Islamic renaissance as a threat.

The practice of Islam: living by the Prophet

Islam is an Arabic word meaning 'submission to God'. It is not just a religion but a total way of life. The main Islamic scripture is the Koran or Quran, the name being taken from the Arabic al-qur'an or 'the recitation'. The Koran is divided into 114 sura, or 'units'. Most scholars are agreed that the Koran was partially written by the Prophet Mohammad. In addition to the Koran there are the hadiths, from the Arabic word hadith meaning 'story', which tell of the Prophet's life and works. These represent the second most important body of scriptures.

The practice of Islam is based upon five central tenets, known as the Pillars of Islam: Shahada (profession of faith), Salat (worship), Zakat (charity), saum (fasting) and Haj (pilgrimage). The mosque is the centre of religious activity. The two most important mosque officials are the imam (leader) and the khatib (preacher) who delivers the Friday sermon.

The **Shahada** is the confession, and lies at the core of any Muslim's faith. It involves reciting, sincerely, two statements: 'There is no god, but God', and 'Mohammad is the Messenger [Prophet] of God'. A Muslim will do this at every **Salat**. This is the daily prayer ritual which is performed five times a day, at sunrise, midday, mid-afternoon, sunset and at night. There is also the important Friday noon worship. The Salat is performed by a Muslim bowing and then prostrating himself in the direction of Mecca (in Malaysian kiblat, in Arabic qibla). In hotel rooms throughout there is nearly always a little arrow, painted on the ceiling – or sometimes inside a wardrobe – indicating the direction of Mecca and labelled kiblat. The faithful are called to worship by a mosque official. Beforehand, a worshipper must wash to ensure ritual purity. The Friday midday service is performed in the mosque and includes a sermon given by the khatib.

A third essential element of Islam is **Zakat** – charity or alms-giving. A Muslim is supposed to give up his 'surplus'; through time this took on the form of a tax levied according to the wealth of the family. In Malaysia there is no official Zakat as there is in Saudi Arabia, but good Muslims are expected to contribute a tithe to the Muslim community.

The fourth pillar of Islam is **saum** or fasting. The daytime month-long fast of Ramadan is a time of contemplation, worship and piety – the Islamic equivalent of Lent. Muslims are expected to read one-thirtieth of the Koran each night. Muslims who are ill or on a journey have dispensation from fasting, but otherwise they are only permitted to eat during the night until "so much of the dawn appears that a white thread can be distinguished from a black one".

The **Haj** (Pilgrimage to the holy city of Mecca in Saudi Arabia) is required of all Muslims once in their lifetime if they can afford to make the journey and are physically able to. It is restricted to a certain time of the year, beginning on the eighth day of the Muslim month of Dhu-l-Hijja. Men who have been on the Haj are given the title Haji, and women hajjah.

The Koran also advises on a number of other practices, in particular the prohibitions on usury, the eating of pork, the taking of alcohol, and gambling. There is quite a powerful Islamic revival in Malaysia. The use of the veil is becoming increasingly de rigeur in Malaysia. The Koran says nothing about the need for women to veil, although it does stress the necessity of women dressing modestly.

In Siddhartha's footsteps: a short history of Buddhism

Buddhism was founded by Siddhartha Gautama, a prince of the Sakya tribe of Nepal, who probably lived between 563 and 483 BC. He achieved enlightenment and the word buddha means 'fully enlightened one', or 'one who has woken up'. Siddhartha Gautama is known by a number of titles. In the West, he is usually referred to as The Buddha, ie the historic Buddha (but not just Buddha); more common in Southeast Asia is the title Sakyamuni, or Sage of the Sakyas (referring to his tribal origins).

Over the centuries, the life of the Buddha has become part legend, and the Jataka tales which recount his various lives are colourful and convoluted. But, central to any Buddhist's belief is that he was born under a sal tree (Shorea robusta), that he achieved enlightenment under a bodhi tree (Ficus religiosa) in the Bodh Gaya Gardens, that he preached the First Sermon at Sarnath, and that he died at Kusinagara (all in India or Nepal).

The Budda was born at Lumbini (in present-day Nepal), as Queen Maya was on her way to her parents' home. She had had a very auspicious dream before the child's birth of being impregnated by an elephant, whereupon a sage prophesied that Siddhartha would become either a great king or a great spiritual leader. His father, being keen that the first option of the prophecy be fulfilled, brought him up in all the princely skills (at which Siddhartha excelled) and ensured that he only saw beautiful things, not the harsher elements of life.

Despite his father's efforts Siddhartha saw four things while travelling between palaces – a helpless old man, a very sick man, a corpse being carried by lamenting relatives, and an ascetic, calm and serene as he begged for food. These episodes made an enormous impact on the young prince, and he renounced his princely origins and left home to study under a series of spiritual teachers. He finally discovered the path to enlightenment at the Bodh Gaya Gardens in India. He then proclaimed his thoughts to a small group of disciples at Sarnath, near Benares, and continued to preach

On Fridays, the Muslim day of prayer, Malaysian Muslims congregate at mosques in their 'Friday best'. The 'lunch hour' starts at 1130 and runs through to about 1430 to allow Muslims to attend the mosque; in big towns and cities, Friday lunchtimes are marked by traffic jams. In the fervently Islamic east coast states, Friday is the start of the weekend. Men traditionally wear songkoks (black velvet hats) to the mosque and often wear their best sarung (sometimes songket) over their trousers. Those who have performed the Haj pilgrimage to Mecca wear a white skullcap. However, at least until recently (see below), Malaysia's Islam has been moderate by Middle Eastern standards. Traditionally, for example, women were not required to wear the head scarf (tudung).

But Malaysia has emerged as an outspoken defender of Muslims and Islamic values around the world. On occasions, former prime minister Mahathir has made outspoken attacks on Western attitudes towards Islam, in which, he says, Muslims are cast as pariahs and bogeymen. Partly this can be viewed as part of his efforts to polish his own Islamic credentials. At home, the BN feels threatened by the rise of fundamentalist sentiments – particularly in the northeastern state of Kelantan, where the Islamic government has approved a bill calling for the introduction of a strict Islamic penal code (see page 297). Hard-line Islam is perceived as a threat to secular society in Malaysia. The former deputy Prime Minister, Anwar Ibrahim – once a young and attract followers until he died at the age of 81 at Kusinagara.

In the First Sermon at the deer park in Sarnath, the Buddha preached the Four Truths, which are still considered the root of Buddhist belief and practical experience. These are the 'Noble Truth' that suffering exists, the 'Noble Truth' that there is a cause of suffering, the 'Noble Truth' that suffering can be ended, and the 'Noble Truth' that to end suffering it is necessary to follow the 'Noble Eightfold Path' – namely, right speech, livelihood, action, effort, mindfulness, concentration, opinion and intention.

Soon after the Buddha began preaching, a monastic order – the Sangha – was established. As the monkhood evolved in India, it also began to fragment as different sects developed different interpretations of the life of the Buddha. An important change was the belief that the Buddha was transcendent: he had never been born, nor had he died; he had always existed and his life on earth had been mere illusion. The emergence of these new concepts helped to turn what up until then was an ethical code of conduct, into a religion. It eventually led to the appearance of a new Buddhist movement, Mahayana Buddhism which split from the more traditional Theravada 'sect'.

Despite the division of Buddhism into two sects, the central tenets of the religion are common to both. Specifically, the principles pertaining to the Four Noble Truths, the Noble Eightfold Path, the Dependent Origination, the Law of Karma and nirvana. In addition, the principles of non-violence and tolerance are also embraced by both sects. In essence, the differences between the two are of emphasis and interpretation. Theravada Buddhism is strictly based on the original Pali Canon, while the Mahayana tradition stems from later Sanskrit texts. Mahayana Buddhism also allows a broader and more varied interpretation of the doctrine. Other important differences are that while the Thervada tradition is more 'intellectual' and self-obsessed, with an emphasis upon the attaining of wisdom and insight for oneself, Mahayana Buddhism stresses devotion and compassion towards others.

Islamic firebrand himself – became during his time in office an eloquent proponent of Islamic moderation. He appealed in articles submitted to international newspapers for less rhetoric in the name of political expediency from Muslim leaders around the world and for greater understanding of Islam in the West.

All of this, of course, has taken on even greater significance in the light of the events of September 11 (see the discussion above, under Politics). But it is worth remembering that the debate over the role and place of Islam in modern Malaysia dates back before the attacks in New York and Washington.

In 1994, then prime minister Mahathir was forced to clamp down on a fundamentalist Islamic sect known as Al Arqam with 10,000 followers, an estimated 200,000 sympathizers, and assets of RM15mn in businesses ranging from property firms to textile factories. Ashaari Muhammed, the leader of the sect, was arrested after being deported from Thailand and then held in detention under the Internal Security Act. Unlikely liberals leapt to defend Mr Ashaari who taught that women should be kept in their place, and operated his sect almost like a secret society. Why there was an order for Mr Ashaari's arrest was a point of dispute. The Prime Minister's office maintained that the sect's teachings were 'deviationist' – as also argued by the National Fatwah Council – and that he threatened state security. To begin with the government even suggested that the sect had a 313-man 'death squad'. Opponents maintained that his arrest was more to do with domestic politics: Al Arqam was attracting middle class Malays, just the sort of people who are the bedrock of UMNO's support. The arrest was not, in their view, anything to do with religion, but a great deal to do with politics. Nonetheless the government were able to get Ashaari Muhammed to renounce his teachings on television, thereby preventing him becoming a martyr.

Mahathir was concerned that radical Islam might destabilize Malaysia's delicate racial and religious cocktail. Sects like Al Arqam, and the spread of Shia theology, are closely watched by a government that wishes to maintain its secular credentials and to control what has been termed 'creeping Islamization'. In mid-1997, Mahathir showed his displeasure at the enforcement of a fatwa in the state of Selangor banning all beauty contests. In June, three Malay contestants were arrested and handcuffed on stage after they had competed in the Miss Malaysia Petite contest. The prime minister rebuked the religious officials who had exceeded their 'little powers'. Earlier he had set in motion a wide-ranging review of Islamic jurisprudence (fiqh). In confronting the clerics and their supporters Mahathir took on a powerful conservative group closely allied with the opposition PAS and, until September 11th, there were those who wondered whether the ulamas (Muslim theologians) might successfully challenge the Prime Minister for the hearts and minds of ordinary Malaysians. But events since then have played into Mahathir's hands (again, see above).

Buddhism

While Buddhism is the formal religion of most of Malaysia's Chinese population, many are Taoists, who follow the teachings of the three sages – Confucius, Mencius and Lao Tse. Taoism is characterized by ancestor worship and many deities. As with Islam, this has been mixed with animist beliefs and spirit worship forms a central part of the faith.

Hinduism

Hindu (and Buddhist) religions were established on the Malay peninsula long before the religion of Islam arrived. Remains of ancient Hindu-Buddhist temples dating from the kingdom of Langkasuka in the early years of the first millennium have been found in the Bujang Valley, at the foot of Gunung Jerai (Kedah Peak) in Kedah. The majority of Malaysia's Indian population is Hindu, although there are also many Indian Muslims.

Religion in Borneo

In Sabah and Sarawak, apart from the Malays, Bajaus, Illanuns and Suluks, who accepted Islam, all the inland tribes were originally animists. The religion of all the Dayak tribes in Borneo boiled down to placating spirits, and the purpose of tribal totems, images, icons and statues was to chase bad spirits away and attract good ones, which were believed to be capable of bringing fortune and prosperity. Head-hunting (see page 388) was central to this belief, and most Dayak tribes practised it, in the belief that freshly severed heads would bring blessing to their longhouses. Virtually everything had a spirit, and complex rituals and ceremonies were devised to keep them happy. Motifs associated with the spirit world – such as the hornbill bird – dominate the artwork and textiles and many of the woodcarvings for sale in art and antique shops in the country had religious significance. Islam began to spread to the tribes of the interior from the late 15th century, but mostly it was confined to coastal districts or those areas close to rivers like the Kapuas and Barito where Malays penetrated into the interior to trade. Christian missionaries arrived with the Europeans but did not proselytize seriously until the mid-19th century. The Dutch, particularly, saw missionaries fulfilling an administrative

Malay magic and the spirits behind the prophet

Despite the fact that all Malays are Muslims, some traditional, pre-Islamic beliefs are still practised by Malays – particularly in the northeast of the peninsula, the conservative Islamic heartland. The bomoh – witch doctor and magic-man – is alive and well in modern Malaysia. The use of ilmu (the malay name for magic), which is akin to voodoo, is still widely practised and bomohs are highly respected and important members of kampong communities. They are often called in to perform their ancient rituals – to bring rain or to determine the site of a new house; on other occasions to make fields (or married couples) fertile or to heal sickness. The healing ceremony is called the main puteri: there are certain illnesses which are believed to be caused by spirits – or hantu – who have been offended and must be placated.

The bomoh's job is to get the protective, friendly spirits on his side, in the belief that they can influence the evil ones. He knows many different spirits by name; some are the spirits of nature, others are spirits of ancestors. Many bomohs are specialists in particular fields. Some, known as pewangs, traditionally concentrated on performing spells to ensure fruitful harvests or safe fishing expeditions. Bomohs are still consulted and contracted to formulate herbal remedies, charms, love potions and perform traditional massage (urut). The belian – or shaman – specializes in more extreme forms of magic conducting exorcisms and spirit-raising seances, or berhantu. In Kelantan, a bomoh who acts as a spirit medium is known as a Tok Peteri and once a spirit has entered him, during a seance, his assistant, called the Tok Mindok, is required to question the spirit, present offerings and address the spirit in a secret language of magic formulae. Seances are always held in front of the whole village after evening prayers.

Manipulation of the weather is one area where the magic is still widely used. In 1991 actors from Kuala Lumpur's Instant Café Theatre Company called on a bomoh to ensure their open-air production of A Midsummer Night's Dream was not washed out. The only occasion on which rain interrupted the play was during an extra performance, not covered in the bomoh's contract.

All natural and inanimate objects are also capable of having spirits and Malays often refer to them using the respectful title Datuk. Other spirits, like the pontianak (the vampire ghost of a woman who dies in childbirth) are greatly feared. Any suspicion of the presence of a pontianak calls for the immediate intervention of a belian, who is believed to inherit his powers from a hantu raya – great spirit – which attaches itself to a bloodline and is subsequently passed from generation to generation.

function, drawing the tribal peoples close to the Dutch and, by implication, away from the Muslim Malays of the coast: it was a policy of divide and rule by religious means. Both Christianity and Islam had enormous influence on the animist tribes, and many converted en masse to one or the other. Despite this, many of the old superstitions and ceremonial traditions, which are deeply ingrained, remain a part of Dayak culture today. (The traditional beliefs of Kalimantan's Dayaks is formalized in the Kaharingan faith, which, despite the in-roads made by Christianity and Islam, is still practised by some Mahakam and Barito river groups. The Indonesian government recognizes it as an official religion.)

Land and environment

Geography

Malaysia covers a total land area of 329,054 sq km and includes Peninsular Malaysia (131,587 sq km) and the Borneo states of Sarawak (124,967 sq km) and Sabah (72,500 sq km). Geologically, both the peninsula and Borneo are part of the Sunda shelf, although the mountains of the peninsula were formed longer ago than those in Borneo. This 'shelf', which during the Pleistocene ice age was exposed forming a land bridge between the two halves of the country, was inundated as the glaciers of the north retreated and sea levels rose.

The **Malay peninsula** is about 800 km north-south, has a long narrow neck, a tapered tail and a bulging, mountainous, middle. The neck is called the Kra Isthmus, which links the peninsula to the Southeast Asian mainland. The isthmus itself is in southern Thailand – Peninsular Malaysia comprises only the lower portion of the peninsula and covers an area larger than England and a little smaller than Florida. Nestled into the southernmost end of the peninsula is the **island of Singapore**, separated from the peninsula by the narrow Strait of Johor. The thin western coastal plain drains into the Strait of Melaka, which separates the peninsula from Sumatra (Indonesia) and is one of the oldest shipping lanes in the world. The eastern coastal lowlands drain into the South China Sea.

The **Barisan Titiwangsa (Main Range)** comprises the curved jungle-clad spine of Peninsular Malaysia. It is the most prominent of several, roughly parallel ranges running down the peninsula. These subsidiary ranges include the Kedah-Singgora Range in the northwest; the Bintang Range (stretching northeast from Taiping), the Tahan Range (which includes the peninsula's highest mountain, Gunung Tahan, 2,187m). In the northern half of the peninsula, the mountainous belt is very wide, leaving only a narrow coastal strip on either side.

The Main Range – or Barisan Titiwangsa – runs south from the Thai border for nearly 500 km, gradually receding as it approaches the coastal plain, near Melaka. The average elevation is about 1,000m and there are several peaks of more than 2,000m. The southern end of the range is much narrower and the mountains, lower; the most prominent southern 'outlier' is Gunung Ledang (Mount Ophir) in Johor. Until just over a century ago, when William Cameron first ventured into the mountains of the Main Range, this was uncharted territory – British colonial Malaya was, in fact, little more than the west coastal strip. Not only was the west coast adjacent to the important trade routes (and therefore had most of the big towns), its alluvial deposits were also rich in tin. Because roads and railways were built along this western side of the peninsula during the colonial period, it also became the heart of the plantation economy.

In addition to the mountain ranges, the Malay peninsula also has many spectacular limestone outcrops. These distinctive outcrops are mainly in the Kuala Lumpur area, such as Batu Caves and those in and around Templer Park, and in the Kampar Valley near Ipoh, to the north. The erosion of the limestone has produced intricate solution-cave systems, some with dramatic formations. The vegetation on these hills is completely different to the surrounding lowland rainforest.

Malaysia's year-round rainfall has resulted in a dense network of rivers. The peninsula's longest river is the Sungai Pahang, which runs for just over 400 km. Most rivers flood regularly, particularly during the northeast monsoon season, and during the heavy rain the volume of water can more than double in the space of a few hours. It is thought that the flooding of Malaysian rivers has become more pronounced due to logging and mining. Waterfalls are very common features in

Peninsular Malaysia; these occur where rivers, with their headwaters in the hills, encounter resistant (usually igneous) rocks as they cut their valleys.

Borneo Three countries have territory on Borneo, but only one of them, the once all-powerful and now tiny but oil-rich sultanate of Brunei, is an independent sovereign state in itself. It is flanked to the west by the Malaysian state of Sarawak and to the east by Sabah. Sarawak severs and completely surrounds Brunei. Sabah, formerly British North Borneo, and now a Malaysian state, occupies the northeast portion of Borneo. The huge area to the south is Kalimantan, Indonesian Borneo, which occupies about three-quarters of the island.

Borneo is the third largest island in the world after Greenland and New Guinea covering almost 750,000 sq km. During the Pleistocene period, Borneo was joined to mainland Southeast Asia, forming a continent which geologists know as Sundaland. The land bridge to mainland Asia meant that many species, both flora and fauna, arrived in what is now Borneo before it was cut off by rising sea levels. Borneo is part of the Sunda shelf. Its interior is rugged and mountainous and is dissected by many large rivers, navigable deep into the interior. The two biggest rivers, the Kapuas and Mahakam, are both in Kalimantan, but there are also extensive river systems in the East Malaysian states of Sabah and Sarawak. About half of Borneo's land area is under 150m, particularly the swampy south coastal region.

Borneo's highest mountain, Gunung Kinabalu in Sabah (4,101m) is often declared the highest mountain in Southeast Asia. Despite this claim being repeated so many times that it has taken on the status of a truth, it isn't: there are higher peaks in Indonesia's province of Irian Jaya and in Myanmar (Burma). Kinabalu is a granite mound called a pluton, which was forced up through the sandstone strata during the Pliocene period, about 15 million years ago. The mountain ranges in the west and centre of the island run east-to-west and curve round to the northeast. Borneo's coal, oil and gas-bearing strata are Tertiary deposits which are heavily folded; most of the oil and gas is found off the northwest and east coasts. The island is much more geologically stable than neighbouring Sulawesi or Java – islands in the so-called 'ring of fire'. Borneo only experiences about four mild earthquakes a year compared with 40-50 on other nearby islands. But because there are no active volcanoes, Borneo's soils are not particularly rich.

Climate

The Malay peninsula has an equatorial monsoon climate. Temperatures are uniformly high throughout the year, as is humidity, and rainfall is abundant and well distributed, although it peaks during the northeast monsoon period from November to February.

Mean annual temperature on the coastal lowlands is around 26°C. The mean daily minima in the lowlands is between 21.7°C and 24.4°C; the mean daily maxima is between 29.4°C and 32.8°C. The maxima are higher and the minima, lower, towards the interior. In the Cameron Highlands, the mean annual temperature is 18°C. Temperatures dip slightly during the northeast monsoon period. The highest recorded temperature, 39.4°C, was taken on Pulau Langkawi in March 1931. The lowest absolute minimum temperature ever recorded on the peninsula was in the Cameron Highlands in January 1937 when the temperature fell to 2.2°C. The Cameron Highlands also claims the most extreme range in temperature – the absolute maximum recorded there is 26.7°C.

Thunderstorms provide most of Malaysia's rainfall. In the most torrential downpour ever recorded in Kuala Lumpur 51mm of rain fell in 15 minutes. Heavy rain like this causes serious soil erosion in areas which have been cleared of vegetation.

The developed west coast of the peninsula is sheltered from the northeast monsoon which strikes the east coast with full force between November and February. The east coast's climatic vagaries have reinforced its remoteness: it is particularly wet and the area north of Kuantan receives between 3,300mm and 4,300mm a year. About half of this falls in the northeast monsoon period. The northwest coast of the peninsula is also wet and parts receive more than 3,000mm of rain a year. Bukit Larut (Maxwell Hill), next to Taiping has an annual rainfall of more than 5,000mm. The west coast receives its heaviest rainfall in March and April. October and April are the transitional months between the southwest and northeast monsoons.

In the more heavily populated coastal districts of the peninsula, the temperature is ameliorated by sea breezes which set in about 1000 and gather force until early afternoon. In the evenings, a land breeze picks up. These winds are only felt for distances up to 15 km inland. Another typical weather feature on the Malay peninsula is the squall, which is a sudden, violent storm characterized by sharp gusts of wind. These can be very localized in their effect, very unpredictable and, from time to time, very hazardous to light fishing vessels. Squalls are caused by cool air either from sea breezes in the late morning or land breezes in the evening undercutting warmer air; squall lines are marked by stacks of cumulo-nimbus clouds. Most squalls occur between May and August; the ones that develop along the west coast between Port Klang and Singapore during this period are called 'Sumatras' and produce particularly violent cloudbursts. Most Sumatras occur at night or in the early morning, while squalls between November and February usually occur in the afternoon.

Borneo

Borneo has a typical equatorial monsoon climate: the weather usually follows predictable patterns, although in recent years it has been less predictable, a phenomenon some environmentalists attribute to deforestation and others to periodic changes to the El Niño Southern Oscillation. Temperatures are fairly uniform, averaging 23-33°C during the day and rarely dropping below 20°C at night, except in the mountains, where they can drop to below 10°C. Most rainfall occurs between November and January during the northeast monsoon; this causes rivers to burst their banks, and there are many short, sharp cloudbursts. The dry season runs from May to September. It is characterized by dry south-easterly winds and is the best time to visit. Rainfall generally increases towards the interior; most of Borneo receives about 2,000-3,000 mm a year, although some upland areas get more than 4,000 mm.

Flora and fauna

Originally 97 per cent of Malaysia's land area was covered in closed-canopy forest. According to the government, about 56 per cent of Malaysia is still forested – although it is difficult to ascertain exactly how much of this is primary rainforest. Only five per cent of the remaining jungle is under conservation restrictions. The Malaysian jungle, which, at about 130 million years old, is believed to be among the oldest forests in the world, supports more than 145,000 species of flowering plant (well over 1,000 of which are already known to have pharmaceutical value), 200 mammal species, 600 bird species and countless thousands of insect species. The rainforest is modified by underlying rock-type (impervious rocks and soils result in swamp forest) and by altitude (lowland rainforest gives way to thinner montane forest on higher slopes). All the main forest types are represented on the peninsula; these include mangrove swamp forest, peat swamp forest, heath forest, lowland and hill mixed Dipterocarp forest and montane forest. Where primary forest has been logged,

burned or cleared by shifting cultivators or miners, secondary forest grows up quickly.
The fields cultivated by shifting cultivators are known as swiddens – a word which is derived from an old English term meaning 'burnt field'. In Malaysia, the secondary regrowth is known as belukar. It can take up to 250 years before climax rainforest is re-established. The pioneer plant species colonizing abandoned ladang (sites cleared by shifting cultivators) is called lalang (elephant grass).

Borneo's ancient rainforests are rich in flora and fauna, including over 9,000-15,000 species of seed plants (of which almost half may be endemic), 200 species of mammals, 570 species of birds, 100 species of snake, 250 species of freshwater fish and 1,000 species of butterfly. The theory of natural selection enunciated by Victorian naturalist Alfred Russel Wallace – while that other great Victorian scientist Charles Darwin was coming to similar conclusions several thousand miles away – was influenced by Wallace's observations in Borneo. He travelled widely in Sarawak between 1854 and 1862.

Flora

As late as the middle of the 19th century, the great bulk – perhaps as much as 95 per cent – of the land area of Borneo was forested. Alfred Russel Wallace, like other Western travellers, was enchanted by the island's natural wealth and diversity: "ranges of hill and valley everywhere", he wrote, "everywhere covered with interminable forest". But Borneo's jungle is disappearing fast and since the mid-1980s there has been a mounting international environmental campaign against deforestation. The campaign has been particularly vocal in Sarawak but other parts of the island are also suffering rapid deforestation, notably Sabah and also Indonesia's province of East Kalimantan. Harold Brookfield, Lesley Potter and Byron state in their hard-headed book *In place of the forest* (1995): Concerning those large areas of forest that have been totally cleared and converted to other uses or that lie waste [in Borneo] A great resource has been squandered, and the major part of the habitat of a great range of plant and animal species has been destroyed. Moreover, this has been done with far less than adequate economic return to the two nations [Malaysia and Indonesia] concerned.

How extensive has been the loss of species as a result of the logging of Borneo's forests is a topic of heated debate. Brookfield et al in the volume noted above suggest that there "is very little basis in firm research for the spectacular figures of species loss rates that appear not infrequently in sections of the conservationist literature and that readily attract media attention". But they do admit that the flora and fauna of Borneo is especially diverse with a high degree of endemism and that there has been a significant loss of biodiversity as a result of extensive logging. It has been estimated that 32 per cent of terrestrial mammals, 70 per cent of leaf beetles, and 50 per cent of flowering plants are endemic to Borneo; in other words, they are found nowhere else.
The best-known timber trees fall into three categories, all of them hardwoods. Heavy hardwoods include selangan batu and resak; medium hardwoods include kapur, keruing and keruntum; light hardwoods include madang tabak, ramin and meranti. There are both peat-swamp and hill varieties of meranti, which is one of the most valuable export logs. Belian, or Bornean iron wood (Eusideroxylon zwageri) is one of the hardest and densest timbers in the world. It is thought that the largest belian may be 1,000 years or more old. They are so tough that when they die they continue to stand for centuries before the wood rots to the extent that the trunk falls. On average, there are about 25 commercial tree species per ha, but because they are hard to extract, 'selective logging' invariably results in the destruction of many unselected trees.

The main types of forest include: **lowland rainforest** (mixed dipterocarp) predominates up to 600m. Dipterocarp forest is stratified into three main layers, the top one rising to heights of 45m. In the top layer, trees' crowns interlock to form a closed canopy of foliage. The word 'dipterocarp' comes from the Greek and means 'two-winged fruit' or 'two [di]-winged [ptero] seed [carp]'. The leaf-like appendages of the mature dipterocarp fruits have 'wings' which makes them spin as they fall to the ground, like giant sycamore seeds. Some species have more than two wings but are all members of the dipterocarp family. It is the lowland rainforest which comes closest to the Western ideal of a tropical 'jungle'. It is also probably the most species rich forest in Borneo. A recent study of a dipterocarp forest in Malaysia found that an area of just 50 ha supported no less than 835 species of tree. In Europe or North America a similar area of forest would support less than 100 tree species. The red resin produced by many species of dipterocarp, and which can often be seen staining the trunk, is known as damar and was traditionally used as a lamp 'oil'. Another characteristic feature of the trees found in lowland dipterocarp rainforest is buttressing, the flanges of wood that protrude from the base of the trunk. For some time the purpose of these massive buttresses perplexed botanists who arrived at a whole range of ingenious explanations. Now they are thought, sensibly, to provide structural support. Two final characteristics of this type of forest are that it is very dark on the forest floor (explaining why trees take so long to grow) and that it is not the impenetrable jungle of Tarzan fantasy. The first characteristic explains the second. Only when a gap appears in the forest canopy, after a tree falls, do light-loving pioneer plants get the chance to grow. When the gap in the canopy is filled by another tree, these grasses, shrubs and smaller trees die back once more.

Many of the rainforest trees are an important resource for Dayak communities. The jelutong tree, for example, is tapped like a rubber tree for its sap ('jungle chewing gum') which is used to make tar for waterproof sealants – used in boat-building. It also hardens into a tough but brittle black plastic-like substance used for parang (machete) handles.

Montane forest occurs at altitudes above 600m, although in some areas it does not replace lowland rainforest until considerably higher than this. Above 1,200m mossy forest predominates. Montane forest is denser than lowland forest with smaller trees of narrower girth. Moreover, dipterocarps are generally not found while flowering shrubs like magnolias and rhododendrons appear. In place of dipterocarps, tropical latitude oaks as well as other trees that are more characteristic of temperate areas, like myrtle and laurel, make an appearance. Other familiar flora of lowland forest, like lianas, also disappear while the distinctive pitcher plant (Nepenthes) become common.

The low-lying river valleys are characterized by **peat swamp** forest, where the peat is up to 9m thick, which makes wet-rice agriculture impossible. **Heath forest** or kerangas – the Iban word meaning 'land on which rice cannot grow' – is found on poor, sandy soils. Although it mostly occurs near the coast, it is also sometimes found in mountain ranges, but almost always on level ground. Here trees are stunted and only the hardiest of plants can survive. Some trees have struck up symbiotic relationships with animals – like ants – so as to secure essential nutrients. Pitcher plants (Nepenthes) have also successfully colonized heath forest. The absence of bird calls and other animal noises make heath forest rather eerie, and it also indicates their general biological poverty.

Along beaches there are often stretches of **casuarina forest**; the casuarina grows up to 27m, and looks like a conifer, with needle-shaped leaves. **Mangrove** occupies tidal mud flats around sheltered bays and estuaries. The most common mangrove tree is the bakau (Rhizophora) which grows to heights of about 9m and has stilt roots to trap sediment. Bakau wood is used for pile-house stilts and for charcoal. Further upstream, but still associated with mangrove, is the nipah palm (Nipa fruticans), whose light-green leaves come from a squat stalk; it was traditionally of great importance as it provided roofing and wickerwork materials.

Fauna

Mammals The continual development of forested areas has destroyed many habitats in recent years. The biggest mammal in Malaysia and Asia is the Asiatic elephant. Adult elephants weigh up to three to four tonnes; they are rarely seen, although the carnage caused by a passing herd can sometimes be seen in Taman Negara National Park. Borneo's wild elephants until recently posed a zoological mystery. They occur only at the far northeast tip of the island, at the furthest possible point from their Sumatran and mainland Southeast Asian relatives. No elephant remains have been found in Sabah, Sarawak or Kalimantan. It is known that some animals were introduced into Sabah – then British North Borneo – by early colonial logging concerns and certainly that there were already populations established in the area. Another theory has it that one of the sultans of Sulu released a small number of animals several centuries ago. The difficulty with this explanation is that experts find it difficult to believe that just a handful of elephants could have grown to the 2,000 or so that existed by the end of the last century. Some zoologists speculate that they were originally introduced at the time of the Javan Majapahit Empire, in the 13th and 14th centuries. Antonio Pigafetta, an Italian historian who visited the Sultanate of Brunei as part of Portuguese explorer Ferdinand Magellan's expedition in July 1521, tells of being taken to visit the sultan on two domesticated elephants, which may have been gifts from another ruler.

Borneo's male elephants are up to 2.6m tall; females are usually less than 2.2m. Males' tusks can grow up to 1.7m in length and weigh up to 15 kg each. Mature males are solitary creatures, only joining herds to mate. The most likely places to see elephants in the wild are the Danum Valley Conservation Area and the lower Kinabatangan basin, both in Sabah. See also box, page 457.

Orang utan (Pongo pygmaeus): Walt Disney's film of Rudyard Kipling's Jungle Book made the orang utan a big-screen celebrity, dubbing him "the king of the swingers" and "the jungle VIP". Borneo's great red-haired ape is also known as 'man of the jungle', after the translation from the Malay: orang (man), utan (jungle). The orang utan is endemic to the tropical forests of Sumatra and Borneo although at the beginning of the historic period it was distributed from tropical China to Java. The Sumatran animals tend to keep the reddish tinge to their fur, while the Bornean ones go darker as they mature. It is Asia's only great ape; it has four hands, rather than feet, bow-legs and has no tail. The orang utan moves slowly and deliberately, sometimes swinging under branches, although it seldom travels far by arm-swinging. Males of over 15 years old stand up to 1.6m tall and their arms span 2.4 m. Adult males (which make loud roars) weigh 50-100 kg – about twice that of adult females (whose call sounds like a long, unattractive belch). Orang utans are said to have the strength of seven men but they are not aggressive. They are peaceful, gentle animals, particularly with each other. Orang utans have bluey-grey skin and their eyes are close together, giving them an almost human look. Males develop cheek pouches when they reach maturity, which they fill with several litres of air; this is exhaled noisily when they demarcate territory.

Orang utans mainly inhabit riverine swamp forests or lowland dipterocarp forests. Their presence is easily detected by their nests of bent and broken twigs woven in much the same fashion as a sun bear's, in the fork of a tree. They are solitary animals and always sleep alone. Orang utans have a largely vegetarian diet consisting of fruit and young leaves, supplemented by termites, bark and birds' eggs. They are usually solitary but the young remain with their mothers until they are five or six years old. Two adults will occupy an area of about 2 sq km and are territorial, protecting their territory against intruders. They can live up to 30 years and a female will have an average of three to four young during her lifetime. Females reach sexual maturity between seven and nine years, and the gestation period is nine months. Female orang utans usually have only one young at a time although twins and even triplets have been recorded. After giving birth, they do not mate for around another seven years.

The penis of the proboscis monkey is almost as obvious as its nose – the proboscis male glories in a permanent erection, which is probably why it is rarely displayed in zoos...

Estimates of the numbers of orang utan vary considerably. One puts the figure at 10,000-20,000 animals; another at between 70-100,000 in the wild in Borneo and Sumatra. Part of the difficulty is that many are thought to live in inaccessible and little researched areas of peat swamp. But this is just a very rough estimate, based on one ape for each 1½ sq km of forest. No one, so far, has attempted an accurate census. What is certain is that the forest is disappearing fast, and with it the orang utan's natural habitat. Orang utans' favoured habitat is lowland rainforest and this is particularly under threat from logging. The black market in young apes in countries like Taiwan means that they fetch relatively high returns to local hunters. At the village level an orang utan might command US$100; in local markets, around US$350; and at their international destination, along with all the necessary forged export permits, travel costs and so on, from US$5,000 to as much as US$60,000.

Monkeys: the five species of monkeys found in Malaysia are the long-tailed macaque, pig-tailed macaque, and three species of leaf monkey (langur) – the banded, dusky and silvered varieties. Malaysia's cutest animal is the little slow loris, with its huge sad eyes and lethargic manner; among the most exotic is the flying lemur, whose legs and tail are joined together by a skin membrane. It parachutes and glides from tree to tree, climbing each one to find a new launch-pad.

The **proboscis monkey** (Nasalis larvatus) is an extraordinary-looking animal, endemic to Borneo, which lives in lowland forests and mangrove swamps all around the island. Little research has been done on proboscis monkeys; they are notoriously difficult to study as they are so shy. Their fur is reddish-brown and they have white legs, arms, tail and a ruff on the neck, which gives the appearance of a pyjama-suit. Their facial skin is red and the males have grotesquely enlarged, droopy noses; females' noses are shorter and upturned. The male's nose is the subject of some debate among zoologists: what ever else it does, it apparently increases their sex-appeal. To ward off intruders, the nose is straightened out, "like a party whoopee whistle", according to one description. Recently a theory has been advanced that the nose acts as a thermostat, helping to regulate body temperature. But it also tends to get in the way: old males often have to resort to holding their noses up with one hand while stuffing leaves into their mouths with the other.

Proboscis monkeys' penises are almost as obvious as their noses – the proboscis male glories in a permanent erection, which is probably why they are rarely displayed in zoos. The other way the males attract females is by violently shaking branches and making spectacular – and sometimes near-suicidal – leaps into the water, in which they attempt to hit as many dead branches as they can on the way down, so as to make the loudest noise possible. The monkeys organize themselves into harems, with one male and several females and young – there are sometimes up to 20 in a group. Young males leave the harem they are born into when the adult male becomes aggressive towards them and they rove around in bachelor groups until they are in a position to form their own harem.

Proboscis monkeys belong to the leaf monkey family, and have large, pouched stomachs to help digest bulky food – they feed almost entirely on the leaves of one tree – the Sonneratia. The proboscis is a diurnal animal, but keeps to the shade during the heat of the day. The best time to see them is very early in the morning or around dusk. They can normally be heard before they are seen: they make loud honks, rather like geese; they also groan, squeal and roar. Proboscis monkeys are good swimmers; they even swim underwater for up to 20m – thanks to their partially webbed feet. Males are about twice the size and weight of females. They are known fairly ubiquitously (in both Malaysian and Indonesian Borneo) as 'Orang Belanda', or Dutchmen – which is not entirely complimentary. In Kalimantan they also have other local names including Bekantan, Bekara, Kahau, Rasong, Pika and Batangan.

Other monkeys found in Borneo include various species of leaf monkey – including the **grey leaf monkey, the white-fronted leaf monkey**, and the **red leaf monkey**. One of the non-timber forest products formerly much prized was bezoar stone which was a valued cure-all. Bezoars are green coloured 'stones' which form in the stomachs of some herbivores, and in particular in the stomachs of leaf monkeys. Fortunately for the leaf monkeys of Southeast Asia though, these stones – unlike rhino horn – are no longer prized for their medicinal properties. One of the most attractive members of the primate family found in Borneo is the tubby slow loris or kongkang. And perhaps the most difficult to pronounce – at least in Dusun – is the tarsier which is locally known as the tindukutrukut.

The ape family includes the **white-handed gibbon** (known locally as wak-wak), the dark-handed gibbon (which is rarer) and siamang, which are found in more mountainous areas.

Rhinoceros: the two-horned Sumatran rhinoceros, also known as the hairy rhinoceros, is the smallest of all rhinos and was once widespread throughout Sumatra and Borneo. The population has been greatly reduced by excessive hunting. The horn is worth more than its weight in gold in Chinese apothecaries, and that of the Sumatran rhino is reputedly the most prized of all. But the ravages of over-hunting have been exacerbated by the destruction of the rhino's habitat. Indeed, until quite recently it was thought to be extinct on Borneo. Most of Borneo's remaining wild population is in Sabah, and the Malaysian government is attempting to capture some of the thinly dispersed animals to breed them in captivity, for they remain in serious danger of extinction (see page 451).

Other mammals: one of the strangest Malayan mammals is the **tapir**, with its curled snout – or trunk – and white bottom. The starkly contrasting black and white is good camouflage in the jungle, where it is effectively concealed by light and shade. Young tapirs are dark brown with light brown spots, simulating the effect of sun-dappled leaf-litter.

Other large mammals include the **common wild pig** and the **bearded pig**, and the seladang (or gaur) wild cattle; the latter live in herds in deep jungle. There are two species of deer on the Malay peninsula: the **sambar** (or rusa) and the **kijang** (barking deer); the latter gets its English name from its dog-like call. The **mouse deer** (kanchil and napoh) are not really deer; they are hoofed animals, standing just 20 cm high. The mouse deer has legendary status in Malay lore – for example, the Malay Annals tell of Prince Parameswara's decision to found Melaka on the spot where he saw a mouse deer beat off one of his hunting dogs (see page 205). Despite their reputation for running, they are also a favoured source of protein.

Malaysia's most famous carnivore is the **tiger** – harimau in Malay. Tigers still roam the jungle in the centre of the peninsula, and on several occasions have made appearances in the Cameron Highlands, particularly during the dry season, when they move into the mountains to find food. Other members of the cat family are the clouded leopard and four species of wild cat: the leopard cat, the golden cat, the flat-headed cat and the marbled cat. Other jungle animals include the Malayan sun bear (which have a penchant for honey), the serigala (wild dog), civet cats (of which there are many different varieties), mongooses, weasels and otters.

Malaysia has several species of fruit bats and insect-eating bats, but the best-known insect-eater is the **pangolin** (scaly anteater), the animal world's answer to the armoured car. Its scales are formed of matted hair (like rhinoceros horn) and it has a long thin tongue which it flicks into termite nests. More common jungle mammals include rodents, among which are five varieties of **giant flying squirrels**. Like the **flying lemur**, these glide spectacularly from tree to tree and can cover up to about 500m in one 'flight'.

Birds

In ornithological circles, Malaysia is famed for its varied bird-life. The country is visited by many migratory water birds, and there are several wetland areas where the Malayan Nature Society has set up birdwatching hides; the most accessible to Kuala Lumpur is the Kuala Selangor Nature Park (see page 90). Migratory birds winter on Selangor's mangrove-fringed mudflats from September to May. There are also spectacular birds of prey, the most common of which are the **hawk eagles** and **brahminy kites**. Among the most fascinating and beautiful jungle species are the **crested firebacks**, a kind of pheasant; the kingfisher family, with their brilliantly coloured plumage; the hornbills (see below); **greater racquet-tailed drongos** – dark blue with long, sweeping tails; and **black-naped orioles**, saffron-coloured lowland residents. There are also **wagtails, mynas, sunbirds, humming birds (flower-peckers), bulbuls, barbets, woodpeckers** and **weaver-birds**.

Hornbill There are nine types of hornbill on Borneo, the most striking and biggest of which is the rhinoceros hornbill (Buceros rhinoceros) – or kenyalang. They can grow up to 1.5m long and are mainly black, with a white belly. The long tail feathers are white too, crossed with a thick black bar near the end. They make a remarkable, resonant "GERONK" call in flight, which can be heard over long distances; they honk when resting. Hornbills are usually seen in pairs – they are believed to be monogamous. After mating, the female imprisons herself in a hole in a tree, building a sturdy wall with her own droppings. The male bird fortifies the wall from the outside, using a mulch of mud, grass, sticks and saliva, leaving only a vertical slit for her beak. She remains incarcerated in her cell for about three months, during which the male supplies her and the nestlings with food – mainly fruit, lizards, snakes and mice. Usually, only one bird is hatched and reared in the hole and when it is old enough to fly, the female breaks out of the nest hole. Both emerge looking fat and dirty.

The 'bill' itself has no known function, but the males have been seen duelling in mid-air during the courting season. They fly straight at each other and collide head-on. The double-storeyed yellow bill has a projection, called a casque, on top, which has a bright red tip. In some species the bill develops wrinkles as the bird matures: one wrinkle for each year of its life. For this reason they are known in Dutch, and in some eastern Indonesian languages as 'year birds'. The hornbill is the official state emblem of Sarawak.

Most Dayak groups consider the hornbill to have magical powers and the feathers are worn as symbols of heroism. In tribal mythology the bird is associated with the creation of mankind, and is a symbol of the upper world. The best place to see hornbills is near wild fig trees – they love the fruit and play an important role in seed dispersal. The helmeted hornbill's bill is heavy and solid and can be carved, like ivory. These bills were highly valued by the Dayaks, and have been traded for centuries. The third largest hornbill is the wreathed hornbill which makes a yelping call and a loud – almost mechanical – noise when it beats its wings. Others species on Borneo include the wrinkled, black, bushy-crested, white-crowned and pied hornbills.

Reptiles

The kings of Malaysia's reptile population are the giant **leatherback turtles** (see page 274), **hawksbill** and **green turtles**; there are several other species of turtle and three species of land tortoise. The most notorious reptile is the **estuarine crocodile** (Crocodilus porosus) – which can grow up to 8 m long. The largest population of estuarine crocodiles are found in the lower reaches of Borneo's rivers. However, they have been so extensively hunted that they are rarely a threat, although people do very occasionally still get taken. The **Malayan gharial** (Tomistoma schlegeli) is a fish-eating, freshwater crocodile which grows to just under 3m.

Lizards include common house geckos (Hemidactylus frenatus – or cikcak in Malay), green-crested lizards (Calotes cristatellus), which change colour like chameleons, and flying lizards (Draco), which have an extendable undercarriage allowing the lizard to glide from tree to tree. Monitors are the largest of Malaysian lizards, the most widespread of which is the common water monitor (Varanus salvator), which can grow to about 2½ m.

The Malaysian jungles also have 140 species of frogs and toads, which are more often heard than seen. Some are dramatically coloured, such as the appropriately named **green-backed frog** (Rana erythraea) and others have particular skills, such as **Wallace's flying frog** (Rana migropalmatus) which parachutes around on its webbed feet.

Of Malaysia's 100-odd land snakes, only 16 are poisonous; all 20 species of sea snake are poisonous. There are two species of python, the **reticulated python** (Python reticulatus) – which can grow to nearly 10m in length and has iridescent black and yellow scales – and the **short python** (Python curtus), which rarely grows more than 2.5m and has a very thick, rusty-brown body. Most feared are the venomous snakes, but the constrictors can also pose a threat to humans.

Among the most common non-poisonous snakes is the dark brown **house snake** (Lycodon aulicus) which likes to eat geckos, and the common **Malayan racer** (Elaphe flavolineata), which grows to about 2 m and is black with a pale underbelly. The most beautiful non-poisonous snakes are the **paradise tree snake** (Chrysopelea paradisi), which is black with an iridescent green spot on every scale and the **mangrove snake** (Boiga dendrophilia) which grows to about 2 m long and is black with yellow stripes. The former is famed for its gliding skills: it can leap from tree-to-tree in a controlled glide by hollowing its underbelly, trapping a cushion of air below it. In the jungle it is quite common to see the dull brown **river snake** which goes by the unfortunate name of the dog-faced water snake (Cerberus rhynchops); it has an appetite for fish and frogs.

The most feared venomous snake is the **king cobra** (Naja hannah) which grows to well over 4m long and is olive-green with an orange throat-patch. They are often confused with non-poisonous rat snakes and racers. The king cobra eats snakes and lizards – including monitor lizards. Its reputation as an aggressive snake is unfounded but its venom is deadly. Both the king cobra and the common cobra (Naja naja) are hooded; the hood is formed by loose skin around the neck and is pushed outwards on elongated ribs when the snake rears to its strike posture.

Other poisonous snakes are the **banded krait** (Bungarus fasciatus) with its distinctive black and yellow stripes and the **Malayan krait** (Bungarus candidus) with black and white stripes. Kraits are not fast movers and are said to bite only under extreme provocation. **Coral snakes** (of the genus Maticora) have extremely poisonous venom, but because the snake virtually has to chew its victim before the venom can enter the bite (its poison glands are located at the very back of its mouth), there have been no recorded fatalities. **Pit vipers** have a thermo-sensitive groove between the eye and the nostril which can detect warm-blooded prey even in complete darkness. The bite of the common, bright green **Wagler's pit viper** (Trimeresurus wagleri) is said to be extremely painful, but is never fatal. They have broad, flattened heads; adults have yellow bars and a bright red tip to the tail.

Insects

Malaysia has a literally countless population of insect species; new ones are constantly being discovered and named. There are 120 species of butterfly in Malaysia. The king of them is the male **Rajah Brooke's birdwing** (Troides brookiana) – the national butterfly – with its iridescent, emerald zig-zag markings on jet-black velvety wings. It was named by Victorian naturalist Alfred Russel Wallace after his friend James Brooke, the first White Rajah of Sarawak (see page 384). The males can be found along rivers while the much rarer females (which are less spectacularly coloured), remain out of sight among the treetops.

There are more than 100 other magnificently coloured butterflies, including the black and yellow common birdwing, the swallowtails and swordtails, the leaf butterflies (which are camouflaged as leaves when their wings are folded) such as the blue and brown saturn and the rust, white and brown tawny rajah. Among the most beautiful of all is the delicately patterned Malayan lacewing (Cethosia hypsea) with its jagged markings of red, orange, brown and white. There are several butterfly farms around the country, including in Kuala Lumpur (see page 89), Penang (see page 165) and the butterfly capital of Malaysia, the Cameron Highlands (see page 130).

The most spectacular moths are the huge atlas moth (Attacus atlas) and the swallow-tailed moth (Nyctalemon patroclus); these can be found on exterior walls illuminated by strip-lights late at night, particularly in remoter parts of the country.

The Malaysian beetle population is among the most varied in the world. The best known is the **rhinoceros beetle** (Oryctes rhinoceros), which can grow to nearly 6cm in length and is characterized by its dramatic horns. The empress cicada (Pomponia imperatoria) is the biggest species in Malaysia and can have a wingspan of more than 20cm. The male cicada is the noisiest jungle resident. The incredible droning and whining noises are created by the vibration of membranes in the body, the sound of which is amplified in the body cavity.

One of the most famous insects is the **praying mantis**. In *Malayan animal life*, MWF Tweedie wrote: "They owe their name to the deceptively devotional appearance of their characteristic pose, with the fore legs held up as if in prayer. In reality the mantis is, of course, waiting for some unwary insect to stray within reach; if it does, the deadly spined fore limbs will strike and grasp and the mantis will eat its victim alive, daintily, as a lady eats a sandwich." There are several other species of mantis, and the most intriguing is the flower mantis (Hymenopus coronatus) which is bright pink and can twist and extend itself to resemble a four-petalled flower, a camouflage which protects it from predators, while attracting meals such as bees.

Of the less attractive insect life, it is advisable to be wary of certain species of wasps and hornets. The most dangerous is the slender banded hornet (Polistes sagittarius) which is big (3cm long) and has a black and orange striped abdomen. Its nests are paper-like, and hang from trees and the eaves of houses by a short stalk. They are extremely aggressive and do not need to be provoked before they attack. The golden wasp (Vespa auraria) is found in montane jungle – notably the Cameron Highlands, and, like the hornet above, will attack anything coming near its nest. The wasp is a honey-gold colour, it nests in trees and shrubs and its sting is vicious. There are several other wasp species which attack ferociously, and stings can be extremely painful. One of the worst is the night wasp (Provespa anomala), which is an orangy-brick colour and commonly flies into houses at night, attracted by lights. Bee stings can also be very serious, and none more so than that of the giant honey bee, which builds pendulous combs on overhanging eaves and trees. It is black with a yellow mark at the front end of the abdomen; multiple stings can be fatal.

Another insect species to be particularly wary of is the fire ant (Tetraponera rufonigra). It has a red body and a big black head; it will enthusiastically sting anything it comes into contact with, and the pain is acute. Weaver ants (Oecophylla smaragdina) are common but do not sting. Instead, their powerful jaws can be used as jungle sutures to stitch up open wounds. The bites alone are very painful, and the ant (which is also known as the kerengga) adds insult to injury by spitting an acidic fluid on the bite. It is difficult to extract the pincers from the skin, and once attached, the ant will not let go. The biggest of all ants, the giant ant (Camponotus gigas), can be nearly 3cm in length; (it is also variously known as the elephant ant and the 'big-bum ant'). They are largely nocturnal, however, so tend to cause less trouble in the jungle.

Other jungle residents worth avoiding are the huge, black, hairy Mygalomorph spiders, whose bodies can be about 5 cm long. Their painful bites cause localized swelling. Scorpions are dangerous but not fatal. The biggest scorpion, the wood scorpion (Hormurus australasiae) can grow to about 1 6cm long; it is black, lives under old logs and is mainly nocturnal. In rural areas, the particularly paranoid might shake their shoes for the spotted house-scorpion (Isometrus maculatus), which is quite common. Centipedes (Chilopoda) have a poisonous bite and can grow up to about 25cm in length.

The environmental costs of growth

As Malaysia has become more wealthy, and the middle class has burgeoned, so environmental concerns have gained greater prominence. In 1993 the Department of the Environment released figures revealing that of Peninsular Malaysia's 116 major rivers, 85 were either 'biologically dead' or 'dying'. Air quality is also a source of concern, especially in the Klang Valley, an agglomeration of industrial activity around Kuala Lumpur. Environmental Impact Assessments (EIAs) are now, in theory, compulsory for every development project, but most companies undertake to do them only grudgingly, if at all. The claim that, as a developing country, Malaysia can ill-afford the 'luxury' of such things is wearing very thin as wealth spreads with each year of eight per cent growth. The government recognizes that the environment is fast becoming a political issue, and like any good political party is trying to climb aboard the bandwagon.

Most accounts of Malaysia's environmental problems – some would characterize it as a 'crisis' – concentrate on the East Malaysian states of Sarawak and Sabah. In a sense the peninsula is a lost cause: deforestation has been so extensive that the only large areas remaining are already gazetted as national parks. In East Malaysia, though, there is a sense that if only logging could be better controlled then the natural wealth of Malaysian Borneo could be preserved.

The haze

For years now, Malaysia (and Singapore) has had to deal with what is locally called 'the haze': a choking fog that reduces visibility to no more than a few metres and causes severe health problems. (The Air Pollution Index reached 851 on September 24, 1997; a figure of 300 is considered 'hazardous'.) The source of the haze is the fires that seasonally devastate huge areas of Sumatra and Indonesian Borneo. These were most serious in 1997, but have returned, at varying levels of seriousness, almost every year since.

In 1997 the government seriously contemplated evacuating the entire population of the East Malaysian state of Sarawak – more than two million people – but wondered where to put them. The airport in Kuching was closed and residents rushed to stockpile water and basic necessities. Schools, factories and government offices stayed shut as the smog became a threat to health. Fishermen did not venture out on the seas. Visibility became so bad that people stopped using their vehicles. A state of emergency was declared and people advised to stay indoors.

The source of the fires is Indonesia where loggers, estate managers and shifting cultivators use burning to clear land for cultivation. Though this is now illegal the Indonesian government lacks the resources to police. The failure to introduce a coherent zoning policy or to control car emissions has been attacked. There is little doubt that the pollution from cars and industry has combined with the smoke from the fires to produce a particularly unpleasant concoction leading to eye irritation, asthma attacks, headaches and breathing difficulties. In 1994 the Malaysian cabinet was presented with a Clean Air Action Plan but it was rejected because of fears that it might undermine the country's industrialization efforts. During the fires of 2000 Malaysian Environment Minister, Datuk Law Hieng Ding, asked the local media not to dwell upon the air-quality index because it might keep tourists away. While the Malaysian government may have been in denial, many residents were dusting off their face masks and visibility in the Straits of Melaka was so poor that the Malaysian marine police put out navigation warnings.

What may be remarkable to many westerners was the time it took before the politics of blame took hold. Former President Suharto of Indonesia apologized to his fellow Asean nations at an environment conference in September 1997, but criticism from Malaysia and Singapore, the two countries most affected after Indonesia, was astonishingly muted. It was the media in the two countries, chivvied on by an irate public making their feelings known through newspaper letter columns and radio talk shows, that encouraged the governments of Malaysia and Singapore to take a more forthright stance.

Nothing much changes, it seems, when it comes to the haze. In July 2001 the haze was back – albeit not as seriously as during 1997 – and new Forestry Minister Marzuki Usman was saying much the same as his predecessors: Indonesia doesn't have the money, the personnel or the plans to deal with the fires. The inaction and the lack of accountability is beginning to get to Indonesia's neighbours.

Books

Malaysia

Novels

Burgess, Anthony. Burgess lived in Malaysia between 1954 and 1957, learnt Malay, and mixed with the locals to a far greater extent than Maugham or Conrad, and this is reflected in a much more nuanced understanding of the Malay character. After leaving Malaya in 1957, he taught in Brunei until 1960. Among his books are *Time for a Tiger* (1956), *The Enemy in the Blanket* (1958) and *Beds in the East* (1959) which were later published together by Penguin as *Malayan Trilogy*.

Conrad, Joseph: Perhaps the finest novelist of the Malay archipelago, books include *Lord Jim*, the tale of Jim, who abandons his ship and seeks refuge from his guilt in Malaya, earning in the process the sobriquet Lord, and *Victory*, arguably Conrad's finest novel, based in the Malay Archipelago. Both are widely available in paperback editions from most bookshops. Also worth reading is *The Rescue*, Penguin: London. Set in the Malay Archipelago in the 1860s; the hero, Captain Lingard, is forced to choose between his Southeast Asian friend and his countrymen.

Keith, Agnes *Land below the Wind* (1969) Ulverscroft: Leicester. Perhaps the best-known English language book on Sabah.

Maniam, KS *The Return* (1983) Skoob Books: London. The novel, by a Indian Malaysian, is about the difficulties a Hindu has in finding a home in Malaysia, especially since the Indian in question is educated at a British colonial school.

Maugham, William *Somerset Maugham's Malaysian Stories* (1969) Heinemann: London and Singapore. Another English novelist who wrote extensively on Malaysia. These stories are best for the insight they provide of colonial life, not of the Malay or Malay life.

Theroux, Paul *The Consul's File* (1979) Penguin. A selection of short stories based on Malaysia.

Travel

Bird, Isabella *The Golden Chersonese* (1883 and reprinted 1983) Murray: London, reprinted by Century paperback. The account of a late 19th century female visitor to the region who shows her gumption facing everything from natives to crocs.

Bock, Carl *The Headhunters of Borneo* (1985, first published 1881) OUP: Singapore. Bock was a Norwegian naturalist and explorer and was commissioned by the Dutch to make a scientific survey of southeastern Borneo. His account, though, makes much of the dangers and adventures that he faced, and some of his 'scientific' observations are, in retrospect, clearly highly faulty. Nonetheless, this is an entertaining account.

Charles, Hose *The Field Book of a Jungle Wallah* (1985, first published 1929) OUP: Singapore. Hose was an official in Sarawak and became an acknowledged expert on the material and non-material culture of the tribes of Sarawak. He was one of that band of highly informed, perceptive and generally benevolent colonial administrators.

King, Victor T (edit) *The Best of Borneo Travel* (1992) OUP: Oxford. A compilation of travel accounts from the early 19th century through to the late 20th. An excellent companion to take while exploring the island. Published in portable paperback.

Mjoberg, Eric *Forest Life and Adventures in the Malay Archipelago*, OUP: Singapore.

O'Hanlon, Redmond *Into the Heart of Borneo* (1984) Salamander Press: Edinburgh. One of the best recent travel books on Borneo. This highly amusing and perceptive romp through Borneo in the company of poet and foreign correspondent James Fenton, includes an ascent of the Rejang River and does much to counter the more romanticized images of Bornean life.

History

Harrisson, Tom *World Within* (1959) Hutchinson: London. During the Second World War, explorer, naturalist and ethnologist Tom Harrisson was parachuted into Borneo to help organize Dayak resistance against the occupying Japanese forces. This is his extraordinary account.

Barber, Noel *The War of the Running Dogs: Malaya 1948-1960* (1971) Arrow Books. This is one of numerous accounts of the Malayan Emergency and the successful British efforts to defeat the Communist Party of Malaya.

Turnbull, Mary C *A History of Malaysia, Singapore and Brunei* (1989) Allen and Unwin. A very orthodox history of Malaysia, Singapore and Brunei, clearly written for a largely academic/student audience.

Chapman, F Spencer *The Jungle is Neutral*. An account of a British guerrilla force fighting the Japanese in Borneo – not as enthralling as Tom Harrisson's book, but still worth reading.

Payne, Robert *The White Rajahs of Sarawak*. Readable account of the extraordinary history of this East Malaysian state.

Natural history

Briggs, John *Mountains of Malaysia: a Practical Guide and Manual* (1988) Longman: London. Briggs has also written Parks of Malaysia, useful for anyone intending to especially visit the country's protected areas (Longman: Kuala Lumpur).

Cranbrook *Earl of Riches of the Wild: Land Mammals of South-East Asia* (1987) Ox ford University Press.

Cubitt, Gerald and Payne Junaidi *Wild Malaysia* (1990) London: New Holland. Large format, coffee table book, lots of wonderful colour photos, reasonable text, short background piece on each national park.

Hanbury-Tenison, Robin *Mulu, the Rain Forest* (1980) Arrow/Weidenfeld. This is the product of a Royal Geographical Society trip to Mulu in the late 1970s; semi-scholarly and useful.

Payne, Junaidi et al *Pocket Guide to Birds of Borneo, World Wildlife Fund/Sabah Society*.

Payne, Junaidi et al *A Field Guide to the Mammals of Borneo*, World Wildlife Fund/Sabah Society. Good illustrations, reasonable text, but very dry.

Tweedie, MWF and Harrison, JL *Malayan Animal Life* (1954 with new editions) Longman.

Wallace, Alfred Russel *The Malay Archipelago*(1869). A classic of Victorian travel writing by one of the finest naturalists of the period. Wallace travelled through all of island Southeast Asia over a period of some years. The original is now re-printed.

Other books

Leee, Kit *Adoi* (1989) Times Books: Singapore. An amusing book of Malaysian attitudes to most things.

Craig, Jo Ann *Culture Shock Malaysia*. One in a series of Culture Shock books, this examines and assesses the do's and don'ts of Malaysian and Singapore society. Useful for those going to live or spend an extended period in the region.

Lat: Lat is Malaysia's foremost cartoonist. His images of the effects of social and economic change on a simple kampong boy are amusing and highly perceptive. His cartoons are compiled in numerous books including *Kampong boy* and *Town boy*, published by Straits Times Publishing.

Books on Malaysia and the wider Southeast Asian region

Buruma, Ian *God's Dust*, (1989), Jonathan Cape: London. Enjoyable journey through Burma, Thailand, Malaysia and Singapore along with the Philippines, Taiwan, South Korea and Japan; journalist Buruma questions how far culture in this region has survived the intrusion of the West.

Caufield, C *In the Rainforest*, (1985) Heinemann: London. This readable and well-researched analysis of rainforest ecology and the pressures on tropical forests is part-based in the region.

Dingwall, Alastair *Traveller's Literary Companion to South-east Asia*, (1994) In Print: Brighton. Experts on Southeast Asian language and literature select extracts from novels and other books by Western and regional writers. The extracts are brief, but it gives a good overview of what is available.

Fraser-Lu, Sylvia *Handwoven Textiles of South-East Asia*, (1988), OUP: Singapore. Well-illustrated, large-format book with informative text.

King, Ben F and Dickinson, EC *A Field Guide to the Birds of South-East Asia*, Collins: London. (1975). Best regional guide to the birdlife of the region.

Osborne, Milton *Southeast Asia: an Introductory History*, (1979), Allen & Unwin: Sydney. Good introductory history, clearly written, published in a portable paperback edition and recently revised and reprinted.

Pentes, Tina and Truelove, Adrienne (1984) *Travelling with Children to Indonesia and South-East Asia*, Hale & Iremonger: Sydney.

Reid, Anthony *Southeast Asia in the Age of Commerce 1450-1680*, Yale University Press: New Haven. (1988 and 1993). Perhaps the best history of everyday life in Southeast Asia, looking at such themes as physical well-being, material culture and social organization; meticulously researched.

Sesser, Stan *The Lands of Charm and Cruelty: Travels in Southeast Asia*, Picador: Basingstoke. (1993). A series of collected narratives first published in the New Yorker including essays on Singapore, Laos, Cambodia, Burma and Borneo. Finely observed and thoughtful, the book is an excellent travel companion.

Young, Gavin *In Search of Conrad*, Hutchinson: London. (1991). This well-known travel writer retraces the steps of Conrad; part travel-book, part fantasy, it is worth reading but not up to the standard of his other books.

Singapore

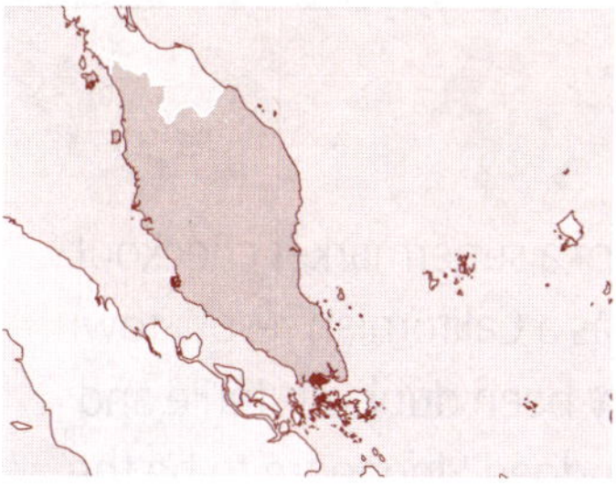

Footprint features

Introduction

To some, it has all the ambience of a supermarket checkout lane. It has even been described as a Californian resort-town run by Mormons. It has frequently been dubbed sterile and dull - a report in The Economist judged Singapore to be the most boring city in the world and for those who fail to venture beyond the plazas that line Orchard Road, or spend their 3½ days on coach-trips to the ersatz cultural extravaganzas, this is not surprising. But there is a cultural and architectural heritage in Singapore beyond the one which the government tries so hard to manufacture. Despite its brash consumerism and toy town mentality, Singapore is certainly not without its charm.

Singapore is difficult to fathom, especially from afar. Beneath its slick veneer of westernized modernity, many argue that its heart and soul are Asian. Behind the computers, hi-tech industries, marble, steel and smoked-glass tower blocks, highways and shopping centres is a society ingrained with conservative Confucian values.

For those stopping over in Singapore for just a few days – en route, as most of the island's tourists are, to somewhere else – there are several key sights that should not be missed. Many who visit, however, consider that it is far more important to enjoy the food. The island has an unparalleled variety of restaurants to suit every palate and wallet. Hawker centres in particular are a highly recommended part of the Singapore epicurean experience – they are inexpensive, and many are open into the early hours.

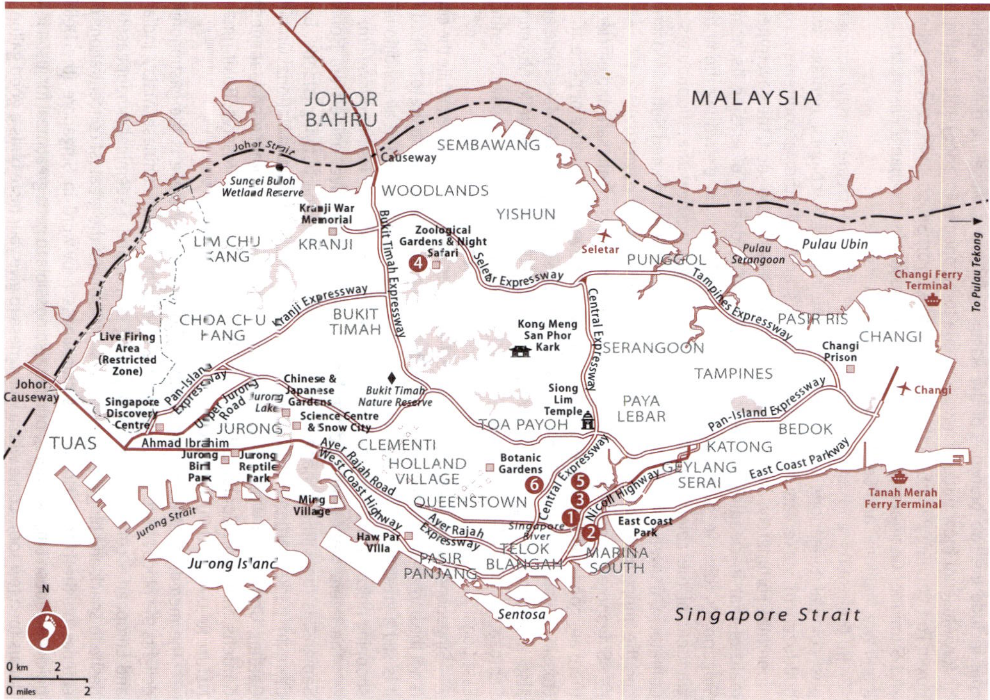

★ Don't miss ...

1. **Singapore Sling** Be a cliché, and order this colonial cocktail at the Raffles Hotel, page 562.
2. **Singapore River** Enjoy the city's lights on a night cruise and make faces at the curious Merlion, page 570.
3. **Arab Street** Delve into piles of rich fabrics – batik, lace and silk organza - in Kampong Glam, page 583.
4. **Night Safari** Feel the flap of a giant fruit bat's wings while exploring the zoo after dark, page 594.
5. **Little India** Smell the spices and order a dosa masala in Komala Vilas – Singapore's legendary South Indian restaurant, page 607.
6. **Orchard Road** The queen of all shopping streets, the perfect place to join Singaporeans in their national pastime, page 616.

Planning your trip

Where to go

Singapore is a city state with a land area of just under 650 sq km. Moreover, public transport in the city is impeccably quick and efficient, so nowhere is exactly 'off the beaten track'. It is possible to get a good feel for the place and to enjoy many of Singapore's places of interest on a week-long stay. That said, if you stop over for just a weekend, expect to leave wondering why you didn't plan to remain a little longer. Singapore is also a nifty jumping off point for exploring neighbouring Malaysia and Indonesia. Indeed, parts of Peninsular Malaysia, including the historic city of Melaka and the Indonesian islands of the Riau archipelago, are accessible on a day trip. Below is a slightly contrived – and by no means exhaustive – attempt to pigeonhole and categorize Singapore's attractions.

The popular image of Singapore as a city state is that it is so well managed that it has lost its charm and erased its history. This is not true and there is a great deal here to interest those with a historic bent. The best historic sights in the central colonial core include the two branches of the Asian Civilisations Museum, the Singapore History Museum (now under renovation, due to be opened in 2006) and the Battle Box in Fort Canning Park. Slightly further afield are Fort Siloso, Images of Singapore and Surrender Chambers, which are all on Sentosa Island. Changi Prison and the Kranji War Memorial and Cemetery are also worth visiting.

In the 1960s and 1970s, as its leaders tried to create a new, modern post-colonial Singapore, a large slice of the republic's colonial heritage was bulldozed to make way for apartment blocks and the other accoutrements of modernity. Fortunately, and not a demolition ball's swing too soon, the government realized that in cleaning up the city it was also in danger of erasing its heart. Singapore's diverse architectural styles are reflected in everything from the grandeur of the colonial core to skyscrapers towering over the shophouses of Chinatown, as well as individual buildings like the golden-domed Sultan Mosque and the impressively garish Kong Meng San Phor Kark (see page 592).

Singapore is a great place to bring young children. It is clean, safe and efficient, there are good hospitals, you can drink the water, drivers take notice of pedestrian crossings – all in all it is a child-friendly and parent-soothing place to visit. There are also a multitude of places to see, including the Singapore Philatelic Museum, Sentosa, Haw Par Villa, Jurong Bird Park, Science Centre, Singapore Discovery Centre, East Coast Park, Singapore Zoological Gardens and the Night Safari.

Singaporeans have taken shopping to their hearts and to new heights. While the city is not the bargain basement place it was – don't come with suitcases waiting to be filled – it is still a great place to browse and buy with care. The advent of the air-conditioned shopping plaza means there is no need to work up a sweat while losing your wealth.

The tigers have gone and the largest creature left alive, aside from Homo Sapiens, is the wild pig, hanging on by its trotters on some outlying islands. But there are parks, gardens and a great zoo; the Botanic Gardens and National Orchid Garden, Underwater World, Sentosa, Jurong Bird Park, the Chinese and Japanese Gardens, Singapore Zoological Gardens, Sungei Buloh Nature Reserve, Bukit Timah Nature Reserve and Pulau Ubin.

The memory that lingers most with visitors after they leave is the gastronomic delights the place has to offer. With such a medley of people – Chinese, Malay, Indian and European – considerable victual buying power, and a seemingly unappeasable desire to snack and binge, Singapore must have one of the greatest concentrations of eateries on the planet. Not only is cleanliness a by-word in Singapore (the Delhi quickstep doesn't make it here), but it is also possible to get a great meal for just a few dollars (or a few 100). Come with a willingness to give your taste buds a good gallop.

When to go

There is no best season to visit Singapore and it is hot throughout the year. It gets even stickier before the monsoon breaks in November, while the hottest months are July and August. The wettest months are November, December and January, during the period of the north-east monsoon, when it is also coolest – but even 'cool' days are hot by most temperate people's standards. As one would expect, the hottest time of day is early afternoon when the average temperature is around 30°C, but even during the coolest time of the day, just before dawn, the temperature is still nearly 24°C.

For daily weather reports, T65427788 and http://app.nea.gov.sg/data/mss/docs/ncastmap.htm

Finding out more

The **Singapore Tourism Board** is a useful place to contact. It produces a good free official guide called Visitor's Guide to Singapore as well as plenty of pamphlets detailing hotels, restaurants and so on. Its website has regularly updated information on hotels, festivals and other tourist-related information – www.visitsingapore.com Its 24-hour toll-free information number is 1800 736 2000.

Websites offer a whole range of information on a vast variety of topics. Below is only a selection. Note that websites in Asia are multiplying like rabbits and this makes searching a sometimes frustrating business.

www.sg The Singapore Infomap site which has website directories covering everything from leisure and entertainment to the economy, and from the National Heritage Board to Singapore's limitless choice of cuisine.

Www.asiatravel.com/singapore.html Asia Travel's website is useful for hotel reservations, weather reports, the very latest travel information and exchange rates, and also has a map detailing some places of interest.

http://asnic.utexas.edu/asnic.html The website for the Asian Studies Network Information Center at the University of Texas has information on the history and politics of Singapore.

http://eatshiokshiok.com/ An average site with food and entertainment listings and some general information in transport.

www.aseansec.org Home page of the Asean Secretariat, the Southeast Asian regional organization of which Singapore is a founder member. Lots of government statistics, acronyms etc.

www.singstat.gov.sg/ For the truly pedantic – a site devoted to statistics regarding Singapore.

http://straitstimes.asia1.com.sg/ The website of Singapore's strait-laced English daily. It requires registration but that is free.

http://www.visitorsguide.com.sg/ Published by the city state's yellow pages, this website has tourist information and business contacts.

Http://www.singaporeexpats.com/ A portal geared at expats. Browse through condos for rent, check entertainment listings, and even search online for a partner.

Language

Mandarin is the national language, although English or rather Singlish is spoken by almost everybody. Singlish is a love-it-or-loathe-it 'musical' variant of English, that despite sharing 98% of its vocabulary with the Queen's tongue sounds remarkably different – sentences typically end in 'ok lah!' Different Chinese groups will speak various dialogues including Cantonese, Hakka and Hokkien and of course Malay, Tamil and Hindi are also widely spoken by members of their respective ethnic groups. For an entertaining look at Singlish and its vocabulary see the following websites: www.geocities.com/Tokyo/4883/singlish.html Or log on to the satirical website www.talkingcock.com and follow the links to the Coxford Singlish Dictionary.

Specialist travel

Disabled travellers

The **National Council for Social Services** publishes Access Singapore, a guidebook especially for physically impaired visitors. There is also an online version of the guide at http://www.dpa.org.sg/access/contents.htm or call T1800-8380100 for more information. The guide lists taxi and van services designed for wheelchair use (public transport is not wheelchair friendly) and lists hotels with facilities for the disabled. Additional information can be found at the **Global Access-Disabled Travel Network Site**, www.geocities.com/Paris/1502

Singapore is the most wheel-chair friendly city in Southeast Asia.

Gay and lesbian travellers

Singapore is a pretty straight place. There are two clauses in Singapore's penal code that deal with homosexual sex, namely: Section 377: 'Whosoever voluntarily has carnal intercourse against the order of nature with any man, woman or animal, shall be punished with imprisonment for life, or with imprisonment for a term which may extend to 10 years, and shall also be liable to a fine'; and Section 377(a): 'Any male person who, in public or private, commits or abets the commission of or procures the commission by any male person of, any act of gross indecency with another male person, shall be punished with imprisonment for a term which may extend to two years'.

However, it is not illegal to be gay. The law only criminalizes the homosexual act. And, despite the law and the city's surface conservatism, the government appears to be actively courting the pink dollar. This is based on the theory that encouraging a more cultured and creative environment that is tolerant of homosexuality will improve a city's economy. There are plenty of openly gay and lesbian bars and clubs around town, a bloom of gay saunas and big gay events such as – The Nation Party in the summer, gay and lesbian film festivals and tons of gay-themed theatre. Look out for the rainbow flag which is often but not always hung outside a gay establishment. Ironically, one of the most closed states in Asia has the most vibrant gay scenes. In summer 2004, the state's tourism office produced their "Pink Guide to Singapore" – a big spread-out map with adverts for gay saunas, escort services and bars. The best professional website for events and contacts is the Singapore-based www.fridae.com. Also check out www.plu-singapore.com (a site with lots of background information on homosexuality in Singapore, but not much on the gay scene).

Student travellers

Student travellers will find Singapore a generally expensive place and not one where being a student will lead to great savings on entrance fees or public transport.

Travelling with children

Singapore is one of the most child-friendly cities in Asia. Not only is it safe and clean, with world-class medical facilities, but there are also lots of things for children to do. With stacks of places to eat, drink and snack, a very efficient transport system and lots of air-conditioned refuges to cool off, you shouldn't be put off bringing little people to the miniscule republic. Just bear in mind that if children are not used to the tropical heat it can be exhausting – so don't expect them to keep going for a full day, and make sure they are regularly topped up with fluids and coated in sun protection.
The attractions that children are likely to find most enthralling are: the Big Splash; Sentosa (especially Underwater World and Fantasy Island); the Haw Par Villa (gruesome and weirdly entertaining for quirkier children); the Jurong Bird Park (excellent); the Science Centre (lots of hands-on exhibits and a great movie theatre); the Singapore Discovery Centre (not bad, especially for those who like martial toys);

the superb Singapore Zoological Gardens and Night Safari; and the Singapore Philatelic Museum (for stamp-mad youngsters). Another good site is Travel for Kids at www.travelforkids.com/Funtodo/Singapore/singapore

Women travellers

Singapore is safe and it is rare for women to be harassed. Unlike some neighbouring countries, it is not considered peculiar for young women to travel alone. Apart from entering temples, there's no conservative dress code here. It is not unusual to see local women wear fairly revealing clothes (for Asia) on the street. Take the usual precautions.

Before you travel

Visas and immigration

Visitors must possess a passport valid for at least six months, a confirmed onward/return ticket, sufficient funds to support themselves in Singapore and, where applicable, a visa. For all of the latest visa information, you should check http://app.ica.gov.sg/travellers/entry/visa_requirements.asp

No visa is required for citizens of the Commonwealth, USA or Western Europe. On arrival in Singapore by air, citizens of these countries are granted a one-month visitor's permit. Tourists entering Singapore via the causeway from Johor Bahru in Malaysia or by sea are allowed to stay for 14 days. Nationals of most other countries (except India, China and the Commonwealth of Independent States) with confirmed onward reservations may stop over in Singapore for up to 14 days without a visa. It is necessary to keep the stub of your immigration card until you leave.

Visas can be extended for up to three months at the **Visitor Services Centre**, Immigration & Checkpoints Authority, 4/F, 10 Kallang Road, Singapore, next to Lavender MRT, 24-hour hotline on T6391 6300. Application takes around a day and costs S$40. It can be just as easy to nip across the causeway to Johor Bahru (in Malaysia) and then re-enter Singapore on a two-week permit. **Singapore Immigration Head Office**, Singapore Immigration Building, 10 Kallang Road, Singapore 208718, T6391 6100.

Customs, duty-free and export restrictions

Singapore is a duty-free port. The duty-free allowance is one litre of liquor, one litre of wine and one litre of beer or stout provided you are not arriving from Malaysia, from where there is no duty free allowance. Note that because of the government's strict anti-smoking policy, there is no duty free allowance for tobacco.

There is no limit to the amount of Singapore and foreign currency or travellers' cheques you can bring in or take out.

There is no export duty, but export permits are required for arms, ammunition, explosives, animals, gold, platinum, precious stones and jewellery, poisons and drugs. No permit is needed for the export of antiques.

Tax Visitors can claim back their 5% Goods and Services Tax (GST) from shops displaying the 'Tax Free for Tourists' sign when they spend S$300 or more (or S$300 in accumulated receipts each one a minimum of S$100). Ask for a Global Refund Cheque when you pay and this is then presented at customs on leaving the country, when visitors are reimbursed minus a handling fee. It is also possible to claim by post; the refund is paid either by bank cheque or to a credit card account. The Singapore Tourism Board publishes a brochure, Tax refund for visitors to Singapore.

Prohibitions Narcotics are strictly forbidden in Singapore and, as in neighbouring Malaysia, trafficking is a capital offence which is rigorously enforced. Dawn hangings at Changi prison are regularly reported and Singapore has the highest execution rate per head of population in the world. Trafficking in more than 30 g of morphine or cocaine, 15 g of heroin, 500 g of cannabis or 200 g of cannabis resin, 250 g of ice (methamphetamine hydrochloride) and 1.2 kg of opium is punishable by death. Those convicted of lesser drug-related offences face 20-30 years in Changi prison and 15 strokes of the rotan, a punishment devised by the British colonial administration. Passengers arriving from Malaysia by rail may have to march, single-file, past sniffer dogs.

In 1992, the Singapore government banned the importation and sale of chewing gum, after the MRT Corporation claimed the substance threatened the efficient running of its underground trains. Chewing tobacco, toy currency, pornographic material and seditious literature are also prohibited items.

Vaccinations

Certificates of vaccination against cholera and yellow fever are necessary for those coming from endemic areas within the previous six days. Otherwise, no certificates are required for Singapore. There is no longer any malarial risk on the island, although sometimes there are outbreaks of dengue fever. Vaccination services are available at the **Tan Tock Seng Hospital**, Moulmein Road, T63595958 (telephone beforehand for a doctor's appointment, but there is a walk-in vaccination service).

What to take

It is not necessary to arrive in Singapore laden down with products that you think will be unavailable. With one or two exceptions, like chewing gum and toy guns, everything is easily purchased in Singapore and, more often than not, more cheaply than at home. Treat travelling to Singapore as you would travelling to Munich, Manchester, Minneapolis or Melbourne. Bring what you seriously shouldn't leave behind, but don't consider bringing the kitchen sink let alone a six-month supply of dental floss.

Money

Currency

Local currency is dollars and cents. Bank notes are available in denominations of S$2, 5, 10, 20, 50, 100, 500, 1,000 and 10,000. Coins are in 1, 5, 10, 20 and 50 cent and 1 dollar denominations. In March 2005, the Singapore dollar was valued at S$1.65 to US$1. Brunei currency is interchangeable with Singapore currency; the Malaysian Ringgit is not, it is roughly 2 ringgit to the S$.

Exchange

It is possible to change money at banks, licensed money changers and hotels – although a service charge may be added. Licensed money changers often give better rates than banks. Singapore is one of the most plastic-friendly countries in the region and there are ATMs (cashpoint machines), seemingly, on every street corner. Cash can be withdrawn using a credit card or Cirrus card providing you have a PIN. Singapore is a major regional banking centre, so it is relatively easy to get money wired from home. Bank opening hours: 0930-1500 Mon-Fri, 0930-1130 Sat. There is no black market.

Credit cards Most of Singapore's hotels, shops, restaurants and banks (and even some taxis) accept the major international credit cards, and many cash machines allow you to draw cash on Visa or MasterCard. After bargaining, expect to pay at least 3% for credit card transactions; most shops insist on this surcharge although you do not have to pay it. **Notification of credit card loss** American Express, T68801111; MasterCard, T800 110 0113; Visa Card, T800 448 1250.

Cost of living

Singapore is a thoroughly first world city. It is an expensive place to live, particularly when compared to its neighbours in Southeast Asia, but with wages more or less in line with costs, most Singaporeans enjoy a high standard of living. The average monthly salary for a doctor is S$7,886, while a receptionist – one of the lowest paid jobs - earns S$1,486. While poverty still exists, it is hard to find as the government has systematically cleared slums and built housing estates offering low cost public flats.

Cost of travelling

Even though Singapore is a comparatively more expensive place to live than its neighbours in Southeast Asia, the Lion City is apparently getting cheaper – relatively speaking. While accommodation along with hotel rooms are pricey (although there is now a glut in rock bottom budget hostels in the city), and fine dining and alcohol will burn a hole in your pocket, no frills food (which is still great) and transport is relatively cheap. You can feast at a hawker stall for around S$5 (although this is still twice the price of an equivalent slap up meal in Malaysia).

Getting there

Air

Changi Airport is the region's busiest and best connected and most major airlines fly here. Over 70 airlines service Singapore, connecting the city state with 160 cities in 53 countries. As well as major long haul airlines including British Airways, Virgin Atlantic, Cathay Pacific, Singapore Airlines, Quantas and American Airlines, Changi is a hub for cheap budget Asian airlines including AirAsia, Tiger Airways and Valuair which connect Singapore with cities in Thailand, Indonesia and Malaysia and with Macau. The airport has two terminals, but a third, costing S$1.5 billion, is currently under construction and due to open in early 2008.

For airport information see page 31.

If you want to work out connections with specific cities, the Changi website has a useful flight planning facility. Type in your city of origin and it will show the flights, airlines and routes available: www.changi.airport.com.sg, under flights click on passenger flight planner.

From Southeast Asia As an international crossroads, Singapore is within easy reach of all key points in the region and there are flights to Changi Airport from destinations throughout Southeast Asia. It is possible to get special deals to selected destinations from discount travel agents and Singapore's Yellow Pages, but tickets bought in **Bangkok** and **Penang** are generally cheaper. The most competitive deals are with the budget airlines – AirAsia, Tiger Airways and Valuair. For return flights to Kuala Lumpur, buy a single ticket as it is cheaper to purchase tickets in Malaysia, unless you fly with a budget airline. Malaysia's AirAsia flies between Singapore and Bangkok, and has cheap deals between Johor Bahru just across the causeway from Singapore with most major cities in Malaysia. **AirAsia** tickets must be bought direct from their website (www.airasia.com), via their call centre (T67339933), from their office directly or from the post office (S$5 surcharge). Some travel agencies sell AirAsia tickets with a small surcharge. **Valuair** tickets can be booked online, through their call centre (T62298338) or via a selected agencies, see www.valuair.com.sg/agents.html. Valuair flies between Singapore and **Hong Kong, Bangkok, Jakarta** and **Perth**. **Tiger Airways** in December 2004, flew to **Bangkok, Hat Yai** and **Phuket** from Singapore. Book online (www.tigerairways.com), through its call centre (T1800 388 8888) or in post offices. While you may not get the cheapest price of the no frills services (you normally have to book weeks in advance for this), they are always cheaper than the standard airlines.

If you can afford the time, then it is usually cheaper to take a bus or train to Kuala Lumpur in Malaysia and buy long-haul flights there. It is also much cheaper when flying between Singapore and other points in Malaysia to use Johor Bahru's airport across the causeway. Johor Bahru is well connected to the Malaysian domestic network. Chartered express coaches ply between Singapore and JB airport; they leave Singapore from the Novotel Orchid Inn on Dunearn Road, but are reserved for MAS passengers only, S$12 (adult), S$10 (children). The courier ensures express clearance of Malaysian customs and immigration. Details from **MAS** office in Singapore: 190 Clemenceau Avenue, T63366777. Likewise, for those wishing to fly to destinations in Indonesia, it is cheaper to take the ferry to the Indonesian island of Batam (see page 541) and then catch a domestic flight from there. However, for most people the saving in fares will probably not outweigh the additional hassle.

Rail

The Tanjong Pagar Railway Station is on Keppel Road, T62213390 to the south of the city centre. Singapore is the last port of call for the Malaysian railway system (Keretapi Tanah Melayu – KTM).

Visitors have to clear Singaporean immigration at the Woodlands and then continue for another 30 minutes, before clearing Malaysian immigration and customs at Tanjong Pagar. For an explanation as to why, see Sights.

There are two main lines connecting Singapore and Malaysia: one up the west coast to **KL** and another line which goes through the centre of Peninsular Malaysia and on to **Kota Bharu** on the northeast coast. Three fully air-conditioned express trains make the trip daily between Singapore and Kuala Lumpur, 6½ hours (S$34-68, and S$19 for third class seat), departing at 0830, 1525 and 2205. The overnight sleeper arrives in Kuala Lumpur at 0625 There is no through train to the north, you will need to change in KL. It is possible to take a train (for S$2.90) to Johor Bahru – just across the border in Malaysia – and then catch a (much cheaper) connection further north, but it requires a wait. Trains are clean and efficient and overnight trains have cabins in first class, sleeping berths in second class, and restaurants. The service to Kota Bharu takes 13 hours (S$41-51 and S$33 for third class seat). It leaves daily at 2000.

Transport to town From the station, bus 10 travels up Robinson Road, past Collyer Quay to Empress Place and the Nicoll Highway; bus 100 goes up Robinson, Fullerton and Beach roads; bus 30 travels west; bus 84 goes to HarbourFront; and buses 97 and 131 travel through the centre of town and then up Serangoon Road and through Little India.

Road

From Malaysia Bus There are bus services to Singapore from a number of towns in Malaysia. These include: **Kuala Lumpur** (S$23), **Melaka** (S$18), **Butterworth** (S$36), **Mersing** (S$30), **Kuantan** (S$50), **Ipoh** (S$31) and **Genting** (S$30). (The fares quoted here are from Singapore – tickets bought in Malaysia are cheaper.) Malaysian long-distance buses arrive at the Lavender Street Terminal at the junction of Lavender Street and Kallang Bahru, while tour group buses (including those from Thailand) arrive outside the Golden Mile Tower on Beach Road. From Singapore it is cheaper to buy a ticket from the Malaysian buses on Lavendar Road (for KL, Mersing, and Melacca). **Golden Mile** buses are more expensive as they are organised by tour agencies. **Transnasional** (for **KL, Genting, Terengganu**, and **Mersing**) has a booking office at Lavendar Road, or T64163948 or T62947034.There are three bus companies leaving at least every 10 minutes between Johor Bahru's Larkin Bus Terminal and Singapore. Boarding in JB is only permitted at Larkin and at immigation. The service crosses the Tuas Causeway, pauses at the Woodlands immigration point for customs formalities, stops at Singapore's Ban San Terminal at the northern end of Queen Street (at the junction with Arab Street; see map, page 584) or Kranji MRT station. The journey from JB takes about an hour , including customs and immigration formalities at the border. The non a/c SBS No 170 runs every 15 minutes from Singapore's Ban San Terminal, between Queen Street and Rochor Canal Road. Tickets are all priced around RM2 from JB, or S$2 (twice as much) from Singapore. The **Johor Singapore Express** is a/c and is slightly more frequent and also leaves from Ban San. The yellow **Causeway Link** bus with a smiley face runs between Kranji MRT station in Singapore and the Larkin terminal. It only takes 20 minutes from the border to the MRT station. All three buses require you to get off twice - for the Malay border point and its Singaporean counterpart. You have to take all your luggage with you since the bus does not wait for you. You wait for the next bus to come along; each bus has its own stop after exiting immigration. Keep your ticket or you will have to buy a new one. Also have a pen handy to fill in immigration forms as they are not provided.

If leaving Singapore for destinations in Malaysia then note that buses to more distant destinations like Butterworth, Terengganu and Ipoh tend to leave in the late afternoon. It is best to book tickets a few days ahead of departure, especially if intending to travel over a holiday period.

Long-distance bus companies are: **Singapore-Johor Bahru Express**, T62928149; **Kuala Lumpur-Singapore Express**, T62928254; **Malacca-Singapore Express**, T62935915.

Taxis Rather than taking a bus, it is possible to catch a long-distance taxi from Malaysia to Singapore. However, this usually requires a change of vehicle in **Johor Bahru**. (In other words, it is necessary to take a taxi from, say, Melaka, Kuantan, KL or Butterworth to JB, and then another taxi on to Singapore.) From JB there are scores of taxis to the Rochor Road terminus (S$6 per person, but if you need a full cab, S$24).

From Thailand As well as buses from destinations in Malaysia, there are also long-distance services from **Bangkok** and **Hat Yai** in Thailand. These obviously route their journeys through Malaysia. Services from Thailand arrive outside the Golden Mile Tower on Beach Road and fares from Singapore are S$41 to Hat Yai and S$70 to Bangkok. There are scores of agents selling tickets close to the station. Note that if you are leaving Singapore for Thailand, then it is cheaper to book a ticket to Hat Yai and then pay for the rest of the journey in Thai baht; or even cheaper still to catch a bus to JB, one from JB to Hat Yai, and then a third from Hat Yai to Bangkok.

Sea/River

A small fraction of Singapore's visitors arrive in the world's busiest port by ship. Passenger lines serve Singapore from **Australia, Europe, USA, India** and **Hong Kong**. Ships either dock at the Singapore Cruise Centre at HarbourFront (formerly the World Trade Centre) or anchor in the main harbour with a launch service to shore. Entry requirements are the same as those described on page 537. **Star Cruises**, T62230002, are one of the biggest companies operating in the region. **Orient Lines**, P&O Travel Singapore T63172800 and **Silversea Cruises**, T62763556 also dock at Singapore. A timetable of all shipping arrivals and departures is published daily in the Shipping Times (a section of the Business Times). According to some travellers, freighter operators are reasonably amenable to marine hitchers who want lifts to Vietnam (although it is difficult to enter Vietnam by sea), the Philippines or Indonesia.

From Indonesia and Malaysia There are regular high-speed ferry connections between Singapore and **Indonesia's Riau islands** of Batam (Sekupang and Batu Ampar) and Bintan (Tanjung Pinang and Loban). Return fares to Batam (around S$27 , 45 minutes journey time), ferries leave from the Singapore Cruise Centre at HarbourFront, south of town, just a short walk from the HarbourFront MRT. Ferries to Bintan leave from Tanah Merah ferry terminal (East Coast), and cost S$34 return (1½ hours). From the Riau islands it is possible to travel by boat to Sumatra or by air to many other destinations in Indonesia (cheaper than flying direct from Singapore). It used to be possible to take a ferry from Tanah Merah to Pulau Tioman off the east coast of Peninsula Malaysia, but because of a lack of demand the service has been scrapped. It may be relaunched by the time this book goes to press. Check with Penguin Ferries. Ferry operators have their offices in the Singapore Cruise Centre, on the second level of the HarbourFront Tower, and include **Dino Shipping**, T62702228; **Penguin Ferries**, T62714866; and **WaveMaster**, T62722192. Penguin and **Bintan Resort Ferries** (T65424369) are the two companies that operate ferries to Bintan. Intending passengers should arrive at the terminal one hour before departure if they do not already have a booked ticket.

If travelling from Tanjung Belungkur to Singapore, fares are considerably cheaper (payable in Ringgit).

There is also a ferry from Changi Ferry Terminal to **Tanjung Belungkor**, east of Johor Bahru in Malaysia. Most people use this service to get to the beach resort of Desaru. Passengers S$16 (S$22 return); journey time 30 minutes. Ferry times 0715, 1000, 1700 and 2000 on Fri-Sun, 1000, 17000 and 2000 Mon-Thur Singapore to Tanjung Belungkur; 0815, 1530 and 1845, Tanjung Belungkor to Singapore. Contact **Cruise Ferries**, T65468518 for reservations. The ferries are passengers only. To get to the terminal, take bus 2 to Changi Village and then a taxi.

It is possible to enter Singapore from Malaysia by bumboat from **Johor Bahru** (S$5), **Tanjung Pengileh** or **Tanjung Surat** (S$6) in southern Johor to Changi Point, on the northeast tip of Singapore – a good way of beating the bottleneck at the causeway. First boat 0700, last at 1600. Boats depart as soon as they have a full complement of 12 passengers.

Touching down

Airport information

Almost all visitors arrive at Singapore's Changi Airport – regularly voted the world's leading or favourite airport. Changi airport is at the extreme eastern tip of the island, about 20 km from town. There are two terminals, divided between airlines (all clearly indicated). A third terminal is currently under construction, but will not be completed until early 2008. The airport's stress-free terminals belie its status as one of the world's most hectic transit hubs. It processes around 26 million passengers a year – around seven times more than the population of Singapore. About 80% of Singapore's tourists arrive by air and it takes only 20 minutes from touchdown to baggage claim – characteristically called 'accelerated passenger through flow'.

Flight information, (toll-free number) T1800 542 4422 (give flight number). Changi airport: www.changiairport.com.sg/

Changi's facilities are excellent and include banks, hotel reservations and Singapore Tourist Board desks, a medical centre, business centre, children's discovery corner, free internet centre, day rooms, restaurants, left-luggage facilities, mail and telecommunications desks, shopping arcades, supermarkets, sports facilities (health centre and swimming pool), hairdresser, nature trails in seven different themed gardens, a movie theatre and accommodation. Everything is clearly signposted in English and the two terminals are connected by a monorail. There is an excellent canteen/food centre in Terminal 2, reached via the multi-deck car park. A tourist information pack is available just after Immigration, near the Customs Hall.

Airport information AL **Changi Village**, 1 Netheravon Rd, T63797111, www.changivillage.lemeridien.com Very well run, first class hotel, situated on Changi Beach, just north of the airport. Recommended for efficiency. C **Transit Hotel 1**, Level 3 Changi Airport Terminal 1, T65425538 , www.airport-hotel.com.sg Short-term rate quoted (6 hrs). A good place to take a break if you are stuck at Changi for an extended period and no need to clear immigration. C **Transit Hotel 2**, departure/transit

Touching down

Business hours: Normal banking hours are 0930-1500 Monday-Friday, 0930-1130 Saturday. Some do not offer foreign exchange dealings on Saturday, although money changers operate throughout the week and for longer hours. Most shops in the tourist belt open around 1030 and close at 2100. Sunday is a normal working day around Orchard and Scotts roads.

Directory enquiries: T103.

Electricity: 220-240 volts, 50 cycle AC; most hotels can supply adapters.

Emergencies: Police: T999. Ambulance/Fire brigade: T995.

IDD code for Singapore: 65.

Time: Eight hours ahead of GMT.

Weights and measures: Metric.

lounge south, Terminal 2, T65428122, www.airport-hotel.com.sg Excellent hotel on the airport property, with short stay facility (price quoted is for six hours). Booking is recommended. It also provides a 'freshen up' service including up-service of showers, sauna and gym from S$8.40.

Seletar Airport This is a military airport, but is also used for connections with **Pulau Tioman** off Malaysia's east coast and for some charter flights. Although the authorities do not allow photographs on the tarmac, checking-in is all very relaxed and informal – very different from the rather brusque efficiency of Changi. There are no public buses to Seletar, most people take taxis, and as at Changi there is a S$3 surcharge. When a scheduled flight is arriving from Tioman the airline usually calls so that the required number of taxis are waiting.

Airport tax Payable on departure – S$21 for all flights to all countries (but many tickets already have this included in their price). A PSC (Passenger Service Charge) coupon can be purchased at most hotels, travel agencies and airline offices in town before departure, which saves time at the airport. The 5% **Goods and Sales tax** (GST) is refundable at the airport for goods bought (over US$300) with appropriate receipts.

Transport to town

Hotels will only meet guests with a previous arrangement; some charge, but others offer the service free. The car pick-up area is outside the arrivals halls of both terminals. A number of **buses** run between the airport and nearby bus interchanges. Bus 36 loops along Orchard Road passing many of the major hotels including the YMCA.The service runs from 0600 until 2300; fare is less than S$2. **Airport shuttle**: between 0600 and midnight, every 15 minutes and every 30 minutes (0600-1800), adults S$7, children S$5, booking counters in arrivals halls. These minibuses will drop off at any destination within the central business district. Note that if you are in a group of three or four, it is probably cheaper to take a taxi (see below).

The airport is now connected to the **MRT underground line.** Trains to the centre of Singapore take approximately 30 minutes. The fare is S$1.40 Trains runs every 12 minutes between 0530 and 2320.

Taxis queue up outside the arrival halls. They are metered but there is an airport surcharge of S$3, which increases to S$5 on Fri, Sat and Sun and after 1700. A trip to the centre of town should cost about S$20 including the surcharge. Most taxi companies operate a **limousine service** (London cab or Mercedes) with a flat rate of S$35. To book limousine service from your hotel, call **City Cab**, T64542222, **Comfort**, T65521111, or **TIBS**, T65558888. **Avis**, T67371668 or **Hertz**, T1800-7344646.

Car hire Avis (T65428855) and Hertz (T65425300) desks are in Terminals 2's arrival hall (from 0700 to 2300).

Tourist information

Singapore Tourism Board, Tourism Court, 1 Orchard Spring Lane, T1800-7362000 (toll-free in Singapore), www.visitsingapore.com, 0800-2230 daily. Other offices at: Liang Court Shopping Centre, 177 River Valley Road, Level 1 T63362888, 1030-2200 daily; Plaza Singapura, 68 Orchard Road Level 1, T63329298, 1000-2200 daily. Changi Airport, arrivals halls 1 and 2, 0600 to 0200 daily; The Galleria at Suntec City Mall, T6333825, 1000-1800 daily and The InnCrowd Backpacker's Hostel, 73 Dunlop St,Little India, T62964280, 1000-2200 daily. All are good sources of brochures and maps. Complaints can also be registered at these offices. There is a 24-hour Touristline which gives automated information in English, Mandarin, Japanese and German, T1800-7362000. (toll free in Singapore). Indonesian Tourist Board, T67377422. Malaysian Tourist Board, Ocean Building, 11 Collyer Quay, T65326351.

Local customs and laws

Clothing Singapore dress is smart but casual. It is rare to find places insisting on jacket and tie, although jeans and T-shirts are taboo at some nightclubs.

Conduct in private homes Most Singaporeans remove their shoes at the door – more out of a keen sense of cleanliness than any deep religious conviction. No host would insist on visitors doing so, but it is the polite way to enter a home.

Eating Chinese meals are eaten with chopsticks and Malays and Indians traditionally eat with their right hands. It is just as acceptable, however, to eat with spoons and forks. In Malay and Indian company, do not use the left hand for eating.

Prohibitions There are several rules and regulations visitors should note: smoking is discouraged and prohibited by law in many public places, such as buses, taxis, lifts, government offices, cinemas, theatres, libraries and department stores and shopping centres – and all air-conditioned restaurants. First offenders can be fined up to S$1,000 for lighting up in prohibited places. Many hotels now provide non-smoking floors. Littering may incur a fine of up to S$1,000 for first time offenders and up to S$2,000 for repeat offenders, with the added prospect of corrective work of some kind. Although jaywalking is less rigorously enforced than it used to be, crossing the road within 50 m of a pedestrian crossing, bridge or underpass could cost you S$500.

Safety Singapore is probably the safest big city in Southeast Asia. Women travelling alone need have few worries. It is wise, however, to take the normal precautions and not wander into lonely places after dark.

Tipping Tipping is virtually non-existent and any attempt will be met with a bewildered stare. Most hotels and restaurants add 10% service charge and 5% government tax to bills. In general, only tip for special personal services.

Getting around

In an attempt to discourage Singaporeans from clogging the roads with private cars, the island's public transport system was designed to be cheap and painless. Buses go almost everywhere, and the **Mass Rapid Transit (MRT)** underground railway provides an extremely efficient subterranean back-up. A useful guide to Singapore's transport system is the annual pocket-sized and pocket-priced (S$3.50) TransitLink Guide, listing all bus and MRT routes and stops, available at news outlets, bookshops and MRT stations, as well as at many hotels.

Boat

Ferries to the southern islands – Sentosa, Kusu, St John's etc – leave from HarbourFront (formerly the World Trade Centre) or it is possible to hire a sampan from Jardine Steps on Keppel Road or Clifford Pier. Boats for the northern islands go from Changi Point or Ponggol Point.

Bus

For anyone visiting Singapore for more than a couple of days, the bus must be the best way of getting around. **SBS** (Singapore Bus Service) and **TIBS** (Trans-Island Bus Services) are efficient, convenient and cheap. Routes for all the buses are listed (with a special section on buses to tourist spots) in the aforementioned Transit Link Guide. If you intend to do much bus travel, then this guide is well worth buying.

All buses are operated by a driver only, so it is necessary to have the exact fare to hand. Fares range from 70¢ (non a/c) to S$1.70 and buses run daily from 0600 to 2400. For those intending to use the bus system extensively, it is well worth considering purchasing an ez-link card, a stored value smartcard which can be used on buses, the MRT and LRT. Buy the card for S$15 (S$3 refundable deposit, $5 card cost and S$7 travel value) at MRT stations.

The sightseeing **Singapore Explorer** trolley (T63396833) travels between Orchard Road, the river, Chinatown, Raffles Hotel, Boat Quay, Clarke Quay, Suntec City all day. Buy tickets from the driver or some hotels also sell tickets; S$9 for adults, S$7 for children, provides you with unlimited rides throughout the day.

Car hire

This is one of the most expensive ways to get around. It is not worth it unless you are travelling to Malaysia as parking is expensive in Singapore (parking coupons can be bought in shops and daily licence booths). If travelling to Malaysia, it is cheaper, in any case, to hire a car in Johor Bahru, Malaysia. Rental agencies require a licence, passport and for the driver to be over 20. Car rental cost is anything from S$60 to S$350 per day, depending on size and comfort, plus mileage. Vans and pick-ups are much cheaper as they are classified as commercial vehicles and are taxed at a lower rate. Driving is on the left, the speed limit 50 km per hour (80 km per hour on expressways) and wearing a seat belt is compulsory. Avoid bus lanes (indicated by an unbroken yellow line) during rush hour. Remember that to drive into the restricted zone a licence must be purchased (S$3). In addition to car hire counters at the airport and booking offices in top hotels, the *Yellow Pages* lists scores of local firms under 'Motorcar Renting and Leasing'.

Cycling

This is not a bicycle-friendly city. Bicycles are available for hire at a number of public parks and other quieter spots on the island, including East Coast Parkway, Sentosa, Pasar Ris, Bishan and Pulau Ubin. Expect to pay S$3-8 per hour or around S$20 per day; some outfits also ask for a deposit.

East Coast Bicycle Centre, East Coast Parkway, bikes for rent including tandems (S$3 per hour), open 0800-1830. **Sentosa Island Bicycle Station,** near Ferry Terminal, S$3 per hour, Monday-Friday 0900-1800, Saturday and Sunday 0900-1900.

Hitchhiking

The idea is an anathema to most Singaporeans and those trying are unlikely to have much success.

Mass Rapid Transit (MRT)

Singapore has one of the most technologically advanced, user-friendly light railway systems in the world – about a third of the system is underground. The designer-stations of marble, glass and chrome are cool, spotless and suicide-free, thanks to the sealed-in, air-conditioned platforms. Nine of the underground stations serve as self-sufficient, blast-proof emergency bunkers for Singaporeans, should they ever need them. Smoking is strictly banned on all public transport – transgression is punishable by a large fine. Eating or drinking inside stations is also strictly forbidden. There are now three MRT lines – the new North-East line runs from HarbourFront through Chinatown, Little India to Punggol in the north-east. The North-South line runs from Jurong East (for the Singapore Science Centre) in a loop north passing Kranji (for buses to Johor Bahru in Malaysia) and down to Marina Bay passing through Orchard Rd, City Hall and Raffles Places. The East-West line runs from Pasir Ris in the west through City Hall, Bugis and onto Changi Airport. The main interchanges are at Outram Park, Raffles Place and City Hall. The MRT's 106 fully automated trains operate every 2½-8 minutes, depending on the time of day, between 0600 and 2400. A new Circle Line is under construction. The S$6.7 billion line will run from Dhoby Ghaut on Orchard Rd linking with the other three lines and end up at HarbourFront. It is due to be finished in 2010.

See the MRT map at the end of the book. For more information, call T1800-336-8900 (toll free, Singapore only), or see www.smrt.com.sg

Fare stages are posted in station concourses, and tickets dispensed, with change, from the vending machines. Fares range from 80¢ to S$1.80.

Taxis

Taxis are cheap and the fastest and easiest way to get around the island in comfort. There are more than 15,000 taxis, all of them metered and air-conditioned, which ply the island's roads. Taxis can only be hailed at specified points; it's best to go to a taxi stand or about 50 m from traffic lights. The taxis' bells are an alarm warning cabbies they've exceeded the 80 km per hour expressway speed limit, but drivers rarely pay attention to this. Fares start at S$2.40 for the first 1 km, and rise 10¢ for every subsequent 240 m up to 10 km, after which they rise by 10¢ every 225 m. 10¢ is also added for every 30 seconds waiting time. There is a peak period surcharge of S$1 for trips commencing between 0730 and 0930 Monday-Saturday, between 1630 and 1900 Monday-Friday, and from 1130 to 1400 on Saturday. These surcharges do not apply on public holidays. A surcharge of S$1.50 is levied on all trips beginning from the Central Business District (CBD) between 1630 and 1900 on weekdays, and between 1130 and 1400 on Saturday (except on public holidays). If this surcharge is levied then the peak period surcharge does not apply. If there are more than two passengers there is a 50¢ surcharge; luggage costs S$1 extra and there's a 50% 'midnight charge' from 2400 to 0600. There is also a S$3 surcharge for journeys starting from (but not going to) Changi International Airport or Seletar Airport, and a S$3.20 flat fee for calling a radio taxi, which rises to S$5.20 if booked more than 30 minutes in advance. Trips paid for with credit cards incur a 10% surcharge on top of the fare, and taxis hired between 1800 on the evening before a public holiday and 2400 on the day of the public holiday also get hit with a S$1 surcharge. TIBS taxis now has a fleet of London cabs which may be hired by the hour, and have the advantage of accommodating five passengers. There's a surcharge here too though, of S$1. Even with this veritable extravaganza of surcharges, Singapore's taxis are still excellent value for money and are definitely the best way to get around. They accept credit and debit cards. Not only do they provide a view of Singapore which is absent from the MRT (at least in the city centre), but taxi drivers, like their brothers (and a few sisters) in most cities, are a great source of information, from political opinion to tourist practicalities. They are also impeccably polite and will even round down fares to the nearest dollar. Unlike most of the rest of Asia, language is not a barrier to communication.

Don't try to flag down a taxi at night in busy places - even at taxi ranks. You will have to call them by phone.

The CBD area scheme restricts all cars and taxis from entering the area 0730-1900 Monday-Friday, 0730-1015 Saturday, unless they purchase an area licence (S$3 cars, $1 for motorbikes). Passengers entering the restricted zone are liable unless the taxi is already displaying a licence. Taxis displaying red destination labels on their dashboards are going home and are only required to take passengers in the direction they are going. Taxis are usually plentiful; there are stands outside most main shopping centres and hotels. Smoking is illegal in taxis.

For taxi services ring: **Comfort**, T65521111; **City Cab**, T65522222; **TIBS**, T65558888.

Trishaws

Descendants of the rickshaw, trishaws have all but left the Singapore street scene. A few genuine articles can still be found in the depths of Geylang or Chinatown, but the biggest population of trishaws is to be found off New Bugis Street, by the Albert Centre (see Little India map, page 581) and lingering outside the Raffles Hotel; they cater for tourists only these days and charge accordingly, making trishaws the most expensive form of public transport in town. As ever, agree a price before climbing in and expect to pay about S$30 for a 45-minute ride. Top hotels offer top-dollar trishaw tours. **Trishaw Tours**, T63396833, also offers trishaw tours starting from Chinatown.

Maps and guides

A plethora of city maps are available free from STB offices and many hotels. The best street map to Singapore is the Periplus Map, available at bookshops. Other useful maps are the Secret Map of Singapore; Secret Food Map of Singapore; Singapore Street Directory. The Singapore Tourism Board (STB) produces a profusion of guides to the city, including the general official guide which is updated each month. It is worth making a visit to one of the STB offices or pick up brochures and maps on arrival at Changi Airport. Other free maps are available and can be picked up from hotels and tourist offices. Invaluable for making the most of Singapore's incomparable public transportation is the annual TransitLink Guide, which lists all bus and MRT routes and stops. A snip at S$3.50.

Sleeping

Many of the excellent international class hotels are concentrated in the main shopping and business areas, including Orchard and Scotts roads, and near Raffles City and the Marina complexes. They are all run to a very high standard and room rates range between S$250 and S$650, although discounts are almost always on offer and few people pay the full rate. Enquire at the airport hotel desk on arrival whether there are any special offers. After a room glut in the early 1980s, Singapore's hotel industry is now suffering a shortage and when a large convention or two hits town, rooms can be hard to find.

Taxes of 10% (government) plus 5% (goods) plus 1% (services) are added to bills in all but the cheapest of hotels.

Singapore offers an excellent choice of hotels in our upper categories, from luxury to tourist class. Though rooms may be more expensive than equivalent classes of hotels elsewhere in the region, they try to make up for this in terms of service. It is rare to stay in a hotel that does not offer attentive and professional care. Budget hotels are scarce and not most backpackers would describe as 'budget'. However, there are a few cheaper places to stay and dorm beds can be had for S$12 or so.

Eating

Eating is the national pastime in Singapore and has acquired the status of a refined art. The island is a tropical paradise for epicureans of every persuasion and budget. While every country in the region boasts national dishes, none offers such a delectably wide variety as Singapore. Fish-head curry must surely qualify as the

Hotel price codes and facilities

LL (S$400+) and **L** (S$300-400) Singapore has some of the very best hotels in the world. These offer unrivalled personal service, sumptuous extras, luxury rooms and bathrooms, and just about every amenity that you can think of. Most of the top hotels now provide two in-room phone lines (for modems and calls), 24-hour business facilities, several pools, jacuzzis, health spas, tennis courts, numerous restaurants, and much else besides.

AL (S$200-300) Most of the middle to upper range hotels in this category will provide a business centre (although it is worth checking whether these operate around the clock). Coupled with this, there will be an executive floor or two, with a lounge for private breakfast and evening cocktails, or for entertaining clients. Most of these hotels will also provide a personal safe in each room. There will be a fitness centre and swimming pool, and they may have a health centre as well as several restaurants.

A (S$150-200) and **B** (S$100-150) Hotels in this category will range from very comfortable to functional. Rooms in the 'A' category will have most extras – like a minibar, TV and tea and coffee-making facilities. They may also have a swimming pool, but it is likely to be small. They will have a coffee shop and perhaps a restaurant. Rooms in the 'B' category may be lacking some, or most, of these amenities, but should still be clean, comfortable and serviceable.

C (S$50-100) There are not many hotels in this category. Rooms may be air-conditioned with a hot water shower attached; there might also be a coffee shop. These are no-frills, functional affairs. There are some bargains to be had, but there are also hotels in this category which are pretty sordid.

D (S$25-50) and **E** (less than S$25) Hotels and guesthouses in these two categories (and there aren't many) are basic places, with shared bathroom facilities and box-like rooms. There are a few that are clean and perfectly adequate and these are the registered establishments; others are squalid. The places on third or fourth floors of apartment buildings usually have no licence, and they are often the dirtiest and least well run. Most of these places provide a basic breakfast.

national dish, but you can sample 10 Chinese cuisines, North and South Indian, Malay and Nonya (Straits Chinese) food, plus Indonesian, Vietnamese, Thai, Japanese, Korean, French, Italian (and other European), Russian, Mexican, Polynesian and Scottish. There's a very respectable selection of Western food at the top end of the market, a few good places in the middle bracket, and swelling ranks of cheaper fast food restaurants like Kentucky Fried Chicken and McDonald's and an explosion of pizza outlets. For young, trendy Singaporeans, coffee culture has replaced food court fare, and the favoured spots are places like *The Coffee Bean, Delifrance, Spinelli's* and *Starbuck's*, which are giving a buzz to thousands.

Do not be put off by characterless, brightly lit restaurants in Singapore; the food can be superb. Eating spots range from high-rise revolving restaurants to neon-lit pavement seafood extravaganzas. A delicious dinner can cost as little as S$3 or more than S$100, and the two may be just yards away from each other. For example, it is possible to have a small beer in one of the bars of the *Raffles Hotel* for S$8, or more, and then stagger 10 m across the road and indulge in a huge plate of curry and rice for S$3.

For a listing of over 100 more pricey restaurants, *Singapore's Best Restaurants* is worth purchasing; it gives a description of the food and a price guideline and is available from most bookstores for $10.30. It is updated annually. The *Secret Food Map*, available at most bookstores for S$5, is also a good buy. Another book worth getting is *Good Food, 500 Great Eating Places Near the MRT Station*, produced by the MRT and MPH Publishers. For short descriptions of Singapore's varied cuisines see the food glossaries, Footnotes.

Coffee shops

Mainly family concerns, traditional Singaporean coffee shops or *kopi tiam* are in the older part of the city, usually in old Chinese shophouses. They serve breakfast, lunch and dinner, as well as beer, at prices only slightly higher than those at hawker centres.

Fast food cafés

Despite Singapore's gourmet delights, fast food outlets do a roaring trade in Singapore. As well as the standard names in fast food fare, there are now chains of more sophisticated 'cafés', selling a wider range of European food. In particular, there is *Spinelli's*, who provide a very good range of fresh coffees (ground or beans), and *Delifrance*, known for its freshly-baked croissants, danish pastries and filled baguettes. Check the Yellow Pages for branch addresses of the various fast food restaurants. They include: A&W (which in 1968 became the first fast-feeder in town), Burger King, Denny's, KFC, McDonald's, Milano Pizza, Orange Julius, Pizza Hut, Shakey's Pizza and one called Fat Mama. Delifrance has probably expanded fastest with restaurants at Clifford Centre, Marina Square, The Dynasty, Wisma Atria, The Promenade, Holland Village and Changi Airport. They also run bistros at Holland Village and Tanglin Mall.

Hawker centres and food courts

The government might have cleared hawkers off the streets, but there are plenty of hawker centres in modern Singapore. Food courts are the modern, air-conditioned, sanitized version of hawker centres. They provide the local equivalent of café culture and the human equivalent of grazing. Large numbers of stalls are packed together under one roof. Hawker centres are found beneath HDB blocks and in some specially allocated areas in the city; while food courts are usually in the basement of shopping plazas. The seats and tableware may be basic, but the food is always fresh and diners are spoilt for choice. Customers claim a table, then graze their way down the rows of Chinese, Malay and Indian stalls. It is not necessary to eat from the stall you are sitting next to. Most are self-service but vendors will deliver to your table when the food is ready and payment is on receipt. The food is cheap and prices are non-negotiable. Two of the best are the Lau Pa Sat Festival Market and the massive Newton Circus.

Drink

Every hawker centre has at least a couple of stalls selling fresh fruit juice, a more wholesome alternative to the ubiquitous bottles of fizzy drink. A big pineapple or papaya juice costs S$2. You can choose any combination of fruits to go in your fruit punch. Freshly squeezed fruit juices are widely available at stalls and in restaurants. Fresh lime juice is served in most restaurants, and is a perfect complement to the banana-leaf curry, tandoori and dosai. Carbonated soft drinks, cartons of fruit juice and air-flown fresh milk can be found in supermarkets. For local flavour, the Malay favourite is *bandung* (a sickly sweet, bright pink concoction of rose essence and condensed milk), found in most hawker centres, as well as the Chinese thirst quenchers, soya bean milk or chrysanthemum tea. Red Bull (Krating Daeng), the Thai energy tonic, is also widely available and is the toast of Singapore's army of Thai building site labourers.

Tiger and Anchor beers are the local brews and Tsingtao, the Chinese nectar, is also available. Tiger Beer was first brewed at the Malayan Breweries with imported

 Dutch hops and yeast on Alexandra Road in 1932, and was the product of a joint venture between Singapore's Fraser & Neave and Heineken. Recently, Tiger Beer has produced two new brews: Tiger Classic is a strong bottled beer and Tiger Light, which is now available on draught in some bars. Anchor was the result of German brewers Beck's setting up the rival Archipelago Brewery. Because of its German roots, Archipelago was bought out by Malayan Breweries in 1941 and is today part of the same empire. Some bars (such as Charlie's at Changi) specialize in imported beers, but even local beer is expensive (around S$8 a bottle in hawker centres and S$10 a glass in bars and pubs). There is an international selection of drinks at top bars, but they're often pricey. Coffee houses, hawker centres and small bars or coffee shops around Serangoon Road, Jalan Besar and Chinatown have the cheapest beer. Expect to pay around S$12 for a half pint of beer in most smart bars. Most bars and restaurants do have a happy hour (or hours) though, where bargains can be had.

There is no shortage of wine available in Singapore, but it is expensive; Australian wines are generally a better deal than imported European ones. Supermarkets all have good wines and spirits sections.

The Singapore Sling is the island's best known cocktail. It was invented in the Raffles Hotel in 1915 and contains a blend of gin, cherry brandy, sugar, lemon juice and angostura bitters.

Festivals, events and public holidays

Singapore's cultural diversity gives Singaporeans the excuse to celebrate plenty of festivals, most of which visitors can attend. The Singapore Tourist Board produces a brochure every year on festivals, with their precise dates, or check the STBs website (www.visitsingapore.com).

January

New Year's Day (**1 January** – public holiday).

February

Chinese New Year (movable – public holiday). This five-day lunar festival is celebrated in **January** or **February**. Each new year is given the name of an animal in 12-year rotation and each has a special significance. The seasonal Mandarin catchphrase is *Gong Xi Fa Chai* (Happy New Year).

Thaipusam (movable – in the Hindu month of Thai, usually **February**). In honour of the Hindu deity Lord Subramaniam, or Murgham, the son of Lord Siva. Held during the full moon in the month of Thai, it is a festival of penance and thanksgiving with a procession from the Chettiars' Temple on Tank Road to the Vinayagar Temple on Keong Saik Road. The highlight of Thaipusam is the second day, when devotees assemble in their thousands at the Sri Perumal Temple on Serangoon Road. Devotees pay homage to Lord Subramaniam by piercing their bodies, cheeks and tongues with sharp skewers (vel) and hooks, weighted with oranges and carrying steel structures bearing the image of Lord Subramaniam.

Hari Raya Haji (movable – public holiday, falls on the 10th day of Zulhiah, the 12th month of the Muslim calendar). This festival honours Muslims who have made the pilgrimage to Mecca. The feast day is marked by prayers at mosques and the sacrificial slaughter of goats and buffalo for distribution to the poor as a sign of gratitude to Allah.

Jade Emperor's Birthday (movable) Crowds converge on the Giok Hong Tian Temple on Havelock Road to celebrate the Jade Emperor's birthday. A Chinese opera is performed in the courtyard of the temple and lanterns are lit in the doorways of houses.

T'se Tien Tai Seng's (the Monkey God's) Birthday (movable – but celebrated twice a year, in Feb and Oct) Participants go into a trance and pierce their cheeks and tongues with skewers before handing out paper charms. Celebrated at the Monkey God Temple, Eng Hoon Street, near Seng Poh market, Tiong Bahru Road, South Chinatown.

March-April

Kwan Yin's Birthday (movable) Chinese visit temples dedicated to the goddess of Mercy (like the one on Waterloo Road). Childless couples come to pray for fertility.
Qing Ming (movable – **early April**) A Chinese ancestor-worship extravaganza in which family graves are spruced up and offerings of food and wine placed on tombs to appease their forebears' spirits.
Tamil New Year (**movable April/May**) Begins at the start of the Hindu month of Chithirai. Pujas are held at Singapore's main temples to honour Surya, the sun god. An almanac containing the Hindu horoscope is published at this time.
Easter (movable – Good Friday is a public holiday) Services are held in the island's churches. There is a candlelit procession in the grounds of St Joseph's Catholic Church, Victoria Street.

May-June

Labour Day (**1 May**, public holiday)
Vesak Day (movable – public holiday, usually in **May**, on the full moon of the fifth lunar month) Commemorates the Buddha's birth, death and enlightenment and is celebrated in Buddhist temples everywhere. Kong Meng San Phor Kark See Temple in Bright Hill Drive and the Temple of a Thousand Lights in Race Course Road are particularly lively. In Singapore celebrations begin before dawn, monks chant sutras (prayers) and lanterns and candles are lit to symbolize the Buddha's enlightenment.

August-September

National Day (**9 August**, public holiday) To celebrate the Republic's independence in 1965. The highlight of the day is the military parade, air force fly-past and carnival procession on and around the Padang and National Stadium.
Festival of the Hungry Ghosts (Yu Lan Jie) (movable – runs for 30 days after the last day of the sixth moon) Banquets are given by stallholders, lavish feasts are laid out on the streets and there are roving bands of Chinese street opera singers, puppet shows and lotteries. Then there is the ritual burning of huge incense sticks and paper 'hell money' to appease the spirits, who are believed to wander around on earth for a month after the annual opening of the gates of hell.
Mooncake or Lantern Festival (movable – mid-way through the Chinese eighth moon) This Chinese festival commemorates the overthrow of the Mongul Dynasty in China. Children parade with elaborate candlelit lanterns and eat mooncakes filled with lotus seed paste. According to Chinese legend, secret messages of revolt were carried inside these cakes and led to the uprising which caused the overthrow of their oppressors. A gentler interpretation is that the round cakes represent the full moon, the end of the farming year and an abundant harvest – a bucolic symbolism that must be lost on most city-born Singaporeans.
Navarathri Festival (movable) Nine days of prayer (navarathiri means 'nine lights'), temple music and classical dance honour the consorts of Siva, Vishnu and Brahma (the Hindu trinity of Gods). Music and dance performances can be viewed at all Hindu temples from around 1930-2200 each night of the festival. The festival is celebrated notably at the Chettiar Temple on Tank Road, ending with a procession on the 10th day along River Valley Road, Killiney Road, Orchard Road, Clemenceau Avenue and returning to the temple.

October-November

Deepavali (movable – public holiday, usually in **October** or **November** in the Hindu month of Aipasi). The Hindu festival of lights commemorates the victory of Lord Krishna over the demon king Narakasura, symbolizing the victory of light over darkness and good over evil. Every Hindu home is brightly lit and decorated for the occasion. Shrines are swamped with offerings and altars piled high with flowers. Row upon row of little earthen oil lamps are lit to guide the souls of departed relatives in their journey back to the next world, after their brief annual visit to earth during Deepavali.
Thimithi Festival (movable, in the Hindu month of Aipasi). This Hindu festival, in honour of the goddess Draupadi, often draws a big crowd to watch devotees fulfil their vows by walking over a 3 m long pit of

burning coals in the courtyard of the Sri Mariamman Temple on South Bridge Road. Fire walking starts at around 1600 on the arrival of the procession from Perumal Temple on Serangoon Road.

December

Hari Raya Puasa or **Aidil Fitri** (movable – public holiday). Marks the end of Ramadan, the month of fasting for Muslims and is a day of celebration. Once the Muftis have confirmed the new moon of Syawal, the 10th Islamic month, Muslims don traditional clothing and spend the day praying in the mosques and visiting friends and family. During Ramadan, Muslims eat at stalls after dark; Geyland Serai and Bussorah Street (near Arab Street) are favourite makan stops, see page 583.

Christmas Day (**25 December**, public holiday) Christmas here is a spectacle of dazzling lights, the best along Orchard Rd, where trees are bejewelled with fairy lights. Shopping centres and hotels compete to have the year's most extravagant or creative display. These seasonal exhibitions are often conveniently designed to last through to Chinese New Year. It would not be untypical, for example, to find Santa riding on a man-eater in the year of the tiger. In shopping arcades, sweating tropical Santa Clauses dash through the fake snow. Choirs from Singapore's many churches line the sidewalks and Singaporeans go shopping.

Shopping

GST (Goods and Service Tax) Tourist Refund Scheme See page 537.

Singapore is a shopper's paradise. There is an endless variety of consumer goods and gimmicks. The choice seems almost unlimited. But don't be deluded that there are bargains galore with rock-bottom prices to match the variety. Singapore's retailers have had to weather several years of stagnant demand. Local shoppers seem to be spending their disposable income in other ways (or themselves go shopping abroad) and tourists no longer come with empty suitcases to stuff them full of goodies. Even the people who used to come here from places like Manila, Bangkok and Jakarta can buy just about everything at home. That said, there are some good buys and sales can throw up the odd bargain.

Probably the best area for window shopping is around Scotts and Orchard roads, where many of the big complexes and department stores are located (see page 580). This area comes alive after dark and most shops stay open late. The towering Raffles City Complex, Parco at Bugis Junction, Suntec City and Marina Square are the other main shopping centres. Serangoon Road (or Little India), Arab Street and Chinatown offer a more exotic shopping experience with a range of 'ethnic' merchandise.

Tips/trends

Singapore has all the latest electronic gadgetry and probably as wide a choice as you will find anywhere. It also has a big selection of antiques (although they tend to be overpriced), arts and crafts, jewellery, silks and batiks. For branded goods, Singapore is still marginally cheaper than most other places, but for Asian-produced products it is no longer the cheapest place in the region.

Singapore Gold Circle Gold Circle has been set up by the Singapore Tourism Board, as a mark of quality assurance; shops who are members of SGC display a gold and black symbol.

Small Claims Tribunal Feel you've been unfairly ripped off? Then contact the Small Claims Tribunal on the fifth floor of the Apollo Centre, Havelock Road, T64356922, F64355994. There's a fast track claims mechanism where visitors, after paying a S$10 fee, can have their cases against errant retailers heard, often within 24 hours.

Touts Although the government has come down hard on copy-watch touts, tourists can still be accosted (and ripped off), particularly along Orchard Road and China Town.

Tips on buying

It doesn't take long to get the feel of where you can bargain and where you cannot. Department stores are fixed-price, but most smaller outfits - even those in smart shopping complexes - can sometimes be talked into discounts. As ever, it is best not to buy at the first shop; compare prices; get an idea of what you should be paying from big department stores - *Tang's Department Store* on Orchard Road is a good measuring rod - which you can nearly always undercut. In ordinary shops, 20-30% can be knocked off the asking price, sometimes more. Keep smiling, joking and teasing when bargaining, and never believe a shopkeeper who tells you they are giving you something at cost or is not making a profit. The golden rule is to keep a sense of humour. Bargaining occurs especially in Chinatown and you are in a strong negotiating position if you are the first customer of the day. The Chinese believe it is very inauspicious for the first customer of the day to leave their shop without buying something!

For big purchases, ask for an international guarantee (they are often extra), although sometimes you will have to be content with Singapore-only guarantees. Generally once goods are sold they are not returnable, unless faulty; make sure you keep your receipt. Deposits, not usually more than 50% of the value of the goods, are generally required when orders are placed for custom-made goods. Make sure electrical goods are compatible with the voltage back home.

Complaints about retailers (who from time to time exhibit aggressive tendencies when selling merchandise to tourists) can be registered at the **Consumers' Association of Singapore**, T62224165. Or contact the **Retail Information Centre**, Block 528, Ang Mo Kio Ave 10, #02-2387, T64502114.

Antiques

Singapore's antique shops stock everything from opium beds, planters' chairs, gramophones, brass fans, porcelain, jade, Peranakan marble-top tables and 17th-century maps, to smuggled Burmese Buddhas, Sulawesian spirit statues and Dayak masks. There are few restrictions on bringing antiques into Singapore or exporting them. Many of the top antique shops are in the Tanglin Shopping Centre, Orchard Road. *A Guide to Buying Antiques, Arts and Crafts in Singapore* by Anne Jones is recommended, available in most bookshops.

Art galleries

With the arrival of both Christie's and Sotheby's and the increased interest in home decorating, art has taken on a new meaning for Singaporeans. For information on contemporary art shows, contact the **Art Galleries Association** (T62354113, www.agas.org.sg), which represents the interests of 15 commercial galleries.

Batik and silk

Malaysian and Indonesian batiks are sold by the metre or in sarong lengths. Arab Street and Serangoon Road are the best areas for batik and silk lengths; big department stores usually have batik ready-mades. Ready-made Chinese silk garments can be found all over Singapore in Chinese emporia. If you want silk without the hassle, at reasonable prices, big department stores (such as *Tang's*, on Orchard Road) have good selections. *China Silk House* designers come up with new collections every month.

Cameras

There are several places dedicated to electronics and they usually house camera shops. *Cathay Photo, Marina Square, Max Photo* on third floor of Centrepoint (Orchard Road) or *Peninsula Plaza* (colonial core), provide a good range and good advice.

Children

Singapore is now a great place to shop for children, from cheap knick-knacks in the markets of Little India or Chinatown, to the chi chi boutiques in the shopping malls. The best choice of children's clothes is to be found at *The Forum*, corner of Cuscaden and Orchard roads, where there are at least 20 shops selling children's clothes. *Tanglin Mall* also has a good smattering of shops, see Shopping, Orchard Road.

Clothes

Singapore boasts all the international designer labels, and many of the lesser high street chains too (including *Warehouse* and *Top Shop*) - many of the shops are strung out along Orchard Road, with the *Paragon Shopping Centre* having the largest selection of designer stores together with the *Japanese Metro* department store and a basement full of a wide variety of eateries. There are now also quite a few shops in *Millennia Walk, Marina Square* and *Suntec City*. Designer fashion comes a bit cheaper in Singapore than other Southeast Asian capitals, as no duty is levied. Locally designed clothes keep up with the trends and are very reasonably priced. For exceptional value, slightly damaged clothes and factory seconds can be purchased from the *Fashion Export*, which has branches in Tanglin Mall and in Holland Village and F.O.S which has branches in Holland Village, Millenia Walk and Specialist Shopping Centre.

Electronic goods

Singapore has all the latest electronic equipment, hot from Japan at duty free prices. Prices are still cheaper than in Europe, but can vary enormously. Check that items come with an international guarantee. The centres for electronic goods are Sim Lim Tower (corner of Jalan Besar, Little India) and Sim Lim Square (corner of Rochor Canal Road, south of Little India). Although be warned you need to know exactly what you want otherwise you will come away with something that may only half meet your requirements. The Japanese *Best Denki* stores are in most of the shopping centres or Singapore's *Harvey Norman* stores also offer a wide variety of electronic goods in a more conventional manner still at competitive prices.

Furniture

Singapore now has a good range of old (or distressed) and new furniture. Antique furniture in varying states of decay can be found at Upper Paya Lebar Road, just north of Macpherson Road; *Chin Yi Antique House, Mansion Antique House* and *Tech Huat Antique House* can all be found here. *Just Anthony* is also on this road, south of Upper Serangoon Road; it sells antique and reproduction furniture. River Valley Road, just up from Tank Road, has several antique and second-hand furniture dealers. Reproduction antique furniture can also be found on Kelantan Lane.

Interior decorating

There is now fantastic choice for kitting out your home, from small to large pieces, most of it imported from around the region (or further afield). Park Mall on Penang Road (running parallel to Orchard Road) offers an electic mix of Asian inspired furniture and lighting designs. Also *The John Erdos Gallery*, Kim Yam Road at the corner of Moh'd Sultan Road and *The Shophouse* in Gillman Village are popular choices for the expats furnishing their homes.

Jewellery

Gold (mostly Asian - 18, 22 or 24 carat), precious stones and pearls (freshwater and cultured) are all easily found in Singapore and are of good value. Styles and designs are quite different from the west. Gold is a good buy, but it too looks different. The Singapore Assay Office uses a merlion head as a hallmark. Most of the jewellery shops are in South Bridge Road; see Shopping, Chinatown.

Shopping centres and plazas

- **The Bencoolen** Bencoolen St, just south of Sim Lim Square, this is a great centre to buy watches and Chinese artifacts.
- **Chinatown Point** Eu Tong Sen St, Chinatown, specializes in handicrafts.
- **Funan Centre** Squeezed in between the Excelsior and Peninsula hotels in the colonial core, with five floors of shops is a good place for electrical equipment; in particular, notebooks and software. It has one of the best and biggest food courts in the area in the basement. A huge screen in the central atrium shows cartoons, opera and pop concerts.
- **Fortune Centre** Middle Road is a great place for alternative medicine.
- **Great World City** Zion Rd. *GV Grand Cinema* on the top floor, *Barang Barang* interiors, and several shoe and clothes shops.
- **Marina Square, Suntec City and Millenia Walk** A huge area of shops with a wide range of designer labels.
- **Parco Bugis Junction** This trendy, air-conditioned shophouse mall is on Victoria Street, north of the colonial core. It is packed with international names, as well as some quirky little shops and cafés.
- **Pidemco Centre** South Bridge Rd, Chinatown, for traditional jewellery.
- **Raffles City Complex** Opposite the Raffles Hotel, this huge, complex holds all the international labels - including *M&S*, *Body Shop*, *Nine West*, *Esprit* and *Knickerbox* and *Robinsons* Department store.
- **Sim Lim Tower and Sim Lim Square** Both these are on the edge of Little India on Jalan Besar and both sell electrical equipment. The difference is that Sim Lim tower, the older of the two, sells more technical equipment (GPS, electrical testers etc), whilst the Square is five floors of electrical goods from TVs to DVDs. Food court in the basement.
- **Suntec City** A handful of children's stores are here, including *Growing Fun* and *Oshkosh B'Gosh*, many designer label outlets, a wide choice of restaurants and a large food court looking onto the spectacular fountain (laser shows every 15 minutes, 2000-2200).

For details of shopping plazas on Orchard Road, see page 617

Sports goods

Plenty of branded goods, one of the most popular choices is the *Royal Sporting House* in many of the malls. The *Queensway Shopping centre* on Alexandra Road has a great selection of branded sports footwear at very competitive prices.

Tailoring

Quick, efficient and usually high-quality tailoring can be found in most shopping centres. The tailors in the main tourist shopping belt along Orchard and Scotts roads, notably *Far East Plaza* and *Lucky Plaza*, are as good a bet as any. You can design virtually what you want for yourself, but it is worth shopping around for the best deal. For more upmarket tailoring, hotel tailors are recommended.

Watches

A huge range of watches are available at duty-free prices in most shopping centres. Copy watches do not officially exist in Singapore, where most people prefer the real thing. The government frequently takes steps to eliminate the trade in copies now often taking a hard line against the purchaser as well as the trader.

Wet markets

The most accessible market of interest is the *Zhujiao (formerly KK) Market*, on the corner of Bukit Timah and Serangoon roads, at the southern end of Little India. It is a hive of activity and sells everything from flowers to fish and meat to spices, and every conceivable vegetable and fruit. There's also a good hawker centre here. An excellent Sunday market is on Seng Poh Road, Tiong Bahru, between Tiong Bahru and Outram Road MRT stations - worth taking in if you go to see the 'Singing Birds'. A good place to buy orchids is the small Holland Village wet market; it is much cheaper than the more touristy flower shops downtown and will pack them for shipment.

Health

The water in Singapore, most of which is pumped across the causeway from Johor, Malaysia, and treated in Singapore, is clean and safe to drink straight from the tap.

Medical facilities Singapore's medical facilities are amongst the best in the world. See the Yellow Pages for listing of public and private hospitals. **Gleneagles**, at the western end of Orchard Road, is probably the best place to go in an emergency. As well as a large A & E department, it has a 24-hour medical clinic, with a price list provided, for longer care. **Mount Elizabeth Hospital** also has a very good reputation. Most big hotels have their own doctor on 24-hour call. Other doctors are listed under 'Medical Practitioners' in the Yellow Pages. Pharmaceuticals are readily available over the counter and registered pharmacists work 0900-1800. The **Traveller's Health and Vaccination Clinic** at the Tan Tock Seng Hospital (Level 1, 11 Jalan Tan Tock Seng, T63572222, www.ttsh.gov.sg) provides specialist advice and treatment for travel-related illnesses and a vaccination service. Open 0800-1700 Mon-Fri, closed 1300-1400 for lunch, 0800-1100 Sat. It offers a walk-in service for vaccinations, but appointments must be made to consult a doctor (S$50.90 consultation fee).

Keeping in touch

Communications

Internet Singapore is one of the most wired and internet savvy places in the world, so there are loads of internet cafés. Internet cafés include: T2, Changi International Airport (Level 3). **Internet Shop**, 57B Pagoda St, above the Chinese pharmacy, Chinatown. **Winware LabsCafé**, 72 Dunlop St, Little India. **Cyber Planet91**, Bencoolen St. Dark games room, but also has fast Internet service. **Cyber Dome**, Orchard Plaza. **Chills Cafe**, 39 Stamford Road. **Internet Point**, 11 Stamford Rd, Capitol Building, open 0900-2330, S$3.50 per hour, fast connection. **Internet café** (no name), foodcourt in the Meridien Shopping Centre, S$4.80 per hour.

Post The main post office is the **Singapore Post Centre** at number 8, 10 Eunos Road (take Paya Lebar MRT), open 0900-2100, Mon-Fri, 0900-1800 Sat, and 0900-1600 Sun. There are 1,300 other postal outlets. Post Office opening hours are 0900-1700 Monday-Friday, 0900-1400 Saturday. A few open later. The Killiney Road branch (just off Orchard Road near Somerset MRT) opens 0900-2100 Monday-Saturday, 0900-1700 Sunday. Changi Airport (departure hall, terminal 2), 0800-2100 daily. Local **postal charges** start at 23¢ (20 g). International postal charges are 50¢ (postcard), 50¢ (aerogramme), S$1 (letter, 20 g). For the latest charges see www.singpost.com The Singapore Post Office provides four sizes of sturdy carton, called Postpacs, for sending parcels abroad. These can be bought cheaply at all post offices. Note: AirAsia and Tiger Airways flights can be booked and paid for at most post offices. There is a S$5 handling fee.

Telephone In public payphones the minimum charge is 10¢ for three minutes. Card phones are quite widespread – cards can be bought in all post offices as well as in supermarkets and newsagents, and come in units of S$5, S$10, S$20 and S$50.

Singapore has three **mobile phone** networks (CDMA, GSM900 and GSM1800), and three mobile phone providers (SingTel, M1 and Starhub). Access codes are: SingTel, 001; for M1, 002; and Starhub, 008. Temporary, pre-paid SIM cards can be bought from money changers, 7-Elevens, and many other stores, starting at S$15.

Singapore's IDD code is 65. For details on country codes, dial 162.

International calls can be made from most public phones; phones take 50¢ and S$1 coins or phonecards. International Phone Home Cards are available at all post offices and come in units of S$10 and S$20. The most widely available card is Singtel's Worldcard, but there are many other brands which often have cheaper IDD rates. Credit card phones are also available. IDD calls made from hotels are free of any surcharge.

Media

The two main media organisations, Singapore Press Holdings and Mediacorp merged their mass-market TV and free newspaper operations in late 2004, narrowing the choice for readers and viewers somewhat.

Newspapers and magazines The press is privately owned and legally free, but is carefully monitored and strictly controlled. It runs on Confucianist principles – respect for one's elders – which translates as unwavering support of the government. In the past, papers that were judged to have overstepped their mark, such as the former *Singapore Herald*, have been shut down. The *Straits Times* has been likened to Beijing's *People's Daily* for the degree to which it is a mouthpiece of the government.

The English language dailies are the *Straits Times* (and *Sunday Times*), which runs better foreign news pages than any other regional newspaper (http://straits times.asia1.com.sg/); the *Business Times* (http://business-times.asia1.com.sg/); and the *New Paper*, Singapore's very own tabloid (http://newpaper.asia1.com.sg/). The *Today* is a freebie.

Radio English language radio stations are easy listening **Gold** (90.5FM), **Class** (95FM) for yuppies, **Perfect Ten** (98.7FM) for teens, **NewsRadio** (93.8FM), and **Symphony** (92.4FM) with classical offerings. **Radio Singapore International** (6080KHZ shortwave) has English news broadcasts. In late 2004, Mediacorp was planning to relaunch **Lush** (99.5FM) with alternative musical genres including new age and acid jazz. The **International Channel** (96.3FM) caters to French, German and Japanese expats. The **BBC World Service** broadcasts 24 hours a day on 88.9FM. In addition to English language stations, there are also local Chinese, Indian and Malay language stations. These are listed on www.mediacorpradio.com/

Television English language channels are **Channel 5**, which shows imported shows from the US, movies and the homegrown (and dreadful) "Singapore Idol"; **Central** has arts-related and more edgier programmes in the evening and British comedies like *The Office*; and **Channel News Asia** is a 24-hour news channel on the CNN model. Many hotels receive **STARHUB** cable TV which shows *HBO, StarTV, MTV, Discovery, CNN, BBC* and *ESPN* among others. Programmes are listed in the daily newspapers.

Sights

The city's main attraction, particularly for Asian tourists, is its shopping. For air conditioned malls head to Orchard Road, while the more aromatic market bargaining experience can be found at stalls in Little India, Chinatown and Arab Street. The city state's colonial core stretches from the world famous Raffles hotel to stately government and court buildings near the river. The river itself is lined with restaurants, bars and leafy walkways. For fun day trips head north of the city for Jurong Bird Park, the zoo, the night safari and Japanese gardens. South, Sentosa Island is linked to the mainland by a cable car and offers beaches, an oceanarium, a fun park and a trapeze. » *For Sleeping, Eating and other listings, see pages 596-620.*

Colonial core

Situated to the north of the Singapore River, the colonial core is bordered to the northeast by Rochor Road and Rochor Canal Road, to the northwest by Selegie Road and Canning Hill, and to the southeast by the sea. The area is small enough to walk around – just. To walk from the Singapore Art Museum in the far northwest corner of this area to the mouth of the Singapore River shouldn't take more than 30 minutes. You may want to take a cab to get over to Fort Canning Park if it is a particularly hot and humid day.

The Padang

The Padang ('playing field' in Malay), the site of most big sporting and other events in Singapore – including the National Day parades – is at the centre of the colonial area. Many of the great events in Singapore's short history have been played out within sight or sound of the Padang. It was close to here that Stamford Raffles first set foot on the island on the morning of 28 January 1819, where the Japanese surrendered to Lord Louis Mountbatten on 12 September 1945, and where Lee Kuan Yew, the first Prime Minister of the city state, declared the country independent in 1959.

The Padang originally fronted on to the sea, but due to land reclamation now stands a kilometre inland. After the founding of Singapore in 1819, English and Indian troops were quartered here and the area was known as 'The Plain'. The name was only later changed to Padang. In 1942, when Singapore fell to the invading Japanese, all the European population of the colony were massed on the Padang before the troops were marched away to prisoner-of-war camps, some to camps in Malaya and Siam (where they helped to build the infamous Bridge over the River Kwai), others to Changi (see page 592). The **Cricket Club**, at the end of the Padang, was the focus of British activity. A sports pavilion was first constructed in 1850 and a larger Victorian clubhouse was built in 1884 with two levels, the upper level being the ladies' viewing gallery. The **Singapore Recreation Club** (the SRC) building, at the northern end of the Padang, has been built on the site of a former club built in 1883 by the Eurasian community, who were excluded from the Cricket Club. The newish building is a modern, green-glass affair with polished brown columns: a nouveau antidote to the venerable Cricket Club at the other end of the Padang. In 1963 the club lifted its membership restrictions and allowed anyone to join, and today fewer than a fifth of the members are Eurasian.

Use City Hall MRT for the Padang and Raffles City. For the Singapore Art Museum, History Museum (closed for renovations until 2006) or Fort Canning Park, use Dhoby Ghaut MRT

Flanking the Padang are the houses of justice and government: the domed **Supreme Court** (formerly the Hotel de l'Europe) and the City Hall. The neo-classical

City Hall, ⓘ *enter via the lower entrance at the front. Hearings usually start at 1000 and the public are allowed to sit at the back and hear cases in session,* was built with Indian convict labour for a trifling S$2m and was finished in 1929. The Japanese surrendered here to Lord Louis Mountbatten and on the same spot, Lee Kuan Yew declared Singapore's independence. Today it contains law courts – the overflow from the Supreme Court next door.

On the seaward side of the Padang from the City Hall is **Tan Kim Seng's Fountain**. Along the base the following words are inscribed: "This fountain is erected by the municipal commissioners in commemoration of Mr Tan Kim Seng's donation towards the cost of the Singapore Water Works". This tells only part of the story for the fountain is a remnant of pristine Singapore's filthy past. Mr Tan, a prosperous Straits Chinese, made a gift of S$13,000 in 1857 to finance the island's first municipal water works on the condition that the water be available to all, free of charge. At the time it was just beginning to be recognized that Singapore's appallingly high mortality rate – which was higher than the island's birth rate (only immigration kept the population growing) – was linked to dirty water. Unfortunately, the terms of Mr Tan's gift were not adhered to; indeed, some people question whether the money ever went on improving Singapore's water supply at all and instead suggest that it was, so to speak, syphoned off for some other nefarious purpose. Certainly, it was not for another 60 years that mortality rates declined significantly, especially among Singapore's Chinese, Indian and Malay communities. Perhaps the city fathers erected this fountain when their guilt got the better of them.

Esplanade and the river

Stretching right along the seafront, looking like a pair of giant metal durians, is the **Esplanade-Theatres on the Bay** ⓘ *www.esplanade.com; walk along the underground shopping centre of CityLink Mall (from City Hall MRT)*, the centre of Singapore's performing arts scene, completed in 2002. Within the durians there's a 1,800-seater concert hall, a 2,000-seat theatre, and various outdoor performing spaces and, of course, a shopping plaza.

Between High Street and Singapore River there are a number of architectural legacies of the colonial period: **Old Parliament House**, the **Victoria Theatre**, and **Empress Place**. It was in this area that the Temenggongs, the former Malay rulers of Singapore, built their kampong; the royal family was later persuaded to move out to Telok Blangah. The **Victoria Theatre** was originally built as the Town Hall in 1856, but was later adapted by Swan and Maclaren to celebrate Queen Victoria's jubilee, integrating a new hall (the Memorial Hall) and linking the two with a central clock tower. During the Japanese Occupation the clock, like those in other occupied countries, was set to Tokyo time. The buildings are still venues for Singapore's multi-cultural dance, drama and musical extravaganzas. The Victoria Concert Hall (the right-hand section of the building) is the home base of the Singapore Symphony Orchestra.

In front of the theatre is the original **bronze statue of Sir Thomas Stamford Raffles**, sculpted in bronze by Thomas Woolner in 1887. There is a story that the statue was saved from destruction at the hands of the invading Japanese by a cunning curator, who hid it away. It seems, however, that the truth is rather more banal: the colonnade previously surrounding the statue was destroyed during the fall of Singapore and the statue was removed to the National Museum for the duration of the Occupation. When Lee Kuan Yew first came to power in 1965, his Dutch economic adviser Dr Albert Winsemius told him to get rid of the Communists but to "let Raffles stand where he is today. Say publicly that you accept the heavy ties with the West because you will very much need them in your economic programme".

Old Parliament House, built in 1827, is the oldest government building in Singapore. Designed by George Coleman, it was originally intended as a residence for the wealthy Javanese merchant John Maxwell, who was appointed by his friend

Singapore centre

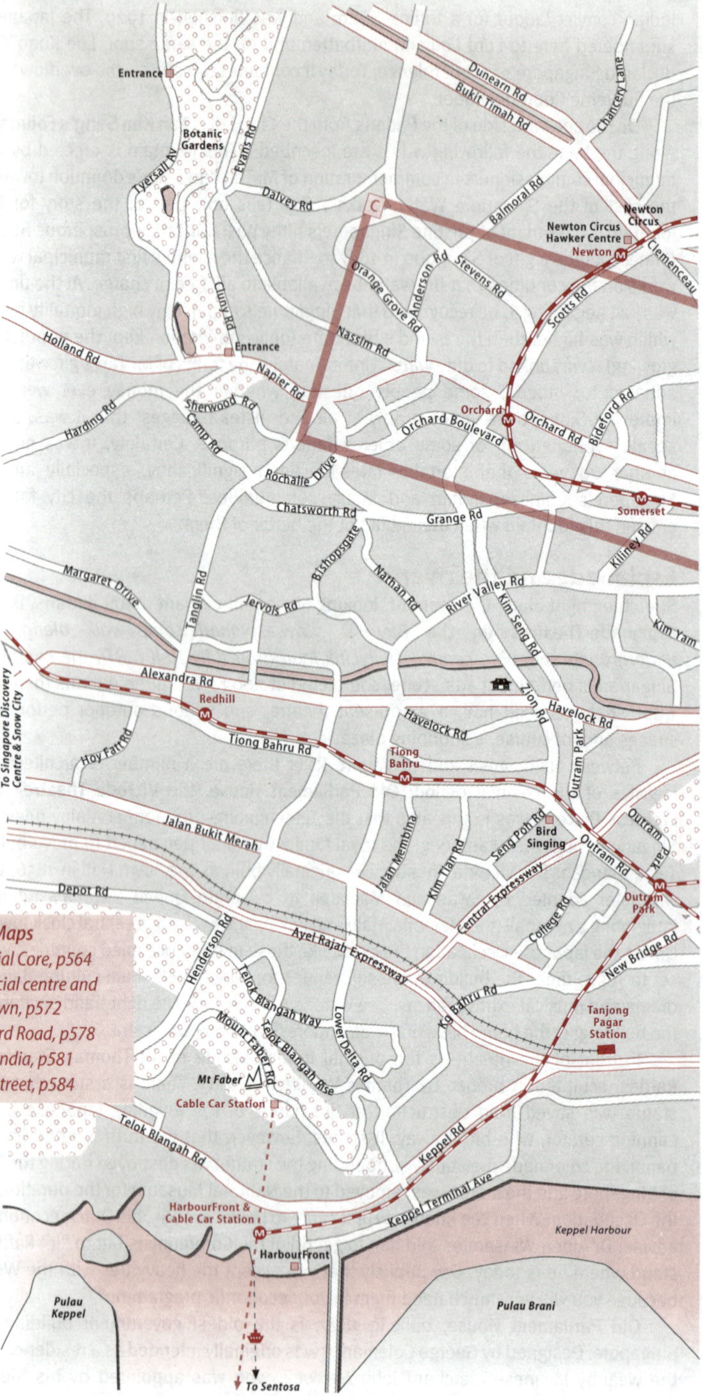

Detail Maps
A Colonial Core, p564
B Financial centre and Chinatown, p572
C Orchard Road, p578
D Little India, p581
E Arab Street, p584

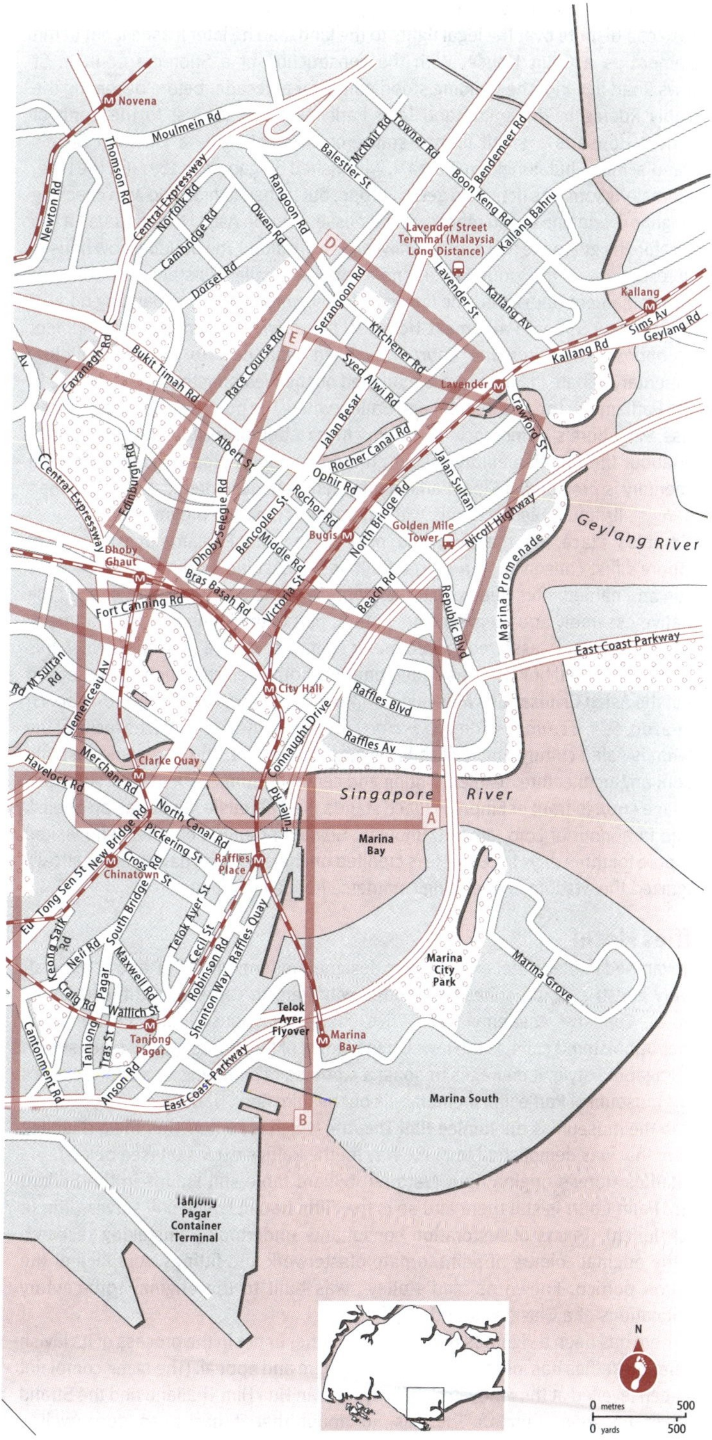
Novena
Moulmein Rd
Thomson Rd
Newton Rd
Central Expressway
Norfolk Rd
Cambridge Rd
Owen Rd
Rangoon Rd
Balestier St
McNair Rd
Towner Rd
Bendemeer Rd
Boon Keng Rd
Kallang Bahru
Lavender Street Terminal (Malaysia Long Distance)
Dorset Rd
Lavender St
Kallang Av
Kallang
Sims Av
Geylang Rd
Kallang Rd
Serangoon Rd
Kitchener Rd
Race Course Rd
Cavanagh Rd
Bukit Timah Rd
Syed Alwi Rd
Lavender
Crawford St
Jalan Besar
Rocher Canal Rd
Albert St
Edinburgh Rd
Ophir Rd
Jalan Sultan
Rochor Rd
Bencoolen St
Dhoby Selegie Rd
Middle Rd
Bugis
North Bridge Rd
Golden Mile Tower
Nicoll Highway
Geylang River
Marina Promenade
Dhoby Ghaut
Bras Basah Rd
Victoria St
Beach Rd
Fort Canning Rd
Republic Blvd
East Coast Parkway
Rd
M Sultan Rd
Clemenceau Av
City Hall
Raffles Blvd
Connaught Drive
Raffles Av
Merchant Rd
Clarke Quay
Havelock Rd
Singapore River
A
North Canal Rd
New Bridge Rd
Pickering St
Fullerton Rd
Marina Bay
Raffles Place
Chinatown
Cross St
Eu Tong Sen St
South Bridge Rd
Telok Ayer St
Cecil St
Raffles Quay
Keong Saik Rd
Neil Rd
Maxwell Rd
Robinson Rd
Marina City Park
Marina Grove
Craig Rd
Wallich St
Shenton Way
Telok Ayer Flyover
Marina Bay
Cantonment Rd
Tanjong Pagar
Tras St
Anson Rd
East Coast Parkway
Marina South
B
D
E
Tanjong Pagar Container Terminal
N
0 metres 500
0 yards 500

 Raffles as one of Singapore's first three magistrates. He never lived here, however, because of a dispute over the legal rights to the land, and he later leased it out to the government as a Court House. With the construction of a Supreme Court in St Andrews Road in 1939, the building stood empty for a decade, before becoming the Assembly Rooms in the 1950s and later Parliament House. Just to the north of Parliament House is a small bronze statue of an **elephant** – a gift from Siam's (Thailand's) King Chulalongkorn, Rama V, who visited Singapore in 1871. (At the time, King Chulalongkorn was itching to get to Europe, but he had to make do with checking out Singapore and one or two other colonial possessions in Asia. He had to wait a few years before he got to the real centre of *siwilai* – civilization.) The building now houses a Thai restaurant on the ground floor, and a small arts gallery upstairs.

Old Parliament House became too small to accommodate the expanding body of MPs and a new S$80m **Parliament House** ⓘ *the public entrance is on Parliament Place, opposite the Supreme Court*, has been built next to the old building. Parliamentary debate in Singapore is modelled on the Westminster system and, as in the Old Parliament, there is a Strangers' Gallery where the public – and visitors – can witness Singapore's democracy in action. In an attempt to educate Singapore's youth about their parliamentary system, there is a sound-proofed gallery where a commentary is provided, a Moot Parliament where schoolchildren can sharpen their debating skills and a History Corner with interactive computer programmes.

Empress Place, on the river and near to the Old Parliament, was one of Singapore's first conservation projects. Built as the East India Company courthouse in 1865 and named after Queen Victoria, Empress of the Empire, it later housed the legislative assembly and then became, in turn, part of the immigration department, the offices of other assorted government agencies, and a museum. Now this thoroughly confused building has undergone yet another reincarnation as the second wing of the **Asian Civilisations Museum**, ⓘ *Mon 1300-1900, Tue-Sun 0900-1900, Fri 0900-2100, S$5, free admission 1900-2100 Fri*. As its name suggests, the focus of the museum is Asian culture and civilization – 5,000 years of it. The 10 galleries explore religion, art, architecture, textiles, writing and ceramics from China to West Asia. See also page 566). In front of Empress Place stands the **Dalhousie Memorial**, an obelisk erected in honour of Lord James Dalhousie, Governor-General of India, who visited Singapore for three days in 1850. He is credited on the plaque as having emphatically recognized the wisdom of liberating commerce from all restraints.

Raffles Hotel

The revamped Raffles Hotel – with its 875 designer-uniformed staff (a ratio of two staff to every guest) and 104 suites (each fitted with Persian carpets), eight restaurants (and a Culinary Academy) and five bars, playhouse and custom-built, leather-upholstered cabs, is the jewel in the crown of Singapore's tourist industry. In true Singapore-style, it manages to boast a 5,000 sq m shopping arcade and there's even a museum of Rafflesian memorabilia on the third floor, ⓘ *daily 1000-1900, free*. Next to the museum is the **Jubilee Hall Theatre**, which is named after the old Jubilee Theatre that was demolished to make way for the Raffles extension (see below).

Raffles Hotel's original (but restored) billiard table still stands in the Billiard Room. Palm Court is still there and so is the Tiffin Room, which still serves tiffin (a snack/lunch). Teams of restoration consultants undertook painstaking research into the original colours of paint, ornate plasterwork and fittings. A replica of the cast-iron portico, known as 'cad's alley', was built to the original 19th-century specifications of a Glasgow foundry.

There has been a vigorous debate over whether or not in the process of its lavish restoration Raffles has lost some of its atmosphere and appeal. (The same complaint has been levelled at the renovated Railway Hotel in Hua Hin, Thailand and the Strand Hotel in Rangoon, Burma.) There is no doubt that it has been done well –

24 hours in Singapore

Breakfast at one of the streetside cafés or hawker centres along Orchard Road. After fueling, pick from a selection of Singapore's finest malls here to window shop, or spend money – Tanglin Shopping Mall is famous for Persian carpets, Forum has a giant toy store, while Palais Renaissance crackles with designer labels.

End your shopping spree with a gentle walk around the Botanic Gardens. Hop across the river to Chinatown for a tour of the city state's backbone Chinese community – there are traditional medicine shops, funeral stores and streets of shuttered traders' homes, now beautifully restored. On nearby Neil Road, you can enjoy a delicate Chinese brew at the Tea Chapter.

It's a few stops on the MRT line to Little India, whose muddle of streets are packed with astrologers, tailors, spice sellers, gaudy jewellers, stalls of sequinned fabrics, thumping Bollywood DVD stores and vendors of Hindu paraphernalia.

A few streets east and you are in the very un-Singapore market warren of Bugis Street – the place to buy pirated goods, bling bling, t-shirts and snacks.

As dusk falls head to the Singapore River, and enjoy dinner and a cocktail at one of the waterside restaurants.

Dinner does not spell the end of the night, however. Take a taxi to Singapore's Night Safari for a tour of the zoo in the dark – the lions will roar and the bats will flap.

The city has tried hard to pump life into its party scene, to some success. If you feel like dancing and you have the cash, head to *Zouk, Liquid* or *Centro* - all very cool clubs that attract international djs.

On your way home, chat to your taxi driver, who, in perfect Singlish will no doubt extol the virtues of his clean, ordered city.

architecturally it can hardly be faulted, and the lawns and courtyards are lush with foliage. There is also no doubt that it is an immensely comfortable and well-run hotel. But critics say they've tried a little too hard. The month after it reopened (on former Prime Minister Lee Kuan Yew's birthday, 16 September 1991), *Newsweek* said that in trying to roll a luxury hotel, a shopping mall and a national tourist attraction into one, "The result is synergy run amok ... great if you need a Hermes scarf, sad if you'd like to imagine a tiger beneath the billiard table."

Cathedrals and churches

South of Raffles lies **St Andrew's Cathedral,** ⓘ *there are several services a day in different languages (see the notice board in the northwest corner of the plot for times of service)*, designed by Colonel Ronald MacPherson and built in the 1850s by Indian (Tamil) convict labourers in early neo-gothic style. Its interior walls are coated with a plaster called Madras chunam, a decorative innovation devised by the Indian labourers to conceal the deficiencies of the building materials. The recipe for Madras chunam was egg white, egg shell, lime and a coarse sugar (called jaggery), mixed with coconut husks and water into a paste. Once the paste had hardened, it was polished to give a smooth surface, and moulded to give many of the buildings their ornate façades. Note the window commemorating Raffles as the founder of modern Singapore. The cathedral is often packed – 7% of Singapore's population over 15 are Christian.

Built in 1835 (the spire was added in 1850), the **Armenian Church of St Gregory the Illuminator** (the first monk of the Armenian church) on Hill Street is the island's oldest church and was designed by Irish architect George Coleman. This diminutive church seats 50 people at a squeeze. The design is said to have been influenced by London's St Martin-in-the-Fields and Cambridge's Round Church. The construction of the church was largely funded by Singapore's small Armenian community, although a number of non-Christian Asians also contributed. Agnes Joaquim is buried here – she discovered what is now the national flower of Singapore, the Vanda Miss Joaquim orchid. On the other side of the road from the church is a strange pagoda-roofed block – the **Singapore Chinese Chamber of Commerce & Industry** building. This rather

Colonial core

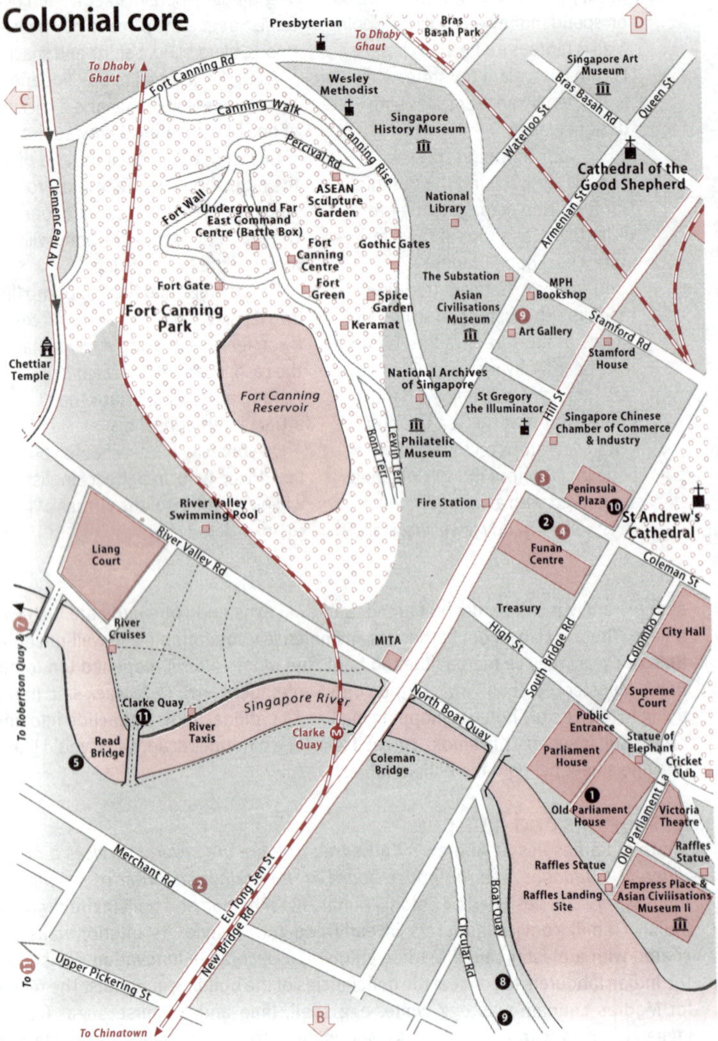

Sleeping
Conrad 1
Gallery 7
Grand Copthorne Waterfront 11
Grand Plaza 3
Mayfair City Boarding House 9
Metropole 10
Peninsula Excelsior 4
Raffles 5
Ritz-Carlton Millenia 6
Swissotel Merchant Court 2
Swissotel The Stamford 8

Eating
1827 1
Al Dente Trattoria 9
Annalakshmi 2
Bobby Rubinos 3
Bologna 4
Brewerkz 5
Bukhara 11

N
0 metres 100
0 yards 100

unhappy edifice was erected in 1964. Two stone lions imported from mainland China guard the entrance and the murals on either side of the gate are copies of similar murals in Beijing.

One of George Coleman's pupils, Denis McSwiney, designed the **Roman Catholic Cathedral of the Good Shepherd**, on the junction of Queen Street and Bras Basah Road. It was used as an emergency hospital during the Second World War. The building has been gazetted as a national monument, but still looks like it needs a lick of paint.

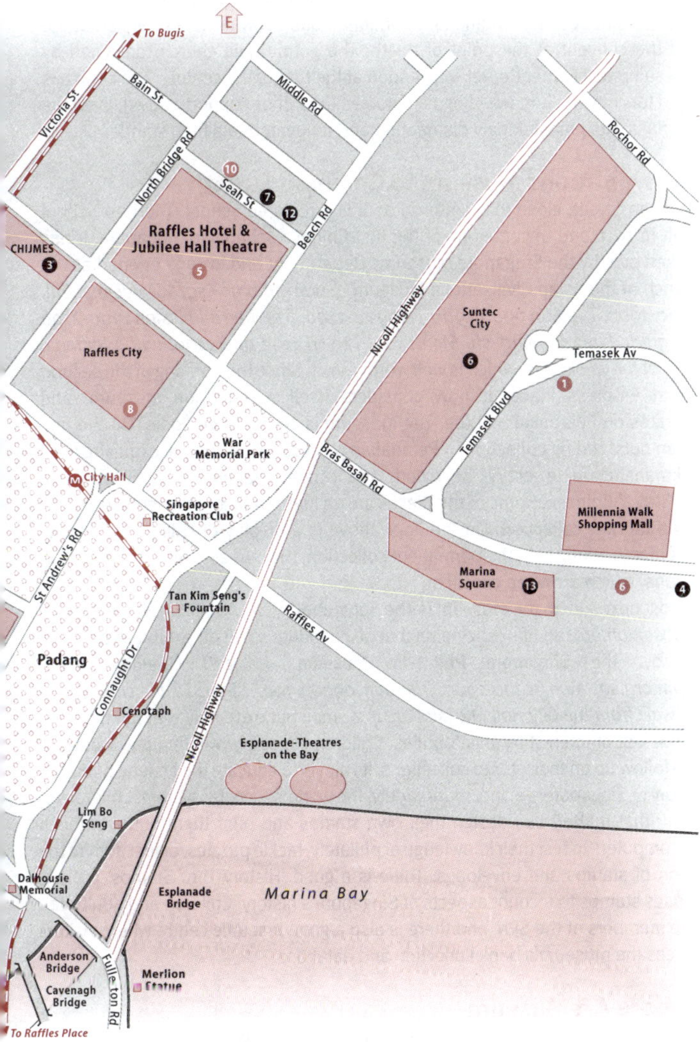

Café Iguana **5**
Chinese Feasts **6**
Ganges **10**
Gatsby **3**
Grappas **3**
Hai Tien Lo **13**
House of Sundanese Food **9**
Imperial Herbal **7**
Inle **10**
Kinara **8**
Komala's Fast Food **10**
La Cave **3**
Lei Garden **3**
Lotus **11**
Maison de Fontaine **3**
Moghul Mahal **11**
Moomba **9**
Ocho Tapas **3**
Riverside Indonesian **5**
Soup **12**
Sukhothai **9**

Route of Thaipusam procession

CHIJMES or the **Convent of Holy Infant Jesus**, opposite the Cathedral on Victoria Street, is a complex consisting of the convent, chapel and **Caldwell House** (designed by George Coleman). It has been redeveloped by a French architect into a sophisticated courtyard of handicraft shops – selling goods from Indonesia, Thailand, the Philippines, the Peranakan region, Mexico and Turkey! – as well as bars and restaurants including an Irish pub and a tapas garden. Originally, the convent was run by four French Catholic nuns, opening its doors to 14 fee paying pupils, nine boarders and 16 orphans in 1854. As well as being an orphanage and school for older girls, the convent became a home for abandoned babies, who were often left at the gates of the convent at the point of death. The gothic-style church, designed by French Jesuit priest Father Beurel, was added at the turn of the century. The church is now used for concerts and wedding ceremonies (and photo opportunities). Even the stained glass was painstakingly dismantled and renovated to a high standard.

Asian Civilisations Museum to Coleman Street

On Armenian Street, close to Stamford Road, is a restored school. Tao Nan School was built in 1910 and became one of the first Chinese schools in Singapore. It has been taken over by the Singapore Museums Department and in 1997 opened as the first branch of the Asian Civilisations Museum ⓘ *www.nhb.gov.sg/ACM/acm.shtml, Mon 1300-1900, Tue-Sun 0900-1900, Fri 0900-2100, S$3, free admission 1900-2100 Fri, free guided tours in English, Mon 1400, Tue-Fri 1100 and 1400, and additional 1530 tour at the weekends*, which is well worth a visit. Since the opening of the second branch at Empress Place, it now considers itself a 'boutique museum' and concentrates on Peranakan culture. The museum is set on three floors. On the first floor is an outstanding collection of Peranakan pieces, displaying the exquisite level of workmanship in jewellery, beadwork and ceramics achieved by Singapore's original 'Baba' Chinese. Some of the pieces are on loan, while the museum gradually builds up its own collection. On the floor above is a display of calligraphy and its accoutrements. Along with the permanent collection, the museum displays travelling exhibitions, which are often excellent.

Almost next door to the museum is **The Substation** ⓘ *45 Armenian St, T63377535, www.substation.org*, an offbeat cinema that also mounts small art exhibitions.

Nearby, the **Singapore Philatelic Museum** ⓘ *23B Coleman Street, www.spm.org.sg, Mon 1300-1900, Tue-Sun 0900-1900, S$3 (S$2 for children); a 10-min walk from the City Hall MRT station*, is a small but extremely well-run museum and is not just of interest to philatophiles. Children especially will find it a wonderful place to follow up on their stamp collections. Its aim is to educate the general public on the history of Singapore's – and, more widely, the world's – postal system. Children (or adults for that matter) can design their own stamps and print them out, use touch screen computers to test their knowledge of philately, tackle puzzles, or just admire the collection of stamps and envelopes. There is a good 'History Thru Stamps' Gallery, which uses stamps to recount aspects of Singapore's history. Children and adults can become members of the SPM and there is also a good resource centre where visitors can access the museum's book collection and database.

Singapore Art Museum

Bras Basah Road was so-called because wet rice – *bras basah* in Malay – was dried here on the banks of the Sungai Bras Basah (now Stamford Canal). The former Catholic boys school St Joseph's Institution, opposite the RC Cathedral at 71 Bras Basah Road, is another good example of colonial religious architecture. Built in 1867, it is now home to the **Singapore Art Museum** ⓘ *www.nhb.gov.sg/SAM, daily 1000-1900, Fri 1000-2100, S$3 adults, S$1.50 children and senior citizens, free on Fri 1800-2100; free guided tours at 1400 Mon, 1100 and 1400 Tue-Fri, and an additional tour at 1530 on Sat and Sun*, where there are travelling exhibitions every month or so, both modern and classical. The Singapore Art Museum's own collection is modest and, understandably, predominantly features Singaporean and Malaysian artists' work. There are always pieces from the collection on show providing an interesting insight into how Singaporean and Malaysian artists have selectively absorbed Western and Eastern influences. While St Joseph's was being renovated, a feature wall was discovered behind a row of built-in cupboards. Two supporting columns bear an entablature emblazoned with the words Santa Joseph Ora Pro Nobis (Saint Joseph pray for us) and it is presumed that the school chapel was located here.

Singapore History Museum

ⓘ *Mon 1300-1900, Tue-Sun 0900-1900, Fri 0900-2100, S$2, free after 1800 on Fri. During the week it is closed for two hours every morning and afternoon for school groups. At the time of writing the museum was closed for extensive redevelopment, which is not expected to be finished until 2006.*

Across the green on Stamford Road is this museum, which, until a few years ago, was the only national museum in Singapore. It promises to be twice the size when it eventually reopens. The idea of setting up a museum was first mooted by Stamford Raffles in 1823; it was finally built in 1887 and named the Raffles Museum. Some of the museum's exhibits are now on show at Riverside Point, 30 Merchant Rd, between Ord Bridge and Read Bridge on the Singapore River. The main showpiece is called Rivertales and it charts the history of island from the 14th century to modern day. The attached **Children's Gallery** has changing exhibits, full of hands-on activities, every six months. There is plenty of hands-on activity for children.

Fort Canning Park

Behind the Singapore History Museum is Fort Canning Park. The British called it Singapore Hill, but its history stretches back centuries earlier. It is known as Bukit Larangan, or Forbidden Hill, by the Malays, as this was the site of the ancient fortress of the Malay kings and reputedly contains the tomb of the last Malay ruler of the kingdom of Singapura, Sultan Iskandar Shah. Archaeological excavations in the area have uncovered remains from the days of the Majapahit Empire. It is thought that the palace was built in the early 14th century and then abandoned in 1396 in the wake of Siamese (Thai) and Majapahit (Javanese) attacks. Furthermore, when Raffles and his companions landed in 1819, it is said that Malay oral history still recalled the former 14th-century palace and its sultans and would not accompany the British up the hill for fear of the spirits. In a letter written to Sir William Marsden at the time of his first landing on Singapore, Raffles mentions the ruins of the Malay fortress. The name Canning Hill was given to this slight geological protuberance in the 1860s in honour of the first Viceroy of India, Viscount George Canning.

Over the last few years Canning Hill has evolved into something a little more ambitious than just a park. The **Battle Box**, ⓘ *1000-1800 daily, last admission 1700 S$8 (S$5 children). Dhoby Ghaut is the nearest MRT*, opened in 1997, is a museum contained within the bunker where General Percival directed the unsuccessful campaign against the invading Japanese in 1942. Visitors are first shown a 15-minute video recounting the events that led up to the capture of Singapore. They are then led into the Malaya Command headquarters – the Battle Box – where the events of the final historic day, 15 February 1942, are re-enacted. Visitors are given earphones and are then taken from the radio room, to the cipher rooms and on to the command room, before arriving at the bunker where Percival gathered his senior commanders for their final, fateful, meeting. It is very well done with a good commentary, figures and film. The bunker is also air conditioned, a big plus after the hot walk up. During the Second World War, though, it was stiflingly hot – air was inefficiently re-circulated in case of gas attack. There is also a small traditional museum and a souvenir shop.

Above the Battle Box are the **ruins of Fort Canning** – the Gothic gateway, derelict guardhouse and earthworks are all that remain of a fort which once covered 3 ha. There are now some 40 modern sculptures here. Below the sculpture garden to the south is the renovated **Fort Canning Centre** (built 1926), which is the home venue of Theatre Works and the Singapore Dance Theatre. In front of Fort Canning Centre is an old Christian cemetery – **Fort Green** – where the first settlers, including the architect George Coleman, are buried. The graves of these early settlers have been exhumed but the gravestones remain, embedded in the boundary wall. Along with George Coleman, there is a Russian and, unusually, a Chinese – for this was a Christian burial ground – and it may indicate an early convert to Christianity. While Sir Stamford Raffles may have lived here, he did not die here. He fell out with the East India Company, and died of a presumed brain tumour the day before his 45th birthday. His funeral in North London went unnoticed by London society, and it was only later that he was reburied in Westminster Abbey.

Chettiar Temple

ⓘ *Many Hindu temples close in the heat of the day, so are best seen before 1100 and after 1500.*

Below Canning Hill, on Clemenceau Avenue, is the Hindu **Chettiar Temple**, also known as the **Sri Thandayuthapani Temple**. The original temple on this site was built in the 19th century by wealthy Chettiar Indians (money lending caste). It has been superseded by a modern version, finished in 1984, and is dedicated to Lord Subramaniam (also known as Lord Muruga). The ceiling has 48 painted glass panels, angled to reflect sunset and sunrise. Its gopuram, the five-tiered entrance, aisles, columns and hall all sport rich sculptures depicting Hindu deities, carved by sculptors trained in Madras. This Hindu temple is the richest in Singapore – some argue, in all of Southeast Asia. It is here that the spectacular Kavadi procession of the Thaipusam festival culminates (see page 52).

Singapore River and the City

The mouth of the river is marked by the bizarre symbol of Singapore – the grotesque Merlion statue, half lion, half mermaid. The financial heart of the city is just south of here – tall towers cast shadows on streets which on weekdays are a frenzy of suited traders, bankers and office workers. The most pleasant area by far is along the river which offers peaceful walks along its banks. The riverside is punctuated with pockets of restaurants and bars making it a lively place at night.

Merlion

Standing guard at the mouth of the **Singapore River** – though rather dwarfed now by a new bridge – is the mythical **Merlion**, half-lion, half-fish, the grotesque saturnine symbol of Singapore. The statue was sculpted by local artist Lim Nang Seng in 1972 and stands in the miniscule **Merlion Park**, an unaccountably popular stop for tour groups, where there is a souvenir shop which is sometimes rather ambitiously billed a museum. The Merlion is best viewed from the Padang side of the river. It is inspired by the two ancient (Sanskrit) names for the island: Singa Pura meaning 'lion city', and Temasek meaning 'sea-town'. The confused creature is emblazoned on many a trinket and T-shirt. In a bizarre move, the 8.6 metre symbol was shifted 120 metres in 2002 to a finger of reclaimed land, still in the park, in front the The Fullerton Hotel. The relocation was the combined efforts of a barge, two 500-tonne lifting capacity cranes and a team of 20 engineers.

Directly behind the Merlion stands the imposing, recently converted, **Fullerton Hotel** (see page 597), in prime position, overlooking the mouth of the river, formerly the General Post Office. Until 1873 this site was occupied by Fullerton Fort, built to defend the Singapore River from seaborne attack. Fullerton Building was erected in 1925-28 by a firm of Shanghai-based architects. The heavy, almost Scottish, design seems a little out of place in tropical Singapore and, perhaps appropriately, the firm left the colony in the early 1930s after they had been struck off the architect's register for professional misconduct.

Cavenagh Bridge, erected in 1869 by convict labourers (the last big project undertaken by convicts here), was originally called Edinburgh Bridge to commemorate the visit of the Duke of Edinburgh. It was later renamed Cavenagh in honour of Governor WO Cavenagh, the last India-appointed governor of Singapore. The bridge was constructed from steel shipped out from Glasgow (supplied by the same company that furnished the Telok Ayer Market), and was built to provide a link between the government offices on the north side of the river and Commercial Square to the south. However, it was apparently built without a great deal of thought to the tides: tongkangs, the lighters that transferred cargo from ships to the godowns (warehouses) at Boat Quay, and vice versa, could not pass under the bridge at high tide and would have to wait for the water level to drop. It became a footbridge in 1909 when the Anderson Bridge superseded it, but it still bears its old sign that forbids bullock carts, horses and heavy vehicles from crossing.

One of the more striking buildings on the river, for its sheer size, is the headquarters of the **United Overseas Bank** (UOB) backing onto Chulia Street, which towers to the maximum permissible height of 280 m (to avoid collision with low-flying aircraft). The octagonal tower is said to represent a pile of coins, although this seems simply too crass to believe. Below, in the open under-court area, is a large bronze statue by **Salvador Dalí** entitled Homage to Newton, cast in 1985. A bronze statue of a squat bird, by **Fernando Botero**, sits on the waterfront, while behind the UOB, on Chulia Street and next to the OCBC Centre, is a giant reclining figure by Henry Moore.

Boat Quay

Along the south bank of the river, facing Empress Place, is Boat Quay – commercially speaking, one of the most successful restoration projects of the Urban Redevelopment Authority (URA). In the early 19th century this part of the river was swamp and the original roomah (rumah means house) rakits were rickety, stilted affairs, built over the mud. However, by the mid-1850s Boat Quay had emerged as the centre of Singapore River's commercial life, with three-quarters of the colony's trade being transferred through the godowns here. The opening of the Suez Canal in 1869 increased trade still further, but the development of the steamship around the same time threatened the commercial vitality of the area: vessels became too large to dock here. Merchants, worried that shipping companies would move their business to the new port of Tanjong Pagar which opened in 1852, began to use lighters, or tongkangs, to load and unload ships moored outside the river. Tongkangs, (lighters), barges and sampans once littered the river, but they were cleared out to Marina Bay, or destroyed and scuttled, as part of the government's river-cleaning programme over a period of 10 years during the 1990s. Singapore River is now said to be 'pollution-free' (although it only takes a quick glance to see that this is blatant rubbish), but what it gained in cleanliness it has lost – some would argue – in aesthetics.

Boat Quay has become, for tourists, one of the most popular places to eat or drink in Singapore.

With technological advances threatening to undermine Boat Quay's vitality, it is perplexing that the area's merchants didn't sell up and move on. One popular explanation is that the curve of the river made it look like the belly of a carp – a sure indicator of commercial success according to chinese folk wisdom. The wealthier the merchant the higher their godowns were constructed, giving the frontage an attractively uneven appearance. By the time the URA announced its conservation plans in 1986, Boat Quay had fallen on hard times. The original inhabitants were encouraged to leave, the shophouses and godowns were restored and renovated, and a new set of owners moved in. The strip now provides a great choice of drinking holes and restaurants for Singapore's upwardly mobile young, expats and tourists alike, although the area's hipness has faded in recent years and is predominantly patronised by tourists only.

Elgin Bridge marks the upriver end of Boat Quay. The bridge was built in 1929 to link the community of Chinese merchants settled on the south side of the river with the Indian traders of the High Street on the north side, and was named after Lord Elgin, Governor-General of India. It is, in fact, the fifth bridge to be built on this site. The first was constructed in 1819 and was the only bridge across the river at that time. Note the roundels depicting the Singapore lion, which are under a palm tree on the bases of each cast-iron lamp at either end of the bridge. They were designed by Cavalieri Rodolofo Nolli.

Clarke Quay

Further upriver, Clarke Quay has also been renovated and is lined with swanky shops, bas and restaurants which are particularly popular with the large expat crowd. This was once godown country – in colonial days, the streets around the warehouses would have been bustling with coolies. It is now a pleasant pedestrian area, with 150-odd shops, restaurants and bars. Clarke Quay has a slightly different feel to Boat Quay; while the latter consists of individual enterprises, the former is controlled by a single company that keeps close tabs on which shops and food outlets open. The atmosphere is more contrived, more managed and controlled. In the pedestrian lanes, overpriced hawker stalls and touristy knick-knack carts set up from lunchtime onwards, selling all manner of goods that people could do without. Despite this, it is still a lot of fun, especially at night, and unlike Boat Quay it is possible to snack from stalls while wandering the alleys of the area. It is also the site of Singapore's first bungy, the G-Max. Daredevils are strapped into a chair to be launched 60 metres in the air at 200km per hour. The screams can be heard from across the river! On Sundays there is a flea market here during daylight hours.

A good way of seeing the sights along Singapore River is on a **bumboat cruise**, which can be taken from Clarke Quay or Boat Quay. A rather banal recorded commentary points out the godowns, shophouses, government buildings and skyscrapers lining the river bank. ⓘ *Bumboats operate 0900-2300, S$12 (S$6 for children), 30 mins. A river taxi operates from here, S$1 (morning) and S$3 (afternoon).*

Riverside Point

Spanning the river at Clarke Quay is a pedestrian bridge, **Read Bridge**, erected in the 1880s and named after a famous businessman of the day. The antique lamps have been recently added to a structure which, when it was built, looked more modern than it does now. Read Bridge leads to **Riverside Point**, an arcade of upmarket shops and restaurants. The History Museum has set up a temporary base here while its main building is renovated. Across Merchant Road via an aerial walkway is yet another shopping centre-cum-restaurant complex – **Riverside Village** – with its component parts, **Merchant Square** and **Central Mall**. This was reputedly once a centre of prostitution and racketeering, which is hard to believe now that fornication and fraud have given way to fusion cuisine and fashion. At the northwest corner of the complex is the attractive **Tan Si Chong Su Temple**, which has successfully resisted attempts at modernization. The temple was built in 1876 as an ancestral temple and assembly hall of the Hokkien Tan clan. The money was donated by Tan Kim Cheng (1829-92) and Tan Beng Swee (1828-84), sons of the wealthy philanthropist Tan Tock Seng. The temple faces the Singapore River – as feng shui (geomancy) dictates – and it is particularly rich in carvings and other decoration. The series of two courtyards and two altar halls symbolizes li, the admired characteristic of humbling oneself in deference to others. The dragon-entwined columns, round windows and granite panels are comparatively unusual. Above the main altar table are four Chinese characters that translate as 'Help the world and the people'.

A little further south is **Clifford Pier**, which was built in the 1930s. It is possible to hire rather expensive boats here to cruise up and down the river and around Marina Bay. Bumboats and junks also take visitors on longer watery tours to Pulau Kusu and the islands of the south. It is possible to hire a bumboat yourself, but expect to pay around S$60 per hour.

Financial centre

ⓘ *Raffles Place MRT station is in the heart of the financial district, just south of the Singapore River. Buses 124 and174 run direct from Orchard Road. Tanjong Pagar is the nearest MRT stop to the Tanjong Pagar container terminal. It is best to explore this from Cavenagh Bridge near the mouth of the Singapore River to Clarke Quay takes about 20 minutes.*

Shenton Way (Singapore's equivalent of Wall Street), **Raffles Place**, **Robinson Road** and **Cecil Street**, all packed tight with skyscrapers, form the financial heart of modern Singapore. These streets contain most of the buildings that give the city its distinctive skyline, and it is best seen from the **Benjamin Sheares Bridge** or from the boat coming back from Batam Island. The first foreign institutions to arrive on the island still occupy the prime sites: the Hong Kong and Shanghai Banking Corporation and Standard Chartered Bank. A short walk away down Philip Street is the small **Wak Hai Cheng Bio Temple**, built in 1826, looking particularly diminutive against the buildings around it. The name means 'Guangdong [Canton] Province Calm Sea Temple' and the purpose is pretty clear: to ensure that Chinese immigrants making the voyage through the dangerous South China Seas arrived safely. The two key gods depicted here are Xuan Tien Shang Di (the Heavenly Father) in the right-hand hall and Tien Hou (the Heavenly Mother) in the left. Tien Hou (Tin Hau) is a particular favourite of sailors. The figures on the roof are extremely vivid and so is some of the carving inside.

Another piece of old Singapore amidst the new is the **Lau Pa Sat Festival Market**, once known as Telok Ayer, between Robinson Road and Raffles Quay. This was the first municipal market in Singapore. The first market here was commissioned by Stamford Raffles in 1822, but the present structure was designed by James MacRitchie and built in cast-iron shipped out from a foundry in Glasgow in 1894. (The same foundry cast the iron for Cavenagh Bridge.) It is said to be the last remaining Victorian cast-iron structure in Southeast Asia and was declared a national monument in 1973, but was dismantled in 1985 to make way for the MRT, before being rebuilt. It is now a thriving food centre.

Chinatown

The area known as Kreta Ayer encompasses Smith, Temple, Pagoda, Trengganu and Sago streets. This was the area that Raffles marked out for the Chinese kampong and it became the hub of the Chinese community, deriving its name from the ox-drawn carts that carried water to the area. Renovation by the URA has meant that these streets still retain their characteristic baroque-style shophouses, with weathered shutters and ornamentation.

History

After Raffles' initial foray to Singapore in 1819, he left the fledgling colony in the hands of Major Farquhar with instructions on how it should be developed. When Raffles returned for a shufti in October 1822, he was horrified to find his instructions being ignored and the city expanding in an alarmingly haphazard fashion. He promptly

Financial centre & Chinatown

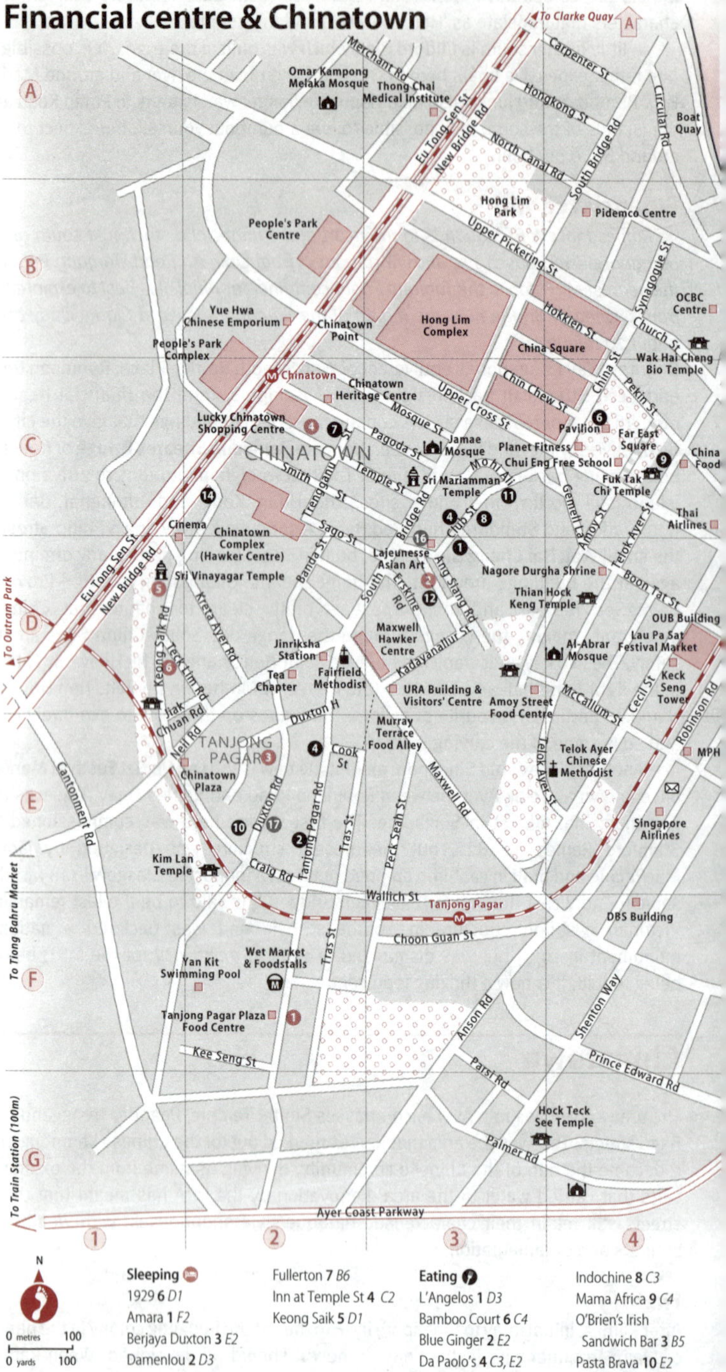

Sleeping
1929 **6** *D1*
Amara **1** *F2*
Berjaya Duxton **3** *E2*
Damenlou **2** *D3*
Fullerton **7** *B6*
Inn at Temple St **4** *C2*
Keong Saik **5** *D1*

Eating
L'Angelos **1** *D3*
Bamboo Court **6** *C4*
Blue Ginger **2** *E2*
Da Paolo's **4** *C3, E2*
Indochine **8** *C3*
Mama Africa **9** *C4*
O'Brien's Irish Sandwich Bar **3** *B5*
Pasta Brava **10** *E2*

countermanded Farquhar's plans and orders and established a committee with even more explicit instructions. The committee allocated an area to each ethnic group and the Chinese were awarded this slice of land, southwest of the river.

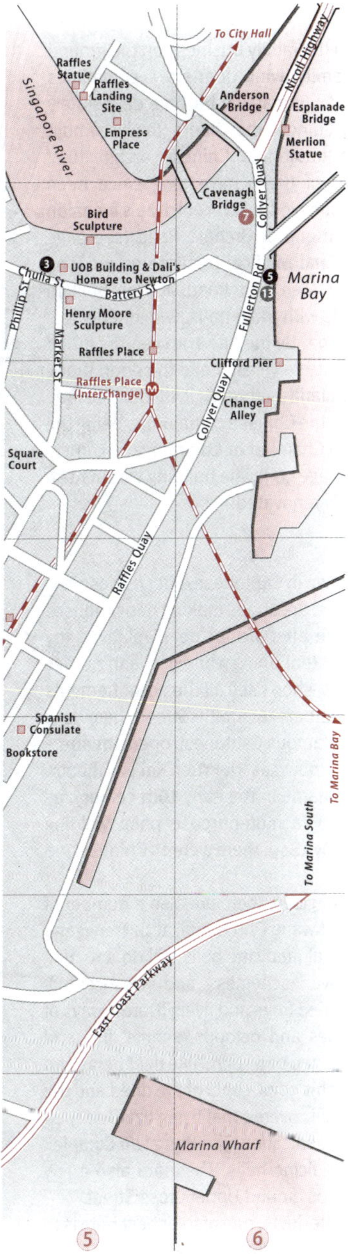

Pierside **5** *B6*
Senso **11** *C3*
Swee Kee **12** *D3*
Tiong Shiang **14** *C2*
Wan Tang Eating House **7** *C2*

Bars & clubs
Beaujolais Winebar **16** *D3*
Centro **13** *B6*
JJ Mahoney's **17** *E2*

Immigrants from China settled in Singapore in the latter half of the 19th century and recreated much of what they had left behind. Clan groups began migrating from the southern provinces of China to the Nang Yang or 'Southern Seas' in successive waves from the 17th century. By 1849 the Chinese population had reached 28,000, but the area they inhabited was largely confined to a settlement between Telok Ayer and Amoy streets. The greatest numbers migrated in the 40 years after 1870, mostly coming from the southeastern coastal provinces, with the Hokkiens forming the majority. Each dialect group established their own temple. The Hokkiens founded **Thian Hock Keng** in 1821, the Cantonese established **Fu Tak Chi** on Telok Ayer Street around the same time, as did the Teochews who built **Wak Hai Cheng Bio** on Philip Street. Streets, too, were occupied by different Chinese groups, with clubs and clan houses (*kongsi*) aiding family or regional ties. The *kongsi* were often affiliated with secret societies, (*tongs*), which controlled the gambling and prostitution industries and the drug trade.

Expansion of the financial district meant that Chinatown was being demolished so rapidly that by the time the authorities realized that tourists actually wanted to see its crumbling buildings, many of the streets had already been destroyed. In any case, Chinatown had become a slum, with overcrowding and poor sanitation being very real problems. A clean-up campaign was undertaken; its markets were cleared out, shops and stalls relocated, shophouses refurbished and the smells and noises of Chinatown banished to a world that only a few confused grandparents care to remember. Many residents have moved out to new, modern flats in HDB (Housing Development Board) estates scattered around the island. To preserve what was left of the city's architectural history, the Urban Redevelopment Authority (URA) was established in the 1970s to list old buildings and provide a framework for restoration and conservation.

Chinatown architecture

The typical Straits Chinese house accommodated the family business on the ground floor, leaving the second and third floors as family living quarters – sometimes accommodating two families (and in later years, as Chinatown became desperately overcrowded, up to five families). A few wealthy Chinese merchants (*towkays*) built their houses according to traditional Chinese architectural conventions, but almost all of these have long since been demolished. One which has survived is **Tan Yeok Nee's mansion** on Tank Road, at the eastern end of Orchard Road (see page 580). Another is the **Thong Chai Medical Institute** on Eu Tong Sen Street, at the corner of Merchant Road. It was built in southern Chinese palace style with three halls, two inner courts and ornamental gables, and was completed in 1892. By the late-19th century it had become a centre for traditional medicine, offering its services free to the poor; thong chai means 'benefit to all'. In 1911, during a malaria outbreak, it distributed free quinine. The building also became a focal point for the Chinese community, being the headquarters for the Chinese guilds. The Chinese Chamber of Commerce began life here (its headquarters are now on Hill Street, see page 564). The building was made a national monument in 1973 and has been expertly renovated.

Chinatown is served by its own MRT station on the north-east line. Buses 124, 143, 174 run through the area and 190 operates direct from Orchard Road.

Chinatown streets

In **Sago Street** (or 'death house alley' as it was known in Cantonese, after its hospices for the dying), **Temple Street** and **Smith Street**, there are shops making paper houses and cars, designed to improve the quality of the after-life for dead relatives (by burning the models after the funeral, it is believed that one's worldly wealth hurries after you into the next world). Also on these streets, shops sell all the accoutrements needed for a visit to a Chinese temple. At Number 36 Smith Street there is a three-storey building that was originally home to a famous Cantonese opera theatre – Lai Chun Yen – and formerly Smith Street was also known as 'Hei Yuen Kai', or Theatre Street. The English probably gave Sago Street its name in the early 19th century, as Singapore became a centre of high-quality sago (a muti-purpose palm yielding starch) production for export to India and Europe. By 1849, there were 15 Chinese and two European sago factories here.

Perhaps because death and health go hand-in-glove, there are also a number of **Chinese medicine shops** in this area – for example, Kwang Onn Herbal at 14 Trengganu Street and others on Sago Street. Chinese traditional medicine halls still do a roaring trade, despite the advantages of Medisave schemes and 21st-century pharmaceuticals. On show are antlers and horns, dried frogs and flying lizards, trays of mushrooms and fungi, baskets of dried seahorses and octopus, sharks' fins and ginseng. Presumably rarer, and because they are illegal, body parts like tiger penis and ground rhino horn are kept out of sight. Looking at this cornucopia of the dried and the pickled, it is easy to wonder how the Chinese ever discovered that flying lizard seeped in tea is good for athlete's foot. It shows enormous dedication. The **Hong Lim Complex** on **Upper Cross Street** has several more such medicine halls. There are also a few skilled Chinese calligraphers still working from shops around Upper Cross Street.

For anyone looking for a full range of Chinese products, one of their best bets is to visit the **Yue Hwa Chinese Emporium** on the corner of Eu Tong Sen and Upper Cross streets. Yue Hwa is an Aladdin's Cave of Chinese goodies, from silk camisoles, to herbal medicines, to beaded bags and Chinese tea. Just north of here, between Upper Pickering Street and North Canal Road, is a small area of green called **Hong Lim Park**.

Sri Mariamman Temple

As if to illustrate Singapore's reputation as a racial and religious melting-pot, the Hindu Sri Mariamman Temple is situated nearby at 244 South Bridge Road. There was a temple on this site as early as 1827, making it Singapore's oldest Hindu place of worship. Stamford Raffles is said to have granted the land to Narian Pillai, a Tamil who accompanied Raffles to Singapore during his second visit on board the *Indiana*, and set up Singapore's first brickworks. The basic layout of the present, gaudy Dravidian (South Indian) structure dates from 1843, although it has been much renovated and extended over the years. The temple shop is piled high with books on Hindu philosophy and cosmology and, unsurprisingly, is run by a Chinese family. The building is dedicated to Sri Mariamman, a manifestation of Siva's wife Parvati. (She is believed to be particularly good at curing epidemics and other major health scares, which at that time in Singapore were the norm rather than the exception.) The gopuram, or tower, here is particularly exuberant and the sacred cows seated along the top of the boundary wall add a rather pleasing bucolic touch to the affair. The temple is the site of the annual Thimithi festival, which takes place at the end of October or the beginning of November. Devotees cleanse their spirits by fasting beforehand and then show their purity of heart by walking over hot coals (see page 551). To the north of the temple, also on South Bridge Road, is the **Jamae Mosque**, built in 1826 by the Chulias from southern India. It harnesses an eclectic mix of Anglo-Indian, Chinese and Malay architecture.

Chinese temple-carvers still live on **Club Street**, which also has a number of *kongsi* along it. Many of the buildings along **Mosque Street** were originally stables. It was also home to Hakkas, who traded in second-hand paper and scrap metal – today it is better known for its Chinese restaurants. Number 37 Pagoda Street was one of the many coolie quarters in the area – home to Chinese immigrants, who lived in cramped conditions, sleeping in bunk spaces.

Also on Pagoda Street is the new **Chinatown Heritage Centre** ⓘ *www.chinatownheritage.com.sg/, Mon-Thu 0900-1800, Fri-Sun, 0900-2100, S$8.80, S$5.30 children*, which is well worth a visit. The centre evocatively captures the lives of early Chinese settlers with mock ups of boats, coffee houses, opium dens, and squalid housing through the ages including kitchens, bedrooms, and even a prostitute's boudoir. Everything is captured right down to the finest detail including fake cockroaches in the kitchens and soiled toilets. Electonic sensors which switch on swinging lamps and start taps make the experience a little creepy.

Telok Ayer Street

This street is full of shophouses and fascinating temples of different religions and was once one of the most important in Singapore. The city's oldest Chinese temple, the Taoist **Thian Hock Keng** Temple, or Temple of Heavenly Happiness, is a gem (notwithstanding the naff fibreglass wishing well in one corner). The temple is also very popular; the coaches lined up outside give the game away – but don't let this put you off. Telok Ayer Street was the perfect place for merchants and traders to establish themselves, as it was right on the seafront. (It also became notorious for its slave trade in the 1850s.) The temple was funded by a wealthy merchant of the same name and building commenced in 1839. Skilled craftsmen and materials were all imported from China, the cast-iron railings came from Glasgow and the decorative tiles from Holland. The building was modelled on 19th-century southern Chinese architectural traditions, with a grouping of pavilions around open courtyards, designed to comply with the dictates of geomancy (feng shui).

The main deity of the temple is Tien Hou (Tin Hau), the Goddess of Seafarers, and she is worshipped in the central hall. The image here was imported from China in the 1840s and the temple soon became a focal point for newly arrived Hokkien immigrants who would gather to thank Tien Hou for granting them a safe journey. In the left-hand hall there is an image of the Lord of Laws (Fa Zhu Gong), while in the right, is the Prince of Prominence, Zai Si Xian He. The ubiquitous Kuan Yin, the Goddess of Mercy, also makes an appearance. The temple's position on the waterfront quickly came to an end, in the 1880s, when one of Singapore's first land reclamation projects moved the shore several blocks east. Well worth a visit.

A little way north of Thian Hock Keng is another much smaller Chinese temple, the Fuk Tak Chai temple. This is situated in an area that has been gentrified and is now known as **Far East Square**. Within the square is a jumble of renovated shophouses, with bars and bistros and a handful of shops. The two buildings of interest here are the **Chui Eng Free School**, 131 Amoy Street, one of the first free schools in Singapore – although sadly only the façade remains – and the **Fuk Tak Chai Temple**, now a museum, ⓘ *76 Telok Ayer Street, daily 1000-2200, free*, one of the oldest of Singapore's temples, restored in 1998. Coolies arriving in Singapore made this their first stop, giving thanks for safe arrival. This modest but elegantly proportioned temple, with just one court and shrine room, was built in 1824 by the Hakkas and Cantonese. Telok Ayer means water bay in Malay; before land reclamation, this temple stood on the waterfront and was constantly under attack from processes of coastal erosion. It's a little oasis of calm amidst the frenetic life of the city and holds a limited display of exhibits, including some Peranakan jewellery, Chinese stone inscriptions, a pair of porcelain pillows, a model of a Chinese junk and an excellent 'diorama' of Telok Ayer Street, as it must have been in the mid-1850s. **The Pavilion**, also within the square, is on the site where Chinese opera was once performed and is now used as a centre for the performing arts.

The Al-Abrar Mosque, also on Telok Ayer Street, was built between 1850 and 1855 by Indian Muslims, who were also responsible for the fancy turrets of the **Nagore Durgha Shrine** – a little further up the street – which was built in 1829. Designated a national monument, the shrine is a blend of architectural styles – Palladian doors and Doric columns combined with more traditional Indian-Islamic touches like the perforated roof grilles...and then there are the fairy lights. An intriguing architectural sight is the **Telok Ayer Chinese Methodist Church**, 235 Telok Ayer Street. The church was built in 1924 and combines a mixture of Eastern and Western influences. There is a flat roof with a Chinese pavilion and a colonnaded ground floor. It is all rather odd. During the Second World War it was used as a refugee camp.

Tea Chapter

ⓘ *9 Neil Road, www.tea-chapter.com.sg/, daily 1100-2300.*

One of Chinatown's more interesting places to visit is the Tea Chapter where visitors are introduced to the intricacies of tea-tasting in elegant surroundings. Visitors are invited to remove their shoes (sometimes an aromatic experience in itself) and can choose either to sit in one of their special rooms or upstairs on the floor. Relaxing Chinese plink-plink music, muffled feet, a tiny cup of delicious Supreme Grade Dragon Well, Scarlet Robe or Green Iron Goddess of Mercy at your lips and the cool atmosphere (it's air conditioned upstairs) all add towards a soothing experience. As the brochure rather extravagantly puts it: "It is a mythical dream come true for those seeking solace from a harsh and unfeeling existence". This is a popular place for young Singaporeans to visit on a Sunday afternoon. There is also a range of teas available to buy in the shop.

Jinriksha Station

The white building on the corner of Tanjong Pagar and Neil Road was the Jinriksha Station, built in 1903, and now the *Dragontown Seafood Restaurant*. It served as the administration centre for the jinriksha pullers. Jinrickshas (rickshaws) arrived from Japan via Shanghai in the 1880s and soon became the most popular way to travel. By 1888 there were 1,800 in use, pulled by immigrants who lived in Sago and Banda streets. At the turn of the century, the fare for a 30-minute trip would have been 3 cents, 20 cents for an hour.

Row upon row of thrushes, merboks and sharmas sing their hearts out, in antique bamboo cages with ivory and porcelain fittings, hung from lines...

West and south of Chinatown

On Sunday mornings, bird lovers gather at the corner of **Tiong Bahru** and Seng Poh roads for **traditional bird singing competitions**, where row upon row of thrushes, merboks and sharmas sing their hearts out, in antique bamboo cages with ivory and porcelain fittings, hung from lines. The birds are fed on a carefully controlled diet to ensure the quality of their song. Owners place their younger birds next to more experienced songsters, to try to improve their voices and pick up new tunes. Birds start twittering at 0730 and are spent by 1000. On the opposite side of the road, there's a shop selling everything you need for your pet bird – including porcelain cage accoutrements. Come here early and combine a visit to hear the birds with breakfast in one of the traditional coffee shops nearby: fresh baked *roti* washed down with sweet black or milky coffee. If you walk on down Seng Poh Road you will come to a fabulous **wet market**; every conceivable vegetable, fruit, fish, meat, beancurd you could ever want to purchase is available here. ⓘ *MRT to Tiong Bahru or Outram Park, or the bus stops right opposite this spot – bus nos 16 (stop outside YMCA) and 33 (stop outside CJIMES).*

The domed **Railway Station** – apparently inspired by Helsinki's – opened in 1932 and was renovated in 1990, though you wouldn't know it. The design, with its rubber-covered walls and their images of rubber tappers, tin miners and other Malay scenes, was heralded when it opened. Also notable are the four fine Art Deco images on the front of the station depicting commerce, agriculture, industry and shipping – suitably industrious for the new, as well as the old, Singapore. The station is notable in another respect too: the building and the land are Malaysian, not Singaporean. This was contrived as part of the deal when Singapore left the Malaysian Federation in 1965 and Malaysia ended up controlling the KTM. The two countries have been wondering how to handle this oddity of history ever since. In August 1998, Singapore moved its immigration officials from the Tanjong Pagar station to new purpose-built facilities at Woodlands, near the causeway on the Straits of Johor. But Malaysia refused to do the same. They are still trying to sort out their differences.

Orchard Road and Botanic Gardens

Orchard Road is a long curl of air-conditioned malls, the spine of modern day Singapore and home to its national pastime – shopping. This glass-fronted materialism is nicely juxtaposed at its western edge with the Botanic Gardens, an elegant park planted with rubber trees, hundreds of orchids, and popular with joggers and stretching tai chi practitioners.

Ins and outs

There are 3 **MRT** stations on, or close to, Orchard Rd. Dhoby Ghaut MRT station lies at the eastern end of Orchard Rd, close to the northwest corner of the colonial core. The Somerset MRT stop is on Somerset Rd, which runs parallel to Orchard Rd. The

Orchard MRT station is at the intersection of Orchard Rd and Scotts Rd, towards the western end of the strip and close to the main concentration of hotels. A profusion of **bus** services run eastwards along Orchard Rd – at last count, some 20 in all. For routes west, walk 1 block south of Orchard Rd. To walk Orchard Road from end to end is quite a slog – from Dhoby Ghaut to the north-western end of Orchard Road past Scotts Road is around 2½ km. This is fine if you're taking it slowly, stopping off for brief respites in one of the many air-conditioned shopping arcades. Otherwise, consider hopping on a bus or taking the MRT.

Botanic Gardens and National Orchid Garden

ⓘ *T64719933, daily 0500-2400, free. A map can be acquired from the Ranger's office, 5 mins' walk into the garden. Lots of buses run past the Botanic Gardens including nos 7, 77, 105, 106, 123 and 174, alighting at the junction of Cluny and Napier roads, next to Gleneagles Hospital. Suitable for wheelchairs. T64717361 for further information.*

At the western end of Orchard Road are the Botanic Gardens, on Cluny Road, not far from Tanglin. The gardens contain almost 500,000 species of plants and trees from around the world in its 47 ha of landscaped parkland, primary jungle, lawns and lakes. In 1963 former Prime Minister Lee Kuan Yew launched the successful Garden City campaign and most of the trees lining Singapore's highways were supplied by the Botanic Gardens. The gardens now cater for the recreational needs of modern Singapore. Every morning and evening, the park fills with joggers and Tai Chi fanatics. During the day, wedding parties pose for pictures among the foliage. The bandstand in the centre of the gardens is used for live music performances at the weekends.

Orchard Road

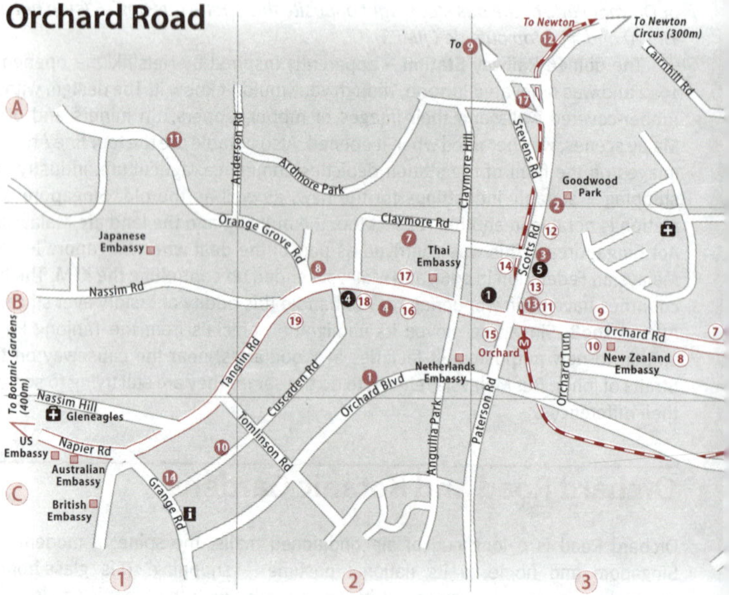

Sleeping
Four Seasons **1** *B2*
Goodwood Park **2** *A3*
Grand Hyatt **3** *B3*
Hilton **4** *B2*
Le Meridien **5** *B5*
Lloyd's Inn **6** *C5*
Meritus Negara **7** *B2*
Metropolitan YMCA **9** *A3*
Orchard **8** *B2*
Regent **10** *C1*
Shangri-La **11** *A1*
Sheraton Towers **12** *A3*
Singapore Marriott **13** *B3*
Traders **14** *C1*
VIP **17** *A3*
YMCA International House **15** *B6*
YWCA **16** *C6*

Eating
Blood Café **3** *B4*
Esmirada's **2** B5
Hard Rock Café **4** B2
Le Viet **5** *B3*
Les Amis **1** *B3*
Orchard Maharajah **6** B5

The Botanic Gardens were founded by an agri-horticultural society in 1859. In the early years they played an important role in fostering agricultural development in Singapore and Malaya, as successive directors collected, propagated and distributed plants with economic potential, the most famous of which was rubber. Henry Ridley, director of the gardens from 1888 to 1912, pioneered the planting of the Brazilian para rubber tree (*Hevea brasiliensis*). In 1877, 11 seedlings brought from Kew Gardens in London were planted in the Singapore gardens. An immediate descendant of one of the 11 originals is still alive in the Botanic Gardens today, near the main entrance. By the lake at the junction of Tyersall and Cluny roads, there is a memorial to Ridley on the site where the original trees were planted. Ridley was known as 'Mad Ridley' because of the proselytizing zeal with which he lobbied Malaya's former coffee planters to take up rubber instead.

The Botanic Gardens also house the **National Orchid Garden**, ⓘ *daily 0830-1900 daily, last ticket sales at 1800, admission S$5, S$1 children. The closest entrance to the Botanic Gardens for the Orchid Garden is on Tyersall Avenue*, where 700 species and 2,100 hybrids of Singapore's favourite flower are lovingly cultivated. It is billed as the 'Largest Orchid Showcase in the World'. The gardens began to breed orchids back in 1928 and those on show include Singapore's national flower, Miss Vanda Joaquim orchid, discovered in the late-19th century by the eponymous Miss Joaquim in her garden. The Mist House contains a collection of rare orchids, whilst the Yuen-Peng McNeice Bromeliad Collection houses 300 species and 500 hybrids from Central and South America.

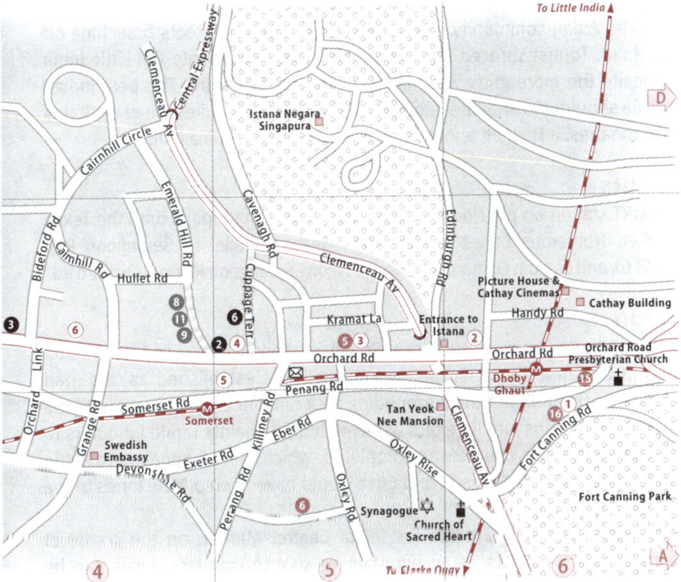

Sushi Tei **3** *B4*

Bars & clubs

Ice Cold Bar **8** *B4*

No 5 Emerald Hill **9** *B4*

Que Pasa Bar **11** *B4*

Shopping

Park Mall **1** *C6*

Plaza Singapura **2** *B6*

Meridien **3** *B5*

Centrepoint **4** *B5*

Specialists' Centre **5** *B5*

Heeren **6** *B4*

Paragon **7** *B4*

Ngee Ann City **8** *B3*

Lucky Plaza **9** *B3*

Wisma Atria **10** *B3*

Tang's **11** *B3*

Scotts **12** *B3*

Far East Plaza **13** *B3*

Shaw House **14** *B3*

Wheelock Place **15** *B3*

Hilton Shopping Plaza **16** *B2*

Palais Renaissance **17** *B2*

Forum **18** *B2*

Tanglin **19** *B2*

Emerald Hill, Dhoby Ghaut and Goodwood Park

Emerald Hill was laid out by 30 different owners between 1901 and 1925; conforming to the established theme was considered good manners, which has resulted in a charming street of Peranakan (Straits Chinese) shophouses. These have been carefully restored to their original condition and combine European and Chinese architectural elements.

At the end of Orchard Road is Dhoby Ghaut, which got its name from the Bengali and Madrasi dhobis who used to wash the clothes of local residents in the stream which ran down the side of Orchard Road and dry them on the land now occupied by the YMCA. Ghaut is a Hindi word meaning landing place or path down to a river, while dhoby is from the Sanskrit word dhona, meaning to wash. The dhobis would walk from house to house collecting their clients' washing, noting each piece down in a little book using a series of marks (they were illiterate). Dhoby Ghaut MRT is now an interchange linking the northeast with City Hall. A mess of construction works still surrounds the station as part of the MRT's Circle Line project.

Apart from Raffles, this is the only other colonial hotel in Singapore. It has had a chequered history, beginning life in 1856 as the German Recreation Club, the *Teutonia*. During the First World War it was declared enemy property and was seized by the government. In 1929 it was converted into a hotel, but then during the Second World War it was occupied by the Japanese. After the war it became a War Crimes Trial Court and did not resume functioning as a hotel until 1947.

Little India

The city's South Asian community has its roots in the grid of streets branching off Serangoon Road. Tourist-spruced handicraft shops are packed into the Little India Arcade opposite the more gritty wet market of the Tekka Centre. The best Indian restaurants lie shoulder to shoulder along Race Course Road, while a bit of exploring will unearth theatres, a Bengali temple and a hand-operated spice mill.

Ins and outs

Little India **MRT** station on the North-East line has an exit that opens onto the Tekka Centre market. Numerous buses run up Jalan Besar (parallel to Serangoon Rd), including nos 64 and 65 from Orchard Rd, 139 runs along Serangoon Rd from Orchard Rd.

Serangoon Road

Serangoon Road was named after the Rongong stork which used to inhabit swampland in the area. By 1828, Serangoon Road was established as 'the road leading across the island', but the surrounding area remained swampland until the 1920s when its brick kilns and lime pits attracted Indian (mainly Tamil) labourers to the area. In 1840 the race course was completed, which drew Europeans to settle here. (The road names Cuff, Dickson and Clive would have been private lanes to the European residences.)

Wet markets The lively **Zhujiao** (or Tekka Centre) **Market**, on the corner of Buffalo and Serangoon roads, is an entertaining spot to wander. Spices can be ground to your own requirements. Upstairs there is a maze of shops and stalls; the wet market is beyond the hawker centre, travelling west along Buffalo Road. New legislation introduced in 1993, which ruled that no animals could be slaughtered on wet market premises, saw the end of the chicken-plucking machine. It used to do the job in 12.4 seconds.

Kandang Kerbau – Malay for corral – was the centre of Singapore's cattle-rearing area in the 1870s. The cattle trade was dominated by Indians and among them was IR Belilios, a Venetian Jew from Calcutta who gave his name to a

Little India

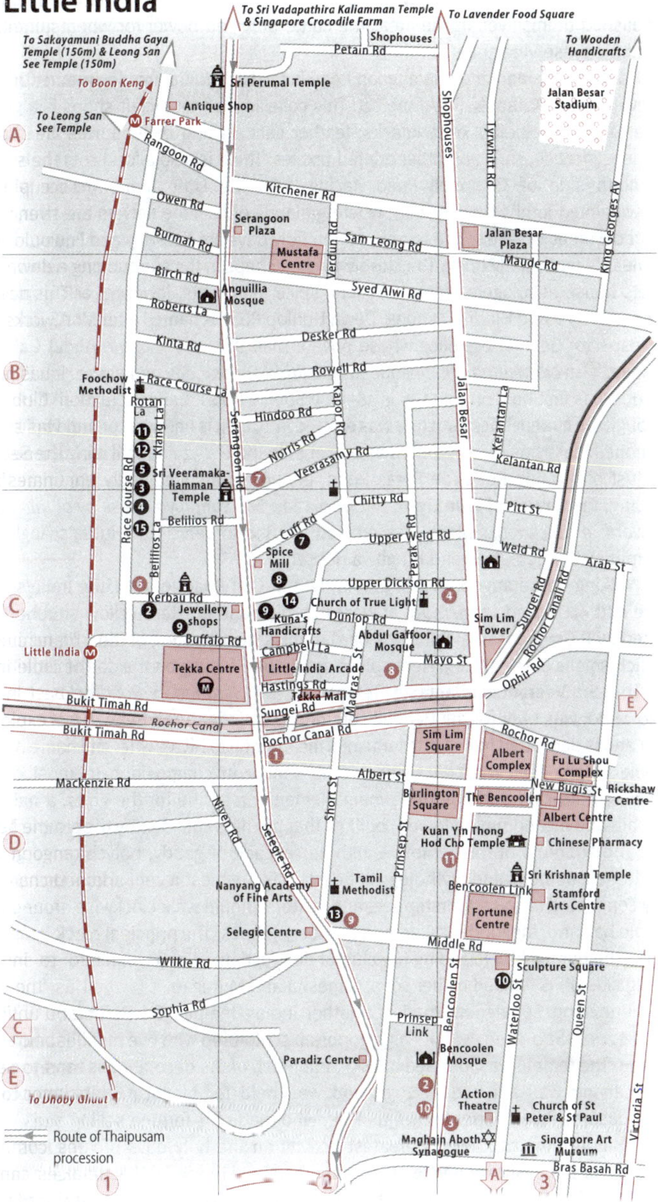

N

0 metres 100

0 yards 100

Sleeping

Albert Court & restaurants **1** *D2*

Bencoolen **2** *E2*

City Bayview **3** *E3*

Dickson Court **4** *C3*

Hotel 81 **10** *E2*

Kerbau **6** *C1*

Little India Guesthouse **7** *B2*

Perak Lodge **8** *C2*

Summer View **11** *D3*

Sun Sun **9** *D2*

Eating

Andhra Curry **2** *C1*

Banana Leaf Apolo **3** *C1*

D'Deli **4** *C1*

Delhi **5** *B1*

Jaggi's **15** *C1*

Kamal's Vegetarian **7** *C2*

Komala's Fast Food **8** *C2*

Komala Vilas **9** *C1, C2*

La Fête du Cuisinier **10** *E3*

Muthu's Curry **11** *B1*

Our Makan Shop **12** *B1*

Rocher Beancurd **13** *D2*

Woodlands **14** *C2*

road nearby. The roads around Zhujiao have names connected to the trade: Lembu (cow) Road and Buffalo Road. With the boom in the cattle trade, related activities established themselves in the area; the cattle provided power for wheat-grinding, pineapple preserving and so on.

Opposite the market on Serangoon Road is the **Little India Arcade**, another Urban Redevelopment Authority (URA) project. This collection of handicraft shops is a great place to pick up Indian knick-knacks: leather sandals and bags, spices and curry powders, incense, saris and other printed textiles. There is also a food court here. On the north side of Campbell Road, facing onto the Little India Arcade is the yellow-painted Jothi's Flower Shop, where garlands of jasmine flowers are strung for Hindu devotees to take to the temple. Hindu holy days are Tuesday and Friday, when business is particularly brisk. The closely-packed shops in the surrounding network of streets house astrologers, framers, tailors, spice merchants, jewellers and pumping Bollywood DVD and Hindi CD shops. Down Dunlop Road – named after Mr AE Dunlop, the Inspector General of Police whose private road this was – is the **Abdul Gaffoor Mosque,** ⓘ *avoid visiting the mosque during Friday prayer day and in the evenings*. A mosque was first built on this site in 1859 by Sheikh Abdul Gaffoor bin Shaikh Hyder, although the current brick structure was erected in 1910. It is hardly a splendid building, but nonetheless has been gazetted as one of Singapore's 32 national monuments.

Just off Dunlop Road, on Perak Road, is another architecturally unremarkable building, the **Church of True Light**, ⓘ *0900-1300 Sat-Sun; if you pass by at this time it's worth a quick look*, which was erected in 1850 to serve Little India's Anglican community of Hock Chew and Hinghwa descent.

Walking up Serangoon Road, take a right at Cuff Road to see Little India's last **spice mill** ⓘ *Closed 1300-1400*, at work in a blue and mustard yellow shophouse, owned by P Govindasamai Pillai. It's hard to miss the chugging of the mill, let alone the rich smells of the spices. Here spices are ground for use on the day of cooking.

The **Sri Veeramaka-liamman Temple** ⓘ *on Serangoon Road, closed daily 1230-1600*, was built for the Bengali community by indentured Bengali labourers in 1881 and is dedicated to Kali, the ferocious incarnation of Siva's wife. The name of the temple means 'Kali the courageous'. It is similar in composition to most other temples of its kind and has three main elements: a shrine for the gods, a hall for worship and a goporum (or tower), built so that pilgrims can identify the temple from afar. The goporum of this temple – with its cascade of gaudy, polychromed gods, goddesses, demons and mythological beasts – is the most recent addition and was only completed in 1987. Worshippers and visitors should walk clockwise around the temple hall and, for good luck, an odd number of times. The principal black image of Kali in the temple hall (clasping her club of destruction – not a woman to get on the wrong side of) is flanked by her sons, Ganesha and Murugan.

Further up Serangoon Road is another Indian temple, **Sri Perumal**, ⓘ *daily 0630-1200, 1800-2100*, with its high goporum sculptured with five manifestations of Vishnu. The temple was founded in 1855, but much of the decoration is more recent. This carving was finished in 1979 and was paid for by local philanthropist P Govindasamy Pillai, better known as PGP, who made his fortune selling saris. Like other Hindu temples, there is greatest activity on the holy days of Tuesdays and Fridays. For the best experience of all, come here and to the Sri Veeramakaliamman and Hindu Chettiars (see page 582) temples during the two-day festival of **Thaipusam** – generally held in January (see page 52) – which celebrates the birthday of Murugan, one of Kali's sons.

Sakayamuni Buddha Gaya Temple

ⓘ *Daily 0730-1645; remove shoes before entering.*

Further north at 366 Race Course Road (parallel to Serangoon Road) is the Buddhist Sakayamuni Buddha Gaya Temple – or Temple of One Thousand Lights – dominated by a 15 m-high, 300 tonne, rather crude, statue of the Buddha surrounded by 987 lights (the lights are turned on if you make a donation). The image is represented in the attitude of subduing Mara – the right hand touches the ground, calling the Earth Goddess to witness the historic Buddha's resistance of the attempts by Mara to tempt him with her naked dancing daughters. At the back of the principal image is a smaller reclining Buddha. Devotees come here to worship the branch of the sacred Bodhi tree – under which the Buddha gained enlightenment – and a replica mother-of-pearl footprint of the Buddha showing the 108 auspicious signs of the Enlightened One. Across the road is the Chinese Mahayana Buddhist **Leong San See Temple** – or Dragon Mountain Temple – with its carved entrance (where you don't have to remove your shoes). It is dedicated to Kuan Yin (the goddess of mercy) who had 18 hands, which are said to symbolize her boundless mercy and compassion. The principal image on the altar shows her modelled, as usual, in white, surrounded by a mixed bag of Chinese Mahayana folk gods and Theravada images of the Buddha.

Arab Street

The smallest of Singapore's ethnic quarters, Arab Street is a pedestrianised tourist market strip with shops hawking all manner of Middle Eastern and Islamic goods - prayer rugs, Egyptian perfume bottles, baskets, rattan, silk, velvets and jewellery. There are also great Middle Eastern canteens and the imposing golden-domed Sultan Mosque. Remember to dress modestly.

History

Originally this area was a thriving Arab village known as Kampong Glam (Glam Village). There is some disagreement over the origins of this name. Some commentators have attributed it to the Gelam tribe of sea-gypsies who once lived in the area. More likely, it refers to the glam tree from which Bugis seafarers extracted resin to caulk their ships.

Bugis MRT station, near SW edge of Arab Street. No 7 is the only bus direct from Orchard Rd with stops along Victoria Street.

Singapore's Arabs were among the area's earliest settlers, the first being a wealthy merchant called Syed Mohammad bin Harum Al-Junied who arrived in 1819, a couple of months after Stamford Raffles. The Alkaffs were another important local Arab family, who built their ostentatious mansion on Mount Faber. Arab merchants began settling in the area around Arab Street in the mid-19th century.

Mosques

0900-1300, 1400-1600. Visitors in shorts, short skirts or sleeveless T-shirts will not be permitted to enter.

The **Sultan Mosque** with its golden domes, on North Bridge Road, attracts thousands of the faithful every Friday. Completed in 1928 and designed by colonial architect Denis Santry of Swan & Maclaren, it is an eclectic mixture of classical, Moorish and Persian. The original building, constructed in the 1820s, was part of a deal between the Temenggong of Johor and the East India Company, in which the company donated S$3,000 towards its construction and the Temenggong leased the land to the trustees of the mosque. Next door is the old **Kampong Glam Istana**, built in the early 1840s as the Temenggong Ali Iskander Shah's palace.

Stalls and shops

In the maze of side streets around the Sultan Mosque, there is a colourful jumble of Malay, Indonesian and Middle Eastern merchandise. Excellent selections of batik (which is sold in sarong lengths of just over 2 m) jostle for space with silk and Indian textiles (especially along Arab Street), wickerware, jewellery, perfumes and religious paraphernalia. In the weeks before Hari Raya Puasa, which marks the end of the fasting month of Ramadan (see page 54), Bussorah Street is lined with stalls selling all kinds of traditional muslim and Malay foods – after dark it is a favourite haunt of famished Muslims. Bussorah Street has been gentrified as part of the URA's redevelopment efforts: it is now a pedestrianized, tree-lined street of elegant shophouses. Tombstone-makers are based along Pahang Street.

Bugis Street

Bugis Street is southwest of Arab Street, right across the road from the Bugis Street MRT station. It is packed with stalls selling cheap T-shirts, copy watches and handicrafts – like a street market you might see in Thailand or Malaysia, but something that seems rather out of place in modern day Singapore. For those who like to see Singapore not just as a giant shopping plaza but also as a real life experiment in ersatz existence, then Bugis Street offers more than keyrings and Oriental flim-flam. The whole street has been re-created from a road that was demolished to make way for the MRT in the mid-1980s. Some people maintain that the reason it was demolished, and then brought back from the dead, sums up Singapore's approach to life. On the opposite side of Victoria Street is the new **Parco Bugis Centre**, a high-tech shopping plaza (in reconstructed air-conditioned shophouses) bustling with life, and containing restaurants, shopping malls and one of Singapore's fabulous fountains.

Temples

Waterloo Street, much of which has been pedestrianized, cuts across New Bugis Street and is also worth a modest detour. The **Sri Krishnan Temple** at 152 Waterloo

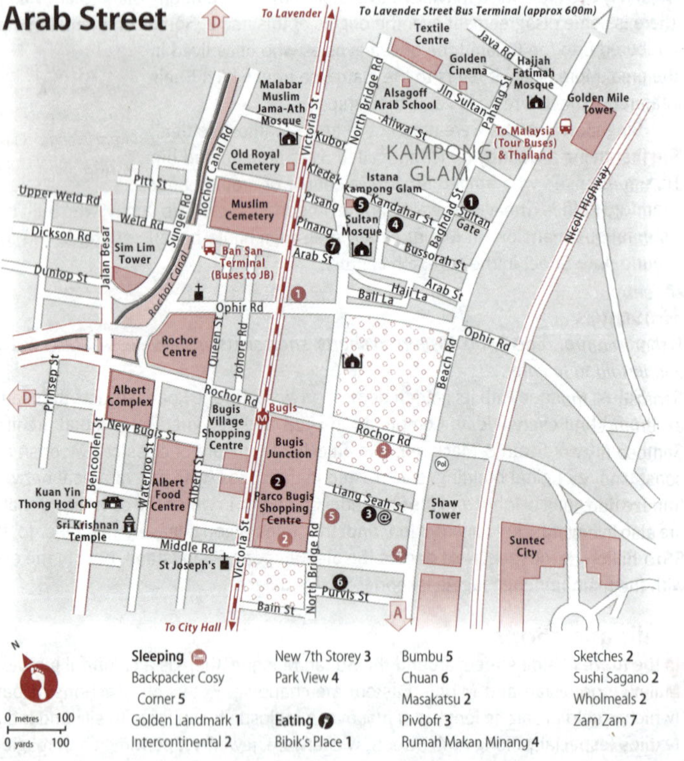

Street dates back to the 1870s, when a simple attap hut protected two Hindu images (Krishna didn't arrive until the 1880s). Over the years it has been expanded and refined as the Hindu population of the surrounding area has prospered. Almost next door is a large, modern Mahayana pagoda, dedicated to **Kuan Yin** – the **Kuan Yin Thong Hod Cho Temple**. This temple is particularly popular – try visiting around lunchtime (1200-1300) when scores of worshippers come here to pray for good fortune. The central image is of multi-limbed Kuan Yin, while on either side are Ta Ma Tan Shith and Hua Tua. The latter was an important Han Dynasty figure (third century BC) who is now the patron saint of Chinese medics.

Perhaps not coincidentally, on the other side of the street in Cheng Yan Court is a collection of **traditional Chinese pharmacies**, selling the usual range of dried fungi, antlers, bones, herbs, roots like ginseng, dessicated sea horses and other unidentified body parts.

HarbourFront and Sentosa

To the west of Tanjong Pagar port (see page 569), on Keppel Road, is HarbourFront (formerly the World Trade Centre). Most people visit the centre either to get to Sentosa, to take the boat to Batam and Bintan islands in Indonesia's Riau Archipelago (see page 541), or to use the cable car which connects Sentosa with Mount Faber.

All visitors get an excellent map of the sites and modes of transport.

Opposite HarbourFront's exhibition halls lies the **Telok Blangah Johor State Mosque**, dating from the 1840s. It was the focal point of the pre-Raffles Malay royalty in Singapore. Nearby is the tomb of the Temenggong Abdul Rahman (the Tanah Kubor Rajah or Tanah Kubor Temenggong), who was partly responsible for negotiating Singapore's status as a trading post with Stamford Raffles. The Johor royal family lived at Telok Blangah until 1855, when the town of Iskandar Putri was founded on the other side of the straits; it was renamed Johor Bahru in 1866.

Sentosa Island

ⓘ *Daily 0900-2100. Many attractions close before 2100 – many at 1800 or 1900. Basic admission is S$2, but there is a charge for each attraction. There are various combination tickets that include admission to Sentosa and to selected attractions. It is slightly cheaper to buy tickets this way at HarbourFront or on Mount Faber at the cable car entrance, rather than purchasing tickets at individual attractions after arrival (see each entry for admission charges). The disadvantage of purchasing tickets in this way is that it commits you before seeing what is on offer. Some combination tickets also tie you in to a tour. Apart from battling with the hordes of people, another downside to Sentosa is that a day here tends to be an expensive, as well as an entertaining, experience. A family of four can easily get through S$200.*

Sentosa is a tourist resort island with a three beaches stretching along its southern coast and various ersatz activities including a man-made volcano, a pizza and trapeze ride, lazer-lit merlion statue, an oceanarium, and World War II museum. There are also five-star resorts and a couple of golf courses. The government has launched a S$10 billion development plan for the island that includes building a monorail link with the mainland, private housing, and a tourism academy.

The word bogey is said to be derived from bugis, and was first used in 1836 as another term for the devil. Thackeray wrote: "The people are all naughty and bogey carries them off". In 1865 the word was bastardized once more into bugbear, a hobgoblin reputed to devour naughty children.

Ins and outs **Tandems** and **trishaws** are for hire from the ferry terminal and near Palawan Beach, open 1000-1800. For cycling enthusiasts, there is a 6 km **cycle track** around the island. The Sentosa **bus** operates from the HarbourFront Bus Terminal to Sentosa from 0700-2300 Sun-Thu, 0700-0030 Fri and Sat. HarbourFront has its own MRT station. Ticket costs S$3 (includes S$2 Sentosa entrance fee).

On Sentosa, there are six **free buses** and the **monorail**. The blue line (from 0700-2300 Sun-Thu, until 0030 on Fri and Sat) does a loop from the Visitor Arrival Centre past the Merlion to Underwater World and Siloso Beach. The green line (from 0900-2100 daily) runs between the Ferry Terminal, the cable car and Underwater World. The yellow line (from 0700-2300 Sun-Thu, until 0030 on Fri and Sat) links the Visitor Arrival Centre with Dolphin Lagoon. The red line (from 1000-1830 daily) links Underwater World with Dolphin Lagoon. The Siloso Beach line (from 1000-1900 daily) runs between Siloso Beach and the Visitor Arrival Centre, while the Beach Line (open 0900-2100 daily) shuttles between the three beaches. Finally the Monorail (open 0900-2200 daily) links all the main sites with the Ferry Terminal.

The **cable car** operates daily 0830-2100. There are 3 stops: Mount Faber (the highest point in Singapore, with scenic views and seafood restaurants – worthwhile), the Cable Car Tower adjacent to the HarbourFront and the Cable Car Plaza on Sentosa. Fares are S$19.80 return, S$9.80 child. Admission to Sentosa is included in these fares. Taxis are charged a toll of S$3 and can only drop off/pick up at the hotels on Sentosa.

Travelling anti-clockwise around the island, the first attraction of interest is the **Underwater World**, ⓘ *www.underwaterworld.com.sg/, 0900-2100, S$17.30, S$11.20 children's ticket which includes entry to Dolphin Lagoon*, the largest walk-through oceanarium in Asia. It is highly recommended and is the highlight of any visit to Sentosa. A 100 m tunnel, with a moving conveyor, allows a glimpse of some of its 350 underwater species and 5,000 specimens. Giant rays glide overhead, while thick-lipped garoupa and spooky moray eels hide in caves and crevices. The 'creatures of the deep' tank, with giant octopus and spider crabs, is impressive. Other smaller tanks house cuttlefish, turtles, reef fish, sawfish, corals, sea urchins and other marine creatures. There is also a touch pool where the curious can prod star fish and baby sharks.

Fort Siloso, ⓘ *1000-1800, S$8 adult, S$5 children*, on the westernmost point, is Singapore's only preserved coastal fort, built in the 1880s to guard the narrow western entrance to Keppel Harbour. It provides an informative visit, especially if you are interested in the fall of Singapore. It is possible to explore the underground tunnels, artillery nests and bunkers, experience a mock firing of a seven-inch gun, run riot over the assault course and play various interactive computer games with a martial tinge. The fort was built to guard against a seaward attack, but, as every amateur student of Singapore's wartime history knows, the Japanese assault was from the north. The guns of Fort Siloso were turned landwards, but could do little to thwart the Japanese advance. When news of the surrender came through, the soldiers of the Royal Artillery (many from the Indian subcontinent) sabotaged the guns to prevent them falling into enemy hands.

Float through the air with the greatest of ease on **Sentosa's Flying Trapeze** which offers heart-stopping swings at S$10 a pop. ⓘ *Mon-Fri 0900-1800, Sat, Sun and public holidays 0900-1900, S$10 per swing, S$20 for three swings. Children under 4 and pregnant women are not allowed to take part. Daredevils wear safety harnesses.*

The **Butterfly Park and Insect Kingdom Museum** ⓘ *0900-1830, S$10 (S$6 children)*, is a 1-ha park containing 1,500 butterflies from 50 species at all stages in their life cycle. Also here is a rather antiseptic museum of dead butterflies and insects.

The **Sijori WonderGolf** course is fun: 45 mini-holes each, with some novel obstruction to surmount. ⓘ *0900-1900, S$8, S$4 children.*

Poking up like a giant needle, the crassly-named **Carlsberg Sky Tower**, ⓘ *0900-2100, last entry 2030, a seven-minute ride costs S$10 adults, S$6 children*, next to the cable car station, has a small glass-sided cabin which rotates at 131 m above sea level giving good views of the island. The tower itself is tackily covered in adverts for said beer.

The **Musical fountain** ⓘ *30 minute shows at 1700, 1730, 1940, and 2040*, is a disco-lit fountain which gyrates, together – with a rather unorchestrated laser light show – to everything from Joan Jett and the Blackhearts to the 1812 Overture. The later two shows have additional laser effects emitted from the 37 m, 12 storey-tall **Merlion**. This stupendous, laser-emitting symbol of Singapore joins with the fountains to create the 'Musical Fountain and Rise of the Merlion Show'. At other times of day, the Merlion can be climbed either up to its mouth or its crown for views over Sentosa, the city and port, ⓘ *1000-2000, last admission 1930, S$8, S$5 children*. There is a shop here – since nothing can be built on Sentosa without some merchandising outlet – that is themed as a Bugis shipwreck. The Bugis were the feared Malay seafarers who sailed from Sulawesi and controlled the seas of the Malay archipelago before the European period. They have often been likened to the Vikings and, like the Vikings, they were famed for their fearlessness and for their seafaring skills – and for the terror they instilled in the hearts of coastal communities.

Images of Singapore, Pioneers of Singapore and the **Surrender Chambers** was closed for renovation at the time of writing; it is due to reopen in June 2005. It offers a well-displayed history of Singapore, focusing on key figures from the origins of the city state as an entrepôt through to the modern period, and also telling the traumatic Second World War story. The wax models are not up to Madame Tussaud's standard, but the history is well told for those interested in such things.

The southwest 'coast' of the island has been redeveloped, with tens of thousands of cubic metres of golden sand shipped in from Indonesia, along with 300 mature coconut palms and over 100 ornamental shrubs and flowering trees. Three **beaches** have been created here: Palawan, Siloso and Tanjong. The Beach Train runs between all three beaches. The **Dolphin Lagoon**, ⓘ *Ticket price includes entry into Underwater World, 1030-1800, S$17.30, S$11.20 children*, near Tanjong Beach, provides 'Meet the Dolphin' sessions at 1100, 1330, 1530 and 1730.

So-called pink (although they are more white in colour) Indo-Pacific humpback dolphins have been trained to do rather banal and demeaning tricks.

Volcanoland, ⓘ *1300-1800, volcano erupts every 30 mins, S$10, S$6 children*, a 'multimedia entertainment park', takes you on a subterranean journey into the earth and is supposed to trace the evolution of life – although your children will pass no exams with this rubbish. The main show is entertaining enough, but the rest of the complex is rather disappointing and, as with so much on Sentosa, the visitor exits from the multimedia extravaganza – no doubt filled with grand, but erroneous, thoughts about the origins of life – straight into a shop.

The **Sentosa Orchid Gardens**, ⓘ *0930-1830*, very close to the ferry terminal, have 10,000 plants and over 200 species of orchid. Within the gardens is a restaurant, a fish pond with koi carp, a Japanese tea room and various other gazebos, boulders and associated paraphernalia, and – yes, you've guessed it – a souvenir shop.

Cinemania, ⓘ *Show every 30 mins, 1100-2000, S$12.50, S$8 children*, a high-tech movie extravaganza. Combining high definition film with state-of the-art sound and seats, raised on hydraulic jacks, it creates what is rather ambitiously called hyper reality. The blurb warns that you should give this a miss if you have back, neck or heart problems, are pregnant, suffer from epileptic fits or have a surname beginning with B.

Golf, ⓘ *contact Sentosa Golf Club, T62750022, 0700-1900*, on one of two courses – Serapong or Tanjong.

Singapore West

Haw Par Villa

ⓘ Daily 0900-1900, free. Do not even think about visiting Haw Par Villa over Chinese New Year – each year about 12,000 people saunter around it in the space of about four days. MRT westbound to Buona Vista, then bus 200.

The gloriously tacky Haw Par Villa (formerly **Tiger Balm Gardens**) is at 262 Pasir Panjang Road, on the way out to Jurong. Built by Aw Boon Haw and Aw Boon Par, brothers of Tiger Balm fame, it was their family home until they opened it to the public. The delightful estate was finally sequestrated by the Singapore government in 1985 and turned into a theme park. Boon Haw originally designed the gardens for his family's enjoyment. But his gory sculptures have instilled a sense of traditional morality in generations of Singaporeans. Sequences depict wrongdoers being punished in creative ways, most notably in the Ten Courts of Hell (newly refurbished in 2004): one is having his tongue cut out, another is galled by a spear, others are variously impaled on spikes, gnawed by dogs, boiled in oil, bitten by snakes, sliced in two, drowned in the Filthy Blood Pond or ground into paste by enormous millstones. Some of the allegories and stories are obscure to say the least: a pig dressed in what appears to be a forerunner to the 'Y' front; acrobatic mermaids; and tango-ing fowl. Though doubtless highly significant to the cognoscenti of Chinese mythology, many of the stories will be lost on the uninitiated.

The MRT West line runs from the city to Boon Lay. Some sights are far from an MRT station, so take a bus or taxi.

Its 9-ha site is five times the size of the original villa and its grounds. There is a large section on ancient China, with pagoda-roofed buildings, arts and crafts shops and restaurants serving authentic cuisine, as well as traditional theatre – in which lion dances and wayangs are performed. The 'Creation of the World Theatre' tells classic tales from the Qin Dynasty; in the 'Legends and Heroes Theatre', a life-like robot is programmed to relate stories; and a video in the 'Spirit of the Orient Theatre' explains Chinese folklore, customs, traditions and festivals. A new museum examining the arrival of Chinese immigrants to Singapore has been added.

Holland Village

ⓘ Take the MRT to Buona Vista and then walk up Commonwealth Ave to Holland Ave (about 15 mins), or take bus 106 from Orchard Rd (stop outside YMCA).

This is really a residential area – and was once the home to the British forces barracked in Singapore – but it also developed into one of the trendier parts of suburban Singapore and is a very pleasant area to explore. It is very popular with expats, especially at weekends. There are restaurants and bars, small craft and antique shops, and a good wet market – Pasar Holland. The Holland Village Shopping Centre, on the first floor of Holland Avenue, is a good stop for Asian arts and crafts and there are ample places to eat (see page 609) and relax while exploring the area.

Jurong Bird Park

ⓘ Daily 0900-1800, T62650022. S$14, S$7 children under 12. There are several bird shows every hour. MRT westbound to Boon Lay then SBS bus 194 or 251 from Boon Lay MRT interchange. There is a monorail service round the park for those who find the heat too much, S$4, S$2 for children. There is an all-in-one ticket for S$30, which allows you entrance to Jurong Bird Park, Singapore Zoo and the Night Safari.

Situated on Jalan Ahmad Ibrahim, Jurong Bird Park (www.birdpark.com.sg) is a beautifully kept 20-ha haven for more than 8,000 birds of 600 species from all over

Haw Par Villa is the island's most revolting theme park, a gaudy adventureland of Chinese folklore and the biggest Chinese mythological theme park in the world.

the world, including a large collection of Southeast Asian birds. As it is now difficult to see most of these birds in the wild in Southeast Asia, a trip here is well worthwhile. Highlights include the world's largest collection of Southeast Asian hornbills and South American toucans and an entertaining air-conditioned penguin corner, complete with snow. Another main attraction is one of the largest walk-in aviaries in the world, with a 30 m-high man-made waterfall and 1,500 birds. There is also an interesting nocturnal house, with owls, herons, frogmouths and kiwis and bird shows throughout the day (the birds of prey show – at 1000 and 1600 – is particularly good).

Kids will love 'Breakfast with the birds' an ornithological buffet extravaganza on Sundays at 0900, S$20 a head for all you can eat.

Chinese and Japanese Gardens

ⓘ *Daily 0600-1900, T62613632, free except for the Bonsai Garden, S$5, S$3 children. MRT to Chinese Gardens (W10) and then walk the 200 m across the open-grassed area to the east gate.*

On Yuan Ching Road are these gardens, which extend over 13 ha on two islands in Jurong Lake. The Chinese garden (Yu-Hwa Yuan) is said to be modelled on an imperial Sung Dynasty garden and specifically on the classical style of Beijing's Summer Palace. There are artfully scattered boulders, Chinese pavilions and a brace-and-a-half of pagodas to give it that Oriental flavour, but it is hard to believe that the Sung emperors would have been happy with this. Rather more refined is the Penjing Garden (Yun Xiu Yuan – or Garden of Beauty), a walled bonsai garden, which reputedly cost S$6mn to develop. The garden contains 3,000 miniature potted *penjing* (bonsai) trees, sourced from all over Asia. The two outside the entrance are said to come from Sichuan and to be over almost 300 years old. They symbolize male and female lions guarding the entrance, but just in case these arboreal defenders should fail, there is also a pair of stone lions to act as back-up. Close to the main entrance is a large statue of the sage Confucious (551-479 BC), looking suitably studious and wise, and a stone boat craftily concealing a food outlet. On a small rise in the middle of the Chinese garden is the main pagoda, which towers up through six levels. It is possible to sweat your way to the top for a great view of HDB blocks.

The Science Centre

ⓘ *Tue-Sun 1000-1800, S$6, S$3 children, www.science.edu.sg To get there, take bus no 335 from Jurong East MRT, or it's a 10-minute walk from the station.*

This centre, on Science Centre Road, might be aimed more at children than adults – it is usually packed with schoolchildren enjoying a few hours away from cramming – but there is plenty of fun for grown-ups too. The central hub of the museum has a figure of Einstein talking in a rather forced German accent, hatching chicks and various other exhibits, including a computer screen where it is possible to conduct plastic surgery on your face. From this hub radiates the Hall of Life Sciences, a Virtual Science Centre, the Aviation Centre, a children's Discovery Centre and a Physical Science Hall. In the Aviation Centre, where Changi Airport makes a predictably significant appearance, visitors are guided around the wonders of flight by Archie the Archaeopteryx – a sort of avine dinosauric maître d'. For an extra charge it is possible to fly a simulator. The Hall of Life Science's theme is humanity's impact on the earth and here there are some live animals along with a few talking dummies, including a dinosaur (spouting surprisingly unscientific rubbish) and Charles Darwin (far too thin) talking with an American-accented gorilla. Disney's *Jungle Book* has a lot to answer for. Overall, the centre succeeds in its mission to make science come alive, with plenty of gadgets and hands-on exhibits. It makes most sense to come here with children who will be able to spend several hours having fun and maybe even learn something.

In the **Omni-theatre** next door ⓘ *T64252500, Tue-Sun 1000-2000, S$10, S$5 children*, the marvels of science, technology and the universe can be viewed in a

284-seat amphitheatre, with a huge hemispherical (3-D) screen and a 20,000 watt sound system. Films have a scientific, geographical or natural history flavour – usually space exploration, an underwater journey or a flying adventure over some geological marvel. Excellent films and very popular.

Ming Village

ⓘ *32 Pandan Road, T62657711, daily 0900-1730, free admission and guided tour,. MRT to Clementi, then bus 78 or 32 to Pandan Road.*

This is one of the last factories in the world that faithfully reproduces Chinese porcelain antiques using traditional methods – from mould-making to hand-throwing – dating from Sung, Yuan, Ming and Qin dynasties. All the pieces are painted by hand and the factory blurb maintains that traditional methods of craftsmanship are scrupulously followed. It is possible to take a guided tour around the factory premises and seeing the work that goes into the pots certainly helps explain why the prices are so high in the showroom. The shop has an export department which will pack items for shipment. The village also runs traditional pottery and painting classes for long-stay and short-stay group visitors. The **Pewter Museum,** which has moved to the Ming Village, has daily demonstrations of traditional pewter-making processes.

Singapore Discovery Centre

ⓘ *T67926188, www.sdc.com.sg; westbound MRT to Boon Lay (W12) and then connecting bus nos 182 or 193.*

Located at the western end of the island, the Singapore Discovery Centre was currently being redeveloped at the time of writing. The new SDC promises to have a dome theatre, a 3-D cinema and new exhibitions centred on major events for the city-state.

Snow City

ⓘ *www.sdc.com.sg/, Tue-Sun 1030-1830, one-hour S$12 inlcudes rental of jacket and boots; take bus no 335 from Jurong East MRT, or a 10-minute walk from the station.*

Sun-bound Singapore now has its own indoor snow centre at Snow City, next to the Singapore Science Centre. Visitors can snow-board, snow-tube or ski up and down slopes covering 1,200 square metres with walls rather kitschly painted with alpine snow scenes.There is an airlock at 10 degrees to get you acclimatized to the -5 degree environment of the snow slopes. There's also a giant (so-called life-sized – how do they know?) model of the Yeti, slides for children and permission to have snowball fights. Snow is made with an aptly named snow gun where water is shot out and cooled with liquid nitrogen. Around 15 tons of the white stuff are made every week to keep the slopes topped up with around 40-cm depth of crunchy snow.

East Coast

Katong and Geylang Serai

ⓘ *Take the MRT to Eunos and then bus 15 or a taxi, or take bus No 33 from Orchard Rd.*

Katong is an enclave of Peranakan architecture and there are still streets of well-preserved shophouses and terraced houses in their original condition. Restaurants in Katong serve some of the best Peranakan food in Singapore, including delicious pastries and sweets. **Joo Chiat Road**, which runs south down to the sea, is interesting for its unchanged early 20th-century shophouse fronts. The extravagant façades, found both here and on Koon Seng Road, are an excellent example of the Singapore Eclectic Style which evolved in the 1920s and 1930s. This whole area was originally a coconut plantation owned by a family of Arab descent – the Alsagoffs. A portion was purchased by a

The MRT East line runs all the way to Pasir Ris. For the coast it is best to take a bus (No 16 from Orchard and Bras Basah rds) or taxi.

wealthy Chinese, Chew Joo Chiat, after whom a number of the roads are named (not just Joo Chiat Road; also Joo Chiat Lane, Joo Chiat Terrace and Joo Chiat Place). While most of the traditional businesses here have closed down or moved out, there are still some candlemakers struggling to make a living and a few other craftspeople.

Peter Wee's Katong Antique House, at 208 East Coast Road, is well worth a visit if you are in the area, with its unsurpassed collection of Peranakan antiques and an owner who is probably the most knowledgeable person in Singapore on the Peranakan culture.

East Coast Park

ⓘ *Open 24 hours, the park is lit from 1900-0700, free; bus No 16 from Orchard Rd and get off at Marine Terrace and walk under the underpass.*

This popular recreation area has beaches and gardens, as well as a tennis centre, driving range, sailing centre, food centre and the **Big Splash**, ⓘ *902 East Coast Parkway, T63456762, daily 0900-1800; there's a free shuttle service from from MacDonald House bus stop near Dhoby Ghaut MRT else Orchard Road bus No 36, or 401*, seawater swimming pool with slides, beach bar, kayak and diving courses. In fact, there are assorted sports and entertainment facilities strung out over several kilometres – although they are largely patronized by locals rather than foreign visitors. The sand along these beaches was imported from nearby Indonesian islands. The **East Coast Recreation Centre**, in East Coast Park, has the usual array of crazy golf, foodstalls, cycling, canoes and fun rides. A good half-day excursion, especially if you are with children, is to hire bicycles and ride along the track that winds its way up the East Coast. There are no hills and lots of food and drink stops. It's more fun than battling with the crowds and cars, and also comparatively quiet during the week.

The **Crocodilarium**, ⓘ *730 East Coast Parkway, daily 0900-1700, S$2, S$1 children, T4473722. No direct buses; take the MRT to Paya Lebar or Eunos and then take a taxi*, has over 1,200 inmates, bred in pens. Note that it is a commercial operation, not a zoological centre, and the animals here will end up as shoes and handbags. The best time to visit is at feeding times (1100 Tuesday, Thursday and Saturday). The Crocodilarium also stages crocodile-wrestling bouts; ring for times. Crocodile-skin goods are for sale.

East Coast

Sleeping
Betel Box Hostel 4
Gay World 1
Hotel 81-Joo Chiat 2
Malacca 3

Eating
House of Sundanese Food 1
Peranakan Inn 1

The **Singapore Crocodile Farm** ⓘ *790 Upper Serangoon Road, daily 0830-1730; buses 81, 84, 97, 111 and 153 all run along Upper Serangoon Rd and stop opposite the farm*, is, like the Crocodilarium on the East Coast, a commercial set-up. Here, visitors can learn about skinning techniques and various other methods of transforming scary reptiles into quiescent handbags and shoes. This farm, with its population of about 800 crocodiles, has been on the same site since 1945, importing crocodiles from rivers in Sarawak.

Changi Prison

ⓘ *Upper Changi Road, T621424521, daily 0930-1700, free; MRT to Tanah Merah and then bus 2.*

The prison, as featured on the 'Go to Jail' square in the Singapore version of Monopoly, is where Singapore's hangman dispenses with drug traffickers – with gruesome regularity. It was originally built to house 600 prisoners, but during the war more than 3,500 civilians were incarcerated here. In 1944, POWs were moved into the prison, and 12,000 American, Australian and British servicemen were interned in and around it. It is mostly visited by Second World War veterans – there is a small museum with reproductions of WRM Haxworth's paintings and the then 17-year-old trooper George Aspinall's photographs, which record the misery of internment. A replica of the atap-roofed Changi Prison chapel stands in the prison yard. The memorial chapel's original altar cross, whose base was made from a Howitzer shell casing, was returned to the chapel in 1992. The Chapel holds a service on Sunday morning at 0945, T65458727. The Prison Museum has an interesting display.

James Clavell's novel King Rat is more enlightening than a visit to Changi

North of the island

Siong Lim Temple

ⓘ *Take the MRT to Toa Payoh. Then take bus 8 or 26, getting off at HDB block 195, one stop past the Toa Payoh stadium.*

This temple at 184 Jalan Toa Payoh lies due north of the city, within the modern suburb of Toa Payoh. This Fujian temple's full name is Lian Shan, Shuang Lin – which means Lotus Hill, Twin Groves – referring to the sal grove in Kunisnara, near Patna, where the Buddha attained enlightenment. It is the largest Buddhist temple in Singapore and was originally built between 1898 and 1905. However, since then Singapore's urban expansion has enveloped it. Chunks of its original 4 ha area have been chipped away for housing development and, perhaps to atone for the effrontery, the Singapore Tourist Board gave the temple its own Suzhou-style rock garden. Despite the redevelopments, the temple retains its excellent wood carvings and some fine Thai images of the Buddha. There is also a statue of Kuan Yin and a corpulent image of the Maitreya Buddha.

The MRT North-South line loops right around this part of the island and has 23 stops. TIBS buses – the Trans-Island Bus Service – are also useful.

Kong Meng San Phor Kark

ⓘ *Get off at Bishan MRT station and take bus No 410.*

This Chinese Temple Complex (Bright Hill Drive) has, since its construction in 1989, grown into a sprawling, million dollar religious centre whose golden roofs spread over 7½ ha. Fed up with tastefully mouldering 19th-century Chinese temples? Then this is

Kong Meng San Phor Kark has been the backdrop for many kung-fu movies and is one of the largest such complexes in Southeast Asia.

the place for you. This is Chinese temple garishness on a truly gargantuan scale; restrained was clearly not a word in the architect's vocabulary. From the main entrance on Sin Ming Avenue, pilgrims climb up through a series of halls with images of the historic Buddha and various other gods and goddesses from Chinese Mahayana Buddhism's extensive repertoire. There are halls for prayer and meditation, a pool containing thousands of turtles, a Buddhist library, an old people's home (and, appropriately, a crematorium), as well as a 9 m-high marble statue of Kuan Yin, the 15-headed goddess of mercy, carved by Italian sculptors. At one end of the complex is The Temple of a Thousand Buddhas surmounted by a large gold stupa. There are great views from the roof.

Singapore Zoological Gardens

ⓘ 80 Mandai Lake Road, T62693411, www.zoo.com.sg, daily 0830-1800, S$14, S$7 for children. There is an all-in-one ticket for S$30, which allows you entrance to Jurong Bird Park, Singapore Zoo and the Night Safari. Combined Zoo and night safari ticket, S$24, S$12 children; MRT to Ang Mo Kio and then bus No 138 from the station.

These zoological gardens have one of the world's few open zoos – with moats replacing bars – making it also one of the most attractive zoos, with animals in environments vaguely reminiscent of their habitats. Only the polar bears and the tigers seem unhappy in their surroundings. It contains over 170 species of animals (about 2,000 actual animals), some of them rare – like the dinosauric Komodo dragons and the golden lion tamarin – as well as many endangered species from Asia, such as the Sumatran tiger and the clouded leopard. The pygmy hippos are

North of the Island

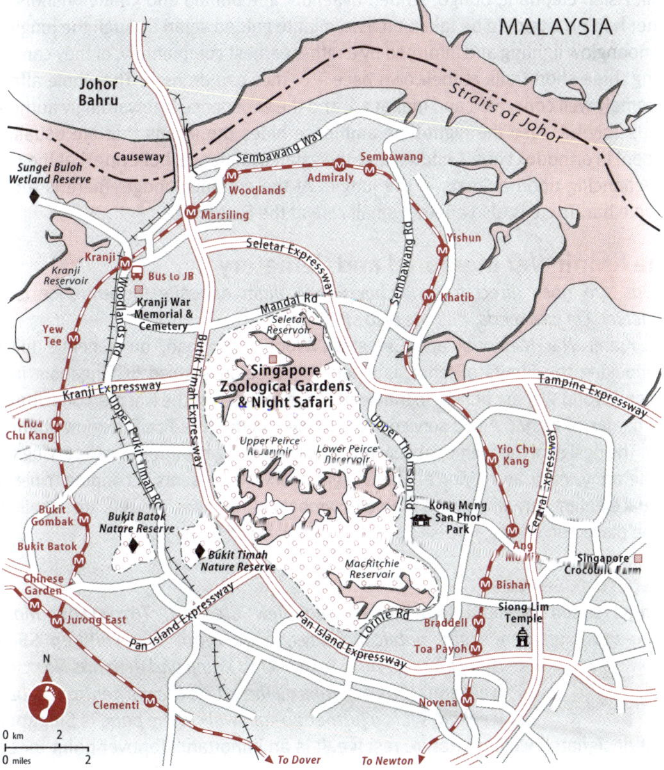

relatively recent newcomers; they live in glass-fronted enclosures (as do the polar bears), so visitors can watch their underwater exploits. Animals are sponsored by companies; Tiger Beer, for example, sponsors the tigers and Qantas the kangaroos.

There are animal shows throughout the day carrying a strong ecological message: elephants (at 1130 and 1530) and sealions (at 1430, extra show at 1700 at weekends). Animal feeding times are provided upon arrival. There is a Treetops Trail, where visitors can view primates, crocodiles, squirrels and pheasants from a 6 m-high boardwalk. There is a children's area too, with farm animals, a miniature train and play equipment. There are tram tours for those too weary to walk (S$4 and S$2), with recorded commentaries, and several restaurants. Elephant, camel and pony rides are on offer at various times each afternoon. A shop sells environmentally sound T-shirts and cuddly toy animals. Overall, it is a well-managed and informative zoo; it's well worth the trip out there.

Night Safari

ⓘ *www.nightsafari.com.sg, 1930-2400, S$18, children S$12. Tram ride is an extra S$6 for adults, S$3 for children. The last tram leaves at 2315. No flash cameras permitted; get off at Ang Mo Kio MRT station and then board the SBS No 138. A taxi from the city will cost around S$15-20 and takes 30 mins. There is an all-in-one ticket for S$30, which allows you entrance to Jurong Bird Park, Singapore Zoo and the Night Safari.*

The unique Night Safari is situated adjacent to the zoo, covering 40 ha of secondary growth tropical forest. The area has been cunningly converted into a series of habitats, populated with wildlife from the Indo-Malayan, Indian, Himalayan and African zoogeographical regions. The park supports 1,200 animals belonging to 110 species, including the tiger, Indian lion, great Indian rhinoceros, fishing cat, Malayan tapir, Asian elephant, bongo, striped hyaena, Cape buffalo and giraffe. Visitors can either hop on a tram to be taken on a 40-minute guided safari through the jungle, lit by moonglow lighting and informed by a rather earnest commentary, or they can walk along three short trails at their own pace – or they can do both. The whole affair is extremely well conceived and managed, and the experience is rewardingly authentic – possibly because the night-time ambience hides the seams that are usually so evident in orthodox zoos. Children love the safari experience, believing that they truly are chancing upon animals in the jungle. At the entrance 'lodge' there is a good noodle bar. There is also another small café at the East Lodge.

The Kranji War Memorial and Cemetery

ⓘ *Bus 170 goes direct from Rochor Road; alight opposite the entrance to the cemetery. On weekends, bus 181 also stops here.*

The Kranji War Memorial and Cemetery, Woodlands Road, on a gentle hillside overlooking the Straits of Johor, is where Allied soldiers killed in Singapore in the Second World War are buried. In the heart of the cemetery is the war memorial, bearing the names of 24,346 Allied servicemen who died in the Asia-Pacific region during the war. The design of the memorial is symbolic, representing the three arms of the services – the army, navy and airforce. The upright section represents a conning-tower, the lateral elements are wings, and the walls symbolize army lines. Flowers are not allowed to be placed on graves, in case tiger mosquitoes breed in the jars.

Nature reserves

Sungei Buloh Wetland Reserve, ⓘ *Neo Tiew Crescent, T67941401, Mon-Fri 0730-1900, weekends and public holidays, 0700-1900, S$1, children S$0.50. Binoculars for hire. Take MRT to Kranji and then bus No 925. On weekends, bus 925 runs all the way to the park entrance, but on weekdays it is a further 20-min walk to the park,* is Singapore's first designated wetland nature reserve. It is an important stopover point for birds

The best time to visit the park is in November.

migrating along the East Asian Flyway. Carefully constructed hides throughout 87 ha provide excellent observation points for visitors, to view birds like sea eagles, kites and blue herons. There is also a mangrove swamp to walk through.

Bukit Timah Nature Reserve, ⓘ *Hindhede Drive off Upper Bukit Timah Road, T4709900, 0830-1830. The nature reserve is at its quietest and coolest in the early mornings. Though the visitors' centre isn't open until 0830, it is possible to enter the reserve earlier. Entrance to the reserve is free and is on Upper Bukit Timah Rd, opposite Courst furniture store, down Hindhede Drive; from Newton MRT station take bus Nos 67, 170 or 171,* nestles in the centre of the island and has a resident population of wild monkeys, pythons and scorpions. It was one of the first Forest Reserves, established in 1883 for the purposes of protecting the native flora and fauna. The naturalist Alfred Russel Wallace collected beetles at Bukit Timah in 1854. Jungle trails go through the forested terrain (130 million-year-old tropical rainforest) that once covered the whole island. The artificial lakes supply the city with much of its water. Clearly marked paths (one of them metalled) in the 81-ha reserve lead to Singapore's highest point (164 m) for scenic views. A visitors' centre includes an informative exhibition on natural history.

Bukit Batok Nature Park ⓘ *0700-1900, the park is a five-minute walk from Bukit Gombak MRT Station,* is a very beautiful secondary forest with trails leading up the main hill. It was developed around an abandoned quarry – the quarry has been filled in to create a small lake. There is a durian orchard (so pungent during durian season) and picnic areas. At the top of Batok hill are the remains of two Japanese war memorials.

Pulau Ubin

ⓘ *For more information on the island, T65424108, www.nparks.gov.sg; from Changi Point it costs S$2 to go to Pulau Ubin; bumboats go when they're full – very frequently at the weekends – and operate between 0600 and 2300. It is possible to charter the whole vessel if you want to be alone, or are bored waiting for the boat to fill up. (For transport to and from Changi Village, see page 592.)*

The source of granite for the causeway and Singapore's earlier buildings and skyscrapers, the name Pulau Ubin derives from the Javanese word for 'squared stone'. Ubin village affords a taste of Singapore in bygone days, with dilapidated wooden shophouses, coffee-shops and community spirit. The island, with its beaten-up cars and old taxis, quarry pits, jungle tracks, hills, beaches and challenging trails, is a mountain-biker's paradise and has become a popular destination for that reason, as the trails are quite challenging; it is possible to hire bicycles in the village. There is also an **outward bound centre** ⓘ *T65461197,* on the island and students come here to experience outdoor living. Wildlife on the island includes the red jungle-fowl (from which domesticated chickens are descended), straw-headed bulbul, Brahminy kites, white-bellied fish eagles, mangrove pitta, flying fox bats, fruit bats and tomb bats, the Oriental whip snake (an unmissable bright yellow colour), long-tailed macaques, house musang, civet and wild pigs. The hill in the centre of the island provides great views over to Singapore. There are some sandy beaches on the north shore – though they can be dirty at low tide.

The Urban Redevelopment Authority (URA) has also published plans to reclaim an additional 2,694 ha on Pulau Ubin and Pulau Tekong (the majority on Tekong, which houses a military training camp and is not open to the public).

Canoes, kayaks and mountain bikes are all available for hire on the island. Mountain bikes can also be hired from Changi Village – S$20 per day (S$10 returnable deposit).

Sleeping

Most budget accommodation is to be found in the Little India and Arab Street areas to the north of town.

Colonial core *p558, map p564*

LL Conrad, 2 Temasek Blvd, Marina Bay, T63348888, www.conradhotelsl.com.sg Close to Suntec City, and good for the business traveller. A total of 509 beautifully designed contemporary-style rooms, with lots of space, big windows and a large desk. Superb service, excellent meeting rooms and an impressive mezzanine level for functions. US$1.3 mn has been invested in almost 3,000 artworks throughout the hotel. Decent sized pool for lengths and adequate fitness centre. Recommended.

LL Raffles, 1 Beach Rd, T63371886, www.raffleshotel.com Singapore's most famous hotel and, despite criticisms, it is still a great place to stay – if you can afford it. There are 9 restaurants and a Culinary Academy, 5 bars (see entries under Eating and drinking, page 602) and is surrounded by 70 shops, including the offbeat *Evolution* which sells big price tag fossils. The 103 suites have been immaculately refurbished, with wooden floors, high ceilings, stylish colonial furniture and plenty of space. Bathrooms are the ultimate in luxury and the other facilities are excellent – a peaceful rooftop pool with Jacuzzis, (although the gym is rather small), both 24 hr. Very exclusive and highly recommended.

LL Ritz-Carlton Millenia, 7 Raffles Ave, Marina Bay, T63378888, www. Ritzcarlton. com/hotels/singapore Both this hotel and the *Conrad* were designed by US Hirsch Bedner. Very contemporary furnishings; considerable investment in artworks (notably the Frank Stella and the Dele Chihuly glass balls below the lobby area); rooms are very attractive, with wooden floors and big bathrooms that provide stunning views of the harbour and river. Large pool area with Jacuzzi in well landscaped grounds, huge fitness centre. Good business facilities. Recommended.

L Swissotel The Stamford (formerly Westin Stamford and Westin Plaza) , 2 Stamford Rd, T63388585, www. Swissotel-thestamford. com Listed in the *Guinness Book of Records* as the tallest hotel in the world, this 2-tower complex was designed by Chinese architect IM Pei, who also designed the futuristic Bank of China building in Hong Kong. Haze permitting, the *Compass Rose Restaurant* on the top floor can provide stunning views over 3 countries – Singapore, Malaysia and Indonesia. There are 13 restaurants, an attractive triple circular pool (great for children) and a high-tech fitness centre. But with over 2,000 rooms and a vast echoing lobby, it is all a little overwhelming – and too large for that personal touch. However, it has a good reputation in the business world.

L-AL Grand Plaza, 10 Coleman St, T63363456, www.grandplaza.singapore. parkroyalhotels.com This marble-cladded monster has a huge echoing lobby and dreamy spa. Despite its size (340 rooms), it feels quite intimate. There are 2 restaurants, an attractive but smallish pool and Jacuzzi, gym and health spa, all on the third floor. It also has a large ballroom and 2 smaller meeting rooms, business centre. Recommended.

AL Peninsula Excelsior, 5 Coleman St, T63372200, www.ytchotels.com.sg This newly renovated hotel which fused two hotels together still has a dated feel. Although the facilities have improved, including a glass-sided swimming pool which faces onto the lobby, the rooms have not been upgraded.

C Metropole, 41 Seah St, T63363611, www.metrohotel.com A smallish business hotel with 54 rooms and no frills, good location for the price.

D Mayfair City Boarding House, 40 Armenian St, T90012526. Great location facing the Asian Civilizations Museum in the heart of Singapore. Rooms are nothing glam, but are large and serviceable with attached bathrooms. Singles, doubles and triples available. Backpacker friendly with an information board and cheery staff. All rooms have windows, and the ones in the front have good views of leafy Armenian St. Recommended.

Singapore River and the City *p568*

AL-L Grand Copthorne Waterfront, 392 Havelock Rd, T67330800, www.grandcopthorne.com.sg This rather overblown monster has a rambling, disjointed lobby, a good gym, 2 tennis courts and a small but attractive pool (all on the 6th floor), extensive business services, a sushi bar and a fusion restaurant . With 338 rooms, there's no sense of intimacy here, but it seems to be doing a roaring trade, so they must have got something right.
AL Fullerton, 1 Fullerton Square, T67338388, www.fullertonhotel. com Great position at the head of the Singapore River, this is Singapore's 5-star newcomer. It has 399 rooms in Phillipe Stark style, very functional and well equipped, but slightly on the small side compared (say) with the Ritz Carlton. The restaurants are excellent: the *Chinese Jade*; international *Town Club*; and seafood *Post Bar*. The infinity swimming pool is stunning with views directly over the Singapore River, with the high-rise CBD on one side and Boat Quay on the other.
AL Swissotel Merchant Court, 20 Merchant Rd, T63379993, www.swissotel.com This 500-room hotel, is a welcome addition to the mid-range bracket of hotels, many of which are looking rather tired. Attractive freeform pool in rooftop garden setting with slides and a separate Jacuzzi overlooking the river. Excellent fitness centre managed by Lifestyles. Great location makes it an appealing choice.
AL-A The Gallery, 76 Robertson Quay, T68498686, www.galleryhotel.com.sg Marketed as the 'First hip hotel in Singapore', this Philip Stark-styled hotel provides 222 minimalist rooms, divided between 3 ultra-modern blocks. Brightly coloured cushions provide some light relief from the austerity in the standard rooms; showers only in these rooms. There is free internet access in all rooms, and "smart wired rooms" have their lighting and air-conditioning controlled with sensors, offering such cool features as guiding lights to the bathroom at night without having to press a switch. The fifth floor pool is certainly different, with glass on all sides. A thoroughly funky choice. The hotel has chillout lounges and bars including the very popular 4,000 sq-foot *Liquid Room club*.

Chinatown *p571, map p572*

Chinatown accommodation has more individuality, but can be on the small side.
L Berjaya Duxton, 83 Duxton Rd, T62277678, www.berjayaresorts.com Intimate, stylish 50-room hotel in row of refurbished shophouses. Deluxe rooms are split level, but even these are small at this price. Restaurant (*L'Aigle d'Or*, page 604). Mainly frequented by business people as it's convenient for the financial district. Its ambience and size make it stand out among Singapore's other luxury hotels. Overpriced on the published rate, but good discounts available either from hotel or from travel agents. Recommended.
AL Amara, 165 Tanjong Pagar Rd, T68792555, www.amarahotels.com Well maintained, with 380 average-sized rooms and good extras such as self-service launderette. Several restaurants (with one of the best Thai restaurants in town – *Thanying*, see page 605) and a coffee shop serving a good buffet spread (mid-range), decent sized pool, with café area for steamboat and barbecues. Four tennis courts, jogging track and a gym. Business centre. Good location to explore Chinatown or for business visitors.
B Hotel 1929 , 50 Keong Saik Rd, T63471929, www.hotel1929.com Singapore's newest funky boutique hotel. The owners have used their own collection of retro and designer furniture for this quirkily restored shophouse. The 32 rooms are small, but so chic that size does not matter for once. There's no pool or gym, but a small Jacuzzi, free internet and in-room safes. Recommended.
B-C Damenlou, 12 Ann Siang Rd, T62211900, yokewong12@hotmail.com Marked by a quaint entranceway, this small establishment remains a great place to stay for budget travelers. A/c, attached bathroom, TV, minibar; cheaper rooms are very small but neat and clean, and well presented. Very friendly management and located in an attractive street of shophouses, 1st floor Cantonese restaurant. Recommended.
B-C The Inn at Temple Street, 36 Temple St, T62215333, www.theinn.com.sg Billing itself as a boutique hotel, the 42 rooms here do have a certain charm, being well appointed with safes, TVs, Peranakan-style furniture

(made in Indonesia) and attached shower (in the standard rooms) or bath (in the deluxe rooms). On the downside, the rooms are very small; not even the deluxe rooms have space for a desk (except in the few single rooms), which will put off business travellers.

C **Keong Saik**, 69 Keong Saik Rd, T62230660, keongsaik@pacific.net.sg An intimate little 'business' hotel in a sensitively restored shophouse, with 25 a/c immaculately presented rooms containing attractive all-wood furniture. It is let down by small room size, with little space for anything other than the bed. Standard rooms have no windows or skylights (attic rooms).

Orchard Road and Botanic Gardens *577, map p578*

There is little to differentiate between the numerous 4- and 5-star hotels strung out along the road, concentrated towards the western end.

LL **Four Seasons**, 190 Orchard Blvd, T67341110, www.fourseasons.com Hard to beat, this intimate hotel of 254 rooms (and more than 300 staff) provides exceptional personal service. Rooms are elegantly decorated in traditional European style, with feather pillows, writing desk, multi-disc player, and spacious bathrooms. The hotel has a unique Asian art collection, with attractive artwork in all the rooms. There are 2 pools – one is for lengths – and the hotel boasts the only a/c tennis courts in Singapore, a golf simulator and a well-equipped health and fitness centre, with attendants on hand all day. Restaurants include Cantonese and contemporary American cuisine, with lunchtime buffet. Although, primarily a business hotel, children are well catered for. Recommended.

LL **Goodwood Park**, 22 Scotts Rd, T67377411, www.goodwoodparkhotel.com.sg Apart from Raffles, this is the only other colonial hotel in Singapore. The exterior is looking a little scruffy and the lobby area isn't very encouraging, but the rooms are exceptional. Of the 234 rooms, there is a choice of colonial or modern style. The former have ceiling fans and windows that can be opened, with very stylish minimalist decor and lots of space. The modern rooms are slightly smaller, but they overlook the Mayfair pool and some rooms on the ground level lead straight out poolside. All rooms are fitted with the latest electronic equipment. There is a lovely pool area, set in a garden with pagodas, and another larger pool for lengths. It has several restaurants (see Eating, page 602). Recommended.

LL **Grand Hyatt**, 10-12 Scotts Rd, T67381234, www.singapore.grand.hyatt.com Owned by the Sultan of Brunei, this hotel has larger than average rooms – all with an alcove sitting area (some with poolside view) – and separate showers. Its selling point must be its garden and fitness facilities. There is a spectacular large fifth floor garden, with a roaring waterfall and very attractive pool area, poolside bar and restaurant. The executive class rooms have their own private Balinese garden (good for families), while those on the fifth floor open out onto a large terrace area. There are also squash courts, 2 tennis courts, huge fitness centre with aerobics classes, fabulous Jacuzzi and sauna. In the basement is a very popular bar, *Brannigans*, while on the mezzanine level is a good restaurant, *Mezza9*. This is mainly a hotel for corporate clients, but good discounts available. Recommended.

L **Hilton**, 581 Orchard Rd, T67372233, www.hilton.com The first international hotel in Singapore. It has 434 average-sized rooms and despite its age it maintains a good reputation. Particularly popular with business people (with its function rooms constantly in demand) and with Japanese tour groups. The *Kaspia Bar* has the largest range of vodkas in Singapore and live jazz. Small, rather dated pool, good fitness centre.

L **Le Meridien**, 100 Orchard Rd, T67338855, www.lemeridien.com Open-plan lobby, with 4 terraces of rooms and garlands of orchids. Good sized rooms (corner rooms are larger) with queen sized beds and attractive decor; ask for a room overlooking the pool, as these have a balcony. Good pool for lengths, but barren seating area. Fitness centre.

L **Meritus Negara**, 10 Claymore Rd, T67370811, www.meritus-negara.com This 198-room hotel, quieter and away from the crowds, prides itself on an intimate atmosphere. It pampers business visitors with a personalized service (no reception counters here) and a very high standard throughout. There are no 'club' floors; but rooms are unusual and larger than average. Bathrooms are spacious and there are separate showers. There is a large pool (but rather exposed sitting area), a very sophisticated fitness centre and Jacuzzi. Recommended.

L Orchard, 442 Orchard Rd, T67347766, www.orchardhotel.com.sg Rooms are decent sized and the bathrooms have separate showers; a luxury in Singapore. Large pool but no shade, excellent fitness centre and sauna. Its claim to fame is its magnificent ballroom, which seats 1,000 for dinner and 1,500 for conferences.

L Regent, 1 Cuscaden Rd, T67338888, www.regenthotels.com.sg Huge ostentatious lobby with bubble lifts and a rather sterile atmosphere, reminiscent of tenement blocks. Situated in a quiet location at western end of Orchard Rd, this hotel is notable for its excellent service and attention to detail. Gloomy corridors and 440 large but quite plain rooms. There is an excellent fitness centre, but a boring circular pool and barren sunbathing area.

L Shangri-La, 22 Orange Grove Rd, T67373644, www.shangri-la.com This is one of Singapore's finest hotels, set in a beautifully maintained, spacious landscaped garden. There are more than 700 rooms, recently very stylishly refurbished; those in the refined and relaxed Valley Wing are superior and the service is exceptional. The excellent leisure facilities include a spacious pool area surrounded by greenery and waterfalls, Jacuzzi, indoor pool, good fitness centre, squash and tennis courts, and a 3-hole pitch and putt golf 'course'. Possibly the best conference facilities in town. There are 3 good restaurants: *Shang Palace* for dim sum, the Japanese *Nadamon* and the outstanding *Blu*, a Californian-French restaurant on the top floor. Winner of Singapore Tourism Board's award for best hotel year after year. Recommended.

L Sheraton Towers, 39 Scotts Rd, T67376888, www.sheratonsingapore.com Quietly sophisticated lobby, with waterfalls and beautiful flowers everywhere, 400 plus rooms with bare corridors but good rooms. The more expensive rooms provide an exceptional service, with lots of extras thrown in. The Cabana rooms on the rooftop overlook the pool. Attractive pool area with bar. Popular with US visitors and 80% business guests. Italian restaurant open evenings only and exclusive Chinese restaurant.

AL Singapore Marriott, 320 Orchard Rd, T67355800, www.marriott.com/sindt Another 380-room monster. Its distinguishing feature is its rather ridiculous pagoda 'hat' at the top of the tower block. The lobby has a library-feel to it. Good fitness centre, large swimming pool with separate whirlpool and *Garden Terrace Café*. Extensive business services, efficient but unwelcoming, very central.

AL Traders, 1A Cuscaden Rd, T67382222, www.shangri-la.com Lavish pots of orchids at the entrance makes it feel special, but there isn't much to mark this hotel apart from the competition. It has 547 rooms and about three-quarters of its guests are business people. The rooms are average, but there is an attractive pool area with a large pool. It has a fitness centre, a business centre and 3 restaurants. Nothing special and a bit stuck out on its own near the western section of Orchard Road opposite the Singapore Tourism Board office.

B Lloyd's Inn, 2 Lloyd Rd, T67377309, www.lloydinn.com A/c, restaurant, scrupulously clean, well-appointed rooms – if a little cramped – quiet location in suburban road near River Valley Rd/Somerset MRT, off Killiney Rd.

B VIP, 5 Balmoral Crescent, T62354277, www.hotel-vip.com Situated in quiet area of the city close to *Garden Hotel* and west of the Newton MRT station. A/c, restaurant, pool, good rooms with TV, minibar etc.

B-C Metropolitan YMCA, 60 Stevens Rd, T68398333, www.mymca.org.sg. All rooms are a/c, a newly renovated no frills place, providing efficient service and clean serviceable rooms. The added bonus is a large swimming pool. Very good value. Recommended.

B-C YWCA Fort Canning Lodge, 6 Fort Canning Rd, T63384222, www.YWCAfclodge.org.sg Large new building with 200 plus rooms, pool, tennis courts, ballroom, exhibition hall. Despite being a YWCA – it is not your average youth hostel. Dorms available.

C **YMCA International House**, 1 Orchard Rd, T63366000, www.ymca.org.sg Facilities are well above the usual YMCA standards, a/c, restaurant, rooftop pool, squash courts, badminton, billiards and fitness centre. Grotty from the outside, but it is very clean and efficient. Good value for this location, S$29 for 4 bed a/c dorm. Non-YMCA or non-YWCA members need to pay a small fee of S$3.15 for the first night. Recommended. The old YMCA which stood on Stamford Rd was used by the Japanese during the war as their dreaded interrogation and torture centre.

Little India *p580, map p581*

A **Albert Court**, 180 Albert St, T63393939, www.albertcourt.com.sg. An unusually designed hotel (a mixture of Western and Peranakan), lying behind a courtyard of renovated shophouses. This is an intimate place built to high specifications, with attractive extras. Ask for a room with big windows. Right next to a good range of restaurants in Albert Court. Recommended.

B **Kerbau**, 54/63 Kerbau Rd, T62976668, kerbauinn@pacific.net.sg. A/c, small hotel in modernized shophouse on this quiet street. The rooms are nothing special, but clean with attached showers, and if you get one looking out onto Kerbau Rd it is possible to open the shutters in the evening and watch Indian life from above. Good value.

B-C **Bencoolen**, 47 Bencoolen St, T63360822, bencolen@pacific.net.sg This hotel is basic and uninspired, but rooms are clean and the bathrooms are larger than average for this price range. There's a tiny plunge pool and sunbathing area on the second floor. Complimentary continental breakfast at the café on the street.

B-C **City Bayview**, 30 Bencoolen St, T63372882, www.citybayview.com.sg This newly-renovated hotel is an excellent three star choice. There are no grand restaurants or business facilities, but there's a leafy rooftop pool, gym and sauna. Altogether, a neat little hotel block with personal safes, attentive and friendly service, and popular with tour groups. The rooms are smallish, but the hotel is competitively priced and well run.

B-C **Perak Lodge**, 12 Perak Rd, T62997733, www.peraklodge.net A small boutique hotel, with just 34 rooms in a restored and protected building. The rooms are small but clean and tastefully furnished and come with a/c, TV, attached shower, safe and complimentary tea and coffee-making gear. Service is friendly.

B-C **Summer View**, 173 Bencoolen Street, T63381122, www.summerviewhotel.com.sg. A good value basic hotel with comfortable-looking rooms with bath tub and complimentary breakfast.

C **Dickson Court**, 3 Dickson Rd, T62977811, www.dicksoncourthotel.com.sg A surprising little enclave in this bustling street. New, smart, clean and simple, with friendly management. Good value.

C **Hotel 81**, 41 Bencoolen St, T63368181, www.hotel81.com.sg. A chain of 17 no frills hotels, which are great value for the budget traveller. Rooms are clean and well equipped with basics you expect from any hotel including attached bathub, cable TV, coffee and tea making equipment. Had a slightly seedy reputation as an hourly love hotel, but has now spruced up its image. There's another branch in Chinatown. The Bencoolen hotel is closer to Orchard Road. Recommended.

D **Little India Guesthouse**, 3 Veerasamy Rd, T62942866, www.singapore-guesthouse.com Some a/c, no private bathrooms, but spotless male/female shower areas and fairly clean rooms. No food served here, but plenty on the street. Good location in the heart of Little India and all in an attractive salmon-pink shophouse. Recommended.

Arab Street *p583, map p584*

In Arab Street, budget accommodation in Rochor Rd and North Bridge Rd on the corner of Liang Seah St, is nicely juxtaposed with the bustling upmarket Parco Bugis shopping complex and the glitzy *Intercontinental*.

L **Intercontinental**, 80 Middle Rd, Bugis Junction, T63387600, http://singapore.intercontinental.com/ This beautifully designed hotel is one of the best in Singapore. It is situated at the edge of the colonial core in the Arab St area, in an attractively renovated and extended block of Art Deco shophouses, with a high rise block behind. It has over 400 good sized rooms with spacious bathrooms and every luxury provided, attractive rooftop pool with Jacuzzi and well-equipped fitness centre. Business centre with small meeting room. The Shophouse Room is the hotel's showpiece and costs an extra S$60 – for which you get original colonial furniture and parquet flooring.

AL **Golden Landmark**, 390 Victoria St, T62972828, www.goldenlandmark.com.sg This 400-room tower block (with Arabic overtones) is looking older than its 1980s birthdate would indicate. It has an Indonesian restaurant, a big pool, corporate floors and a business centre. It caters mainly for tours and corporate clients – not many Europeans stay here.

B-C **Park View**, 81 Beach Rd, T63388558, www.parkview.com.sg A/c, medium-sized hotel. No pool or gym, but the well-appointed rooms - the deluxe rooms - are a good size and better value than the cramped standard (no windows) and superior rooms.

C-E **New 7th Storey Hotel**, 2/F, 229 Rochor Road, T63370251, www.nsshotel.com This friendly place is well-run with more than 40 rooms ranging from 4-bedroom a/c dorms to big doubles with attached bathroom, fridge, TV and DVD player. The lift is ancient and a tad scary, but all rooms look clean and well kept. Recommended.

D-E **Backpacker Cosy Corner** , 2/F, 490 North Bridge Rd, T62246859, A newly-renovated guest house above a series of Muslim and Indian restaurants on North Bridge Rd, just south of Liang Seah St. After its spruce up this place is a good backpacker choice with clean, simple rooms and dorms with shared bathrooms only and nice touches like free internet and breakfast.

Harbour Front and Sentosa

p585

Staying in these three hotels, as Stan Sesser put it in his New Yorker piece on Singapore, is rather like being a prisoner in a theme park.

L-LL **Sentosa Resort and Spa**, 2 Bukit Manis Rd, T62750331, www.thesentosa.com A/c, restaurants, large (33 m) pool, gym, tennis courts, archery, volley ball court, squash courts, access to the 18-hole Tanjong golf course, luxurious spa and 27 acres of grounds. The most refined of the hotels on Sentosa, smaller, quieter and more elegant than the Rasa Sentosa, with excellent service.

AL **Shangri-La Rasa Sentosa**, 101 Silosa Rd, T62750900, www.shangri- la.com At the western tip of the island, facing the beach, a/c, restaurant, free-form pool, sports facilities, creche, clean beach (sterilized sand imported from Indonesia) with water OK for swimming. Built in a curve, behind Fort Siloso, this hotel has first-class facilities and an unsurpassed view of the oil refinery just across the water, competitive weekend package deals available – though it can get very busy then.

A **Sijori Resort**, 23 Beach View, T62712002, situated close to the action by the 37 m-high Merlion. This hotel/resort opened in early 1997 and is clearly positioned to tempt those people who wish to make full use of Sentosa's attractions.

East Coast

p590, map p591

C **Hotel 81-Joo Chiat**, 305 Joo Chiat Rd, T63488181, www.hotel81.com.sg Good value place to stay for business visitors on a budget. An attractive shophouse hotel with reasonable rooms. *Hotel 81* has a spread of cheap, clean and efficient hotels in the eastern area.

C **Malacca**, 97 Still Rd, T63457411, www.malacca.com.sg. Another good value business hotel in this area of town, 20 mins' walk from nearest MRT station (Eunos). Rooms are very well appointed at the price, with a/c, TV, and attached bathrooms; payment in cash only.

C-D **Gay World Hotel**, 115 Geylang Rd, T67458884. Small hotel just 15 minutes by taxi from the airport. Credit cards accepted. Convenient for business visitors needing somewhere cheaper and out of town centre. Use Kallang MRT.

E **BetelBox Hostel**, 200 Joo Chiat Rd, T62477340, www.betelbox.com. A joint venture by a Singporean and a Dutch former backpacker based in a converted shophouse. The owners have used Aisan-style furnishings. There's a large lounge and kitchen area, breakfast is free. Dorms only available, with shared hot water showers. Free internet and lots of free tours organised. Comes highly recommended. Take bus No 24 from terminal 2 at the airport, get off at Joo Chiat complex, from here it's a 7-min walk. Closest MRT is Payar Lebar, and then a 15-min walk.

Eating

Colonial core *p558, map p564*

1827, Old Parliament House, 1 Parliament Lane, T63371871. Elegant Thai restaurant on the ground floor of the beautifully renovated Parliament House. Great ambience.

Annalakshmi, 02-10 Excelsior Hotel and Shopping Centre, 5 Coleman St, T63399993. North and South Indian vegetarian cuisine. Run on the same basis as Kuala Lumpur's *Annapoorna* – staffed by unpaid housewives, with profits going to the Kalamandhir Indian cultural group. The health drinks are excellent – especially Mango Tharang (mango juice, honey and ginger) and Annalakshmi Special (fruit juices, yoghurt, honey and ginger). The restaurant, which sprawls out onto the verandah overlooking the tennis courts, closes at 2130. Recommended.

Bobby Rubinos, Fountain Court, CHIJMES, 30 Victoria St, T63375477. International; good menu of ribs, burgers and chicken. Booking recommended.

Chinese Feasts, Suntec City Mall, 3 Temasek Blvd, T63376921. Traditional Sichuan fare served in grand surroundings next to Suntec's fountain. Spicey hot pots are their specialty.

Doc Cheng's, Raffles Shopping Arcade, 1 Beach Road, T64121264. New Asian (so-called "trans-ethnic") gives an unusual combinations of flavours. The food, of course, is excellent.

Gatsby, Fountain Court, CHIJMES. Extensive menu of international seafood, meat dishes and salad, and a choice for children too.

Grappas, CHIJMES, Gallery Floor, 30 Victoria St, T63349928. Large Italian restaurant in this trendy courtyard. Extensive menu, with mostly pasta and risotto dishes as well as some meat entrees; booking advisable. Recommended.

Hai Tien Lo, Pan Pacific Hotel, 37th Floor, Marina Square, T68268338. Cantonese restaurant in elegant surroundings, with stunning views of the city. Sharks' fins, steamed lobster and Kobe beef are specialities. Dim sum lunches on Sun.

Jaan, Swissotel The Stamford, 2 Stamford Rd, T68373322 Great venue for a romantic dinner or business lunch atop Singapore's tallest hotel building and features visiting international chefs with "an altitude". Adjoining *Equinox* bar is an atmospheric place for a drink with a view.

Lei Garden, Gallery Floor, CHIJMES, 30 Victoria St, T63393822. A menu which is said to comprise 2,000 dishes. Outstanding Cantonese food: silver codfish, emperor's chicken and such regulars as dim sum and Peking duck. Dignatories, royalty and film stars dine here. Tasteful decor and a 2-tier aquarium displaying the day's offerings. Despite seating for 250, you need to book in advance. Worth every penny. Recommended.

Maison de Fontaine, Gallery Floor, CHIJMES, 30 Victoria St, T63347663. Excellent, sophisticated French restaurant in an attractive setting.

Raffles Grill, Raffles Hotel, 1 Beach Rd (main building, lobby), T64121185. Excellent French cuisine in elegant colonial surroundings, with silver plate settings, chandeliers and reproduction Chippendale furniture.

Ristorante Bologna, Marina Mandarin Hotel, 6 Raffles Blvd, Marina Square, T68451113. Award-winning Italian restaurant, house specialities include spaghetti alla marinara and baked pigeon. Diners lounge amidst sophisticated decor whilst wandering minstrels strum.

Empire Café, Ground Floor, Raffles Hotel, 1 Beach Rd. International food served; not bad for pork chops and oxtail stew, prepared by Chinese cooks and served on marble-topped tables. Also serves chicken rice, burgers and ice creams. *Ah Teng's Bakery* adjoins, selling pricey pastries, pies and biscuits – mostly local favourites.

House of Sundanese Food, several outlets spread around town, eg, Suntec City Marina Square. Typical Sundanese dishes from West Java, with a real home-cooked taste including spicy salad (*keredok*), charcoal-grilled seafood (*ikan Sunda* and *ikan mas*) and curries. Simply decorated non-a/c restaurant.

Imperial Herbal, Hotel, 3rd Floor, 41 Seah St, T63370491. Unusual, delicately flavoured

Chinese food. A resident in-house herbalist takes your pulse (for a fee) and recommends a meal with the appropriate rejuvenating ingredients to balance your yin and yang. Booking recommended for dinner.

La Cave, B1-10 Fountain Court, CHIJMES, 30 Victoria St, T63379717. Fusion cuisine with good servings and a lovely ambience. Good value and excellent service. There is also a bar here, open 1700-2300, with food served from 1900.

Ocho Tapas Bar, Gallery Floor, CHIJMES, 30 Victoria St. Funky little tapas bar with Spanish and Mexican dishes. Also has tables outside in pleasant setting. Good place for a margherita. Friendly service.

Soup Restaurant, 39 Seah Street. A chain of very popular Cantonese restaurants serving herbal soups and Guangdong favourites.

Inle, Peninsula Plaza, Basement, Coleman St. One of Singapore's rare Burmese restaurants. Simple canteen style, with Burmese coffee and Shan noodles.

Komala's Fast Food, Peninsula Plaza, Basement, Coleman St. One of Komala's fast food outlets, serving good South Indian delicacies including thalis, masala dosas and idlis, served at competitive prices; a/c. Next door is the more upmarket **Ganges Restaurant**, which lays on a good lunchtime Indian vegetarian buffet spread.

Cafés and bakeries

Ah Teng's Bakery, Raffles Arcade. Pricey, but it has all the goodies you dream about at the end of a long trip away from home. **Café Aria**, Young Musicians' Society Arts Centre, Waterloo St. Popular for a coffee stop. **Dôme**, just in front of the YMCA on Penang Road. Delicious focaccia sandwiches, patisseries and some of the best coffee in town, good café atmosphere and a pleasant stop for a mid-morning break. Complimentary second cup of coffee. **Seah Street Deli**, Ground Floor, Raffles Hotel, North Bridge Rd. New York-style deli, serving everything from corned beef and smoked salmon to cheesecakes and Turkish pastries.

Hawker centres and food courts

Fountain Terrace, Suntec City, Marina Square. Trendy food court situated under the enormous fountain. **Funan Centre**, South Bridge Rd. This big shopping plaza contains one of the better food courts in Singapore in its basement, with a huge range of foods to choose from; in particular, an excellent Indian stall. **Water Court**, basement of Raffles City. Sophisticated food court, mostly frequented by business people with a penchant for extravagant sandwiches and patisseries – no chicken rice or mutton biryani here.

Tiffin

Tiffin Room, Raffles Hotel, 1 Beach Rd (main building, ground floor). Tiffin curry buffet (plus à la carte menu) in pristine white, overlit, ersatz Victorian grandeur. The food is good, but at S$35 for the buffet, you're paying a lot more for the surroundings than for the curry. Reservation recommended, no sleeveless T-shirts or shorts.

Singapore River and the City

p568, maps p564 and p572

Al Dente Trattoria , 71 Boat Quay. Good pizza and lobster pasta. Also has a Holland Village branch.

Brewerkz, Riverside Point, opposite Clarke Quay, T64382311. This very popular American-style restaurant and bar provides most of its seating under awnings by the riverfront. Great place for lunch, with a menu of satay, buffalo wings, nachos, burgers, steaks and pizza. Also has a children's menu.

Kinara, 57 Boat Quay, distinctive wooden doors at the entrance. North Indian frontier cuisine, good choice of tandoori-baked meat or vegetarian alternatives. Equally atmospheric Fez bar upstairs.

Moomba, behind Penny Black, on Circular Rd. Australian food and a good selection of wine (to take out); also sells wine fridges – a must for anyone residing here!

O'Brien's Irish Sandwich Bar, UOB Building, on the waterfront (just east of Boat Quay). A very popular lunch spot for business people, serving international food.

Pierside, One Fullerton, T61380400 Mainly seafood and some fusion dishes. The main attraction here is the alfresco dining with views of Marina Bay. Try the spiced crab cakes.

Sukhothai, 47 Boat Quay, T65382422. Extensive Thai menu, but the food can be a little hit and miss; booking recommended.

¥¥ **Aburiya**, 60 Robertson Quay, T67354862. Japanese barbecued meat. Quiet location just in front of the Gallery Hotel.

¥¥ **Bukhara**, Block 3C, River Valley Rd, Clarke Quay, T63381411. This award-winning restaurant, named after an Uzbek city, dishes up west Asian cuisine, Singapore style. Its creamy chicken kebab comes recommended. The menu derives from food typically eaten by nomads – meat barbecued over a clay oven.

¥¥ **Café Iguana**, Riverside Point, opposite Clarke Quay. A funky bar and restaurant with a classic choice of Mexican dishes and a good choice of margaritas, try the horny toad.

¥¥ **Lotus**, No.3 Clarke Quay, just next to the G-Max bungy jump, T63367993. A slickly organised restaurant serving a mix of Asian food. Seems to be popular, as the garden alongside the river is regularly packed.

¥¥ **Moghul Mahal**, Shophouse Row, Clarke Quay, T63386907. Northern Indian fare. Service fairly mediocre, but the restaurant is open onto the street, although there's no view of the river. Try the leg of lamb served in flaming rum.

¥¥ **Riverside Indonesian Restaurant**, Riverside Point, opposite Clarke Quay. Bright functional interior, with some alfresco dining overlooking the river, serving Indonesian food: baked pomfret, chilli crabs, grilled chicken. An attractive location.

¥¥ **Tamade**, 60 Robertson Quay, T68368950. Said with the right tones, the name of this restaurant is a very rude insult in Chinese! In spite of, or because of this, this place is popular with its red and white decor, fusion food with major Japanese influence.There's curried lamb shank and wicked chocolate pudding.

¥ **House of Sundanese Food**, 55 Boat Quay. Typical Sundanese dishes, with a real home-cooked taste from West Java including spicy salad (*keredok*), charcoal-grilled seafood (*ikan Sunda* and *ikan mas*) and curries. Simply decorated non-a/c restaurant.

Cafés and bakeries

Dome, in the UOB Building, to the east of Boat Quay. **The Book Cafe** , 20 Martin Road. Just behind The Gallery Hotel. Sandwiches, soups and rich desserts in a relaxing lounge setting with free books to browse.

Hawker centres and food courts

Food Court, Basement of Liang Court, next door to Clarke Quay. Good choice of Asian stalls, Burger King and a play area for children. **Lau Pa Sat Festival Market** (formerly the Telok Ayer Food Centre), at the Raffles Quay end of Shenton Way in the old Victorian market (see page 571). Good range of food on offer: Chinese, Indian, Nonya, Korean, Penang, ice creams, fruit drinks – best in the evening when Boon Tat St is closed off and satay stalls serve up cheap, tasty sticks of chicken, beef, mutton or prawns washed down with jugs of Tiger beer. **Satay Club**, evening stalls in the pedestrian streets of Clarke Quay. The food is good but, being a tourist trap, it's almost double the price of other food courts.

Chinatown *p571, map p572*

The last couple of years has seen a burgeoning of restaurants along Club St. All are top-end eateries, catering for city business people, and all seem to be vying to create the most ostentatious menu (foie gras, venison and seafood are standard fare). Having said this, the standard of cuisine is extremely high.

¥¥¥ **Blue Ginger**, 97 Tanjong Pagar Rd, T62223925. In restored shophouse, good home-cooked Nonya (Peranakan) food and relaxed atmosphere.

¥¥¥ **Da Paolo's**, 80 Club St, (see map, page 574, for location). There are 5 Da Paolo's in Singapore, of which 2 are in Chinatown, in restored shophouses decorated in contemporary fashion. Popular with expats, Italian homemade pasta, but overpriced.

¥¥¥ **Indochine**, 49B Club St, T63230503. Indochinese food; plenty of fish on the menu here, from squid to mussels to tiger prawns, the ground floor is the *Sa Vanh Bar*, ethnically decorated with a laidback feel, whilst dining is on the upper floor. Running water on both levels adds to the serene atmosphere, but they have undermined this a tad by arranging the tables too close together for comfort. The bar is open 1700-0300. The restaurant has sister establishments at Wisma Atria on Orchard Road and on Clarke Quay.

¥¥¥ **L'Aigle d'Or**, Duxton Hotel, 83 Duxton Rd, T62277678. A few Oriental touches and a good vegetarian selection, extensive, expensive French menu with wine list to match, sophisticated atmosphere, popular as a business venue at lunchtime, booking recommended.

L'Angelos, Club St. Another contender for the 'richest menu on Club Street' contest, with foie gras, duck, pork tripe and veal – classic French food, run by a Frenchman.

Mama Africa, 88 Telok Ayer St, T65329339, on the eastern edge of Far East Square. A diverse and quirky menu; oysters or standloper snoekfish, ostrich or venison. Surround yourself in African memorabilia and transport yourself from Asia to the dark continent, if only for an hour or two.

Senso, 21 Club St. An all-Italian experience, with 'neo-classical Italian cooking'. Superb cuisine, great atmosphere, sophisticated London-style joint.

Thanying, Amara Hotel, T62277856. Provides the best Thai food in town, extensive menu and superb food (the 15 female chefs are all said to have trained in the royal household in Bangkok). Specialities include deep fried garoupa, *yam som-o* (spicy pomelo salad), *khao niaw durian* (durian served on a bed of sticky rice – available from May-Aug), as well as such classics as *tom yam kung* (spicy prawn soup with lemongrass); booking necessary. Recommended.

Bamboo Court, 130 Amoy St, Far East Square. A Thai-Chinese eatery set in former temple grounds. There's an a/c section or tables in the garden around a pleasant fountain.

Pasta Brava, 11 Craig Rd, Tanjong Pagar. Tastiest Italian in town in an equally tasty shophouse conversion; fairly expensive, but good choice of genuine Italian fare. Recommended.

Sanur, 3rd Floor, 133 New Bridge Rd. Malay/Indonesian restaurant, one of a chain, specialities include fish-head curry and spicy grilled chicken.

Swee Kee, 12 Ann Siang Rd, T2228926. This first-floor Chinese restaurant has acquired some degree of local renown due to the owner Tang Kwong Swee – known to his friends as 'Fish-head' – having run the same place for 60 years (although the location has changed). Recommended are the deep-fried chicken, Hainanese style, fish-head noodle soup and prawns in magi sauce; very popular.

Tiong Shiang, corner of Keong Saik and New Bridge roads. Very popular Hainanese corner café, with tables spilling out onto the street.

Wan Tang Eating House, 2 Trengganu St. A rowdy Cantonese restaurant serving seafood and cheap Tiger beer with tables on the street at the corner of Trengganu and Pagoda Sts. Popular.

Cafes and bakeries

Beans & Bread, 57-58 Amoy St. A friendly little café with old movie star posters serving cakes, pastries and sandwiches. **Tea Chapter**, 9A-11A Neil Rd, Chinatown, T62261175. An excellent little place on 3 floors with a choice of seating (on the floor or at tables), a peaceful atmosphere, plenty of choice of teas as well as sweet and savoury snacks, games for those who want to tarry, and the director, Lee Peng Shu, and his wife enthusiastically talk you through the tea tasting ceremony (if you wish). Recommended.

Hawker centres and food courts

Amoy Street Food Centre, just south of Al-Abrar Mosque at southern end of Amoy St. Excellent little centre, worth a graze. **Chinatown Complex Hawker Centre**, Block 335, 1st Floor, Smith St. Recommended stall: Ming Shan (No 179), for its *kambing* (mutton) soup; famed for decades, though a pretty scruffy food centre. A pleasant place to snack at night is along Trengganu Street where hawkers set up stalls. **Murray Terrace Food Alley**, for a strip of cheap Chinese and Malay restaurants. **Tanjong Pagar Plaza Food Centre**, Tanjong Pagar Rd, southern end.

Orchard Road and Botanic Gardens *p577, map p578*

Au Jardin, EJH Corner House, Singapore Botanic Gardens Visitors' Centre, 1 Cluny Rd, T64668812. Situated in the former garden director's black and white bungalow, with only 12 tables, this French restaurant is elegant and sophisticated, with a menu which is changed weekly. Booking essential.

Blu, Shangri-La Hotel, 22 Orange Grove

Rd, T62134598. Situated on the 24th floor, Blu provides stunning views, great service and excellent Californian food. Recommended.

TTT **Esmirada's**, corner of Peranakan Place and Orchard Rd, T67353476. Mediterranean food in Spanish-style taverna, good salads, paella, couscous. Always packed, reservations recommended.

TTT **Gordon Grill**, Lobby, Goodwood Park Hotel, 22 Scotts Rd, T67301744. One of the last grills in town, Singapore's only Scottish restaurant with haggis on the menu – at 24 hrs advance notice. Plenty of choice cuts of meat to choose from. Superb desserts.

TTT **Harbour Grill and Oyster Bar**, Hilton Hotel, 581 Orchard Rd, T67303393. Contemporary surroundings with nautical theme, serving international food. Delicacies include caviar and smoked salmon; monthly guest chef. Impeccable service.

TTT **Kintamani**, Novotel Apollo, 405 Havelock Rd, T67396463. Balinese-style interior, extensive buffet spread available at lunch and dinner.

TTT **Les Amis**, Shaw Centre, 1 Scotts Rd, T67332225. Great French food, excellent service and extensive wine list. Closes at 2200.

TTT **Mezza9**, Grand Hyatt Hotel, 10-12 Scotts Rd, T64167189. Incorporates Western Grill, Japanese food, Chinese, a salad bar and a patisserie. A la carte during the week and a set-price buffet brunch on Sun 1100-1500.

TTT **Min Jiang**, Goodwood Park Hotel, 22 Scotts Rd, T67301704. Large, noisy room, expansive Szechuan menu, with excellent reputation – delicious hot and sour soup, and good choice of seafood, 7 private rooms as well, booking recommended.

TTT **Nanbantei**, 5/F Far East Plaza, 12 Scotts Rd, T67335666. Japanese eatery, famous for its yakitori. Tables divided by shoji screens.

TTT **Pete's Place**, Grand Hyatt, Scott's Rd, basement, T64167113. One of the oldest Italian restaurants in Singapore, huge helpings, popular set price Sun brunch.

TTT **Seasons**, Four Seasons Hotel, 190 Orchard Blvd, T67341110. Sophisticated surroundings and unusual international food combinations make this a relaxed and pleasurable gastronomic experience. At weekends they cater for children.

TTT **Shahi Maharani**, 25 Scotts Rd, T62358840. North Indian tandoor – especially good seafood dishes. Live performances during dinner; a cosy place.

TTT **Top of the M**, Meritus Mandarin Hotel, 39/F, 333 Orchard Rd, T68316258. A revolving restaurant with good views of the city. Tuck into steaks while serenaded by wandering guitarists. A novel experience.

TT **Blood Café**, 290 Orchard Rd, Paragon, T67356765. Funky café with style and fashion magazines to browse behind the *ProjectShockBloodBrothers* clothes shop on the second floor. Relaxing place, with an inventive menu featuring couscous, roasted vegetables and chunky sandwiches. Very hip and healthy. Good veggie choices. Recommended.

TT **Hard Rock Café**, 02-01 HPL House, 50 Cuscaden Rd. One of the best bets for international food: a decent steak, buffalo wings or a bacon cheeseburger, open until 0200.

TT **Lei Garden**, Orchard Shopping Centre, 321 Orchard Rd, T67343988, and Orchard Plaza, 150 Orchard Rd, T67382448. Another branch of this famous Cantonese restaurant. Book in advance. Recommended.

TT **Orchard Maharajah**, 27 Cuppage Terr, T67326331. Excellent North Indian food – tandoori and Kashmiri – 7 different types of bread to choose from. Conveniently located in a converted shophouse close to some good bars. Another branch at 41 Boat Quay.

TT **Sakura**, 2/F and 5/F Far East Plaza. Packed restaurant with no pretensions serving Halal Thai-Chinese fare. If the crowds are anything to go by, then it's worth a try.

TT **Sanur**, 17/18, 4th Floor, Centrepoint, 176 Orchard Rd, T67343434. Cramped Malay/Indonesian restaurant ideally placed for shoppers, specialities including fish-head curries and spicy grilled chicken or fish.

TT **Singapore Polo Club**, 80 Mount Pleasant Rd (just off Thomson Rd). If you're not put off by the polo set or visiting sultans, the Polo Club is a great place to dine (or drink Pimms) on the verandah – especially on match days (Tue, Thu and Sat) when there's plenty to look at. There is a snack menu (steak sandwich, fish and chips etc) for the verandah overlooking the turf and a smarter restaurant inside.

TT **Sushi Tei**, Paragon, 290 Orchard Rd. Japanese; great conveyor-belt sushi.

TT **Tambuah Mas**, 4th Floor, Tanglin

Shopping Centre, T67333333 (another branch at The Paragon, on the corner of Bridge and Orchard Rds). Very popular and cramped a/c Indonesian restaurant. What it lacks in ambience, it more than makes up for with the food; specialities include *ayam goreng istimewa* (marinated fried chicken). Recommended.

Le Viet, 14 Scotts Rd, opp Hyatt Grand, T67337100. A fairy-lit street side Vietnamese café with nightly live band. Wonderfully tacky.

Cafés

Checkers Deli, Hilton Hotel, Orchard Rd, for a fabulous selection of cheesecakes, cakes and pastries. **Dôme**, Lane Crawford House, Orchard Rd and The Promenade on Orchard Rd. Delicious focaccia sandwiches, patisseries and some of the best coffee in town, good café atmosphere and a pleasant stop for a mid-morning break. **Goodwood Park Hotel**, Scotts Rd. Sophisticated buffet tea, served on the lawn by the pool. **Rose Veranda**, Shangri-La Hotel, 22 Orange Grove Rd, said to offer the best tea in town. **Spinelli Coffee**, The Heeren, Orchard Rd. Relaxing coffee shop with outdoor seating and friendly staff.

Hawker centres and food courts

Newton Circus, Scotts Rd, north of Orchard Rd. Despite threats of closure by the government, this huge food centre of over 100 stalls is still surviving and dishing up some of the best food of its kind. Open later than others so very popular with tourists. **Taman Serasi**, Cluny Rd, opposite entrance to Botanic Gardens, small centre but well known for roti John and superb satay; mainly Malay stalls, excellent fruit juice. Many of the plazas along Orchard Rd provide foodcourts in their basements. Convenient and cheap.

Little India *p580, map p581*

Restaurants here range from sophisticated a/c places to the simplest of banana plate eateries. For North Indian cuisine, the best option is to trot down to the southern end of Race Course Rd, where there are 6 good restaurants in a row, all competing for business, including the *Banana Leaf Apolo*, *Delhi* and, most famous of all, *Muthu's*. Some of the best vegetarian restaurants – South Indian particularly – are found on the other side of Serangoon Rd, along Upper Dickson Rd.

La Fête du Cuisinier, 161 Middle Rd, T63330917, on the corner of Waterloo St and Middle Rd. A surprising location for one of the more sophisticated restaurants in town. Exquisite French Creole cuisine – a lavish menu of foie gras, oysters and crab (and that's only the starters). Attractive setting, elaborate French decor in Marie Antoinette style.

Andhra Curry, 41 Kerbau Rd. South Indian cuisine, popular place in the heart of things.

Banana Leaf Apolo, 56-58 Race Course Rd. North Indian food, another popular fish-head curry spot, a/c and more sophisticated than the name might imply – although the food is still served on banana leaves to justify the name. Recommended.

D' Deli, 60 Race Course Rd. North Indian, Mughlai and Kashmiri, under same management as *Delhi* just up the road, with a similar good reputation.

Delhi, Race Course Rd. North Indian food including chicken tikka, various tandooris, as well as creamy Kashmiri concoctions. Popular and award-winning restaurant.

Jaggi's, 34 Race Course Rd. North Indian cuisine, immaculately clean and extremely popular.

Komala Vilas, 76-78 Serangoon Rd, T62936980, and 12 Buffalo Rd. South Indian thalis and masala dosas, bustling café, with a little more room upstairs. Recommended.

Muthu's Curry, corner of Rotan Lane and Race Course Rd, T62937029. North Indian food, reckoned by connoisseurs to be among the best banana leaf restaurants in town; Muthu's fish-heads are famous. Recommended.

Our Makan Shop, Race Course Rd. Sparse looking place, but extremely popular – so they must be doing something right; another excellent Indian joint.

Kamal's Vegetarian, Cuff Rd. Vegetarian restaurant; excellent paper and masala dosas.

Komala's Fast Food, Upper Dickson Rd. This is the fast food end of the Komala empire – South Indian delicacies including thalis, masala dosas and idlis are served in an a/c restaurant. Very popular and recommended.

ᛉ **New Delhi**, Broadway Hotel, 195 Serangoon Rd. Good, cheap vegetarian and non-vegetarian North Indian food, specialities are chicken and almond, and seafood curries.

ᛉ **Ponthuk Bawean Restaurant**, Dunlop Rd (at Jln Besar end). Simple, open-air Malay restaurant in a wonderfully gaudy shophouse, serving such dishes as beef rendang, chilli eggs and spicy beans.

ᛉ **Rocher Beancurd**, corner of Middle Rd and Short St. Popular noodle joint.

ᛉ **Woodlands**, 12 Upper Dickson Rd (off Serangoon Rd), T62971594. Thalis, masala dosa and vegetarian curries, good and cheap. Recommended.

Hawker centres and food courts

Albert Centre, between Waterloo and Queen streets. There's a huge area of hawker stalls here. **Lavender Food Square**, Lavender Rd, north of Little India. Is one of the best hawker centres in town. **Paradiz Centre Basement Food Centre**, 1 Selegie Rd, recommended stall: Mr Boo's Teochew Mushroom Minced Meat Mee (No 34). **Zhujiao or Kandang Kerbau (KK) Food Centre**, on the corner of Buffalo and Serangoon roads. Wide range of dishes, and the best place for Indian Muslim food: curries, rotis, dosai and murtabak are hard to beat (beer can be bought from the Chinese stalls on the other side).

Cafés and bakeries

Café Oriel, Ground Floor of Selegie Arts Centre, off Prinsep St. Popular for its pizzas. **Zhong Guo Hua Tuo Guan**, 52 Queen St (name above the tea house is in Chinese characters), just by the Albert and Waterloo streets roadside market. This traditional Chinese tea house has quite a few outlets, including this atmospheric one. It sells Hua Tuo's ancient recipes, helpful for 'relieving of heatiness' and 'inhibiting the growth of tumor cells,' amongst other things. Very friendly proprietress will introduce you to wild ginseng and showfrog or longan (a fruit like a lychee) herbal jelly, and tell you why you will feel better (that's if you can get any of the concoctions down!).

Arab Street *p583, map p584*

Arab St is the best area for Muslim food of all descriptions – Malay, Indonesian, Indian or Arabic. There are some good restaurants around the Sultan Mosque and many more on noisy North Bridge Rd. Try the Parco Bugis Shopping Centre for non-Muslim restaurants including good Italian ones, and New Bugis St for simple open-air fare and jugs of cold beer.

ᛉᛉᛉ **Bumbu**, 44 Kandahar St, T63928628. Beautifully decorated with Peranakan antiques and screens. Fare is a Thai and Indonesian mix, famous for its deep fried fish.

ᛉᛉᛉ **Masakatsu**, Ground Floor, Parco Bugis Shopping Centre, 80 Middle Rd, T63348233. Japanese. Known for its hotpot. Book at weekends.

ᛉᛉᛉ **Olive Tree Restaurant and Café**, Intercontinental Hotel, 80 Middle Rd, T64311061. The café is situated in the Parco Bugis shopping mall, whilst the restaurant is cosier and separate from all those frantic shoppers. Both serve the same good Mediterranean food – there's a good buffet.

ᛉᛉᛉ **Pasta Fresca da Salvatore**, Shaw Centre. Fresh Italian food; tasty pizzas and a good range of pasta dishes, open 24 hrs.

ᛉᛉᛉ **Pimai Thai**, Intercontinental Hotel, 80 Middle Rd, T64311064. Excellent Thai menu with unusually extensive dessert buffet.

ᛉᛉ **Bibik's Place**, Pahang St. Upmarket little place in a renovated shophouse, excellent Nonya dishes.

ᛉᛉ **Chuan**, 9 Purvis St, T63384755. Sichuan hotpot that promises to set your mouth on fire.

ᛉᛉ **Pivdofr**, 1 Liang Seah St, T63362995. A shophouse café serving classic international fare such as pizza, macaroni cheese or pork chops. Good service.

ᛉᛉ **Sketches**, Parco Bugis Shopping Centre, 80 Middle Rd, T63398386. A novel approach to ordering Italian, with boxes to tick for 9 types of pasta, 8 sauces and some garnishes. Quick and fairly basic food.

ᛉᛉ **Sushi Sagano**, Parco Bugis Shopping Centre, Victoria St, T63376766. Japanese; the set menu is affordable, seafood is good as is the sashimi.

ᛉᛉ **Wholmeals**, Parco Bugis Shopping Centre, 200 Victoria St, T63379257. All food is low fat and low salt. Good set lunch with choice of four main courses. Fab juice drinks too.

Ұ **Rumah Makan Minang**, Kandahar St (facing onto the Istana Kampong Glam). Small restaurant serving cheap Padang (West Sumatran) dishes, including beef rendang (dry beef curry), spicy grilled fish and kangkung.

Ұ **Zam Zam Restaurant**, junction of Arab St and North Bridge Rd. Muslim Malay-Indian dishes served in busy and chaotic coffee shop. Very popular and recommended for a taste of the other Singapore – spicy meats, chargrilled seafood, creamy curries.

Harbour Front and Sentosa

p585

ҰҰҰ **Long Beach Seafood**, 31 Marina Park, Marina South, T63232222. One of the island's most famous seafood restaurants, specializing in pepper and chilli-crabs, drunken prawns and baby squid cooked in honey.

ҰҰҰ **Prima Tower Revolving Restaurant**, 201 Keppel Rd, T62728822. Revolving restaurant atop a huge silo looks out over the harbour and city, established 20 years ago with the same chef still working here. Beijing cuisine, particularly good Peking duck, book in advance.

ҰҰҰ **The Cliff** at the **Sentosa Resort & Spa**, T62750331, which has good sea views from dining perches. It's worth splashing out on the buffet at the adjoining terrace.

Ұ **Dotty Café**, Bukit Chermin Rd, off Keppel Marina, T62708575, and Telok Blangah Rd, just west of where the cable car goes over the road. Call Dorothy before you go and plan your seafood menu to get the best catch of the day. Eat under fairy lights, right on the sea, and admire yachts moored next door, very quiet and peaceful.

Ұ **Han's**, 8 branches around the city including HarbourFront. This chain of restaurants is Singapore's answer to the Greasy Spoon – cafes without the acute accent on the 'e', single dish Chinese meals, simple (largely fried) breakfasts, some European food including such things as steaks, burgers and fries, all served in large helpings at very competitive prices.

Hawker centres and food courts

The **Sentosa Food Centre**, close to the ferry terminal, is a squeaky-clean hawker centre, serving Malay, Chinese, Peranakan, Indian and Western cuisine. The dishes are pricier than elsewhere in Singapore and the food is sometimes disappointing; open 1100-2200.

Singapore West *p588*

ҰҰҰ **Au Petit Salut**, Jl Merah Saga, Holland Village, T64751976. French patisserie-style restaurant. Some main course dishes, but come here for the pastries and cakes.

ҰҰҰ **Brazil Churrascaria**, 14-16 Sixth Av (off Bukit Timah Rd), T64631923. If carnivore-style is your thing, this Brazilian restaurant – with its huge skewers of barbecued (churrascaria is Portuguese for barbecue) meat – is for you; as much meat as you can eat.

ҰҰҰ **Cha Cha Cha**, 35 Lorong Mambong, Holland Village, T64621650. Small and informal Mexican restaurant, with some outdoor seating and an extensive menu. Always bustling with locals. Food is reputedly more authentic than the adjoining Mexican place which sports poncho tablecloths.

ҰҰҰ **Da Paolo**, Jl Merah Saga, Holland Village, T64761332. Italian restaurant with indoor or terrace dining. The most sophisticated restaurant on this strip, with food to match.

ҰҰҰ **Lucerne**, Pasir Panjang Village, T67761221. Sophisticated Swiss restaurant.

ҰҰҰ **Michelangelo's**, Jl Merah Saga, Holland Village, T64759069. Under same management as Sistina and Original Sin, Italian, range of pasta dishes and other specialities. Pleasant surroundings (both indoor or terrace seating), fairly average food for the price. Booking recommended, especially at the weekend.

ҰҰҰ **Original Sin**, Jl Merah Saga, Holland Village, T64755605. Mediterranean vegetarian restaurant, with some really intriguing dishes. Try the Lentil Tower, packed with lentils, eggplants, roasted peppers and haloumi cheese. Indoor or terrace dining. Booking recommended, especially at the weekend. Recommended.

ҰҰҰ **Shayray**, Lorong Mambong, Holland Village. North Indian, tandoori. Recommended.

Sistina, Jl Merah Saga, Holland Village, T64767782. Under same management as Michelangelo's and Original Sin, this place is primarily a pizza joint. Attractive location, with indoor or outdoor dining. Booking recommended, especially at the weekend.

Sukhothai, Lorong Mambong, Holland Village. Thai, authentic and recommended.

Sushi Tei, 20 Lorong Mambong, Holland Village. Japanese sushi bar, where you grab food from a conveyor belt as it glides by.

Wala-Wala, 31 Lorong Mambong, Holland Village, T64624288. Buzzy atmosphere and pretty tiles on the tables in this Mexican restaurant; good, honest, no pretentions.

Westlake Eating House, Empress Dr, off Farrer Rd, 1st flr of an HDB block. Big indoor and outdoor restaurant serving Singapore-Chinese food. Extensive menu, including delicious black-peppered prawns and baby kailan; great value for money.

NYDC, 30 Lorong Mambong, Holland Village. Stands for New York Dessert Café, this is the place to come for your sugar fix, with cheesecake to die for. Also serves savoury food.

Qhue, 242 Pasir Panjang Rd, T64716501. Fusion cuisine with indoor or outdoor seating. Excellent choice of food and good atmosphere.

Samy's Curry Restaurant, Civil Service Club, Dempsey Rd. A wonderful Indian establishment where food is served at your table on a banana leaf – you pay for what you take – great value and very atmospheric. Highly recommended, especially by Indians.

East coast *p590, map p591*

The east coast is a particularly good place to experience seafood in one of the large, casual-style restaurants, where customers pick their own fish from tanks and then choose how they'd like it cooked.

Al Forno East Coast, 400 East Coast Rd, T63488781. Authentic Italian cuisine with fine, but pricey Italian wine to match.

Casa Bom Vento, 467 Joo Chiat Rd, T63487786. Eurasian and Peranakan cuisine. Famous for its Katong jelly drink – unique to this restaurant.

Chao Phaya Thai Seafood, Block 730, 2nd flr, Ang Mo Kio Ave 6, T64560118. Enormous informal restaurant with huge choice of authentic Thai dishes, including chilli crab, tom yam kung and green, yellow or red curried fish.

Granita's, 17 Crescendo Building, Upper East Coast Rd, T62421353. Californian-Mediterranean cuisine in intimate restaurant.

The Olea, 158 Upper East Coast Rd, T4493880. Authentic Greek cuisine, classics such as tzatziki and souvlaki lamb. Also has a deli which sells range of olives, taramasalata, etc.

AJ's Tandoori, 328 Joo Chiat Rd, opposite Hotel 81, T64401257. Typical North Indian menu; Kashmiri chicken is good.

Bernie's, 961A Upper Changi Rd, T65422232. American fare in a laid-back setting, with friendly staff and big American-style helpings.

International Seafood Centre, East Coast Parkway, provides trolleys to choose your fish pre-cooked. Not for the squeamish. Recommended.

Kim's Seafood Restaurant, 477 Changi Rd, T67421119. Claypot pepper crabs are the speciality in Mr Tan's cheap and informal seafood restaurant, open to 0130 weekdays and 0230 on Sat.

Palm Beach Seafood Restaurant, Kallang Leisure Park, 1st and 2nd floors, 5 Stadium Walk, T63443088. Located near the International Building and the National Stadium, spread over 4 a/c floors, basic decor; tiled flooring and melamine crockery, good shellfish at a fair price – the chilli crab is a speciality.

Peranakan Inn, 210 East Coast Rd. Prompt service in this popular restaurant, selling classic Peranakan food such as galangal, *ayam buah keluak*, *chap chye* and *itek tim*.

UDMC Seafood Centre, 1000 East Coast Parkway. There are 10 outlets here and they're all good. In particular: **Gold Coast Live Seafood**, T64482020, and **Jumbo Seafood**, East Coast Parkway, T64423435. Serving Singapore specialities like chilli crabs and black pepper crayfish.

Charlie's, Block 2, 01-08, Changi Village, T65420867. Charlie's folks, who were first generation immigrants from China, set up the Changi Milk Bar in the 1940s, then Charlie's Corner became the favoured watering hole and makan stop for sailors and riggers for decades. His mum still fries up the chips that gave them the reputation as the best chippies east of London's Isle of Dogs, excellent chilli-dogs, spicy chicken wings and other international food, as well as 70 beers to choose from, closed weekends. Recommended. Bus to Changi Point from Tampines MRT.

House of Sundanese Food, 218 East Coast Rd, T63455020. Typical Sundanese dishes from West Java include spicy salad (*keredok*), charcoal-grilled seafood (*ikan sunda, ikanemas*) and curries, a/c restaurant with real home-cooked food, small portions.

Bars and clubs

Most big hotels have discos, cover charge usually S$25-30.

Colonial core *p558, map p564*

Bar and Billiard Room, Raffles Hotel, Beach Rd. Relocated from its original position, the bar is lavishly furnished with teak tables, oriental carpets and two original billiard tables.

Brauhaus, United Square, 101 Thomson Rd. Micro brewery serving a massive range of beers to business folk. German sausage and other Teutonic delicacies in a pleasant underground garden.

China Jump, Fountain Court, CHIJMES, Victoria St. This bar and restaurant has outdoor seating and some booths inside. The menu is hardly revolutionary and the name should really be USA Jump, since it serves the usual American bistro-style food of burgers, salads, generic Mexican and a few adapted Asian dishes to give it a drizzle of local ambience. Food is good despite the lack of culinary inspiration. Cocktails and beer.

Equinox, atop Swissotel Stamford, the cocktail lounge is situated in the Stamford Tower and provides a good choice of bevvies.

Father Flannagan's Irish Pub, CHIJMES, Fountain Court, 30 Victoria St. Ersatz Irish pub with Irish beer on tap and a high density of local business people. Some Irish food (stews etc) also available.

Lock, Stock and Barrel Pub, 29 Seah St. This dark bar/pub with juke box is popular with expats on a budget and backpackers. Extended happy hour from 1600 to 2000.

Rascals, Pan Pacific Hotel, Marina Square, 6 Raffles Blvd. Open 1800-0300, disco, extended happy hour, Sun is gay night.

Reading Room, Marina Mandarin Hotel, Marina Square, is a smart, expensive and pretentious disco which attracts a younger crowd.

Scandals, Westin Plaza Hotel, Raffles City Complex, popular hotel disco.

The Long Bar, Raffles Hotel, 1-3 Beach Rd. The home of the Singapore Sling, originally concocted by bartender Ngiam Tong Boon in 1915 (see page 550), now on 2 levels and extremely popular with tourists and locals alike, gratuitous tiny dancing mechanical punkah-wallahs sway out of sync to the cover band.

Writers' Bar, Raffles Hotel, 1 Beach Rd (just off the main lobby). In honour of the likes of Somerset Maugham, Rudyard Kipling, Joseph Conrad, Noel Coward and Herman Hesse, who were said either to have wined, dined or stayed at the hotel. Bar research indicates that other literary luminaries from James A Michener to Noel Barber and the great Arthur Hailey are said to have sipped Tigers at the bar – as the bookcases and momentoes suggest.

Singapore River and the City *p568*

There are lots of bars on Boat and Clarke quays; those at the former are wilder and less packaged, although the last few years has seen a slight deterioration in quality as locals have moved on and tourists have become the dominant clientele. One of the more dramatic changes over the past couple of years is the development along the riverfront westwards. Both Robertson's Walk and The Quayside are gradually filling up with shops and restaurants, and the nearby Mohammed Sultan Rd has become an extremely popular watering hole; the entire street is lined with bars and clubs. The west side is a row of restored shophouses, whilst the east is a modern high-rise block.

1NiteStand, 3A River Valley Rd, Clarke Quay. Big, dark bar with regular comedy nights, variety shows and nightly in-house band.
BB's, The Bungy Bar, 3E River Valley Rd, Clarke Quay. Busy bar facing the bungy jump. Drink your pints and enjoy the screams.
BQ Bar, 39 Boat Quay. The most popular bar on Boat Quay, which still attracts an evening crowds of expats.
Brewerkz, Riverside Point. One of the micro breweries which are all the rage in Asia. Good beer, but pricey.
Centro, One Fullerton, T63338117. Great club with views of Marina Bay. Attracts international DJs and is one of Singapore's top clubbing venues.
Coco Carib, 3C River Valley Rd, Clarke Quay. Lively and fun Caribbean bar with nightly music.
Crazy Elephant, Clarke Quay, T63371190. Live music, graffiti scrawled walls, popular place for a drink following a meal.
Dbl O (pronounced 'Double O'), Robertson Walk, 11 Unity St. New posh dance club, with a spacious dance floor and 10 m-high ceilings. Open 2000 to 0300; happy hour 2000-2200.
Hard Landers, 231 River Valley Rd, on the eastern corner of Mohammed Sultan Rd. Fashioned after a Chinese Huay Quan or clan house. Open 1700-0300, with happy hour from 1700-2100 daily.
Harry's Bar, 28 Boat Quay. Large bar with seating outside overlooking the river, popular with City boys, serves pricey food on the 1st floor, jazz band.
Liquid Room, Gallery Ev@son, 76 Robertson Quay. Hi-tech disco. On two floors, with different music on each, the Sound Bar is open from 1900-0300 daily, whilst the Liquid Room is open from 2230-0300. Happy hour is from 1900-2100.
Molly Malone's, 42 Circular Rd (behind Boat Quay). Irish pub, complete with stout and Irish folk music (also serves food).
Penny Black, 26 Boat Quay. A stylized English Victorian London pub, with some classic English food.
Rootz, 20 Upper Circular Rd, behind Boat Quay. Soul and groove music. Open 1800-0300, happy hour 1800-2200.
Siam Supperclub, Mohammed Sultan Rd. A tastefully decorated place (with a reputed 56 Buddha images on display), spirit mixes such as 'Buddha jumps over the wall' available.
Sugar, 13 Mohammed Sultan Rd. Cushioned walls and deeply cool.
Tajie, 27 Mohammed Sultan Rd. Varied music and popular with the younger crowd. Open 1800-0300, happy hour Mon-Thu 1800-2130.
The Yard, 294 River Valley Rd. The Singaporean version of a London pub, complete with darts, dominos, fish 'n' chips and Newcastle Brown Ale.
Trader Vics, 5th Floor, New Otani Hotel, River Valley Rd. Hawaii 5-0 décor and Chin-Ho's favourite cocktails – try a few goblets of Tikki Puka Puka for something violently different.
Velvet Underground, 17 Jiak Kim St (off Kim Seng Rd), next door to Zouk and under the same management. Small nightclub, open until 2100-0300 Tue-Sat, cover S$25, free for women on Wed nights. Recommended. Often has gay or lesbian parties.
Wong San's, Mohammed Sultan Rd. One on both sides of the street, the Eastside version is also a sushi bar.
Zouk, 17 Jiak Kim St, opp the Concorde Hotel. Huge quirky club, with a fun design. Described as the place for hard clubbing.

Chinatown *p571, map p572*

There are several quiet bars on Duxton Hill, Chinatown, in a pleasant area of restored shophouses – a retreat from the hustle and bustle of Boat Quay or the city. Duxton Road and Tanjong Pagar Road also provide a dozen or so bars in restored shophouses.
Beaujolais Winebar, 1 Ann Siang Hill, T62242227. Very pleasant wine bar in restored shophouse, serves reasonably priced wine, candles in wine bottles on the window-sills, atmospheric, good cheese and charcuterie platters. Recommended.
Boom Boom Boom, Far East Square, 130 Amoy St. Open until 0200.
Carnegie's, Far East Square, Pekin St, has 366 shooters to choose from.
Fluid, 11 Purvis St, has 100 shooters and a range of vodkas available.
JJ Mahoney's, 55 Duxton Rd, T62256225, is not quite the Irish bar the name might suggest; beer and karaoke.

Orchard Road and Botanic Gardens *p577, map p578*

Peranakan Place just off Hollywood Road is home to a string of funky New York-style bars carved out of restored shophouses. You are looking at S$15 a pint, these places are not cheap, but they are very stylish, albeit poseury.

Acid Bar, 180 Orchard Rd, Peranakan Place, T67388828. Big lounge-style bar, chilled atmosphere, and mammoth mirrors to make the place look cavernous.

Alley Bar, 1 Emerald St, T67388818. Faux alleyway with clever lighting, hip music, and scarey bar bills.

Aquadisiac Club, Wisma Atria, T62383452. Pretentious club with a massive aquarium running along one wall.

Brannigan's (basement of Grand Hyatt), 10/12 Scotts Rd. Open until 0100, 0200 on Fri and Sat, American style, touristy bar with loud live music and video screens, haunt of the infamous SPG (Singapore Party Girl), very popular.

Hard Rock Café, HPL House, 50 Cuscaden Rd, west end of Orchard Rd. Complete with limo in suspended animation and queues to enter.

Ice Cold, 9 Emerald Hill. If you like a slightly anarchic feel to your bars, with loud music and darts, then this is a good place. In an old shophouse at the top of the pedestrianized section of Emerald Hill, good place for a drink away from Orchard Rd, popular with locals, 35 beers to choose from, Happy Hours 1700-2100.

Kaspia Bar, Hilton Hotel, Orchard Rd. For the widest selection of vodkas in Singapore and live jazz.

Mezza9, Grand Hyatt Hotel, Orchard Rd, provides a selection of 30 Martinis.

Muddy Murphy's, Orchard Hotel Shopping Arcade, rowdy Irish pub full of tourists and expats.

Number 5, 5 Emerald Hill. Happy hours 1200-2100 Mon-Sat, 1700-2100 Sun, at the top of the pedestrianized section of Emerald Hill, retro-chic restored shophouse bar and restaurant (upstairs), popular with young expats and Chuppies (Chinese yuppies), great music. Recommended.

Observation Lounge, Mandarin Hotel, 333 Orchard Rd. Circular cocktail bar on the 38th floor.

Que Pasa, 7 Emerald Hill. This is a wine bar in a converted shophouse, with a small snack menu of tapas, oysters and olives and an extensive wine menu. It is near the top of the pleasant pedestrianized section of Emerald Hill and next door to the slightly wilder Ice Cold Bar.

Ridleys, ANA Hotel, Nassim Hill. Another good club, open 1800-0300, 1930-0300 weekends, happy hour 1800-2200.

Roar, 15 Cairnhill Rd. A new dance club with lots of space – 7,000 sq ft – 2 bars and a dance floor. Open 1800-0300 weekdays and 2000-0300 Sat. Happy hour 1800-2100.

Sparks, Level 7, Ngee Ann City, Orchard Rd. The biggest disco in all of Asia, very glitzy with KTV rooms and jazz bar, packed at weekends, open 1900-0300, happy hour 1900-2100 daily. Cover: S$15 Mon-Thu, S$20 Fri-Sun.

The Dubliner, Winsland Conservation House, 165 Penang Rd, T67352220. Irish pub set inside a beautifully restored colonial house. Very friendly, good hearty Irish food as well as the compulsory pints of Guinness and Kilkenny. Recommended.

Top Ten Club, Orchard Towers, 400 Orchard Rd. Huge converted cinema, often has live black-American or Filipino disco bands. Recommended.

Venom, Pacific Plaza, Scott's Rd, a recent addition, glamorous and exclusive.

Woodstock, Rooftop, Far East Plaza, 14 Scotts Rd. Take the bullet lift up the outside of the building, expect to hear hard rock, open until 0200.

Harbour Front and Sentosa *p585*

Sunset Bay, Siloso Beach. Quintessential beach bar with a fun crowd.

Singapore West *p588*

There are a number of pubs and bars in a row of restored shophouses in Pasir Panjang Village, along what is known as **The Pub Row**.

East coast *p590, map p591*

Changi Sailing Club, Changi Village, pleasant and, surprisingly, one of the cheapest places for a quiet beer, overlooking the Strait of Johor.

Charlie's, Block 2, 01-08, Changi Village. Charlie Han describes his bar as 'the pulse of the point', tucked away behind the local hawker centre, he is a teetotaller but serves 70 brands of beer from all over the world, which you can sip as you watch the red-eyes touchdown on runway one; Charlie's is best known for its fish and chips; see above. Closed weekends. Recommended.

Gay and lesbian venues

Regular parties for gay and lesbians are held throughout the month, usually at *Zouk, Centro*, and *Why Not*. Check www.fridae.com for an update or ask at one of the establishments listed below.

Backstage, 13A Trengganu St, T62271712. A funky chillout bar for men, very boutiquey with drapes and candlesticks.

Cow & Coolies, 30 Mosque St, T62211239. A scruffy karoake pub for lesbians.

Mad Monks, 20 Upper Circular Road, opposite Clarke Quay next to Clarke Quay MRT. Lesbian parties held most Fri nights. Attracts a younger crowd of girls.

Mox Bar, 21 Tanjong Pagar, T63239438. Retro lounge bar, that has a no smoking policy - you have to retreat to the balconies if you want to light up. Very kitsch with 70s' furniture, a lovers' swing and a piano. Friendly crowd. Recommended.

Sky Bar, 27 Neil Rd, T62247441. A lesbian pub with a pool table, karoake and not much seating.

Why Not, 56-58 Tras Street, Tanjong Pagar. A disco karaoke bar with a small stage. Mainly gay male crowd.

Entertainment

Cinema

The *Straits Times Life* section publishes listings daily. With more than 50 cinemas, Singapore gets most of the blockbusters soon after their release in the US. Tickets cost about S$8-9 and shows continue all the day, with late night viewing at weekends. Censors have relaxed in recent years; there's a new RA category for those over 21 years old, which means a little more sex and violence hits the screens. When the *Cathay*, at the southeastern end of Orchard Road, opened in 1939 and became the first a/c public building in Singapore, local celebrities turned up in fur coats. It has sadly recently stopped screening films.

The new cinema experience can be had at **GV Grand**, top floor of Great World City, Zion Rd, T67358484, booking recommended. You can relax in an easy chair and eat a meal at the same time. There are several other multiplex cinemas, including: **Parco Bugis Junction** on Victoria St, opposite Bugis MRT, the **Lido Cineplex** at the Shaw Centre, **Orchard Rd** and **Suntec City**, Marina Square.

Classical, opera and other music

Chinese classical and folk music are organized by the **Nanyang Academy of Fine Arts** (NAFA), T63376636 for performance details.

Most classical music performances are held at The **Singapore Cultural Theatre** and the **Victoria Hall** – the Singapore Symphony Orchestra gives regular performances and there are often visiting orchestras, quartets and choirs. The Singapore Symphony Orchestra also performs in many free open-air shows in the Botanic Gardens. The National Theatre Trust promotes cultural dance performances and local theatre as well as inviting international dance and theatre groups to Singapore.

Kala Mandhir, Temple of Fine Arts, 1st Flr, Excelsior Hotel Shopping Centre, T63390492. Classes available in dance, instrumental music, percussion and singing. Fabulous array of Indian instruments. It might be possible to take a one-week course here, although most are longer.

Chinese Street Opera (Wayang) Traditional Chinese street operas (wayang) mostly take place during the 7th lunar month, following the Festival of the Hungry Ghosts (see page 54). They are regularly staged on makeshift wooden platforms which are erected in vacant lots all over the city. To the sound of clashing cymbals and drums, the wayang actors – adorned in ornate costumes and with faces painted – act out the roles of gods, goddesses, heroes, heroines, sages and villains from Chinese folklore.

Live music

Brannigan's, Basement, Hyatt Regency Hotel, 10/12 Scotts Rd. Popular American-style, touristy bar with loud live music and video screens. Open until 0100, 0200 on Fri and Sat.
Crazy Elephant, Clarke Quay. House band, mostly covers.
Fabrice's World Music Bar, Basement, Singapore Marriott Hotel, 320 Orchard Rd. Good bands from around the world.
Hard Rock Café, HPL House, 50 Cuscaden Rd: AOR covers (Boston, Chicago and the like); forget conversation. Queues to get in.
Harry's Quayside, 28 Boat Quay. Jazz Wed-Sat, blues on Sun.
Kaspia Bar, Hilton Hotel, Orchard Rd. Jazz.
Studebakers, Penthouse of Pacific Plaza, Orchard Rd. Live performances and dancing.
Molly Malone's, 42 Circular Rd (behind Boat Quay). Irish folk.
Somerset's, Westin Stamford Hotel, Raffles City. Large and pleasant bar with frieze of the Padang in the days before Raffles City, with live jazz music.
Top Ten Club, Orchard Towers, 400 Orchard Rd. Good black American or Philippine disco funk bands, some soul as well.

Theatre, dance and comedy

Most theatrical and dance performances are held at the Esplanade or Victoria Hall. Tickets for many performances can be bought from **SISTIC** (T63485555, www.sistic.com.sg) as well as from the box offices themselves.
Action Theatre, Waterloo St, next to the Synagogue. Provides small scale productions either on an outdoor stage or in a small auditorium.
Boom Boom Room, 3 New Bugis St, T63398187. Cabaret and stand-up comedy shows. Popular with locals; tame by international standards. Cabaret Tue-Thu 2230-0100 and until 0200 on the other nights. No happy hour.
Raffles Jubilee Hall, 328 North Bridge Rd, T63311732, holds occasional theatrical performances.
Sculpture Square, 155 Middle Rd. Open 1100-1800 Mon-Fri and 1200-1800 weekends. Housed in Middle Rd church, which has been converted to a light and airy exhibition space, this is a centre for 3D work, with changing exhibitions.
Stamford Arts Centre, 155 Waterloo St. A centre for the performing arts, with Chinese opera, Nrityalaya performances, and traditional Indian dance and drama. China Theatre Circle, 5A Smith St, Chinatown, T63234862.
The Esplanade: theatres on the Bay The majority of performances will be held here in the theatres enclosed in a pair of what looks like giant durians.
The Substation, 45 Armenian St, www.substation.org, set up in a former power station, T63377800. The latest offering on the thespian and artistic scene, this venue has an intimate small theatre where it stages plays and shows avant garde films. It also holds drama workshops.

Shopping

The colonial core *p558, map p564*

Art galleries

Many contemporary galleries have opened up and whilst some can be found in the Tanglin Shopping centre there are also the following specialising in contemporary asian art. **Gajah Gallery**, MICA Building, 140 Hill St, T67374202, www.gajahgallery.com for contemporary Southeast Asian art and there are a few others within the same building.

Books

National Museum Shop, 53 Armenian St. Next to The Asian Civilisations Museum. Excellent Source Of Asian Art Books.

Electronic goods

Funan Centre, North Bridge Rd, and Peninsula Plaza, next to Grand Plaza Hotel, Coleman St. Both have dozens of shops dedicated to cameras, phones, Walkmans, video cameras and computers etc.

Furniture

Pacific Link Shopping Centre, Marina Square. Shops here sell a range of contemporary furniture and furnishings.

Pennsylvania House, Stamford House, Stamford Rd. New England furniture and small items (also now has a contemporary section).

Peter Hoe, CHIJMES, 30 Victoria St, T/F63396880. An interesting assortment of small-scale pieces: kitchenware, candlesticks, mirrors etc; mostly Indonesian.

Handicrafts

Natraj's Arts & Crafts, 03-202 Marina Square Shopping Centre, in a row of Far Eastern handicraft shops. By far the best shop for Indian exotica, Natraj's specialities are the papier maché Bharata Natayam dancing girl dolls, which wobble and shake just like the real thing.

The Substation, 45 Armenian St. Arts and crafts for sale at the market here on the last Sun of every month.

Singapore River and the City

p568

Handicrafts

Flea market every Sun at Clarke Quay, where anyone can hire a pitch for S$25 for the day; it's possible to find some bargains.

Chinatown *p571, map p572*

Handicrafts

Shops on Smith and Sago streets sell assorted Chinese knick-knacks, including kites, lanterns, silk dressing gowns, opera masks, incense sticks, candle holders, lucky money and all the paraphernalia required for visiting a Chinese temple and attending a funeral. It is cheap and prices are not negotiable. **People's Park Complex**, Eu Tong Sen St. One of the biggest Chinese emporia. **Singapore Handicraft Centre**, Chinatown Point Shopping Centre, New Bridge Rd. Specializes in small handicrafts, all a bit naff, but a good place to browse for small Asian gifts.

Orchard Road *p577, map p578*

Antiques

Many of the top antique shops are to be found on levels 2 and 3 of the Tanglin Shopping Centre. They include the old map shop, **Antiques of the Orient**, level 2, T67349351. This is probably the best place to buy antique maps and prints in Southeast Asia and is a wonderful place to browse. It also has a library. **Apsara** for lacquerware chests. **Tiepolo**, T67327924, was established over 20 years ago and David Mun has a fabulous range of Chinese and Indonesian porcelain, wooden pieces and bronze. This is well worth a visit and Mr Mun is a mine of information and fascinating to talk with. Kensoon has exclusive Asiatic pieces. **Tatiana**, on the floor above, is a long established treasure trove of mostly 'primitive' art. A considerable proportion is from Indonesia: antiques, great wooden sculptures and textiles, baskets, Vietnamese drums and jewellery. **Spiritual Antique Land** for quality Tibetan and Chinese furniture and accessories with the main shop on the 1st floor. **Lopburi**, on the ground floor of Tanglin Place, Orchard Rd, sells a good range of Thai art and antiquities. For general antiques, there are shops dotted around Cuppage Terrace behind Centrepoint (upstairs, above Saxophone, there are several good shops, selling antique Melaka furniture, porcelain, and Peranakan pieces). There are also some good shops (selling antiques and restored/imitation items) at Binjai Park, off Bukit Timah Rd, which is rather off the beaten track to the north of Orchard Road.

Art galleries

Gauguin Gallery, Orchard Hotel Shopping Arcade, 442 Orchard Rd, T67334268, mounts changing exhibitions of international artists. **Tzen Gallery**, Tanglin Shopping Centre, 19 Tanglin Rd, T67344339, shows mainland Chinese watercolours and pen and ink drawings, and has a wide selection of scrolls, reasonable prices. Also check out the **Mekong Gallery** and **HaKaren ART gallery** on the 2nd floor.

Books

Borders Books & Music, Ground Floor of Wheelock Place, Orchard Rd. The best place to browse, with 140,000 titles, books that are not sealed in polythene, a café and seating. **Tango Mango**, 3rd floor, Tanglin Mall, sells a selction of local interest books and **Kinokuniya** in Ngee Ann City. **Select**

Books, Tanglin Shopping Centre, Orchard Rd, sell a good range of coffee table glossies of the region.

Ceramics

Boon's Pottery, level 1, Tanglin Mall, Orchard Rd. An outlet for 50 or so local artists. Some are pretty ghastly, but there's something here to suit most tastes. There is a larger storage area in Tanglin Place, almost next door, on the lower ground level.

Children

The Forum, corner of Orchard Rd and Cuscaden Rd. An entire shopping plaza for children, with Toys 'R' Us on the top floor and lots of other individual shops on the other 3 floors. The best choice of children's clothes is to be found at The Forum, corner of Cuscaden and Orchard roads, where there are at least 20 shops selling children's clothes.
Tanglin Mall, at the western end of Orchard Rd, also has several excellent little shops for children; eg a great beanie baby and wooden toy shop on the ground floor. Another beanie shop is at **Beanie Barn**, 1st Floor of Wheelock Place, Orchard Rd. **Magic Wand**, Orchard Point, Orchard Rd. A treasure trove of goodies. Tanglin Mall also has a good smattering of shops, eg **Bamboozle**, with brightly coloured clothes reminiscent of the Balinese Kuta Kidz (in fact, though the clothes are locally made, the block prints are Indonesian). Eg **British India**, **Dune** maternity wear and **Mothers at Work** all do childrens clothes. For swimwear, try **Ocean Paradise** on the ground floor and **Q'tees**, good for babies' clothes and shoes. **Birkenstock** shops are also here, the latter stocking a good range of brightly coloured sandals for children, also check out **Nicole Boutique.**

Chinese porcelain

Ju-I Antiques and **Moon Gate**, both at Tanglin Shopping Centre (Orchard Rd) are good shops for porcelain.

Electronic goods

Lucky Plaza, Orchard Rd, and **Far East Plaza**, Scotts Rd. Both have many electronics shops.

Furniture

Renee Hoy Fine Arts, 1st Floor, Tanglin Shopping Centre, 19 Tanglin Rd (western end of Orchard Rd), T62351596. A wide choice of Korean chests and some Thai **furniture.** Babazar, 31-35A Cuppage Terrace, off Orchard Rd, T62. An excellent selection of beautiful Indian furniture. **A2 Atelier**, Le **Meridien Sho**pping Centre, 100 Orchard Rd, **375081. An** extensive choice of reproduction furniture, including 4-poster beds and some attractive chairs and chests. **Barang Barang**, Tang lin Mall, Orchard Rd. A considerable range of contemporary furnishings, from bedding to kitchenware to sitting rooms or the garden.

Handicrafts

Singapore Handicrafts, in the rather down-at-heel Tudor Court, the far western end of Orchard Rd.

Jade

Kwok Gallery, Far East Shopping Centre, Orchard Rd.

Music

The Heeren, on the corner of Cairnhill Rd and Orchard Rd. Four floors of HMV. CDs are well worth buying here as they are good value.

Persian rugs

The Orientalist at 1 Nassim Rd, corner with Orchard Rd has a huge showroom. **Pardisan**, Orchard Shopping Centre, Orchard Rd. Good selection of rugs. **Salam Carpets**, 2nd floor, The Tanglin Mall. **Mohammed Akhtar**, Tanglin Shopping Centre, Orchard Rd. **Hassan's Carpets**, Tanglin Shopping Centre, Orchard Rd also has an extensive range.

Shoes

Birkenstock shop, Tanglin Mall, Orchard Rd **Hush Puppies** to name but a few in Centrepoint Shopping centre.

Shopping centres on Orchard Road

Numbers after the shopping centre correspond to the Orchard Road map. **Centrepoint** (4), dominated by *Robinsons department store, Mothercare, Lacoste, Times Bookshop* and *M&S* and a host of small clothes boutiques.

Far East Plaza (13), Scotts Road: one of the older plazas with a maze of small boutiques, plenty of shops selling electronic goods, cameras and watches. Money changers, tailors and a small food court.
Forum (18), predominantly children's clothes and a *Toys R Us* on the upper floor.
Heeren (6), dominated by *HMV* store, also good sandwich joint - *Fiddleheads*.
Hilton Shopping Plaza (16), connects Hilton and Four Seasons Hotel - top haute couture designers. Escalators state 'Ladies watch your gowns'.
Lucky Plaza (9), one of Singapore's oldest plazas, rather downmarket. Good selection of electronic goods (including CD Walkmans, mini DVDs, Gameboys, cameras), loads of jewellery shops, cheap clothing and opticians along the road frontage offer some good deals. Furtive selling of copy watches.
Meridien (3), by Meridien Hotel, *DFS Collections* in basement for duty free goods, large, very good quality furniture store - old and new wooden products.
Ngee Ann City (8), this massive complex houses the Takashimaya department store, and over 100 speciality stores, mainly fashion boutiques - *Burberrys, Louis Vuitton, Tiffanys, Chanel, Charles Jourdain* - and several restaurants. Sparks disco is on the top floor. Popular with the rich and famous and a hang-out for the young and trendy.
Palais Renaissance (17), hideously trendy design, the best in designer-boutiques and branded goods (*Versace, DKNY* etc).
Paragon (7). Newly expanded to included Japanese department store *Metro* and numerous designer labels, good bag shop (*Furla*), *M&S, Ferragamo, Gucci* and *Dunhill*, also houses the Metropolitan Art Museum shop. Sculptures outside the plaza by Taiwanese sculptor Sun Yu-Li, inspired by rock paintings in Mongolia.
Park Mall (1), Penang Rd, one of the newer plazas, full of interior design items: furniture, textiles, lamps. Food in basement.
Plaza Singapura (2). *Carrefour's* second hypermarket, *John Little* department store, *M&S, Times book shop, Spot light, Best Denki* and numerous eateries together with a multi screen cinema complex. Right next door to Dohby Ghaut MRT.
Scotts (12), 6 Scotts Road: department store, 'Picnic' food court in basement, smart female boutiques with contemporary designers. Good electronics shops.
Shaw House (14), Isetan shopping centre and a cinema complex.
Specialists' Centre (5), just across from Centrepoint; downmarket department store.
Tanglin Shopping Centre (19), top end of Orchard Road, a treasure trove of Asian antiques and curios, Persian rugs, closes between 1800 and 1900.
Tang's (11), next to Marriott Hotel. Very smart department store; the Harrods of Singapore.
Wisma Atria (10), one of the best places for boutique browsers, though not necessarily top brands. With a spectacular marine aquarium in the basement.
Wheelock Place (15), *M&S* on the lower floors, *Borders bookshop* dominates the ground level, also houses a Nike sports store, a Café Dome, a Nooch Noodles bar and a couple of children's toy shops. Large Clarins on top floor.

Silk
If you want silk without the hassle, at reasonable prices, big department stores (such as **Tang's** on Orchard Rd) have good selections. The best known of the silk boutiques, with fine silks at high prices, is **China Silk House**, which has shops in Tanglin, Scotts and Centrepoint shopping centres on Orchard Rd. There is also a **Jim Thompson** Thai Silk shop in Palais Renaissance centre at the top of orchard road.

Tailoring
Far East Plaza and **Lucky Plaza**, along Orchard and Scotts roads.

Textiles
Spotlight. The large Australian owned shop is on the 5th Floor of Plaza Singapura.

Little India *p580, map p581*

Department stores
Mustufa Centre department store on corner of Serangoon road and Styed Alwi Road is popular for cheap electronics, clothes, textiles, gold and household goods.

Computers

Sim Lim Tower (upper floors) and the nearby Albert Complex, both just off Bukit Timah on Rochor Canal Rd.

Electronic goods

Sim Lim Tower and **Sim Lim Square.** Of these two, Sim Lim Tower does not have a very good reputation.

Handicrafts

Kuna's, Buffalo Rd. Sells Indian handicrafts. There are other shops around here where Indian knick-knacks can be found.

Textiles

Serangoon Rd is one of the best areas for reasonably priced batik and silk lengths, but you should bargain.

Arab Street *p583, map p584*

Textiles

Arab Street is one of the best areas for reasonably priced batik and silk lengths, but you should bargain.

Singapore West *p588*

Antiques

Dempsey Road, off Holland Road, is a great place to browse amongst the furniture warehouses in some of the old army barracks there (though it's a bit of a tourist trail these days). Furniture from Indonesia, plantation chairs, opium couches, Burmese Buddhas and so on are all available. Warehouse shops include: **Asian Passion**, Block 13, T64731339, good for tables and cabinets; **Woody Antique House,** blk7 01-01 Dempsey Rd; **Eastern Discoveries**, Block 26, T64751814, for wooden sculptures amongst other things; **Journey East**, Block 13, T64731693, for chests, planters chairs - old and new; **Pasardina**, Block 13, T64720228, good range of new and old cabinets, planters chairs, beds and some small-scale Indonesian pieces (spice boxes and baskets); **Renaissance**, Block 15, T64740338, range of restored Chinese furniture.

Chinese porcelain

At **Ming Village**, 32 Pandan Road, visitors can watch reproduction Ming vases being made Holland Village, west of the Botanic Gardens, has quite a number of porcelain shops.

Handicrafts

Holland Village Shopping Centre, Holland Av. An excellent place for Asian arts and crafts, Vietnamese lacquerware, Balinese goods etc. **Lim's**, also here, see below.

Linen

Lim's, 1st floor, Holland Village Shopping Centre, Holland Av.

Persian rugs

Hedgers Carpet Gallery, 24a Lorong Mambong Holland Village.

Textiles

Mountain Looms, Block 16 Dempsey Rd, T64767629. Very fine pieces of cloth from all over the region.

East Coast *p590, map p591*

Antiques

Geylang has a number of good antique junk shops where occasional treasures can be found. Peter Wee's **Katong Antique House** (aka Katong Antiques House, at 208 East Coast Road (half museum, half shop), has one of the best selections of Peranakan antiques. The shop has been established for 20 years and has become a focal point for Peranakan culture. He has established a Peranakan Association and publishes a newsletter. Groups from the National Museum visit him. He has a considerable collection of beaded shoes and holds classes on how to make them every Wed.

Directory

Embassies and consulates

Australia (High Commission), 25 Napier Rd, T68364100. **Austria**, 600 North Bridge Rd, T63966350. **Belgium**, 8 Shenton Way, 1401 Temasek Tower, T62207677. **Canada (High**

Commission), 1400 Fuji Xerox Towers, 80 Anson Rd, T63253200. **Denmark**, 1301 United Square, 101 Thomson Rd T63555010. **France**, 101-103 Cluny Park Rd T68807800. **Germany**, 1200 Singapore Land Tower, 50 Raffles Place, T65336002. **Israel**, 24 Stevens Close, T62350966. **Italy**, 101 Thomson Road, No 27-02 United Square, T62506022. **Japan**, 16 Nassim Rd, T62358855. **Malaysia (High Commission)**, 30 Hill St, T62350111. **Netherlands**, 1301 Liat Towers, 541 Orchard Rd, T67371155. **New Zealand** (High Commission), 391A Orchard Rd, T62359966. **Norway**, 1401 Hong Leong Building, 16 Raffles Quay, T62207122. **South Africa** (High Commission), 15th Floor, Odeon Towers, 331 North Bridge Road, T63393319. **Spain**, 3900 Suntec Tower One, 7 Temasek Boulevard, T63333035. **Sweden**, 111 Somerset Rd, T64159720. **Thailand**, 370 Orchard Rd, T67372158. **UK (High Commission)**, 100 Tanglin Rd, T64244270. **USA**, 27 Napier Rd, T64769100.

Medical facilities

Alexandra, 378 Alexandra Rd, T4755222. **East Shore**, 321 Joo Chiat Pl, T3447588. **Gleneagles**, 6A Napier Rd, T4737222. **Mount Alvernia**, 820 Thomson Rd, T2534818. **Mount Elizabeth**, 3 Mount Elizabeth, T7372666. **National University**, 5 Lower Kent Ridge Rd, T7795555. **Singapore General, Outram Rd**, T2223322. **Traveller's Health and Vaccination Clinic**, Tan Tock Seng Hospital Medical Centre, Level 1, 11 Jalan Tan Tock Seng, T63572222, www.ttsh.com.sg

Footnotes

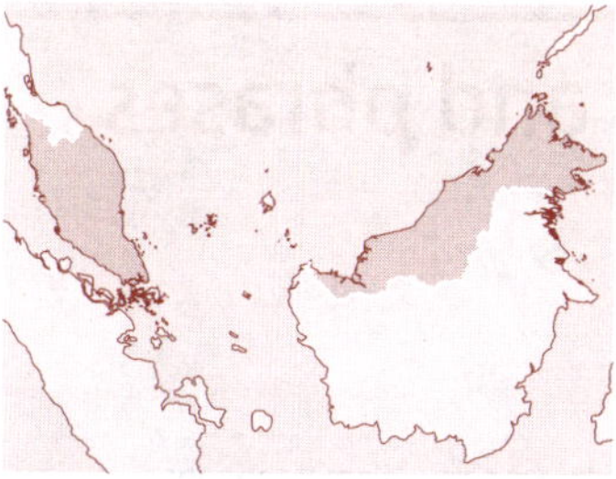

Malaysian words and phrases

Basic phrases

Yes/No ia/tidak
Thank you Terimah kasih
You're welcome Sama-sama
Good morning/Good afternoon (early) Selamat pagi/Selamat tengahari
Good afternoon (late)/Good evening/night Selamatpetang/Selam at malam
Welcome Selamat datang
Goodbye (said by the person leaving/said by the person staying) Selamat tinggal/Selamat jalan
Excuse me/sorry Ma'af saya
Where's the...? Dimana...
How much is this...? Ini berapa?
I [don't] understand Saya [tidak] mengerti
I want.../I don't want Saya mahu/Saya tak mahu
My name is... Nama saya...
What is your name? Apa nama anda?
Bon Appetit! Selamat makan!

Sleeping

How much is a room? Bilik berapa?
Does the room have air-conditioning? Ada bilik yang ada air-con-kah?
I want to see the room first please Saya mahu lihat bilik dulu
Does the room have hot water? Ada bilik yang ada air panas?
Does the room have a bathroom? Ada bilik yang ada mandi-kah?

Travel

Where is the railway station? Stesen keretapi dimana?
Where is the bus station? Stesen bas dimana?
How much to go to...? Berapa harga ke...?
I want to buy a ticket to... Saya mahu beli tiket ke...
How do I get there? Bagfaimanakah saya
Is it far? Ada jauh?
Turn left / turn right Belok kiri /belok kanan
Go straight on! Turus turus!

Time and days

Monday Hari Isnin (Hari Satu)
Tuesday Hari Selasa (Hari Dua)
Wednesday Hari Rabu (Hari Tiga)
Thursday Hari Khamis (Hari Empat)
Friday Hari Jumaat (Hari Lima)
Saturday Hari Sabtu (Hari Enam)
Sunday Hari Minggu (Hari Ahad)

Today Hari ini
Tomorrow Esok
Week Minggu
Month Bulan
Year Tahun

Numbers

1 satu
2 dua
3 tiga
4 empat
5 lima
6 enam
7 tujuh
8 lapan
9 sembilan
10 sepuluh
11 se-belas
12 dua-belas...etc
20 dua puluh
21 dua puluh satu...etc
30 tiga puluh
100 se-ratus
101 se-ratus satu
150 se-ratus limah puluh
200 dua ratus...etc
1,000 se-ribu
2,000 dua ribu...
100,000 se-ratus ribu
1,000,000 se-juta

Basic vocabulary

a little sedikit
a lot banyak
all right/good baik
and dan
bank bank
bathroom bilek mandi
beach pantai
beautiful cantik
bed sheet cadar
big besar
boat perahu
broken tak makan/rosak
bus bas
bus station setsen bas
buy beli
can boleh
cannot tak boleh
cheap murah
chemist rumah ubat
cigarette rokok
clean bersih
closed tutup
cold sejuk
crazy gila
day hari
delicious sedap
dentist doktor gigi
dirty kotor
doctor doktor
eat makan
excellent bagus
expensive mahal
food makan
he/she dia
hospital rumah sakit
hot (temperature) panas
hot (chilli) pedas
I/me saya
ice air batuais
island pulau
male lelaki
man laki
market pasar
medicine ubat ubatan
more lagi/lebeh
open masuk
please sila
police polis
police station pejabat polis
post office pejabat pos
railway station stesen keretapi/tren
restaurant restoran/kedai makanan
room bilik
sea laut
ship kapal
shop kedai
sick sakit
small kecil
stand berdiri
stop berhenti
taxi teksi
they mereka
that itu
ticket tiket
toilet (female) tandas perempuan
toilet (male) tandas lelaki
town bandar
trishaw beca
very sangat
wait tunggu
water air
we kami
what apa
when bila
woman perempuan
you awak/anda

A practical alternative

Malaysian English, which has been dubbed 'Manglish', as opposed to Singaporean English ('Singlish'), has evolved its own usages, abbreviations and expressions. Its very distinctive pronunciation can be almost unintelligible to visitors when they first arrive. The first thing many visitors notice is the use of the suffix lah which is attached to just about anything and means absolutely nothing. English has been spoken in the Malay world since the late 18th century, but over time, it has been mixed with local terms. The converse has also happened: English has corrupted Malay to such a degree that it is now quite common to hear the likes of 'you pergi-mana?' for 'where are you going?' In abbreviated Malaysian- Chinese English, can is a key word. 'Can-ah?' (inflection) means 'may I?'; can-lah means yes; cannot means no way; also can means 'yes, but I'd prefer you not to' and how can? is an expression of disbelief.

The man who first applied the term Manglish to mangled Malaysian English was Chinese-Malaysian satirist Kit Leee, in his book *Adoi* (which means ouch). It gives an uncannily accurate and very humorous pseudo-anthropological rundown on Malaysia's inhabitants. His section on Manglish, which should be pronounced exactly as it is written, is introduced: Aitelyu-ah, nemmain wat debladigarmen say, mose Malaysians tok Manglish... Donkair you Malay or Chinese or Indian or everyting miksup... we Malaysians orways tok like dis wan-kain oni. Below are extracts from his glossary of common Manglish words and phrases (which will help decipher the above).

atoyu (wat) gentle expression of triumph: 'What did I tell you?'
baiwanfriwan ploy used mainly by shop assistants to promote sales: 'If you buy one you'll get one free'.
betayudon mild warning, as in 'You'd better not do that'.
debladigarmen contraction of 'the bloody government'; widely used scapegoat; for all of life's disappointments, delays, denials, and prohibitions.
hauken another flexible expression applicable in almost any situation, eg 'That's not right!', 'Impossible!' or 'Don't tell me!'.
izzenit from 'isn't it?' but applied very loosely at the end of any particular statement to elicit an immediate response, eg Yused you will spen me a beer, izzenit?
kennonot request or enquiry, contraction of 'can or not': 'May I?' or 'Will you?' or 'Is it possible?'
nola a dilute negative, used as a device to interrupt, deny or cancel someone else's statement.
oridi contraction of already.
sohau polite interrogative, usually used as a greeting, as in 'Well, how are things with you?'
tingwat highly adaptable expression stemming from 'What do you think?'
wan-kain adjective denoting uniqueness; contraction of 'one of a kind'. Sometimes rendered as wan-kain oni ('only').
watudu rhetorical question: 'But what can we do?'
yala non-committal agreement, liberally used when confronted with a bore.
yusobadwan expression of mild reproach: 'That's not very nice!'

With thanks to Kit Leee and his co-etymologists: Rafique Rashid, Julian Mokhtar and Jeanne MC Donven. Leee, Kit (1989) *Adoi*, Times Books International: Singapore)

Glossary

A

Adat custom or tradition
Amitabha the Buddha of the Past (see Avalokitsvara)
Atap thatch
Avalokitsvara also known as Amitabha and Lokeshvara, the name literally means 'World Lord'; he is the compassionate male Bodhisattva, the saviour of Mahayana Buddhism and represents the central force of creation in the universe; usually portrayed with a lotus and water flask

B

Bahasa language, as in Bahasa Malaysia
Barisan Nasional National Front, Malaysia's ruling coalition comprising UMNO, MCA and MIC along with seven other parties
Batik a form of resist dyeing common in Malay areas
Becak three-wheeled bicycle rickshaw
Bodhi the tree under which the Buddha achieved enlightenment (Ficus religiosa)
Bodhisattva a future Buddha. In Mahayana Buddhism, someone who has attained enlightenment, but who postpones nirvana in order to help others reach the same state
Brahma the Creator, one of the gods of the Hindu trinity, usually represented with four faces, and often mounted on a hamsa
Brahmin a Hindu priest
Budaya cultural (as in Muzium Budaya)
Bumboat small wooden lighters, now used for ferrying tourists in Singapore
Bumiputra literally, 'sons of the soil'; Malays as opposed to other races in Malaysia

C

Cap batik stamp
Chedi from the Sanskrit cetiya (Pali, caitya) meaning memorial. Usually a religious monument (often bell-shaped) containing relics of the Buddha or other holy remains. Used interchangeably with stupa
Cutch see Gambier

D

Dalang wayang puppet master
DAP Democratic Action Party, Malaysia's predominantly Chinese opposition party
Dayak/Dyak collective term for the tribal peoples of Borneo
Dharma the Buddhist law
Dipterocarp family of trees (Dipterocarpaceae) characteristic of Southeast Asia's forests
Durga the female goddess who slays the demon Mahisa, from an Indian epic story

E

Epiphyte plant which grows on another plant (but usually not parasitic)

F

Feng shui the Chinese art of geomancy

G

Gambier also known as cutch, a dye derived from the bark of the bakau mangrove and used in leather tanning
Gamelan Malay orchestra of percussion instruments
Ganesh elephant-headed son of Siva
Garuda mythical divine bird, with predatory beak and claws, and human body; the king of birds, enemy of naga and mount of Vishnu
Gautama the historic Buddha
Geomancy or feng shui, the Chinese art and science of proper placement
Godown Asian warehouse
Goporum tower in a Hindu temple
Gunung mountain

H

Hamsa sacred goose, Brahma's mount; in Buddhism it represents the flight of the doctrine
Hinayana 'Lesser Vehicle', major Buddhist sect in Southeast Asia, usually termed Theravada Buddhism

I

Ikat tie-dyeing method of patterning cloth

Indra the Vedic god of the heavens, weather and war; usually mounted on a three headed elephant

J

Jataka(s) birth stories of the Buddha, of which there are 547; the last 10 are the most important

K

Kajang thatch

Kala (makara) literally, 'death' or 'black'; a demon ordered to consume itself; often sculpted over entranceways to act as a door guardian, also known as kirtamukha

Kampung or *Kampong*, village

Kerangas from an Iban word meaning 'land on which rice will not grow'

Keraton see kraton

Kinaree half-human, half-bird, usually depicted as a heavenly musician

Kongsi Chinese clan house

Kris traditional Malay sword

Krishna an incarnation of Vishnu

Kuti living quarters of Buddhist monks

L

Laterite bright red tropical soil/stone sometimes used as a building material

Linga phallic symbol and one of the forms of Siva. Embedded in a pedestal shaped to allow drainage of lustral water poured over it, the linga typically has a succession of cross sections: from square at the base through octagonal to round. These symbolize, in order, the trinity of Brahma, Vishnu and Siva

Lintel a load-bearing stone spanning a doorway; often heavily carved

Lokeshvara see Avalokitsvara

Lunggyi Indian sarong

M

Mahabharata a Hindu epic text written about 2,000 years ago

Mahayana 'Greater Vehicle', major Buddhist sect

Mandi Malay bathroom with water tub and dipper

Maitreya the future Buddha

Makara a mythological aquatic reptile, somewhat like a crocodile and sometimes with an elephant's trunk; often found, along with the kala, framing doorways

Mandala a focus for meditation; a representation of the cosmos

MCA Malaysian Chinese Association

Meru the mountain residence of the gods; the centre of the universe, the cosmic mountain

MIC Malaysian Indian Congress

Mudra symbolic gesture of the hands of the Buddha

N

Naga benevolent mythical water serpent, enemy of Garuda

Naga makara fusion of naga and makara

Nalagiri the elephant let loose to attack the Buddha, who calmed him

Nandi/Nandin bull, mount of Siva

NDP New Development Policy

Negara kingdom and capital, from the Sanskrit

Negeri also negri, state

NEP New Economic Policy

Nirvana 'enlightenment', the Buddhist ideal

O

Orang Asli indigenous people of Malaysia

P

Paddy/padi unhulled rice

Pantai beach

Pasar market, from the Arabic 'bazaar'

Pasar malam night market

Perahu/prau boat

Peranakan 'half caste', usually applied to part Chinese and part Malay people

Pradaksina pilgrims' clockwise circumambulation of a holy structure

Prang form of stupa built in the Khmer style, shaped rather like a corncob

Prasat residence of a king or of the gods (sanctuary tower), from the Indian prasada

Pribumi indigenous (as opposed to Chinese) businessmen

Pulau island

Pusaka heirloom

R

Raja/rajah ruler
Raksasa temple guardian statues
Ramayana the Indian epic tale

Ruai common gallery of an Iban longhouse, Sarawak
Rumah adat customary or traditional house

S

Sago multi-purpose palm
Sal the Indian sal tree (Shorea robusta), under which the historic Buddha was born
Sakyamuni the historic Buddha
Silat or bersilat, traditional Malay martial art
Singha mythical guardian lion
Siva one of the Hindu triumvirate, the god of destruction and rebirth
Songket Malay textile interwoven with supplementary gold and silver yarn
Sravasti the miracle at Sravasti when the Buddha subdues the heretics in front of a mango tree
Sri Laksmi the goddess of good fortune and Vishnu's wife
Stele inscribed stone panel or slab
Stucco plaster, often heavily moulded
Stupa see chedi
Sungai river

T

Tamu weekly open-air market
Tanju open gallery of an Iban longhouse, Sarawak
Tara also known as Cunda; the four-armed consort of the Bodhisattva Avalokitsvara
Tavatimsa heaven of the 33 gods at the summit of Mount Meru
Theravada 'Way of the Elders'; major Buddhism sect also known as Hinayana Buddhism ('Lesser Vehicle')
Tiffin afternoon meal – a word that was absorbed from the British Raj
Timang Iban sacred chants, Sarawak
Tong or towkay, a Chinese merchant
Totok 'full blooded'; usually applied to Chinese of pure blood
Towkay Chinese merchant
Triads Chinese mafia associations
Tunku also Tuanku and Tengku, prince

U

Ulama Muslim priest
Ulu jungle
UMNO United Malays National Organization
Urna the dot or curl on the Buddha's forehead, one of the distinctive physical marks of the Enlightened One
Usnisa the Buddha's top knot or 'wisdom bump', one of the physical marks of the Enlightened One

V

Vishnu the Protector, one of the gods of the Hindu trinity, generally with four arms holding the disc, the conch shell, the ball and the club

W

Waringin banyan tree
Warung a foodstall – a simple place to eat on the street – the alernative Malay name is Kedai Makan. The word originally comes from Indonesia.
Wayang traditional Malay shadow plays

Malay food glossary

assam sour
ayam chicken
babi pork
belacan hot fermented prawn paste
buah fruit
daging meat
Es avocado chilled avocado shake
Es delima dessert of water chestnut in sago and coconut milk
Gado-gado cold dish of bean sprouts, potatoes, long beans, tempeh, bean curd, rice cakes and prawn crackers, topped with a spicy peanut sauce
garam salt
gula sugar
Ice kachang similar to *chendol* (see Chinese food) but with evaporated milk instead of coconut milk
ikan fish
ikan bilis anchovies
ikan panggang spicy barbecued fish
kambing mutton
Kepala ikan fish head, usually in curry or grilled
kerupak prawn crackers
ketupat cold, compressed rice
kopi coffee
kueh cakes
lemang glutinous rice in bamboo
limau lime
manis sweet
mee noodles
minum drink
roti canai pancakes served with lentils and curry
roti john baguette filled with sardine/egg mixture
roti kosong plain pancake
sambal spicy paste of pounded chillis, onion and tamarind
sayur manis sweet vegetables
sayur masak lemak deep fried marinated prawns
sejuk crab
soto ayam spicy chicken soup
sotong squid
susu milk
tahu beancurd
telur egg
udang prawn

Rice dishes

nasi campur Malay curry buffet of rice served with meat, fish, vegetables and fruit.
nasi goreng rice, meat and vegetables fried with garlic, onions and sambal.
nasi lemak a breakfast dish of rice cooked in coconut milk and served with prawn sambal, ikan bilis, a hard boiled egg, peanuts and cucumber.
nasi padang plain rice served with a selection of dishes.
nasi puteh plain boiled rice.
nasi dagang popular on the east coast for breakfast; glutinous rice cooked in coconut milk and served with fish curry, cucumber pickle and sambal.

Soup

soto ayam popular for breakfast in Johor and Sarawak, a spicy chicken soup served with rice cubes, chicken and vegetables.
lontong popular in the south, particularly for breakfast. Cubed compressed rice served with mixed vegetables in coconut milk. Sambal is the accompaniment.

Meat

satay chicken, beef or mutton marinated and skewered on a bamboo, barbecued over a brazier. Usually served with ketupat.

Noodles

kway teow flat noodles fried with seafood, egg, soy sauce, beansprouts and chives.
laksa johor noodles in fish curry sauce and raw vegetables.
mee goreng fried noodles.
mee jawa noodles in gravy, served with prawn fritters, potatoes, tofu and beancurd.
mee rebus noodles with beef, chicken or prawn with soybean in spicy sauce.

Curries

rendang dry beef curry (a Sumatran dish).
longong vegetable curry made from rice cakes cooked in coconut, beans, cabbage and bamboo shoots.

Salad

rojak Malaysia's answer to Indonesia's gado gado – mixed vegetable salad served in peanut sauce with ketupat.

Vegetables

kang-kong belacan water spinahc fried in chilli shrimp paste
sayur manis sweet vegetables; vegetables fried with chilli, belacan and mushrooms.

Sweets (kueh)

apam steamed rice cakes.
pulut inti glutinous rice served with sweetened grated coconut.
nyonya kueh Chinese kueh, among the most popular is yow cha koei – deep-fried kneaded flour.

For more information on cuisine, see Eating, Essentials, page 45.

Asian food glossary

Chinese and local food

Bak chang local rice dumpling filled with savoury or sweet meat and wrapped in leaves
Bak choy Chinese cabbage
Bak kut the local pork rib soup, with garlic and Chinese five spice
Belachan fermented prawn paste
Bird's nest edible nest of the swiftlet, made from glutinous secretions of their salivary glands
Char kway teow broad rice noodles fried with sweet sauce and additions of cockels, Chinese sausage, bean sprouts or fish cake
Char siew Sweet barbecued pork slices
Chendol a dessert: a cone of ice shavings topped with coloured syrups, brown syrup, coconut milk, red beans, attap seeds and jelly
Cheng ting a Chinese dessert of a bowl of syrup with herbal jelly, barley and dates
Chicken rice rice in chicken stock and ginger, served with steamed chicken slices
Chilli padi an extremely hot variety of chilli
Choi sum Chinese vegetable served steamed with oyster sauce
Claypot rice rice cooked in a clay casserole with pieces of chicken, Chinese mushroom, Chinese sausage and soy sauce
Congee Chinese porridge
Dian sin/dim sum Chinese sweet and savoury dumplings served at breakfast and lunch
Dow see Chinese fermented salted black beans
Fish sauce known as *nampla* in Thai, a brown sauce made from salted dried fish, used as a salt seasoning
Garoupa white fish popular in Asia
Gula malacca coarse palm sugar sold in lumps, from the sap of the Palmyra palm
Hainanese chicken rice chicken served with spring onions, ginger dressing, soup and rice boiled in chicken stock or coconut milk
Hoisin sauce Chinese thick seasoning with a sweet-spicy flavour
Hokkien mee yellow noodles fried with sliced meat, squid, prawns and garnished with strips of fried egg
Kang kong a Chinese vegetable – water convolvulus
Kway teow broad rice noodles
Laksa spicy coconut soup of thin white noodles garnished with bean sprouts, quail's eggs, prawns, shredded chicken and dried bean curd
Lor mee a dish of noodles served with slices of meat, eggs and a dash of vinegar in a dark brown sauce
Rojak salad of cucumber, pineapple, turnip, fried beancurd tossed in a prawn paste with peanuts, tamarind and a sugary sauce
Sio bee a pork filling ina paper-thin wrapping
Tau hui a dessert made from a by-produt of soya bean, served with syrup
Teh tarek tea made with evaporated milk
Yu char kway deep-fried Chinese breadsticks

Indian

Aloo gobi potato and cauliflower dish
Bhindi okra or lady's fingers
Biryani North Indian dish of basmati rice and meat, seafood and vegetables
Brinjal aubergine or eggplant
Daun pisang a Malay/South Indian thali – curry and rice, with poppadoms and chutneys all served on a banana leaf.
Dhal pureed lentils

Dhosas large crispy pancakes served with potatoes, onions and spices
Gulab jumun fried milk balls in syrup
Idli steamed rice cake
Keema spicy minced meat
Kofta minced meat or vegetable ball
Lassi yoghurt based drink
Murgh chicken
Murtabak roti (bread) which has been filled with pieces of mutton, chicken or vegetables
Nasi biriyani rice cooked in ghee, spices and vegetable, served with beef or chicken.
Nasi kandar Mamak's version of nasi campur.
Pakora vegetable fritter
Pilau rice fried in ghee and mixed with nuts, then cooked in stock
Pudina mint sauce
Raita side dish of cucumber, yoghurt, mint
Rogan josh spicy lamb curry with yoghurt
Roti prata flat round pancake-like bread
Saag spinach
Sambar fiery mixture of vegetables, lentils and split peas
Tandoori style of cooking: meat is marinated in spicy yoghurt and then baked in a clay oven
Tikka small pieces of meat or fish served off the bone, marinated in yoghurt and baked

Nyonya

kapitan chicken cooked in coconut milk.
otak otak minced fish, coconut milk and spices, steamed in a banana leaf.
laksa rice noodles in spicy coconut milk and prawn-flavoured gravy blended with spices and served with shellfish, chicken, beancurd and belacan.
assam laksa the specialized Penang version – rice noodles served in fish gravy with shredded cucumber, pineapple, raw onions and mint.

Sabahan

hinava marinated raw fish.
sup manuk on hiing chicken soup with rice wine.
tapai chicken cooked in rice wine.
pakis ferns, which are fried with mushrooms and belacan. Sometimes ferns are eaten raw, with a squeeze of lime (sayur pakis limau).
sup terjun jumping soup – salted fish, mango and ginger.
hinompula a dessert made from tapioca, sugar, coconut and the juice from screwpine leaves.

Sarawakian

Ternbok fish, either grilled or steamed.
pan suh manok chicken cooked in bamboo cup, served with bario (Kelabit mountain rice).
Lontong rice cakes in a spicy coconut-milk topped with grated coconut and sometimes bean curd and egg
Manis sweet
Mee rebus yellow noodles served in a thick sweet sauce made from sweet potatoes. Garnished with sliced hard-boiled eggs and green chillies
Mee siam white thin noodles in a sweet and sour gravy made with tamarind
Nasi biryani saffron rice flavoured with spices and garnished with cashew nuts, almonds and raisins
Rijsttafel Indonesian meal consisting of a selection of rice dishes, to which are added small pieces of meat, fish, fruit and pickles
Sambal spicy paste of pounded chillis, onion and tamarind
Sayur masak lemak deep fried marinated prawns
Tempeh preserved deep fried soya bean

Thai

Gai haw bai toey fried chicken in pandanus leaves
Gai tom kla chicken and coconut soup
Kaeng jud soup
Kaeng paad curry
Kaeng phet kai hot chicken curry
Kai tom kha lemon grass chicken soup with coconut milk
Khao rice
Larb minced chicken or pork flavoured with spices, herbs and lime
Mi krob crisp thin noodles with shrimp, egg and sweet and sour sauce
Pak krasan a cabbage-like vegetable
Phrik chillies
Pla thot sam rot fried garoupa with sweet and sour sauce
Poo paad gari curried crab
Tom kam kung hot and sour spiced seafood soup
Yam salad

Index

T

U

V

W

Y

Map index

Advertisers' index

Map symbols

Administration

- Capital city
- Other city/town
- International border
- Regional border
- Disputed border

Roads and travel

- National highway, motorway
- Main road
- Minor road
- Track
- Footpath
- Railway with station
- Airport
- Bus station
- Metro station
- Cable car
- Funicular
- Ferry

Water features

- River, canal
- Lake, ocean
- Seasonal marshland
- Beach, sand bank
- Waterfall

Topographical features

- Contours (approx)
- Mountain
- Volcano
- Mountain pass
- Escarpment
- Gorge
- Glacier
- Salt flat
- Rocks

Cities and towns

- Main through route
- Main street
- Minor street
- Pedestrianized street
- Tunnel
- One way street
- Steps
- Bridge
- Fortified wall
- Park, garden, stadium
- Sleeping
- Eating
- Bars & clubs
- Entertainment
- Building
- Sight
- Cathedral, church
- Chinese temple
- Hindu temple
- Meru
- Mosque
- Stupa
- Synagogue
- Tourist office
- Museum
- Post office
- Police
- Bank
- Internet
- Telephone
- Market
- Hospital
- Parking
- Petrol
- Golf
- A Detail map
- A Related map

Other symbols

- Archaeological site
- National park, wildlife reserve
- Viewing point
- Campsite
- Refuge, lodge
- Castle
- Diving
- Deciduous/coniferous/palm trees
- Hide
- Vineyard
- Distillery
- Shipwreck
- Historic battlefield

Acknowledgements

Dinah Gardner would like to thank Pearlyn Ng for soup and support in Singapore and the following were also a massive help: in KL - Doreen Lim, David Bowden and Kevin the pixel miner; elsewhere - Jodi Smith, Chwee Sze Foong, Carey Walker, Narelle at Langkawi's Bon Ton Resort, Kieth Sarson, Mark Elliot, the crazy boys at Uncle Tan's in Sabah, and last but not least, Andrew Paterson, who knows what he did. Also thank you to everyone who sent in comments and updates on the previous edition.

Dinah and Footprint would also like to thank Joshua Eliot and Jane Bickersteth for all their work on the previous four editions of this guide. Thanks also to Rebecca Wharton for reviewing the Singapore shopping section; to Charlie Easmon for the Health section, and to Beth Tierney for the Diving section.

Credits

Footprint credits

Editor: Claire Boobbyer
Map editor: Sarah Sorensen
Picture editor: Kevin Feeney

Publisher: Patrick Dawson
Editorial: Alan Murphy, Sophie Blacksell, Sarah Thorowgood, Angus Dawson, Felicity Laughton, Laura Dixon, Nicola Jones
Cartography: Robert Lunn, Claire Benison, Kevin Feeney, Angus Dawson
Series development: Rachel Fielding
Cover design: Robert Lunn
Design: Mytton Williams and Rosemary Dawson (brand)
Advertising: Debbie Wylde
Finance and administration: Sharon Hughes, Elizabeth Taylor

Photography credits

Front cover: Eye Ubiquitous (Penang door painting)
Back cover: Powerstock (Kuala Lumpur skyline at night)
Inside colour section: Alamy, Eye Ubiquitous, Jamie Marshall, Powerstock, Robert Harding, Travel Ink.

Print

Manufactured in India by Nutech Photolithographers. Pulp from sustainable forests

Footprint feedback

We try as hard as we can to make each Footprint guide as up to date as possible but, of course, things always change. If you want to let us know about your experiences – good, bad or ugly – then don't delay, go to **www.footprintbooks.com** and send in your comments.

Publishing information

Footprint Malaysia & Singapore
5th edition

March 2005

ISBN 1 904 777 33 3
CIP DATA: A catalogue record for this book is available from the British Library

Published by Footprint

6 Riverside Court
Lower Bristol Road
Bath BA2 3DZ, UK
T +44 (0)1225 469141
F +44 (0)1225 469461
discover@footprintbooks.com
www.footprintbooks.com

Distributed in the USA by

Publishers Group West

Neither the black and white nor coloured maps are intended to have any political significance.

Every effort has been made to ensure that the facts in this guidebook are accurate. However, travellers should still obtain advice about travel and visa requirements before travelling. Hotel and restaurant price codes should only be taken as a guide to the prices and facilities offered by the establishment. It is with the discretion of the owners to vary them from time to time. The authors and publishers cannot accept responsibility for any loss, injury or inconvenience however caused.

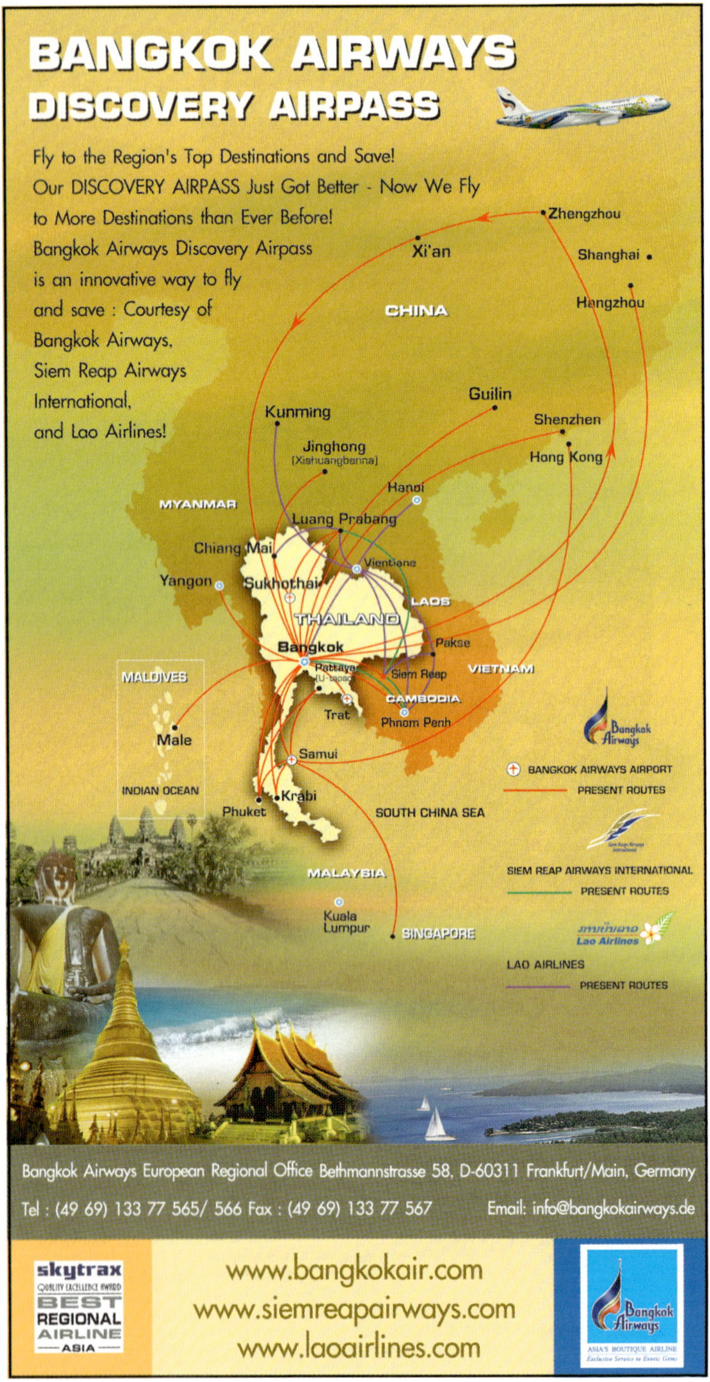
BANGKOK AIRWAYS
DISCOVERY AIRPASS
Fly to the Region's Top Destinations and Save!
Our DISCOVERY AIRPASS Just Got Better - Now We Fly to More Destinations than Ever Before!
Bangkok Airways Discovery Airpass is an innovative way to fly and save : Courtesy of Bangkok Airways, Siem Reap Airways International, and Lao Airlines!
Zhengzhou
Xi'an
Shanghai
Hangzhou
CHINA
Guilin
Kunming
Shenzhen
Hong Kong
Jinghong
(Xishuangbanna)
Hanoi
MYANMAR
Luang Prabang
Chiang Mai
Vientiane
Yangon
Sukhothai
LAOS
THAILAND
Bangkok
Pakse
VIETNAM
MALDIVES
Pattaya
(U-tapao)
Siem Reap
CAMBODIA
Trat
Phnom Penh
Male
Samui
BANGKOK AIRWAYS AIRPORT
PRESENT ROUTES
INDIAN OCEAN
Krabi
Phuket
SOUTH CHINA SEA
MALAYSIA
SIEM REAP AIRWAYS INTERNATIONAL
PRESENT ROUTES
Kuala Lumpur
SINGAPORE
Lao Airlines
LAO AIRLINES
PRESENT ROUTES
Bangkok Airways European Regional Office Bethmannstrasse 58, D-60311 Frankfurt/Main, Germany
Tel : (49 69) 133 77 565/ 566 Fax : (49 69) 133 77 567
Email: info@bangkokairways.de
skytrax
QUALITY EXCELLENCE AWARD
BEST
REGIONAL
AIRLINE
ASIA
www.bangkokair.com
www.siemreapairways.com
www.laoairlines.com
Bangkok Airways
ASIA'S BOUTIQUE AIRLINE

Malaysia

THAILAND
1
Kangar
Alor Star
Georgetown
Penang
Andaman Sea
Ipoh
Cameron Highlands
Barisan Titiwangsa
Kota Bharu
Kuala Terengganu
PENINSULAR MALAYSIA
2
Kuantan
Strait of Melaka
KUALA LUMPUR
Seremban
Segamat
Melaka
Johor Bahru
SINGAPORE
SUMATRA (INDONESIA)
South China Sea
Kepelauan Natuna
Kepelauan Anambas
3
EAST MALAYSIA
Bintulu
Sibu
SARAWAK
Kuching
Bandar Sri Aman
4
BANDAR SERI BEGAWAN
BRUNEI
Kota Kinabalu
Gunung Kinabalu
SABAH
Sandakan
Tawu
PHILIPPINES
Sulu Sea
Celebes Sea
KALIMANTAN (INDONESIA)
Altitude in metres
4000+
3000
2000
1000
500
200
100
0
Neighbouring country
National highway
Primary road
Secondary road
Track
10 Route number
Railway
N
0 km 100
0 miles 100

Map 1

THAILAND
Padang Besar
Kaki Bukit
Sungai Korok
PERLIS
Arau
Bukit Kayu Hitam
Kangar
Kuala Perlis
Chinchin Straits
Padang Lalang
Pulau Langgun
Pulau Langkawi
Belanga Beach
Pulau Rebak Besar
Kuah
Pulau Timun
Pulau Tuba
Pulau Singa Besar
Pulau Dayang Bunting
Taluk Air Pedu
Sungai Kedah
Jitra
Taluk Air Muda
Alor Star
Kuala Kedah
KEDAH
Andaman Sea
Sungai Muda
Gurun
Gunung Jerai (1,206m)
Bujang Valley
Sungai Petani
Betong
PENANG
Batu Ferringhi
Georgetown
Butterworth
Penang
Bukit Mertajam
Kulim
Batu Muang
Pulau Jerejak
Grik
Taluk Temengor
Tesuk Kenering
Gunung Inas (1,801m)
Bintang Mountains
Kubuh Gajah
Parit Buntar
Bukit Merah
PERAK
Bukit Larut (Maxwell Hill)
Kuala Sepetang
Taiping
Sungai Siput
Kuala Kangsar
Straits of Melaka
Gunung Korbu (2,183m)
Sungai Perak
Gunung Tasek
Tanjung Rambutan
Sungai Kinta
Perak Tong Temple
Ipoh
Brinchang (2,031m)
Cameron Highlands
Sam Poh Tong
Beremban (1,840m)
Brinchang
Batu Gajah
Kellie's Castle
Tanah Rata
Taluk Ringlet
Ringlet
Pulau Pangkor
Bukit Pangkor
Lumut
Pulau Pangkor Laut
Teluk Batik
Tapah
Tapah Road
Sungai Perak
Teluk Intan
North-South Highway
Belanga Bay
Sungai Bernam
Tanjung Malim
SELANGOR
A
B
C
1
2
3

South China Sea
A
B
C
N
0 km 20
0 miles 20
Tumpat
Pantai Cinta Berahi
Kampung
Wakaf Bharu
Kota Bharu
Pasir Mas
Rantau Panjang
Pantai Dalam Rhu
Pulau Perhentian Kecil
Pulau Perhentian Besar
Pulau Lang Tengah
Tanah Merah
Sungai Kelantan
Pasir Puteh
Kuala Besut
Jerteh
Pulau Redang
Pulau Lima
Pulau Pinang
Pulau Ekor Tibu
Pulau Bidong Laut
Penarek
Merang
Batu Rakit
Kuala
Gunung Noring Timor
Dabong
Bukit Abu
Gunung Lawit (1,519m)
Kuala Terengganu
Cendering
Pulau Kapas
Marang
Sungai Terengganu
Sungai Marang
KELANTAN
Gunung Chirgoi (863m)
Taluk Kenyir
Kuala Berang
Sekayu Falls
To Pulau Tenggol (26km)
Gua Musang
TERENGGANU
Rantau Abang
Sungai Dungun
Kuala Abang
Kuala Dungun
Gunung Perlis (1,279m)
Gunung Gagau (1,377m)
Gunung Mandi Angin (1,473m)
Gunung Padang
Gunung Tahan (2,187m)
Taman Negara National Park
Kerteh
Kampung Kuala Tahan
Park HQ
Kemasik
Kemasik Pantai
Gunung Dulang (1,063m)
Kenong Rimba National Park
Kampung Kuala Kenong
Sungai Tembeling
Kuala Lipis
Kemaman
Map 2
Sungai Jelai
Kampung Cherating
Kuala Tembeling
Gunung Tapis Park
Gunung Tapis (1,512m)
Kampung Sungai Ular
PAHANG
Sungai Kuantan
Charah Caves
Jerantut
Kampung Sungai Karang
Sungai Lembing
Beserah
Fraser's Hill
Sungai Pahang
Kuantan
Gunung Benom (2,107m)
4
5
6
3
8
14
2

Map 2

Tapah
Tapah Road
Teluk Intan
Sungai Perak
Sungai Bernam
Kuala Lipis
Kampung Kuala Kenong
Sungai Jelai
Sungai Tembeling
Tembeling
Jerantut
Sungai Pahang
Fraser's Hill
Gunung Benom (2,107m)
PAHANG
Tanjung Malim
Kuala Kubu Bahru
Barisan Titiwangsa
SELANGOR
North-South Highway
Mentakab
Temerloh
Genting Highlands
Kanching Falls
Sungai Selangor
Batang Berjuntai
Kuala Selangor
Kuala Selangor Nature Park
Rawang
Orang Asli Museum
Templer Park
Batu Caves
FRIM (Canopy Walkway)
Jinjang
Gombak
Jeram
Triang
KUALA LUMPUR
Ampang
Kapar
Meru
Ulu Langat
Kemayan
Petaling Jaya
Pulau Ketam
Pulau Klang
Klang
Shah Alam
Cheras
NEGERI SEMBILAN
Port Klang
Sungai Klang
Serdang Baharu
Kajang-Sungai Chua
Pulau Lumut
Mines Wonderland
Semeyih
Kampong Dengkil
Bangi
Jenjarom
Telok Datok
Sungai Langat
Bahau
Ladang Geddes
Morib
Banting
Salak
Seremban
Kuala Pilah
KLIA
Sri Menanti
Rembau
Gemas
Port Dickson
Tampin
Simpang Empat
Cape Rachado
North-South Highway
Gunung Ledang (Mt Ophir 1,276m)
Tanjung Bidara
Ayer Keroh
MELAKA
Tanjung Kling
Melaka
Pulau Besar
Muar
Strait of Melaka
SUMATRA (INDONESIA)
A
B
C
1
2
3

Kemaman
Kampung Cherating
Kampung Sungai Ular
Kampung Sungai Kerang
Beserah
Teluk Chempedak
Kuantan
Gunung Tapis National Park
Gunung Tapis (1,512m)
Caras Caves
Sungai Kuantan
Sungai Lembing
Map 1
Maran
Sungai Pahang
Kampung Chini
Tasek Chini
Kampung Pahang
Pekan
Nenasi
South China Sea
Kampung Gading
Sungai Rompin
Kuala Rompin
Padang Endau
Bukit Keryon Kecil
Monkey Bay
Kampong Tekek
Pulau Tioman
Kampong Juara
Bukit Seperok
Kampong Mukut
Pulau Seri Buat
Endau Rompin National Park
Sungai Endau
Segamat
Labis
Bukit Kepong
Gunung Bekok (962m)
Mersing
Pulau Pemanggil
Pulau Rawa
Pulau Tengah
Pulau Babi Besar
Pulau Aur
Pulau Tinggi
Pulau Sibu
JOHOR
Kahang
Jemaluang
North-South Highway
Yong Peng
Kluang
Ayer Hitam
Batu Pahat
Gunung Muntahak
Lombong
Teluk Mahkota (Jason's Bay)
Teluk Mahkota
Kota Tinggi
Kulai
Gunung Pulai (660m)
Sungai Johor Bahru
Johor Lama
Johor Bahru
Pontian Kecil
Desaru
Kukup
Bukit Timah
Semagoon
Pulau Ubin
Johor Strait
Queenstown
SINGAPORE
Sentosa
Singapore Strait
N
0 km 20
0 miles 20
A
B
C
4
5
6

Map 3

A
B
C
1
2
3
N
0 km
30
0 miles
30
South China Sea
Mukah
Sungai Mukah
Sungai Igan
R Balin
Sibu
Sarikei
Kanowit
Tanjung Datu National Park
Telok Datu
Damai Peninsula
Sematan
Gunung Gading National Park
Damai Beach
Santubong
Gunung Santubong
Pulau Lakei
Bako National Park
Lundu
Kampung Telaga Air
Buntal
Bako
Muara Tebas
Kubah National Park
Sibu Salak
Sarawak Mangrove Reserve
Kuching
Batu Kawa
Kuap
Kota Samarahan
Bau
Semonggoh Orang Utan Sanctuary
Siburan
Serian
Anna Rais
Gunung Penrissen
Lupar
Bukit Saban Resort
Sungai Skrang
Lanjak-Entimau Wildlife Sanctuary
Betong
Bandar Sri Aman
Batang Ai National Park
Batang Ai Reservoir
Hilton Longhouse Resort

LABUAN
Muara
BANDAR SERI BEGAWAN
BRUNEI & MUARA
Brunei
Tutong
Limbang
Lumut
Kuala Belait
Seria
Lutong
Miri
Kuala Baram
Baram
TUTONG
BRUNEI
Labi
Teraja
BELAIT
Sungai Belait
Ladan Hills
Sungai Limbang
Marudi
Lambir Hills National Park
Gunung Mulu (2,376m)
Gunung Mulu National Park
Long Terawan
Sungai Tutoh
Long Seridan
Batu Niah
Niah National Park
Niah Caves
Loagan Bunut National Park
Bukit Bat (2,082
Sungai Baram
Sungai Patah
Sungai Tinjar
Map 4
Similajau National Park
Bintulu
Sungai Kemena
Tatua
Gunung Skalap
Long Peran
Sungai Belepeh
Long Muma
Belaga
Long Murum
Long Linau
Sungai Kakus
Lirong Amo
Long Sah
Long Dungan
Long Geng
Long Pangai
Sungai Murum
Sungai Rejang
Gunung Mersing
SARAWAK
Sungai Balui
Gunung Batu (2,012m)
Pelagus Rapids
Long Ayak
Song
Sungai Rejang
Kapit
Sungai Baleh
Sungui Mengiong
KALIMANTAN (INDONESIA)
A
B
C
4
5
6

Map 4

To Pulau Layang Layang
A
B
C
1
2
3
N
0 km
30
0 miles
30
South China Sea
Tempasuk (Bird Sanctuary)
Kota Belud
Surusup
Gunung Kinabalu National Park
Tuaran
Tamparuli
Mengkabong
Tunku Abdul Rahman Park
Telipok
Mesilau Nature Resort
Kota Kinabalu
Pulau Gaya
Tanjung Aru
Putatan
Penampang
Kundasan
Rafflesia Forest Reserve
Kinarut
Gunung Alab (1,964m)
Pulau Tiga National Park
Papar
Manggis
Sungai Papar
Mawar Waterfall
Patau
Tambunan
Kuala Penyuh
Gunung Trusmadi (2,642m)
Crocker Range National Park
LABUAN
Pulau Labuan
Menumbok
Beaufort
Keningan
Melalap
Agricultural Research Station, Orchid Centre
Tenom
Telok Brunei
Sipitang
Sindumin
BANDAR SERI BEGAWAN
Muara
BRUNEI & MUARA
Merapok
Lawas
Gunung Lumaku (1,966m)
Tomani
Tutong
Brunei
Labu
Limbang
Bangar
Kampong Batong Duri
Sapulut
Lumut
Lutong
Kuala Belait
Seria
TUTONG
Miri
Kuala Baram
BRUNEI
TEMBURONG
Partit Baru Amo
Baram
Sungai Trusan
Labi
Ladan Hills
Teraja
BELAIT
Sungai Belait
Sungai Limbang
Long Semado
Map 3
Lambir Hills National Park
Marudi
Gunung Mulu (2,376m)
Gunung Mulu National Park
Long Seridan
Long Terawan
Sungai Tutoh
Gunung Murudi (2,423m)
Niah National Park
Niah Caves
KALIMANTAN (INDONESIA)
Bukit Batu Bali (2,082m)
Kelabit Highlands
Loagan Bunut National Park
Bario
Sungai Baram
Sungai Patah
Sungai Tinjar
SARAWAK
Gunung Skalap
Long Peran
Sungai Belepeh
Long Muma
Long Murum

Pulau Balambangan
Pulau Banggi
Pulau Malawali
Kudat
Sikuati
Rungas
Pulau Jambongan
Sumangat
Kota Marudu
Sulu Sea
A
Gunung Tambuyukon (2,759m)
Hot Springs
Poring
Ranau
Ling Kabau
Telok Labuk
Pulau Selingan
Pulau Gulisaan
Pulau Libaran
Pulau Langkayan
Turtle Islands National Park
Tanjung Pisau
Tanjung Lari Lari
PHILIPPINES
Samawang
Pulau Berhala
Sandakan
Sepilok Orang Utan Rehabilitation Centre
Sandakan Harbour
Tanjung Aru
Tanjung Bidadari
Segaliud
Sekong Bay
Mangrove
Abai
Sekong
Sua Lamba
Telupid
Sukau
Sungai Kinabatangan
Batangan
Lamag
Bilit
Malapi
Gomantong Caves
SABAH
Batu Tulug
Sungai Segama
Sungai Kinabatangan
Tabin Wildlife Reserve
Pinangah
B
Lahad Datu
Tungku
Sungai Kuamut
Danum Valley Conservation Area
Lotung (1,667m)
Telok Lahad Datu
Gunung Silam
Luasong
Kunak
Madai Caves
Pulau Timbun Mata
(1,006m)
Batu Punggul
Baturong Caves
Gunung Magdalena (1,347m)
Semporna
Tawau Hill National Park
Pulau Mabul
Sebatik Island
Tawau
Sebuku Bay
Pulau Kapalai
Nunukan
Pulau Sipadan Marine Reserve
C
Celebes Sea
4
5
6

Kuala Lumpur Rail Transit System

Singapore MRT System

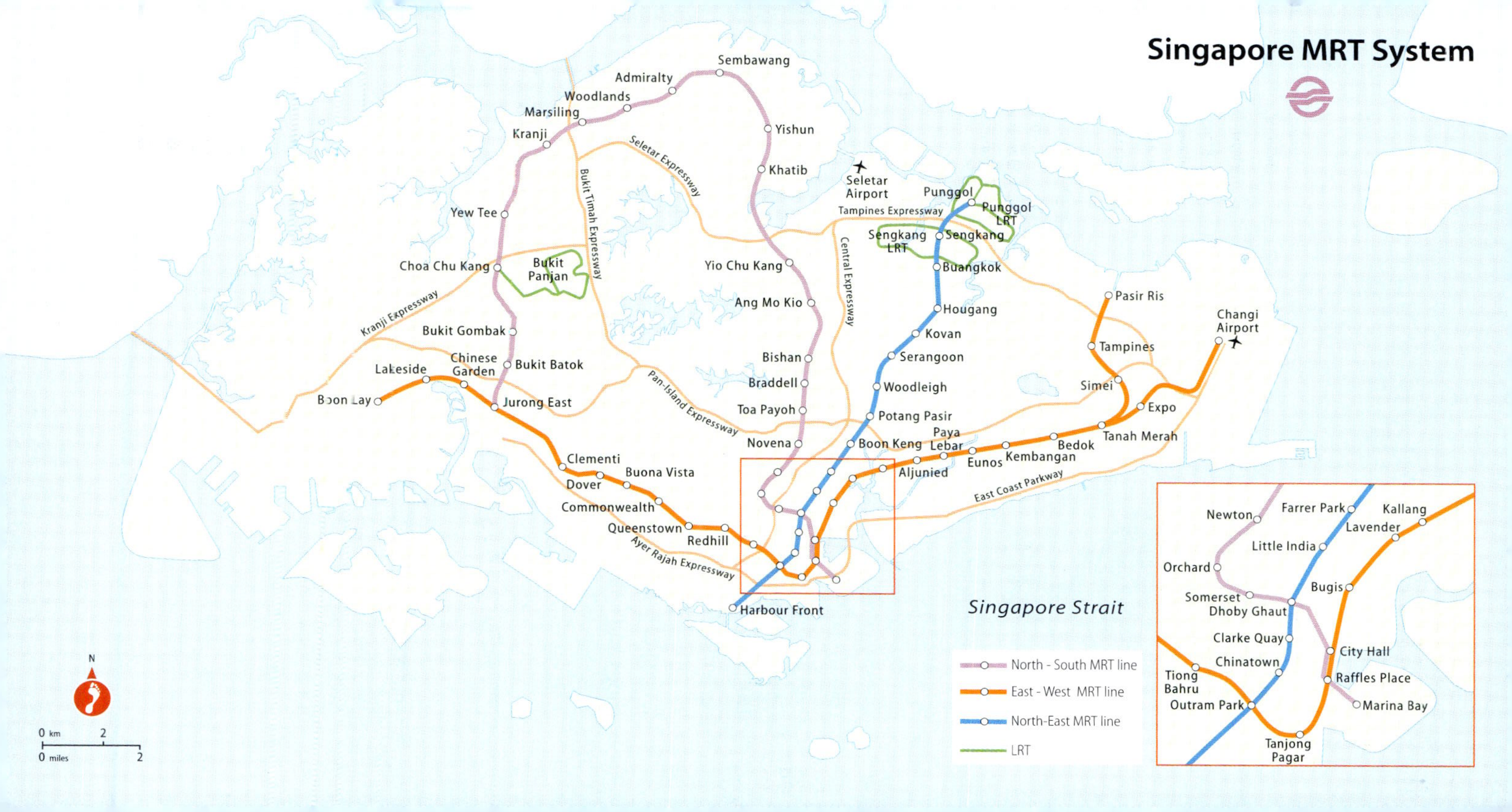

Complete title listing

Footprint publishes travel guides to over 150 destinations worldwide. Each guide is packed with practical concise and colourful information for everybody from first-time traveller to travel aficionados. The list is growing fast and current titles are noted below.

Available from all good book shops and online

www.footprintbooks.com

(P) Denotes pocket guide

Latin America & Caribbean

Antigua & Leeward Islands (P)
Argentina
Barbados (P)
Belize, Guatemala and Southern Mexico
Bolivia
Brazil
Caribbean Islands
Central America & Mexico
Chile
Colombia
Costa Rica
Cuba
Cusco & the Inca Trail
Dominican Republic (P)
Ecuador & Galápagos
Guatemala
Havana (P)
Mexico
Nicaragua
Patagonia
Peru
Peru, Bolivia and Ecuador
Rio de Janeiro (P)
St Lucia (P)
South American Handbook
Venezuela

North America

Vancouver (P)
New York (P)
Western Canada

Africa

Cape Town (P)
East Africa
Egypt
Libya
Marrakech (P)
Morocco
Namibia
South Africa
Tunisia
Uganda

Middle East

Dubai (P)
Israel
Jordan
Syria & Lebanon

Asia

Bali
Bangkok & the Beaches
Cambodia
Goa
Hong Kong (P)
India
Indian Himalaya
Indonesia
Laos
Malaysia
Myanmar (Burma)
Nepal
Northern Pakistan
Pakistan
Rajasthan & Gujarat
Singapore
South India
Sri Lanka
Sumatra
Thailand
Tibet
Vietnam

Australasia

Australia
East Coast Australia
New Zealand
Sydney (P)
West Coast Australia

Europe

Andalucía
Barcelona (P)
Berlin (P)
Bilbao (P)
Bologna (P)
Britain
Cardiff (P)
Copenhagen (P)
Croatia
Dublin (P)

Edinburgh (P)
England
Glasgow (P)
Ireland
Lisbon (P)
London
London (P)
Madrid (P)
Naples (P)
Northern Spain
Paris (P)
Reykjavík (P)
Scotland
Scotland Highlands & Islands
Seville
Spain
Tallin (P)
Turin (P)
Turkey
Valencia (P)
Verona (P)

Lifestyle guides

Surfing Europe
Surfing Britain